New SAT Guide, Edition 2.3

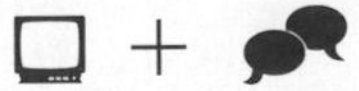

Resources & Downloads:

IVYGLOBAL.COM/STUDY

New SAT Guide, Edition 2.3

This publication was written and edited by the team at Ivy Global.

Editor-in-Chief: Sarah Pike
Producers: Lloyd Min and Junho Suh

Editors: Sacha Azor, Corwin Henville, Nathan Létourneau, and Kristin Rose

Contributors: Sarah Atkins, Amanda Bakowski, Sabrina Bartlett, Spencer Bass, Stephanie Bucklin, Alexandra Candib, Ho-Jae Cha, Shavumiyaa Chandrabalan, Beini Chen, Natalia Cole, Elizabeth Cox, Shayna Darling, Lisa Faieta, Howard Fung, Aleah Gornbein, Yvonne Greenen, Keven Gungor, Elizabeth Hilts, Helen Huang, Lei Huang, Caroline Incledon, Keven Ji, Caroline Jo, Lana Lam, Somin Lee, James Levine, Lucy Liu, Amelia McLeod, Mark Mendola, Casey O'Leary, Laurel Perkins, Michael Protacio, Julia Romanski, Martha Schabas, Meena Sundararaj, Yolanda Song, Nathan Tebokkel, and Kalden Tsung

About the Publisher

Ivy Global is a pioneering education company that delivers a wide range of educational services.

E-mail: publishing@ivyglobal.com
Website: http://www.ivyglobal.com

Contents

Chapter 1: Introduction

Chapter 2: Reading

Chapter 3: Writing

Chapter 4: Essay

Chapter 5: Math

Chapter 6: Practice Tests

Chapter 7: Answers

Introduction

Chapter 1

Section 1

About This Book

Welcome, students and parents! This book is intended to help students prepare for the SAT, a test created and administered by the College Board.

Many colleges and universities in the United States require the SAT as part of the application process. It is our goal to demystify the SAT by offering you tips, tricks, and plenty of practice to help you do your best. This book will help you turn this challenging admissions requirement into an opportunity to demonstrate your skills and preparation to colleges.

We'll provide you with you with a comprehensive breakdown of the new SAT and proven test-taking strategies for the different sections and question types. There are chapters about the new SAT's Reading Test, Writing and Language Test, Essay, and Math Test, as well as multiple practice tests. Here is what's inside:

- Key test-taking strategies
- A breakdown and detailed review of the content of each section
- Lists of SAT word roots to build vocabulary
- 3 full-length practice tests and more than 450 practice problems and drills
- Answer keys at the back of this book, and full answer explanations and scoring online

The first key to succeeding on the SAT is knowing the test, so the rest of this chapter provides details about its structure, format, and timing along with key strategies to use in all sections. Chapters 2-5 delve into the question types and content you will encounter in each section. We recommend working through these chapters, taking the practice exams in Chapter 6, and then reviewing any challenging material.

Check out our website for additional resources, including review of foundational concepts, extra practice, answer explanations, and online scoring sheets. You'll also find information about upcoming tests, tutoring services and prep classes, and other tips to help you do your best. Good luck studying!

For additional resources, please visit **ivyglobal.com/study**.

What is the SAT?

Part 1

Introduction

The SAT is a standardized examination designed to measure students' abilities in three areas: reading, writing, and mathematical reasoning. The SAT is written and administered by the College Board. Many American colleges and universities require SAT scores for admission and consider these scores an important factor in assessing applications.

Why do colleges care about the SAT? Since grading standards vary from one high school to another, it can be hard for colleges to know whether two applicants with the same grades are performing at the same level. Therefore, having everyone take the same standardized test gives colleges another metric for comparing students' abilities.

Of course, SAT scores aren't the only things that colleges consider when assessing applicants. Your high school grades, course selection, extracurricular activities, recommendation letters, and application essays are all factors that colleges will use to decide whether you are a good fit for their school. However, in today's highly competitive admissions process, a solid SAT score may provide you with the extra edge needed to be successful.

What's New?

The College Board is implementing significant changes to the SAT that will take effect in the spring of 2016. If you're already familiar with the old SAT, you should review the table below about the differences. If this is your first time learning about the SAT, skip ahead to The New SAT in Detail.

The Old SAT vs. The New SAT		
Category	Old SAT	New SAT
Timing	• 3 hours 45 minutes	• 3 hours 50 minutes (including the optional 50 minute Essay)
Sections	• Critical Reading • Writing (includes the Essay) • Math	• Evidence-Based Reading and Writing • Math • Essay (optional and separate from the Writing Test)
Areas of Emphasis	• General reasoning skills • Understanding challenging vocabulary used in limited contexts • Using logic to solve unfamiliar and abstract math problems	• Applying reasoning and knowledge to real-world situations • Using reading, writing, and math skills to analyze evidence • Understanding vocabulary and word choice in a greater range of contexts • Demonstrating core applied reasoning skills in algebra and data analysis
Question Types	• 161 multiple choice • 10 grid-in	• 141 multiple choice • 13 grid-in
Answer Choices	• 5 answer choices (A to E) for multiple choice questions	• 4 answer choices (A to D) for multiple choice questions
Penalty	• Guessing penalty: quarter-point deduction for wrong answers	• No penalty for wrong answers
Scoring	• Total scaled score from 600 to 2400, comprised of area scores from 200-800 in Critical Reading, Mathematics, and Writing • Essay score factored into Writing scaled score	• Total scaled score from 400 to 1600, comprised of area scores from 200-800 in Math and in Evidence-Based Reading and Writing • Essay score reported separately • Subscores and cross-test scores based on demonstration of skills in more specific areas

The New SAT in Detail

Part 2

Understanding the format and scoring of the new SAT will help you pick appropriate strategies and know what to expect on test day.

The Format

The SAT is 3 hours long (plus 50 minutes for the optional Essay). It is composed of the following sections:

- 100-minute Evidence-based Reading and Writing section
    - Reading Test (65 minutes, 52 questions)
    - Writing and Language Test (35 minutes, 44 questions)
- 80-minute Math section
    - Calculator allowed section (55 minutes, 38 questions)
    - No-calculator allowed section (25 minutes, 20 questions)
- Optional Essay-writing section (50 minutes)

The Scoring System

The new SAT will have three **test scores** on a scale from 10 to 40. There will be one test score for each test: the Reading Test, the Writing Test, and the Math Test. The Reading Test score and the Writing and Language Test score will be added together and converted to a single **area score** in Evidence-Based Reading and Writing; there will also be an area score in Math based on the Math Test Score.

The area scores will be on a scale from 200 to 800. Added together, they will form the **composite score** for the whole test, on a scale from 400 to 1600. The Essay will be scored separately and will not affect your scores in other areas.

SAT Scoring	
Test Scores (10 to 40)	• Reading Test • Writing Test • Math Test
Area Scores (200 to 800)	• Evidence-Based Reading and Writing • Math
Composite Score (400 to 1600)	• Math (Area Score) + Evidence-Based Reading and Writing (Area Score)
Essay Scores (1 to 4)	• Reading • Analysis • Writing
Cross-test Scores (10 to 40)	• Analysis in Science • Analysis in History/Social Studies
Subscores (1 to 15)	• Words in Context • Command of Evidence • Expression of Ideas • Standard English Conventions • Heart of Algebra • Problem Solving and Data Analysis • Passport to Advanced Math

The College Board will also be reporting new types of scores. **Cross-test scores** for **Analysis in Science** and **Analysis in History/Social Studies** will be based on performance on specific questions across different tests relating to specific types of content. For example, your cross-test score in Analysis in Science will be based on your performance on questions relating to science passages on the Reading Test as well as questions using scientific data on the Math Test. These scores will be on a scale from 10 to 40.

There will also be seven **subscores** based on particular question types within each test section. Subscores will be reported on a scale from 1 to 15. Four will be related to particular questions in the Reading and Writing Test: Words in Context, Command of Evidence, Expression of Ideas, and Standard English Conventions. The other three relate to specific types of questions on the Math Test: Heart of Algebra, Problem Solving and Data Analysis, and Passport to Advanced Math. You'll learn more about what these subscores are measuring in the chapters explaining what these questions are like.

Taking the SAT

Part 3

Now that we've covered the format and content of the new SAT, let's talk about how you go about taking the exam. The SAT is administered at standard testing dates and locations worldwide throughout the academic year. These standard dates fall in January, March, May, June, October, November, and December, but the March test date is only available in the United States. You can see the upcoming dates in your location on the College Board website: sat.collegeboard.org.

How Do I Register?

The easiest way to sign up for the exam is on the College Board website: sat.collegeboard.org. You'll need to fill out a personal profile form and upload a recognizable photo, which will be included on your admission ticket.

You can also register by mail. To do this, ask your school counselor for *The Student Registration Guide for the SAT and SAT Subject Tests*, which includes a registration form and a return envelope. You'll need to enclose a photo with this paper registration form.

When you register, you can sign up for your preferred date and location. However, testing centers often run out of room, so make sure you sign up early in order to reserve your place! There is also a cut-off for registrations a month before the test date, after which you'll need to contact the College Board to see if late registration or standby testing is an option.

The new SAT will be first administered in spring 2016. If you are registered for an exam that will be administered before then, you will be taking the old SAT exam.

When Should I Take the SAT?

Typically, students take the SAT during 11th grade or the beginning of 12th grade. However, you should plan to take the exam when you feel most prepared, keeping in mind when colleges will need your scores.

Almost all schools will accept scores through December of your 12th grade year. After December, it really depends on the school to which you are applying. If you are planning to apply for Early Admission to any school, you'll need to take the test by November of 12th grade at the very latest.

Can I Re-Take the SAT?

Yes! The College Board has no limits on how many times you can take the SAT. Many students take the exam two or three times to ensure their scores represent the best they can do. However, we don't recommend taking the exam more than two or three times, because you'll get fatigued and your score will start to plateau. Prepare to do your best each time you take the test, and you shouldn't have to re-take it too many times.

In order to give yourself the option to re-take the test, it is always wise to choose a first testing date that is earlier than you need. That way, if you decide you'd like to re-take the test you won't miss any deadlines.

How Do I Send My Scores to Colleges?

When you sign up for the SAT, you can select which schools you'd like to receive your scores. You can also do this after taking the SAT by logging onto your account on the College Board website. If you have taken the SAT more than once, the College Board's "Score Choice" program allows you to choose which test results you would like to report to schools. You can't "divide up" the scores of different tests—all sections of the SAT from a single test date must be sent together.

However, certain schools don't participate in the "Score Choice" program. These schools request that applicants send the results of every SAT test they have taken. Even so, most schools have a policy of only considering your highest scores. Some schools will take your best overall score from a single administration while others will mix and match your best scores for your entire test history, called a "Superscore." You can see how your prospective schools consider your scores by visiting their admissions websites.

How Do I Improve My Score?

The key to raising your SAT score is to adopt a long-term strategy. Score improvement on the SAT occurs only after consistently practicing and learning concepts over a long period of time. Early on in your high school career, focus on building vocabulary and improving essay-writing skills. Read as much as you can beyond your school curriculum—materials like novels, biographies, and current-event magazines. Keep up with the math taught in your classes and ask questions if you need help.

In addition to keeping up with the fundamental concepts and skills tested on the SAT, you'll need to learn how to approach the specific types of questions included on the exam. In the next section, we'll talk about some general test-taking strategies that will help you tackle the format of the SAT as a whole. Then, you can work through Chapters 2-5 to learn specific strategies for the SAT Reading, Writing, Essay, and Math Tests. In Chapter 6, you'll be able to apply these strategies to 3 full-length practice tests.

With enough practice, you'll be prepared to score your personal best on test day! Let's get started.

Section 2

Approaching the SAT

In this section, we will help you prepare for the SAT with effective ways to approach studying and test taking. We will cover some tips to keep in mind before test day, essential strategies to tackle the test, and what to keep on your radar after you walk out of that test center.

Test-Taking Basics

Part 1

Now that you're familiar with the SAT, there are a few more things you need to know about how to take the test. These strategies include knowing what you're going to see on the test, managing your time, guessing effectively, and entering your answers.

Know the Test

The first step to tackling the SAT is to know the test. Because it is a standardized exam, the format of the SAT is the same every time it's administered. By knowing the time limit, number of questions, and directions for each section, you will be ahead of the game. Review these key details for each portion of the test until you know them inside out. On test day, you'll save time by skipping over the directions, and can relax knowing there won't be any surprises!

It is also important to know that the SAT is not like certain tests that require you to show your work or explain your answers. Except for the optional essay, you will enter all of your answers on an answer sheet that will be graded by a machine. Thus, it is important to correctly enter your answer choices on your answer sheet; otherwise, you will not receive credit for them.

Also remember that there is a set time limit. Even though the test is broken up into multiple parts, you do not have control over how to divide the total time among the individual sections. Once time is up for a certain section, you have to move on and can't work on previous sections.

Manage Your Time

Similarly, to do well on the SAT, you need to know the length of the test, the time allowed for each section, and the time allotted for snack/bathroom breaks so you can work strategically and be prepared for test day.

Unlike a normal hour-long high school test, the SAT runs between three and four hours long—so you'll want to practice building your stamina! Doing timed practice tests or timed sections will help you learn to stay focused for the duration of the test.

Remember that time between sections isn't transferable; you're given a set amount of time for each section and you can't proceed to the next section or look at previous sections if you finish early. Time yourself while practicing in order to develop a sense of what "a quarter-of-the-way through" and "halfway through" feels like in each section. Finished early? Use that leftover time to go over your answers and make sure you entered them correctly.

To maximize your time, it's important not to get too stuck on any single question and to move through the test at a steady pace. Don't waste 10 minutes on a question that stumps you, only to find that you do not have enough time to answer the things you know inside out. Each question is only worth one point, regardless of its difficulty. If you are stuck on a problem, you should make your best guess and move on quickly. Circle the problem in your question booklet so you can look at it again if you have time. You don't want to leave any question unanswered, as there's no penalty for guessing!

You should try to answer every question because you have nothing to lose—just more points to gain! At the same time, you should strike a balance between quality and quantity. Budget your time so you can get to every or almost every question, but you also have the opportunity to read each question carefully and consider each answer choice.

Guess Effectively

The new SAT will no longer deduct a quarter point for each wrong answer choice. That means that there is no downside to guessing! You should always guess on any questions you cannot answer with certainty.

But how can you guess to maximize your chances of gaining a few extra points? First, attempt each question using the processes discussed below and in the chapters that follow. Even if a question is difficult, eliminating any wrong answers will improve your odds of guessing correctly.

If you aren't sure of the answer, bubble in a guess on your answer sheet, circle the question in your test booklet, and return to it later. Once you have attempted all the other questions in the section, come back to any circled questions and re-read them carefully. Then, try again to answer them. Eliminate any wrong answers, and see if you want to change the answer you originally guessed.

It is possible you will not have time to attempt every question in a section. Because of this, it is a good idea to choose a letter beforehand that you will always use when guessing. This will save you from spending time deciding what answer choice to pick, and makes it easier to bubble in guesses. For any questions you do not have time to answer, simply fill in your bubble sheet using your chosen answer choice. Make sure you have time to enter a guess for every question you do not attempt before time is up for that section.

Write and Bubble Clearly

As noted above, except for the Essay, all of your work on the SAT will be graded by a machine. What you write in your answer sheet determines whether you'll get a point or not, so you don't want to make a mistake when it comes to bubbling your answers!

Always mark your answer in your answer sheet. Your exam booklet will not be graded, but this will provide you with a reference so you can correctly and confidently transfer your responses to your answer sheet. Make sure to fill in each bubble completely using only a No. 2 pencil. Also, always make sure you are filling in the correct section of the answer sheet. Before beginning each section, double check that you are working on the corresponding section of the answer sheet.

You can either bubble your answers in after every question, or bubble them in in groups. If you bubble your answers in groups, you may disrupt your concentration less and be more efficient. Fill in your answers after completing a specific portion of the test, such as all of the questions on one or two pages, or after finishing all the questions for a Reading passage. If you are feeling frustrated during the test, you can also take a quick 'break' to fill in your answers and clear your head, and then return to the questions feeling refreshed.

When you write your essay, write as legibly as you can. Even though you're trying to write quickly, your readers need to be able to read your handwriting in order to give you points. Remember to write your essay only in the lines of the lined pages provided in your answer sheet—your readers won't be able to see anything you write outside of these margins! Don't write any part of your essay in your test booklet, though you can use this space for jotting down notes or an outline for your essay.

While you are not given credit for anything written in your test booklet, you are not penalized either. The test booklet is yours to use how you choose, so mark it up however will help you do your best. Cross out answer choices you know are wrong. Use margins and blank space in the test booklet to work out math problems and outline your essay. Underline key words, phrases, or sections of reading passages.

Key Strategies

Part 2

In addition to learning the material tested on the SAT, to perform your best you must also use the best strategies for tackling the questions. Below we outline four key techniques that we call the **4 Ps**. They can be used across the test to help you choose answers confidently and improve your score. The strategies are:

- Plugging in Options
- Pencil on Paper
- Process of Elimination
- Pick and Skip

Plugging in Options

Even if you're not sure how to approach a multiple choice question, because you are given 4 answer options you will always have somewhere to start—you can plug in the answer choices to see which might work.

This can be especially helpful in the Math Test, where plugging in answer choices can often help you avoid completing long calculations. When you use this strategy, it is best to start with choice (B) or (C), as most answer choices are listed in increasing or decreasing numerical order. If you start with (B) or (C), you may be able to eliminate multiple answers based on the result. For example, if the answers increase in value from (A) to (D) and you determine that choice (C) is too small, you can eliminate choices (A), (B), and (C).

You can see the value of this approach with an example math problem:

Example

$$\frac{9}{4x} = \frac{3}{8}$$

What is the value of x?

A) 2 B) 4 C) 6 D) 8

To solve by testing answer choices, start with (B) or (C). If you start with (B), then substitute 4 for x:

$$\frac{9}{4 \times 6} = \frac{9}{16}$$

Next, check your answer with the question:

$$\frac{9}{16} \neq \frac{3}{8}$$

Your answer $\frac{9}{16}$ does not reduce to $\frac{3}{8}$, so (B) is not the right answer. However, you can use this to eliminate more than one answer choice. $\frac{9}{16}$ is greater than $\frac{3}{8}$, so you know that 4 is too small a value of x. Therefore, you can also eliminate any other values smaller than 4, such as answer choice (A).

Next, try (C), substituting 6 for x:

$$\frac{9}{4 \times 6} = \frac{9}{24}$$

This fraction can be simplified by dividing both the numerator and denominator by three. Checking this with the original answer:

$$\frac{9}{24} = \frac{3}{8}$$

Since $\frac{9}{24}$ can be reduced to $\frac{3}{8}$, (C) is the correct answer.

On the Writing Test, you can also apply this strategy by plugging each answer choice in to the original passage, and reading the resulting sentence in your head. Even if you can't say exactly what the error is, your everyday English skills can help you to eliminate choices that clearly sound wrong. Consider the following example:

Example

Yesterday, John ran the store until 5:00, then Lisa <u>will take</u> over.

A) NO CHANGE

B) took

C) is taking

D) DELETE the underlined portion

This type of error is called an "inappropriate shift in verb tense." "John ran the store" is in the past tense, and since Lisa took over at 5:00 yesterday, that should also be in the past tense. But even if you can't quite articulate all of that using your explicit knowledge of the rules of English, you can probably guess that (D) is wrong by imagining the sentence with that option plugged in: "John ran the store until 5:00, then Lisa over." The phrase "then Lisa over" doesn't really make any sense, because there's no verb.

You might also be able to eliminate (A) and (C) by noticing that they just don't sound right. (B) solves the error, sounds right, and is the correct answer. This is a fast and easy way of handling many Writing Test problems, but be careful: if you only go by what sounds right, and you're never sure exactly what sort of errors you're looking at, then it's possible that you'll make a careless mistake by picking something that sounds okay but is technically wrong, or vice versa. You'll have a chance to learn about specific grammar errors in Chapter 3, Section 3.

This same technique can be used on the Reading Test for questions that ask you about the meaning of words in the passage. These questions are called Words in Context questions, and are discussed further in Chapter 2, Section 4. To answer these questions, you can sub the answer choices back in to the original sentence to see what choice works best in context. Consider the following example, taken from Charles Dickens's *Great Expectations*:

Example

Ours was the marsh country, down by the river, within, as the river wound, twenty miles of the sea. My first most vivid and broad impression of the identity of things seems to me to have been gained on a memorable raw afternoon towards evening. At such a time I found out for certain that this place overgrown with nettles was the churchyard; and that Philip Pirrip, late of this parish, and also Georgiana, wife of the above, were dead and buried.

1

As used in line 6, "raw" most nearly means

A) uncooked.

B) bleak.

C) passionate.

D) inexperienced.

Though all four choices could be synonyms of raw, only answer choice (B) makes sense when we plug it into the original sentence. An afternoon cannot be "uncooked," or "inexperienced," so (A) and (D) are incorrect. While an afternoon could be "passionate" this word does not match with the tone of the surrounding lines, which are describing a graveyard. Thus, (C) is also incorrect.

Pencil on Paper

When you take the SAT, you don't want to passively read the information presented to you, but rather you want to engage with and understand it. The best way to do this is to be an **active reader** and interact with the passages and questions to find and understand the information you will be tested on. You can use your pencil to mark up or add information in your test booklet.

In the Reading Test, you can be an active reader by using your pencil to **mark up** passages as you read them by underlining important parts of the text and adding your own notes to emphasize key information. This will help you stay focused, understand what you read, and make it easy to find ideas in the passage when you refer back to it. Active reading will be discussed further in Chapter 2, Section 2.

Here's how a reading passage may look once it has been marked up. Aim to circle or underline two to three **main ideas** per paragraph that relate to the **5 *w's*:** "who," "what," "where," "when," and "why."

This passage is adapted from Daniel Zalewski, "Under a Shroud of Kitsch May Lie a Master's Art." ©2001 by The New York Times Company.

Tommaso Strinati clambers to the top of the rickety scaffold and laughs. "It's a good thing that all this Baroque work is so unimpressive," he says, pointing at the clumsy trompe l'oeil painting covering the wall in front of him. "Otherwise, we might not have been allowed to scrape it off!"

A 28-year-old art historian, he is standing 16 feet above the marble floor of San Pasquale Baylon chapel, a long-neglected nook of Santa Maria in Aracoeli, a Franciscan basilica in the center of Rome. Last year, Mr. Strinati, who is still a graduate student, began studying the church's history. Records suggested that the Roman artist Pietro Cavallini—a painter and mosaicist whose greatest works have been destroyed—spent years decorating Aracoeli toward the end of the 13th century. Yet only one small Cavallini fresco, in the church's left transept, remained visible. Mr. Strinati wondered: had other Cavallini frescoes been painted over with inferior work? And if so, could modern restorers uncover them?

"The answer to both questions was yes," Mr. Strinati says. A close-up examination of the chapel's walls last summer revealed ghostly images lying

You can use a similar approach for the Writing Test. Some questions will ask you about the main point, examples, or errors in the passage. To read actively, you should focus on identifying a main point or conclusion (if there is one) and any examples. Some portions of the passage will already be underlined. You will be asked to replace the underlined portion if it contains an error or can be improved, or leave it as-is if it does not need to be changed. It can therefore help to circle or underline the parts of a sentence that seem related to an error, as in the following example.

Example

While he claimed to have a wealth of relevant experience, he had neither served in an elected office nor business management.

A) NO CHANGE

B) even business management

C) even managed a business

D) even the management of a business

The error in this problem is related to "parallel structure." "Neither" and "nor" are a common word pair. These sorts of word pairs are called "correlative conjunctions," but even if you haven't memorized this term, you might still know that they are frequently paired. Underlining important features can help you work out this subtle error; we've circled "neither" and "nor" because they're a common word pair and "nor" comes right before the underlined portion. We've also underlined "served in elected office," because that comes right after "neither." As you read through the answer options, notice that only (C) has the same structure as the part of the sentence following "neither:" a verb and its object.

Some passages will be missing information or have sentences that are in the wrong place in the paragraph. These parts of the passage might sound a little funny to you, so don't be surprised if this happens. If you can identify these types of errors while you're reading, selecting the correct answer choice will be much easier!

In the Math Test, you can use active reading techniques by underlining what the question is asking you to find. This will help you focus on solving the problem rather than being distracted by details.

You can also actively use your pencil by drawing a diagram for questions where no diagram is provided, or where it is labeled as not to scale. Here's an example:

Example

A square and a rectangle have the same perimeter. The square has a length and width of 4 and the rectangle has a length of 5. What is the area of the rectangle?

A) 3 B) 6 C) 15 D) 30

First, draw a diagram of the square and rectangle:

Since the perimeter of the square is $4 \times 4 = 16$, the perimeter of the rectangle is also 16. The perimeter is $2 \times 5 + 2x$, so you can set this expression equal to 16 and solve for x:

$$2 \times 5 + 2x = 16$$

$$10 + 2x = 16$$

$$2x = 6$$

$$x = 3$$

Remember that you are solving for the area, not x! From the diagram, you can calculate the area as $3 \times 5 = 15$, so (C) is the correct answer.

To check this answer, you can use the figures you drew. The area of the rectangle is close to the area of the square. None of the other answer choices are close to 15.

This technique can even be helpful on the Essay. You can use your pencil to mark up ideas or information in the prompt that you wish to analyze in your essay. You'll learn more about this in Chapter 4, Section 3.

Process of Elimination

Sometimes the easiest way to answer a question is by finding the wrong answers. You may have used the Process of Elimination before; it's a great technique to narrow down your possible answer choices.

As you read through the answer choices, don't select an answer on your first read-through. Assess each answer choice one by one. If you know an option is incorrect, knock it out of consideration and strike it through or mark it with an X in your test booklet. If an answer choice seems possible, leave it open to reconsider. Once you have assessed all of the answer choices, compare any that you left open and select the best one. In some cases you may even be able to knock out every answer except for one. In this case, you will have found the correct answer!

Let's look at how this works with an example math problem:

Example

If $y = x^2$ and $-1 < x < 1$, which of the following could be a possible value for y?

A) $-\frac{5}{4}$ B) $-\frac{1}{4}$ C) $\frac{1}{4}$ D) $\frac{5}{4}$

If you think about this equation a bit, you'll see that there are some choices you can eliminate immediately. The equation says that y is the square of x. Think about what happens when you square a positive or negative number—the result is always positive! Therefore, choices (A) and (B) are impossible—if x is a real number, then x^2 can't be a negative number. You can knock out (A) and (B) right away.

A) ~~$\frac{5}{4}$~~ B) ~~$\frac{1}{4}$~~ C) $\frac{1}{4}$ D) $\frac{5}{4}$

Now you're left with (C) and (D). If you're short on time, you could guess and you'd have a 50-50 chance of gaining a point. Or, you could look at the given information again and reason that because x is a fraction greater than -1 and less than 1, x^2 can't be greater than 1. This means that you can eliminate choice (D) as well, leaving you with the correct answer: (C).

You can use this same approach in the Reading and Writing Tests as well. In the Reading Test, you can immediately knock out any answers that contradict information given in the passage. Next, you can knock out any answers that could generally be true, but aren't supported by information in the passage.

On the Writing Test, you can use the Process of Elimination in two ways. First, you should eliminate answer choices that don't correct the error in the underlined section. Then, you should eliminate answer choices that correct the error but introduce new errors. Because the correct answer has to be the *best* version of the underlined portion, any answers that have grammatical or stylistic errors cannot be the correct choice and should be eliminated.

Let's see how the process of elimination can lead to the correct answer in the Writing question below:

Example

The Iron Age and the Middle Ages bookend the classical cultures of Greece and Rome. For over a thousand years, Greek and Roman societies were the center of achievement in the **2** Mediterranean, in fact, the political, philosophical, and scientific roots of our own modern society were formed from Greek and Roman culture.

2

A) NO CHANGE

B) Mediterranean. In fact, the political philosophical and scientific

C) Mediterranean, in fact, the political philosophical and scientific

D) Mediterranean. In fact, the political, philosophical, and scientific

In this example, the original sentence is a run-on sentence, which needs to be divided into two separate sentences (you can read more about run-on sentences in Chapter 3, Section 3). First, eliminate any choices that don't correct this error. You can eliminate choices (A) and (C) because neither of those choices correct the run-on sentence. Only choices (B) and (D) split it into two separate sentences.

You're left with two possible choices that correct the run-on sentence: choices (B) and (D). Now, check to see whether one of these choices introduces new errors. Choice (B) corrects the run-on sentence by adding a period to separate the underlined portion into two sentences. However, choice (B) also takes away the commas between "political, philosophical, and scientific," which the sentences need. Therefore, you can eliminate choice (B) because it introduces a new error. You are now only left with choice (D), which is the correct answer! Choice (D) corrects the original error by separating the sentences without adding any new errors.

Next, take a look at the following Reading example, taken from Teddy Roosevelt's speech "Citizenship in a Republic."

Example

Strange and impressive associations rise in the mind of a man from the New World who speaks before this august body in this ancient institution of learning. Before his eyes pass the shadows of mighty kings and war-like nobles, of great masters of law and theology; through the shining dust of the dead centuries he sees crowded figures that tell of the power and learning and splendor of times gone by; and he sees also the innumerable host of humble students to whom clerkship meant emancipation, to whom it was well-nigh the only outlet from the dark thraldom of the Middle Ages.

3

Roosevelt uses language like "kings," "nobles," and "dead centuries" in order to

A) emphasize the high class of men who make up the institution.

B) call to mind the age and venerability of the university.

C) equate the institution of learning with a medieval castle.

D) flatter the professors and administrators he is addressing.

Here, read the full paragraph in order to understand the context. Based on clues in the text, such as "ancient institution of learning," "masters of law and theology," and "host of humble students," you can conclude that Roosevelt is discussing a school or university. From there, consider why Roosevelt would use language like "kings," "nobles," and "splendor." These references and adjectives are creating a positive description.

Answer choices (A) and (D) can be eliminated, since nowhere does the paragraph indicate that Roosevelt is trying to focus on or flatter the men he is addressing; instead, he is describing the history of the school itself. Choice (C) can also be eliminated as too literal. We are then left with choice (B), which gets to Roosevelt's purpose in including this language—specifically, bringing to mind the long and impressive history of the institution.

Pick and Skip

Working strategically doesn't only apply to individual questions; you should be clever in your approach to each section as a whole. Remember that every question on the SAT is worth one point, no matter how easy or difficult it is. That means it can be to your advantage to work on questions that are easier for you first, and leave more challenging or time-consuming questions for later. If after doing some timed practice you sense you need to improve your speed, you can apply this strategy. However, be sure to use it with caution, as it can increase your chances of making errors when bubbling in your answers.

On the Reading and Writing Tests, you might apply this strategy by first reading passages on topics that are the most interesting or familiar to you. If the first passage to appear doesn't fit this description, move on to other passages and come back later.

You can also attempt the questions for each passage out of order. On the Reading Test, you may answer more specific questions first, especially those that provide line references. As you learn more about the passage by answering these questions, you may feel more confident in answering the general questions about the passage. Citing Textual Evidence questions (discussed further in Chapter 2, Section 4) ask you to provide support for your answer to a previous question, and should thus always be answered after the preceding question.

On the Writing Test, most questions about parts of speech, punctuation, and sentence combination can be answered right after you read the appropriate sentence. When a word or short phrase is underlined in a sentence, you may be able to correct it as you read it. Try to anticipate the correct answer and then compare it to the available revisions.

However, for other questions you'll need to read other sentences in the paragraph to make your answer choice. For example, you may be asked to select the best version of a word to match the author's tone. You may also be asked to add, delete, or move sentences within a paragraph. Wait to answer these questions until after you have read the whole paragraph.

Finally, some questions are related to the passage as a whole. For example, a question may ask you to insert new information to support the passage's main idea or additional evidence to support a conclusion. Wait to answer these questions until after you have read the whole passage.

On the Math Test, you can also do the questions out of order by skipping over those that are the most challenging or time-consuming to complete. If you attempt questions out of order, be sure to circle those you are skipping in your test booklet, so you know to come back to them after. Also remember to guess on every question, in case you don't have time to attempt it later.

As you practice for the SAT, you are bound to figure out the kinds of questions you can answer quickly versus those that take some time, so it will become easier to apply this strategy. If you wish, you can skim through each section and answer the questions you can handle easily first, then move on to the types of questions that you tend to find more difficult or time-consuming. Remember to make a guess and circle any questions that you skip.

Create a Study Schedule

Part 3

To prepare to do your best on test day, you'll need to organize your time leading up to the exam. First, you'll need to assess your strengths and weaknesses in order to figure out *what* to study. Then, you'll need to organize *how* you will study in order to make the best use of your time before your test date.

Identify Your Strengths and Weaknesses

To determine your areas of strength and weakness and to get an idea of which concepts you need to review, work through some practice questions. You can try out the questions for the Reading, Writing, Essay, and Math tests in Chapters 2-5 of this book, or you can take one of the full-length practice tests in Chapter 6.

Then, check your answers against the correct answers. Write down how many questions you missed, and note the topics or types of questions you found most difficult. What was challenging for you? What did you feel good about? Did you get questions wrong because you made an avoidable error, or did you get questions wrong because you did not know how to solve them? Reflecting on these questions will help you determine your individual strengths and weaknesses, and will help you decide what to focus on before your test date.

Plan Your Study Time

After determining your areas of strength and weakness, create a study plan and schedule for your SAT preparation. Work backward from your test date until you arrive at your starting point for studying. The number of weeks you have until your exam will determine how much time you can (and should) devote to your preparation. Make sure you leave enough time to review and practice each concept you'd like to improve—remember, practice is the most important!

To begin, try using this sample study plan as a model for your own personalized study schedule.

My test date is: ______________________.

I have ______ weeks to study. I will make an effort to study ______ minutes/hours every day/week, and I will set aside extra time on ______________________ to take timed sections.

I plan to take ______ full-length tests between now and my test date. I will study for ______ weeks and then take a practice test. My goal for this test is to improve my score in the following specific areas:

____

____

____

____

____

If I do not make this goal, then I will spend more time studying.

Study Schedule

Date	Plan of Study	Time Allotted	Goal Reached?	Further Action
Jan 1	Review 10 vocabulary words and quadratic equations	1 hr	Yes, I know these 10 words and feel comfortable with quadratic equations.	
Jan 3	Review the next 10 vocabulary words and parts of speech	1 hr	I know these 10 words, but I'm still a bit shaky on parts of speech.	I'll review this again tomorrow and ask my English teacher for advice.

Test Day

Part 4

After you've prepared by reviewing and practicing each area you need to improve, you're ready for test day! Here are some tips to make sure you can do your best.

Before the Test

On the night before the test, review only lightly, if at all. You can review a few concepts you find challenging, but don't try to learn anything new. Pick out what you are going to wear to the test—try wearing layers in case the exam room is hotter or colder than you expect. Organize everything you need to bring. Know where the test center is located and how long it will take to get there. Have a nutritious meal and get plenty of sleep!

On the morning of the exam, let your adrenaline kick in naturally. Eat a good breakfast and stay hydrated; your body needs fuel to help you perform. Allow enough time for traveling to the test center, and be sure to follow your admissions ticket for directions on how early you should arrive. Remember to bring the following items with you:

Test Day Checklist

- Admission ticket
- Approved photo ID
- No. 2 pencils and erasers
- Calculator with new batteries and back-up batteries
- Non-beeping watch
- Snack and water bottle
- Directions to the test center and instructions for finding the entrance

Make sure you set your alarm and plan a time to leave that allows for delays. You need to be on time, or you can't take the test!

During the Test

During the test, you cannot overestimate the importance of a positive outlook. You have spent months preparing for the SAT—now it is time to be confident in the work you have done and in the knowledge you have acquired. Stay confident. Trust yourself, your abilities, and all of your preparation. Walk into the test room with every expectation that you will do well.

Stay focused. This is your time to show colleges what you are capable of. Keep your mind on the task at hand, which should be nothing but the question in front of you. If you find your mind wandering, pull your focus back to the test. Don't look around the room to compare your progress to that of your neighbors. Everyone works at their own pace, and you have no idea which particular part of the section your neighbors are working on.

Remember the test-taking strategies that you've practiced. Read and think carefully. Be sure to read each question in its entirety, and consider each answer choice. Work at a good, even pace, and keep moving. Keep an eye on your time throughout each section (and make sure your watch's time matches the proctor's clock). Frequently double check that you are bubbling answers in the correct section of your answer sheet.

Make educated guesses and remember to utilize the 4 Ps and other relevant strategies. Use your test booklet to cross out answers that you know are wrong, work out math problems, and annotate reading passages. Answer the easy questions first, and make a guess for those you're not sure of. Be sure to mark questions where you guessed so that you can quickly turn back to them after you finish all the other questions in the section.

Take a deep breath and remember: you are smart and accomplished! Believe in yourself and you will do well.

After the Test

First things first: give yourself a pat on the back! You have just completed a huge step in your educational career. Take some time to relax and unwind with friends or family.

Your score report should become available to you about two to four weeks after you take the test. This score report will contain your composite score, area scores, test scores, subscores, and cross-test scores. While these scores are important, remember to keep things in perspective. College applications will also entail submitting essays, letters of recommendation, high school grades, an activities list, and more. Even if you feel that your SAT scores are not an accurate reflection of your capabilities, you have many opportunities to shine in the other areas of your applications.

Remember that you can also retake the SAT. After you take the SAT the first time, you can pinpoint which areas you need to practice more. Students often improve their scores after taking the test a second time.

Either way, congratulate yourself on completing this challenge!

Reading

Chapter 2

Section 1

Introduction to the Reading Test

The SAT Reading Test is a test of advanced reading comprehension. You will be given a variety of reading passages, and asked questions about each one. While the passages and questions will be new every time, the structure of the SAT Reading test will always be the same. By learning about it now, you can make sure you will not encounter any surprises on test day!

The Basics

You will have 65 minutes to complete the SAT Reading Test, which is composed of four individual passages and one pair of passages. You will learn more about passage pairs in Section 6. Each passage or pair will be between 500 and 750 words, about one to one and a half pages.

Each passage or pair will have 10 or 11 questions, for a total of 52 questions. There will also be two passages with accompanying graphics in every SAT Reading Test. You will be asked questions about these graphics and how they relate to the passage.

SAT Reading Test by the Numbers

- 65 minutes to complete section
- 4 single passages and 1 passage pair
- 500-750 words per passage or pair for a total of 3250 words
- 10-11 questions per passage or pair for a total of 52 questions
- 2 passages with 1 or more accompanying graphics

Scoring

You will receive several different scores based on your answers on the Reading Test.

You will receive an individual **test score** for Reading, from 10-40. You will also receive an **area score** for Evidence-Based Reading and Writing, which combines your scores from the Reading and Writing Tests. You will receive an Evidence-Based Reading and Writing score from 200-800, making up half of your total **composite score** on the SAT.

Questions from the Reading Test will contribute to two **cross-test scores**, which evaluate your skills in Analysis in History/Social Studies and Analysis in Science by looking at your performance on questions across different sections of the SAT. Your answers on the Reading Test will also contribute to two of your **subscores** on the SAT: Command of Evidence and Words in Context.

Passages

All passages in the SAT Reading Test will come from previously published sources, and may represent a variety of tones and styles. The passages will contain all of the information needed to answer the questions on the test; you will never need to rely on any prior knowledge about the material to answer questions. The chart below shows the specific passage types that you will see in each Reading Test.

Passage Breakdown

Passage Type	Topics	Number of Passages
Literature	Classic and contemporary literature from the United States and around the world	1
History and Social Studies	Topics from history and social studies, including anthropology, communication studies, economics, education, geography, law, linguistics, political science, psychology, and sociology	1
Founding Document or Great Global Conversation	Historically important, foundational texts from the United States (Founding Documents); other historically and culturally important works dealing with issues at the heart of civic and political life (Great Global Conversation)	1
Science	Both basic concepts and recent developments in the natural sciences, including Earth science, biology, chemistry, and physics	2

The passages will not be presented in order of difficulty. As you learned in Chapter 1, you can choose to read them out of order, such as by tackling passages with familiar subjects first.

Questions

The questions associated with the passages will assess whether or not you understand information and ideas in the text, and are able to analyze the author's use of persuasive language and argument. You will also be tested on combining information from the two passages of the passage pair, as well as from passages and their accompanying graphics.

The questions will be presented in a consistent order. However, they are not presented in order of difficulty. You will first be asked more general questions about central ideas, themes, points of view, and the overall text structure. These will be followed by more specific questions about the meaning of a particular word or phrase, or specific evidence that supports a claim. Many of these questions will have line references, which will point you to the material being discussed in the question.

Although you'll see a variety of questions on the Reading Test, two question types will appear with every passage or pair: Words in Context and Command of Evidence questions. Both of these question types will be discussed further in Section 4 of this chapter.

The rest of this chapter will introduce you to all of these concepts in more detail, and will teach you strategies for approaching the passages and correctly answering questions. Reading comprehension is something you can improve with practice, so take your time to work through all of the lessons and exercises in this chapter. You can also improve your reading speed and comprehension by reading every day. You can find a reading list organized by grade and subject matter in the supplementary materials online.

For additional resources, please visit **ivyglobal.com/study**.

Section 2

Approaching the Reading Test

In this section, you'll first learn what to look for in a passage, how to be an active reader, and how to summarize paragraphs to better understand what you read. Then, you'll learn how to read the questions and answer them efficiently and accurately. You'll practice with individual questions, and then have a chance to put everything you've learned into action with full-length practice passages at the end of the section.

Reading a Passage
Part 1

You will encounter different types of passages on the SAT Reading Test, just as you encounter various types of content in your everyday reading. While the different kinds of passages will be explored further in Section 3, the basic strategy for reading a passage will remain the same regardless of its content.

What Makes the SAT Different?

The SAT requires a different kind of reading than what you may do in your everyday life. Normally when you read, you are probably focused on the content of the text, rather than on how an author has organized her writing, or why she chooses certain words.

However, the techniques, evidence, and structure an author uses are all things you are likely to be asked about on the SAT Reading Test. Thus, when you read SAT passages you will need to understand their content and also *how* and *why* the author organized that content in a certain way.

Questions on the SAT Reading Test will go beyond basic comprehension to test how different parts of the passage relate to each other, how the author makes her point or persuades the reader, and the opinions of the author and other people discussed in the passage. If you are already looking for these things as you read, answering the questions will be faster and easier.

Plan Your Approach

1. **Read one at a time.** Read only one passage or pair at a time, and try to answer all the related questions before moving on to the next passage. Switching between passages will make it harder to recall what you have read.
2. **Read the passage introductions.** Read any bolded information at the beginning of a passage. This can include details about the passage such as its author, intended audience, date, topic, and other important information to help you understand the passage.
3. **Pick and Skip.** As you learned in Chapter 1, you are free to answer questions in the order that works best for you. The reading passages are not presented in order of difficulty, so you may choose to read passages that seem easier or more familiar to you first. If you do this, be sure to bubble in your answers on the correct part of your answer sheet!
4. **Read the whole passage**. You may have heard you can avoid reading the full passage by reading just the lines each question asks about. However, not all questions will have line references, and some questions will require you to understand the passage as a whole. You

will answer questions more accurately when you read the entire passage. One exception to this rule is if the five-minute warning has been called or you do not have time to read another passage. In that case, you may look for a question that gives you a line reference, read that portion of the passage, and attempt the question.

Make sure to give yourself time to read the passage and not just skim it! You need to understand the passage to accurately answer questions. A good guideline is to split your time almost equally between reading a passage and answering its questions, with a bit more time devoted to the questions. The chart below offers you some ideas for how to pace yourself. Remember that you have 65 minutes for the entire Reading Test.

Pacing Yourself			
Reading Speed	Minutes Spent Reading Passage	Minutes Spent Answering Questions	Total Minutes Per Passage
Fast	5	8	13
Medium	6	7	13

Mark Up the Passage

On the SAT, you know you will be tested about the content you read, so you want to make an effort to understand as you go, rather than trying to make sense of ideas only once you reach the questions. As you learned in Chapter 1, you can achieve this by using the Pencil on Paper strategy. This will help you to be an **active reader**, by encouraging you to interact with the passages to find and understand the information you will be tested on.

Specifically, the best way to be an active reader is to use your pencil to **mark up** the passage as you read by underlining text, and adding your own notes and symbols to highlight what is important. The goals of marking up the passage are to help you stay focused, understand what you read, and make it easier to find key ideas in the passage when you refer back to it.

Use your pencil to circle or underline two to three **main ideas** per paragraph. Main ideas are those that relate to the **5 w's:** "who," "what," "where," "when," and "why." Stay focused on the bigger picture by making sure the main points you identify help answer the following questions:

1. **Who** is involved in this passage? Look for the people being discussed (artists, scholars, scientists, politicians) or the characters in a literature passage, and think about who might be writing the passage.
2. **What** is being discussed in this passage? Are specific events, theories, or ideas discussed? Look for the major concepts in each section of the passage.

3. **Where** are the events in the passage taking place? This can mean a specific location (one science laboratory) or a general setting (schools in North America).
4. **When** are the events in the passage taking place? It is usually more important to know the order in which things occur than to know specific dates.
5. **Why** is the information in this passage important? How are the ideas in the passage connected, and what is the author's purpose for writing the passage?

Let's look at the first few paragraphs from a reading passage and see how it might look if we mark it up using these ideas.

Example

This passage is adapted from Daniel Zalewski, "Under a Shroud of Kitsch May Lie a Master's Art." ©2001 by The New York Times Company.

<u>Tommaso Strinati</u> clambers to the top of the rickety scaffold and laughs. "It's a good thing that all this <u>Baroque work</u> is so <u>unimpressive</u>," he says, pointing at the clumsy trompe l'oeil painting covering the wall in front of him. "Otherwise, we might not have been allowed to <u>scrape it off</u>!"

A 28-year-old <u>art historian</u>, he is standing 16 feet above the marble floor of San Pasquale Baylon chapel, a long-neglected nook of <u>Santa Maria in Aracoeli</u>, a Franciscan basilica in the center of <u>Rome</u>. Last year, Mr. Strinati, who is still a graduate student, began studying the church's history. <u>Records suggested</u> that the <u>Roman artist Pietro Cavallini</u>—a painter and mosaicist whose greatest works have been destroyed—spent <u>years decorating Aracoeli</u> toward the <u>end of the 13th century. Yet only one</u> small Cavallini <u>fresco</u>, in the church's left transept, remained visible. Mr. Strinati wondered: had other Cavallini frescoes been <u>painted over</u> with inferior work? And if so, could modern restorers uncover them?

"The answer to both questions was yes," Mr. Strinati says. A close-up examination of the chapel's walls last summer revealed ghostly <u>images lying beneath the surface</u>. The entire chapel, it seemed, was a painted palimpsest. And when a heavy altarpiece was removed from one wall, a remarkably <u>tender portrait</u> of the Madonna and Child was <u>found hidden</u> behind it.

Let's see how these key words helped us locate the 5 w's for this passage:

1. **Who** is involved in this passage?
   - The art historian Tommaso Strinati
   - The Roman artist Pietro Cavallini
2. **What** is being discussed in this passage?
   - How Strinati discovered Cavallini frescos that had been painted over
3. **Where** are the events in the passage taking place?
   - Santa Maria in Aracoeli, the basilica in Rome where Cavallini's art was found
4. **When** are the events in the passage taking place?
   - Cavallini painted the frescos at the end of the 13th century

- The passage is written in the present tense and modern English, so we can assume the discovery of the frescos was fairly recent.

5. **Why** is the information in this passage important?
   - The information we underlined in the second paragraph shows a surprising contrast between ideas. If Cavallini spent years painting the basilica, why is there only one fresco? This sets up a bit of a mystery, which Strinati begins to solve in the third paragraph.

Though it can be tempting, don't go overboard with your active reading! If you mark up your entire passage, nothing will stand out as important, and you won't be able to find anything.

Exercise on Marking Up a Passage

Now that you've seen how to mark up a text, practice marking up the rest of the Cavallini passage below. This passage contains a lot of information, but not all of it contributes to the main ideas of the paragraph. Remember to stay focused on the 5 w's! When you are finished, compare your work with the fully marked-up version of this passage in the answer key at the end of the book.

Tommaso Strinati clambers to the top of the rickety scaffold and laughs. "It's a good thing that all this Baroque work is so unimpressive," he says, pointing at the clumsy trompe l'oeil painting covering the wall in front of him. "Otherwise, we might not have been allowed to scrape it off!"

A 28-year-old art historian, he is standing 16 feet above the marble floor of San Pasquale Baylon chapel, a long-neglected nook of Santa Maria in Aracoeli, a Franciscan basilica in the center of Rome. Last year, Mr. Strinati, who is still a graduate student, began studying the church's history. Records suggested that the Roman artist Pietro Cavallini—a painter and mosaicist whose greatest works have been destroyed—spent years decorating Aracoeli toward the end of the 13th century. Yet only one small Cavallini fresco, in the church's left transept, remained visible. Mr. Strinati wondered: had other Cavallini frescoes been painted over with inferior work? And if so, could modern restorers uncover them?

"The answer to both questions was yes," Mr. Strinati says. A close-up examination of the chapel's walls last summer revealed ghostly images lying beneath the surface. The entire chapel, it seemed, was a painted palimpsest. And when a heavy altarpiece was removed from one wall, a remarkably tender portrait of the Madonna and Child was found hidden behind it.

After months of careful paint-peeling, what has been uncovered are dazzling fragments of a late-medieval masterpiece completed shortly after 1285. Although the Aracoeli fresco is not signed, the figures strongly resemble those in a surviving Cavallini work, the resplendent "Last Judgment" fresco at nearby Santa Cecilia.

Mr. Strinati has grand ambitions for his discovery. He hopes that in a few years the fully restored fresco will not only rescue Cavallini's name from obscurity, but also upend the widespread notion that the first flowers of the Renaissance budded in Florence, not Rome. For the fresco's lifelike figures—in particular, an impish Christ child with charmingly flushed cheeks—suggest to Strinati that Cavallini may have anticipated some of the extraordinary naturalistic innovations that have long been credited to the Florentine artist Giotto.

Moreover, the Aracoeli fragments may provide a critical new clue in a decades-old battle concerning the "St. Francis Legend," the 1296 fresco cycle at Assisi, universally recognized as one of the foundations of the Renaissance. For centuries, the 28-scene cycle—which recounts the life of the saint with a narrative zest and compositional depth that leave the flat tableaus of the Byzantine era far behind—was attributed to Giotto. But since the 1930's, various scholars have questioned this judgment, claiming that the Assisi cycle doesn't resemble Giotto's other work. Now, the Aracoeli discovery is ammunition for Italian art historians who believe that Cavallini might actually be the primary creative force behind the "St. Francis Legend."

The growing debate about Cavallini's importance was the occasion for a symposium in Rome in November. *La Republicca*, an Italian daily, has cast the debate as "War Between Rome and Florence." Mr. Strinati is enjoying the ruckus. "I had a hunch that there was more Cavallini lurking around here," he says of the Aracoeli basilica. "But I didn't expect to find an exquisite work that could shake up the history of art."

Summarize

Another good way to be an active reader is to summarize as you read the passage. Summarizing helps ensure that you understand what you read, and that you stay focused throughout the passage rather than "zoning out." This way you can avoid the dreaded feeling of finishing a passage and wondering what you just read!

Summarizing also makes long passages easier to manage. Breaking passages up into smaller pieces to analyze is easier than trying to make sense of the entire passage all at the end.

As you read, make a summary after each paragraph. Use the words you have underlined to help you. Your summaries should be short and snappy and cover only main ideas, not details or specific examples. Try to keep your summaries three to six words long, like a newspaper headline. Summarize in your own words. That helps you to understand the paragraph, and remember key information.

Let's refer back to our passage about Cavallini, and see how we could summarize the main ideas in the second paragraph.

A 28-year-old art historian, he is standing 16 feet above the marble floor of San Pasquale Baylon chapel, a long-neglected nook of Santa Maria in Aracoeli, a Franciscan basilica in the center of Rome. Last year, Mr. Strinati, who is still a graduate student, began studying the church's history. Records suggested that the Roman artist Pietro Cavallini—a painter and mosaicist whose greatest works have been destroyed—spent years decorating Aracoeli toward the end of the 13th century. Yet only one small Cavallini fresco, in the church's left transept, remained visible. Mr. Strinati wondered: had other Cavallini frescoes been painted over with inferior work? And if so, could modern restorers uncover them?

While there is a lot of information in this paragraph, the most important idea is about Cavallini's "missing" art. He reportedly spent a lot of time painting the basilica, so Strinati wonders why there is only one Cavallini fresco. To capture this we might write something as simple as "Seems could be more Cavallini." You might also choose to abbreviate the names of people mentioned in a passage using their initials or something else. So another summary for this paragraph might read "T.S. thinks hidden P.C. frescos."

Exercise on Summarizing

Now that you've seen how to make a good summary, you can practice with the rest of the Cavallini passage. Remember to keep your summaries short! The first three paragraphs have summaries. Write your own summaries for paragraphs four through seven, and compare them to the answer key at the end of this book.

Tommaso Strinati clambers to the top of the rickety scaffold and laughs. "It's a good thing that all this Baroque work is so unimpressive," he says, pointing at the clumsy trompe l'oeil painting covering the wall in front of him. "Otherwise, we might not have been allowed to scrape it off!"

#1 T.S. glad remove Baroque

A 28-year-old art historian, he is standing 16 feet above the marble floor of San Pasquale Baylon chapel, a long-neglected nook of Santa Maria in Aracoeli, a Franciscan basilica in the center of Rome. Last year, Mr. Strinati, who is still a graduate student, began studying the church's history. Records suggested that the Roman artist Pietro Cavallini—a painter and mosaicist whose greatest works have been destroyed—spent years decorating Aracoeli toward the end of the 13th century. Yet only one small Cavallini fresco, in the church's left transept, remained visible. Mr. Strinati wondered: had other Cavallini frescoes been painted over with inferior work? And if so, could modern restorers uncover them?

#2 Continued on next column...

#2 T.S. thinks hidden P.C. frescos

"The answer to both questions was yes," Mr. Strinati says. A close-up examination of the chapel's walls last summer revealed ghostly images lying beneath the surface. The entire chapel, it seemed, was a painted palimpsest. And when a heavy altarpiece was removed from one wall, a remarkably tender

#3 Found P.C. frescoes

portrait of the Madonna and Child was found hidden behind it.

After months of careful paint-peeling, what has been uncovered are dazzling fragments of a late-medieval masterpiece completed shortly after 1285. Although the Aracoeli fresco is not signed, the figures strongly resemble those in a surviving Cavallini work, the resplendent "Last Judgment" fresco at nearby Santa Cecilia.

Mr. Strinati has grand ambitions for his discovery. He hopes that in a few years the fully restored fresco will not only rescue Cavallini's name from obscurity, but also upend the widespread notion that the first flowers of the Renaissance budded in Florence, not Rome. For the fresco's lifelike figures—in particular, an impish Christ child with charmingly flushed cheeks—suggest to Strinati that Cavallini may have anticipated some of the extraordinary naturalistic innovations that have long been credited to the Florentine artist Giotto.

Moreover, the Aracoeli fragments may provide a critical new clue in a decades-old battle concerning the "St. Francis Legend," the 1296 fresco cycle at Assisi, universally recognized as one of the foundations of the Renaissance. For centuries, the 28-scene cycle—which recounts the life of the saint with a narrative zest and compositional depth that leave the flat tableaus of the Byzantine era far behind—was attributed to Giotto. But since the 1930's, various scholars have questioned this judgment, claiming that the Assisi cycle doesn't resemble Giotto's other work. Now, the Aracoeli discovery is ammunition for Italian art historians who believe that Cavallini might actually be the primary creative force behind the "St. Francis Legend."

The growing debate about Cavallini's importance was the occasion for a symposium in Rome in November. *La Republicca*, an Italian daily, has cast the debate as "War Between Rome and Florence." Mr. Strinati is enjoying the ruckus. "I had a hunch that there was more Cavallini lurking around here," he says of the Aracoeli basilica. "But I didn't expect to find an exquisite work that could shake up the history of art."

Part 1 Practice: Reading a Passage

Use your active reading techniques to read and mark up the following passage. Also write a short summary for every paragraph as you read. Use the answer key at the end of this book to check your work.

This passage is adapted from Glenn Hubbard, "The Unemployment Puzzle: Where Have All the Workers Gone?" ©2014 by Dow Jones & Company.

The unemployment rate, the figure that dominates reporting on the economy, is the fraction of the labor force (those working or seeking work) that is unemployed. This rate has declined slowly since the end of the Great Recession. What hasn't recovered over that same period is the labor force participation rate, which today stands roughly where it did in 1977.

Labor force participation rates increased from the mid-1960s through the 1990s, driven by more women entering the workforce, baby boomers entering prime working years in the 1970s and 1980s, and increasing pay for skilled laborers. But over the past decade, these trends have leveled off. At the same time, the participation rate has fallen, particularly in the aftermath of the recession.

In one view, this decline is just a temporary, cyclical result of the Great

Recession. If so, we should expect workers to come back as the economy continues to expand. Some research supports this view. A 2013 study by economists at the Federal Reserve Bank of San Francisco found that states with bigger declines in employment saw bigger declines in labor-force participation. It also found a positive relationship between these variables in past recessions and recoveries.

But structural changes are plainly at work too, based in part on slower-moving demographic factors. A 2012 study by economists at the Federal Reserve Bank of Chicago estimated that about one-quarter of the decline in labor-force participation since the start of the Great Recession can be traced to retirements. Other economists have attributed about half of the drop to the aging of baby boomers.

Reading the Questions

Part 2

You can answer every question on the SAT Reading Test with information from the passage. Don't answer the questions using outside knowledge or opinions. Applying all the strategies you learned for understanding passages is the first step to answering questions quickly and correctly. Keep reading for more strategies to help you conquer reading questions.

Refer Back to the Passage

For every question, the correct answer will be based on something stated explicitly in the passage, or that can be inferred by reading between the lines of the text. Take advantage of the fact that in the SAT Reading Test, you can refer back to the material you are being asked about!

Don't answer the questions by memory alone, and don't rely on your own knowledge or opinion of the subject, which might lead you to the wrong answer. You should always be able to support your answer choice with specific lines or words in the text, even if none are specified in the question.

Some questions use **line references** to indicate which part of the passage they are asking you about. When you are given a line reference, always return to the passage to review that line, as well as two to three lines before and after the one you are asked about. This helps you understand the context of the line in question, and there are often clues there that will help you find the correct answer.

Let's see how this works with a line reference question from the Cavallini passage.

Example

The author mentions "an impish Christ child with charmingly flushed cheeks" (lines 54-55) in order to

A) provide an example of the fresco's lifelike figures.

B) describe Giotto's naturalistic style.

C) rescue Cavallini's name from obscurity.

D) suggest that it could help solve the "St. Francis Legend."

You may not remember this line from the passage, but if you refer back to the text, you can easily answer this question. Here is the paragraph:

> Mr. Strinati has grand ambitions for his discovery. He hopes that in a few years the fully restored fresco will not only rescue Cavallini's name from obscurity, but also upend the widespread notion that the first flowers of the Renaissance budded in Florence, not Rome. For the fresco's lifelike figures—in particular, an impish Christ child with charmingly flushed cheeks—suggest to Strinati that Cavallini may have anticipated some of the extraordinary naturalistic innovations that have long been credited to the Florentine artist Giotto.

If you read the lines referenced and skim the two lines above and below it, you learn that this fresco has particularly lifelike figures and is a good indicator of the naturalistic innovations in Cavallini's work. Thus, only answer choice (A) matches the passage.

The other answer choices are all ideas mentioned at different points of the passage, but not in reference to the painting of the child or in the lines you were asked about. Therefore, you know they do not match and you can eliminate them.

When you answer questions that do not provide line references, you should still refer back to the passage. Because you will have marked up your passage, you will likely know where to find the evidence you need. If a question asks you something general about the passage, you can refer back to the summaries you made while reading, and any notes you made in the margins.

Pick & Skip

Generally, the question set will begin with more general questions on central ideas, tone, and structure, and then move onto more detailed questions that follow the order of the passage. However, just like the passages themselves, the questions will not necessarily be presented in order of difficulty. As you learned in Chapter 1, if you are unsure of the answer to any one question, you can mark it in your test booklet, bubble in your best guess, and come back to it later if you have time.

Part 2 Practice: Reading the Questions

Consider how you will approach the passage and questions below. Think about what strategies you might use if you cannot answer a question. Practice marking up this passage and making paragraph summaries the way you learned to earlier in this section.

This passage is adapted from Robert Lee Hotz, "A Wandering Mind Heads Straight Toward Insight." ©2009 by Dow Jones & Company.

In our fables of science and discovery, the crucial role of insight is a cherished theme. To these epiphanies, we owe the concept of alternating electrical current, the discovery of penicillin, and on a less lofty note, the invention of Post-its, ice-cream cones, and Velcro. The burst of mental clarity can be so powerful that, as legend would have it, Archimedes jumped out of his tub and ran naked through the streets, shouting to his startled neighbors: "Eureka! I've got it."

In today's innovation economy, engineers, economists, and policy makers are eager to foster creative thinking among knowledge workers. Until recently, these sorts of revelations were too elusive for serious scientific study. Scholars suspect the story of Archimedes isn't even entirely true. Lately, though, researchers have been able to document the brain's behavior during Eureka moments by recording brain-wave patterns and imaging the neural circuits that become active as volunteers struggle to solve anagrams, riddles, and other brain teasers.

Following the brain as it rises to a mental challenge, scientists are seeking their own insights into these light-bulb flashes of understanding, but they are as hard to define clinically as they are to study in a lab.

To be sure, we've all had our "aha" moments. They materialize without warning, often through an unconscious shift in mental perspective that can abruptly alter how we perceive a problem. "An 'aha' moment is any sudden comprehension that allows you to see something in a different light," says psychologist John Kounios at Drexel University in Philadelphia. "It could be the solution to a problem; it could be getting a joke; or suddenly recognizing a face. It could be realizing that a friend of yours is not really a friend."

These sudden insights, they found, are the culmination of an intense and complex series of brain states that require more neural resources than methodical reasoning. People who solve problems through insight generate different patterns of brain waves than those who solve problems analytically. "Your brain is really working quite hard before this moment of insight," says psychologist Mark Wheeler at the University of Pittsburgh. "There is a lot going on behind the scenes."

1

Which of the following can be inferred from the passage about anagrams, riddles, and other brain teasers?

A) It is possible to experience insight while solving them.

B) They can only be solved through insight.

C) They are best solved by thinking analytically.

D) They are best solved in a lab setting.

2

The purpose of the first paragraph (lines 1-12) is to

A) highlight the inventions created through insight.

B) introduce the general concept of insight.

C) describe the story of Archimedes.

D) explain the origin of the phrase "Eureka!"

3

As used in line 50, "resources" most nearly means

A) capital.

B) energy.

C) resort.

D) finances.

4

The author quotes John Kounios in order to

A) prove that numerous scientists are studying insight.

B) suggest that research on insight is very basic.

C) offer a definition and examples of insight.

D) demonstrate that people often do not recognize insight.

Selecting Your Answers

Part 3

Now that you have learned how to effectively read passages, you are ready to tackle some different techniques for answering questions. Make sure to always refer back to the passage when selecting your answer choices!

Think for Yourself

One of the best ways to answer reading questions is by **thinking for yourself** rather than relying on the answer choices. Three of the four answer choices will be incorrect, and may be designed to trick you; simply reading them without knowing what you are looking for is not the best strategy. Because you have already done a lot of work to understand the passage, you will likely already be able to figure out how to answer a question without even looking at the answer choices.

Once you read a question, try to come up with your own answer based on the knowledge you gathered when you read the passage. You can refer back to your paragraph summaries, and to the words and ideas you circled and underlined. Then, imagine an answer in your own words. Practice covering up the answer choices to be sure you are coming up with your own answer rather than using the given choices as a crutch.

Let's practice using this technique with a question about the Cavallini passage, which you can refer back to in Part 1 of this Section:

Example
The primary purpose of the passage is to

Based on your summaries and marking of the passage, what do you think it was trying to do? The passage explained how Strinati correctly guessed that Cavallini's work was covered over in the basilica. It then discussed the lost frescos Strinati was able to reveal, and the potentially major implications of Cavallini's work for art history.

We might summarize that as "explaining big artistic finding." Now let's look for an answer choice that matches our prediction.

The primary purpose of the passage is to

A) explain an exciting discovery.

B) describe Cavallini's artistic style.

C) emphasize the importance of art history.

D) discuss Giotto's role in the Renaissance.

Does one answer choice jump out at you right away? Answer choice (A) is almost an exact match with what you predicted! The other options are not focused on the main ideas and purpose of the passage, so you can be confident in ruling them out. Doing the mental work of answering the question in your own words pays off when you can make your choice and gain a point so quickly.

Process of Elimination

If you are unsure of an answer, you may want to use the **Process of Elimination,** which you learned about in Chapter 1. Feel free to review that information to refresh your memory. Because there is only one correct answer for each question, it can be helpful to eliminate the choices you know are wrong.

Make sure you only eliminate answer choices you are certain are wrong, either because they are directly contradicted by the passage, or because there is no information in the passage to support them. You can eliminate answers by crossing them out in your test booklet.

Let's put this to use with a question from the Cavallini passage:

Example

Based on the passage, which choice best describes the relationship between the fresco cycle titled the "St. Francis Legend" and the artist Giotto?

A) The fresco cycle established Giotto as the founder of the Renaissance.

B) Cavallini was originally thought to be the fresco cycle's artist, but many art historians now believe it was Giotto.

C) Giotto was originally thought to be the fresco cycle's artist, but some art historians now believe it was Cavallini.

D) Giotto painted the fresco cycle to capture the story of his life with narrative zest.

Refer back to the sixth paragraph, which discusses the "St. Francis Legend," and compare it to the answer choices to see if they are supported. Here is the sixth paragraph:

> Moreover, the Aracoeli fragments may provide a critical new clue in a decades-old battle concerning the "St. Francis Legend," the 1296 fresco cycle at Assisi, universally recognized as one of the foundations of the Renaissance. For centuries, the 28-scene cycle—which recounts the life of the saint with a narrative zest and compositional depth that leave the flat tableaus of the Byzantine era far behind—was attributed to Giotto. But since the 1930's, various scholars have questioned this judgment, claiming that the Assisi cycle doesn't resemble Giotto's other work. Now, the Aracoeli discovery is ammunition for Italian art historians who believe that Cavallini might actually be the primary creative force behind the "St. Francis Legend."

Answer choice (A) goes too far, as the passage never states that Giotto was the founder of the Renaissance. It only states that the "St. Francis Legend" is a foundational piece of art in the Renaissance, which is not the same. You can knock it out. Answer choice (B) contradicts the passage, which says, "For centuries, the 28-scene cycle … was attributed to Giotto." You can knock it out.

Answer choice (C) matches the passage, so we can keep it open for now. Answer choice (D) contradicts the passage, as the paintings depict the life of St. Francis, not the life of Giotto. You can knock it out, and choose answer choice (C) as your correct response.

The Process of Elimination cannot always help you knock out all the wrong answers, but it is always helpful to have fewer answer choices to consider. Be sure to use it whenever you get stuck!

Best Choices

Remember that every question has only one correct answer. For many questions it will be clear that only one answer relates to the passage, as the others contain information not mentioned in the passage, or contradict information given in the passage.

However, other questions may have more than one answer option that could potentially be true. Remember you are looking for the **best choice**, which means the answer that most directly and completely answers the question, and is most supported by the passage. The best way to ensure that you select the best answer choice is to make sure you can find a word, line, or selection of lines in the text that support your answer.

Here is another example question from the Cavallini passage:

Example

The passage most strongly suggests that the Renaissance

A) began in the 1930s.

B) had roots in neither Rome nor Florence.

C) began in numerous Italian cities simultaneously.

D) featured naturalistic styles of painting.

First, use the Process of Elimination to knock out any answer choices you know are wrong. Both answer choice (A) and answer choice (B) contradict the passage, so you can eliminate them.

Answer choices (C) and (D) do not contradict the passage, so you can now consider each one more closely. Which answer choice has more support from the passage?

While answer choice (C) doesn't contradict the passage, there is nothing in the text to indicate that the Renaissance started in multiple places simultaneously. Remember you cannot use outside information to answer questions, or make assumptions. You must find support for your answers in the passage itself.

On the other hand, you can find specific evidence to support answer choice (D). Lines 56-57 talk about how Cavallini's lifelike figures are evidence that he "may have anticipated some of the extraordinary naturalistic innovations" of the Renaissance. Line 34 also describes a Cavallini portrait as "remarkably tender." While answer choice (C) could potentially be true, answer choice (D) can be proven true by the passage, and is therefore the best choice for this question.

What should you do if it seems that you can support two separate answer choices with information from the passage? First, make sure that the evidence supports the answer choice in the way you think it does. For example, some answer choices may use the same words as the passage, but in a way that means something different than the original text.

Second, for questions that ask what you can infer about the passage by reading between the lines, be sure to look for the most likely, or plausible, conclusion you can reach. Try to make as few leaps between ideas as possible. If your answer choice feels like a stretch, requires making a lot of assumptions, or relies on information or ideas not found in the text, it is likely incorrect. Avoid using your outside knowledge and stick to what is on the page.

Finally, if you really can't decide between options, it's okay to make your best guess and move on.

Part 3 Practice: Selecting Your Answers

Practice marking up this passage and making paragraph summaries the way you learned earlier in this section.

This passage is adapted from Nina Teicholz, "The Questionable Link Between Saturated Fat and Heart Disease." ©2014 by Dow Jones & Company.

After the AHA[1] advised the public to eat less saturated fat and switch to vegetable oils for a "healthy heart" in 1961, Americans changed their diets. Now these oils represent 7% to 8% of all calories in our diet, up from nearly zero in 1900, the biggest increase in consumption of any type of food over the past century.

This shift seemed like a good idea at the time, but it brought many potential health problems in its wake. In those early clinical trials, people on diets high in vegetable oil were found to suffer higher rates not only of cancer but also of gallstones. And, strikingly, they were more likely to die from violent accidents and suicides. Alarmed by these findings, the National Institutes of Health convened researchers several times in the early 1980s to try to explain these "side effects," but they couldn't. (Experts now speculate that certain psychological problems might be related to changes in brain chemistry caused by diet, such as fatty-acid imbalances or the depletion of cholesterol.)

We've also known since the 1940s that when heated, vegetable oils create oxidation products that, in experiments on animals, lead to cirrhosis of the liver and early death. For these reasons, some midcentury chemists warned against the consumption of these oils, but their concerns were allayed by a chemical fix: oils could be rendered more stable through a process called hydrogenation, which used a catalyst to turn them from oils into solids.

From the 1950s on, these hardened oils became the backbone of the entire food industry, used in cakes, cookies, chips, breads, frostings, fillings, and frozen and fried food. Unfortunately, hydrogenation also produced trans fats, which since the 1970s have been suspected of interfering with basic cellular functioning and were recently condemned by the Food and Drug Administration for their ability to raise our levels of "bad" LDL cholesterol.

Yet paradoxically, the drive to get rid of trans fats has led some restaurants and food manufacturers to return to using regular liquid oils—with the same long-standing oxidation problems. These dangers are especially acute in restaurant fryers, where the oils are heated to high temperatures over long periods.

[1]The American Heart Association

Think about the primary purpose of this passage, and try to put it in your own words. Consider the author's tone. If you can, analyze the individual parts of the passage and try to figure out why the author included certain bits of information. For example, in lines 41-43, the author lists the types of foods that use hydrogenated oils in order to demonstrate how widespread the use of hardened hydrogenated oils has become.

For the following questions:

- Note which answers you can eliminate using the Process of Elimination, and why you know they are wrong.
- Note why the answer you selected is the best one, using words and lines from the passage to support your answer choice.

1

The author of the passage would probably agree with which of the following statements?

A) While trans fats are unhealthy, they are preferable to saturated fats.

B) Using large amounts of vegetable oil is safe as long as the oil is not hydrogenated.

C) Americans' attempt to avoid saturated fats has had unhealthy consequences.

D) The process of hydrogenation eliminates the only problem with vegetable oils.

2

It can reasonably be inferred from the passage that it is best to consume vegetable oils

A) in regular liquid form, in large quantities.

B) in regular liquid form, lightly heated.

C) in solid form after hydrogenation.

D) in small amounts or not at all.

3

Which of the following situations is most analogous to the problem presented in the passage?

A) Drivers are advised to avoid a certain highway because it has a lot of traffic, but the other road they take is backed up because of an accident.

B) Doctors prescribe an effective medicine for an illness, although it causes side effects for a small percentage of patients.

C) Shoppers frequent a local grocer, but when it closes they are forced to buy food at a more expensive market.

D) Farmers have a problem with frequent pests, but when they use a new harvesting technique fewer crops are eaten by insects.

Practice Set

Part 4

This passage is adapted from Richard Halloran, "Tapping Ocean's Cold For Crops." ©1990 by The New York Times Company.

On a wind-swept point of black lava jutting into the Pacific Ocean, a small band of scientists and entrepreneurs is generating electricity, raising lobsters, and growing strawberries using cold water from the depths of the sea. Eventually, they say, they hope the techniques they are devising here may increase food supplies and produce energy without pollution and without the use of fossil fuels. For now, however, "cold water is the resource we're selling," said Thomas H. Daniel, technical director of the Natural Energy Laboratory of Hawaii, where the projects are under way.

That water, pumped from a depth of 2,000 feet, comes up at a nearly constant temperature of 6 degrees Celsius, or 43 degrees Fahrenheit. It has a high concentration of nutrients like nitrates, phosphates, and silicates that foster the growth of plants and algae. And it is pure, having been out of contact with the surface for centuries as it drifted slowly along the bottom, and thus is free of the pathogens that carry diseases.

When the laboratory began the project about 10 years ago, scientists here were confident it would be possible to put the water to profitable use. While profits have so far been elusive, the researchers have demonstrated the feasibility of several ideas, solved formidable engineering problems, and produced a wealth of data.

The lab, which operates on a budget of $1.5 million a year and has a staff of 20, began by seeking to use the differences in temperature between surface and deep sea water to produce electricity in a process called ocean thermal energy conversion. But it is the other projects developed on this 322-acre site that seem more promising today: growing lobsters in half the time it takes in their natural habitat along the coast of Maine; raising flounder, sea urchins, and salmon; distilling fresh water and cooling buildings and industrial plants.

Next to the energy lab is the Hawaii Ocean Science and Technology park, a 547-acre site set aside by the state for commercial development of the laboratory's findings. Once a project developed at the lab becomes profitable, it must move out, either to the park or elsewhere. Aquaculture Enterprises has already moved to the park. The company has been experimenting since 1987 with lobsters and has begun test sales locally. The lobsters are raised in shallow tanks under green tents that block the heat of the sun. They are kept in separate pans so they will not eat each other. Joseph Wilson, a partner in the enterprise, said that by mixing cold and warm sea water to maintain a steady temperature of 22 degrees Celsius, researchers have eliminated the near-hibernation of the lobsters in winter. That has cut growing time to less than four years from the seven and a half years it takes in nature. As they learn more about the lobsters' environment, nutrition, and genetics, he said, "we think that could be cut again to 30 months." But the cold water also finds uses on land. Run through pipes the energy laboratory has laid in strawberry, lettuce, and flower beds, the cold water keeps the plants at the cool temperature they like and causes fresh water to condense on the pipes. The fresh water drips from the pipes to water the plants. "When we want the strawberries to think it's winter," Mr. Daniel said, standing under a tropical sun, "we just run the cold water faster." Strawberries with five times more sugar than those in nature have been produced.

1

This passage is primarily concerned with

A) describing a new alternative source of energy.

B) advocating alternatives to fossil fuels.

C) discussing new applications of a natural resource.

D) explaining the challenges of food production.

2

The purpose of the second paragraph (lines 15-25) is to

A) describe the beneficial properties of cold ocean water.

B) explain how nitrates, phosphates, and silicates foster plant and algae growth.

C) convey the author's interest in the numerous uses of cold ocean water.

D) explore the process used to move cold water up to the ocean surface.

3

Based on the passage, which choice best describes the relationship between the electricity and food production projects involving cold ocean water?

A) The food production projects are more successful than the electricity project.

B) The food production projects are less profitable than the electricity project.

C) The food production projects depend on the electricity projects.

D) The food production projects undermine the electricity projects.

4

Which choice provides the best evidence for the answer to the previous question?

A) Lines 6-10 ("Eventually … fossil fuels")

B) Lines 26-29 ("When … profitable use")

C) Lines 39-41 ("But it … today")

D) Lines 56-58 ("The lobsters … sun")

5

As used in line 33, "wealth" most nearly means

A) investment.

B) fortune.

C) means.

D) abundance.

6

As used in line 75, "condense" most nearly means

A) compress.

B) squeeze.

C) form.

D) consolidate.

7

Based on the passage, the interviewed scientists' attitude toward their current agriculture projects could best be described as

A) optimistic.

B) contemptuous.

C) skeptical.

D) disappointed.

8

Which choice provides the best evidence for the answer to the previous question?

A) Lines 29-33 ("While profits … data")

B) Lines 54-56 ("The company … locally")

C) Lines 60-64 ("Joseph Wilson … winter")

D) Lines 67-70 ("As they … months")

9

According to the passage, the growing time for lobsters can be reduced by

A) eliminating cold temperatures to prevent their near-hibernation.

B) preventing them from eating one another.

C) running cool water over them at a faster rate.

D) providing them with a high concentration of nutrients like nitrates.

10

What is the most likely reason the author describes Mr. Daniel as "standing under a tropical sun" (lines 78-79)?

A) To contrast the local weather with the cold conditions created for the strawberries

B) To give the reader a sense of place through vivid description

C) To indicate that tropical locations are the usual growing region for strawberries

D) To suggest that the local weather could pose a threat to the success of the strawberry crop

This passage is adapted from Sir Arthur Conan Doyle, *A Study in Scarlet*, originally published in 1887. Here, the narrator, Dr. John Watson, describes the detective Sherlock Holmes.

His very person and appearance were such as to strike the attention of the most casual observer. In height he was rather over six feet, and so excessively lean that he seemed to be considerably taller. His eyes were sharp and piercing, save during those intervals of torpor to which I have alluded; and his thin, hawk-like nose gave his whole expression an air of alertness and decision. His chin, too, had the prominence and squareness which mark the man of determination. His hands were invariably blotted with ink and stained with chemicals, yet he was possessed of extraordinary delicacy of touch, as I frequently had occasion to observe when I watched him manipulating his fragile philosophical instruments.

The reader may set me down as a hopeless busybody, when I confess how much this man stimulated my curiosity, and how often I endeavoured to break through the reticence which he showed on all that concerned himself. Before pronouncing judgment, however, be it remembered, how objectless was my life, and how little there was to engage my attention. My health forbade me from venturing out unless the weather was exceptionally genial, and I had no friends who would call upon me and break the monotony of my daily existence. Under these circumstances, I eagerly hailed the little mystery which hung around my companion, and spent much of my time in endeavouring to unravel it.

He was not studying medicine. He had himself, in reply to a question, confirmed Stamford's opinion upon that world. Yet his zeal for certain studies was remarkable, and within eccentric limits his knowledge was so extraordinarily ample and minute that his observations have fairly astounded me. Surely no man would work so hard or attain such precise information unless he had some definite end in view. Casual readers are seldom remarkable for the exactness of their learning. No man burdens his mind with small matters unless he has some very good reason for doing so.

His ignorance was as remarkable as his knowledge. Of contemporary literature, philosophy and politics he appeared to know next to nothing. Upon my quoting Thomas Carlyle, he inquired in the naivest way who he might be and what he had done. My surprise reached a climax, however, when I found incidentally that he was ignorant of the Copernican Theory and of the composition of the Solar System. That any civilized human being in this nineteenth century should not be aware that the earth travelled round the sun appeared to be to me such an extraordinary fact that I could hardly realize it.

"You appear to be astonished," he said, smiling at my expression of surprise. "Now that I do know it I shall do my best to forget it."

"To forget it!"

"You see," he explained, "I consider that a man's brain originally is like a little empty attic, and you have to stock it with such furniture as you choose. A fool takes in all the lumber of every sort that he comes across, so that the knowledge which might be useful to him gets crowded out, or at best is jumbled up with a lot of other things so that he has a difficulty in laying his hands upon it. Now the skillful workman is very careful indeed as to what he takes into his brain-attic. He will have nothing but the tools which may help him in doing his work, all in the most perfect order. It is a mistake to think that that little room has elastic walls and can distend to any extent. There comes a time when for every addition of knowledge you forget something that you knew before. It is of the highest importance, therefore, not to have useless facts elbowing out the useful ones."

"But the Solar System!" I protested.

"What the deuce is it to me?" he interrupted impatiently; "you say that we go round the sun. If we went round the moon it would not make a pennyworth of difference to me or to my work."

11

Watson's attitude toward Sherlock in the passage is best described as

A) impatient.

B) disdainful.

C) adoring.

D) fascinated.

12

Which choice provides the best evidence for the answer to the previous question?

A) Lines 19-24 ("The reader … himself")

B) Lines 36-38 ("He had … world")

C) Lines 43-45 ("Surely … in view")

D) Lines 59-63 ("That any … it")

13

The primary purpose of the first paragraph (lines 1-18) is to

A) provide a description of Sherlock.

B) explain why Watson is interested in Sherlock's strange mannerisms.

C) describe Sherlock's delicacy in using his instruments.

D) introduce the tools Sherlock uses to solve mysteries.

14

Watson sees a surprising contrast between

A) Sherlock's expertise in some subjects and unfamiliarity with others.

B) his impression of Sherlock and Sherlock's attitude toward him.

C) Sherlock's motivations and enthusiasm for learning.

D) his own intellect and that of Sherlock.

15

Which choice provides the best evidence for the answer to the previous question?

A) Lines 1-3 ("His … casual observer")

B) Lines 47-49 ("No … doing so")

C) Lines 50-51 ("His ignorance … knowledge")

D) Lines 53-55 ("Upon my … done")

16

As used in line 17, "manipulating" most nearly means

A) exploiting.

B) tricking.

C) tampering.

D) handling.

17

The second paragraph (lines 19-35) suggests that Watson feels his interest in Sherlock is

A) understandable, but something for which he may be judged.

B) routine, but something that he indulges too frequently.

C) embarrassing, as it fails to break the monotony of his existence.

D) acceptable, as it allows him to unravel the mystery surrounding the detective.

18

As used in line 24, "pronouncing" most nearly means

A) uttering.

B) passing.

C) reciting.

D) declaring.

19

Once Watson learns Sherlock is unfamiliar with the Solar System, he

A) mocks him for his lack of education.

B) explains the concept to him.

C) asks Sherlock about his opinion on human memory.

D) decides it is not as important as he originally thought.

20

Which hypothetical situation involves the same form of expertise demonstrated by Sherlock?

A) A librarian is familiar with all types of media, both modern and antiquated.

B) A highly accomplished classical musician can play few other types of music.

C) A carpenter works with numerous types of wood but prefers one.

D) A new art student has been studying theory but has not yet created anything.

21

According to the passage, Sherlock believes the brain is like an attic because

A) a room can only hold so many items, similar to how human memory is not unlimited.

B) the human brain cannot grow, similar to how the walls of a room cannot be extended.

C) a person cannot store endless memories, similar to how a skillful workman carefully chooses his projects.

D) a cluttered mind makes it difficult to recall important information, similar to how a crowded room can become dangerous.

Section 3

SAT Passage Types

Now that we've outlined the basic strategies that you'll use to approach the Reading section, let's talk about the passages. In this section, we'll show you how to approach each type of SAT passage. You'll learn what types of passages you will see, what to expect in each type of passage, and how to apply the skills we've already reviewed to each type of passage.

As you saw in Section 1 of this chapter, there are five passages in the Reading section. These passages fall into three domains: one passage will be in the Literature domain, two will be in the Science domain, and two will be in the History/Social Studies domain.

There are also a couple of special passage types: passages with graphics (like charts, graphs, or diagrams), and passage pairs. One of the two Science passages will include a graphic, and one of the two History/Social Studies passages will include a graphic. One passage will actually be a set of two shorter, paired passages.

In this section we're going to highlight some important elements that you'll want to keep an eye out for in each type of passage. Then, we'll give you a chance to practice your skills.

Literature Passages

Part 1

There is one Literature passage in the Reading section of the SAT. It will usually be an excerpt from a novel or short story. Sometimes it will be taken from a recently published source, and other times it may be taken from an older source. Passages from older sources might contain some phrases that you're not familiar with, but most of the language will be understandable to modern readers. Literature passages will never include graphics, and will not be presented as passage pairs.

Literature passages will usually tell a story, or describe a scene, object, or character—often with an underlying message that is implied rather than stated directly. With Literature passages, your goals are to follow the details of what is actually being described, to try to understand any underlying message of the passage, and to pay attention to how the author uses language and literary techniques to convey that message. The tips that follow will help you put Pencil on Paper and use your active reading skills to accomplish those goals.

You won't be tested on your knowledge about specific works, but you will need to be comfortable reading various types of literature. The best way to increase your familiarity with literature is to read it; once you've finished the practice exercises in this book, go online to see our reading list with recommended literature passages listed by grade.

For additional resources, please visit **ivyglobal.com/study**.

Important Details in Literature Passages

As we mentioned in Section 2, you should pay special attention to important details in a passage as you're reading it. Which details are the most important will depend largely on what type of passage you're reading. The following are important elements to keep in mind when reading Literature passages.

Figurative Language

Literature passages often contain **figurative language**, which is language that's used in some creative or unusual way. Figurative language often doesn't mean exactly what it says, but instead has a second meaning. The SAT will often ask you to interpret specific pieces of figurative language, or to analyze how they affect the passage or why the author chose to use them.

There are five basic kinds of figurative language:

Types of Figurative Language		
Hyperbole	Hyperbole is language that involves major exaggeration.	I ate about ten tons of candy last Halloween.
Idioms	An idiom is a phrase that has meaning beyond what the words themselves mean (although it might also be literally true).	That's not exactly brain surgery.
Personification	Personification is language that ascribes human characteristics, like personality traits, intentions, or human-like actions, to non-human things.	As we approached the mouth of the cavern, it belched out a noxious breath, and its foul exhalation warned of a deadly distaste for intruders.
Metaphor	Metaphor is language that uses one thing to represent another thing or an idea, especially when they aren't very much alike.	Luke was adrift on a sea of opportunities, with no current to direct his course.
Simile	A simile is language that compares two things of different kinds, using the words "like" or "as."	With the children finally all away at school, Sally's home was as vast and empty as a starless sky.

Correctly identifying figurative language can give you a lot of insight into the meaning of a story. You won't need to categorize these elements in order to understand the story, but you will need to analyze how they're being used in the passage—so pay attention to them, and to the effect that they have in the passage.

Take a look at the following example:

Example

This passage is adapted from Tom Gallon, *Tinman*, originally published in 1907.

In all that I shall set down here, in telling the strange story of my poor life, I shall write nothing but the truth. It has been written in many odd times and in many odd places: in a prison cell, on paper stamped with the prison mark; on odd scraps of paper in a lonely garret under the stars, with a candle-end for light—and I, poor and old and shivering—scrawling hastily because the time was so short. I have been at once the meanest and the greatest of all men; the meanest—because all men shuddered at the mere mention of my name, and at the thought of what I had done; the greatest—because one woman loved me, and taught me that beyond that nothing else mattered. I have lived in God's sunlight, and in the sunlight of her eyes; I have gone down into the Valley of the Shadow of Death, and have not been afraid; I have been caged like a wild beast, until I forgot the world, just as the world forgot me. In a mere matter of the counting of years I am but little past forty years of age; yet I am an old man, and I have lived two lives—just as, when my time comes, I shall have died two deaths. I have

The author uses metaphors here to represent a state of being.

Here, the author uses a simile, which can be spotted with the clue word *like*.

The author here uses personification to attribute human characteristics, such as lips and hands, to Love and Misery.

touched the warm lips of Love; I have clasped the gaunt hands of Misery. I have warmed both hands at the fire of Life; but now the fire has gone out, and only the cold grey ashes remain. But of all that you may read, just as I have written it, and as the memory of it has come back to me. Roll up the curtain—and see me as I was—and judge me lightly.

Here, the author includes an idiom as the narrator invites readers to look more deeply into his life.

What sorts of figurative language does the author use in this passage? You might note that he uses similes such as "I have been caged like a wild beast" and personification such as "the warm lips of Love" and "the gaunt hands of Misery." Consider the author's purpose in using this language. How does it set the scene or provide insight into the narrator's character? Here, you will notice that the narrator is using such description to set the scene and convey the highs and lows of his own life.

Characterization

The people in stories, plays, and novels are characters. **Characterization** is the process where the author gives the reader new information about the characters.

Writers can use a number of techniques for characterization. Here are some of the big ones:

Techniques for Characterization		
Type	Definition	Example
Description	An author might use physical details to suggest something about the character's life or personality.	She wore an expensive business suit, diamond earrings, and an elegant gold watch.
Dialogue	The style or content of a character's speech can reveal what the character believes or how he feels.	He stammered, "W-would you, um, I mean, would you like to maybe, uh, go out with me sometime?"
Action	The way an author describes a character's actions can tell you more than just what the character is doing.	As the time drew closer to her audition, she reviewed her script over and over, biting her nails.
Internal Speech	An author might state or paraphrase a character's inner monologue to let the reader know what the character is thinking.	She smiled and thanked her boss, privately thinking that she was looking forward to the day she never had to see his smug face again.
Responses	The way other characters respond to someone can give you clues about that character's situation.	When he walked into the guidance counselor's office, the secretary raised an eyebrow and said, "Again?"

Paying attention to how the author uses these techniques will help you to answer questions about characters and their relationships, and about the author's purpose. Keep an eye out for characterization, and pay attention to how it shapes individual characters, their relationships to one another, and their role in the story.

Let's look at another excerpt from the story *Tinman*. Take a look at the following portion, when the narrator goes to meet his guardian.

This passage is adapted from Tom Gallon, *Tinman*, originally published in 1907.

I was beginning to feel uncomfortable when at last he dropped the paper-knife, and stood up to shake hands with me. "So you are Charles Avaline?" he said. "I'm glad to see you. How old are you? I forget times and dates."

"I shall be twenty in a month," I replied, "but I feel much older."

"Most people do at your age," he retorted. "Well—there are certain arrangements to be made about your future—your income, and so on"—he was looking down at the desk, and shifting some papers about uneasily there—"and perhaps it would be better if you came round to my rooms to-night to see me. I've got an old-fashioned place in Bloomsbury; perhaps you'll dine with me there. I'll write the address down for you; seven sharp, please."

Now, take a look at the following question:

Fxample

Based on the passage, it can best be concluded that the narrator's guardian is

A) thrilled to finally meet his charge.
B) disappointed by the narrator's greed.
C) surprised by the narrator's young age.
D) apprehensive about news he has to deliver.

How would you go about answering this question? The passage does not directly state that the guardian is thrilled, disappointed, surprised, or apprehensive. Instead, it is important to pay attention to the different techniques for characterization employed by the author in order to draw a conclusion. Here, the guardian's dialogue and responses provide insight into his attitude. He mentions "certain arrangements to be made" about the narrator's future before "shifting some papers about uneasily," suggesting that he needs to have an uncomfortable conversation with the narrator. Thus, answer choice (D) is best supported by the passage.

As you continue to read and practice with a variety of sources, you'll become an expert at recognizing these techniques.

The Structure of a Literature Passage

As you read the passage, you should pay attention to how it's structured, meaning the focus of different parts of the passage and how they fit together.

Some Literature passages will be mostly narrative, which means that they focus on telling a story. A narrative passage describes events that happen in a certain order. Others will be mostly **descriptive**, which means that they focus on describing an important person, place, or thing in detail. For example, the excerpt of *Tinman* above, showing the meeting between the narrator and his guardian, is mostly narrative, while the first excerpt of *Tinman*, a broader paragraph about the narrator's life, is mostly descriptive.

Many of the passages you encounter will mix some narrative and descriptive elements. In these passages, the two kinds of elements are usually intended to support one another. Descriptive elements in a narrative passage often provide additional details about an important figure in the story, while narrative elements in a descriptive passage often help characterize the subject that the passage is describing.

Part 1 Practice: Literature Passages

Below is an example passage. Read the passage, paying special attention to the elements we have discussed, and then answer the accompanying practice questions.

This passage is adapted from Jerome K. Jerome, *Three Men in a Boat (to Say Nothing of the Dog)*. Originally published in 1889.

We were planning supplies for our trip. George said:

"Begin with breakfast." (George is so practical.) "Now for breakfast we shall want a frying-pan"—(Harris said it was indigestible; but we merely urged him not to be a fool, and George went on)—"a tea-pot and a kettle, and an ethanol stove.

"No oil," said George, with a significant look; and Harris and I agreed. We had taken an oil-stove on a boat trip once, but "never again."

It had been like living in an oil-shop that week. It oozed. I never saw another thing ooze like kerosene oil. We kept it in the nose of the boat, and, from there, it oozed down to the rudder, impregnating the whole boat and everything in it on its way, and it oozed over the river, and saturated the scenery and spoilt the atmosphere. Sometimes a westerly oily wind blew, and at other times an easterly oily wind, and sometimes it blew a northerly oily wind, and maybe a southerly oily wind; but whether it came for the Arctic snows, or was raised in the waste of the desert sands, it came alike to us laden with the fragrance of kerosene oil. And that oil oozed up and ruined the sunset; and as for the moonbeams, they positively reeked of kerosene.

We tried to get away from it at Marlow. We left the boat by the bridge, and took a walk through the town to escape it, but it followed us. The whole town was full of oil. We passed through the church-yard, and it seemed as if the people had been buried in oil. The High Street stunk of oil; we wondered how people could live in it. And we walked miles upon miles out Birmingham way; but it was no use, the country was steeped in oil.

At the end of that trip we met together at midnight in a lonely field, under a blasted oak, and took an awful oath (we had been swearing for a whole week about the thing in an ordinary, middle-class way, but this was a swell affair)—an awful oath never to take kerosene oil with us in a boat again.

And so for this trip, we confined ourselves to an ethanol stove. Even that is bad enough. You get ethanol pie and ethanol cake. But ethanol is more wholesome than kerosene, and much less persistent.

1

The main purpose of this passage can best be described as

A) suggesting that planning an adventure might be more fun than going on one.

B) telling the story of how a group of friends learned from a past mistake.

C) describing the process of planning and preparing to go on a trip.

D) explaining why it is important to avoid using certain types of fuel in enclosed spaces.

2

Based on the passage, we can most reasonably infer that Harris, George, and the narrator are

A) recent acquaintances planning a trip to get to know one another.

B) traveling companions who first met during an unfortunate journey by boat.

C) seasoned adventurers who regularly travel great distances.

D) old friends planning a trip similar to one they had taken before.

3

The author's purpose in describing how the oil affected the sunset and moonbeams (lines 30-33) is mainly to

A) describe the widespread pollution that the boys encountered as they travelled down the river.

B) contrast the environment of the boat with the lonely field the boys would visit later.

C) suggest that the smell of kerosene was so overwhelming that it tainted every other experience.

D) relate the specific event that finally persuaded the friends never to bring kerosene again.

Science Passages

Part 2

There are two Science passages in the SAT Reading Test. The Science passages you encounter on the SAT will usually come from magazines, newspapers, or non-fiction books on popular science. Science passages will almost always be from contemporary sources, which means they're current science. Science passages will be about natural or physical sciences—physics, biology, astronomy, chemistry, or similar fields.

You won't be tested on your knowledge of science, but you will have to be comfortable reading passages that use scientific language. Check out our reading list online for some recommended reading in science, including sources that will help familiarize you with this type of writing.

For additional resources, please visit **ivyglobal.com/study**.

One of the Science passages will include one or two graphics, which we cover in Part 4 of this chapter. One of the Science passages might actually be a passage pair, which we cover in Part 5.

With Science passages, your goal is to identify the main topic or argument, and understand how the additional information and evidence provided explains the topic or supports the argument. The tips that follow will help you to accomplish that goal.

Important Details in Science Passages

Science passages will focus on communicating specific facts, either to help the reader understand a broader topic or to build an argument in support of the author's opinion on a scientific issue. You need to pay special attention to data and experimental evidence, and to the elements of the argument presented in a passage.

Elements of an Argument

Often, Science passages build an argument that shows, using evidence and logic, why the author believes that some basic idea is true.

Keep an eye out for all of the following elements of an argument in Science passages:

Elements of an Argument	
Category	**Definition**
Thesis	The main idea that the author is defending with her argument. There may be a sentence near the beginning that clearly states the thesis. However, there may not be one; be careful not to assume that whatever idea is mentioned earliest is the thesis. Look instead for the idea that the passage as a whole supports.
Claims	Claims are statements that the author says are true, or that we know she wants us to believe are true based on the surrounding context.
Supporting Evidence	Supporting evidence is the information that an author provides to back up her claims. It can take the form of data from studies, quotes from experts, historical examples, or other claims or facts that you might already agree with.
Counterclaims and Refutations	Counterclaims are claims that disagree with or contradict claims made elsewhere in the passage, and refutations are statements intended to disprove other statements.
Conclusion	Persuasive passages often end with a concluding statement that restates the thesis. This is more than just repetition; the concluding statement is usually stronger than the thesis statement, and often includes a summary of the evidence presented in the text.

Below is an example. Read the passage, paying special attention to the elements we have discussed:

Example

Europa, a moon of Jupiter, is the place where we are most likely to find extraterrestrial life in our own solar system. Liquid water is widely considered to be one of the most important preconditions for life, and there are likely vast oceans of liquid water beneath Europa's surface. Certain organic chemicals are also considered necessary precursors for life, and we have reason to believe that natural processes on Europa's surface create them in abundance.

Given that sunlight is the main source of energy for life on Earth, it may seem that Europa's thick icy crust, which prevents any sunlight from reaching the ocean, would make life on the moon impossible. But there is an alternative source of energy on Europa: tidal flexing, a process in which gravitational tugs cause Europa's oceans to slosh about, generating heat and energy.

With its suitable environment, and sources of the chemicals and energy necessary for life, it would be more surprising to find that Europa was barren than to discover life beneath its crust.

The first paragraph begins with a clear statement of the thesis. It proceeds to offer a couple of pieces of supporting evidence. The second paragraph then raises a counterclaim, but only for the purpose of refuting it. Finally, the third paragraph concludes with a summary of the evidence and a restatement of the thesis.

Reading about Experiments

Science passages will often discuss specific experiments. Sometimes details about an experiment may be offered as supporting evidence, and other times an experiment may be the main subject of the passage. To be sure that you understand Science passages, you should make sure that you're familiar with some basic facts about how experiments are conducted and what they mean.

The Basic Idea

Experiments measure one thing: the interaction between cause and effect. Experiments measure whether a change in one thing causes a change in another, and what kind of change occurs.

To start, scientists identify the **variables**—things or circumstances which might change or can be changed—that might have some influence on the relationship they want to test. You can get a good idea of what any experiment is about by paying attention to just two pieces of information: which variables the scientists *change* (independent variables), and which they *measure* (dependent variables).

There may also be a **control variable**. This is a variable that will be left unchanged, so that scientists can be sure it is not affecting their results, or so they can compare it to a variable that has been manipulated.

Experiments are designed to measure the effect of the variable that scientists change on the variable that they measure. Let's look at an example:

Example

Using timed growth lights, scientists provided 12 hours of light to plants in Group 1 and 4 hours of light to plants in Group 2. Scientists controlled for the effects of nutrition and hydration by using identical soil sources and equal amounts of water and fertilizer to all plants. Growth was measured by periodically recording the height and leaf size of plants, and weighing the pots.

We can see that the variable that changed (independent variable) was the amount of light plants received, and the variable that was measured (dependent variable) was growth. By looking at which variable scientists changed and which they measured, we can conclude that the experiment was designed to measure the effect of light exposure on plant growth. We can also tell that scientists were *not* interested in measuring the effects of hydration or nutrition; the use of "controlled" indicates that soil type, water, and fertilizer are all control variables.

Drawing Conclusions

Whether a passage describes an experiment in detail or only talks about the results of an experiment, there are some important things to keep in mind when drawing conclusions from experimental evidence.

Experiments only demonstrate very specific relationships. You can make some inferences about what else an experiment *suggests*, and what other ideas an experiment *supports*, but not what is *demonstrated* beyond the very specific relationship tested. This relationship will be between the independent variable—what is changed or manipulated—and the dependent variable, or what is measured.

Summarizing a Science Passage

Just as Literature passages could be divided into two basic categories, narrative or descriptive, we can generally split Science passages into two broad categories as well. Being able to identify which type of passage you're reading will help you to answer questions about the main idea and about the author's purpose.

Explanatory passages will provide information about a topic. Their purpose is simply to inform the reader. These passages will not support any particular side of an issue, although they might describe the positions taken about the issue by other people.

Persuasive passages will take a certain position on an issue, and provide additional information as evidence to support that position. The purpose of a persuasive passage is to build support for the author's position using specific evidence and logical arguments.

Pay attention to the author's position and to the balance of evidence to help you decide what type of passage you're reading. Knowing whether a passage is explanatory or persuasive will help you answer questions about the author's purpose, or the main purpose of the passage. Be sure to also pay attention to the elements of specific paragraphs and to identify their purpose, as you might be asked about the purpose of only a part of the passage.

Part 2 Practice: Science Passages

Below is an example passage. Read the passage, paying special attention to the elements we have discussed, and then answer the accompanying practice questions.

This passage is adapted from Joseph Heremans, "Magnetic Fields Can Control Heat and Sound." ©2015 by Joseph Heremans.

Sound is carried by periodic vibrations of atoms in gases, liquids, and solids. When we talk to each other, the vocal chords of the speaker vibrate, causing the air coming from his lungs to vibrate as well. This creates sound waves, which then propagate through the air until they hit a listener's eardrums and make them vibrate as well. From these vibrations, the listener can then reconstruct the speaker's words.

Sound is affected by the surroundings in which it travels and by the frequency of the sound waves. We design musical instruments to manipulate the sound waves they produce. Further, we know that there are sound waves that are outside the range of human hearing, such as those produced by a dog whistle. As physicists have researched sound both inside and outside the range of human hearing, interesting properties have been discovered.

More than a hundred years ago, physicists understood that heat is simply the energy stored in the vibrations of atoms, and therefore realized that heat and sound are related. Now my lab has shown for the first time that these atomic vibrations have magnetic properties too.

Physicists called the sound wave particles "phonons," derived from the Greek word for sound. In the March 23 issue of *Nature Materials*, we offer experimental proof that sound waves interact with external magnetic fields.

The experiment was carried out on a large, single crystal of a very pure semiconductor, indium antimonide, which had been cut into two unequal sections and then cooled to about –445°F (–265°C). A controlled amount of heat was made to flow in each section separately.

At these temperatures, the phonons can be thought of as individual particles, like runners on a racetrack each carrying a little bucket of heat.

In the small section, the phonons often run into the walls, which slows them down. The small section is used as a reference, to make the experiment independent of the other properties of the solid that might interfere. In the large section, the phonons can go faster, and they don't run into the walls as much as into each other. When we apply a magnetic field, they tend to run into each other more frequently. Because the magnetic field increases the number of collisions, it also slows the phonons down and lowers the amount of heat they carry by 12%.

We think this is due to the electrons that rotate in orbits around each atom in the solid. The orbital motion of these electrons emits a very small intrinsic magnetic field that interacts with the externally applied field—an effect called "diamagnetism." This property exists even in substances we don't traditionally think of as magnetic, such as glass, stone, or plastic. When the atoms vibrate due to the passing of the phonons, this interaction creates a force on the atoms that makes the phonons collide with each other more often.

At this point, we've just described a new concept, something that had never been thought of before. Engineers can perhaps use this concept to control heat and sound waves magnetically. Sound waves can be effectively steered already by using multiple sources of sound, as is done in ultrasound imaging systems, but controlling heat conduction is much harder.

Conversion of heat into electrical or mechanical power, as is done in engines and in power stations, supplies over 90% of the energy humanity uses. Therefore, being able to control heat conduction could have an enormous impact on energy production, though, obviously, applications of this emergent concept are still quite a way in the future.

1

The main purpose of this passage is to

A) suggest new technologies that could be developed from recent breakthroughs.

B) describe a new discovery by the author's lab and its implications for the field.

C) compare the magnetic and thermodynamic properties of sound.

D) educate readers about the different way sound waves are measured.

2

The author includes the paragraph on diamagnetism (lines 61-73) to

A) establish his authority as a specialist in diagmagnetic properties of sound waves.

B) suggest a new area for research on magnetic waves and phonons.

C) provide background on the structure and function of magnetic fields.

D) propose a theory to explain some of his research team's results on phonons.

3

Based on information in the passage, it can be inferred that the author believes that the evidence about the magnetic properties of sound waves

A) is a fascinating but unsupported theoretical claim.

B) requires additional research to prove results were not an anomaly.

C) is a groundbreaking result ripe for further exploration.

D) ignores other essential properties of waves that should be investigated.

Social Studies and Historical Passages
Part 3

There are two Social Studies/History passages on the SAT. One of these two passages will resemble a Science passage, as it will have a similar structure and focus, and will ask similar types of questions. It will probably come from a magazine, newspaper, or non-fiction book, and it will be from a contemporary source. However, it will be from a field in the social sciences rather than the natural or physical sciences. The social sciences include fields like economics, psychology, linguistics, and history. This passage will likely include a graphic. You can approach a Social Studies passage on one of these subjects much like you would approach a Science passage.

The other Social Studies/History passage will be very different, and will be the focus of this part of this section. On each SAT, there will be one historical document that fits into one of two categories: either the Founding Documents of the United States or the Great Global Conversation.

Founding Documents are those documents that shaped the history of the United States. This category includes documents like the Declaration of Independence, the U.S. Constitution, and the Bill of Rights. The Great Global Conversation refers to the ongoing global conversation about civic life. This category could include a Winston Churchill speech, a passage from a work written by Nelson Mandela, a letter from Gandhi, or a wide variety of other historically important documents and speeches. This category could also include passage pairs, where one author responds directly to another, or two authors write on similar themes.

Founding Documents or Great Global Conversation passages are most often **persuasive**: the author or speaker attempts to persuade the reader or listener to agree with their position using techniques besides evidence and logical arguments. Persuasive passages might also use **appeals to emotion**, in which the author makes statements designed to make you *feel* that they are right, rather than providing evidence on which to build their argument.

In such passages, you should aim to identify the thesis, and how each portion of the passage works to support that thesis—either by providing evidence, or by using rhetorical techniques that have a compelling emotional effect on the reader. Examine how the author or speaker uses language, evidence, and arguments to emphasize certain points.

Historical documents frequently use dated language that might not be very familiar. They also address complex topics: the nature of liberty, the role of government, the relationship between individuals and society, and so on. Check out our reading list online for some recommended material to help you practice.

For additional resources, please visit **ivyglobal.com/study**.

They're not exactly light reading, but don't worry! With practice, you can develop all the skills that you need to tackle these challenging passages.

Active Reading with Historical Passages

As with literature and science passages, you want to pay attention to claims and facts in the passage, as the author or speaker of the passage may be building an argument. But in historical passages, you are going to want to pay special attention to the way that the speaker or author uses **rhetoric**, or language which is designed to have a persuasive effect on a listener or reader. The techniques employed will vary and will depend upon the author's overall purpose. Analyzing these techniques will help you pinpoint the author's main argument and supporting points.

In historical passages, you should keep an eye out for all of the following elements:

Common Rhetorical Techniques		
Type	Description	Example
Rhetorical Emphasis	There are several techniques that speakers and authors might use to add emphasis to a point. They might repeat an important phrase or word several times, use several words in a row that all mean roughly the same thing, ask questions which they themselves answer, or use unusual or repetitive sentence structures to emphasize important points.	Were the original documents provided? No. Were uncensored copies provided? No. Was any reasonable effort made to share key information about the contents of the documents? No. Each and every request for additional information was totally and completely ignored.
Juxtaposition	Juxtaposition is used in order to highlight the contrast between the things being compared. A speaker or writer might place two very different things close together in a passage or speech, or provide a real-world example where two very different things meet.	In the shadow of scrap-heaps piled high with the discarded luxuries of the world's richest economies, there live and work some of the poorest people in the developing world.

Analogies	In addition to using devices like metaphors and similes, the speaker or author in a Historical passage might employ analogies to compare the relationships between different sorts of things. Unlike metaphors and similes, however, analogies are often used to imply that if the things being compared are alike in some ways, they may also be alike in other ways. Analogies can also be used to make complex ideas easier to understand.	The government is like a pair of work boots: it protects us from injury and discomfort, but only if it is properly fitted. A pair of work boots which is too large or too small may do more harm than good, and had better be replaced.

Part 3 Practice: Social Studies and Historical Passages

Below is an example passage. Read the passage, paying special attention to the elements we have discussed, and then answer the accompanying practice questions.

This passage is adapted from John F. Kennedy, "Speech on His Religion," originally delivered to the Greater Houston Ministerial Association on September 12, 1960. President John F. Kennedy was the first Catholic to be elected president of the United States. During the campaign for the presidency, Kennedy faced attacks over the positions of the Catholic Church, and charges that as president he would "take orders from the Pope." In this speech, Kennedy addresses the "religious issue."

While the so-called "religious issue" is necessarily and properly the chief topic here tonight, I want to emphasize from the outset that I believe that we have far more critical issues to face in the 1960 election: the spread of Communist influence, until it now festers 90 miles off the coast of Florida; the humiliating treatment of our president and vice president by those who no longer respect our power; the hungry children I saw in West Virginia; the old people who cannot pay their doctors' bills; the families forced to give up their farms; an America with too many slums, with too few schools, and too late to the moon and outer space.

These are the real issues which should decide this campaign. And they are not religious issues—for war and hunger and ignorance and despair know no religious barriers. But because I am a Catholic, and no Catholic has ever been elected president, the real issues in this campaign have been obscured—perhaps deliberately, in some quarters less responsible than this.

So it is apparently necessary for me to state once again not what kind of church I believe in—for that should be important only to me—but what kind of America I believe in. I believe in an America where the separation of church and state is absolute, where no Catholic prelate would tell the president (should he be Catholic) how to act, and no Protestant minister would tell his parishioners for whom to vote; where no church or church school is granted any public funds or political preference; and where no man is denied public office merely because his religion differs from the president who might appoint him or the people who might elect him.

I believe in an America that is officially neither Catholic, Protestant, nor Jewish; where no public official either requests or accepts instructions on public policy from the Pope, the National Council of Churches, or any other ecclesiastical source; where no religious body seeks to impose its will directly or indirectly upon the general populace or the public acts of its officials; and where religious liberty is so indivisible that an act against one church is treated as an act against all.

For while this year it may be a Catholic against whom the finger of suspicion is pointed, in other years it has been, and may someday be again, a Jew, or a Quaker, or a Unitarian, or a Baptist. It was Virginia's harassment of Baptist preachers, for example, that helped lead to Jefferson's statute of religious freedom. Today I may be the victim, but tomorrow it may be you—until the whole fabric of our harmonious society is ripped at a time of great national peril.

Finally, I believe in an America where religious intolerance will someday end; where all men and all churches are treated as equal; where every man has the same right to attend or not to attend the church of his choice; where there is no Catholic vote, no anti-Catholic vote, no bloc voting of any kind; and where Catholics, Protestants, and Jews, at both the lay and the pastoral level, will refrain from those attitudes of disdain and division which have so often marred their works in the past, and promote instead the American ideal of brotherhood.

That is the kind of America in which I believe. And it represents the kind of presidency in which I believe: a great office that must neither be humbled by making it the instrument of any one religious group, nor tarnished by arbitrarily withholding its occupancy from the members of any one religious group.

I believe in a president whose views on religion are his own private affair, neither imposed by him upon the nation, nor imposed by the nation upon him as a condition to holding that office.

1

Kennedy's main purpose in this passage is to

A) urge Americans to reconsider their religious views, in light of the many issues facing society.

B) argue against providing government funds to religious organizations.

C) express his view that religion and politics should be strictly separated.

D) suggest that since all churches are equal they deserve equal representation in government.

2

Kennedy's tone in lines 6-8 ("the spread ... Florida") suggests that he feels that "Communist influence" is

A) slowly decaying until it finally disappears.

B) an offensive problem about which too little has been done.

C) an unpleasant but mostly harmless irritation.

D) the cause of most of the other problems in the United States.

3

Lines 64-68 ("Today I ... peril") are most likely intended to suggest that

A) when one religious group is treated unfairly, others are more likely to be treated unfairly in the future.

B) people are most likely to discriminate on the basis of religion during times of crisis.

C) religious diversity and political harmony cannot exist in the same society.

D) religious discrimination could lead to divisions which harm all Americans.

Section 4

Understanding the Facts

In this section, you will learn about some common question types associated with every passage. These question types fall under the category of **Information and Ideas**, which means that they require you to understand the facts of the passage. This includes understanding specific lines from a passage, identifying main ideas, and analyzing how parts of the text relate to one another. In this section, we will cover questions on:

- Words and Phrases in Context
- Explicit and Implicit Meaning
- Central Ideas and Relationships
- Command of Evidence
- Analogical Reasoning

We'll describe each question type and the strategies for answering it, followed by practice exercises so you can try questions on your own. At the end of this section you will have a chance to apply what you've learned to full-length practice passages.

Words in Context

Part 1

Every passage or pair of passages will be accompanied by one or two **Words in Context** questions. These questions will give you a word or phrase from the passage and ask you to select the answer choice that could best replace it. Some answer choices will be valid synonyms of the word or phrase you are asked about, but only one will make sense in the original sentence. Other words may work in the context of the sentence, but don't convey the exact same meaning or have the same connotation.

Example

Margaret runs a very successful business, yet still finds time to volunteer in the community.

1

As used in line 1, "runs" most nearly means

A) operates.

B) jogs.

C) flees.

D) functions.

This question is asking you to identify the word that could best replace "runs" in the original sentence. Notice that all of the answer choices are possible meanings of "runs"—your job is to find the meaning that is closest to what the author of the passage intended. Here are some strategies to help you identify this meaning.

Think for Yourself

As you learned in Section 2, it is helpful to think for yourself when answering questions. You should use this approach for Words in Context questions. Refer back to the passage, and try thinking of a suitable word or phrase to replace the one you are asked about. Be sure to read the full sentence in which the word or phrase appears. You can also read a few lines above and below to help you understand the context in which the word or phrase is being used.

Margaret runs a very successful business, yet still finds time to volunteer in the community.

1

As used in line 1, "runs" most nearly means

A) operates.

B) jogs.

C) flees.

D) functions.

What is a word you can think of to define "runs" in this sentence? Perhaps something like "manages," as the sentence refers to a business that Margaret is in charge of. Now you can compare this idea to the answer choices. The word "operates" is closest to your word "manages," and is the only answer that captures the right meaning for the sentence.

(B) and (C) refer to the physical act of running. (D) refers to the way something works, as in "The car only runs/functions if it is filled with premium gas." Notice that these are all valid ways you can use the word "runs," but only the first answer would make sense in the original sentence.

Plugging In Options

As you learned in Chapter 1, you can test each answer choice by plugging it back into the original sentence to see what choice works best in context. Remember that the correct answer must provide nearly the same meaning as the original word. Compare your choice to the original sentence and ensure it matches the context of the lines above and below in order to be sure of your answer.

If you weren't sure of your answer for the example question above, you could try plugging each answer choice into the original sentence to see which one makes sense:

- ✓ Margaret operates a very successful business …
- X Margaret jogs a very successful business …
- X Margaret flees a very successful business …
- X Margaret functions a very successful business …

Only answer choice (A) makes sense when you plug it into the original sentence, so you know (A) must be the correct answer.

Part 1 Practice: Words in Context

For each question below, choose the answer choice that most nearly means the same thing as the word or phrase specified in each question.

The safety of the nation has been threatened, and it is imperative that we respond. Though we do not go lightly into this conflict, we go with the certainty that to act is to protect our great country. We will call upon our citizens to act bravely in this time of need. Sacrifices will need to be made, but we are confident that our citizens are ready and able to take on these challenges.

1

As used in line 6, "call upon" most nearly means

A) shout at.

B) visit briefly.

C) appeal to.

D) cry for.

Before they set out, Charu provided her companions with some practical advice about hiking in Death Valley. She warned them not to bring overly heavy packs, and to make sure that they wore shoes that were comfortable and broken in. A few of her companions asked her about food and water, and Charu explained that, on the route they were taking, they would only be gone for a maximum of five hours and should pack accordingly.

2

As used in line 2, "practical" most nearly means

A) functional.

B) applied.

C) useful.

D) grounded.

The lab has produced some groundbreaking research in recent years. A significant amount of press has been devoted to their results, leading to a significant influx of donors. But the most intriguing aspect of this new scholarship is its synthesis of modern and traditional techniques.

3

As used in line 7, "synthesis" most nearly means

A) fusion.

B) alloy.

C) conflation.

D) overlap.

Hank arrived at the party a little late, and hurried to hang up his coat and hat and join the rest of the guests. He found, to his embarrassment, that he was underdressed, and spent the first hour pressed against the back wall sipping his drink. The hostess, his cousin's college friend, eventually pulled him into a conversation with a viscount and an earl. Hank was not used to being in the company of such refined individuals, and strove to choose his words and references carefully.

4

As used in line 11, "refined" most nearly means

A) developed.

B) unadulterated.

C) cultured.

D) delicate.

The doctor suggested an aggressive treatment plan upon learning of her patient's rare diagnosis. She explained the various options open to him, and provided an analysis of the drawbacks and benefits of each one. After, she encouraged her patient to follow up with her if he had any other questions.

5

As used in line 1, "aggressive" most nearly means

A) intensive.

B) violent.

C) militant.

D) enterprising.

Today's economists are quick to point out that constant spending on consumer goods could leave you saddled with debt. Even with salaries increasing in numerous fields, consumer spending is vastly outpacing income. Worse is when you use credit cards to pay for new goods, and then delay paying off the debts for these new items; interest quickly accrues and you end up spending nearly double the cost of the original item.

6

As used in lines 3-4, "saddled with" most nearly means

A) burdened by.

B) packed with.

C) freighted by.

D) strained with.

Explicit and Implicit Meaning

Part 2

All passages will usually have questions that ask you about specific ideas discussed in the text. These questions can come in two forms: Explicit Meaning and Implicit Meaning questions.

Explicit Meaning

Explicit Meaning questions ask you about something stated more or less directly in the passage. "Explicit" means direct or fully expressed. To answer these questions, you will need to refer back to the text and read closely to understand what the author wrote. Use the Process of Elimination to knock out any answers that contradict what the author wrote, or any answers that are not directly stated in the passage. You are looking for ideas the author has stated directly.

Here are some ways that Explicit Meaning questions might be phrased:

- According to the passage, which choice best describes …
- The author suggests that …
- The narrator indicates that …

Remember the passage about the artist Cavallini from Section 2? Let's have a look at it again and see how an Explicit Meaning question about that passage would work.

This passage is adapted from Daniel Zalewski, "Under a Shroud of Kitsch May Lie a Master's Art." ©2001 by The New York Times Company.

Tommaso Strinati clambers to the top of the rickety scaffold and laughs. "It's a good thing that all this Baroque work is so unimpressive," he says, pointing at the clumsy trompe l'oeil painting covering the wall in front of him. "Otherwise, we might not have been allowed to scrape it off!"

A 28-year-old art historian, he is standing 16 feet above the marble floor of San Pasquale Baylon chapel, a long-neglected nook of Santa Maria in Aracoeli, a Franciscan basilica in the center of Rome. Last year, Mr. Strinati, who is still a graduate student, began studying the church's history. Records suggested that the Roman artist Pietro Cavallini—a painter and mosaicist whose greatest works have been destroyed—spent years decorating Aracoeli toward the end of the 13th century. Yet only one small Cavallini fresco, in the church's left transept, remained visible. Mr. Strinati wondered: had other Cavallini frescoes been painted over with inferior work? And if so, could modern restorers uncover them?

"The answer to both questions was yes," Mr. Strinati says. A close-up examination of the chapel's walls last summer revealed ghostly images lying beneath the surface. The entire chapel, it seemed, was a painted palimpsest. And when a heavy altarpiece was removed from one wall, a remarkably tender portrait of the Madonna and Child was found hidden behind it.

After months of careful paint-peeling, what has been uncovered are dazzling fragments of a late-medieval masterpiece completed shortly after 1285. Although the Aracoeli fresco is not signed, the figures strongly resemble those in a surviving Cavallini work, the resplendent "Last Judgment" fresco at nearby Santa Cecilia.

Mr. Strinati has grand ambitions for his discovery. He hopes that in a few years the fully restored fresco will not only rescue Cavallini's name from obscurity, but also upend the widespread notion that the first flowers of the Renaissance budded in Florence, not Rome. For the fresco's lifelike figures—in particular, an impish Christ child with charmingly flushed cheeks—suggest to Strinati that Cavallini may have anticipated some of the extraordinary naturalistic innovations that have long been credited to the Florentine artist Giotto.

Moreover, the Aracoeli fragments may provide a critical new clue in a decades-old battle concerning the "St. Francis Legend," the 1296 fresco cycle at Assisi, universally recognized as one of the foundations of the Renaissance. For centuries, the 28-scene cycle—which recounts the life of the saint with a narrative zest and compositional depth that leave the flat tableaus of the Byzantine era far behind—was attributed to Giotto. But since the 1930's, various scholars have questioned this judgment, claiming that the Assisi cycle doesn't resemble Giotto's other work. Now, the Aracoeli discovery is ammunition for Italian art historians who believe that Cavallini might actually be the primary creative force behind the "St. Francis Legend."

The growing debate about Cavallini's importance was the occasion for a symposium in Rome in November. *La Republicca*, an Italian daily, has cast the debate as "War Between Rome and Florence." Mr. Strinati is enjoying the ruckus. "I had a hunch that there was more Cavallini lurking around here," he says of the Aracoeli basilica. "But I didn't expect to find an exquisite work that could shake up the history of art."

According to the passage, Cavallini

A) was widely known before the recent discovery of his frescos.

B) was the undisputed creator of the "St. Francis Legend."

C) painted frescos exclusively in Roman churches.

D) had some of his work painted over by later artists.

To answer this question, see which choice is supported by information clearly stated in the text. Answer choice (A) directly contradicts the passage, as we're told that Mr. Strinati wants to "rescue Cavallini's name from obscurity" (line 49). Answer choice (B) also contradicts the passage, as lines 71-79 state that "since the 1930's, various scholars have questioned" whether Giotto painted the "St. Francis Legend." Therefore, you can eliminate both (A) and (B).

Answer choice (C) is simply not supported by the passage. While the passage lists two churches in which Cavallini frescoes have been found, you are not given any other information about where else he may have painted. Remember that explicit meaning questions are asking about what is presented in the passage, so avoid making assumptions. You can eliminate answer choice (C).

You are left with answer choice (D), which matches exactly the information from the passage. In the first paragraph, Strinati points to a "clumsy trompe l'oeil painting" in front of him while discussing unimpressive Baroque art. This is the type of art he was removing to reveal Cavallini's frescoes, so it must have been painted later. Because (D) is the only answer stated directly in the passage, it is the correct answer.

Implicit Meaning

Implicit Meaning questions ask you about ideas that are presented more subtly in the text. "Implicit" means implied rather than stated directly. For these questions you will need to read between the lines or combine clues from different parts of the text to understand what the author is suggesting. In some passages this may mean understanding literary devices such as metaphor. These concepts will be discussed further in Section 5.

Here are some ways that Implicit Meaning questions might be phrased:

- It can reasonably be inferred from the passage that …
- The passage most strongly suggests that …
- In lines 30-31 the phrase "better late than never" implies that …

Be careful not to take everything the author says too literally when answering Implicit Meaning questions. In real life, you are probably good at picking up on implied meanings. For example, if your friend says she is "thrilled" to take out the trash but rolls her eyes as she says it, you know she is being sarcastic. Similarly, things like the tone and structure of a passage can help indicate what an author really means.

Let's look at another question about the Cavallini passage to see how Implicit Meaning questions work.

Example

The passage most strongly suggests that

A) Strinati believes Cavallini to be a superior artist to Giotto.

B) similarities between paintings can be used to determine who painted them.

C) Baroque artwork is considered less impressive than Renaissance pieces.

D) Renaissance frescoes were frequently painted over in Italian churches.

Which of these ideas are suggested by the passage? While answer choice (A) may be true, there is no information in the passage to support this idea. We know that Strinati thinks highly of Cavallini's work because of the adjectives he uses, like when he calls it "exquisite" at the end of the passage. However, he never compares Cavallini to Giotto.

Answer choices (C) and (D) are similarly not things that you could reasonably conclude on the basis of the passage. You are not given wider information about the Renaissance or about Baroque artwork in general; the passage only discusses the artwork at the Aracoeli basilica. While implied meaning questions require you to extrapolate slightly from the passage, you must still have evidence in the text to support your answer! Be careful of answers like these that are too broad.

Answer choice (B) can be supported by two different portions of the text. First, lines 71-79 indicate some historians believed Giotto had painted the "St. Francis Legend," but they began to question this because it does not resemble his other work. Lines 40-45 suggest that the Aracoeli frescoes are likely Cavallini's because they do resemble his other work. These both indicate that historians look at similarities between paintings to help determine if the same person painted them. Therefore, (B) is the correct answer.

Part 2 Practice: Explicit and Implicit Meaning

Review the techniques we discussed in Section 2, and mark up and summarize this passage excerpt. Then, answer the Explicit and Implicit Meaning questions using the strategies you just learned.

This passage is adapted from Steve Lohr, "The Vaccination Effect: 100 Million Cases of Contagious Disease Prevented." ©2013 by The New York Times Company.

Vaccination programs for children have prevented more than 100 million cases of serious contagious disease in the United States since 1924, according to a new study published in *The New England Journal of Medicine*. The research, led by scientists at the University of Pittsburgh's Graduate School of Public Health, analyzed public health reports going back to the 19th century. The reports covered 56 diseases, but the article in the journal focused on seven: polio, measles, rubella, mumps, hepatitis A, diphtheria and pertussis, and whooping cough.

Researchers analyzed disease reports before and after the times when vaccines became commercially available. Put simply, the estimates for prevented cases came from the falloff in disease reports after vaccines were licensed and widely available. The researchers projected the number of cases that would have occurred had the pre-vaccination patterns continued as the nation's population increased.

The University of Pittsburgh researchers also looked at death rates, but decided against including an estimate in the journal article, largely because death certificate data became more reliable and consistent only in the 1960s, the researchers said. But Dr. Donald S. Burke, the dean of Pittsburgh's Graduate School of Public Health and an author of the medical journal article, said that a reasonable projection of prevented deaths based on known mortality rates in the disease categories would be three million to four million.

1

All of the following are directly addressed in the passage EXCEPT

A) how researchers estimated the preventative impact of vaccinations.

B) why the researchers did not include death rate estimates in the journal article.

C) some diseases for which vaccines became commercially available.

D) why death certificate data only become reliable in the 1960s.

2

Which of the following statements is supported by the passage?

A) Childhood vaccination programs can be effective at preventing certain contagious diseases.

B) Without the effect of successful vaccinations, the American population would have soared.

C) It is difficult for researchers to obtain reliable death certificate data.

D) Vaccinations for certain diseases are much more effective than vaccinations for other diseases.

3

It can reasonably be inferred from the passage that

A) most vaccines were very expensive when first introduced.

B) some vaccines became commercially available around the 1920s.

C) American public health reports only date back to the 19th century.

D) it is impossible to accurately predict the effect of disease on population growth.

4

The passage most strongly suggests that

A) the mortality rates for all diseases are well-known today.

B) scientists may choose not to publish all data estimates they make.

C) researchers always struggle to create accurate predictions when working with historical data.

D) the diseases the scientists focused on in their publication were those with the highest mortality rates.

Summarizing, Central Ideas, and Relationships

Part 3

There are several types of questions on the SAT Reading Test that require you to summarize ideas in the text, identify central ideas of the whole text, and examine relationships among these ideas. Be sure you are using the active reading and summarizing strategies discussed in Section 2 as you read each passage. Referring to the summaries you have already made will make these questions much easier!

Summarizing

Summarizing questions ask you to identify a reasonable summary of specific parts of the passage. This will require you to paraphrase certain lines from the text, which means to provide a short, clear restatement of what you have read. The techniques you learned about summarizing in Section 2 will help you to paraphrase concisely and accurately, so review that section for guidance.

If you are asked for a summary of a paragraph you can also refer to your notes and paragraph summaries. Then, compare your summary to the answer choices. Be sure you select an answer that is focused on the most important ideas of the paragraph. Make sure your answer contains ideas discussed within the paragraph in question rather than elsewhere in the passage, and make sure it is truly the focus of the paragraph and not merely a detail.

Here are some ways that Summarizing questions might be phrased:

- Which best summarizes lines 63-82?
- Which choice best summarizes the first paragraph of the passage?
- Which choice best summarizes the passage?

Example

Moreover, the Aracoeli fragments may provide a critical new clue in a decades-old battle concerning the "St. Francis Legend," the 1296 fresco cycle at Assisi, universally recognized as one of the foundations of the Renaissance. For centuries, the 28-scene cycle— which recounts the life of the saint with a narrative zest and compositional depth that leave the flat tableaus of the Byzantine era far behind—was attributed to Giotto. But since the 1930's, various scholars have questioned this judgment, claiming that the Assisi cycle doesn't resemble Giotto's other work. Now, the Aracoeli discovery is ammunition for Italian art historians who believe that Cavallini might actually be the primary creative force behind the "St. Francis Legend."

3

Which best summarizes lines 60-79?

A) The Aracoeli discovery has contributed to the debate about who painted the "St. Francis Legend."

B) The "St. Francis Legend" is important as an example of early Renaissance work.

C) Many scholars doubt that Giotto was the artist responsible for the "St. Francis Legend."

D) Cavallini was almost certainly the artist who painted the "St. Francis Legend."

Here, only answer choice (A) provides an overall summary of the paragraph. Answer choices (B) and (C) are too narrowly focused, and answer choice (D) makes a judgment that goes beyond what can be supported by the passage.

Central Ideas

Determining Central Ideas and Themes questions ask you about the central ideas that are the focus of the text. We'll call these "Central Ideas" questions. To answer them, review the paragraph summaries you created to come up with an overall summary or to spot recurring themes in the passage. Then look for the answer choice that best matches your prediction.

You can also use Process of Elimination to knock out incorrect answer choices. Check each option to be sure it meets the following two criteria: it is true according to the passage and it deals with most of the passage.

Making sure your answer is true according to the passage helps you knock out answer choices that mention new information or go beyond the passage. For example, just because a passage suggests that a new technology is a good idea does not mean that the author believes it is the best solution to a problem, unless that is stated in the text. Be wary of answer choices that include stronger opinions than the passage itself.

Ensuring your answer to a Central Ideas question deals with most of the passage helps you stay focused on the big picture of the passage, rather than details. Just because something is mentioned in the passage does not necessarily mean it is a main idea! Look for ideas that are mentioned multiple times or are discussed in-depth across multiple lines and paragraphs.

Here are some ways that Central Ideas questions might be phrased:

- The passage primarily focuses on …
- What is the author's main point about …
- The central claim of the passage is that …

With these ideas in mind, let's look at a Central Ideas question about the Cavallini passage. You can find it in Part 2 of this chapter if you need to refresh your memory.

Example

The events presented in the passage are best described as

A) a potential solution to the mystery of who painted a specific work of art.

B) one researcher's quest which is of little interest to other historians.

C) the painstaking removal of certain artwork to reveal more valuable pieces.

D) a new discovery with potentially major implications for art history.

Answer choice (A) demonstrates the second type of wrong answer discussed above, as it does not deal with the entire passage. While the mystery of who painted the "St. Francis Legend" is important, it is too specific to be considered the main idea of the passage as a whole. Rather, it serves as one example of how the discovery of Cavallini's work might impact art history in Italy. Answer choice (C) is also too narrow, because it only discusses events in the first few paragraphs of the passage.

Answer choice (B) does not meet our first criterion, as it is not true according to the passage. Strinati's discovery and attempts to rescue Cavallini's work are described as having a big impact on other art historians and leading to many important debates. Therefore, they *are* of interest to other historians.

Answer choice (D) captures all of the main ideas of the passage. It first mentions discovery, which relates to the first half of the passage about Cavallini's hidden frescoes. It also notes how this will impact the art world, which is what the author discusses in the final three paragraphs. You've found your answer!

Relationships

Some questions will ask you to describe the ways parts of the passage relate to one another. **Understanding Relationships** questions will ask you to identify relationships between individuals, events, or ideas in a passage. We'll refer to these as "Relationship" questions. These relationships may be explicitly stated, or may be implied and require you to read between the lines.

To answer these questions, consider what elements you are asked about and put the relationship between them into your own words. As always, this ensures that you know what you are looking for and will be precise when selecting your answer.

To figure out the relationship between elements, look back to the passage. Where are the people or ideas mentioned, and what is said about them? You can also refer back to any important parts of the passage you marked up, or the summaries you made for each paragraph.

Here are some ways that Relationships questions might be phrased:

- Based on the passage, which choice best describes the relationship between …
- The author's statement in lines 29-31 implies that purines and pyrimidines …
- The author indicates that, in comparison to individuals, traditional organizations have tended to be …

Let's look at a Relationship question about the Cavallini passage to practice these strategies.

Example

Based on the passage, which choice best describes the relationship between Cavallini and Giotto?

A) Giotto may have anticipated Cavallini's work.

B) Cavallini may have anticipated Giotto's work.

C) Giotto is a more contemporary artist than Cavallini.

D) Giotto is a less contemporary artist than Cavallini.

First, try to think of what you know about these two artists from the passage. You know that they worked around the same time period and have both been credited with the same work of art. New discoveries about Cavallini suggest he may have anticipated some of Giotto's techniques. Now see which answer choice best matches what you know.

You can use the Process of Elimination to knock out choices (C) and (D) because you know the artists painted around the same time. There is nothing in the passage to support answer (A). However, answer choice (B) matches what you know about the artists, and is the correct response!

Try another Relationship question from this passage:

Example

Based on the passage, which choice best describes the relationship between Florence's and Rome's role in the Renaissance?

A) Florence is usually credited with following Rome in adopting Renaissance styles.

B) Florence is usually credited with pioneering Renaissance styles that Rome adopted.

C) Rome and Florence are credited with simultaneously launching Renaissance art.

D) Florence is usually credited with abandoning Renaissance styles before Rome.

Here, only answer choice (B) is supported by the passage. Remember that Strinati is trying to "upend the widespread notion that the first flowers of the Renaissance budded in Florence" (lines 50-52). Therefore, you can infer that it is generally believed that Florence started the Renaissance and other cities followed. Choices (A) and (C) directly contradict the idea that Florence started the Renaissance, while choice (D) talks about the abandonment instead of the adoption of Renaissance styles, which is unsupported by the passage.

Part 3 Practice: Summarizing, Central Ideas, and Relationships

Review the techniques we discussed in Section 2, and mark up and make summaries for this passage excerpt. Then, answer the Summarizing, Central Ideas, and Relationships questions using the strategies you just learned.

This passage is adapted from Robert Lee Hotz, "A Neuron's Obsession Hints at Biology of Thought." ©2009 by Dow Jones & Company.

Neurons process and transmit information through electrical and chemical signals, and researchers have discovered neurons that respond only to certain famous figures.

Probing deep into human brains, a team of scientists discovered a neuron roused only by Ronald Reagan, another cell smitten by the actress Halle Berry, and a third devoted solely to Mother Teresa. Testing other single human neurons, they located a brain cell that would rather watch an episode of "The Simpsons" than Madonna.

In one sense, these findings are merely noise. They arise from rare recordings of electrical activity in brain cells, collected by neuroscientists at the University of California, Los Angeles, during a decade of experiments with patients awaiting brain surgery for severe epilepsy. These tingles of electricity, however, gave the researchers the opportunity to locate neurons that help link our perceptions, memories and self-awareness.

In their most recent work this year, the research team reported that a single human neuron could recognize a personality through pictures, text, or the sound of a name—no matter how that person was presented. In tests, one brain cell reacted only to Oprah Winfrey; another just to Luke Skywalker; a third singled out Argentine soccer star Diego Maradona.

Each neuron appeared to join together pieces of sensory information into a single mental impression. The researchers believe these cells are evidence that it only takes a simple circuit of neurons to encode an idea, perception, or memory.

"These neurons will fire to the person no matter how you present them," says bioengineer Rodrigo Quian Quiroga at the U.K.'s University of Leicester who studied the neurons with colleagues at UCLA and the California Institute of Technology. "All that we do, all that we think, all that we see is encoded by neurons. How do the neurons in our brain create all our perceptions of the world, all our emotions, all our thinking?"

1

Which of the following best summarizes lines 27-36?

A) Individual neurons can identify personalities presented in different forms.

B) Individual neurons combine different pieces of information using a simple circuit.

C) Every neuron in the human brain is capable of identifying different celebrities.

D) Famous personalities can be presented in a variety of ways and still be recognizable.

2

The passage primarily focuses on which of the following characteristics of neurons?

A) Their ability to recognize people and personalities

B) Their involvement in conditions like epilepsy

C) Their ability to be recorded during rare forms of research

D) Their profound effect on all human perceptions

3

Based on the passage, which choice best describes the relationship between neurons and celebrities?

A) Every neuron can recognize all celebrities.

B) Every neuron can recognize one celebrity.

C) A single neuron can recognize a single celebrity.

D) All celebrities are recognized by all neurons.

Command of Evidence

Part 4

As we discussed in Section 2, you should always be able to support any answer you choose by referring to words or lines in the passage. On the redesigned SAT Reading Test, there are also questions in each passage that explicitly test this skill—two **Command of Evidence** questions that ask you to identify the support for your answer to another question. We'll refer to these as "Evidence" questions.

Evidence questions will list four different selections from the passage, and ask which one provides the best evidence to support your answer to the previous question. You should be sure you have answered the previous question before you attempt an Evidence question. Evidence questions are always worded as follows:

- Which choice provides the best evidence for the answer to the previous question?

Refer Back

Once you see that you are being asked an Evidence question, refer back to your answer to the previous question and consider why you selected it. Find the paragraph or lines that supported your choice. Then, look at each answer choice for the Evidence question. Look for the choice that is a match for the paragraph or lines you identified, or for a choice that could be another piece of evidence for your answer to the previous question. Be sure to read each line reference you are given in its original context in the passage.

Example

This passage is adapted from Daniel Zalewski, "Under a Shroud of Kitsch May Lie a Master's Art." ©2001 by The New York Times Company.

Tommaso Strinati clambers to the top of the rickety scaffold and laughs. "It's a good thing that all this Baroque work is so unimpressive," he says, pointing at the clumsy trompe l'oeil painting covering the wall in front of him. "Otherwise, we might not have been allowed to scrape it off!"

A 28-year-old art historian, he is standing 16 feet above the marble floor of San Pasquale Baylon chapel, a long-neglected nook of Santa Maria in Aracoeli, a Franciscan basilica in the center of Rome. Last year, Mr. Strinati, who is still a graduate student, began studying the church's history. Records suggested that the Roman artist Pietro Cavallini—a painter and mosaicist whose greatest works have been destroyed—spent years decorating Aracoeli toward the end of the 13th century. Yet only one small Cavallini fresco, in the church's left transept, remained visible. Mr. Striani wondered: had other Cavallini frescoes been painted over with inferior work? And if so, could modern restorers uncover them?

"The answer to both questions was yes," Mr. Strinati says. A close-up examination of the chapel's walls last summer revealed ghostly images lying beneath the surface. The entire chapel, it seemed, was a painted palimpsest. And when a heavy altarpiece was removed from one wall, a remarkably tender portrait of the Madonna and Child was found hidden behind it.

After months of careful paint-peeling, what has been uncovered are dazzling fragments of a late-medieval masterpiece completed shortly after 1285. Although the Aracoeli fresco is not signed, the figures strongly resemble those in a surviving Cavallini work, the resplendent "Last Judgment" fresco at nearby Santa Cecilia.

Mr. Strinati has grand ambitions for his discovery. He hopes that in a few years the fully restored fresco will not only rescue Cavallini's name from obscurity, but also upend the widespread notion that the first flowers of the Renaissance budded in Florence, not Rome. For the fresco's lifelike figures—in particular, an impish Christ child with charmingly flushed cheeks—suggest to Strinati that Cavallini may have anticipated some of the extraordinary naturalistic innovations that have long been credited to the Florentine artist Giotto.

Moreover, the Aracoeli fragments may provide a critical new clue in a decades-old battle concerning the "St. Francis Legend," the 1296 fresco cycle at Assisi, universally recognized as one of the foundations of the Renaissance. For centuries, the 28-scene cycle—which recounts the life of the saint with a narrative zest and compositional depth that leave the flat tableaus of the Byzantine era far behind—was attributed to Giotto. But since the 1930's, various scholars have questioned this judgment, claiming that the Assisi cycle doesn't resemble Giotto's other work. Now, the Aracoeli discovery is ammunition for Italian art historians who believe that Cavallini might actually be the primary creative force behind the "St. Francis Legend."

The growing debate about Cavallini's importance was the occasion for a symposium in Rome in November. *La Republicca*, an Italian daily, has cast the debate as "War Between Rome and Florence." Mr. Strinati is enjoying the ruckus. "I had a hunch that there was more Cavallini lurking around here," he says of the Aracoeli basilica. "But I didn't expect to find an exquisite work that could shake up the history of art."

4

The passage most strongly suggests that the discovery of Cavallini's work

A) was a fortuitous accident.

B) will impact art history broadly.

C) is one of many discoveries in the Aracoeli basilica.

D) was a shocking surprise for Tommasso Strinati.

5

Which choice provides the best evidence for the answer to the previous question?

A) Lines 28-31 ("A close-up … surface")

B) Lines 37-40 ("After months … 1285")

C) Lines 65-71 ("For centuries … Giotto")

D) Lines 80-82 ("The growing … November")

First select your answer to the implicit meaning question. Which one can you support with information from the passage? Answer choices (A) and (D) contradict the passage, as you are told that Strinati had a hunch that he would find more work by Cavallini, and worked purposively to uncover this work. Answer choice (C) could be true, but the passage never discusses other discoveries in the Aracoeli basilica, so you cannot support this answer.

Answer choice (B) is supported in the passage by several ideas, such as the reconsideration of the "St. Francis Legend," Mr. Strinati's "grand ambitions," and other lines in the final three paragraphs. Therefore, (B) is the correct answer.

With this answer in mind, look at the options for the Evidence question. Remember that you are looking for the lines that most strongly suggest that Cavallini's work will have an impact on art history. Here is the question again:

Which choice provides the best evidence for the answer to the previous question?

A) Lines 28-31 ("A close-up ... surface")
B) Lines 37-40 ("After months ... 1285")
C) Lines 65-71 ("For centuries ... Giotto")
D) Lines 80-82 ("The growing ... November")

Here, none of the answers mention the "St. Francis Legend," or quote Strinati. But remember that there can be lots of ways to support an answer choice! Answer choice (D) also suggests that the Cavallini discovery is making waves, as a symposium (a meeting to discuss a topic) was held to discuss how important this discovery might be. (D) is the correct response.

The other answer choices do not relate to the impact of the Cavallini discovery. Answer choice (C) is about Giotto, not Cavallini, so you can eliminate it. Answer choices (A) and (B) relate to characteristics of the Cavallini discovery but don't address the impact or importance the discovery may have for art history. You can knock them out as well.

Using the Evidence Question to Answer the Previous Question

If you're having trouble with an Evidence question, keep in mind that the lines that best support a given answer choice could be anywhere in the passage. An argument made in the second paragraph may be backed up by data or reasoning in the third or fourth paragraph, rather than appearing immediately after the argument.

If none of the answer choices seem to support your previous answer, take another look at each option and see if they might work in a creative or unexpected way. If they still don't seem to work, review the previous question. It is possible your original answer choice was incorrect and therefore does not match with the lines given in the Evidence question! If you ever change your answer to a question that precedes an Evidence question, be sure to redo the accompanying Evidence question as well. On the other hand, if you are stumped on a question that precedes an Evidence question, you may be able to look ahead to the line references for clues as to which answer will make sense.

Part 4 Practice: Evidence in a Passage

Review the techniques we discussed in Section 2, and mark up and make summaries for this passage excerpt. Then, answer the questions using the evidence strategies you just learned.

This passage is adapted from Kelly Crow, "Colombia's Art Scene Heats Up." ©2014 by Dow Jones & Company.

Across Colombia—from the walled coastal city of Cartagena to the sugar-cane fields outside Cali—there's a palpable feeling of flux, of a society shaking off its solitude and stretching out. Crime and poverty persist, but a measure of peace is making it safer to travel and do business across the region. This calm is also allowing Colombia to export greater supplies of oil, gas, sugar, and cut flowers, boosting the pace of its economic growth. Last year alone, the country attracted nearly $16 billion in foreign investments. Luxury malls and beach resorts are sprouting up to cater to the country's 36,000 high-net-worth individuals. Tourism campaigns cheekily play down Colombia's war-torn reputation with slogans such as "The only risk is wanting to stay."

Similar wealth booms have recently helped transform China and Brazil into global art hubs, so it makes sense to see international curators and dealers booking trips to Colombia now. New York's Museum of Modern Art, Houston's Museum of Fine Arts, and London's Serpentine Galleries, among others, have all recently sent delegations of curators and patrons to scout art in Colombia. Pablo León de la Barra, a curator for New York's Solomon R. Guggenheim Museum, was among the early explorers, and the art he's uncovered since is impressive, he says. "For some, art has become a way of working through the communal trauma, but the younger ones are trying to use art as an instrument of usefulness for something else. There are many things at play, but one of them is a desire for normalization."

Whenever curators and collectors start sniffing around a new region, dealers and auctioneers invariably follow, eager to pounce on whatever the tastemakers discover. (A similar phenomenon has lately pushed up prices for China's Zeng Fanzhi and Brazil's Beatriz Milhazes.) In the past year, these market movers have begun championing a potential poster boy for Colombia's rise in Oscar Murillo, the 28-year-old son of Cali sugar-cane farmers who now lives in London. Three years ago, Murillo's frenetic paintings—often made with the help of relatives using dust and debris from his studio floor—were selling for as little as $10,000 apiece.

But last fall, Phillips in New York auctioned off one of the artist's 2011 canvases, Untitled (Drawings Off the Wall), for $401,000, or 10 times its highest estimate.

1

The passage most strongly suggests that

A) most Colombian artists now earn high prices for their work.

B) Colombia was not always as stable a country as it is now.

C) Colombian art has a long history of engaging dangerous themes.

D) Colombian art will become less popular at the initial interest subsides.

2

Which choice provides the best evidence for the answer to the previous question?

A) Lines 6-8 ("Crime … the region")

B) Lines 12-14 ("Last … investments")

C) Lines 31-35 ("Pablo … he says")

D) Lines 43-47 ("Whenever … tastemakers discover")

3

Based on the passage, which choice best describes the relationship between national prosperity and art?

A) Increased wealth in a nation leads to higher prices on the work of its oldest artists.

B) When a nation becomes less prosperous, it uses art to work through the trauma.

C) Economic prosperity can attract art buyers and collectors to a previously overlooked country.

D) As a country grows wealthier, its artists feel more encouraged to create.

4

Which choice provides the best evidence for the answer to the previous question?

A) Lines 9-12 ("This calm … growth")

B) Lines 14-17 ("Luxury malls … individuals")

C) Lines 21-25 ("Similar wealth … now")

D) Lines 60-64 ("But last … estimate")

Analogical Reasoning

Part 5

Analogical Reasoning questions ask you to find an answer choice that is analogous to (the same as) an idea or relationship presented in the passage. An **analogy** is an extended comparison between two things or situations. For example, if a character in a literature passage lies to a friend about a surprise party for them, you would look for an answer choice that presents an analogy for that situation—such as another situation where someone is harmlessly deceived for their own benefit.

These questions can be phrased in a variety of ways:

- Which of the following situations is most analogous to the problem presented in the passage?
- Which hypothetical situation involves the same paradox discussed by the author?
- The principle illustrated in lines 16-19 ("By ... life") is best conveyed by which additional example?

Your job is to identify the situation that follows a similar pattern as an idea or relationship from the passage. The content or topics of the answer choices do not matter. Just because a passage is about cancer research does not mean the right answer will also be about cancer research, or scientific research at all. It might be about music, or politics, or any other subject, as long as it illustrates the same idea or reasoning as the original passage.

Use Your Own Words

To answer these questions, refer back to the passage and restate the idea, principle, or relationship you are asked about in your own words. Then look for an answer choice that matches your description.

Example

A 28-year-old art historian, he is standing 16 feet above the marble floor of San Pasquale Baylon chapel, a long-neglected nook of Santa Maria in Aracoeli, a Franciscan basilica in the center of Rome. Last year, Mr. Strinati, who is still a graduate student, began studying the church's history. Records suggested that the Roman artist Pietro Cavallini—a painter and mosaicist whose greatest works have been destroyed—spent years decorating Aracoeli toward the end of the 13th century. Yet only one small Cavallini fresco, in the church's left transept, remained visible. Mr. Strinati wondered: had other Cavallini frescoes been painted over with inferior work? And if so, could modern restorers uncover them?

6

Which of the following situations is most analogous to the mystery presented in lines 15-22?

A) A muralist spent weeks sketching and eventually completed a beautiful design.

B) A lawmaker took less time than originally expected to draft a bill.

C) Dancers took a few minutes to practice but did not master new choreography.

D) A chef developed recipes for years but few survive today.

To answer this question, first put the "mystery" from the referenced lines into your own words. Cavallini spent years decorating Aracoeli, and yet there is very little art by him in the basilica. We would expect there to be a lot of Cavallini paintings in Aracoeli. You might phrase this "mystery" more generally as "spent lots of time but little to show for it" or "less work than expected."

Which answer choice best matches your description of these lines? Only answer choice (D) shows another scenario where someone produced "less work than expected." Notice that this answer choice does not need to be about art to be analogous to the idea from the passage. However, it closely mirrors the situation in lines 15-22, and even hints that there was more work at some point that was destroyed or lost, just as with Cavallini's art in the passage.

Answer choice (A) is about art but does not match the passage, because here the amount of effort seems to match the output. Answer choice (C) also doesn't match the passage—it is not surprising that dancers did not improve during only a few minutes. Choice (B) is almost the opposite of the passage, as more work was accomplished than expected. Therefore, none of these situations would be a good analogy for the mystery in the passage.

Part 5 Practice: Analogical Reasoning

Answer the following analogical reasoning questions using the approach you have just learned.

According to scientists, the relationship between sugar and adult-onset diabetes is different from what the population generally believes it to be. Most people believe that a high sugar diet leads directly to adult-onset diabetes. In reality, eating a diet high in refined sugar can lead to excess weight, and being overweight can predispose individuals to adult-onset diabetes.

1

Which of the following situations is most analogous to the relationship between sugar and adult-onset diabetes?

A) Increased exercise can lead to both improved mood and lower cholesterol over time.

B) Studying leads to increased comprehension, and increased comprehension always ensures a higher grade.

C) Advertising can cause companies to grow rapidly, and expanding companies are more prone to mistakes.

D) Having a father who is colorblind can predispose a child to colorblindness.

As a new yoga instructor, Juri faced a challenge: guiding her students into the right alignment in their poses. As creative as she was in her descriptions of each position, it seemed they did not help her students recreate them. One day she began adopting the poses herself at the front of the class, hoping she could better describe them by focusing on her own muscle movements. Instead, she looked up and saw her students perfectly copying her form on their own mats.

2

Which hypothetical situation involves the same approach ultimately used by the yoga instructor?

A) A rugby coach uses a video of professional games to explain a new strategy.

B) An electrician demonstrates to an assistant the process of rewiring.

C) Violin teachers have their students sing a melody before they attempt to play it.

D) A public speaker suggests a list of books to read for inspiration.

When the scandal came to light I must admit I was hardly surprised; the mayor did, after all, have a reputation for deception and bending the truth. In a way, then, I felt the journalists were nearly equally to blame. After all, was it not their job to investigate the credibility of claims, especially those coming from such an untrustworthy figure? Instead of uncovering his secrets they had been busy propagating the mayor's lies.

3

The narrator's attitude towards the journalists is most similar to which example?

A) The advertisers who overlooked a key defect in a car they are promoting are nearly as responsible as the engineers who built it incorrectly.

B) Police officers who arrest criminals on the wrong charges should be reprimanded for their mistake.

C) It is not a driver's fault if she gets lost because the map she is using is outdated.

D) A mail officer who delivers a package to the wrong address is more responsible than the sender who miswrote the address.

Practice Set

Part 6

The following passages have been designed to test the question types you learned about in this section. Review the techniques we discussed in Section 2, and mark up and make summaries for this passage. Then, answer the questions using the strategies you just learned.

This passage is adapted from Gretchen Reynolds, "This Is Your Brain on Coffee." ©2013 by The New York Times Company.

For hundreds of years, coffee has been one of the two or three most popular beverages on earth. But it's only recently that scientists are figuring out that the drink has notable health benefits. In one large-scale epidemiological study from last year, researchers primarily at the National Cancer Institute parsed health information from more than 400,000 volunteers, ages 50 to 71, who were free of major diseases at the study's start in 1995. By 2008, more than 50,000 of the participants had died. But men who reported drinking two or three cups of coffee a day were 10 percent less likely to have died than those who didn't drink coffee, while women drinking the same amount had 13 percent less risk of dying during the study. It's not clear exactly what coffee had to do with their longevity, but the correlation is striking.

Perhaps most consequential, animal experiments show that caffeine may reshape the biochemical environment inside our brains in ways that could stave off dementia. In a 2012 experiment at the University of Illinois at Urbana-Champaign, mice were briefly starved of oxygen, causing them to lose the ability to form memories. Half of the mice received a dose of caffeine that was the equivalent of several cups of coffee.

After they were reoxygenated, the caffeinated mice regained their ability to form new memories 33 percent faster than the uncaffeinated. Close examination of the animals' brain tissue showed that the caffeine disrupted the action of adenosine, a substance inside cells that usually provides energy, but can become destructive if it leaks out when the cells are injured or under stress. The escaped adenosine can jump-start a biochemical cascade leading to inflammation, which can disrupt the function of neurons, and potentially contribute to neurodegeneration or, in other words, dementia.

In a 2012 study of humans, researchers from the University of South Florida and the University of Miami tested the blood levels of caffeine in older adults with mild cognitive impairment, or the first glimmer of serious forgetfulness, a common precursor of Alzheimer's disease, and then re-evaluated them two to four years later. Participants with little or no caffeine circulating in their bloodstreams were far more likely to have progressed to full-blown Alzheimer's than those whose blood indicated they'd had about three cups' worth of caffeine.

There's still much to be learned about the effects of coffee. "We don't know whether blocking the action of adenosine is sufficient to prevent or lessen the effects of dementia," says Dr. Gregory G. Freund, a professor of pathology at the University of Illinois who led the 2012 study of mice. It is also unclear whether caffeine by itself provides the benefits associated with coffee drinking or if coffee contains other valuable ingredients. In a 2011 study by the same researchers at the University of South Florida, for instance, mice genetically bred to develop Alzheimer's and then given caffeine alone did not fare as well on memory tests as those provided with actual coffee. Nor is there any evidence that mixing caffeine with large amounts of sugar, as in energy drinks, is healthful. But a cup or three of coffee "has been popular for a long, long time," Dr. Freund says, "and there's probably good reasons for that."

1

The passage suggests the author would most likely agree with which of the following?

A) Current research does not yet show convincing health benefits of coffee.

B) The historical popularity of coffee is enough to demonstrate that its health benefits are significant.

C) It would be beneficial to conduct further research on the health benefits of coffee.

D) Doctors must begin advising patients at risk for dementia to increase their coffee intake.

2

Which choice provides the best evidence for the answer to the previous question?

A) Lines 20-23 ("Perhaps most … dementia")

B) Lines 57-58 ("There's still … coffee")

C) Lines 72-74 ("Nor … is healthful")

D) Lines 74-77 ("But … for that")

3

It can reasonably be inferred from the passage that

A) caffeine consumption is a major cause of Alzheimer's disease.

B) caffeine may stimulate memory formation under certain conditions.

C) once it is better understood, coffee will provide a cure for Alzheimer's disease.

D) coffee consumption will increase once its health benefits are publicized.

4

Based on the passage, which choice best describes the relationship between caffeine and coffee?

A) Coffee is only healthful when it contains caffeine.

B) Coffee may be healthier than isolated caffeine.

C) Coffee may be less healthy than isolated caffeine.

D) Coffee is most healthful when supplemented with additional caffeine.

5

Which choice provides the best evidence for the answer to the previous question?

A) Lines 27-29 ("Half of … coffee")

B) Lines 51-56 ("Participants with … caffeine")

C) Lines 58-63 ("We don't … mice")

D) Lines 66-72 ("In … actual coffee")

6

According to the "large-scale epidemiological study" (lines 5-6) cited in the passage, women participants who were coffee drinkers

A) were more likely to drink two to three cups of coffee a day than men.

B) were less likely to drink two to three cups of coffee a day than men.

C) were less likely to die than women who did not drink coffee.

D) were more likely to die than men who drank coffee.

7

Which of the following is most analogous to the description in lines 35-38 ("adenosine … under stress")?

A) Antibiotics are often helpful in fighting infections, but only if they are used consistently.

B) Even a small amount of arsenic can be dangerous, but consuming large amounts is deadly.

C) Humor gives an essay character, but can detract from the argument if used in the wrong context.

D) Operating power tools is very risky, except when done by trained professionals.

8

As used in line 49, "precursor" most nearly means

A) model.

B) prototype.

C) predecessor.

D) harbinger.

9

As used in line 70, "fare" most nearly means

A) travel.

B) survive.

C) perform.

D) happen.

This passage is adapted from Matt Ritchel, "The Search for Our Inner Lie Detectors." ©2014 by The New York Times Company.

Is a job applicant lying to you? What about your boss, or an entrepreneur who is promising to double your investment? Most of us are bad at spotting a lie, at least consciously. New research, published last month in *Psychological Science*, suggests that we have good instincts for judging liars, but that they are so deeply buried that we can't get at them.

This finding is the work of Leanne ten Brinke, a forensic psychologist. "Perhaps our own bodies know better than our conscious minds who is lying," explained Dr. ten Brinke, now at the Haas School of Business at the University of California, Berkeley.

It's well accepted that most of us are no better than a flip of the coin at seeing a lie. A classic experiment involves showing study subjects videotapes of people, some of whom are lying, who say they did not steal $100; the subjects correctly guess the liars about half the time. Dr. ten Brinke and her collaborators at Haas built on that experiment, with a twist: after the subjects watched the video and made their conscious assessments of who was lying, the researchers tried to measure the subjects' unconscious reactions.

To do so, the researchers flashed images of someone already seen in the videotape—but this time in milliseconds, indiscernible consciously. The subjects then completed a word task that involved placing "truth" words (like truthful, honest, valid) and "lie" words (dishonest, invalid, deceitful) into their proper categories. When study subjects were flashed a picture of a liar, they were significantly slower to lump words like truthful or honest into the "truth" category, but faster to lump words like deceitful into the "lie" category. The opposite was true when the subjects saw a truthful person. So, in general, the same people seemed better at detecting lies unconsciously than consciously. By scientific measures, the size of the effect was decidedly non-trivial, but not overwhelming.

There are many theories about why the ability to pick out liars gets lost in translation to consciousness. Dr. ten Brinke speculated that we tell one another little lies all the time—for survival, reproductive strategy, and so on—and that part of getting along socially is being able to let those harmless lies escape notice.

Is it possible to tap into the unconscious ability? "It's the million-dollar question," she said. The study fits into a rich history of lie-detection research, with some researchers saying they can read lies in facial expressions, and others arguing that liars just don't give off enough clear signals to allow detection. "The cues are so faint," said Dr. Bella DePaulo, a visiting professor of psychology at University of California, Santa Barbara and an expert in the science of lie detection. She said that there was some evidence, including her own research, that supported the idea of unconscious or indirect lie detecting, but she doubted that it would ever become a truly effective system. Dr. ten Brinke has started a new experiment, one that she hopes will offer concrete tactics to help us identify liars. It entails measuring physiological symptoms like blood flow and perspiration in study subjects who are listening to a liar. That, too, is a twist. The traditional lie-detector test makes similar measures of a person suspected of lying. Maybe the better detector will be the person listening, at least if the conscious mind can be left out of it.

10

The passage serves mainly to

A) discuss ongoing scientific research.

B) resolve a longstanding debate.

C) suggest a definitive solution to a problem.

D) describe breakthroughs in treating a disease.

11

Based on the passage, which choice best describes the relationship between lying and detection?

A) It is easiest to detect lies using the unconscious mind.

B) We unconsciously detect lies more accurately than we're aware of.

C) We can most accurately detect lies using the conscious mind.

D) We can most accurately detect lies when the liar is unconscious of their lie.

12

The passage most strongly suggests that

A) there is still no consensus on the best way to catch liars.

B) in the future there will be methods to detect lies with very high accuracy.

C) humans' accuracy in distinguishing lies from truth is improving.

D) there are fewer studies about lying conducted now than in the past.

13

Which choice provides the best evidence for the answer to the previous question?

A) Lines 41-43 ("So … than consciously")

B) Lines 56-60 ("The study … detection")

C) Lines 71-74 ("It entails … a liar")

D) Lines 77-79 ("Maybe … of it")

14

The results of the "classic experiment" (lines 17-22) most strongly suggest that

A) people are more successful in guessing if someone is lying to them than in actively trying to figure it out.

B) making a random guess would be about as accurate as consciously trying to figure out if someone is lying.

C) people are such poor judges of lying they are better off guessing if they are being deceived.

D) most of the time people assume that they are not being lied to.

15

Which of the following experiments would be most similar to the experiment described in lines 28-35?

A) An image of a clean or messy place is flashed for a few milliseconds and subjects are asked to complete word sets with clean or messy sounding words.

B) An image of a person is flashed for a few milliseconds and subjects are asked to say whether they've met that person before.

C) Subjects are allowed to examine the face of a person and then guess whether they will be likely to lie in the future.

D) Subjects are asked to examine an image of a house and then match the image with the most accurate descriptive words.

16

According to Dr. ten Brinke, humans' inability to spot lies may

A) be remedied with her current techniques.

B) help us study the brain.

C) serve a social purpose.

D) be overcome through concentration.

17

Which choice provides the best evidence for the answer to the previous question?

A) Lines 5-9 ("New research … them")

B) Lines 17-22 ("A classic … time")

C) Lines 48-53 ("Dr. ten Brinke … escape notice")

D) Lines 69-71 ("Dr. ten Brinke … identify liars")

18

As used in line 37, "lump" most nearly means

A) group.

B) congregate.

C) accumulate.

D) trudge.

19

As used in line 71, "concrete" most nearly means

A) specific.

B) established.

C) physical.

D) realistic.

Section 5

Persuasive Language

Passages on the SAT Reading Test will use a variety of techniques, devices, and language to communicate ideas to the reader. The questions that test these techniques fall under a category that the College Board calls **Rhetoric**. This section will cover the types of questions you will be asked about these types of persuasive language and how to answer them.

First, you'll learn how to analyze word choice as well as the overall structure of a text. Next, you'll learn how to decipher the point of view and purpose of a passage. Finally, you'll learn how to assess arguments made by the author. There will be practice exercises for you to try along the way, and two passages at the end of the section where you will put together everything you've learned.

Analyzing Word Choice
Part 1

Analyzing Word Choice questions ask you how specific words, phrases, or patterns shape the meaning and tone of the text. They will often require you to read between the lines and decipher the passage beyond a literal understanding of what is being said.

Here are some ways that Word Choice questions might be phrased:

- The author uses the phrase "is written in" (line 6) most likely to …
- The analogy in the final sentence of Passage 2 has primarily which effect?
- What main effect do the quotations by Andrews in lines 10-18 have on the tone of the passage?

Rhetorical Devices

You may be asked what certain rhetorical devices are achieving in the text. Remember that **rhetorical devices** are tools that the author uses to convey her argument, such as repetition, metaphor, or simile. You can refer back to Section 3 for a review of these devices. However, you don't need to know the definitions of rhetorical devices in order to answer these questions. Instead, you'll need to know how rhetorical devices shape the text.

For example, repetition is often used to make or emphasize a point. Metaphors and similes are often used to describe or explain an interesting concept. To understand specific metaphors and similes, think about what is being used as a comparison. For example, birds are free to fly wherever they like, so comparing something to a bird is often meant to indicate freedom. Referring to a caged animal might suggest the opposite. Be careful of choosing an answer that is too literal when answering questions about these devices.

Let's see what a Word Choice question might look like for the following paragraph, taken from John F. Kennedy's inaugural address.

Example

In the long history of the world, only a few generations have been granted the role of defending freedom in its hour of maximum danger. I do not shrink from this responsibility—I welcome it. I do not believe that any of us would exchange places with any other people or any other generation. The energy, the faith, the devotion which we bring to this endeavor will light our country and all who serve it—and the glow from that fire can truly light the world.

1

The reference to "light" and "glow" in lines 10-11 mainly have which effect?

A) To argue for citizen involvement to bring electricity to other nations

B) To suggest that the action of citizens can benefit their country and the world

C) To persuade listeners that they must share their resources with others

D) To imply that all Americans have benefited from the actions of previous generations

Be wary of interpreting the images of light and fire literally. Here, Kennedy is using a metaphor to make a point about the power of citizen action. This is clearer when you read the entire paragraph, so always be sure to read the lines surrounding a Word Choice question. Also consider the author's main purpose, or the structure of the overall passage, to help you determine how the figurative language functions within it. Answer choice (B) demonstrates that the light represents how the actions of the listeners will benefit the United States and the rest of the world. Therefore, (B) is the correct answer.

You can use Process of Elimination to rule out the other answer options. Answer choices (A) and (C) interpret the imagery too literally, so they can be knocked out. Answer choice (D) talks about action being taken, but the paragraph refers to the energy and faith of those listening, not of a previous generation.

Tone

Word Choice questions may also ask you to analyze how certain words or lines shape the tone of a text, or to describe the tone of a passage overall. **Tone** refers to the feeling or attitude the author demonstrates in his writing. You can determine the tone of a passage by paying attention to the words the author uses, and to how you feel as you read the passage. Adjectives in particular help shape the tone of a text, so look out for them as you read. Refer back to the notes you made when marking up the passage, as discussed in Chapter 1 and Section 2 of this chapter as part of the Pencil on Paper strategy.

The following words may be used by the SAT to describe the tone of the passage, or the attitude of someone mentioned in the text. This is only a partial list—the SAT may use a number of different words to describe an author's tone.

Tone Words	
Positive	Captivated, Effusive, Enthusiastic, Engaged, Excited, Humorous, Intrigued, Laudatory, Reverent , Whimsical
Neutral	Academic, Candid, Contemplative, Detached, Dispassionate, Impartial, Judicious, Pragmatic, Scholarly
Negative	Apathetic, Caustic, Condescending, Contemptuous, Cynical, Derisive, Disparaging, Flippant, Grudging, Skeptical, Vindictive

When you answer a tone question, think back to your impression of the passage, or the section you are asked about. How did it make you feel? Think of your own word to describe the tone of the text. If you cannot think of a specific word, try to think more generally about the tone. Was it strong or neutral? Positive or negative? Happy or sad? Then, compare your prediction to the answer choices.

Let's look at a tone question about the excerpt from John F. Kennedy's speech to see how this works.

Example

In the long history of the world, only a few generations have been granted the role of defending freedom in its hour of maximum danger. I do not shrink from this responsibility—I welcome it. I do not believe that any of us would exchange places with any other people or any other generation. The energy, the faith, the devotion which we bring to this endeavor will light our country and all who serve it—and the glow from that fire can truly light the world.

2

The tone of the paragraph is best described as

A) uncertain.

B) confident.

C) biting.

D) delicate.

How would you describe the tone of these lines? The word "devotion" demonstrates Kennedy's strong commitment, and stating, "the glow from that fire can truly light the world" suggests he's convinced that things will move forward in a positive way. You might choose a word like "encouraging" or "optimistic" to describe this tone. Once you compare this word to the answer choices, (B) is the only option that is close to your prediction.

Answer choice (A) is nearly the opposite of what you are looking for, as the declarative language in the paragraph reflects Kennedy's sure attitude ("I do not shrink...I welcome...I do not believe"). (C) is too negative to describe the lines in question, since Kennedy talks here about faith, devotion, light, and freedom. (D) is a poor fit as Kennedy's words are decisive and bold.

Part 1 Practice: Analyzing Word Choice

Review the techniques we discussed in Section 2, and mark up and make summaries for this passage excerpt. Then, answer the Analyzing Word Choice questions using the strategies you just learned.

This passage is adapted from Kate Chopin, *The Awakening and Selected Short Stories*, first published in 1899.

Edna often wondered at one propensity which sometimes had inwardly disturbed her without causing any outward show or manifestation on her part. At a very early age—perhaps it was when she traversed the ocean of waving grass—she remembered that she had been passionately enamored of a dignified and sad-eyed cavalry officer who visited her father in Kentucky. She could not leave his presence when he was there, nor remove her eyes from his face, which was something like Napoleon's, with a lock of black hair falling across the forehead. But the cavalry officer melted imperceptibly out of her existence.

At another time her affections were deeply engaged by a young gentleman who visited a lady on a neighboring plantation. It was after they went to Mississippi to live. The young man was engaged to be married to the young lady, and they sometimes called upon Margaret, driving over some afternoons in a buggy. Edna was a little miss, just merging into her teens; and the realization that she herself was nothing, nothing, nothing to the engaged young man was a bitter affliction to her. But he, too, went the way of dreams.

1

The main rhetorical effect of the repeated word in lines 28-29 is to

A) underscore how frequently Edna had felt ignored in her teens.

B) suggest that Edna often had to remind herself of her proper place.

C) emphasize how little Edna mattered to the young man.

D) imply that Edna lacked self-confidence around the young man and Margaret.

2

The author's tone is best described as

A) apologetic.

B) disturbed.

C) invigorated.

D) reflective.

Analyzing Text Structure

Part 2

Analyzing Text Structure questions ask you about the structure of the text as a whole, or about the relationship between the whole text and a specific part of the text, such as one sentence or paragraph.

Analyzing Text Structure questions might be phrased as follows:

- Which choice best reflects the overall sequence of events in the passage?
- Which choice best describes the structure of the first paragraph?
- Over the course of the passage, the focus shifts from …

Use Your Summaries

Referring back to the summaries you made while reading the passage can help you answer Analyzing Text Structure questions. Reading these summaries will help you understand how the paragraphs relate to one another, and can help you figure out the relationship between a specific part of the text and the text as a whole. Look for points where certain ideas were introduced or where the focus of the passage changed. You can then describe the structure of the passage in your own words and compare it to the answer choices.

Let's see how this works with a question about the overall structure of a passage. Remember the summaries you wrote for the Cavallini passage in Section 2? Here is the passage and the paragraph summaries again:

Example

This passage is adapted from Daniel Zalewski, "Under a Shroud of Kitsch May Lie a Master's Art." ©2001 by The New York Times Company.

Tommaso Strinati clambers to the top of the rickety scaffold and laughs. "It's a good thing that all this Baroque work is so unimpressive," he says, pointing at the clumsy trompe l'oeil painting covering the wall in front of him. "Otherwise, we might not have been allowed to scrape it off!"

#1 T.S. glad remove Baroque

A 28-year-old art historian, he is standing 16 feet above the marble floor of San Pasquale Baylon chapel, a long-neglected nook of Santa Maria in Aracoeli, a Franciscan basilica in the center of Rome. Last year, Mr. Strinati, who is still a graduate student, began studying the church's history. Records suggested that the Roman artist Pietro Cavallini—a painter and mosaicist whose greatest works have been destroyed—

#2 Continued on next column…

#2 T.S. thinks hidden P.C. frescos

spent years decorating Aracoeli toward the end of the 13th century. Yet only one small Cavallini fresco, in the church's left transept, remained visible. Mr. Strinati wondered: had other Cavallini frescoes been painted over with inferior work? And if so, could modern restorers uncover them?

#3. Found P.C. frescoes

"The answer to both questions was yes," Mr. Strinati says. A close-up examination of the chapel's walls last summer revealed ghostly images lying beneath the surface. The entire chapel, it seemed, was a painted palimpsest. And when a heavy altarpiece was removed from one wall, a remarkably tender portrait of the Madonna and Child was found hidden behind it.

#4. Resemble other P.C. work

After months of careful paint-peeling, what has been uncovered are dazzling fragments of a late-medieval masterpiece completed shortly after 1285. Although the Aracoeli fresco is not signed, the figures strongly resemble those in a surviving Cavallini work, the resplendent "Last Judgment" fresco at nearby Santa Cecilia.

#5. P.C. maybe anticipated Giotto/ Renaissance

Mr. Strinati has grand ambitions for his discovery. He hopes that in a few years the fully restored fresco will not only rescue Cavallini's name from obscurity, but also upend the widespread notion that the first flowers of the Renaissance budded in Florence, not Rome. For the fresco's lifelike figures—in particular, an impish Christ child with charmingly flushed cheeks—suggest to Strinati that Cavallini may have anticipated some of the extraordinary naturalistic innovations that have long been credited to the Florentine artist Giotto.

#6. Cont. on next column...

#6. P.C. maybe painted "St. F"

Moreover, the Aracoeli fragments may provide a critical new clue in a decades-old battle concerning the "St. Francis Legend," the 1296 fresco cycle at Assisi, universally recognized as one of the foundations of the Renaissance. For centuries, the 28-scene cycle—which recounts the life of the saint with a narrative zest and compositional depth that leave the flat tableaus of the Byzantine era far behind—was attributed to Giotto. But since the 1930's, various scholars have questioned this judgment, claiming that the Assisi cycle doesn't resemble Giotto's other work. Now, the Aracoeli discovery is ammunition for Italian art historians who believe that Cavallini might actually be the primary creative force behind the "St. Francis Legend."

#7. P.C. causing art history debates

The growing debate about Cavallini's importance was the occasion for a symposium in Rome in November. *La Republicca*, an Italian daily, has cast the debate as "War Between Rome and Florence." Mr. Strinati is enjoying the ruckus. "I had a hunch that there was more Cavallini lurking around here," he says of the Aracoeli basilica. "But I didn't expect to find an exquisite work that could shake up the history of art."

3

Which of the following best describes the structure of the passage as a whole?

A) The passage introduces a scholar, and then focuses on a discovery he has made.

B) The passage introduces an artist, and details a new discovery of his art.

C) The passage makes an argument about an artist, then supports it with historical evidence.

D) The passage considers both sides of an issue, yet reaches no conclusion.

The summaries for the Cavallini passage show that the first paragraph is about Strinati, and the second and third paragraphs introduce the Cavallini frescoes Strinati discovered. The rest of the passage is focused on

Cavallini's work and the impact it might have on theories of art history. Answer choice (A) matches this progression, as Strinati is an art historian, and the remainder of the passage discusses the Cavallini discovery. Therefore, answer (A) is correct.

Answer choice (B) is close, but the passage does not begin by introducing the reader to the artist Cavallini. It introduces Strinati, who is an academic and not an artist; this answer is therefore incorrect. Answer choice (C) is incorrect because the passage as a whole isn't focused on one argument about Cavallini. Instead, there are several smaller arguments supported with historical evidence in individual paragraphs, such as the "St. Francis Legend" in the sixth paragraph. Thus, (C) does not represent the structure of the passage as a whole. Answer choice (D) is also incorrect, as the passage does not debate two sides of an issue throughout.

Mark Up the Structure

To help you get a better sense of the structure of a passage, you can also build upon the techniques you learned in Section 2 and mark up additional items in your passage. You can look for transition words, evidence, and examples in the passage.

Marking up Passage Structure

Concept	Importance	How to mark it in the passage
Transition words	Indicate a change in direction of author's reasoning or argument	Circle the word
Examples or evidence	Clarify concepts discussed by the author; can reveal how an author has supported his or her argument	Note "e.g." for examples or "e.v." for evidence in the margin

Here are a few paragraphs from the Cavallini passage. We've marked up transition words, evidence, and examples to show you how this works.

Example

Moreover, the Aracoeli fragments may provide a critical new clue in a decades-old battle concerning the "St. Francis Legend," the 1296 fresco cycle at Assisi, universally recognized as one of the foundations of the Renaissance. For centuries, the 28-scene cycle—which recounts the life of the saint with a narrative zest and compositional depth that leave the flat tableaus of the Byzantine era far behind—was attributed to Giotto. But since the 1930's, various scholars have questioned this judgment, claiming that the Assisi cycle doesn't resemble Giotto's other work. Now, the Aracoeli discovery is ammunition for Italian art historians who believe that Cavallini might actually be the primary creative force behind the "St. Francis Legend."

The growing debate about Cavallini's importance was the occasion for a symposium in Rome in November. La Republicca, an Italian daily, has cast the debate as "War Between Rome and Florence." Mr. Strinati is enjoying the ruckus. "I had a hunch that there was more Cavallini lurking around here," he says of the Aracoeli basilica. "But I didn't expect to find an exquisite work that could shake up the history of art."

By noting the transition words, you can see how parts of the paragraph relate to one another, and also how assertions are supported with evidence and examples. For example, lines 71 to 79 provide evidence against the previous assertion about Giotto. It also provides the reason for questioning whether he was the original artist of the "St. Francis Legend."

Part 2 Practice: Analyzing Text Structure

Review the techniques we discussed in Section 2, and mark up and make summaries for this passage excerpt. Then, answer the Analyzing Text Structure questions using the strategies you just learned.

This passage is adapted from Matt Ridley, "The World's Resources Aren't Running Out." ©2014 by *Dow Jones & Company.*

How many times have you heard that we humans are "using up" the world's resources, "running out" of oil, "reaching the limits" of the atmosphere's capacity to cope with pollution or "approaching the carrying capacity" of the land's ability to support a greater population? The assumption behind all such statements is that there is a fixed amount of stuff—metals, oil, clean air, land—and that we risk exhausting it through our consumption. "We are using 50% more resources than the Earth can sustainably produce, and unless we change course, that number will grow fast—by 2030, even two planets will not be enough," says Jim Leape, director general of the World Wide Fund for Nature International (formerly the World Wildlife Fund). But here's a peculiar feature of human history: we burst through such limits again and again. After all, as a Saudi oil minister once said, the Stone Age didn't end for lack of stone. Ecologists call this "niche construction"—that people (and indeed some other animals) can create new opportunities for themselves by making their habitats more productive in some way. Agriculture is the classic example of niche construction: we stopped relying on nature's bounty and substituted an artificial and much larger bounty.

1

Which of the following best describes the general organization of the passage?

A) A problem is introduced, the evidence supporting it is questioned, and then the author concludes the problem is solvable.

B) A problem is introduced with evidence to support it, and then the author introduces a competing argument.

C) Evidence is introduced, a problem is identified, and then the author offers additional information.

D) A problem is introduced, a solution is proposed, and then the author offers an alternative solution.

2

The author's statement in lines 20-21 ("we … and again) serves primarily to

A) introduce new evidence for his conclusion.

B) provide support for an earlier argument.

C) summarize the passage.

D) introduce his main argument.

3

The author discusses "niche construction" (line 24) in order to

A) help explain his claim that humans can overcome the limits of existing resources.

B) counter the argument that humans are rapidly consuming resources.

C) provide an example of how humans can reduce their usage of limited resources.

D) suggest that the earlier claim that certain resources are limited is false.

Point of View and Analyzing Purpose

Part 3

Just like all texts you read, the passages on the SAT Reading Test were written from a specific point of view and for a specific reason. You may be asked two different kinds of questions about this: **Point of View** questions and **Analyzing Purpose** questions.

Here are some ways Point of View questions might be phrased:

- The passage is written from the perspective of someone who is …
- Over the course of the passage, the narrator's attitude shifts from …
- The author's attitude toward Dr. Brown's discovery is best described as …

Here are some ways Analyzing Purpose questions might be phrased:

- The passage serves primarily to …
- The most likely purpose of the parenthetical information in lines 63-64 is to …
- The author of Passage 2 refers to the novel *War and Peace* primarily to suggest that …

Point of View

Point of View questions ask you to determine the point of view or attitude of the author. This may involve determining what the author's attitude is towards a specific subject, or describing how the author approached writing the text overall. These questions can sometimes be similar to Word Choice questions about tone, which you learned about earlier in this section.

One good place to find the author's point of view or opinion is through certain adjectives she may use. Adjectives can be simple and descriptive, such as "the sky is blue," or can demonstrate how we feel about something, such as "Brussel sprouts are delicious." When you see adjectives that convey an opinion in the text, and they are not attributed to another person or character in the passage, you can assume they represent the point of view of the author.

There may be passages with very few strong adjectives or statements by the author that indicate her opinion. In that case, do not make assumptions that go beyond what is stated in the passage. Be wary of answer choices that state the author's opinion too strongly, or use absolute language like "best" or "worst" that doesn't fit with the passage.

Let's look at a Point of View question to see how this works:

Example

Dr. Chabra has found a way to help serious athletes recover more quickly from the stiffness caused by heavy training. Like any new medical intervention, Dr. Chabra's novel approach to treating muscle soreness has been met with some skepticism and a lot of questions. Still, many of her colleagues praised the innovative treatment; they rightly recognized the valuable impact it could have on athletic performance.

4

The author's attitude toward Dr. Chabra's new treatment is best described as

A) uncertain.

B) relieved.

C) disparaging.

D) approving.

While the second sentence of this paragraph indicates that there has been some skepticism about Dr. Chabra's treatment, it does not appear to be the author's attitude. Instead, the author aligns herself with Dr. Chabra's colleagues who have "rightly" praised the treatment, which indicates a positive attitude. The adjectives "innovative" and "valuable" are also very complimentary and suggest the author thinks highly of Dr. Chabra's discovery. Answer (D) is therefore the correct response.

Answer choice (A) does not work, as the author is not hesitant about Dr. Chabra's work. Neither is the author disparaging; while some "skeptics" are mentioned the author does not count himself among them, and does not make any negative or derogatory statements about Dr. Chabra's research. Thus, answer choice (C) can also be eliminated. Answer choice (B) does not make sense in the context of the passage, as nothing indicates that the author was previously worried and then consoled once she learned of Dr. Chabra's discovery.

Analyzing Purpose

Analyzing Purpose questions ask you about the purpose of either an entire passage or specific lines or paragraphs. To answer these questions you need to analyze what the author was trying to achieve with his writing.

For questions that ask you about the purpose of the passage as a whole, you will want to choose a "big-picture" answer. Ask yourself why the passage was written. Was it to persuade the reader of something, to argue against a previously held idea, or just to introduce a new concept? Describe the goal of the passage in your own words before looking at the answer choices.

Here's an example of an Analyzing Purpose question from the Cavallini passage that you already tackled in Section 2:

Example

The primary purpose of the passage is to

A) explain an exciting discovery.
B) describe Cavallini's artistic style.
C) emphasize the importance of art history.
D) discuss Giotto's role in the Renaissance.

Here, answers (B) and (D) are too narrow, and answer choice (C) is not discussed at all in the passage. Therefore, (A) is the correct answer as the passage discusses the discovery of the hidden frescoes.

You may also be asked about the purpose of individual lines or paragraphs. Again, try to think of what the author is trying to achieve with the portions of text you are asked about. Is she introducing or summarizing concepts? Providing arguments or counterarguments? Presenting a contrast for emphasis? Review your summaries and notes on the passage to see how the section you are analyzing relates to other parts of the text.

Remember that you are being asked about the role of a certain part of the passage, and not just what it says. You may need to read critically to understand the author's intent or goal! Be sure to carefully analyze persuasive language, and look at the lines before and after the ones you are asked about for clues as to the author's intent.

Part 3 Practice: Point of View and Purpose

Review the techniques we discussed in Section 2, and mark up and make summaries for this passage excerpt. Then, answer the Point of View and Purpose questions using the strategies you just learned.

This passage is adapted from Charles Dickens, *Great Expectations*, first published in 1861.

Dinner done, we sat with our feet upon the fender. I said to Herbert, "My dear Herbert, I have something very particular to tell you."

"My dear Handel," he returned, "I shall esteem and respect your confidence."

"It concerns myself, Herbert," said I, "and one other person."

Herbert crossed his feet, looked at the fire with his head on one side, and having looked at it in vain for some time, looked at me because I didn't go on.

"Herbert," said I, laying my hand upon his knee, "I love—I adore—Estella."

Instead of being transfixed, Herbert replied in an easy matter-of-course way, "Exactly. Well?"

"Well, Herbert? Is that all you say? Well?"

"What next, I mean?" said Herbert. "Of course I know that."

"How do you know it?" said I.

"How do I know it, Handel? Why, from you."

"I never told you."

"Told me! You have never told me when you have got your hair cut, but I have had senses to perceive it. You have always adored her, ever since I have known you. You brought your adoration and your portmanteau here together. Told me! Why, you have always told me all day long. When you told me your own story, you told me plainly that you began adoring her the first time you saw her, when you were very young indeed."

1

The primary purpose of lines 26-31 is to

A) explain how Herbert knows that Handel loves Estella.

B) introduce the fact that Handel has loved Estella for a long time.

C) highlight Herbert's keen powers of perception.

D) suggest that many people must be aware of Handel's love for Estella.

2

The passage serves mainly to

A) describe the relationship between one friend and another.

B) recount a conversation between two friends.

C) reveal a mysterious character's secret motives.

D) foreshadow an upcoming action in a story

Analyzing Arguments

Part 4

Analyzing Arguments questions ask you to analyze the way the author of the passage makes and supports her arguments. You may be asked to identify claims or counterclaims in a passage, whether explicit or implicit. You may also be asked to assess an author's reasoning and evidence.

Here are some ways Analyzing Arguments questions might be phrased:

- In lines 6-10 the author argues that …
- In Passage 2, the author claims that ...
- The authors most likely use the examples in lines 1-9 of the passage to ...
- An unstated assumption made by the author is that …
- In the passage, the author anticipates which of the following objections to her argument?

Analyzing Claims and Counterclaims

Analyzing Claims and Counterclaims questions, or "Claims" questions, ask you to locate arguments the author makes. An **argument** is an idea that the author believes is true or is trying to persuade the reader to believe, and it is usually supported by evidence.

To find an author's argument, look for what the passage is trying to persuade you to believe. This may be clearly defined as a thesis statement, or may require you to read between the lines. Look for statements that are not necessarily factual, that make judgments, or that suggest a particular course of action should be taken.

A **counterclaim** or counterargument is an argument that goes against a previous argument in the passage. A counterclaim may disprove another person's claim that was previously mentioned by the author. It could also offer an alternative to an argument made by the author, showing that he recognizes the limitations of his earlier claim. The author may then conclude with this new argument, or present evidence to refute it and stand by what he had originally asserted.

Take a look at the following example.

Example

This passage is adapted from Diane Lewis, "The Toxic Brew in Our Yards." ©2014 by The New York Times Company.

A study by the United States Geological Survey released in 1999 found at least one pesticide, and often more than one, in almost every stream and fish sample tested, and in about half of the samples drawn from wells throughout the country. These pesticides are going from our lawns and gardens into our drinking water and into our bodies.

The amounts of these chemicals are small and often considered "acceptable," but scientists now know that they have a cumulative effect. Many chemicals that we use very casually on our lawns cause long-term health problems in ways that have only recently been understood. They "disrupt," or throw out of whack, the endocrine system, made up of glands and hormones that control almost every aspect of our bodies' functions.

Can you spot the counterargument in this excerpt? Consider the author's main point and arguments, and how she structures her evidence. You should notice that, in the second paragraph, the author mentions that "the amount of these chemicals are small and often considered 'acceptable,'" before explaining why this fact is actually not enough to discredit her larger claim. Even though the chemical amounts are small, the author explains, they still cause long-term health problems.

If you have trouble identifying arguments, ask yourself what the author seems sure about, or what he is trying to persuade you to believe.

Now let's practice by answering a Claims question about the paragraph below, from a speech by Anna Howard Shaw. Focus on identifying her argument as you read.

Example

This passage is adapted from a speech by Anna Howard Shaw, "The Fundamental Principle of a Republic." Delivered during the New York State equal suffrage campaign on June 21, 1915.

Now if we should take a vote and the men had to read their ballot in order to vote it, more women could vote than men. But when the government says not only that you must be twenty-one years of age, a resident of the community, and native born or naturalized, those are qualifications, but when it says that an elector must be a male, that is not a qualification for citizenship; that is an insurmountable barrier between one half of the people and the other half of the citizens and their rights as citizens. No such nation can call itself a Republic. It is only an aristocracy. That barrier must be removed before the government can become a Republic, and that is exactly what we are asking right now, that this great state of New York shall become in fact as it is in theory, a part of a government of the people, by the people, and for the people.

1

In lines 13-17 the author argues that

A) a Republic is the only acceptable form of government.

B) only those who can read should be allowed to vote in a Republic.

C) a true Republic must allow both women and men to vote.

D) a Republic is necessary to allow women to vote.

In this paragraph, Shaw is speaking about republics in order to make a point about women's right to vote. Her comments about women and men in the earlier lines of the paragraph help make this clear, even though the heart of the argument is in lines 13-17. When Shaw says "that barrier must be removed," she is referring to women's inability to vote, as stated in lines 8-13. Only answer choice (C) sums up this argument.

You can knock out answer choice (A) since it is too strong; you only know that Shaw is in favor of a true republic. As she doesn't discuss other forms of government, we can't be sure that she thinks republics are the best possible form. (B) refers to something mentioned in the first line, which is also not an argument but an observation. Answer choice (D) is almost the inverse of Shaw's argument—she never says that having a republic is the only way to grant women the right to vote.

Assessing Reasoning

Assessing Reasoning questions ask you to follow an author's line of reasoning, analyze whether an author's reasoning makes sense, or determine why an author used a certain type of reasoning. If you are asked why an author used a certain type of reasoning, you can use a similar approach as you learned for Purpose questions earlier in this section. Focus on what the author's overall goal or purpose is for the lines you are asked about, so you can determine how the reasoning the author uses lines up with what she is trying to prove.

To assess if an author's reasoning makes sense, look at whether the evidence she has given truly supports or matches up with the argument she is trying to make. This may require looking at evidence over more than one paragraph, and combining it in ways that allow you to draw new conclusions.

Let's look again at an excerpt from the Cavallini passage.

Example

Mr. Strinati has grand ambitions for his discovery. He hopes that in a few years the fully restored fresco will not only rescue Cavallini's name from obscurity, but also upend the widespread notion that the first flowers of the Renaissance budded in Florence, not Rome. For the fresco's lifelike figures—in particular, an impish Christ child with charmingly flushed cheeks—suggest to Strinati that Cavallini may have anticipated some of the extraordinary naturalistic innovations that have long been credited to the Florentine artist Giotto.

Moreover, the Aracoeli fragments may provide a critical new clue in a decades-old battle concerning the "St. Francis Legend," the 1296 fresco cycle at Assisi, universally recognized as one of the foundations of the Renaissance. For centuries, the 28-scene cycle—which recounts the life of the saint with a narrative zest and compositional depth that leave the flat tableaus of the Byzantine era far behind—was attributed to Giotto. But since the 1930's, various scholars have questioned this judgment, claiming that the Assisi cycle doesn't resemble Giotto's other work. Now, the Aracoeli discovery is ammunition for Italian art historians who believe that Cavallini might actually be the primary creative force behind the "St. Francis Legend."

Consider the author's statement that the Aracoeli discovery may suggest Cavallini painted the "St. Francis Legend." Does this argument make sense?

It does if we consider information the author has introduced over the previous two paragraphs. The author states that Cavallini's work may have been done before some of Giotto's, and thus may have been important to the start of the Renaissance. The "St. Francis Legend" is also described as a foundation of the Renaissance, but doesn't look like Giotto's other work. It would therefore make sense that Cavallini, who was painting during the early Renaissance before Giotto and may have been one of its leaders, could be the artist behind the painting.

When answering Assessing Reasoning questions, think critically about whether the author has supported his point, and whether you are convinced by the type of evidence he has used.

Some questions will ask you about what kinds of evidence the author uses to support her arguments, or whether she fails to use any. These are called **Analyzing Evidence** questions. Some kinds of evidence are more common in certain contexts. For example, an argument about the increasing infection rates for a certain disease would be better proven by data than by a personal anecdote. To answer these questions, first locate the author's argument, and then ask yourself what he did to prove it. Keep in mind that an author may use multiple types of evidence, which may appear either before or after the argument itself.

Part 4 Practice: Analyzing Arguments

Review the techniques we discussed in Section 2, and mark up and make summaries for this passage excerpt. Then, answer the Analyzing Arguments questions using the strategies you just learned.

This passage is adapted from Dayo Olopade, "Africa's Tech Edge." ©2014 by *The Atlantic Monthly Group.*

It's a painfully First World problem: splitting dinner with friends, we do the dance of the seven credit cards. No one, it seems, carries cash anymore, so we blunder through the inconvenience that comes with our dependence on plastic. Just as often, I encounter a street vendor or taxi driver who can't handle my proffered card and am left shaking out my pockets and purse.

When I returned to the United States after living in Nairobi on and off for two years, these antiquated payment ordeals were especially frustrating. As I never tire of explaining to friends, in Kenya I could pay for nearly everything with a few taps on my cellphone.

Every few weeks, I'd pull cash out of my American bank account and hand it to a contemplative young man stationed outside my local greengrocer. I'd show him my ID and type in a PIN, and he'd credit my phone number with an equivalent amount of digital currency.

Through a service called M-Pesa, I could store my mobile money and then, for a small fee, send it to any other phone number in the network, be it my cable company's, a taxi driver's, or a friend's. Payments from other M-Pesa users would be added to my digital balance, which I could later withdraw in cash from my local agent.

For me, M-Pesa was convenient, often simpler than reaching for my credit card or counting out paper bills. But for most Kenyans, the service has been life-changing. Kenya has one ATM for every 18,000 people—the U.S., by contrast, has one for every 740—and across sub-Saharan Africa, more than 75 percent of the adult population had no bank account as of 2011. When Safaricom, the major Kenyan telecommunications firm, launched M-Pesa in 2007, pesa—Swahili for "money"—moved from mattresses to mobile accounts virtually overnight. Suddenly, payment and collection of debts did not require face-to-face interactions. Daylong queues to pay electric- or water-utility bills disappeared. By 2012, 86 percent of Kenyan cellphone subscribers used mobile money, and by 2013, M-Pesa's transactions amounted to some $35 million daily. Annualized, that's more than a quarter of Kenya's GDP.

M-Pesa isn't the first mobile-money service. The Philippines has had at least rudimentary mobile money-transfer systems since 2001, but nine years later, fewer than 10 percent of Filipino mobile users without bank accounts actively used them, while the long tail of mobile-payment systems has already transformed Africa. Parrot programs like Paga, EcoCash, Splash Mobile Money, Tigo Cash, Airtel Money, Orange Money, and MTN Mobile Money have sprung up in several African countries. Even government has elbowed its way in: the Rwanda Revenue Authority has introduced a service that allows citizens to declare and pay taxes right from their cellphones.

1

The author makes which of the following arguments?

A) Americans should begin implementing and using M-Pesa.

B) M-Pesa is more convenient than most forms of payment in the United States.

C) Making easy payments is now only a problem in the United States.

D) Mobile money was difficult to introduce in Kenya.

2

The author supports the claim that M-Pesa "has been life-changing" (lines 37-38) by

A) explaining how M-Pesa works.

B) describing some common financial transactions in Kenya.

C) offering statistics about the use of mobile money services in the United States.

D) citing statistics about the use of M-Pesa in Kenya.

3

In lines 58-65, the author uses the example of the Filipino mobile money services to

A) suggest mobile money services do not work well in all types of economies

B) contrast the limited success of mobile money services in the Philippines with the huge impact of mobile money systems in African countries

C) provide evidence that M-Pesa was not the first mobile money service to be widely used

D) imply that mobile payment services will continue to spread to new places in the coming years

Practice Set

Part 5

The following passages have been designed to test the question types you learned about in this section. Review the techniques we discussed in Section 2, and mark up and make summaries for this passage. Then, answer the questions using the strategies you just learned.

This passage is adapted from a speech delivered to the United States Senate by Senator Robert La Follette on October 6th, 1917, shortly after the US entered the First World War.

I think all men recognize that in time of war the citizen must surrender some rights for the common good that he is entitled to enjoy in time of peace. But the right to control their own Government according to constitutional forms is not one of the rights that the citizens of this country are called upon to surrender in time of war.

Rather in time of war the citizen must be more alert to the preservation of his right to control his Government. He must be most watchful of the encroachment of the military upon the civil power. He must beware of those precedents in support of arbitrary action by administrative officials, which excused on the plea of necessity in war time, become the fixed rule when the necessity has passed and normal conditions have been restored.

More than all, the citizen and his representative in Congress in time of war must maintain his right of free speech. More than in times of peace, it is necessary that the channels for free public discussion of governmental policies shall be open and unclogged. I believe that I am now touching upon the most important question in this country today—and that is the right of the citizens of this country and their representatives in Congress to discuss in an orderly way frankly and publicly and without fear, from the platform and through the press, every important phase of this war: its causes, the manner in which it should be conducted, and the terms upon which peace should be made. The widespread belief that this most fundamental right is being denied to the citizens of this country is a fact the tremendous significance of which those in authority have not yet begun to appreciate. I am contending for the great fundamental right of the sovereign people of this country to make their voice heard and have that voice heeded upon the great questions arising out of this war, including not only how the war shall be prosecuted but the conditions upon which it may be terminated with a due regard for the rights and the honor of this nation and the interests of humanity.

I am contending for this right because the exercise of it is necessary to the welfare of this Government, to the successful conduct of this war, and to a peace that shall be enduring and for the best interest of this country.

Suppose success attends the attempt to stifle all discussion of the issues of this war, all discussion of the terms upon which it should be concluded, and all discussion of the objects and purposes to be accomplished by it. If we then concede to the demand of the war-mad press and war extremists, who monopolize the right of public utterance upon these questions unchallenged, what would be the consequences to this country, not only during the war but after the war?

Our Government, above all others, is founded on the right of the people freely to discuss all matters pertaining to their

Government, in war not less than in peace, for in this Government the people are the rulers in war no less than in peace. Though the right of the people to express their will by ballot is suspended during the term of office of the elected official, nevertheless the duty of the official to obey the popular will continues throughout this entire term of office. How can that popular will express itself between elections except by meetings, by speeches, by publications, by petitions, and by addresses to the representatives of the people? Any man who seeks to set a limit upon those rights, whether in war or peace, aims a blow at the most vital part of our Government. And then as the time for election approaches and the official is called to account for his stewardship the people must have the right to the freest possible discussion of every question upon which their representative has acted, of the merits of every measure he has supported or opposed, of every vote he has cast and every speech that he has made. And before this great fundamental right every other must, if necessary, give way, for in no other manner can representative government be preserved.

1

The main purpose of the passage is to

A) explain the responsibilities of citizens.

B) suggest that people should be allowed to have new rights.

C) advocate for the protection of traditional freedoms.

D) seek the middle ground between two extreme positions.

2

Which of the following best characterizes the overall structure of the passage?

A) An idea is introduced and then supported with arguments.

B) Competing claims are described, the first is criticized, and the second is praised.

C) A claim is presented and its supporting evidence is refuted.

D) A proposal is outlined, its impact is analyzed, and an alternative is proposed.

3

La Follette's tone throughout the passage can best be described as that of a

A) neutral observer.

B) reluctant supporter.

C) determined advocate.

D) unrelenting critic.

4

In this passage, La Follette argues that the public must be more protective of its right to free speech during wartime because

A) free public discussion is necessary to ensure that the war is conducted properly.

B) the military is more likely than the government to violate citizens' rights.

C) people's right to express their will through their vote is suspended during wartime.

D) government officials have not yet recognized the growing belief that certain rights are being ignored.

5

The first sentence of the passage (lines 1-4) serves to

A) establish the position that La Follette will proceed to argue against.

B) define a concept that will be crucial to La Follette's claim.

C) express a general idea that La Follette will describe in greater detail.

D) state a general principle to which La Follette will discuss an exception.

6

La Follette claims that the right to free speech

A) should only be maintained as long as a number of other rights are guaranteed as well.

B) is the most important right for the proper functioning of democratic government.

C) must sometimes be limited in order for other rights to be upheld.

D) is the only protection necessary in a free society.

7

Which choice provides the best evidence for the answer to the previous question?

A) Lines 9-11 ("Rather ... Government")

B) Lines 21-25 ("More than ... unclogged")

C) Lines 75-79 ("How can ... people")

D) Lines 90-94 ("And before ... preserved")

8

The list of activities included in lines 86-90 ("every question…made") is most likely included to

A) describe the important public work that is done by La Follete and other representatives.

B) imply that La Follette's colleagues fear public discussion because they have acted improperly.

C) emphasize the broad scope of the public's right to speak about their representatives.

D) explain the limits of the public's right to speak about the government during wartime.

This passage is adapted from Patricia Hampl, *I Could Tell You Stories: Sojourns in the Land of Memory.* ©1999 by W.W. Norton.

When I was seven, my father, who played the violin on Sundays with a nicely tortured flair which we considered artistic, led me by the hand down a long, unlit corridor in St. Luke's School basement, a sort of tunnel that ended in a room full of pianos. There many little girls and a single sad boy were playing truly tortured scales and arpeggios in a mash of troubled sound. My father gave me over to Sister Olive Marie, who did look remarkably like an olive.

Her oily face gleamed as if it had just been rolled out of a can and laid on the white plate of her broad, spotless wimple. She was a small, plump woman; her body and the small window of her face seemed to interpret the entire alphabet of olive: her face was a sallow green olive placed upon the jumbo ripe olive of her black habit. I trusted her instantly and smiled, glad to have my hand placed in the hand of a woman who made sense, who provided the satisfaction of being what she was: an Olive who looked like an olive.

My father left me to discover the piano with Sister Olive Marie so that one day I would join him in mutually tortured piano-violin duets for the edification of my mother and brother who sat at the table meditatively spooning in the last of their pineapple sherbet until their part was called for: they put down their spoons and clapped while we bowed, while the sweet ice in their bowls melted, while the music melted, and we all melted a little into each other for a moment. But first Sister Olive must do her work. I was shown middle C, which Sister seemed to think terribly important. I stared at middle C and then glanced away for a second. When my eye returned, middle C was gone, its slim finger lost in the complicated grasp of the keyboard. Sister Olive struck it again, finding it with laughable ease. She emphasized the importance of middle C, its central position, a sort of North Star of sound. I remember thinking, "Middle C is the belly button of the piano," an insight whose originality and accuracy stunned me with pride. For the first time in my life I was astonished by metaphor. I hesitated to tell the kindly Olive for some reason; apparently I understood a true metaphor is a risky business, revealing of the self. In fact, I have never, until this moment of writing it down, told my first metaphor to anyone.

Sunlight flooded the room; the pianos, all black, gleamed. Sister Olive, dressed in the colors of the keyboard, gleamed; middle C shimmered with meaning and I resolved never—never—to forget its location: it was the center of the world.

Then Sister Olive, who had had to show me middle C twice but who seemed to have drawn no bad conclusions about me anyway, got up and went to the windows on the opposite wall. She pulled the shades down, one after the other. The sun was too bright, she said. She sneezed as she stood at the windows with the sun shedding its glare over her. She sneezed and sneezed, crazy little convulsive sneezes, one after another, as helpless as if she had the hiccups.

"The sun makes me sneeze," she said when the fit was over and she was back at the piano. This was odd, too odd to grasp in the mind. I associated sneezing with colds, and colds with rain, fog, snow, and bad weather. The sun, however, had caused Sister Olive to sneeze in this wild way, Sister Olive who gleamed benignly and who was so certain of the location of the center of the world. The universe wobbled a bit and became unreliable. Things were not, after all, necessarily what they seemed. Appearance deceived: here was the sun acting totally out of character, hurling this woman into sneezes, a woman so mild that she was named, so it seemed, for a bland object on a relish tray.

9

The main purpose of the passage is to

A) explain the narrator's love for a particular instrument.

B) provide a description of the narrator's family.

C) argue that the world is not always as it appears.

D) share a certain memory from the narrator's childhood.

10

Which of the following best characterizes the overall structure of the passage?

A) A story is told, using vivid descriptions of the setting and characters to illustrate the thoughts and memories of the narrator.

B) A mysterious character's past is explored by recounting the events from the point of view of a child.

C) A story is told as a series of initially separate events that are tied together in the end.

D) A location is described and a story is told about the location to explain its importance in the life of the narrator.

11

Which of the following best describes the narrator's first impression of Sister Olive?

A) She did not seem interesting because she resembled a dull food.

B) She seemed trustworthy because her appearance matched her name.

C) She seemed competent because she could quickly and easily identify middle C.

D) She seemed reliable because the narrator's father left the narrator in her care.

12

The third paragraph serves primarily to

A) emphasize the musical skill of the narrator's father.

B) introduce a new character.

C) describe one goal of the narrator's new lessons.

D) speculate about the most likely outcome of current events.

13

The effect of the phrase "we all melted a little into each other" (lines 33-34) is mainly to

A) suggest that when they performed music together her family members were equal in talent.

B) show how the family was as sweet as the pineapple sherbet that was melting in their bowls.

C) express that the musical performance brought the family closer together.

D) provide a vivid description of the melting sound of the performance.

14

The narrator had been reluctant to tell anyone about her first metaphor because

A) she only realized that it was a metaphor once she was older.

B) she understood that a metaphor can expose a person's private thoughts and feelings.

C) she had used the metaphor to remember the place of middle C, and did not want to reveal her trick.

D) she has always preferred to express herself through her music.

15

Which choice provides the best evidence for the answer to the previous question?

A) Lines 1-6 ("When I ... pianos")

B) Lines 19-23 ("I trusted ... olive")

C) Lines 49-52 ("I hesitated ... self")

D) Lines 61-65 ("Then Sister ... wall")

16

What is the main rhetorical effect of the repetition of the word "sneezed" in lines 67-69?

A) To denote the exact number of occurrences of a particular action

B) To subtly shift the meaning of the word in each iteration

C) To imply that there was no discernible difference between a set of incidents

D) To emphasize the frequency and extent of an action

17

The narrator comes to believe that "Things were not, after all, necessarily what they seemed" (lines 82-83) because

A) Sister Olive looked like an olive but was actually a regular person.

B) although Sister Olive was mild-mannered, she had a wild sneezing fit.

C) middle C seemed to disappear when she briefly looked away.

D) sunshine was the opposite of bad weather, yet still made Sister Olive sneeze.

Section 6

Combining Ideas

This section on Combining Ideas covers **Synthesis** questions, which you will encounter in certain passage sets. To **synthesize** means to combine, and Synthesis questions ask you to integrate information from more than one source to discover new insights and arrive at an answer. These question types appear only when you are dealing with passage pairs or passages with graphics.

In this section, you will learn how to tackle both paired passages and passages with graphics, and you will practice what you've learned with exercises along the way. There are also full-length passages for you to test your skills at the end of the section.

Paired Passages

Part 1

One of the five sets of questions on the Reading section of the SAT will be about a set of two short passages, rather than one long one.

In many ways, these paired passages can be treated as a single passage of a special type. Combined, the two passages in the pair are the same length as a single regular passage, have the same number of questions as a single regular passage, and—most importantly—are worth *the same number of points* as a single regular passage. Approach them as though they are just a special passage type that presents two points of view.

Each passage pair will always be of the same type—either Science or Social Studies—and about the same general subject. The passages might agree with one another, or they might disagree. They might just explore different aspects of the same subject, without directly agreeing or disagreeing with one another at all.

You should treat each of the two short passages the same way that you treat other passages of that type. But remember to also pay attention to the relationship between the two passages.

Look for Similarities and Differences

Paired passages always have some similarities. There will also always be some differences between them. Look for similarities and differences in:

- **Main Ideas:** Pay attention to the main ideas in each passage, and consider how they compare. Do they agree? Disagree? Are they talking about *exactly* the same thing, or only related things?
- **Purpose:** Look for differences in the purpose of the passages. Is one author trying only to provide information about the subject, while the other is expressing an opinion?
- **Claims:** Pay attention to what the authors claim is true. See which claims the authors seem to agree about, which ones they disagree about, and which ones are addressed by only one author.
- **Style and Tone:** Pay attention to how the passages are alike or different in style and tone. Do they both contain dry, slightly boring exposition? Is one an exciting story about football, while the other is an impassioned argument against allowing high-school students to play such a dangerous sport?
- **Focus:** Even if the passages are about the same main topic, they might focus on slightly different aspects of that topic. It might be that both passages are about tax policy, but one focuses on the effects of tax policy on the government's ability to raise revenues while the other focuses on the effects of tax policy on individuals and businesses.

Summarizing Paired Passages

When summarizing paired passages, start by jotting down summaries of each passage in the pair as you read them—just as you would with regular passages. Then, consider the relationship between the two passages, and think of a quick summary about how they relate to one another.

This summary won't usually be as simple as "Authors 1 and 2 agree" or "Authors 1 and 2 disagree." If that's all that comes to mind, you might want to think for just a moment longer; there's usually something subtler going on. Consider the elements that are most different and most similar between the two passages, and make a note about them.

Finding Repeated Ideas

To figure out the relationship between two passages, pay attention to information that appears in both. Remember the Pencil on Paper strategy mentioned in Chapter 1 and earlier in this chapter—you want to make sure you engage with and interact with the text. Mark up the passage and add your own notes to emphasize key information.

In addition to your usual notes and markings on passages, you can note ideas or important words in the second passage that are repeated from the first passage. You can also note any contrasts or opposites that you find as you read the second passage. This will help you easily find these lines if you are asked about any of these concepts.

Let's see how this works with an example of two short passage excerpts:

Example

Passages 1 and 2 are adapted from Daniela Dimitrova Russo, Todd Myers, "Should Cities Ban Plastic Bags?" ©2012 by Dow Jones & Company.

Passage 1

Bags env. problem

Plastic pollution is the nexus of some of the major environmental challenges facing us today. Discarded plastic bags float in the ocean, they tumble in the desert, they are found in riverbeds and dams. They kill off marine animals that confuse the bags with plankton and jellyfish; they end up calcified in the stomachs of animals on land.

But the greatest damage is economic—the cost of cleaning up all that waste. That's why dozens of countries and cities around the world, including 47 municipalities in California alone, have adopted ordinances banning plastic bags.

Bags banned

Passage 2

Across the world, cities are joining the latest environmental fad—banning plastic grocery bags. Activists think banning the bags is a simple and environmentally responsible approach. Some ban supporters claim plastics harm human health, even when studies from organizations like the Environmental Protection Agency, the Centers for Disease Control and Prevention, and Pacific Northwest National Labs show these claims are false or exaggerated.

Bags fad, harm exaggerated

Passage 1 shows the main ideas marked up using the 5 w's you learned about in Section 2. Passage 2 also has main ideas underlined in its second paragraph, as these are new ideas that are not related to Passage 1.

However, some ideas in the first paragraph of Passage 2 overlap with ideas from Passage 1, and we've underlined these overlapping ideas with a wavy line. The idea of "banning plastic grocery bags" is underlined because it is repeated from lines 15-16 in Passage 1. The term "environmental fad" is underlined because it suggests the issue is not serious, which is the opposite of the idea of "major environmental challenges" (line 2) in Passage 1.

By noting how the passages overlap, you can see how they fit together. You can tell that the author of Passage 2 disagrees with the author of Passage 1 over whether plastic bags are a major environmental issue. Passage 2 also discusses other topics like human health that Passage 1 does not address.

Approaching the Questions

Analyzing Multiple Texts questions ask you about both passages in a pair. We will refer to these as "Multiple Texts" questions. These questions will require you to consider elements from both passages at once. This can mean comparing the information from the passages, as well as their structure, tone, or way of making an argument.

To answer these questions, look for the element you are asked about in each individual passage first. For example, if you are asked about bird flight patterns, identify what each passage says about that topic. If you are asked about something more general, like tone, use your notes and summaries to determine the tone of each passage first. Then you can combine or compare these ideas to find your answer.

Let's see how this works with a question about the plastic bag passage excerpts from above. Read the longer excerpts of the passages below and mark up the repeated and contrasting ideas. Then attempt the question that follows.

Example

The following passages are adapted from Daniela Dimitrova Russo, Todd Myers, "Should Cities Ban Plastic Bags?" ©2012 by Dow Jones & Company.

Passage 1

Plastic pollution is the nexus of some of the major environmental challenges facing us today. Discarded plastic bags float in the ocean, they tumble in the desert, they are found in riverbeds and dams. They kill off marine animals that confuse the bags with plankton and jellyfish; they end up calcified in the stomachs of animals on land.

But the greatest damage is economic—the cost of cleaning up all that waste. That's why dozens of countries and cities around the world, including 47 municipalities in California alone, have adopted ordinances banning plastic bags.

Communities don't have much of a choice if they leave things as they are: They either drown in plastic bags or spend millions of dollars to clean up the mess—tax dollars that should go toward infrastructure, education and libraries.

San Jose, Calif., reports that it costs about $1 million a year to repair recycling equipment jammed with plastic bags. San Francisco estimates that to clean up, recycle and landfill plastic bags costs as much as 17 cents a bag, or approximately $8.5 million a year.

Elsewhere in the world, Bangladesh banned plastic bags because they clog storm-drain systems and cause major flooding, which in turn has significant economic cost. Ireland's PlasTax was prompted by the cost of litter. The United Arab Emirates plans to eliminate the use of conventional plastic bags by 2013.

Passage 2

Across the world, cities are joining the latest environmental fad—banning plastic grocery bags. Activists think banning the bags is a simple and environmentally responsible approach.

Some ban supporters claim plastics harm human health, even when studies from organizations like the Environmental Protection Agency, the Centers for Disease Control and Prevention, and Pacific Northwest National Labs show these claims are false or exaggerated.

Consider a study from the U.K. Environment Agency that found plastic grocery bags have the lowest environmental impact in "human toxicity" and "marine aquatic toxicity" as well as "global-warming potential" even after paper bags are used four times and reusable cotton bags are used 173 times. Why? Largely because paper and cotton bags come from crops that require fertilizer, pesticides, herbicides and the like.

Critics also say that ban opponents ignore the environmental impact of bags over the course of their lifetime. But many studies do just that. The U.K. Environment Agency's study, for instance, compared the energy expended in creating, using and disposing of plastic, paper and reusable bags to arrive at its figures. Consumers would have to use a cotton bag 173 times before they match the energy savings of one plastic bag, assuming 40% of bags are reused—a percentage that's actually lower than the rate in some cities.

Some critics say we need to ban bags because voluntary take-back programs don't work. But the point of the programs is simply to reuse bags, and consumers already reuse bags to hold garbage or pick up after pets. As for the idea that plastic bags cost consumers more, the reason grocery stores use plastic instead of paper or other bags is that they cost less and hold more. Reusable bags are even more expensive.

1

Passage 2 differs from Passage 1 in that only Passage 2

A) discusses the impact of alternative types of bags.

B) mentions types of costs associated with plastic bags.

C) uses quantitative information to support its claims.

D) provides examples of places that have banned plastic bags.

To answer this question, you can refer back to the things you underlined and noted in the passages. Pay particular attention to ideas that overlap between the two passages. This can help you select the correct answer choice, (A), as lines 73-78 describe a concept that is not repeated from Passage 1.

You can use Process of Elimination to knock out incorrect answer choices. For this question, answers are incorrect if they mention something not covered in Passage 2, or something that is mentioned in Passage 1.

You can therefore eliminate answer choice (B), as cost appears in both passages, though in different ways. Passage 1 discusses the cost of cleaning up bags, and Passage 2 discusses the cost to the consumer. Answer choice (C) is incorrect, as both passages use numbers to bolster their arguments; you may have noted this in lines 23-30 and 73-78. You can knock out choice (D) because only Passage 1 lists places that have banned plastic bags, and the question is asking about an idea only present in Passage 2.

Part 1 Practice: Paired Passages

Below is an example passage. Read the passage, paying special attention to the elements we have discussed, and then answer the accompanying practice questions.

Passages 1 and 2 are adapted from Steven W. Lockley, Jane Orient, "Should Medical Residents Be Required to Work Shorter Shifts?" ©2012 by Dow Jones & Company.

Resident physicians are physicians who have graduated from a medical school and are continuing their professional training by performing supervised work in a medical care facility.

Passage 1

At Brigham and Women's Hospital, we quantified the effects of work hours on medical error rates in a group of first-year residents who worked in intensive-care units under two sets of conditions: a traditional schedule with 24- to 30-hour shifts every other shift, and a schedule with 16-hour limits. On the former schedule, the residents made 36% more serious medical errors than on the latter, and inadvertently fell asleep on duty twice as often on overnight duty. Longer shifts affect not just the safety and health of patients but that of physicians as well. In surveys conducted by our group, residents working 24 or more hours in a row reported sticking themselves with needles 60% more often, and had more than double the odds of having a car crash on the drive home from work as compared with shorter shifts. In a 2010 review of 23 studies on the effects of reducing resident work hours, all but one showed an improvement or no change in patient care or resident sleep or quality of life. There were no objective data showing that shorter work hours were worse for patients or physicians.

Despite the increasing emphasis on evidence-based decision-making in medicine, these data have often been met with a negative response. Those who oppose stricter work-hour limits say continuity of care demands long shifts. But even with 30-hour shifts, care of a patient eventually has to be handed over to another team. Medicine is also increasingly filled with specialists, a development requiring a team approach to deliver the best care. So we need to find better ways for teams to communicate and to transfer information, rather than insist that doctors risk their own and their patients' health by working beyond their biological limits.

Doctors are not immune to biology. While we appreciate their dedication and sacrifice, we cannot allow them to harm others or themselves with the outdated and unnecessary "rite of passage" of 24-hour shifts.

Passage 2

For a half-dozen years, the Accreditation Council for Graduate Medical Education has experimented with reduced work hours for physicians-in-training. The current limit is no more than 80 hours per week. Now some want to reduce this even further.

I think we should challenge the whole idea of having a central committee dictate work limitations for all residency programs.

Treating new physicians like shift workers is destroying the individual patient-physician relationship. Having shorter shifts means more frequent "handoffs," which disrupts both education and patient care. Those who favor shorter shifts, and thus more handoffs, may argue that quality of handoffs matters more than quantity. But quantity matters too. The shift-work culture means working until time is up, rather than until work is done. The incentive is to leave problems for the next shift rather than to find and address them as early as possible. Patients are now the collective responsibility of the team, rather than primarily the responsibility of "their doctor." In the old system, the patient's doctor was expected to take care of anticipated problems as well as possible before signing out. It is also more efficient for the doctor who already knows the patient to order the fever work-up, talk to the family, or assess progress and the potential need for a change in the treatment.

In the old days, it was understood that residency would be grueling. A surgical residency was specifically compared with becoming a Marine. The enemy was disease or death or human suffering, and the schedule of fighting was determined by the enemy, not by a central committee.

1

Both passages suggest which of the following is a main reason to be concerned about shift-length during residency?

A) Freedom of choice for doctors

B) The quality of medical care

C) The safety of doctors

D) Preserving traditional training methods

2

Which of the following types of evidence is used in Passage 1, but NOT in Passage 2?

A) An appeal to emotions with the illustration of a specific case

B) Quotations from sleep experts about the requirements of proper rest

C) Personal anecdotes about the author's own experience as a resident

D) Data from studies on the effects of resident working hours on performance

3

The author of Passage 2 would most likely respond to the argument in lines 30-34 ("Those who … team") by

A) arguing that fewer hand-overs are still preferable, even if some are unavoidable.

B) suggesting that doctors should continue to work until patients recover.

C) pointing out that specialist training would not be possible with shorter shifts.

D) proposing that we should develop a better system for hand-overs.

Passages with Graphics

Part 2

Two reading passages on the SAT will include graphics. One of the passages will be a Science passage, and the other will be a Social Studies passage. There will be one or two graphics accompanying each passage. The graphics will contain additional information that supplements the passage, and will always be related to the main topic of the passage. Most often, the graphics will be representations of statistical data—including bar graphs, tables, and pie charts.

Graphics may provide supporting evidence for the passage, with accompanying questions that require you to correctly interpret the graphic in relation to the passage. You may also be asked questions that will require you to interpret information presented *only* in the graphic.

Reading the Graphics

Graphs can contain a lot of information. Here are some of the key elements to look for.

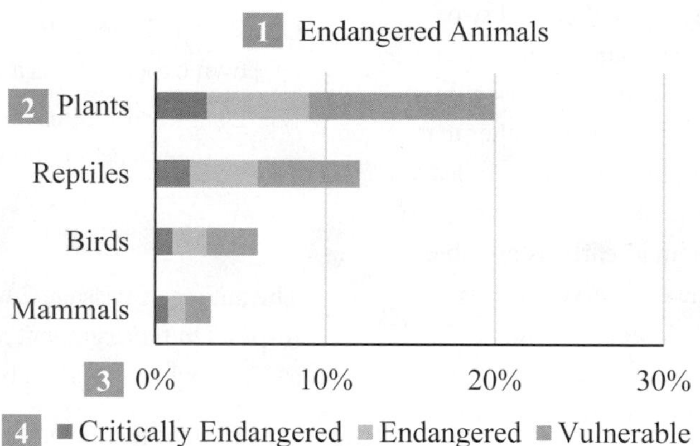

5 This chart shows the percentage of various species, by group, on the IUNC Red List as of 2007. The Red List is an online listing of endangered species categorized by taxonomy, type of threat and other criteria.

1 **Title.** The title of a graphic usually tells you what the graphic is intended to show.

2 **Labels.** Be sure to read all of the labels in a graphic, and make sure that you understand which elements they refer to and what they say about them.

3 **Units.** Be sure you know what units a graphic is using for data. The number ten will mean something very different on a chart showing distances in feet than on one showing distance in *thousands* of feet.

4 **Legend.** A legend is a guide to the graphic that shows you what different shades, images, or patterns mean in the image. Always read legends carefully when they're available.

5 **Caption.** If there's a caption below the graphic, read it carefully. The captions often provide directions for how to properly read the graphic, and extra details about the information provided in the graphic.

6 **References in the Passage.** If the passage refers to the graphic, or to information in the graphic, pay attention to which information the passage is referring to and how the author is using the information from the graphic in the passage.

Sometimes, a graphic might contain a lot of information. You don't need to scrutinize every detail: just try to understand the graphic's relationship to the passage, and look for the essential elements described above so that when you need to check the graphic to get a specific piece of information, you'll be able to find it quickly.

Analyzing Quantitative Info

Be careful not to make any assumptions about information that you are not given, or to assume that trends presented in the graphic will remain true for other scenarios.

Let's look at an example to see how this works.

Example

Temperatures in Singapore		
Month	Record High °F	Average High °F
Jan	93.7	86.2
Feb	95.4	88.2
Mar	96.8	88.9
Apr	96.4	89.1
May	95.7	88.9
Year	96.8	86.2

This chart shows temperatures in Singapore for the years 1929–1941 and 1948–2011.

2

Which claim about Singapore's weather is supported by the graphic?

A) January is on average the coldest month of the year in Singapore.

B) There have been higher record temperatures in April than in March.

C) The average high in March is lower than the yearly average.

D) The average high in March is higher than the yearly average.

Here only answer choice (D) is actually supported by the chart. You can easily compare the average temperatures for given for March and fir the year overall, and see that 88.9 is higher than 86.2. Answer choice (C) gives the opposite answer, so you know it is incorrect.

You can also use the Process of Elimination to knock out answer choice (A) because even though January is the coldest month according to the chart, the chart does not include data for the entire year.

Answer choice (B) can be eliminated as it confuses average temperature for the record temperature; the record high for March is higher than that for April.

Relating Graphics to Passages

To relate a graphic back to information in the passage, look for lines in the passage that discuss the same subjects being measured and presented in the graphic. You may have marked up these lines as you first read the passage. Then, compare the information from the passage to what is presented in the graphic. You can underline or circle the items on the graphic that you are asked about or that are repeated from the passage.

The graphic may present slightly different information than the passage, and you may need to combine these two sources of information in order to reach a broader conclusion than what you could support from just one source.

Let's look at an example of a passage excerpt and graphic to see how this works.

Example

Gross domestic product (GDP) is the market value of all goods and services produced within a country in a year. GDP is an aggregate figure, which does not consider the differing sizes of nations. Therefore, GDP can be stated as GDP per capita, in which the total GDP is divided by the resident population on a given date. GDP per capita is not a measure of personal income, as it is measured by dividing the total amount of GDP equally among all citizens. However, a high GDP per capita is generally considered an indicator of the economic health of a nation and the living standards of its citizens generally.

GDP per Capita in US Dollars		
Year	United States	United Kingdom
2008	46,760	43,147
2009	45,305	35,331
2010	46,612	36,238
2011	48,112	38,974
2012	49,641	39,090

3

It can reasonably be inferred from the passage and graphic that

A) the United States produced more goods and services than the United Kingdom for all years measured.

B) the United Kingdom produced more goods and services than the United States for all years measured.

C) the United States likely experienced better economic health than the United Kingdom for all years measured.

D) the United Kingdom had a lower GDP than the United States in 2008.

To answer this question, you need to combine information given in the chart with information stated in the text of the passage. Only answer choice (C) is supported by information from both sources. The chart shows you that the United States had a higher GDP per capita, and the passage tells you this is usually "considered an indicator of the economic health of a nation" (lines 14-15). By combining these pieces of information, you can select this answer.

Answer choice (A) is contradicted by information in the passage, which clarifies that GDP per capita does not measure total goods and services, but divides that number by the number of total citizens. Without knowing the population of the two countries for the years measured, it is not possible to determine which country produced more goods and services. There is a similar issue with answer choice (B). Answer choice (D) is incorrect as the chart only indicates GDP per capita, which is different from regular GDP as defined by the passage.

Part 2 Practice: Passages with Graphics

Below are two example passages. Read the passages, paying special attention to the elements we have discussed, and then answer the accompanying practice questions.

This passage is adapted from Justin Gillis, "Heat-Trapping Gas Passes Milestone, Raising Fears." ©2013 by The New York Times Company.

The level of the most important heat-trapping gas in the atmosphere, carbon dioxide, passed a long-feared milestone, scientists reported in May 2013, reaching a concentration not seen on the earth for millions of years.

Scientific instruments showed that the gas had reached an average daily level above 400 parts per million—just an odometer moment in one sense, but also a sobering reminder that decades of efforts to bring human-produced emissions under control are faltering.

"It symbolizes that so far we have failed miserably in tackling this problem," said Pieter P. Tans, who runs the monitoring program at the National Oceanic and Atmospheric Administration (NOAA) that reported the new reading.

Ralph Keeling, who runs another monitoring program at the Scripps Institution of Oceanography in San Diego, said a continuing rise could be catastrophic. "It means we are quickly losing the possibility of keeping the climate below what people thought were possibly tolerable thresholds," he said.

China is now the largest emitter, but Americans have been consuming fossil fuels extensively for far longer, and experts say the United States is more responsible than any other nation for the high level.

The new measurement came from analyzers atop Mauna Loa, the volcano on the big island of Hawaii that has long been ground zero for monitoring the worldwide trend on carbon dioxide, or CO_2. Devices there sample clean, crisp air that has blown thousands of miles across the Pacific Ocean, producing a record of rising carbon dioxide levels that has been closely tracked for half a century.

Carbon dioxide above 400 parts per million was first seen in the Arctic last year, and had also spiked above that level in hourly readings at Mauna Loa.

But the average reading for an entire day surpassed that level at Mauna Loa for the first time in the 24 hours that ended at 8 p.m. Eastern Daylight Time on Thursday, May 9, 2013. The two monitoring programs use slightly different protocols; NOAA reported an average for the period of 400.03 parts per million, while Scripps reported 400.08.

Carbon dioxide rises and falls on a seasonal cycle, and the level will dip below 400 this summer as leaf growth in the Northern Hemisphere pulls about 10 billion tons of carbon out of the air. But experts say that will be a brief reprieve—the moment is approaching when no measurement of the ambient air anywhere on earth, in any season, will produce a reading below 400.

From studying air bubbles trapped in Antarctic ice, scientists know that going back 800,000 years, the carbon dioxide level oscillated in a tight band, from about 180 parts per million in the depths of ice ages to about 280 during the warm periods between. The evidence shows that global temperatures and CO_2 levels are tightly linked.

For the entire period of human civilization, roughly 8,000 years, the carbon dioxide level was relatively stable near that upper bound. But the burning of fossil fuels has caused a 41 percent increase in the heat-trapping gas since the Industrial Revolution, a mere geological instant, and scientists say the climate is beginning to react, though they expect far larger changes in the future.

Indirect measurements suggest that the last time the carbon dioxide level was this high was at least three million years ago, during an epoch called the Pliocene. Geological research shows that the climate then was far warmer than today, the world's ice caps were smaller, and the sea level might have been as much as 60 or 80 feet higher.

Countries have adopted an official target to limit the damage from global warming, with 450 parts per million seen as the maximum level compatible with that goal. "Unless things slow down, we'll probably get there in well under 25 years," Ralph Keeling said.

Yet many countries, including China and the United States, have refused to adopt binding national targets. Scientists say that unless far greater efforts are made soon, the goal of limiting the warming will become impossible without severe economic disruption.

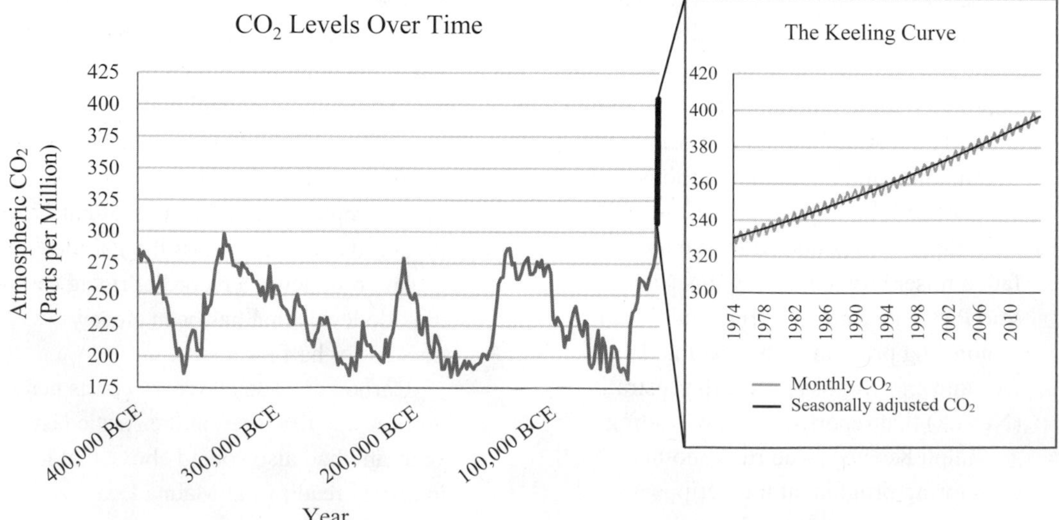

1

The passage indicates that, during the winter, which of the following is true?

A) Dropping temperatures will also cause a drop in carbon dioxide levels.

B) Atmospheric sampling is less likely to produce accurate results.

C) Atmospheric carbon dioxide levels are higher than at other times in the year.

D) Scientists are able to sample air bubbles trapped in ice.

2

Based on information from the passage and graph, carbon dioxide levels

A) never reached 400 parts per million before the Industrial Revolution.

B) never reached levels as high as today in the preceding 400,000 years.

C) have been as high as 400,000 parts per million in the past.

D) are usually around 200 parts per million.

3

Information from the graph best supports which of the following statements?

A) From 1974 to 2010, carbon dioxide levels rose more slowly but to a higher point than at any other time in the past 400,000 years.

B) Seasonally adjusted carbon dioxide levels have been above 300 parts-per-million for more than 200,000 years.

C) Due to increasing carbon dioxide, sea levels in 2010 most likely rose to levels similar to those in the Pliocene.

D) Between 1974 and 2010, carbon dioxide levels sometimes dropped from month-to-month, but seasonally adjusted levels rose steadily.

This passage is adapted from "Age Invaders." ©2014 by The Economist.

According to the UN's population projections, the standard source for demographic estimates, there are around 600 million people aged 65 or older alive today. That is in itself remarkable; the author Fred Pearce claims it is possible that half of all the humans who have ever been over 65 are alive today. But as a share of the total population, at 8%, it is not that different to what it was a few decades ago.

By 2035, however, more than 1.1 billion people—13% of the population—will be above the age of 65. This is a natural corollary of the dropping birth rates that are slowing overall population growth; they mean there are proportionally fewer young people around. The "old-age dependency ratio"—the ratio of old people to those of working age—will grow even faster. In 2010 the world had 16 people aged 65 and over for every 100 adults between the ages of 25 and 64, almost the same ratio it had in 1980. By 2035 the UN expects that number to have risen to 26.

In rich countries it will be much higher. Japan will have 69 old people for every 100 of working age by 2035 (up from 43 in 2010), Germany 66 (from 38). Even America, which has a relatively high fertility rate, will see its old-age dependency rate rise by more than 70%, to 44. Developing countries, where today's ratio is much lower, will not see absolute levels rise that high, but the proportional growth will be higher. Over the same time period, the old-age dependency rate in China will more than double from 15 to 36. Latin America will see a shift from 14 to 27.

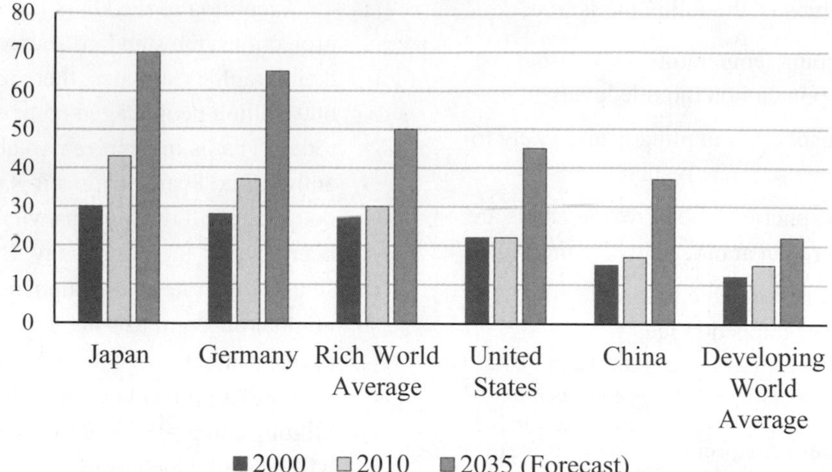

Adapted from "Age Invaders." ©2014 by The Economist

4

It can reasonably be inferred from the passage and graphic that

A) Latin America will have a lower old-age dependency ratio than the rich world average in 2035.

B) Latin America had a lower old-age dependency ratio than the developing world average in 2000.

C) Japan will have 70 old people for every 100 of working age by 2040.

D) the United States will never have as high an old-age dependency ratio as Germany.

5

Which claim about old-age dependency is supported by the graphic?

A) Japan has historically had a lower old-age dependency ratio than the United States.

B) The developing world will have a lower old-age dependency ratio than China in 2035.

C) The developing world had a higher old-age dependency ratio than China in 2010.

D) Germany's growing old-age dependency ratio is representative of rich countries overall.

Practice Set

Part 3

The following passages have been designed to test the question types you learned about in this section. Review the techniques we discussed in Section 2, and mark up and make summaries for these passages. Then, answer the questions using the strategies you just learned.

Passages 1 and 2 are adapted from Richard G. Little, Wenonah Hauter, "Are We Better Off Privatizing Water?" ©2012 by Dow Jones & Company.

Passage 1

Our nation's aging drinking-water systems will require staggering amounts of investment in the coming decades—as much as $1 trillion over the next 25 years, the American Water Works Association estimates. As things stand now, this burden will fall mostly on the public water utilities that serve about 80% of the U.S. population.

But these bodies don't have the money to pay such bills. Many of them already have put off necessary improvements for years due to insufficient public funding. And there is little chance of meaningful federal aid, given the national focus on debt reduction. The root of the problem is the artificially low rates the public utilities have charged for years. These rates, kept low for political purposes, don't come close to supporting the long-range capital investment we would expect of any well-run business.

Is privatization the solution in every case? Of course not. We must strive to find what works best for the customers in a specific situation. Mismanagement is not a problem limited to private operators, just as good management is not intrinsic to public systems. But private management can be successful much more often than its critics would like to believe. Private-sector managers focus on the cost of service and return on capital. The new and innovative technologies in which they invest may have a higher initial cost, but they offer savings, too, which can be shared with customers while improving service and quality.

Ultimately, the best water provider is the one that is best able to deliver safe, reliable, and accessible service. If the provider can also make a profit, that should be of less concern than its ability to deliver safe and affordable drinking water.

Passage 2

Privatization is not the solution for deteriorating public water systems already feeling the double-pinch of dwindling local and federal funds. Private companies that operate water systems have appalling track records of rate increases, poor system maintenance, faulty billing practices and other failures, sometimes even jeopardizing the health and safety of local residents.

Some municipalities have taken their water systems back from private water providers. Indeed, some are realizing what cities like New York, Baltimore, and Boston realized a century ago—that water is best controlled by an entity that is accountable to the public, not outside shareholders.

Water service isn't a business enterprise; it's a basic human right, and what privatization proponents refer to as "political pressure" is actually our democratic processes at work. Our elected leaders should absolutely respond to public concern about the affordability of their water service. The provision of water service is a natural monopoly, and the public can exercise choice only at the ballot box through the election of the officials who oversee the service. How government-run utilities decide to allocate costs among different users is a local decision that should be made in an open and democratic manner.

Rather than privatizing water systems or asking household users to pay more, why not ask commercial and industrial water users to pay more for the services they profit from? We should also ask the federal government to establish a dedicated source of federal funding in the form of a clean-water trust fund, similar to the program that provides funding for highways. This would provide a guaranteed source of funding for replacing and maintaining public infrastructure systems, thereby alleviating communities of the burden of having to finance improvement projects on their own. When it comes to efficiently and affordably providing water to our communities, public control trumps private profits.

1

Both passages are primarily concerned with

A) how to charge individuals for drinking water.

B) investing in new infrastructure for public water systems.

C) privatizing public water systems.

D) regulating American's drinking-water system.

2

Which of the following best describes the relationship between the two passages?

A) Passage 2 advocates a different solution to the same problem discussed in Passage 1.

B) Passage 2 provides a more detailed explanation for the situation described in Passage 1.

C) Passage 2 offers alternative evidence in support of the argument made in Passage 1.

D) Passage 2 focuses on a narrow aspect of the problem defined in Passage 1.

3

The authors of both passages agree that water service should be

A) priced to discourage excessive use.

B) financially profitable for public operators.

C) priced differently for industrial use than for common use.

D) affordable for all water consumers.

4

Unlike the author of Passage 2, the author of Passage 1

A) appeals to emotion by invoking the idea of human rights.

B) refers to the argument of the opposing side in order to refute it.

C) uses specific data to demonstrate the seriousness of the problem.

D) provides evidence to show that privatization of water services has been successful in the past.

5

The author of Passage 1 would most likely respond to Passage 2's claim that private water systems "have appalling track records of rate increases" (lines 46-47) by

A) demonstrating that rate increases best allow water providers to invest in future projects and other industries.

B) stating that public utility rates are too low and that raising them is necessary to ensure long-term sustainability.

C) explaining that high prices are, unfortunately, necessary due to dwindling federal aid for public works.

D) countering that political pressure will prevent prices from rising even if water companies are privatized.

6

What would the author of Passage 1 most likely think about the "clean-water trust fund" (line 79) proposed by the author of Passage 2?

A) That it is unlikely to be established while the federal government is trying to reduce its debt

B) That it would likely prohibit spending on vital technological development

C) That it is a good first step towards revitalizing struggling water systems and helping them to remain public

D) That it would be a risky investment because no similar fund has ever existed

7

Which best describes the difference between the main focus of Passage 1 and the main focus of Passage 2?

A) Passage 1 is focused on how water utilities might turn a profit, while Passage 2 is focused on how citizens can campaign for better water use rates.

B) Passage 1 is focused on how utilities fund infrastructure and innovation, while Passage 2 is focused on consumers' right to affordable water.

C) Passage 1 is focused on the danger posed to water utilities by political corruption, while Passage 2 is focused on the maintenance of a free public debate over water use.

D) Passage 1 is focused on the difficulties water utilities will face in the future, while Passage 2 is focused on the causes for these problems.

8

How would the author of Passage 2 most likely respond to the assertion in Passage 1 that current rates for water service are too low to support necessary investments (lines 14-20)?

A) By arguing that it is not necessary to invest additional funds in water services

B) By suggesting that price increases should be avoided because they are undemocratic

C) By observing that public utilities are able to invest in water services without raising rates

D) By conceding that some price increases may be necessary, but should fall on commercial water users

This passage is adapted from Olga Khazan, "How We Get Tall." ©2014 by The Atlantic.

Last year, Tim Hatton, an economist at the University of Essex in the U.K., rounded up data on the heights of European 21-year-olds dating from 1860 to about 1980. The results, published in the Oxford Economic Papers, were impressive: The average European man became about 11 centimeters taller between 1870 and 1970, gaining about a centimeter per decade. A mid-19th century British man stood just five feet, four inches tall, but he was five-foot-ten by 1980.

While about 80 percent of height is determined by genes, auxologists (those are height scientists) now believe that nutrition and sanitation determine much of the rest. As the New Yorker's Burkhard Bilger put it in 2004: "Height variations within a population are largely genetic, but height variations between populations are mostly environmental, anthropometric history suggests. If Joe is taller than Jack, it's probably because his parents are taller. But if the average Norwegian is taller than the average Nigerian it's because Norwegians live healthier lives."

Hatton and his colleagues, Roy E. Bailey from the University of Essex and Kris Inwood from the University of Guelph, created a database of 2,236 British soldiers who served in World War I, and then they looked up their birth records. The soldiers were relatively representative of the male population as a whole—about two-thirds of the 1890 British male birth cohort* enlisted. It turns out that subtle differences in their heights hinted at their origins.

The more kids there were in a household, the shorter they were. Not only because there was less food to go around, but also because it made it more likely that there were more people in each bedroom. "Crowding can help spread respiratory and gastrointestinal infections," Hatton said. "People sneezing on each other, that sort of thing."

People from industrial districts were shorter than those from agricultural areas. Regardless of income, the Dickensian living conditions of 19th century British cities suppressed height by about nine-tenths of an inch. On top of being hit with factory pollution, urban dwellers were packed into filthy, disease-ridden slums. As Kellow Chesney described in *The Victorian Underworld*, "Hideous slums, some of them acres wide, some no more than crannies of obscure misery, make up a substantial part of the metropolis … In big, once handsome houses, thirty or more people of all ages may inhabit a single room."

But as the 20th century wore on, that description became less and less apt. Tenements and slums were replaced with better housing; sewage systems and running water became standard. Women attended school in greater numbers and went from having five children, on average, to two. The 20th century was when Europeans achieved modernity, and as a result, it seems, they had to buy longer pants. "Together these developments help to explain the apparent puzzle of rapid improvement in average health status during a period of war and depression that predates the advent of universal health services," Hatton and his colleagues wrote.

For centuries, Americans were the NBA players of the world. We were two inches taller than the Red Coats we squared off against in the American Revolution. In 1850, Americans had about two and a half inches on people from every European country. But our stature plateaued after World War II, and since then, other countries shot past us. Now, the Dutch are the tallest, at an average of six feet for men and five-foot-seven for women. They've come a long way: In 1848, a quarter of Dutch men were rejected from military service because they didn't meet the five-foot-two height limit. "Today, fewer than one in 1,000 is that short," the Associated Press noted in 2006.

The Danes, Norwegians, and Germans stack up right under the Dutch. American men and women, meanwhile, measure just 5'9" and 5'4", respectively, barely edging out the

Southern Europeans. John Komlos, an economic historian who has studied height extensively, thinks we Americans lost our height advantage because of poorer overall healthcare and nutrition compared to Europe. Our social shortcomings, he believes, are literally making us come up short. "American children might consume more meals prepared outside of the home, more fast food rich in fat, high in energy density, and low in essential micronutrients," he and co-author Benjamin E. Lauderdale of Princeton University wrote in 2006. "Furthermore, the European welfare states provide a more comprehensive social safety net including universal health care coverage."

*A "birth cohort" is the group of people born during a specified period of time.

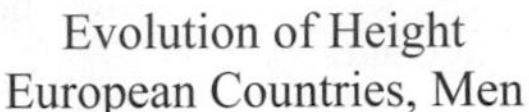

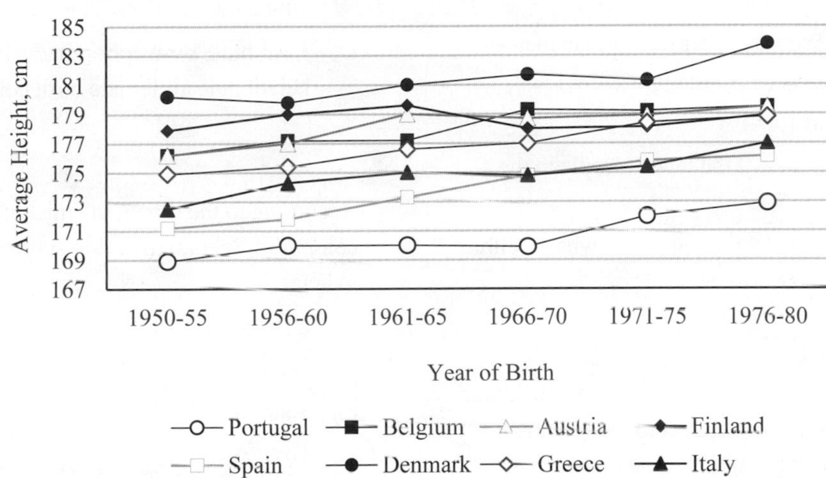

Country	Average Height of Birth Cohort, 1950-55 (cm)		Average Height of Birth Cohort, 1976-80 (cm)		Annual Growth Rate in Average Cohort Heights, %	
	Men	Women	Men	Women	Men	Women
Austria	176.3	165.6	179.6	167.1	0.07	0.04
Belgium	176.2	163.4	179.5	167.8	0.07	0.11
Denmark	180.3	167.2	183.7	168.6	0.07	0.03
Finland	177.8	164.3	178.7	165.9	0.02	0.04
Greece	174.7	163.3	178.6	165.9	0.09	0.06
Ireland	174.9	162.7	177.4	164.4	0.06	0.04
Italy	172.5	161.4	177.1	166.5	0.10	0.12
Portugal	168.8	158.9	172.9	162.5	0.10	0.09
Spain	171.3	160.4	176.1	165.5	0.11	0.12

Adapted from Jaume Garcia, Universitat Pompeu Fabra, "The Evolution of Adult Height in Europe: A Brief Note." ©2007 by Economics and Human Biology.

9

According to the table, graph, and passage, which of the following groups had the lowest average height?

A) Women born in Denmark in 1950-55

B) Women born in Austria in 1976-80

C) Men born in Portugal in 1966-70

D) Men born in Greece in 1950-55

10

It can reasonably be inferred from the passage and the graph that

A) all Greek men are taller than Italian men.

B) a man born in Finland in 1968 is taller than one born in 1964.

C) Danish people are the tallest people in the world.

D) conditions in Belgium are somewhat healthier than those in Portugal.

11

Based on the passage and the graph, in which pair of countries would you expect to find the most similar living conditions?

A) Austria in 1976-80 and Belgium during the same period

B) Belgium in 1976-80 and Spain during the same period

C) Italy in 1950-55 and Spain in 1976-80

D) Denmark in 1950-55 and Spain during the same period

12

Based on the passage and the table, which of the following statements is true?

A) Women in Ireland gained an average of .04 centimeters in height between 1950 and 1980.

B) Men in Spain got 11% taller between 1860 and 1980.

C) Women in Greece got 0.06% taller each year, on average, between 1950 and 1980.

D) Women born in Europe in 1960 were 1 cm taller than those born in 1950.

13

Based on information in the table, which of the following statements is true for every country included in the data presented?

A) The tallest individual man in any birth cohort was no taller than 183.7 cm.

B) The average height of the female birth cohort was lower but increased at a greater rate than the male birth cohort.

C) Male birth cohorts had a higher average height and higher average increase in height than female birth cohorts between 1950 and 1980.

D) Each male birth cohort had a higher average height than all female birth cohorts.

14

According to the graph, in which period's birth cohort did Belgian men first surpass Finnish men in height?

A) 1956-60

B) 1961-65

C) 1966-70

D) 1971-75

15

According to the table, which pair of groups saw the same annual increase in average height between 1950 and 1980?

A) Italian men and Italian women

B) Belgian women and Spanish men

C) Finnish women and Greek women

D) Greek men and Spanish men

Section 7

Vocabulary Building

The SAT's Reading and Writing Tests assess your ability to understand advanced reading material and vocabulary. In this section, we've provided a list of **roots, prefixes, and suffixes** to help you tackle this challenge. Learning these word parts is one of the fastest ways to quickly increase your ability to understand a wide variety of words, even if you haven't seen them before. Work through the lists to help build your vocabulary.

You can also access additional resources to further your study on our website. You'll find reading lists organized by grade level and subject, and a vocabulary list covering the difficulty level and content areas that are most likely to appear on the SAT.

For additional resources, please visit **ivyglobal.com/study**.

Working through these materials will not only help you with your SAT score, but will also help you to become a better student in high school and college.

SAT Vocabulary

Part 1

The SAT's Reading and Writing Tests assess your knowledge of college-level vocabulary—the kinds of words that you will need to know in order to understand academic writing, as well as words that have different meanings in different contexts.

Building your vocabulary will help you not only on the SAT, but also in your future studies. In this part, we have included lists of common word parts to help you learn new vocabulary.

Word Roots, Prefixes, and Suffixes

Many words can be broken into basic parts. Roots carry the basic meaning of a word, prefixes come before roots and alter their meaning, and suffixes come after roots and alter either their meaning or their part of speech. Because English is related to French, German, Spanish, Latin, and Greek, many of these word parts will look familiar if you know one of those languages.

The lists below contain some of the most common English roots, prefixes, and suffixes. Start learning these basic parts to help you break down unfamiliar words and speed up your vocabulary-building process for the SAT.

Common Roots					
Root	Definition	Example	Root	Definition	Example
ag, act	do	action, activity, agent	*belli*	war	belligerent, rebellious, bellicose
ambul	walk, move	ambulance, ambulatory, amble	*ben, bene*	good	benefactor, beneficial, benevolence
ami, amo	love	amiable, amorous	*biblio*	book	bibliography, Bible
anim	mind, soul, spirit	animal, animate, unanimous	*bio*	life	biography, biology
anthro	human	anthropology, philanthropy	*carn*	flesh, meat	carnivore, carnal, incarnate
aud, audit	hear	audible, auditorium, audience	*chron*	time	chronic, chronology, synchronize
auto	self	automobile, autobiography, autograph	*cid, cis*	cut, kill	incision, homicide, insecticide

civi	citizen	civilization, civilian, civil	*omni*	all	omniscient, omnipotent, omnivorous
corp	body	corporation, corporeal, corpse	*pac, pas, pax*	peace	pacify, pacific, pacifist, passive
dem	people	democracy, demographic	*path, pass*	disease, feeling	pathology, sympathetic, apathy, antipathy
dic, dict	speak	dictate, contradict, prediction, verdict	*phil*	love	philanthropist, philosophy, philanderer
domin	master	dominant, domain, domineering	*port*	carry	portable, porter, transport, export
err	wander	error, erratic, errand	*poten*	able, powerful	potential, omnipotent, potentate, impotent
eu	good, beautiful	eulogize, euphoria, euphemism	*psych*	mind	psyche, psychology, psychosis, psychopath
fall, fals	deceive	fallacious, infallible, falsify	*reg, rect*	rule	regicide, regime, regent, insurrection
fid	faith	fidelity, confide, confidence	*sacr, secr*	holy	sacred, sacrilegious, sacrament, consecrate
graph, gram	writing	grammar, telegram, graphite	*scribe, script*	write	scribe, describe, script
loqu, locut	talk	soliloquy, loquacious, elocution	*somn*	sleep	insomnia, somnolent, somnambulist
luc	light	elucidate, lucid, translucent	*spec, spic*	see, look	spectators, spectacles, retrospect, conspicuous
magn	great	magnify, magnate, magnanimous	*tang, tact, ting*	touch	tactile, tangent, contact, contingent
mal	bad	malevolent, malediction, malicious	*terr*	land	terrain, terrestrial, subterranean
mori, mort	die	mortuary, immortal, moribund	*urb*	city	urban, urbane, suburban
morph	shape, form	amorphous, metamorphosis	*vac*	empty	vacation, vacuous, evacuate, vacant
nat	born	innate, natal, nativity	*ver*	truth	veracity, verify, veracious
nom	name	misnomer, nominal	*verb*	word	verbose, verbatim, proverb
nov	new	novice, innovate, renovate, novelty	*viv, vit*	alive	revival, vivacious, vitality

Common Prefixes					
Prefix	Definition	Example	Prefix	Definition	Example
ambi, amphi	both	ambidextrous, ambiguous, ambivalent	*mis*	bad, hatred	misdemeanor, mischance, misanthrope
an, a	without	anarchy, anemia, amoral	*mono*	one	monarchy, monologue, monotheism
anti	against	antibody, antipathy, antisocial	*pan*	all, every	panacea, panorama, pandemic
circum	around	circumnavigate, circumspect, circumscribe	*peri*	around, near	perimeter, periphery, periscope
co, col, com, con	with, together	coauthor, collaborate, composition, concurrent	*poly*	many	polygon, polygamist, polyglot
contra, contro	against	contradict, contravene, controversy	*post*	after	postpone, posterity, postscript, posthumous
di, dif, dis	not, apart	digress, discord, differ, disparity	*pre*	before	preamble, prefix, premonition, prediction
dia	through, across	diagonal, diameter, dialogue	*pro*	forward, for, before	propulsive, proponent, prologue, prophet
dys	abnormal, bad	dysfunction, dyslexia, dystopia	*re, retro*	again, back	reiterate, reimburse, react, retrogress
e, ex, extra, extro	out, beyond	expel, excavate, eject, extrovert	*sub, suc, sup, sus*	under, less	subway, subjugate, suppress
in, il, im, ir (2)	in, upon	invite, incite, impression, illuminate	*syn, sym, syl, sys*	with, together	symmetry, synchronize, synthesize, sympathize
inter	between, among	intervene, international, interjection, intercept	*trans*	across	transfer, transport, transpose
intra	within	intramural, introvert, intravenous	*un*	not	unabridged, unkempt, unwitting

Common Suffixes					
Suffix	Definition	Example	Suffix	Definition	Example
able, ible	ADJ: capable of	edible, presentable, legible	*fy*	V: to make	magnify, petrify, beautify
ac, ic, ical	ADJ: like, related	cardiac, mythic, dramatic, musical	*ism*	N: doctrine, belief	monotheism, fanaticism, egotism
acious, icious	ADJ: full of	malicious, audacious	*ist*	N: dealer, doer	fascist, realist, artist
ant, ent	ADJ/N: full of	eloquent, verdant	*ize, ise*	V: make	victimize, rationalize, harmonize
ate	V: make, become	consecrate, enervate, eradicate	*logy*	N: study of	biology, geology, neurology
en	V: make, become	awaken, strengthen, soften	*oid*	ADJ: resembling	ovoid, anthropoid, spheroid
er (1)	ADJ: more	bigger, wiser, happier	*ose, ous*	ADJ: full of	verbose, lachrymose, nauseous, gaseous
er (2)	N: a person who does	teacher, baker, announcer	*osis*	N: condition	psychosis, neurosis, hypnosis
cy, ty, ity	N: state of being	democracy, accuracy, veracity	*tion, sion*	N: state of being	exasperation, irritation, transition, concession
ful	ADJ: full of	respectful, cheerful, wonderful	*tude*	N: state of	fortitude, beatitude, certitude

Writing

Chapter 3

Section 1
Introduction to the Writing Test

Writers are always looking to make their writing clear and effective while following the standard rules of written English. On the Writing and Language Test, you will answer multiple choice questions that prompt you to revise and edit text from a range of content areas. Your job is to decide whether passages can be improved by making changes, and which changes best improve the passage.

First, let's go over some basic facts about the Writing Test.

The Basics

The SAT Writing Test is made up of four passages and 44 multiple choice questions. You will have 35 minutes to read the passages and answer the questions in this section.

The topics in the passages include Careers, Social Studies/History, Humanities, and Science. The passages will be 400-450 words in length, and broken up into sections across several pages. At least one passage will also contain an informational graphic. The graphic may be a table, graph, or chart that conveys information that is related to the passage topic.

Unlike on the Reading Test, the passages on the Writing and Language Test contain errors. The questions in this section challenge you to revise an underlined portion of the passage in order to make it better. Some questions may deal with one word in the passage, while other questions involve many words or many sentences within a paragraph. Some questions ask specifically about certain goals and how to achieve them. However, most questions on the Writing and Language Test don't actually "ask" a question; rather, a portion of the passage is underlined, and you will be asked to determine whether or not any of the answer options would improve the passage if they were to replace the underlined part. No matter what the question looks like, it should always be your goal to select the best option.

Scoring

The questions on the Writing Test contribute to several different scores on the SAT.

- **Writing Test Score**—this takes into account your answers to the questions on the Writing Test itself. Your Writing Test score will be reported as a number between 10 and 40.
- **Area Score for Evidence-Based Reading and Writing**—this combines your scores from the Reading and Writing Tests. Your Evidence-Based Reading and Writing Score will be reported as a number between 200 and 800, and will be half of your total Composite Score on your SAT.
- **Cross-Test Scores**—two cross-test scores combine scores from Reading, Writing, and Math to assess your skills in Analysis in History/Social Studies and Analysis in Science.
- **Subscores**—the Writing Test will also contribute to four subscores on the SAT: Command of Evidence, Words in Context, Expression of Ideas, and Standard English Conventions.

The Questions

Unlike on the Reading Test, the passages in the Writing and Language Test contain errors. The questions in this section will ask you to choose the answer that corrects those errors or improves a passage.

Here is an example of what a single question might look like:

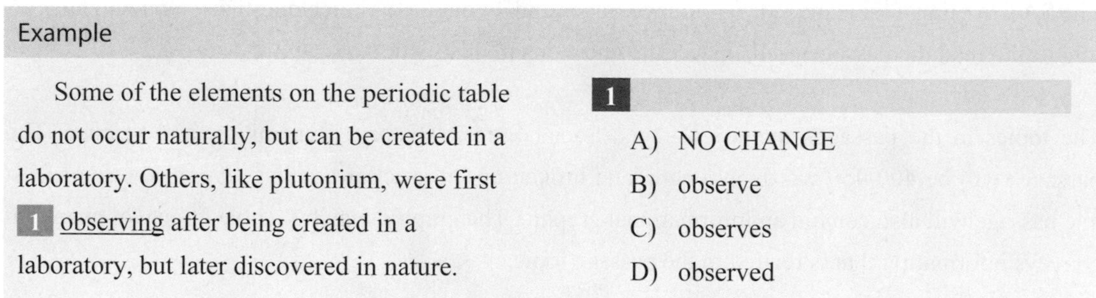

Example

Some of the elements on the periodic table do not occur naturally, but can be created in a laboratory. Others, like plutonium, were first [1] observing after being created in a laboratory, but later discovered in nature.

1

A) NO CHANGE
B) observe
C) observes
D) observed

The first answer choice (NO CHANGE) indicates that the underlined portion of the passage shouldn't be changed. The second, third, and fourth answer choices provide different versions of the underlined portion of the passage. This question is asking you to select the best option for the underlined portion of the sentence, either by replacing it with one of the different versions provided, or by leaving it as it is. Here, the correct answer is (D).

Some questions may ask about one word in the passage, while other questions involve many words or many sentences within a paragraph. Sometimes, questions will ask more specific questions about what needs to be changed in the corresponding section. No matter what the question looks like, it should always be your goal to select the best option.

The Format

Below is an example of what the SAT Writing Test will look like. Notice that as you read through the passage, you will encounter numbers; when you reach a number, refer to the column on the right to find the question paired with the number. Many question numbers in the passage are followed by underlined portions of the passage. Usually, the answer options presented in the right-hand column are options for completely replacing the underlined portion. Sometimes, a question is asked about the underlined portion.

Questions 1-5 are based on the following passage.

Athens in the Peloponnesian War

The city of Athens, one of the two main actors in the Peloponnesian War, experienced a "golden age" prior to the war. Athens's access to the Aegean Sea allowed for trade routes to develop, bringing goods, language, and culture to Athenian society. The trade routes [1] ensured that essential grain and wheat [2] are imported while native fields cultivated more specialized crops, such as olives and grapes. At the beginning of the Peloponnesian War, Athenian power was rooted in the nation's ability to defeat [3] enemies at sea. Its power was also rooted in its ability to transport necessary supplies to Athens through the sea trade.

1

A) NO CHANGE

B) secured

C) assured

D) confirmed

This is the most common question format. The number corresponds to a number in the passage. Answer choices replace the underlined portion.

2

A) NO CHANGE

B) were

C) is

D) was

3

Which choice best combines the sentences at the underlined portion?

A) enemies at sea, however, its power also came from transporting

B) enemies at sea; additionally, its power also came from transporting

C) enemies at sea and transport

D) enemies and sea and rooted in transporting

Sometimes, there's actually a question being asked. Pay attention and do what the question says; don't just pick the choice that looks best in context.

When you see sentence numbers like this, it means that a question will appear later that refers to the numbered sentences. Don't count sentences; use these numbers.

[1] Athens's primary strategy was to avoid land battles and instead rely on this sea power. [2] This strategy served them well during the first half of the war. [3] However, this early advantage would not be enough to secure Athens's victory. **4** [4] Athens was struck by a plague, further weakening the Athenian effort. [5] Sparta was then able to use its naval resources to threaten and attack the supply of grain and silver going into the port at the city of Amphipolis, delivering a final blow to the Athenian war fund. **5**

There won't always be an underlined portion: sometimes, it's because a question asks about inserting something "here" or "at this point." That means inserting it at the place where the number of the question appears in the passage.

Notice how question 4 asks you to insert a sentence between sentences 3 and 4? After you answer that, which one is the real sentence 4? The one that's labeled sentence 4! Always use the sentence numbering.

Sometimes when there's no underlined portion, it's because the question is referring to numbered sentences in the passage. These questions can ask about whole paragraphs, or even the passage as a whole.

4

Which choice, inserted here, best develops the series of events described in the passage?

A) The Peloponnesian War would ultimately become the longest war in Greek history.

B) As the war continued, Sparta secured funds from Persia to improve the Spartan navy and close the gap with Athens.

C) During the war, soothsayers interpreted omens in order to provide advice to commanders.

D) Because accounts of the Peloponnesian War come mainly from Thucydides, an Athenian, there may be an Athenian bias.

5

The writer is considering deleting one of the sentences in this paragraph in order to improve the focus of the passage. Which sentence should be deleted in order to accomplish this goal?

A) Sentence 1

B) Sentence 2

C) Sentence 4

D) Sentence 5

Section 2

Approaching the Writing Test

In Section 1, you saw what the passages and questions on the Writing Test look like. Now we will discuss some strategies you can use to tackle these passages and questions.

In this section, you'll learn how to read the passages in the most efficient way. Then you'll learn how to work through the questions and choose the best answer. There are a few different kinds of questions on the Writing Test, so we will discuss how to deal with these using context clues and Process of Elimination. We'll also review general strategies for completing the Writing Test, including guessing and time management.

Reading the Passages

Part 1

Strategies

The first step in the Writing Test is to read the passages. Here are some strategies to help you read the passages effectively.

1. **Read the whole passage.** On the Writing Test, every sentence is important. Even if sentences don't have underlined portions, they may give you valuable information that you will use to answer the questions. Don't skip portions of the passage just because they don't include questions.
2. **Work on one passage at a time**. Make sure you attempt all questions for a passage before moving on. It is easiest to answer the questions while the passage is fresh in your mind. If you're not sure about a question, circle it in your test booklet and enter a guess on your answer sheet. That way, you can easily go back to the question if you have extra time to check your answers.
3. **Put your Pencil on Paper.** Mark up the passages in your test booklet as you read them to help keep track of important elements that will help you correctly answer questions.
4. **You're allowed to read passages out of order.** This is a helpful strategy if you feel rushed. Skim the first paragraph of each passage, and start with the passage that seems most interesting or least difficult. Taking the passages out of order can make it easy to make avoidable mistakes, so always be sure that you're bubbling in for the correct number on your answer sheet.

The practice tests at the back of this book will help you determine which strategies work best for you.

Pacing

No matter which strategies you choose to use, make sure to give yourself enough time to read the passage and answer the questions before moving on to the next passage. You have 35 minutes for the entire Writing Test. This is about 8.5 minutes per passage but it's not a deadline: don't panic if you spend more than 8.5 minutes per passage, but try not to spend more than 10 minutes on a single passage. When you have spent 10 minutes on a passage, it's time to move on to the next passage. Skim the rest of the passage you're working on, take the time to answer easy questions, bubble in your best guesses for harder questions, and circle problems that you guessed on in your booklet so that you can come back to them later if you have time.

However, keep in mind that it's always better to answer a question than to leave it blank: try to answer every question carefully, but bubble in a guess for every question before time is up for that section.

Reading the Questions

Part 2

While you are reading the passages, you will come across underlined portions with question numbers next to them. As we saw in Section 1, these numbers signal that the question will ask you to revise the underlined section. You might need to revise words, phrases, or whole sentences in the passage. Depending on what part of the passage the question is asking about, you may want to pick certain questions or skip others.

Question Types Matter

There are two basic types of questions on the SAT Writing Test: questions of **Conventions**, and questions of **Expression**. Understanding which type of question you're looking at helps you to understand how to identify the correct answer.

Questions of Conventions are about the basic rules of English. There will be grammar or punctuation errors in the underlined portion, the answer choices, or both. Your task on a question of Conventions is simply to select the option that correctly follows the rules, or conventions, of standard written English. There will only ever be one choice on this type of question that is entirely free of errors, and that is always the correct choice.

You can always use Process of Elimination on this type of question by knocking out options that include errors.

Questions of Expression are about issues of logic, style, and tone. Neither the underlined portion nor any of the answer choices will contain errors of English. It's always important to pay attention to the type of question that you're answering: you don't want to come across a question of Expression and carelessly select "NO CHANGE" because the underlined portion is grammatically correct. The underlined portion may be grammatically correct, but not the best way of expressing the ideas in the passage. Your task on these questions is either to select the option that is the most clear, logical, and appropriate in the context of the passage, or to satisfy the requirements of a specific goal or question spelled out in the exam.

You can't necessarily use Process of Elimination to confidently eliminate every incorrect choice on this type of question. Instead, you have to compare your choices and select the best option. The best approach can often be to Plug In Options and consider how each choice sounds in context.

Decoding the Questions

A lot of students approach questions on the SAT Writing Test by thinking only about how each option sounds in context, and choosing the one that sounds best. We call that Plugging In Options: that is a quick way of approaching the questions, and can work for some types of errors. However, if you're not sure what type of problem you're supposed to be correcting, then it can be difficult to select the correct answer—and easy to make avoidable errors. In order to really be sure that you're picking the right answers, you have to know just what sort of questions you're answering.

Some questions on the Writing and Language Test have prompts, and you should carefully read these prompts to make sure that you know what the question is asking you to do. Most questions, however, don't clearly state exactly what you have to correct in the question. For these questions, you should look at the differences between answer options and the context of the question in order to determine what the question is asking about. Consider the following examples.

Example

Labradors are known for being **1** friendly; outgoing, and playful, but they are also known for their tendency to chew objects.

1

A) NO CHANGE
B) friendly—outgoing—and playful, but
C) friendly, outgoing, and playful, but
D) friendly outgoing and playful, but

In this question, (A), (B), (C), and (D) all use the same words. The only difference is punctuation. Most of the punctuation comes between items in a list, so this is a question about how to punctuate lists. This is a question of Conventions.

Items in a list should be separated by commas (or sometimes semicolons). (A) incorrectly uses a semicolon, (B) unnecessarily separates "outgoing" from the rest of the list with em-dashes, and (D) doesn't separate the items in the list at all. Only (C) punctuates the list correctly.

Example

Synthetic fibers are often **2** inequitably criticized as being cheap and inferior alternatives to natural fibers, even though many modern synthetics have useful characteristics not present in natural fibers.

2

A) NO CHANGE
B) unevenly
C) unfairly
D) dishonorably

In this question, the difference between the underlined portion and the answer choices is the choice of a single word. All of these choices are adverbs, and any of them would be grammatically correct choices. The task here is to select the word that is most appropriate in context. This is a question of Expression.

To figure out which word is best in context, we need to think about the meaning, tone, and connotations of each word. All of the words have similar meanings. (A) means "in a biased way," (B) means "in an irregular or unbalanced way," (C) means "in a way that isn't fair," and (D) means "in a way that isn't honorable." Honor doesn't seem to be involved, so we can cross out (D). There's no mention of criticisms of other kinds of fabrics, or of why critics might be biased, but there is a suggestion that synthetic fibers have some virtues which make the criticisms untrue or unfair. The comparisons suggested by (A) and (B) don't make as much sense in context as (C).

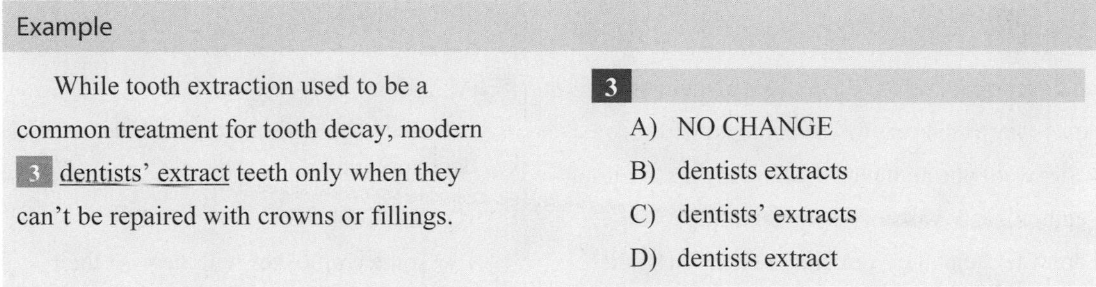
Example

While tooth extraction used to be a common treatment for tooth decay, modern **3** dentists' extract teeth only when they can't be repaired with crowns or fillings.

3

A) NO CHANGE
B) dentists extracts
C) dentists' extracts
D) dentists extract

In this question, we're looking at both wording and punctuation differences. (A) and (C) both use apostrophes, making the noun possessive instead of plural, while (B) and (D) both use the non-possessive plural form. However, the verbs are also different. This question is asking about two concepts. That might seem to make it more complicated, but it actually helps you out: using Process of Elimination, you can take the rules one at a time and rule out answer options if they break even one rule.

Let's say you rule out the options that punctuate the noun incorrectly: after that, you only have to consider two options when you're figuring out which verb agrees with the subject. This is a question of Conventions.

We need to use the plural, non-possessive form of "dentist," so we can eliminate (A) and (C). We also need to use for the form of "extract" that agrees with the plural noun "dentists," and that is "extract." We can therefore rule out (B), and that leaves us with (D) as the correct answer.

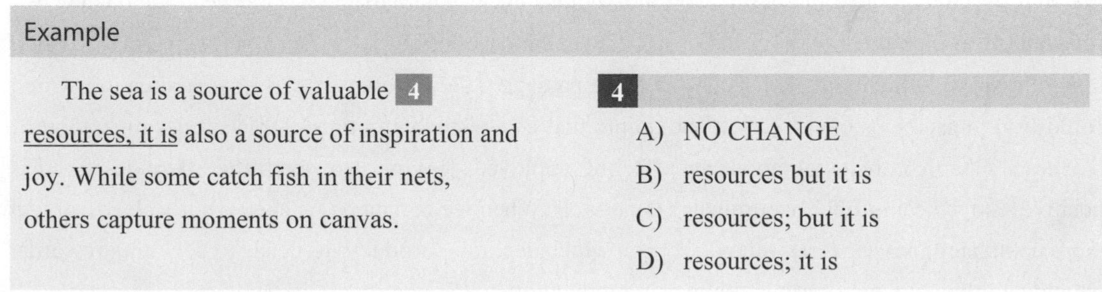
Example

The sea is a source of valuable **4** resources, it is also a source of inspiration and joy. While some catch fish in their nets, others capture moments on canvas.

4

A) NO CHANGE
B) resources but it is
C) resources; but it is
D) resources; it is

Here's another question with punctuation and wording differences. (A) and (D) don't have a conjunction, but (B) and (C) do. In this case, the question is asking about how to correctly join two clauses. However, the same two clauses might be able to be joined with a conjunction or without one, depending on how punctuation is used. That means that you have to consider punctuation and wording together, not separately, to answer the question correctly. This is a question of Conventions.

The two parts of the sentence here are independent clauses. We can either join them with a semicolon, or with a comma and a conjunction. (A) uses a comma but no conjunction; (B) uses a conjunction but no comma; (C) uses a semicolon, but also incorrectly adds a conjunction. Only (D) correctly joins the two clauses.

Example

Poor labor relations can lead to a vicious cycle, in which two forces continuously aggravate one another—making the situation continuously worse. When some employees don't feel that they're being treated fairly, the productivity of the workforce as a whole tends to decline. Facing declining productivity, some employers may invest less in rewarding their workforce. Confronted with declining rewards, **5** <u>more employees may feel that they're being treated unfairly, leading to additional declines in productivity.</u>

5

Which example best completes the description of a vicious cycle?

A) NO CHANGE

B) some employees will increase their productivity, improving conditions for the workforce.

C) some employees might look for jobs elsewhere.

D) less productive employees will seek other jobs, increasing the overall efficiency of the workforce.

This question tells us about a specific goal, and asks how best to accomplish that goal. All of the choices provided create a grammatically complete and correct sentence. Questions with written prompts like this are always questions of Expression. We have a very specific task with these questions: satisfying the stated goal of the question. Usually, the answer that best satisfies that goal also sounds best. Sometimes, an incorrect choice might be tempting because it seems more concise or more interesting, but if it doesn't accomplish the stated goal then it isn't correct.

We're trying to complete the description of a vicious cycle. The passage has defined "vicious cycle," so we need to pick the situation that best matches the description. (B) describes a situation in which things improve, which isn't consistent with the passage's definition. (C) describes a situation which could lead to a vicious cycle, so let's hold onto that as a plausible option. (D) is similar to (C), but it reaches a specific conclusion about the effect of employees leaving. However, the effect described is positive—so we can probably eliminate (D) as well. When we compare (A) and (C), it's clear that (A) more completely describes a vicious cycle, in which declining productivity leads to declining rewards, which leads back to even further declines in productivity.

Part 2 Practice: Reading the Questions

Let's look again at the passage that we reviewed when discussing the format of the exam. We've changed a couple of the questions and inserted follow-up questions. Follow-up questions will not appear on the SAT Writing section, but will help you to practice decoding the questions. For follow-up questions 1a, 2a, and 4a, select the option that best identifies the type of the preceding question and best poses the question. For questions 3a and 5a, select the choice that best describes why your answer choice is correct. Use the answer key at the end of this book to check your work.

Questions 1-4 are based on the following passage.

Athens in the Peloponnesian War

The city of Athens, one of the two main actors in the Peloponnesian War, experienced a "golden age" prior to the war. Athens was located fairly centrally among the ancient Greek city states, with ready access to the Aegean sea. Access to the Aegean allowed for trade routes to develop, bringing goods, language, and culture to Athenian society. The trade routes **1** ensured that essential grain and wheat

1

A) NO CHANGE
B) secured
C) assured
D) established

1a

A) Conventions. Which choice corrects the sentence fragment by adding a verb?
B) Conventions. Which choice of verb uses the correct tense and agrees with its subject?
C) Expression. Which word choice most precisely expresses the main idea of the sentence?
D) Expression. Which word choice best maintains the pattern established in the previous sentence?

2 are imported, while native fields cultivated more specialized crops, such as olives and grapes.

At the beginning of the Peloponnesian War, Athenian power was rooted in the nation's ability to defeat **3** enemies at sea. Its power was also rooted in its ability to transport necessary supplies to Athens through the sea trade.

2

A) NO CHANGE

B) were

C) is

D) was

2a

A) Conventions. Which choice corrects the sentence fragment by adding a verb?

B) Conventions. Which choice of verb uses the correct tense and agrees with its subject?

C) Expression. Which word choice most precisely expresses the main idea of the sentence?

D) Expression. Which word choice best maintains the pattern established in the previous sentence?

3

Which choice best combines the sentences at the underlined portion?

A) enemies at sea, however, its power also came from transporting

B) enemies at sea; additionally, its power also came from transporting

C) enemies at sea and transport

D) enemies at sea, and rooted in transporting

3a

My choice is correct because it

A) uses the transitional word that best expresses the relationship between the two clauses in the sentence.

B) concisely combines the two sentences without any unnecessary words.

C) correctly combines the two sentences while making the fewest wording changes.

D) uses the transitional word that best emphasizes the most important part of the sentence.

[1] Athens's primary strategy was to avoid land battles and instead rely on this sea power. [2] This strategy served them well during the first half of the war. [3] However, this early advantage would not be enough to **4** <u>secure Athen's</u> victory. [4] As the war continued, Sparta secured funds from Persia to improve the Spartan navy and close the gap with Athens. [5] Athens was struck by a plague, further weakening the Athenian effort. [6] Sparta was then able to use its naval resources to attack the supply of grain and silver going into the port at the city of Amphipolis, delivering a final blow to the Athenian war fund. **5**

4

A) NO CHANGE

B) secured Athen's

C) secured Athens's

D) secure Athens's

4a

A) Conventions. Which choice uses the correct verb tense and possessive noun?

B) Conventions. Which choice uses the verb and object that agree with the subject?

C) Expression. Which choice best expresses the relationship between Athens and victory?

D) Expression. Which choice best helps the reader to understand when the events took place?

5

The writer is considering deleting one of the sentences in this paragraph in order to improve the focus of the passage. Which sentence should be deleted in order to accomplish this goal?

A) Sentence 1

B) Sentence 2

C) Sentence 4

D) Sentence 5

5a

My choice is correct because it

A) deletes a sentence that repeats an idea expressed in another sentence.

B) shortens the passage by removing the greatest number of words.

C) removes an idea that does not develop the main point of the paragraph.

D) deletes contradictory information.

Answering the Questions
Part 3

You should use the approaches we just discussed to read the passages and the questions effectively. Once you have read the passage and the questions, you will be ready to choose an answer. When choosing the best answer, you can also use the strategies presented below, including Plugging In Options, Process of Elimination, choosing (A) appropriately, and guessing wisely.

Use Context

Questions that require information from a whole paragraph or the whole passage are often more challenging and time-consuming to answer than those which require you to read only a single sentence. While it may seem tedious to read through many paragraphs to answer questions about one part of a sentence, the test writers have actually crafted the test in this way to help you! Full paragraphs give you access to examples of the author's style and clues to the meaning and usage of words.

In other words, full paragraphs allow you to use other sentences in the paragraph to help you answer questions. When you use other sentences in this way, you are relying on **context.** When you look at sentences in context, think about not only that sentence but also the ones before and after it. Context will help you to determine the author's tone and intention, the logical order of the passage, the style of writing and evidence, and the appropriate usage of words or phrases.

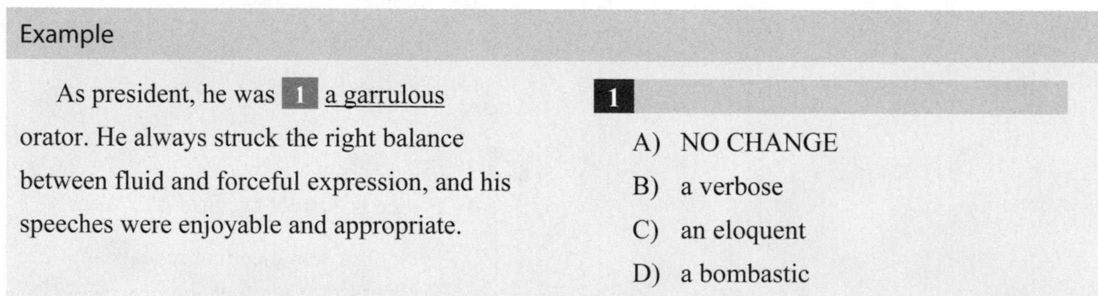

Example

As president, he was **1** a garrulous orator. He always struck the right balance between fluid and forceful expression, and his speeches were enjoyable and appropriate.

1

A) NO CHANGE
B) a verbose
C) an eloquent
D) a bombastic

To answer this question, you need to use context clues to help you. If you only read the first sentence, every answer choice could be correct! To get the context, you need to read the next sentence as well. The second sentence tells you that the president had "fluid and forceful expression," and his speeches were "enjoyable and appropriate."

Now you can tell that garrulous is not the right word because it means extremely talkative, and you want something that means fluid, forceful, enjoyable, and appropriate. Looking at the answer choices, you can see that "eloquent" is the best answer choice because its definition matches our context clues which describe the president as a talented speaker—not unnecessarily long-winded.

You will not only be asked if certain *words* are used correctly in context, but also if entire *sentences* make sense based on their place in the passage. You may be asked to move a sentence to another location or add new information to support an idea—things that you can only do if you have a good understanding of the passage as a whole!

Plugging In Options

Before bubbling in an answer, plug in your choice. Re-read the sentence, but substitute your answer choice for the underlined portion. The new sentence should make sense. Remember: the best version of a sentence or paragraph will correct any original errors and avoid any new errors. Furthermore, always consider options exactly as they are worded. If a choice seems like it might be the best option because all you would really need to do to make it perfectly correct is toss in a conjunction, then it's not correct. To avoid careless errors, plug in each of your answer choices before bubbling in—even when you're pretty confident.

Example

Amelia Earhart was a female aviation pioneer. **2** <u>She set numerous aviation records, she</u> was not able to be located after her plane failed to reach its destination.

2

A) NO CHANGE
B) Having set numerous aviation records, she and her partner
C) After setting numerous aviation records, she
D) She set numerous aviation records and then she

In the original passage, the second sentence is incorrect because it connects two independent clauses using only a comma. This is called a "comma splice." We will discuss this topic in detail in Section 3.

To revise the sentence, you will either need to change the underlined portion to include a dependent clause—a clause that could not stand by itself as a sentence—or use an appropriate method for connecting two independent clauses. Choice (B) corrects the problem by changing the beginning phrase to "Having set numerous aviation records," so you may be tempted to choose this answer. Remember to plug it back into the sentence! When you do so, it reads:

> "<u>Having set numerous aviation records, she and her partner</u> was not able to be located after her plane failed to reach its destination."

You have now introduced a *new* error in the second half of the sentence. It is incorrect to say "she and her partner was not able to be located" because "she and her partner" is a plural subject and "was not able" is a singular verb. Therefore, choice (B) cannot be the answer.

Answer choice (D) uses a conjunction to connect the two clauses, but when connecting two independent clauses with a conjunction you also need to use a comma, so (D) isn't correct either.

The correct answer is choice (C), because it makes the appropriate revision and does not introduce any new errors. Remember, you should always check your answer by inserting it into the complete sentence to check that it is correct in context.

Choosing "NO CHANGE"

Much of this chapter will be focused on how to spot and correct errors in the passages on the Writing Test. However, some portions of the passages will need no correction. In these cases, the correct answer will be (A) NO CHANGE.

When questions have (A) NO CHANGE as a possible answer, you should not be afraid to pick it! Many students are hesitant to pick (A) because it seems "too easy." However, there *are* portions of the passage that are already in their best form. Remember to read the underlined portion using context and anticipation and go through the answer choices using Process of Elimination. If you do this and still think that the portion is best unchanged, then it probably is! Go ahead and bubble in (A) NO CHANGE as your answer.

Example

He was nearly forty years younger, yet his writing **3** <u>was stronger and more popular than his mentor's writing</u>.

3

A) NO CHANGE
B) was stronger and more popular than his mentor.
C) was stronger and more popular then his mentor's writing.
D) was stronger and more popular then his mentor.

This sentence doesn't have any grammatical or stylistic errors, so the original version is correct. However, you also want to check the other answer choices to make sure that (A) is the best answer before you select it. Answer choice (B) compares unlike things ("his writing" and "his mentor"), (C) incorrectly uses "then" instead of "than," and (D) makes both errors, so none of those options are correct. Therefore, you would choose (A) NO CHANGE.

You may find that (A) is the answer for more than one question in a single passage. Again, don't second-guess your answer just because you think there isn't an error. Follow the strategies above and feel confident in your choice!

Guessing

In Chapter 1, you learned that there is no penalty to guessing on the new SAT, so you should always guess if you don't know the correct answer.

If you get to the end of a passage and are unsure about one or more questions, make a temporary guess on the answer sheet, and circle the question in your test booklet. Once you have completed all of the passages, you can use any remaining time to go back to your circled questions. See if you can eliminate any more answers and make a better guess. However, make sure you always bubble in your guesses on your answer sheet—you don't want to run out of time and leave a question blank!

Part 3 Practice: Answering the Questions

Read the passage below and answer the questions. For follow-up questions 1a, 3a, 4a, and 5a, select the option that best identifies the type of the preceding question and best poses the question. For question 2a, select the choice that best describes why your choice of answer is correct. Use the answer key at the end of this book to check your work.

Questions 1-5 are based on the following passage.

The Three Fates

According to Greek mythology, the Fates had the power to decide a person's destiny. They controlled each person's "thread of life." Clotho was the spinner of the thread,  she chose when people were born. Lachesis was the

1

A) NO CHANGE

B) one choose

C) who chose

D) they chose

1a

A) Conventions. Which choice corrects the subject-verb disagreement by inserting both a subject and a verb that agree with one another?

B) Conventions. Which choice corrects the comma splice by changing the second clause into a dependent clause?

C) Expression. Which choice most nearly matches the pattern established in the preceding sentences?

D) Expression. Which word choice best emphasize Clotho's role as just one of the three Fates?

measurer, who chose a person's "lot" in life. **2** Lachesis had an iconic measuring rod. With her measuring rod, Lachesis measured the thread of life. Atropos was responsible for cutting the thread of life, choosing the time of a person's death.

The Fates **3** were independent by the other gods and goddesses, controlling mortal threads

2

Which choice best combines the sentences at the underlined portion?

A) Lachesis had a measuring rod; it was iconic, and with it she

B) With her iconic measuring rod, Lachesis

C) Using her measuring rod, which was iconic, Lachesis

D) Lachesis both had and used an iconic measuring rod, with which she

2a

My choice is correct because it…

A) emphasizes the importance of Lachesis's measuring rod.

B) expresses the idea that Lachesis had to possess the rod in order to use it.

C) places all of the information about Lachesis's rod into a single, concise introductory clause.

D) eliminates unnecessary description in favor of a concise, factual expression.

3

A) NO CHANGE

B) was independent of

C) was independent by

D) were independent of

3a

A) Conventions. Which choice uses both a verb that agrees with its subject and the correct preposition?

B) Conventions. Which choice corrects the subject-verb disagreement by inserting both a subject and a verb that agree?

C) Expression. Which transitional phrase best expresses the relationship between the Fates and other gods and goddesses?

D) Expression. Which word choice is most consistent with the style and tone of the passage as a whole?

of life without **4** <u>interference</u>. The Fates are often described as stern and severe. They are usually depicted holding representative items, such as a spindle, staff, or cutting shears. The Fates are referenced in several ancient works, **5** <u>including *The Iliad* and *The Odyssey*, which are works of Homer.</u>

4

A) NO CHANGE

B) static

C) distortion

D) invasion

4a

A) Conventions. Which choice of noun correctly agrees with the number of other nouns in this sentence?

B) Conventions. Which choice of noun best agrees with the verb that takes it as an object?

C) Expression. Which choice of transitional word best expresses the relationship between the Fates and the other gods and goddesses?

D) Expression. Which word choice most precisely expresses the main idea of this sentence?

5

A) NO CHANGE

B) such as *The Iliad* and *The Odyssey*, which are two works of Homer.

C) including Homer's *The Iliad* and *The Odyssey*.

D) including two ancient works of Homer: *The Iliad* and *The Odyssey*.

5a

A) Conventions. Which choice corrects the comma splice by changing the final clause into a dependent clause?

B) Conventions. Which choice correctly punctuates the list of Homer's works?

C) Expression. Which choice arranges the information in the underlined portion in the clearest and most concise fashion?

D) Expression. Which choice best develops the ideas in the sentence by separating unique ideas and placing them in the most logical order?

Section 3
SAT Grammar

Before we can talk about grammar questions you'll have to tackle on the SAT, we're going to go through a quick review of basic grammar concepts. Don't be scared by the technical names for these concepts—the SAT won't test you on any technical grammar terms. However, knowing these concepts will help you to understand and correct the grammar errors in SAT questions. In this section, you will review common grammar errors that you might see on the Writing and Language Test, and learn how to correct them.

In order to work with all of the materials in this chapter, you will need to have some foundational skills. Additional materials are available online at ivyglobal.com/study. If you need extra review of any of the following concepts, please refer to the supplemental materials online and work through the practice exercises.

- **Nouns and pronouns:** concrete and abstract nouns, proper and improper nouns, possessive nouns, pronouns and antecedents
- **Verbs:** verb number and tense, action verbs and linking verbs
- **Adjectives and adverbs**
- **Sentences:** subject and objects, direct and indirect objects, clauses, subordination and coordination, conjunctions
- **Punctuation:** using colons and semicolons, using commas

For additional resources, please visit **ivyglobal.com/study**.

Common Grammar Errors

Part 1

Let's take a look at some of the specific kinds of errors the SAT will ask you to correct. We'll begin with some of the more straightforward error types that the SAT will include in its Writing and Language Test passages. Though the SAT will try to trick you by disguising these errors, most of them will be fairly easy to spot once you know what to look for. Many of them will sound wrong to your ear, or they would if you spoke them out loud.

Complete Sentences and Their Boundaries

Some of the errors you'll have to correct on the SAT will ask you to rearrange or combine **clauses** in order to fix a sentence that is incorrectly structured.

You may encounter sentence fragments on the SAT. A **fragment** is a set of words or clause that cannot stand on its own, but that a writer has tried to use as a complete sentence.

Example

X Emma didn't show up until 9 PM. Even though she said she'd arrive at 7.

Although the second "sentence" has a subject and a verb, it is not complete. You can see that it is a dependent clause. To fix this problem, you can attach it to the first sentence with a comma.

✓ Emma didn't show up until 9 PM, even though she said she'd arrive at 7.

Sometimes phrases will occur as fragments as well. A **phrase** isn't even a clause—it doesn't have both a subject and a verb.

Example

X She said she got stuck in traffic, but tried her hardest to get there. Driving like a maniac and weaving in and out of traffic.

You'll notice that the second "sentence" here doesn't have a subject. In general, if you see a "sentence" whose verbs are all in "-ing" form, chances are there is a problem with it. To fix the sentence in this example, you have a couple of options. Attaching it to the main sentence with a comma makes it clear that "she" was the one driving like a maniac and weaving in and out of traffic:

✓ She said she got stuck in traffic, but tried her hardest to get there, driving like a maniac and weaving in and out of traffic.

You can also resolve it by making the fragment into a stand-alone sentence:

✓ She said she got stuck in traffic, but tried her hardest to get there. She drove like a maniac and weaved in and out of traffic.

The second sentence now has a subject ("she") and two verbs that agree with it ("drove" and "weaved"). Both are appropriately in the past tense, since the narrator is describing a completed past event.

Some sentences you encounter on the SAT will try to pack *too much* into one sentence. These include **run-on sentences**, which occur when two independent clauses are mashed together without proper conjunctions or punctuation.

Example

X My cat is very mischievous she likes to climb where she's not supposed to be.
X My cat is very mischievous, she likes to climb where she's not supposed to be.

These sentences are both wrong because they combine two independent clauses in an inappropriate way. With no punctuation, the sentence is a run-on. With just a comma, it is a **comma splice**. In either case, the SAT will ask you to correct the mistake. Look for multiple-choice options that accomplish the following changes.

You can break a run-on into two sentences:

✓ My cat is very mischievous. She likes to climb where she's not supposed to be.

You can also split it up with a semicolon:

✓ My cat is very mischievous; she likes to climb where she's not supposed to be.

You can also make one of the clauses into a dependent clause:

✓ Because my cat is very mischievous, she likes to climb where she's not supposed to be.

Be especially careful with **introductory** and **transitional** words. Most transitional words, like "however," "consequently," and "nevertheless," are adverbs. Sometimes, in informal conversation, they can sound like conjunctions—but they don't do the job of a conjunction in a formal English sentence.

Example

X I needed to get a 97 on the exam to pass the course, consequently, I studied for weeks.

This is a comma splice. The word "consequently" is an adverb, which modifies the verb "studied." A new independent clause begins between the words "course" and "consequently," so you must split this sentence with a period or semicolon, or correctly join the clauses with a conjunction.

✓ I needed to get a 97 on the exam to pass the course; consequently, I studied for weeks.
✓ I needed to get a 97 on the exam to pass the course, and, consequently, I studied for weeks.

Verb and Pronoun Shifts

Some words in English change their form depending on certain factors. We will pay particular attention here to verbs and pronouns. When verbs or pronouns change their form because of other words in the sentence, this is called **agreement**. Some questions on the Writing and Language Test will test your ability to tell if verbs and pronouns correctly agree with other words in the sentence.

Subject-verb agreement is one of the forms of agreement the SAT will test. As the name implies, verbs must always agree with their subjects. Luckily, in English, this process is fairly simple. Verbs only have to agree with their subjects in number.

Most verbs do not change form in the present tense, except when the subject could be replaced with the pronouns "he," "she," or "it." For example, see these present-tense forms of the verb "to dance":

To Dance (Present Tense)			
Singular	I dance	You dance	He/she/it dances
Plural	We dance	You dance	They dance

When speaking and writing in English, most native speakers are unlikely to make mistakes with subject-verb agreement. However, the SAT will sometimes try to trick you by putting a lot of extra words between the subject and verb, making it unclear what the actual subject is. You must be a sleuth and find the verb's true subject!

Example

? The artist in the studio by the warehouse full of robots draw/draws all day.

Reading this sentence quickly, you might see the noun "robots" next to the verb "draw(s)" and assume that "robots" is the subject, making the verb "draw." However, the correct verb is actually "draws." You can solve this question by asking yourself: "What noun is actually *doing* the verb here?" In this sentence, who was drawing? The *artist* was. Artist is singular, so the correct verb is "draws."

✓ The artist in the studio by the warehouse full of robots draws all day.

The SAT may also try to trick you with subjects that are ambiguously singular or plural. This can happen when parts of the subject are connected by "and" or "or."

Subjects with "and" are always plural.

✓ The bowl and the spoon are in the cabinet.

When the subject uses "or," the verb agrees with the *closer* word.

Example

? Either Brian or his colleagues is/are bringing donuts.

Since the subject is "Brian or his colleagues," the verb has to agree with the closer part of the subject. In this case, that's "colleagues."

✓ Either Brian or his colleagues are bringing donuts.

Certain pronouns can also make it difficult to figure out whether the subject is singular or plural.

Example

? Neither of my sisters is/are good at sports.

? Each of the princes has/have a chance to take the throne.

In these cases, it may be tempting to use the plural verb form, especially if you think that the plural nouns ("sisters" or "princes") are the subjects. However, those plural nouns are both objects of the preposition "of," which means that they can't be the subjects. The true subjects here are the pronouns "neither" and "each," which are both singular.

✓ Neither of my sisters is good at sports.
✓ Each of the princes has a chance to take the throne.

Here are some other pronouns that are always singular:

Singular Pronouns	
Pronoun	Example
Either	Either of those gifts is a good choice.
Someone	I hope someone brings the cake!
Anyone	If anyone speaks, we will lose the game.
Somebody	Somebody always forgets to close the garage.
Nobody	By the time I got there, nobody was awake.
Everything	Everything in the kitchen seems clean.
Anybody	Let me know if anybody finds my keys.
Everyone	Everyone in my town loves football.

You will also need to watch out for **pronoun agreement**. Pronouns need to have the same number and gender as the nouns they are referring to (their antecedents). The SAT may try to trick you by changing a pronoun inappropriately or by making it unclear what noun it is referring to.

Avoid changing the pronoun you are using partway through the sentence:

Example
X If one changes pronouns midsentence, you are doing it wrong.

If you start a sentence with one pronoun, stick with it all the way through.

✓ If you change pronouns midsentence, you are doing it wrong.

Similarly, if you are using one pronoun to refer to something in one sentence, do not change to a different pronoun in the next sentence.

Example

X If a doctor prescribes too many antibiotics, he or she risks creating antibiotic-resistant strains of bacteria. However, they must also consider the welfare of patients in the here and now.

Instead, use the same pronoun in both sentences:

✓ If a doctor prescribes too many antibiotics, he or she risks creating antibiotic-resistant strains of bacteria. However, he or she must also consider the welfare of patients in the here and now.

Note that the correct sentence uses "he or she" as the pronoun. This is because the pronoun is replacing "a doctor," which is a singular noun. The plural pronoun "they" should be used only to replace plural nouns.

If it is unclear what the pronoun is referring to, then you need to fix the sentence:

Example

X Carlos and Michael were neck-and-neck at the end of the race, but, in the end, he finished first.

Who is "he?" That pronoun could refer to Carlos, Michael, or someone else who beat them both! Choose multiple-choice options that eliminate these kinds of unclear situations.

Last but not least, watch out for pronouns that are far away from the nouns they are referring to.

Example

? The best part of living in a major urban center, like New York or Los Angeles, is that they have/it has a lot of concerts, art exhibitions, and other cultural events to enjoy.

Reading this sentence quickly, you might see multiple cities mentioned ("New York or Los Angeles") and think the pronoun and verb should be plural ("they have"). However, try removing the part of the sentence that is set off between two commas. As we discussed in Part 2, material set off by commas in this way is often additional information that can be removed. You are left with:

? The best part of living in a major urban center is that they have/it has a lot of concerts, art exhibitions, and other cultural events to enjoy.

The pronoun refers to the "urban center," which is singular. This means the pronoun and its verb should also be singular.

✓ The best part of living in a major urban center, like New York or Los Angeles, is that it has a lot of concerts, art exhibitions, and other cultural events to enjoy.

Tense, Voice, and Mood Shifts

In Part 2, we talked about verb tense and voice. Some of the questions on the SAT will ask you to find the correct version of a verb based on its place in the sentence. As you've seen, many sentences involve more than one clause. Clauses presented one after another form a **sequence**, and the verbs in these sequences have to be in the correct tense and voice.

Verb tenses reflect changes in time. Many tense mistakes involve the past tenses:

Example

X Patty began high school thirty years after her mother graduates from college.

If one of the events happened before the other one—it's farther in the past—then you can use the remote past tense to help make the order of events more clear. In this sentence, Patty's mother graduated college before Patty began high school, so you should use the past tense of "graduate:"

✓ Patty began high school thirty years after her mother graduated from college.

You should also watch out for verb tense in conditional sentences. **Conditional sentences** have a "condition" clause that starts with "if" or "when," connected to a "result" clause that gives the result of the condition. You use conditional sentences to talk about imaginary or possible situations.

If the result clause has "will," the condition clause should use the present tense of the verb.

Example

X If she trains rigorously, she will be able to run the marathon.

If the result clause has "would," the condition clause should use the past tense of the verb.

✓ If she trained rigorously, she would be able to run the marathon.

What if the imaginary part has already happened? If the result clause has "would have," use the remote past tense of the verb:

✓ If she had trained rigorously, she would have been able to run the marathon.

Let`s take a look at another example:

Example

X If you study more, you would get better grades.
✓ If you studied more, you would get better grades.
✓ If you had studied more, you would have gotten better grades.

In Part 2, you also learned about the voice of a verb. You may remember that the active voice is usually preferable. However, the most important thing is to keep the voice of your verbs the same within a sentence—that is, use a **consistent voice**:

Example

X The clown makes balloon animals for adults, and children are entertained by him.

This sentence uses both the active voice ("makes") and the passive voice ("are entertained"). Shifting voice in a sentence can be confusing. Be sure to keep the voice of verbs the same.

✓ The clown makes balloon animals for adults, and he entertains the children.

Another feature of verbs that can shift is the mood. The **mood** tells you if a sentence is a statement, question, command, suggestion, or desire. Just like voice, mood needs to be consistent within a sentence or group of sentences:

Example

X Bring in the groceries. After that, you should walk the dog.

If the first sentence is a command, the second sentence should also be command.

✓ Bring in the groceries. After that, walk the dog.

Part 1 Practice: Common Grammar Errors

1 Carolyn Doty has loved baking since she was a child. When she spent weekends and vacations at her grandparents' farm. "My grandmother cooked every meal we ate and she did all of her own baking," Doty explained. "I spent a lot of time in her kitchen, where she **2** teach me how make cookies, cakes, pies, and bread." Doty, inspired to take what **3** they had learned from her grandmother to the next **4** level, decided to make baking her career. She attended a culinary institute, graduating with a bachelor's degree in pastry arts. Now, she works as a pastry chef in one of America's best restaurants, a job **5** one loves.

1

A) NO CHANGE

B) When she spent weekends and vacations at her grandparents' farm; Carolyn Doty has loved baking since she was a child.

C) Carolyn Doty has loved baking since she was a child, and when she spent weekends and vacations at her grandparents' farm.

D) Carolyn Doty has loved baking since she was a child, when she spent weekends and vacations at her grandparents' farm.

2

A) NO CHANGE

B) is teaching

C) teaches

D) taught

3

A) NO CHANGE

B) them

C) she

D) those

4

A) NO CHANGE

B) level. Decided

C) level and decided

D) level, and decided

5

A) NO CHANGE

B) she loves

C) they love

D) she loved

Nevertheless, she has decided that she wants to use her expertise to become a food entrepreneur. She has permission to use the kitchen at her restaurant for her own projects, and the many pieces of large-scale cooking equipment in the restaurant's kitchen **6** makes it possible for her to cook large batches of cookies and pies, which **7** is sold by Doty at the local farmer's market. Now, she wants to make this her full-time job. Doty is taking courses in food entrepreneurship offered by her **8** alma mater, during which she is learning more about how to scale up her baking business, find financial backers, and market her products effectively.

6

A) NO CHANGE

B) make

C) has made

D) is making

7

A) NO CHANGE

B) has been sold by Doty

C) Doty sells

D) is sold by Doty

8

A) NO CHANGE

B) alma mater. During which

C) alma mater; during which,

D) alma mater and during which

Harder Grammar Errors

Part 2

The errors discussed in this part may be a little more difficult for you to spot. In fact, some of them may not sound wrong when you read through them in your head! Nevertheless, our tips will help you detect and correct these errors when you see them on the SAT.

Parallel Structure

Some sentences in the Writing and Language Test passages will be missing parallel structure. **Parallel structure** is a way of constructing a sentence so that different parts of the sentence all have the same grammatical structure. Parallel structure makes long sentences easy to read and gives them a natural flow. On SAT questions, you will sometimes be asked to change a part of a sentence to fix a broken parallel structure. Let's take a look at some examples.

Example

✓ After a long day, I like listening to music, reading, and talking with friends.

This sentence has three elements listed in a series: "listening to music," "reading," and "talking with friends." Each of these elements is an "-ing" form of a verb: "listening," "reading," and "talking." Because they are all in the same form, this sentence has parallel structure. Here is the same sentence with a broken parallel structure:

X After a long day, I like listening to music, reading, and to talk with friends.

Now the three elements in the list are in different forms. "Listening" and "reading" are in "-ing" forms, but "to talk" is not. To answer parallel structure questions, you will need to identify the odd man out and find the multiple choice option that puts all the elements in the same form. Let's look at another example:

Example

X Whether you fight with Ron or giving him the silent treatment, you're going to have to resolve the argument eventually.

This example is a little less obvious than the last one we looked at. What elements are being listed here? If you're not sure, try looking for key words like "and" or "or" that suggest that things are being put together or compared. Here, we find that our options for how to deal with Ron are being contrasted: we can "fight" or "giving him the silent treatment." You may already see the problem: "fight" is a present-tense verb, while "giving" is an "-ing" form. To fix this sentence, let's bring them in line with each other.

✓ Whether you fight with Ron or give him the silent treatment, you're going to have to resolve the argument eventually.

This is better. Now both elements being compared are present-tense verbs. Let's try out one more example:

Example

X Discipline is necessary for anyone who wants to train for a marathon; being motivated is also a requirement.

Where's the parallelism here? This sentence probably doesn't sound obviously wrong at first. Let's look more closely at this sentence's structure. The sentence is made up of two independent clauses joined by a semicolon. The first clause is "discipline is necessary." This has the structure "[noun] is [adjective]." The second clause is "being motivated is also a requirement." This has the structure "[-ing form] is [noun]." We need to put these clauses in the same form.

✓ Discipline is necessary for anyone who wants to train for a marathon; motivation is also required.

Now both clauses are in the form "[noun] is [adjective]." There are other ways you could fix this parallelism, such as "Discipline and motivation are necessary for anyone who wants to train for a marathon."

Finally, sentences must always have the same structure following each conjunction in a pair of **correlative conjunctions**. These are conjunctions that work together to connect two parallel parts of a sentence. These conjunctions include the following pairs:

Conjunction Pairs	
Both...and	Either...or
Neither...nor	Not only...but also
Not...but	Whether...or

Here is an example of a sentence that fails to use parallel structure around a pair of conjunctions:

Example
X I not only enjoy <u>swimming</u>, but also <u>to read</u>.

Notice that this is incorrect because "swimming" is not in the same form as "to run." However, look at the following example:

? I not only enjoy swimming, but also reading.

What do you think of this one?

It sounds a little better, and this is how we often use correlative conjunctions in casual conversation. However, this is technically incorrect. That's because we've got the verb "enjoy" sitting *after* the phrase "not only," and the word "reading" is not parallel with the phrase "enjoy swimming." To fix this, we need to put the verb "enjoy" in front of "not only."

✓ I enjoy not only swimming, but also reading.

We are allowed to have a verb after correlative conjunctions, but we have to make sure that there is a verb after each conjunction in the pair—and if it's the same verb, it's better just to put it in front of the first conjunction. Here are some correct examples:

✓ This weekend, I will either swim in the pool or read a book.
✓ A good workout stimulates both the body and the mind.

Misplaced Modifiers

The SAT will also ask you to move or revise misplaced modifiers. **Misplaced modifiers** are phrases or clauses that are separated from the words they are meant to describe, creating ambiguities or mistaken meanings. Let's take a look at an example:

Example
X While biking to work this morning, an odd thought struck Alanna.

What this sentence *means* to say is that Alanna was the one biking to work, but the misplaced modifier "While biking to work this morning" creates the impression that the "odd thought" was actually biking. We know this can't be true, so it must be a misplaced modifier.

We have a couple of options for how to fix misplaced modifiers. The general rule is that we need to reorder the sentence so that the modifier is as close as possible to the word it's meant to modify.

✓ While biking to work this morning, Alanna was struck by an odd thought.
✓ An odd thought struck Alanna while she was biking to work this morning.

You'll notice that for these types of questions, you'll often need to change more than just a word or two. Often, entire clauses or the sentence as a whole will need to be reorganized or rewritten.

Usually, these modifying phrases will contain verbs in their "-ing" or "-ed" forms. Here's an example of a misplaced modifier sentence with an "-ed" form verb:

Example

X Seasoned with many spices, Sam's mouth burned when he ate a bite of the curry.

This sentence makes it sound like Sam's mouth was seasoned with many spices, which is not too likely. The modifier is meant to refer to the hot curry, so we'll need to rearrange the sentence to reflect that.

✓ Sam's mouth burned when he ate a bite of the curry, which was seasoned with many spices.
✓ Seasoned with many spices, the curry burned Sam's mouth when he ate a bite of it.

You have multiple options when fixing a misplaced modifier, depending on how much you want to change the sentence. Some multiple-choice options on the SAT will make relatively minor changes, whereas others will overhaul the sentence. Make sure that the answer you choose doesn't introduce any new mistakes.

Logical Comparison Errors

Errors in logical comparison can be some of the trickiest mistakes to spot on the SAT. **Logical comparison errors** occur when two unlike elements of a sentence are compared.

Example

X Picasso's paintings are even stranger than Dalí.

Though it seems like this sentence is just comparing two artists, it actually compares two unlike things: "Picasso's paintings" (the artworks) and "Dalí" (the person). While the artwork might indeed be stranger than the person, we need to compare paintings to paintings.

✓ Picasso's paintings are even stranger than Dalí's paintings.

We can also write this more concisely:

✓ Picasso's paintings are even stranger than Dalí's.

Let's take a look at another example:

Example

X France's poets challenged artistic conventions, unlike writing anywhere else.

This sentence also compares two unlike things: "France's poets" (the people) and "writing" (the activity). This mistake can also be corrected with a minor change.

✓ France's poets challenged artistic conventions, unlike those writing anywhere else.

The pronoun "those" indicates that we are comparing France's poets to poets elsewhere. This makes the comparison logical.

Confused Words and Idioms

English is a difficult language to master. In fact, even native speakers confuse English words with each other. Sometimes this is because two words that sound or are spelled the same have different meanings. Other times, two similar sounding words are simply misused.

The table below shows some commonly misused words:

	Definition	Correct Usage
Accept vs. Except	**Accept** – to receive or take as payment **Except** – with the exclusion of	We **accept** credit cards for purchases **except** those under five dollars.
Affect vs. Effect	**Affect** (verb) – to influence or change; the object is the thing that is changed. **Affect** (noun) – emotion or feeling **Effect** (noun) – a result **Effect** (verb) – to cause a change; the object is the change.	The rain did not **affect** our crop yield. This was not the expected **effect.** Bill sought to **effect** changes in environmental policy. Laura claimed indifference, but displayed an excited **affect.**

Precede vs. Proceed	**Precede** – to come before **Proceed** – to move forward	A loud noise **preceded** the fireworks. The officers told us to **proceed** with caution.
Than vs. Then	**Than** – a conjunction used to compare **Then** – next or soon after	I told her I liked peas more **than** candy. **Then** she really thought I was lying!
Too vs. To	**Too** – in addition, also, or excessively **To** – a preposition used to show direction toward a point	Please drive **to** the market this afternoon. Make sure you bring the coupons, **too**: you don't want to spend **too** much.
Wary vs. Weary	**Wary** – cautious; alert **Weary** – tired	The **weary** hikers were glad to make camp, and promptly retired to their sleeping bags; however, being **wary** of bears and other scavengers, they first tied their food safely out of reach on the limb of a tree.

There are also some words that are commonly confused but have specific grammatical rules that you can try to remember:

	Rule	Correct Usage
Among vs. Between	Use **between** only for relationships of two. Use **among** for relationships of more than two.	It was hard to choose **between** the red and pink scarves. **Among** the four gloves, the silk ones were best.
Less vs. Fewer	Use **fewer** for people or things you can count. Use **less** for things that can't be counted or don't have a plural.	**Fewer** people are opening their own businesses these days. Unfortunately, this means **less** money is being spent locally.
Its vs. It's	**Its** is the possessive form of "it." **It's** means "it is."	**It's** hard to tell when the baby will start crying. **Its** arched brows make it always appear upset!
Their vs. They're	**Their** is the possessive form of "they." **They're** means "they are."	The team practiced all year, and **their** hard work paid off. **They're** going to the championship.
Whose vs. Who's	**Whose** is the possessive form of "who." **Who's** means "who is."	**Who's** going to the store with me? Judy is. Now **whose** car should we take?
Your vs. You're	**Your** is the possessive form of "you." **You're** means "you are."	**You're** too talented to give up acting. Plus, **your** voice is incredible!
Who vs. Whom vs. Which	**Who** and **whom** both refer to people; who is used as subject pronoun, and whom is used as an object pronoun. **Which** refers to things or groups.	**Who** brought the salad? To **whom** should I return the bowl? The bowl, **which** has a beautiful pattern on the inside, looks like it might be expensive.

Part 2 Practice: Harder Grammar Errors

From 1812 to 1815 the United States and Great Britain fought the War of 1812. The War began because of American anger over trade issues, the taking—or "impressment"—of U.S. sailors to serve on British ships, and British support of Indian attacks on U.S. colonies on the western frontier. During the conflict, the U.S. invaded the British colony of Canada, British forces crossed the border to fight on U.S. soil, **[1]** <u>and capital cities had been burned by both sides.</u>

In April of 1813, U.S. forces invaded the capital city of York (better known today as Toronto). During the invasion, an explosion of ammunition in one of the city's magazines killed 300 Americans. Nevertheless, U.S. forces were successful in capturing York. Following the battle, the U.S. army **[2]** <u>burned York's provincial parliament, looted homes, and destroyed the press at the Printing Office.</u>

A series of other battles followed. Besieged by Bristish and Native American forces, American forces successfully defended their position at Fort Meigs, in Ohio. American forces defeated British forces at the naval Battle of Lake Erie. British and Canadian forces defeated a larger American force at the Battle of Crysler's farm. **[3]** <u>Chafing under wartime taxes, the war was becoming increasingly unpopular with the British public.</u> Peace negotiations began in August, 1814.

1

A) NO CHANGE

B) and capital cities by both sides had been burned.

C) and, by both sides, capital cities had been burned.

D) and both sides burned capital cities.

2

A) NO CHANGE

B) burned, looted, and destroyed York's parliament, homes, and press at the Printing Office.

C) burned York's provincial parliament, had looted homes, and destroyed the press at the Printing Office.

D) burned York's provincial parliament, looted homes, and had destroyed the press at the Printing Office.

3

A) NO CHANGE

B) The war, chafing under wartime taxes, was becoming increasingly unpopular with the British public.

C) The war was, chafing under wartime taxes, becoming increasingly unpopular with the British public.

D) The war was becoming increasingly unpopular with the British public, who were chafing under wartime taxes.

The negotiations did not begin a cease-fire, however; people continued to suffer the terrible **4** effects on the war. Later that month, British troops captured Washington, D.C. Just as **5** American forces had done in York, Britain looted and burned numerous buildings in Washington.

In spite of the attack on the U.S. Capitol, the British and Americans continued treaty negotiations, and had a complete treaty by December, 1814. The final treaty **6** granted neither the main American demands, nor granted the main demands of the British, yet most of the causes of the war had been resolved by its end. Since the end of the War of 1812, Britain and America have enjoyed more than 200 years of peaceful relations.

4

A) NO CHANGE
B) affects on
C) effects of
D) affects of

5

A) NO CHANGE
B) American forces had done in York, British forces
C) American had done in York, British
D) America had done in York, British forces

6

A) NO CHANGE
B) granted neither the main demands of the Americans, nor the main demands of the British
C) neither granted the main American demands, nor the main demands of the British
D) neither the main American demands, nor the main British demands

Practice Set
Part 3

Patti Smith: Punk Poet Laureate

Patti Smith is a modern Renaissance woman. She wrote and recorded what many claim was the first true "punk" song in 1974, was a performance poet, starred in a play she co-wrote with Sam Shepard, wrote two memoirs and multiple volumes of **1** poetry: and, she is now turning her attention to fiction. However, Smith originally set out to become a high school art teacher, a goal she abandoned **2** on principal when school administrators objected to her focus on obscure and experimental artists.

After moving to New York City in 1967, Smith met the photographer Robert Mapplethorpe, with whom she had a short-lived romance that evolved into a deep friendship. Their relationship was the topic of her National Book Award-winning memoir, *Just Kids.* By 1974, Smith had become a well-known figure in the New York arts scene.

3 After recording her famous "first punk rock song," a grassroots audience flocked to Smith. Arista Records offered her a recording contract after Bob Dylan attended one of her concerts. Her debut album, *Horses*, **4** meet with huge critical and commercial success when it was released in 1975. That album, considered the definitive early punk rock album, frequently appears on lists of the best albums of all time.

1

A) NO CHANGE
B) poetry, and she
C) poetry and she,
D) poetry; and she

2

A) NO CHANGE
B) in principle
C) on principle
D) principally

3

A) NO CHANGE
B) A grassroots audience flocked to Smith after recording her famous "first punk rock song."
C) After recording her famous "first punk rock song," Smith was flocked by a grassroots audience.
D) A grassroots audience flocked to Smith after she recorded her famous "first punk rock song."

4

A) NO CHANGE
B) meets
C) met
D) is meeting

Smith had another megahit with "Because the Night," a song she co-wrote with Bruce Springsteen. It was a surprising collaboration because **5** Smith's music was always more alternative than Springsteen's. By 1980, Smith retreated from the music scene after marrying Fred Smith, the legendary guitarist in the band MC5; the couple moved to Detroit where they raised their two children. Following her husband's death in 1994, Patti Smith returned to the public arena where she is **6** writing, performing, and has recorded albums.

5

A) NO CHANGE

B) Smith's music was always more alternative than Springsteen

C) Smith was always more alternative than that of Springsteen

D) Smith's music was always more alternative than the music of Springsteen

6

A) NO CHANGE

B) writing, performing, and is recording albums

C) writing, performing, and recording albums

D) writes, performs, and records albums

Section 4

Expression of Ideas

On the SAT Writing Test, in addition to answering questions about the standard conventions of English, you will need to answer questions about how a writer can best and most logically express ideas. Expression of Ideas questions don't ask you to correct straightforward errors of English, and an answer choice isn't correct just because it doesn't include any such errors. While Standard English Conventions questions generally ask you to make only small changes to wording or punctuation, Expression of Ideas questions may ask you to add information to the passage, revise the presentation of information, or even delete some portions altogether.

These questions are concerned with three distinct categories: Development of Ideas, Organizing Ideas, and Effective Language Use. Each category contains specific elements, which we will review in this section, and your task is always to select the choice that creates the best version of the passage.

Development of Ideas

Part 1

Effective development is key to any passage; successful writing depends in large part on the writer's ability to present the content clearly, appropriately, and in sufficient detail.

Because answering questions about effective development often depends on recognizing the style and purpose of a passage, it is important to be able to identify which style a writer is using. There are three passage styles that will appear on the SAT Writing Test:

- **Informative passages** will focus on presenting accurate information and may include summaries of data, research, or instructions. One or two passages will be written in this style.
- **Argumentative passages** will present the writer's position on an issue and use argument and evidence to support that position. One or two passages will be written in this style.
- **Nonfiction Narrative passages** tell a true story, but use many of the same techniques as fictional writing. One passage will be written in this style.

Informative and Argumentative passages are discussed in more detail in Chapter 2: Reading. Nonfiction Narrative passages are not specifically discussed in that chapter, but they may contain elements of both informative passages—like data, or quotes from experts—and literature passages—like metaphor.

Passage Styles		
Style	Goal	Examples
Informative	Give accurate information	Research, summaries, instructions
Argumentative	Persuade the reader	Opinions, debates, editorials
Nonfiction narrative	Tell a true story	Biographies, anecdotes, narrative journalism

Proposition

A **proposition** is a central idea, claim, or counterclaim. The main proposition in a passage is sometimes expressed in a single sentence, or thesis statement, while the main points of individual paragraphs are often expressed as topic sentences.

Questions relating to propositions in a passage may take a number of forms. You may be asked to add a thesis statement, or revise sentences to introduce or explain the main idea of an entire passage. You may also be asked to add, delete, or revise topic sentences for individual paragraphs.

When answering questions about propositions, it's important to remember that propositions should:

- ✓ express the main idea of the passage as a whole or a portion of the passage.
- ✓ be expressed clearly and concisely.
- ✓ maintain the tone of the writer and style of the passage.
- ✓ agree with other information in the passage.

Look at the following example of a proposition question:

Example

[1] <u>Traveling by train is more fun than driving</u>. All motorized travel has environmental impacts, but the amount of CO_2 emitted per passenger by a train is about half of the amount from car travel, and can be as little as a tenth of the amount from air travel. Furthermore, much of the impact of electric trains come from burning fuel for electricity—so if we move to cleaner power sources, electric trains will become cleaner even without changes to their design. Finally, trains are less disruptive to wildlife than is a highway.

1

Which choice best establishes the main point of the paragraph?

A) NO CHANGE

B) For passengers, trains are significantly safer than other forms of travel.

C) Until its environmental impacts are adequately addressed, train travel may not be a better option than the alternatives.

D) Train travel has significant environmental benefits over other modes of travel.

You need to read the entire paragraph in order to answer this question. The writer is providing information about train travel, and specifically about the environmental impact of train travel. Furthermore, the balance of the evidence offered suggests that the writer favors train travel. In this example, (A) and (C) each say something positive about train travel, but don't specifically address its environmental advantages. (B) does address the "environmental impacts" of trains, but it's not consistent with evidence that puts trains in a positive light. Only (D) best states the main point of this paragraph.

Support

In any passage, the main point is not enough to make a paragraph complete. Each paragraph will have **supporting information**—facts, statistics, examples, opinions, and anecdotes—that strengthens the main point. In some questions, you will be asked to support claims with additional evidence. Often, this means adding relevant information to strengthen a claim or clarify a point.

In questions about support, the key idea is whether the material strengthens a writer's claims through facts, details, examples, or explanations. Most of the questions related to support will ask you to revise sentences that provide supporting information; some answer choices will provide new facts, but the correct answer choice will always contain evidence that best supports the sentence or sentences before it.

Example

Humans only landed a spacecraft on an asteroid for the first time in 2014, and the prospect of capturing asteroids and mining them for resources is still a long way off. But while it's still a distant prospect, asteroid mining might someday bring real wealth back to Earth. **2** Considering its potential, perhaps it should be unsurprising that the U.S. Congress is already considering legislation to promote asteroid mining.

2

The writer wants to add evidence supporting the idea that asteroid mining could bring wealth to Earth. Which choice best accomplishes this goal?

A) Asteroids have collided with Earth in the past, with devastating consequences.

B) Astronauts could hollow out asteroids and ride inside of them for protection against cosmic rays.

C) A single large asteroid could contain more gold than has ever been mined.

D) The costs of asteroid mining are great, but its benefits could be even greater.

(A) discusses asteroids and Earth, but doesn't directly support the idea that asteroids could bring wealth to Earth; rather, it suggest that they could bring devastation. (B) discusses potential benefits from asteroids, but not in terms of wealth on Earth. (D) explicitly states that asteroids could have great benefits, but it doesn't actually provide evidence. Only (C) provides an additional fact as evidence in support of the claim that asteroids could bring wealth to Earth, in the form of gold.

Focus

Focus questions ask you to consider specific information in the context of the passage or paragraph as a whole. For example, a sentence may be included that provides irrelevant facts or evidence that goes against the main point or goal of the passage, taking away from the **focus** of the paragraph. Focus questions will either ask you to identify and delete irrelevant information or they will ask you to consider whether information is relevant enough to be added to a passage.

Example

It's generally agreed that design choices about color and decorations can have an effect on mood, but which choices are best probably depends on the setting. Warm colors, like red or orange, are stimulating, and might be a good choice when designing a high-energy office. Cool colors, like blue or green, are calming, and might be a good choice when designing a more mellow office. **3** <u>Noise levels also have an effect on mood and concentration.</u> Posters and artwork are generally reported to make the workplace more pleasant, but also to make work tasks seem more challenging. That suggests that artwork might be distracting, so it might not be the best choice for a setting in which high levels of focus are required.

3

The writer is considering deleting the underlined sentence. Should the writer make this change?

A) Yes, because it is not relevant to the main idea of the passage.

B) Yes, because it contradicts information elsewhere in the passage.

C) No, because it provides a specific detail that supports the main point of the paragraph.

D) No, because it provides important information about the main topic of the passage.

(A) is correct. The paragraph as a whole is about how color choices and decorations affect mood. Additional details about noise levels may be interesting, but are not relevant to that main idea.

(B) suggests deleting the underlined sentence, but the rationale that it provides for deleting the sentence is incorrect. The information in the underlined sentence doesn't contradict the rest of the passage because it doesn't come up anywhere else. The sentence is simply not relevant.

(C) suggests keeping the sentence, on the grounds that it provides a specific detail supporting the main point of the paragraph. We can imagine what a specific, relevant detail might be. For example, "A study conducted at a large insurance agency showed that employees working in its offices with blue and green color schemes reported much lower levels of stress than those working in its white and grey offices." That provides a specific example supporting the general idea that blue and green are calming colors, and the main point that color choices can affect mood. A detail about noise levels doesn't accomplish that, because the main point of the passage is that color and decoration affect mood—not that noise does so.

(D) suggests keeping the sentence because it provides important information about the main topic. We also imagine important information about the main topic would look like. For example, "Studies suggest that red might have a negative impact on test performance, perhaps because it disrupts concentration, so it's probably not a great choice for a study area." That's relevant to the main topic of the effect of color and design choices on mood. Noise levels are not relevant to the main topic, though, so (D) is not the correct choice.

Quantitative Information

Some passages in the Writing test will include graphical representations of evidence, which may include graphs, charts, tables, or other types of graphics. **Quantitative Information** questions on the Writing Test don't test math skills; rather, the focus is on your understanding of both the text and the graphic. However, common graphics are discussed in detail in the Math chapter, in Section 6. Be sure to review that section carefully, because graphics will appear in every section of the SAT.

Sometimes, you might also run into unusual graphics that are not discussed in the Math chapter. Instead of using a common graphic type, the writer of a passage might devise a special kind of graphic to present supporting information. Consider the following example:

Example

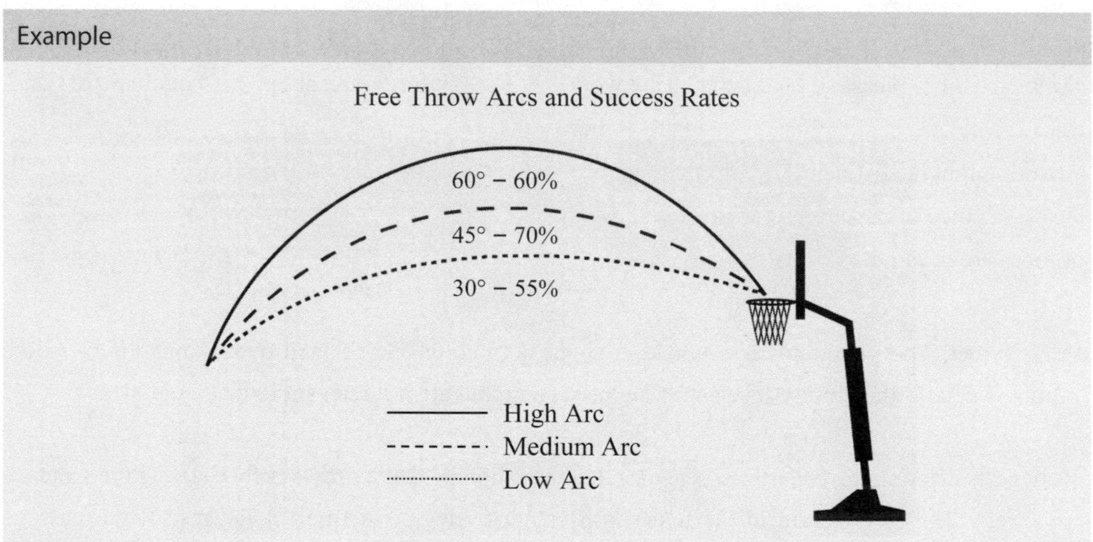

The above graphic sorts free throws into low, medium, or high arc height categories, and presents the average angle of arc for each category and the average success rate of shots in that arc category for a high school basketball team.

When a graphic isn't a common type, look for common features to help you decipher it: data labels, a legend or key, units, and a caption that might explain the information in the graphic.

In the example above, we can figure out several pieces of important information from these features. The key tells us which line represents which arc category, that we have two different units (degrees and percentages), and the position of the labels in the graphic tells us which units go with which line. The caption explains what the units mean: degrees represent the "angle of arc" for shots in a category, and percentages represent the "success rate" for shots in a category. Even without a passage to accompany the graphic, from that information we can conclude that shots with a medium arc of 45 degrees had the highest success rate.

When passages contain a graphic, it will be your job to choose the answer that best translates the graphic into text. Look out for the following common mistakes when you're selecting the best choice.

- **Misreading Units:** If a passage discusses average travel in miles, and has an accompanying graph that shows travel distance in *hundreds* of miles, one or more answer options might use the numbers for "hundreds of miles" in sentences that express them in "miles."
- **Misreading Axes:** Pay attention to what the axes measure. A chart that shows class attendance could have an axis labeled "total attendance" or one labeled "total absences." A line that moved up over time on the first graph would indicate *increasing* participation, while the same line on the second graph would indicate *decreasing* participation.
- **Confusing Labels:** You might see a graphic that has numbers in a different place from data labels, and answer choices that use numbers that actually appear in the graphic but pair them with the wrong items. Pay close attention for a legend or key, and make sure that you're picking options that correctly pair numbers with the items they represent.
- **Picking Irrelevant Data:** Sometimes an answer choice is perfectly consistent with the graphic, but still incorrect. It expresses the right quantities in the right units for the right data points; it just doesn't have anything to do with the rest of the sentence or paragraph. Irrelevant data can be tempting if you're only looking for a correct reading of the graphic. Make sure that your answer choice not only agrees with the graphic, but also makes sense in the context of the passage.
- **Making Bad Inferences:** Some answers are wrong because they go beyond the scope of the passage and graphic. Remember that you can't determine certain things based on the information in a graphic. Don't pick an answer option that says that one thing in the graphic is caused by another unless there's supporting information in the passage. Don't pick an answer choice that makes inferences about data that's not presented in the graphic unless there's supporting information in the passage.

Example

People are terrified of shark attacks, even though they are enormously unlikely. Comparing the odds of being attacked by a shark to other unlikely or even implausible fates has become a cliché. Shark attacks aren't just less common than many other accidents: with advances in emergency medicine, they've also been getting less deadly over time.

As more people live near coasts, the total number of shark attacks has increased—but the percentage of fatal attacks has decreased. As a result, **4** the number of fatal shark attacks has increased over time, even though the number of non-fatal shark attacks has not.

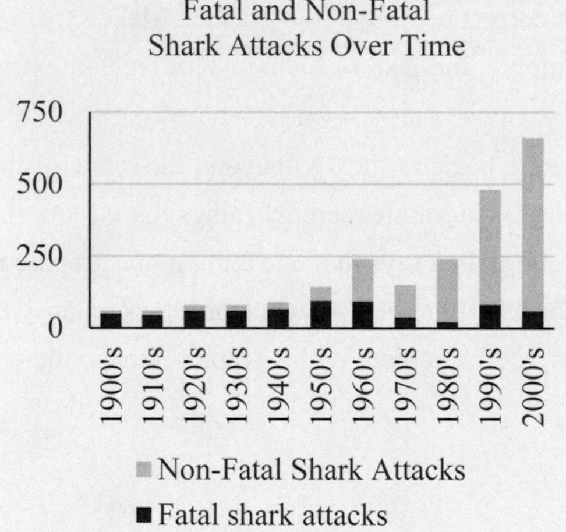

4

Which choice offers an accurate interpretation of the data in the graph?

A) NO CHANGE

B) about the same percentage of attacks are fatal today, even though the rate of attacks increased over 600%.

C) more attacks occur today mainly because people are able to survive multiple attacks.

D) while the total number of shark attacks has greatly increased over time, the number of fatal shark attacks has not.

(A) is incorrect because it mixes up the data labels: it confuses fatal and non-fatal shark attacks. It also doesn't agree with information in the previous sentence, which is a strong clue that it's not the most accurate interpretation of the graph. (B) is wrong because it misreads the units, and misinterprets the numbers on the y-axis of the graphic as percentages. (C) is incorrect because it draws a conclusion which is beyond the scope of the information presented in the graphic. Sometimes, these sorts of speculative conclusions might seem plausible—but they don't accurately interpret information directly from the graphic. Only (D) offers an accurate interpretation of the data in the graph.

Part 1 Practice: Development of Ideas

Read the passage excerpt below and answer the questions that follow. Use the answer key at the end of this book to check your work.

Questions 1-4 are based on the following passage.

Have you ever heard that elephants never forget? Well, elephants aren't the only animals with exceptional memories. When compared with other bird species, the Clark's Nutcracker has been determined to have remarkable memory skills. Scientists have studied the Clark's Nutcracker and found that they perform better on memory tasks and have larger hippocampi, regions of the brain that are associated with memory. Why does the Clark's Nutcracker have such a good memory? [1] It seems that Clark's Nutcrackers have developed exceptional memory skills in order to survive in their environment.

The environment of Clark's Nutcrackers forces them to store seeds away for the winter months. Clark's Nutcrackers mainly live in mountains and rely on seeds of pines as their primary food source. [2] Nutcrackers typically nest in the early spring. Clark's Nutcrackers collect and store large amounts of seeds in the ground during the growing season. They then recover them with incredible accuracy when

1

Which choice most effectively establishes the main topic of the passage?

A) NO CHANGE

B) Not only do Clark's Nutcrackers have better memories, they also have larger brain structures that support memory.

C) Years of practice on experimental memory tasks have allowed the Clark's Nutcracker to develop their exceptional memories.

D) Scientists argue that the memory of the Clark's Nutcrackers affects their ability to reproduce.

2

The writer is considering deleting the underlined sentence. Should the writer do this?

A) Yes, because it contradicts information elsewhere in the passage.

B) Yes, because it provides an irrelevant detail that diminishes the focus of the passage.

C) No, because it explains why Clark's Nutcrackers are able to store seeds before winter.

D) No, because it establishes the sequence of events that is the main focus of the passage.

winter arrives. **3** In contrast, squirrels—also famous for storing food over winter—typically recover **4** <u>between 30% and 100% of their caches</u>.

Approximate Cache Recovery Rates: Squirrels Vs. Nutcrackers

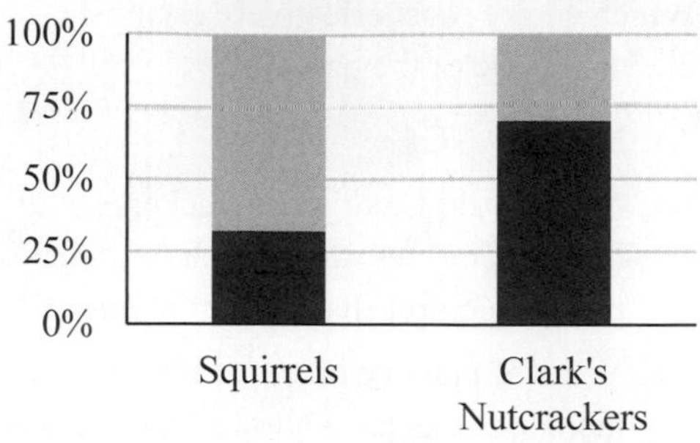

3

At this point, the writer is considering adding the following sentence.

> Typically, the Nutcrackers recover over 70% of their cached pine seeds.

Should the writer make this addition here?

A) Yes, because it supports the main claim of the passage and completes a contrast that follows.

B) Yes, because it introduces information which is necessary to determine whether the Nutcrackers recover enough seeds to survive the winter.

C) No, because the claim is an inaccurate interpretation of information from the graph.

D) No, because it undermines the passage's central claim about Nutcrackers' memory skills by suggesting that many of the seeds are not recovered.

4

A) NO CHANGE

B) Up to 100% of their caches

C) Only about 30% of their caches

D) Approximately 70% of their caches

Organizing Ideas

Part 2

The effective expression of ideas relies on how well a writer organizes and connects ideas so that passages and paragraphs make sense to the reader. Questions related to the organization of ideas will focus on issues of the **Logical Sequence** of information and how the writer connects the ideas in the text with **Introductions**, **Transitions**, and **Conclusions**.

Signal Words

Some questions will ask you to choose a **signal word** or phrase that expresses the most logical relationship or transition between two or more pieces of information in a passage.

Signal words and phrases express the relationship between two or more pieces of information. The chart below provides a handy guide to some common signal words.

Common Signal Words		
Type of Signal Word	When to Use	Examples
Examples	When introducing a specific piece of information to support a more general point	For example, much like, specifically, for instance
Continuations	When introducing additional information that supports the same point as earlier examples, or continuing a description of a series of events	Moreover, also, additionally, similarly, furthermore, next
Change	When introducing a contrasting piece of information, or to signal a shift in emphasis within a text	While, in spite of, yet, however, although
Conclusion	When introducing the last event or piece of information in a text, or concluding an argument	As a result, finally, therefore, consequently, hence

Consider the way that signal words are used in the following example:

> Many tenants have long complained about conditions in the building. For example, tenants are upset about the frequent lack of hot water. Furthermore, the building heat is often turned off during cold weather. Finally, some tenants' doors do not lock properly. While the building owners have often promised to address the problems, they have failed to actually make repairs. When pressed, the owners claim that they lack the funds for repairs. However, they have made significant investments in renovating vacant apartments. As a result, some of the tenants are now planning to sue the owners.

Now, try to pick the best signal word in the following example question:

Example

Some people say that the Steelhead Trout is a kind of salmon. **1** As a result, that's not exactly true: as its name indicates, it is a trout.

1

A) NO CHANGE
B) For example
C) Furthermore
D) However

(A) is a conclusion word, but the fact that "some people say" doesn't *cause* it to be "not exactly true," so that's not the best choice. The fact that it's not exactly true that the Steelhead Trout is not a kind of salmon isn't an example of people saying that it is, so (B) isn't the best choice. (C) doesn't work very well, because saying that an idea isn't true isn't just a continuation of the idea—it's a contrasting idea. Only (D) correctly signals that "that's not exactly true" contrasts with the first sentence, and is therefore the correct choice.

Introductory, Transitional, and Concluding Sentences

Writers often choose to begin a passage with an **introductory sentence** that introduces some of the ideas that will be discussed. An introductory sentence doesn't necessarily spell out the whole main idea; it might just provide some basic facts that prepare the reader to understand the main idea. Sometimes, a writer might even ask a question as an introductory sentence, so that they can answer that question in the rest of the passage.

As the writer moves through the passage, they will need to shift focus between different ideas. To accomplish that, they will use **transitional sentences**. A typical transitional sentence will bridge two ideas by explaining their relationship. Sometimes, instead of explaining the relationship between two ideas, a transitional sentence will just explain why the focus of the passage is shifting from one idea to another.

Finally, writers usually end a passage on a strong **concluding sentence**. An effective concluding sentence ties together the ideas in the passage, usually by offering a summary of the key ideas and the conclusion of the writer's argument.

Consider the following example:

Example

Pigeons are often regarded as unusually dirty birds. Some city-dwellers even refer to them as "rats with wings." In reality, pigeons could hardly be more different than rats: rats directly transmit a wide array of diseases, while pigeons generally don't carry any diseases that are directly transmissible to humans. It's true that pigeon droppings can pose a small health risk, and it's true that people should generally avoid direct contact with any wild animal. **2** <u>I wish people would just leave the birds alone!</u>

2

Which choice most effectively concludes the paragraph?

A) NO CHANGE

B) However, pigeons are actually cleaner and safer than other urban wildlife; they certainly don't deserve their dirty reputation.

C) Pigeons have even been raised as gourmet poultry, while rats are generally not regarded as a delicacy.

D) That said, I'm still not planning to sit under a pigeon's perch.

This question is asking for an effective concluding sentence. An effective concluding sentence usually states the conclusion of the writer's argument, and summarizes key facts. Let's consider our choices: (A) is somewhat consistent with the writer's argument, but it doesn't effectively conclude it. We can tell that the writer disagrees with the idea that pigeons are dirty birds, and seems to be basically pro-pigeon; however, (A) doesn't summarize any key ideas or directly address the main point of the writer's argument that pigeons are not the dirty "rat with wings" that people say they are.

(C) introduces a new fact that supports the writer's argument, but introducing a new fact doesn't effectively conclude the argument.

(D) actually diminishes the strength of the writer's argument; if you're tempted by (D), then it might be because it's succinct and sort of entertaining, but remember: you shouldn't just pick the choice that sounds best to you. You need to pick the one that best answers the question being posed.

Only (B) summarizes and concludes the writer's main argument: pigeons don't deserve their dirty reputation, because they're actually not as dirty as the animals that people compare them to.

Logical Order

On the Writing Test, some questions will ask about moving a sentence from one place to another within a paragraph, ask where a new sentence should be added in a paragraph, or even ask about rearranging paragraphs within a passage as a whole.

In order to answer these questions, you should first identify what a sentence is *doing* in the paragraph. Is it a main point, evidence, example, or conclusion? Once you know what the sentence is doing, you will be able to determine the best location for it within the paragraph.

There are three important kinds of clues to help you order sentences correctly:

1. **Signal words**: if a sentence contains a signal word that expresses a specific type of relationship to another sentence, it should always be adjacent to—and should usually follow—the sentence to which it is related.
2. **References**: references within sentences to other information in a passage can be a big clue about where the sentence belongs. Sentences that refer to ideas that haven't been introduced yet should be moved so that they follow the sentences that introduce them; sentences that introduce ideas should be moved so that they come before sentences that refer to them.
3. **Purpose**: the purpose of a sentence isn't *always* clear when you're reading it out of context, but when the purpose is clear it's usually a very good clue about where the sentence belongs. Sentences that are designed to introduce the main idea of a paragraph usually come first, or near the beginning. Sentences that provide supporting information usually come in the middle. Sentences that provide a conclusion, or summarize the paragraph, usually come at the end.

Let's look at an example, to see how these clues can help us find the right spot for a sentence.

Example

[1] Workplace wellness initiatives include health screenings and health education, along with changes to the workplace environment to facilitate healthy behavior. [2] Some also offer discounted gym memberships and access to programs to assist those who want to quit smoking. [3] As a result, employees enjoy healthier lives, and employers enjoy a reduction in sick days and disability claims. [4] Many workplaces are now introducing workplace wellness initiatives, which provide benefits to both the employees and the company. [5] Those reductions translate to reduced costs. **3**

3

To make this paragraph most logical, sentence 4 should be

A) placed where it is now.
B) placed before sentence 1.
C) placed before sentence 2.
D) placed after sentence 5.

This question is asking about sentence 4: "Many workplaces are now introducing workplace wellness initiatives, which provide benefits to both the employees and the company."

You may have noticed that sentence 4 breaks up two sentences that should be linked (sentences 3 and 5). Sentence 5 refers to the reductions mentioned in sentence 3, and sentence 4 is disrupting the connection. If you see a sentence that breaks an important link, you should move that sentence to another location in the paragraph—so we can rule out (A).

Now, are there any relevant signal words or phrases? Yes: sentence 2 includes the word "also," signaling that it continues an idea from the previous sentence. Sentence 1 discusses some of the specific benefits offered by workplace wellness initiatives, and so does sentence 2—so that transition makes sense. Sentence 4 doesn't express exactly the same idea, so the signal word in sentence 2 wouldn't make sense if we chose (C).

Finally, what's the purpose of the sentence? This sentence is a general statement that is supported by the facts and examples in the other sentences, and could serve to introduce the main idea of the paragraph. This type of sentence is a main point, and should be placed at or near the beginning of the paragraph. We can therefore eliminate (D), and select (B).

When you answer questions about logical order, make sure that you test your choice by placing it back in the paragraph. Before you bubble in your answer, re-read the paragraph with the sentence in its new location. Correct answers may involve keeping the sentence where it is, moving it to a new location, or deleting it altogether.

Part 2 Practice: Organizing Ideas

Read the passage excerpt below and answer the questions that follow. Use the answer key at the end of this book to check your work.

Questions 1-3 are based on the following passage.

[1] 1 While sign language is sometimes perceived as only an alternative to vocal speech, it's a complete language in its own right. [2] Some researchers have studied deaf children and compared those children who were exposed to sign language instruction and those who weren't. [3] They found that even without instruction, the children developed pointing and gestures that were very similar to those common to various sign languages. [4] Sometimes these gestures were even complex. [5] The children lacking instruction also shared other similarities with the children who had received instruction. [6] 2 Therefore, both groups of children relaxed their hands between "sentences," signaling an intuitive break in thought. 3

1

Which choice best introduces the main idea of this paragraph?

A) NO CHANGE

B) Because sign language is used by only a fraction of the population, it is of special interest to researchers.

C) Researchers have found compelling evidence that some elements of sign language may emerge from a set of innate gestures.

D) Sign language is used by both children and adults, but children learn it more quickly than adults.

2

A) NO CHANGE

B) For example,

C) As a result,

D) Finally,

3

To make this paragraph most logical, sentence 4 should be

A) placed where it is now.

B) placed after sentence 1.

C) placed after sentence 5.

D) placed after sentence 6.

Effective Language Use

Part 3

Have you ever read something that was difficult to understand because it was too wordy or vague, or because the writer didn't seem to be using exactly the right words? These types of mistakes occur when writers use language ineffectively. Just as the order of sentences within a paragraph can help a writer express her ideas, so can the proper use of words and phrases.

On the Writing Test, you will be asked to revise the language the writer uses to more effectively convey her ideas. You can do this by making sentences **precise**, using exactly the right words, and **concise**, not using too many words, while matching the style and tone of the passage.

Precision

Mark Twain once claimed that, "The difference between the right word and the wrong word is the difference between lightning and a lightning bug." In other words, **precision** matters.

Some Writing Test questions concerned with precision will ask you to replace vague or unclear language that does not precisely express the writer's meaning. All of your options will be the same part of speech, and any of them would make a complete and grammatical sentence, but only one will clearly express the correct idea.

Consider the following example:

Example

I was so distracted by the delicious smell wafting from the tray that I forgot to put on an oven mitt. The result was my first—and a very painful—burn. The skin surrounding the area was red and tender to the touch. I immediately covered it with a bandage so that I would not further [4] <u>provoke</u> the burn.

4

A) NO CHANGE
B) frustrate
C) alleviate
D) aggravate

Using the context of the paragraph, you can tell that the burn is painful, red, and tender. In the final sentence, the writer uses the word "further" to suggest that the bandage is being used to prevent more pain, redness, and tenderness. In order words, the bandage will prevent it from becoming more irritated. You want to choose an answer that means something like "irritate" or "make worse."

The correct answer is (D) aggravate, which means "to make worse or more serious." Answers (A) "provoke" and (B) "frustrate" are synonyms of aggravate, but don't fit in the sentence; "provoke" means to cause a response or to make angry, and "frustrate" means to prevent. The writer wouldn't "provoke" the burn, nor would she "frustrate" the burn. Answer (C), "alleviate," means "to ease or improve," so it is an antonym of aggravate.

To do your best on precision questions, you need to really flex your vocabulary. If you're having trouble with precision questions, then work on expanding your vocabulary. You can use the common word roots discussed in the Reading chapter, and go online for extra vocabulary lists.

For additional resources, please visit **ivyglobal.com/study**.

Concision

The Writing Test will require you to consider whether a writer has expressed her ideas concisely. This means providing information without being redundant, using two or more words that each express the same idea, or wordy, using extra words and phrases where they aren't necessary.

Some **concision** questions will ask you to consider the passage as a whole and determine if the writer makes the same point more than once. Other questions will be concerned with single sentences that may include empty words, words that don't improve the sentence or add information. With concision questions, shorter is usually better, but not always: sometimes cutting out words also cuts out the main idea of the sentence, and that's not the correct way to make sentences more concise. You should pick the shortest option that effectively expresses the key idea.

Consider the following example:

Example

X He is <u>a man who is always busy</u>. He often switches <u>in a hasty manner</u> from one task to the next.

X He is <u>a man</u>. He often switches from one task to the next.

✓ He is <u>always busy</u>. He often switches <u>hastily</u> from one task to the next.

The first example is unnecessarily long. The phrase "a man who is" is redundant, because it only repeats the meaning of "he is," so we can cut that. "In a hasty manner" uses empty words; it can be more concisely written using the adverb "hastily." However, in the second example, we've cut too much. The main idea being expressed is that this man is so busy that he's always switching tasks; cutting out all of the descriptive words totally eliminates that meaning. We should just cut out empty or redundant words.

Always carefully consider the meaning of all of the words in a sentence, and keep an eye out for redundant phrases.

Consider the following example:

Example

X Novice drivers <u>who don't have much experience driving</u> are more likely to be involved in car accidents.

✓ Novice drivers are more likely to be involved in car accidents.

In the first sentence, "who don't have much experience driving" is unnecessary because you already know they are "novice drivers." "Novice" means "lacking experience," so the writer does not need to repeat this using a phrase.

One final way you will be asked to make passages more concise is by combining sentences.

Example

? Certain dog breeds have been bred as herding dogs. These breeds include sheepdogs and collies.

✓ Certain dog breeds, such as sheepdogs and collies, have been bred as herding dogs.

When you combine two short sentences using a phrase, you can keep the meaning the same but express an idea more concisely. Often, the correct answer will combine the two sentences by turning one sentence into a modifier or dependent phrase.

Style and Tone

Both style and tone are ways a writer develops her "voice" in a piece of writing. **Style** involves the techniques the writer uses and the purpose of the passage. **Tone** relates to the way that a passage feels, or how it is supposed to feel.

To correctly answer questions about style and tone, you will need to consider what the writer is trying to accomplish in the passage and what techniques the writer uses to achieve her goal. A writer trying to express her own emotional experience might use the first-person voice ("I," "me"), very expressive language with strong positive or negative connotations ("ecstatic," "sorrowful"), expressive punctuation ("!"), and personal opinion. In contrast, a writer who is describing a recent experiment to inform readers might instead use the third-person voice ("he," "she," "they"), and avoid language with strong connotations, expressive punctuation, or personal opinions.

Many questions will focus on the differences between formal and informal style and tone. Formal writing is straightforward: it uses clear, concise wording. Formal writing usually favors words with neutral tone. Slang is never used in formal writing. Informal writing might use slang phrases like "that's really cool" or "she was like, 'what?'" Most passages on the Writing Test have a formal style and tone.

When you are asked to revise a section to better match the tone of the passage, choose the answer that continues the writer's style and tone, and uses techniques that match those used elsewhere in the passage. Ask yourself, does this fit in with the rest of the passage? Would the writer express this thought in this way? Is there a similar choice somewhere else in the passage?

Example

One of Jane Goodall's first observations about chimpanzees was that they possessed the ability to make and use tools. Previously, many scientists assumed only humans had this capability. Goodall observed chimpanzees creating rods out of grass; the chimpanzees would then use these rods to collect termites from a termite hole and lick the termites from the rod. **5** Chimpanzees are obviously as intelligent as humans.

5

Which choice is most consistent with the rest of the paragraph?

A) NO CHANGE

B) Those scientists who originally disagreed were totally not as observant as Goodall.

C) She determined that chimpanzees possess similar tool-making abilities to humans.

D) I will always admire Jane Goodall for her work in expanding our knowledge of chimpanzee abilities.

This paragraph is describing a discovery Jane Goodall made while living with chimpanzees. The paragraph primarily gives facts and uses descriptions to inform the reader.

The final sentence of the paragraph breaks the tone by introducing an opinion. The word "obviously" has strong connotations, and the use of an opinion is not consistent with the rest of the paragraph. (B) also introduces an opinion, and uses "totally" in an informal way, so it does not match the style or tone of the rest of the passage. (D) switches to first person, while the paragraph is written in third person. Only (C) continues the same tone by introducing a new fact about Goodall's conclusion from her discovery.

Syntax

Syntax refers to the arrangement of words and clauses within sentences. On the Writing Test, you will sometimes be asked to choose between different ways of ordering the parts of sentences in order to clearly express ideas.

Effective use of syntax means ordering the elements of a sentence in a clear and straightforward manner. Usually, it's best to place the subject before the verb, the object after the verb, and any modifiers directly next to the element that they modify.

Consider the following example:

Example

? Which choice best combines the underlined sentences?

X <u>Colin and Zach were driving down the road. Colin and Zach saw a kangaroo.</u>

X Driving down the road were Colin and Zach, who saw a kangaroo.

X Colin and Zach were driving down the road, at which time they saw a kangaroo.

X They saw a kangaroo, Colin and Zack did, while they were driving down the road.

✓ Colin and Zach saw a kangaroo while they were driving down the road.

The incorrect choices don't sound quite right, but they aren't grammatically incorrect. These sentences just order the parts of the sentence in ways that introduce a variety of problems. Some of them use the passive voice, while others use parenthetical elements to clarify ideas that could be expressed clearly without them.

Part 3 Practice: Effective Language Use

Read the passage below and answer the questions that follow. Use the answer key at the end of this book to check your work.

Questions 1-4 are based on the following passage.

Imagine you're doing your favorite activity. You might be playing baseball, piano, or chess. You might be painting, singing, or dancing. **1** <u>When you do this activity, is time lost track of by you? Do you feel energized?</u> If this happens to you, you are probably experiencing what is called "flow."

1

Which choice most effectively combines the underlined sentences?

A) Do you lose track of time when you do this activity, and also feel energized when you do it?

B) Do you, when you're doing this activity, feel energized, and lose track of time?

C) When you're doing this activity, do you feel energized and lose track of time?

D) Is time lost track of by you, and do you feel energized when you do this activity?

You experience flow when you are completely involved in an activity. **2** <u>An individual experiencing flow perceives the activity as both challenging and pleasant.</u> Flow involves intense and focused concentration on an activity. **3** <u>Due to the fact that</u> this activity is rewarding, you may feel as if time is flying or forget other worries. In order to continue to experience flow, you must **4** <u>unceasingly</u> seek new challenges. For example, if you achieve flow through sports, you should practice a few times every week and regularly establish new goals.

2

Which choice is most consistent with the style of the passage as a whole?

A) NO CHANGE

B) Flow is awesome: you're in the zone, challenged but happy.

C) Challenge and pleasure together is what makes for flow.

D) During flow, you are challenged but still have a pleasant experience.

3

A) NO CHANGE

B) Since you may feel like

C) Because of the fact that

D) Because

4

A) NO CHANGE

B) consistently

C) seldom

D) incessantly

Essay
Chapter 4

Section 1

Introduction to the SAT Essay

Unlike the other portions of the SAT discussed in this book, the Essay portion of the SAT is optional. If the schools you are applying to do not require the Essay, you can choose to not write it. There are, however, some compelling reasons to write the Essay even if the schools you want to attend don't require it.

Most important is that the Essay gives you a chance to demonstrate your skills in reading, analysis, and writing—all of which provide evidence of your readiness for college, and may help you decide if there are skills you still need to work on. Further, it is possible that you may later decide to apply to more schools than you originally anticipated, including schools that require the Essay. As you cannot take the Essay separately from the rest of the SAT, it makes the most sense to write the Essay the first time you write the test so your bases are covered.

Some things to bear in mind about the Essay portion include:

- **Order:** The Essay is administered at the end of the SAT, after the multiple-choice sections of the test.
- **Time**: You will have 50 minutes to complete the SAT Essay.
- **Prompt**: There is a single SAT Essay prompt that asks you to read and analyze one provided passage. The prompt itself is nearly the same on every exam—it is the passage that varies from test to test.
- **Task**: The SAT Essay asks you to analyze how the author of the passage builds an argument to persuade an audience. In other words, your task is to write a rhetorical analysis, focusing on how the author uses specific techniques and elements to create a specific effect. You will not be asked to take a stance on or form an opinion about an issue. Rather, the focus is on your ability to comprehend source material, analyze how the author presents her argument, and use textual evidence from the passage to support your position about how the author builds her argument.

Essay Scoring

The SAT Essay is evaluated based on three specific criteria: Reading, Analysis, and Writing. Each of these criteria will be scored on a scale of 1-4; because two raters will consider your essay, you will receive a score of 2-8 for each criterion for an overall score of 6-24. Your Essay score will not affect your score on other sections of the SAT. Below is a breakdown of what each of these scores means and what the College Board expects to see in your essay. They are explored in more detail in Section 4 of this chapter.

- **Reading:** The College Board wants to see evidence in your essay that you read and understood the passage. The best way to prove that you understood all the nuances of the passage is to use pieces of it effectively in your essay. We'll show you how to do this in Section 3.
- **Analysis:** The College Board wants to see that you can analyze the elements of someone else's argument and use this analysis to craft an argument of your own. You can achieve this by coming up with interesting, supportable claims and selecting strong, relevant evidence to support them. We will also be showing you how to do this in Section 3.
- **Writing:** The College Board wants to see evidence that you can not only come up with a good analysis, but that you can also effectively convey it to your reader. The scorers are evaluating your ability to organize your writing, use varied sentence structures, and make good word choices. You have likely learned many of these skills in school, but we'll still do some practice in the coming sections to reinforce them.

Sample Essay Prompt

Here is a sample essay prompt and passage. The prompt preceding the passage will always be the same; the instructions for your specific essay will appear after the passage.

This is the standard prompt.

As you read the next passage, consider how Yvon Chouinard uses

- evidence, such as facts or examples, to support claims.
- reasoning to develop ideas and to connect claims and evidence.
- stylistic or persuasive elements, such as word choice or appeals to emotion, to add power to the ideas expressed.

This is the passage you need to read and analyze in your essay.

Adapted from "Tear Down 'Deadbeat' Dams" by Yvon Chouinard. ©2014 by the New York Times Company. Originally published May 7, 2014.

1 Of the more than 80,000 dams listed by the federal government, more than 26,000 pose high or significant safety hazards. Many no longer serve any real purpose. All have limited life spans. Only about 1,750 produce hydropower, according to the National Hydropower Association.

2 In many cases, the benefits that dams have historically provided—for water use, flood control, and electricity—can now be met more effectively without continuing to choke entire watersheds.

3 Dams degrade water quality, block the movement of nutrients and sediment, destroy fish and wildlife habitats, damage coastal estuaries, and in some cases rob surrounding forests of nitrogen. Reservoirs can also be significant sources of greenhouse gas emissions.

4 Put simply, many dams have high environmental costs that outweigh their value. Removing them is the only sensible answer. And taking them down can often make economic sense as well. The River Alliance of Wisconsin estimates that removing dams in that state is three to five times less expensive than repairing them.

5 The message has been slowly spreading around the country. More and more communities and states have reclaimed rivers lost to jackhammers and concrete. Last year, 51 dams in 18 states were taken down, restoring more than 500 miles of streams, according to the group American Rivers. Nearly 850 have been removed in the last 20 years, and nearly 1,150 since 1912.

6 But the work is far from done. I was disappointed to see the Energy Department release a report last week on the potential to develop new "sustainable" hydroelectric dams on rivers and streams across the country. The report follows President Obama's signing of two laws last year to encourage small hydro projects and revive nonproducing dams.

7 New dams are a bad idea. We've glorified them for decades, but our pride in building these engineering marvels has often blinded us to the environmental damage they cause. The consequences run the length of the river and beyond. Our many complex attempts to work around these obstacles would make Rube Goldberg proud. Interventions like fish elevators and trap-and-haul programs that truck fish around impoundments don't lead to true recovery for wild fish populations or reverse the other environmental problems caused by blocking a river's flow.

8 But we do know that removing dams brings streams and rivers back to life and replenishes our degraded aquifers.

9 A case in point is the Elwha River on the Olympic Peninsula in Washington, where two hydroelectric dams built early in the last century exacted huge environmental costs but were no longer important as power generators. Salmon runs that once reached about 400,000 fish a year dropped to fewer than 3,000. A year after the Elwha Dam was removed, Chinook salmon returned to the river in numbers not seen in decades, with three-quarters of them observed spawning upstream of the former dam site. Today, the river runs free from its headwaters in Olympic National Park to the Strait of Juan de Fuca, and a terrible wrong imposed on the salmon-dependent Lower Elwha Klallam tribe has been righted.

10 President Obama should learn from that example. Most urgently, he should turn his attention to the Snake River in eastern Washington, where four dams along its lower reaches provide marginal (and replaceable) electricity generation that is outweighed by the opportunities for the revival of endangered salmon populations, plus the jobs and communities a healthy salmon fishery would support. Those deadbeat dams should be taken down and added to the list of dams in the process of being removed along the White Salmon River in Washington, the Penobscot in Maine, and the Klamath in southern Oregon.

11 I've been working to take down dams for most of my life. The idea, once considered crazy, is gaining momentum. We should seize it and push for the removal of the many dams with high costs and low or zero value. The environmental impacts are too enormous.

12 Time and again, I've witnessed the celebration that comes with the removal of an unnecessary dam. After a river is restored and the fish have returned you never hear a single person say, "Gee, I wish we had our dam back."

These are the specific instructions for what your essay should accomplish.

> Write an essay in which you explain how Yvon Chouinard builds an argument to persuade his audience that obsolete dams should be removed. In your essay, analyze how Chouinard uses one or more of the features listed in the box above (or features of your own choice) to strengthen the logic and persuasiveness of his argument. Be sure that your analysis focuses on the most relevant features of the passage.
>
> Your essay should not explain whether you agree with Chouinard's claims, but rather explain how Chouinard builds an argument to persuade his audience.

Now that you've reviewed some basic information and a sample passage, we'll move on to more specific advice. We'll refer back to this example as we continue. In this chapter, we will cover:

- Some overall basics and tips to help you prepare for the Essay portion of the SAT
- What the College Board looks for in a good essay
- How to analyze someone else's argument
- How to use your time wisely
- How to put this all together to write a strong essay

Section 2

Approaching the Essay

Now that we've gone over the format of the SAT Essay, we're going to give you some tips for writing your essay. In this section, we're going to go over some basic strategies, and the broad picture of how you should plan and organize your essay.

SAT Essay Basics

Part 1

Because writing an SAT essay has a lot in common with writing assignments you may have received in school, some of the following guidance will be familiar. However, some of our tips will be quite specific to the SAT and what the College Board is looking for in an essay.

Use the Answer Sheet and Your Test Booklet

Write only in the designated section of the exam booklet. Use only the four lined pages provided for your essay. Remember, the only portion of your essay that the graders will see is what you write within the available lines; they won't see anything you write in the margins.

Write neatly. Unlike the other computer-graded sections of the SAT, the essay has to be read by another human being, which makes the legibility of your writing very important. Ensure that your grader sees the greatness of your essay by writing neatly and legibly. Don't use small handwriting to save space: bigger letters are easier to read.

Use your test booklet for outlining and notes. As you read, it's a good idea to underline or note the line number of quotes you'd like to use, and start outlining your essay in the margins.

Write as Much as Possible

Filling up as many of the answer pages as possible tells your graders that you have taken the time to write a thorough, well-argued essay. You have plenty of space to write; use as much of it as possible to develop your argument.

Write six full paragraphs. Fifty minutes is plenty of time to outline and write an introduction, four body paragraphs, and a conclusion. Writing six paragraphs will properly break up four pages of writing and make it easier for your graders to follow your argument; one long run-on paragraph or many short paragraphs can be difficult to follow.

Be Explicit

State your argument (which is, again, a claim about how the author built an argument, not an opinion about the subject of the author's essay) as clearly as possible. When you are writing it's easy to think that the main point of your argument is abundantly clear throughout your essay. However, your graders are going to need help following your argument. Make it easy for them by re-emphasizing your main point at the beginning and end of every paragraph.

Refer back to the provided text. One of the purposes of the SAT essay is to test your ability to read as well as write. There is no better way to demonstrate that you properly understood the passage than by quoting it throughout your analysis. Having the passage right in front of you provides you with abundant evidence to use in your essay—take advantage of it! Your test booklet notes will help you quickly and easily find quotes that support your argument.

Revise

Fifty minutes gives you plenty of time to go back and read over your essay after you've finished writing. Graders can penalize you for grammatical or spelling errors, particularly if they make your essay difficult to read. So once you've finished writing, take time to read over your essay and fix any spelling or grammatical mistakes or to make revisions.

Structuring an Essay

Part 2

The best way to showcase your argument is by using effective **external** and **internal structure**. External structure means properly arranging the introduction, body paragraphs, and conclusion; internal structure means properly structuring each paragraph. This section will show you the best ways to structure your SAT essay.

External Structure

The external structure of your essay should make it easy for your graders to follow your argument. The chart below illustrates the structure you should aim for and provides estimates of how much time you should spend on each section, including reading and analyzing the passage and proofreading your essay.

Analyze Passage (*10 minutes*)

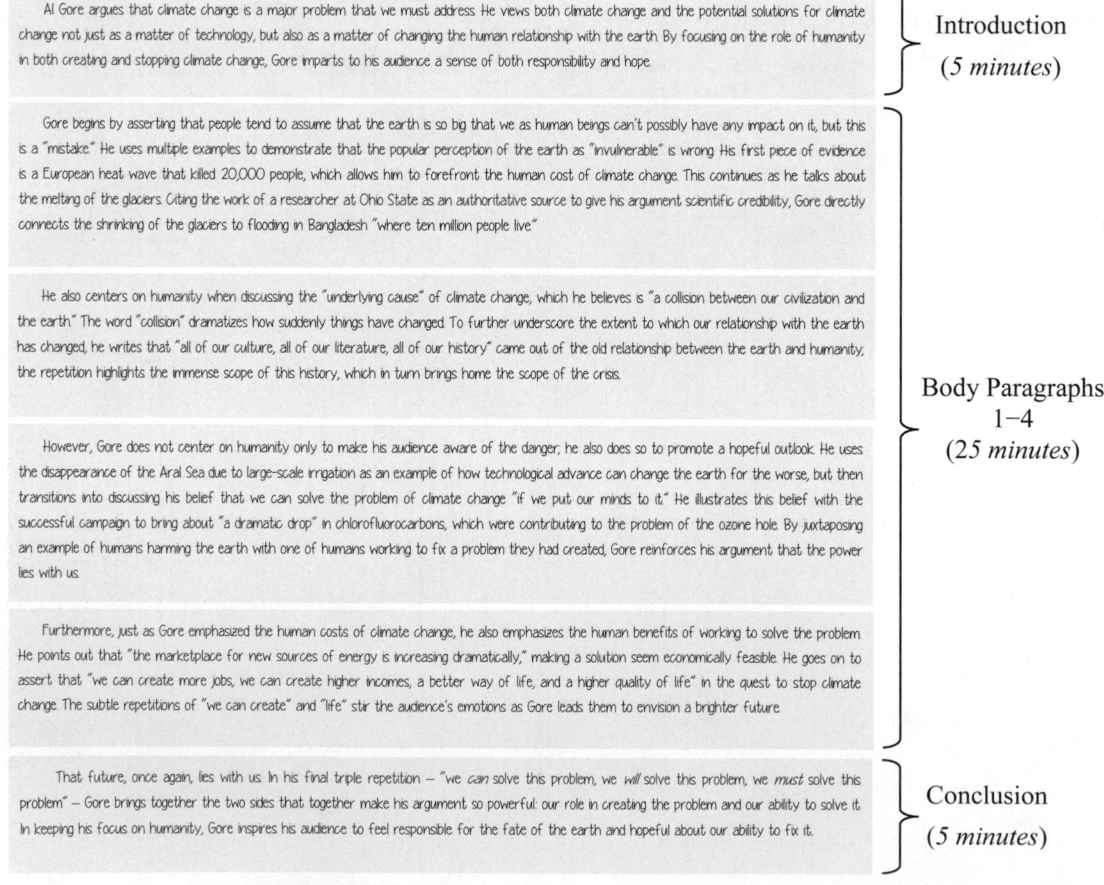

Al Gore argues that climate change is a major problem that we must address. He views both climate change and the potential solutions for climate change not just as a matter of technology, but also as a matter of changing the human relationship with the earth. By focusing on the role of humanity in both creating and stopping climate change, Gore imparts to his audience a sense of both responsibility and hope.

Gore begins by asserting that people tend to assume that the earth is so big that we as human beings can't possibly have any impact on it, but this is a "mistake." He uses multiple examples to demonstrate that the popular perception of the earth as "invulnerable" is wrong. His first piece of evidence is a European heat wave that killed 20,000 people, which allows him to forefront the human cost of climate change. This continues as he talks about the melting of the glaciers. Citing the work of a researcher at Ohio State as an authoritative source to give his argument scientific credibility, Gore directly connects the shrinking of the glaciers to flooding in Bangladesh "where ten million people live."

He also centers on humanity when discussing the "underlying cause" of climate change, which he believes is "a collision between our civilization and the earth." The word "collision" dramatizes how suddenly things have changed. To further underscore the extent to which our relationship with the earth has changed, he writes that "all of our culture, all of our literature, all of our history" came out of the old relationship between the earth and humanity; the repetition highlights the immense scope of this history, which in turn brings home the scope of the crisis.

However, Gore does not center on humanity only to make his audience aware of the danger; he also does so to promote a hopeful outlook. He uses the disappearance of the Aral Sea due to large-scale irrigation as an example of how technological advance can change the earth for the worse, but then transitions into discussing his belief that we can solve the problem of climate change "if we put our minds to it." He illustrates this belief with the successful campaign to bring about "a dramatic drop" in chlorofluorocarbons, which were contributing to the problem of the ozone hole. By juxtaposing an example of humans harming the earth with one of humans working to fix a problem they had created, Gore reinforces his argument that the power lies with us.

Furthermore, just as Gore emphasized the human costs of climate change, he also emphasizes the human benefits of working to solve the problem. He points out that "the marketplace for new sources of energy is increasing dramatically," making a solution seem economically feasible. He goes on to assert that "we can create more jobs, we can create higher incomes, a better way of life, and a higher quality of life" in the quest to stop climate change. The subtle repetitions of "we can create" and "life" stir the audience's emotions as Gore leads them to envision a brighter future.

That future, once again, lies with us. In his final triple repetition – "we *can* solve this problem, we *will* solve this problem, we *must* solve this problem" – Gore brings together the two sides that together make his argument so powerful: our role in creating the problem and our ability to solve it. In keeping his focus on humanity, Gore inspires his audience to feel responsible for the fate of the earth and hopeful about our ability to fix it.

Proofread (*5 minutes*)

Internal Structure

The internal structure—how you build the individual paragraphs—is integral to writing an essay that expresses your argument in a clear and straightforward manner.

Introduction

Your introduction will set the tone for your essay and provide graders with their first impression of your writing. It's important that your introduction be clear because it's hard to structure a good, coherent essay if the introduction doesn't make any sense.

The best way to make your introduction clear is to keep it brief and straightforward. Your goal is to get to your point as quickly as possible so you can spend the bulk of your time focusing on your body paragraphs.

Start with a brief statement or two relevant to the prompt, demonstrating that you've read the passage and understood the author's claim. It's a good idea to refer to the title of the passage and introduce the author (by full name the first time; when you reference the author later, use her last name *only*), paraphrase the author's central claim, and describe the evidence the author uses to support that claim. Then move directly to your thesis, the sentence where you will lay out the main point of your essay and make a claim about the author's use of rhetorical devices that establishes a context for your analysis.

Body Paragraphs

In your body paragraphs, you will elaborate on the different points that you mentioned in your thesis statement and link them together to create your overall analysis.

Each body paragraph is like a mini-essay. Each paragraph should start with a **topic sentence**. A topic sentence is like a mini-thesis statement: it states what the rest of the paragraph is going to be about.

Following the topic sentence should be 3-4 **supporting sentences**. In these sentences, you should analyze evidence (including appropriate quotes) you have found in the passage and explain how it supports the argument you made in your topic sentence. Use effective transitions that link your ideas together. This helps your reader follow your argument. In the following sentences, the words in italics are examples of transitions:

- *However*, the author does not rely on personal experience alone.
- The author *also* builds her argument by using scientific evidence.
- *Furthermore*, the author uses vivid language to appeal to her readers' emotions as well as their intellect.

Finally, use a **concluding sentence** that summarizes the point you have made in your body paragraph so that you leave the reader with a solid foundation for going on to your next point.

Conclusion

Your conclusion sums up the argument you have been making throughout your entire essay so that your graders know exactly what your argument is. Therefore, it is very important that your conclusion be clear and, like your introduction, brief. Resist the urge to add new arguments in your conclusion; instead, just summarize the arguments you have already made.

The first sentence of your conclusion should rephrase the thesis statement you wrote in your introduction. Don't rewrite it word for word (your graders will notice), but generally restate the ideas present in the thesis. The purpose of this sentence is to show how you have proven the arguments of your thesis statement.

Following this restatement of purpose, you should say something about the importance or implications of your analysis. Does the passage make you think about the issue in a different way? Would the passage have been less effective if the author hadn't used the devices that you analyzed? Does your analysis reveal some flaws in the ways the author made and supported her argument?

Practice Set

Part 3

Read the sample introduction from a student essay below. Then, identify the different elements that make it effective at introducing the student's claims. Ask a trusted reader to check your work.

In "Tear Down 'Deadbeat' Dams," Yvon Chouinard makes a compelling argument for why the United States government should remove ineffective, environmentally harmful dams. Four distinct features make Chouinard's argument so compelling: his use of impressively large statistics, his employment of specific examples, his telling of personal anecdotes, and the logical organization of his argument. These features in combination make Chouinard's essay very convincing.

1. How does the student demonstrate that he has read the passage and understood the author's claim?

2. What is the student's thesis statement?

3. How does the student describe the supporting arguments that he will be making in the essay?

Read the sample body paragraph below. Then, identify the components that make it effective at conveying its topic. Ask a trusted reader to check your work.

One feature of Chouinard's essay that makes it convincing is the effective use of evidence, particularly undeniably large numbers. For example, in the very first paragraph, Chouinard cites that "[o]f the more than 80,000 dams listed by the federal government, more than 26,000 pose high or significant safety hazards." Safety hazards numbering in the tens of thousands are difficult to ignore. Chouinard utilizes large-number statistics later when describing the example of the Elwha River: "Salmon runs that once reached about 400,000 fish a year dropped to fewer than 3,000." Again, a 397,000 drop in salmon in a single river makes a fairly compelling case for dam removal. Chouinard's skillful employment of large, eye-grabbing statistics gives his obscure topic more force and makes his argument more powerful.

4. What is the student's topic sentence?

5. How does the student analyze evidence from the passage in order to support the argument in his topic sentence?

6. What is the student's concluding sentence?

Read the sample conclusion below. Then, identify the components that make it effective at summarizing the student's argument. Ask a trusted reader to check your work.

> Chouinard utilizes many strategies to make his argument convincing, among them eye-grabbing statistics, specific examples, personal anecdotes, and logical organization. Together these strategies form a compelling claim for dam removal. Using these strategies is especially important in promoting a relatively low-profile environmental cause such as this.

7. How does the student re-state the ideas present in his thesis?

8. How does the student explain the importance or implications of his argument?

Section 3

Analyzing an Argument

The Essay is not just a test of your writing ability—it's also a test of your reading ability. The assignment doesn't ask you to write about the topic presented in the provided passage; instead, you need to write about how the author builds her argument in the passage. That means you can't write a great essay without first solidly understanding and analyzing the passage.

The first step to writing your essay is to read the prompt carefully. Use the Pencil on Paper strategy from Chapter 1 to be an active reader and mark up the provided passage. This way, you can easily refer back to the techniques the author uses to construct her argument. Those techniques are what the bulk of your essay should be about.

In this section, we're going to go over three different aspects of a passage you can examine when you're looking for ways to analyze the author's argument: language, organization, and evidence. We'll discuss how to write about these areas, as well as how to fully support your claims so that your essay is both insightful and thorough.

Language

Part 1

Authors choose every word carefully. The decision to use a certain word or phrase can tell you more than just the information the author is trying to get across. It can convey the author's opinion or add layers of emotion to what could have been just a statement of fact.

This might sound complicated, but you choose your words instinctively all the time. You use different vocabulary around your teachers than you do around your friends, or even around different groups of friends.

Example

After sleeping through his alarm, Carlos *ran* all the way to school.
After sleeping through his alarm, Carlos *sprinted* all the way to school.

The information in these sentences is the same: Carlos slept through his alarm and headed to school quickly. The difference is in the language. By using "sprinted," the second sentence implies that Carlos was not only running, but was running as fast as he could, which conveys a greater sense of urgency.

The same principles will apply to the passage you'll be reading. When you see a word that sticks out to you, ask yourself how that word relates to the author's argument. What are the connotations of the words the author chooses? What rhetorical devices does he use to support his ideas?

Connotations

It can be useful to think about a word's **connotations**—ideas that might not be part of its dictionary definition, but are implied when people use that particular word. To identify the connotations of a word, think about how you usually hear people use it. A word that people generally use to describe something they don't like has a negative connotation; a word that people use for something they like has a positive connotation. If an author has chosen a word with a negative connotation, she is trying to paint what she's describing in a negative light.

Rhetorical Devices

A **rhetorical device** is a tool the author uses to persuade the reader to agree with his argument. Rhetorical devices aren't just about the literal meaning of the words; they're about how those words are used to make an argument more vivid or appeal to the reader's emotions.

For example, an author who is concerned about losses in the bee population could write, "Bees are dying in North America, South America, and Europe." However, she might also choose to write: "Bees are dying in North America. They're dying in South America. They're dying in Europe." That author would be using the rhetorical device of **repetition** to make her point more dramatic and persuade her reader to care.

Figurative language is another common rhetorical device for authors who want to spice up their arguments and make them more compelling. For example, let's say the author writes, "Bees are as important to the planet as bones are to the human body." This is an example of **figurative language**. In this case the author is using a **simile**, a comparison of two unlike things using the words "like" or "as." Comparing bees to human bones emphasizes how necessary bees are—without bones, the human body would collapse, so she's implying that without bees the planet would collapse. You can learn more about specific types of figurative language in Chapter 2 or online.

Remember that it is not enough just to identify tools the author uses. You must also pinpoint where the author uses these tools *and* state clearly how these tools contribute to the author's argument.

Example

Our nation's trees are crying out for relief from air pollution.

Trees don't cry; by giving a human characteristic to something that is not human, this sentence is using **personification**. However, your graders will not be impressed if you only write, "The author uses personification." You must be specific about where the author uses it, what it accomplishes, and, if possible, how it contributes to the overall argument: "The author states that our nation's trees are 'crying,' thus using personification to rouse the reader's sympathy. This gives emotional weight to her argument that we must work to end air pollution soon."

Suppose that in a passage arguing that it is important to preserve playgrounds, an author writes:

Example

Neglected playgrounds become dangerous playgrounds, and for most parents the risks posed by a dangerous playground are worse than no playground at all. Do we want future generations to grow up without memories of going down slides or playing on the swings?

The second sentence is a **rhetorical question**—not a question the author thinks needs to be answered, but a question used to make a point. Once again, it's not enough to write, "The author uses a rhetorical question," or even "The author uses a rhetorical question to support his point." A better claim to make about this would be: "By posing a rhetorical question about 'future generations,' the author invites the reader to imagine those generations growing up without safe playgrounds."

An author might also use a passing reference to a literary or artistic work, person, or event to illustrate a point.

Example

Regulatory agencies are often established to oversee potentially hazardous industries. But even if they are well-designed, well-intentioned, and staffed by competent employees, funding remains their Achilles heel. After high-profile regulatory legislation is passed, a budget can be quietly passed that strips funding from the regulatory agency.

In this example, the author refers to an "Achilles heel." This is a reference, or **allusion**, to the story of Achilles, a mythic Greek hero whose weakness was his heel. You might not always recognize allusions, but you should point them out when you do.

Part 1 Practice: Language

In the selection below, we've underlined writing choices you could address to analyze how the author uses language to add weight to his argument—that we should remove dams instead of building new ones. Choose four of these words or phrases and write a couple sentences explaining why the author has made these particular language choices. Remember to quote from the text and connect your examples to the author's purpose. Have a trusted reader check your work.

Example Essay Adapted from "Tear Down 'Deadbeat' Dams" by Yvon Chouinard. © 2014 by the New York Times Company. Originally published May 7, 2014.

1 New dams are a bad idea. We've glorified them for decades, but our pride in building these engineering marvels has often blinded us to the environmental damage they cause. The consequences run the length of the river and beyond. Our many complex attempts to work around these obstacles would make Rube Goldberg proud. Interventions like fish elevators and trap-and-haul programs that truck fish around impoundments don't lead to true recovery for wild fish populations or reverse the other environmental problems caused by blocking a river's flow.

2 But we do know that removing dams brings streams and rivers back to life and replenishes our degraded aquifers.

1. The first word or phrase I am analyzing:

   Why has the author chosen this word or phrase to use?

2. The second word or phrase I am analyzing:

   Why has the author chosen this word or phrase to use?

3. The third word or phrase I am analyzing:

   Why has the author chosen this word or phrase to use?

4. The fourth word or phrase I am analyzing:

   Why has the author chosen this word or phrase to use?

Evidence

Part 2

The author of the passage will use different kinds of evidence to support her point. In this part, we'll take a look at some of the evidence that an author might decide to use. The table below shows some common ways authors support their arguments.

Types of Evidence		
Type of Evidence	**Definition**	**Example**
Data or Quantitative Evidence	Uses statistics, percentages, or other kinds of numbers	We should be doing more to preserve wildlife habitats. Though it is common to lose one to five species each year, we are now losing species at an accelerated rate of 200 to 2000 a year.
Expert Opinion	Relies on the opinion or ideas of scholars, researchers, or other people with expert knowledge on the topic	The proposal to teach astronomy to young students is a good one. Dr. Yaskin, an astronomy researcher, believes it will drastically increase interest in the field.
Personal Example	Uses a personal experience or situation encountered by the author	Tourists are often unaware of local etiquette in the places they visit. I witnessed this first-hand on a recent trip to Guatemala.
Comparison	Compares an idea being discussed to something else to clarify or make a point	This engineering project is a poor idea. Building new bridges in small cities with few cars is like buying designer running shoes for toddlers; it is better to wait until they are big enough to need them.
Appeal to Emotion	Creates feelings in the reader to persuade them of an argument	This policy cannot be maintained if we are to consider ourselves a just nation. After all, how dispirited would you feel if your property, acquired through hard work over time, was taken from you without explanation?

Types of Sources

As demonstrated in the chart above, both personal and more expert sources can be used as effective evidence. However, these types of support may be used in different contexts and have different impacts.

Personal evidence often makes a topic more immediate for a reader. It can illustrate what a large issue looks like in someone's day-to-day life. Authors sometimes also use it to make themselves seem relatable and therefore trustworthy. For example, in the passage we've been using, Yvon Chouinard writes, “Time and again, I’ve witnessed the celebration that comes with the removal of an unnecessary dam.” This enables the reader to attach a specific image to a larger situation.

On the other hand, authors can build credibility by drawing on an authoritative source, especially when using data. Governmental organizations (”the Bureau of Labor Statistics”), professional bodies (“the American Medical Association”), and international organizations (“the World Health Organization”) are all examples of authoritative sources.

A source might also be authoritative because of where it was first presented, such as in a reputable publication like the *New England Journal of Medicine*. You can also look for the names of universities, which usually signal an authoritative source.

A source’s expertise might also be established through other means. Someone might have written a book related to the subject (“Michelle Alexander, whose recently published *The New Jim Crow: Mass Incarceration in the Age of Colorblindness* deals with this topic…”). An expert might also have won a distinguished prize in his field (“Steven Chu, who received the 1997 Nobel Prize in Physics…”). Someone also might just have an extremely respected position that automatically lends her authority (“Supreme Court Justice Sonia Sotomayor has stated…”).

Writing about Evidence

As we discussed above, identifying types of evidence is only the first step. It’s crucial that when you bring up evidence in your essay, you spell out how the author uses it to support her broader argument. Let’s look at an example:

Example

Recently, researchers at the University of Pennsylvania have found that sleep deprivation causes permanent brain damage in mice. This should give us pause as we contemplate the trade-offs of encouraging young people to achieve success at the expense of resting their bodies.

You could write, “The author uses an authoritative source to show that sleep deprivation causes brain damage in mice,” and it would be accurate. However, it would not be sufficient, because the mice aren’t central to the author’s main point: the author is using this evidence to discuss the effects of sleep deprivation on people. A better way to discuss this would be, “The author cites research on mice from The University of Pennsylvania, an authoritative source which gives scientific credibility to her argument that we should be concerned about the physical dangers of sleep deprivation in people.”

The key thing to notice is that we made the link between what the author did (use an authoritative source) and why the author did it (to support the passage’s broader argument). Don’t assume this connection is obvious to your reader; while it may be, you need to prove that *you* see that connection, too.

Part 2 Practice: Evidence

As you read the following selection, look for different ways the author uses evidence to support his argument that old dams should be torn down and new dams should not be built. Identify four pieces of evidence, along with their sources, and describe how this evidence supports the author's argument. Have a trusted reader check your work, and go online for some examples of possible answers.

Adapted from "Tear Down 'Deadbeat' Dams" by Yvon Chouinard. ©2014 by the New York Times Company. Originally published May 7, 2014.

1 Of the more than 80,000 dams listed by the federal government, more than 26,000 pose high or significant safety hazards. Many no longer serve any real purpose. All have limited life spans. Only about 1,750 produce hydropower, according to the National Hydropower Association.

2 Last year, 51 dams in 18 states were taken down, restoring more than 500 miles of streams, according to the group American Rivers. Nearly 850 have been removed in the last 20 years, and nearly 1,150 since 1912.

3 A case in point is the Elwha River on the Olympic Peninsula in Washington, where two hydroelectric dams built early in the last century exacted huge environmental costs but were no longer important as power generators. Salmon runs that once reached about 400,000 fish a year dropped to fewer than 3,000. A year after the Elwha Dam was removed, Chinook salmon returned to the river in numbers not seen in decades, with three-quarters of them observed spawning upstream of the former dam site.

4 Time and again, I've witnessed the celebration that comes with the removal of an unnecessary dam. After a river is restored and the fish have returned you never hear a single person say, "Gee, I wish we had our dam back."

1. The first piece of evidence I am analyzing:

   Its source:

   How it supports the author's argument:

2. The second piece of evidence I am analyzing:

   Its source:

   How it supports the author's argument:

3. The third piece of evidence I am analyzing:

   Its source:

   How it supports the author's argument:

4. The fourth piece of evidence I am analyzing:

   Its source:

   How it supports the author's argument:

Organization and Reasoning

Part 3

How authors choose to structure and reason through their arguments can be just as important as the language and facts they use to make them. We are now going to show you how to recognize the methods authors use to organize their arguments and how to write about them effectively.

Logical Structure

Picking out the logical structure of a piece of writing might sound difficult, but in fact our brains do it subconsciously all the time. We are geared to find patterns in everything around us in order to make sense of them.

Example

- Annie put a bandage on her scrapes.
- Annie fought with her mother about wearing knee pads while skating.
- Annie skated over some gravel and fell.
- Annie ignored her mother and went skating without knee pads.

On the first reading, these sentences don't make any sense at all, right? The events are out of order, and our brains pick up on that immediately. We might even try to start reorganizing the sentences without thinking about it (the correct order is 2, 4, 3, 1).

The SAT also tests this pattern-finding skill in the Writing Test, using multiple choice questions that ask you to select the best order for certain sentences. On the Essay, you'll be recognizing the organization on your own, rather than picking it up from a line-up of potential options, and you'll be writing about how that organization affects the author's argument.

Tracking the Author's Argument

The easiest way to think about organization and logical reasoning is to think about how the author moves from one point to another. As you read the following selection, let's track the different ways the author uses evidence to support his argument that we should remove obsolete dams.

Adapted from "Tear Down 'Deadbeat' Dams" by Yvon Chouinard, 2014, The New York Times Company.

1 Of the more than 80,000 dams listed by the federal government, more than 26,000 pose high or significant safety hazards. Many no longer serve any real purpose. All have limited life spans. Only about 1,750 produce hydropower, according to the National Hydropower Association.

The author begins his argument with several statements about the negative effects of dams. This establishes the harm posed by dams, setting up the author to propose a solution.

2 In many cases, the benefits that dams have historically provided—for water use, flood control, and electricity—can now be met more effectively without continuing to choke entire watersheds.

The author further establishes his argument by showing how dams are no longer useful.

"Now" is a word that can signal a logical contrast (ie. while something was like this then, now it is different).

3 Put simply, many dams have high environmental costs that outweigh their value. Removing them is the only sensible answer. And taking them down can often make economic sense as well. The River Alliance of Wisconsin estimates that removing dams in that state is three to five times less expensive than repairing them.

The author summarizes his prior points and shapes them into a coherent thesis statement. He also provides his solution: remove the deadbeat dams.

4 The message has been slowly spreading around the country. More and more communities and states have reclaimed rivers lost to jackhammers and concrete. Last year, 51 dams in 18 states were taken down, restoring more than 500 miles of streams, according to the group American Rivers. Nearly 850 have been removed in the last 20 years, and nearly 1,150 since 1912.

The author broadens his argument from a personal opinion to a national "message," giving his argument greater clout.

5 But the work is far from done. I was disappointed to see the Energy Department release a report last week on the potential to develop new "sustainable" hydroelectric dams on rivers and streams across the country. The report follows President Obama's signing of two laws last year to encourage small hydro projects and revive nonproducing dams.

"But" is another organizational signpost that signals a logical turn.

The author maintains the urgency of his argument by pointing out that there is still much work to be done in removing dams.

6 New dams are a bad idea. We've glorified them for decades, but our pride in building these engineering marvels has often blinded us to the environmental damage they cause. The consequences run the length of the river

The author moves to another point in his argument about dams: we shouldn't build any new ones. This both reinforces the points the author made earlier in the passage and allows him to introduce new evidence against dams.

and beyond. Our many complex attempts to work around these obstacles would make Rube Goldberg proud. Interventions like fish elevators and trap-and-haul programs that truck fish around impoundments don't lead to true recovery for wild fish populations or reverse the other environmental problems caused by blocking a river's flow.

7 But we do know that removing dams brings streams and rivers back to life and replenishes our degraded aquifers.

After showing how bad dams are, the author shows us the other side of his argument—the many benefits of dam removal.

8 A case in point is the Elwha River on the Olympic Peninsula in Washington, where two hydroelectric dams built early in the last century exacted huge environmental costs but were no longer important as power generators. Today, the river runs free from its headwaters in Olympic National Park to the Strait of Juan de Fuca, and a terrible wrong imposed on the salmon-dependent Lower Elwha Klallam tribe has been righted.

The author supports this logical turn with a specific example about the Elwha River. Again, the author uses a now/then contrast to illustrate the benefits of removing dams.

9 I've been working to take down dams for most of my life. The idea, once considered crazy, is gaining momentum. We should seize it and push for the removal of the many dams with high costs and low or zero value. The environmental impacts are too enormous.

The author brings the argument back to his personal perspective, using his authority as a life-long fighter of dams to make his argument even more credible.

The author summarizes his prior points and shapes them into a coherent thesis statement. He also provides his solution: remove the deadbeat dams.

10 Time and again, I've witnessed the celebration that comes with the removal of an unnecessary dam. After a river is restored and the fish have returned you never hear a single person say, "Gee, I wish we had our dam back."

The author concludes the passage with a statement that reinforces the apparent obviousness of his argument—who would ever want a dam back when its removal clearly provided so much good?

Following an author's argument is much like reading a roadmap: once you get used to the signs, it's easy to follow. But identifying the author's organizational and logical methods is only half of the job. You also need to be able to write about them effectively.

Writing about Structure

After you have tracked the author's main argument through the passage, you'll need to figure out how to write about that structure. The easiest way to do this is to ask the question "Why?" Why does the author move from a certain point to another? Why does she use a certain kind of logical reasoning to connect these points? Answering these "why" questions will enable you to write about how these organizational decisions on the author's part did or did not aid her argument.

Take the first organizational turn we noticed in our example passage.

Example

In many cases, the benefits that dams have historically provided—for water uses, flood control, and electricity—can now be met more effectively without continuing to choke watersheds.

We identified that the author places a turn in the middle of the sentence. The author acknowledges why we have built dams in the past, but then points out their current ineffectiveness. Why does the author do this? There are a few things we could write about to answer that question:

- First, acknowledging the past benefits of dams makes the author's argument seem more balanced and fair.
- Second, showing that these benefits can be provided by other more efficient mechanisms makes dams seem unnecessary.
- Third, showing that these other methods are more environmentally friendly makes dams seem unnecessary *and* bad.

And just like that, we have a paragraph's worth of writing about one small part of the passage's logical organization.

Part 3 Practice: Organization and Reasoning

Now it's your turn. Below are some more organizational and logical turns from the "'Deadbeat' Dams" passage. Explain why the author included these turns and how they help or hurt his argument. Have a trusted reader check your work, and go online for some examples of possible answers.

1 And taking them down can often make economic sense as well. The River Alliance of Wisconsin estimates that removing dams in that state is three to five times less expensive than repairing them.

1. Why did the author include this turn?

2. How does it help or hurt his argument?

1 New dams are a bad idea. We've glorified them for decades, but our pride in building these engineering marvels has often blinded us to the environmental damage they cause.

3. Why did the author include this turn?

4. How does it help or hurt his argument?

Putting It Together

Part 4

Now that we've gone over how to analyze an author's language, evidence, and organization, it's time to put them all together. In the sample passage below, we've marked up the full sample text we've been using with the kinds of observations you might use in your essay.

Sample Passage Analysis

As you read the passage below, consider how Yvon Chouinard uses

- evidence, such as facts or examples, to support claims.
- reasoning to develop ideas and to connect claims and evidence.
- stylistic or persuasive elements, such as word choice or appeals to emotion, to add power to the ideas expressed.

Adapted from "Tear Down 'Deadbeat' Dams" by Yvon Chouinard, 2014, The New York Times Company.

1 Of the more than 80,000 dams listed by the federal government, more than 26,000 pose high or significant safety hazards. Many no longer serve any real purpose. All have limited life spans. Only about 1,750 produce hydropower, according to the National Hydropower Association.

2 In many cases, the benefits that dams have historically provided—for water use, flood control, and electricity—can now be met more effectively without continuing to choke entire watersheds.

3 Dams degrade water quality, block the movement of nutrients and sediment, destroy fish and wildlife habitats, damage coastal estuaries and in some cases rob surrounding forests of nitrogen. Reservoirs can also be significant sources of greenhouse gas emissions.

(1) Yvon Chouinard uses evidence from an authoritative source (the federal government) to support his claim that dams pose serious dangers. Placing this statistic in the first sentence adds urgency to his pleas.

(2) The author uses evidence from another authoritative source (the National Hydropower Association) to show that many more dams pose serious hazards than produce hydropower, suggesting that the dangers outweigh the benefits.

(3) The author acknowledges that dams "originally provided" specific benefits and suggests that there are now better ways of meeting these needs without negative consequences. The author demonstrates that he is knowledgeable about several sides of the issue.

(4) Vivid word choices such as "degrade" and "destroy" dramatize the effect of dams on the environment. The word "rob" heightens their menace, implying that dams are stealing nitrogen that rightly belongs to forests.

4 Put simply, many dams have high environmental costs that outweigh their value. Removing them is the only sensible answer. And taking them down can often make economic sense as well. The River Alliance of Wisconsin estimates that removing dams in that state is three to five times less expensive than repairing them.

5 The message has been slowly spreading around the country. More and more communities and states have reclaimed rivers lost to jackhammers and concrete. Last year, 51 dams in 18 states were taken down, restoring more than 500 miles of streams, according to the group American Rivers. Nearly 850 have been removed in the last 20 years, and nearly 1,150 since 1912.

6 But the work is far from done. I was disappointed to see the Energy Department release a report last week on the potential to develop new "sustainable" hydroelectric dams on rivers and streams across the country. The report follows President Obama's signing of two laws last year to encourage small hydro projects and revive nonproducing dams.

7 New dams are a bad idea. We've glorified them for decades, but our pride in building these engineering marvels has often blinded us to the environmental damage they cause. The consequences run the length of the river and beyond. Our many complex attempts to work around these obstacles would make Rube Goldberg proud. Interventions like fish elevators and trap-and-haul programs that truck fish around impoundments don't lead to true recovery for wild fish populations or reverse the other environmental problems caused by blocking a river's flow.

8 But we do know that removing dams brings streams and rivers back to life and replenishes our degraded aquifers.

(5) After listing concrete examples of the damage caused by dams, the author summarizes his point that dams are harmful and not worth the environmental cost, and then concisely states his solution.

(6) The author uses statistics from another authoritative source (the River Alliance of Wisconsin) to support his claim that removing dams makes economic sense as well.

(7) By claiming that his solution is increasing in popularity, the author portrays his argument as viable, since communities and states have already adopted it.

(8) Careful word choice makes his cause seem righteous. Saying communities have "reclaimed" rivers that were "lost" positions dams as an injustice to the communities and environment.

(9) The author uses specific statistics as evidence to back up his claim that the removal of dams is already in process.

(10) The author clarifies that although his plan for dam removal is in some ways already in motion, the situation is still urgent.

(11) Referring to a specific event from as recently as a week ago makes the subject seem very timely.

(12) The author suggests that the appeal of new dams lies in our pride in building them rather than in anything they actually accomplish.

(13) Rube Goldberg was a cartoonist famous for drawings of gadgets that performed simple tasks in extremely complicated ways. By saying that our attempts to minimize the damage of dams would "make Rube Goldberg proud," the author is implying that we are doing many unnecessarily complicated things while overlooking the obvious solution.

(14) The author elaborates on the comparison he just made by naming some of those unnecessarily complicated interventions and stating that they are not effective.

(15) The author positions removing dams as the obvious solution being overlooked even though we already know that it is the one guaranteed solution.

9 A case in point is the Elwha River on the Olympic Peninsula in Washington, where two hydroelectric dams built early in the last century exacted huge environmental costs but were no longer important as power generators. Salmon runs that once reached about 400,000 fish a year dropped to fewer than 3,000. A year after the Elwha Dam was removed, Chinook salmon returned to the river in numbers not seen in decades, with three-quarters of them observed spawning upstream of the former dam site. Today, the river runs free from its headwaters in Olympic National Park to the Strait of Juan de Fuca, and a terrible wrong imposed on the salmon-dependent Lower Elwha Klallam tribe has been righted.

10 President Obama should learn from that example. Most urgently, he should turn his attention to the Snake River in eastern Washington, where four dams along its lower reaches provide marginal (and replaceable) electricity generation that is outweighed by the opportunities for the revival of endangered salmon populations, plus the jobs and communities a healthy salmon fisher would support. Those deadbeat dams should be taken down and added to the list of dams in the process of being removed along the White Salmon River in Washington, the Penobscot in Maine, and the Klamath in southern Oregon.

11 I've been working to take down dams for most of my life. The idea, once considered crazy, is gaining momentum. We should seize it and push for the removal of the many dams with high costs and low or zero value. The environmental impacts are too enormous.

12 Time and again, I've witnessed the celebration that comes with the removal of an unnecessary dam. After a river is restored and the fish have returned you never hear a single person say, "Gee, I wish we had our dam back."

(16) This specific example of the dams on the Elwha River underscores his points with vivid descriptions. The descriptions reinforce the idea of dams being obsolete, because these dams were no longer producing significant amounts of power. The descriptions also emphasize the harmfulness of dams, because of the large drop in salmon population. Finally, this case study also exemplifies the author's point that removing dams is an easy, obvious solution, since it only took a year after their removal to see dramatic positive results.

(17) The author portrays the dams as a terrible injustice to the environment—this time especially to a particular local tribe—and says the removal of these dams is necessary to restoring justice.

(18) Invoking the most powerful official in the country (President Obama) makes it clear that this is a national issue, lending the argument urgency and importance because of its national scope.

(19) The author makes clear that removing the dams in question would benefit both salmon (who would see their numbers replenished) and humans (who would see job creation opportunities).

(20) The author uses specific examples to restate his point that removing dams is something more and more communities are already choosing to do.

(21) By stating he has been active in this cause for a long time, the author grants himself the legitimacy of a firsthand witness to support his claim that the idea of taking down dams is gaining support.

(22) After several specific, concrete examples, the author summarizes his argument again for emphasis.

(23) The author ends the article by using his personal experience to position himself as a legitimate authority on the benefits of removing dams. A colloquial expression ("gee") gives it a personal feel.

We've annotated this text to illustrate the kin ds of elements you should look out for when you read the passage. You can see that we don't focus on just one kind of tool. Instead, we look at different tools the author wields from a variety of angles. It's important to show that you can recognize a diverse set of strategies.

However, finding these strategies is only the first step. If you were to read our notes like an essay, it would be a mess: totally disorganized, hard to follow, and lacking a clear thesis. In order to turn your thoughts into an essay, you'll need to identify the passage's overarching themes. Then you'll use those themes to organize your essay.

Identify Themes

For the sample text that we've provided, you could pull out the following three themes. Pay attention to the way the author uses multiple strategies to develop each one.

Theme 1: Dams pose a problem that is both serious and urgent. This is the problem the author is trying to demonstrate.

- He uses authoritative sources to provide evidence that dams are harmful, including the federal government and the National Hydropower Association. Statistics support his claims that dams are dangerous. The example of the Snake River makes it easier for readers to visualize the damage dams cause. In addition, he highlights different *kinds* of harm that dams cause, including depleting the salmon population, destroying wildlife habitats, and hurting the Lower Elwha Klallam tribe.
- He chooses strong words to bring the tragedy to life. Dams don't just block watersheds, they *choke* them. The word "choke" suggests violence. The salmon population in the Elwha River didn't just decrease, it *dropped*. The word "dropped" makes it sound drastic and shocking.
- He emphasizes that this is a problem right *now*. The Energy Department report from the previous week shows that the fight is far from over. By naming President Obama, he implies this issue that must be dealt with immediately, not in the future.

Theme 2: Removing dams is the most logical solution. This is what the author is trying to persuade his audience to believe.

- He identifies several benefits of dam removal. He uses the Elwha River example to show how removing a dam can revive the local salmon population, which benefits the environment. He points out that more salmon would provide job opportunities for local residents, which benefits the community. He uses an authoritative source to show that removing harmful dams is cheaper than fixing them, which benefits the economy.
- He addresses counterarguments that others might make, suggesting that there are no downsides to his plan. He states that there are better ways to accomplish what dams provide. He points out that we could find a way to replace the electricity generated by the dams on Snake River. He also claims that he has never seen anyone regret that a dam has been taken down.

- He argues that removing dams is becoming more popular. This suggests that its effects are positive enough to win people over to his side. He admits that the idea was "once considered crazy," which implies it has become common for people to change their minds about it.

Theme 3: Unnecessary dams are an injustice that must be corrected. This theme is crucial for taking our analysis to the next level. The previous two themes lay out the facts of the author's argument: what is happening (dams pose a problem) and what we should do about it (tear them down). This theme is about why his argument matters—basically, why we should care. Here, he appeals to the reader's emotions and sense of justice.

- He uses language to frame the damage dams cause in moral terms. Dams "rob" forests of nitrogen, making them sound criminal. When communities take dams down, they "reclaim" rivers once "lost," suggesting that they have restored the natural order of things.
- He explicitly states that the loss of the salmon population of the Elwha River was a "terrible wrong" done to the Lower Elwha Klallam tribe, which was "righted" by removing the dam.
- He refers to dams which are deeply harmful and marginally beneficial as "deadbeat dams," using an adjective with a connotation that suggests a moral failing.

Notice that the author does not lay out these themes in order, detailing one in full and then abandoning it for the next. Instead, he weaves them together throughout the essay. By the time he gets to the example of the Elwha River, he can use it to make all of these ideas come together. This is important to watch out for as you plan your essay—remember that you might be drawing from different parts of the passage to fully support one of your points.

Part 4 Practice: Putting It Together

We've gone over how to structure your essay so that it's clear and easy to read. We've also given you the tools you need to analyze the different ways an author builds his argument, and write about it so that your own argument will be compelling. Now it's time to put these skills to work and write the essay we've been working on in this chapter. We've provided the prompt again below. Because we've already read and analyzed the passage and discussed how to identify the author's use of language and evidence, aim to complete this practice essay in under 50 minutes. There are additional prompts later in this chapter you should use for timed practice. Have a trusted reader check your work.

As you read the passage below, consider how Yvon Chouinard uses

- evidence, such as facts or examples, to support claims.
- reasoning to develop ideas and to connect claims and evidence.
- stylistic or persuasive elements, such as word choice or appeals to emotion, to add power to the ideas expressed.

Adapted from "Tear Down 'Deadbeat' Dams" by Yvon Chouinard, 2014, The New York Times Company

1 Of the more than 80,000 dams listed by the federal government, more than 26,000 pose high or significant safety hazards. Many no longer serve any real purpose. All have limited life spans. Only about 1,750 produce hydropower, according to the National Hydropower Association.

2 In many cases, the benefits that dams have historically provided — for water use, flood control, and electricity — can now be met more effectively without continuing to choke entire watersheds.

3 Dams degrade water quality, block the movement of nutrients and sediment, destroy fish and wildlife habitats, damage coastal estuaries, and in some cases rob surrounding forests of nitrogen. Reservoirs can also be significant sources of greenhouse gas emissions.

4 Put simply, many dams have high environmental costs that outweigh their value. Removing them is the only sensible answer. And taking them down can often make economic sense as well. The River Alliance of Wisconsin estimates that removing dams in that state is three to five times less expensive than repairing them.

5 The message has been slowly spreading around the country. More and more communities and states have reclaimed rivers lost to jackhammers and concrete. Last year, 51 dams in 18 states were taken down, restoring more than 500 miles of streams, according to the group American Rivers.

6 Nearly 850 have been removed in the last 20 years, and nearly 1,150 since 1912.

7 But the work is far from done. I was disappointed to see the Energy Department release a report last week on the potential to develop new "sustainable" hydroelectric dams on rivers and streams across the country.

8 The report follows President Obama's signing of two laws last year to encourage small hydro projects and revive nonproducing dams.

9 New dams are a bad idea. We've glorified them for decades, but our pride in building these engineering marvels has often blinded us to the environmental damage they cause. The consequences run the length of the river and beyond.

10 Our many complex attempts to work around these obstacles would make Rube Goldberg proud. Interventions like fish elevators and trap-and-haul programs that truck fish around impoundments don't lead to true recovery for wild fish populations or reverse the other environmental problems caused by blocking a river's flow.

11 But we do know that removing dams brings streams and rivers back to life and replenishes our degraded aquifers.

12 A case in point is the Elwha River on the Olympic Peninsula in Washington, where two hydroelectric dams built early in the last century exacted huge environmental costs but were no longer important as power generators. Salmon runs that once reached about 400,000 fish a year dropped to fewer than 3,000. A year after the Elwha Dam was removed, Chinook salmon returned to the river in numbers not seen in decades, with three-quarters of them observed spawning upstream of the former dam site. Today, the river runs free from its headwaters in Olympic National Park to the Strait of Juan de Fuca, and a terrible wrong imposed on the salmon-dependent Lower Elwha Klallam tribe has been righted.

13 President Obama should learn from that example. Most urgently, he should turn his attention to the Snake River in eastern Washington, where four dams along its lower reaches provide marginal (and replaceable) electricity generation that is outweighed by the opportunities for the revival of endangered salmon populations, plus the jobs and communities a healthy salmon fishery would support. Those

deadbeat dams should be taken down and added to the list of dams in the process of being removed along the White Salmon River in Washington, the Penobscot in Maine, and the Klamath in southern Oregon. I've been working to take down dams for most of my life. The idea, once considered crazy, is gaining momentum. We should seize it and push for the removal of the many dams with high costs and low or zero value. The environmental impacts are too enormous.

14 Time and again, I've witnessed the celebration that comes with the removal of an unnecessary dam. After a river is restored and the fish have returned you never hear a single person say, "Gee, I wish we had our dam back."

Write an essay in which you explain how Yvon Chouinard builds an argument to persuade his audience that obsolete dams should be removed. In your essay, analyze how Chouinard uses one or more of the features listed in the box above (or features of your own choice) to strengthen the logic and persuasiveness of his argument. Be sure that your analysis focuses on the most relevant features of the passage.

Your essay should not explain whether you agree with Chouinard's claims, but rather explain how Chouinard builds an argument to persuade his audience.

Section 4

Essay Rubric and Examples

Grading the Essay is more difficult than grading the rest of your practice exam. Unfortunately, there's no answer key for the Essay. Instead, you need carefully evaluate your own work or have a trusted reader evaluate your essay and provide honest feedback. In this section, we provide guidance about the College Board's grading rubric to help you understand how the College Board will evaluate your work, and how you can evaluate your own work or the work of others.

The College Board's Rubric

Part 1

In this section, we will look at the rubric for each grading criterion—Reading, Analysis, and Writing—used by the College Board graders in assessing your essay. We'll use examples from the annotated passage that we reviewed in Section 3, "Tear Down 'Deadbeat' Dams," by Yvon Chouinard.

Reading

In the reading category, your graders are evaluating how well you show that you understand the prompt passage, including its main argument, the important details, and how those details are related to the argument.. Here are some examples of what they'll be looking for.

What College Board Wants	Good Example	Bad Example
Get the main idea. Even though the prompt gives you a version of the main idea of the passage, the College Board wants to see evidence that you have accurately and comprehensively understood and interpreted the passage.	In this passage, Yvon Chouinard argues that dams have a negative impact on the environment and generally should be removed.	In this passage, Yvon Chouinard talks about his own personal agenda that has something to do with dams.
Use the evidence. The College Board is looking for references to the passage through quotes or paraphrasing that support your interpretation of the passage.	Chouinard supports his claim with statistics, such as the fact that "[o]f the more than 80,000 dams listed by the federal government, more than 26,000 pose high or significant safety hazards."	Chouinard talks about how lots of dams are doing bad things.
Use the evidence correctly. Use the evidence accurately, both by citing it correctly and by using it in the same spirit as the author.	Chouinard supports his claim with statistics, such as the fact that "[o]f the more than 80,000 dams listed by the federal government, more than 26,000 pose high or significant safety hazards."	Chouinard doesn't cite good facts to support his argument. For example, he states that only 20,000 of the more than 80,000 dams listed by the federal government pose significant safety hazards, which is not that many.

Analysis

In the Analysis category, your graders are evaluating how well you analyze an author's argument. They want you to evaluate the effectiveness of the author's use of evidence, reasoning, and rhetorical elements, not to give your own opinion. These are some things the graders will be looking at to determine your score.

What College Board Wants	Good Example	Bad Example
Analyze, don't respond to, the passage. Your job is to analyze the author's argument, *not* respond to it with your own opinions.	Chouinard utilizes a combination of statistical evidence, personal examples, and appeals to authority to make the argument that harmful dams should be removed.	Chouinard really doesn't know what he's talking about; in my opinion, dams are super helpful.
Pick good elements to write about. Read the passage, identify what tools the author uses to make her argument, and evaluate the effectiveness of the author's use of evidence, reasoning, and rhetorical elements.	Chouinard's use of strong numerical evidence shores up his argument and makes the issue seem more important and urgent.	Chouinard writes really well and thus makes a good argument.
Pick the right support for those elements. Pick the strongest, most relevant parts of the passage to support your claims.	For example, Chouinard uses statistics about the decreasing number of salmon in the Elwha River (400,000 down to fewer than 3,000) to demonstrate the negative effects dams have on wildlife.	Chouinard cites lots of statistics to support his argument. For example, he states once a dam is taken down, "you never hear a single person say, 'Gee, I wish we had our dam back.'" That's some strong statistical evidence.

Writing

In the Writing category, your graders are evaluating how well you structure your essay and how effectively you use language to express your ideas. Here are some things you should keep in mind.

What College Board Wants	Good Example	Bad Example
Make a precise claim. When you write an essay, you have to have some sort of claim or argument. This claim should be expressed as a clear, concise thesis statement.	Chouinard uses statistical evidence, personal examples, and appeals to authority to build his argument that removing harmful dams is necessary to restore justice.	This is an interesting article about dams.

Organize your argument. Write an effective introduction, develop your argument using body paragraphs that show a deliberate and clear progression of your ideas, and provide a clear conclusion.	See Section 2, Part 2 earlier in this chapter.	See Section 2, Part 2 earlier in this chapter.
Switch up your sentences. Don't just use simple sentences—mix it up!	Though some of Chouinard's evidence comes in the form of personal anecdotes, much of it comes from authoritative sources. This combination of evidence makes his argument more well-rounded as well as easier to read.	Chouinard is a good writer. He makes good points. He uses good evidence.
Choose precise words. Try to include higher caliber words in your sentences. However, never use words whose meanings you don't entirely understand. This can actually hurt your essay.	Chouinard appeals to the federal government when he directly addresses President Obama.	Chouinard pretends he's talking to President Obama to make a point.
Use an academic tone. For an academic essay, you should always use a formal and objective tone—avoid slang or informal language.	Although Chouinard can be didactic at times, overall he effectively argues for the removal of dams.	Even though this guy is pretty boring sometimes, you can really understand where he's coming from.
Use good grammar, spelling, and punctuation. Be sure to read over your essay at least once after you've finished writing to catch any mistakes.	Chouinard argues that there are many reasons to close down deadbeat dams.	Chouinard argues "there are many reasons closing down Deadbeat Dams"

Sample Essays

Part 2

In this section we apply the College Board's grading criteria to two student essays written in response to the prompt below. Recall that each criterion will be graded on a scale of 1-4. The sample essays demonstrate Reading, Analysis, and Writing scores of 2 and 4 respectively.

Your essays may merit different scores in each category. Additional sample essays are available online, including samples that demonstrate mixed scores and an example of how an incomplete essay would be scored.

For additional resources, please visit **ivyglobal.com/study**.

Essay Prompt

As you read the passage below, consider how Al Gore uses

- evidence, such as facts or examples, to support claims.
- reasoning to develop ideas and to connect claims and evidence.
- stylistic or persuasive elements, such as word choice or appeals to emotion, to add power to the ideas expressed.

Adapted from former Vice President Al Gore's 2004 speech "The Climate Emergency," collected in Red, White, Blue, and Green: Politics and the Environment in the 2004 Election (2004), edited by members of Yale School of Forestry & Environmental Studies, James R. Lyons, Heather S. Kaplan, Fred Strebeigh, and Kathleen E. Campbell.

1 The environment is often felt to be relatively invulnerable because the earth is so big. People tend to assume that the earth is so big that we as human beings can't possibly have any impact on it. That is a mistake.

2 In Europe during the summer of 2003, we experienced an extreme heat wave that killed an estimated 20,000 people, and many predict such events will be much more commonplace as a result of increasing temperatures. The anomaly was extreme, particularly in France, with consequences that were well reported in the press. Year-to-year, decade-to-decade there's variation, but the overall upward trend worldwide since the American Civil War is really clear and really obvious, at least to me.

3 If you look at the glaciers around the world, you see that many are melting away. A friend of mine named Lonnie Thompson of Ohio State studies glaciers, and he reports that 15 to 20 years from now there will be no more snows of Kilimanjaro. This shrinking of glaciers is happening all

around the world, including Latin America, China, and the U.S. In our own Glacier National Park, all of the glaciers are predicted to be gone within 15 to 20 years.

4 An area of Bangladesh is due to be flooded where ten million people live. A large area of Florida is due to be flooded. The Florida Keys are very much at risk. The Everglades are at risk.

5 The trend is very clear. What's behind it all? I've come to believe that global warming, the disappearance of the ocean fisheries, the destruction of the rain forests, the stratospheric ozone depletion problem, the extinction crisis, all of these are really symptoms of an underlying cause. The underlying cause is a collision between our civilization and the earth. The relationship between the human species and our planet has been completely changed. All of our culture, all of our literature, all of our history, everything we've learned, was premised on one relationship between the earth and us, and now we have a different one.

6 Think about the subsistence that we have always drawn from the earth. The plow was a great advance, as was irrigation. But then we began to get more powerful with these tools. At the Aral Sea in Russia, something as simple as irrigation on a large scale led to the virtual disappearance of the fourth largest inland body of water in the world. We're changing the surface of the earth, and technology sometimes seems to dwarf our human scale. We now have to try to change this pattern.

7 There's another assumption that needs to be questioned. In contrast to the idea that the earth is so big that we can't have any impact on it, there are others who assume that the climate change problem is so big we can't solve it. I, however, believe that we can if we put our minds to it. We had a problem with the ozone hole, a big global problem that seemed too big to solve. In response, we had political leadership and the world passed a treaty outlawing chlorofluorocarbons, the chemicals that caused this problem. The United States led the way, and we brought about a dramatic drop in CFCs and are now in the process of solving that problem. We now have the ability to buy hybrid cars like the Toyota Prius and the marketplace for new sources of energy is increasing dramatically. We're also seeing new efficiencies with energy savings. If we have political leadership and the collective political will to say it is important to solve this problem, we can not only solve it, we can create more jobs, we can create higher incomes, a better way of life, and a higher quality of life by solving the problem.

8 Everything we have ever known—and Carl Sagan made a beautiful long statement about this—all the wars, all the heartbreak, all the romance, every triumph, every mistake, everything we've ever known is contained in this small planet. If we keep the right perspective and keep our eyes on the prize, we can solve this problem, we will solve this problem, we must solve this problem. It really is up to you.

Write an essay in which you explain how Al Gore builds an argument to persuade his audience that climate change is a serious problem we must address. In your essay, analyze how Gore uses one or more of the features listed in the box above (or features of your own choice) to strengthen the logic and persuasiveness of his argument. Be sure that your analysis focuses on the most relevant features of the passage.

Your essay should not explain whether you agree with Gore's claims, but rather explain how Gore builds an argument to persuade his audience.

Sample Essay #1

Al Gore says that we need to take better care of the earth. If we don't, things will get worse, and things are already pretty bad. "In Europe during the summer of 2003, we experienced an extreme heat wave that killed an estimated 20,000 people, and many predict such events will be much more commonplace as a result of increasing temperatures." The earth is in bad shape, we need to fix it.

One example Al Gore uses is the glaciers. The glaciers is melting, according to his friend Lonnie, and that's a big problem. If there are no more glaciers, that will mean we no longer have Glacier National Park. This is a big problem. "The trend is very clear." Rain forests are being destroyed, fisheries are disappearing from the oceans. This situation could be deadly.

Things are basically different than they've ever been before. Humans used to be farmers, so they didn't need technology. Now we have made enormous technological advances, but their bad for the planet. All the machines that we use are causing global warming.

But don't worry, there is some hope. We can still stop this menace if we get to work right now. There is other new technology that is making things better. For example, the Toyota Prius is a hybrid car which is are better for the environment. The United States is striving to improve and lead the way. Right now. We need politicians to step up. "If we have political leadership and the collective political will to say it is important to solve this problem," we can get it done. Al Gore thinks that we can solve the problem and have "a higher quality of life by solving the problem." This means that things can only get better for us from hear on out, if we listen to what he says. We made this problem, but we can fix it.

Score Breakdown: Essay #1

Reading Score: 2. The writer demonstrates limited comprehension of the source text's central ideas.

The writer understands Gore's central argument—that we need to address a serious environmental problem—but she does not grasp the nuances of his argument about the relationship between humans and technology. Furthermore, she does not connect important details to how Gore uses them. For example, she highlights his example of glaciers melting, but does not link it to the mass flooding of areas where many people live, which is what makes this example significant in context.

Although the writer does not make any overt errors in referring to the passage, her discussion is not always precise. She does quote from the source text, but she does not provide context for the quotes, or explain why they are important. She also makes some unsupported claims.

Analysis Score: 2. The writer shows that she understands she is supposed to write about the passage, not the topic. However, her analysis lacks depth, and she often writes as if she is discussing her own opinion rather than Gore's argument.

The writer summarizes her perception of Gore's thesis, but she does not examine how he builds his argument. She discusses some of the most relevant features of Gore's argument (such as his example of the heat wave), but misses others (such as the changing relationship between humans and the planet). When she does refer to Gore's use of evidence, she does not always do so effectively and she does not provide any analysis of his reasoning or stylistic elements.

The writer does provide evidence for some of her claims, such as when she supports the statement that the earth is in bad shape by talking about the glaciers melting. However, other claims are both broad and not supported by the text.

Writing Score: 2. The writer demonstrates limited mastery of language and organization.

The tone in this essay is not conversational. However, the style is quite simple, and occasionally too casual for formal writing. Sentences vary in structure, but only slightly. There are also some errors in grammar and usage, including run-on sentences.

The writer does make a central claim—"The earth is in bad shape, and we need to fix it"— but it is not focused on the passage, which is what an essay's thesis should focus on. There is a clear series of ideas in the essay, but they are not well connected; the ideas do not build upon each other, and there is only one clear transition. Furthermore, although the essay is structured in distinct paragraphs that each has a clear topic, the sentences within those paragraphs are not clearly ordered to develop a point.

Student Sample Essay #2

Al Gore argues that climate change is a major problem that we must address. He views both climate change and the potential solutions for climate change not just as a matter of technology, but also as a matter of changing the human relationship with the earth. By focusing on the role of humanity in both creating and stopping climate change, Gore imparts to his audience a sense of both responsibility and hope.

Gore begins by asserting that "people tend to assume that the earth is so big that we as human beings can't possibly have any impact on it," but this is a "mistake." He uses multiple examples to demonstrate that the popular perception of the earth as "invulnerable" is wrong. His first piece of evidence is a European heat wave that killed 20,000 people, which allows him to foreground the human cost of climate change. This continues as he talks about the melting of the glaciers. Citing the work of a researcher at Ohio State as an authoritative source to give his argument scientific credibility, Gore directly connects the shrinking of the glaciers to flooding in Bangladesh "where ten million people live." Once more, he emphasizes the human cost of climate change as he is establishing the severity of the crisis.

He also centers on humanity when discussing the "underlying cause" of climate change, which he believes is "a collision between our civilization and the earth." The word "collision" dramatizes how suddenly things have changed. To further underscore the extent to which our relationship with the earth has changed, he writes that "all of our culture, all of our literature, all of our history" came out of the old relationship between the earth and humanity; the repetition highlights the immense scope of this history, which in turn brings home the scope of the crisis.

However, Gore does not center on humanity only to make his audience aware of the danger; he also does so to promote a hopeful outlook. He uses the disappearance of the Aral Sea due to large-scale irrigation as an example of how technological advance can change the earth for the worse, but then transitions into discussing his belief that we can solve the problem of climate change "if we put our minds to it." He illustrates this belief with the successful campaign to bring about "a dramatic drop" in chlorofluorocarbons, which were contributing to the problem of the ozone hole. By juxtaposing an example of humans harming the earth with one of humans working to fix a problem they had created, Gore reinforces his argument that the power lies with us.

Furthermore, just as Gore emphasized the human costs of climate change, he also emphasizes the human benefits of working to solve the problem. He points out that "the marketplace for new sources of energy is increasing dramatically," making a solution seem economically feasible. He goes on to assert that "we can create more jobs, we can create higher incomes, a better way of life, and a higher quality of life" in the quest to stop climate change. The subtle repetitions of "we can create" and "life" stir the audience's emotions as Gore leads them to envision a brighter future.

That future, once again, lies with us. In his final triple repetition—"we can solve this problem, we will solve this problem, we must solve this problem" —Gore brings together the two sides that together make his argument so powerful: our role in creating the problem and our ability to solve it. In keeping his focus on humanity, Gore inspires his audience to feel responsible for the fate of the earth and hopeful about our ability to fix it.

Score Breakdown: Essay #2

Reading Score: 4. The writer demonstrates a clear and nuanced understanding of different aspects of Gore's argument, and states them in her introduction.

The writer focuses on details relevant to the passage and highlights their importance to Gore's argument. She consistently uses evidence from the text to support her claims. She also provides both context and explanation for the quotes she uses.

Analysis Score: 4. The writer clearly understands the assignment, structuring her essay entirely around her own analysis of Gore's speech. Her thesis is both specific and clear.

The writer analyzes the role that evidence plays in Gore's argument in ways that are relevant to her own thesis about his speech. She also analyzes how both organizational choices and stylistic tools contribute to the aspect of Gore's argument she has chosen to focus on. She develops each of her claims using evidence from the text.

Writing Score: 4. The writer demonstrates exceptional mastery of language and strong organization.

The writer states her central claim clearly in her introduction, and develops it throughout the essay. Her essay is effectively organized, with focused paragraphs in a logical order so that each one builds on the point the previous one made. At the end of each paragraph, she makes its relationship to her main argument clear. She also uses transitions to make her argument easy to follow.

The tone is consistent and academic. The style is sophisticated, employing a variety of sentence structures and vocabulary that allows her to be specific and concise. She demonstrates full proficiency in grammar and usage.

Section 5

Sample SAT Essay Prompts

Here are five essay prompts to practice the strategies you learned in this chapter. Answer each prompt within a 50-minute time limit, and ask a trusted reader to check your work. In the chart below, we've also given you a checklist of questions you can ask yourself as you're reviewing your work.

Criteria	Checklist
Reading	✓ Did I show that I understand the passage's argument? (Remember that the prompt summarizes it for you!) ✓ Did I connect important details to the main idea? ✓ Did I use evidence from the text to support my claims?
Analysis	✓ Is my essay about the passage, *not* about the topic of the passage? ✓ Did I analyze the author's use of evidence, reasoning, and style, using specific examples from the text? ✓ Did I explain how my examples were relevant to my argument?
Writing	✓ Do I have a clear thesis statement? ✓ Do my paragraphs have topic sentences and transitions? ✓ Are my sentences grammatically correct?

Essay Prompt #1

Part 1

As you read the passage below, consider how Rodrigo A. Medellín, Don J. Melnick, and Mary C. Pearl use

- evidence, such as facts or examples, to support claims.
- reasoning to develop ideas and to connect claims and evidence.
- stylistic or persuasive elements, such as word choice or appeals to emotion, to add power to the ideas expressed.

Adapted from Rodrigo A. Medellín, Don J. Melnick, and Mary C. Pearl, "Protect Our Bats." © 2014 by the New York Times Company. Originally published May 11, 2014.

1 Disease and heedless management of wind turbines are killing North America's bats, with potentially devastating consequences for agriculture and human health.

2 We have yet to find a cure for the disease known as white-nose syndrome, which has decimated populations of hibernating, cave-dwelling bats in the Northeast. But we can reduce the turbine threat significantly without dismantling them or shutting them down.

3 White-nose syndrome (also known as W.N.S.) was first documented in February 2006 in upstate New York, where it may have been carried from Europe to a bat cave on an explorer's hiking boot. In Europe, bats appear to be immune. But in North America, bats are highly susceptible to the cold-loving fungus that appears in winter on the muzzle and other body parts during hibernation, irritating them awake at a time when there is no food. They end up burning precious stores of energy and starve to death.

4 The consequences have been catastrophic. A 2011 study of 42 sites across five Eastern states found that after 2006 the populations of tri-colored and Indiana bats declined by more than 70 percent, and little brown bats by more than 90 percent. The population of the northern long-eared bat, once common, has declined by an estimated 99 percent and prompted a proposal from the United States Fish and Wildlife Service to list it as an endangered species. Other species of hibernating cave-dwelling bats have declined precipitously as well.

5 Whether these bats will recover or go extinct is unclear. Meanwhile, W.N.S. continues to spread rapidly. On the back of this year's extremely cold winter, it moved into Michigan and Wisconsin. It is now confirmed in 23 states and five Canadian provinces.

6 Tree-dwelling bats don't seem to be affected by W.N.S., since they don't hibernate in caves. But wind farms are killing them. Wind turbines nationwide are estimated to kill between 600,000 and 900,000 bats a year, according to a recent study in the journal BioScience. About half of those lost to turbines are hoary bats, which migrate long distances seasonally throughout North America. Eastern red and silver-haired bats, commonly seen in Central Park in New York City hunting insects at night, are also being killed by turbines by the tens of thousands.

7 We can't afford to lose these creatures. In the Northeast, all of our native bat species eat insects. One little brown bat can eat 1,000 mosquitoes in an hour, reducing the potential for mosquito-borne diseases. A colony of 150 big brown bats can protect crops from up to 33 million rootworms over a growing season. The Mexican free-tailed bats of Bracken Cave in south-central Texas consume about 250 tons of insects every summer night. The natural pest control provided by that species across eight Texas counties has been valued at nearly $750,000 as it protects the $6 million summer cotton crop. Nationwide, the value of bats as pest controllers is estimated to be at least $3.7 billion and possibly much more.

8 Today, genetic engineering may seem to provide an effective way to protect crops from insects, but pests have already developed resistance to some of these products. Insects also readily evolve resistance to chemical insecticides, and increased use of these chemicals would come at a great cost to human health. But bats have shared the night skies with insects for at least 50 million years, and they know how to hunt and eat them.

9 Fortunately, we can reduce the mortality caused by wind farms, which are often located on windy routes favored by some migratory bats. Wind turbines usually switch on automatically at wind speeds of about 8 to 9 miles per hour, speeds at which insects and bats are active. But if, during times of peak bat activity, energy companies recalibrated their turbines to start at a wind speed of about 11 miles per hour, which is too windy for insects and bats to fly, turbine-related deaths could be reduced by 44 to 93 percent, according to a 2010 study published in the journal Frontiers in Ecology and the Environment. The effect on power output would be negligible—less than 1 percent annually.

10 Threats to bats also threaten us. We should step up research on the prevention and cure of white-nose syndrome. And we should require energy companies to take steps to protect bats from collisions with wind turbines. It is foolish to spend enormous sums to create pesticides and transgenic crops to fight insects, while investing little to protect bats, our most efficient insect fighters.

Write an essay in which you explain how Rodrigo A. Medellín, Don J. Melnick, and Mary C. Pearl build an argument to persuade their audience that we need to protect North America's bat population. In your essay, analyze how the authors use one or more of the features listed in the box above (or features of your own choice) to strengthen the logic and persuasiveness of their argument. Be sure that your analysis focuses on the most relevant features of the passage.

Your essay should not explain whether you agree with Medellín, Melnick, and Pearl's claims, but rather explain how the authors build an argument to persuade their audience.

Essay Prompt #2

Part 2

As you read the passage below, consider how Timothy D. Wilson uses

- evidence, such as facts or examples, to support claims.
- reasoning to develop ideas and to connect claims and evidence.
- stylistic or persuasive elements, such as word choice or appeals to emotion, to add power to the ideas expressed.

Adapted from Timothy D. Wilson, "Stop Bullying The 'Soft' Sciences." © 2012 by the Los Angeles Times. Originally published July 12, 2012.

1 Once, during a meeting at my university, a biologist mentioned that he was the only faculty member present from a science department. When I corrected him, noting that I was from the Department of Psychology, he waved his hand dismissively, as if I were a Little Leaguer telling a member of the New York Yankees that I too played baseball.

2 There has long been snobbery in the sciences, with the "hard" ones (physics, chemistry, biology) considering themselves to be more legitimate than the "soft" ones (psychology, sociology). It is thus no surprise that many members of the general public feel the same way. But of late, skepticism about the rigors of social science has reached absurd heights.

3 The U.S. House of Representatives recently voted to eliminate funding for political science research through the National Science Foundation. In the wake of that action, an opinion writer for the Washington Post suggested that the House didn't go far enough. The NSF should not fund any research in the social sciences, wrote Charles Lane, because "unlike hypotheses in the hard sciences, hypotheses about society usually can't be proven or disproven by experimentation."

4 This is news to me and the many other social scientists who have spent their careers doing carefully controlled experiments on human behavior, inside and outside the laboratory. What makes the criticism so galling is that those who voice it, or members of their families, have undoubtedly benefited from research in the disciplines they dismiss.

5 Most of us know someone who has suffered from depression and sought psychotherapy. He or she probably benefited from therapies such as cognitive behavioral therapy that have been shown to work in randomized clinical trials.

6 Ever hear of stereotype threat? It is the double jeopardy that people face when they are at risk of confirming a negative stereotype of their group. When African American students take a difficult test, for example, they are concerned not only about how well they will do but also about the possibility that performing poorly will reflect badly on their entire group. This added worry has been shown time and again, in carefully controlled experiments, to lower academic performance. But fortunately, experiments have also showed promising ways to reduce this threat. One intervention, for example, conducted in a middle school, reduced the achievement gap by 40%.

7 If you know someone who was unlucky enough to be arrested for a crime he didn't commit, he may have benefited from social psychological experiments that have resulted in fairer lineups and interrogations, making it less likely that innocent people are convicted.

8 An often-overlooked advantage of the experimental method is that it can demonstrate what doesn't work. Consider three popular programs that research psychologists have debunked: Critical Incident Stress Debriefing, used to prevent post-traumatic stress disorders in first responders and others who have witnessed horrific events; the D.A.R.E. anti-drug program, used in many schools throughout America; and Scared Straight programs designed to prevent at-risk teens from engaging in criminal behavior.

9 All three of these programs have been shown, with well-designed experimental studies, to be ineffective or, in some cases, to make matters worse. And as a result, the programs have become less popular or have changed their methods. By discovering what doesn't work, social scientists have saved the public billions of dollars.

10 To be fair to the critics, social scientists have not always taken advantage of the experimental method as much as they could. Too often, for example, educational programs have been implemented widely without being adequately tested. But increasingly, educational researchers are employing better methodologies. For example, in a recent study, researchers randomly assigned teachers to a program called My Teaching Partner, which is designed to improve teaching skills, or to a control group. Students taught by the teachers who participated in the program did significantly better on achievement tests than did students taught by teachers in the control group.

11 Are the social sciences perfect? Of course not. Human behavior is complex, and it is not possible to conduct experiments to test all aspects of what people do or why. There are entire disciplines devoted to the experimental study of human behavior, however, in tightly controlled, ethically acceptable ways. Many people benefit from the results, including those who, in their ignorance, believe that science is limited to the study of molecules.

Write an essay in which you explain how Timothy D. Wilson builds an argument to persuade his audience that the “soft” sciences are real sciences and should be funded. In your essay, analyze how Wilson uses one or more of the features listed in the box above (or features of your own choice) to strengthen the logic and persuasiveness of his argument. Be sure that your analysis focuses on the most relevant features of the passage.

Your essay should not explain whether you agree with Wilson’s claims, but rather explain how Wilson builds an argument to persuade his audience.

Essay Prompt #3

Part 3

As you read the passage below, consider how Tom Vanderbilt uses

- evidence, such as facts or examples, to support claims.
- reasoning to develop ideas and to connect claims and evidence.
- stylistic or persuasive elements, such as word choice or appeals to emotion, to add power to the ideas expressed.

Adapted from Tom Vanderbilt, "When Pedestrians Get Mixed Signals." © 2014 by the New York Times Company. Originally published February 1, 2014.

1 Let's put aside the tired trope that no one walks in Los Angeles—Ray Bradbury nailed that one with his 1951 short story "The Pedestrian," about a man picked up by the police for the suspicious activity of walking. In fact, Los Angeles has many places that are quite pleasant for walking.

2 Take the Silver Lake neighborhood: It does not even rank among the city's top 20 "most walkable" areas, according to the website Walk Score, yet still wins 75 points ("most errands can be accomplished on foot")—a number that puts many American cities to shame. In 2012, the city hired its first "pedestrian coordinators."

3 But then came the surest indication of a walking resurgence in Los Angeles: It suddenly had a pedestrian problem. As The Los Angeles Times reported, the Police Department was targeting people for a variety of pedestrian violations in downtown Los Angeles. "We're heavily enforcing pedestrian violations because they're impeding traffic and causing too many accidents and deaths," said Lt. Lydia Leos of the Los Angeles Police Department.

4 Thus a familiar pattern reasserts itself: The best way to reduce pedestrian deaths is to issue tickets to pedestrians. A similar dynamic can be seen in recent weeks after a spate of pedestrian deaths in New York City, where Mayor Bill de Blasio has endorsed more aggressive enforcement by the New York Police Department against jaywalkers. Enforcement against jaywalking varies between states, but it is an infraction in most, even a misdemeanor in some.

5 But neither enforcement nor education has the effect we like to think it does on safety. Decades of graphic teenage driving safety films did not bring down teenage driving deaths; what did was limiting the age and conditions under which teenagers could begin to drive. Similarly, all the "awareness campaigns" on seatbelt usage have had a fraction of the impact of simply installing that annoying chime that impels drivers to buckle up.

6 If tough love will not make pedestrians safer, what will? The answer is: better walking infrastructure, slower car speeds and more pedestrians. But it's easier to write off the problem as one of jaywalkers.

7 Nowadays, the word connotes an amorphous urban nuisance. In fact, the term once referred to country bumpkins ("jays"), who came to the city and perambulated in a way that amused and exasperated savvy urban bipeds. As the historian Peter Norton has documented, the word was then overhauled in the early part of the 20th century. A coalition of pro-automobile interests Mr. Norton calls "motordom" succeeded in shifting the focus of street safety from curbing the actions of rogue drivers to curbing rogue walkers. The pedestrian pushback was shortlived: An attempt to popularize the term "jay driver" was left behind in a cloud of exhaust.

8 Sure, we may call an errant driver, per the comedian George Carlin, an "idiot" or a "maniac," but there is no word to tar an entire class of negligent motorists. This is because of the extent to which driving has been normalized for most Americans: We constantly see the world through what has been called the "windshield view."

9 Those humans in Los Angeles who began walking a second or two after the light was blinking were, after all, violating the "Vehicle Code." Note that cars, apparently, do not violate a "Human Code."

10 As for pedestrian safety, which is the typical stated purpose of jaywalking crackdowns, more pedestrians generally are killed in urban areas by cars violating their right of way than are rogue pedestrians violating vehicles' right of way. Then there are those people struck on sidewalks, even inside restaurants. What do we call that? Jay-living?

11 Pedestrians, who lack air bags and side-impact crash protection, are largely rational creatures. Studies have shown that when you shorten the wait to cross a street, fewer people will cross against the light. When you tell people how long they must wait to cross, fewer people will cross against the signal.

12 When you actually give people a signal, more will cross with it. As the field of behavioral economics has been discovering, rather than penalizing people for opting out of the system, a more effective approach is to make it easier to opt in.

13 The Los Angeles Police Department may be patrolling on foot in downtown Los Angeles, but it is still looking through the windshield.

Write an essay in which you explain how Tom Vanderbilt builds an argument to persuade his audience that penalizing jaywalking will not increase pedestrian safety. In your essay, analyze how Vanderbilt uses one or more of the features listed in the box above (or features of your own choice) to strengthen the logic and persuasiveness of his argument. Be sure that your analysis focuses on the most relevant features of the passage.

Your essay should not explain whether you agree with Vanderbilt's claims, but rather explain how Vanderbilt builds an argument to persuade his audience.

Essay Prompt #4

Part 4

As you read the passage below, consider how Alfie Kohn uses

- evidence, such as facts or examples, to support claims.
- reasoning to develop ideas and to connect claims and evidence.
- stylistic or persuasive elements, such as word choice or appeals to emotion, to add power to the ideas expressed.

Adapted from Alfie Kohn, "Do Our Kids Get Off Too Easy?" © 2014 by the New York Times Company. Originally published May 3, 2014.

1 The conventional wisdom these days is that kids come by everything too easily— stickers, praise, A's, trophies. It's outrageous, we're told, that all kids on the field may get a thanks-for-playing token, in contrast to the good old days, when recognition was reserved for the conquering heroes.

2 Most of all, it's assumed that the best way to get children ready for the miserable "real world" that awaits them is to make sure they have plenty of miserable experiences while they're young. Conversely, if they're spared any unhappiness, they'll be ill-prepared. This is precisely the logic employed not so long ago to frame bullying as a rite of passage that kids were expected to deal with on their own, without assistance from "overprotective" adults.

3 In any case, no one ever explains the mechanism by which the silence of a long drive home without a trophy is supposed to teach resilience. Nor are we told whether there's any support for this theory of inoculation by immersion. Have social scientists shown that those who are spared, say, the rigors of dodge ball (which turns children into human targets) or class rank (which pits students against one another) will wind up unprepared for adulthood?

4 Not that I can find. In fact, studies of those who attended the sort of nontraditional schools that afford an unusual amount of autonomy and nurturing suggest that the great majority seemed capable of navigating the transition to traditional colleges and workplaces.

5 But when you point out the absence of logic or evidence, it soon becomes clear that trophy rage is less about prediction— what will happen to kids later—than ideology —how they ought to be treated now. Fury over the possibility that kids will get off too easy or feel too good about themselves seems to rest on three underlying values.

6 The first is deprivation: Kids shouldn't be spared struggle and sacrifice, regardless of the effects. The second value is scarcity: the belief that excellence, by definition, is something that not everyone can attain. No matter how well a group of students performs, only a few should get A's. Otherwise we're sanctioning "grade inflation" and mediocrity. To have high standards, there must always be losers.

7 But it's the third conviction that really ties everything together: an endorsement of conditionality. Children ought never to receive something desirable—a sum of money, a trophy, a commendation—unless they've done enough to merit it. They shouldn't even be allowed to feel good about themselves

without being able to point to tangible accomplishments. In this view, we have a moral obligation to reward the deserving and, equally important, make sure the undeserving go conspicuously unrewarded. Hence the anger over participation trophies. The losers mustn't receive something that even looks like a reward.

8 A commitment to conditionality lives at the intersection of economics and theology. It's where lectures about the law of the marketplace meet sermons about what we must do to earn our way into heaven. Here, almost every human interaction, even among family members, is regarded as a kind of transaction.

9 Interestingly, no research that I know of has ever shown that unconditionality is harmful in terms of future achievement, psychological health or anything else. In fact, studies generally show exactly the opposite. One of the most destructive ways to raise a child is with "conditional regard."

10 Over the last decade or so, two Israeli researchers, Avi Assor and Guy Roth, and their colleagues in the United States and Belgium, have conducted a series of experiments whose consistent finding is that when children feel their parents' affection varies depending on the extent to which they are well behaved, self-controlled or impressive at school or sports, this promotes "the development of a fragile, contingent and unstable sense of self."

11 Other researchers, meanwhile, have shown that high self-esteem is beneficial, but that even more desirable is unconditional self-esteem: a solid core of belief in yourself, an abiding sense that you're competent and worthwhile—even when you screw up or fall short. In other words, the very unconditionality that seems to fuel attacks on participation trophies and the whole "self-esteem movement" turns out to be a defining feature of psychological health. It's precisely what we should be helping our children to acquire.

Write an essay in which you explain how Alfie Kohn builds an argument to persuade his audience that parents should show unconditional acceptance for their children. In your essay, analyze how Kohn uses one or more of the features listed in the box above (or features of your own choice) to strengthen the logic and persuasiveness of his argument. Be sure that your analysis focuses on the most relevant features of the passage.

Your essay should not explain whether you agree with Kohn's claims, but rather explain how Kohn builds an argument to persuade his audience.

Math

Chapter 5

Section 1

Introduction to the Math Test

The new SAT Math Test will test certain topics in math as well as your ability to use reasoning and critical thinking to solve real-world problems. These concepts and skills provide the foundations for the math you will learn in college and use in everyday life. The SAT groups these concepts into four major areas that you will see on the Math Test: Heart of Algebra, Problem Solving and Data Analysis, Passport to Advanced Math, and Additional Topics in Math.

In this chapter, we will review all of the topics that you may see on the Math Test. We will also practice strategies for solving different types of questions and for tackling difficult or unfamiliar problems. But first, let's look at the format of the Math Test.

The Basics

The SAT Math Test includes two sections and a total of 58 questions. You can use your calculator on only one of the sections:

Section	Number of Questions	Amount of Time
Calculator Section	38 questions	55 minutes
No-Calculator Section	20 questions	25 minutes

In the Calculator Section, you'll have about 1.5 minutes to answer each question. In the No-Calculator Section, you'll have 1.25 minutes to answer each question. This might not seem like a lot of time, but reviewing and practicing the concepts in this chapter will help you apply your knowledge quickly and efficiently on test day! We'll talk about time management and other test-taking strategies in Section 2 of this chapter.

Topics

There are four main content areas covered by the Math Test. Here is a breakdown of the topics and number of questions in each content area:

Content Area	Topics Covered	Number of Questions	
		Calculator	No-Calculator
Heart of Algebra	Fundamental concepts in algebra involving linear equations and inequalities	11	8
Problem Solving and Data Analysis	Interpreting qualitative and quantitative data, analyzing relationships	17	0
Passport to Advanced Math	More advanced concepts in algebra, including quadratic and higher-order equations	7	9
Additional Topics in Math	Geometry, trigonometry, complex numbers	3	3
Total		**38**	**20**

Sections 3-6 cover the topics in each of these content areas in depth. Fundamental math skills that apply to all of these topics are covered online.

For a fundamental review, please visit **ivyglobal.com/study**.

Questions

Both sections on the Math Test will have two types of questions: multiple choice questions and student-produced response questions. In total, you will see 45 multiple choice questions and 13 student-produced response questions on the Math Test.

Each section will start with the multiple choice questions, then progress to the student-produced response questions.

Within each section, the multiple choice questions will be ordered by difficulty, and so will the student-produced response questions. For example, in the Calculator Section, you will see 30 multiple choice questions ordered from easy to difficult, then 8 student-produced response questions. The No-Calculator Section has 15 multiple choice questions and 5 student-produced response questions.

Some of the questions will include real-world contexts in areas such as science and social studies. These questions will require you to apply reasoning and critical thinking skills to analyze situations, create mathematical models, and find relevant solutions. You will also see graphs, charts, and diagrams in some of the problems and answer choices.

Scoring

Each question is worth one point. The number of points you receive on each section will contribute to your raw score, which will be scaled to give you your final math score from 200-800. The Calculator Section has nearly twice the weight of the No-Calculator Section in determining your score. Here is a chart that shows the scoring breakdown for each question type:

Section	Problem Type	Points	Percentage of Math Score	
Calculator	Multiple Choice	30	52%	66%
	Student-Produced Response Questions	8	14%	
No-Calculator	Multiple Choice	15	26%	34%
	Student-Produced Response Questions	5	8%	
Total		**58**	**100%**	**100%**

In the next section, we will discuss the different question types on the Math Test and learn strategies for approaching and solving each type of question. The rest of the chapter provides an in-depth review of the topics covered on the Math Test. To practice applying your knowledge, make sure to do the practice exercises for each section. Let's get started!

Section 2

Approaching the Math Test

To succeed on the SAT Math Test, you need to know specific math concepts and math skills. The good news is that the redesigned SAT Math Test evaluates math skills that you have learned in your high school classes. You just need to learn which skills the SAT tests, and what strategies you can use to apply your knowledge during the test.

In this section, you will learn about approaching problems, entering your answers, and using problem-solving strategies for the Math Test. You'll see how these techniques can be applied to sample math questions and practice using them.

Once you have mastered these strategies, you'll be ready to review the math concepts on the exam. All of these concepts are covered in Sections 3-6 of this chapter. If you feel comfortable with some or all of the material, you can complete the practice sets at the end of each section to determine which topics you should review.

Plan Your Approach

Part 1

When you take the SAT Math Test, you can reduce your stress by planning ahead. Know what the directions say, how you will approach each question, and how to pace yourself. We'll go through these steps with an example below.

Know the Directions

You will be given directions and reference information at the beginning of each math section of the SAT. The directions contain important information about the types of questions you will see and how much time you have to complete them. Make sure to read the directions before starting the problems so you know what to expect in each section.

The "Notes" section at the beginning of each math section will look similar to the one below. This section will tell you whether you can use a calculator on that section. It also gives you information about the figures and functions you will see and use on the test.

NOTES

1. You **may not** use a calculator.
2. Variables and expressions represent real numbers unless stated otherwise.
3. Figures are drawn to scale unless stated otherwise.
4. Figures lie in a plane unless stated otherwise.
5. The domain of a function f is defined as the set of all real numbers x for which $f(x)$ is also a real number, unless stated otherwise.

The Reference section contains important formulas and facts. To use this information to your advantage, be familiar with what formulas are provided. Use this reference information when practicing for the SAT. Remember that this information is only helpful if you know how to use it to solve problems.

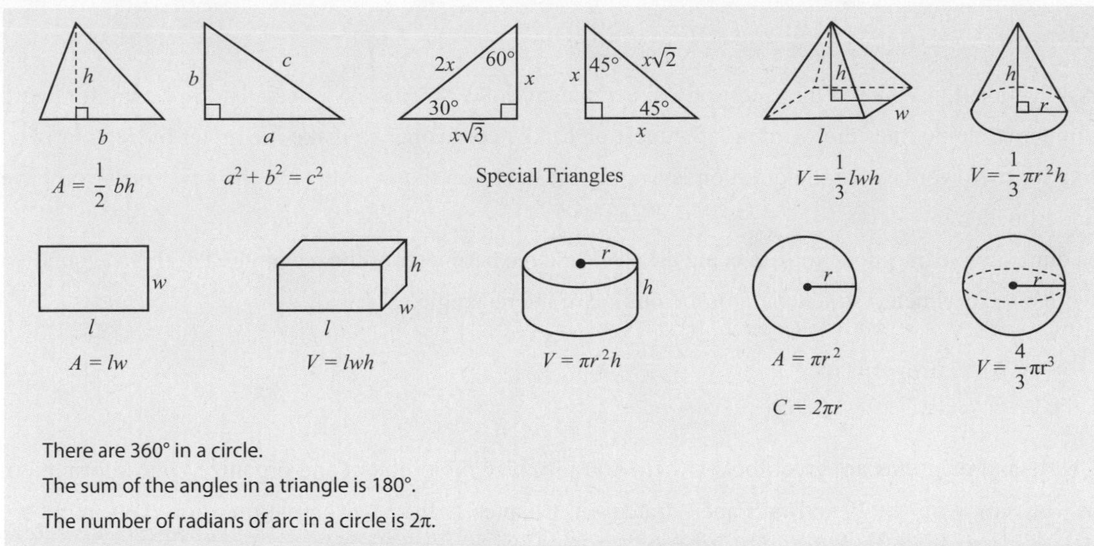

Read the Question Carefully

Read through the whole question. Don't assume you understand the question just by reading the first few words! Reading the whole question will help you avoid making assumptions that can lead to careless errors.

If you see unfamiliar or difficult-looking material, stay calm and keep reading until the end of the question. There might be more information in the question that will help you figure out the solution. If you still think a question is too difficult after you have finished reading the whole thing, you should make your best guess, circle it in your question booklet, and come back to it if you have time.

Underline Key Words

Underline or circle any information given in the question that will help you solve it. Here's an example:

Example

The width of a rectangular field is one-quarter its length. If the length is 16, what is the perimeter of the field?

A) 4 B) 24 C) 36 D) 40

Identify What the Question is Asking

Ask yourself, "What is the question asking me to solve?" This is especially important for word problems. Sometimes the wording of a question can be confusing, so make it simpler by summarizing in your own words what the question is asking for. Focus on the meanings of the key words you have underlined.

In our example question, you are being asked to find the perimeter of the rectangle. Put this in your own words: the perimeter is the length of the outline of the rectangle.

Draw a Chart or Diagram

Charts and diagrams are great tools to help you visualize the problem and organize your information, as you saw with the Pencil on Paper strategy in Chapter 1. In our example question, you might try drawing a quick sketch of a rectangle. Fill in any information given in the question:

width $= \frac{1}{4}$ length

length = 16

Come up With a Strategy

Strategize the best way to solve the question. Think about all of the information provided in the question and how it is related. Think about where you have seen this type of question before, and what methods you have used to solve similar types of questions. If there is a formula you know that could help, write it down.

Here's a strategy we could use to solve our example question.

- We know: length = 16

$$\text{width} = \frac{1}{4} \text{ of length} = \frac{1}{4} \times 16 = \frac{16}{4} = 4$$

- We want: the perimeter of the whole rectangle
- Our strategy: we can use a formula that relates a rectangle's perimeter to its length and width

$$\text{perimeter} = (2 \times \text{length}) + (2 \times \text{width})$$

We can now plug in the values and solve:

$$\text{perimeter} = (2 \times 16) + (2 \times 4) = 32 + 8 = 40$$

Is our solution one of the answer choices? It is indeed! The answer is (D) 40.

Check Your Answer

Always check your work to make sure that you picked the best answer among all of the answer choices. Double-check your arithmetic to make sure that you didn't make any avoidable errors. Check that you solved for what the question was asking. For example, if the question asked you to solve for a perimeter, make sure you didn't solve for area.

Try to determine whether or not your answer seems reasonable based on context. For example, if the length of one side of the rectangle is 16, the perimeter of the whole rectangle has to be greater than twice the length, or 32. Answers (A) and (B) in the example are less than 32, so they are unreasonable.

Finally, check that you bubbled in the answer on your answer sheet correctly. It would be a shame to have solved the question correctly and not get credit! Take a look at Part 2 to learn how to enter your answers correctly.

Pace Yourself

Remember that you will be answering questions under a time limit, and you need to leave yourself enough time to attempt every question on the test. One way to save time during the test is to be familiar with the format and instructions before the test day. Be aware of the number and types of sections that you will see. Before starting a section, look at the number of questions you will be answering and the time you have to answer them.

Here is a chart showing how many minutes you should average per question on each section of the Math Test. The questions in the multiple choice section are ordered from easy to difficult. Plan to spend less time on the early questions so that you have enough time for the more challenging ones at the end of the section.

Pacing on the Math Test			
Section	Total Time	Total Questions	Time Per Question
Calculator Section	55 minutes	38 questions	1.4 minutes per question
No-Calculator Section	25 minutes	20 questions	1.25 minutes per question

Finally, remember that every question is worth the same number of points. If you get stuck on any problem, make a guess and return to that question if you have time at the end. You don't lose points for guessing, so you should never leave a question blank. In Part 3, we'll talk about some strategies for guessing efficiently on the SAT Math Test.

Entering Your Answers

Part 2

As we saw in Section 1, questions on the Math Test come in two types: regular multiple-choice questions and student-produced response questions. The **multiple-choice questions** ask you to choose an answer from four possible choices, but the **student-produced response questions** require you to come up with your own answer and enter it into a special grid.

For both question types, you'll need to bubble in your answer on your answer sheet. For a review of how to bubble in your answers to multiple-choice questions, see Chapter 1. Here, we'll discuss how to "grid in" your answers for the student-produced response questions. The gridding process can be confusing, so you should practice thoroughly before the test day. This will help you avoid mistakes, save time, and build confidence.

Gridding In

You will see directions for gridding answers immediately before the grid-in problems. Practice gridding answers before the test so you can skip the directions and have more time to work on the problems.

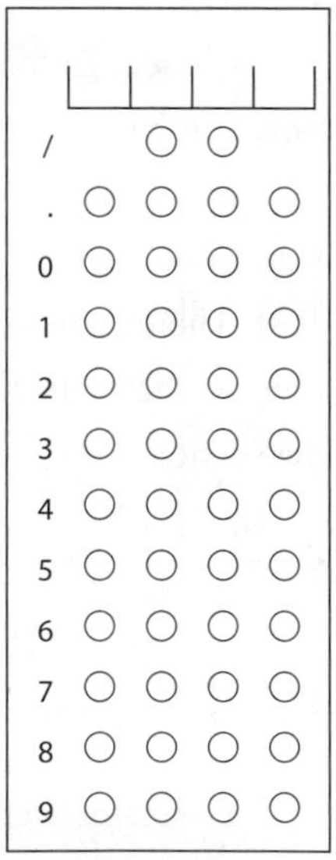

You will enter your answers to student-produced response questions in a grid like the one shown here. The grid has four columns, and in each column you can enter a digit from 0-9, a decimal point, or a fraction bar (/). This way, you can enter any whole number between 0 and 9,999. You can also enter fractions or decimal numbers.

The machine will score the bubbles you fill in on the grid. Make sure to fill in bubbles completely and mark no more than one circle in any column. Completely erase any stray marks in the grid.

Answers written in the boxes above the grid are *not* scored. You can write your answer into those boxes as a guide when you bubble in your answers, and it is a good idea to use the boxes to avoid bubbling errors. However, remember that you always need to bubble your answers as well!

Placement

You can start your answer in any column as long as you can fit in the whole answer. You may leave columns blank if the answer is fewer than four characters. For example, 64 can be gridded in the three ways shown below; all are correct.

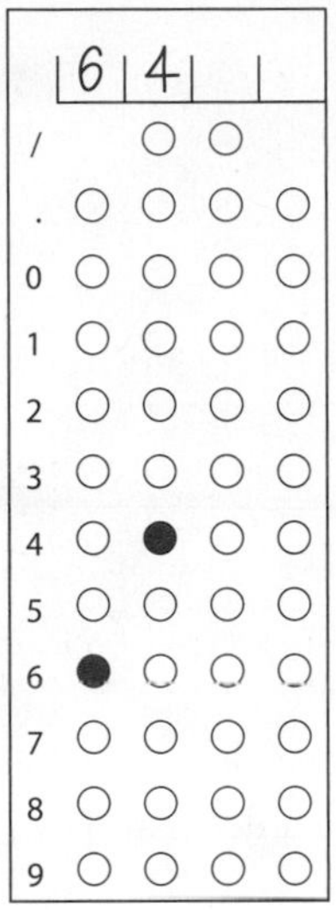

6	4		

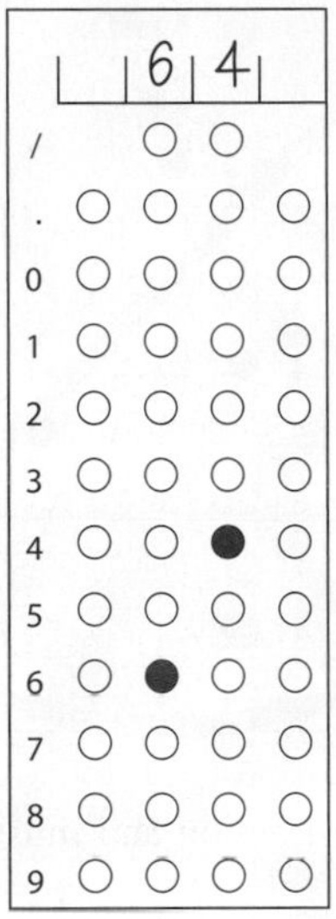

	6	4	

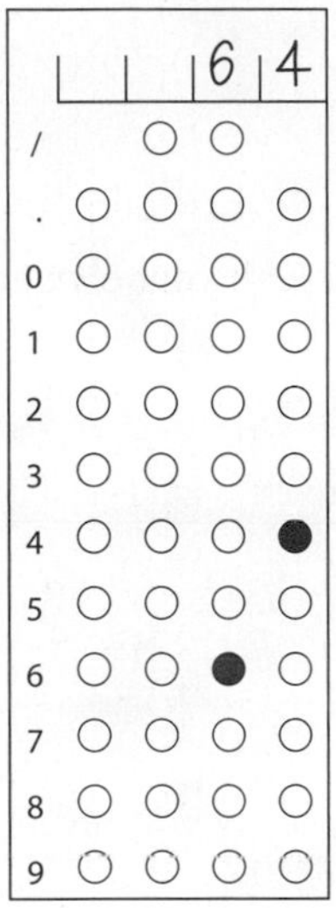

		6	4

Signs

There is no negative sign in the grid, so all answers will be positive numbers or zero. If you get a negative number for an answer, either you have made a mistake or there are other possible answers. Check your work and rework the problem if necessary.

Fractions and Decimals

Grid-in responses may contain fractions or decimals. You can write these answers in either fraction or decimal form as long as you follow the rules below.

You can grid proper and improper fractions, but *not* mixed numbers. If the answer is a mixed number, you must convert it to an improper fraction or a decimal. For example, the answer $4\frac{1}{5}$ must be gridded as 21/5 or 4.2 as shown in the following grids.

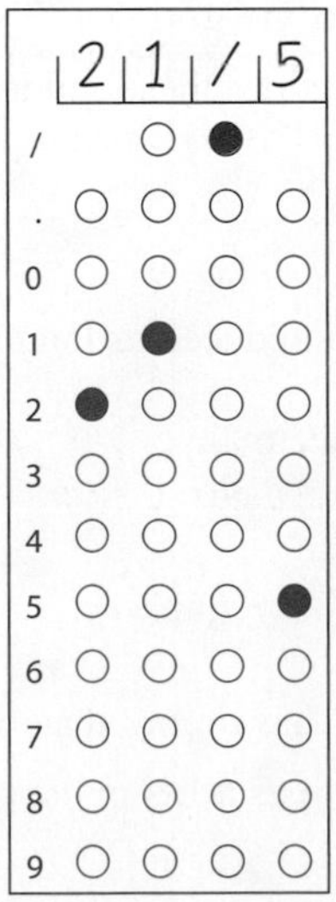

2	1	/	5

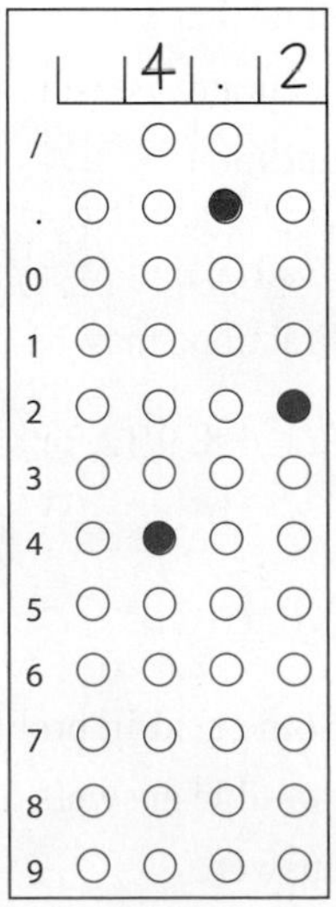

	4	.	2

If you grid the answer as the mixed number 4 1/5 like the example below, the machine will read it as $\frac{41}{5}$, which is incorrect.

Some answers will not fit in the grid as a fraction and must be converted to a decimal. For example, $\frac{1}{100}$ must be gridded as .01 because 1/100 will not fit.

Decimals must be as accurate as possible. If a decimal is longer than four characters, grid the first four characters (including the decimal point) or it may be marked incorrect. For example, $\frac{4}{7}$ should be written as .571 with no zero before the decimal point. The response .57 may be scored as incorrect because it is less accurate than .571.

You do not have to follow rounding rules when shortening your answer. If you round, do so at the last digit that you can fit in the grid. 8.127 can be bubbled as 8.12 or 8.13, but not as 8.1, which is less accurate. Be sure to follow these guidelines, unless specific rounding instructions are given in the question.

Fractions may be left unreduced as long as they fit in the grid. If an answer was $\frac{3}{4}$, you could grid it as 3/4, 6/8, 9/12, or as a decimal.

Multiple Correct Answers

Some grid-in problems have more than one correct answer. In those cases, you may grid in any of the possible answers as long as it fits in the grid. There may also be multiple methods to arrive at a correct answer.

Math Strategies

Part 3

In Chapter 1, we reviewed general strategies that you can use on all parts of the SAT, such as Plugging in Options and Process of Elimination. In this section, we will review additional strategies that apply specifically to mathematics questions. These strategies will help you use your time and resources, like your calculator and the testing materials, to answer questions quickly, and will reduce your chance of making mistakes.

Use your Calculator

The Math Test is divided into a Calculator Section and a No-Calculator Section. Every math problem on the SAT can be solved without a calculator, but when you're allowed to use a calculator, it can help you save time and avoid errors.

You must provide your own calculator. A scientific or graphing calculator is recommended. You cannot use calculators with keypads, styluses, touchscreens, internet access, cellular access, or power cords. You also cannot use calculators that can play or record audio, video, or images. Your calculator can't make noise, and you can't use a laptop, tablet, or phone as a calculator. For a list of acceptable calculators, see ivyglobal.com/study/links/#calculator.

Make sure to practice using the calculator that you plan to bring to the SAT so you are familiar with it. Before the test, make sure your calculator is working properly and has fresh batteries. Consider bringing a spare set of batteries or a back-up calculator.

Don't rely too much on your calculator when you take the test. On some problems, using a calculator can slow you down. When starting a problem, think about how you will solve it and whether you need to use a calculator. Look for ways to simplify the problem that will make the calculation easier, such as factoring.

Write down calculations and scratch work in the test booklet. This will help you avoid calculator errors and makes it easier to check your work and find errors. Also, remember that every problem can be solved without a calculator. If you find yourself doing complicated or tedious calculations, there is likely a simpler method to find the answer.

Look for Shortcuts

None of the problems should require time-consuming calculations. If your solution strategy is long or complicated, look for a simpler method or a trick to solve the problem more quickly. Also double-check to make sure you are solving for the correct variable or value.

There are often multiple ways to solve a problem, so look for shortcuts or tricks that will save you time and unnecessary work. When possible, simplify equations and expressions.

Example

$$\frac{10x}{y} \times \frac{3}{4} \times \frac{2}{5} \times \frac{1}{6} =$$

A) $\frac{x}{3y}$ B) $\frac{x}{2y}$ C) $\frac{x}{y}$ D) $\frac{2x}{y}$

You could solve this problem by finding the product of all the terms. However, this is not the best approach. Instead, try to cancel as many factors as possible. The 3 × 2 in the numerator cancels the 6 in the denominator. You can rewrite the 4 × 5 in the denominator as 2 × 10 and cancel that 10 with the 10 in the numerator.

$$\frac{10x}{y} \times \overset{6}{\cancel{\frac{3}{4}} \times \cancel{\frac{2}{5}}}_{2\times 10} \times \frac{1}{6} = \frac{\cancel{10} \times \cancel{6} \times x}{2 \times \cancel{10} \times \cancel{6} \times y} = \frac{x}{2y}$$

Now you are left with $\frac{x}{2y}$, which gives you the correct answer, (B).

This approach reduces the chance of making an arithmetic or calculator error. In fact, it eliminates the need to use a calculator at all. If this question were on the no-calculator section, this approach is faster and safer than multiplying all the factors out by hand.

Use Figures

Any figure provided in the Math Test will be accurate unless noted otherwise. If an angle looks like a right angle, you can assume that it is one. It is safe to assume other features like parallel or perpendicular lines and relative angles or lengths. Charts, graphs, and gridded figures are always accurate.

Although you are not allowed to use a ruler, you can measure lengths by using the side of your answer sheet. Place the corner of the sheet at one point and mark the distance to another point. This strategy may help you eliminate answer choices or check your answer, although there will always be a way to solve these problems without measuring lengths.

Some figures may not show all of the lines that you need to solve the problem. You should add any necessary lines as accurately as possible.

Example

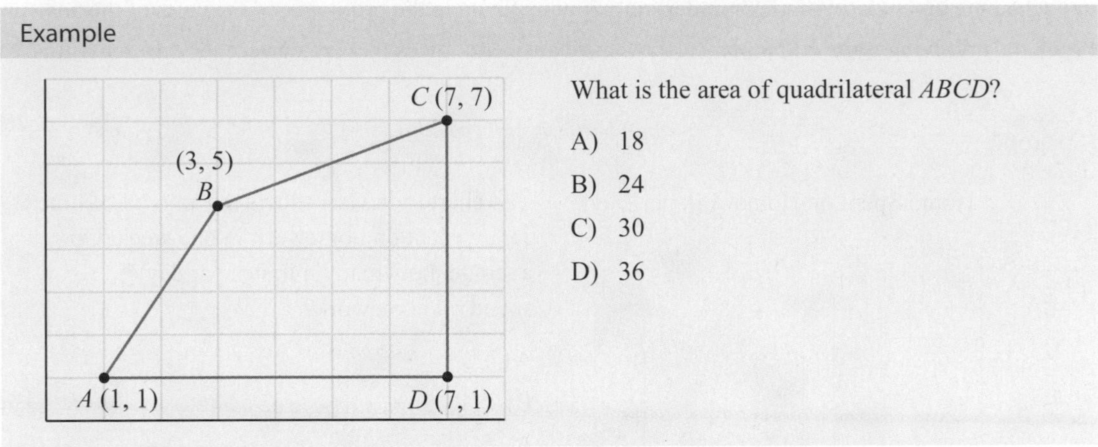

What is the area of quadrilateral *ABCD*?

A) 18

B) 24

C) 30

D) 36

Since quadrilateral *ABCD* is irregular, you cannot easily find the area. However, if you draw a line between *B* and *D*, you will have two triangles whose areas you can calculate:

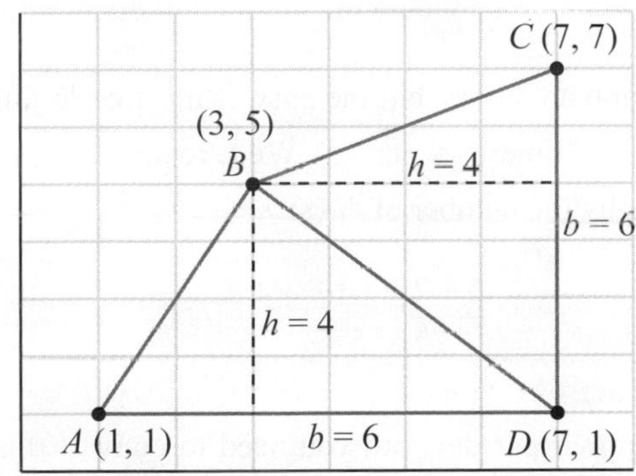

Define the base of triangle *ABD* to be $\overline{AD}$ and the base of triangle *BCD* to be $\overline{CD}$. The height of each triangle is the line segment from the base to the opposite vertex, perpendicular to the base. The bases and heights are labelled in the diagram.

We can use the formula $A = \frac{1}{2}bh$ to find the areas of each of these triangles. The area of triangle *ABD* is $\frac{1}{2}(6)(4) = 12$, and the area of triangle *BCD* is $\frac{1}{2}(6)(4) = 12$. Therefore, the area of quadrilateral *ABCD* is 24, which is answer choice (B).

Draw a diagram if a figure is not provided for a geometry problem, as you learned in Chapter 1. Figures may also be helpful for solving other types of problems. You might draw a number line, graph, or quick sketch of a situation. Keep your diagrams simple and accurate.

Pay Attention to Units and Variables

When choosing an answer, double check that it is in the correct units. The answer may have different units than the given data. Circle or underline any units given in the problem and the units of the answer. Problems involving units will almost always have answer choices that are correct for different units.

Example

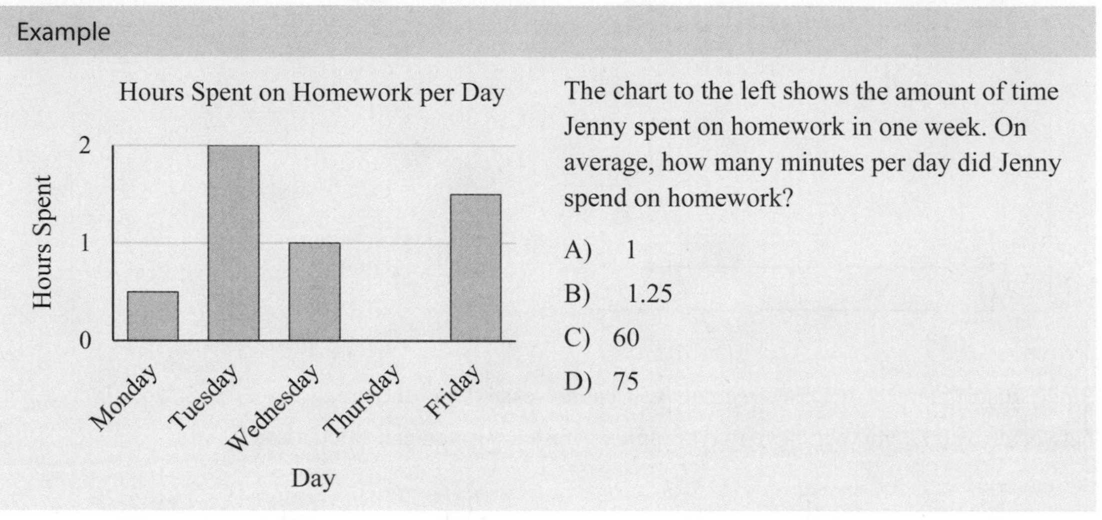

The chart to the left shows the amount of time Jenny spent on homework in one week. On average, how many minutes per day did Jenny spend on homework?

A) 1

B) 1.25

C) 60

D) 75

Notice that the units of the graph are hours, but the answer must be in minutes. First, find the average number of hours Jenny spends on homework per day. We take the average by adding together her hours for each day and then dividing by the number of days:

$$\frac{.5+2+1+0+1.5}{5}=1$$

Jenny spends an average of 1 hour per day, but you need to convert this into minutes. There are 60 minutes in 1 hour, so answer choice (C) is correct.

Check Your Answers

Before starting to work on a problem, make sure you know what the problem is asking. On problems that take multiple steps, double check that your final solution is the answer to the problem, not an intermediate step.

Watch out for answer choices that are factors, multiples, or other variations of your answer. You may have forgotten a final step or gone too far in your calculation.

Example

An isosceles triangle has a perimeter of 16. Two legs have length L and the other leg has a length of 6. What is the area of the triangle?

A) 4 B) 5 C) 6 D) 12

First, draw a diagram of the triangle:

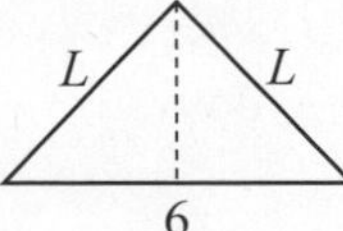

Next, find the value of L using the equation for the perimeter:

$$2L + 6 = 16$$

$$2L = 10$$

$$L = 5$$

Notice that answer choice (B) is 5, but that is *not* the answer to the question, which asks for area, not L.

To find the area, we must find the height shown by the dashed line. Notice that if we divide the triangle into two halves at the dashed line, it becomes two right triangles. We know that L, the hypotenuse, is 5, and the base of each new triangle is $6 \div 2 = 3$.

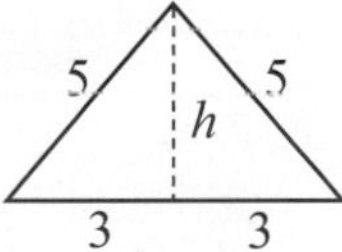

We can use the Pythagorean Theorem to find the height, which we've labelled h:

$$3^2 + h^2 = 5^2$$

$$9 + h^2 = 25$$

$$h^2 = 16$$

$$h = 4$$

Be careful—this is another intermediate solution! Now we can find the area of the original triangle using our values for base and height:

$$A = \frac{1}{2}bh$$

$$A = \frac{1}{2}(6)(4) = 12$$

(D) 12 is the correct answer.

If you have extra time at the end of a section, double-check your answers, especially for grid-in problems. Try to use a different process to find the answer to avoid making the same mistake twice. Write out your calculations when solving problems to make it easier to find your mistakes. Remember to always guess on problems that you cannot solve.

Section 3

Heart of Algebra

The **Heart of Algebra** questions on the SAT test your fundamental algebra skills. Algebra is one of the most important "languages" of math, and is something you use every day—maybe even without knowing it. Using simple letters, numbers, and signs, you can represent a vast range of situations. Let's say, for example, you went out to dinner with six friends and wanted to split your $50 bill equally among you; how much should each person pay? Using algebra you can determine that each person should pay the total cost of the meal ÷ the number of people. This can be rewritten as the amount each person should pay $50 ÷ 6 people = $8.33 per person. The language of algebra allows you to create mathematical models for real world situations.

On the new SAT, a solid understanding of algebra is very important. Out of the 58 questions on the Math Test, 19 involve the Heart of Algebra topics. In this section you will learn how to use algebra to analyze, solve, and create linear equations, inequalities, and systems of equations. In addition to developing mathematical tools, you learn how to apply these principles to real world examples from science and social science.

The concepts covered in this section are:

- Algebraic Expressions
- Linear Equations
- Inequalities
- Absolute Value
- Functions
- Interpreting Equations
- Graphing Equations and Inequalities

Algebraic Expressions

Part 1

An algebraic **expression** is a mathematical "phrase" containing numbers, variables, and operations. A **variable** stands for an unknown number, and is usually represented by a letter. Any letter—x, y, z, N, A—can be used to represent a number that is unknown. The opposite of a variable is a **constant**, which is an unchanging number in an expression.

An algebraic expression is made up of **terms**, which are variables or numbers multiplied together. When a number is right in front of a variable, it means the variable is being multiplied by that number. This number is called the **coefficient**.

$$\text{Coefficient} \longleftarrow \underbrace{\mathbf{9x}}_{\text{Term}} \longrightarrow \text{Variable}$$

When a variable does not have a written coefficient, it has a coefficient of one. For example, the term x is the same as $1x$.

Any expression with two or more terms is called a **polynomial**. An expression with one term only, like the one above, is called a **monomial**. The expression $4x + 6$ has two terms and is called a **binomial**.

Like Terms

You can simplify an algebraic expression by adding or subtracting like terms. **Like terms** have the same variable and are raised to the same power. For example, $4x$ and $6x$ are like terms. However, $3y$ and $3x$ are not like terms because they contain two different variables.

To add or subtract like terms, add or subtract their coefficients:

$$5x + 6x = 11x$$

If you have more than one term, add or subtract the like terms, and leave any remaining terms as they are.

Example

Add $(P + Q + 6)$ and $(2P - 4)$.

The two groups of like terms are P and $2P$, and 6 and –4. Add these like terms together, and leave Q as it is:

$$P + Q + 6 + 2P - 4$$

$$(P + 2P) + (6 - 4) + Q$$

$$3P + 2 + Q$$

Distributive Property

You can also simplify expressions by multiplying and dividing. To multiply or divide like terms, multiply or divide their coefficients:

$$\frac{4x}{2x} = 2$$

The distributive property can help you multiply and divide expressions with more than one term. Remember that according to the **distributive property**, multiplying a number by a sum of two other numbers in parentheses is the same as multiplying it by each number separately and then adding:

$$a(b + c) = ab + ac$$

$$6(x + 2y) = 6x + 12y$$

The distributive property also works for division. Dividing a sum of two numbers by another number is the same as dividing each number separately and then adding:

$$\frac{b + c}{a} = \frac{b}{a} + \frac{c}{a}$$

$$\frac{2x + 3y}{5} = \frac{2x}{5} + \frac{3y}{5}$$

Factoring

Factoring is the opposite of distributing. You can factor out numbers or variables from expressions. When **factoring** an expression, find the greatest common factor that all of your terms have in common. Then, work backwards to take this factor out of your expression.

Example
$5x + 5y - 10$

The greatest common factor is 5, so you can factor it out of each term in the expression. Factoring out 5 from $5x$ gives you x, 5 from $5y$ gives you y, and 5 from 10 gives you 2:

$$5x + 5y - 10 = 5(x + y - 2)$$

You can always check that you have factored correctly by distributing and checking that your answer matches the original expression.

Part 1 Practice: Algebraic Expressions

1

$$x + 3x$$

Which of the following correctly combines the like terms for the expression above?

A) $4x$

B) $3x$

C) $3x^2$

D) $x + 3x$

2

Which of the following expressions is equivalent to $17 - 6h - 23 + 2h$?

A) $40 - 4h$

B) $40 - 8h$

C) $-6 - 8h$

D) $-6 - 4h$

3

$$6x - 2y - x + 5y = P$$

Given the equation above, which of the following could be the value of P?

A) $5x + 3y$

B) $5x - 7y$

C) $7x + 3y$

D) $7x + 7y$

4

If twelve more than three times x equals y, which of the following is the expression for y?

A) $3x + 12$

B) $3x + 15$

C) $3x + 24$

D) $3x + 36$

5

Which of the following expressions is equal to $2\left(a - \frac{a}{2} + 3b\right)$?

A) $a + 3b$

B) $a + 6b$

C) $2a + 3b$

D) $2a + 6b$

Questions 6 and 7 refer to the following information.

$$4x + 16 - 2y$$

6

Which of the following is equivalent to the expression above?

A) $2(x + 4 - y)$

B) $2(2x + 4 - y)$

C) $2(2x + 8 - y)$

D) $4(x + 4 - y)$

7

If the expression is multiplied by 4, resulting in $ax + b - cy$, what is the value of $a + b - c$?

A) 64

B) 72

C) 80

D) 88

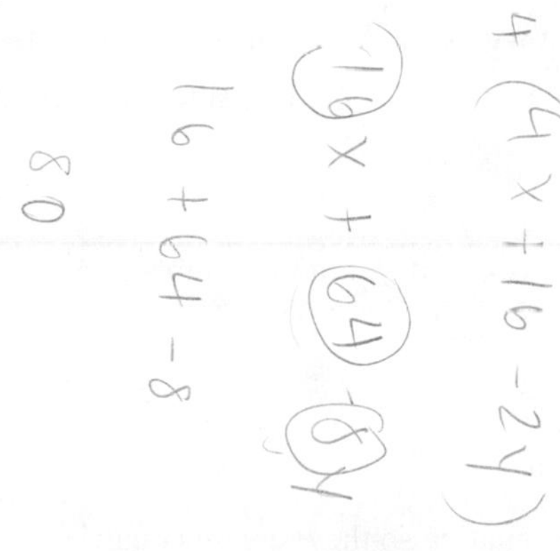

8

If $3g - 11 = 3y$, what is the value of y when g is 12?

25/3

9

$$3y - 15xy + 21x = a(y - 5xy + 7x)$$

What is the value of a in the equation above?

10

A politician estimates that her support in two districts can be approximated by the expression $3x + 12y$, where x represents the number of people, in thousands, who vote in the first district and y represents the number of people, in thousands, who vote in the second district. The politician's adviser says that two thousand people will vote in the first district, and one thousand people will vote in the second district. If this is true, what would be the greatest common factor of the estimated support in the two districts, in thousands of people?

Linear Equations
Part 2

An algebraic **equation** tells you that two expressions are equal to each other.

You can use an equation to say that $9x$ is equal to 36:

$$9x = 36$$

Often, you will be asked to solve an algebraic equation. If you are asked to "solve for x," you need to find a value for x that makes the equation true. For the equation above, you may know right away that $x = 4$ because $9 \times 4 = 36$.

Manipulating Equations

For more complicated algebraic equations, you may not be able to figure out the answer in your head. You will need to use a method to manipulate the equation and solve for the unknown variable. Your goal is always to **isolate** your variable—to get it by itself on one side of the equation. To do this, you can work backwards to "undo" all of the operations that are being performed on your variable until you can get it by itself.

There's one important rule to remember when working with equations: whatever you do to one side of the equation, you must also do to the other! If you violate this rule, the two sides of your equation will no longer be equal.

You know the equation $4 = 4$ is a true statement. However, if you add a number to one side of the equation but not to the other, the two sides are no longer equal:

$$4 + 2 \neq 4$$

You need to add the same number to both sides of the equation so they remain equal:

$$4 + 2 = 4 + 2$$

Let's see how this works with the following algebraic equation:

Example

$$3x - 2 = 13$$

On the left side of the equation, x is being multiplied by 3, and 2 is being subtracted from the product. You need to "undo" each of these operations by adding numbers to and dividing numbers from both sides of your equation. First, work with the operations that don't involve the variable. In this case, you can undo the subtraction by adding 2 to each side:

$$3x - 2 + 2 = 13 + 2$$

$$3x = 15$$

Then, undo the multiplication by dividing each side by 3:

$$\frac{3x}{3} = \frac{15}{3}$$

$$x = 5$$

What if the equation has variables on both sides? First, get all of the variables onto one side of the equation and combine like terms. Then, isolate the variable like you just did above.

Example

$$5a - 7 = 2a - 1$$

First, get all of your variables on one side of the equation by subtracting $2a$ from each side and combining like terms:

$$5a - 2a - 7 = 2a - 2a - 1$$

$$3a - 7 = -1$$

Then, undo the subtraction by adding 7 to each side:

$$3a - 7 + 7 = -1 + 7$$

$$3a = 6$$

And finally, undo the multiplication by dividing each side by 3:

$$\frac{3a}{3} = \frac{6}{3}$$

$$a = 2$$

To test if you got the right answer, you can plug this number back into the original equation:

$$5a - 7 = 2a - 1$$

$$5 \times 2 - 7 = 2 \times 2 - 1$$

$$10 - 7 = 4 - 1$$

$$3 = 3$$

More Complicated Equations

Some equations will look much more complicated than the ones above. Don't let this scare you! You will always use the same process for solving linear equations with one variable. Work carefully through each step. Get your variable on one side and then undo the operations.

Example

$$\frac{5(x+7)}{4} = \frac{100-5x}{5}$$

You can see there are a lot of operations in this equation. You need to get the variable x on one side, but you'll have to do some other operations first. First, cross-multiply and use the distributive property:

$$(5 \times 5)(x+7) = 4(100 - 5x)$$

$$25x + 175 = 400 - 20x$$

Then, undo the operations to get your variable on one side of the equation and your constant on the other side:

$$25x + 175 + 20x = 400 - 20x + 20x$$

$$45x + 175 = 400$$

$$45x + 175 - 175 = 400 - 175$$

$$45x = 225$$

Finally, divide by 45 on both sides to completely solve for x.

$$\frac{45x}{45} = \frac{225}{45}$$

$$x = 5$$

Equations with Two Variables

Sometimes you will see an equation that has two different variables in it, such as $y = 2x + 6$. You will not be able to find an exact number for x or y without more information, as we will see in Part 5. However, you can solve for one variable *in terms of* the other. This means that your answer will still contain a variable.

To solve for one variable in terms of the other, use the same steps as for single-variable equations and treat the second variable as if it were a number. For the equation above, let's solve for x in terms of y.

Because you're solving for x, you need to get x by itself. Start by subtracting 6 from both sides, and then divide by 2:

$$y = 2x + 6$$

$$y - 6 = 2x + 6 - 6$$

$$\frac{y-6}{2} = \frac{2x}{2}$$

$$\frac{y-6}{2} = x$$

$\frac{y-6}{2}$ is how you would represent x in terms of y.

You may also be asked to use an equation to solve for another algebraic expression.

Example

If $6x + 2y = 24$, what is the value of $3x + y$?

At first it might seem like you cannot find the answer without solving for x and y individually. Luckily, there is another way. We are looking for $3x + y$, not x or y alone. Look closely at the left side of the equation. You may notice that $6x + 2y$ divided by 2 gives you $3x + y$—the exact expression we are looking for! Therefore, divide both sides of the equation by 2:

$$\frac{6x}{2} + \frac{2y}{2} = \frac{24}{2}$$

$$3x + y = 12$$

$3x + y$ is equal to 12.

Part 2 Practice: Linear Equations

1

If $a + 20 = 5$, what is the value of a?

A) –25

B) –15

C) –4

D) 25

2

If $2x + 8 = 14$, what is the value of x?

A) –3

B) 1

C) 3

D) 6

3

$$2(x + 3) = y + 6$$

Given the expression above, which of the following expresses x in terms of y?

A) $\frac{y}{2}$

B) y

C) $2y$

D) $3y$

4

If 1 divided by $3x$ is equal to 4 divided by $7y$, which of the following expresses x in terms of y?

A) $\frac{7y}{12}$

B) $\frac{12y}{7}$

C) $7y$

D) $12y$

5

If $y = \frac{2(x+10)}{3}$, which of the following represents $2x$ in terms of y?

A) $\frac{3y}{2} - 10$

B) $\frac{3y}{2} - 5$

C) $3y - 10$

D) $3y - 20$

Questions 6 and 7 refer to the following information.

The number of cows, c, and the number of ducks, d, a farmer has in his 4 acres of land is represented by the equation $\frac{2c}{3} + \frac{4d}{12} = 4$.

6

Given the equation above, what is $6c$ in terms of d?

A) $2d$

B) $36 - 3d$

C) $3d$

D) $48 - 4d$

7

If there are 6 ducks, how many cows does the farmer have?

A) 2

B) 3

C) 4

D) 5

8

If $3x - 5 = 7$, what is the value of x?

9

Charles' Law defines the relationship between the volume of a confined gas, V, and its temperature, T. When the temperature changes to a different temperature, D, the volume of the gas also changes to another volume, A. These relationships are defined as $\frac{V}{T} = \frac{A}{D}$. To start, V is 3 and the temperature is 2. If the temperature, T, is increased by 3, what will be the value of the new volume, A?

10

If $5j + z = 3$ is equal to $2z = a - bj$, what is $a + b$?

Inequalities

Part 3

An **inequality** is a mathematical statement comparing two quantities that are not the same. Inequalities can be represented with these symbols:

Inequality Symbols	
Symbol	Meaning
$>$	greater than
$<$	less than
$\geq$	greater than or equal to
$\leq$	less than or equal to

An algebraic inequality states that a certain algebraic expression is greater than or less than another quantity. For example, $x < 3$ means "an unknown quantity, x, is less than 3." There are many possible solutions for this inequality. The variable x may equal 1, 2, 0.5, –4, –6, 0, or any other number that is less than three.

To solve a more complex inequality, treat it like an equation—manipulate the inequality to isolate your variable. You'll end up with a range of solutions that can satisfy the inequality.

Example

$$4x \geq 24$$

Isolate your variable by dividing both sides by 4:

$$\frac{4x}{4} \geq \frac{24}{4}$$

$$x \geq 6$$

If $4x$ is greater than or equal to 24, then x can be any value greater than or equal to 6.

Rules for Inequalities

Just as with an equation, you can add or subtract the same number from both sides of an inequality and the inequality will be **preserved** (the inequality symbol will stay the same).

Example

$$x + 3 > 7$$

To solve, subtract 3 from both sides of the inequality:

$$x + 3 - 3 > 7 - 3$$

$$x > 4$$

You have to be more careful when multiplying or dividing. Multiplying or dividing both sides of an inequality by a positive number preserves the inequality, but multiplying or dividing by a negative number *reverses* the inequality. When you multiply or divide by a negative number, you have to flip the sign. Consider the true inequality $7 > 2$. You can multiply both sides of this inequality by a positive number, and the inequality is still true:

$$7 \times 4 > 2 \times 4$$

$$28 > 8$$

However, if you multiply both sides by a negative number, you get a false result:

$$7 \times (-4) > 2 \times (-4)$$

$$-28 > -8$$

Wrong!

Therefore, you need to reverse the inequality when multiplying or dividing by a negative number:

$$7 \times (-4) < 2 \times (-4)$$

$$-28 < -8$$

Let's try a more complex example:

Example

$$-4x + 1 > 3$$

First, undo the addition by subtracting 1 from both sides:

$$-4x + 1 - 1 > 3 - 1$$

$$-4x > 2$$

Then, undo the multiplication by dividing both sides by –4. Remember to reverse the inequality sign because you are dividing by a negative number!

$$\frac{-4x}{-4} < \frac{2}{-4}$$

$$x < -\frac{1}{2}$$

Now you know x can be any number less than $-\frac{1}{2}$. You can check your solution by picking a possible value for x and plugging it back into the original inequality. Let's try –1:

$$-4x + 1 > 3$$

$$(-4 \times (-1)) + 1 > 3$$

$$4 + 1 > 3$$

$$5 > 3$$

Because 5 is greater than 3, you know your solution was correct.

Inequalities on a Number Line

Algebraic inequalities are sometimes shown using lines, line segments, and circles on a number line. A shaded line segment represents all of the possible solutions for the inequality. Circles show whether numbers at the end of a line segment are part of the solution set. If a circle is shaded in completely, it means the number is included in the solution set: it is a possible solution for the inequality. If a circle is unshaded, it means the number is excluded from the solution set: it is not a possible solution for the inequality.

For example, the number line below shows the possible solutions for $x > 1$:

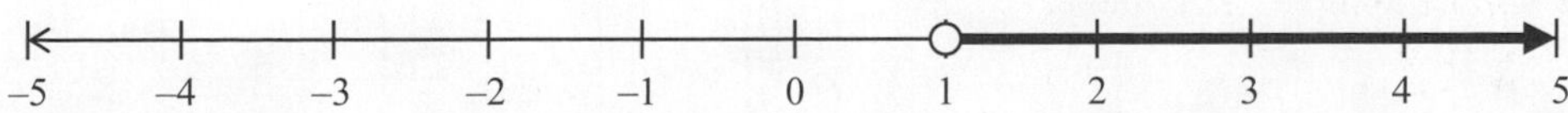

All numbers greater than 1 are possible solutions for this inequality, so a shaded line extends to the right of 1. The number 1 is not a possible solution for this inequality, so there is an unshaded circle over the number 1.

Example

What inequality is represented by the number line below?

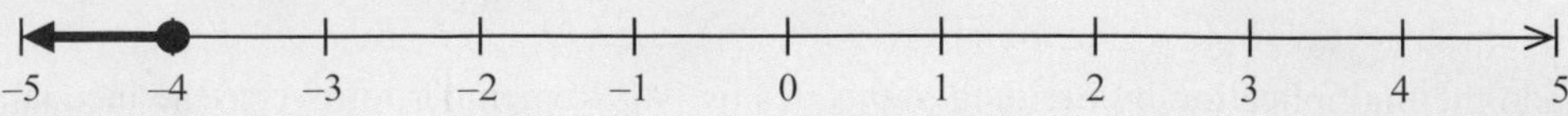

The shaded line segment to the left of –4 means that all numbers less than –4 are possible solutions for this inequality. The shaded circle over –4 means that –4 is a possible solution for this inequality. The inequality would therefore be written as:

$$x \leq -4$$

Inequalities with Two Variables

Sometimes you will see an inequality that has two different variables in it, such as $y < -4x - 5$. Just like you saw with equations in Part 2, you will not be able to find an exact number for x or y without more information. You can, however, solve for x in terms of y. Follow the same steps as you did for equations, but remember to be careful of the inequality sign.

For the inequality above, let's see how you would solve for x in terms of y. Start by adding 5 to both sides, then divide by –4 and reverse the inequality sign.

$$y < -4x - 5$$

$$y + 5 < -4x - 5 + 5$$

$$\frac{y+5}{-4} > \frac{-4x}{-4}$$

$$\frac{y+5}{-4} > x$$

Part 3 Practice: Inequalities

1

The inequality $-x > y$ is divided by negative one on both sides. Which of the following represents the correct result of this division?

A) There is no change in the original inequality.

B) $x > -y$

C) $-x < y$

D) $x < -y$

Questions 2 and 3 refer to the following information.

A geologist decides to use number line charts to determine whether a rock is the appropriate weight for his study, as shown below. He measures the rocks he excavates against a rock that has worked before in testing. The numbers on his line represent weight difference, in ounces, between his sample rock and his excavated rocks.

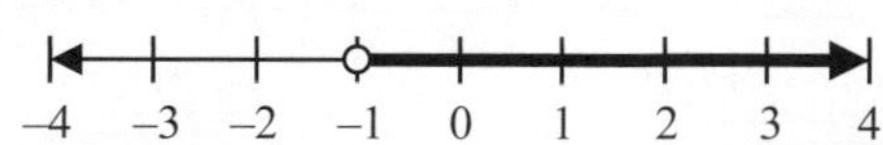

2

If the weight difference between the geologist's sample rock and an excavated rock is represented by w, which of the following represents his number line?

A) $w > -1$

B) $w \geq -1$

C) $w < -1$

D) $w \leq -1$

3

After further testing, the geologist determines that his initial number line is not correct. He sketches a number line, shown below, to reflect his new results.

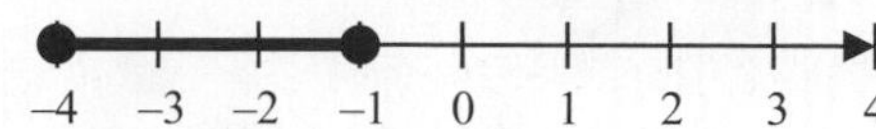

Which of the following expresses w in relation to this new inequality?

A) $-4 > w > -1$

B) $-4 \geq w \geq -1$

C) $-4 < w < -1$

D) $-4 \leq w \leq -1$

4

Jonas must score at least 79 on his next physics exam out of a maximum 100 points in order to pass his class. Which of the following inequalities models all the possible scores, x, that he could receive in order to pass the class?

A) $79 < x < 100$

B) $79 \leq x < 100$

C) $79 < x \leq 100$

D) $79 \leq x \leq 100$

5

If $23 \leq 7x + 2 \leq 37$, what is one possible value for x?

A) 2

B) 4

C) 6

D) 8

Questions 6 and 7 refer to the following information.

A sandwich shop sells all its subs, s, for \$15 each and its drinks, d, for \$3 each. The first customer of the day, Bonnie, has a budget of \$45 to purchase drinks and subs at the shop.

6

Which of the following inequalities represents the number of drinks that Bonnie can purchase, in terms of the number of subs that she can purchase?

A) $d \geq 5s - 15$

B) $d \leq 5s + 15$

C) $d \geq -5s + 15$

D) $d \leq -5s + 15$

7

If she buys 2 subs, what is the maximum number of drinks she can purchase without spending more than \$45?

A) 0

B) 3

C) 5

D) 9

8

If Larissa's GPA is somewhere between 3.8 and 3.9, what is one possible value for her GPA?

9

If $3x - 7 \geq x + 1$, what is one possible value of x?

10

$-2a + 10 > 4b$, and a is an integer. What is the maximum value of a if b is 1?

Absolute Value

Part 4

The **absolute value** of a number is its distance away from zero on a number line. To represent the absolute value of a quantity, you write two vertical bars around the quantity.

$|-5|$ represents the absolute value of –5, or the distance between –5 and zero on a number line. –5 is 5 units away from zero, so its absolute value is 5:

$$|-5| = 5$$

The absolute value of any number or expression will always be a positive number or zero.

Example

What is $|4-7|$?

This question is asking you to find the absolute value of the expression 4 – 7. First, you need to solve for the quantity within the absolute value bars:

$$|4-7| = |-3|$$

Now, you need to find the absolute value of –3. –3 is 3 units away from zero, so its absolute value is 3:

$$|-3| = 3$$

Equations with Absolute Value

On the SAT, you may need to solve an absolute value equation using algebra. Here is an important rule to remember:

If $|x| = a$, then $x = a$ or $x = -a$.

Example

If $|x| = 4$, then what values are possible for x?

This question is asking you to find any values of x that have an absolute value of 4. You know that 4 is a possible value. However, the value –4 is also possible. Think about it: both of these numbers are 4 units away from zero on the number line. Therefore, they both have an absolute value of 4.

$$\text{If } |x| = 4, \text{ then } |x| = 4 \text{ or } x = -4.$$

Example

If $|x - 5| = 4$, what are the possible values for x?

You know that both 4 and –4 have an absolute value of 4. Therefore, the quantity $x - 5$ could either be equal to 4 or –4. You can set up two equations and solve each separately to find the two possible values of x:

$x - 5 = 4$	$x - 5 = -4$
$x = 9$	$x = 1$

You have two solutions: $x = 1$ or $x = 9$.

Absolute Value Inequalities

You may also need to solve an absolute value inequality on the SAT. Here are two rules for absolute value inequalities:

$$\text{If } |x| < a, \text{ then } -a < x < a.$$

$$\text{If } |x| > a, \text{ then } x < -a \text{ or } x > a.$$

Example

If $|x| \le 3$, then what values are possible for x?

The inequality tells you that the distance between x and 0 is less than or equal to 3. All numbers between –3 and 3, including –3 and 3, have a distance from zero that is 3 units or less. If you were to graph the range of solutions for this inequality on a number line, it would look like this:

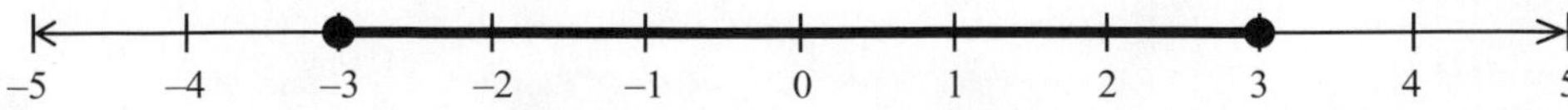

Therefore:

$$\text{If } |x| \le 3, \text{ then } -3 \le x \le 3.$$

You can always check your answer by making sure that a value from your solution set makes the original inequality true. For example, –2 is a value from your solution set. Is $|-2| \leq 3$? The absolute value of –2 is 2, and 2 is certainly less than 3.

$$|-2| \leq 3$$

$$2 \leq 3$$

Example

What values for x satisfy the inequality $|x-2|+1>3$?

First, you need to get the absolute value by itself. To do that, subtract 1 from each side:

$$|x-2|+1-1>3-1$$

$$|x-2|>2$$

You know that all quantities less than –2 and greater than 2 have an absolute value greater than 2. Remember, when using the "greater than" sign to solve for an absolute value inequality, you need to set up two inequalities and solve:

$$x-2>2 \qquad\qquad x-2<-2$$

$$x>4 \qquad\qquad x<0$$

The values of x that satisfy the inequality $|x-2|>2$ are any values greater than 4 or less than 0. In other words, they are any values more than 2 units away from 2 on the number line.

Part 4 Practice: Absolute Value

1

Which of the following is equal to $|-3|$?

A) –9

B) –3

C) 3

D) 9

2

Which of the following is the absolute value of a number x that is 7 less than 2?

A) –9

B) –5

C) 5

D) 9

3

$$-|a-5|=-2$$

Based on the equation above, what is one possible value of a?

A) -3

B) -7

C) 3

D) There are no solutions.

4

$$\left|\frac{5a}{3}\right| = 10$$

Which of the following provides all possible values of a in the equation above?

A) 2

B) 6

C) 2 and -6

D) 6 and -6

5

If $-|b-3|<-5$, which of the following is true about b?

A) $b<-2, b>8$

B) $-2<b<8$

C) $b<-8, b>2$

D) $-8<b<2$

Questions 6 and 7 refer to the following information.

Camille's AP English class is scheduled to start at 10:00 A.M. Because there is another class directly before, the earliest she can enter is at 9:50 A.M.

6

If Camille's teacher marks all students who arrive after 10:10 A.M. as late, which of the following inequalities models the time in hours, t, that Camille can enter the class *and* be considered on time?

A) $|t-10| \leq \frac{1}{6}$

B) $|t-10| \leq \frac{1}{3}$

C) $|t-10| \leq 10$

D) $|t-10| \leq 20$

7

If Camille arrives at 10:15 A.M., by how many hours is she late?

A) $\frac{1}{12}$

B) $\frac{1}{6}$

C) 5

D) $\frac{5}{12}$

8

The average helicopter is 12.5 m long. If a Tyrannosaurus is thought to have been about 15.2 m long, what is the absolute value of the difference between the lengths of a helicopter and a Tyrannosaurus?

9

$$|b-9| \leq 0.2$$

A construction company produces cold-drawn steel bars that must be 9 inches in length with a tolerance of 0.2 inches as shown above. What is one possible length for one of their steel bars, *b*, that conforms with the requirements?

10

$$\frac{|7a-2|}{3}+5=9$$

In the equation above, what is the positive solution for the value of *a*?

Systems of Equations and Inequalities

Part 5

A **system of equations** is a group of equations that share like terms. On the SAT, you may see systems of two equations. Even though you now have to deal with two equations instead of one, systems of equations help simplify more complicated problems and are actually very useful! If you have two equations and two variables, you can use both equations to find the value of x and y.

Example

$$x + y = 3$$

$$2x - y = 12$$

You can use two methods to solve this system of equations: substitution and elimination.

Substitution

The **substitution method** allows you to solve for one variable at a time by substituting an equivalent equation for one variable. First, choose a variable to isolate in either equation. Let's try isolating y in the first equation. To isolate y, subtract x from both sides of the equation:

$$x + y - x = 3 - x$$

$$y = 3 - x$$

You now know that y is equal to the value of $3 - x$. Now, substitute this value into the second equation by writing $3 - x$ instead of y:

$$2x - y = 12$$

$$2x - (3 - x) = 12$$

Now you have a single equation with only one variable, so you can solve this equation for x:

$$2x - (3 - x) = 12$$

$$3x - 3 = 12$$

$$3x = 15$$

$$x = 5$$

Now that you know that $x = 5$, you can plug this value of x into either of the original two equations to solve for y. Let's plug this into the first equation:

$$x + y = 3$$

$$5 + y = 3$$

$$y = -2$$

You've found that $x = 5$ and $y = -2$. You can check that you've solved this system of equations correctly by plugging these values back into the original two equations and verifying that they are true:

$$5 + (-2) = 3$$

$$2 \times 5 - (-2) = 12$$

Elimination

You can also solve this system of equations using the elimination method. The **elimination method** allows you to cancel variables by adding or subtracting the two equations. In the example above, if you add the two equations together, the y's will cancel each other out:

$$\begin{array}{r} x + y = 3 \\ +\ 2x - y = 12 \\ \hline 3x \quad\ \ = 15 \end{array}$$

You now have one single equation in which you can solve for x:

$$3x = 15$$

$$x = 5$$

Then, you can plug this value for x back into one of the two original equations to solve for y, following the same steps you used above.

$$x + y = 3$$

$$5 + y = 3$$

$$y = -2$$

How do you know when to use substitution and when to use elimination? If one of the equations involves variables without coefficients (like $x + y = 3$) or could be easily simplified by dividing (like $2x + 2y = 8$), then substitution may be easier. However, some systems of equations are more effectively solved using elimination, even if they don't look like it at first. You may have to transform equations in order to use elimination.

Transforming Equations

Some systems of equations don't seem like they can be solved using elimination at first.

Example

$$6x + 3y = 18$$

$$2x + 5y = 14$$

You can transform one of the equations so that you can use elimination to solve the equations. To **transform** an equation, you multiply or divide both sides of the equation by the same number. Since you want to be able to eliminate one variable, you should choose a number that will change your equation so that it can be easily added to or subtracted from the other equation.

In the example above, you can transform the second equation by multiplying both sides by 3. Why? Because multiplying the equation by 3 gives you $6x + 15y = 42$. You can now use subtraction to eliminate the $6x$'s.

$$\begin{array}{r} 6x + 3y = 18 \\ -\ (6x + 15y = 42) \\ \hline -12y = -24 \end{array}$$

$$\frac{-12y}{-12} = \frac{-24}{-12}$$

$$y = 2$$

Now plug y into one of the original equations to solve for x:

$$6x + 3(2) = 18$$

$$6x + 6 = 18$$

$$6x = 12$$

$$x = 2$$

Systems of Inequalities

On the SAT, you may also see **systems of inequalities**. You may be asked to solve for values of x that satisfy both inequalities.

Example

$$7x \geq 21$$

$$2x < 10$$

In order to find the values of x that would satisfy both inequalities, you need to solve each inequality, determine if there is any overlap, and create a range of possible values. For the example above, first solve each inequality individually:

$$\frac{7x}{7} \geq \frac{21}{7} \qquad\qquad \frac{2x}{2} < \frac{10}{2}$$

$$x \geq 3 \qquad\qquad x < 5$$

In order for a value of x to satisfy both inequalities, x must be greater than or equal to 3, but also less than 5. Therefore, you can write a range of values that represents the possible solutions to both inequalities:

$$3 \leq x < 5$$

You can check your answer by plugging in a value of x from your solution set into both equations. Let's try 4:

$$7(4) \geq 21 \qquad\qquad 2(4) < 10$$

$$28 \geq 21 \qquad\qquad 8 < 10$$

Part 5 Practice: Systems of Equations and Inequalities

1

$$5x = 5$$
$$x + y = 5$$

In the system of equations above, what are the values of x and y?

A) $x = 1, y = -4$
B) $x = 1, y = 4$
C) $x = 1, y = 6$
D) $x = 1, y = -6$

2

$$2m = 3$$
$$4m + n = y$$

Given the system of equations above, which of the following is equal to y?

A) $3n$
B) $6n$
C) $6 + n$
D) $6 + 3n$

3

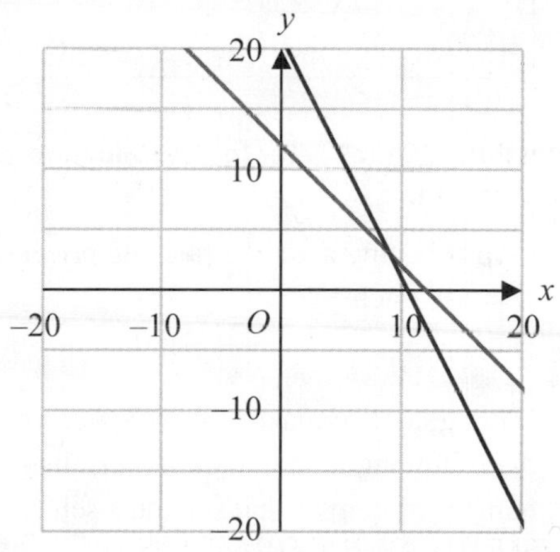

The graphs of $2x + y = 21$ and $3x + 3y = 36$ are shown above. Which of the following are the values for the point (x, y) where the two lines intersect?

A) $(-9, 3)$
B) $(-9, -3)$
C) $(9, 3)$
D) $(3, 9)$

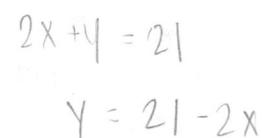

4

Bullets travel at least ten times the speed of an average arrow. If the fastest bullet travels at 4,100 ft/s and the average arrow travels at 250 ft/s, which of the following systems of inequalities expresses all possible values of a bullet's speed, x?

A) $2500 < x \leq 4100$

B) $2500 < x \leq 4100$

C) $2500 \leq x < 4100$

D) $2500 < x < 4100$

5

$$x - 4 > 8$$
$$3x \leq 39$$

In the system of inequalities above, which of the following models all the possible values of x?

A) $12 \leq x \leq 13$

B) $12 \leq x < 13$

C) $12 < x \leq 13$

D) $12 < x < 13$

Questions 6 and 7 refer to the following information.

Victoria is having a garage sale and prices all items at $15 each.

6

If her goal is to make at least $800, which of the following inequalities models the number of items x that she must sell?

A) $60 \leq x$

B) $800 \leq 15x$

C) $60 \leq x \leq 800$

D) $800 \leq 15 + x$

7

What is the minimum number of items Victoria must sell in order to achieve her goal?

A) 52

B) 53

C) 54

D) 55

8

If $5p - 2q = 16$ and $4p + q = 5$, what is the value of $p - q$?

9

$$4x - 13 > 7$$
$$2x + 4 \geq 4x - 8$$

Given the system of inequalities above, what is one possible value of x that satisfies the relationship?

10

A pet store sells its puppies for $400 each and adult dogs for $300 each. If the store collected $5000 from a total of 15 puppies and adult dogs last month, how many adult dogs did the pet store sell?

Linear Functions

Part 6

A **function** is a relationship between inputs and outputs. A function shows how an "input" value is transformed into an "output" value. The input, x, will produce an output, $f(x)$, according to the rules of the function. The notation $f(x)$ is read as "f of x." Functions are most often referred to by f, but you may also see other letters such as g, h, or A. You can think about a function like a recipe for a cake: the inputs are your flour, egg, sugar, and butter, the "rules" of the function are your recipe, and your output, $f(x)$, is the cake itself.

Function Notation

The notation $f(x)$ is another way of representing the y-value in a function. For example, $f(x) = 2x - 3$ is the same thing as $y = 2x - 3$.

The function $f(x) = 2x - 3$ means that for any input x, the function assigns it the output $2x - 3$. Therefore:

$$f(2) = 2(2) - 3$$

$$f(2) = 1$$

This is how you **evaluate** a function—just replace the variable in the function with the given input value and solve. What if $x = a + b$?

$$f(a + b) = 2(a + b) - 3$$

$$f(a + b) = 2a + 2b - 3$$

The chart below represents the value of the input, x, and output, $f(x)$, for the function $f(x) = 2x - 3$. You can see how the function acts as a rule for what happens to the input to generate the output. You multiply each input by 2 and then subtract 3.

$f(x)$	–1	1	3	5
x	1	2	3	4

The following graph also represents $f(x) = 2x - 3$. Because the graph is a line, we call this a linear function. We will talk about how to graph linear functions in Part 8, but you can use this graph to visualize what the function means. You can see that when the input (x) is at 2, the output (y) is at 1—just like we found when we were evaluating the function.

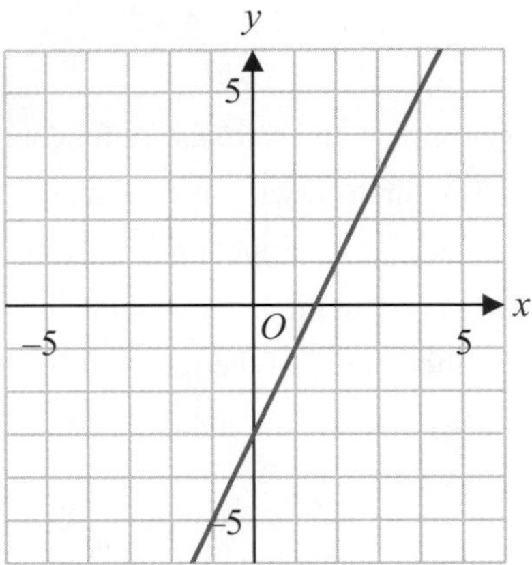

Domain and Range

Every linear function has a domain and range. The **domain** is the set of all values for which the function generates an output. The **range** is the set of all values that could be the output of the function.

Domain $\longrightarrow$ Function $\longrightarrow$ Range

Often, the domain of a linear function is "all real numbers." This is because most linear equations can use any input and still be defined. For example, in the function $f(x) = -2x - 3$, you'll get an output for any real number that you plug in for x. The exception is a function that produces a vertical line, which only has one possible x value.

The range of a linear function is also typically "all real numbers." Most lines can extend infinitely in both directions, so there are no limits to the range of y values that can be generated. The exception is a function that produces a horizontal line, which only has one possible y value.

Combining Functions

On the SAT, you might see functions combined through a notation like $f(g(x))$. This notation means that you need to take the output of $g(x)$, and use it as the input of $f(x)$. You would read this as "f of g of x."

Example

If $f(x) = 3x - 4$ and $g(x) = 8x$, what is the value of $f\left(g\left(\frac{1}{2}\right)\right)$?

Start by working from the inside out. First, find $g\left(\frac{1}{2}\right)$. Then, use that answer and plug it into $f(x)$:

$$g\left(\frac{1}{2}\right) = 8\left(\frac{1}{2}\right) = 4$$

$$f(4) = 3(4) - 4 = 8$$

There are many other things to learn about functions, such as how to graph and transform them. We will cover these topics in Part 8.

Part 6 Practice: Linear Functions

1

$f(x)$	x
3	1
5	2
9	4
13	6
?	34

The table above shows a linear function of $f(x)$. Which of the following is the value of $f(x)$ when x is 34?

A) 35

B) 47

C) 59

D) 69

2

If $h(x) = 5x + 3$, what is $h(x + 2)$?

A) $5x + 5$

B) $5x + 6$

C) $5x + 13$

D) 18

3

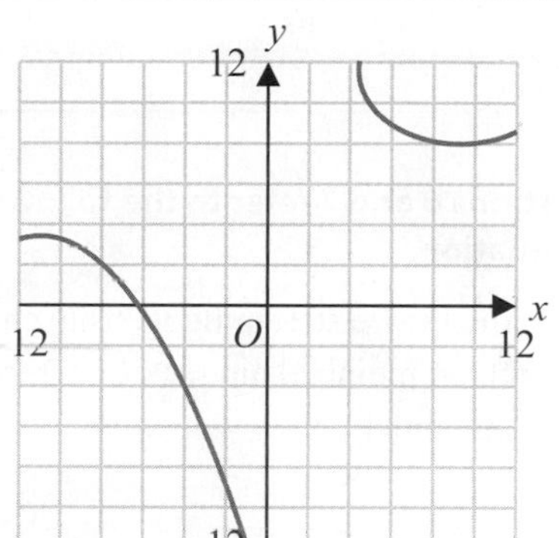

If the figure above shows the graph of $g(x)$, what is the value of $g(10)$?

A) 5

B) 8

C) –8

D) 10

4

$$f(x) = 3x - 2$$

Which of the following is the domain of $f(x)$ above?

A) All real numbers

B) All positive integers

C) All negative integers

D) No solution

5

$$m(v) = 3v$$

The momentum of a 3 kg object is provided by the function above, where v is the velocity in meters per second at which the object travels. If the object is traveling at a constant velocity of 5.5 m/s, which of the following is the value of the object's momentum?

A) 14.0 kg · m/s

B) 14.5 kg · m/s

C) 15.0 kg · m/s

D) 16.5 kg · m/s

Questions 6 and 7 refer to the following information.

An online movie streaming website charges a one-time $5 membership fee and $2 for every movie streamed.

6

If Leah rents x number of movies, which of the following functions models the total cost she will be charged?

A) $f(x) = 10x$

B) $f(x) = 2x$

C) $f(x) = 2x + 5$

D) $f(x) = 2x + 10$

7

If Leah joins the website in October and her budget for the month is $24, what is the maximum number of movies she can rent?

A) 9

B) 10

C) 11

D) 12

8

If $g(x) = | x - 3 | - 2$, what is $g(-2)$?

9

$$g(x) = 5x$$
$$h(x) = x - 5$$

Given $g(x)$ and $h(x)$ above, what is the value of $g(h(5))$?

10

A jeweler can cut x gems into $f(x) = \frac{x}{2} + 10$ usable pieces and creates $g(x) = \frac{2x}{5} + 4$ pieces of jewelry from those pieces. If the jeweler has 10 gems, how many pieces of jewelry can he make?

Interpreting Equations

Part 7

In the previous parts of this section, you learned how to work with the "vocabulary" of the language of algebra. For example, you learned how to solve linear equations and inequalities and perform operations on functions. Now, you need to learn how to interpret the vocabulary and create your own "sentences" with linear equations. In this part, we will discuss what the different parts of linear equations mean and how to use them in word problems.

Variables and Constants

In Part 1, you learned that both variables and constants represent values in algebraic expressions. The difference is that constants represent values that can't change, while variables represent values that can change.

Example

Jeannie's phone company charges her a flat rate of $40 per month plus $8 per 500 MB of data usage. If Jeannie uses 3.5 GB of data in January, how much will her phone company charge her for that month?

You can use an equation to solve this problem. Jeannie is charged $40 per month—this is a flat rate, so it is unchanging. She is also charged an unchanging rate of $8 per 500 MB of data. Therefore, $40 and $8 are constants. What will determine how much Jeannie's phone company charges her? How much data she uses. That is a variable, which you could decide to call *d*. You are looking for her total monthly charge, which you could call *c*. Using these variables, you could write the equation:

$$c = 8d + 40$$

This means that Jeannie's monthly phone bill is found by multiplying her total data usage by $8 and adding $40. Jeannie uses 3.5 GB, or 3500 MB, of data in January, so you can plug in $\frac{3500}{500} = 7$ for d:

$$c = 8 \times 7 + 40 = 96$$

Jeannie's phone company will charge her $96 for the month of January.

Translating from Words to Math

As you've seen in the examples above, to solve any word problem on the SAT, all you have to do is "translate" the words in the problem into letters and operations. Here is a chart you can use to translate between words and math:

Words	Meaning
Is, was, will be, has	Equals (=)
More, older, total, increased by, exceeds, gained, further, greater, sum	Addition (+)
Fewer, younger, less, decreased by, gave away, lost, difference	Subtraction (−)
Of, each, product	Multiplication (×)
For, per, out of, quotient	Division (÷)
At least	Greater than or equal to (≥)
At most	Less than or equal to (≤)
What, how many	Variable (*x*, *y*, etc.)

Example

The sum of Jake's and Amy's ages is 17. If A is Amy's current age, which expression represents Jake's age in 3 years, in terms of A?

The question tells you that A stands for Amy's current age. If you let J stand for Jake's current age, then you can use addition to represent the total of their ages right now:

$$J + A = 17$$

Then, you can isolate J to find an expression for Jake's age right now:

$$J + A = 17$$
$$J = 17 - A$$

However, the question isn't asking you for Jake's age right now—you need to find his age 3 years from now. Translating into math, you need to find the value of $J + 3$. To do this, add 3 to both sides of your equation:

$$J = 17 - A$$
$$J + 3 = 17 - A + 3$$
$$J + 3 = 20 - A$$

The expression $20 - A$ represents Jake's age three years from now.

Interpreting Absolute Value

You may also need to translate a word problem into an absolute value equation.

> **Example**
>
> A candle factory has machines that cut wax into candles. Each candle is supposed to be 6 inches long. If a candle differs from this length by more than 0.25 inches, it will be rejected. What absolute value inequality represents the lengths of the products that will be rejected?

Candles will be rejected if they are 0.25 inches greater or less than the target of 6 inches. This means any candles greater than 6.25 inches or less than 5.75 inches will be rejected. You can use an absolute value inequality to represent all values that are more than 0.25 units away from 6 on a number line:

$$|x-6| > 0.25$$

The absolute value sign works here because it allows you to take into account candles that are greater than the target size and also those less than the target size. The amount that candles can differ from the target size is on the right side. The absolute value expression on the left represents the difference between the size of any candle and the target size.

To check that your inequality is correct, solve for x using the rules you learned in Part 5:

$$x-6 > 0.25 \qquad\qquad x-6 < -0.25$$

$$x > 6.25 \qquad\qquad x < 5.75$$

Your inequality generated all values greater than 6.25 and less than 5.75. You know that these are the lengths of candles that will be rejected, so your inequality is correct.

Creating a System of Equations

Some word problems will require you to create a system of equations.

> **Example**
>
> In a school cafeteria, students can either buy sandwiches or salads for lunch. Sandwiches cost \$5.50 and salads cost \$5.00. On one day, a total of 557 lunches were served for a total of \$3036. Which set of equations could be used to solve for the number of sandwiches, x, and the number of salads, y, served that day?

The question tells you that the total number of lunches served was 557, so the sum of sandwiches, x, and salads, y, must be 557:

$$x + y = 557$$

You also know that the total cost was \$3036. Sandwiches cost \$5.50, so the cost of all the sandwiches would be \$5.50 multiplied by the number of sandwiches purchased (\$5.50x). Similarly, the cost of all the salads would be \$5.00 multiplied by the number of salads purchased (\$5.00y). The total cost is the sum of the sandwich cost and the salad cost:

$$5.50x + 5y = 3036$$

You have now found a system of equations that would allow you to solve for x and y:

$$x + y = 557$$

$$5.50x + 5y = 3036$$

Part 7 Practice: Interpreting Equations

1

Wendy has \$10 and receives an additional \$10 per week for her allowance. If she doesn't spend any of her money, which of the following equations expresses the total amount m she will have saved up at the end of w weeks?

A) $m = 10w$

B) $m = 10 + 10w$

C) $m = 100w$

D) $10m = 10w$

2

If Joy sells c number of cupcakes for \$5 each, which of the following expresses the total revenue?

A) $5c$

B) $\frac{5}{c}$

C) $\frac{c}{5}$

D) $c + 5$

3

When 6 is subtracted from four times a number L, the result is 26. Which of the following equations represents the relationship?

A) $6 - 4L = 26$

B) $4L - 6 = 26$

C) $(4 - 6)L = 26$

D) $(6 - 4)L = 26$

4

The height of the players on High Ridge Elementary School's basketball team is shown below. Based on the table, which of the following inequalities represents all possible values for height h of the students?

Height (in meters)

1.65	1.69	1.58
1.48	1.40	1.63
1.78	1.73	1.8

A) $|1.6 - h| \leq 0.2$

B) $|1.6 + h| \leq 0.2$

C) $|1.6 - h| \geq 0.2$

D) $|1.6 + h| \geq 0.2$

5

If a certain medication is exposed to a temperature less than 55°F or greater than 85°F, it must be discarded. Which of the following inequalities models all temperatures x at which the medication does NOT need to be discarded?

A) $|70 - x| \leq 15$

B) $|70 + x| \leq 15$

C) $|70 - x| \geq 15$

D) $|70 + x| \geq 15$

Questions 6 and 7 refer to the following information.

Adult tickets for an event are \$10 each and student tickets are \$8 each. The ticket office has sold 77 tickets totaling \$686.

6

Which of the following systems of equations can be used to find the number of adult tickets, a, and student tickets, s, sold?

A) $10a + 8s = 686$
$a + s = 77$

B) $10a + 8s = 77$
$a + s = 686$

C) $18as = 686$
$as = 77$

D) $18as = 77$
$as = 686$

7

Which of the following is the value of a?

A) 25

B) 32

C) 35

D) 42

8

If Irene runs two miles every morning, how many days would it take for her to run 26 miles?

9

If Jessica triples a number and divides the result by 2 to get 9, what is her original number?

10

There is a total of 15 cows and chickens on a farm. If the total number of legs for these animals equals 42, how many cows are on the farm?

Graphing Equations

Part 8

In the previous parts of this section, you learned how to solve equations, inequalities, absolute values, and systems of equations algebraically. While knowing how to solve these types of problems algebraically is essential, you also need to know how to solve them graphically on the SAT Math Test.

Graphing Linear Equations

Linear equations can be graphed as lines on a coordinate plane. Some equations represent horizontal or vertical lines.

- The equation of a **horizontal line** is $y = b$, where b represents the point where the line crosses the y-axis.
- The equation of a **vertical line** is $x = a$, where a represents the point where the line crosses the x-axis.

$y = 3$

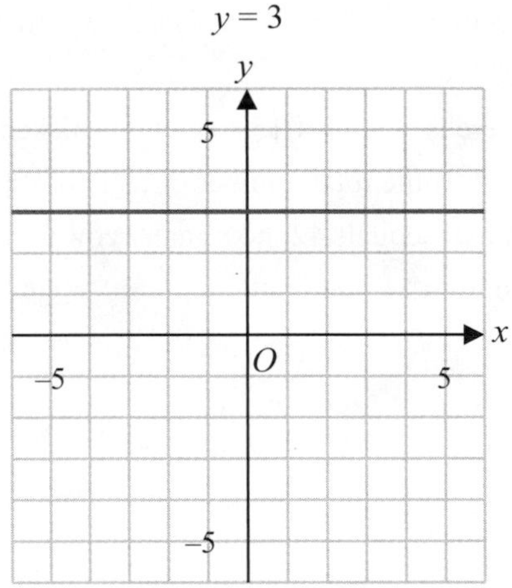

$x = 4$

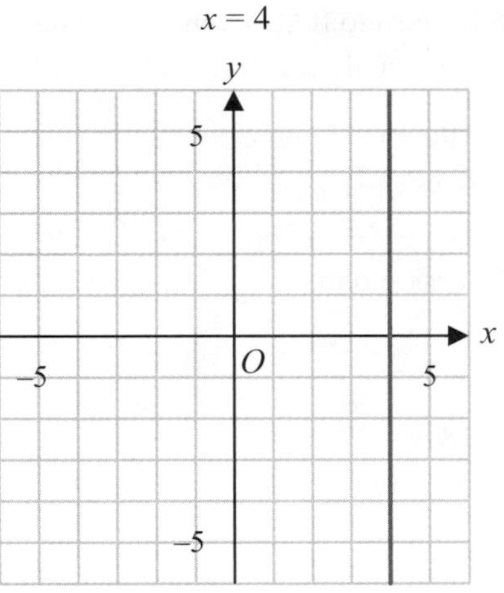

You can also graph equations with two variables. The **standard equation** of a line can be represented as:

$$y = mx + b$$

Each part of this equation tells you something about how the line looks on the graph. The letter m represents the **slope**—how steep the line is. The letter b represents the ***y*-intercept**—the point where the line crosses the y-axis. Here is the graph of the line $y = 2x + 6$:

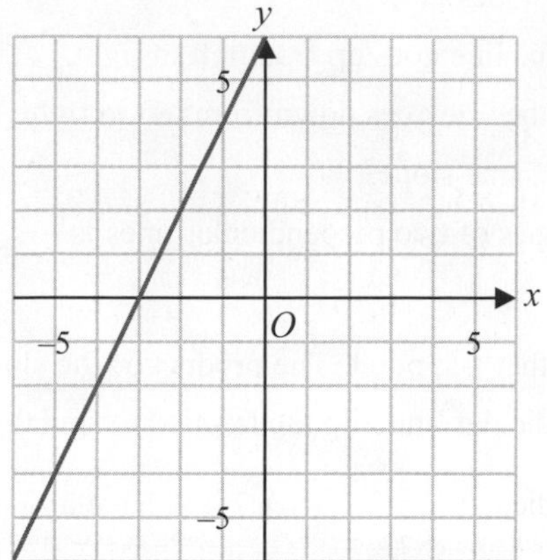

You can see that the line crosses the y-axis at 6. The equation also tells you that the slope of the line is 2. Let's see what that means.

Slope

The **slope** of a line tells you how steep it is—in other words, how quickly y is increasing for every unit that x increases. The equation of the line above tells us that the slope is 2. If you look at the graph, you can also see that y increases 2 units for every unit that x increases.

The SAT won't always give you the equation for a line. You might need to find the slope of a line using a graph. Choose any two points on the line and plug their coordinates into the slope formula. If the first point has the coordinates (x_1, y_1) and the second point has the coordinates (x_2, y_2), the slope formula tells you:

$$m = \frac{y_2 - y_1}{x_2 - x_1}$$

You might have also learned the slope formula as "rise over run." The "rise" between two points is the same thing as the vertical difference between their two y-coordinates, and the "run" is the horizontal difference between their two x-coordinates. Therefore, "rise over run" is the same as the formula above.

Let's test this formula by plugging in some points from the line graphed above. You can see that the line contains the points (–3, 0) and (0, 6). If you plug in these values for the formula for slope, you get:

$$m = \frac{y_2 - y_1}{x_2 - x_1} = \frac{6 - 0}{0 - (-3)} = \frac{6}{3} = 2$$

This formula tells us that the slope of the line is 2.

Here are a few important facts about slope:

- Vertical lines have undefined slopes.
- Horizontal lines have slopes of 0.
- A slope is positive if the line goes up from left to right.
- A slope is negative if the line goes down from left to right.
- Parallel lines have the same slope.
- The product of the slopes of two perpendicular lines is –1.

Let's talk a little bit more about that last point. The product of the slopes of two perpendicular lines is –1. To find the slope of a perpendicular line, flip the fraction to find the reciprocal, and then reverse the sign. For example, a line perpendicular to $y = -\frac{3}{4}x + 7$ will have a slope of $\frac{4}{3}$.

Graphing Inequalities

Graphing inequalities is similar to graphing equations. Start by graphing the inequality as if it were a linear equation. Use a solid line for $\leq$ or $\geq$, and a dashed line for $<$ or $>$. Then, shade in the solution area. For "greater than" inequalities, shade *above* the line. For "less than" inequalities, shade *below* the line.

Example

$$y \leq \frac{1}{2}x + 3$$

Start by graphing the line $y = \frac{1}{2}x + 3$. The line crosses the y-axis at 3. The slope of the line is $\frac{1}{2}$, so y increases 1 unit for every 2 units that x increases. Because the inequality uses the symbol $\leq$, you'll want to graph a solid line:

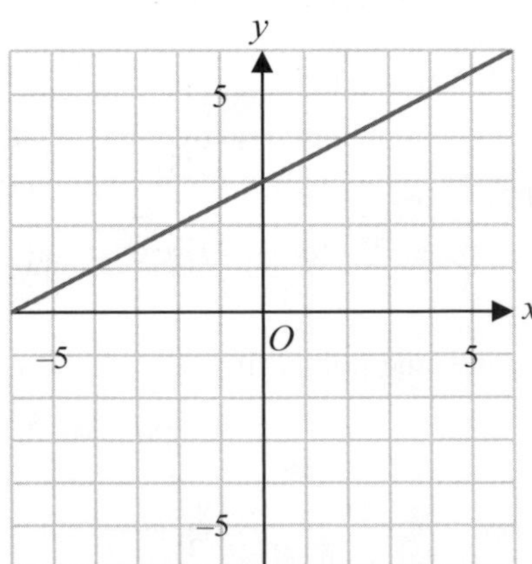

Next, shade in the solution area. Because this is a "less than" inequality, shade below the line.

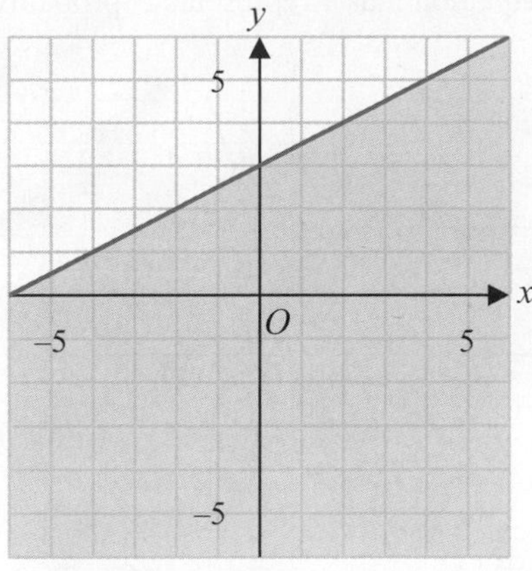

Graphing Absolute Values

In order to graph absolute values, you want to recall what the absolute value means. The absolute value of a number is its distance away from zero on a number line. Here is the graph of $y = 3x$.

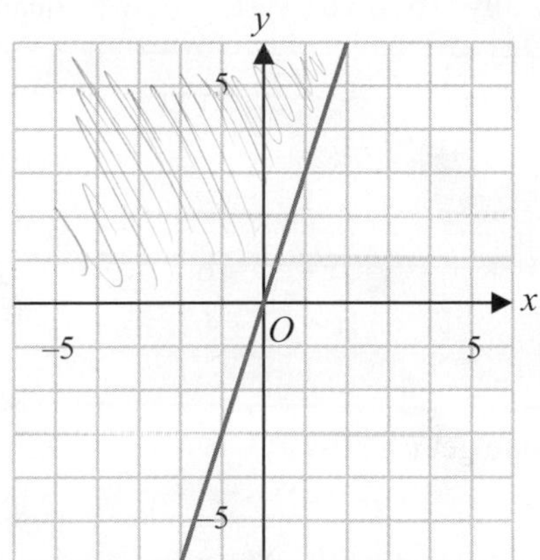

What about the graph of $y = | 3x |$? For every positive value of x, the graph will stay the same. However, for negative values of x, the absolute value will be positive—so the left side of the graph needs to have positive values for y.

Absolute-value equations often give you a graph that looks like the "V" shape below. If you are given a graph like this on the SAT, the equation that it represents is probably an absolute value.

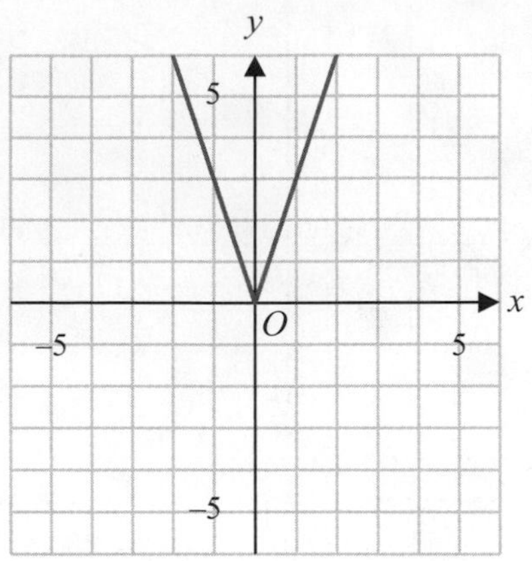

Graphing Systems of Equations

In Part 5, you learned how to solve for variables in a system of equations algebraically. You can also solve systems of equations graphically. To solve a system of two equations, graph the lines and find the point where they cross.

Example

$$2x - 3y = 6$$
$$4x = 12 - 4y$$

Start by rearranging each equation to get y by itself:

$$y = \frac{2}{3}x - 2$$

$$y = -x + 3$$

Now, graph each line using the slopes and y-intercepts:

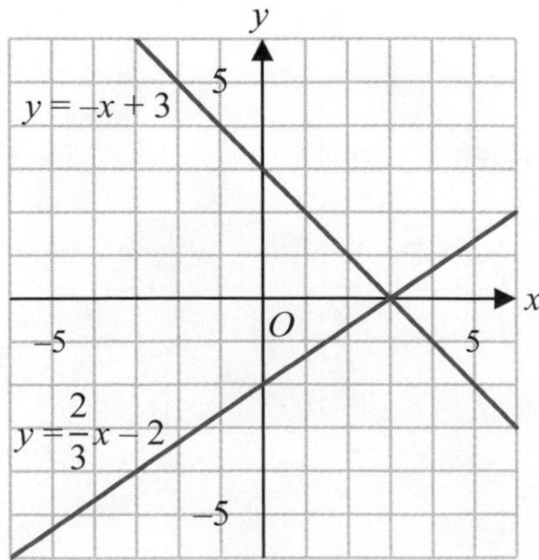

The lines cross at the point (3, 0), so the solution for the system of equations is $x = 3$, $y = 0$. You can always check your answer by plugging the values into the original equations and confirming that they are both true.

Graphing Functions

Linear functions are graphed just like linear equations. You simply treat $f(x)$ as your y variable. Therefore, the graph of $f(x) = -2x - 3$ is the same as the graph of $y = -2x - 3$:

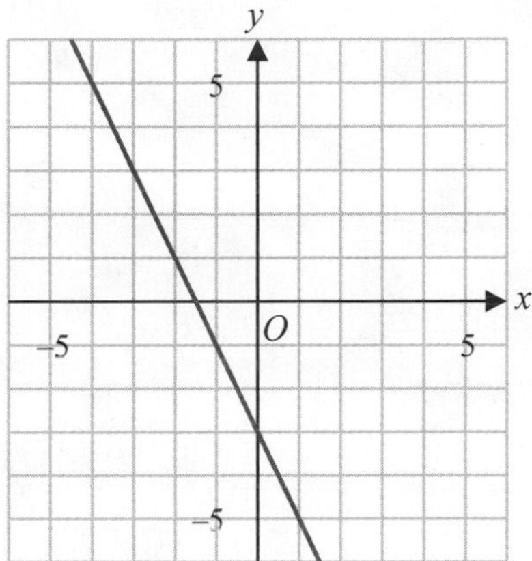

Some questions on the SAT will require you to create or recognize the transformation of a linear function. If you start with the function $f(x) = ax$, you can shift the function vertically b units by adding b to the right side of the function:

$$f(x) = ax + b$$

If b is positive, the function shifts b units up. If b is negative, the function shifts b units down.

The graphs below show the function $f(x) = 2x$ and the same function shifted 3 units up:

$f(x) = 2x$

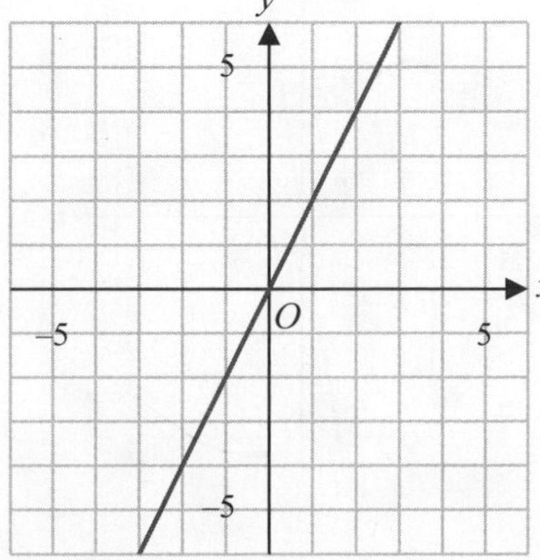

$f(x) = 2x + 3$

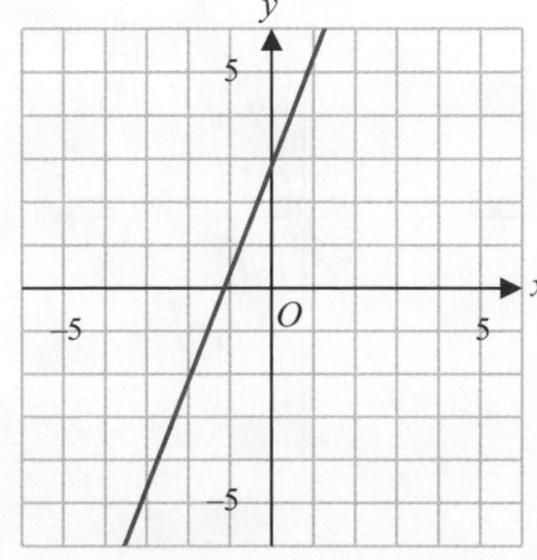

If you start with the function $f(x) = ax$, you can shift the function horizontally b units by taking the function of $x + b$:

$$f(x + b) = a(x + b)$$

If b is positive, the function shifts b units to the left. If b is negative, the function shifts b units to the right.

The graphs below show the function $f(x) = 2x$ and the same function shifted 1 unit to the left:

$f(x) = 2x$

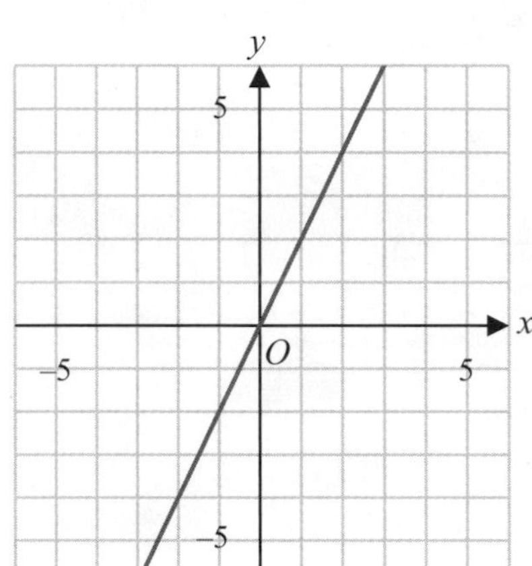

$f(x + 1) = 2(x + 1)$

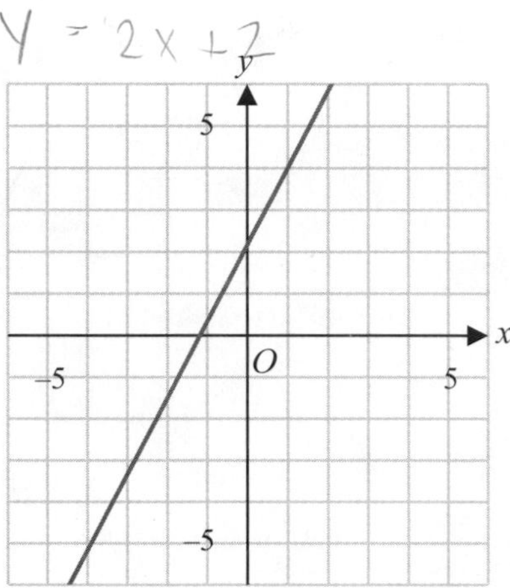

If you start with the function $f(x) = ax$, you can stretch the function by multiplying it by b:

$$b \times f(x) = b \times ax$$

For a linear function, this means the slope of the line is multiplied by b.

The graphs below show the function $f(x) = 2x$ and the same function stretched by a factor of 3:

$f(x) = 2x$

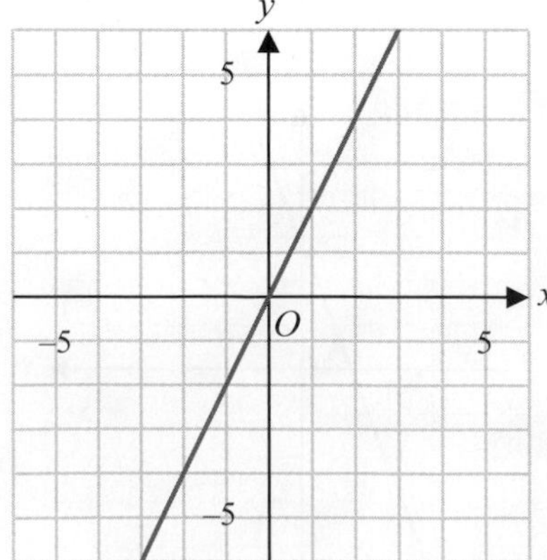

$3f(x) = 3 \times 2x$

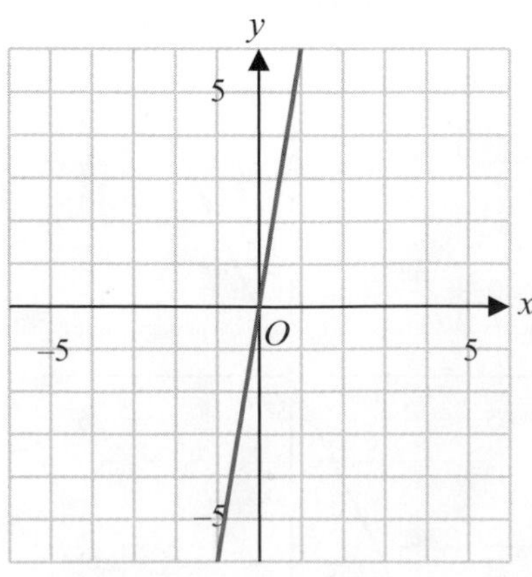

To reflect a function about the x-axis, multiply the whole function by -1.

The graphs below show the function $f(x) = \frac{1}{2}x + 1$ and the same function reflected about the x-axis:

$f(x) = \frac{1}{2}x + 1$

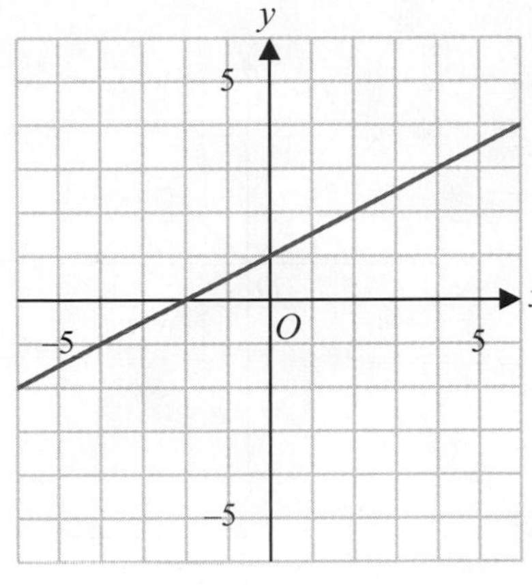

$-f(x) = -\left(\frac{1}{2}x+1\right)$

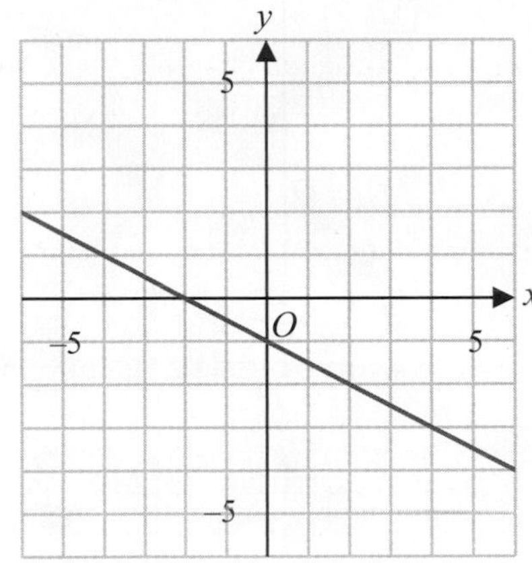

To reflect a function about the y-axis, take the function of $-x$.

The graphs below show the function $f(x) - \frac{1}{2}x + 1$ and the same function reflected about the y-axis:

$f(x) = \frac{1}{2}x + 1$

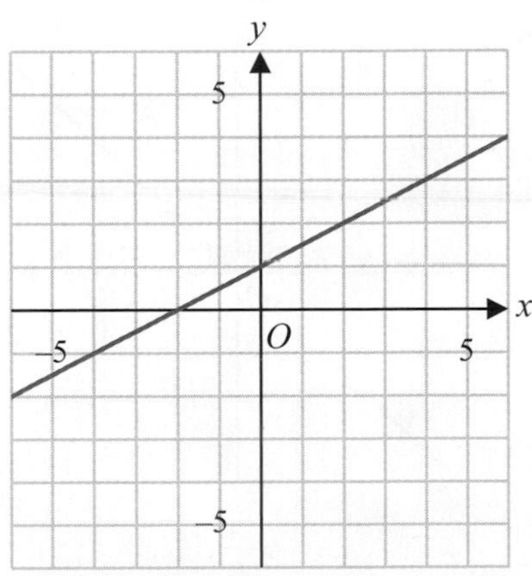

$f(-x) = -\frac{1}{2}x + 1$

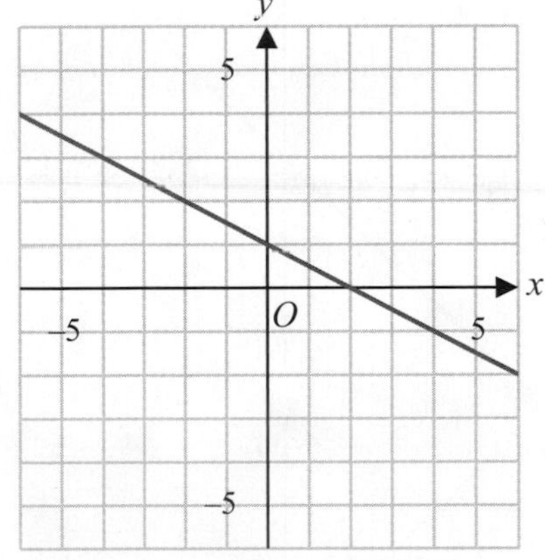

Part 8 Practice: Graphing Equations

1

Which of the following is the graph of $y = 3$?

A)

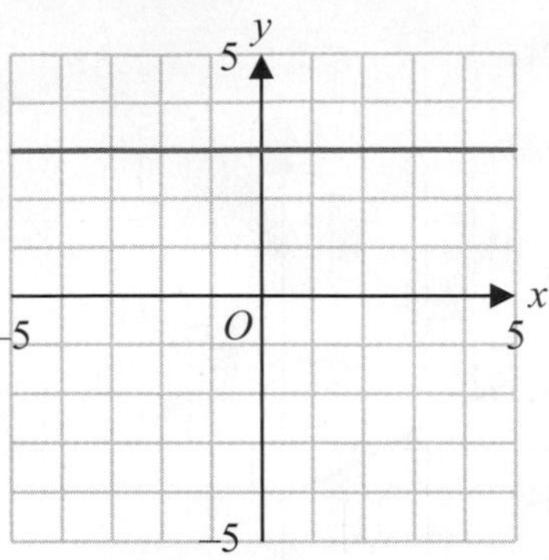

B)

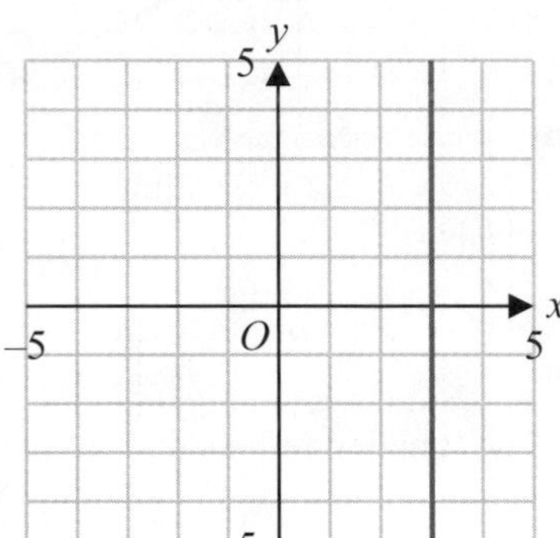

C)

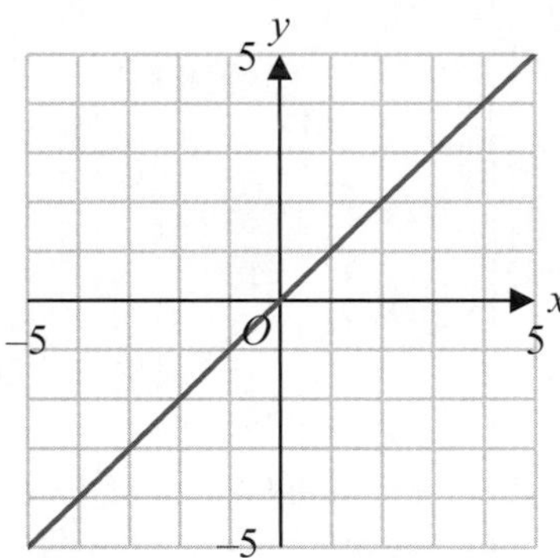

D)

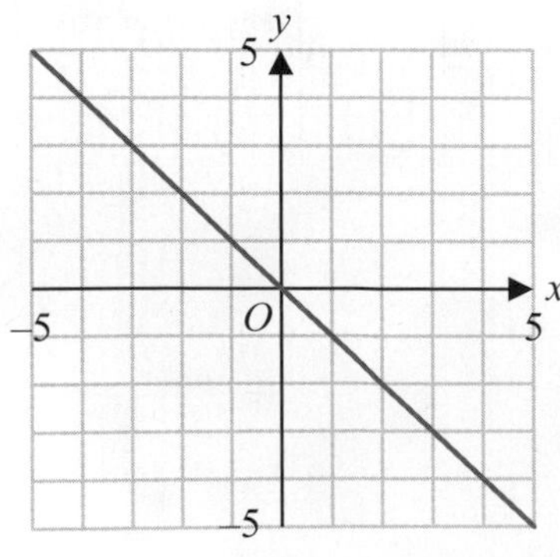

2

As the volume of a gas increases, its pressure decreases. Which of the following could be the graph of volume-pressure relationship?

A)

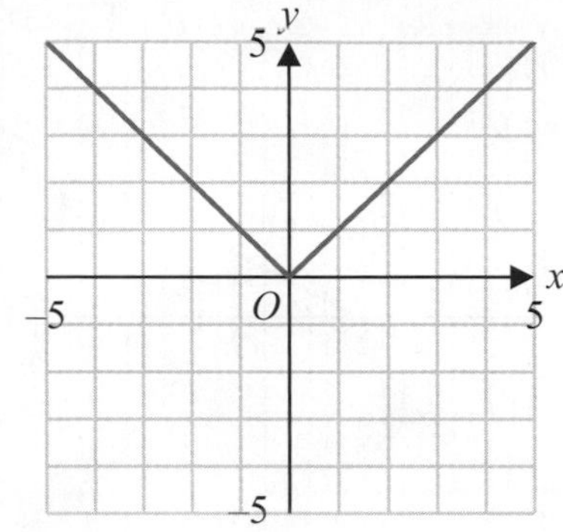

B)

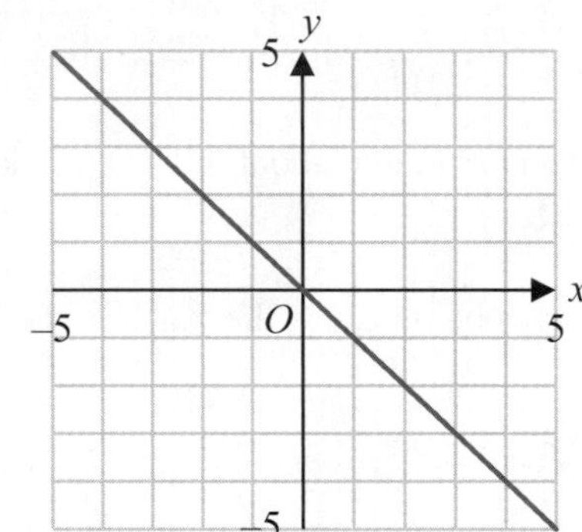

C)

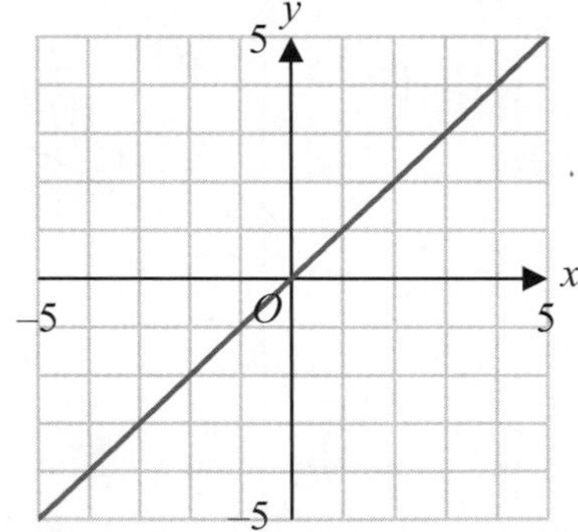

D)

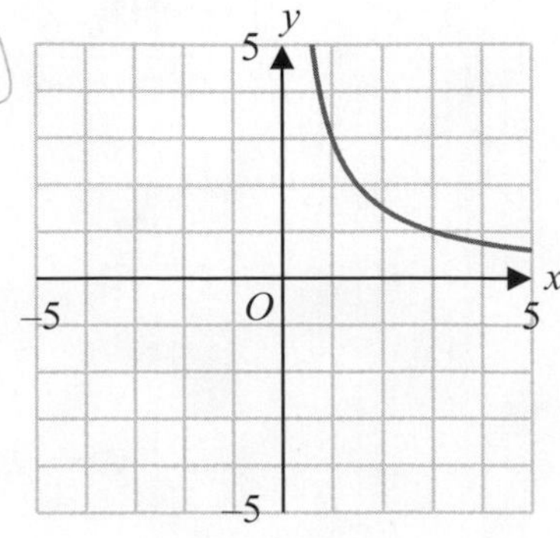

3

If $y = \frac{x}{2} - 3$, which of the following is the slope multiplied by the y-intercept?

A) $-\frac{3}{2}$

B) -3

C) $\frac{3}{2}$

D) 3

4

Which of the following is the graph of $y = |2x - 2|$?

A)

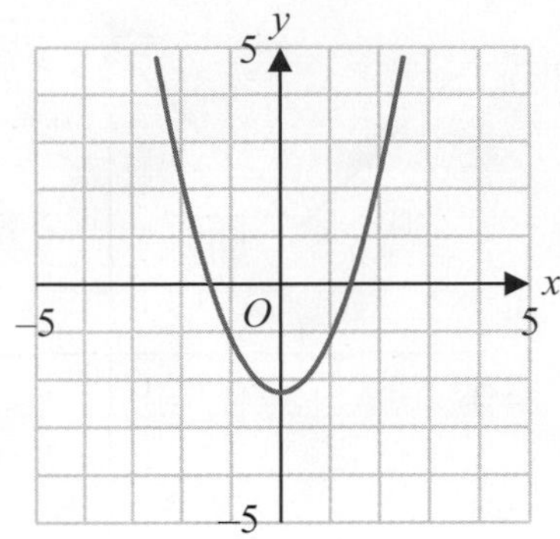

B)

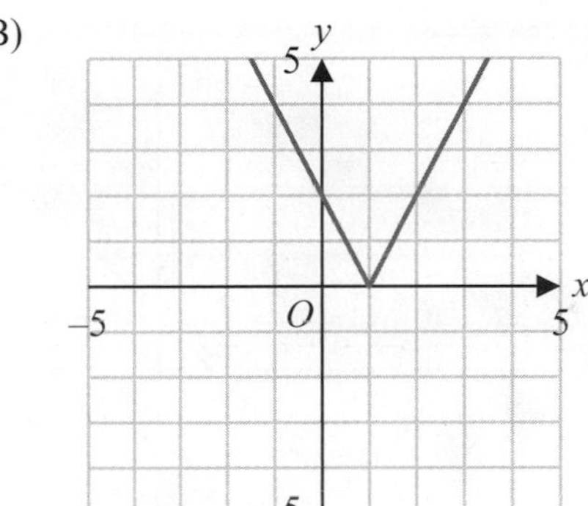

C)

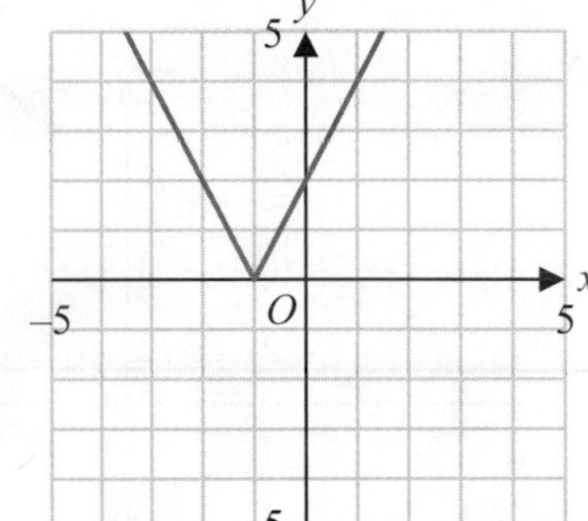

D)

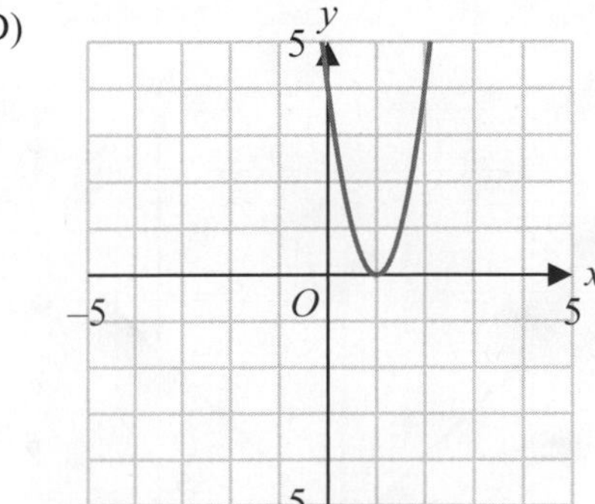

5

Which of the following is the graph of $y \geq |x+3| - 2$?

A)

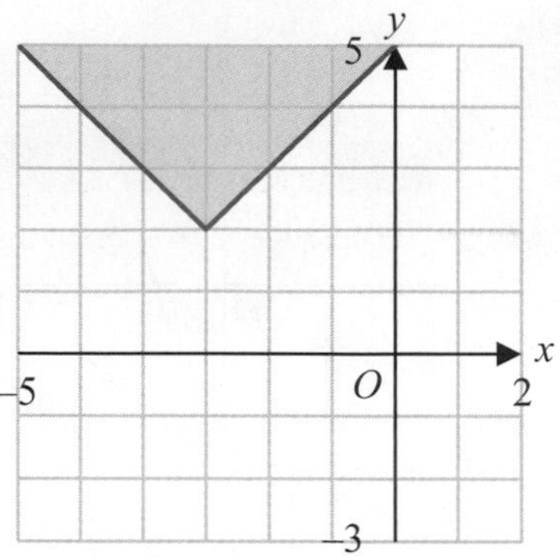

B)

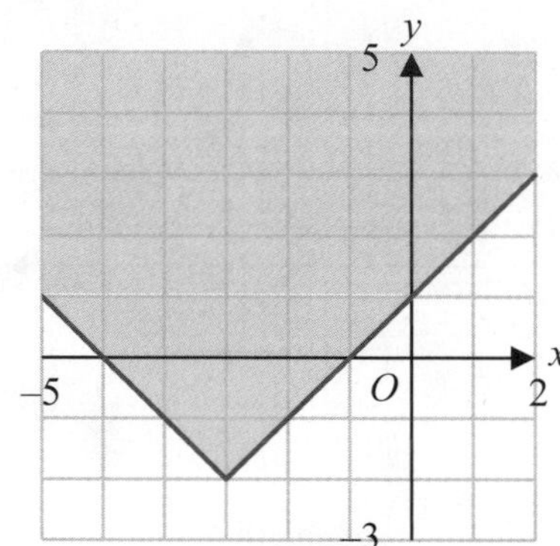

C)

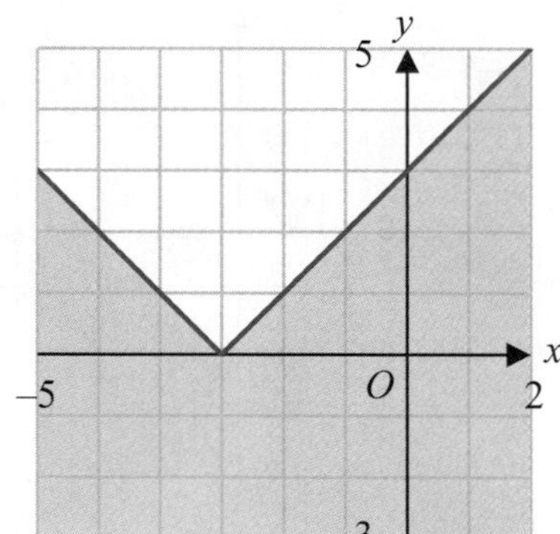

D)

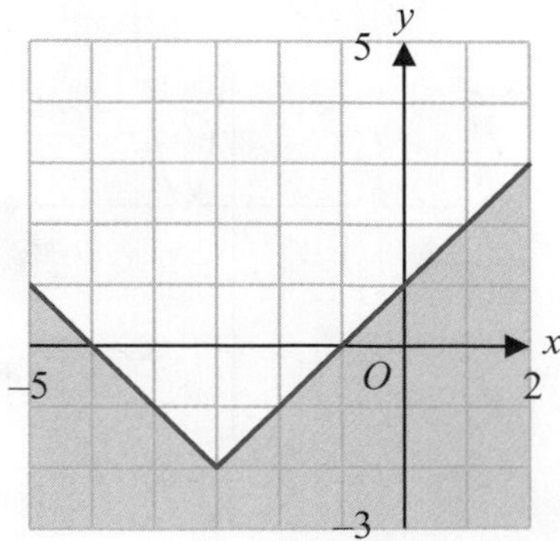

For questions 6-7, use the graph below.

6

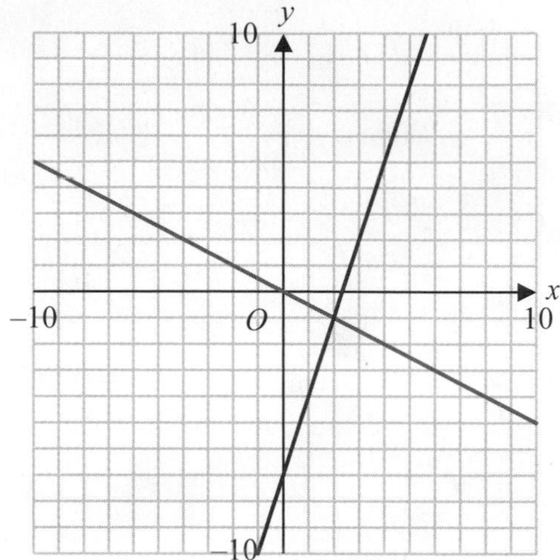

According to the graph above, which of the following represents the coordinates of the point where the two lines intersect.?

A) (–2, 1)

B) (–1, 2)

C) (1, –2)

D) (2, –1)

7

According to the graph, what is the product of the two x-intercepts?

A) 4

B) 2

C) 0

D) Cannot be determined from the information given.

8

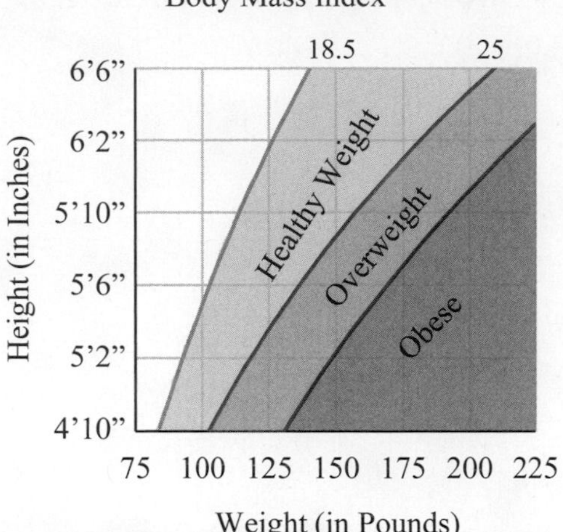

The graph above shows an adult's BMI based on height and weight. If an individual who is 5' 8" is categorized as "overweight," what is one possible value for his weight?

9

Line L has an equation of $3 - 5x = 2y$. If Line M is drawn perpendicular to Line L, what is the slope of Line M?

10

If the graph below is reflected about the x-axis, what is the value of y-intercept in the new line?

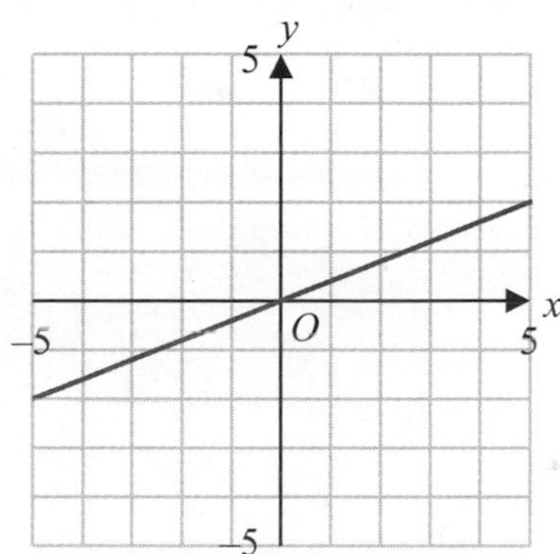

Section 4

Passport to Advanced Math

The **Passport to Advanced Math** questions cover important topics for college-level math, focusing on expressions, equations, and functions. You might think that this content seems similar to Heart of Algebra; it is in some ways, but with one major difference—every question uses higher order math. Whether calculating trajectories in astrophysics, the path of subatomic particles in quantum mechanics, or the chemical composition of fertilizer for high-yield crops, this math is the foundation for engineering, the social sciences, and the pure sciences. On the SAT, there will be sixteen Passport to Advanced Math questions: seven in the Calculator Section and nine in the No Calculator Section. In this section, we'll go over the following topics:

- Polynomial expressions
- Factoring polynomials
- Quadratic equations
- Quadratic functions and their graphs
- Advanced equations
- Applications of functions

Polynomial Expressions

Part 1

A **polynomial** is an expression that is a sum of one or more terms. Each **term** consists of one or more variables multiplied by a coefficient. Coefficients can be negative, so don't be surprised if you see a minus sign in a polynomial—that just means there's a term with a negative coefficient.

Here are some examples of polynomials:

$$5x^2$$

$$3x^3 + 2xy - y$$

$$-3x^2 + 6x - 7$$

Polynomials are classified by the number of terms they have when they are expressed in their simplest form. A **monomial** has one term, a **binomial** has two terms, and a **trinomial** has three. $3x + 2$ is a binomial, because it has two terms. $x^2 - 4x + 2$ is a trinomial, because it has three terms. It is important to notice that something like $3x + 2x$, while it looks like a binomial, is a monomial because it can be simplified to one term, $5x$.

Polynomials are also classified by their degree. The **degree** of a term is the sum of the exponents of its variables. The **degree of a polynomia**l is the same as its highest degree term. For example, $x^2 + 3$ is a second-degree polynomial because its highest exponent is 2. The expression $x^3 + x^2 + 2x + 1$ is a third-degree polynomial because its highest exponent is 3.

Certain polynomials have special names determined by their degree:

Degree	0	1	2	3
Name	Constant	Linear	Quadratic	Cubic
Example	5	$x + 7$	$x^2 + 9$	$2x^3 + 19x^2 - 6x + 13$

Polynomials can be added, subtracted, and multiplied, just like regular numbers. Next up, we'll cover how to do this, and will also look at some basic techniques for polynomial division.

Adding Polynomials

To add two polynomials, you need to combine the like terms. **Like terms** have the same variables raised to the same powers. So $5x^3y^2z$ and $7x^3y^2z$ are like terms because each term has x cubed, y squared, and z. However, $5x^3y^2z$ and $7xyz$ are not like terms, because although they have the same variables, the variables are not raised to the same powers.

Let's say you want to find the sum of $3m^2 + 2m + 6$ and $m - 9$. You can join them with a plus sign:

Example

$$3m^2 + 2m + 6 + m - 9$$

Then, put like terms next to each other. Remember to pay attention to the signs!

$$3m^2 + 2m + m + 6 - 9$$

Finally, add and subtract the like terms, including the constants:

$$3m^2 + 3m - 3$$

Subtracting Polynomials

Subtracting polynomials is very similar to adding them: join the expressions and combine like terms. However, with subtraction, you first have to take care of the signs.

Example

What is the value of $4p^3 + 6p^2 - 8p + 11$ minus $3p^3 - 2p^2 + 12p - 3$?

Just like with addition, you'll need to join the like terms. With subtraction, however, you need to put the second term in parentheses:

$$4p^3 + 6p^2 - 8p + 11 - (3p^3 - 2p^2 + 12p - 3)$$

Then, distribute the negative sign across the parentheses:

$$4p^3 + 6p^2 - 8p + 11 - 3p^3 + 2p^2 - 12p + 3$$

Now you're ready to combine like terms for your result:

$$p^3 + 8p^2 - 20p + 14$$

Multiplying Polynomials

To multiply two monomials, use exponent rules.

Example

$$(5x^3y^5z^2)(2x^6y^8z)$$

Remember that when you multiply two expressions with the same base, you can add their exponents. Don't forget to multiply the coefficients!

$$5x^3y^5z^2 \times 2x^6y^8z = 10x^{3+6}y^{5+8}z^{2+1}$$

Once you do the arithmetic, you're left with:

$$10x^9y^{13}z^3$$

When you multiply polynomials with more terms, you will need to use the Distributive Property, which we talked about in Section 4, Part 1. Take a moment to review the Distributive Property, and then look at this example:

Example

$$2x(x + 3)$$

Using the Distributive Property, you can rewrite the expression like this:

$$2x \times x + 2x \times 3$$

Then, simplify to get your solution:

$$2x^2 + 6x$$

When you're multiplying more than one polynomial with multiple terms, the idea is the same: use the Distributive Property and simplify. You just have to make sure you've multiplied every term in one polynomial by every term in the other. Luckily, for multiplying two binomials, there's an easy way to keep everything straight. The **FOIL method** tells you to multiply the **F**irst terms, the **O**uter terms, the **I**nner terms, and the **L**ast terms. Always remember to combine like terms when you've finished.

Example

$$(x + 3)(2x + 5)$$

You need to multiply both terms in the first binomial by both terms in the second, like this:

$$(x + 3)(2x + 5)$$

The FOIL method makes this simple. Multiply together the *first* terms in the parentheses (x and $2x$), then the *outer* terms (x and 5), then the *inner* terms (3 and $2x$), and finally the *last* terms (3 and 5):

$$(x \times 2x) + (x \times 5) + (3 \times 2x) + (3 \times 5)$$

Then, simplify and combine like terms:

$$2x^2 + 5x + 6x + 15$$

$$2x^2 + 11x + 15$$

Dividing Polynomials

To divide polynomials, you can use the same techniques you learned for factoring expressions.

Example

$$\frac{2x^3 + 4x^2 - 6x}{2x}$$

This operation is asking you to divide each term of the polynomial by $2x$. Remember that dividing two expressions with the same base means you can divide the coefficients and subtract the exponents:

$$\frac{2}{2}x^{3-1} + \frac{4}{2}x^{2-1} - \frac{6}{2}x^{1-1}$$

Carry out that arithmetic, and simplify the coefficients where you can:

$$x^2 + 2x - 3$$

Don't worry if the number you're dividing the coefficients by isn't a common factor. It's fine to leave coefficients as fractions in lowest terms.

Let's look at something a little more complex:

Example

$$\frac{x^3 - x^2 + 3x - 10}{x - 2}$$

This operation is asking you to divide each term of the polynomial by the binomial $x - 2$. Because there are two terms in the denominator, we need to match these with the numerator through a process that looks a lot like long division. First we put the denominator on the left side and the numerator on the right side:

$$x - 2\overline{\smash{)}\,x^3 - x^2 + 3x - 10}$$

Next, create a match with the highest order term in the numerator, x^3, by multiplying the denominator, in this case by x^2:

$$(x - 2) \times x^2 = x^3 - 2x^2$$

Now subtract this result from your numerator:

$$\begin{array}{r l} & x^2 \\ x - 2) & \overline{x^3 - x^2 + 3x - 10} \\ & -(x^3 - 2x^2) \\ \hline & x^2 + 3x - 10 \end{array}$$

Now we match the next highest term, x^2, multiplying $x - 2$ by x:

$$(x - 2) \times x = x^2 - 2x$$

Now subtract this result from your numerator, like before:

$$\begin{array}{r l} & x^2 + x \\ x - 2) & \overline{x^3 - x^2 + 3x - 10} \\ & -(x^3 - 2x^2) \\ \hline & x^2 + 3x - 10 \\ & -(x^2 - 2x) \\ \hline & = 5x - 10 \end{array}$$

Finally, we match the last variable term $5x$ to the denominator, by multiply the denominator by 5:

$$(x - 2) \times 5 = 5x - 10$$

Subtracting this result from the numerator:

$$\begin{array}{r l} & x^2 + x + 5 \\ x - 2) & \overline{x^3 - x^2 + 3x - 10} \\ & -(x^3 - 2x^2) \\ \hline & x^2 + 3x - 10 \\ & -(x^2 - 2x) \\ \hline & 5x - 10 \\ & -(5x - 10) \\ \hline & 0 \end{array}$$

Since we found a value of 0, the numerator is divisible by the denominator. Another way of looking at this is that the denominator is a factor of the numerator. If we had been left with a value different from zero, we would know that the denominator is not a factor of the numerator. The result of our long division, found above the numerator, is $x^2 + x + 5$:

$$\begin{array}{r} x^2 + x + 5 \\ x - 2 \overline{) \, x^3 - x^2 + 3x - 10} \\ \underline{-(x^3 - 2x^2) \qquad\qquad} \\ x^2 + 3x - 10 \\ \underline{-(x^2 - 2x) \qquad} \\ 5x - 10 \\ \underline{-(5x - 10)} \\ 0 \end{array}$$

You can double check your answer by multiplying this result by the denominator $(x^2 + x + 5)(x - 2)$. Since this is equal to $x^3 - x^2 + 3x - 10$, we can confirm that our calculations are correct:

$$\frac{x^3 - x^2 + 3x - 10}{x - 2} = x^2 + x + 5$$

Part 1 Practice: Polynomial Expressions

1

$$x^3 + 2x - 6 + 4x^3 - 5x + 9$$

What is the value of the expression above when $x = 3$?

A) 109

B) 129

C) 159

D) 171

2

If $m^4 + 4m^3 - m^2 + 17m - 2$ is added to $3m^4 - m^3 - 2m^2 + 3m - 8$, which of the following statements is true?

I. The coefficient of its largest term is positive.

II. It has no second-degree term.

III. Its constant term is positive.

A) I only

B) II only

C) I and II

D) I, II, and III

3

Which of the following expressions is equal to $3x + 16 - 2y$ minus $x + 8 - y$?

A) $-2x - 16 + 2y$

B) $-2x - 8 - 3y$

C) $2x + 8 - 3y$

D) $2x + 8 - y$

4

The growth rate of a city's population can be modeled using the equation $p = 4x + 7$, where x represents the number of years since 1900, and p is the increase in the population of the city. If people leave the city at a rate of $2x - 10$ people per year, which of the following expressions accurately models the change in the city's total population in a given year?

A) $-2x - 17$

B) $2x - 3$

C) $2x + 17$

D) $6x - 3$

5

$$12m^2n^7 \times 5m^{10}n^3$$

Which of the following expressions is equivalent to the one shown above?

A) $17m^{12}n^{10}$

B) $17m^{20}n^{21}$

C) $60m^{12}n^{10}$

D) $60m^{20}n^{21}$

Questions 6 and 7 refer to the following information.

The equation below describes the path of a projectile thrown from an initial height of $\frac{9}{4}$ feet, where t is time in seconds and h is the height of the projectile.

$$\frac{-4t^2 + 16t + 9}{4} = h$$

6

What is the height of the projectile, in feet, at two seconds?

A) 2

B) $\frac{25}{2}$

C) 4

D) $\frac{25}{4}$

7

If the projectile is exactly 5.25 feet high in the air, how many seconds could it have elapsed since it was thrown?

A) 4 seconds

B) 2 seconds

C) 1.5 seconds

D) 1 second

8

$$(2x + 5)(11 - x)$$

If $2x + 5 = 11$, what is the value of the expression above?

9

What is the value of $100x^4 + 44x^2$ divided by $4x^2$ when $x = 2$?

10

$$\frac{3x^4 - 36x^3 - 12x^2}{-3x}$$

If $x = -2$, what is the value of the expression above?

Factoring Polynomials

Part 2

In the previous section you learned how to multiply polynomials. With multiplication, you start with two or more factors and find their product. Remember from Section 4 that factoring is the opposite of multiplication: you start with a product and find its factors. In this section, we'll build on what you learned in Section 4 and discuss how to factor quadratic and cubic polynomials. Here's what this relationship looks like:

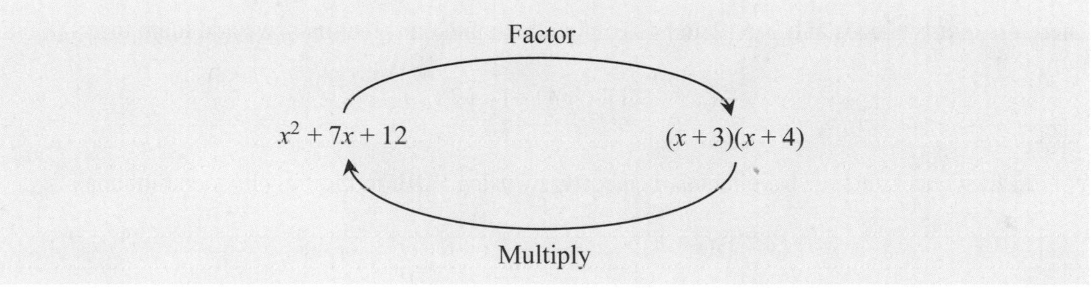

Factoring Quadratic Trinomials

Remember that a quadratic expression has a degree, or highest power, of two, and a trinomial is a polynomial with three terms. Therefore, a quadratic trinomial is a second-degree polynomial with three terms. You can write a general expression for quadratic trinomials like this:

$$ax^2 + bx + c$$

In this form, a is the coefficient of x^2, b is the coefficient of x, and c is the constant. So in the quadratic trinomial $x^2 + 2x - 8$, $a = 1$, $b = 2$, and $c = -8$. Quadratic trinomials where $a = 1$ are a little simpler to factor, so we'll take this one as our first example. To fully factor it, we want to write it as two binomials multiplied together, like this:

$$(x + m)(x + n)$$

How do we find m and n? Well, we can multiply these two binomials using FOIL, and then simplify:

$$x^2 + nx + mx + mn = x^2 + (n + m)x + mn$$

By comparing this to our general expression for quadratic trinomials above, we can see that two things must be true:

$$n + m = b$$

$$m \times n = c$$

In other words, to find m and n, we need to find two numbers that have a sum of b and a product of c. For the trinomial $x^2 + 2x - 8$, that means we're looking for two numbers that add up to 2 and multiply together to –8. First, let's see what numbers multiply to –8:

$$-1 \times 8 = -8$$

$$-8 \times 1 = -8$$

$$-2 \times 4 = -8$$

$$-4 \times 2 = -8$$

Which pair of numbers has a sum of 2? Only –2 and 4:

$$-2 + 4 = 2$$

Therefore, our two constants are –2 and 4. To plug them into our binomials, we add them to x:

$$\big(x + (-2)\big)(x + 4) = (x - 2)(x + 4)$$

We can then check that we have factored correctly by using FOIL to multiply the two binomials:

$$(x - 2)(x + 4) = x^2 + 4x - 2x - 8 = x^2 + 2x - 8$$

Because multiplying leads to the expression we started out with, we know we have factored correctly.

Factoring with Different Values

Now you know how to factor a quadratic trinomial when a—the coefficient of the quadratic term—is equal to 1. But what if a is equal to another number? First, check whether you can factor this number out of the entire expression.

Example

$$5x^2 + 15x + 10$$

Did you notice that every term has a common factor of 5? That means you can start by pulling 5 out of the entire expression:

$$5x^2 + 15x + 10 = 5(x^2 + 3x + 2)$$

Now you can use the method you've just learned to factor the quadratic expression in parentheses. You're looking for two numbers have a product of 2 and a sum of 3. The numbers 1 and 2 fit those requirements:

$$5(x^2 + 3x + 2) = 5(x + 1)(x + 2)$$

You can tell that you've factored correctly because when you multiply these binomials together using **FOIL**, you get the trinomial you were trying to factor:

$$5(x + 1)(x + 2) = 5(x^2 + 3x + 2) = 5x^2 + 15x + 10$$

However, what happens when you can't factor out a from the entire expression? This time, one or both of the x's in the binomials will have a coefficient, marked here by p and q:

$$ax^2 + bx + c = (px + m)(qx + n)$$

We need a few things to happen:

1. $p \times q = a$
2. $m \times n = c$
3. $p \times n + m \times q = b$

Example

$$3x^2 - 5x - 2$$

p and q will multiply to 3 so their values will be 1 and 3. (If a is negative, first factor –1 out of the equation.) Therefore, you know the two binomials will look something like this:

$$3x^2 - 5x - 2 = (3x + m)(x + n)$$

To find m and n, you need values that will multiply to –2. There are two sets of possible values: 1 and –2 or –1 and 2. Which of these values should you pick so that $3 \times n + m \times 1 = -5$? The only option is 1 and –2, because $3 \times -2 + 1 \times 1 = -5$. Therefore, the two binomials must be:

$$(3x + 1)(x - 2)$$

Factoring a Difference of Squares

Expressions that consist of subtracting one perfect square from another, such as $x^2 - 25$, are called a **difference of squares**. Recognizing when a polynomial is a difference of squares will come in handy because these expressions all factor according to a simple formula:

$$a^2 - b^2 = (a + b)(a - b)$$

Here are some examples:

$$x^2 - 4 = (x + 2)(x - 2)$$

$$x^2 - 64 = (x + 8)(x - 8)$$

$$x^2 - y^2 = (x + y)(x - y)$$

$$x^4 - y^4 = (x^2 + y^2)(x^2 - y^2)$$

But wait—notice that in our last example, the second factor is also a difference of squares! We can factor that, too:

$$x^4 - y^4 = (x^2 + y^2)(x + y)(x - y)$$

Factoring a Sum or Difference of Cubes

There are also special formulas for factoring a sum or difference of cubes:

$$a^3 + b^3 = (a + b)(a^2 - ab + b^2)$$

$$a^3 - b^3 = (a - b)(a^2 + ab + b^2)$$

These two formulas look very similar – in fact, the only differences are in the signs. To keep the signs straight, think **SOAP**: "same, opposite, always positive." The first sign is the same as the one in the original expression, the second sign is the opposite, and the last sign is always a plus sign.

Here are some examples:

$$x^3 + 8 = (x + 2)(x^2 - 2x + 4)$$

$$x^3 - 27 = (x - 3)(x^2 + 3x + 9)$$

$$x^6 - 64 = (x^2 - 4)(x^4 + 4x^2 + 16)$$

Did you catch that the first factor in our last example is a difference of squares? You can use the difference of squares formula to further simplify:

$$x^6 - 64 = (x + 2)(x - 2)(x^4 + 4x^2 + 16)$$

Using Factoring to Simplify Rational Equations

On the SAT, you won't have to do complicated division with polynomials. However, you may be asked to look at a rational expression involving polynomials and simplify. In Part 1, you learned about how to do some basic division with polynomials. Your new factoring skills will allow you to divide polynomials with multiple terms in the denominator.

Example

$$\frac{x^2 + 3x + 2}{x + 2}$$

The denominator is a linear expression and can't be factored. However, the numerator is a quadratic trinomial, which you can factor:

$$x^2 + 3x + 2 = (x + 1)(x + 2)$$

Substituting that into the original expression, you can quickly see that one of those factors is a common factor with the denominator:

$$\frac{(x+1)(x+2)}{x+2}$$

As with any rational expression, cancel common factors to simplify:

$$\frac{(x+1)\cancel{(x+2)}}{\cancel{x+2}} = x+1$$

Example

$$\frac{x^2+7x+12}{x^2-9}$$

In this case, both polynomials can be factored (notice that the denominator is a difference of squares):

$$\frac{(x+3)(x+4)}{(x+3)(x-3)}$$

After cancelling out the common factor $(x + 3)$, you're left with:

$$\frac{x+4}{x-3}$$

This can't be simplified any further, so you're all done!

Part 2 Practice: Factoring Polynomials

1

$$x^2 + 3x - 10$$

Which of the following expressions is a factor of the equation above?

A) $x+5$

B) $x-5$

C) $x+2$

D) x

2

$$-9x^2 + 22x + 15$$

Which of the following expressions represents a complete factoring of the expression above?

A) $(-9x+5)(x-3)$

B) $(9x+5)(x-3)$

C) $-(9x-5)(x+3)$

D) $-(9x+5)(x-3)$

3

$$x^2 - 11x - 12$$

If a and b represent the two factors of the expression above, which of the following expressions represents $a + b$?

A) $2x - 13$

B) $2x - 11$

C) $2x + 11$

D) $2x + 13$

4

$$2x^3 + 3x^2 - 3x - 2$$

Which of the following expressions is a factor of the expression above?

A) $2x^2 + 2x + 2$

B) $2x^2 + 5x + 2$

C) $4x^2 - 6x + 2$

D) $8x^2 - 4x - 4$

Questions 5 and 6 refer to the following expression.

$$x^3 - 27$$

5

If the expression above is factored into its simplest form, which of the following statements about the factored form of the expression is true?

A) Both factors are of the first degree.

B) One factor is of the second degree, and one is of the first degree.

C) One factor has four terms, and the other has two.

D) Both factors have two terms.

6

What is the value of the product of all the coefficients of the expression's two factors?

A) 0

B) 1

C) 3

D) 4

7

The number of people with the INS gene, which is associated with diabetes, increases or decreases in a small town depending on the calendar year, according to the expression $4x^2 - 4x - 120$. If x is a positive integer representing the number of years since 2000, in what year was there no increase or decrease in the number of people with the INS gene in the small town?

A) 2004

B) 2005

C) 2006

D) 2007

8

$$-(x^2 - 100)$$

The number of used trucks sold by a car dealership decreases as the price increases according to the expression above, where x represents the price of the truck in thousands of dollars. At what price, in thousands of dollars, will the dealership sell no trucks?

9

$$x^3 - 125$$

If the expression above is represented by $(x - b)[(x + b)(x + b) - xb]$, what is the value for b?

10

$$x^2 - 9x + 18$$

The expression above is factored as $(x - a)(x - b)$. What is the value of ab?

Quadratic Equations
Part 3

Quadratic equations are equations with one variable raised to the second degree. Here's an example:

$$x^2 + 10x + 21 = 0$$

To solve quadratic equations, you can use what you've learned about factoring quadratic polynomials. How? Take a look at the quadratic equation above, and factor the left side:

$$x^2 + 10x + 21 = 0$$

$$(x + 3)(x + 7) = 0$$

On the left side, you now have two factors that have a product of zero. For two numbers to have a product of zero, at least one of them has to be equal to zero. In this equation, there are two ways for that to be true:

$$x + 3 = 0 \qquad\qquad x + 7 = 0$$

$$x = -3 \qquad\qquad x = -7$$

Therefore, this quadratic equation has two possible solutions: $x = -3$ or $x = -7$. These values are known as the **roots** of the equation.

Example

$$2x^2 + 21x + 40 = 13$$

Notice that unlike our first example, this equation is not set up so that one side is equal to zero. You have to gather all your terms on one side. In this case, subtract 13 from both sides to get zero on the right side of the equation:

$$2x^2 + 21x + 27 = 0$$

Now you are ready to factor the left side:

$$(2x + 3)(x + 9) = 0$$

Then, set each factor equal to zero in order to solve for x:

$$2x + 3 = 0 \qquad\qquad x + 9 = 0$$

$$x = -\frac{3}{2} \qquad\qquad x = -9$$

The two roots of the quadratic equation are $-\frac{3}{2}$ and -9.

Word Problems with Quadratic Equations

On the SAT, you may need to solve word problems using quadratic equations.

Example

Patricia throws a tennis ball out of her window. The height h of the ball at time t is given by $h = -t^2 - t + 20$. How many seconds does it take for the tennis ball to fall to the ground?

The height of something measures its distance from the ground. That means that when the tennis ball falls to the ground, its height (h) is zero. You can substitute 0 for h in the equation:

$$-t^2 - t + 20 = 0$$

Now that you have a quadratic equation, you can factor it to find the roots. Notice that right now, the coefficient of the quadratic term, t^2, is -1. Factoring would be simpler if that coefficient were 1. Since any number multiplied by zero equals zero, you can multiply both sides by -1 to get:

$$t^2 + t - 20 = 0$$

Now you have a quadratic polynomial that's easier to factor:

$$(t + 5)(t - 4) = 0$$

You've solved the equation: $t = -5$ or $t = 4$. However, remember that you're not just solving an equation this time; you're answering a word problem. The ball can't fall to the ground twice, so you need to figure out which one of your solutions makes sense for the problem.

This problem is asking you to find a particular time after Patricia throws the ball. Since you know that time is never negative, you can look at your solutions and realize that $t = -5$ doesn't make sense. This makes it an **extraneous solution**: a solution that works mathematically but doesn't make logical sense. This leaves you with only one solution: the tennis ball falls to the ground when $t = 4$.

The Quadratic Formula

Not all quadratic equations can be easily solved by factoring. For quadratic equations that can't be easily factored using the methods we've covered, you can use the Quadratic Formula. The **Quadratic Formula** states that if you have a quadratic equation in the form:

$$ax^2 + bx + c = 0$$

You can solve for x using this formula:

$$x = \frac{-b \pm \sqrt{b^2 - 4ac}}{2a}$$

Example

Solve for x in the equation:

$$x^2 + 17x + 72 = 0$$

In this equation, $a = 1$, $b = 17$, and $c = 72$. Putting these values into the Quadratic Formula gives you:

$$x = \frac{-17 \pm \sqrt{17^2 - 4(1)(72)}}{2(1)}$$

After this, it's just a matter of remembering your order of operations to simplify:

$$x = \frac{-17 \pm \sqrt{289 - 288}}{2}$$

$$x = \frac{-17 \pm \sqrt{1}}{2}$$

$$x = \frac{-17 \pm 1}{2}$$

That ± sign looks strange but just means "plus or minus." In other words, you need to both add those terms and subtract them. Doing so gives you:

$$x = \frac{-16}{2} \quad \text{or} \quad x = \frac{-18}{2}$$

Simplify those fractions for your final solutions:

$$x = -8 \quad \text{or} \quad x = -9$$

The two roots for the quadratic equation are –9 and –8. Take note that while we used the quadratic formula, this equation can also be solved by the factoring technique (try it!).

Irrational and Nonexistent Solutions

There are two types of quadratic equations that the Quadratic Formula is especially useful for. The first is quadratic equations with irrational solutions. Take this equation:

$$x^2 + 5x - 7 = 0$$

Applying the Quadratic Formula gives you:

$$x = \frac{-(5) \pm \sqrt{(5)^2 - 4(1)(-7)}}{2(1)}$$

$$x = \frac{-5 \pm \sqrt{25 + 28}}{2}$$

$$x = \frac{5 \pm \sqrt{53}}{2}$$

This one couldn't be solved by factoring because its roots are irrational, so you needed to use the Quadratic Formula.

The other kind of quadratic equation, the Quadratic Formula, is especially useful for quadratic equations with *no* solutions.

Example

$$x^2 + x + 2 = 0$$

Look what happens when you try to apply the Quadratic Formula:

$$x = \frac{-1 \pm \sqrt{1^2 - 4(1)(2)}}{2(1)}$$

$$x = \frac{-1 \pm \sqrt{1 - 8}}{2}$$

$$x = \frac{-1 \pm \sqrt{-7}}{2}$$

Wait a minute! You can't take the square root of a negative number. That means there is **no solution**: the expression cannot be factored, and there are no values of x that will make the equation true. A quadratic equation will always have zero, one, or two roots, and you can use the Quadratic Formula to figure out how many it has.

Part 3 Practice: Quadratic Equations

1

$$x^2 - 4x - 21 = 0$$

If a and b are the two values of x that satisfy the equation above, what is the value of ab?

A) –21

B) –7

C) 0

D) 21

2

$$4x^2 - 12x + 8$$

Which of the following expressions is equal to the expression above?

A) $(x - 2)(x - 1)$

B) $(x + 2)(x + 1)$

C) $4(x - 2)(x - 1)$

D) $4(x + 2)(x + 1)$

3

(7,0), (5,0)

Which of the following equations contains both of the xy-coordinates of the set shown above?

A) $2x^2 - 70 = y$

B) $2x^2 - 24x + 70 = y$

C) $2x^2 + 24x - 70 = y$

D) $2x^2 + 24x + 70 = y$

4

$$3x^2 + 25x + 42 = 0$$

Which of the following equations is equivalent to the equation above?

A) $(x + 6)(x + 7) = 0$

B) $(3x + 7)(x + 6) = 0$

C) $3(x + 6)(x + 7) = 0$

D) $3(x + 6)(3x + 7) = 0$

5

$$3x^2 - 3x + 8 = 7x$$

Which of the following statements are true about the equation above?

I. Both of its solutions are integers.
II. All of its solutions are positive.
III. It has no real solutions.

A) Only I

B) Only II

C) Both I and II

D) I, II, and III

Questions 6 and 7 refer to the following information.

The number of votes a political candidate receives in a certain district can be predicted by the number of registered voters in that district using the equation $2x^2 + x + 13 = v$, where x represents 100 registered voters, and v represents the number of votes received.

6

If 1,000 voters register for the election, how many votes can this candidate expect to get?

A) 223

B) 200

C) 113

D) 100

7

If the candidate received 313 votes in her last election, how many voters were registered in the district?

A) 100

B) 120

C) 1200

D) 2489

8

$$x^2 - x = 6$$

What is the absolute value of the difference of the solutions for x in the equation above?

9

$$x^2 - 10x = 0$$

What is the sum of the values of x in the equation above?

10

$$3x^2 - 9x + 16 = s$$

The time it takes, in seconds, for a computer algorithm to calculate the average of a set of digits is shown in the expression above, where x represents the number of digits in the set and s represents the number of seconds. If the computer takes 10 seconds to calculate an average of a set of numbers, how many numbers could be in the set?

Quadratic Functions and Graphs

Part 4

So far you have learned about quadratic equations and now we turn our attention to quadratic functions. In Section 4, you learned that a **function** is a formula that turns every "input" value into an "output" value. **Quadratic functions** are simply functions with a variable raised to the second power. Since you are now quadratic experts, we will also take a look at graphs in this section. All of the principles for the graphs of functions will also apply to graphs of equations. Like linear functions, quadratic functions can either be written with the function notation $f(x)$, or with a second variable like y:

$$f(x) = ax^2 + bx + c$$

$$y = ax^2 + bx + c$$

Graphing Quadratic Functions

To graph quadratic functions, let's begin with the simplest quadratic function:

$$f(x) = x^2$$

To start graphing this quadratic function, you can create a chart with some input and output values:

x	−3	−2	−1	0	1	2	3
$f(x)$	9	4	1	0	1	4	9

Then, you can plot these points on a graph:

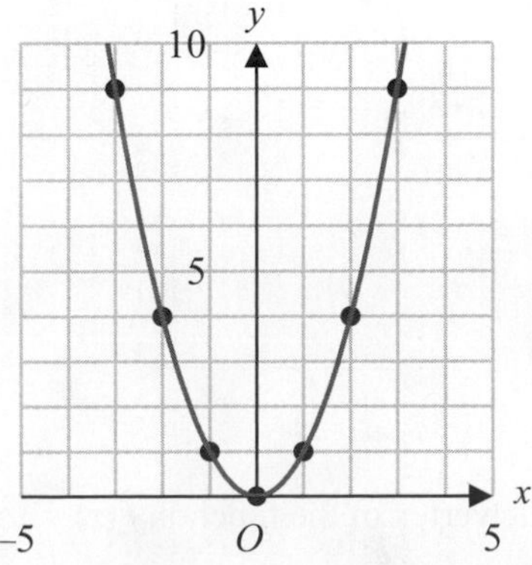

The type of curve created by graphing quadratic functions is called a **parabola**. Parabolas can move up or down, be wider or narrower, or flip upside down, but they will always retain this basic shape.

Notice that the parabola above is symmetric about the y-axis. All parabolas are symmetric about a vertical line drawn through their **vertex**, which is the highest or lowest point. To find the x-coordinate (h) of the vertex (h, k) of any parabola, you can use the following formula:

$$h = \frac{-b}{2a}$$

In the function above, b is equal to zero, so the vertex has the x-coordinate 0. If you plug $x = 0$ into the function, you can find the y-coordinate of the vertex: $f(x) = 0^2 = 0$. Therefore, the parabola's vertex is located at (0, 0)—which you can see on the graph.

What if we had the function $f(x) = x^2 + 4x$? In this case, $b = 4$, so the x-coordinate of the vertex would be $\frac{-b}{2a} = \frac{-4}{2 \times 1} = -2$. You can plug this x value into the function to find the y-coordinate: $f(x) = (-2)^2 + 4 \times (-2) = -4$. Therefore, the vertex is located at the point (–2, –4).

Transformations of Quadratic Functions

Like we saw in Section 4, manipulating a function will move or stretch the graph of the function on the coordinate plane.

If you add a constant to a quadratic function, this moves its vertex up or down. Adding a positive constant moves the vertex up, and adding a negative constant moves the vertex down. For example, if you add 5 to the function $f(x) = x^2$, you'll shift the vertex of the parabola up by 5 units. If you subtract 7, you'll shift the vertex of the parabola down by 7 units:

$f(x) = x^2 + 5$

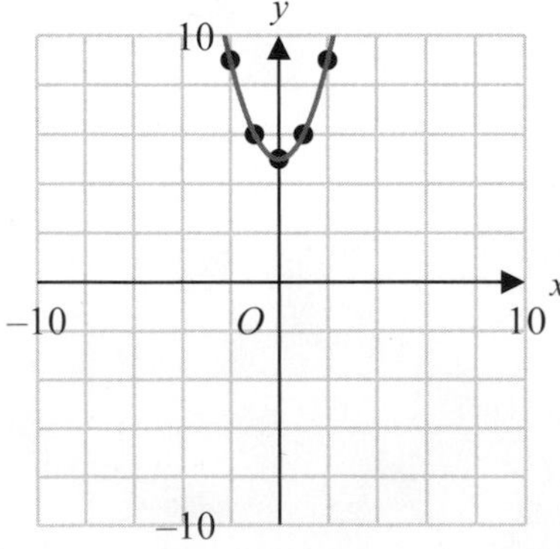

$f(x) = x^2 - 7$

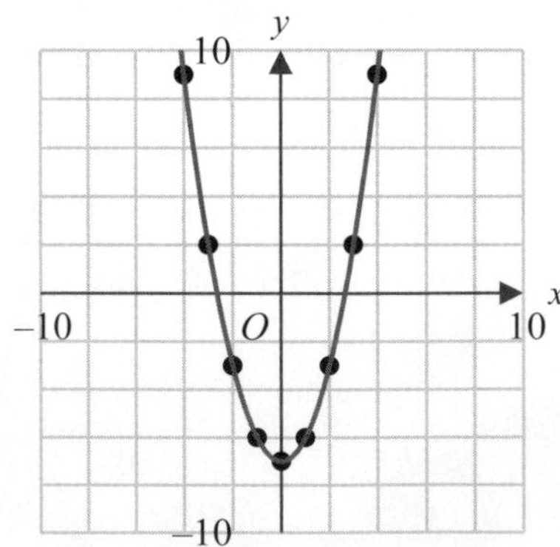

Instead of being located at (0, 0), the vertex of the function $f(x) = x^2 + 5$ is located at (0, 5). The vertex of the function $f(x) = x^2 - 7$ is located at (0, –7).

Just like with linear functions, you can shift a parabola left or right by taking the function of x plus a constant. Taking the function of x plus a constant for parabolas means replacing every x with x plus that constant. Adding a positive constant shifts the parabola's vertex to the left, and adding a negative constant shifts the parabola's vertex to the right. For example, if you take the function of $(x + 2)$, you'll shift the vertex of the parabola left by 2 units. If you take the function of $(x - 1)$, you'll shift the vertex of the parabola right by 1 unit:

$f(x) = (x + 2)^2$

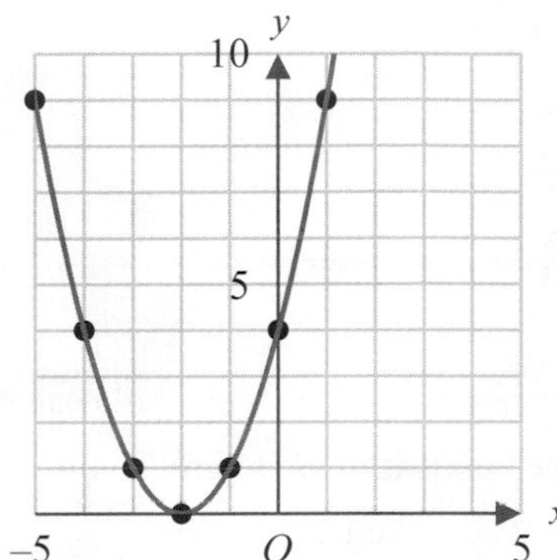

$f(x) = (x - 1)^2$

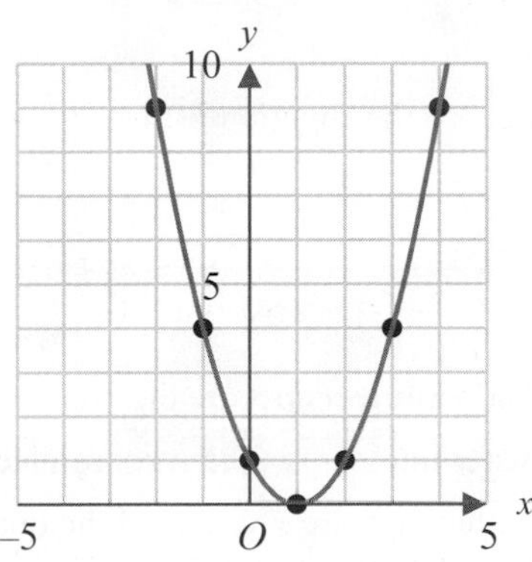

The vertex of the function $f(x) = (x + 2)^2$ is located at (–2, 0). The vertex of the function $f(x) = (x - 1)^2$ is located at (1, 0).

You can "stretch" a quadratic function by changing the value for a. If a is bigger than 1, you'll end up with a narrower parabola. If a is a fraction between 0 and 1, you'll end up with a wider parabola. For example, the function $f(x) = 2x^2$ is stretched so it is narrower, and the function $f(x) = \frac{1}{2}x^2$ is stretched so it is wider:

$f(x) = 2x^2$

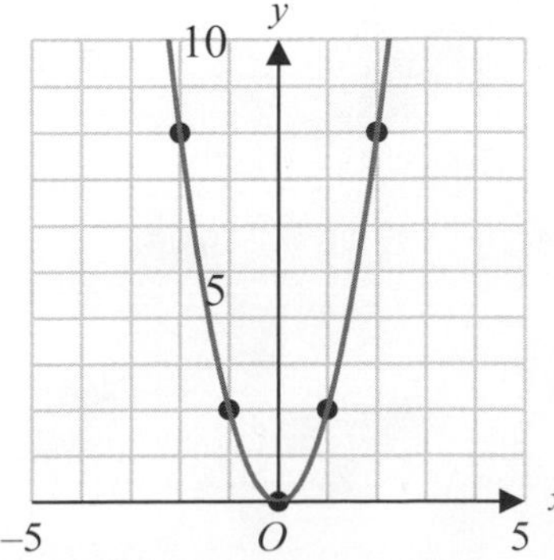

$f(x) = \frac{1}{2}x^2$

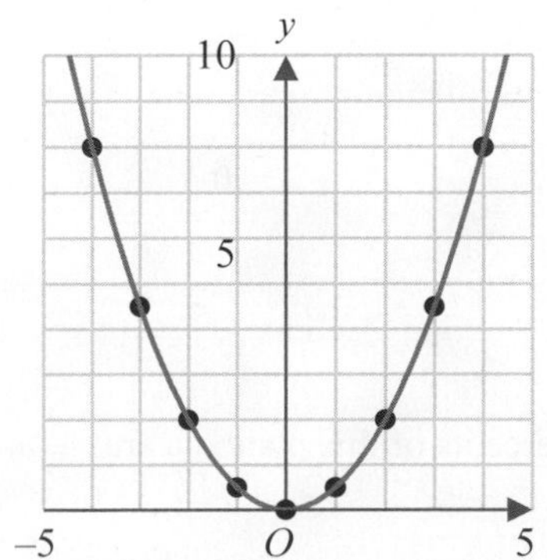

Finally, what about a negative constant? If a is equal to a negative number, the parabola flips upside down. In other words, it's reflected about the x-axis:

$$f(x) = -x^2$$

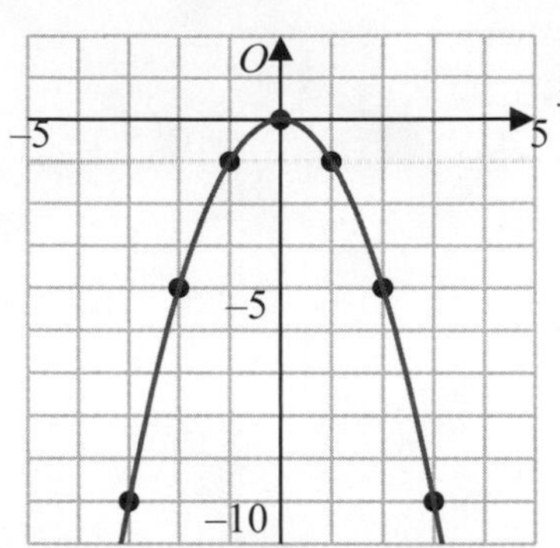

A parabola's ***x*-intercepts** are the points where the parabola meets the x-axis. A parabola can have zero, one, or two x-intercepts. The y-coordinate for any point on the x-axis is always zero, so the coordinates for the x-intercepts are x values of the quadratic function that will make y equal to 0.

You already know how to find the values of x that will make a quadratic function equal to 0—this is the same as finding the roots of any quadratic equation! Just set the quadratic function equal to zero, and then factor it into two binomials.

Example

$$f(x) = 6x^2 - 19x - 36$$

First, set this function equal to zero. Then, use the method you learned in Part 3 to factor and solve for x:

$$6x^2 - 19x - 36 = 0$$

$$(3x + 4)(2x - 9) = 0$$

$$3x + 4 = 0 \qquad\qquad 2x - 9 = 0$$

$$x = -\frac{4}{3} \qquad\qquad x = \frac{9}{2}$$

The x-intercepts of this parabola are $-\frac{4}{3}$ and $\frac{9}{2}$.

Systems of Equations

On the SAT, you might see systems of linear and quadratic equations. Since a linear equation represents a line and a quadratic equation represents a parabola, the solution to a system of a linear and a quadratic equation represents where that line and that parabola meet.

Systems of linear and quadratic equations can have zero, one, or two solutions. If there are no solutions, the line and the parabola do not intersect at all. If there is only one solution, the line is **tangent** to the parabola, touching it at exactly one point. If there are two solutions, the line intersects the parabola at two points.

To solve a system of equations consisting of one quadratic equation and one linear equation, you'll use substitution, just like with systems of linear equations.

Example

$$y + 30 = x^2 + 3x$$
$$y - 5x = 90$$

In order to substitute, you need to first solve for y in terms of x. Add $5x$ to both sides of the second equation:

$$y - 5x = 90$$
$$y = 5x + 90$$

Plug this value for y into the first equation:

$$y + 30 = x^2 + 3x$$
$$5x + 90 + 30 = x^2 + 3x$$

Then, solve this equation. Add and subtract like terms until one side is equal to zero:

$$5x + 90 + 30 = x^2 + 3x$$
$$x^2 - 2x - 120 = 0$$

Now you just need to use one of your strategies for solving quadratic equations. This one factors to:

$$(x + 10)(x - 12) = 0$$
$$x = -10 \quad \text{or} \quad x = 12$$

You're not done yet! You need to solve for both variables. Substitute these x values into either equation to find the corresponding y values. Both equations will give you the same values, so pick the easiest one to handle—usually the linear equation. Plug both x values into this equation:

$y = 5(-10) + 90$ $\qquad$ $y = 5(12) + 90$

$y = 40$ $\qquad$ $y = 150$

The parabola and the line intersect at two points: (–10, 40) and (12, 150).

Part 4 Practice: Quadratic Functions and Graphs

1

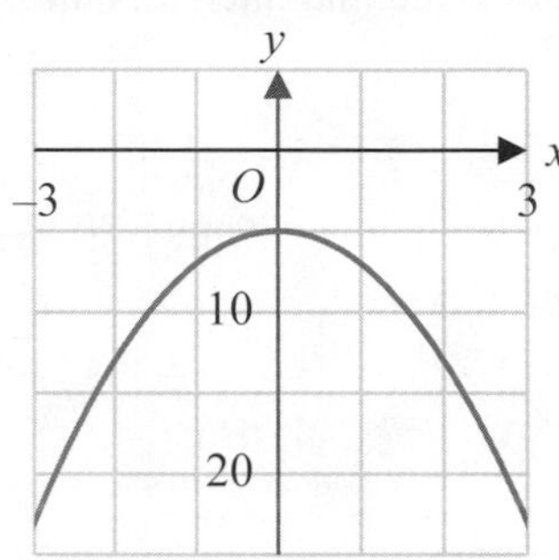

Which of the following functions could match the graph above?

A) $f(x) = -x^2 - 5$

B) $f(x) = x^2 - 5$

C) $f(x) = -2x^2 - 5$

D) $f(x) = 2x^2 - 5$

2

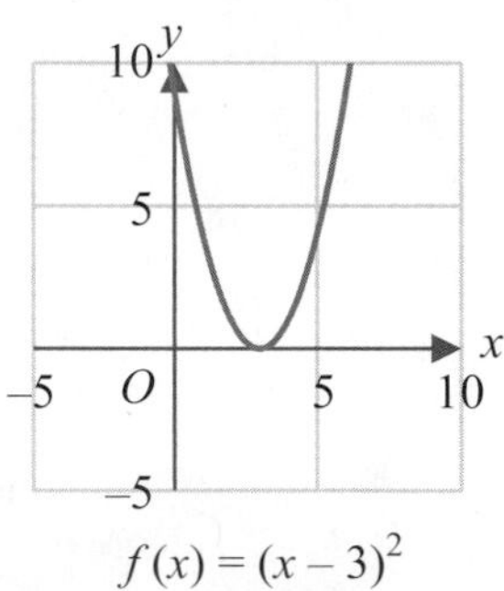

$f(x) = (x - 3)^2$

Which of the following statements is true about the graph of the function above?

A) It has a vertex at $x = -3$.

B) It has a vertex at $x = 3$.

C) It has no x-intercepts.

D) It has two x-intercepts.

3

Which of the following graphs could represent $f(x) = x^2 - 3$?

A)

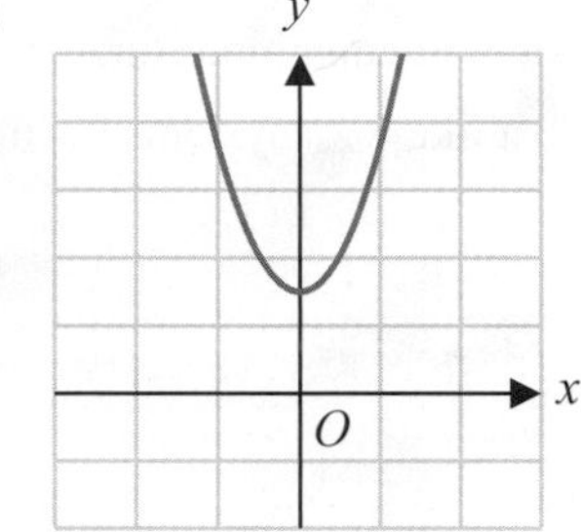

B)

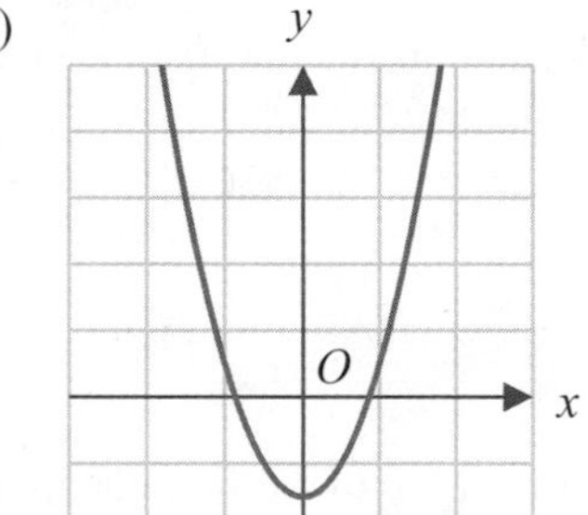

C)

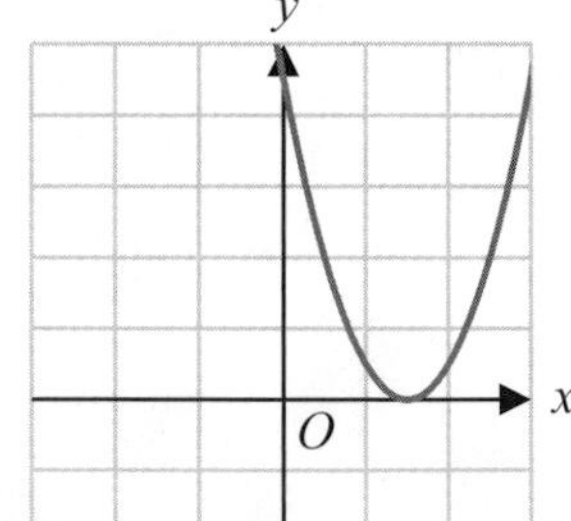

D)

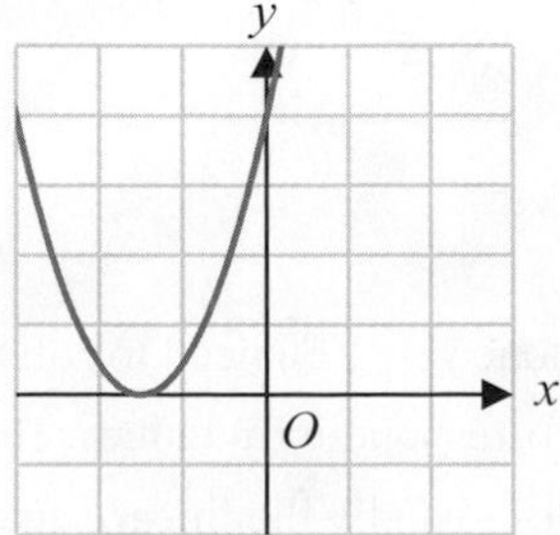

4

$$y = x^2 + 10x$$

$$y = 3x$$

At what value(s) of x do the two equations shown above intersect?

A) Only 0

B) Only –7

C) –7 and 0

D) 0 and 7

5

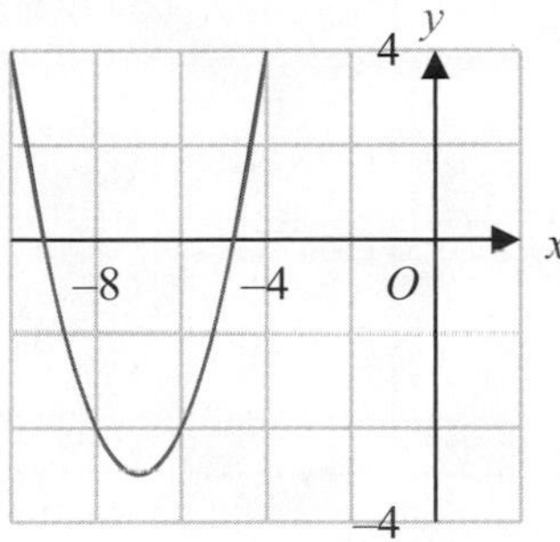

Which of the following functions models the graph above?

A) $f(x) = (x - 7)^2 - 3$

B) $f(x) = (x + 7)^2$

C) $f(x) = (x + 7)^2 - 3$

D) $f(x) = (x + 7)^2 + 3$

Questions 6 and 7 refer to the following information.

The Gross Domestic Product of a country (GDP) is the total goods and services produced by a country during a year. The GDP of Country A changes according to the equation $y = x^2 - 10x + 100$, where x represents the number of years since 2000, and y represents the country's GDP, in billions of dollars.

6

In what year does the equation predict that Country A's GDP will be 75 billion dollars?

A) 2005

B) 2006

C) 2007

D) 2008

7

The GDP of Country B changes according to the equation $y = 5x + 50$. In what year will Country A's GDP equal Country B's GDP?

A) 2007

B) 2008

C) 2009

D) 2010

8

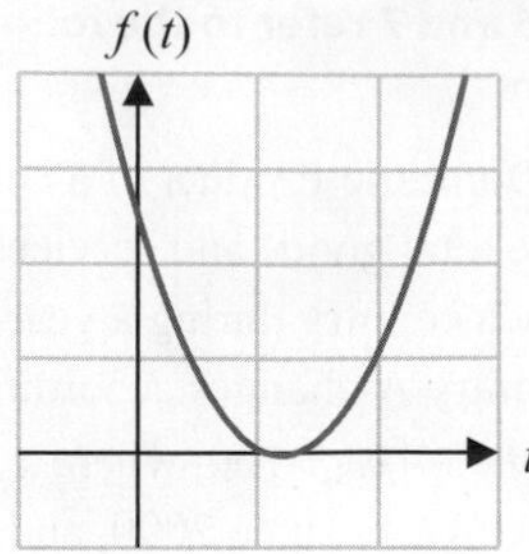

Alex throws a ball from the top of his house. The ball's motion can be modeled using the function $f(t) = t^2 - 14t + 49$, where t represents the number of milliseconds that have passed since Alex threw the ball. This function is shown above on the xy-axis. How many milliseconds will it take for the ball to hit the ground?

9

$$f(x) = x^2 - 8x + 16$$

What is the sum of the x-intercepts of the function above?

10

$$f(x) = x^2 - 6x + 8$$

What is the product of the x-intercepts in the function above?

Advanced Equations

Part 5

In this section, you'll learn about some more kinds of equations you might see on the SAT: exponential equations, rational equations, and radical equations.

Exponential Equations

In an **exponential equation**, the variable you are solving for is part of an exponent.

Example

$$2^x = 8$$

One way of putting this equation into words is, "2 raised to what power equals 8?" If you don't know off the top of your head, you can use trial and error:

$$2^1 = 2$$

$$2^2 = 4$$

$$2^3 = 8$$

Since $2^x = 8$ and $2^3 = 8$, you know that $x = 3$.

Sometimes the exponent will be a little more complicated:

Example

$$4^{2x-6} = 16$$

You know that $16 = 4^2$. Replacing 16 with 4^2 in the equation gives you:

$$4^{2x-6} = 4^2$$

Using exponent rules, since the bases are the same, you know that the exponents must also be the same. You can write an equation using only the exponents to solve for x:

$$2x - 6 = 2$$

$$x = 4$$

It's a good idea to check your work by plugging the value you found for x into the original equation:

$$4^{2(4)-6} = 4^{8-6} = 4^2 = 16$$

Since this gives you the same value, you know that x is equal to 4.

Rational Equations

A **rational equation** is one in which one or more terms are in the form of a fraction.

Example

$$\frac{x}{3} = \frac{1}{5}$$

You can cross-multiply to solve for x:

$$5 \times x = 1 \times 3$$

$$x = \frac{3}{5}$$

Now let's try something a little more complicated:

Example

$$\frac{1}{x+1} = \frac{2}{3x}$$

The idea is the same. You simply cross-multiply and divide to solve for x:

$$3x \times 1 = (x + 1) \times 2$$

$$3x = 2x + 2$$

$$x = 2$$

You have solved for x, and determined that it is equal to 2. But you're not quite done. When dealing with rational equations, you have to check that the solution was allowed by the original equation, which had some restrictions.

Restrictions are rules that limit the values that your variable is allowed to take. In the original equation, x can't be equal to negative 1 or 0 because this would mean you are dividing by zero. However, it isn't an issue if x is equal to 2—this isn't one of the restrictions of the equation. Therefore, you can now confidently say that $x = 2$.

Radical Equations

A **radical equation** is an equation where the variable is inside a radical.

Example

$$\sqrt{x} = 5$$

To solve this equation, you need to square both sides:

$$(\sqrt{x})^2 = 5^2$$
$$x = 25$$

You have determined that x is equal to 25.

What if the equation is a little more complicated?

Example

$$2\sqrt{x+8} - 4 = x + 1$$

Squaring both sides right away would lead to something very messy and unproductive. To save time and hassle, first isolate the radical by adding 4 to both sides:

$$2\sqrt{x+8} = x + 5$$

Now you can square both sides:

$$\left(2\sqrt{x+8}\right)^2 = (x+5)^2$$
$$4\,(x+8) = x^2 + 10x + 25$$
$$4x + 32 = x^2 + 10x + 25$$

Move everything to one side and combine like terms. Then, solve by factoring:

$$4x + 32 = x^2 + 10x + 25$$
$$x^2 + 6x - 7 = 0$$
$$(x+7)(x-1) = 0$$
$$x = -7 \quad \text{or} \quad x = 1$$

You have found that x is equal to -7 or 1, but you are not quite done. Squaring both sides of an equation can introduce extraneous solutions, so you need to check whether your values for x are real solutions of the equation. You can do this by plugging the solutions into both sides of the original equation and seeing if they match. Start with $x = -7$:

$$2\sqrt{-7+8} - 4 = -7 + 1$$

$$2 - 4 = -6$$

$$-2 = -6$$

Wrong!

Since the two sides are not equal, $x = -7$ is an extraneous solution. You have found that your solution for x doesn't include -7.

The fact that you ruled out one solution as extraneous doesn't necessarily mean the other solution is valid, so make sure to repeat the check with $x = 1$:

$$2\sqrt{1+8} - 4 = 1 + 1$$

$$2 \times 3 - 4 = 2$$

$$2 = 2$$

In this case, the two sides of the original equation match, so you can say that $x = 1$. This is the only solution for your equation.

Part 5 Practice: Advanced Equations

1

$$\frac{17}{2} = \frac{x}{5}$$

What is the value of x in the equation above?

A) $\frac{17}{5}$

B) $\frac{34}{5}$

C) $\frac{85}{4}$

D) $\frac{85}{2}$

2

$$\frac{x-2}{6} = \frac{x}{12}$$

Given the equation above, what is the value of $\frac{x}{3}$?

A) $\frac{2}{3}$

B) $\frac{4}{3}$

C) 2

D) 4

3

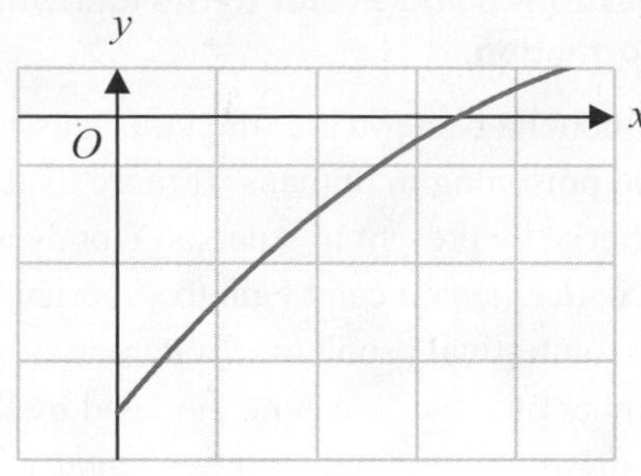

Which of the following equations could match the graph above?

A) $f(x) = \dfrac{1}{x} - 6$

B) $f(x) = 6x - 6$

C) $f(x) = \sqrt{x} - 6$

D) $f(x) = \sqrt{x} + 6$

4

$$\frac{5}{x} = \frac{4}{x-1}$$

Which of the following statements is true about the equation above?

I. It has no real solutions.
II. Its domain includes all real numbers except for 0 and 1.
III. It has one real solution.

A) I only
B) II only
C) I and II
D) III only

5

$$f(x) = \sqrt{-x} - 9$$

Which of the following graphs could represent the equation above?

A)

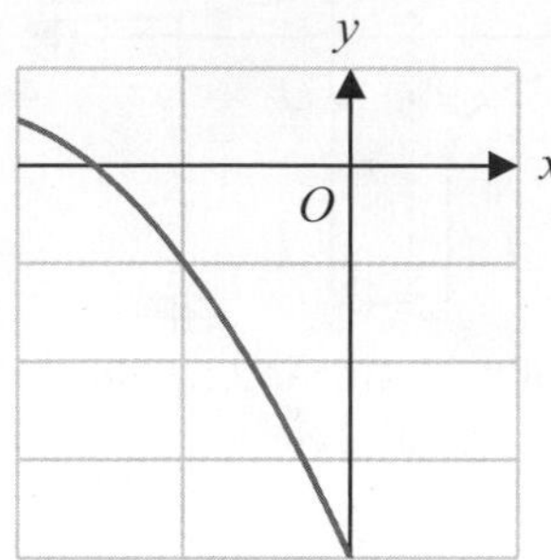

B)

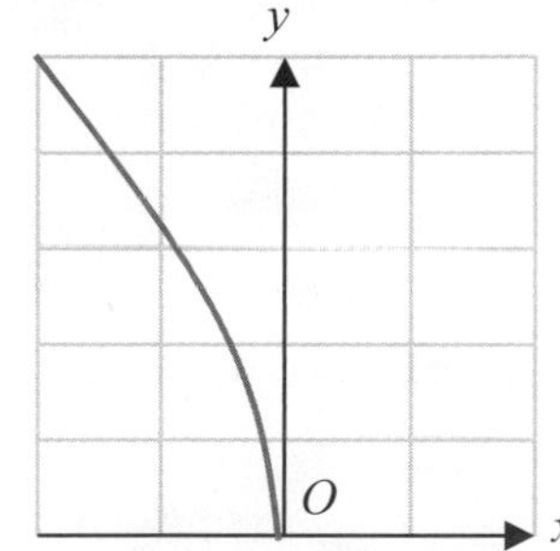

C)

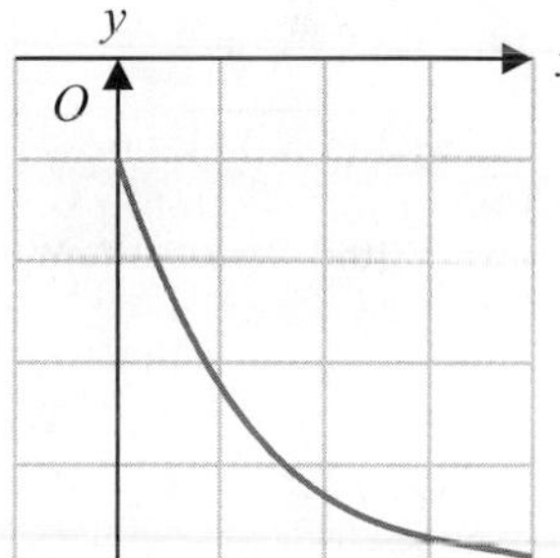

D)

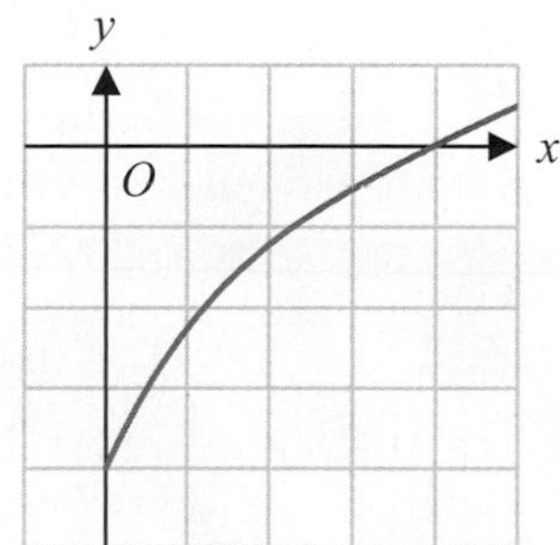

6

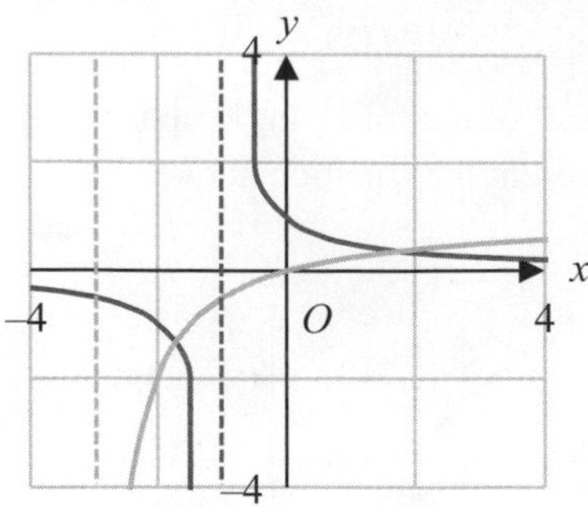

Which of the following equations could match the graph above?

A) $\frac{1}{x+1} = \frac{x}{x+3}$

B) $\frac{1}{x+1} = \frac{x}{x-3}$

C) $\frac{1}{x-1} = \frac{1}{x-3}$

D) $\frac{x}{x-1} = \frac{1}{x+3}$

7

$$\sqrt{2(x+15)} = 6$$

Based on the equation above, what is the value of $(4+x)^2$?

A) –4

B) 16

C) 36

D) 49

Questions 8 and 9 refer to the following information.

Salmonella bacteria are often the cause of food poisoning in humans. If more than 64 bacteria are present in a person's body at once, that person can begin to experience mild gastrointestinal problems. In Person A, the number of bacteria can be modeled by the equation $f(t) = 2^t$, where t represents the number of minutes since the first bacterium enters the person's body.

8

How many minutes will it take for this person to begin experiencing gastrointestinal issues?

9

In another person, whose body is less resistant to salmonella bacteria, the bacteria's growth can be modeled using the equation $f(t) = 16^{t-3}$. How many minutes earlier will this person begin to experience gastrointestinal problems?

10

The median household income of Country A grows according to the equation $f(t) = \sqrt{3t-5}$, where t represents the number of years since 2010. The median household income of Country B grows according to the equation $f(t) = t - 3$. In what year will the two countries have the same median household income?

Applications of Functions

Part 6

The functions discussed in this chapter have several real-world applications. In this section you'll get a look at applications that you might see on the SAT.

Zeroes and Intercepts

Recall that the zeroes of a function are the places where its graph intersects the x-axis. This can also be used in real-world applications.

Example

Juana throws a paper airplane. Its height h meters above the ground at time t seconds is given by $h = -t^2 + 3t + 10$. At what time does it fall to the ground?

When the airplane falls to the ground, you know that its height above the ground is zero. Since you know that $h = 0$, you can write the function as:

$$0 = -t^2 + 3t + 10$$

Now you're back in familiar territory. Factoring out the negative sign will give you:

$$0 = t^2 - 3t - 10$$

From here we can find the factors of the equation:

$$0 = (t + 2)(t - 5)$$

As an equation, this has the solutions $t = -2$ or $t = 5$. However, you're looking for a specific time, and you know that a real quantity such as time can never be negative. This means that you know that the paper airplane hits the ground at $t = 5$ seconds.

Other Problems with Quadratics

The SAT may also ask you to find particular points in a function that show you understand its structure. Let's use the same paper airplane to solve a different problem:

Example

Juana throws a paper airplane. Its height h above the ground at time t seconds is given by $h = -t^2 + 3t + 10$. At what time after it is thrown is its height the same as the height at which Juana threw it?

To solve this problem, you need to understand that when Juana threw the airplane, its time t was 0. You can find its height by plugging that value in for t:

$$h = -(0^2) + 3(0) + 10$$

$$h = 10$$

Now you want to find the other value of t that gives h a value of 10, which you can do by setting h equal to 10 and factoring.

$$10 = -t^2 + 3t + 10$$

$$0 = -t^2 + 3t + 10 - 10$$

$$0 = -t^2 + 3t$$

$$0 = (-t)(t - 3)$$

Factoring reveals that $t = 0$ or $t = 3$. In this case, you know that $t = 0$ when Juana threw the airplane, which means we want the other value. The airplane reaches the same height it was thrown from when $t = 3$.

Exponential Growth

One common use of exponential functions is to model the growth of particular populations. **Exponential growth** occurs when a quantity increases by the same factor over a particular period of time.

Example

A colony of bacteria that begins with 100 specimens doubles in size every hour. What function models the colony's rate of growth?

If the colony begins with 100 specimens, the equation after it has doubled in size can be given by:

$$y = 100 \times 2$$

That's the number that will double in the next hour, meaning that after two hours, the number of bacteria will be:

$$y = 100 \times 2 \times 2$$

Following this pattern, you can see that you are multiplying the original number by increasing powers of 2. You can create a general function for this that looks like this:

$$y = 100 \times 2^x$$

Where x stands for the number of hours the bacteria have been multiplying.

Exponential functions create graphs that look like this:

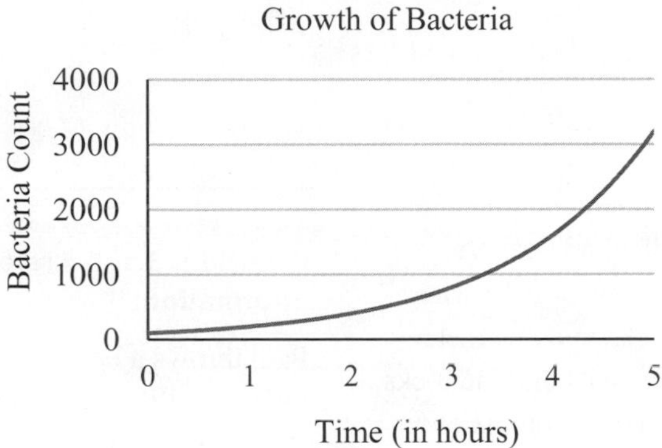

Exponential curves look similar to one half of a parabola. They're smooth curves that curve up slowly at first and become increasingly steep. They also don't reverse direction; one end is always going up and the other is always going down. If you see this shape on the SAT you'll know it represents exponential growth.

Equation Comparison

Linear, quadratic, and exponential functions can all be used to model situations. Here is a table and a graph comparing examples of the first few values of each of these types:

x	0	1	2	3	4	5
Linear: $y = 3x + 5$	5	8	11	14	17	20
Quadratic: $y = x^2 + 5$	5	6	9	14	21	30
Exponential: $y = 2^x + 4$	5	6	8	12	20	36

Notice that the linear function grows the fastest at the start, and the quadratic function catches up first. But, by the end, the exponential function is both the biggest and growing the fastest. The following graph shows the comparison of these three equation types:

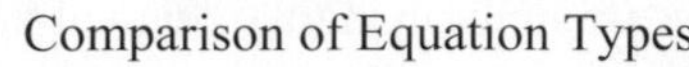

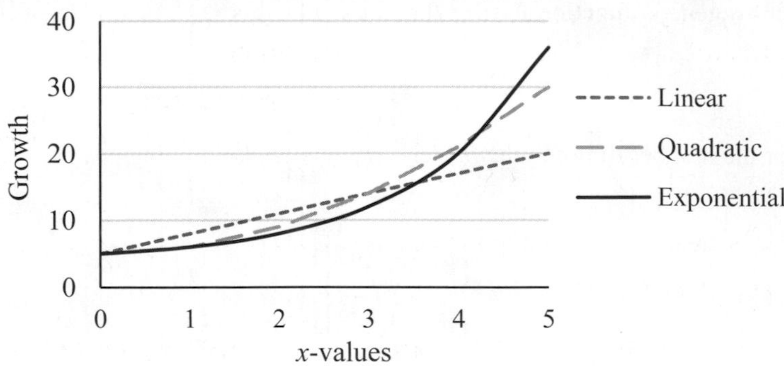

Part 6 Practice: Applications of Functions

1

Rocks are falling and fill a large cavern according to the equation $c = 2^s + 2s$, where c is the volume of the rocks in cubic meters and s is the number of seconds that the rocks have been falling. What is the volume of rocks in the cavern, in cubic meters, after 4 seconds?

A) 4

B) 8

C) 24

D) 32

2

Bacteria triple every hour in a petri dish. If there are 2 colonies to begin with, which of the following functions could represent these bacteria's growth?

A) $b(t) = t^2 + 3$

B) $b(t) = \frac{t}{3} + 2$

C) $b(t) = 2(3^t)$

D) $b(t) = 3(2^t) + 2$

Questions 3 and 4 refer to the following information.

Paul throws a book straight up in the air. The height h of the book at time t is given by $h = -t^2 + 3t + 4$, where h is measured in meters.

3

There are approximately 3.281 feet in a meter. How many feet from the floor was Paul holding the book when he threw it?

A) 4.0 feet

B) 6.562 feet

C) 9.843 feet

D) 13.124 feet

4

Which of the following plots could show the trajectory of the book?

A)

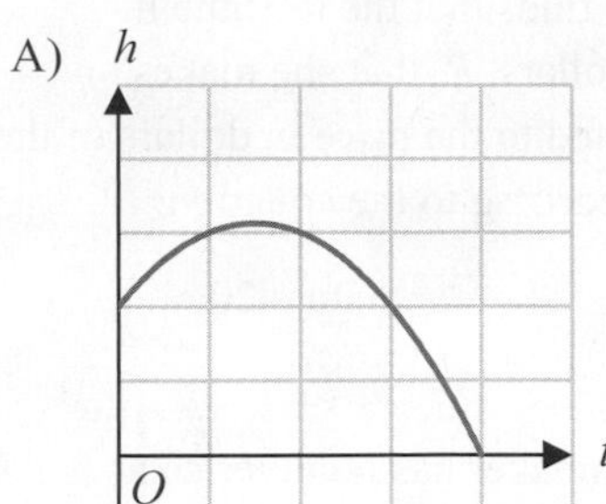

B)

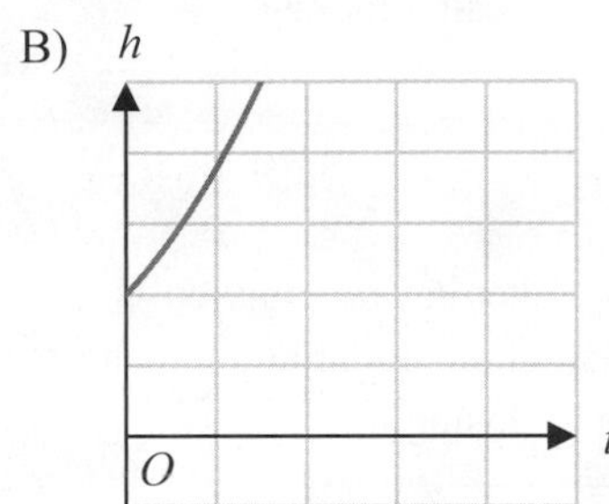

C)

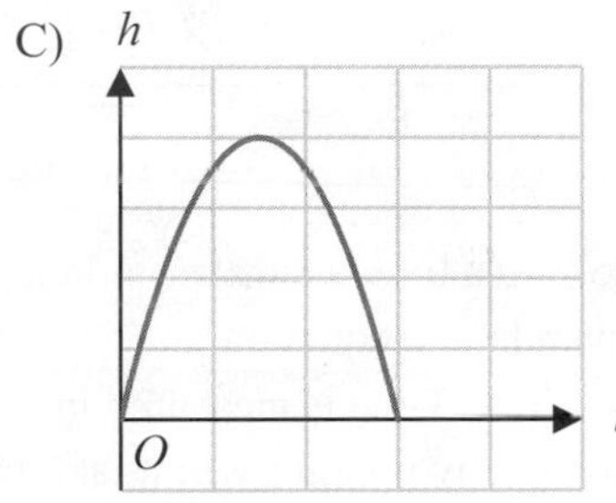

D)

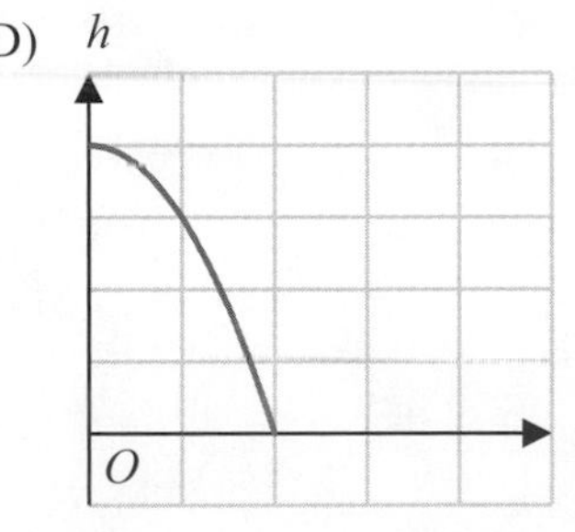

Questions 5 and 6 refer to the following information.

For the past 10 years since the opening of City X's subway system, annual ridership has been 1.2 times larger than it was the year before. The city develops a subway model where each rider represents one thousand people.

5

If there were originally 4000 subway riders in their model, what is the equation that expresses this pattern if t represents the number of years since the subway's opening?

A) $f(t) = 1.2^t + 4000$

B) $f(t) = 4000(1.2)^t$

C) $f(t) = 4000^t$

D) $f(t) = 4000^{1.2t}$

6

City Y's subway ridership grows according to the equation $f(t) = 60t + 1000$, and City Z's subway ridership grows according to the equation $f(t) = 10t^2 + 2000$. Which of the following options correctly orders their growth rates from smallest to largest?

A) City Y, City X, City Z

B) City X, City Z, City Y

C) City Z, City X, City Y

D) City Y, City Z, City X

7

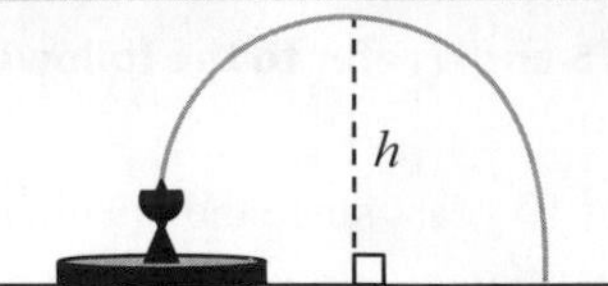

From its base, a fountain shoots water up to 25 feet into the air, as shown above. If the water takes 5 seconds to fall back to the ground from its highest point, which of the functions below models the water's height h at time t?

A) $h(t) = -t^2 + 25$

B) $h(t) = -t^2 + 10t + 25$

C) $h(t) = t^2 - 10t - 2$

D) $h(t) = 10t - t^2$

Questions 8 and 9 refer to the following information.

A watchmaker finds that the revenue in thousands of dollars, R, that she makes on watches is related to the price in dollars of the watches, p, according to the equation:

$$R = -p^2 + 9p - 20$$

8

If the watchmaker has no other costs, what is the lowest whole dollar amount she can charge without losing money?

9

If the watchmaker has no other costs, what is the highest whole dollar amount she can charge without losing money?

10

The volume V of a basin of water, in liters at time t, is given by the equation $V = t^2 - 24t + 144$. Time is measured in seconds. How many minutes will it take for the basin to be empty?

Section 5

Problem Solving and Data Analysis

What do music, football, and chemistry have in common with politics and the economy? Aside from improving college applications, all of these subjects can be analyzed in numbers, tables, and graphs. How many people who play football like to sing opera? Where do these people reside, and what kind of food do they eat—how is this food prepared, packaged and brought to their markets? In this section, we'll talk about how to measure and convert information, how to look at it in various forms, and what it all means. This section will show you how to analyze ideas and theories using numbers, text, tables, and different types of diagrams.

We will cover the following topics:

- Measurements and Units
- Properties of Data
- Ratios, Rates, and Proportions
- Probability and Statistics
- Modeling Data
- Using Data as Evidence

Measurements and Units

Part 1

You use **units** in your life every day. The distance you travel to school, the time you spend studying, and the price of this book are all described in terms of units. Units like miles, feet, and meters are units of distance. Seconds, days, and years are units of time. Dollars and cents are units of currency. A dozen is a unit that refers to a group of 12 things.

There are two systems of units frequently used to measure mass, length, and volume. The **imperial system** is used frequently in the United States. While these units appear on the SAT regularly, they are always accompanied by their conversion values. The following table summarizes common units in imperial units of measurement:

Weight	Length	Volume
Ounce	Inch	Cup
Pound: 16 ounces	Foot: 12 inches	Pint: 2 cups
Ton: 2000 pounds	Yard: 3 feet	Quart: 2 pints (4 cups)
	Mile: 1760 yards (5280 feet)	Gallon: 4 quarts (16 cups)

The **metric system** is commonly used internationally and in the scientific community. This system also appears frequently on the SAT. However, their conversion values are not provided and must be memorized. In the metric system, mass is measured in grams (g), length is measured in meters (m), and volume is measured in liters (l).

The metric system uses prefixes, or different word beginnings, to indicate multiples of 10. These prefixes can be combined with any of the units (grams, meters, or liters). Each prefix has a short form that is combined with the unit abbreviation. The following table summarizes the metric system:

Factor	1,000	100	10	0.1	0.01	0.001
Prefix	Kilo	Hecto	Deca	Deci	Centi	Milli
Short Form	K	h	D	d	c	m

For example, a kilogram (kg) is 1,000 grams, a centimeter (cm) is 0.01 meters, and a milliliter (ml) is 0.001 liters.

Here's a quick way to remember the correct order of prefixes. If you write out the prefix abbreviations from biggest to smallest, you'll get:

k h D d c m

A common phrase to remember this order is **K**ing **H**enry **D**ied **D**rinking **C**hocolate **M**ilk.

Conversions

Some problems on the SAT will require you to convert between different units. To do this, set up a ratio between the two units so that the numerator and the denominator are equal. For example, let's look at converting kilometers (km) to meters (m). Since 1 km = 1,000 m, the ratio of meters to kilometers is:

$$\frac{1{,}000 \text{ m}}{1 \text{ km}}$$

This can also be written as a ratio of kilometers to meters:

$$\frac{1{,}000 \text{ m}}{1 \text{ km}} = \frac{1 \text{ km}}{1{,}000 \text{ m}}$$

The ratio between two units is called a **conversion factor**. Conversion factors are always equal to 1 because the numerator is equal to the denominator.

To convert a measurement into a different value, multiply it by the conversion factor with the desired units on top and the current units on the bottom. When you multiply a measurement by a conversion factor, the old units cancel out in the numerator and denominator. You are left with the new units:

$$\frac{16 \cancel{\text{km}}}{1} \times \frac{1{,}000 \text{ m}}{1 \cancel{\text{km}}} = 16{,}000 \text{ m}$$

Always check that the units cancel out correctly. You should be able to cancel out all units in the conversion except for the units of the answer.

You may also have to convert between units in different systems on the SAT. The SAT problems will give you the necessary conversion factors.

Example

Approximately how many centimeters are in half a mile? (Assume that 1 mile is equal to 1.6 kilometers.)

This problem requires multiple conversions. First, convert 0.5 miles to kilometers:

$$0.5 \text{ miles} \times \frac{1.6 \text{ km}}{1 \text{ mile}} = 0.8 \text{ km}$$

Now convert 0.8 kilometers to centimeters. It may be easiest to convert first to meters, then centimeters like this:

$$0.8 \text{ km} \times \frac{1{,}000 \text{ m}}{1 \text{ km}} \times \frac{100 \text{ cm}}{1 \text{ m}} = 80{,}000 \text{ cm}$$

Half a mile is equal to 80,000 centimeters.

Compound Units

A car's speedometer measures its speed in miles per hour and kilometers per hour. Gas mileage is measured in miles per gallon. These quantities have **compound units**, or units that combine multiple measurements. Speed depends on measurements of both distance and time. Gas mileage depends on measurements of distance and volume of gas consumed.

When you use or convert compound measurements, pay extra attention to the units of quantities and answers. Convert one unit at a time. For example, speed is always distance divided by time. When you convert speed using different units, check that the new units are also distance over time.

Example

What is 15 m/s in km/hr?

You can solve this using the same conversion method you practiced earlier:

$$\frac{15 \text{ m}}{\text{s}} \times \frac{1 \text{ km}}{1{,}000 \text{ m}} \times \frac{60 \text{ s}}{1 \text{ min}} \times \frac{60 \text{ min}}{1 \text{ hr}} = \frac{54 \text{ km}}{\text{hr}}$$

15 m/s is equal to 54 km/hr. Both m/s and km/hr are correct units of speed because they are units of distance over time.

Word Problems

Units and measurements often appear in SAT word problems. Some of the problems will involve conversions and compound units. Most of the problems that you will solve will be either distance and rate problems, or geometry and measurement problems. Here is an example of a geometry and measurement problem:

Example

A wooden cube has a side length of 20 cm. Its density is 0.65 g/cm^3. What is the mass of the block in kilograms? (Density is equal to mass divided by volume.)

Your first step is finding the volume of the block. The volume of a cube is equal to its side length cubed, so the volume of the block is equal to:

$$\text{volume} = (20 \text{ cm})^3 = 8{,}000 \text{ cm}^3$$

Now you can find the mass of the block through the density formula in the question. You can re-arrange that formula in order to solve for mass:

$$\text{density} = \frac{\text{mass}}{\text{volume}}$$

$$\text{mass} = \text{density} \times \text{volume}$$

Just plug in the values that you have for density and volume:

$$\text{mass} = \frac{0.65\text{g}}{\text{cm}^3} \times 8{,}000 \text{ cm}^3 = 5{,}200 \text{ g}$$

Now you have calculated that the mass of the block is 5,200 grams. The last step is converting the mass of the block from grams to kilograms:

$$5{,}200 \text{ g} \times \frac{1 \text{ kg}}{1{,}000 \text{ g}} = 5.2 \text{ kg}$$

The mass of the block is 5.2 kg.

Now let's take a look at a speed and distance problem:

Example

A train travels from Toronto to Hamilton, a distance of 72 km. The train travels at an average speed of 36 km/hr. How many hours did the trip take?

To solve this problem, all you need to use is the average speed as a conversion factor:

$$72 \text{ km} \times \frac{1 \text{ hr}}{36 \text{ km}} = 2 \text{ hours}$$

Since the kilometer units cancel, you are left with your answer of 2 hours.

Here is an important formula to remember when answering speed and distance questions:

$$\text{distance} = \text{rate} \times \text{time}$$

You could also solve the question above using this formula. Just plug in 72 km for distance and 36 km/hr for rate, and then solve for time:

$$72 \text{ km} = 36 \text{ km/hr} \times \text{time}$$

$$\text{time} = \frac{72 \text{ km}}{36 \text{ km/hr}} = 2 \text{ hours}$$

Using this formula, you get the same answer: the trip took 2 hours.

Part 1 Practice: Measurements and Units

1

How many milliliters are in 0.65 liters?

A) 650
B) 65
C) 6.5
D) 0.65

2

How many meters are there in 18,000 millimeters?

A) 1.8
B) 18
C) 180
D) 1,800

3

Lewis' car is 85 inches wide and he is trying to park in a space with a width of 2.4 yards. Which of the following most accurately states whether Lewis's car will fit in the parking space? (There are 12 inches in a foot and 3 feet in a yard.)

A) The width of Lewis' car will fit in the parking space.
B) Lewis' car is too wide for the parking space.
C) Lewis' car precisely matches the width of the parking space.
D) Lewis cannot compare the width of the car to the width of the parking space.

4

Seconds	$f(s) = sf(m)$
Minutes	$f(m) = mf(h)$
Hours	$f(h) = 0.8$

If s is the number of seconds in a minute and m is the number of minutes in an hour, what is the value of $f(s)$ in the table above?

A) 1.6
B) 2.9
C) 1,440
D) 2,880

5

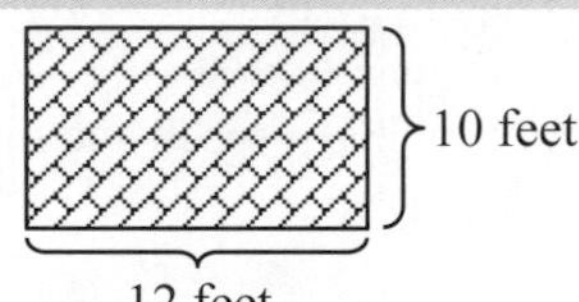

Mr. and Mrs. Liu are covering their living room floor with tiles, as shown in the diagram above. If the tiles cost $5 per square foot, how much will they spend on tiles?

A) $120
B) $240
C) $600
D) $2,400

6

Alex drove 6 miles from his house to the grocery store at an average speed of s mph. On the way back, Alex drove this same distance at an average speed of 33 mph. If Alex's average speed was 27.5 mph, what is the value for s?

A) 33

B) 22

C) 11

D) 10

7

Tyler went for a 20 km bike ride. If he rode for an hour and 20 minutes, what was his average speed, in kilometers per hour?

A) 30

B) 20

C) 16

D) 15

8

To train for an upcoming 10 km race, Mariam ran 5 km to the post office and back. If it took her 25 minutes to run there and 30 minutes to run back, what was her average pace over her whole run, in minutes per kilometer?

Questions 9 and 10 refer to the following information.

A factory produces silver and gold alloys for mass market jewelry stores. Its suppliers measure the silver and gold in grams, but the plant measures the two elements by volume.

9

If the density of silver is 10.5 g/cm^3, what is the mass, in grams, of a rectangular block of silver with the dimensions 2 cm by 5 cm by 10 cm?

10

The density of gold is 19.3 g/cm^3. What volume of gold, rounded to the nearest tenth of a cubic centimeter, has the same mass as 100 cm^3 of silver?

Properties of Data

Part 2

Data sets are just collections of numbers. Without context, they are not very useful. In order to interpret what the numbers mean and to make conclusions based on the data, you need to be able to determine the data's properties.

Let's say that a small group gets scores of 20, 15, 13, 12, 20 and 18 on a test—are these good scores? If the test is out of 20, then perhaps they are, but what if the test is out of 25 or 30? Also, can we say that most of the group did well if the average score is fairly high? If another person, Michael, joins the group and gets a 17 on the same test, is this a good mark compared to the others? Further, how does the addition of Michael's individual score affect the group's overall score?

The properties of data, range, mean, median, mode, and standard deviation will help us to answer these questions. In addition to looking at numbers, you'll also need to be able to interpret data presented visually in a chart or a graph on the SAT. Let's look at these concepts and how to use them.

Range

The **range** of a set of data is the difference between its biggest and smallest values. All data in a set of data fall within the set's range. To find the range of any set of data, put the data in numerical order and subtract the smallest from the biggest value.

Example

Dmitri's History Quiz Scores				
Quiz 1	Quiz 2	Quiz 3	Quiz 4	Quiz 5
87	83	94	87	90

What is the range of Dmitri's quiz scores in the chart above?

To find the range of these scores, let's first put them in numerical order:

83, 87, 87, 90, 94

Dmitri's lowest score was 83 and his highest was 94, so his range is the difference between these two:

$$\text{Range} = 94 - 83 = 11$$

Dmitri's scores fall within a range of 11 points.

Mean

The **mean** (or arithmetic mean) of a set of data is the same as its **average**. To calculate the mean or average of a set of data, add up all of the data values and divide by the total number of data points:

$$\text{Mean} = \frac{\text{Sum of all values in the set}}{\text{Total number of terms in the set}}$$

Example

What is the mean of Dmitri's quiz scores from the previous chart?

First add up all his scores. Then divide by the number of quizzes:

$$\frac{87 + 83 + 94 + 87 + 90}{5} = \frac{441}{5} = 88.2$$

Dmitri's average score is 88.2.

Median

The **median** refers to the value that is exactly in the middle of a set of data. To find the median, put all of the data in numerical order and locate the middle number.

Example

What is the median of Dmitri's quiz scores?

Put the scores in numerical order:

83, 87, 87, 90, 94

The middle number in this data set is 87, so Dmitri's median history quiz score is 87.

What if your data set has an even number of values, so there is no middle number? In this case, the median is the average of the two numbers closest to the middle.

Example

Dmitri is able to score a 99 on his sixth history quiz. What is the median of his new set of scores?

The data set will now be:

83, 87, 87, 90, 94, 99

There is no number in the middle of this set of data, but the two numbers closest to the middle are 87 and 90. To find the median, take the average of these two numbers:

$$\frac{87+90}{2} = 88.5$$

The average of 87 and 90 is 88.5, so 88.5 is the median of Dmitri's six quiz scores.

Mode

The **mode** of a set of data refers to the value that occurs most frequently. A set of data can have one or more modes if there are one or more numbers that occur more frequently than any other number. A set of data may have no mode if all values occur the same number of times.

Example

Dmitri and his classmates received the following scores on their last history quiz: 91, 88, 94, 90, 82, 79, 84, 94, 85, 88, 93, 97, 92, 80, 96. Identify the mode or modes in this data set.

The answer to this question is easiest to find out if we put the data in numerical order:

79, 80, 82, 84, 85, 88, 88, 90, 91, 92, 93, 94, 94, 96, 97

Both 88 and 94 occur two times, and the rest of the values only occur once. Therefore, 88 and 94 are the two modes of these quiz scores.

Standard Deviation

Standard deviation measures how much the values in a set of data vary from its mean. The greater the standard deviation, the farther the data points are from the mean. For example, take a look at these two lists of data:

List A: 1, 2, 3, 10, 17, 18, 19

List B: 7, 8, 9, 10, 11, 12, 13

Although these two lists both have a mean of 10, List A has a higher standard deviation because the points are more spread out.

While you will most likely not need to calculate standard deviation on the SAT directly, standard deviation can be found with the following expression, where m is the mean of the data set, n is the number of data points, and each value of x represents an individual data point:

$$\sqrt{\frac{(x_1-m)^2+(x_2-m)^2+(x_3-m)^2+\ldots+(x_n-m)^2}{n}}$$

To use this formula, first square the difference between each data point and the mean. Then, add together these squares, divide by the number of data points, and take the square root of the result.

Example

What is the standard deviation of the data set $\{1, 3, 6, 8, 12\}$?

First, calculate the mean:

$$m = \frac{1 + 3 + 6 + 8 + 12}{5}$$

$$m = 6$$

For each data point, find its difference from the mean, square this difference, and add together the squares:

$$= (1 - 6)^2 + (3 - 6)^2 + (6 - 6)^2 + (8 - 6)^2 + (12 - 6)^2$$

$$= 25 + 9 + 0 + 4 + 36$$

$$= 74$$

Then, take the average of the differences by dividing the sum by the number of data points:

$$\frac{74}{5} = 14.8$$

And finally, take the square root:

$$\sqrt{14.8} \approx 3.85$$

The standard deviation of this data set is about 3.85.

You can also say that a data point is a certain number of standard deviations away from the mean. For example, let's look at the first number in the data set above—the number 1. The mean of the data set is 6, so 1 is 5 units away from the mean. In order to express this difference in terms of standard deviations, just divide by the standard deviation of the data set, which is 3.85:

$$\frac{5}{3.85} \approx 1.3$$

1 is approximately 1.3 standard deviations from the mean.

Charts

One way to make properties of data easy to see is to display them as a chart or graph. When you see a question with a chart or graph, examine it carefully to make sure you understand it. Ask yourself the following questions:

- What is the main purpose of this chart or graph?
- What is being measured?
- What is the **scale**, or what units are being used?

Let's use these questions to analyze the chart below:

Population (in thousands) by Town, 1960-2000			
Town	1960	1980	2000
Cedarville	72	83	104
Franklin	80	82	73
Pine Ridge	121	136	143

- What is the main purpose of this chart or graph? From the title, you can tell that the chart above shows the population of several towns from 1960 to 2000.
- What is being measured? The chart is comparing the population of these three different towns (Cedarville, Franklin, and Pine Ridge) at three different dates (1960, 1980, and 2000).
- What is the scale, or what units are being used? The numbers give the population of each town for each year. Notice that the data is represented in thousands.

Now that you are familiar with this data in chart format, let's take a look at how it might be represented in different types of graphs. The most common types of graphs on the SAT include pie charts, bar graphs, line graphs, and histograms.

Pie Charts

A **pie chart** compares different sections of data as fractions out of a whole. A circle represents the total amount, and differently sized sections of that circle represent parts out of the total amount. A legend or labels on the chart will explain what data each section represents.

Let's look again at the populations of Cedarville, Franklin, and Pine Ridge in 1960. Here is a representation of the data as a pie chart:

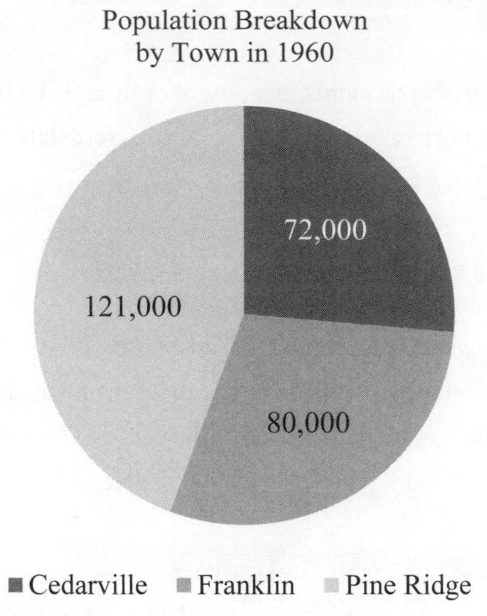

The title of this graph tells you that you are looking at the population of the three towns in 1960. The legend tells you that each of the slices in this pie chart represents a town, and the entire pie chart represents the total population of all three towns. The data labels for each slice also tell you exactly how many people lived in each town.

You can also estimate the relative proportion of residents by looking at the sizes of their slices in the pie chart. You can tell that slightly more than a quarter of the people lived in Cedarville, slightly less than a third lived in Franklin, and slightly less than half lived in Pine Ridge.

Bar Graphs

A **bar graph** uses bars of different lengths to compare different categories of data. Bar graphs represent data along two axes, using vertical or horizontal bars. If a bar graph uses differently colored or patterned bars, the legend will explain what other variables these colors or patterns represent.

The data from the chart we saw earlier can be represented in a bar graph:

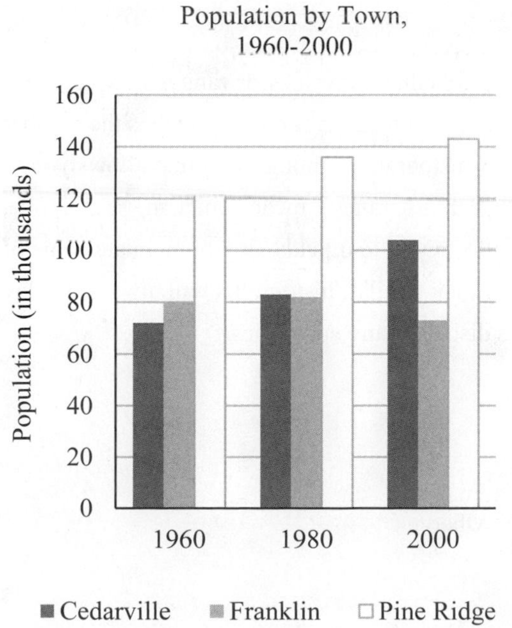

In this graph, the legend tells you that the different-colored bars represent different towns. These are grouped together at each date along the horizontal axis. The vertical axis displays what is being measured: population. Again, you are told that the units are in thousands.

Because numbers are given in thousands, each tick mark along the vertical axis represents 20,000 people. With these tick marks, you can tell that the population of Pine Ridge in 1960 was about 120,000, and by 1980 it had grown by about 15,000. You can also tell that the populations of Cedarville and Franklin were relatively similar in 1960 and 1980, but they differed by about 30,000 people in 2000.

Line Graphs

A **line graph** uses a line or several lines to represent changes in amounts, usually over time. Like bar graphs, line graphs also represent data along two axes. The horizontal x-axis displays different dates or time periods, and the vertical y-axis displays the amounts being measured.

Here is the population data for Cedarville, Franklin, and Pine Ridge as a line graph:

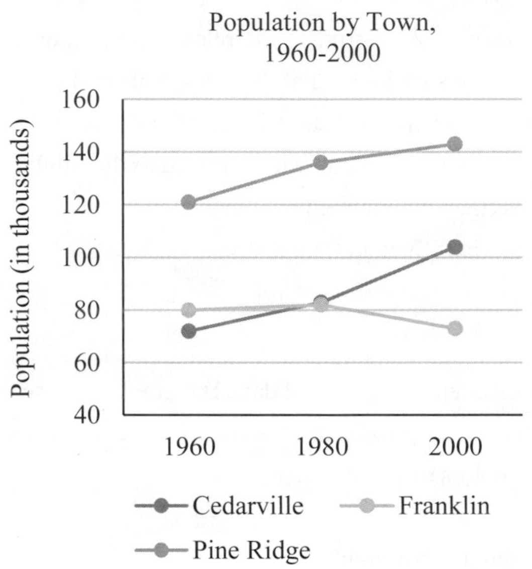

The legend tells you that each line on this graph represents the population of a different town. Just like our bar graph, the scale of the y-axis tells us that each tick mark represents 20,000 people.

Because this graph displays lines across the whole time period, you can use the graph to make estimates about population at specific years. For example, you don't know the exact population of Pine Ridge in 1970, but by looking at the middle of the line drawn from 1960 to 1980, you can estimate that the population was around 130,000. You can also use the slopes of line segments to determine the rate of change between two data points.

Histograms

A **histogram** is a graphical distribution of data, grouped together by values or ranges of values. By grouping the data together, a histogram displays the **frequency** of those groupings, which is the number of times those values or ranges occurred in the data set. A histogram is another tool that allows you to graphically calculate specific statistical information such as range, mean, median, and mode. Furthermore, the graphical representation of data often allows you to quickly find or estimate some of this information without calculation. Note that while they look similar, histograms will always display frequencies of one individual category, while bar graphs display many categories.

Here is an example of a histogram:

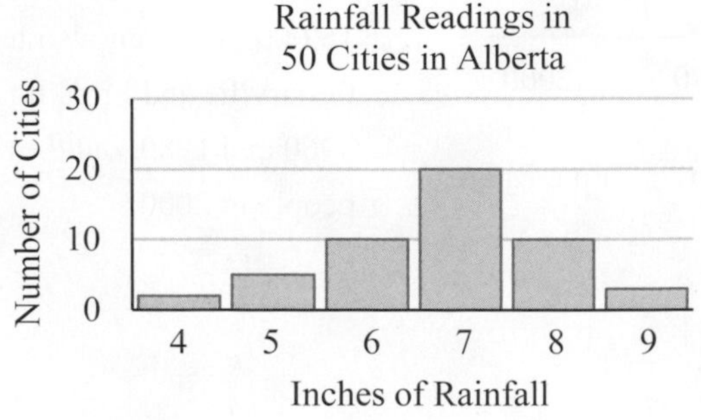

The x-axis displays the different rainfall readings (in inches) that were recorded. The y-axis displays the number of cities that recorded each reading. This information tells you the frequency with which each reading occurred. For example, the graph shows that 20 cities recorded 7" of rainfall, but only about 2 cities recorded 4" of rainfall.

It is easy to find the mode and the range of the data from the histogram. 7" was the most frequent value recorded, so 7 is the mode of this data. To find the range of this data, subtract the smallest rainfall reading (4") from the largest (9"): $9 - 4 = 5$. The range of the data is 5.

You can use the histogram to calculate the mean. First, you need to multiply each grouping by its frequency and add those products together:

$$(4 \times 2) + (5 \times 5) + (6 \times 10) + (7 \times 20) + (8 \times 10) + (9 \times 3) = 340$$

You can find the total number of readings in the graph by adding together all of the frequencies for each rainfall reading:

$$2 + 5 + 10 + 20 + 10 + 3 = 50$$

Finally, divide the sum of all of the data by the number of values:

$$\frac{340}{50} = 6.8$$

The mean rainfall reading in this data is 6.8 inches.

You can also find the median from the histogram. Because the median is the middle number in a data set, you need to find which rainfall reading would represent the middle number if all 50 readings were arranged in order from least to greatest. Because you have 50 readings, the middle number would be the average of the 25th and 26th readings.

Which group on the histogram would contain the 25th reading? To find this, start adding up the frequencies of each grouping, from left to right, and stop when you get above 25. There were 2 readings of 4", 5 readings of 5", and 10 readings of 6". This is 17 readings total, which is still less than 25. However, there were 20 readings of 7", which brings you to 37 readings total. Therefore, the 25th and 26th readings must both be in the 7" group. You can conclude that the median rainfall reading is 7".

Part 2 Practice: Properties of Data

1

A set of five numbers had an average of 14. When two of these numbers were removed, the remaining three numbers had an average of 13. What is the sum of the two numbers that were removed?

A) 1

B) 13.5

C) 15

D) 31

2

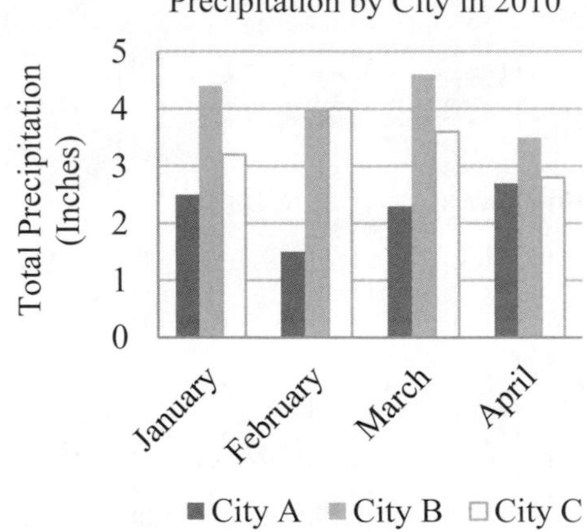

According to the graph above, during which month did City B experience about twice as much precipitation as City A?

A) January

B) February

C) March

D) April

3

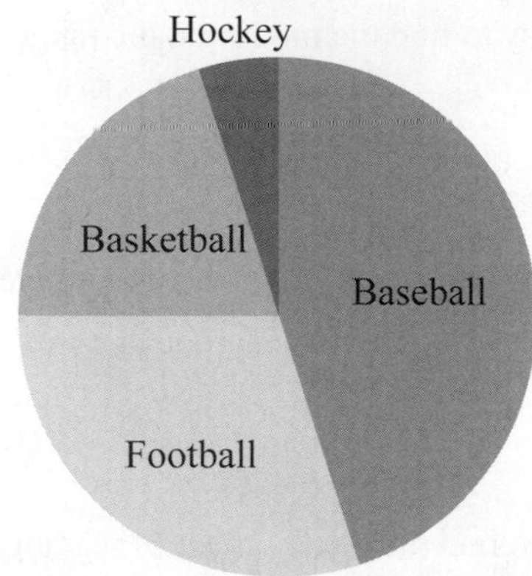

According to the diagram above, approximately how many surveyed students reported either hockey or basketball as their favorite sport?

A) 25

B) 50

C) 100

D) 200

Questions 4 and 5 refer to the following information.

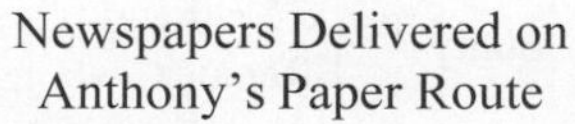

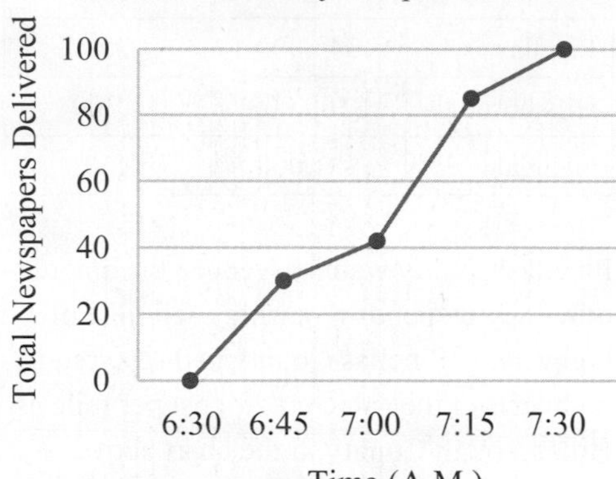

4

Which of the following is the best estimate for the number of newspapers that Anthony delivered between 7:15 and 7:30 A.M.?

A) 15

B) 45

C) 75

D) 100

5

Over which 15-minute time period did Anthony deliver newspapers at the fastest rate?

A) 6:30 A.M.-6:45 A.M.

B) 6:45 A.M.-7:00 A.M.

C) 7:00 A.M.-7:15 A.M.

D) 7:15 A.M.-7:30 A.M.

Questions 6-7 refer to the following information.

The histogram below shows the test scores of students in a writing class.

Test Scores in a Writing Class

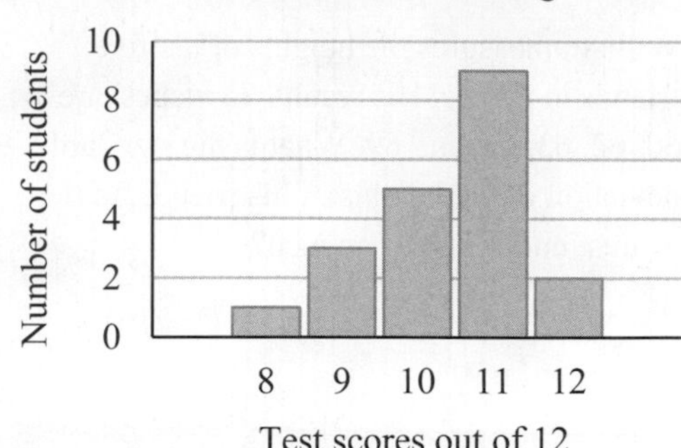

6

What is the median test score?

A) 1.05

B) 10

C) 10.4

D) 11

7

What is the mode of this data set?

A) 1.05

B) 10

C) 10.4

D) 11

8

What is the mean of the data for the set {–4, 8, 2, 6}?

9

William measures the heights of his five friends in inches. His results, in inches, are 60, 62, 63, 66, and 69. What is the standard deviation of the heights of his friends, to the nearest hundredth of an inch?

10

Highway Repair Costs by County in 2011

County	Highway Repair Costs	Miles of Highway in County
Pinellas	\$45,000	300
Hillsborough	\$169,000	1,300
Glendale	\$81,000	450

Pinellas County wants to reduce the amount of money it spends repairing each mile of highway. If Pinellas County had repaired its highways at the same repair cost per mile as Hillsborough County in the chart above, how much money, in dollars, would Pinellas County have saved in 2011? (Note: disregard the \$ sign when gridding your answer.)

Ratios, Percentages, Proportions, and Rates

Part 3

Ratios, percentages, proportions, and rates compare two or more quantities, either by comparing parts to a whole or by representing a relationship between the quantities. In Section 3, we covered some basic properties of these topics. However, some of the problems involving these topics on the SAT will require more steps or more complex algebra than the examples in Section 3. Let's see what this looks like.

Fractions and Proportions

Word problems with fractions and proportions will often require you to multiply a number by a proportion or to find an equivalent proportion. To find a fraction of a number, multiply the number by the fraction:

$$\frac{3}{8} \text{ of } 24 = \frac{3}{8} \times 24 = 9$$

You can find equivalent proportions by setting them equal to each other. For example, if 12 is $\frac{3}{4}$ of x, you can find x by setting up the equivalent proportions:

$$\frac{12}{x} = \frac{3}{4}$$

Which you can solve by cross-multiplying:

$$3x = 4 \times 12$$

$$x = 16$$

Example

Four friends ate a whole pizza. Shelley had $\frac{1}{5}$ of the pizza, Ming had 4 slices, Lily had 3 slices, and Adam had 1 slice. How many slices did Shelley have?

To find the number of slices that Shelley had, you first need to find the total number of slices in the pizza. The four friends ate the whole pizza, and Shelley ate $\frac{1}{5}$, so Ming, Lily, and Adam must have eaten

$1 - \frac{1}{5} = \frac{4}{5}$ of the pizza. This means that $4 + 3 + 1 = 8$ slices make up $\frac{4}{5}$ of the pizza. You can write this as a proportion:

$$\frac{\text{8 slices}}{\text{Total slices}} = \frac{4}{5}$$

Then, cross-multiply to find the total slices in the pizza:

$$\text{40 slices} = 4 \times \text{Total slices}$$

$$\text{Total slices} = 10$$

Now, you can calculate the number of slices that Shelley ate by setting up a proportion and cross-multiplying:

$$\frac{\text{Shelley's slices}}{\text{10 total slices}} = \frac{1}{5}$$

$$5 \times \text{Shelley's slices} = 10$$

$$\text{Shelley's slices} = 2$$

Shelley ate 2 slices of pizza.

Ratios

Ratio problems will involve applying ratios to quantities or finding ratios from quantities. It is important to remember that ratios are different than fractions or proportions: they compare a part to a part instead of a part to a whole. To find the whole, add all of the parts. For example, the ratio 2:5:3 has a whole of $2 + 5 + 3 = 10$.

Remember that you can convert ratios to fractions. Each part of the ratio becomes a numerator, and the denominator is the whole. If your ratio is 1:3:6, for example, the denominator will be $1 + 3 + 6 = 10$ and the fractions would be $\frac{1}{10}$, $\frac{3}{10}$, and $\frac{6}{10}$.

It may help to use variables when working with ratios. If you know the total quantity that the ratio describes, you can write it as the sum of each part multiplied by a variable.

Example

The measures of the two acute angles of a right triangle have the ratio 11:4. What is the difference between the two angle measures?

To solve this problem, you need to recall some geometric properties of triangles. First, the sum of the angle measures in a triangle is 180°. Since this is a right triangle, one of those angles is 90°, so the remaining acute angles must have a sum of $180° - 90° = 90°$.

You also know that one angle measure is equal to 11 times an integer, and the second angle measure is equal to 4 times the same integer. If you call the unknown integer x, you could represent the two angle measures as $11x$ and $4x$. Because you know that the two angles add to 90°, you can set up an equation to solve for x:

$$11x + 4x = 90°$$

$$15x = 90°$$

$$x = \frac{90°}{15}$$

$$x = 6°$$

Now, you can plug the value of x back into your expressions for each angle measure: $11x = 66°$ and $4x = 24°$. The question asks for the difference between these two angle measures:

$$66° - 24° = 42°$$

Your answer is 42 degrees.

Percentages

These word problems will give you a mix of percentages and quantities. If you have to find a percent of a whole number, like 12% of 4, multiply the percentage by the whole: $4 \times 0.12 = 0.48$.

If you are given a quantity that is a percent of a whole, divide the quantity by the percentage to get the whole. For example, if 3 is 5% of x, then $x = \frac{3}{0.05} = 60$.

Example

Two sweaters have the same original price. One sweater is then marked up 20% and the other is put on sale for 20% off. The difference between the new prices is $9.60. What was the original price of each sweater?

Let's say that p represents the original price of each sweater. The marked-up price of the first sweater is 20% greater, so you could represent this by $1.2p$. The sale price of the second sweater is 20% less, so you could present this by $0.8p$. You know that the difference between these prices is $9.60, so you can set up an equation to solve for p:

$$1.2p - 0.8p = 9.60$$
$$0.4p = 9.60$$
$$p = \frac{9.60}{0.4}$$
$$p = 24$$

The original price of each sweater was \$24.

Rates

Rate problems appear frequently on the SAT. Remember that rates compare two related quantities, like distance and time. You can often set up rate problems as equivalent proportions. Be sure to write the proportions so that the two rates have the same units, and make sure that your answer is in the correct units as well.

Example

Paola is training for a 10 km race. She can run 5 miles in 36 minutes. If she keeps this pace, what will her race time be? (1 mile is equal to approximately 1.6 kilometers).

First you should find Paola's pace in minutes per mile:

$$\frac{36 \text{ min}}{5 \text{ miles}} = \frac{7.2 \text{ min}}{1 \text{ mile}}$$

Since the length of the race is in kilometers, you need to convert the pace to minutes per kilometer:

$$\frac{7.2 \text{ min}}{1 \text{ mile}} \times \frac{1 \text{ mile}}{1.6 \text{ km}} = \frac{4.5 \text{ min}}{1 \text{ km}}$$

Finally, to find the time it would take Paola to run 10 km, multiply her pace in minutes per km by the distance of the race:

$$10 \text{ km} \times \frac{4.5 \text{ min}}{1 \text{ km}} = 45 \text{ min}$$

Paola's race time will be 45 minutes.

For some rate problems, you will have to combine rates. To combine rates, first make sure that they have the same units. Then add them together in their fraction form with a common denominator. The units of the new rate will be the same as the units of each individual rate.

Example

Rachel can grade 5 tests in 6 minutes and Sebastian can grade 2 tests in 3 minutes. Rachel and Sebastian have 21 tests to grade. If they work together, how long will it take them to grade the tests?

First, you need to find the rate at which Rachel and Sebastian can grade tests separately. Divide the number of tests by the number of minutes: Rachel's rate is $\frac{5}{6}$ tests/min and Sebastian's rate is $\frac{2}{3}$ tests/min.

Then, to find their combined rate, you need to add the two rates:

$$\frac{5}{6} + \frac{2}{3} = \frac{5}{6} + \frac{4}{6} = \frac{9}{6} = 1.5$$

Rachel and Sebastian have a combined rate of 1.5 tests per minute. Now you can use this rate to find the time it would take Rachel and Sebastian to grade the 21 tests. Remember to flip the rate so that the unit "tests" cancels:

$$21 \text{ tests} \times \frac{1 \text{ min}}{1.5 \text{ tests}} = 14 \text{ min}$$

It will take Rachel and Sebastian 14 minutes to grade the tests if they work together.

Part 3 Practice: Ratios, Percentages, Proportions, and Rates

1

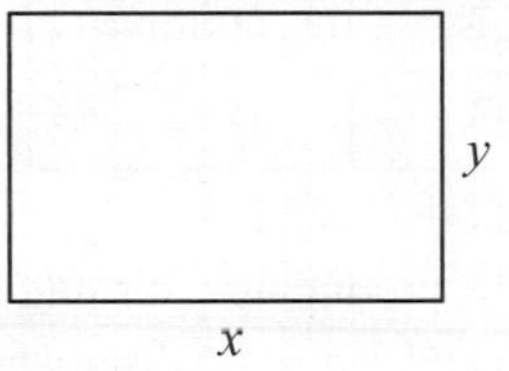

When the width x is doubled and the height y is tripled, the rectangle above becomes a square. Which of the following expresses x in terms of y?

A) $\frac{2}{3}y$

B) $\frac{3}{2}y$

C) $2y$

D) $3y$

2

If $2x = 5y$ and $4y = 3z$, what is the ratio of x to z?

A) 8:15

B) 10:12

C) 12:10

D) 15:8

3

If Antony buys an $80 guitar on sale for 10% off and pays 8% sales tax on the reduced price, how much does he pay for the guitar?

A) $66.24

B) $72.00

C) $77.76

D) $86.40

4

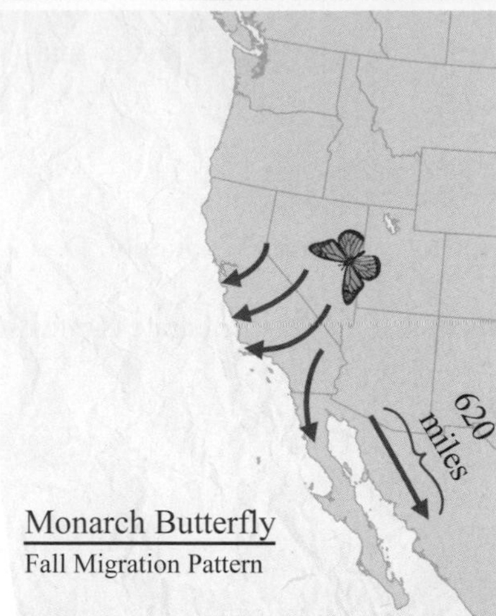

The migratory routes of a population of Monarch butterflies on the west coast is shown in the graph above. If the butterflies travel an average of 5 miles per hour for 12 hours each day, how many days will it take for the Monarchs in the southern-most migratory route to reach their destination?

A) 8

B) 11

C) 12

D) 20

5

A store sells CDs at 20% off the displayed price. The store buys CDs for $12 each. If the store owner wants to make a 10% profit on the CDs, what price should she display for each CD?

A) $13.20

B) $15.60

C) $16.50

D) $17.80

6

Antja's Quizzes	Grade
Exam 1	85
Exam 2	93
Exam 3	91
Exam 4	97

The table above shows Antja's exam scores in her geometry class. The first exam had 20 questions and each additional exam had 20 more than the previous exam. What percent of the total number of questions did Antja get correct? (Note: Round your answer to the nearest percent.)

A) 84%

B) 86%

C) 88%

D) 93%

7

Factory Production Schedule

	Monday	Tuesday
Nails	30 tons	90 tons
Screws	18 tons	54 tons

A factory, producing nails and screws on Monday and Tuesday, discovers that 4% of the nails produced are defective, and 6% of the screws are defective. If nails and screws are produced in the ratio represented by its production schedule shown above, what percent of the total nails and screws produced are defective?

A) 3.8

B) 4.75

C) 5.25

D) 38

8

Mark's car has a gas mileage of 36 miles per gallon. If gas costs $2.40 per gallon and he drives 120 miles, how much gas money will Mark pay for his trip? (Note: Disregard the $ sign when gridding your answer.)

9

A jar of buttons contains purple, red and black buttons. The ratio of purple to black buttons is 12:7. If there are 5 red buttons for every 4 purple buttons that are in the jar, what fraction of the buttons is purple?

10

Person	Rate of Filing Papers
Lily	4 papers/16 seconds
Arjun	x papers/ 4 seconds
Emily	2 papers/ 8 seconds

Lily, Arjun, and Emily are filing papers at the rates represented by the chart above. Together, Lily, Arjun, and Emily can file 3 papers every 4 seconds. If Arjun works at the same rate, how many minutes would it take him, working alone, to file 60 papers?

Probability and Statistics

Part 4

If you've ever used a weather forecast or looked up the chance that your favorite sports team will win a game, you have used **probability**. Probability describes how likely something is to happen. On the SAT, you will use probability to solve word problems and problems involving data in charts or graphs. First, let's look at some important terms.

A **set** is a group of things, often numbers. Each number or thing in a set is called an **element**. Sets are often written inside brackets, like this: {–3, 0, 2, 6.6, 100}.

A useful tool for working with sets of numbers is the **Venn diagram**. A Venn diagram uses overlapping circles to demonstrate relationships between sets of numbers. Here is an example of a Venn diagram of two sets:

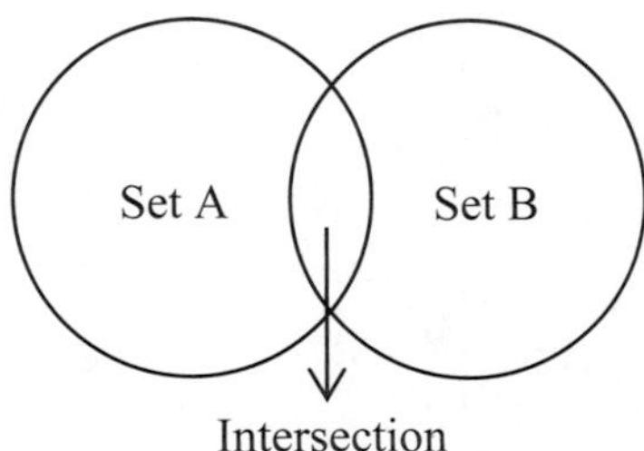

Each set is represented by a circle. If the sets share elements, those elements go in the portion of the Venn diagram where the circles overlap: this portion is called the **intersection** of the sets.

If you combine all the numbers in the Venn diagram, you will get the union of the sets. The **union** of two or more sets contains all the elements of all the sets.

Example

At Forestview High School, 60 students are taking math, science, or both. If 50 of these students are taking math and 30 students are taking science, how many are taking both?

You may have noticed that $50 + 30$ is more than 60. This reminds us that some students are taking both math and science, so they are counted in both categories. These students represent the intersection of the two sets. Let's represent the intersection with the variable x. Our Venn Diagram then looks like this:

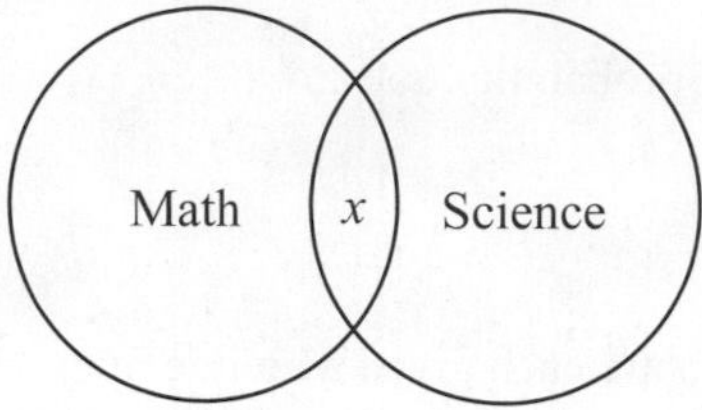

Since 50 students are taking math, you know that the total students in the "MATH" circle must be 50. Since there are x students overlapping both circles, the students only taking math is $50 - x$ because:

$$x + (50 - x) = 50$$

Notice that 50 are all the students in "MATH", and that this number also includes the students in both "MATH and SCIENCE" (your x variable).

In the same way, the number of students only taking science is $30 - x$. Our updated Venn diagram is:

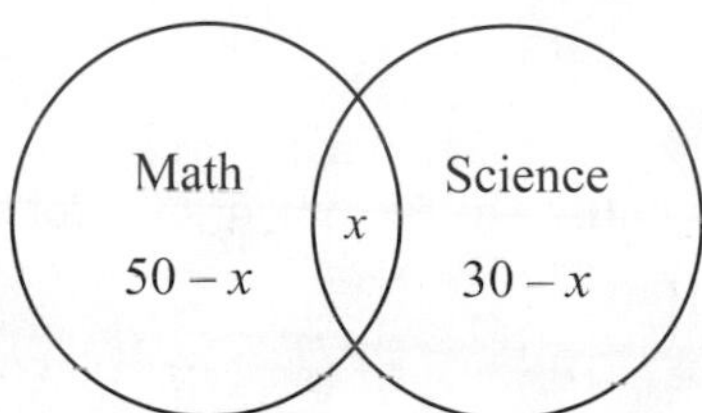

You know that the total number of students is 60. Since this number represents the union of the two sets, it equals the number of students in the three areas:

$$(50 - x) + x + (30 - x) = 60$$

Now you can solve for x:

$$80 - x = 60$$

$$x = 20$$

You have found that the number of students taking both math and science is 20.

Probability

Probability is the likelihood that something will happen. Scientists and mathematicians can make educated predictions about the future by analyzing data and using the principles of probability. For example, weather forecasters use probability to predict the chance of rain tomorrow, and medical researchers use probability to predict people's chance of developing heart or lung disease.

The formula to calculate probability is:

$$\text{Probability} = \frac{\text{Number of ways to get a certain outcome}}{\text{Number of possible outcomes}}$$

Let's take a look at a common SAT probability question:

Example

There is a group of six people who are each given a unique integer from 1 through 6. If one person is randomly selected from the group, what is the probability that they were given an even number?

Since one person is selected at random, there is an equal chance that they have any integer from 1 to 6. Therefore, there are six equal possible outcomes. To find the probability that they have an even number, you divide the number of even-number outcomes (3) by the number of possible outcomes (6):

$$\text{Probability of an even number} = \frac{3}{6} = \frac{1}{2}$$

The probability that the person has an even number is $\frac{1}{2}$. You can also state this as a decimal (0.5) or as a percent (50%).

Some problems will give you a probability and ask you to solve for numbers:

Example

A biologist is studying a pond of 40 frogs. If the probability of choosing a black frog is $\frac{1}{4}$, how many black frogs are in the pond?

The question tells us that there is a $\frac{1}{4}$ or 25% probability of choosing a black frog. You're told that the number of total frogs is 40. Let's write the probability of choosing a black frog using our formula:

$$\text{Probability of choosing a black frog} = \frac{\text{Number of black frogs}}{40} = \frac{1}{4}$$

Now all you need to do is solve by cross-multiplying your proportion:

$$\frac{x}{40} = \frac{1}{4}$$

$$40 = 4x$$

$$x = 10$$

The number of black frogs in the pond is equal to 10.

Understanding Probability

Probabilities are written as fractions or decimals between 0 and 1, or as percentages between 0% and 100%. The lower the probability, the less likely an event is to occur. The higher the probability, the more likely an event is to occur.

A probability of 0 means an event is impossible and will never occur.

Example

A group of six people are each given a unique integer from 1 through 6. If one person is randomly selected, what is the probability that they were given a 7?

There are six possible outcomes, but no one in the group was given the number 7. Therefore, there are zero ways that one person was given a 7. If you plug this into our formula, you get:

$$\text{Probability of a 7} = \frac{0}{6} = 0$$

The probability of selecting someone with a 7 is 0, so there is a no chance that the person will have a 7. This event is impossible.

On the other hand, a probability of 1 or 100% means that an event is absolutely certain to happen.

Example

A group of six people are each given a unique integer from 1 through 6. If one person is randomly selected, what is the probability that they were given a positive number?

There are six possible outcomes, and all six of these numbers are positive numbers. Therefore, there are also six ways to get a positive number outcome:

$$\text{Probability of a positive number} = \frac{6}{6} = 1$$

The probability of that the person has a positive number is 1, so this event is always going to happen.

Since a probability of 1 means an event will always happen, you will never get a probability greater than 1 or 100%.

If you know the probability of getting a certain outcome, you can also calculate the probability of *not* getting that outcome. These two possibilities are called **complementary events**. If you add the probabilities of complementary events, you will get 1. This means that every outcome will be one of the two complementary events.

Example

A group of six people are each given a unique integer from 1 through 6. If one person is randomly selected, what is the probability that they do not have a 4?

Someone having a 4 and not having a 4 are complementary events. Since the probability of selecting someone with a 4 is $\frac{1}{6}$, the probability of not selecting someone with a 4 is:

$$1 - \frac{1}{6} = \frac{5}{6}$$

There is a $\frac{5}{6}$ chance of not selecting someone with a 4, but of selecting someone with any of the other possible numbers (1, 2, 3, 5, or 6).

Two events are **mutually exclusive** if it is impossible for both of them to happen at the same time. For example, if you select one person from a group of six people who are all given unique integers from 1 through 6, it is impossible that the person will have both the number 5 and the number 3. They will either have one number or the other. Complementary events are always mutually exclusive.

You can find the chance of one event *or* another event occurring by adding together their individual probabilities:

Example

A group of six people are each given a unique integer from 1 through 6. If one person is randomly selected, what is the probability that they have a 5 or a 6?

The probability that they have 5 is $\frac{1}{6}$ and the probability that they have 3 is also $\frac{1}{6}$. To find your chances that they have a 5 or a 3, add their probabilities together:

$$\text{Probability of a 5 or 3} = \frac{1}{6} + \frac{1}{6} = \frac{1}{3}$$

If you add together the probabilities of all of the possible mutually-exclusive outcomes of an event, you will get the number 1. For example, there is a probability of 1 that your selected person will have a 1, 2, 3, 4, 5, or 6 if there are six people who are each given unique integers from 1 to 6.

Conditional Probability

Conditional probability is the probability that an event occurs given that another event has already occurred. Questions dealing with conditional probability are often phrased as, "If X is true, what is the probability of P?" This is the most important form of probability in the SAT. It pops up frequently in tables and in statistics. Since you are dealing with multiple events, you need to figure out what relationship the events have to each other.

If there are multiple events whose outcomes do *not* depend on each other, they are called **independent events**. The probability of multiple independent events is simply the product of their separate probabilities. If Event A has a probability of 0.7, and Event B has a probability of 0.2, the probability of both Event A and Event B occurring is:

$$0.7 \times 0.2 = 0.14$$

Events are **dependent** if one event affects the probability of the other event occurring. If two events are dependent, you need to figure out what happens to the probability of the second event after the first one has taken place:

Example

Janice, a geologist, is cataloguing the composition of a sample of 52 rocks. She selects her first rock and then sets it aside before selecting a second rock. If rocks with the same composition are always found in groups of four, what is the probability that both rocks are made of granite?

The probability for the first rock is easy: there are 52 rocks and 4 of them are granite, so Janice has a $\frac{4}{52}$ or $\frac{1}{13}$ chance of selecting a granite rock.

However, now that she has removed one rock, the number of rocks in the sample has changed. She now has only 51 rocks in her sample. If her first rock was made of granite, there are only 3 granite rocks left. Therefore, the probability that her second rock will also be made of granite is $\frac{3}{51}$. You've figured out the probability of the first event, and how the probability of the second event will be affected if the first event takes place. You can now multiply these probabilities together to find the probability of both events occurring:

$$\text{Probability of selecting two granite rocks} = \frac{1}{13} \times \frac{3}{51} = \frac{3}{663} = \frac{1}{221}$$

If Janice is selecting two rocks one at a time, the probability that she will pick two granite rocks is 1 out of 221.

Analyzing Two-Way Tables

Conditional probability may also be used to analyze two-way tables. This is by far the most frequent use of probability on the SAT exams.

Example

	Classical	Rock	Pop	Total
9th grade	50	21	39	110
10th grade	63	22	20	105
11th grade	3	90	19	112
12th grade	47	12	44	103
Total	163	145	122	430

The table on the left summarizes students' preferences for music. If one student out of 430 students surveyed is randomly selected, what is the probability that the student is in the 9th grade?

This is a regular probability question. There are 110 9th graders out of 430 total students, so the probability that the student is in the 9th grade is $\frac{110}{430}$, or $\frac{11}{43}$, or approximately 26%.

A more complicated question for the same table is:

Example

What is the probability that a student prefers rock music given that he is in the 11th grade?

This is a conditional probability question, since you are only looking at the students in 11th grade. There are 90 students who prefer rock music out of the 112 students in 11th grade, so the probability is $\frac{90}{112} = \frac{45}{56}$, or approximately 80%.

Making Predictions

You can use samples of data to make predictions about larger populations or groups. The accuracy of these estimates depends on properties of the sample data such as size and selection process. You will discuss how to evaluate sample data in Part 6.

In order to make an estimate for a population based on sample data, you treat the sample data as proportional to the entire population. This allows us to use proportions and percentages to make estimates for the whole population.

Example

	For Mandatory Math	Against Mandatory Math	Total
Male	126	42	168
Female	81	69	150
Total	207	111	318

Jaetown surveyed residents about their opinion on mandatory math education. The results are summarized in the chart on the left. Jaetown has a population of 12,000 female residents and 13,000 male residents. Based on the survey results, how many female residents would the city predict to support the policy?

The question asks for the number of female residents who are "for" the policy. The survey found that $\frac{81}{150} = 54\%$ of the women surveyed supported mandatory math education. Multiply the percent of women supporting the policy in the survey by the total number of female residents in the city:

$$12{,}000 \times 0.54 = 6{,}480$$

Our estimate is that around 6,480 of the female residents in Jaetown support mandatory math education.

Part 4 Practice: Probability and Statistics

1

Lawyers who have debt cases

Lawyers who have criminal cases

40 10 35

5

10 15

25

Lawyers who have insurance cases

According to the Venn Diagram above, how many lawyers have both debt and criminal cases, but do not have insurance cases?

A) 10

B) 15

C) 25

D) 75

2

The Instruments that Students Play

Instrument	Number of Students
Piano	52
Violin	30
No Instrument	24

The results of a survey of students who play an instrument are shown above. If there were 100 students surveyed, how many students play both the piano and the violin?

A) 3

B) 6

C) 12

D) The answer cannot be determined from the information given.

Questions 3 and 4 refer to the following information.

Two cities compared how many hours their population exercised over a one-month period. The results, measured according to the age and hours of exercise, are summarized in the table below.

Monthly Average Number of Hours

Age of Population	Georgetown	Lakeview
18 years or younger	40	20
19 to 25 years	20	40
26 to 34 years	28	40
35 to 45 years	40	28
46 to 55 years	20	12
56 years or older	12	20

3

According to the data, if one Georgetown resident from each age group were compared with one Lakeview resident from each age group, which of the following is true?

A) The six Georgetown residents would most likely exercise more than the six Lakeview residents.

B) The six Georgetown residents would most likely exercise less than the six Lakeview residents.

C) Both the six Georgetown and six Lakeview residents would most likely exercise a similar amount.

D) There is not enough information to compare the residents from Georgetown and Lakeview.

4

Three 36-year-old residents are randomly selected from Georgetown and from Lakeview. If one 36-year-old person is randomly picked from the group of 6 people, how many hours would they most likely exercise in a month?

A) 20

B) 28

C) 34

D) 40

5

The weatherman of Romley County predicts that there will be a 20% chance of rain on Tuesday if the northern winds increase beyond 15 miles per hour on Monday. If his satellite imagery indicates there is a 75% chance that the northern winds will increase to 16 miles per hour, what is the probability that rain will fall on Tuesday in Romley County?

A) 26.66%

B) 21.33%

C) 20%

D) 15%

Questions 6 and 7 refer to the information below.

Repairs During the Year 2010 by Car Model

Car Model	Repaired	Not Repaired	Total
N-Model	397	305	702
K-Model	322	226	548
Total	719	531	1250

6

Based on the table above, what is the percent probability that a car is N-model given that it underwent a repair in 2010?

A) 31.8%

B) 55.2%

C) 56.2%

D) 56.6%

7

There were a total of 3000 K-model cars in 2010. Based on the table above, approximately how K-model cars would be expected to have been repaired in 2010?

A) 773

B) 1237

C) 1343

D) 1762

8

Two colonies of bacteria are grown in two separate petri dishes. There is a one in three chance that a colony of *E. coli* bacteria grows in either of the petri dishes. If a colony of *E. coli* bacteria grows in the first dish, what is the percent probability that it will grow in the second? (Note: Disregard the % sign when gridding your response.)

9

In the United States, about 40% of people will be diagnosed with cancer in their lifetime. If two people are randomly chosen from the United States, what is the percent probability that both of them will be diagnosed with cancer in their lifetime? (Note: Disregard the % sign when gridding your response.)

10

The male Satin Bowerbird builds a nest from twigs and blue objects to attract a mate. Males who build a larger nests area have a proportionately larger chance of attracting a mate. In the figure above, two nests are compared. The area of the smaller nest is the square root of the area of larger nest. If a mate is nine times more likely to choose the male who built the larger nest than the male who built the smaller nest, what is the size of the smaller nest, in square units?

Modeling Data

Part 5

When scientists or researchers collect data, they look for relationships between different variables. For example, imagine Mario is running a lemonade stand. He wants to know if there is a relationship between the temperature and the amount of lemonade he sells. He collects the following information over a series of days:

Average Temperature (°F)	76	89	68	82	91	74	84
Cups Sold	19	54	12	25	61	23	41

One way to find trends in data is to create a scatterplot. A **scatterplot** is a graph of two variables compared against each other; these types of graphs are commonly found on the SAT. It is the most common means of analysis because you can visually see patterns, or **trends** of data. Here is a scatterplot of Mario's data:

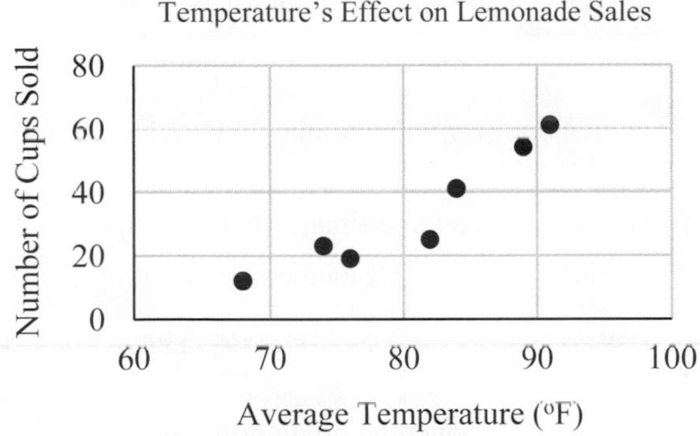

From this scatterplot, you can see that the number of cups of lemonade sold tended to be higher on days with a higher temperature. The trend is not a perfect line or curve, but you can estimate an equation that will approximate these data: this is called **modeling data**. Modeling data allows us to find an equation for the relationship between two pieces of information and to make estimates or predictions.

To model the data from Mario's lemonade stand, you first need to decide what type of curve best models the relationship between the temperature and the number of cups sold. This relationship could be linear, quadratic, polynomial, or exponential. The data in Mario's scatterplot appears to follow a linear trend.

Now you need to draw a trend line or a line of best fit. A **trend line** or **line of best fit** is a line that best approximates all the scatterplot data. It should be as close to *all* the points as possible, but it does not have to pass through all—or any—of the actual data points. The line of best fit of Mario's data is:

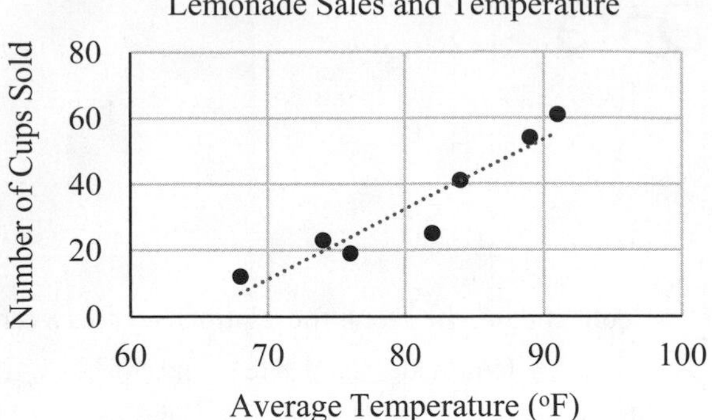

Estimating Using a Trend Line

You can estimate the equation of the trend line by using two points on the line. Make sure you do *not* use the experimental data points unless they fall exactly on the line!

Pick values that are easy to estimate from the graph. For example, you could use (70, 12) and (90, 54) from the trend line above. This would give us the equation:

$$y = 2.1x - 135$$

In this equation, y represents the number of cups sold and x is the temperature. If you wanted to predict how many cups of lemonade would be sold if the temperature were 80°F, for example, you would plug 80 into the formula:

$$\text{Cups Sold} = 2.1 \times 80 - 135 = 33$$

Based off of your line of best fit, you could estimate that 33 cups would be sold at an average temperature of 80°F. You can similarly predict all temperatures within the range of 68°F to 91°F this way.

The SAT may also include quadratic or exponential prediction models.

Example

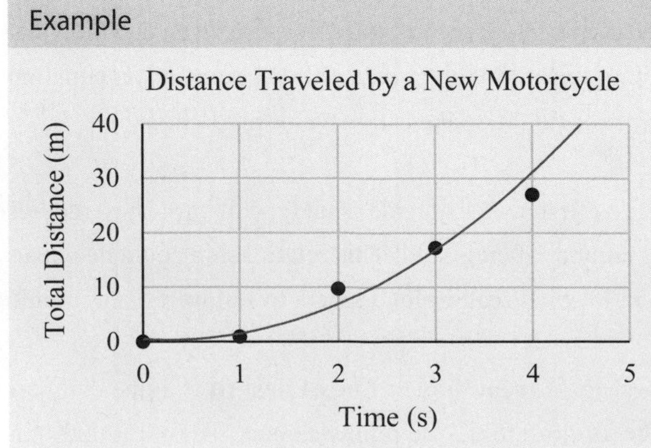

Motorcycle manufacturers are measuring the acceleration of a new motorcycle. They record the cumulative distance traveled in intervals of one second. Their data are plotted on the graph to the left. Based on the trend line, how many seconds would it take for the new motorcycle to travel 10 meters? (Round to the nearest tenth of a second.)

You need to find the point where the trend line reaches 10 meters. This occurs at the second tick mark after 2 seconds. Since there are 5 tick marks between each second, each tick mark represents 0.2 seconds. Therefore, the time it takes for the motorcycle to reach 10 meters is about 2.4 seconds.

Example

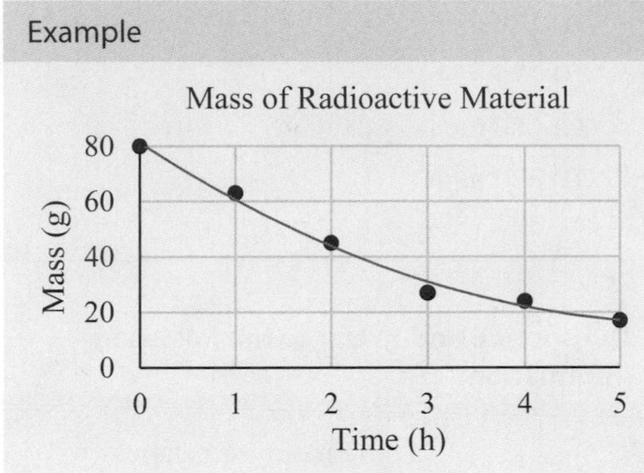

A researcher collects data on a mass of a radioactive material at different times and displays the results in the scatterplot on the right. Based on the graph, how long will it take the material to decrease to one quarter of its original mass? (Round to the nearest quarter of an hour.)

The original mass is 80 grams, so one quarter of the original mass is 20 grams. The trend line reaches 20 grams about half way between 4 and 5 hours, so our estimate is 4.5 hours.

Part 5 Practice: Modeling Data

1

Temperature (°C)	Reaction Time (s)
20	13.5
24	11
28	7.9
32	3.6
36	2.1
40	1.3

A chemist measures the reaction time of an experiment at different temperatures. The results are summarized in the chart above. If these data are displayed as a scatterplot, will the slope of the trend line be positive, negative, or zero?

A) Positive

B) Negative

C) Zero

D) The answer cannot be determined from the information given.

Questions 2 and 3 refer to the following information.

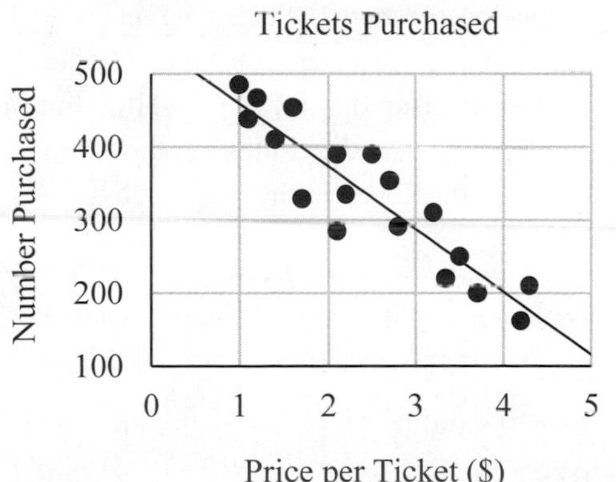

2

According to the data above, how many tickets would you expect to be purchased if the price is $3.00?

A) 250

B) 290

C) 310

D) 350

3

If tickets are sold at $4.00 each, approximately how much is the total ticket revenue?

A) $400
B) $680
C) $740
D) $800

Questions 4 and 5 refer to the following information.

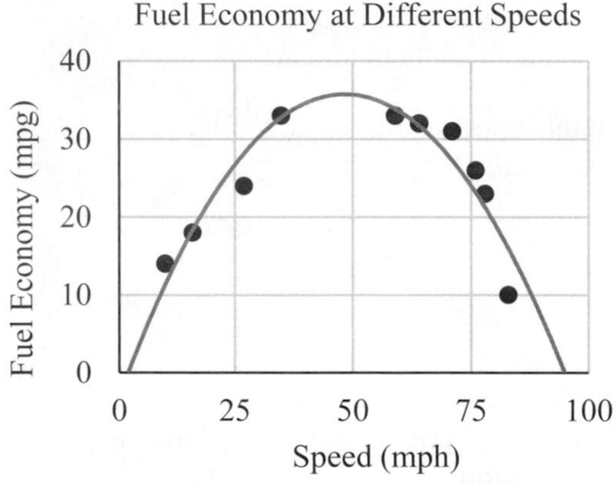

A group of researchers collects data on the fuel economy of a car at different speeds. The fuel economy is measured in miles per gallon (mpg) and speed is measured in miles per hour (mph). The data are displayed in the graph above.

4

Which of the following is the best estimate for the maximum fuel economy of this car?

A) 30 mpg
B) 32 mpg
C) 35 mpg
D) 82 mpg

5

The car has a fuel economy of 18 mpg at a speed of 18 mph. At which other speed should the car have the same fuel economy?

A) 70 mph
B) 75 mph
C) 80 mph
D) 90 mph

Questions 6 and 7 refer to the following information.

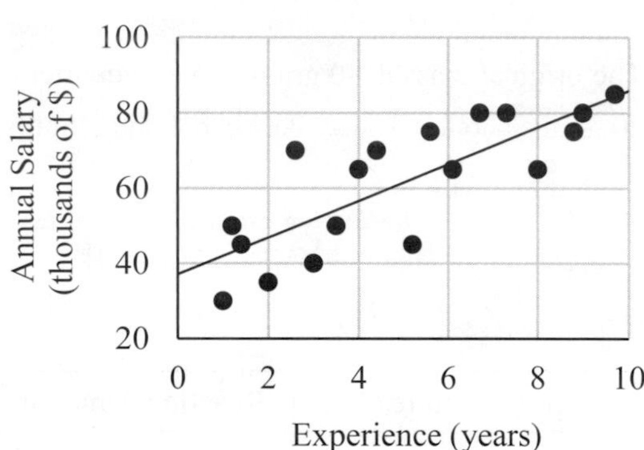

The graph above shows data collected on employees' salaries in relation to their experience. The data are modeled as a linear relationship where e is the employee's experience in years and S is their annual salary in thousands of dollars.

6

Which of the following best estimates the annual salary of an employee with 4 years of experience?

A) $55,000
B) $60,000
C) $65,000
D) $75,000

7

Which of the following best models the graph's trend line?

A) $S = 5e + 38$

B) $S = e + 38$

C) $S = \frac{1}{5}e + 38$

D) $S = -\frac{1}{5}e + 38$

8

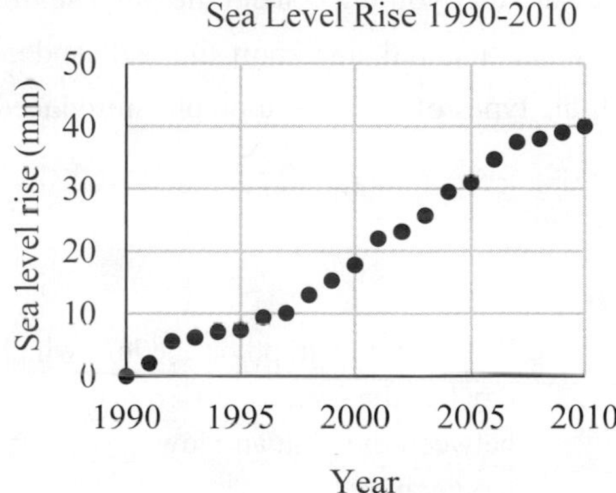

According to the graph above, how much did the sea level rise per year between 1990 and 2010? Round to the nearest millimeter.

Questions 9 and 10 refer to the following information.

Time (hours)	Number of Bacteria
0	20
1	43
2	71
3	100
4	144
5	230

A biologist is growing a culture of bacteria in his lab. He records the population at different times and displays the data in the chart above.

9

Based on the table above, to the nearest hour, what is the hour in which the population grows to seven times its original size?

10

The biologist determines that the equation for the trend line is modeled by $N = 46t - 8$, where t is time and N is the number of bacteria. According to the equation, approximately how many times greater is the number of bacteria after 11 hours than the number after 2 hours? Round your answer to the nearest whole number.

Using Data as Evidence

Part 6

In Section 5, we've covered many topics related to data analysis. In this part, you'll learn how these topics will appear on the SAT. Data analysis questions will test your ability to read different types of charts and graphs, interpret data and trends, make conclusions and predictions from data sets, and analyze data.

Reading Charts and Graphs

To solve any data analysis problem, you must first make sure that you understand the purpose of the graph. Ask yourself which quantities are being measured and compared, and know the scale and units of those quantities. Make sure that you are familiar with the types of charts and graphs introduced in Part 2.

Example

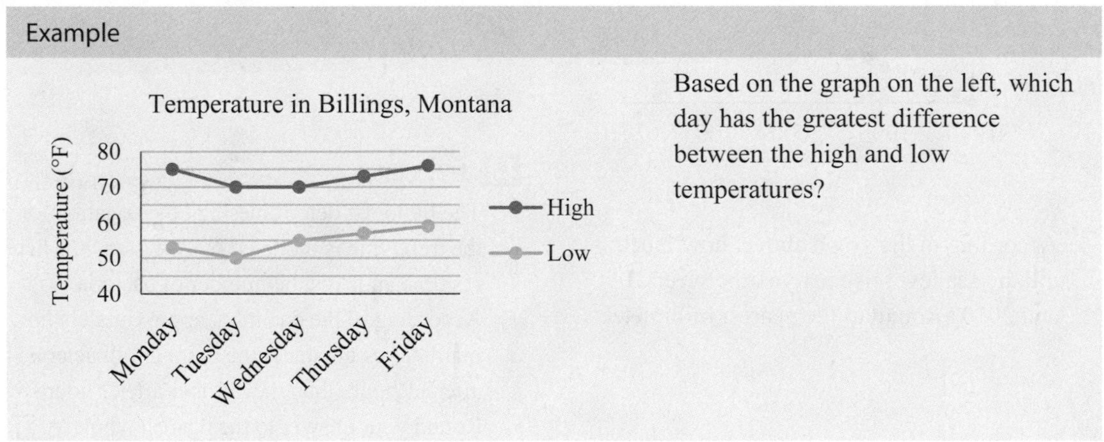

Based on the graph on the left, which day has the greatest difference between the high and low temperatures?

To solve the problem, you need to look at the graph and compare the high and low temperatures for each day. Monday and Tuesday have the widest gap between the high and low temperatures, so we should compare those more closely. There is a difference of about 22° between Monday's temperatures and only a 20° difference between Tuesday's temperatures, so the answer is Monday.

Interpreting Data

In some cases, you will need to use data in the chart or graph to find information that is not part of the data you are given. You will have to do calculations with the data you are given or make estimates and predictions based on data or trends.

Some of these questions might ask you to use data from a sample group to make predictions for a larger population. For these problems, you can use fractions or percentages to compare the sample group to the larger population.

Example

GPA of Graduating Students	
GPA	Number of Students
3.5-4.0	25
3.0-3.4	37
2.5-2.9	24
2.0-2.4	14

The chart on the left shows a random sample of GPAs from a high school's graduating students. The entire graduating class contains 600 students. Based on the data, which is the best estimate for the number of students in the graduating class who had a GPA of 3 or higher?

A) 62 B) 150 C) 222 D) 372

We can use percentages to solve this problem. First, find the percentage of students in the sample who had a GPA of 3.0 or higher. This is 25 + 37 students out of 100 total students, so 62%. Now, multiply this percentage by the number of students in the graduating class:

$$600 \times 0.62 = 372 \text{ students}$$

The best estimate for the number of students in the graduating class who had a GPA of 3 or higher is 372 so (D) is the correct answer.

You may also be asked to model data or to use a model to make predictions. The scatterplot is often used in these types of questions; you could be asked, for example, to estimate the slope or to find the function that best models the data. These problems will look like the examples and practice exercises in Part 5.

Example

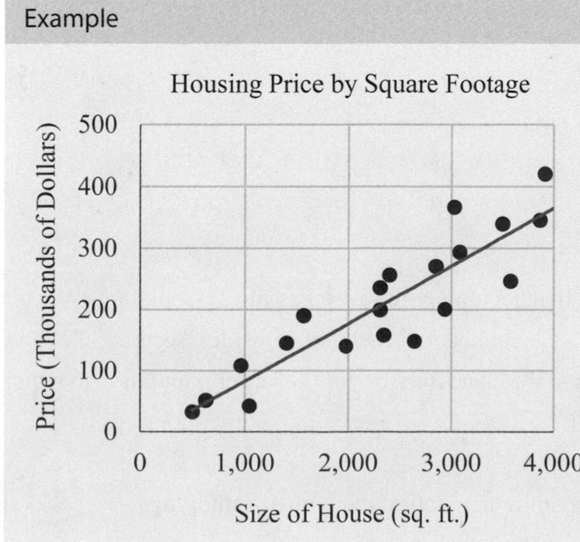

The graph on the left is a scatterplot of the size and price of houses. Based on the trend line, which of the following is the best estimate for the price per square foot of a 2,000 sq. ft. house?

A) 10 B) 70 C) 90 D) 180

Since the question asks us to use the trend line, find the price that corresponds to 2,000 sq. ft. on the trend line. This is approximately 180 thousand dollars. Make sure to check your units – \$180 will give a much different answer than \$180,000! To find price per sq. ft., divide \$180,000 by 2,000 sq. ft. to get 90, which is choice (C).

Data analysis questions will ask you to find or compare the mean, median, mode, range, or standard deviation of data sets. These problems might include raw data sets, tables of values, or bar graphs, so you should be familiar with finding statistical quantities from these types of graphics.

Example

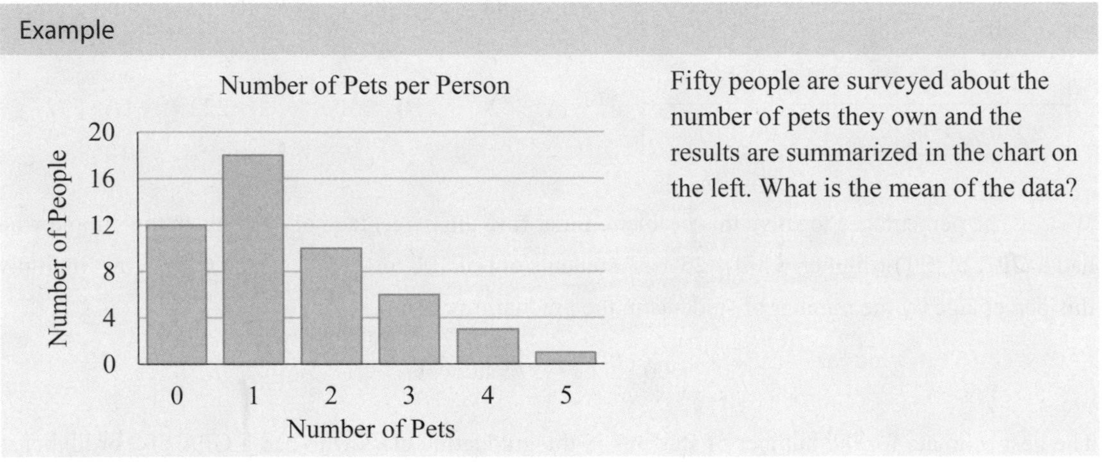

Fifty people are surveyed about the number of pets they own and the results are summarized in the chart on the left. What is the mean of the data?

To find the mean from a bar graph, multiply each possible number of pets by the number of people who own that number, then add them together:

$$(0 \times 12) + (1 \times 18) + (2 \times 10) + (3 \times 6) + (4 \times 3) + (5 \times 1) = 73$$

This is the total number of pets owned by the 50 people. Now divide by the number of people, 50, to find the mean:

$$\frac{73}{50} = 1.46$$

The mean is 1.46.

Data Collection Methods

The goal of data collection is to get information that accurately reflects the entire population. When a question on the SAT asks you to evaluate a data collection method, consider factors like how participants are selected, the size of the data set, and the characteristics of the larger population to which you are comparing your sample.

In order to be accurate, your data must reflect the entire population that you are studying.

Consider the map below:

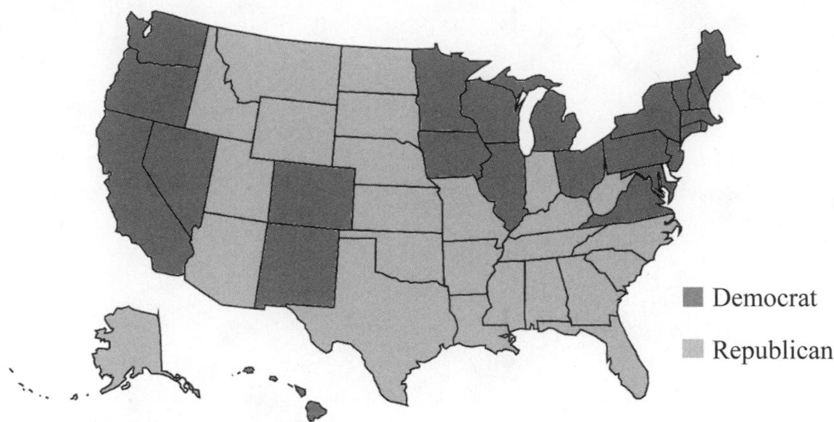

If you only surveyed people from the Northeast, you would get very different results than if you only surveyed people from southern states. Neither group would give you results that reflect the political preference of all U.S. residents.

The *type* of data that you are collecting also determines what makes a good sample. A sample group that includes only college students, for example, is a great sample group if you are studying college students. It is not, however, a good sample group to represent the entire population of the U.S.

When evaluating a sample selection, consider how well it represents the entire population and how that may affect results.

The *size* of the sample also affects the accuracy of data. If you only collect a few data points, they will not reflect the entire population as well as many data points.

Imagine you are rolling a six-sided number cube numbered 1 through 6 and recording the results. You would expect each number to be rolled about $\frac{1}{6}$ or 17% of the time. If you only rolled the cube 5 times, your data would look something like this:

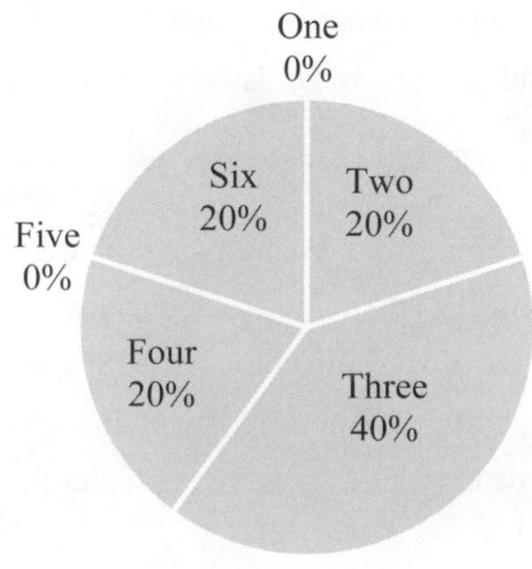

This data is not very accurate because the sample size is so small. If you rolled the number cube 50 or 100 times, you would get results that are much more accurate:

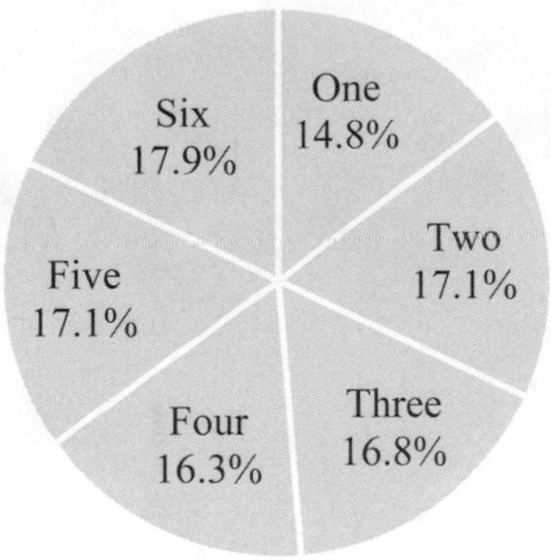

This principle is true for all kinds of data collection: the bigger the sample size, the better the chance it will give accurate results.

Measuring Error

Researchers can estimate the accuracy of their data with a margin of error or a confidence interval. You will not have to calculate margins of error or confidence intervals on the SAT, but you need to understand what these mean and know how to use them to analyze data.

A **margin of error** measures how well a sample group represents the entire population. Consider the chart below:

Pre-Election Survey			
Candidate	Jones	Liu	Albini
Percent of Votes (± 3%)	28%	37%	35%

The chart gives a margin of error of 3%. This means that the actual percentages may vary as much as 3% in either direction. Jones could have anywhere between 25% and 31% of the votes. Similarly, Liu's range is between 34% and 40%, and Albini's range is between 32% and 38%. These ranges are called confidence intervals.

The margin of error affects how we analyze the data. Notice that Liu has 2% more of the votes than Albini. However, the margin of error tells us that the percentages can vary up to 3%. This means that Liu could actually have 34% of the votes or Albini could have 38% of the votes, which would put Albini in the lead. A good rule is that if the difference between two numbers or percentages is smaller than the margin of error, you cannot conclude that one is greater or smaller than the other.

Margins of error and confidence intervals can also be represented visually on a graph. Confidence intervals are shown as vertical bars like the ones in the following graph.

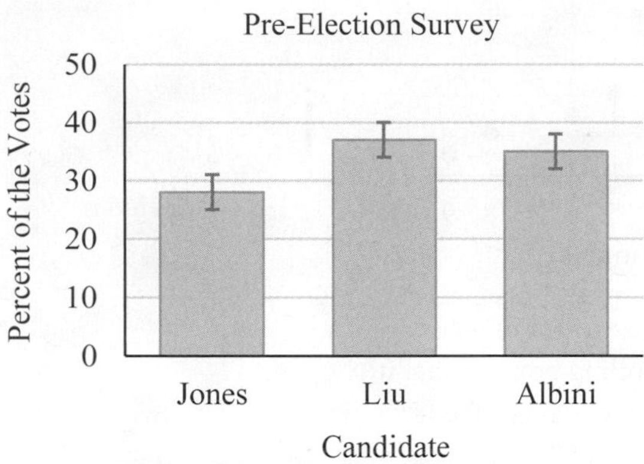

Since the margin of error is 3%, each confidence interval extends 3% above and below the measured percentage. You can see that the confidence intervals for Liu and Albini overlap, which tells you that you don't know for sure which candidate has a larger percentage of votes.

Part 6 Practice: Using Data as Evidence

Questions 1 and 2 refer to the following information.

1

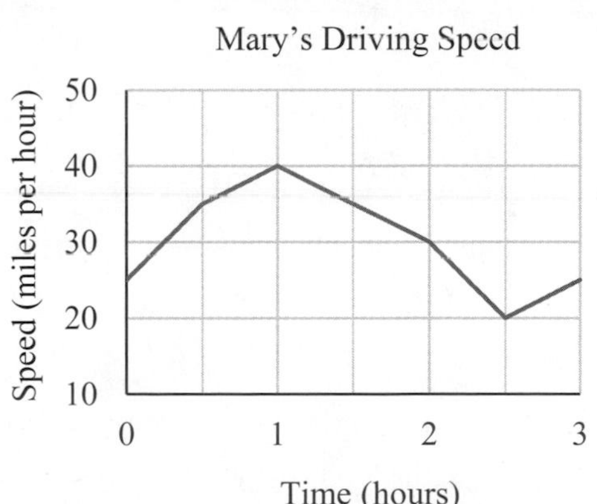

Which of the following is the value of the difference between Mary's fastest and slowest speed over the three-hour period?

A) 15

B) 20

C) 25

D) 30

2

According to the graph, how many miles did Mary cover between hours 1 and 2?

A) 30

B) 33

C) 35

D) 40

3

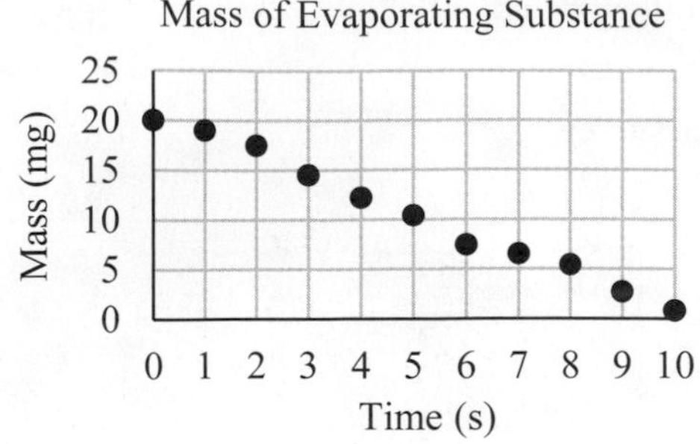

Susanne conducts an experiment in which she heats a solid to its boiling point so that it evaporates. She records the mass of the remaining solid every second. The plot above shows her resulting data.

If the data is modeled as the linear function $M = 20 + at$, where M is the mass of the substance in milligrams, t is time in seconds, and a is a constant, which of the following is the best estimate for a?

A) –2

B) –1

C) 1

D) 2

4

Product	Average Rating	Standard Deviation
A	4	0.43
B	3	0.76

Customers rate two products on a scale of 1-5. The chart above summarizes statistics from these reviews. Which of the following statements can you conclude from the information given?

A) More customers rated Product B than Product A.

B) All of the ratings for Product A were a 3, 4, or 5.

C) The ratings for Product B were more varied than for Product A.

D) The range of the ratings for Product B is larger than that for Product A.

5

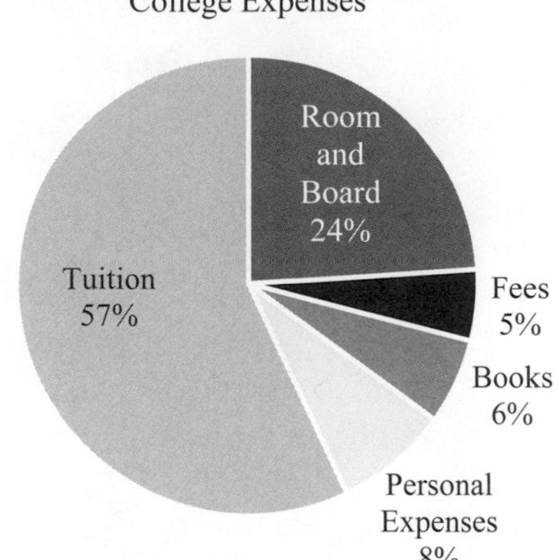

The chart above is a summary of Malik's expenditures for his first year in college. If Malik's total expenditure for the year is \$30,000, how much more did Malik spend on tuition than on the other categories combined?

A) \$2,100

B) \$4,200

C) \$12,900

D) \$17,100

Questions 6 and 7 refer to the following information.

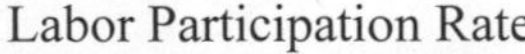

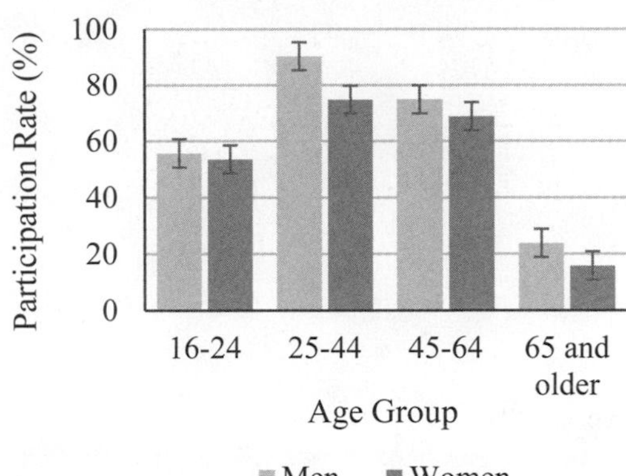

6

Which of the following conclusions can you make from the graph above?

A) A higher percentage of men ages 16-24 work than the percentage of women ages 16-24.

B) Between 70% and 80% of women ages 25-44 work.

C) The margin of error is ±10%.

D) There are more men ages 65 or older than women ages 65 or older.

7

200 men ages 25-44 who took the original survey are selected for a second survey. Incorporating margin of error, what are the maximum and minimum number of men that you would expect to work in this age group?

A) 95 and 85

B) 115 and 105

C) 190 and 170

D) 200 and 180

8

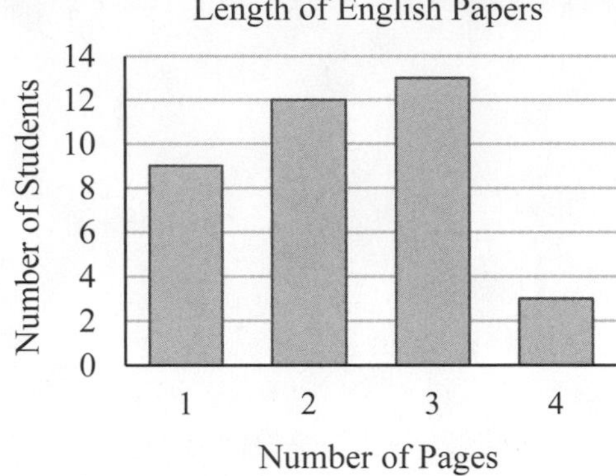

If the histogram above shows the length of 37 students' English papers, what is the median paper length?

Questions 9 and 10 refer to the following information.

November Sales Report

Store	Price of Product	Number Sold
A	\$99	15
B	\$85	21
C	\$110	18

The chart above is a report on the sale of a product in three stores.

9

What is the value of the difference in sales between Store A and Store B?

10

If the product costs \$80 for the stores to purchase, what is the combined total profit from the product's sales at all three stores?

Section 6

Additional Topics

The **Additional Topics** questions on the SAT test various advanced topics in geometry, trigonometry, and complex numbers. Although a variety of topics fall under this content area, Additional Topics questions make up the smallest portion of the Math Test. You'll only see a total of 6 questions on these topics: 2-4 in the Calculator Section and 2-4 in the No-Calculator Section. You'll want to ensure you understand the introductory concepts of lines, triangles, quadrilaterals, polygons, and circles. If you need to go over these concepts, you can find a thorough review online.

For additional resources, please visit **ivyglobal.com/study**.

In this section, we will cover the following material tested in the Additional Topics questions:

- Angles and Volumes of Shapes
- Right Triangles
- Radians and Degrees
- Circles
- Complex Numbers

Angles and Volumes of Shapes

Part 1

All geometric shapes have **dimensions**, or distances you can measure. Shapes with one dimension, like simple lines, can only be measured by length. Two dimensional shapes can be measured two ways, by length and width. Shapes in three dimensions can be measured three ways—by length, width, height or depth. Since lines and two-dimensional shapes are covered in our online review, we'll start by discussing angles, and then we'll talk about three-dimensional shapes.

Angles

An **angle** is formed when two lines or line segments intersect. Angles are measured in degrees from 0° to 360°, which represents the angle of a full circle. Angles are classified according to their degree measurements:

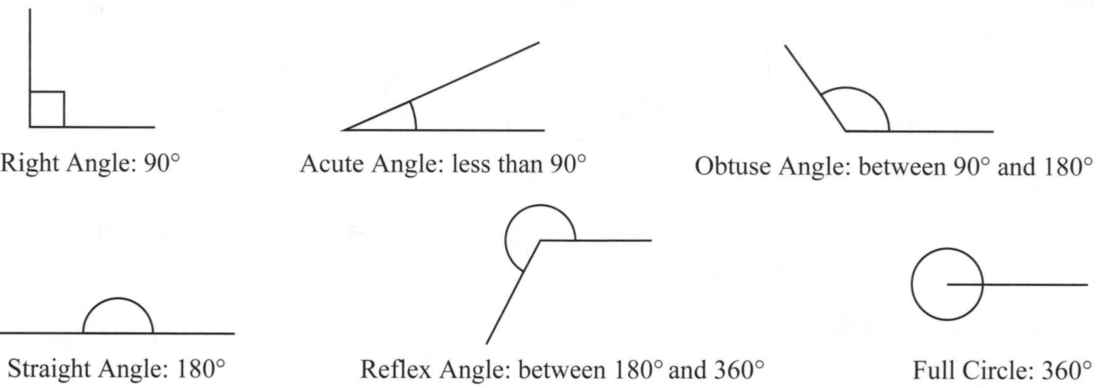

Pairs of angles can also be classified by comparing their degree measurements. **Complementary** angles are a pair of angles that add up to 90°. **Supplementary** angles are a pair of angles that add up to 180°. **Congruent** angles are a pair of angles that have equal measures.

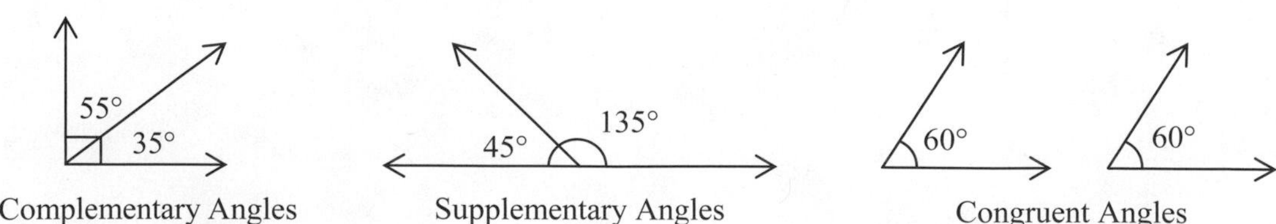

A line that **bisects** an angle divides it into two equal parts. In the figure on the right, line $\overleftrightarrow{BD}$ bisects $\angle ABC$ and divides it into two congruent angles, $\angle ABD$ and $\angle DBC$:

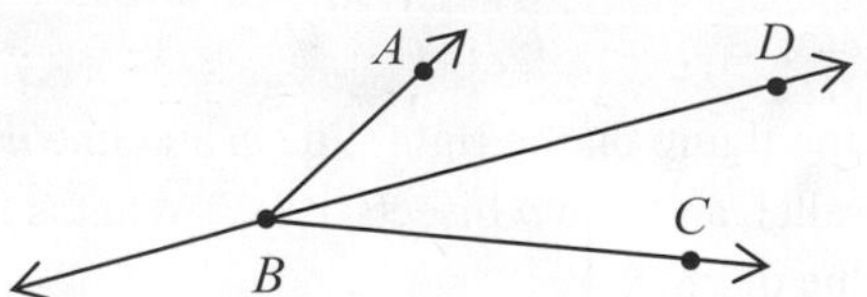

Intersecting Lines and Angles

Two lines are **perpendicular** if they intersect to form right angles. If two lines are **parallel**, then they will never intersect.

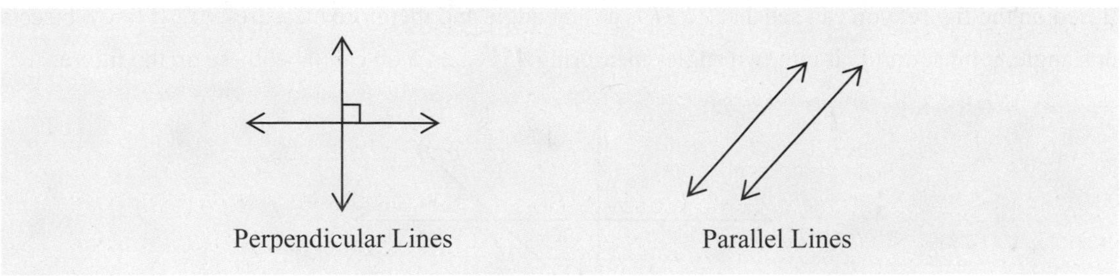

When one line intersects with another line, they form two sets of **vertical angles**. Vertical angles are congruent. In the figure below, $a = d$ and $b = c$.

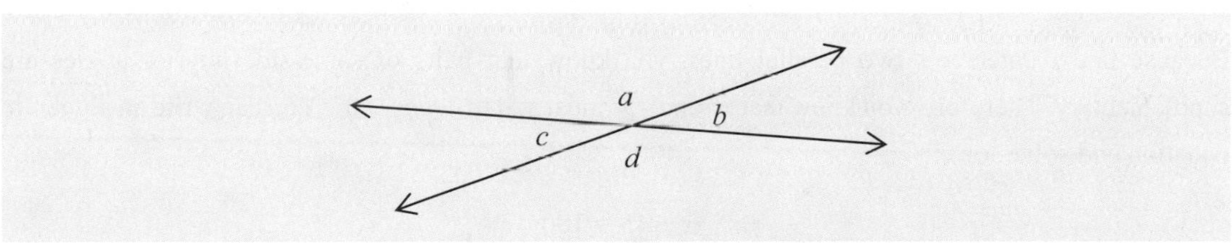

If a third line, or a **transversal**, intersects a pair of parallel lines, it forms eight angles:

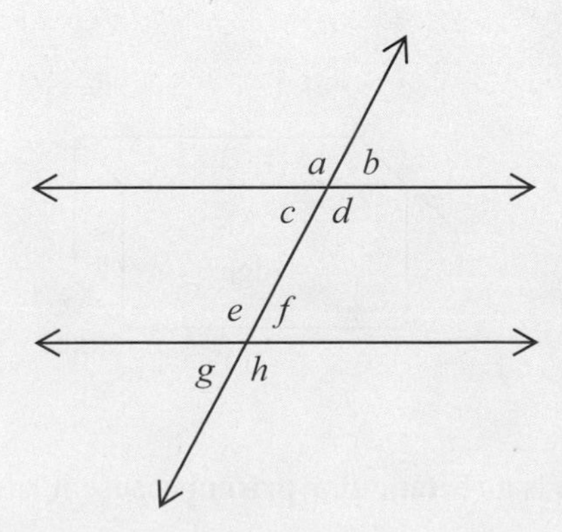

Here are some properties of transversals:

- The pairs of **corresponding angles** are congruent: $a = e$, $b = f$, $c = g$, and $d = h$.
- The pairs of **alternate interior angles** are congruent: $c = f$ and $d = e$.
- The pairs of **alternate exterior angles** are congruent: $a = h$ and $b = g$.
- The pairs of **same side interior angles** are supplementary: $c + e = 180°$ and $d + f = 180°$.

Example

In the figure on the right, line m and line n are parallel, and line p bisects $\angle RST$. What is the value of x?

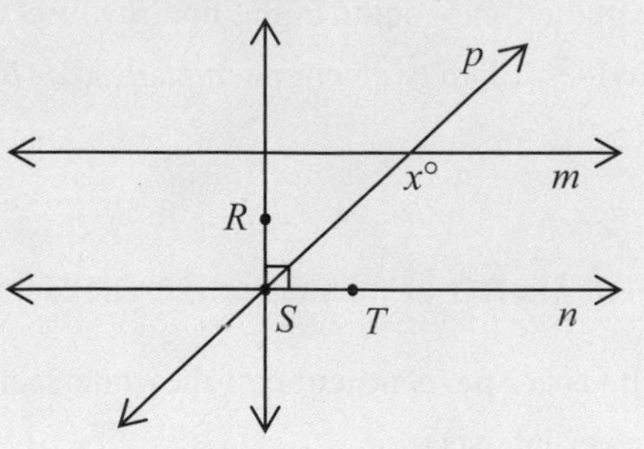

Based on the figure, you can see that $\angle RST$ is a right angle and therefore measures 90°. If line p bisects this angle, it must divide it into two angles measuring 45° each. You can label these on the figure:

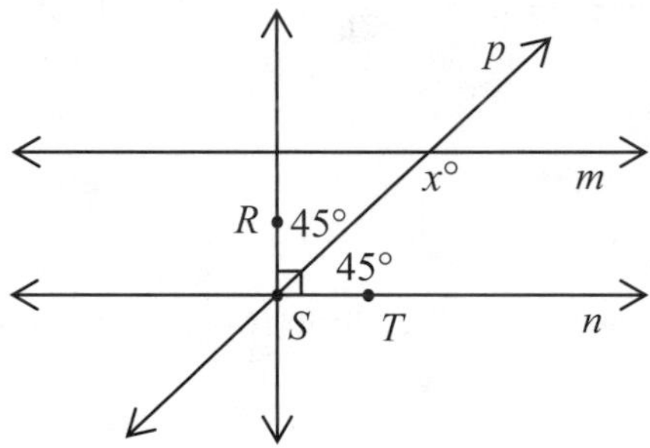

Because line p intersects two parallel lines, you know that pairs of same-side interior angles are supplementary. Therefore, you know that $x°$ and 45° must add to equal 180°. You can write an algebraic equation and solve for x:

$$x + 45 = 180$$

$$x + 45 - 45 = 180 - 45$$

$$x = 135$$

Prisms

A **solid** is a three-dimensional shape. A **prism** is a solid with two congruent polygons, called **bases**, joined by perpendicular rectangles. Each exterior surface of a prism is called a **face**, the lines where these faces intersect are called **edges**, and the points where these edges intersect are called **vertices** (singular: vertex).

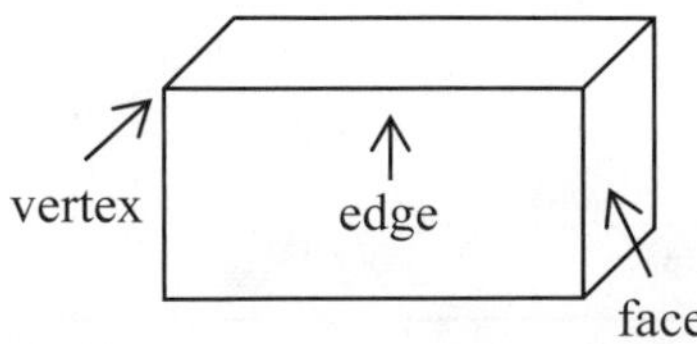

Prisms are named for the shape of their bases. The prism above is a **rectangular prism** because it has a rectangular base—in other words, it's a box.

The volume of a prism is the space contained within the prism. To find the volume of a rectangular prism, multiply its length by its width by its height. For example, the prism to the right has a volume of 40 units cubed:

$$\text{Volume} = \text{length} \times \text{width} \times \text{height} = 5 \times 4 \times 2 = 40$$

A rectangular prism whose edges are all the same length is called a cube. The volume of a cube is equal to the length of one of its edges cubed. For example, the cube to the right has a volume of 64 units cubed:

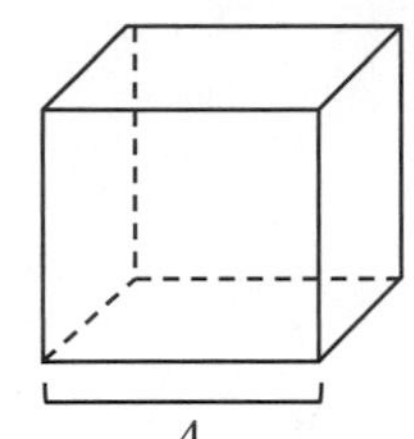

$$\text{Volume} = \text{edge}^3 = 4^3 = 64$$

The volume of any other type of prism can be found by multiplying the area of one of its bases by its length, or the edge perpendicular to its bases. For example, the triangular prism to the right has a volume of 150 cubed units:

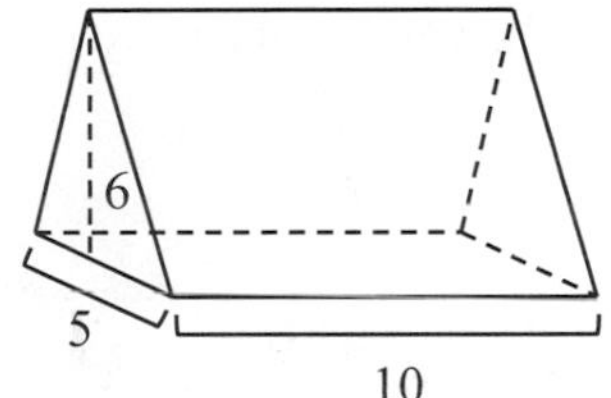

$$\text{Volume} = \text{base} \times \text{length} = \frac{6 \times 5}{2} \times 10 - 150$$

The surface area of any prism can be found by adding together the areas of its faces.

Example

The adjacent figure shows the dimensions of a cardboard box. If there are no overlapping sides, how many square inches of cardboard are needed to make this box?

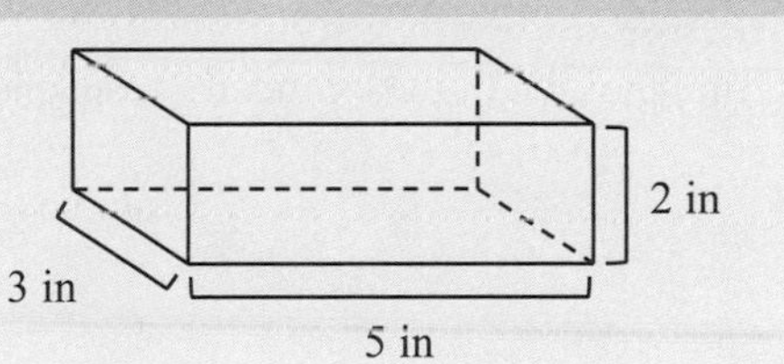

This question is asking you to find the surface area of a rectangular prism with a height of 2 inches, a width of 3 inches, and a length of 5 inches. To find how many square inches of cardboard make up the exterior of the box, you need to find the area of each rectangular face and then add these areas together.

The top and bottom faces each have an area of $5 \text{ in} \times 3 \text{ in} = 15 \text{ in}^2$. The front and back faces each have an area of $5 \text{ in} \times 2 \text{ in} = 10 \text{ in}^2$. The left and right faces each have an area of $3 \text{ in} \times 2 \text{ in} = 6 \text{ in}^2$. To find the total surface area of the box, add together the areas of each of these faces:

$$(2 \times 15 \text{ in}^2) + (2 \times 10 \text{ in}^2) + (2 \times 6 \text{ in}^2) = 62 \text{ in}^2$$

If you wanted to build this box, you would need 62 in^2 of cardboard.

Cylinders

A **cylinder** is like a prism, but its base is a circle instead of a polygon. Two circular bases connected by a perpendicular curved surface form a cylinder:

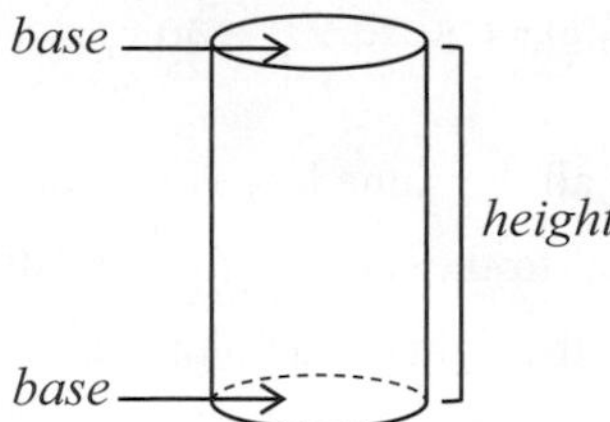

The volume of a cylinder is equal to the area of its base multiplied by its height. The area of the cylinder's base is equal to π times the radius of the cylinder squared, so you can use the formula below to find the volume of any cylinder:

$$\text{Volume} = \pi \times \text{radius}^2 \times \text{height}$$

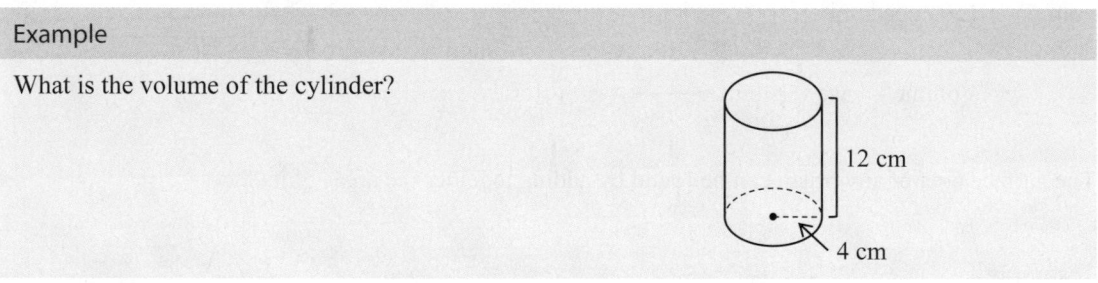
Example

What is the volume of the cylinder?

First, find the area of the cylinder's base, and then multiply by its height:

$$\begin{aligned}\text{Volume} &= \pi \times \text{radius}^2 \times \text{height}\\ &= \pi \times 4^2 \times 12\\ &= \pi \times 16 \times 12\\ &= 192\pi\end{aligned}$$

The volume of the cylinder is 192π cubic centimeters.

To find the surface area of a cylinder, imagine that the cylinder was sliced along its height and "unfolded" on a flat surface. You would then have two circular bases and one rectangle that wraps around the bases. To find the surface area of the cylinder, you need to add up the areas of the bases and the area of this rectangle.

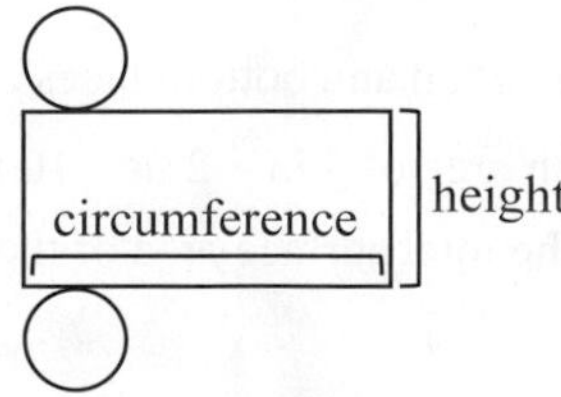

This rectangle has a length that is equal to the circumference of one of the bases, and a width that is equal to the height of the cylinder. Therefore, to find the area of this rectangle, you would multiply the cylinder's circumference by its height. You would then add this number to the area of the two bases to find the total surface area of the cylinder:

$$\text{surface area} = (\text{area of bases}) + (\text{circumference} \times \text{height})$$

Example

Find the surface area of the cylinder.

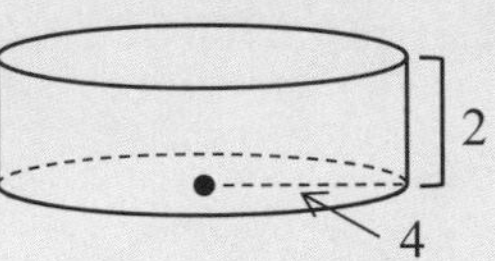

First, find the area of the bases:

$$\text{Area of each base} = \pi \times 4^2 = 16\pi$$

Then, find the circumference:

$$\text{Circumference} = 2 \times \pi \times 4 = 8\pi$$

Finally, add the area of the bases to the product of the circumference and the height:

$$\begin{aligned}\text{Surface area} &= (\text{area of bases}) + (\text{circumference} \times \text{height})\\ &= (2 \times 16\pi) + (8\pi \times 2)\\ &= 32\pi + 16\pi\\ &= 48\pi\end{aligned}$$

The total surface area of the cylinder is 48π square units.

Spheres

A **sphere** is like a three-dimensional circle: the surface of the sphere is a collection of points that are all the same distance away from the center. As in a circle, the line segment drawn from the center to a point on the sphere's surface is called the sphere's radius, and all radii of a sphere are equal lengths.

The volume of a sphere is equal to $\frac{4}{3}\pi$ times its radius cubed. For example, the sphere to the right has a volume of $\frac{32}{3}\pi$ units cubed:

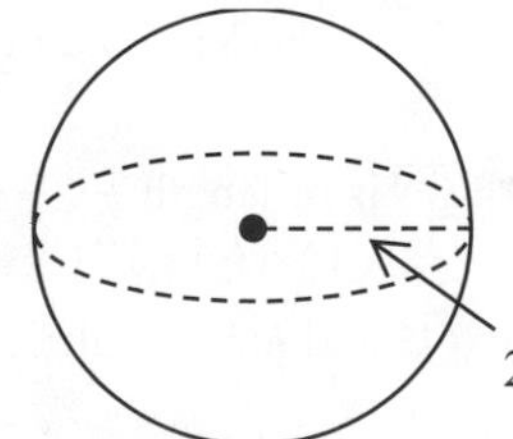

$$\text{volume} = \frac{4}{3}\pi r^3 = \frac{4}{3}\pi \times 2^3 = \frac{4}{3}\pi \times 8 = \frac{32}{3}\pi$$

You don't need to memorize this formula because it's included in the reference section of the SAT Math Test. You should, however, be familiar with how to use it; the less you have to flip back and forth from the reference section to your question, the more time you will be able to spend on the question!

In this part, we reviewed some properties of lines, angles, quadrilaterals, triangles, and circles. We also reviewed some properties of solids, such as prisms, cylinders, and spheres. During the rest of the section, we'll build on these simple concepts in order to solve some of the more complex Additional Topics questions on the SAT.

Part 1 Practice: Angles and Volumes of Shapes

1

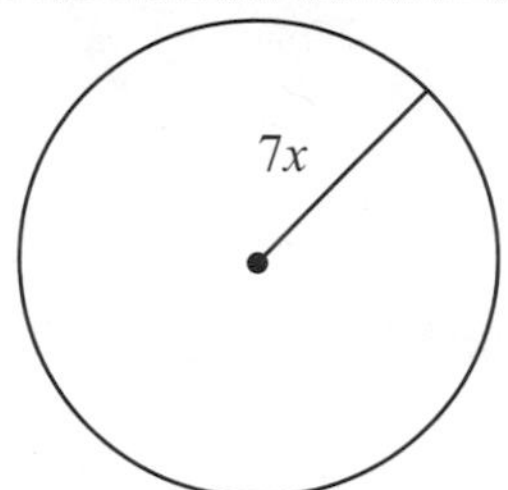

What is the area of the circle above, in terms of x?

A) $7\pi x^2$

B) $49\pi x$

C) $49\pi^2 x$

D) $49\pi x^2$

2

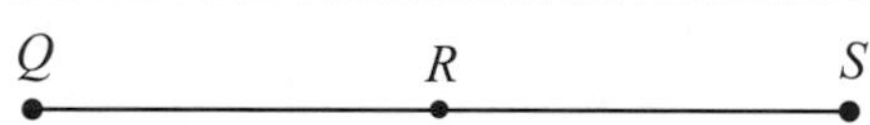

In the figure above, R is the midpoint of $\overline{QS}$. If $\overline{QR} = \frac{3}{4}$, which of the following statements must be true?

A) $\overline{QR}$ is longer than $\overline{RS}$.

B) $\overline{QR}$ and $\overline{QS}$ are both of length $\frac{3}{4}$.

C) $\overline{QS}$ is of length $\frac{3}{2}$.

D) $\overline{QS}$ and $\overline{RS}$ have the same length.

3

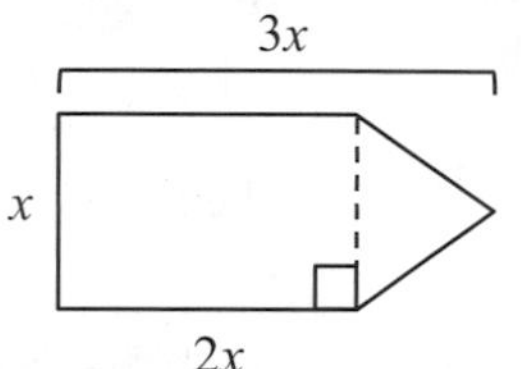

What is the area of the polygon shown above, in terms of x?

A) $\frac{3x^2}{2}$

B) $2x^2$

C) $\frac{5x^2}{2}$

D) $3x^2$

4

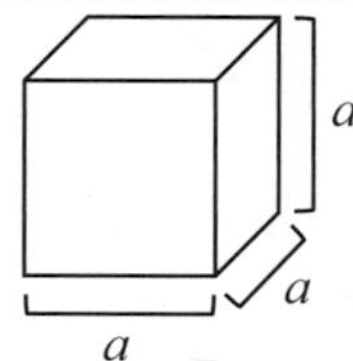

The surface area of the rectangular prism above, in squared units, is equal to its volume, in cubed units. Which of the following equations is true for the prism?

A) $a = 3$

B) $a = 6$

C) $a^2 = 6$

D) $a^3 = 6$

5

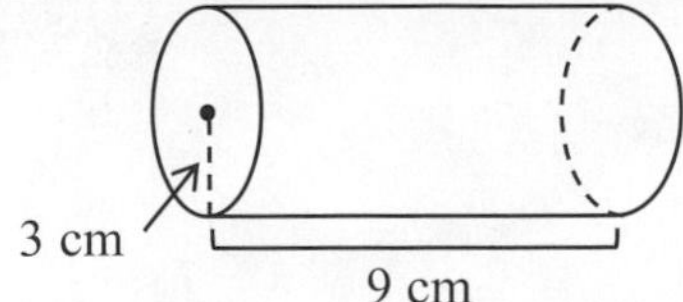

A food company wants to sell tomato sauce in a can whose shape is shown above. It costs the company two cents per cm^3 to produce and package the tomato sauce, and it sells the cans for $7.00. How much profit does it make per can, rounded to the nearest cent?

A) $0.63

B) $1.91

C) $2.76

D) $5.30

Questions 6 and 7 refer to the following information.

The volume of a sphere is 36π centimeters cubed. Its volume with a radius r and volume v is calculated according to the equation $v = \frac{4}{3}\pi r^3$.

6

What is the sphere's radius?

A) 3 cm

B) 6 cm

C) 9 cm

D) 24 cm

7

If the sphere has a density of $\frac{4 \text{ g}}{\pi \text{ cm}^3}$, what is its mass, in grams?

A) 9

B) 72

C) 144

D) 388

8

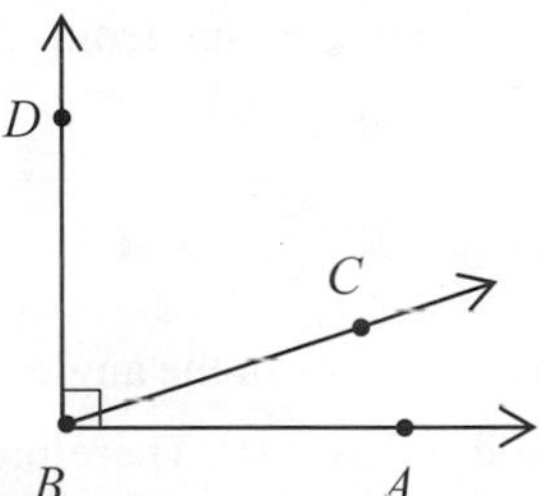

In the figure above, angles ABC and CBD are complementary. If $\angle CBD$ measures 70°, what is the measure of $\angle ABC$? (Ignore the degree symbol when gridding your response.)

9

If the area of a square is 81 m^2, what is the length of one of the square's sides, in meters?

10

If the area of a circle is 64π, what is its diameter?

Right Triangles

Part 2

The basic properties of triangles, their side lengths, perimeters, and areas, are covered in our online material. The SAT will ask questions about these properties, but in the context of a more complex situation. Specific rules that the SAT lists in their reference section include the Pythagorean theorem $c^2 = a^2 + b^2$, and the special right triangles with angles of 30-60-90 and 45-45-90 degrees. In this section we will cover this reference material as we look at right triangles and see how you can use their special properties to find angles and lengths.

Angles of Right Triangles

In a **right triangle**, one of the angles is always 90°. As discussed in the online review, the interior angles of any triangle add to 180°. Therefore, the sum of the two acute angles of a right triangle is always equal to 180 – 90 = 90°. You can use this information to find unknown angles in a right triangle.

Example

Find the value of the angle x.

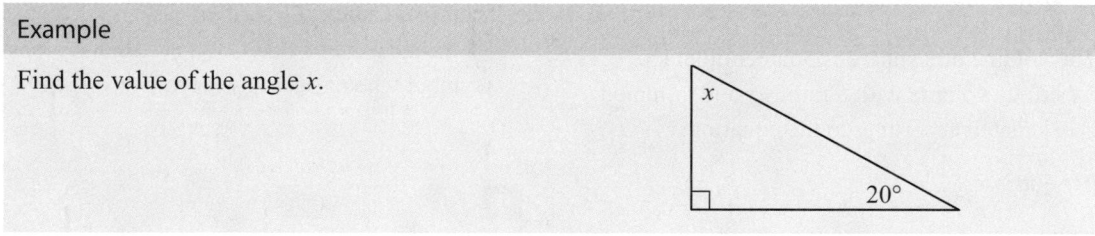

Because this is a right triangle, you know that the sum of the two acute angles is 90°. You can write an equation to solve for x:

$$20° + x = 90°$$

$$x = 90° - 20°$$

$$x = 70°$$

The angle x is 70°.

Pythagorean Theorem

We've seen how to find a missing angle of a right triangle. Now we are going to look at how to find a missing side length of a right triangle.

The sides of a right triangle have special names. The **hypotenuse** of a right triangle is the side opposite the right angle, and the other two sides of a right triangle are called its **legs**. The Pythagorean theorem gives us a formula to solve for the side lengths of a right triangle. According to the **Pythagorean theorem**, if a and b are the lengths of the triangle's legs and c is the length of its hypotenuse, then a squared plus b squared equals c squared.

This is the Pythagorean theorem:

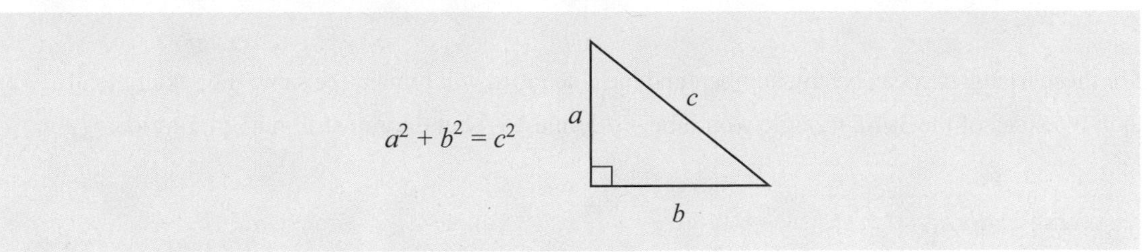

Example

What is the value of x in the adjacent figure?

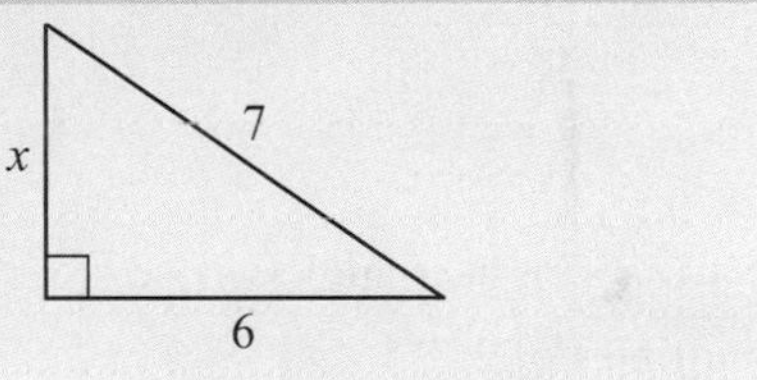

To find the length of the missing side, plug the lengths of the two sides given into the Pythagorean theorem and solve for x. The sum of the lengths of our two sides squared ($x^2 + 6^2$) is equal to the length of the hypotenuse squared (7^2):

$$x^2 + 6^2 = 7^2$$

$$x^2 + 36 = 49$$

$$x^2 = 13$$

$$x = \sqrt{13}$$

13 isn't a perfect square, so you can't simplify this expression further. For calculator grid-in questions on the SAT, you may occasionally be asked to calculate this as $x = 3.61$. Most often, however, you will find a multiple-choice answer in the form of $x = \sqrt{13}$.

Special Triangles

While the Pythagorean theorem can help you find the sides of a right triangle, many triangles don't need so much calculation. The SAT is full of **special triangles**—triangles whose three side lengths have fixed ratios. These include 3-4-5 triangles, 5-12-13 triangles, 30-60-90 triangles, and 45-45-90 triangles. Recognizing a special triangle reduces the time you need to calculate the missing sides.

3-4-5 and 5-12-13 triangles are named for the ratios of their side lengths. **3-4-5 triangles** have side lengths in the ratio of 3:4:5, and **5-12-13 triangles** have side lengths in the ratio of 5:12:13.

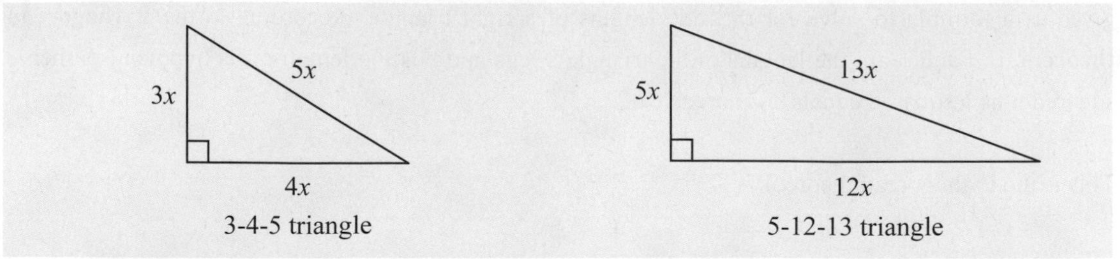

3-4-5 triangle

5-12-13 triangle

For these triangles, x can be any number, and the side ratios will remain the same. For example, if $x = 3$, then the sides of the 3-4-5 triangle would be 9, 12, and 15—but they're still in a 3:4:5 ratio.

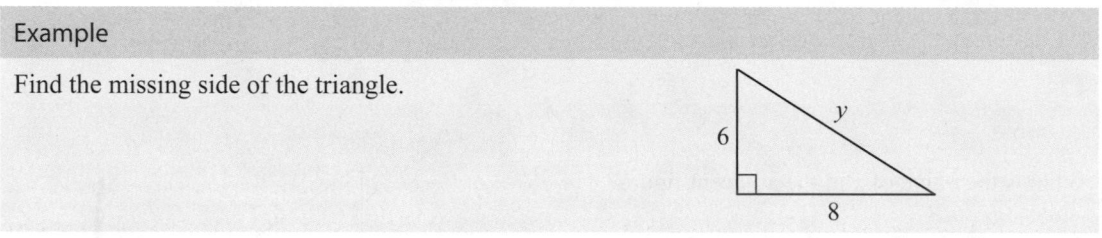

This is a right triangle whose sides have a common factor of 2. You can re-write the side lengths as multiples of 2:

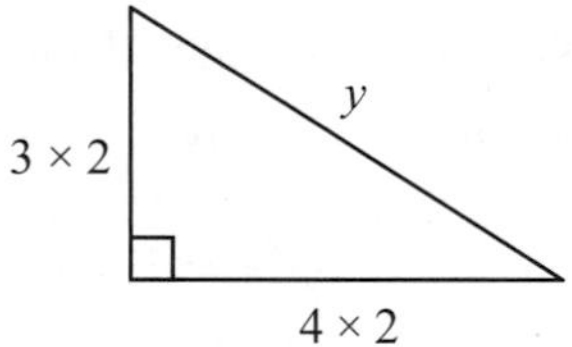

Now you see that these sides are in the ratio of 3:4, and you can use your knowledge of the 3-4-5 special triangle to calculate the missing side. If the lengths of the two legs are 3×2 and 4×2, then the length of the hypotenuse must be 5×2:

$$y = 5 \times 2 = 10$$

The missing side is equal to 10.

30-60-90 triangles and 45-45-90 triangles are named for their angles. **30-60-90 triangles** have angles measured 30°, 60°, and 90°, and side lengths in a ratio of $1:\sqrt{3}:2$. **45-45-90 triangles** have angles measured 45°, 45°, and 90°, and side lengths in a ratio of $1:1:\sqrt{2}$.

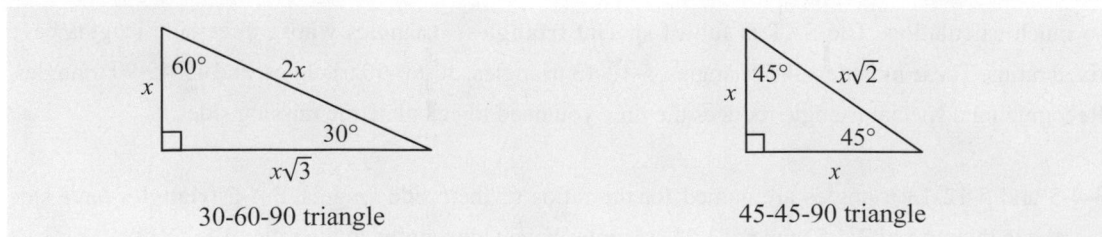

30-60-90 triangle

45-45-90 triangle

Example

What are the values of x and y in the triangle?

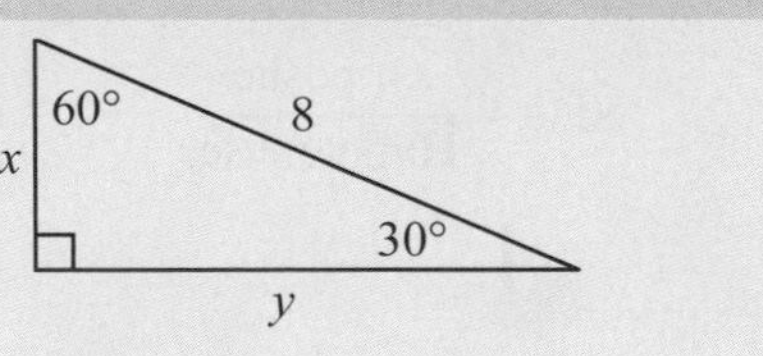

Using what you know about 30-60-90 triangles, you can easily find x and y. You know that x is half of the value of the hypotenuse because it is located opposite the 30 degree angle:

$$x = 8 \div 2 = 4$$

Now that you have the value of x, you can find y by multiplying x by $\sqrt{3}$:

$$y = 4 \times \sqrt{3} = 4\sqrt{3}$$

An easy way to remember the side lengths of these triangles is by thinking about their angles. The triangle with two different angles has a side length of the square root of two, and the triangle with three different angles has a side length of the square root of three. Knowing the value of just one side and one angle (other than the right angle) of a 30-60-90 triangle allows you to find the values for all three sides!

Trigonometry

Trigonometry is a more specialized type of math that deals with relationships between sides and angles in right triangles. In addition to using the Pythagorean theorem and special triangle ratios, you can use trigonometry to calculate the length of sides in right triangles.

In trigonometry, the relationships between sides and angles of right triangles can be written as ratios with specific names. The three ratios you will find on the SAT are sine (abbreviated sin), cosine (abbreviated cos), and tangent (abbreviated tan). These ratios need to be memorized, and are not provided in the SAT's reference material. We will now take a look at what these ratios mean and review an easy way to remember them.

You can find the **sine** of an angle by dividing the length of the side opposite to the angle by the length of the triangle's hypotenuse. You can find the **cosine** by dividing the length of the side adjacent to the angle by the length of the hypotenuse. You can find the **tangent** by dividing the length of the opposite side by the length of the adjacent side. These ratios are summarized in the following formulas, where x stands for the measure of any angle in the triangle:

$$\sin(x) = \frac{\text{opposite}}{\text{hypotenuse}} \qquad \cos(x) = \frac{\text{adjacent}}{\text{hypotenuse}} \qquad \tan(x) = \frac{\text{opposite}}{\text{adjacent}}$$

In order to help you remember these ratios, we recommend you memorize the acronym **SOHCAHTOA**:

$$\text{Sine} = \frac{\textbf{O}\text{pposite}}{\textbf{H}\text{ypotenuse}} \qquad \text{Cosine} = \frac{\textbf{A}\text{djacent}}{\textbf{H}\text{ypotenuse}} \qquad \text{Tangent} = \frac{\textbf{O}\text{pposite}}{\textbf{A}\text{djacent}}$$

Example

What is the sine of $x°$?

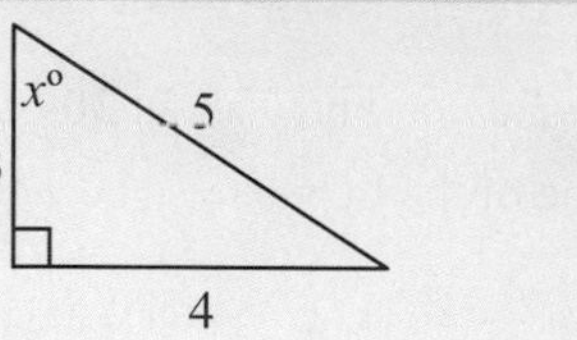

In order to calculate the sine for angle x in this triangle, first locate the side opposite to $x°$. The opposite side has a length of 4. Then, plug this value into the formula for sine:

$$\sin(x°) = \frac{\text{opposite}}{\text{hypotenuse}} = \frac{4}{5}$$

The sine of $x°$ is $\frac{4}{5}$.

You can use your knowledge of sine, cosine, and tangent to solve for the length of one of the sides of a triangle. For example, let's look at the following question:

Example

In the adjacent triangle, what is the value of B?

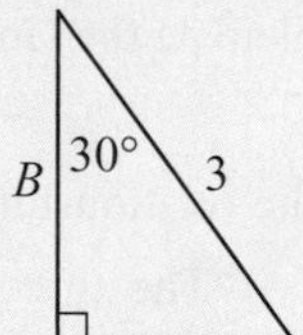

In this triangle, you know the measure of an angle and the length of the hypotenuse. You need to find the length of the side adjacent to the angle. "**SOHCAHTOA**" reminds us that the cosine of an angle compares the adjacent side with the hypotenuse. You can plug the values from the triangle into the cosine ratio formula:

$$\cos(x) = \frac{\text{adjacent}}{\text{hypotenuse}}$$

$$\cos(30°) = \frac{B}{3}$$

Then, you can solve for B:

$$B = \cos(30°) \times 3$$

Using trigonometry, you have determined that the length of B is equal to $\cos(30°) \times 3$. On the SAT, the answer will normally remain in this format. You will not be required to memorize trigonometric values such as $\cos(30°)$.

Before you leave this chapter, make sure that you understand how to find the missing angles and sides of right triangles using the Pythagorean theorem and trigonometry. Also remember that many questions on the SAT use special right triangles. By memorizing just a few of their ratios and angles, you will save a lot of time and avoid many complex calculations!

Part 2 Practice: Right Triangles

1

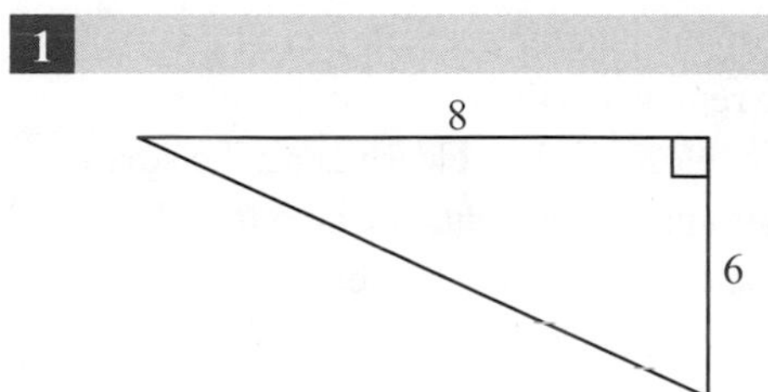

Which of the following triangles is similar to the one above?

A) 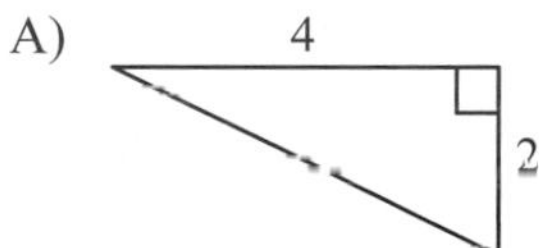

B) 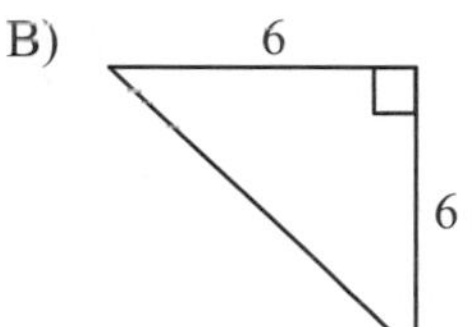

C) 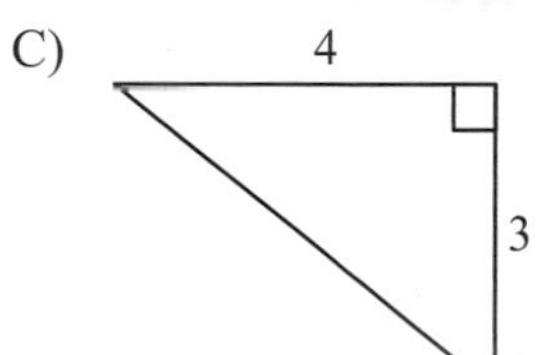

D) 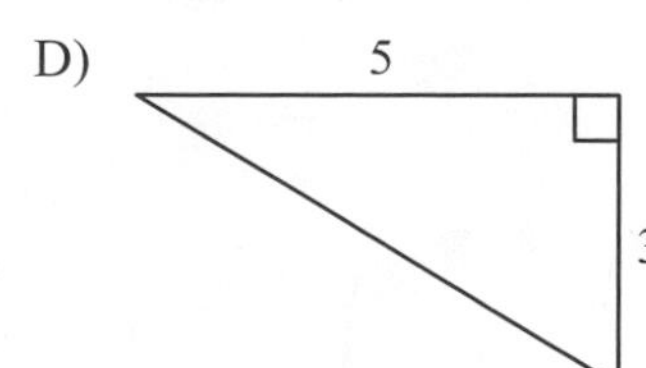

2

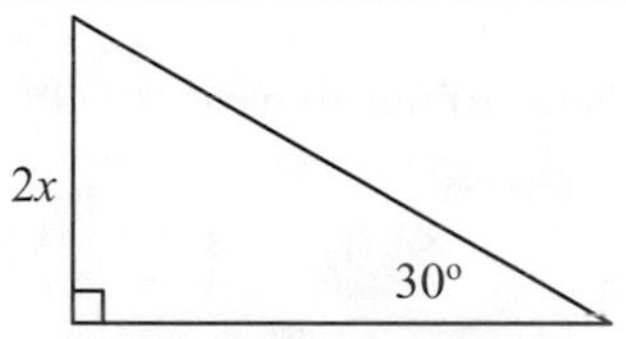

Which of the following expressions correctly represents the length of the hypotenuse of the triangle above?

A) $x\sqrt{3}$

B) $x\sqrt{5}$

C) $4x$

D) $5x$

3

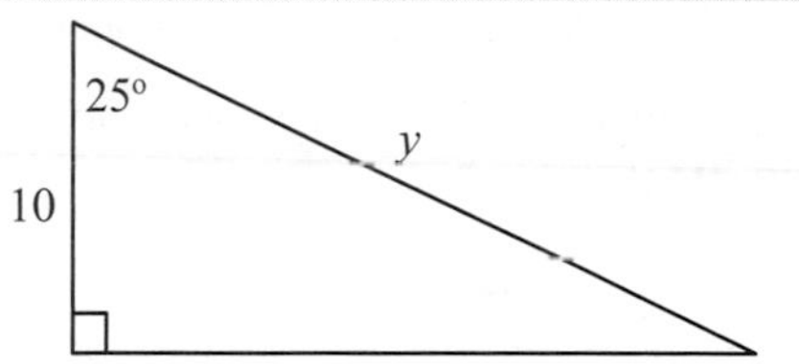

What is the value of y in the triangle above?

A) $\dfrac{10}{\cos(25°)}$

B) $\dfrac{10}{\sin(25°)}$

C) $10\sin(25°)$

D) $\sin(25°)$

4

If you know two side lengths of a right triangle, what other information can you calculate?

I. The length of the third side
II. The sine of every angle in the triangle
III. The cosine of every angle in the triangle

A) I only
B) II only
C) I, II, and III
D) None of the above

5

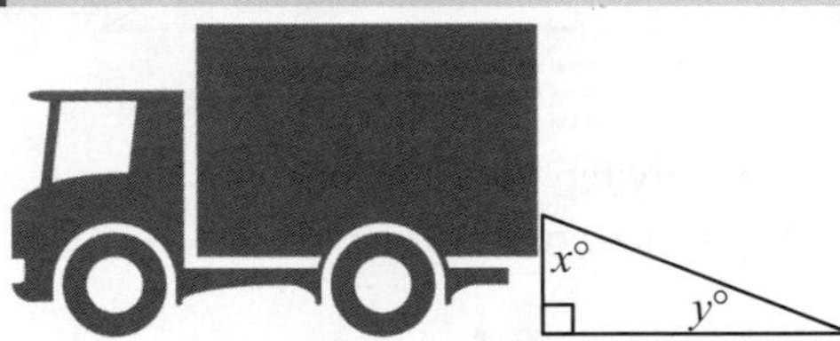

Felicia owns a furniture company and wants to build a ramp to push furniture from her warehouse into a truck, as shown above. Her contractor tells her that he will charge her $10 for every degree of the angle between the floor and the ramp (y). If $\sin(x) = \frac{\sqrt{3}}{2}$, how much money will she have to pay to build the ramp?

A) $150
B) $300
C) $600
D) $900

Questions 6 and 7 use the following information.

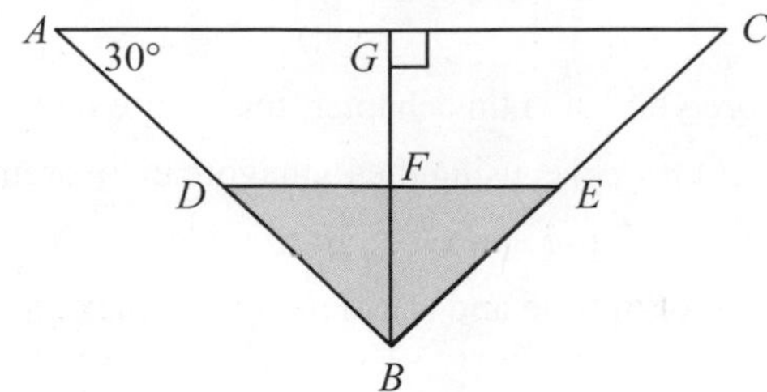

The area that is viewable by an astronomer from a telescope is diagrammed above. The larger triangle represents the area that is viewable from the telescope less clearly, and the smaller shaded triangle represents the area that the telescope can show the most clearly. In the figure above, $\overline{AB} = \overline{BC} = 10$ light years, $\overline{DB} = 4$ light years, and $\overline{DE}$ is parallel to $\overline{AC}$.

6

What is the length of $\overline{BG}$?

A) 2.5 light years
B) 5 light years
C) 10 light years
D) 20 light years

7

What is the length of $\overline{FG}$?

A) 0.25 light years
B) 0.5 light years
C) 2 light years
D) 3 light years

8

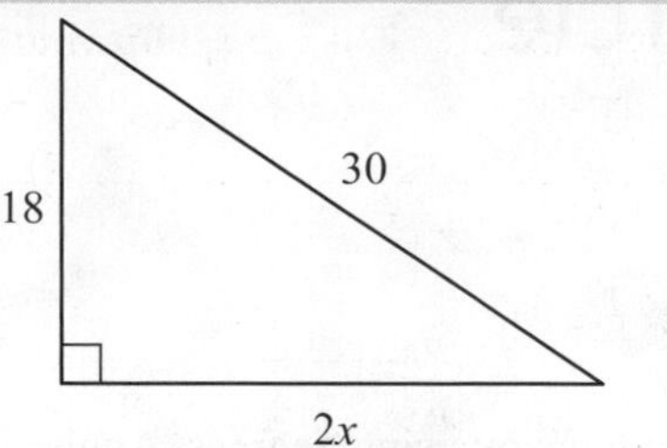

What is the value of x in the triangle above?

9

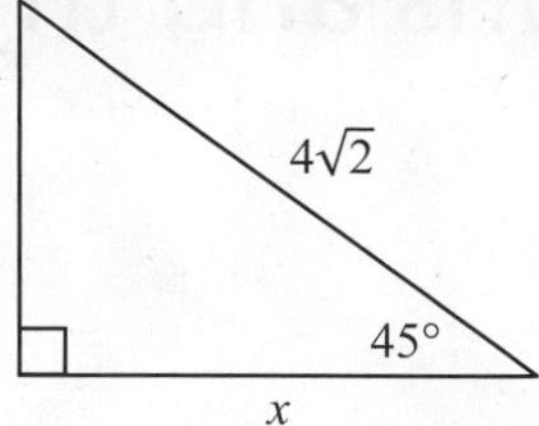

What is the value of x in the triangle above?

10

Tim draws an isosceles right triangle with a hypotenuse of $\sqrt{8}$ in. How many inches long are each of the triangle's legs?

Radians and the Unit Circle

Part 3

So far, we have been measuring angles using lines and polygons by using degrees. Angles can also be measured in another unit called radians. A **radian** is a unit that measures an angle as a part of a circle. Radians are expressed in the unit π. They are used when measuring sectors of the unit circle, a useful tool for looking at the relationship between sine and cosine. The Math test may require you to make a direct conversion of degrees to radians or vice-versa. Knowing how to do this conversion will also help you with figuring out chords and arc lengths, which are covered in part 4.

Measuring Angles

There are 2π radians in a circle, or full rotation. Since both 2π radians and $360°$ are equal to a full rotation, $360° = 2\pi$ radians. You can divide both sides by 2 to get the following equation:

$$180° = \pi \text{ radians}$$

You can use this equation to convert between degrees and radians.

Example
What is 270° in radians?

You know that there are π radians in 180°, so you can convert from degrees to radians by multiplying by the conversion factor $\frac{\pi}{180°}$:

$$270° \times \frac{\pi \text{ radians}}{180°} = \frac{3\pi}{2} \text{ radians}$$

Here is a table of common angles in degrees and radians:

Degrees	30°	45°	60°	90°	180°	270°	360°
Radians	$\frac{\pi}{6}$	$\frac{\pi}{4}$	$\frac{\pi}{3}$	$\frac{\pi}{2}$	π	$\frac{3\pi}{2}$	2π

The Unit Circle

On the SAT, you'll often see questions involving radians and trigonometry. You can solve these questions using a special circle called the unit circle. The **unit circle** is a circle drawn on the *xy*-plane, centered at (0, 0), with a radius of 1 unit:

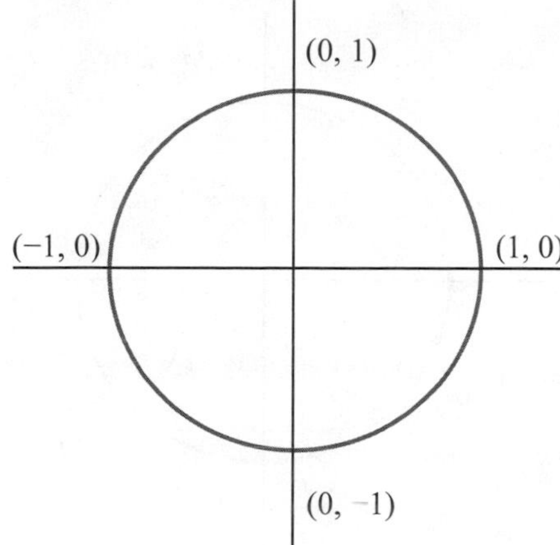

In the unit circle, angles and radians are calculated counterclockwise from the point (1, 0). For example, the angle formed between point (1, 0) and (0, 1) is 90° or $\frac{\pi}{2}$ radians. The angle formed between point (1, 0) and (0, −1) is 270° or $\frac{3\pi}{2}$ radians.

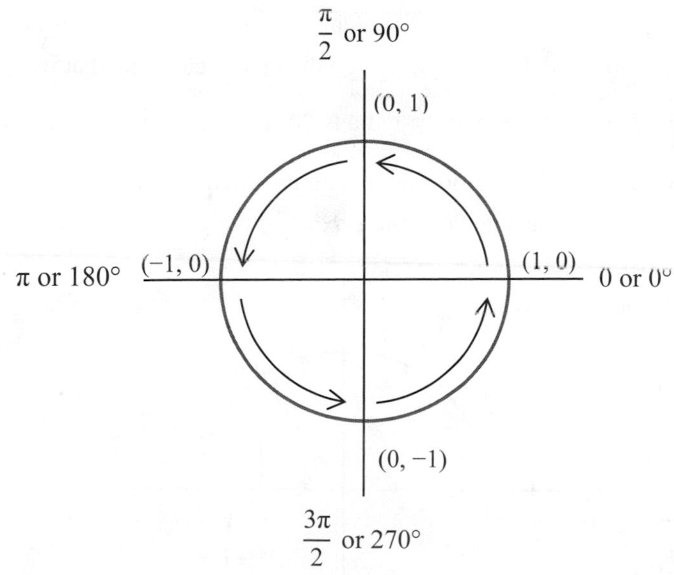

As you move counterclockwise around the unit circle, you can divide it into four quadrants. A **quadrant** is one quarter of the circle. In the diagram below, the labels I, II, III, and IV show you the first, second, third, and fourth quadrants.

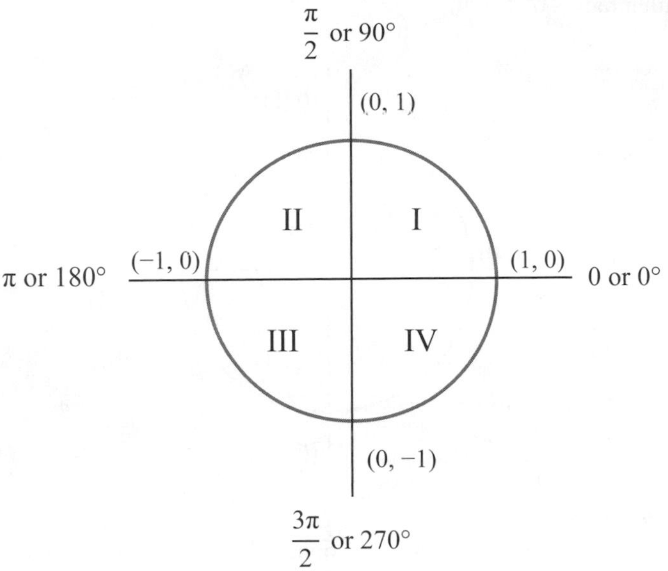

Trigonometry and the Unit Circle

Using the unit circle, you can figure out the sine and cosine of any angle in radians. So far, we've determined where 90°, 180°, and 270° are located on the unit circle. But what if you wanted to draw a different angle, like 60°? 60° is the same as $\frac{\pi}{3}$ radians. Moving counterclockwise from the point (1, 0), you'd draw a line segment that forms a 60° angle with the *x*-axis. You can make a right triangle with this angle by drawing a line segment down to the *x*-axis:

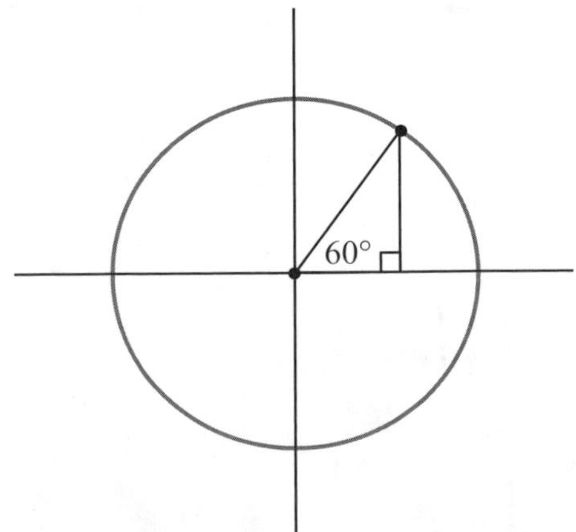

Because you know that the unit circle has a radius of 1, the hypotenuse of the right triangle must be equal to 1. From Part 2, you also know that a right triangle with a 60° angle is a type of special right triangle—a 30-60-90 triangle. Using the formula for the side lengths of 30-60-90 triangles, you can figure out that the lengths of the two sides must be equal to $\frac{1}{2}$ and $\frac{\sqrt{3}}{2}$.

You can then figure out the point where the right triangle intersects the unit circle. It is $\frac{\sqrt{3}}{2}$ units above the x-axis and $\frac{1}{2}$ units to the right of the y-axis, so it must be the point $\left(\frac{1}{2}, \frac{\sqrt{3}}{2}\right)$:

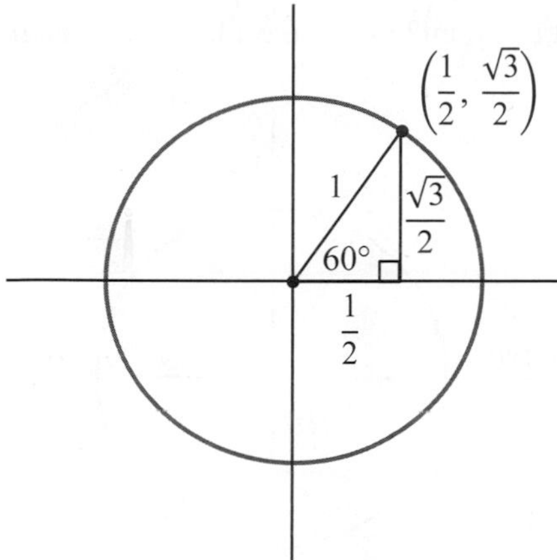

Even though you can calculate the coordinates of this point using 30-60-90 triangles, you actually won't have to do this on the SAT. If you're asked a question about a point on the unit circle, you'll be given its coordinates.

Now that you have all of the side lengths for your right triangle, you can calculate the sine and cosine of 60°, or $\frac{\pi}{3}$ radians. Remember that $\sin(x) = \frac{\text{opposite}}{\text{hypotenuse}}$ and that $\cos(x) = \frac{\text{adjacent}}{\text{hypotenuse}}$. The hypotenuse of the triangle has a length of 1, the side opposite to the 60° angle has a length of $\frac{\sqrt{3}}{2}$, and the side adjacent to the 60° angle has a length of $\frac{1}{2}$. You just have to plug these values into the trigonometric ratios:

$$\sin(60) = \frac{\text{opposite}}{1} = \frac{\sqrt{3}}{2}$$

$$\cos(60) = \frac{\text{adjacent}}{1} = \frac{1}{2}$$

Remember that the point formed by 60° on the unit circle has the coordinates $\left(\frac{1}{2}, \frac{\sqrt{3}}{2}\right)$. The sine of 60° is $\frac{\sqrt{3}}{2}$, which is the y-coordinate of that point. The cosine of 60° is $\frac{1}{2}$, which is the x-coordinate of that point.

Therefore, when you're given a point that corresponds to an angle on the unit circle, you know that:

- The sine of the angle is equal to the y-coordinate.
- The cosine of the angle is equal to the x-coordinate.

Trigonometry and Quadrants

Remember that the unit circle is divided into four quadrants. What if we wanted to find the sine and cosine of an angle in a different quadrant? Let's take a look at the angle 120°, or $\frac{2\pi}{3}$ radians:

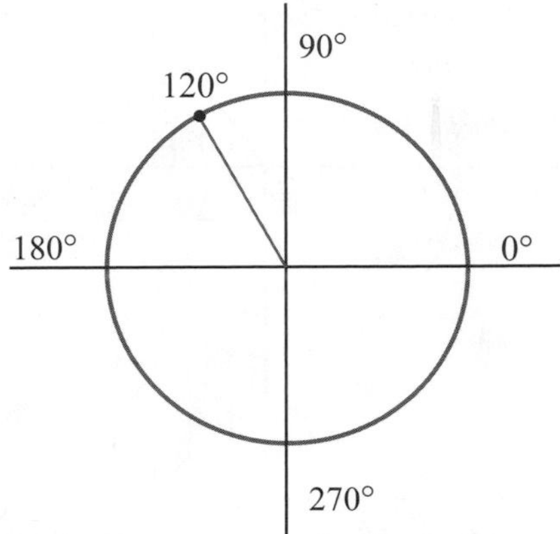

If you draw a line from this point to the x-axis, you'll form another 30-60-90 triangle with side lengths $\frac{1}{2}$ and $\frac{\sqrt{3}}{2}$. The point where this angle intersects the unit circle is $\frac{\sqrt{3}}{2}$ units above the x-axis and $\frac{1}{2}$ units to the left of the y-axis, so it must have the coordinates $\left(-\frac{1}{2}, \frac{\sqrt{3}}{2}\right)$:

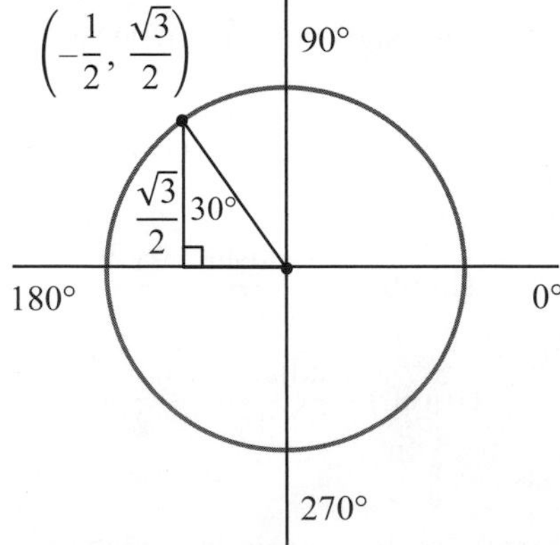

Remember that, for any point corresponding to an angle on the unit circle, the sine of the angle is equal to the y-coordinate and the cosine of the angle is equal to the x-coordinate. Because 120° has the coordinates $\left(-\frac{1}{2}, \frac{\sqrt{3}}{2}\right)$ on the unit circle, you know that:

$$\sin(120°) \text{ equals the } y\text{-coordinate: } \frac{\sqrt{3}}{2}$$

$$\cos(120°) \text{ equals the } x\text{-coordinate: } -\frac{1}{2}$$

In the first quadrant, you saw that both the sine and cosine were positive. Now that you've drawn an angle in the second quadrant, the sine is still positive but the cosine is negative. This is because all of the points in the second quadrant have positive y-coordinates but negative x-coordinates.

While the SAT will not ask you to calculate the coordinates of points on the unit circle, you need to know the signs of both sine and cosine as you move counterclockwise along the unit circle. An easy way of remembering these signs is by thinking of **CAST**. Starting in the fourth quadrant $\cos(x)$ is always positive, in the first quadrant all of the functions are positive, in the second quadrant $\sin(x)$ is positive, and in the third quadrant $\tan(x)$ is positive. All other functions in the quadrants are negative. The diagram below illustrates this acronym:

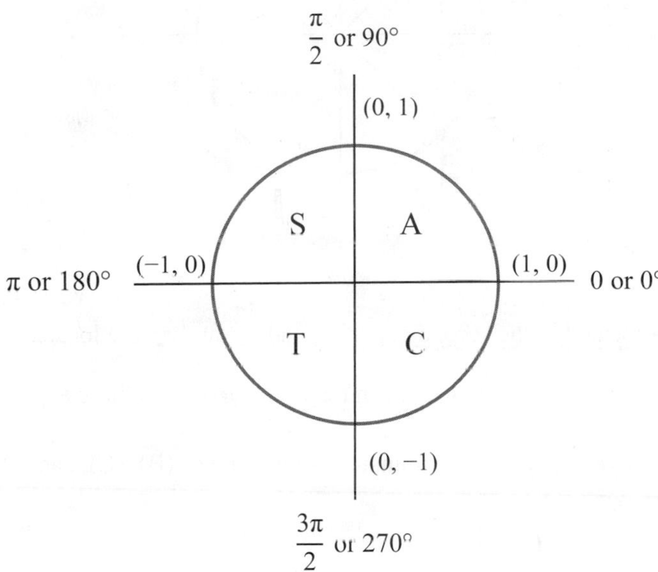

Here is a table to help you remember:

Signs of Sine and Cosine around the Unit Circle				
	Quadrant I	Quadrant II	Quadrant III	Quadrant IV
sine	+	+	−	−
cosine	+	−	−	+

Example

$$\cos(x) = \frac{\sqrt{2}}{2}$$

Which of the following could be a value for x, in radians?

A) $\frac{\pi}{4}$

B) $\frac{3\pi}{4}$

C) $\frac{6\pi}{5}$

D) $\frac{5\pi}{4}$

First, notice that the cosine of the angle is a positive number. Using the unit circle, you know that cosines are only positive for angles in the first or fourth quadrant, where all points have positive x-coordinates. Next, take a look at the answer options, and draw these angles on the unit circle:

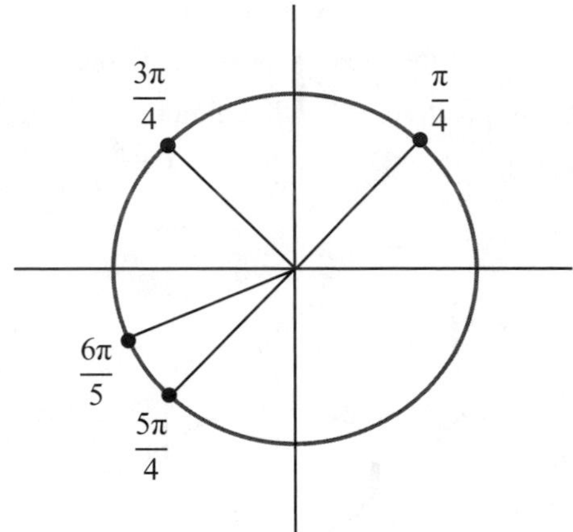

You can see that $\frac{3\pi}{4}$ is located in the second quadrant, and $\frac{5\pi}{4}$ and $\frac{6\pi}{5}$ are located in the third quadrant. You know that cosine is negative in the second and third quadrants, so these angles can't possibly have a cosine equal to $\frac{\sqrt{2}}{2}$. Therefore, you can eliminate answer choices (B), (C), and (D).

Since $\frac{\pi}{4}$ is located in the first quadrant, we know that its cosine is positive. Therefore, (A) is the only possible answer choice that could have a cosine equal to $\frac{\sqrt{2}}{2}$. The correct answer is (A).

Part 3 Practice: Radians and the Unit Circle

1

A woodworker determines that he must drill a hole by spinning a power drill for 3π radians. If one turn of the drill is equal to 360°, how many complete turns must he use to drill the hole?

A) 1

B) 1.5

C) 2

D) 2.5

2

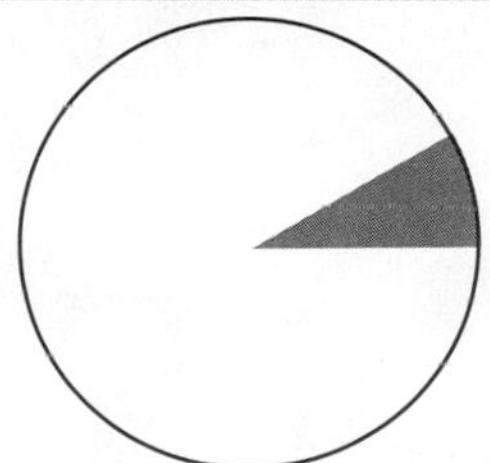

A shaded sector of a circle, with an arc length of $\frac{\pi}{6}$ radians is shown above. What is the arc length, in degrees, of this sector?

A) 20

B) 30

C) 45

D) 60

3

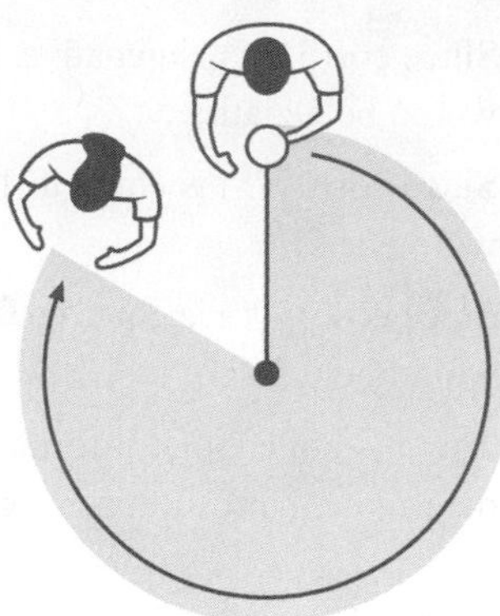

Xiao is playing a game of tether ball with his friend Mei, as shown above. If Xiao needs to hit the ball so that it moves 300° to get to Mei, how many radians must the ball travel?

A) $\frac{5\pi}{3}$

B) $\frac{4\pi}{3}$

C) π

D) $\frac{2\pi}{3}$

4

When evaluating the unit circle on the *xy*-plane, which quadrant does $\frac{\pi}{4}$ fall into?

A) Quadrant I

B) Quadrant II

C) Quadrant III

D) Quadrant IV

5

Cos (32°) is used in a calculation and is multiplied by 13. Which of the following statements is true?

A) Cos(32°) × 13 is negative.

B) Cos(32°) × 13 is positive.

C) Cos(32°) × 13 is equal to sin(32°) × 13.

D) Cos(32°) × 13 cannot be calculated.

6

If cos(217°) is multiplied by 2, which of the following statements is true?

A) Since cos(317°) is negative, the result would be negative.

B) Since cos(317°) is equal to 1, the result would be 2.

C) Since cos(317°) is equal to 0, the result would be 0.

D) There is not enough information to determine the result of this equation.

7

Which of the following is FALSE when considering the value of $\sin\left(\frac{\pi}{2}\right)$?

A) $\sin\left(\frac{\pi}{2}\right)$ is positive.

B) $\sin\left(\frac{\pi}{2}\right) \times \pi = \pi$.

C) $\sin\left(\frac{\pi}{2}\right) \times \cos\left(\frac{\pi}{2}\right)$ is negative.

D) $\sin\left(\frac{\pi}{2}\right) = \sin\left(\frac{5\pi}{2}\right)$.

8

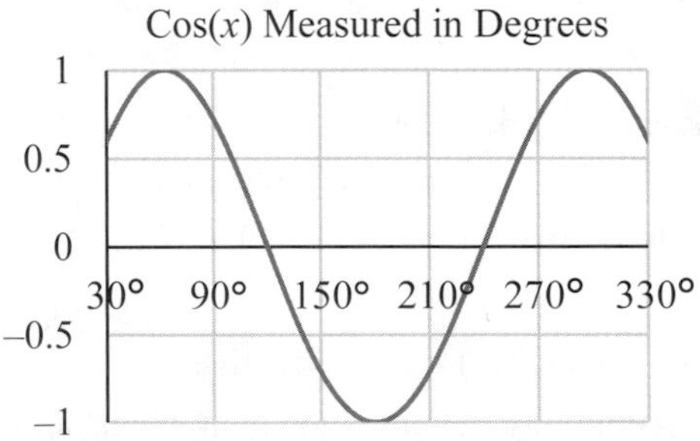

Cos(x) is plotted in xy-space, with the degree value on the x-axis and the value of cos(x) on the y-axis, as shown above. If $\cos\left(\frac{\pi}{6}\right)$ is approximated by $-0.89 \times a$, what is the approximate value of the coefficient of a for $\cos\left(\frac{7\pi}{6}\right)$?

Questions 9 and 10 refer to the following information.

A metal pipe is being cut for use in the manufacturing of sculptural elements for the garden courtyard of a new condominium complex. The engineer has drawn up the transverse of the pipe on an xy-graph, as shown below, in order to calculate where it needs to be cut.

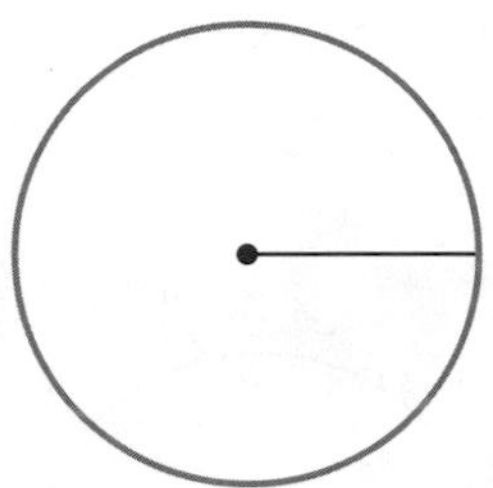

9

One straight horizontal line is drawn from a circle's midpoint to the circle's edge, as shown above. If another line is drawn at an angle of 228° with respect to the first line, which quadrant does this line fall into?

10

The engineer then decides that the pipe should instead be cut at an angle of 179°. Assuming that the first cut is made at an angle of 0°, in which quadrant should the second cut be made?

Circles

Part 4

In Part 1, we discussed how to find the area and circumference of a circle using the circle's radius and diameter. In this part, we'll talk about different parts of circles, and we'll discuss how to find the perimeters and areas of sections within a circle, subjects that frequently appear on the Additional Topics content of the Math test.

Chords

A **chord** is a line segment that connects two different points on the circumference of a circle.

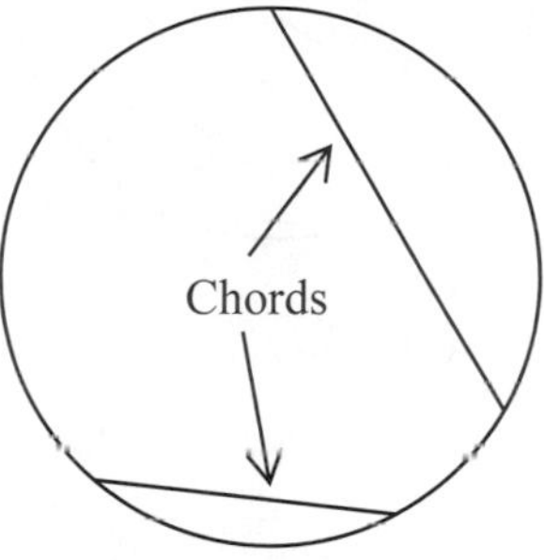

In order to find the length of a chord, you will need to know the circle's radius (r) and the distance from the middle of the chord to the center of the circle (t). You can plug these values into the following formula for chord length:

$$\text{Chord length} = 2\sqrt{r^2 - t^2}$$

You might notice that this formula looks very similar to the Pythagorean theorem. This is because you can derive this formula by using a right triangle. Half of the chord is one leg of the triangle, so in order to find the whole chord, you multiply the leg by two. Can you figure out how to get the rest of the formula from the Pythagorean theorem? Hint: the radius of the circle is the hypotenuse of the right triangle.

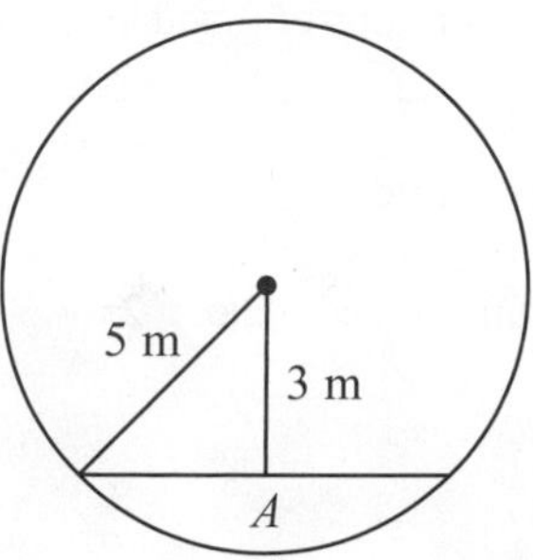

The circle has a radius of 5 m, and chord A is 3 m from the center of the circle. To find the length of chord A, plug these values into the formula for chord length:

$$2\sqrt{(5)^2 - (3)^2} = 2\sqrt{16} = 8$$

The length of the chord is 8 m.

Arcs

An **arc** is a portion of the circumference of a circle. You can think of the arc as being "enclosed" by two radii:

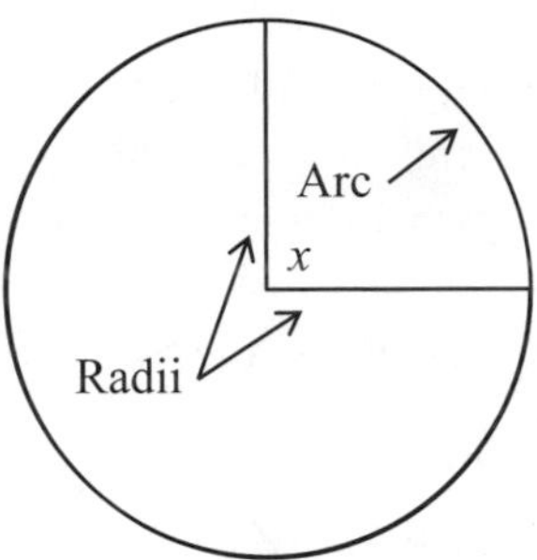

Each arc corresponds to the angle formed between the two radii. The arc in the diagram above corresponds to the angle x.

Arc length is the measure of distance along an arc. The ratio of the arc length to the circumference of the circle is equal to the ratio of the arc angle to the angle of the entire circle, which is 2π radians or 360°.

To calculate the arc length for an arc angle x, use the following proportions:

$$\frac{\text{Arc Length}}{\text{Circumference}} = \frac{x^\circ}{360^\circ}$$

$$\frac{\text{Arc Length}}{\text{Circumference}} = \frac{x \text{ radians}}{2\pi \text{ radians}}$$

Example

What is the arc length for a circle with a radius of 3 and an arc angle of 120°?

First, calculate the circumference of the circle:

$$\text{Circumference} = 2\pi r = 2\pi \times 3 = 6\pi$$

Then, set up the proportion to solve for arc length:

$$\frac{\text{Arc Length}}{\text{Circumference}} = \frac{x^\circ}{360^\circ}$$

$$\frac{\text{Arc Length}}{6\pi} = \frac{120^\circ}{360^\circ}$$

$$\text{Arc Length} = 6\pi \times \frac{120^\circ}{360^\circ}$$

$$\text{Arc Length} = 2\pi$$

The arc length is 2π.

If the arc angle x is in radians, you can manipulate the arc length proportion above to create a very simple formula for arc length. Here's the proportion again:

$$\frac{\text{Arc Length}}{\text{Circumference}} = \frac{x}{2\pi}$$

First, plug in $2\pi r$ for the circumference, and then simplify:

$$\frac{\text{Arc Length}}{2\pi r} = \frac{x}{2\pi}$$

$$\text{Arc Length} = 2\pi r \times \frac{x}{2\pi}$$

$$\text{Arc Length} = r \times x$$

The length of an arc is equal to the radius of the circle multiplied by the arc angle in radians. To solve the example question above, you could also convert 120° into radians and multiply by the radius. 120° is equal to $\frac{2\pi}{3}$ radians, and the radius is 3, so the arc length is equal to:

$$r \times x = 3 \times \frac{2\pi}{3} = 2\pi$$

Sectors

A **sector** is the area enclosed by two radii and the arc that they create. Think of a sector as a slice from a circular pizza.

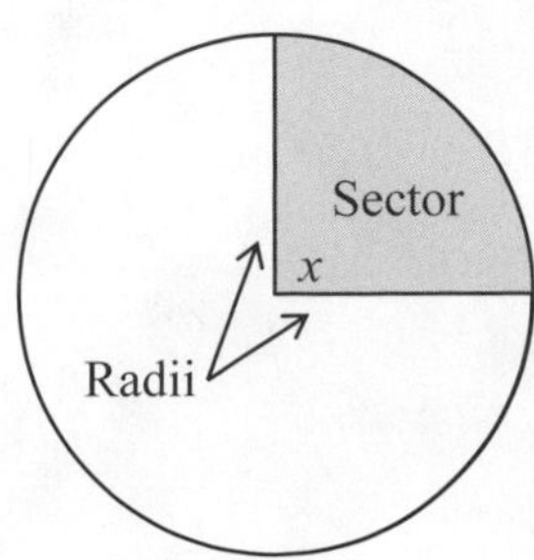

The area of a sector is also determined by the angle x between the two radii. The ratio of the sector area to the area of the circle is equal to the ratio of the sector angle to the angle of the entire circle. To calculate the sector area for a sector angle x, use the following proportions:

$$\frac{\text{Sector Area}}{\text{Circle Area}} = \frac{x°}{360°} \qquad \frac{\text{Sector Area}}{\text{Circle Area}} = \frac{x \text{ radians}}{2\pi \text{ radians}}$$

Example

What is the area of a sector with an angle of 120° and a radius of 3?

First, calculate the area of the circle:

$$\text{Circle Area} = \pi r^2 = \pi \times 3^2 = 9\pi$$

Then, set up the proportion to solve for sector area:

$$\frac{\text{Sector Area}}{\text{Circle Area}} = \frac{x°}{360°}$$

$$\frac{\text{Sector Area}}{9\pi} = \frac{120°}{360°}$$

$$\text{Sector Area} = 9\pi \times \frac{120°}{360°}$$

$$\text{Sector Area} = 3\pi$$

The area of the sector is 3π.

Graphing Circles

Circles can be graphed on the xy-plane. On the SAT, you will need to know the equation of a circle on the xy-plane. You will also need to know how to find the circle's center and radius from its equation or its graph. If you know the central point of the circle and another point on the circumference, you can find the radius of the circle.

The figure below shows a circle with a center at point (h, k). The point (x, y) is found on the circumference of the circle. You can connect these two points with a radius of the circle, and draw a right triangle:

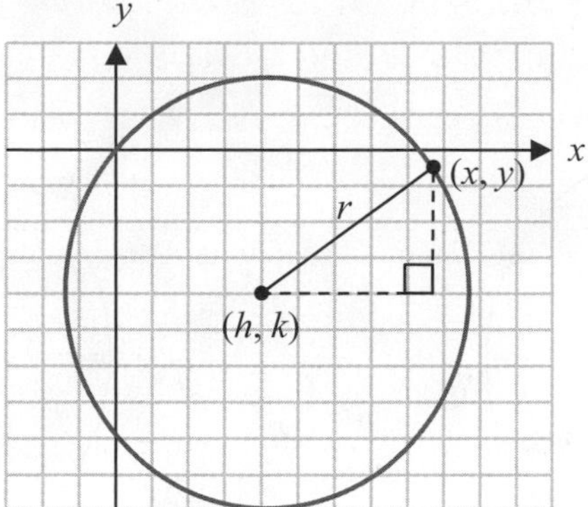

The hypotenuse of this right triangle is the radius of the circle, r. The base of the triangle is equal to the difference between the two x-coordinates of the points: $x - h$. The height of the triangle is equal to the difference between the two y-coordinates: $y - k$.

To set up an equation that describes the relationship between the radius and the two points, you can plug in the lengths for the sides of the triangle into the Pythagorean theorem:

$$(x - h)^2 + (y - k)^2 = r^2$$

This is the standard form for the equation of a circle. This equation tells you that the circle has its center at point (h, k) and a radius with length r.

Example

The equation of a circle is defined by the equation $(x - 2)^2 + (y + 1)^2 = 144$. What are the center and radius of this circle?

In order to find the center and radius of this circle, you'll need to rewrite its equation so it looks like the formula above:

$$(x - 2)^2 + (y - (-1))^2 = 12^2$$

Now that the equation is in standard form, you can see that $h = 2$, $k = -1$, and $r = 12$. Therefore, the circle's center is located at $(2, -1)$, and the circle's radius is 12.

Part 4 Practice: Circles

1

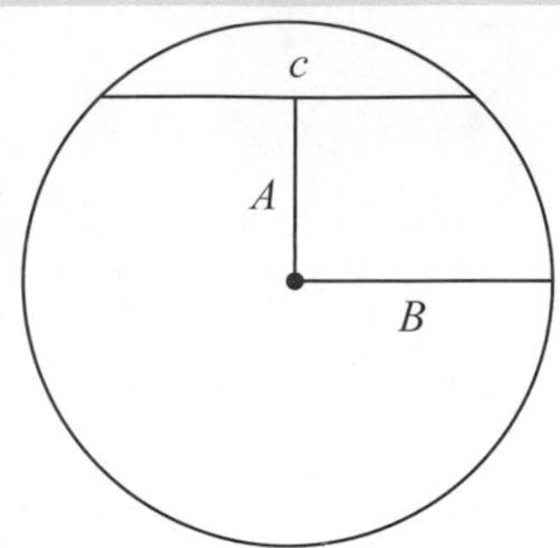

In the figure above, chord c is perpendicular to A and parallel to the radius B. If the length of A is 2 and B is 3, which of the following is the length of chord c?

A) $\sqrt{5}$

B) $2\sqrt{5}$

C) $\sqrt{13}$

D) $2\sqrt{13}$

2

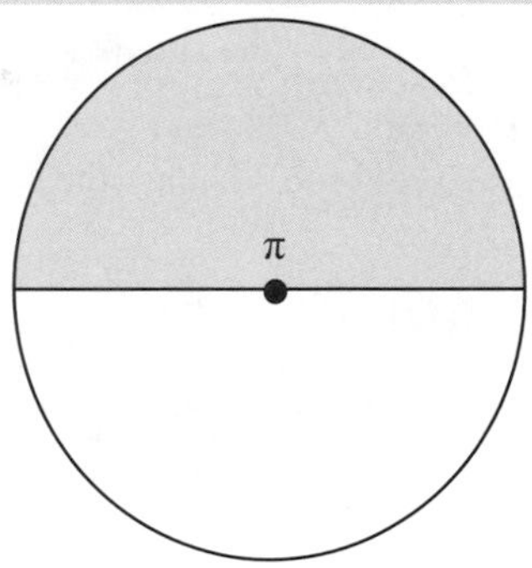

In the figure above the circle's diameter is 20. If the angle of the shaded area is π radians, which of the following is the length of the corresponding arc?

A) π

B) 10

C) 10π

D) 30

3

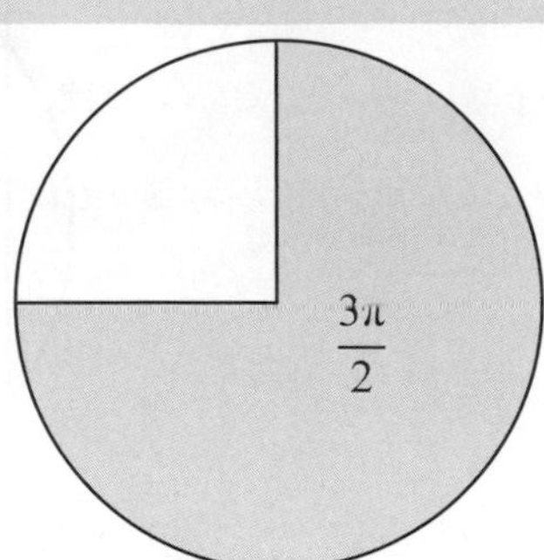

In the circle above, the radius is 4 and the angle of the shaded area is $\frac{3\pi}{2}$ radians. Which of the following is the length of the corresponding arc?

A) 6π

B) 16π

C) 25π

D) 32π

4

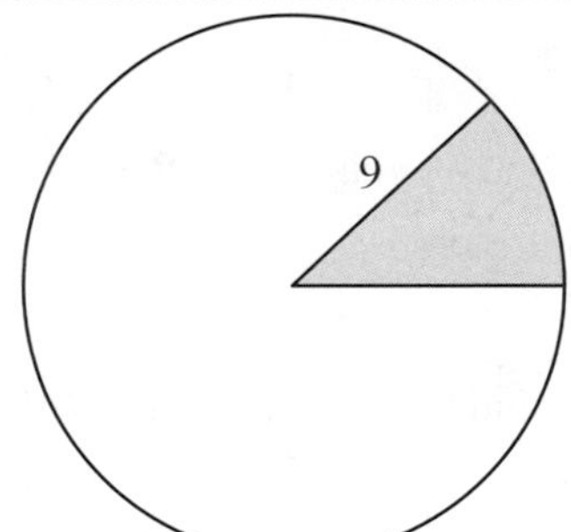

Susan orders a pizza pie that is divided into 8 equally sized slices. If she takes one slice out of the pie as shown above, which of the following is the arc length of the slice?

A) 2π

B) 2.25π

C) 2.5π

D) 4π

Questions 5 and 6 refer to the following information.

The circle below has a radius of 4. Its shaded sector represents $\frac{1}{16}$ of the total area of the circle.

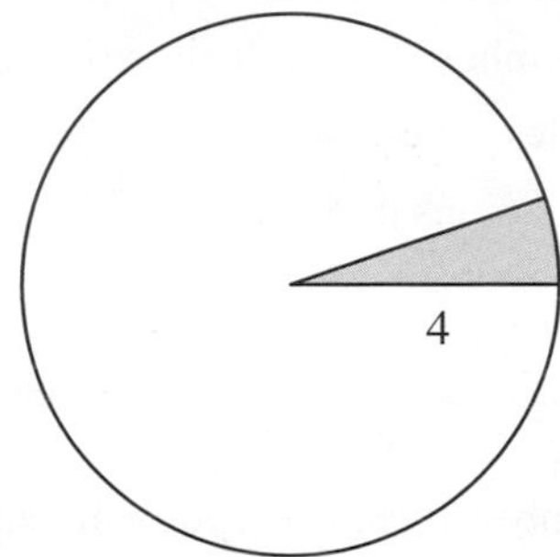

5

According to the figure, which of the following is the value for the area that is twice the shaded sector?

A) π

B) 2π

C) $\frac{3\pi}{2}$

D) 4π

6

Which of the following is the value of the angle, in radians, that corresponds to the shaded sector?

A) $\frac{\pi}{4}$

B) $\frac{3\pi}{8}$

C) $\frac{\pi}{8}$

D) $\frac{\pi}{16}$

7

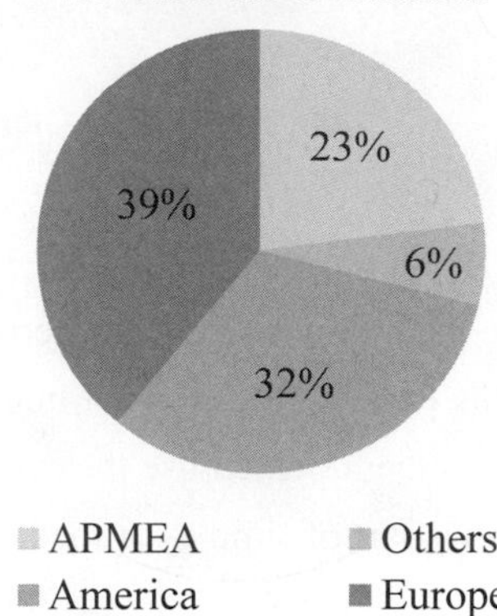

The figure above shows worldwide income distribution for O'Chicken Corporation in 2012. What is the value of the sector angle, in degrees, that corresponds to America?

A) 32

B) 82.8

C) 115.2

D) 140.4

8

If Sector Z of a circle with a diameter of 1 m has an area of 0.5 m^2, what is the value of the sector angle that corresponds to Sector Z to the nearest degree?

9

If a 10 foot long chord is located 12 feet from the center of a circle, what is the value of the circle's radius?

10

$$(x-1)^2+(y-1)^2=9$$

The circle provided by the equation above has radius a, and its center is located at the point (b, c). What is the value of abc?

Complex Numbers

Part 5

So far, we have discussed the properties of real numbers, or any number that can be found on a number line. In this part, we'll see what numbers lie beyond the real numbers. These include imaginary and complex numbers, which use the symbol i and follow special rules. These numbers are often tested in the SAT as a part of simple- or medium-difficulty algebraic expressions or equations.

Imaginary Numbers

Normally, it is impossible to take the square root of a negative number. Even when you square a negative number, you end up with a positive result. Therefore, there isn't a way to work backwards and find a real number that is the square root of a negative number.

However, sometimes it is helpful to "imagine" that we can take the square root of a negative number and use this in our calculations. We can do this by introducing the unit i, which is equal to the square root of -1:

$$i^2 = -1$$

$$i = \sqrt{-1}$$

Because a number like i does not exist in the set of real numbers, we call it an **imaginary number**. In equations and calculations that involve imaginary numbers, we can use i as a placeholder for $\sqrt{-1}$. In questions using imaginary numbers, the SAT Math Test will always provide the equation for i, as shown above.

Simplifying Expressions With *i*

In an expression that involves imaginary numbers, you can simplify the square root of any negative number by using i.

Example

Simplify $\frac{\sqrt{-16}}{2}$ in terms of i.

First, re-write the square root as the product of two square roots:

$$\frac{\sqrt{-16}}{2} = \frac{\sqrt{-1} \times \sqrt{16}}{2}$$

Then, plug in i for $\sqrt{-1}$ and simplify:

$$\frac{\sqrt{-1} \times \sqrt{16}}{2} = \frac{i \times \sqrt{16}}{2} = \frac{4i}{2} = 2i$$

Your final answer is $2i$.

We know that the square of i is -1, but now let's look at what happens when we raise i to another exponent. For example, what happens when you take the cube of i? You can substitute $\sqrt{-1}$ for i in order to work out the equation:

$$i^3 = (\sqrt{-1})^3$$

$$i^3 = \sqrt{-1} \times \sqrt{-1} \times \sqrt{-1}$$

$$i^3 = -1 \times \sqrt{-1}$$

$$i^3 = -1 \times i$$

$$i^3 = -i$$

The square of i is -1, but the cube of i is $-i$.

Using the same method, values of i raised to other common exponents are summarized below:

$i^0 = 1$	$i^1 = i$	$i^2 = -1$	$i^3 = -i$	$i^4 = 1$

You will notice that the values of i^0 and i^4 are the same. This is also true for the values of i^1 and i^5. In fact, there are only four values possible for i raised to an exponent: 1, i, -1, and $-i$; these values always repeat in a pattern of four. Using this table, you can determine the value of i raised to any other power.

Let's see how to figure out the value of i^5.

You know that $i^4 = 1$ and $i^5 = i^4 \times i$. Plugging in these values, you can write:

$$i^5 = 1 \times i = i$$

Therefore, i^5 is the same thing as i, or $\sqrt{-1}$.

Complex Numbers

A **complex number** is the sum of a real number and an imaginary number. Complex numbers are normally written in the form $a + bi$, where a is the real component and bi is the imaginary component. For example, $4 + 2i$ is a complex number with a real component, 4, and an imaginary component, $2i$.

On the SAT, you'll need to know how to simplify expressions with complex numbers by adding, subtracting, and multiplying. These operations are simple if you treat the imaginary variable i like any other variable in an algebraic expression.

To add or subtract expressions with complex numbers, first group together like terms—that is, group real numbers together and group imaginary numbers together. Then, add or subtract the real numbers, and add or subtract the imaginary numbers.

Example

$$(3 + 5i) + (2 + 3i)$$

First, group together the real numbers and the imaginary numbers:

$$3 + 5i + 2 + 3i = (3 + 2) + (5i + 3i)$$

Then, add the like terms:

$$(3 + 2) + (5i + 3i) = 5 + 8i$$

The final answer is $5 + 8i$.

Multiplying complex numbers is similar to multiplying binomials: use the FOIL method to multiply all of the components in the complex numbers. The only difference is that you'll need to simplify i raised to any power greater than 1. See Section 5 for a review of the FOIL method.

Example

$$(3 - 4i)(6 + 2i)$$

Use the FOIL method to multiply out the two binomials:

$$(3 - 4i)(6 + 2i) = 18 + 6i - 24i - 8i^2$$

Then, combine like terms:

$$18 + 6i - 24i - 8i^2 = -8i^2 - 18i + 18$$

Notice that you have i^2 in the answer. Because $i^2 = -1$, you can plug -1 into the answer in place of i^2:

$$-8(-1) - 18i + 18 = 8 - 18i + 18$$

Finally, combine like terms again:

$$26 - 18i$$

The final simplified answer is $26 - 18i$.

Part 5 Practice: Complex Numbers

1

For $i = \sqrt{-1}$, which of the following expresses $\sqrt{-64}$ in terms of i?

A) $-\sqrt{8}i$

B) $\sqrt{-8}i$

C) $8i$

D) $64i$

2

Which of the following expressions is NOT equal to $8\sqrt{-49}$? (Note: $i = \sqrt{-1}$)

A) $\sqrt{3136}i$

B) $7\sqrt{64}i$

C) $\sqrt{56}i$

D) $56i$

3

Which of the following is equal to $(8 + 2i) + (2 + 8i)$? (Note: $i = \sqrt{-1}$)

A) 0

B) $10 + 10i$

C) $10 + 16i$

D) -6

4

If $\frac{5\sqrt{-4}}{2i} = 3w$, what is the value of w? (Note: $i = \sqrt{-1}$)

A) $\frac{3}{5}$

B) $\frac{5}{3}$

C) $\frac{10}{3}$

D) 5

Questions 5 and 6 use the following information.

Measure of impedance in an electrical circuit is commonly calculated in electrical engineering. It is represented, in a simple form, by the equation $Z = C + jL$, where Z is the circuit's impedance, C and L are constants, and j is a function of i. (Note: $i = \sqrt{-1}$)

5

If C is 2, $j = i^3$, and L is 5, which of the following is equal to the circuit's impedance?

A) 7

B) $5i + 2$

C) -7

D) $-5i + 2$

6

If C is 0, $j = i^{10}$, and L is 1, which of the following is NOT equal to the circuit's impedance?

A) i

B) i^2

C) i^6

D) i^{14}

7

If $(1 + i) \times (7 + i) = 2r$ and $i = \sqrt{-1}$, what is the value of r?

A) $4i + 3$

B) $8i + 6$

C) $9i$

D) 7

8

If $(49 - 2i) - (48 - i) = \dfrac{x - 4i}{4}$, what is the value of x? (Note: $i = \sqrt{-1}$)

9

If $(1 + i) \times (1 - i) = 2x$, what is the value of x? (Note: $i = \sqrt{-1}$)

10

If $i = \sqrt{-1}$, what is the value of $(3 + 3i) \times (4 - 4i)$?

Practice Tests

Chapter 6

Practice Test 1

YOUR NAME (PRINT): ____
LAST FIRST MI

SAT

Directions

- Work on just one section at a time.
- If you complete a section before the end of your allotted time, use the extra minutes to check your work on that section only. Do NOT use the time to work on another section.

Using Your Test Booklet

- No credit will be given for anything written in the test booklet. You may use the test booklet for scratch paper.
- You are not allowed to continue answering questions in a section after the allotted time has run out. This includes marking answers on your answer sheet that you previously noted in your test booklet.
- You are not allowed to fold pages, take pages out of the test booklet, or take any pages home.

Answering Questions

- Each answer must be marked in the corresponding row on the answer sheet.
- Each bubble must be filled in completely and darkly within the lines.

- Be careful to bubble in the correct part of the answer sheet.
- Extra marks on your answer sheet may be marked as incorrect answers and lower your score.
- Make sure you use a No. 2 pencil.

Scoring

- You will receive one point for each correct answer.
- Incorrect answers will NOT result in points deducted. Even if you are unsure about an answer, you should make a guess.

DO NOT BEGIN THIS TEST
UNTIL YOUR PROCTOR TELLS YOU TO DO SO

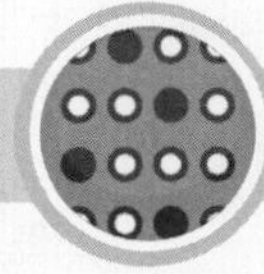

For automatic scoring and scaling, please visit **ivyglobal.com/study**.

Section 1

Reading Test

65 MINUTES, 52 QUESTIONS

Turn to Section 1 of your answer sheet to answer the questions in this section.

DIRECTIONS

Every passage or paired set of passages is accompanied by a number of questions. Read the passage or paired set of passages, then use what is said or implied in what you read and in any given graphics to choose the best answer to each question.

Questions 1-11 are based on the following passage and supplementary material.

This passage is adapted from The Economist, "The U-Bend of Life." © 2014 by The Economist.

Ask people how they feel about getting older, and they will probably reply in the same vein as Maurice Chevalier: "Old age isn't so bad when you consider the alternative." Stiffening joints, weakening muscles, fading eyesight and the clouding of memory, coupled with the modern world's careless contempt for the old, seem a fearful prospect—better than death, perhaps, but not much. Yet mankind is wrong to dread aging. Life is not a long slow decline from sunlit uplands towards the valley of death. It is, rather, a U-bend.

When people start out on adult life, they are, on average, pretty cheerful. Things go downhill from youth to middle age until they reach a nadir commonly known as the mid-life crisis. So far, so familiar. The surprising part happens after that. Although as people move towards old age they lose things they treasure—vitality, mental sharpness and looks—they also gain what people spend their lives pursuing: happiness.

This curious finding has emerged from a new branch of economics that seeks a more satisfactory measure than money of human well-being. Conventional economics uses money as a proxy for utility—the dismal way in which the discipline talks about happiness. But some economists, unconvinced that there is a direct relationship between money and well-being, have decided to go to the nub of the matter and measure happiness itself.

Ask a bunch of 30-year-olds and another of 70-year-olds (as Peter Ubel, of the Sanford School of Public Policy at Duke University, did with two colleagues, Heather Lacey and Dylan Smith, in 2006) which group they think is likely to be happier, and both lots point to the 30-year-olds. Ask them to rate their own well-being, and the 70-year-olds are the happier bunch. The academics quoted lyrics written by Pete Townshend of The Who when he was 20: "Things they do look awful cold / Hope I die before I get old". They pointed out that Mr. Townshend, having passed his 60th birthday, was writing a blog that glowed with good humor.

Mr. Townshend may have thought of himself as a youthful radical, but this view is ancient and conventional. The "seven ages of man"—the dominant image of the life-course in the 16th and 17th centuries—was almost invariably conceived as a rise in stature and contentedness to middle age, followed by a sharp decline towards the grave. Inverting the rise and fall is a recent idea. "A few of us noticed the U-bend in the early 1990s," says Andrew Oswald, professor of economics at Warwick

CONTINUE

Business School. "We ran a conference about it, but nobody came."

Since then, interest in the U-bend has been growing. Its effect on happiness is significant. It appears all over the world. David Blanchflower, professor of economics at Dartmouth College, and Mr. Oswald looked at the figures for 72 countries. The nadir varies among countries—Ukrainians, at the top of the range, are at their most miserable at 62, and Swiss, at the bottom, at 35—but in the great majority of countries people are at their unhappiest in their 40s and early 50s. The global average is 46.

Approximate Age of Minimum Happiness Across Countries

Country Name	Age of Minimum Happiness
All countries	46
Australia	40
Brazil	37
Canada	54
France	62
Mexico	41
Puerto Rico	36
Ukraine	62
United States	40

1

The primary purpose of the passage is to

A) interpret a phenomenon observed by economists.

B) discuss the findings of a group of economists.

C) explore competing measures of happiness.

D) relate an interesting anecdote about happiness and aging.

2

The passage most strongly implies that

A) conventional economic measures of happiness are unsatisfactory.

B) the "seven ages of man" can still describe the lives of some seniors.

C) conventional economists have not previously been interested in happiness.

D) the trend of happiness increasing in old age means people will no longer fear aging.

3

Which choice provides the best evidence for the answer to the previous question?

A) Lines 9-11 ("Life is … death")

B) Lines 17-20 ("Although as … happiness")

C) Lines 24-26 ("Conventional economics … happiness")

D) Lines 30-37 ("Ask … happier bunch")

CONTINUE

4

The passage suggests that the conventional view of aging as a "slow decline" (line 10) from joyful youth to unhappy old age is

A) the opposite of most adults' real experience.

B) basically correct about life through middle age, but not old age.

C) usually correct but with a few notable exceptions.

D) accurate with respect to the elderly but not the young.

5

As used in line 2, "vein" most nearly means

A) style.

B) humor.

C) strain.

D) streak.

6

The Duke University academics most likely quoted Pete Townshend in their study (lines 39-40) in order to

A) support the idea that most 70-year-olds underestimate their happiness.

B) exemplify a typical contrast between expectations and experiences of aging.

C) suggest that most seniors are happier than they expected to be as they aged.

D) explain why a conventional view has often been perceived as radical.

7

Which choice provides the best evidence for the answer to the previous question?

A) Lines 1-4 ("Ask … the alternative")

B) Lines 26-29 ("But some … itself")

C) Lines 40-42 ("They … good humor")

D) Lines 50-53 ("Inverting the … School")

8

The author refers to the "seven ages of man" (line 45) primarily in order to

A) highlight how the definition of happiness has changed over time.

B) suggest that some attitudes about aging have a basis in history.

C) contrast an earlier view of happiness and aging with the one introduced in the passage.

D) emphasize that numerous models exist for predicting happiness during various life stages.

9

As used in line 60, "nadir" most nearly means

A) abyss.

B) low point.

C) zero.

D) bedrock.

CONTINUE

10

The passage and table most strongly support which of the following conclusions?

A) Most Ukrainians are happier at 70 than at 62.

B) Most Ukrainians are at their happiest in their 70s.

C) Few Ukrainians are as happy as the Swiss.

D) Ukrainian 35-year-olds are happier than Swiss 35-year-olds.

11

It can reasonably be inferred from the passage and table that

A) the countries with the happiest citizens also tend to have the earliest ages of minimum happiness.

B) Brazilians tend to be happiest around the age of 36.6, while Mexicans are not at their happiest until 41.4.

C) Australians and Americans experience roughly the same levels of unhappiness during adulthood.

D) after the age of 54, Canadians tend to become happier, while the French tend to become less happy.

Questions 12-21 are based on the following passage.

This passage is adapted from "Address Before the General Assembly of the United Nations on Peaceful Uses of Atomic Energy," a speech given by President Dwight D. Eisenhower to the General Assembly of the United Nations in 1953.

I feel impelled to speak today in a language that in a sense is new—one which I, who have spent so much of my life in the military profession, would have preferred never to use. That new language is the language of atomic warfare.

The atomic age has moved forward at such a pace that every citizen of the world should have some comprehension, at least in comparative terms, of the extent of this development of the utmost significance to every one of us. Clearly, if the peoples of the world are to conduct an intelligent search for peace, they must be armed with the significant facts of today's existence. Atomic bombs today are more than 25 times as powerful as the weapons with which the atomic age dawned, while hydrogen weapons are in the ranges of millions of tons of TNT equivalent. Today, the United States' stockpile of atomic weapons, which, of course, increases daily, exceeds by many times the explosive equivalent of the total of all bombs and all shells that came from every plane and every gun in every theatre of war in all of the years of World War II.

But the dread secret, and the fearful engines of atomic might, are not ours alone. In the first place, the secret is possessed by our friends and allies, Great Britain and Canada, whose scientific genius made a tremendous contribution to our original discoveries, and the designs of atomic bombs. The secret is also known by the Soviet Union. The Soviet Union has informed us that, over recent years, it has devoted extensive resources to atomic weapons. During this period, the Soviet Union has exploded a series of atomic devices, including at least one involving thermo-nuclear reactions.

If at one time the United States possessed what might have been called a monopoly of atomic

CONTINUE

power, that monopoly ceased to exist several years ago. Therefore, although our earlier start has permitted us to accumulate what is today a great quantitative advantage, the atomic realities of today comprehend two facts of even greater significance.

First, the knowledge now possessed by several nations will eventually be shared by others—possibly all others. Second, even a vast superiority in numbers of weapons, and a consequent capability of devastating retaliation, is no preventive, of itself, against the fearful material damage and toll of human lives that would be inflicted by surprise aggression.

The free world, at least dimly aware of these facts, has naturally embarked on a large program of warning and defense systems. That program will be accelerated and expanded. But let no one think that the expenditure of vast sums for weapons and systems of defense can guarantee absolute safety for the cities and citizens of any nation. The awful arithmetic of the atomic bomb does not permit of any such easy solution. Even against the most powerful defense, an aggressor in possession of the effective minimum number of atomic bombs for a surprise attack could probably place a sufficient number of his bombs on the chosen targets to cause hideous damage.

Surely no sane member of the human race could discover victory in such desolation. Could anyone wish his name to be coupled by history with such human degradation and destruction? Occasional pages of history do record the faces of the "Great Destroyers" but the whole book of history reveals mankind's never-ending quest for peace. It is with the book of history, and not with isolated pages, that the United States will ever wish to be identified. My country wants to be constructive, not destructive. It wants agreements, not wars, among nations. It wants itself to live in freedom, and in the confidence that the people of every other nation enjoy equally the right of choosing their own way of life.

So my country's purpose is to help us move out of the dark chamber of horrors into the light, to find a way by which the minds of men, the hopes of men, the souls of men everywhere, can move forward toward peace and happiness and well being.

12

The passage primarily focuses on which of the following characteristics of atomic warfare?

A) The serious threat it poses to the future of humanity

B) Its application to new situations in warfare

C) How recently it became available to Western nations

D) Its advantages over other types of warfare

13

Which choice provides the best evidence for the answer to the previous question?

A) Lines 13-17 ("Atomic … TNT equivalent")

B) Lines 36-39 ("If at … years ago")

C) Lines 59-64 ("Even against … hideous damage")

D) Lines 74-78 ("It wants … of life")

14

Eisenhower's tone is best described as

A) apologetic.

B) exhilarated.

C) concerned.

D) cynical.

CONTINUE

15

The passage most strongly suggests that Eisenhower would wish to pursue which of the following?

A) Expansion of the United States' nuclear weapons production

B) Development of a peaceful nuclear energy program for the United States and other countries

C) Agreements between the United States and other countries to limit nuclear weapons usage

D) The sharing of United States nuclear weapons expertise with other countries

16

Which choice provides the best evidence for the answer to the previous question?

A) Lines 43-45 ("First … all others")

B) Lines 51-53 ("The … defense systems")

C) Lines 54-57 ("But let … nation")

D) Lines 74-75 ("It wants … among nations")

17

The main rhetorical effect of lines 17-23 is to

A) emphasize the unprecedented power of atomic weapons.

B) explain how numerous the weapons of World War II were.

C) provide background information on other types of weaponry.

D) suggest that atomic weapons function in similar ways to older types of arms.

18

As used in line 48, "material" most nearly means

A) physical.

B) essential.

C) relevant.

D) worldly.

19

As used in line 67, "coupled" most nearly means

A) compounded.

B) fused.

C) married.

D) associated.

20

Eisenhower refers to "the book of history" (line 72) in order to suggest that the United States

A) wishes to be associated with seeking peace rather than destruction.

B) is able to shape history through the choices it makes.

C) has sought compromises with other nations to avoid atomic warfare.

D) identifies strongly with the history of warfare.

CONTINUE

21

The final paragraph primarily serves to

A) contradict Eisenhower's earlier statements about peace.

B) offer a concrete strategy for avoiding warfare.

C) suggest how Eisenhower wishes the United States to proceed.

D) encourage other countries to cooperate with the United States.

Questions 22-32 are based on the following passage and supplementary material.

This passage is adapted from Carl Zimmer, "This Is Your Brain on Writing." © 2014 by The New York Times Company.

A novelist scrawling away in a notebook in seclusion may not seem to have much in common with an NBA player doing a reverse layup on a basketball court before a screaming crowd. But if you could peer inside their heads, you might see some striking similarities in how their brains were churning.

That's one of the implications of new research on the neuroscience of creative writing. For the first time, neuroscientists have used fMRI scanners to track the brain activity of both experienced and novice writers as they sat down—or, in this case, lay down—to turn out a piece of fiction. The researchers, led by Martin Lotze of the University of Greifswald in Germany, observed a broad network of regions in the brain working together as people produced their stories. But there were notable differences between the two groups of subjects. The inner workings of the professionally trained writers in the bunch, the scientists argue, showed some similarities to people who are skilled at other complex actions, like music or sports.

To begin, Dr. Lotze asked 28 volunteers to simply copy some text, giving him a baseline reading of their brain activity during writing. Next, he showed his volunteers a few lines from a short story and asked them to continue it in their own words. The volunteers could brainstorm for a minute, and then write creatively for a little over two minutes. Some regions of the brain became active only during the creative process, but not while copying, the researchers found. During the brainstorming sessions, some vision-processing regions of volunteers became active. It's possible that they were, in effect, seeing the scenes they wanted to write.

Other regions became active when the volunteers started jotting down their stories. Dr. Lotze suspects

CONTINUE

that one of them, the hippocampus, was retrieving factual information that the volunteers could use. One region near the front of the brain, known to be crucial for holding several pieces of information in mind at once, became active as well. Juggling several characters and plot lines may put special demands on it.

But Dr. Lotze also recognized a big limit of the study: his subjects had no previous experience in creative writing. Would the brains of full-time writers respond differently? To find out, he and his colleagues went to another German university, the University of Hildesheim, which runs a highly competitive creative writing program. The scientists recruited 20 writers there (their average age was 25). Dr. Lotze and his colleagues had them take the same tests and then compared their performance with the novices'.

As the scientists report in a new study in the journal *NeuroImage*, the brains of expert writers appeared to work differently, even before they set pen to paper. During brainstorming, the novice writers activated their visual centers. By contrast, the brains of expert writers showed more activity in regions involved in speech. "I think both groups are using different strategies," Dr. Lotze said. It's possible that the novices are watching their stories like a film inside their heads, while the writers are narrating them with an inner voice.

When the two groups started to write, another set of differences emerged. Deep inside the brains of expert writers, a region called the caudate nucleus became active. In the novices, the caudate nucleus was quiet. The caudate nucleus is a familiar part of the brain for scientists like Dr. Lotze who study expertise. It plays an essential role in the skill that comes with practice, including activities like board games.

When we first start learning a skill—be it playing a piano or playing basketball—we use a lot of conscious effort. With practice, those actions become more automatic. The caudate nucleus and nearby regions start to coordinate the brain's activity as this shift happens. "I was really happy to see this," said Ronald T. Kellogg, a psychologist who studies writing at Saint Louis University. "You don't want to see this as an analog to what James Joyce was doing in Dublin. But to see that they were able to get clean results with this, I think that's a major step right there." But Steven Pinker, a Harvard psychologist, was skeptical that the experiments could provide a clear picture of creativity. "It's a messy comparison," he said.

Brain Activity in Expert Writers

Area*	Level of Activity
Brainstorming	
Inf. occipital gyrus le	7.51
Inf. occipital gyrus ri	7.47
Inf. frontal gyrus le	6.20
Inf. frontal gyrus ri	5.47
Creative writing	
Inf. occipital le	9.41
Inf. occipital ri	9.15
Inf. frontal gyrus le	9.07
Inf. frontal gyrus ri	6.95
Thalamus le	5.40

*Anatomical description; ri: right; le: left; inf.: inferior.

CONTINUE

22

The stance the author takes in the passage is best described as that of

A) an interested observer.

B) an excited colleague.

C) a skeptical rival scientist.

D) a concerned creative writer.

23

The passage most strongly suggests that

A) writers draw on their own knowledge during creative writing.

B) most people may not realize that creative writing is a learnable skill.

C) it is important for all neuroscience studies to include both experts and novices.

D) all expert writers employ the same approach to writing.

24

Which choice provides the best evidence for the answer to the previous question?

A) Lines 38-40 ("Dr. Lotze … usc")

B) Lines 64-67 ("It's possible … voice")

C) Lines 69-71 ("Deep inside … active")

D) Lines 80-82 ("The caudate … happens")

25

It can reasonably be inferred from the passage that

A) the hippocampus plays a role in memory.

B) the caudate nucleus grows larger as people learn more skills.

C) experts in any field are less likely to rely on their visual centers when writing creatively.

D) most skills activate only a single area of the brain.

26

As used in line 7, "churning" most nearly means

A) producing.

B) working.

C) proceeding.

D) spinning.

27

The first paragraph primarily serves to

A) make a surprising comparison that the rest of the passage will explain.

B) lay out a hypothesis that the passage will prove to be false.

C) describe a question that has long puzzled researchers.

D) prove that a surprising comparison is indeed true.

CONTINUE

28

Based on the passage, which choice best describes the relationship between novice and expert writers?

A) Novices' brains are less active than experts' brains during writing.

B) Novices' brains are more active than experts' brains during writing.

C) Novices' behavior is less automatic than experts' behavior during writing.

D) Novices' behavior is less intense than experts' behavior during writing.

29

Which choice provides the best evidence for the answer to the previous question?

A) Lines 4-7 ("But if … churning")

B) Lines 13-17 ("The researchers … their stories")

C) Lines 30-32 ("Some … researchers found")

D) Lines 77-80 ("When we … effort")

30

As used in line 81, "coordinate" most nearly means

A) match.

B) organize.

C) correlate.

D) negotiate.

31

The passage most strongly suggests that Steven Pinker would agree with which of the following statements?

A) It is impossible for neuroscientists to truly study creativity.

B) Dr. Lotze's results may not support the broad conclusions discussed in the passage.

C) The caudate nucleus does not become more active in the brains of expert writers.

D) Writing is not a skill that can be easily improved.

32

Which of the following statements is supported by the graphic at the end of the passage?

A) Non-expert writers relied mainly on their occipital and frontal lobes when brainstorming.

B) Non-expert writers saw no significant activation in brain regions that were activated in expert writers.

C) Expert writers used more neural energy in creative writing than in brainstorming.

D) Expert writers showed activity in areas including the left inferior frontal gyrus and left thalamus during creative writing.

CONTINUE

Questions 33-42 are based on the following passage.

This passage is adapted from Jerome K. Jerome, *Three Men in a Boat*, originally published in 1889.

It is a most extraordinary thing, but I never read a patent medicine advertisement without being impelled to the conclusion that I am suffering from the particular disease therein dealt with in its most virulent form. The diagnosis seems in every case to correspond exactly with all the sensations that I have ever felt.

I remember going to the British Museum one day to read up on the treatment for some slight ailment of which I had a touch—hay fever, I fancy it was. I got down the book, and read all I came to read; and then, in an unthinking moment, I idly turned the leaves, and began to indolently study diseases, generally. I forget which was the first distemper I plunged into—some fearful, devastating scourge, I know—and, before I had glanced half down the list of "premonitory symptoms," it was borne in upon me that I had fairly got it.

I sat for awhile, frozen with horror; and then, in the listlessness of despair, I again turned over the pages. I came to typhoid fever—read the symptoms—discovered that I had typhoid fever, must have had it for months without knowing it—wondered what else I had got; turned up St. Vitus's Dance—found, as I expected, that I had that too,—began to get interested in my case, and determined to sift it to the bottom, and so started alphabetically—read up ague, and learnt that I was sickening for it, and that the acute stage would commence in about another fortnight. Bright's disease, I was relieved to find, I had only in a modified form, and, so far as that was concerned, I might live for years. Cholera I had, with severe complications; and diphtheria I seemed to have been born with. I plodded conscientiously through the twenty-six letters, and the only malady I could conclude I had not got was housemaid's knee.

I felt rather hurt about this at first; it seemed somehow to be a sort of slight. Why hadn't I got housemaid's knee? Why this invidious reservation? After a while, however, less grasping feelings prevailed. I reflected that I had every other known malady in the pharmacology, and I grew less selfish, and determined to do without housemaid's knee. Gout, in its most malignant stage, it would appear, had seized me without my being aware of it; and zymosis I had evidently been suffering with from boyhood. There were no more diseases after zymosis, so I concluded there was nothing else the matter with me.

I sat and pondered. I thought what an interesting case I must be from a medical point of view, what an acquisition I should be to a class! Students would have no need to "walk the hospitals," if they had me. I was a hospital in myself. All they need do would be to walk round me, and, after that, take their diploma.

Then I wondered how long I had to live. I tried to examine myself. I felt my pulse. I could not at first feel any pulse at all. Then, all of a sudden, it seemed to start off. I pulled out my watch and timed it. I made it a hundred and forty-seven to the minute. I tried to feel my heart. I could not feel my heart. It had stopped beating. I have since been induced to come to the opinion that it must have been there all the time, and must have been beating, but I cannot account for it. I patted myself all over my front, from what I call my waist up to my head, and I went a bit round each side, and a little way up the back. But I could not feel or hear anything. I tried to look at my tongue. I stuck it out as far as ever it would go, and I shut one eye, and tried to examine it with the other. I could only see the tip, and the only thing that I could gain from that was to feel more certain than before that I had scarlet fever.

I had walked into that reading-room a happy, healthy man. I crawled out a decrepit wreck.

CONTINUE

33

Which of the following best describes the passage?

A) An argument about the state of diagnostics in medicine

B) A chilling and cautionary anecdote

C) An entertaining story about false beliefs

D) A description of the symptoms of several common diseases

34

The passage most strongly suggests that the narrator's self-diagnoses of disease are based on

A) his tendency to be swayed by what he reads.

B) changes to his health that he had observed.

C) careful examination by medical professionals.

D) his rigorous study of medicine.

35

Which choice provides the best evidence for the answer to the previous question?

A) Lines 1-5 ("It is ... virulent form")

B) Lines 51-53 ("I thought … a class")

C) Lines 67-69 ("I patted … the back")

D) Lines 73-75 ("I could … fever")

36

The author's approach to retelling this story is best described as

A) reflective.

B) panicked.

C) apologetic.

D) humorous.

37

It can reasonably be inferred from the passage that the narrator

A) somewhat enjoys believing he has many illnesses.

B) is likely to seek medical treatment for his many ailments.

C) has a great respect for the practice of medicine.

D) frequently visits the British Museum.

38

Which choice provides the best evidence for the answer to the previous question?

A) Lines 8-10 ("I remember … it was")

B) Lines 32-34 ("Cholera … born with")

C) Lines 42-44 ("I reflected … housemaid's knee")

D) Lines 71-73 ("I stuck … the other")

39

As used in line 34, "plodded" most nearly means

A) stumbled.

B) blundered.

C) worked.

D) strived.

40

As used in line 39, "slight" most nearly means

A) indignity.

B) criticism.

C) outrage.

D) shame.

CONTINUE

41

The statement "I was a hospital in myself" (line 55) suggests that the narrator

A) suffered from nearly as many diseases as can be found in an entire hospital.

B) had knowledge of so many illnesses that he could run a hospital.

C) was cured of many illnesses, just like patients in a hospital.

D) was typical of patients found in hospitals of the time.

42

The last two lines (76-77) primarily serve to

A) summarize the transformation that the narrator recounts during the passage.

B) suggest that the narrator was permanently changed by his visit to the British Museum.

C) emphasize the severity of the author's many illnesses.

D) demonstrate that the narrator's experience in the British Museum was unusual for him.

Questions 43-52 are based on the following passages.

Passage 1 is adapted from Erik Olsen, "Protected Reef Offers Model for Conservation." © 2010 by The New York Times Company. Passage 2 is adapted from The New York Times Editorial Board, "To Save Fish and Birds." © 2014 by The New York Times Company.

Passage 1

Glover's Reef, about 28 miles from the coast of Belize, is one of the only true atolls in the Atlantic Ocean. It is also the site of Belize's largest "no-take" marine reserve, a 17,500-acre zone where all types of fishing are prohibited. The no-take zone makes up about 20 percent of the wider 87,000-acre Marine Protected Area here. Within 75 percent of the reserve, some types of fishing are allowed, although there are restrictions on the type of gear that can be used.

According to scientists here, the marine reserve at Glover's Reef offers a test case for the viability of similar reserves around the world. They are now hoping to apply some of the conservation strategies here to make other places succeed. "I think Glover's Reef is a model of hope," says Ellen K. Pikitch, a marine biologist at the Stony Brook University School of Marine and Atmospheric Sciences. Dr. Pikitch runs the Institute for Ocean Conservation Science, an organization seeking wider protection for sharks worldwide. She said that the effort at Glover's "shows that marine reserves, even small marine reserves, can work. I think it's very transportable, this concept."

Dr. Pikitch, a self-professed "shark fanatic," has other reasons to be hopeful. She leads the largest shark population study in the Caribbean here at Glover's Reef, now in its 10th year. Shark populations here have remained stable, while others around the world are in severe decline.

The sharks are an integral part of a healthy reef. Along with other top predators they help keep barracuda populations in check, which is important because barracuda consume algae grazers like

CONTINUE

parrotfish that prevent runaway algae growth from choking the corals.

There are still significant challenges. Enforcement remains a problem. The Wildlife Conservation Society shares its home on Middle Caye with an outpost of the Belize Fisheries Department. The department employs four rangers here whose job is to patrol the reef and catch fishermen who violate the fishing ban or who poach undersized conch and spiny lobster outside the no-take zone.

Dr. Pikitch acknowledges that the problems facing reefs here are significant, but she remains optimistic that new information, including data from her shark study, will increase awareness and prompt action to protect reefs. "We are losing coral reefs at an astounding rate," she said. "It's like death by a thousand cuts. So when you have a success like this in a coral ecosystem you say, 'Wow this is great.'"

Passage 2

One of the few bright spots in the struggle to protect the world's fragile oceans has been the rapidly increasing number of "marine protected areas," places where fishing is limited or banned and where, presumably, depleted species can recover by simply being left to themselves. The benefits of hands-off environmental protection may seem self-evident. But creating a preserve and rebuilding a healthy ecosystem are not necessarily the same thing. A recent study published in *Nature* found that, more often than not, marine protected areas don't work as well as they could.

Researchers with the University of Tasmania studied 87 marine protected areas in 40 countries worldwide, and found that 59 percent of the areas were no better off than areas where fishing was allowed. The reasons for failure varied, but they boiled down to this: not all marine protected areas are alike. Some allow fishing; others forbid it. Some are managed well; others are managed badly. Some are relatively intact; others have been left barren by generations of overfishing.

The researchers identified five essential characteristics of the most successful marine protected areas: These areas were designated "no take" (allowing no fishing whatsoever), their rules were well enforced, they were more than 10 years old, they were bigger than 100 square kilometers, and they were isolated by deep water or sand. Compared with regular fished areas, the areas that had four or five of those attributes had a far richer variety of species, five times the biomass of large fish and 14 times the biomass of sharks, which are indicators of ecological health.

Most underachieving marine sanctuaries had only one or two of these magic factors, and thus "were not ecologically distinguishable from fished sites." The four sanctuaries lucky enough to have all five characteristics were isolated areas in the oceans off Costa Rica, Colombia, New Zealand, and Australia. The "coral triangle" of Southeast Asia also got high marks, but it did not have as great an array of large species as its more isolated counterparts.

43

As used in line 24, "transportable" most nearly means

A) addressable.

B) transmittable.

C) easily moved.

D) transferable.

CONTINUE

44

Which of the following situations is most analogous to the role of sharks presented in lines 31-36?

A) Bears contribute to healthy ecosystems by consuming unwanted human trash, which benefits other species.

B) Bears contribute to healthy ecosystems only when their populations are kept low so they do not excessively hunt other animals.

C) Bears contribute to healthy ecosystems by keeping salmon populations under control, which ensures that smaller fish can survive.

D) Bears damage healthy ecosystems by over-fishing salmon populations, which prevents salmon from controlling smaller fish populations.

45

Information from Passage 2 most strongly suggests that designating a reef as a marine protected area

A) is the only way to safeguard the variety of fish species inhabiting the reef.

B) has no effect unless the marine protected area covers more than 100 square kilometers.

C) is less effective than other methods of protecting marine ecosystems.

D) can be an effective method of protecting fish populations if certain standards are met.

46

Which choice provides the best evidence for the correct answer to the previous question?

A) Lines 54-59 ("One of … to themselves")

B) Lines 70-72 ("The reasons … are alike")

C) Lines 83-87 ("Compared with … health")

D) Lines 91-93 ("The four … Australia")

47

The author of Passage 2 would most likely agree with which of the following?

A) Marine protected areas are a poor approach to marine conservation and not worth pursuing.

B) Unsuccessful marine protected areas are often undistinguishable from areas that permit fishing.

C) Even when they meet rigorous standards, marine protected areas are not the best method for protecting marine species.

D) Ocean health cannot be improved by a hands-off approach, so marine protected areas are ineffective.

48

Which choice provides the best evidence for the answer to the previous question?

A) Lines 63-65 ("A recent … could")

B) Lines 66-70 ("Researchers with … allowed")

C) Lines 78-82 ("These areas … sand")

D) Lines 94-96 ("The … isolated counterparts")

49

As used in line 74, "intact" most nearly means

A) solid.

B) faultless.

C) unspoiled.

D) complete.

CONTINUE

50

Both Passage 1 and Passage 2 include

A) statistical information about fish populations.

B) data on the ecological health of various protected sites.

C) information about marine predator populations.

D) a summary of recently published scientific research.

51

Compared to Passage 2, Passage 1 is

A) narrower in its focus.

B) more persuasive in tone.

C) less adamant about its conclusion.

D) more complex in its reasoning.

52

Passage 1 discusses the difficulty of ensuring which of the essential characteristics of marine protected areas discussed in Passage 2?

A) Having areas designated "no-take"

B) Proper enforcement of the rules

C) Being isolated by deep water

D) Placing restrictions on what fishing gear can be used

STOP

If you complete this section before the end of your allotted time, check your work on this section only. Do NOT use the time to work on another section.

Section 2

Writing and Language Test

35 MINUTES, 44 QUESTIONS

Turn to Section 2 of your answer sheet to answer the questions in this section.

DIRECTIONS

Every passage comes with a set of questions. Some questions will ask you to consider how the writer might revise the passage to improve the expression of ideas. Other questions will ask you to consider correcting potential errors in sentence structure, usage, or punctuation. There may be one or more graphics that you will need to consult as you revise and edit the passage.

Some questions will refer to a portion of the passage that has been underlined. Other questions will refer to a particular spot in a passage or ask that you consider the passage in full.

After you read the passage, select the answers to questions that most effectively improve the passage's writing quality or that adjust the passage to follow the conventions of standard written English. Many questions give you the option to select "NO CHANGE." Select that option in cases where you think the relevant part of the passage should remain as it currently is.

Questions 1-11 are based on the following passage.

Decoding Honey Bee Dance Language

If you look inside a bustling honey bee hive, you may see a single bee dancing wildly among a crowd. On the honey bee "dance floor," other bees gather around to watch and [1] imitate the dancing bee. After a few minutes of matching the movements, the bees leave the hive and all take flight in the same direction.

Scientists have studied the dances of [2] honey bees and the scientists then determined that honey bees readily communicate reliable food sources to each other by dancing. How does this process work? First, honey bees called "scouts" go out to find flowers rich

1

A) NO CHANGE
B) impersonate
C) mock
D) duplicate

2

A) NO CHANGE
B) honey bees; then the scientists determined
C) honey bees; then determined
D) honey bees then determining

CONTINUE

with the bees' main source of energy—nectar. 3 At the end of the scout's long day, it returns to the hive to rest and recover for its next trip. The scout dances in quick and deliberate circuits. Forager bees dance behind the scout, "practicing" the scout's dance. The foragers then leave to seek out the nectar and bring it back to the hive.

[1] Researchers have begun to decode the dances by noting what sort of dances scouts perform under varying circumstances. [2] When a nectar source is closer than fifty meters from the hive, scouts perform a "round dance." [3] When the food is farther than seventy-five meters from the hive, scouts perform a "waggle dance." [4] The waggle dance consists of elaborate "figure eight" circuits. [5] The number of dance circuits per fifteen seconds signals how far the nectar source is 4 from the hive, and the angle of the dance tells the forager bees the direction they should fly. [6] For instance, if the nectar source is in the

3

Which choice most effectively sets up the information that follows?

A) NO CHANGE

B) Bees share the nectar by passing it from one worker to another, and eventually storing it as honey.

C) If the flowers are in bloom, the scout should find plenty of nectar.

D) When a scout finds a promising location of nectar, it returns to the hive and "performs" for the other bees.

4

A) NO CHANGE

B) from the hive and the angle of the dance

C) from the hive: and the angle of the dance

D) from the hive; and the angle of the dance

CONTINUE

opposite direction from the sun, the bee **5** <u>will perform at least 180 circuits</u>. [7] The circuits signal important information about the location of food to the rest of the hive. **6**

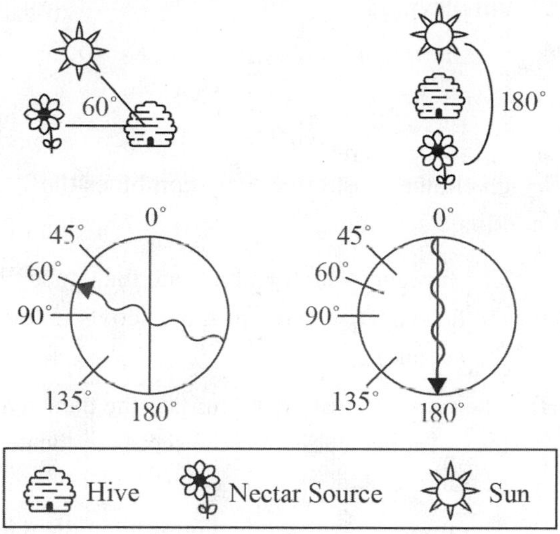

The figure above illustrates the waggle dances performed based on the location of the nectar source (flowers) in relation to the hive and the sun.

5

Which choice offers an accurate interpretation of the data in the graph?

A) NO CHANGE
B) will perform the dance at a 180° angle.
C) will perform the dance at a 60° angle.
D) will perform no circuits.

6

To make this paragraph most logical, sentence 7 should be placed

A) where it is now.
B) before sentence 2.
C) before sentence 4.
D) before sentence 5.

CONTINUE

Both the forager bees and the scout **7** plays important roles in the process of collecting nectar. Scouts must find the best locations for nectar. Scouts must also be cautious of sites with damaged flowers or deceased bees, as these may be signs of predators. **8** The foragers watch and imitate the dance. Then the foragers use the cues from the scouts to locate the nectar site.

7

A) NO CHANGE

B) play

C) is playing

D) am playing

8

Which choice most effectively combines the underlined sentences?

A) The foragers watch and imitate the dance, then the foragers use cues from the scouts to locate the nectar site.

B) The foragers watch and imitate the dance, and they also use cues from the scouts to locate the nectar site.

C) The foragers both watch and imitate the dance of the scouts, and then they use cues to locate the nectar site.

D) After watching and imitating the dance, the foragers use the cues from the scouts to locate the nectar site.

CONTINUE

9 Because bees have small brains relative to humans, they can convey complex and vital information to each other through 10 they're dances. Scientists suggest that the bees "understand" the dance because it elicits a uniform response from the viewers; most forager bees fly to the location encoded in the dance. In this way, honey bees use these dances as 11 tools to both navigate and for communication.

9

A) NO CHANGE
B) Although bees have small brains
C) Without their small brains
D) Insofar as bees have small brains

10

A) NO CHANGE
B) their dances
C) they're: dances
D) their: dances

11

A) NO CHANGE
B) tools for both navigation and to communicate
C) tools for both navigation and communication
D) tools for navigation and for communicating

CONTINUE

Questions 12-22 are based on the following passage.

Maya Angelou: A Voice for Caged Birds

At President Bill Clinton's inauguration, Maya Angelou stands at the podium to recite a poem just as she did when she was a young girl in church. As a child, [12] too nervous to complete her reading in front of her congregation. Now on stage in front of the world, [13] however, Angelou does not resemble that frightened girl at all. She reads "On the Pulse of Morning," a poem she composed that proposes inclusion, change, and progress as America's goals. It is easy to see how her life and journey [14] have not only influenced her work but also embodied the change and progress for which she calls. Passion and courage are evident in her performance, not fear or anxiety. She speaks with a strong voice—a voice that has long touched generations of listeners.

12

A) NO CHANGE

B) she was too nervous. Too nervous to complete her reading

C) she was too nervous, she could not complete her reading

D) she was too nervous to complete her reading

13

A) NO CHANGE

B) for instance

C) therefore

D) moreover

14

A) NO CHANGE

B) have influenced not only her work but also embodied the change

C) have not influenced only her work but embodied also the change

D) not only have influenced her work but also embodied the change

CONTINUE

Angelou faced a difficult childhood. She and her brother, Bailey, were raised for a period of time with their grandmother **15** in Arkansas. It was here that Angelou experienced the devastating effects of racism firsthand. **16** Angelou also struggled with her own insecurities; in her autobiographical work, *I Know Why the Caged Bird Sings*, she notes that her awkward looks brought on ridicule, and she felt she did not fit in with her peers.

15

Which choice most effectively combines the sentences at the underlined portion?

A) in Arkansas, and she experienced

B) and Angelou experienced, in Arkansas,

C) in Arkansas, where Angelou experienced

D) in Arkansas, but experienced

16

At this point, the writer is considering adding the following sentence.

> For example, the white dentist in the town refused to treat Angelou because of her skin color.

Should the writer make this addition here?

A) Yes, because it supports the claim that Angelou experienced the effects of racism with a specific example.

B) Yes, because it explains why Angelou decided to live with her grandmother in Arkansas.

C) No, because the dentist is not a central figure in Angelou's story, and detracts from the focus of the paragraph.

D) No, because the paragraph already states that Angelou experienced the effects of racism.

CONTINUE

17 Angelou first tried her hand at singing and dancing, touring Europe and releasing a musical album. During this time, she gained a sense of confidence and a set of valuable mentors and collaborators. With the help of these connections, she wrote and produced a documentary series and began work on *I Know Why the Caged Bird Sings*. Finally able to shake the insecurities of her youth, Maya Angelou 18 <u>had found her voice.</u>

17

Which sentence, inserted here, would most effectively establish the main topic of the paragraph?

A) Angelou was a pioneer for African American women in film.

B) Angelou was the recipient of many honors and awards for her work in the arts.

C) *I Know Why the Caged Bird Sings* was the first work in Angelou's autobiographical series.

D) Angelou's life changed when she began discovering her creativity.

18

A) NO CHANGE

B) had found, her voice.

C) had found; her voice.

D) had: found her voice.

CONTINUE

Angelou put her voice to use throughout the rest of her life **19** by composing and producing; acting and writing. Her poetry and prose were widely **20** lionized, and her script for the film *Georgia, Georgia* was nominated for a Pulitzer Prize. Much of Angelou's success has been attributed to her ability to connect with her audience through vivid imagery, **21** instigating powerful emotions from her listeners.

In "On the Pulse of Morning," Angelou encourages Americans to have courage to live each day with hope. She invites **22** them to move forward with her into the light of the morning. On stage at the inauguration, she is not a caged bird or a shy little girl; she is a songbird whose melodies echo through television cables and touch hearts across the nation.

19

A) NO CHANGE
B) by composing; producing; acting and writing.
C) by composing, producing, acting, and writing.
D) by composing and producing; and acting and writing.

20

A) NO CHANGE
B) acclaimed
C) prized
D) championed

21

A) NO CHANGE
B) infuriating
C) agitating
D) evoking

22

A) NO CHANGE
B) themselves
C) him or her
D) oneself

CONTINUE

Questions 23-33 are based on the following passage.

Living the Wild Life

Many branches of science are devoted to [23] preserving, protecting, and studying animals, and their habitats. For example, biologists and environmentalists may make observations and collect data to determine the [24] effect's of temperature increase on rainforest wildlife. However, these scientists cannot do their work alone. [25] To help them carry out their projects, scientists often employ assistants. These are called "wildlife technicians." By assisting scientists who study animals and their relationships to the Earth, wildlife technicians enjoy a rewarding career working with both humans and animals.

23

A) NO CHANGE

B) preserving; protecting; and studying animals, and their habitats.

C) preserving, protecting, and studying animals and their habitats.

D) preserving protecting and studying animals, and their habitats.

24

A) NO CHANGE

B) affect's

C) affects

D) effects

25

Which choice most effectively combines the underlined sentences?

A) To help them carry out their projects, scientists often employ assistants; furthermore, these are called "wildlife technicians."

B) To help them carry out their projects, scientists often employ assistants, but they call them "wildlife technicians."

C) To help them carry out their projects, scientists often employ assistants, called "wildlife technicians."

D) To help them carry out their projects, scientists often employ assistants, while the assistants are called "wildlife technicians."

CONTINUE

Wildlife technicians have a variety of responsibilities. Most often, they work directly with animals or natural resources. Wildlife technicians are responsible for collecting data for use in research. Sometimes they collect data **26** by tagging and observing animals; other times, they collect samples or follow trails to determine patterns. Some wildlife technicians are able to perform hands-on work, such as caring for injured animals or restoring areas that have been disturbed or destroyed. Technicians may also use or create maps to help scientists understand patterns of weather or animal migration.

Once they collect data, wildlife technicians then input the data into computer databases to be used as inventories for further research. They may also create reports, develop hypotheses, and make suggestions based on **27** his or her observations. **28** Thus, some wildlife technicians are able to utilize their knowledge of science, math, and statistics to uncover valuable information about environments and the animals that live on earth.

26

A) NO CHANGE
B) by tagging and observing animals, other times, they collect
C) through the use of tagging and observation of animals and other times they collect
D) to tag and observe animals, other times they collect

27

A) NO CHANGE
B) their
C) one's
D) its

28

A) NO CHANGE
B) However,
C) Unfortunately,
D) Conversely,

CONTINUE

29 Many wildlife technicians work in nature parks or nature centers, but others work in harsh and **30** reserved environments, such as the isolated lands of the tundra. In some of these environments, wildlife technicians may encounter uncomfortable weather or dangerous conditions.

29

Which choice, inserted here, would most effectively establish the main topic of the paragraph?

A) Wildlife technicians need several skills to perform their difficult tasks.

B) Some wildlife technicians need to drive large trucks in order to travel.

C) The life of a wildlife technician is not always easy.

D) Wildlife technicians are able to work with a variety of animal species.

30

A) NO CHANGE

B) improbable

C) diffident

D) remote

CONTINUE

Wildlife technicians need a two-year degree to get started, but many **31** chose to pursue a bachelor's degree to obtain the benefits of a more advanced degree. Wildlife technicians study in numerous areas, including biology, ecology, forestry, and zoology. Wildlife technicians need to be skilled in science, math, and computer technology and be comfortable working with animals. Some students develop a focus area in a particular topic, such as aquatic life or resource conservation. **32** Many aspiring wildlife technicians also get involved in relevant extracurricular activities. They might join nature or outdoors clubs or volunteer at local zoos or arboretums.

For nature lovers, the work of a wildlife technician could be an exciting and satisfying job. Wildlife technicians **33** allocate their lives to helping animals and the Earth, and often find fulfillment through their careers.

31

A) NO CHANGE
B) choose
C) will have chosen
D) DELETE the underlined portion

32

The writer is considering deleting the underlined sentence. Should the writer make this change?

A) Yes, because information about extracurricular activities are not pertinent to this passage.
B) Yes, because it does not logically follow from the previous sentence.
C) No, because it does logically follow from the previous sentence.
D) No, because it provides information that sets up the examples that follow.

33

A) NO CHANGE
B) consign
C) dedicate
D) designate

CONTINUE

Questions 34-44 are based on the following passage.

Children of the Industrial Revolution

Imagine this is your daily routine: You wake up at 5:00 A.M. and walk to your job at a coal mine. There you spend fourteen hours in a mine shaft, breaking and collecting rock. At the end of the day, you receive ten cents and return home. Before going to sleep, 34 they put the money in a jar set aside for family expenses.

This was the routine of many children during the Industrial Revolution. The Industrial Revolution marked a dramatic change in the way goods were produced and manufactured, making the processes quicker and easier. Although the gains of the Industrial Revolution were great, the extreme use of child labor casts a shadow of disgrace over the period.

35 Before the Industrial Revolution, many children did work. Some children completed tasks at home or assisted with a family farm or business. 36 But during the Industrial Revolution, the role of the child in the labor force changed dramatically.

34

Which choice best maintains the pattern already established in the passage?

A) NO CHANGE

B) children were asked to put the money in the jar for family expenses.

C) the money is put in a jar for family expenses.

D) you put the money in a jar set aside for family expenses.

35

At this point, the writer is considering adding the following sentence.

Of course, I'm not totally opposed to child labor in all circumstances.

Should the writer make this addition here?

A) Yes, because it serves as an effective introduction for the main idea of the paragraph.

B) Yes, because it clarifies the writer's opinion.

C) No, because child labor is unacceptable in all circumstances.

D) No, because it is inconsistent with the style of the passage as a whole.

36

Which choice, inserted here, would be the most relevant addition to the paragraph?

A) Others still do chores at home in modern times.

B) Some people might consider mandatory school attendance to be a form of labor.

C) The children of affluent families were less likely to perform that sort of work.

D) Other children became apprentices, assistants to workers who would teach them a trade in exchange for labor.

CONTINUE

Young children were allowed to work in many industries, including coal mines, textile mills, tobacco factories, and sweatshops. In fact, children were often the preferred type of employee. Children's pay was much less than **37** adults, even when they produced the same amount of work. They could also perform some tasks that adults could not, like reaching into small compartments under running machines **38** for replace moving parts.

Many accounts of child labor investigations describe horrific and deplorable working conditions. In mills and factories, children were forced to use dangerous equipment. After working more than twelve hours per day, **39** many fatigued children were injured by the machinery. Many child laborers also faced cruel treatment by their supervisors. Children had always received discipline at home, but employers took extreme measures **40** to ensure that the work of the children was happening efficiently.

37

A) NO CHANGE

B) the adults

C) an adult

D) adults' pay

38

A) NO CHANGE

B) while

C) to

D) into

39

A) NO CHANGE

B) many children were fatigued and injured by the machinery.

C) the machinery injured many fatigued children.

D) the machinery injured many of the children who were fatigued.

40

A) NO CHANGE

B) to ensure that the work of the children was efficiently being done.

C) to ensure that the children were working efficiently.

D) in order to ensure that the children's work was being done efficiently.

CONTINUE

One of the most dangerous jobs for **41** children were coal mining. Not only did they face the immediate danger of working underground with heavy machinery, but they also risked chronic health problems. **42** Because mining was so dangerous, boys had to be at least fourteen years old to work underground. However, some parents would create fake birth certificates to allow their young boys to work in the mines.

Overall, the conditions for children during the Industrial Revolution were atrocious. Children were missing out on education and **43** worked in dangerous situations. The increase in productivity did not **44** validate the harms caused to child laborers.

41

A) NO CHANGE
B) children being
C) children was
D) children are

42

Which choice, inserted here, would best support the statement in the previous sentence?

A) During the mining process, coal dust and poisonous gases were released.
B) Mineworkers could develop "black lung," a condition in which coal dust builds up in the lungs causing permanent damage.
C) The emergency medicine of the time was less sophisticated than modern medicine, and injuries were more likely to be fatal.
D) Mining is even considered a dangerous job for adults today.

43

A) NO CHANGE
B) had worked
C) working
D) had been working

44

A) NO CHANGE
B) justify
C) rate
D) corroborate

STOP

If you complete this section before the end of your allotted time, check your work on this section only. Do NOT use the time to work on another section.

Section 3

Math Test – No Calculator

25 MINUTES, 20 QUESTIONS

Turn to Section 3 of your answer sheet to answer the questions in this section.

DIRECTIONS

Questions **1-15** ask you to solve a problem, select the best answer among four choices, and fill in the corresponding circle on your answer sheet. Questions **16-20** ask you to solve a problem and enter your answer in the grid provided on your answer sheet. There are detailed instructions on entering answers into the grid before question 16. You may use your test booklet for scratch work.

NOTES

1. You **may not** use a calculator.
2. Variables and expressions represent real numbers unless stated otherwise.
3. Figures are drawn to scale unless stated otherwise.
4. Figures lie in a plane unless stated otherwise.
5. The domain of a function f is defined as the set of all real numbers x for which $f(x)$ is also a real number, unless stated otherwise.

REFERENCE

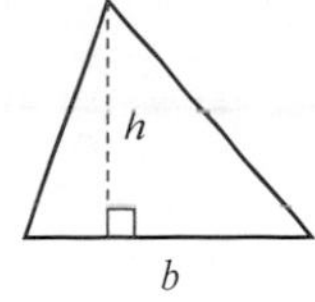

$A = \frac{1}{2}bh$

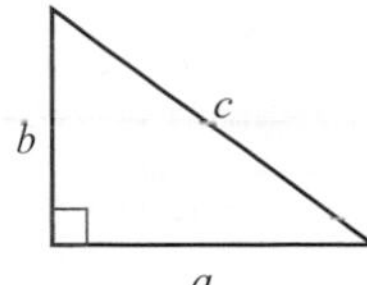

$a^2 + b^2 = c^2$

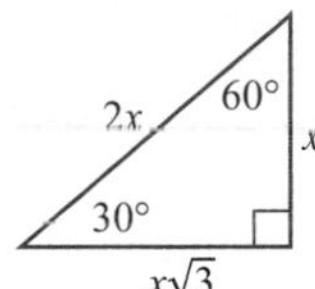

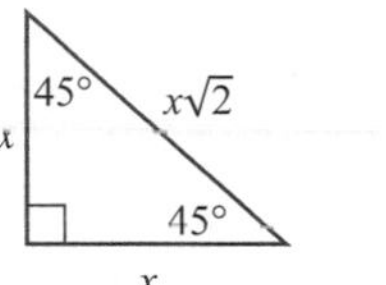

Special Triangles

$V = \frac{1}{3}lwh$

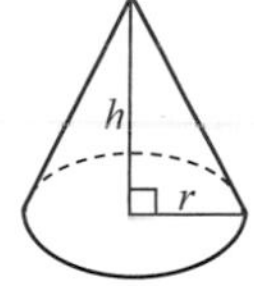

$V = \frac{1}{3}\pi r^2 h$

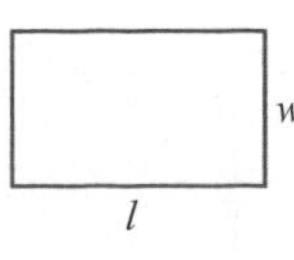

$A = lw$

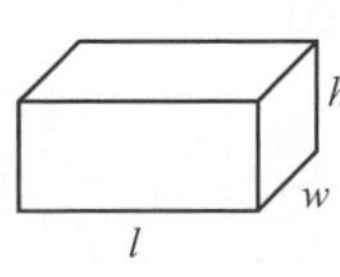

$V = lwh$

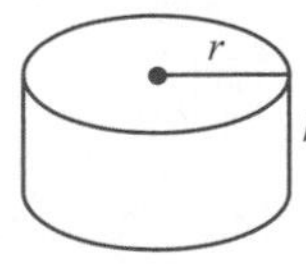

$V = \pi r^2 h$

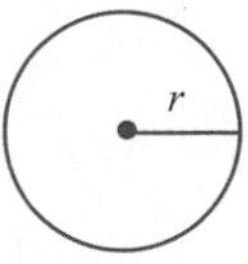

$A = \pi r^2$

$C = 2\pi r$

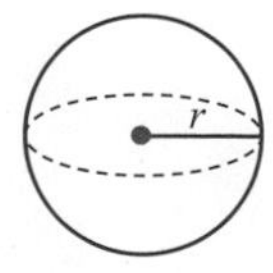

$V = \frac{4}{3}\pi r^3$

There are 360° in a circle.

The sum of the angles in a triangle is 180°.

The number of radians of arc in a circle is 2π.

CONTINUE

3

What is the difference when $-3 + 3x$ is subtracted from $4 - x$?

A) $7 + 2x$

B) $1 + 2x$

C) $7 - 4x$

D) $1 - 4x$

A car lease costs a flat fee of $1000 plus a monthly charge of $100. A 5% tax is applied to the monthly rate. Which of the following expressions represents the total cost, in dollars, if the car is leased for m months?

A) $1.05(100m) + 1000$

B) $1.05(100m + 1000)$

C) $(100 + 0.05m) + 1000$

D) $1.05(100 + 1000)m$

3

If k is a positive integer greater than 2, which of the following could be a graph of $y = \frac{kx}{2}$?

A)

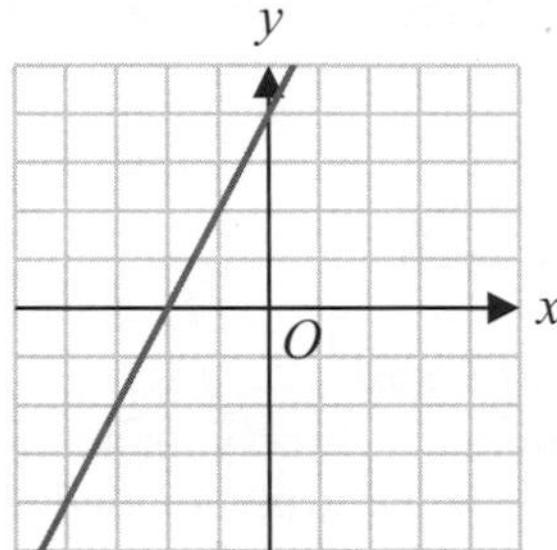

B)

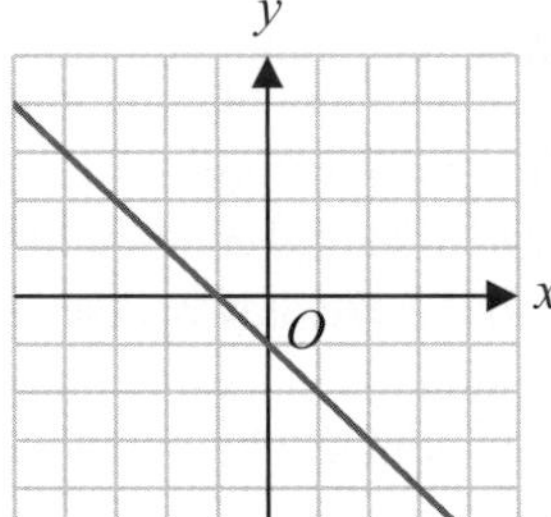

C)

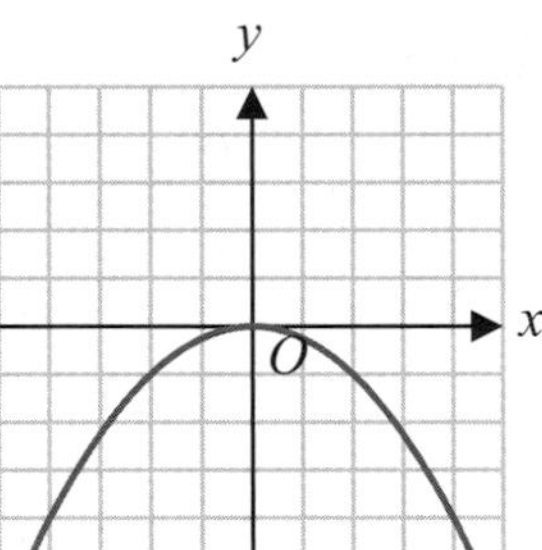

D)

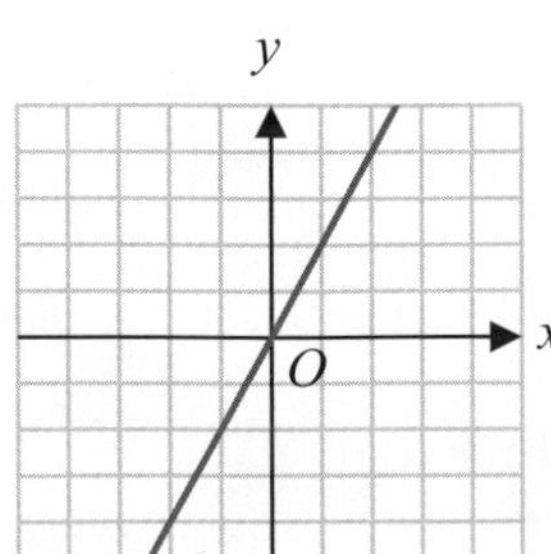

CONTINUE

4

If $-\frac{5}{3} < -2x - 1 < \frac{1}{5}$, what is one possible value of $4x + 2$?

A) -1

B) 0

C) 4

D) 5

5

$$x^2 + y^2 = 25$$
$$y = -2x$$

In the system of equations above, what is the value of x^2?

A) 25

B) $\sqrt{5}$

C) 5

D) 20

6

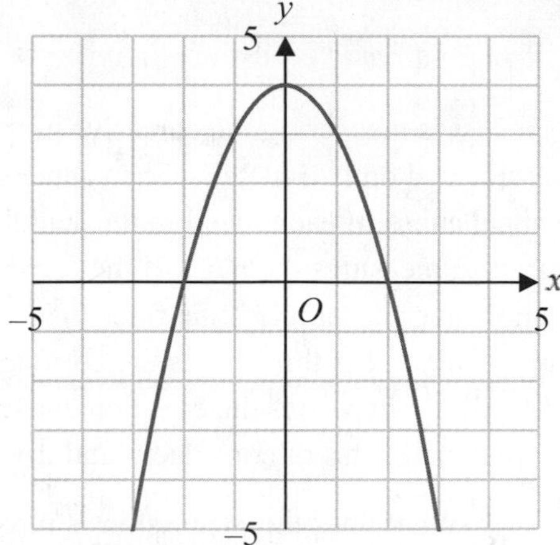

If p represents the product of the x-intercepts in the graph above, what is the value of $\frac{p}{6}$?

A) 2

B) $\frac{2}{3}$

C) $-\frac{1}{3}$

D) $-\frac{2}{3}$

CONTINUE

7

$$m = \frac{1}{x} + \frac{3}{x}$$

A chemist is measuring the corrosive properties of a certain acid on two metals. She submerges identical cubes of each metal in the acid for one hour, then measures the mass of the corroded metal from each sample. She finds that corroded mass of Metal *A* is three times the corroded mass of Metal *B*. She writes the equation above for *m*, the combined mass of corroded metal from both samples. What does the expression $\frac{3}{x}$ represent?

A) The time, in hours, that it will take the acid to corrode all of Metal *A*.

B) The mass of Metal *A* that the acid corroded in one hour.

C) The mass of Metal *B* that the acid corroded in one hour.

D) The rate at which the acid corrodes Metal *B*.

8

If $n^{2+x} = 125$ and $n^0 = x$, what is the value of n?

A) 1

B) 2

C) 3

D) 5

9

$$\frac{L}{W} = 1 + \frac{1}{4}S$$

Mathematical models can be used to predict characteristics of wildfires. Fires tend to take an elliptical shape whose length and width depend on the wind speed. The equation above gives the ratio of the length, *L*, and width, *W*, of the predicted ellipse based on the wind speed, *S*, measured in feet per second. What is the predicted length of a fire with a width of 3,000 ft at a wind speed of 12 ft/s?

A) 12,000 ft

B) 9,000 ft

C) 4,000 ft

D) 1,000 ft

10

$$\frac{1}{4}x - \frac{y}{2} = 4$$
$$ax - 2y = 16$$

If the system of equations above has an infinite number of solutions, what is the value of *a*?

A) 1

B) $\frac{3}{2}$

C) $\frac{1}{4}$

D) 3

CONTINUE

11

$$y = -(ax + c)(ax - c)$$

Which of the following values of c results in the largest range of positive integers for the equation above?

A) -11

B) 0

C) 10

D) It cannot be determined from the information given.

12

$$PV = \frac{\frac{C}{1+r}}{1 - \frac{1+g}{1+r}}$$

The equation above can be used to determine the value of investment returns, PV, on an annual payment, C, which has a rate of return of r and a growth rate of g. Which of the following is an equivalent expression for PV?

A) $\frac{Cr}{r-g}$

B) $\frac{C}{r+g}$

C) $\frac{C}{r-g}$

D) $\frac{C(1+r)}{r+g}$

13

If $\frac{2x^2}{x-1} = \frac{2}{x-1} + M$, what is M in terms of x?

A) $2x - 2$

B) $2x + 2$

C) $2x^2$

D) $2x^2 - 2$

CONTINUE

3

14

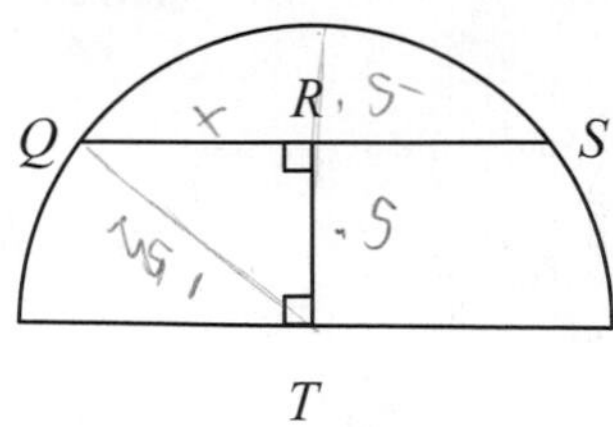

The semicircle above has a diameter of 2. If the length of $\overline{RT}$ is $\frac{1}{2}$, what is the length of the chord $\overline{QS}$?

A) $\frac{\sqrt{2}}{2}$

B) $\frac{\sqrt{3}}{2}$

C) $\sqrt{3}$

D) 2

15

If $0 < x < \frac{\pi}{2}$, what is the value of $\cos(x + \pi)$?

A) $-\frac{\cos x}{2}$

B) $-\cos x$

C) $\frac{\cos x}{2}$

D) $\cos x$

CONTINUE

DIRECTIONS

Questions **16-20** ask you to solve a problem and enter your answer in the grid provided on your answer sheet. When completing grid-in questions:

1. You are required to bubble in the circles for your answers. It is recommended, but not required, that you also write your answer in the boxes above the columns of circles. Points will be awarded based only on whether the circles are filled in correctly.
2. Fill in only one circle in a column.
3. You can start your answer in any column as long as you can fit in the whole answer.
4. For questions 16-20, no answers will be negative numbers.
5. **Mixed numbers,** such as $4\frac{2}{5}$, must be gridded as decimals or improper fractions, such as 4.4 or as 22/5. "42/5" will be read as "forty-two over five," not as "four and two-fifths."
6. If your answer is a **decimal** with more digits than will fit on the grid, you may round it or cut it off, but you must fill the entire grid.
7. If there are **multiple correct solutions** to a problem, all of them will be considered correct. Enter only **one** on the grid.

5/11	8.4	3/7
.422	.326	.125

CONTINUE

16

$$10 = |x - 4|$$

What is the greatest possible integer value for x that satisfies the equation above?

17

If the product of three different positive integers is 48 and the sum of these integers is less than 13, what is the largest of these numbers?

18

If $\frac{1}{4}x + \frac{1}{5}y = 6$, what is the value of $5x + 4y$?

19

$$E = (0.5)4^{\left(\frac{h}{16}\right)}$$

A hospital is studying the effect of the length of resident physicians' work shifts on the physicians' error rate. Researchers collect data and model the physicians' error rate, E, as a function of the length of the shift in hours, h, with the equation above. Based on this model, the physicians' error rate doubles every x hours. What is the value of x?

20

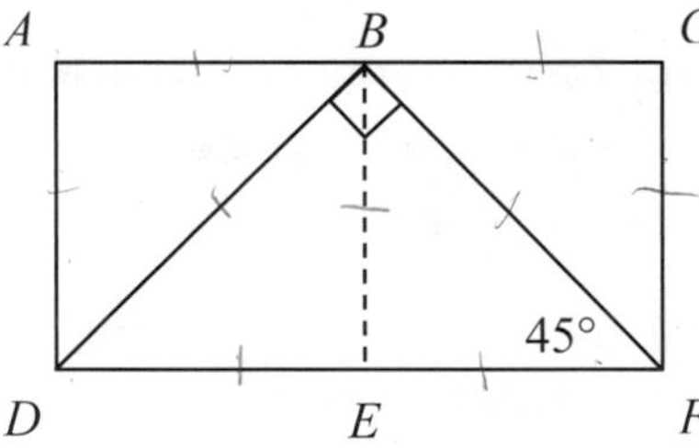

In the diagram above, $2 \times BE = DF$, and $BF = \sqrt{2}$. What is the perimeter of rectangle $ACFD$?

STOP

If you complete this section before the end of your allotted time, check your work on this section only. Do NOT use the time to work on another section.

Section 4

Math Test – Calculator

55 MINUTES, 38 QUESTIONS

Turn to Section 4 of your answer sheet to answer the questions in this section.

DIRECTIONS

Questions **1-30** ask you to solve a problem, select the best answer among four choices, and fill in the corresponding circle on your answer sheet. Questions **31-38** ask you to solve a problem and enter your answer in a grid provided on your answer sheet. There are detailed instructions on entering answers into the grid before question 31. You may use your test booklet for scratch work.

NOTES

1. You **may** use a calculator.
2. Variables and expressions represent real numbers unless stated otherwise.
3. Figures are drawn to scale unless stated otherwise.
4. Figures lie in a plane unless stated otherwise.
5. The domain of a function f is defined as the set of all real numbers x for which $f(x)$ is also a real number, unless stated otherwise.

REFERENCE

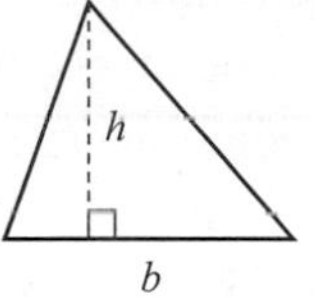

$A = \frac{1}{2}bh$

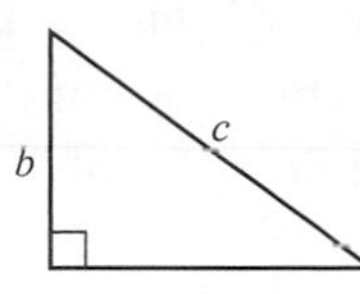

$a^2 + b^2 = c^2$

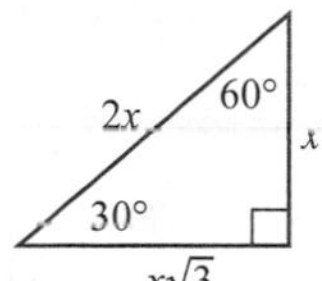

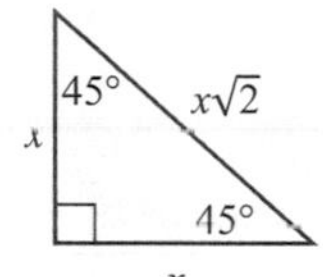

Special Triangles

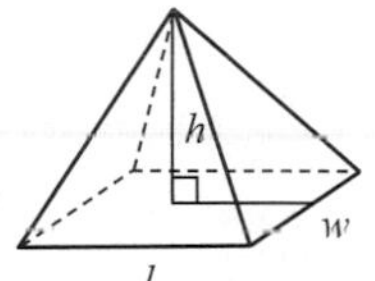

$V = \frac{1}{3}lwh$

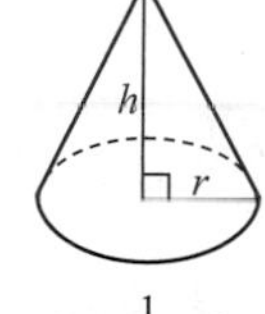

$V = \frac{1}{3}\pi r^2 h$

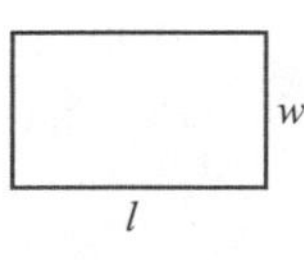

$A = lw$

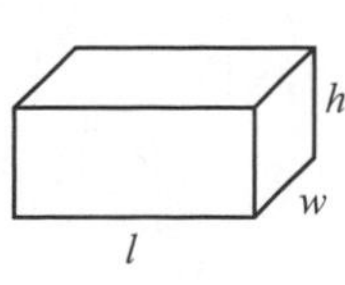

$V = lwh$

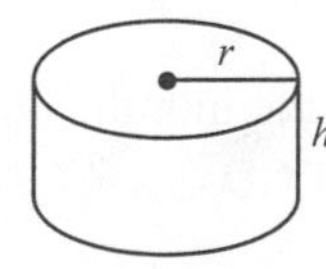

$V = \pi r^2 h$

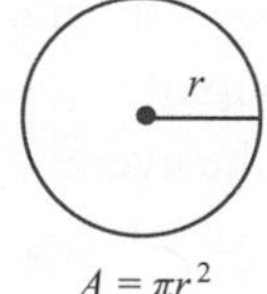

$A = \pi r^2$

$C = 2\pi r$

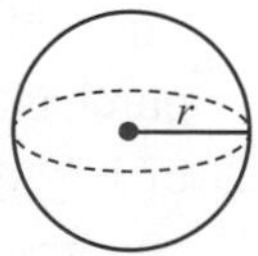

$V = \frac{4}{3}\pi r^3$

There are 360° in a circle.

The sum of the angles in a triangle is 180°.

The number of radians of arc in a circle is 2π.

CONTINUE

1

How much smaller is $p - 3$ than $p + 4$?

A) 1

B) 3

C) 6

D) 7

2

The sum of three consecutive integers is 900. What is the value of the largest of these three integers?

A) 300

B) 301

C) 303

D) 900

3

Peter	Rita	Juan	Isabella	Ming
19	8	9	7	2

The table above shows the number of CDs purchased by a group of students during the month of July. What was the average number of CDs purchased per student?

A) 9

B) 13

C) 17

D) 45

4

The population of Manchester increased by 12.0% between 1990 and 1999, and then decreased by 5.0% between 1999 and 2009. What was the percentage change in Manchester's population between 1990 and 2009?

A) 6.4%

B) 7.1%

C) 16.1%

D) 17.7%

5

The U.S. Department of Health and Human Services determined that the optimal level of fluoride in drinking water is 0.7 mg per liter of water. A county water district requires that the fluoride level should remain within 0.3 mg per liter of the optimal level. If x is the fluoride level per liter of water, which of the following inequalities expresses the range of fluoride levels, in mg per liter, that meet the city's requirements?

A) $|x - 0.3| \geq 0.7$

B) $|x - 0.7| \geq 0.3$

C) $|x - 0.3| \leq 0.7$

D) $|x - 0.7| \leq 0.3$

CONTINUE

6

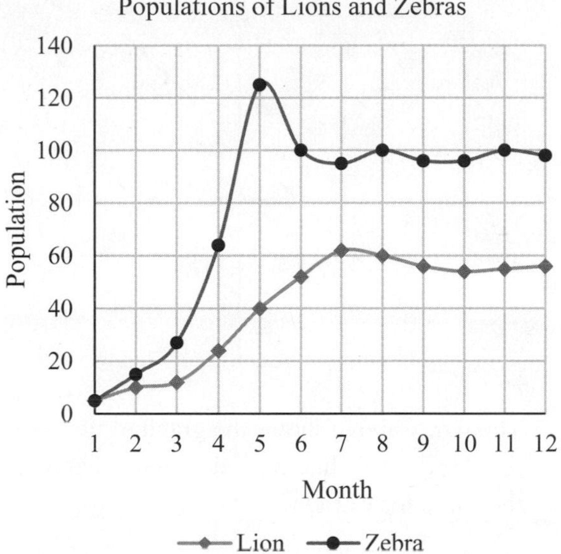

Researchers measured the populations of lions and zebras every month during a one-year period. The population data is fit to a curve, as shown above. Which of the following is a correct interpretation of the data?

A) At the 1st month, the population of lions and zebras is zero.

B) At the 2nd month, the population of lions and zebras is the same.

C) At the 4th month, there are about 3 times more zebras than lions.

D) At the 7th month, the populations of lions and zebras is the closest.

7

What is the slope of the line that connects the points (2, 5) and $\left(-\frac{10}{3}, 1\right)$?

A) $-\frac{2}{9}$

B) $\frac{2}{9}$

C) $\frac{3}{4}$

D) $\frac{4}{3}$

8

$$\frac{2x-1}{3} = 7x - 1$$

What is the value of x in the equation above?

A) $\frac{1}{21}$

B) $\frac{1}{19}$

C) $\frac{2}{19}$

D) $\frac{5}{19}$

CONTINUE

9

If $4^{2y} = 256$, what is the value of y?

A) 1
B) 2
C) 3
D) 4

10

Speed of light in a vacuum	3.0×10^8 m/s
Distance between Earth and Sun	1.5×10^{11} m

A common unit of length used in astronomy is a light year, which is defined as the distance light travels in a vacuum in one year. For smaller distances, astronomers can use units like the light minute, which is the distance light travels in a vacuum in one minute. Based on the table above, what is the approximate distance between the Earth and the Sun, in light minutes?

A) 0.12
B) 8.33
C) 500
D) 30,000

11

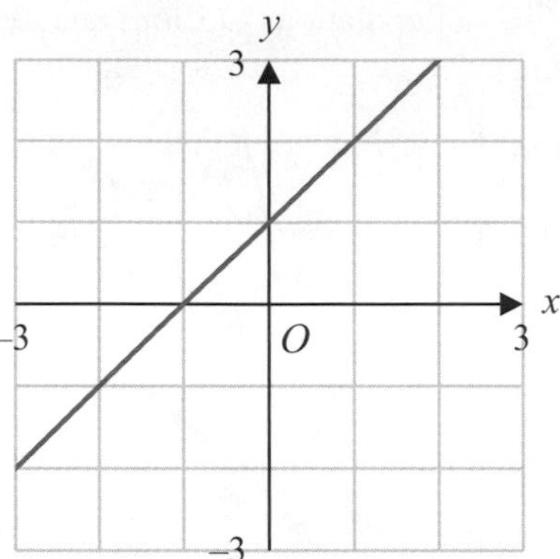

The figure above shows the graph of $y = mx + b$. If the slope of this line were doubled, what would be the value for y at $x = 2$?

A) 5
B) 6
C) 7
D) 8

CONTINUE

12

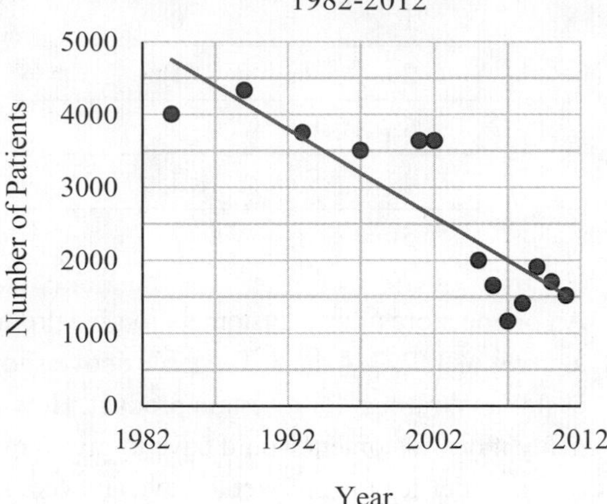

The scatterplot above shows the number of patients treated for chicken pox in a hospital from 1982 to 2012. The line of best fit shown has the equation $y = -120x + 5000$, where x is the number of years since 1982. Which of the following best describes the meaning of the number -120 in the equation of the line of best fit?

A) The average annual change in the number of patients treated for chicken pox between 1982 and 2012

B) The average number of patients treated for chicken pox each year between 1982 and 2012

C) The difference between the number of patients that received treatment for chicken pox in 1982 and 2012

D) The percent decrease in patients treated for chicken pox each year between 1982 and 2012

13

If $x = -2$, what is the value of $|x^3| - x^2 - x$?

A) -14

B) -10

C) 2

D) 6

14

If $f(x) = x^2 + 7$ and $g(x) = -f(x) + 3$, what is $g(4)$?

A) 26

B) 19

C) -1

D) -20

CONTINUE

15

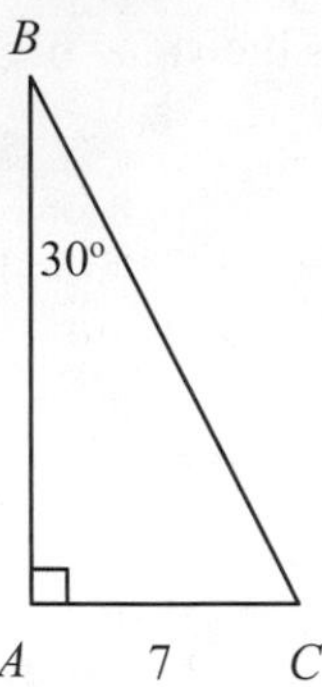

In the figure above, what is the length of $\overline{BC}$?

A) 7

B) 10

C) 11

D) 14

16

Carlos walks at a constant pace of 13 miles per x minutes. How many miles does he walk in 35 minutes, in terms of x?

A) $455x$

B) $\frac{13}{35x}$

C) $\frac{35}{13x}$

D) $\frac{455}{x}$

17

Rating	Number of Customers
1	0
2	1
3	3
4	3
5	2

An online store allows customers to give products a rating of 1, 2, 3, 4, or 5. The table above shows customers' ratings for a certain product. How many more customers would have to give a rating of 5 in order for the product to have an average rating of 4?

A) 3

B) 5

C) 7

D) 9

18

The genetic code in RNA is stored in strings of 3 base nucleotides, called codons. There are 4 base nucleotides, which are represented by U, C, A, and G. Some examples of possible codon sequences are: ACG, CGU, and UCA. How many codon sequences do NOT have any repeated base nucleotides?

A) 4

B) 24

C) 44

D) 64

CONTINUE

Questions 19 and 20 refer to the following information.

A survey on cereal preference was conducted among a random sample of United States citizens in 2010. The table below displays a summary of the survey results.

Favorite Cereal Grain				
	Corn	Oats	Other	Total
18 years or younger	3,401	2,305	2,532	8,238
19- to 44-year-olds	7,325	5,321	8,432	21,078
45- to 64-year-olds	5,643	3,423	9,647	18,713
Total	16,369	11,049	20,611	48,029

19

According to the table, which age group has the greatest percentage of people who prefer corn cereal?

A) 18 years or younger

B) 19- to 44-year-olds

C) 45- to 64-year-olds

D) All the groups' percentages are equal

20

In 2010, there were 81 million 45- to 64-year-olds in the United States. If the sample in the survey accurately reflects the rest of the population, which of the following is the best estimate of the number of 45- to 64-year-olds in the United States who preferred oat cereal?

A) 13 million

B) 15 million

C) 32 million

D) 42 million

CONTINUE

21

List 1	List 2
$-a, a, b, 118$	$a, b, 76$

Two lists of variables and numbers are written in ascending order in the table above. If $a > 42$, which of the following expressions represents the difference between the ranges of List 1 and List 2?

A) 42

B) $a - 42$

C) $a + 42$

D) $2a + 42$

22

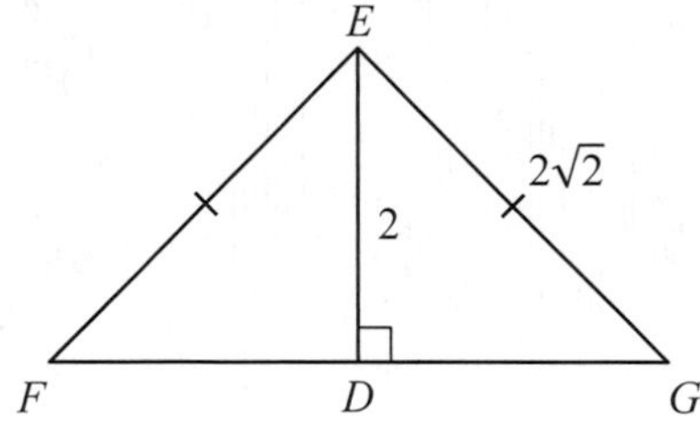

What is the area of the triangle *EFG* above?

A) $\sqrt{2}$

B) 4

C) $4\sqrt{2}$

D) 8

23

There is a 33% chance of rain in Boston and a 62% chance of rain in London. If weather conditions in London are independent of weather conditions in Boston, what is the approximate percent probability that it rains in both Boston and London?

A) 20%

B) 48%

C) 71%

D) 95%

24

$$12x + 15y = 106$$
$$36x + 45y = 6z$$

In the system of equations above, which value of z would result in infinitely many solutions?

A) 318

B) 106

C) 53

D) 18

CONTINUE

25

$$f(x) = \frac{2}{5}x + 1$$

If $g(x) = -2f(x)$, which of the following is the graph of $g(x)$?

A)
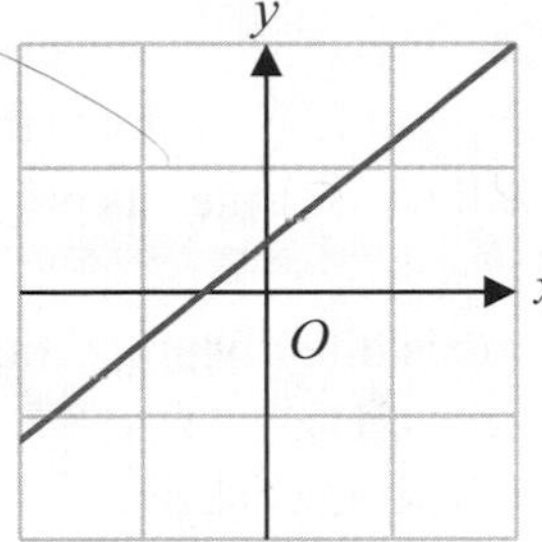

B)
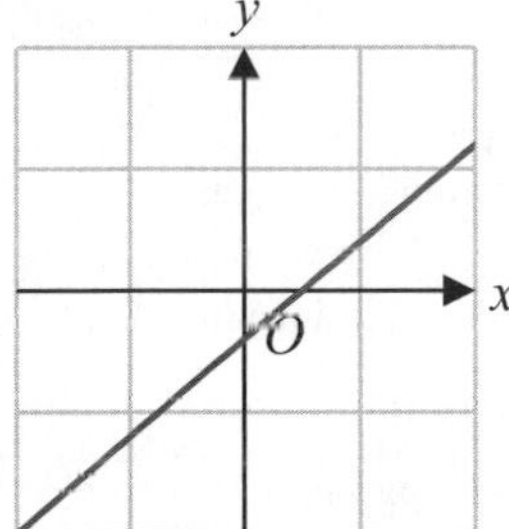

C)
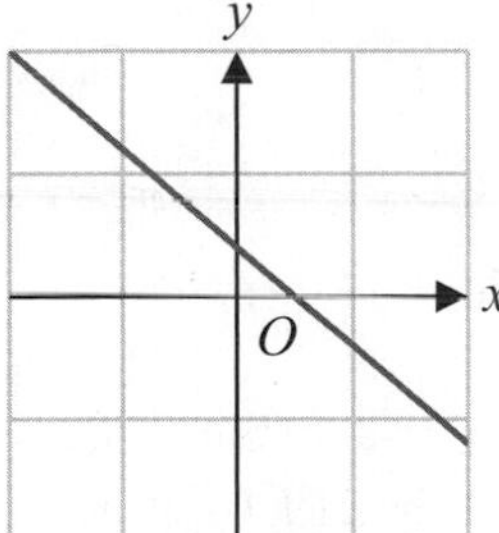

D)
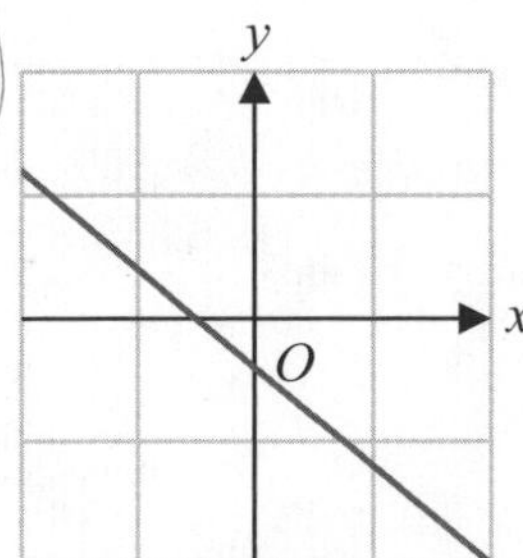

26

The data in List *A* has a standard deviation of 10, and the data in List *B* has a standard deviation of 7. Which of the following statements must be true?

A) The mean for List *A* is different than the mean for List *B*

B) The data for List *A* vary less than the data for List *B*

C) The data for List *A* vary more than the data for List *B*

D) List *A* has more accurate data than List *B*

27

Which of the following expressions is equivalent to $x^3y^3 - 64$?

A) $(xy - 4)(x^2y^2 + 2xy + 12)$

B) $(xy - 4)(x^2y^2 + 4xy + 16)$

C) $(xy - 4)(2x^2y^2 + 4xy + 16)$

D) $(xy - 6)(x^2y^2 + 2xy + 12)$

CONTINUE

28

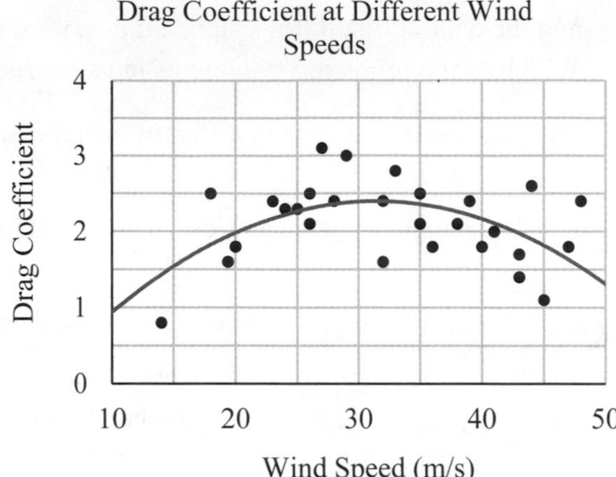

The scatterplot above shows wind speed and drag coefficient data collected in hurricane conditions by meteorologists. The scientists modeled the relationship between wind speed, w, and the drag coefficient, D, using the equation $D = aw^2 + bw + c$, where a, b, and c are constants. The model predicts that the drag coefficient will be equivalent for wind speeds of 24 m/s and 38 m/s. According to the model, what wind speed will give the maximum drag coefficient?

A) 24 m/s

B) 28 m/s

C) 31 m/s

D) 33 m/s

29

The rate of a chemical reaction depends on the concentrations of the reacting substances. The concentration of a substance A is given by $[A]$. The rate of a reaction is $r = k\,[NO]^3[H_2]$, where k is a constant. Based on the equation, which of the following is true?

I. If the concentration of NO is doubled, the reaction rate will be six times its original value.

II. The reaction rate is directly proportional to the concentration of H_2.

III. An increase in the concentration of NO and H_2 will increase the reaction rate.

A) I and II only

B) I and III only

C) II and III only

D) I, II, and III

30

$$f(x) = x^2 - 16$$

The graph of the function above intersects the x-axis at the points $(b, 0)$, and $(c, 0)$. What is the value of $b + c$?

A) −4

B) 0

C) 4

D) 8

CONTINUE

DIRECTIONS

Questions **31-38** ask you to solve a problem and enter your answer in the grid provided on your answer sheet. When completing grid-in questions:

1. You are required to bubble in the circles for your answers. It is recommended, but not required, that you also write your answer in the boxes above the columns of circles. Points will be awarded based only on whether the circles are filled in correctly.
1. Fill in only one circle in a column.
2. You can start your answer in any column as long as you can fit in the whole answer.
3. For questions 31-38, no answers will be negative numbers.
4. **Mixed numbers,** such as $4\frac{2}{5}$, must be gridded as decimals or improper fractions, such as 4.4 or as 22/5. "42/5" will be read as "forty-two over five," not as "four and two-fifths."
5. If your answer is a **decimal** with more digits than will fit on the grid, you may round it or cut it off, but you must fill the entire grid.
6. If there are **multiple correct solutions** to a problem, all of them will be considered correct. Enter only **one** on the grid.

5/11	8.4	3/7
.422	.326	.125

CONTINUE

31

When three times a number is divided by 4, the result is 6. What is the number?

32

The density of lead is 11.3 g per cm^3. A lead pipe weighs 50 kg. What is the volume of the pipe, rounded to the nearest cubic centimeter? (Density is equal to mass/volume.)

33

If $-3 < -4x + 6 < -\frac{2}{3}$, what is one possible value of x?

34

Results of Circuit Voltage Experiment						
Test	1	2	3	4	5	6
Voltage Differential	0.52	0.54	0.56	0.52	0.52	0.55

Students in a physics course are studying electricity. An experiment requires them to find the voltage differential between two points in a circuit. They take multiple measurements to ensure the accuracy of their reading and record the results in the table above. What is the median voltage reading of the students' measurements?

35

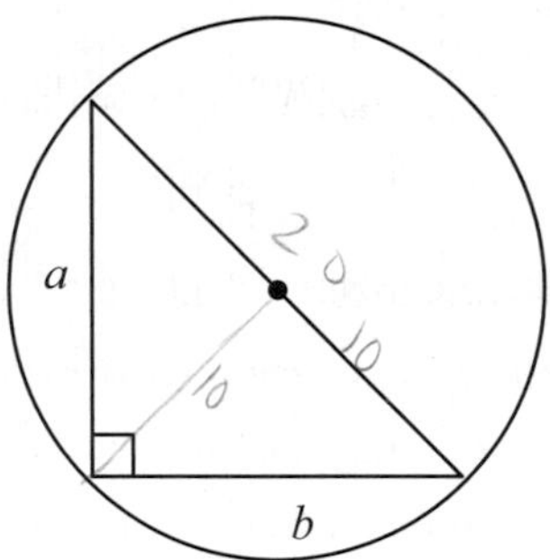

The circumference of the circle above is 20π. What is the value of $a^2 + b^2$?

CONTINUE

36

If $x = 2^{2t} + 5$ and $y = t - 1$, what is the value of $x + y$ when $t = 1.5$?

13.5

Questions 37 and 38 refer to the following information.

Monique is a student who frequently uses her American debit card to make purchases when traveling abroad. When she makes a purchase, the bank converts the purchase price at the daily foreign exchange rate and then charges a 3% fee on the converted cost.

Monique also converts cash from one currency to another at her bank. To convert cash into a different currency, her bank uses the daily foreign exchange rate and charges a 2.5% fee on the converted cost.

37

In Mexico, Monique used her debit card for a purchase that cost 235 pesos. The bank charged her card 18.62 U.S. dollars, including the 3% conversion fee. What foreign exchange rate, in Mexican pesos per U.S. dollar, did the bank use for Monique's purchase? Round your answer to the nearest whole number.

13

38

Before her trip, Monique asked her bank to convert 100 U.S. dollars into Mexican pesos. Monique did not spend any of these pesos during her trip, and she asked her bank to convert them back into U.S. dollars when she returned. If the daily foreign exchange rate stayed the same, how many U.S. dollars did Monique lose after these two conversions? Round your answer to the nearest whole number.

5

STOP

If you complete this section before the end of your allotted time, check your work on this section only. Do NOT use the time to work on another section.

Essay

Essay (Optional)

50 MINUTES

Turn to the lined pages of your answer sheet to write your essay.

DIRECTIONS

This essay is optional. It is a chance for you to demonstrate how well you can understand and analyze a written passage. Your essay should show that you have carefully read the passage and should be a concisely written analysis that is both logical and clear.

You must write your entire essay on the lines in your answer booklet. No additional paper will be provided aside from the Planning Page inside your answer booklet. You will be able to write your entire essay in the space provided if you make use of every line, keep tight margins, and write at a suitable size. Don't forget to keep your handwriting legible for the readers evaluating your essay.

You will have 50 minutes to read the passage in this booklet and to write an essay in response to the prompt provided at the end of the passage.

REMINDERS

- What you write in this booklet will not be evaluated. Write your essay in the answer booklet only.
- Essays that are off-topic will not be evaluated.

As you read the passage below, consider how Theresa Brown uses

- evidence, such as facts or examples, to support claims.
- reasoning to develop ideas and to connect claims and evidence.
- stylistic or persuasive elements, such as word choice or appeals to emotion, to add power to the ideas expressed.

1 We nurses all have stories—if we're lucky, it's just one—about the time we failed a patient. It's usually a problem of being too busy: too many cases, too many procedures to keep track of until one critical step, just one, slips through our frenetic fingers and someone gets hurt.

2 I saw it happen the first time while in nursing school. A patient needed an escalating dose of pain medicine. Her pain eased, but her breathing slowed and her oxygen level dropped. I told her nurse that the patient might need narcan, a reversing agent for opioids.

3 "Narcan?" The nurse didn't have time for that. Caring for eight patients on a busy medical-surgery floor meant that getting through the day's tasks took up all her time. Half an hour later, though, the patient needed an emergency team to revive her.

4 Bedside nurses are the hospital's front line, but we can't do the first-alert part of our jobs if there aren't enough of us on the floor. More demands for paperwork, along with increasing complexity of care, means the amount of time any one nurse has for all her patients is diminishing. And as hospitals face increasing financial pressure, nurse staffing often takes a hit, because nurses make up the biggest portion of any hospital's labor costs.

5 For patients, though, the moral calculus of the nurses-for-money exchange doesn't add up. Pioneering work done by Linda H. Aiken at the University of Pennsylvania in 2002 showed that each extra patient a nurse had above an established nurse-patient ratio made it 7 percent more likely that one of the patients would die. She found that 20,000 people died a year because they were in hospitals with overworked nurses.

6 Research also shows that when floors are adequately staffed with bedside nurses, the number of patients injured by falls declines. Staff increases lead to decreases in hospital-acquired infections, which kill 100,000 patients every year.

7 The importance of sufficient nurse staffing is becoming irrefutable, so much so that the Registered Nurse Safe-Staffing Act of 2013 was recently introduced by Representatives Lois Capps, a Democrat from California and a nurse, and David Joyce, a Republican from Ohio. Concerns over money will determine whether this bill has even a chance at passing.

8 It's hard to do a definitive cost-benefit analysis of a variable as complicated as nurse staffing because health care accounting systems are often byzantine. But data suggest that sufficient staffing can significantly reduce hospital costs.

9 Medicare penalizes hospitals for readmitting too many patients within 30 days of discharge, and a full nursing staff is one way to reduce readmissions. Having enough nurses increases patient-satisfaction scores, which also helps maintain Medicare reimbursement levels. Understaffing leads to burnout and nurses' quitting their jobs, both of which cost money in terms of absenteeism and training new staff. Finally, falls and infections have associated costs.

10 What this discussion of finances misses, though, is that having enough nurses is not just about dollars and cents. It's about limiting the suffering of human beings. When hospitals have insufficient nursing staffs, patients who would have gotten better can get hurt, or worse.

11 Several months ago I started a new job and a few weeks in, I heard my name being called. A patient getting a drug that can cause dangerous reactions was struggling to breathe. I hurried to her room, only to discover that I wasn't needed. The other nurses from the floor were already there, stopping the infusion, checking the patient's oxygen and drawing up the rescue medication. The patient was rattled, but there were enough nurses to respond, and in the end she was completely fine.

12 Now picture the same events in a different hospital, one that doesn't adequately staff, and this time the patient is you. As the drug drips in, you feel a malaise. You breathe deeply but can't quite get enough air. Your thinking becomes confused, your heart races. Terrified, you press the call light, you yell for help, but the too few nurses on the floor are spread thin and no one comes to help in time. A routine infusion ends with a call to a rapid-response team, a stay in intensive care, intubation, ventilation, death.

13 This kind of breakdown is not the nurses' fault, but the system's. We are not an elastic resource. We can be where we are needed, but only if there are enough of us.

Write an essay in which you explain how Theresa Brown builds an argument to persuade her audience that hospitals must have sufficiently large nursing staffs. In your essay, analyze how Brown uses one or more of the features listed in the box above (or features of your own choice) to strengthen the logic and persuasiveness of her argument. Be sure that your analysis focuses on the most relevant features of the passage.

Your essay should not explain whether you agree with Brown's claims, but rather explain how Brown builds an argument to persuade her audience.

Practice Test 2

YOUR NAME (PRINT): ______________________________

LAST FIRST MI

SAT

Directions

- Work on just one section at a time.
- If you complete a section before the end of your allotted time, use the extra minutes to check your work on that section only. Do NOT use the time to work on another section.

Using Your Test Booklet

- No credit will be given for anything written in the test booklet. You may use the test booklet for scratch paper.
- You are not allowed to continue answering questions in a section after the allotted time has run out. This includes marking answers on your answer sheet that you previously noted in your test booklet.
- You are not allowed to fold pages, take pages out of the test booklet, or take any pages home.

Answering Questions

- Each answer must be marked in the corresponding row on the answer sheet.
- Each bubble must be filled in completely and darkly within the lines.

- Be careful to bubble in the correct part of the answer sheet.
- Extra marks on your answer sheet may be marked as incorrect answers and lower your score.
- Make sure you use a No. 2 pencil.

Scoring

- You will receive one point for each correct answer.
- Incorrect answers will NOT result in points deducted. Even if you are unsure about an answer, you should make a guess.

DO NOT BEGIN THIS TEST

UNTIL YOUR PROCTOR TELLS YOU TO DO SO

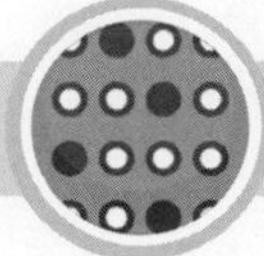

For automatic scoring and scaling, please visit **ivyglobal.com/study**.

Section 1

1	A B C D	12	A B C D	23	A B C D	34	A B C D	45	A B C D
2	A B C D	13	A B C D	24	A B C D	35	A B C D	46	A B C D
3	A B C D	14	A B C D	25	A B C D	36	A B C D	47	A B C D
4	A B C D	15	A B C D	26	A B C D	37	A B C D	48	A B C D
5	A B C D	16	A B C D	27	A B C D	38	A B C D	49	A B C D
6	A B C D	17	A B C D	28	A B C D	39	A B C D	50	A B C D
7	A B C D	18	A B C D	29	A B C D	40	A B C D	51	A B C D
8	A B C D	19	A B C D	30	A B C D	41	A B C D	52	A B C D
9	A B C D	20	A B C D	31	A B C D	42	A B C D		
10	A B C D	21	A B C D	32	A B C D	43	A B C D		
11	A B C D	22	A B C D	33	A B C D	44	A B C D		

Section 2

1	A B C D	10	A B C D	19	A B C D	28	A B C D	37	A B C D
2	A B C D	11	A B C D	20	A B C D	29	A B C D	38	A B C D
3	A B C D	12	A B C D	21	A B C D	30	A B C D	39	A B C D
4	A B C D	13	A B C D	22	A B C D	31	A B C D	40	A B C D
5	A B C D	14	A B C D	23	A B C D	32	A B C D	41	A B C D
6	A B C D	15	A B C D	24	A B C D	33	A B C D	42	A B C D
7	A B C D	16	A B C D	25	A B C D	34	A B C D	43	A B C D
8	A B C D	17	A B C D	26	A B C D	35	A B C D	44	A B C D
9	A B C D	18	A B C D	27	A B C D	36	A B C D		

Section 3 (No-Calculator)

1 A B C D	4 A B C D	7 A B C D	10 A B C D	13 A B C D
2 A B C D	5 A B C D	8 A B C D	11 A B C D	14 A B C D
3 A B C D	6 A B C D	9 A B C D	12 A B C D	15 A B C D

Only answers that are gridded will be scored. You will not receive credit for anything written in the boxes.

	16	17	18	19	20
/	○ ○	○ ○	○ ○	○ ○	○ ○
.	○ ○ ○ ○	○ ○ ○ ○	○ ○ ○ ○	○ ○ ○ ○	○ ○ ○ ○
0	○ ○ ○ ○	○ ○ ○ ○	○ ○ ○ ○	○ ○ ○ ○	○ ○ ○ ○
1	○ ○ ○ ○	○ ○ ○ ○	○ ○ ○ ○	○ ○ ○ ○	○ ○ ○ ○
2	○ ○ ○ ○	○ ○ ○ ○	○ ○ ○ ○	○ ○ ○ ○	○ ○ ○ ○
3	○ ○ ○ ○	○ ○ ○ ○	○ ○ ○ ○	○ ○ ○ ○	○ ○ ○ ○
4	○ ○ ○ ○	○ ○ ○ ○	○ ○ ○ ○	○ ○ ○ ○	○ ○ ○ ○
5	○ ○ ○ ○	○ ○ ○ ○	○ ○ ○ ○	○ ○ ○ ○	○ ○ ○ ○
6	○ ○ ○ ○	○ ○ ○ ○	○ ○ ○ ○	○ ○ ○ ○	○ ○ ○ ○
7	○ ○ ○ ○	○ ○ ○ ○	○ ○ ○ ○	○ ○ ○ ○	○ ○ ○ ○
8	○ ○ ○ ○	○ ○ ○ ○	○ ○ ○ ○	○ ○ ○ ○	○ ○ ○ ○
9	○ ○ ○ ○	○ ○ ○ ○	○ ○ ○ ○	○ ○ ○ ○	○ ○ ○ ○

Section 4 (Calculator)

1 A B C D	7 A B C D	13 A B C D	19 A B C D	25 A B C D
2 A B C D	8 A B C D	14 A B C D	20 A B C D	26 A B C D
3 A B C D	9 A B C D	15 A B C D	21 A B C D	27 A B C D
4 A B C D	10 A B C D	16 A B C D	22 A B C D	28 A B C D
5 A B C D	11 A B C D	17 A B C D	23 A B C D	29 A B C D
6 A B C D	12 A B C D	18 A B C D	24 A B C D	30 A B C D

Section 4 (Continued)

Only answers that are gridded will be scored. You will not receive credit for anything written in the boxes.

31

/
.
0
1
2
3
4
5
6
7
8
9

32

/
.
0
1
2
3
4
5
6
7
8
9

33

/
.
0
1
2
3
4
5
6
7
8
9

34

/
.
0
1
2
3
4
5
6
7
8
9

35

/
.
0
1
2
3
4
5
6
7
8
9

Only answers that are gridded will be scored. You will not receive credit for anything written in the boxes.

36

/
.
0
1
2
3
4
5
6
7
8
9

37

/
.
0
1
2
3
4
5
6
7
8
9

38

/
.
0
1
2
3
4
5
6
7
8
9

Section 5 (Optional)

Important: Use a No. 2 pencil. Write inside the borders.

You may use the space below to plan your essay, but be sure to write your essay on the lined pages. Work on this page will not be scored.

Use this space to plan your essay.

START YOUR ESSAY HERE.

Continue on the next page.

Continue on the next page.

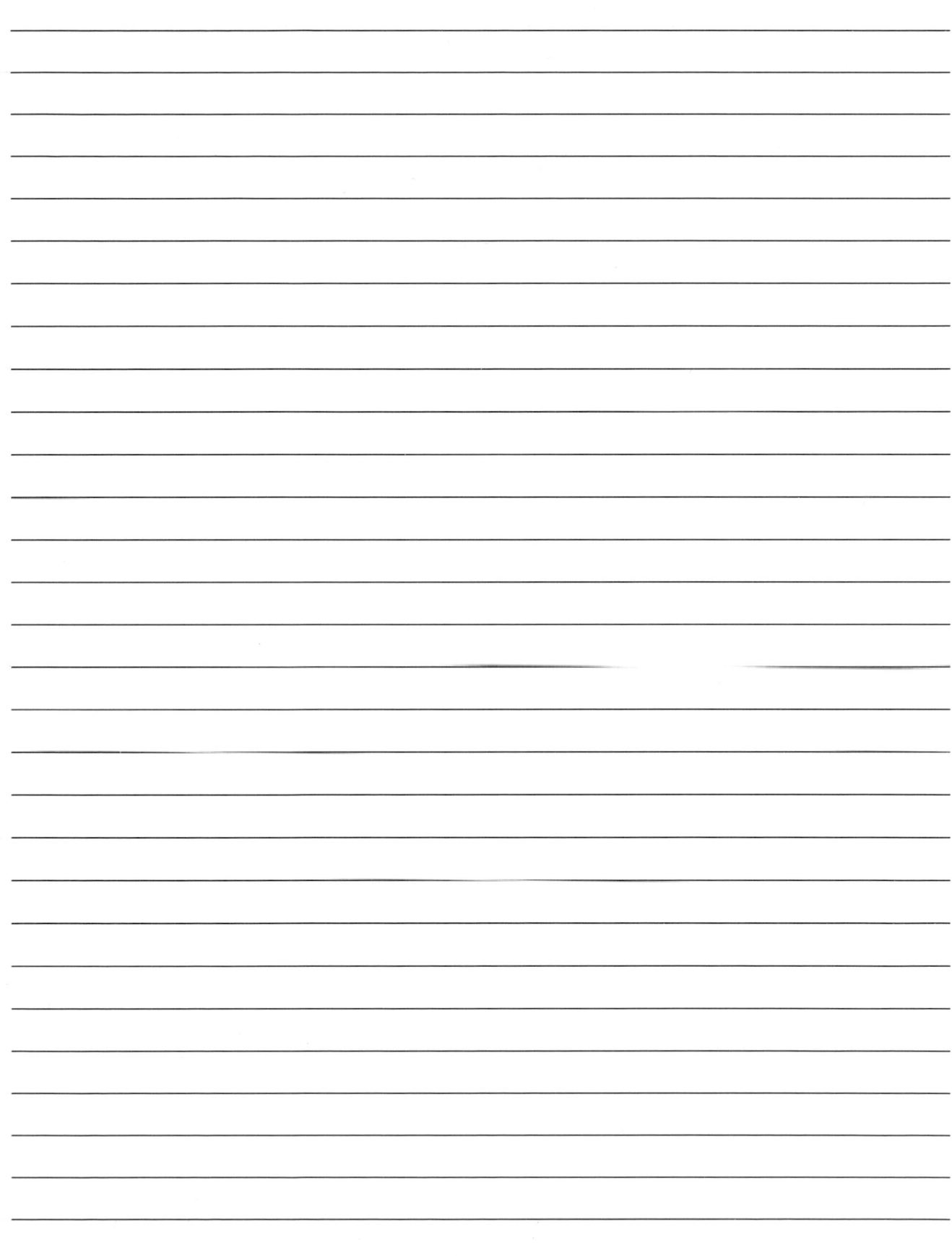

Continue on the next page.

Reading Test

65 MINUTES, 52 QUESTIONS

Turn to Section 1 of your answer sheet to answer the questions in this section.

DIRECTIONS

Every passage or paired set of passages is accompanied by a number of questions. Read the passage or paired set of passages, then use what is said or implied in what you read and in any given graphics to choose the best answer to each question.

Questions 1-11 are based on the following passage and supplementary materials.

This passage is adapted from Adam Minter, "Plastic Arts: What Really Happens to Human Junk." © 2014 by The Economist.

Recycling bins overflow after the holidays, stuffed with gift wrapping and tangled Christmas-tree lights. Rarely does this junk earn a second thought. But where does it all go? Probably Asia, and particularly China, the largest importer of recycling from the rich world. Those broken lights, for example, may turn up in Guangdong province where factories salvage the copper wire and melt the stripped plastic into new slipper soles. China's thriving economy is desperate for stuff that consumers in America and elsewhere carelessly throw away.

The multibillion-dollar recycling trade stands as "one of globalization's great, green successes," writes Adam Minter, an American journalist, in *Junkyard Planet*. It is also a largely unsung one, as under-appreciated as a rusty bike. The industry turns over as much as $500 billion annually, and employs a huge number of people. After years spent traveling the junk heaps of the world, and a decade living in China, Mr. Minter is keen to give the scrap-dealers their due. Son of an American scrap-yard owner, he approaches the industry with affectionate curiosity, marveling at the "groan and crunch" of machines that turn rubbish into usable goods.

When Mr. Minter first moved to Shanghai in 2002, the city had three subway lines; ten years later it boasts one of the world's largest systems, with 11 lines and 270 miles of track. Building booms in the developing world, particularly in China, have caused an explosion of demand for steel, copper, and other resources. Yet China lacks the raw materials it needs, so it imports the metal, often as scrap. This has pushed up prices; a pound of copper has risen from 60 cents in the late 1990s to nearly $3.40 today. Americans, meanwhile, have more scrap than they can handle. Known among scrap traders as the "Saudi Arabia of Scrap," the country lacks real demand for manufacturing materials. American labor costs are too high—and environmental regulations too onerous—for it to be cost-effective to salvage most scrap anyway. For the savvy, fast-talking businessmen of the international scrap trade, this has created a profitable exchange. It has also driven the kind of innovation that diverts more junk from landfills.

For example, people now worry more about the afterlife of their mobile phones than their cars because of the invention of the motor shredder, which turns old vehicles into scrap metal. In 1970, at least 20 million rusting cars were abandoned across

CONTINUE

America. In 2012, America recycled nearly 11.9 million cars. China, the world's biggest car buyer, has become the fastest growing market for shredders. America's trade deficit with China reinforces the two countries' relationship as recycling partners. Americans consume, and therefore dispose of, more goods than their Chinese counterparts. And it is also often cheaper for American scrap-yards to send their goods to China than anywhere else in the world. This is because shipping companies hauling goods to America would rather not return to China empty, and so they offer discounts on what they call their "back-hauls."

Whether Mr. Minter is accompanying a Chinese scrap buyer on a road trip through the American Midwest or trying to sell his old mobile phones in Guiyu, China's controversial electronic-waste recycling zone, he is an authorial, engaging guide through the global trash trade. Dirty, dangerous, cheap to get into and not without romance, the junk business extracts value from what others see as worthless. Mr. Minter is not blind to the grim realities of the industry. Wen'an County in China, a place once known for its fertile soil, clear streams, and peach trees, was the "most polluted place" he ever visited because of its role in the plastics trade.

But any recrimination over these recycling practices is best directed at the rich world and at the increasingly wealthy Chinese who are beginning to match their wasteful, spendthrift counterparts in the West. The recycling industry squeezes value from used goods, but nothing is 100% recyclable. The special chemistry of many products, such as iPhone touchscreens, means they cannot be recycled. Consumers should be more aware of what is harmful, and companies should be nudged to design products that are easier to repair and recycle. In the meantime, a bit more appreciation might be spared for junkyards, without which "the world would be a dirtier and less interesting place."

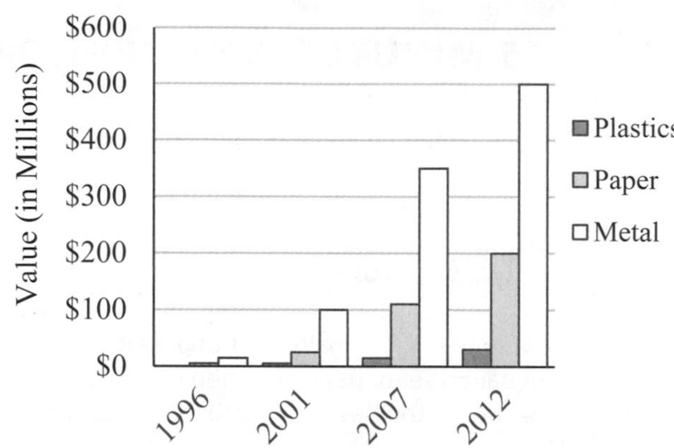

The above chart shows the amount of US scrap exports to China by value over time. Data from the United States International Trade Commission.

1

The main purpose of the passage is to

A) describe the economic relationship between two countries.

B) criticize the environmental policies of a major world power.

C) discuss the virtues of a valuable and growing industry.

D) express an opinion about the rising cost of certain metals.

CONTINUE

2

It can be reasonably inferred from the passage that the author would agree with which statement about the global recycling industry?

A) Its economic importance has been over-emphasized.

B) Its impact on other industries is largely insignificant.

C) It disproportionately benefits already developed economies.

D) Its benefits are often not fully appreciated.

3

Which choice provides the best evidence for the answer to the previous question?

A) Lines 4-6 ("Probably … world")

B) Lines 16-17 ("It is … bike")

C) Lines 22-25 ("Son … goods")

D) Lines 29-32 ("Building … resources")

4

The author's attitude towards Adam Minter's book *Junkyard Planet* could best be described as

A) interested and approving.

B) perplexed and reserved.

C) enthusiastic and worshipful.

D) detached and unimpressed.

5

According to the passage, the rapid expansion of the global recycling trade in the past few decades has been caused mainly by

A) the depletion of natural resources in Asia through environmentally unsafe practices.

B) the increased demand for resources to sustain construction projects in the developing world.

C) the growing innovation in consumer goods that has caused products to become obsolete sooner.

D) the swiftly expanding Chinese population that has created a large new market for American goods.

6

According to the passage, which of the following claims is true about American scrap metal?

A) The price of scrap metal has increased more since the late 1990s than ever before.

B) Scrap metal has been used in the past to construct subway lines in major American cities.

C) It is usually not profitable to recycle scrap metal in America.

D) Safety regulations prevent scrap metal from being recycled for domestic construction projects.

7

Which choice provides the best evidence for the answer to the previous question?

A) Lines 26-29 ("When … track")

B) Lines 33-36 ("This has … today")

C) Lines 39-42 ("American … anyway")

D) Lines 44-46 ("It has … landfills")

CONTINUE

8

As used in line 28, "boasts" most nearly means

A) gloats.

B) exaggerates.

C) brags.

D) features.

9

The purpose of the fourth paragraph (lines 47-64) is to

A) provide evidence to support a claim made in an earlier paragraph.

B) define terms that were introduced in an earlier paragraph.

C) describe a scenario that demonstrates a general rule.

D) articulate the disadvantages of a position that was advocated for in an earlier paragraph.

10

As it is used in line 72, "extracts" most nearly means

A) removes.

B) derives.

C) selects.

D) exacts.

11

Which one of the following claims is supported by the graph?

A) Total United States plastic exports to China reached 200 million tons in 2012.

B) From 1996 to 2012, the value of United States scrap metal exported to China was greater than the value of paper and plastic exports combined.

C) In 2001, China imported less than $50 million worth of scrap paper from around the world.

D) The United States exported a total of $500 million worth of scrap metal in 2012, up from around $200 million in 2001.

CONTINUE

Questions 12-22 are based on the following passages.

Passage 1 and Passage 2 are adapted from Robert S. Blumenthal and Rita Redberg, "Should Healthy People Take Cholesterol Drugs to Prevent Heart Disease?" © 2014 by Dow Jones & Company.

Passage 1

Heart disease is the leading cause of death in the U.S., and people with higher cholesterol are at higher risk for heart attacks. There's good evidence that people who already have heart disease benefit from cholesterol-lowering medications, or statins. Among those people, statin treatment reduces risk of heart attack and may prolong life.

But what about healthy people with high cholesterol? Many doctors have taken the evidence from studies of people with heart disease and made a leap of logic: they've treated millions of healthy people with statins to prevent heart disease.

But there's a serious problem with that logic. For most healthy people, data show that statins do not prevent heart disease, nor extend life or improve quality of life. And they come with considerable side effects. That's why I don't recommend giving statins to healthy people, even those with higher cholesterol.

Despite research that has included tens of thousands of people, there is no evidence that taking statins prolongs life, although cholesterol levels do decrease. Using the most optimistic projections, for every 100 healthy people who take statins for five years, one or two will avoid a heart attack. One will develop diabetes. But, on average, there is no evidence that the group taking statins will live any longer than those who don't.

Some argue that clinical trials of statin use among healthy people haven't demonstrated a reduced mortality rate because each individual trial only follows patients for a few years—not long enough to show a reduction in mortality. Many doctors, including me, believe that we need clinical trials that actually follow healthy people treated with statins for the long term to see if treatment really results in lower mortality. Statin proponents think such trials would be prohibitively expensive. That's a disappointing stance, considering the billions that have already been spent on statin prescriptions and advertising.

Some statin supporters argue that even if the data don't support the benefits of statins in healthy people, they might help and can't hurt. But that's untenable, because statins undeniably harm some people. Besides increasing the risk for developing diabetes, statins can cause memory loss, muscle weakness, stomach distress, and aches and pains. These aren't merely anecdotal results, as some critics assert; they're documented by recent studies.

Passage 2

We don't prescribe drugs to otherwise healthy people without rigorous scientific evidence. And, in this case, there is a mountain of high-quality scientific evidence.

Heart disease is an insidious process that takes decades to manifest itself. Risk factors for developing heart disease often go unrecognized and undertreated until it's too late. So, the first manifestation of cardiovascular disease is often sudden cardiac death, heart attack, or stroke—which may result in disability or death. A little late at that point to start prescribing statins.

Yet critics say we should wait until after a patient has gone through one of these life-shattering events before we prescribe a statin. It makes no sense that a medication that slows the progression of hardening of the arteries would be harmful the day or week before a heart attack, but helpful the day or week after a heart attack.

The totality of the available biologic, observational, and clinical-trial evidence strongly supports the selective use of statin therapy in adults demonstrated to be at high risk for heart disease. Studies have conclusively shown that statins prolong life and reduce the risk of heart attack, stroke, and death in patients with known heart disease. Similarly, they have been shown to do the same in

CONTINUE

patients without heart disease, but who are at high risk of developing heart disease.

For instance, a study of 6,600 Scottish men who hadn't had heart attacks showed a decrease in mortality rates after five years with statin therapy. Likewise, the recent world-wide Jupiter study of men and women without prior heart disease showed statins significantly decreased the risk of death after two years in people with an average age of 66.

Critics raise a number of complaints about these studies—exaggerated, in my view—but many other large prevention trials of people with multiple risk factors have consistently shown reductions in total cardiovascular events of 30% to 40% with the use of a statin.

12

It can be reasonably inferred from Passage 1 that the author would most likely recommend statins for a patient who

A) is male and between the ages of 65 and 74.

B) has an unusually high cholesterol level.

C) is at a higher than average risk of having a heart attack.

D) is already suffering from heart disease.

13

Which choice provides the best evidence for the answer to the previous question?

A) Lines 3-5 ("There's good … statins")

B) Lines 9-12 ("Many doctors … disease")

C) Lines 17-19 ("That's why … cholesterol")

D) Lines 33-37 ("Many … mortality")

14

According to Passage 1, which of the following best describes the relationship between statins and diabetes?

A) People with diabetes are not allowed to take statins.

B) People are more likely to develop diabetes when using statins.

C) Statins are often prescribed for the treatment of diabetes.

D) People are less likely to develop diabetes when using statins.

15

As used in line 31, "individual" most nearly means

A) peculiar.

B) personal.

C) secluded.

D) particular.

CONTINUE

16

Which of the following best summarizes the position held by the author of Passage 2?

A) Since it is unethical to treat people for a disease they don't have, statins should be considered preventative medication and prescribed to anyone who wants them.

B) Since many people with heart disease don't know they have it, doctors should prescribe statins to patients who might have or might develop heart disease.

C) Since statins are not known to prevent the development of heart disease, doctors should only prescribe them to patients at risk for diabetes.

D) Since doctors only prescribe medicines with well-documented records of success, patients should trust their doctors' recommendations.

17

The main rhetorical effect of lines 61-62 ("A little late… statins") is to

A) specify the correct moment for prescribing statins.

B) provide information about when the prescription of statins is most appropriate.

C) portray the opposing argument as nonsensical and dangerous.

D) convey a sense of regret about the preventable death of a patient.

18

As used in line 72, "selective" most nearly means

A) exacting.

B) choosy.

C) judicious.

D) exclusive.

19

The authors of both passages would most likely agree with which of the following statements?

A) Drugs should never be prescribed to healthy patients.

B) Past studies measuring the effects of statin use have been flawed.

C) Statins are effective at treating patients with heart disease.

D) Statins should only be prescribed after a patient has experienced a cardiovascular incident.

20

Which one of the following pieces of evidence is included in Passage 2 but not Passage 1?

A) A discussion of the side effects of cholesterol-lowering medication

B) Statistics from specific scientific studies

C) Information about the prevalence of statin use

D) An analysis of the financial costs of statin use

CONTINUE

21

How would the author of Passage 2 most likely respond to the claim made in lines 29-33 ("Some ... mortality") of Passage 1?

A) By asserting that certain studies have shown a reduction in mortality for healthy patients who use statins

B) By agreeing that more studies need to be conducted that follow patients for longer periods of time

C) By suggesting that scientists should examine the quality of life of statin users rather than just the risk of death

D) By arguing that following patients for only one year is enough to prove reduced mortality in healthy patients who use statins

22

Which choice provides the best evidence for the answer to the previous question?

A) Lines 56-58 ("Risk … late")

B) Lines 65-69 ("It makes … attack")

C) Lines 74-76 ("Studies … disease")

D) Lines 80-82 ("For instance … therapy")

Questions 23-32 are based on the following passage.

This passage is adapted from John Jay, "Concerning Dangers From Foreign Force and Influence," originally published in 1787 in *The Federalist Papers: No. 3*. The Federalist Papers aimed to build support for ratification of the United States Constitution, which would unify the States under a national government.

The just causes of war, for the most part, arise either from violation of treaties or from direct violence. America has already formed treaties with no less than six foreign nations. It is of high importance to the peace of America that she observe the laws of nations towards all these powers, and to me it appears evident that this will be more perfectly and punctually done by one national government than it could be either by thirteen separate States or by three or four distinct confederacies. For this opinion various reasons may be assigned.

The prospect of present loss or advantage may often tempt the governing party in one or two States to swerve from good faith and justice; but those temptations, not reaching the other States, and consequently having little or no influence on the national government, the temptation will be fruitless, and good faith and justice be preserved. The case of the treaty of peace with Britain adds great weight to this reasoning.

If even the governing party in a State should be disposed to resist such temptations, yet as such temptations may, and commonly do, result from circumstances peculiar to the State, and may affect a great number of the inhabitants, the governing party may not always be able, if willing, to prevent the injustice meditated, or to punish the aggressors. But the national government, not being affected by those local circumstances, will neither be induced to commit the wrong themselves, nor want power or inclination to prevent or punish its commission by others.

So far, therefore, as either designed or accidental violations of treaties and the laws of nations afford just causes of war, they are less to be apprehended

CONTINUE

under one general government than under several lesser ones, and in that respect the former most favors the safety of the people.

As to those just causes of war which proceed from direct and unlawful violence, it appears equally clear to me that one good national government affords vastly more security against dangers of that sort than can be derived from any other quarter.

Because such violences are more frequently caused by the passions and interests of a part than of the whole; of one or two States than of the Union. Not a single Indian war has yet been occasioned by aggressions of the present federal government, feeble as it is; but there are several instances of Indian hostilities having been provoked by the improper conduct of individual States, who, either unable or unwilling to restrain or punish offenses, have given occasion to the slaughter of many innocent inhabitants.

Besides, it is well known that acknowledgments, explanations, and compensations are often accepted as satisfactory from a strong united nation, which would be rejected as unsatisfactory if offered by a State or confederacy of little consideration or power.

In the year 1685, the state of Genoa having offended Louis XIV, endeavored to appease him. He demanded that they should send their Doge, or chief magistrate, accompanied by four of their senators, to France, to ask his pardon and receive his terms. They were obliged to submit to it for the sake of peace. Would he on any occasion either have demanded or have received the like humiliation from Spain, or Britain, or any other powerful nation?

23

The main purpose of the passage is to

A) illustrate how a united government should operate.

B) propose a new form of government.

C) explain some of the benefits of united government.

D) recount the recent history of the United States.

24

According to Jay, which of the following would most likely constitute a just cause of war?

A) A country seeks to expand its borders.

B) Treaty negotiations between two countries are stalled by one side's refusal to compromise.

C) One country discovers that its neighbor has been producing weapons and training troops.

D) A country repeatedly violates the terms of a treaty that it has signed.

25

Which of the following choices provides the best evidence for the answer to the previous question?

A) Lines 1-3 ("The just … violence")

B) Lines 4-10 ("It is … confederacies")

C) Lines 39-43 ("As to … quarter")

D) Lines 47-54 ("Not a … inhabitants")

CONTINUE

26

As used in line 10, "distinct" most nearly means

A) separate.

B) prominent.

C) unmistakable.

D) precise.

27

As used in line 12, "prospect" most nearly means

A) hope.

B) candidate.

C) view.

D) possibility.

28

In lines 12-14, Jay raises the concern that individual states, if left to their own devices, might

A) behave improperly towards other nations for their own short-term gain.

B) allow their citizens to over-indulge in pleasurable activities.

C) start practicing a different religion from the rest of the union.

D) attack other nations without the consent of the national government.

29

According to the passage, unlike state governments, a national government is

A) less likely to catch and punish foreign criminals.

B) less likely to be swayed by narrow public interests.

C) more likely to keep its people safe, happy, and obedient.

D) more likely to fund numerous foreign wars.

30

Which of the following choices provides the best evidence for the answer to the previous question?

A) Lines 12-18 ("The prospect … preserved")

B) Lines 18-20 ("The case ... reasoning")

C) Lines 55-59 ("Besides ... power")

D) Lines 65-68 ("They ... nation")

CONTINUE

31

In the sixth paragraph (lines 44-54), Jay implies that the federal government has not provoked conflicts with American Indians because

A) it fears that the nation would suffer serious casualties in the case of war.

B) it is unwilling to punish its citizens for their inappropriate behavior.

C) such conflicts arise from local concerns that are not important to the nation as a whole.

D) such conflicts are best resolved on the local level without federal interference.

32

The final paragraph (lines 60-68) serves to

A) support the claim in the previous paragraph with a historical example.

B) direct the reader's attention to the United States' relationship with France.

C) predict what will happen to the United States if Jay's proposals are not acted upon.

D) illustrate how superior the United States is to Genoa.

Questions 33-42 are based on the following passage and supplementary materials.

This passage is adapted from Gary Marcus and Christof Koch, "The Future of Brain Implants." © 2014 by Dow Jones & Company.

What would you give for a retinal chip that let you see in the dark or for a next-generation cochlear implant that let you hear any conversation in a noisy restaurant, no matter how loud? Or for a memory chip, wired directly into your brain's hippocampus, that gave you perfect recall of everything you read? Or for an implanted interface with the Internet that automatically translated a clearly articulated silent thought ("the French Sun King") into an online search that digested the relevant Wikipedia page and projected a summary directly into your brain?

Science fiction? Perhaps not for very much longer. Brain implants today are where laser eye surgery was several decades ago. They are not risk-free and make sense only for a narrowly defined set of patients—but they are a sign of things to come. Unlike pacemakers, dental crowns or implantable insulin pumps, neuroprosthetics—devices that restore or supplement the mind's capacities with electronics inserted directly into the nervous system—change how we perceive the world and move through it. For better or worse, these devices become part of who we are.

Neuroprosthetics aren't new. They have been around commercially for three decades, in the form of the cochlear implants used in the ears (the outer reaches of the nervous system) of more than 300,000 hearing-impaired people around the world. Last year, the Food and Drug Administration approved the first retinal implant, made by the company Second Sight. Both technologies exploit the same principle: an external device, either a microphone or a video camera, captures sounds or images and processes them, using the results to drive a set of electrodes that stimulate either the auditory or the optic nerve, approximating the naturally occurring output from the ear or the eye.

CONTINUE

Another type of now-common implant, used by thousands of Parkinson's patients around the world, sends electrical pulses deep into the brain proper, activating some of the pathways involved in motor control. A thin electrode is inserted into the brain through a small opening in the skull; it is connected by a wire that runs to a battery pack underneath the skin. The effect is to reduce or even eliminate the tremors and rigid movement that are such prominent symptoms of Parkinson's (though, unfortunately, the device doesn't halt the progression of the disease itself). Experimental trials are now under way to test the efficacy of such "deep brain stimulation" for treating other disorders as well.

Electrical stimulation can also improve some forms of memory, as the neurosurgeon Itzhak Fried and his colleagues at the University of California, Los Angeles, showed in a 2012 article in the *New England Journal of Medicine*. Using a setup akin to a videogame, seven patients were taught to navigate a virtual city environment with a joystick, picking up passengers and delivering them to specific stores. Appropriate electrical stimulation to the brain during the game increased their speed and accuracy in accomplishing the task.

But not all brain implants work by directly stimulating the brain. Some work instead by reading the brain's signals—to interpret, for example, the intentions of a paralyzed user. Eventually, neuroprosthetic systems might try to do both, reading a user's desires, performing an action like a Web search, and then sending the results directly back to the brain.

Behavioral Performance on Spatial Learning Tasks

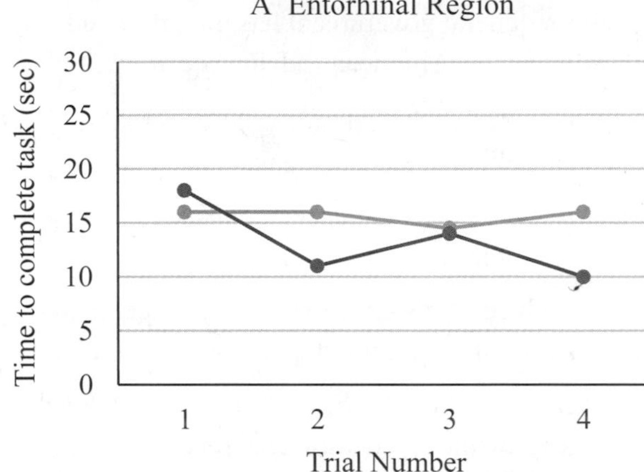

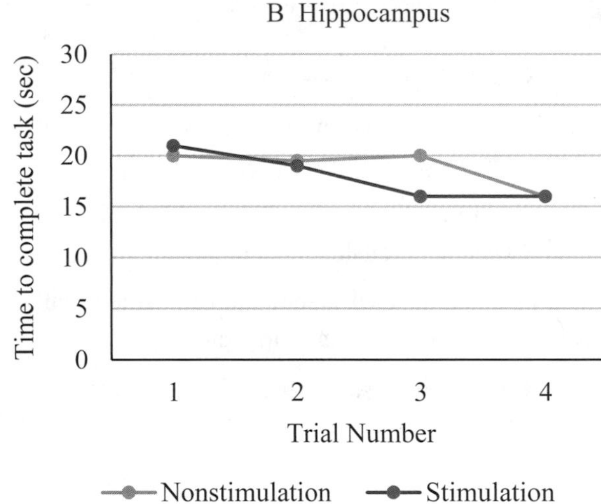

These two graphs show the time it took study participants to complete a memory task when certain brain regions were and were not stimulated with electrodes.

CONTINUE

33

Which one of the following best describes the overall structure of the passage?

A) Disparate facts are joined by a central story.

B) A common misconception is explained and refuted.

C) Speculation about the future is supported with examples.

D) An experiment is discussed to support a prediction.

34

The series of questions in lines 1-11 ("What would … your brain") serves mainly to

A) demonstrate the incredible advances that have been achieved by a new technology.

B) prompt readers to consider the potential value of hypothetical technologies.

C) suggest that technologies that most people desire will soon be available.

D) challenge readers to consider the true costs of future advances in technology.

35

As used in line 15, "defined" most nearly means

A) explained.

B) interpreted.

C) expressed.

D) delineated.

36

The passage most strongly suggests that

A) neuroprosthetics are used exclusively to treat brain disorders.

B) retinal implants are currently used by nearly 300,000 people.

C) cochlear implants represent a significant improvement over pacemakers.

D) neuroprosthetics alter the way in which patients experience the world.

37

It can be reasonably inferred from the passage that cochlear and retinal implants

A) took a long time to become approved by the Food and Drug Administration.

B) attempt to recreate the sensations experienced by the average person.

C) allow the user to see or hear just as well as someone who does not need these implants.

D) are as safe and effective as laser eye surgery.

38

Which choice provides the best evidence for the answer to the previous question?

A) Lines 13-14 ("Brain … ago")

B) Lines 17-22 ("Unlike … through it")

C) Lines 24-28 ("They have … world")

D) Lines 32-37 ("an external … eye")

CONTINUE

39

As used in line 31, "exploit" most nearly means

A) harness.

B) abuse.

C) deceive.

D) contrive.

40

Information provided by the passage suggests that electrical stimulation of parts of the nervous system

A) is currently being used around the world to cure patients with Parkinson's disease and other disorders.

B) could soon become a part of commercially available video games.

C) may have the potential to alleviate the symptoms of patients living with a variety of medical conditions.

D) has been shown to improve memory in the vast majority of patients.

41

Which choice provides the best evidence for the answer to the previous question?

A) Lines 38-42 ("Another … control")

B) Lines 49-51 ("Experimental … well")

C) Lines 60-62 ("Appropriate … task")

D) Lines 64-66 ("Some work … user")

42

Which choice is supported by the passage and by the information in the graph?

A) Memory is stored mostly in the entorhinal region, and response time is governed by the hippocampus.

B) Memory is stored mostly in the hippocampus, and response time is governed by the entorhinal region.

C) Electrical stimulation to the entorhinal region and hippocampus leads to slower processing speeds in the brain.

D) Electrical stimulation to certain regions of the brain can increase the speed of task completion in a game.

CONTINUE

Questions 43-52 are based on the following passage.

This passage is adapted from Arthur Henry Howard Heming, *The Drama of the Forests*, originally published in 1921.

My traveling companion was a "Free Trader," whose name was Spear—a tall, stoop-shouldered man with heavy eyebrows and a shaggy, drooping mustache. The way we met was amusing. It happened in a certain frontier town. His first question was as to whether I was single. His second, as to whether my time was my own. Then he slowly looked me over from head to foot. He seemed to be measuring my stature and strength and to be noting the color of my eyes and hair.

Narrowing his vision, he scrutinized me more carefully than before, for now he seemed to be reading my character—if not my soul. Then, smiling, he blurted out:

"Come, be my guest for a couple of weeks. Will you?"

I laughed.

He frowned. But on realizing that my mirth was caused only by surprise, he smiled again and let flow a vivid description of a place he called Spearhead. It was the home of the northern fur trade. It was the center of a great timber region. It was the heart of a vast fertile belt that was rapidly becoming the greatest of all farming districts. It virtually stood over the very vault that contained the richest veins of mineral to be found in the whole Dominion—at least that's what he said—and he also assured me that the Government had realized it too, for was it not going to hew a provincial highway clean through the forest to Spearhead? Was it not going to build a fleet of steamers to ply upon the lakes and rivers in that section? And was it not going to build a line of railroad to the town itself? In fact, he also impressed upon me that Spearhead was a town created for young men who were not averse to becoming wealthy in whatever line of business they might choose. It seemed that great riches were already there and had but to be lifted. Would I go?

But when I explained that although I was single, and quite free, I was not a businessman, he became crestfallen, but presently revived enough to exclaim:

"Well, what are you?"

"An artist," I replied.

"Oh, I see! Well … we need an artist very badly. You'll have the field all to yourself in Spearhead. Besides, your pictures of the fur trade and of pioneer life would eventually become historical and bring you no end of wealth. You had better come. Better decide right away, or some other artist chap will get ahead of you."

But when I further explained that I was going to spend the winter in the wilderness, that I had already written to the Hudson's Bay Factor at Fort Consolation and that he was expecting me, Spear gloated:

"Bully boy!" and slapping me on the shoulder, he chuckled: "Why, my town is just across the lake from Fort Consolation. A mere five-mile paddle, old chap, and remember, I extend to you the freedom of Spearhead in the name of its future mayor. And, man alive, I'm leaving for there tomorrow morning in a big four-fathom birch bark. Be my guest. It won't cost you a farthing, and we'll make the trip together."

I gladly accepted. Free Trader Spear was a character, and I afterward learned that he was an Oxford University man, who, having failed, left for Canada, entered the service of the Hudson's Bay Company, and had finally been moved to Fort Consolation where he served seven years, learned the fur-trade business, and resigned to become a "free trader," as all fur traders are called who carry on business in opposition to "The Great Company." We were eight days upon the trip, but, strange to say, during each day's travel toward Spearhead, his conversation in reference to that thriving town made it appear to grow smaller and smaller, until at last it actually dwindled down to such a point, that, about sunset on the day we were to arrive, he turned to me and casually remarked: "Presently you'll see Fort Consolation and the Ojibwa village beyond.

CONTINUE

Spearhead is just across the lake, and by the bye, my boy, I forgot to tell you that Spearhead is just my log shack. But it's a nice little place, and you'll like it when you pay us a visit."

43

Which of the following provides the most reasonable summary of the passage?

A) A businessman receives a rare financial opportunity that he finds impossible to pass up.

B) An explorer undertakes a journey that he later regrets.

C) A well-educated fur trader attempts to succeed independently.

D) A man is persuaded into undertaking a trip under false pretenses.

44

Spear's tone can best be described as

A) enthusiastic insistence.

B) reluctant acceptance.

C) zealous conviction.

D) restrained confidence.

45

The suggestion that Spear was reading the narrator's soul (line 13) serves to

A) highlight Spear's mystical inclinations.

B) emphasize the intensity of Spear's visual inspection.

C) imply that the narrator has something to hide.

D) illustrate Spear's ability to judge the character of a stranger.

46

As used in line 25, "richest" most nearly means

A) wealthiest.

B) most opulent.

C) most expensive.

D) most bountiful.

47

Which of the following does Spear assure the narrator that he will gain if he comes to Spearhead?

A) The opportunity to make a great deal of money

B) A life of independence and adventure

C) The reputation of one who opposes The Great Company

D) A tranquility which could not be found in other cities

48

Which choice provides the best evidence for the answer to the previous question?

A) Lines 22-24 ("It was … districts")

B) Lines 46-48 ("Besides … wealth")

C) Lines 58-60 ("A mere … mayor")

D) Lines 74-77 ("We … and smaller")

CONTINUE

49

As used in line 59, "extend" most nearly means

A) expand.

B) increase.

C) proffer.

D) exert.

50

Which of the following best describes the current relationship between Spear and the Hudson's Bay Company?

A) Spear trades in competition with the Hudson's Bay Company.

B) Spear lives in subservience to the Hudson's Bay Company.

C) The Hudson's Bay Company is pointedly disinterested in Spear's activities.

D) The Hudson's Bay Company appreciates the efforts of free traders like Spear.

51

Which choice provides the best evidence for the answer to the previous question?

A) Lines 1-4 ("My traveling … mustache")

B) Lines 20-21 ("It was … fur trade")

C) Lines 39-42 ("But when … are you")

D) Lines 71-73 ("and resigned … Company")

52

The final paragraph of the passage (lines 82-85) serves mainly to

A) describe the town of Spearhead in detail.

B) expose the true intentions of the narrator's companion.

C) reveal how the narrator was misled by his companion.

D) indicate the precise location of the narrator's destination.

STOP

If you complete this section before the end of your allotted time, check your work on this section only. Do NOT use the time to work on another section.

Section 2

Writing and Language Test

35 MINUTES, 44 QUESTIONS

Turn to Section 2 of your answer sheet to answer the questions in this section.

DIRECTIONS

Every passage comes with a set of questions. Some questions will ask you to consider how the writer might revise the passage to improve the expression of ideas. Other questions will ask you to consider correcting potential errors in sentence structure, usage, or punctuation. There may be one or more graphics that you will need to consult as you revise and edit the passage.

Some questions will refer to a portion of the passage that has been underlined. Other questions will refer to a particular spot in a passage or ask that you consider the passage in full.

After you read the passage, select the answers to questions that most effectively improve the passage's writing quality or that adjust the passage to follow the conventions of standard written English. Many questions give you the option to select "NO CHANGE." Select that option in cases where you think the relevant part of the passage should remain as it currently is.

Questions 1-11 are based on the following passage.

Good Work: Praising Effort over Intelligence

Our culture tends to place high value on natural ability as a measure of our potential. We often praise our children more for their talent than for their effort or ambition. We exalt musical or athletic prodigies, whose early successes seem to promise great things for the future, in the sincere belief that we are encouraging them to pursue their potential. [1]

Social science research has indicated that praising children for their talent instead of their effort can cause them to feel constrained by their own perceived limits. An influential study by Stanford psychologist

1

Which choice most effectively sets up the information that follows?

A) Nevertheless, children should be shielded from criticism.

B) Therefore, children should be taught that they can overcome any obstacle through hard work and perseverance alone.

C) However, praising children for talent over effort may actually be stifling their development.

D) Accordingly, we should praise children for recognizing their own strengths and following them.

CONTINUE

Carol Dweck **2** identified the different effects of these two types of praise. Dweck and a colleague, Claudia Mueller, conducted a study with 128 children ranging in age from 10 to 12. Each child was given a set of moderately challenging puzzles. Regardless of **3** they performance on the puzzles, all the children were told that they had done well. Some children **4** were praised in that instance for their intelligence in particular, while others were praised for their effort.

2

Which choice best supports the statement made in the previous sentence?

A) NO CHANGE
B) identified how artistic and athletic prodigies perform in solving puzzles.
C) explored why some kids do well when they get praised for their effort while others don't.
D) identified ways parents can discover what natural talents their children possess.

3

A) NO CHANGE
B) his or her
C) their
D) him or her

4

A) NO CHANGE
B) were praised for their intelligence
C) were praised and complimented for their intelligence
D) were praised for their intellect and intelligence

CONTINUE

After receiving this praise, each child was asked whether he or she wanted to continue working on fairly easy problems or to move on to harder ones that would be 5 educational; but might not make the student "look smart." When presented with this choice, the students who had been praised for their intelligence 6 tend to ask for the easier puzzles. Furthermore, when these children were later presented with harder puzzles, they reported feeling very discouraged if they could not complete them. Dweck and her colleagues believe these children felt that if solving puzzles meant they were smart, 7 failure to solve them would then mean they were not smart. As a result, they avoided 8 risking failure. They were discouraged when they encountered it. The children who had been praised for effort, on the other hand, were more likely to seek out challenging but educational problems, and were less discouraged by failure.

5

A) NO CHANGE
B) educational but, might
C) educational but might
D) educational. But might

6

A) NO CHANGE
B) would have tended
C) will tend
D) tended

7

A) NO CHANGE
B) if they fail to solve them the that would
C) then failing to solve them would
D) failing would

8

Which choice most effectively combines the sentences at the underlined portion?

A) risking failure; they were also observed to be discouraged
B) risking failure; however, they were discouraged
C) risking failure and were discouraged
D) risking failure, but they were discouraged

CONTINUE

Dweck's work has important implications for how parents and teachers should interact with children—even very intelligent ones. In Dweck's study, students who performed very well on the first set of puzzles responded to praise **9** <u>for they're</u> intelligence in the same way as students who performed less well. This means that even students who do **10** <u>manifest awesome promise</u> could be blocked from reaching their full potential by a fear of failure. **11** <u>Conversely, if children are criticized for not making an effort and then fail to make an effort in the future, that could be called a self-fulfilling prophecy.</u>

9

A) NO CHANGE

B) upon their

C) upon they're

D) for their

10

A) NO CHANGE

B) possess exceptional talents

C) develop smarts

D) show a knack for puzzles

11

The writer is considering deleting the underlined sentence. Should the writer do this?

A) Yes, because it contradicts information provided earlier in the passage.

B) Yes, because it needlessly introduces a new and distracting idea at the end of the passage.

C) No, because it suggests a tantalizing possibility for future investigation.

D) No, because it supports the idea that Dweck's research has implications for how parents and teachers should interact with children.

CONTINUE

Questions 12-22 are based on the following passage.

On Exhibit: Museum Professionals

The United States has 35,000 museums. If you visit one of these museums, **12** one can see pieces of art, historical documents, or scientific models. What you may not **13** see are the many people who work behind the scenes to collect, restore, and improve the collections of museums. The dedicated professionals that work for museums are **14** responsible for restoring, preserving, and promoting the treasures that museums hold.

Overseeing the museum's historical archives are its archivists. Archivists take care of records and documents, such as letters, diaries, maps, films, and **15** audio recordings and it is their job to preserve these records so that they can be accessed by both researchers and the general public. To properly preserve documents and records, archivists need to have an understanding of their unique physical properties. An archivist may need to **16** understand, for example, the conditions necessary to safely store papyrus, vellum, paper, or film media. Some archivists also create electronic versions of documents so that the information can be easily distributed. Perhaps most importantly, archivists maintain digital databases that keep track of the documents in a museum and those that are being borrowed. Without this information, it would be impossible to keep track of these valuable pieces of history.

12

A) NO CHANGE
B) one could see
C) you can see
D) someone could see

13

A) NO CHANGE
B) be seeing is
C) see is
D) seeing are

14

A) NO CHANGE
B) culpable
C) accountable
D) sensible

15

A) NO CHANGE
B) audio recordings, it is also their job to preserve
C) audio recordings: and it is their job to preserve
D) audio recordings; it is their job to preserve

16

A) NO CHANGE
B) understand; for example, the
C) understand, for example the
D) understand for example, the

CONTINUE

17 While archivists care for documents in museums, conservators care for objects. The job of a conservator is to preserve and restore important objects. Depending on the museum that they work for, conservators may encounter many different kinds of objects. **18** Because they work with many different types of objects, conservators have to understand both history and chemistry. They have to understand how different materials will **19** decompress over time and what chemicals will best preserve them during this process. Conservators sometimes even use x-rays to determine the best way to protect or restore an aging object.

17

Which choice establishes the most effective transition between paragraphs?

A) NO CHANGE

B) While most people think documents are more important than objects,

C) Even though archivists care only for documents,

D) Since archivists have complete control of documents,

18

Which choice, inserted here, most effectively adds support for the previous sentence?

A) Conservators have to possess a broad range of skills and techniques to satisfy the requirements of their profession.

B) They also have to work with many different populations, including collectors and tourists.

C) A museum's collection might contain ivory carvings, bronze works, paintings, or even pieces of ancient buildings.

D) The objects that conservators work with are often expensive and precious.

19

A) NO CHANGE

B) decompose

C) denude

D) renege

CONTINUE

Conservators may also design replacements for missing parts of an object or create replicas for use in other museums. Some conservators become experts in a specific type of object or material. **20** However, some conservators specialize in restoring and preserving objects made of stone. Expert conservators may be asked to travel around the world in order to protect the world's supply of historical objects.

These are professions for people with a passion for learning and teaching. Most conservator and archivist positions require at least a Master's degree, and archivists and conservators continue to study and learn throughout **21** their life. **22** Many people, including archivists and conservators, enjoy reading books or visiting museums in their spare time.

20

A) NO CHANGE
B) On the other hand,
C) Therefore,
D) For instance,

21

A) NO CHANGE
B) each of their life
C) their lives
D) one's life

22

The writer wants to end the passage with a sentence that supports the central idea of this paragraph without repeating information. Which choice best accomplishes this goal?

A) NO CHANGE
B) Most will take graduate-level courses to enhance their knowledge.
C) Many of them study disciplines that will enable them to expand their opportunities for job growth.
D) They also have the satisfaction of knowing that their jobs help people of all ages learn about history, art, and science.

CONTINUE

Questions 23-33 are based on the following passage.

Flexing Your Brain

Individual practitioners of meditation have long touted its mental benefits, but **23** in recent decades it has now also been a subject of scientific interest—and the evidence suggests that the practice may actually promote brain health. Researchers have been conducting meditation studies since the 1950s, and it is now well-established that meditation can cause people to become more relaxed and that long-term practice can change the way that the brain works. In 2005, a group of scientists at Yale University conducted a study to investigate whether meditation might also **24** affecting the physical growth and development of certain parts of the brain.

[1] Previous studies had demonstrated that the physical structures of the brain **25** are changed by tasks that repeatedly activate specific areas of the brain. [2] In other words, just as muscles grow or shrink in response to use or disuse, different parts of the brain can physically change in response to how frequently they are used. [3] MRI scans reveal thickening of brain tissue in areas of the brain which have been **26** repeatedly activated over and over by stimulation. [4] These changes in brain structure are detectable through the use of magnetic resonance imaging, or MRI, which creates three-dimensional maps of the brain or other organs. [5] The Yale team hypothesized that regular meditation might cause similar thickening. **27**

23

A) NO CHANGE
B) in decades it has
C) in the most recent decades it has now also
D) in recent decades it has also

24

A) NO CHANGE
B) affect
C) effecting
D) effect

25

A) NO CHANGE
B) is changed by
C) was changed by
D) are changing by

26

A) NO CHANGE
B) activated again and again by repeated stimulation.
C) repeatedly activated by stimulation.
D) activated by stimulation.

27

To make this paragraph most logical, sentence 4 should be placed

A) where it is now.
B) before sentence 1.
C) before sentence 3.
D) after sentence 5.

CONTINUE

28 To confirm these findings, the Yale team designed a study to compare the brains of participants from two groups: a control group of non-meditators, and an experimental group of seasoned meditators. The researchers were most concerned with areas of the brain associated 29 with attention and sensory processing, which are activated during meditation. They designated these areas of the brain the "search area," used MRI scans to map out brain tissue thickness in certain search areas of the brain, and compared the brain scans of meditators with 30 the brains of non-meditators.

28

Which choice results in the most effective transition from the previous paragraph?

A) NO CHANGE
B) To verify this result,
C) To test this hypothesis,
D) To learn more about MRIs,

29

A) NO CHANGE
B) in
C) by
D) to

30

A) NO CHANGE
B) non-meditators.
C) the brain scans of non-meditators.
D) the search areas of non-meditators.

CONTINUE

The team's results indicated that tissue in the search area was indeed **31** <u>much less thick</u> overall in meditators' brains than in non-meditators'. Furthermore, while older subjects tended to have thinner brain tissue in the search area, age differences were much less pronounced within the group of meditators. While the study did not follow individuals over time, the differences between these groups do suggest that meditation may help to slow the thinning of brain tissue that takes place throughout the brain as people age.

The study did not determine whether the increased thickness was the result of larger **32** <u>brain cells; new brain cells or the growth</u> of blood vessels in the brain. However, any of these causes would likely be good for brain function. That gives researchers some reason to believe that meditation is likely to help **33** <u>continuously improve brain function over time.</u>

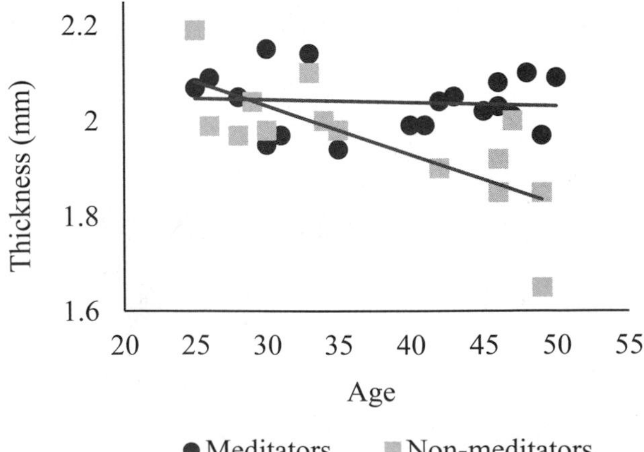

31

Which choice is most consistent with the information provided in the graph?

A) NO CHANGE
B) healthier
C) somewhat thicker
D) somewhat younger

32

A) NO CHANGE
B) brain cells; new brain cells; or the growth
C) brain cells; new brain cells, or the growth
D) brain cells, new brain cells, or the growth

33

Which choice is most consistent with evidence presented earlier in the passage?

A) NO CHANGE
B) generate new brain cells to replace those that die.
C) preserve healthy brain function over time.
D) preserve the function of brain areas even as they become thinner over time.

CONTINUE

Questions 34-44 are based on the following passage.

The Great American Ballet

A lighted Christmas tree grows larger and larger until it fills half the stage. A pugnacious, many-headed mouse is defeated in battle by a living doll. Twenty-foot windows open onto a landscape awhirl with snow.

Every year since 1954, George Balanchine's *The Nutcracker* has delighted the thousands of families who come—some once, some a few times, some annually—to see this hallmark work of American ballet. **34** Performed around Christmas in theaters across the United States, *The Nutcracker* might not seem to be an obvious candidate for the title of "great American ballet." However, both its origins and **35** its reception have marked it as essentially American.

Balanchine choreographed *The Nutcracker* for New York City Ballet, **36** the company he had founded; with Lincoln Kirstein six years earlier. Balanchine was Russian by birth, but **37** Kirstein was an American. Kirstein longed to bring ballet, which was chiefly performed in Europe, to an American audience. Kirstein's love of ballet was kindled when, as a child, he saw the Russian ballerina Anna Pavlova perform on tour in Boston. But as much as he admired them, his hope was not merely to bring European artists to America: he wanted the art form itself to take root in his native soil.

34

Which choice would best support the second part of the sentence?

A) NO CHANGE
B) As the single most popular ballet in the United States
C) Choreographed by a Russian, to Russian music based on a German story
D) Introduced to the United States in San Francisco and made famous in New York

35

A) NO CHANGE
B) their reception have marked them
C) their reception has marked it
D) its reception have marked them

36

A) NO CHANGE
B) the company he had founded with Lincoln Kirstein six years earlier.
C) the company, he had founded with Lincoln Kirstein, six years earlier.
D) the company he had, founded with Lincoln Kirstein six years earlier.

37

Which choice most effectively combines the sentences at the underlined portion?

A) Kirstein, although he was an American, longed
B) Kirstein was an American, and also longed
C) Kirstein was an American who longed
D) American-born Kirstein longed

CONTINUE

[1] Kirstein first saw Balanchine's work in the late '20s in Paris, and he was impressed by **38** its physical vitality and modernism. [2] Balanchine's response, "but, first a school," suited Kirstein's ambitions perfectly. [3] In 1933, he invited the choreographer to move to the United States **39** and had founded an American ballet company. [4] Before staging his ballets with dancers unschooled in European techniques, **40** the dancers needed training. [5] In 1934, Kirstein and Balanchine founded the School of American Ballet, where Balanchine taught a technique that combined elements of the European tradition with **41** backwards notions of his own, many of them inspired by what he saw as the uniquely American qualities of his new ensemble. **42**

38

A) NO CHANGE
B) his
C) their
D) that

39

A) NO CHANGE
B) and found
C) and founding
D) and have founded

40

A) NO CHANGE
B) the dancers needed to train.
C) Balanchine needed to train them.
D) they needed training.

41

A) NO CHANGE
B) shocking thoughts
C) newfangled plans
D) fresh ideas

42

To make this paragraph most logical, sentence 2 should be placed

A) where it is now.
B) before sentence 1.
C) after sentence 3.
D) before sentence 5.

CONTINUE

The pair's attempts at founding a professional company were interrupted by World War II **43** but eventually reached their fruition with the event of the establishment of New York City Ballet in 1948. *The Nutcracker* was not the first ballet Balanchine staged for his new company, but it was his most ambitious project to date. **44** The dances for the children in Balanchine's production of *The Nutcracker* are choreographed to be easier than those of adults, but are still a joy to watch.

43

A) NO CHANGE

B) but reached fruition eventually when New York City Ballet was established at last in 1948.

C) but finally reached fruition with the establishment of New York City Ballet in 1948.

D) but reached their eventual fruition, finally, with New York City Ballet's establishment in 1948.

44

Which choice of conclusion best links the final sentences to the main point of the passage as a whole?

A) NO CHANGE

B) Balanchine would go on to choreograph dozens of other shows for American companies and companies around the world.

C) *The Nutcracker* is a major source of revenue for major American ballet companies today, generating up to 40% of all ticket sales.

D) *The Nutcracker* quickly became an American classic, performed annually not only by New York City Ballet but also by regional companies across the country.

STOP

If you complete this section before the end of your allotted time, check your work on this section only. Do NOT use the time to work on another section.

Section 3

Math Test – No Calculator

25 MINUTES, 20 QUESTIONS

Turn to Section 3 of your answer sheet to answer the questions in this section.

DIRECTIONS

Questions **1-15** ask you to solve a problem, select the best answer among four choices, and fill in the corresponding circle on your answer sheet. Questions **16-20** ask you to solve a problem and enter your answer in the grid provided on your answer sheet. There are detailed instructions on entering answers into the grid before question 16. You may use your test booklet for scratch work.

NOTES

1. You **may not** use a calculator.
2. Variables and expressions represent real numbers unless stated otherwise.
3. Figures are drawn to scale unless stated otherwise.
4. Figures lie in a plane unless stated otherwise.
5. The domain of a function f is defined as the set of all real numbers x for which $f(x)$ is also a real number, unless stated otherwise.

REFERENCE

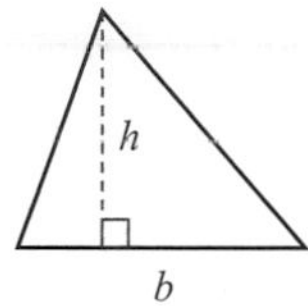

$A = \frac{1}{2}bh$

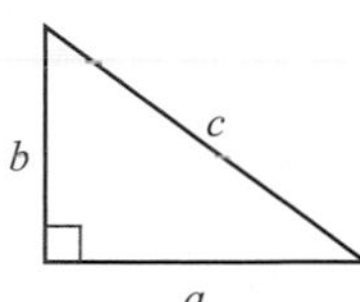

$a^2 + b^2 = c^2$

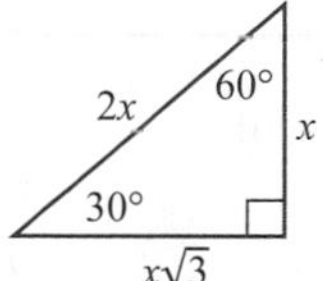

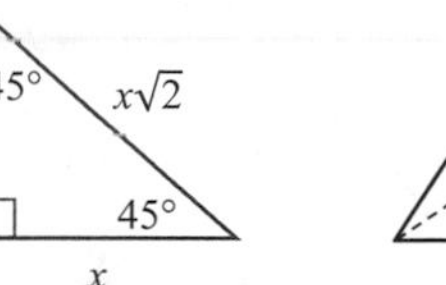

Special Triangles

$V = \frac{1}{3}lwh$

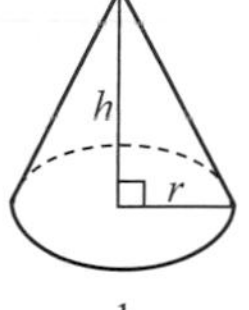

$V = \frac{1}{3}\pi r^2 h$

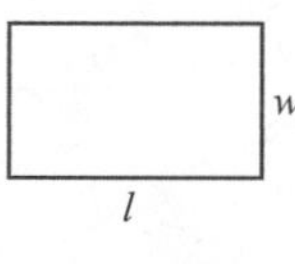

$A = lw$

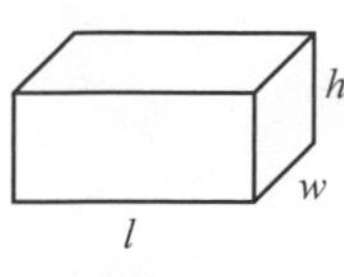

$V = lwh$

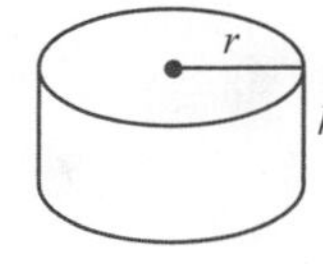

$V = \pi r^2 h$

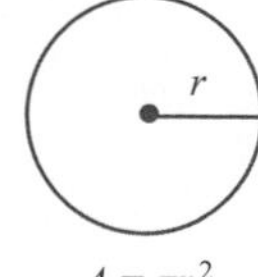

$A = \pi r^2$

$C = 2\pi r$

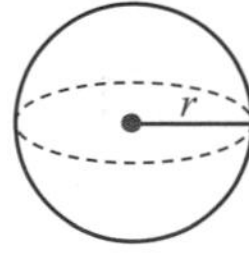

$V = \frac{4}{3}\pi r^3$

There are 360° in a circle.

The sum of the angles in a triangle is 180°.

The number of radians of arc in a circle is 2π.

CONTINUE

1

Which of the following represents the solution set to the inequality $1 \leq -2x + 3$?

A) 

B) 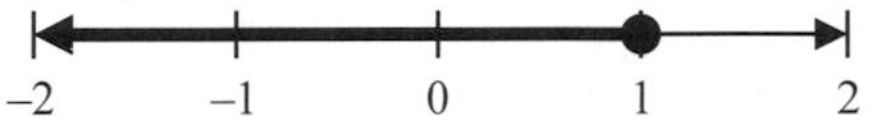 −2 −1 0 1 2

C) 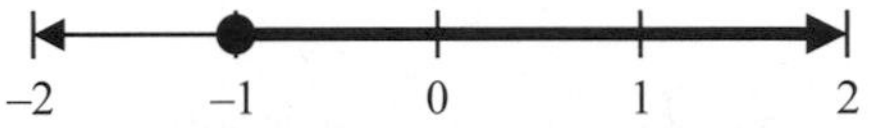 −2 −1 0 1 2

D) 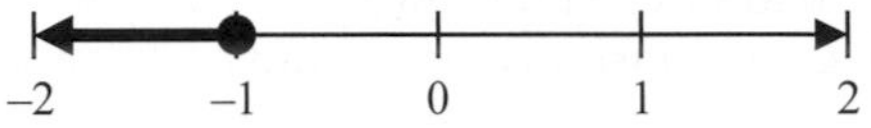 −2 −1 0 1 2

2

The chemical formula for water is H_2O, which indicates that each molecule of water contains two hydrogen atoms and one oxygen atom. A cup of water contains approximately 2.4×10^{25} hydrogen and oxygen atoms combined. How many of these atoms are hydrogen atoms?

A) 8×10^{24}

B) 1.6×10^{25}

C) 2.4×10^{25}

D) 4.8×10^{25}

3

$$3x \geq y - 1$$

Which of the following ordered pairs is NOT a solution to the inequality above?

A) $(-1, -4)$

B) $(0, 0)$

C) $(2, 7)$

D) $(3, 11)$

CONTINUE

4

A gas station charges \$3.39 per gallon of gas and a flat fee of \$2 per transaction. Which of the following graphs represents the cost of a transaction as a function of the number of gallons of gas purchased?

A)

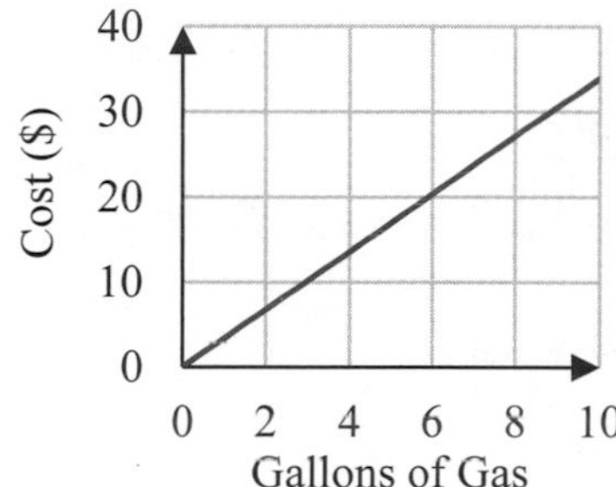

B)

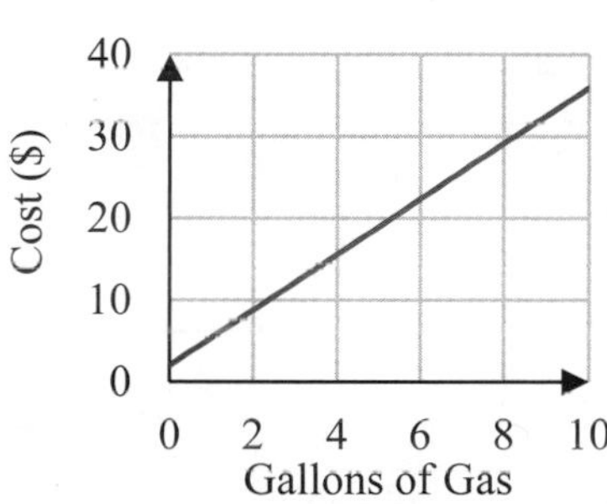

C)

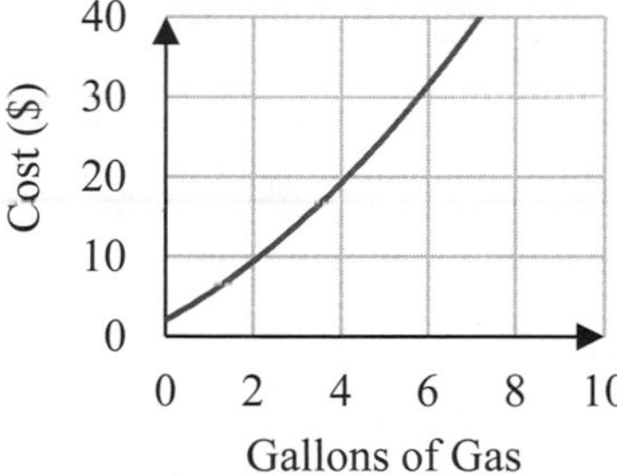

D)

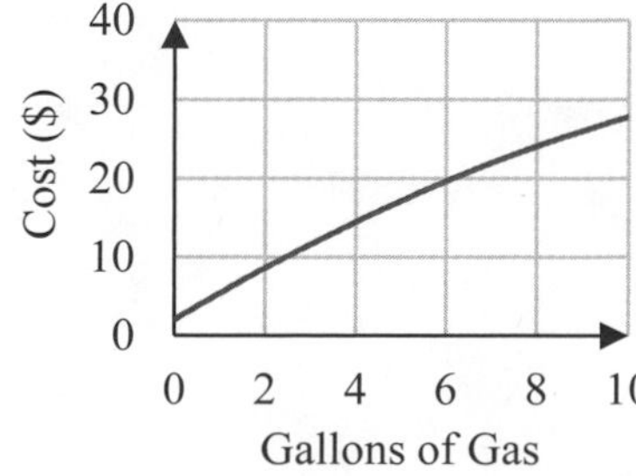

5

100 mg of glucose and 100 mg of compound *A* can be used to create 100 mg glucose-6-p and 100 mg of compound *B*. 100mg of glucose-6-p sells for \$100 and 100mg of *B* sells for \$150. If the lab selling glucose-6-p and compound *B* makes \$2000 of income, how many mg of glucose-6-p does the lab sell?

A) 500

B) 600

C) 800

D) 1,000

6

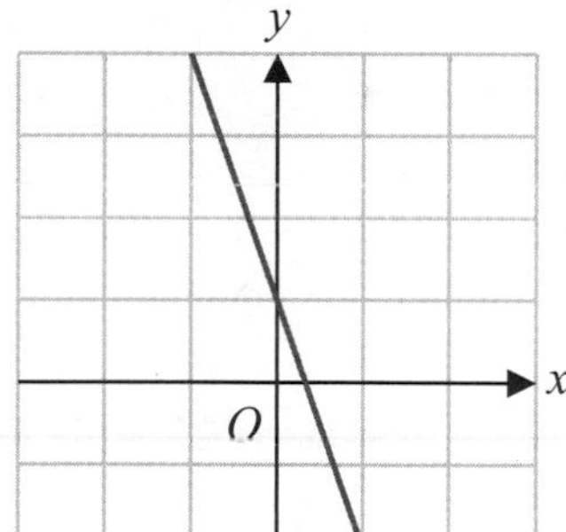

The graph above represents the function $y = mx + b$. Which of the following is the equation for x as a function of y?

A) $x = -my - b$

B) $x = -my + b$

C) $x = \dfrac{y - b}{m}$

D) $x = \dfrac{-y - b}{m}$

CONTINUE

7

	Membership Fee	Locker Rental	Day Fee
Membership	\$100	Free	Free
No Membership	None	\$10	\$7

The table above shows possible rates at a gym. Without a membership, customers pay a fee of \$10 per month for a locker and \$7 per visit. A membership includes a locker and unlimited visits for \$100 per month. How many times per month must a customer go to the gym in order to benefit from purchasing a membership?

A) 13

B) 12

C) 11

D) 2

8

Which of the following equations has exactly one real solution?

A) $x^2 + 6x + 3 = 0$

B) $2x^2 + 6x + 3 = 0$

C) $3x^2 + 6x + 3 = 0$

D) $4x^2 + 6x + 3 = 0$

9

Andre is planning a field trip to a museum for his class of s students. He has \$200 to spend on tickets and meals, and each student gets one meal and one ticket. If tickets cost t dollars each, how much money can Andre spend on each meal?

A) $200 + ts$ dollars

B) $200 - ts$ dollars

C) $\frac{200 + ts}{s}$ dollars

D) $\frac{200 - ts}{s}$ dollars

10

Which of the following expressions is NOT equivalent to the others?

A) $2\sqrt{2x}$

B) $\sqrt{8x}$

C) $\sqrt[4]{16x^2}$

D) $\sqrt[4]{4^2 \times 4x^2}$

CONTINUE

11

For $i = \sqrt{-1}$, which of the following expressions is equivalent to $(5 - i)(2 + 6i)$?

A) $4 + 28i$

B) $11 - 28i$

C) $6 - 28i$

D) $16 + 28i$

12

If $f(x) = \dfrac{x+1}{3x}$ and $g(x) = 2x^2$, what is the value of $f(g(x))$?

A) $\dfrac{2x^2 + 1}{6x^2}$

B) $\dfrac{2y^2 + 1}{6y^2}$

C) $\dfrac{2x^2 + 1}{3x}$

D) $\dfrac{(x + 1)(2y^2)}{3x}$

13

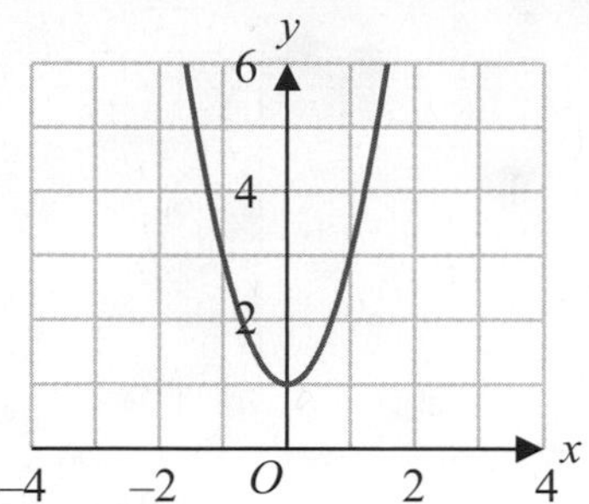

The graph above represents the function $f(x) = ax^2 + c$. This function includes the point (2, 6). If $g(x) = 2f(x)$ and $g(x)$ includes the point (2, b), what is the value of b?

A) 6

B) 12

C) 14

D) 16

CONTINUE

14

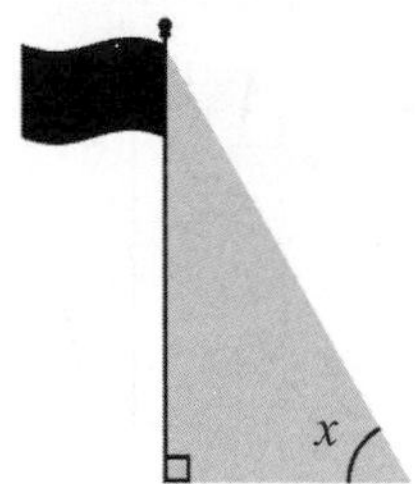

The diagram above shows a flag pole casting a shadow. The distance between the top of the flag pole and end of the shadow is 10. What is the difference between the height of the flag pole and the length of the shadow, in terms of x?

A) $\sin(x) \times 10 - \cos(x) \times 10$

B) $\dfrac{\sin(x)}{10} - \dfrac{\cos(x)}{10}$

C) $\dfrac{2\cos(x) \times 10 - \sin(x) \times 10x^2 + 1}{3x}$

D) $\dfrac{\cos(x)}{10} - \dfrac{\sin(x)}{10}$

15

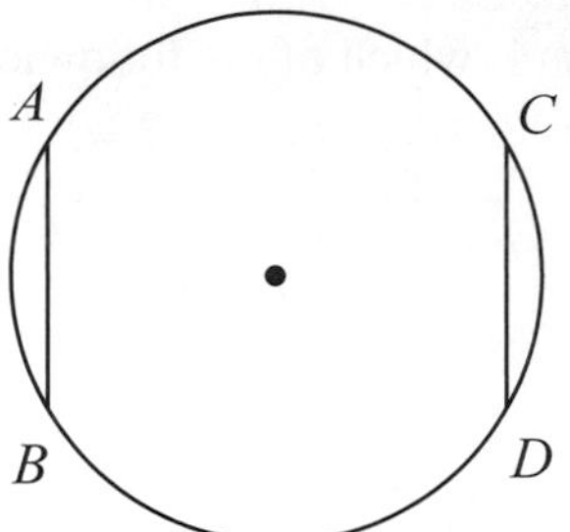

The circle above has a radius r and parallel chords $\overline{AB}$ and $\overline{CD}$. Each chord has a length of r. If a rectangle is formed by connecting the points A, B, C, and D, what is the area of the rectangle?

A) $r\sqrt{3}$

B) $r\sqrt{5}$

C) $r^2\sqrt{3}$

D) $r^2\sqrt{5}$

CONTINUE

DIRECTIONS

Questions **16-20** ask you to solve a problem and enter your answer in the grid provided on your answer sheet. When completing grid-in questions:

1. You are required to bubble in the circles for your answers. It is recommended, but not required, that you also write your answer in the boxes above the columns of circles. Points will be awarded based only on whether the circles are filled in correctly.
2. Fill in only one circle in a column.
3. You can start your answer in any column as long as you can fit in the whole answer.
4. For questions 16-20, no answers will be negative numbers.
5. **Mixed numbers,** such as $4\frac{2}{5}$, must be gridded as decimals or improper fractions, such as 4.4 or as 22/5. "42/5" will be read as "forty-two over five," not as "four and two-fifths."
6. If your answer is a **decimal** with more digits than will fit on the grid, you may round it or cut it off, but you must fill the entire grid.
7. If there are **multiple correct solutions** to a problem, all of them will be considered correct. Enter only **one** on the grid.

5/11	8.4	3/7
.422	.326	.125

CONTINUE

16

Josh has $6.90 in quarters and nickels. If he has the same number of quarters and nickels, how many quarters does Josh have?

17

$$y + 3 = 2x^2 - 5x$$
$$y - 3 = 6x$$
$$x > 0$$

What is a value of x that satisfies the system of equations above?

18

Carlos runs directly towards Xiao at 15 miles per hour. Xiao walks directly toward Carlos at 3 miles per hour. If they meet after 20 minutes, how far apart were they, in miles, before they started moving?

19

$$\sqrt{5x - 4} = 2x - 4$$

What value of x satisfies the equation above?

20

$$2(a^3 + a^2 + 4a - 8) = 2a^3 + 4a^2 - 5a - 1$$

What is one possible value of a for the equation above?

STOP

If you complete this section before the end of your allotted time, check your work on this section only. Do NOT use the time to work on another section.

Section 4

Math Test – Calculator

55 MINUTES, 38 QUESTIONS

Turn to Section 4 of your answer sheet to answer the questions in this section.

DIRECTIONS

Questions **1-30** ask you to solve a problem, select the best answer among four choices, and fill in the corresponding circle on your answer sheet. Questions **31-38** ask you to solve a problem and enter your answer in a grid provided on your answer sheet. There are detailed instructions on entering answers into the grid before question 31. You may use your test booklet for scratch work.

NOTES

1. You **may** use a calculator.
2. Variables and expressions represent real numbers unless stated otherwise.
3. Figures are drawn to scale unless stated otherwise.
4. Figures lie in a plane unless stated otherwise.
5. The domain of a function f is defined as the set of all real numbers x for which $f(x)$ is also a real number, unless stated otherwise.

REFERENCE

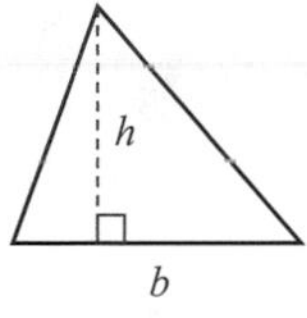

$A = \frac{1}{2}bh$

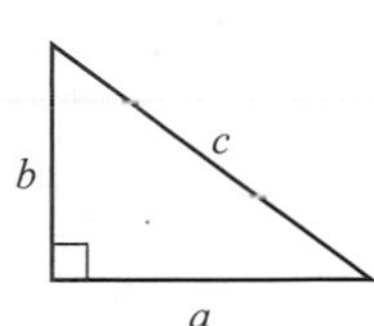

$a^2 + b^2 = c^2$

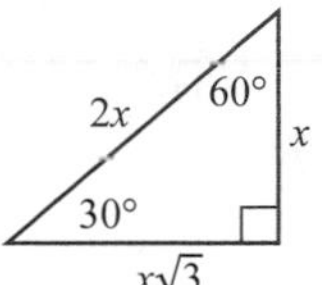

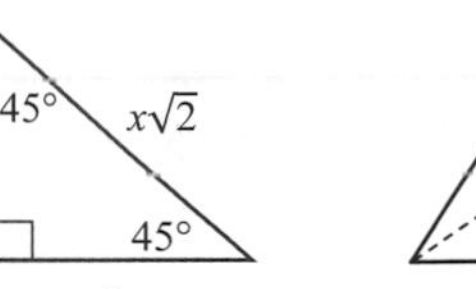

Special Triangles

$V = \frac{1}{3}lwh$

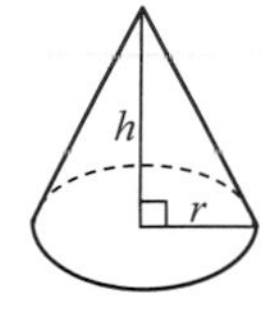

$V = \frac{1}{3}\pi r^2 h$

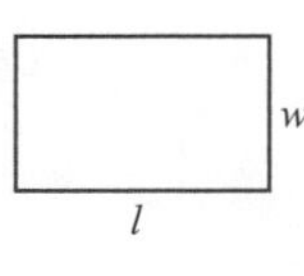

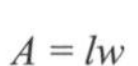

$A = lw$

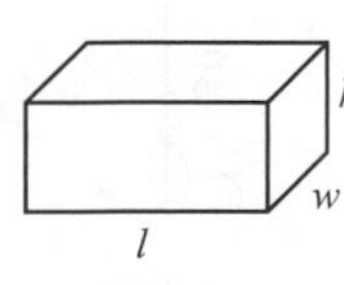

$V = lwh$

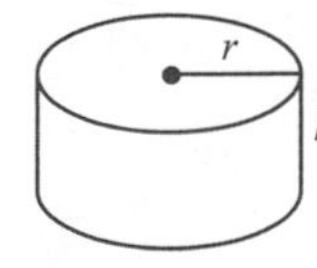

$V = \pi r^2 h$

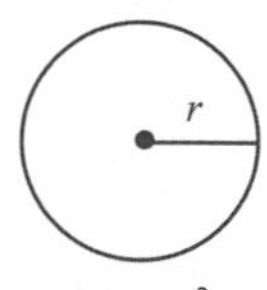

$A = \pi r^2$

$C = 2\pi r$

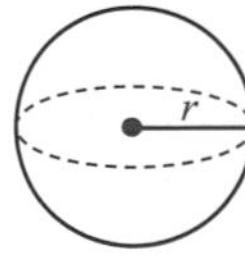

$V = \frac{4}{3}\pi r^3$

There are 360° in a circle.

The sum of the angles in a triangle is 180°.

The number of radians of arc in a circle is 2π.

CONTINUE

1

If $2x - 6 = 4x + 4$, what is the value of x?

A) –5

B) –1

C) 1

D) 5

2

If a and b are both even integers, which of the following must be an odd integer?

I. $(a + 1)(b + 1)$
II. $(a + 1)(b + 2)$
III. $(a - 1)(b + 1)$

A) I and II

B) I and III

C) II and III

D) I, II, and III

3

A tree is planted when it is 3 feet tall. If the tree's growth rate is linear, which of the following graphs could represent its height over time?

A)

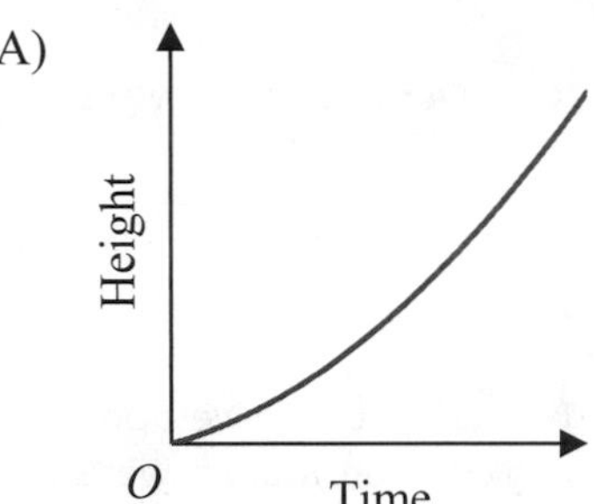

B)

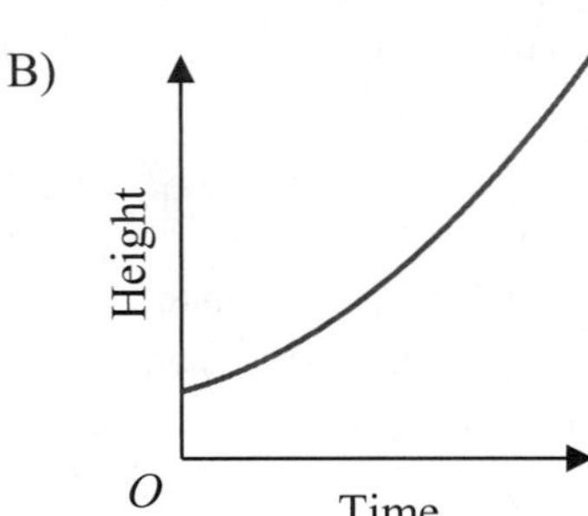

C)

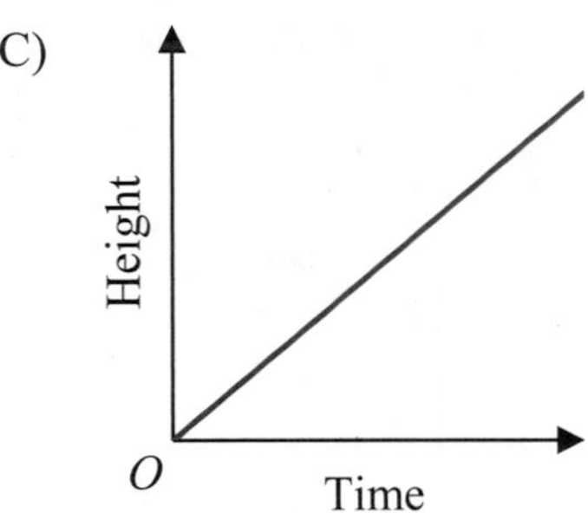

D)

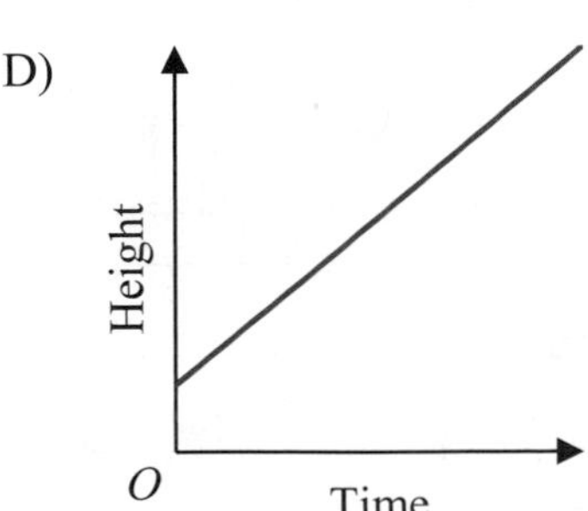

CONTINUE

4

$$3x + y < 8$$

How many pairs of positive integers (x, y) satisfy the inequality above?

A) 1

B) 3

C) 5

D) 7

5

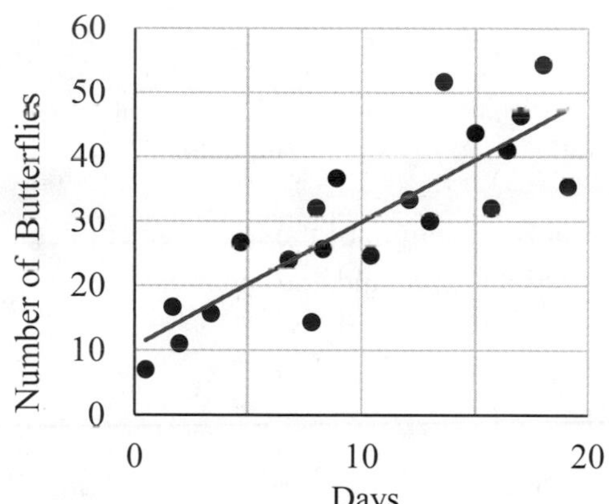

The scatterplot above shows the number of Monarch butterflies over a three-week period. Based on the line of best fit, which of the following values is closest to the average daily increase in the number of Monarch butterflies?

A) 0.5

B) 2

C) 10

D) 40

6

a is 8% of b and b is 150% greater than c. If c is 15, what is the value of a?

A) 4

B) 3

C) 2

D) 1

7

	Symptoms	No Symptoms
Vaccinated	216	1134
Not Vaccinated	584	336

A hospital collected data from patients who were exposed to a certain virus. The hospital recorded whether the patients had been vaccinated for the virus and whether they showed symptoms. The data is summarized in the chart above. What percentage of patients who showed symptoms had been vaccinated?

A) 16%

B) 27%

C) 37%

D) 73%

CONTINUE

8

If $3x = \frac{1}{2}y$, what is $\frac{y}{3}$ in terms of x?

A) $2x$

B) $\frac{3}{2}x$

C) x

D) $\frac{2}{3}x$

9

$$p(x) = |2x - 5|$$

$p(x)$ is defined above. What is the value of $p(2) + p(-2)$?

A) –10

B) –8

C) 8

D) 10

10

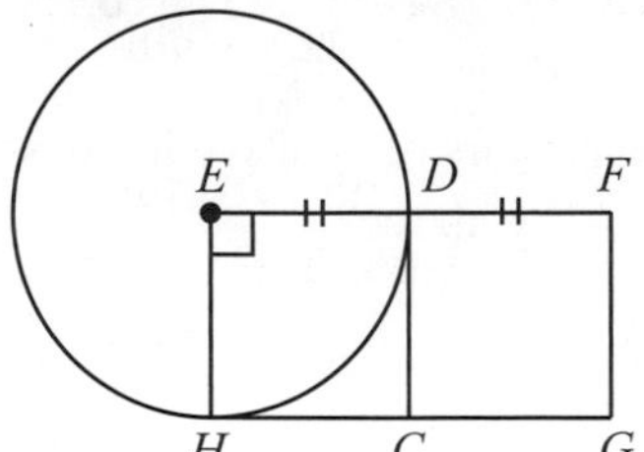

In the diagram above, the circumference of circle E is 6π. What is the area of rectangle $EFGH$?

A) 3π

B) 18

C) 24

D) 12π

11

What is the length of the line segment beginning at the point (–2, 3) and ending at the point (1, 7)?

A) 0.75

B) 3

C) 4

D) 5

CONTINUE

Questions 12 and 13 refer to the following information.

A chemist is working with two groups of elements. He finds that each of the elements has either one, two, or three stable isotopes, which are forms of an element with different numbers of neutrons. He records the data in the charts below.

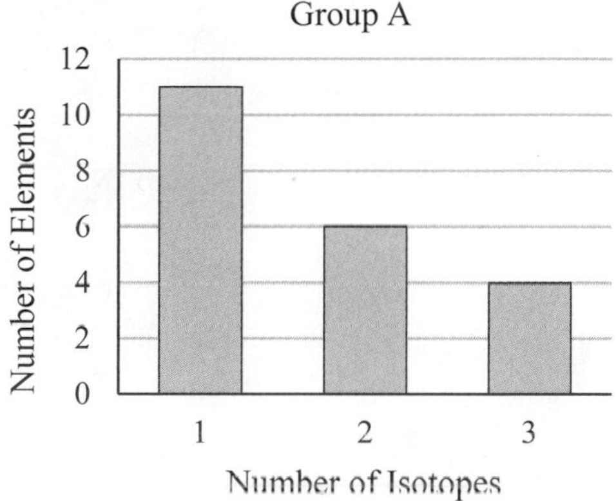

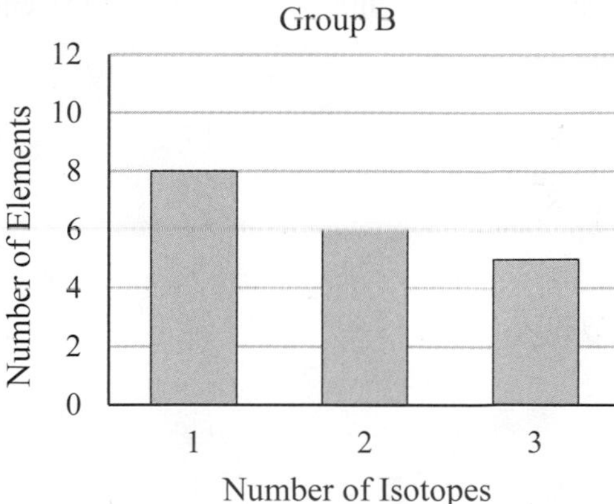

12

Approximately what percentage of elements in Group A have two stable isotopes?

A) 14%

B) 19%

C) 29%

D) 48%

13

Which of the following statements correctly compares the medians and modes of the data from the two groups of elements?

A) Group A's data have a smaller median than Group B's. Group A's data have the same mode as Group B's.

B) Group A's data have a larger median than Group B. Group A's data have the same mode as Group B's.

C) Group A's data have the same median as Group B's. Group A's data have a smaller mode than Group B.

D) Group A's data have the same median as Group B's. Group A's data have a larger mode than Group B's.

CONTINUE

14

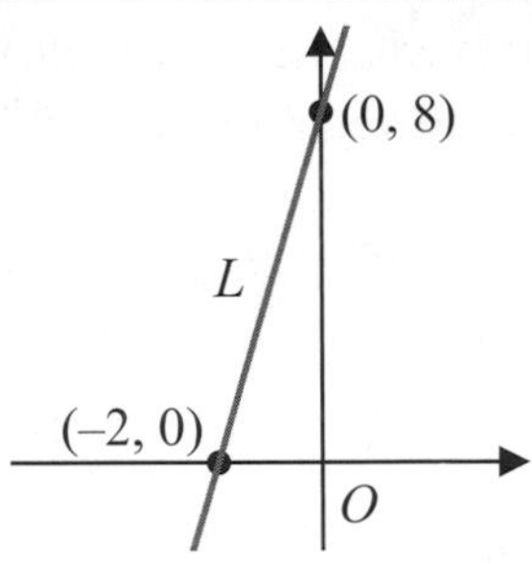

Which of the following equations describes a line that is perpendicular to line L above?

A) $y = 4x + 8$

B) $y = -4x + 8$

C) $y = \frac{1}{4}x + 8$

D) $y = -\frac{1}{4}x + 8$

15

A car dealer buys a car from a manufacturer. The dealer increases the price of the car by 20% to \$36,000. The dealer then sells the car at a 5% discount. What is the dealer's total profit from the sale of the car?

A) \$4,200

B) \$6,000

C) \$7,200

D) \$9,000

16

$$\frac{4(x+1)-1}{3} = \frac{8-(5-x)}{5}$$

What is the value of x in the equation above?

A) $-\frac{24}{17}$

B) $-\frac{6}{17}$

C) $-\frac{24}{23}$

D) $-\frac{6}{23}$

17

Which of the following expressions is NOT equal to $3\sqrt{32x}$?

A) $12\sqrt{2x}$

B) $6\sqrt{8x}$

C) $4\sqrt{12x}$

D) $\sqrt{288x}$

CONTINUE

18

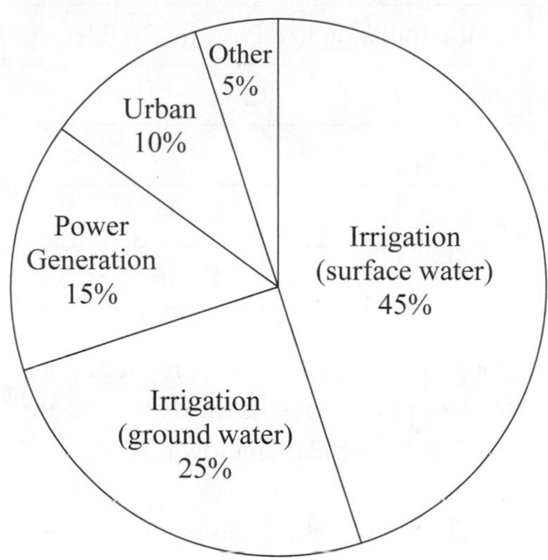

The chart above shows the distribution of water use in the South Platte River Basin. If the total water use is 4 billion gallons per day, how many gallons of water are used for irrigation every week?

A) 1.8 billion

B) 2.8 billion

C) 12.6 billion

D) 19.6 billion

19

Macey and Sam both have \$100 in their bank accounts. Each year Macey's bank increases her balance by \$10, and Sam's bank increases his balance by 10%. If Macey and Sam do not deposit or withdraw any money, what is the difference between Macey's balance and Sam's balance after 5 years?

A) Macey's account will have \$11.05 more than Sam's account.

B) Macey's account will have the same balance as Sam's account.

C) Macey's account will have \$9.05 less than Sam's account.

D) Macey's account will have \$11.05 less than Sam's account.

20

For which of the following functions is $f(2) < f(-2)$?

A) $f(x) = \frac{3}{x}$

B) $f(x) = 3x^2 + 3$

C) $f(x) = 3 - x^3$

D) $f(x) = -3$

CONTINUE

21

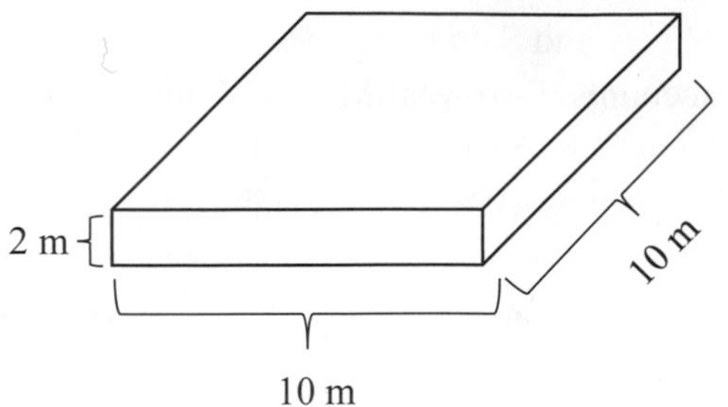

The width, depth, and length of a rectangular pool are shown above. If a pump fills the pool at a rate of 55 gallons per minute, how many hours will it take to fill half of the pool? (1 cubic meter equals approximately 264 gallons.)

A) 8

B) 16

C) 20

D) 30

22

$$y - x = -3x$$

Given the equation above, what is the value of $\frac{x}{y}$?

A) $-\frac{1}{4}$

B) $-\frac{1}{2}$

C) -2

D) -4

23

Wolf Population in a Protected Wilderness Area	
Year	Count of Wolves
0	20
6	27
12	36

A group of scientists have reintroduced a species of wolf into a protected wilderness area and are measuring the population growth, as summarized in the table above. The scientists modeled the population change as increasing at a rate of approximately 5% each year. Which of the following functions approximates the relationship between the wolf population, P, and time in years, t?

A) $P = 20 + 0.05t$

B) $P = 20 \times 1.05 \times t$

C) $P = 20(0.05)^t$

D) $P = 20(1.05)^t$

24

$$P = \frac{V^2}{R}$$

In an electrical circuit, the power, P, of the circuit is related to the voltage, V, and the resistance, R, as shown in the equation above. If both the voltage and the resistance are doubled, what happens to the value of P?

A) P is halved.

B) P is not changed.

C) P is doubled.

D) P is tripled.

CONTINUE

Questions 25 and 26 refer to the following information.

A survey was conducted to determine the types of vehicles owned by people in different age groups. The table below displays a summary of the survey results.

Car Type by Age

Age	SUV/ Minivan	Sedan/ Coupe	Truck	Electric/ Hybrid	None	Total
18-29	9,357	6,980	3,537	3,583	3,498	**26,955**
30-49	11,439	13,476	4,343	3,953	2,309	**35,520**
50-69	10,964	14,055	1,506	1,068	2,004	**29,597**
70+	7,033	15,610	680	792	5,377	**29,492**
Total	**38,793**	**50,121**	**10,066**	**9,396**	**13,188**	**121,564**

25

According to the table, which age group contained the smallest percentage of people who did not own a vehicle?

A) 18-29
B) 30-49
C) 50-69
D) 70+

26

According to the table, what is the approximate percent probability that the owner of a hybrid or electric car is 50 or more years old?

A) 3%
B) 11%
C) 20%
D) 24%

CONTINUE

27

Which of the following is NOT a solution to the equation $\sin(x) = \sin^2(x)$?

A) π

B) $\frac{\pi}{2}$

C) $-\frac{\pi}{2}$

D) $-\pi$

28

A construction worker uses a chain-link fence to completely enclose a rectangular area. The worker has 40 feet of fencing material. Which of the graphs below shows the total enclosed area as a function of the length of one side of the rectangle? (Note: Graphs are not drawn to scale.)

A)
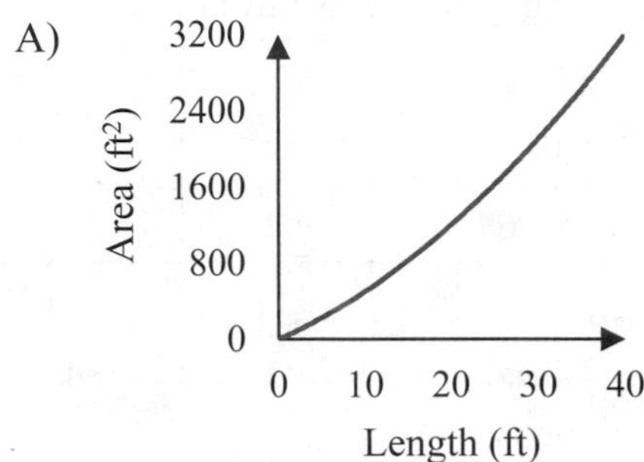

B)
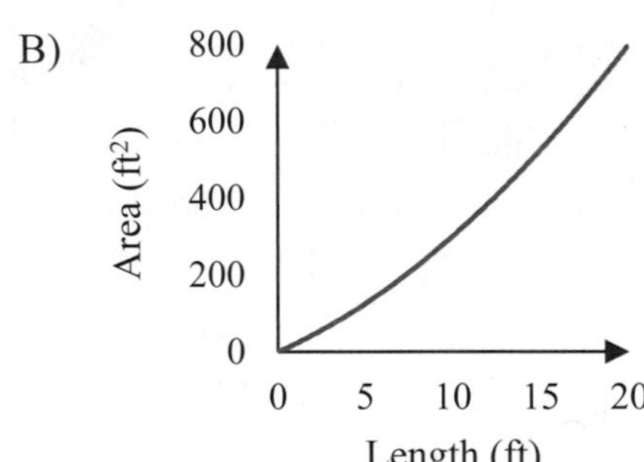

C)
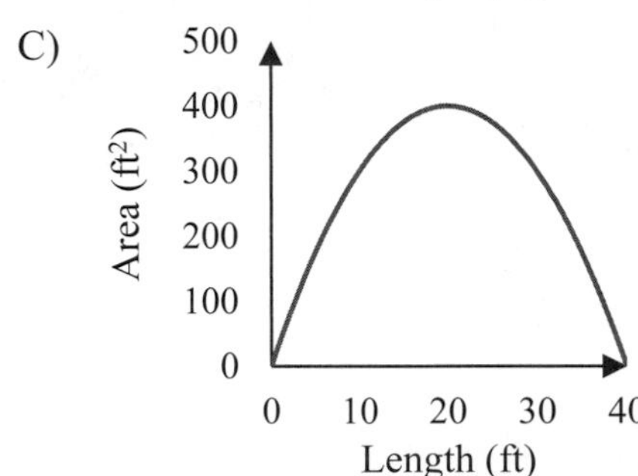

D)
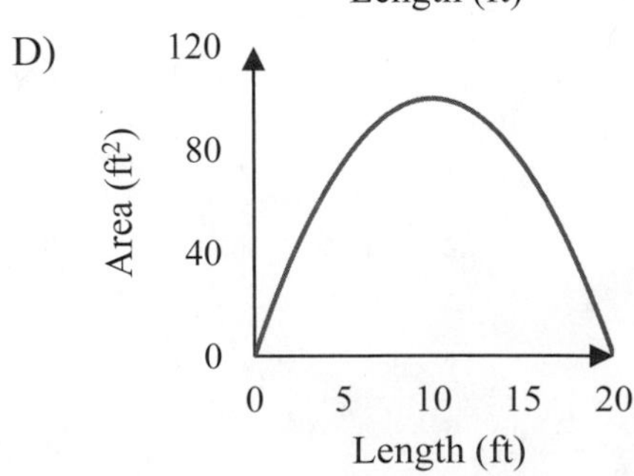

CONTINUE

29

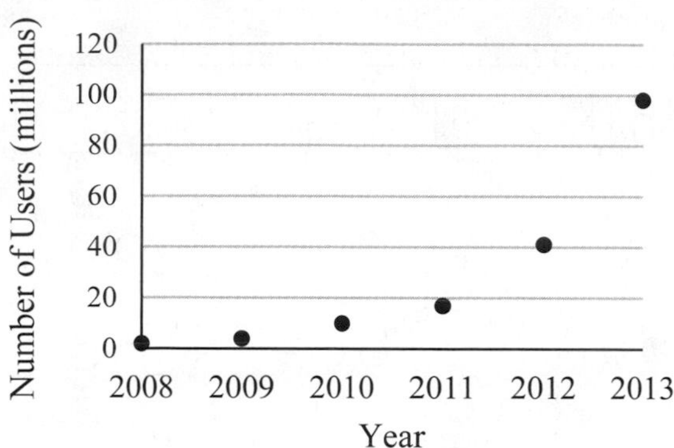

The scatter plot above shows the popularity of a social media site created in 2008. If y is the number of years since the site was founded and N is the number of people, in millions, using the site, which of the following functions best describes the relationship between y and N?

A) $N(y) = 20y$

B) $N(y) = 2.5^y$

C) $N(y) = -15y^2 + 100y$

D) $N(y) = 15y^2 - 100$

30

$\frac{9x^2}{3x+1}$ is rewritten as $A + \frac{1}{3x+1}$. What is A in terms of x?

A) $3x - 1$

B) $3x + 1$

C) $9x - 1$

D) $9x + 1$

CONTINUE

DIRECTIONS

Questions **31-38** ask you to solve a problem and enter your answer in the grid provided on your answer sheet. When completing grid-in questions:

1. You are required to bubble in the circles for your answers. It is recommended, but not required, that you also write your answer in the boxes above the columns of circles. Points will be awarded based only on whether the circles are filled in correctly.
2. Fill in only one circle in a column.
3. You can start your answer in any column as long as you can fit in the whole answer.
4. For questions 31-38, no answers will be negative numbers.
5. **Mixed numbers,** such as $4\frac{2}{5}$, must be gridded as decimals or improper fractions, such as 4.4 or as 22/5. "42/5" will be read as "forty-two over five," not as "four and two-fifths."
6. If your answer is a **decimal** with more digits than will fit on the grid, you may round it or cut it off, but you must fill the entire grid.
7. If there are **multiple correct solutions** to a problem, all of them will be considered correct. Enter only **one** on the grid.

5/11 | 8.4 | 3/7

.422 | .326 | .125

31

A train travels at an average speed of 30 miles per hour. How many minutes will it take the train to travel 75 miles?

32

If $\frac{2}{5}$ of n is 48, what is $\frac{2}{3}$ of n?

33

$$f(x) = x^3 + 3x^2 - 6x + 14$$

Give the equation above, what is the value of $f(-3)$?

34

Kavi takes two buses to get to work. Bus A has an average speed of 20 miles per hour, and Bus B has an average speed of 15 miles per hour. If Kavi takes Bus A for 3 miles and Bus B for 6 miles, how many minutes does Kavi spend on the two buses on his way to work?

35

$$\frac{12}{a-2} + \frac{5}{a+2} = 1$$

If a represents a positive value in the equation above, what is a possible value for a?

CONTINUE

36

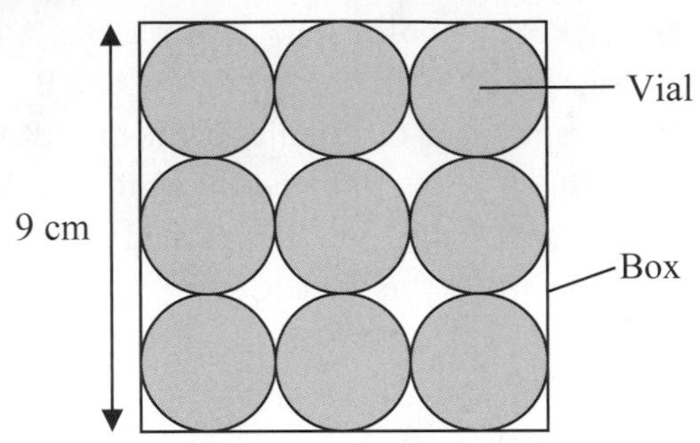

Top view of a box

A biotechnology company has built boxes with square bases that are 5 centimeters high; one side of the box is 9 cm long, as shown. Each box holds 9 cylindrical vials that contain bacteria colonies. The number of colonies initially in each vial is equal to the vial's total volume, in cubic centimeters. If the number of colonies decreases by one third for every hour that they are in storage, how many colonies remain in the box after it has been stored for two hours? (Use the approximation $\pi = 3.14$ and round to the nearest colony.)

Questions 37 and 38 refer to the following information.

Mia is graduating from college in four years. She took out a loan of $2,000 at the beginning of each year to pay for part of her tuition and expenses. The annual interest rate for her loan is 4%, calculated on her total debt at the end of each year. Interest is added to her total debt for that year.

37

What is Mia's total debt with interest at the end of the fourth year? Round to the nearest dollar.

38

Suppose Mia does not borrow more money or pay off any of her debt for two years after graduating. Her interest rate continues to accrue at the same 4% annual rate. At the beginning of her third year after graduating, Mia pays a lump sum of $8,000 toward her loan. After making that payment, how much debt does she still owe? Round to the nearest dollar.

STOP

If you complete this section before the end of your allotted time, check your work on this section only. Do NOT use the time to work on another section.

Essay

Essay (Optional)

50 MINUTES

Turn to the lined pages of your answer sheet to write your essay.

DIRECTIONS

This essay is optional. It is a chance for you to demonstrate how well you can understand and analyze a written passage. Your essay should show that you have carefully read the passage and should be a concisely written analysis that is both logical and clear.

You must write your entire essay on the lines in your answer booklet. No additional paper will be provided aside from the Planning Page inside your answer booklet. You will be able to write your entire essay in the space provided if you make use of every line, keep tight margins, and write at a suitable size. Don't forget to keep your handwriting legible for the readers evaluating your essay.

You will have 50 minutes to read the passage in this booklet and to write an essay in response to the prompt provided at the end of the passage.

REMINDERS

- What you write in this booklet will not be evaluated. Write your essay in the answer booklet only.
- Essays that are off-topic will not be evaluated.

As you read the passage below, consider how David Epstein uses

- evidence, such as facts or examples, to support claims.
- reasoning to develop ideas and to connect claims and evidence.
- stylistic or persuasive elements, such as word choice or appeals to emotion, to add power to the ideas expressed.

1 The national furor over concussions misses the primary scourge that is harming kids and damaging youth sports in America. The heightened pressure on child athletes to be, essentially, adult athletes has fostered an epidemic of hyperspecialization that is both dangerous and counterproductive.

2 Children are playing sports in too structured a manner too early in life on adult-size fields—i.e., too large for optimal skill development—and spending too much time in one sport. It can lead to serious injuries and, a growing body of sports science shows, a lesser ultimate level of athletic success. We should urge kids to avoid hyperspecialization and instead sample a variety of sports through at least age 12.

3 Nearly a third of youth athletes in a three-year longitudinal study led by Neeru Jayanthi, director of primary care sports medicine at Loyola University in Chicago, were highly specialized—they had quit multiple sports in order to focus on one for more than eight months a year — and another third weren't far behind. Even controlling for age and the total number of weekly hours in sports, kids in the study who were highly specialized had a 36 percent increased risk of suffering a serious overuse injury. Dr. Jayanthi saw kids with stress fractures in their backs, arms or legs; damage to elbow ligaments; and cracks in the cartilage in their joints.

4 Some young athletes now face surgeries befitting their grandparents. Young hockey goaltenders repeatedly practice butterfly style—which stresses the developing hip joint when the legs are splayed to block the bottom of the goal. The sports surgeon Marc Philippon, based in Vail, Colo., saw a 25-year-old goalie who already needed a hip replacement.

5 In the Loyola study, sport diversification had a protective effect. But in case health risks alone aren't reason enough for parents to ignore the siren call of specialization, diversification also provides performance benefits.

6 Kids who play multiple "attacking" sports, like basketball or field hockey, transfer learned motor and anticipatory skills—the unconscious ability to read bodies and game situations—to other sports. They take less time to master the sport they ultimately choose.

7 Several studies on skill acquisition now show that elite athletes generally practiced their sport less through their early teenage years and specialized only in the mid-to-late teenage years, while so-called sub-elites—those who never quite cracked the highest ranks—homed in on a single sport much sooner.

8 Data presented at the April meeting of the American Medical Society for Sports Medicine showed that varsity athletes at U.C.L.A.—many with full scholarships—specialized on average at age 15.4, whereas U.C.L.A. undergrads who played sports in high school, but did not make the intercollegiate level, specialized at 14.2.

9 We may prize the story of Tiger Woods, who demonstrated his swing at age 2 for Bob Hope. But the path of the two-time N.B.A. M.V.P. Steve Nash (who grew up playing soccer and didn't own a basketball until age 13) or the tennis star Roger Federer (whose parents encouraged him to play badminton, basketball and soccer) is actually the norm.

10 A Swedish study of sub-elite and elite tennis players—including five who ranked among the top 15 in the world—found that those who topped out as sub-elites dropped all other sports by age 11. Eventual elites developed in a "harmonious club environment without greater demands for success," and played multiple sports until age 14.

11 The sports science data support a "sampling period" through at least age 12. Mike Joyner, a Mayo Clinic physician and human performance expert, would add general physical literacy-building to the youth sports menu: perhaps using padded gymnastics gyms for parkour, which is essentially running, climbing, or vaulting on any obstacle one can find.

12 In addition to athletic diversity, kids' sports should be kid-size. In Brazil, host of this month's World Cup, kids are weaned on "futsal," a lightly structured and miniaturized form of soccer. Futsal is played on tiny patches of grass or concrete or on indoor courts and typically by teams of five players. Players touch the ball up to five times as frequently as they do in traditional soccer, and the tighter playing area forces children to develop foot and decision-making skills under pressure.

13 A futsalization of youth sports generally would serve engagement, skill development and health.

Write an essay in which you explain how David Epstein builds an argument to persuade his audience that kids should avoid specializing in a specific sport too early. In your essay, analyze how Epstein uses one or more of the features listed in the box above (or features of your own choice) to strengthen the logic and persuasiveness of his argument. Be sure that your analysis focuses on the most relevant features of the passage.

Your essay should not explain whether you agree with Epstein's claims, but rather explain how Epstein builds an argument to persuade his audience.

Practice Test 3

YOUR NAME (PRINT): ____

LAST FIRST MI

SAT

Directions

- Work on just one section at a time.
- If you complete a section before the end of your allotted time, use the extra minutes to check your work on that section only. Do NOT use the time to work on another section.

Using Your Test Booklet

- No credit will be given for anything written in the test booklet. You may use the test booklet for scratch paper.
- You are not allowed to continue answering questions in a section after the allotted time has run out. This includes marking answers on your answer sheet that you previously noted in your test booklet.
- You are not allowed to fold pages, take pages out of the test booklet, or take any pages home.

Answering Questions

- Each answer must be marked in the corresponding row on the answer sheet.
- Each bubble must be filled in completely and darkly within the lines.

Correct  Incorrect 

- Be careful to bubble in the correct part of the answer sheet.
- Extra marks on your answer sheet may be marked as incorrect answers and lower your score.
- Make sure you use a No. 2 pencil.

Scoring

- You will receive one point for each correct answer.
- Incorrect answers will NOT result in points deducted. Even if you are unsure about an answer, you should make a guess.

DO NOT BEGIN THIS TEST

UNTIL YOUR PROCTOR TELLS YOU TO DO SO

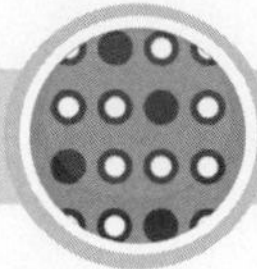

For automatic scoring and scaling, please visit **ivyglobal.com/study**.

Section 1

Question	A	B	C	D
1	○	○	○	○
2	○	○	○	○
3	○	○	○	○
4	○	○	○	○
5	○	○	○	○
6	○	○	○	○
7	○	○	○	○
8	○	○	○	○
9	○	○	○	○
10	○	○	○	○
11	○	○	○	○
12	○	○	○	○
13	○	○	○	○
14	○	○	○	○
15	○	○	○	○
16	○	○	○	○
17	○	○	○	○
18	○	○	○	○
19	○	○	○	○
20	○	○	○	○
21	○	○	○	○
22	○	○	○	○
23	○	○	○	○
24	○	○	○	○
25	○	○	○	○
26	○	○	○	○
27	○	○	○	○
28	○	○	○	○
29	○	○	○	○
30	○	○	○	○
31	○	○	○	○
32	○	○	○	○
33	○	○	○	○
34	○	○	○	○
35	○	○	○	○
36	○	○	○	○
37	○	○	○	○
38	○	○	○	○
39	○	○	○	○
40	○	○	○	○
41	○	○	○	○
42	○	○	○	○
43	○	○	○	○
44	○	○	○	○
45	○	○	○	○
46	○	○	○	○
47	○	○	○	○
48	○	○	○	○
49	○	○	○	○
50	○	○	○	○
51	○	○	○	○
52	○	○	○	○

Section 2

Question	A	B	C	D
1	○	○	○	○
2	○	○	○	○
3	○	○	○	○
4	○	○	○	○
5	○	○	○	○
6	○	○	○	○
7	○	○	○	○
8	○	○	○	○
9	○	○	○	○
10	○	○	○	○
11	○	○	○	○
12	○	○	○	○
13	○	○	○	○
14	○	○	○	○
15	○	○	○	○
16	○	○	○	○
17	○	○	○	○
18	○	○	○	○
19	○	○	○	○
20	○	○	○	○
21	○	○	○	○
22	○	○	○	○
23	○	○	○	○
24	○	○	○	○
25	○	○	○	○
26	○	○	○	○
27	○	○	○	○
28	○	○	○	○
29	○	○	○	○
30	○	○	○	○
31	○	○	○	○
32	○	○	○	○
33	○	○	○	○
34	○	○	○	○
35	○	○	○	○
36	○	○	○	○
37	○	○	○	○
38	○	○	○	○
39	○	○	○	○
40	○	○	○	○
41	○	○	○	○
42	○	○	○	○
43	○	○	○	○
44	○	○	○	○

Section 3 (No-Calculator)

1 A B C D	4 A B C D	7 A B C D	10 A B C D	13 A B C D
2 A B C D	5 A B C D	8 A B C D	11 A B C D	14 A B C D
3 A B C D	6 A B C D	9 A B C D	12 A B C D	15 A B C D

Only answers that are gridded will be scored. You will not receive credit for anything written in the boxes.

16	17	18	19	20
/	/	/	/	/
.	.	.	.	.
0	0	0	0	0
1	1	1	1	1
2	2	2	2	2
3	3	3	3	3
4	4	4	4	4
5	5	5	5	5
6	6	6	6	6
7	7	7	7	7
8	8	8	8	8
9	9	9	9	9

Section 4 (Calculator)

1 A B C D	7 A B C D	13 A B C D	19 A B C D	25 A B C D
2 A B C D	8 A B C D	14 A B C D	20 A B C D	26 A B C D
3 A B C D	9 A B C D	15 A B C D	21 A B C D	27 A B C D
4 A B C D	10 A B C D	16 A B C D	22 A B C D	28 A B C D
5 A B C D	11 A B C D	17 A B C D	23 A B C D	29 A B C D
6 A B C D	12 A B C D	18 A B C D	24 A B C D	30 A B C D

Section 4 (Continued)

Only answers that are gridded will be scored. You will not receive credit for anything written in the boxes.

31

32

33

34

35

Only answers that are gridded will be scored. You will not receive credit for anything written in the boxes.

36

37

38

Section 5 (Optional)

Important: Use a No. 2 pencil. Write inside the borders.

You may use the space below to plan your essay, but be sure to write your essay on the lined pages. Work on this page will not be scored.

Use this space to plan your essay.

START YOUR ESSAY HERE.

Continue on the next page.

Continue on the next page.

Continue on the next page.

STOP.

Section 1

Reading Test

65 MINUTES, 52 QUESTIONS

Turn to Section 1 of your answer sheet to answer the questions in this section.

DIRECTIONS

Every passage or paired set of passages is accompanied by a number of questions. Read the passage or paired set of passages, then use what is said or implied in what you read and in any given graphics to choose the best answer to each question.

Questions 1-10 are based on the following passage.

This passage is adapted from W.E.B. Du Bois, *A Negro Schoolmaster in the New South*, originally published in 1899. In this book, Du Bois describes his experience as a schoolmaster in a rural black community in Tennessee.

There came a day when all the teachers left the Institute, and began the hunt for schools. I learn from hearsay (for my mother was mortally afraid of firearms) that the hunting of ducks and bears and men is wonderfully interesting, but I am sure that the man who has never hunted a country school has something to learn of the pleasures of the chase. I see now the white, hot roads lazily rise and fall and wind before me under the burning July sun; I feel the deep weariness of heart and limb, as ten, eight, six miles stretch relentlessly ahead; I feel my heart sink heavily as I hear again and again, "Got a teacher? Yes." So I walked on and on—horses were too expensive—until I had wandered beyond railways, beyond stage lines, to a land of "varmints" and rattlesnakes, where the coming of a stranger was an event, and men lived and died in the shadow of one blue hill.

Sprinkled over hill and dale lay cabins and farmhouses, shut out from the world by the forests and the rolling hills toward the east. There I found at last a little school. Josie told me of it; she was a thin, homely girl of twenty, with a dark brown face and thick, hard hair. I had crossed the stream at Watertown, and rested under the great willows; then I had gone to the little cabin in the lot where Josie was resting on her way to town. The gaunt farmer made me welcome, and Josie, hearing my errand, told me anxiously that they wanted a school over the hill; that but once since the war had a teacher been there; that she herself longed to learn,—and thus she ran on, talking fast and loud, with much earnestness and energy.

The schoolhouse was a log hut, where Colonel Wheeler used to shelter his corn. It sat in a lot behind a rail fence and thorn bushes. There was an entrance where a door once was, and within, a massive rickety fireplace; great holes between the logs served as windows. Furniture was scarce. A pale blackboard crouched in the corner. My desk was made of three boards, reinforced at critical points, and my chair, borrowed from the landlady, had to be returned every night. Seats for the children were rough plank benches without backs, and at times without legs. They had the one virtue of making naps dangerous—possibly fatal, for the floor was not to be trusted.

It was a hot morning late in July when the school opened. I trembled when I heard the patter of little

CONTINUE

feet down the dusty road, and saw the growing row of solemn faces and bright eager eyes facing me.

There they sat, nearly thirty of them, on the rough benches, their faces shading from a pale cream to a deep brown, the little feet bare and swinging, the eyes full of expectation, with here and there a twinkle of mischief, and the hands grasping Webster's blue-back spelling-book. I loved my school, and the fine faith the children had in my wisdom as their teacher was truly marvelous. We read and spelled together, wrote a little, picked flowers, sang, and listened to stories of the world beyond the hill. At times the school would dwindle away, and I would start out. I would visit the Eddings, who lived in two very dirty rooms, and ask why little Lugene, whose flaming face seemed ever ablaze with the dark-red hair uncombed, was absent all last week, or why the unmistakable rags of Mack and Ed were so often missing. Then their father would tell me how the crops needed the boys, and their mother would assure me that Lugene must mind the baby. "But we'll start them again next week." When the Lawrences stopped, I knew that the doubts of the old folks about book-learning had conquered again, and so, toiling up the hill, I put Cicero's "pro Archia Poeta" into the simplest English, and usually convinced them—for a week or so.

1

Which best describes Du Bois's attitude toward his work as a teacher?

A) He was relieved to have work despite the poor working conditions.

B) He was worried about living up to his students' expectations.

C) He was indifferent toward the simple activities he engaged in with his students.

D) He was proud of his school and felt respected by his students.

2

Which choice provides the best evidence for the answer to the previous question?

A) Lines 40-43 ("My … every night")

B) Lines 49-51 ("I trembled … me")

C) Lines 57-59 ("I loved … marvelous")

D) Lines 63-68 ("I would … missing")

3

Du Bois most likely discusses hunting (lines 2-7) in order to

A) suggest that hunting for schools is more dangerous than hunting game.

B) imply that he used similar techniques in finding a school as hunters use in hunting animals.

C) argue that he enjoyed finding a school more than he would have enjoyed hunting animals.

D) suggest that hunting for a school had its own unique challenges.

4

The rhetorical effect of lines 13-18 is to suggest that the places the narrator had reached

A) were small, isolated communities.

B) were very dangerous.

C) had abnormally high death rates.

D) had never been visited by outsiders before.

CONTINUE

5

As used in line 45, "virtue" most nearly means

A) bravery.

B) character.

C) decency.

D) benefit.

6

Du Bois's reaction to the "patter of little feet" (lines 49-50) most strongly suggests that he felt a sense of

A) anxious anticipation.

B) unconstrained elation.

C) strong nostalgia.

D) unavoidable apathy.

7

The passage most strongly suggests that when students stopped attending school Du Bois was

A) relieved that he would have fewer pupils.

B) compelled to ensure they returned.

C) indifferent about their absence.

D) angry that they did not value their education.

8

Which choice provides the best evidence for the answer to the previous question?

A) Lines 52-57 ("There they … spelling-book)

B) Lines 59-62 ("We read … hill")

C) Lines 62-63 ("At times … start out")

D) Lines 68-71 ("Then … the baby")

9

As used in line 74, "toiling" most nearly means

A) endeavoring.

B) sweating.

C) working.

D) plodding.

10

It can reasonably be inferred from the passage that Cicero's "pro Archia Poeta" (line 75) is

A) a Latin treatise about farming.

B) a short story about life in a small community.

C) a homework assignment that Du Bois's students had not completed.

D) a text that argues for the benefits of education.

CONTINUE

Questions 11-21 are based on the following passage.

This passage is adapted from "We Have Only Just Begun to Fight," a speech given by Franklin D. Roosevelt in Madison Square Garden in 1936. Roosevelt was campaigning for a second term as President after winning the previous election in 1932.

On the eve of a national election, it is well for us to stop for a moment and analyze calmly and without prejudice the effect on our Nation of a victory by either of the major political parties. The problem of the electorate is far deeper, far more than the continuance in the Presidency of any individual. For the greater issue goes beyond units of humanity—it goes to humanity itself.

In 1932 the issue was the *restoration* of American democracy; and the American people were in a mood to win. They did win. In 1936 the issue is the preservation of their victory. Again they are in a mood to win. Again they will win.

More than four years ago in accepting the Democratic nomination in Chicago, I said, "Give me your help not to win votes alone, but to win in this crusade to restore America to its own people." The banners of that crusade still fly in the van of a Nation that is on the march.

It is needless to repeat the details of the program which this Administration has been hammering out on the anvils of experience. No amount of misrepresentation or statistical contortion can conceal or blur or smear that record. Neither the attacks of unscrupulous enemies nor the exaggerations of over-zealous friends will serve to mislead the American people.

What was our hope in 1932? Above all other things the American people wanted peace. They wanted peace of mind instead of gnawing fear.

First, they sought escape from the personal terror which had stalked them for three years. They wanted the peace that comes from security in their homes: safety for their savings, permanence in their jobs, a fair profit from their enterprise.

Next, they wanted peace in the community, the peace that springs from the ability to meet the needs of community life: schools, playgrounds, parks, sanitation, highways—those things which are expected of solvent local government. They sought escape from disintegration and bankruptcy in local and state affairs. They also sought peace within the Nation: protection of their currency, fairer wages, the ending of long hours of toil, the abolition of child labor, the elimination of wild-cat speculation, the safety of their children from kidnappers.

And, finally, they sought peace with other Nations—peace in a world of unrest. The Nation knows that I hate war, and I know that the Nation hates war.

I submit to you a record of peace; and on that record a well-founded expectation for future peace—peace for the individual, peace for the community, peace for the Nation, and peace with the world.

Tonight I call the roll—the roll of honor of those who stood with us in 1932 and still stand with us today. Written on it are the names of millions who never had a chance—men at starvation wages, women in sweatshops, children at looms. Written on it are the names of farmers whose acres yielded only bitterness, business men whose books were portents of disaster, homeowners who were faced with eviction, frugal citizens whose savings were insecure.

Written there in large letters are the names of countless other Americans of all parties and all faiths, Americans who had eyes to see and hearts to understand, whose consciences were burdened because too many of their fellows were burdened, who looked on these things four years ago and said, "This can be changed. We will change it."

We still lead that army in 1936. They stood with us then because in 1932 they believed. They stand with us today because in 1936 they know. And with them stand millions of new recruits who have come to know. Their hopes have become our record.

CONTINUE

We have not come this far without a struggle and I assure you we cannot go further without a struggle. For twelve years this Nation was afflicted with hear-nothing, see-nothing, do-nothing Government. The Nation looked to Government but the Government looked away. Powerful influences strive today to restore that kind of Government with its doctrine that that Government is best which is most indifferent.

For nearly four years you have had an Administration which instead of twirling its thumbs has rolled up its sleeves. We will keep our sleeves rolled up.

11

Based on the passage, which choice best describes how Roosevelt feels about his previous term as president?

A) His term was productive, and his record speaks for itself.

B) His term was productive, but his friends have overstated his success.

C) His term was a struggle that produced few good results.

D) His term has resulted in a deeply divided electorate.

12

Which choice provides the best evidence for the answer to the previous question?

A) Lines 20-24 ("It is … record")

B) Lines 40-42 ("They sought … affairs")

C) Lines 56-58 ("Tonight … us today")

D) Lines 78-80 ("We have … struggle")

13

Based on the passage, which choice best describes the relationship between Roosevelt's previous term and his plans for his next term?

A) He will build upon his previous successes by continuing to pursue the same goals.

B) He will learn from his failures and implement very different policies.

C) He will learn from his failures and help the struggling Americans he previously ignored.

D) He will alter his policies slightly based on the criticisms of voters.

14

In this speech, Roosevelt does which of the following to promote his administration?

A) Contrasts his administration's hard work with the indifference of the previous administration

B) Lists the shortcomings of the opposition party

C) Compares his leadership style favorably to other politicians

D) Offers statistics to demonstrate the effectiveness of his policies

15

Which choice provides the best evidence for the answer to the previous question?

A) Lines 4-6 ("The problem … individual")

B) Lines 24-27 ("Neither … American people")

C) Lines 32-35 ("They wanted … enterprise")

D) Lines 87-89 ("For nearly … sleeves")

CONTINUE

16

The main rhetorical effect of lines 9-13 is to

A) associate Roosevelt's past and future victory with victory for the whole American people.

B) highlight that America's mood has changed due to changing social and political factors.

C) imply that Americans' wishes have shifted from the desire to change society to the desire to preserve the status quo.

D) persuade listeners that the issues facing Americans are different than they were in 1932.

17

In line 28, what is the most likely reason that Roosevelt asks a question?

A) So he can answer it and demonstrate that he achieved what Americans hoped for

B) So he can answer it and argue that Americans' goals can only be accomplished if he is re-elected

C) To force the opposition to answer, and admit that they were ignorant of Americans' hopes

D) To encourage Americans to reflect on what they wanted in the past

18

As used in line 37, "springs" most nearly means

A) leaps.

B) vaults.

C) arises.

D) bounds.

19

It can reasonably be inferred from the passage that the phrase "farmers whose acres yielded only bitterness" (lines 61-62) most likely refers to farmers who

A) had crops that failed and therefore had nothing to harvest.

B) opposed the agriculture policies of the previous administration.

C) opposed Roosevelt's agriculture policies.

D) had crops that were too bitter to eat or sell.

20

Franklin D. Roosevelt uses words like "army" and "new recruits" in lines 73-77 in order to emphasize the

A) military nature of the coming challenges.

B) inner fortitude of his closest followers.

C) growing strength of his supporters.

D) deadly threats of international neighbors.

21

As used in line 86, "indifferent" most nearly means

A) impartial.

B) apathetic.

C) dispassionate.

D) objective.

CONTINUE

Questions 22-31 are based on the following passages.

Passage 1 is adapted from Atul J. Butte, and Passage 2 is adapted from Robert Green, "Should Healthy People Have Their Genome Sequenced At This Time?" © 2013 by Dow Jones & Company.

Passage 1

We live in an amazing time. Very shortly, any individual will be able to know the sequence of his or her whole genome: the genetic recipe that guides the creation and functioning of our bodies. It's just a piece of what makes us unique individuals, but it's a critical piece.

What's to be gained from learning things about our bodies and our health that might scare us, but that we might not do anything about? There are four important ways a healthy person can medically benefit from obtaining his or her whole genome sequence.

Thousands of DNA combinations have been identified as indicators of susceptibility to specific diseases. Some argue that you might go through life worrying needlessly about a disease that never appears. On the other hand, spotting those DNA variants and recognizing whether you are at risk can lead directly to early diagnoses and preventive strategies.

Couples planning families can find out when they carry genetic risks for severe disorders and so make more informed choices: to have a baby together and hope for the best, for example, or to adopt. Doctors can better determine what drugs will be most effective for a patient, at what dose, and what drugs to avoid. Genome sequencing also can help in the diagnosis of illnesses yet to be identified.

Genome sequencing isn't perfect. There are mistakes. But not many. We can currently expect one misread bit of DNA among hundreds of thousands. Other common preventive medical procedures aren't free from errors either: mammography and Pap smears have high overdiagnosis rates, and PSA testing (prostate specific antigen) is unreliable, yet we typically accept these problems. Moreover, continuing research will certainly identify more of the inaccurate and "missing" bits, leading to better clinical interpretations.

There are limits. Despite the incredible science behind sequencing, we won't be able to predict every possible condition in one's lifetime. Behaviors, environment, and other factors are involved. But there are already individuals who have had a whole genome sequenced, and who learned the pharmacological, environmental, medical, or behavioral changes they could make to "compensate" for their genome.

There is no gene for compliance; it can require difficult changes to improve one's health. But for many people, that genome sequence may provide the crucial first step to move from "knowing thyself" to "helping thyself."

Passage 2

Most of us agree that in a few years, affordable genomic and epigenomic analyses of healthy individuals will allow for more individually tailored disease prevention and pharmaceutical treatment. But some serious challenges remain before this can be done safely.

One problem is that medically dangerous genetic mutations are quite rare in healthy individuals, but finding them today would still be enormously expensive. This year an entire genome will cost somewhere around $5,000 to be sequenced, analyzed with bioinformatics, and interpreted. And while there is much to find in each genome that can reflect subtle health risks or aid in reproductive planning, we currently estimate that less than 2% of healthy people will have a dangerous and well-recognized DNA mutation that might cause a doctor to initiate surveillance or treatment. That means spending $250,000 to find even one such individual.

Finding well-recognized disease mutations in healthy people is just the tip of the genomic iceberg. We all have unique or novel mutations in disease-associated genes. I have 14 such mutations in my

CONTINUE

own genome! But the smartest geneticists in the world cannot always agree as to whether a novel mutation is dangerous. If a healthy person without family history has a novel mutation in a cancer predisposition gene, should we take X-rays every year for the cancer that might never appear? Should we do the same for their parents, brothers, sisters, and children that carry the same mutation?

Perhaps we all underestimated how complicated it would be to move genomic knowledge into the practice of medicine and public health. Now is the time to make sure we get this right through rigorous basic and clinical studies that define which mutations are dangerous, and distinguish useful from unnecessary interventions. Soon, genomic insights will give us early warnings about life-threatening illnesses that we may be able to prevent. Soon, standards will be available to guide doctors about which findings are meaningful and which are not. Soon, there may be evidence to support the benefits of screening healthy individuals. But not today.

22

Both passages are primarily concerned with

A) creating new genome sequencing techniques.

B) reducing the existing risks of genome sequencing.

C) whether genome sequencing is ready for widespread use.

D) the costs currently associated with genome sequencing.

23

The author of Passage 1 can best be described as

A) an excited proponent of a new technology who still recognizes its potential limitations.

B) a skeptical critic of a new technology who is unconvinced by current supporting evidence.

C) a biased advocate of a new technology who ignores counterarguments from opponents.

D) a neutral scholar researching a debate over a new technology.

24

The author of Passage 1 supports his assertion that, despite some errors, genome sequencing is already accurate enough to be used by

A) noting that we accept errors in other common preventive tests.

B) discussing the impossibility of error-free tests.

C) disproving that genome sequencing will lead to overdiagnosis.

D) stating that less than 2% of healthy people will have a well-recognized DNA mutation.

25

Which choice provides the best evidence for the answer to the previous question?

A) Lines 34-37 ("Mammography … problems")

B) Lines 41-43 ("Despite the … lifetime")

C) Lines 45-49 ("But there … genome")

D) Lines 51-54 ("But for … thyself")

CONTINUE

26

The author of Passage 1 would most likely agree with the author of Passage 2 about which of the following?

A) Healthy individuals should not have their genomes sequenced.

B) Genome sequencing will be more reliable in the future than it is now.

C) Genome sequencing is currently too expensive to be useful.

D) There is not enough consensus about which DNA mutations are dangerous.

27

Which choice provides the best evidence for the answer to the previous question?

A) Lines 15-17 ("Some argue … appears")

B) Lines 29-30 ("Genome sequencing … mistakes")

C) Lines 37-40 ("Moreover … interpretations")

D) Lines 50-51 ("There is … health")

28

As used in line 68, "reflect" most nearly means

A) reconsider.

B) reveal.

C) mirror.

D) imitate.

29

The author of Passage 2 most likely mentions that his own genome has mutations (lines 77-78) in order to

A) emphasize how common mutations are.

B) prove that most genetic mutations are harmless.

C) give examples of well-recognized gene mutations.

D) urge readers to have their genome sequenced.

30

As used in line 81, "novel" most nearly means

A) innovative.

B) unconventional.

C) unfamiliar.

D) unique.

31

The main rhetorical effect of the repeated words in lines 92-98 is to

A) emphasize that the major benefits of genome sequencing have yet to be realized.

B) imply that further research needs to be undertaken as quickly as possible.

C) suggest that readers should sequence their genomes immediately.

D) indicate that the author is concerned about new developments in genome sequencing.

CONTINUE

Questions 32-41 are based on the following passage and supplementary material.

The following passage is adapted from Saab, A. Joan, "Without a humanistic inquiry, we will lose our creativity." © 2015 by A. Joan Saab.

Today it is hard to imagine that the national government would spend millions of dollars to put unemployed artists to work for the good of the country. But that is precisely what happened in the United States at the height of the Great Depression.

In the 1930s, Harry Hopkins, the head of the Works Progress Administration (WPA), oversaw the Federal Arts Project (FAP), one of the New Deal cultural programs. Hopkins repeatedly stressed "that the objective of this whole project is … taking 3,500,000 off relief and putting them to work."

In the America of the 1930s, artists and their labor were considered to be important cultural assets. In its 8-year existence, the FAP created over 5,000 jobs and funded over 225,000 works of art. The artist George Biddle is credited with writing to his friend and former prep-schoolmate Franklin D. Roosevelt and encouraging him to emulate the Mexican mural program, which he called "the greatest national school of mural painting since the Renaissance."

This type of engagement was crucial to the ideology of the WPA cultural projects. Biddle, Hopkins, and FDR all saw direct links between a strong democratic country and its artwork. They believed that making art was a way of making strong citizens.

Indeed, Biddle advocated for including artists in the national relief program since, he argued, the artist was as valuable a worker to the health of the nation as the "the farmer or the bricklayer." For New Dealers, the arts and the humanities—painting, sculpture, music, theater, and literature—were not only a viable form of labor, they were key to America's past, present, and future success.

Many of the works created on the FAP directly addressed the relationship between manual and intellectual labor. For example, a two-panel series exploring the Life of Action and its corollary, the Life of Contemplation, was painted in 1937 by the local Rochester artist Carl Peters.

Inspired by the monumental Renaissance masterpieces by Michelangelo, Peters broke with his traditional, small-scale easel practice (he was primarily a landscape painter of local scenes) to depict a subject matter that shows the need for balance between doing and thinking.

Peters imagined these classical themes within a visual vocabulary that stressed images of progress through learning and work. By explicitly linking the past to the present, Peters transforms contemplation and its corollaries of education and imagination into an active process. Thus contemplation becomes a form of action akin to the work being performed in its partner panel.

Taken together these works provide an inventory of New Deal imagery: the teacher, the laborer, the architect, the student. They situate Peters, as the artist, as an important cultural laborer. They encapsulate in visual form the ideologies of the New Deal and suggest that art and contemplative labor were valuable forms of work, as important to nation building as building bridges and skyscrapers.

In this way, Peters and other artists used media to help understand the world around them. Peters and his peers on the WPA looked for a balance between action and contemplation, which they accomplished through humanistic inquiry and creative work.

CONTINUE

Total Employment as of November 1, 1936

Fine Arts 49%

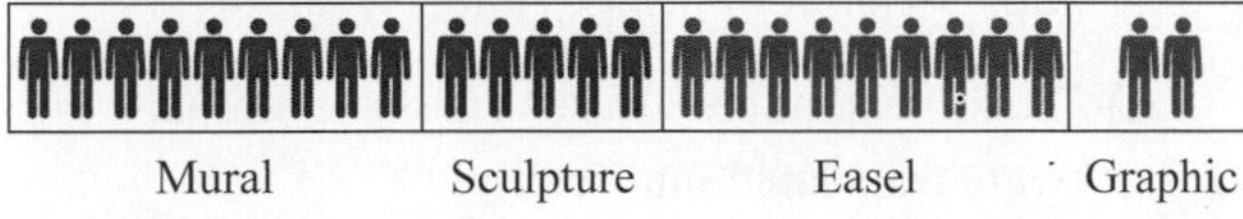

Practical Arts 29%

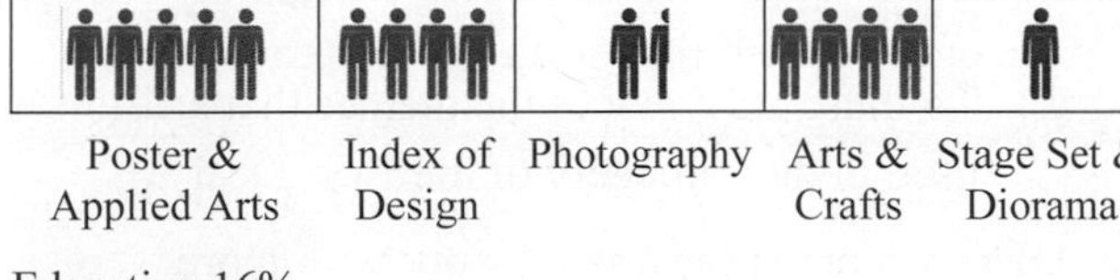

Education 16%

Miscellaneous 6%

*Each Figure Represents 100 Project Workers

32

Which one of the following best describes the organization of the passage?

A) The author discusses a historical government initiative and gives a specific example of what it produced.

B) The author argues in favor of governmental art programs and provides evidence of one's success.

C) The author explains the historical difficulties faced by the arts and suggests potential remedies.

D) The author explores different types of labor during the Depression, then considers one profession more in depth.

33

The passage indicates that, during the Great Depression, artists were considered

A) pitiable charity cases.

B) self-sacrificing heroes.

C) necessary and amusing distractions.

D) valuable community contributors.

34

Which choice provides the best evidence for the answer to the previous question?

A) Lines 6-9 ("In the … programs")

B) Lines 12-14 ("In the … assets")

C) Lines 14-15 ("In its … art")

D) Lines 22-23 ("This type … projects")

35

The passage most directly supports that Franklin D. Roosevelt believed art could

A) help comfort citizens weathering a difficult economic time.

B) inspire thousands of Americans to redouble their efforts in labor.

C) fortify the nation through its cultural products.

D) strengthen the ties between the U.S. and its neighboring countries.

36

Which choice provides the best evidence for the answer to the previous question?

A) Lines 1-4 ("Today … country")

B) Lines 16-21 ("The artist … Renaissance")

C) Lines 25-27 ("They believed … citizens")

D) Lines 28-31 ("Indeed … bricklayer")

CONTINUE

37

As used in line 14, "assets" most nearly means

A) advantages.

B) belongings.

C) estates.

D) resources.

38

As used in line 34, "viable" most nearly means

A) worthwhile.

B) sustainable.

C) possible.

D) attainable.

39

Which of the following could serve as an additional example accomplishing Peters's goal for his mural, as stated in lines 45-47 ("to depict … thinking")?

A) The first panel depicting a teacher, and the second panel depicting a student

B) The first panel depicting a banker, and the second panel depicting a lawyer

C) The first panel depicting an architect, and the second panel depicting a building

D) The first panel depicting a railroad engineer, and the second panel depicting a physics researcher

40

In lines 59-63, what is the most likely reason that the author mentions bridges and skyscrapers?

A) To show that the artists' visions eventually were translated into reality

B) To demonstrate that artists had less selfish motives than some of their industrial counterparts

C) To illustrate a few of the themes that artists used in their imagery of the New Deal

D) To contrast the artists' work with more practical endeavors while arguing that both are essential

41

Which of the following choices is best supported by data in the graphic?

A) The majority of workers in the Great Depression had occupations in the fine arts.

B) More people in the FAP were employed in the creation of murals than in sculpture.

C) 16% of those employed by the FAP were teachers.

D) Over a quarter of workers in the arts program were involved in stage set & drama.

CONTINUE

Questions 42-52 are based on the following passage and supplementary material.

This passage is adapted from Justin Gillis, "A Warming Planet Struggles to Feed Itself." © 2014 by *The New York Times Company*.

For decades, scientists believed that the human dependence on fossil fuels, for all the problems it was expected to cause, would offer one enormous benefit. Carbon dioxide, the main gas released by combustion, is also the primary fuel for the growth of plants. They draw it out of the air and, using the energy from sunlight, convert the carbon into energy-dense compounds like glucose. All human and animal life runs on these compounds.

Humans have already raised the level of carbon dioxide in the atmosphere by 40 percent since the Industrial Revolution, and are on course to double or triple it over the coming century. Studies have long suggested that the extra gas would supercharge the world's food crops, and might be especially helpful in years when the weather is difficult.

But many of those studies were done in artificial conditions, like greenhouses or special growth chambers. For the past decade, scientists at the University of Illinois have been putting the "CO_2 fertilization effect" to a real-world test in the two most important crops grown in the United States.

They started by planting soybeans in a field, then sprayed extra carbon dioxide from a giant tank. Based on the earlier research, they hoped the gas might bump yields as much as 30 percent under optimal growing conditions. But when they harvested their soybeans, they got a rude surprise: the bump was only half as large. "When we measured the yields, it was like, 'wait a minute—this is not what we expected,'" said Elizabeth A. Ainsworth, a Department of Agriculture researcher who played a leading role in the work. When they grew the soybeans in the sort of conditions expected to prevail in a future climate, with high temperatures or low water, the extra carbon dioxide could not fully offset the yield decline caused by those factors.

They also ran tests using corn, America's single most valuable crop and the basis for its meat production and its biofuel industry. While that crop was already known to be less responsive to carbon dioxide, a yield bump was still expected—especially during droughts. The Illinois researchers got no bump.

Their work has contributed to a broader body of research suggesting that extra carbon dioxide does act as plant fertilizer, but that the benefits are less than previously believed—and probably less than needed to avert food shortages. "One of the things that we're starting to believe is that the positives of CO_2 are unlikely to outweigh the negatives of the other factors," said Andrew D. B. Leakey, another of the Illinois researchers.

Other recent evidence suggests that longstanding assumptions about food production on a warming planet may have been too optimistic. Two economists, Wolfram Schlenker of Columbia University and Michael J. Roberts of North Carolina State University, have pioneered ways to compare crop yields and natural temperature variability at a fine scale. Their work shows that when crops are subjected to temperatures above a certain threshold—about 84 degrees for corn and 86 degrees for soybeans—yields fall sharply. This line of research suggests that in the type of climate predicted for the United States by the end of the century, with more scorching days in the growing season, yields of today's crop varieties could fall by 30 percent or more.

CONTINUE

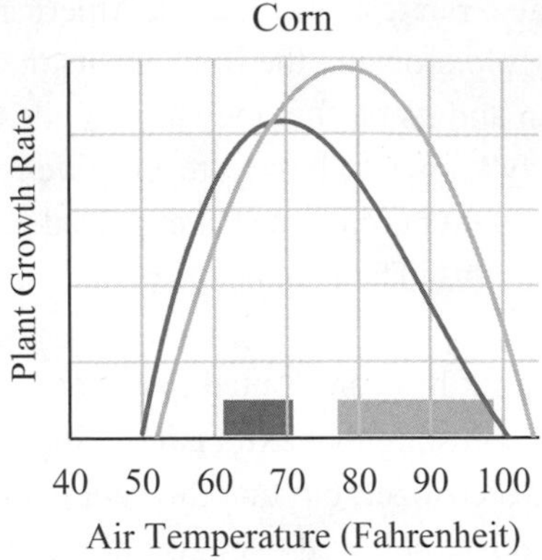

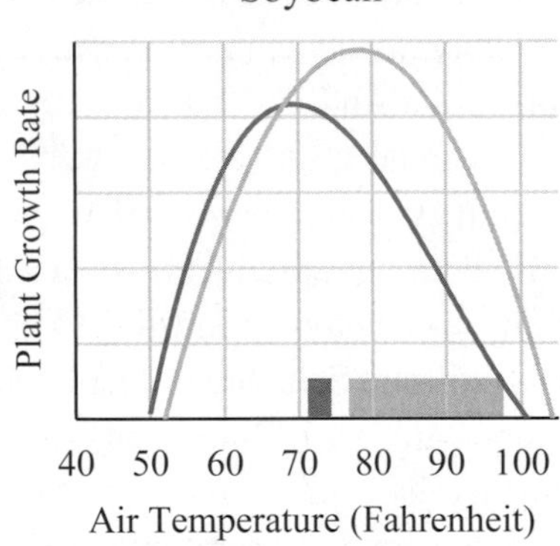

Reproductive Response Curve: temperature range within which plants can produce seed

Optimum Range

Vegetative Response Curve: temperature range within which plants can grow, between germination and flowering

Optimum Range

Corn Failure at 99°F, Soybean Failure at 102°F

Adapted from 2009 report of the US Global Change Research Program, "Global Climate Change Impact in the United States." Agricultural Research Service, USDA.

42

The primary purpose of the passage is to

A) convince readers to change their behavior in response to new scientific evidence.

B) explain how new evidence challenges what scientists previously believed.

C) describe the latest experiments being conducted in a certain scientific field.

D) summarize the challenges facing farmers in the future.

43

The passage most strongly suggests that scientists

A) previously ignored the potentially harmful effects of fossil fuel consumption.

B) had expected to observe at least one benefit from fossil fuel consumption.

C) underestimated the benefits of carbon dioxide for crops.

D) only began studying the effect of carbon dioxide on crops in the last decade.

44

Which choice provides the best evidence for the answer to the previous question?

A) Lines 1-4 ("For decades … benefit")

B) Lines 23-24 ("They started … tank")

C) Lines 45-49 ("Their work … shortages")

D) Lines 54-56 ("Other … too optimistic")

CONTINUE

45

Based on the passage, which choice best describes the relationship between older studies about carbon dioxide's fertilizer effect and newer ones conducted by the Illinois researchers?

A) The newer studies completely confirm the findings of the older studies.

B) The newer studies support the basic findings of previous studies but show a more modest effect than expected.

C) The newer studies totally refute the findings of the older studies.

D) The newer studies partially refute the findings of the older studies by showing a much stronger effect than expected.

46

Which choice provides the best evidence for the answer to the previous question?

A) Lines 19-22 ("For ... United States")

B) Lines 27-29 ("But when … as large")

C) Lines 40-43 ("While … during droughts")

D) Lines 61-64 ("Their … fall sharply")

47

As used in line 35, "prevail" most nearly means

A) win.

B) triumph.

C) impose.

D) predominate.

48

As used in line 49, "avert" most nearly means

A) prevent.

B) turn away.

C) frustrate.

D) help.

49

Lines 49-53 ("One of … researchers") serve primarily to

A) summarize the techniques used by the Illinois researchers.

B) suggest that there is consensus about the future increase in extreme weather.

C) describe the Illinois researchers' predictions for the future based on their research.

D) provide reasons to support undertaking further crop research.

50

It can reasonably be inferred from the passage and graphic that

A) soybeans and corn grow best at very different temperatures, but reproduce in about the same range of temperatures.

B) constant temperatures above 100 degrees Fahrenheit could make it impossible to grow soybeans and corn.

C) soybean and corn yields could best be increased by temperatures below 55 degrees Fahrenheit.

D) soybean and corn yields could best be increased by temperatures above 95 degrees Fahrenheit.

CONTINUE

51

Based on data in the graphics, which of the following temperatures would be optimal for growing both soybeans and corn?

A) 40°F

B) 60°F

C) 80°F

D) 100°F

52

Which claim about crop growth and temperature is supported by the graphics?

A) Soybeans but not corn can grow at 50 degrees Fahrenheit.

B) Corn but not soybeans can grow at 70 degrees Fahrenheit.

C) Neither corn nor soybeans can grow at 50 degrees Fahrenheit.

D) Neither corn nor soybeans can grow at 70 degrees Fahrenheit.

STOP

If you complete this section before the end of your allotted time, check your work on this section only. Do NOT use the time to work on another section.

Section 2

Writing and Language Test

35 MINUTES, 44 QUESTIONS

Turn to Section 2 of your answer sheet to answer the questions in this section.

DIRECTIONS

Every passage comes with a set of questions. Some questions will ask you to consider how the writer might revise the passage to improve the expression of ideas. Other questions will ask you to consider correcting potential errors in sentence structure, usage, or punctuation. There may be one or more graphics that you will need to consult as you revise and edit the passage.

Some questions will refer to a portion of the passage that has been underlined. Other questions will refer to a particular spot in a passage or ask that you consider the passage in full.

After you read the passage, select the answers to questions that most effectively improve the passage's writing quality or that adjust the passage to follow the conventions of standard written English. Many questions give you the option to select "NO CHANGE." Select that option in cases where you think the relevant part of the passage should remain as it currently is.

Questions 1-11 are based on the following passage and supplementary materials.

Conflict and Cooperation: The Robbers Cave

In the 1950s, social scientists were fascinated with group interactions. During this time, many psychologists studied belonging, cooperation, and [1] conflict. They hoped to better understand the sources of prejudice and war. Specifically, they wanted to know what circumstances bring about conflict or cooperation among groups and if it is possible to reproduce these effects in experiments. One such scientist was Muzafer Sherif, who became interested in group interactions after witnessing the violent invasion of his home country, Turkey. In 1954, Sherif published

1

Which choice most effectively combines the sentences at the underlined portion?

A) conflict, and they also hoped to better understand

B) conflict, hoping thereby to reach a better understanding of

C) conflict to better understand

D) conflict, understanding

CONTINUE

his landmark study on group relationships, "The Robbers Cave Experiment."

Sherif's experiment was original in a number of ways. Sherif used a real-world setting by placing twelve-year-old boys at a camp into two groups, the "Eagles" and the "Rattlers." The experiment had three stages. In stage one, the researchers separated the groups, and **2** they enjoyed the first days at the camp, each group unaware of the other. In stage two, the boys were asked to engage in an athletic **3** tournament, it consisted of activities like baseball and tug of war. This competition led to increased hostility and an **4** ascension in physical and emotional conflict. In stage three, the researchers introduced problems for the boys at the camp. **5** For example, the boys were told that the camp's water supply was blocked and that the boys needed to repair it together. The goal of this phase was to encourage cooperation **6** amidst the two groups to solve the problem. Throughout the experiment, the boys were asked questions about members of their own group, the "ingroup," and members of the other group, the "outgroup."

2

A) NO CHANGE
B) they all
C) the researchers
D) the boys

3

A) NO CHANGE
B) tournament consisting of activities
C) tournament; consisting of activities
D) tournament, it consisted of: activities

4

A) NO CHANGE
B) arising
C) expansion
D) increase

5

A) NO CHANGE
B) Successively,
C) Finally,
D) Yet,

6

A) NO CHANGE
B) concerning
C) between
D) through

CONTINUE

The researchers observed changes in the boys' feelings and behavior as the stages progressed. In stage two, the boys developed negative stereotypes of the outgroup and were unlikely to choose friends from among **7** it's members. During the competitions, the boys showed unfriendly and aggressive behavior. Yet after the cooperation in stage three, the boys rated outgroup members more positively and **8** are cooperating with each other more frequently. **9**

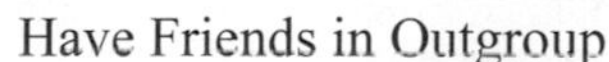

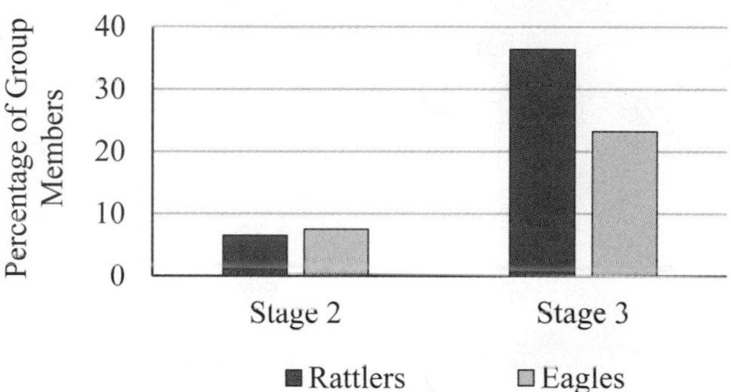

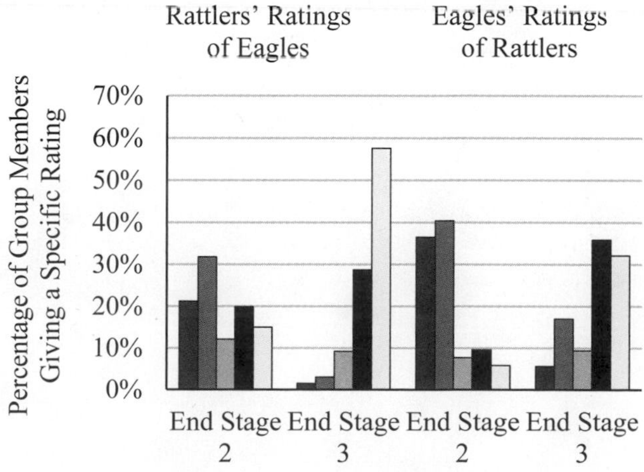

Adapted from Sherif et al. "Intergroup Conflict and Cooperation: The Robbers Cave Experiment." 1954.

7

A) NO CHANGE
B) its members
C) their members
D) there members

8

A) NO CHANGE
B) cooperate with each other
C) will be cooperating with each other
D) cooperated with each other

9

At this point, the writer is considering adding the following sentence.

> The researchers also found that friendships with members of the outgroup increased for both groups between stages two and three.

Should the writer make this addition here?

A) Yes, because it explains how the information in the previous sentence is expressed in the graphs.
B) Yes, because it supplies accurate information from the graphs that supports the main idea of the paragraph.
C) No, because it contradicts the information presented in the graphs.
D) No, because it's excessively redundant to duplicate information from the graphs in the text of the passage.

CONTINUE

[1] From this experiment, Sherif was able to determine that competition tends to fuel conflict, and a **10** public goal tends to increase cooperation. [2] Shared goals also serve to reduce negative stereotypes and increase friendships between groups. [3] Other scientists used similar situations to bring out cooperation and conflict and witnessed the same effect. [4] From his experiment, Sherif concluded that while tension arises when groups form and compete, this tension can be relieved when a common goal is introduced. **11**

10

A) NO CHANGE
B) divided
C) popular
D) common

11

To best improve the focus and organization of this paragraph, sentence 3 should be

A) placed where it is now.
B) placed before sentence 1.
C) placed before sentence 2.
D) DELETED.

CONTINUE

Questions 12-22 are based on the following passage.

Jerome Robbins: Broadway and Beyond

Although Jerome Robbins began his career as a chorus dancer, today he is known as one of the most inventive choreographers in ballet and Broadway. 12 His Broadway shows are still performed around the world. They have remained some of the most beloved and acclaimed productions. Dancers and audiences alike 13 appreciates Robbins' works because of their engaging and dramatic style. During his career, Robbins created hundreds of theatrical masterpieces and captured the essence of American drama and dance in his work.

12

Which choice most effectively combines the sentences at the underlined portion?

A) His Broadway shows are still performed around the world, however, they remain

B) Although his Broadway shows are still performed around the world, they remain

C) His Broadway shows are still performed around the world, and they have also remained

D) His Broadway shows are still performed around the world, remaining

13

A) NO CHANGE

B) appreciate

C) to appreciate

D) appreciating

CONTINUE

In 1940, Robbins joined the American Ballet Theatre and performed there for four years. In 1944, he began choreographing ballets, which he continued to do throughout his career. Robbins was inspired by the American **14** way of life, many of his pieces, highlighted the vitality and diversity of American culture. His first work, *Fancy Free*, was a jazz-inspired ballet about American sailors **15** who enjoy an evening on the town. At its premiere, *Fancy Free* received twenty-two curtain calls. Later that year, Robbins turned his ballet sensation into a musical, *On the Town.* Seamlessly transitioning between ballet and Broadway, **16** storytelling in any form was Robbins's gift.

14

A) NO CHANGE
B) way of life, many of his pieces highlighted
C) way of life many of his pieces highlighted
D) way of life; many of his pieces highlighted

15

A) NO CHANGE
B) who enjoys
C) whom enjoy
D) whom enjoys

16

A) NO CHANGE
B) storytelling in any form was a gift of Robbins.
C) Robbins had a gift for storytelling in any form.
D) any form of storytelling was Robbins's gift.

CONTINUE

[1] In 1957, Robbins choreographed and directed *West Side Story*, which would become an iconic American musical. [2] Inspired by Shakespeare's *Romeo and Juliet, West Side Story* explores the conflicts between ethnic groups in New York City and the trials of young love. [3] However, some critics said the elements of dance **17** <u>was</u> even more compelling than the story itself. [4] The decade following the success of *West Side Story* was a prolific period in Robbins' Broadway career. **18** [5] <u>During this time, Robbins received numerous honors for his work, including several Tony Awards.</u> **19**

17

A) NO CHANGE
B) is
C) were
D) DELETE the underlined portion

18

Which choice best supports the claim made in the previous sentence?

A) NO CHANGE
B) Robbins experimented with the boundaries of dance and storytelling, and achieved wide recognition for his work.
C) With shows like *Moves*, a silent ballet, Robbins explored storytelling through pure movement.
D) Robbins worked on a dozen Broadway productions in this period, including such hits as *Gypsy* and *Fiddler on the Roof.*

19

The writer is considering inserting the following sentence.

> The show received praise for its endearing characters and gripping plot.

Where should the sentence be inserted in the paragraph?

A) Before sentence 1
B) Before sentence 2
C) Before sentence 3
D) Before sentence 4

CONTINUE

20 Conversely, Robbins also took some of his works from the stage to the screen. In 1956, he was asked to recreate his dances for the film *The King and I*. In 1961, he co-directed the film version of *West Side Story*, for which he won two Academy Awards. While Robbins's Broadway shows continued to be produced around the world, his expansion into film 21 condensed his artistic legacy.

Throughout a career lasting more than fifty years, Jerome Robbins created innovative and iconic works in ballet, theater, and film. 22

20

A) NO CHANGE
B) In contrast,
C) Likewise,
D) DELETE the underlined portion.

21

A) NO CHANGE
B) settled
C) solidified
D) toughened

22

The writer wants to conclude the passage with a sentence that restates and affirms the main idea of the passage as a whole. Which choice best accomplishes this goal?

A) The stunning success of *West Side Story* on Broadway and on the big screen remains the greatest example of Jerome Robbins's work.
B) Looking back on his career, we are left with only one question: what masterpiece would Robbins make if he were still alive today?
C) Robbins continued working until the end of his life, staging *Les Noces*, his final project, just two months before his death.
D) Through the widespread success of his works on both stage and screen, Robbins shows himself to be a true master of the dramatic arts.

CONTINUE

Questions 23-33 are based on the following passage.

Physician Self-Referral

To combat the high costs of a medical education and increased reliance on technology, physicians sometimes establish themselves as investors in medical facilities to [23] whom they can refer patients. This arrangement is known as "physician self-referral." Traditionally, the American health care system has given physicians great professional freedom, trusting that they will act not in their narrow financial interests, but [24] thinking about their patients' most important interests. [25] However, health care costs are rising. Regulation aimed at cutting costs will become increasingly important.

23

A) NO CHANGE
B) which
C) who
D) that

24

A) NO CHANGE
B) with their patients' best interests in their minds
C) in their patients' best interests
D) in order to preserve their patients' interests

25

Which choice most effectively combines the sentences at the underlined portion?

A) However, as health care costs are rising, regulation aimed at
B) Although, even though health care costs are rising, regulation aimed at
C) But now we must consider that health care costs are rising, so regulation aimed at
D) Meanwhile, health care costs are rising, even though regulation aimed at

CONTINUE

[26] The physician self-referral system creates incentives for doctors to provide unnecessary health care. In a self-referral arrangement, a physician invests money in another medical facility, such as an imaging center. The physician will make a profit when the imaging center [27] do well. This encourages the physician not only to increase the number of patients he or she refers but also [28] ordering more tests for each patient. For example, the physician may suggest an imaging procedure, such as an MRI, be conducted before completing a simpler, more cost effective test. This phenomenon has been documented in studies showing that self-referring physicians order more unnecessary tests. [29] Therefore, it is clear that the financial incentives created by self-referrals result in excessive use of expensive medical services.

26

Which sentence, inserted here, would most effectively establish the main argument of the passage?

A) Ethical concerns are equally important to financial concerns, and must also become a factor in many regulatory debates.

B) Medical school costs have more than doubled in the last fifty years, contributing to overcharging by physicians.

C) Such cost containment can be achieved in a variety of ways.

D) Regulation of self-referral arrangements has become necessary to reduce excessive service costs and maintain patient safety.

27

A) NO CHANGE

B) does

C) did

D) doing

28

A) NO CHANGE

B) to order more tests for each patient

C) the number of tests ordered for each patient

D) increase the number of tests per patient

29

A) NO CHANGE

B) Surprisingly

C) Nevertheless

D) However

CONTINUE

A physician's financial interest should never be placed above a patient's interest. Physicians typically know a great deal more about medicine **30** <u>then their patients</u>. Because of this, patients are inclined to trust the suggestions of their physician. In self-referral arrangements, physicians are able to take advantage **31** <u>of this asymmetry, they may suggest</u> unnecessary tests that are costly or painful. While many physicians who invest in medical facilities are likely able to uphold their **32** <u>virtuous</u> duty, regulation of physician self-referral is necessary as a protective measure for all patients.

[1] Some argue that self-referrals don't need to be placed under regulatory control. [2] After all, if we trust physicians with our health, why shouldn't we trust them with their own investments? [3] Further, physicians have specialized knowledge of medical services, so they might even seem like the "best" investors. **33** [4] But surely these benefits do not outweigh the risk of a corrupting influence on medical practice, and so it is clear that regulation of self-referral is essential for maintaining standards of practice.

30

A) NO CHANGE
B) than their patients know
C) than that of their patients
D) then their patients know

31

A) NO CHANGE
B) of this asymmetry, and may suggest
C) of this asymmetry they may suggest
D) of this; asymmetry, they may suggest,

32

A) NO CHANGE
B) earnest
C) ethical
D) dispassionate

33

Which choice, inserted here, most effectively adds support for the statement in sentence 3?

A) Nurses also have specialized knowledge of medical services, but generally have less capital with which to invest.
B) Most physicians choose to save their income over time.
C) Many physicians are involved in charities outside of their practice.
D) First-hand knowledge of medical practices allows physicians to invest in the most needed facilities.

CONTINUE

Questions 34-44 are based on the following passage.

Submarine Volcanoes

Volcanic eruptions are remarkable and dangerous natural events. While most well-known eruptions have come from volcanoes on land, volcanoes are also common structures on the ocean floor. These underwater volcanoes, called submarine volcanoes, are often submerged beneath more than 8,500 feet of water but produce about three quarters of the total volcanic output on Earth. **34** Even though they are mostly hidden, submarine volcanoes are part of an interesting and productive system.

Before they were able to detect submarine volcanoes, oceanographers were aware that underwater eruptions were occurring. In the 1990s, scientists created a new system to measure the small earthquakes that accompany underwater eruptions. On land, scientists are able to measure vibrations of the earth's surface to gauge the power of an earthquake. When they need to gauge underwater earthquakes, **35** acoustic waves traveling through the water are measured. To see and explore the submarine volcanoes, oceanographers have utilized new aquatic technology that can handle the extreme heat and pressure around deep-sea volcanoes. **36** For example, scientists use remotely operated vehicles to capture images and video of volcanic structures, underwater eruptions, and the marine life dwelling in the volcanoes' surrounding areas.

34

Which choice most effectively establishes the main point of the passage?

A) NO CHANGE

B) Many varieties of marine life thrive around submarine volcanoes.

C) There are several major distinctions between land and submarine volcanoes.

D) Because submarine volcanoes are more productive than land volcanoes, scientists should conduct more research in this field.

35

A) NO CHANGE

B) the water conducts acoustic waves, which are measured.

C) acoustic waves in the water give the best clues.

D) scientists measure acoustic waves travelling through the water.

36

The writer is considering deleting the underlined sentence to improve the focus of this paragraph. Should the underlined sentence be deleted?

A) Yes, because information about additional techniques used by scientists detracts from the focus on measuring vibrations.

B) Yes, because details about how scientists use various pieces of equipment do not provide information about volcanoes.

C) No, because the use of new technologies has already been mentioned and supporting details are relevant.

D) No, because the sentence helps to establish a focus on the hazards of volcanic environments.

CONTINUE

[1] Using these techniques, scientists have observed the effects of submarine volcanic eruptions. [2] Over time, these eruptions have shaped the sea floor. [3] However, underwater lava behaves differently **37** than observations of terrestrial eruptions. [4] After an eruption, water rushes over **38** the lava, so that it then receives 250 times the pressure of the atmosphere. [5] Underwater, lava typically forms "pillows," whereas lava forms hard blocks on land. [6] Like land eruptions, underwater eruptions eject lava, a type of molten rock. [7] These pillows of lava **39** creates the edges of oceanic plates. [8] Because lava cools and solidifies quickly underwater, some lava turns into volcanic glass. [9] Lava from underwater eruptions also supplies heat and chemicals to unique volcanic ecosystems. **40**

Underwater volcanic ecosystems often form around thermal vents, openings in the Earth's surface that release water heated by volcanic activity. At these vents, water comes in and mixes with natural chemicals, minerals, and bacteria before **41** proceeding to exit the vents at high temperatures.

37

A) NO CHANGE
B) than does the behavior of terrestrial lava.
C) than does terrestrial lava.
D) than does the shaping of land.

38

A) NO CHANGE
B) the lava with
C) the lava, thereby applying
D) the lava, gushing over it with

39

A) NO CHANGE
B) create the edges
C) creating the edges
D) to create the edges

40

To make this paragraph most logical, sentence 6 should be

A) placed where it is now.
B) placed before sentence 3.
C) placed before sentence 5.
D) placed after sentence 7.

41

A) NO CHANGE
B) preceding to exit
C) proceeding exiting
D) preceding exiting

CONTINUE

These ecosystems are home to an abundance of marine life, **42** <u>including mussels, giant clams, and other organisms, that thrive in warm conditions</u>. The unique environment around thermal vents has allowed for an ecosystem of organisms that are able to live without energy from sunlight. **43**

While the recent explorations of submarine volcanoes have given scientists insight into underwater eruptions, **44** <u>it is imperative that more continues to be learned.</u> New technologies may allow scientists to capture and measure eruptions of submarine volcanoes, as well as to study the marine life thriving in volcanic ecosystems.

42

A) NO CHANGE
B) including mussels, giant clams, and other organisms; that thrive in warm conditions.
C) including mussels, giant clams, and other organisms—that thrive in warm conditions.
D) including mussels, giant clams, and other organisms that thrive in warm conditions.

43

Which choice, inserted here, most effectively adds support for the statement in the previous sentence?

A) In fact, some companies are looking to collect the valuable minerals from the floor of the thermal vents.
B) Bacteria use the chemicals from the vents to produce organic material, supplying the necessary energy for other organisms to survive.
C) The chemicals present in the water at thermal vents usually come to the ocean through rain, rivers, or groundwater.
D) The water from the thermal vents range in temperature from 60 to 400°C.

44

A) NO CHANGE
B) I think we should still be learning more.
C) scientists still have more to learn.
D) scientists necessarily need to learn more.

STOP

If you complete this section before the end of your allotted time, check your work on this section only. Do NOT use the time to work on another section.

Section 3

Math Test – No Calculator

25 MINUTES, 20 QUESTIONS

Turn to Section 3 of your answer sheet to answer the questions in this section.

DIRECTIONS

Questions **1-15** ask you to solve a problem, select the best answer among four choices, and fill in the corresponding circle on your answer sheet. Questions **16-20** ask you to solve a problem and enter your answer in the grid provided on your answer sheet. There are detailed instructions on entering answers into the grid before question 16. You may use your test booklet for scratch work.

NOTES

1. You **may not** use a calculator.
2. Variables and expressions represent real numbers unless stated otherwise.
3. Figures are drawn to scale unless stated otherwise.
4. Figures lie in a plane unless stated otherwise.
5. The domain of a function f is defined as the set of all real numbers x for which $f(x)$ is also a real number, unless stated otherwise.

REFERENCE

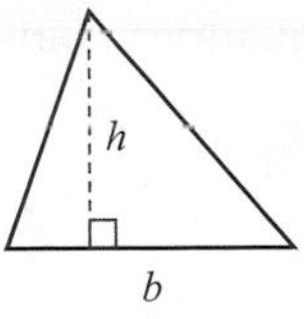

$A = \frac{1}{2}bh$

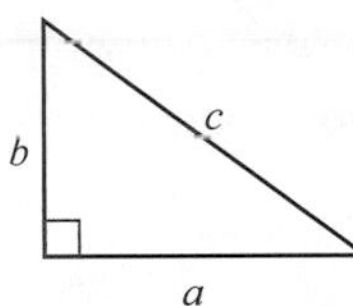

$a^2 + b^2 = c^2$

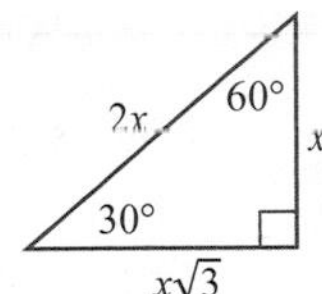

Special Triangles

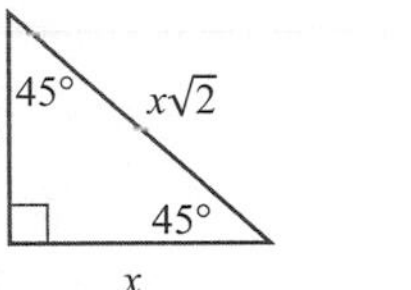

$V = \frac{1}{3}lwh$

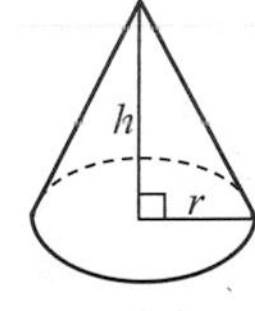

$V = \frac{1}{3}\pi r^2 h$

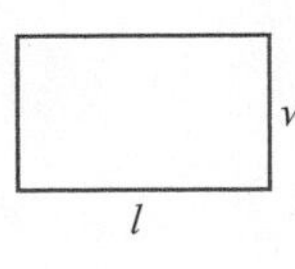

$A = lw$

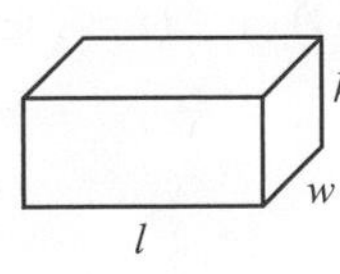

$V = lwh$

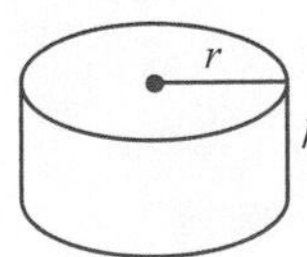

$V = \pi r^2 h$

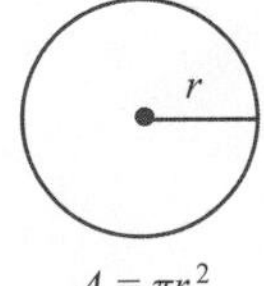

$A = \pi r^2$

$C = 2\pi r$

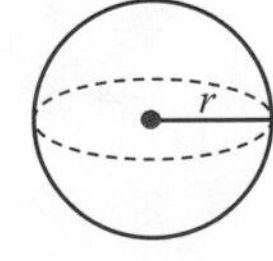

$V = \frac{4}{3}\pi r^3$

There are 360° in a circle.

The sum of the angles in a triangle is 180°.

The number of radians of arc in a circle is 2π.

CONTINUE

1

If $f(x) = x^2 + 1$, what is the value of $f(3x)$?

A) $3x^2 + 1$

B) $3x^2 + 3$

C) $9x^2 + 1$

D) $9x^2 + 3$

2

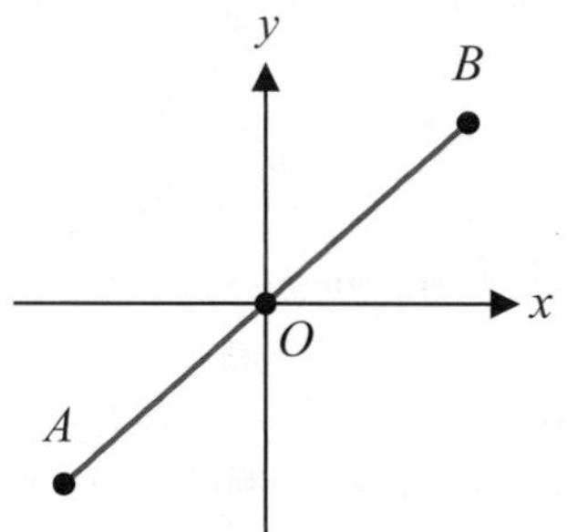

The coordinates of point B in the figure above are (c, d), where $c > d$. Which of the following could be the slope of $\overline{AB}$?

A) $-\frac{1}{2}$

B) 0

C) $\frac{3}{4}$

D) $\frac{4}{3}$

3

If $|2x - 4| \leq 6$, which of the following inequalities represents all possible values of x?

A) $-1 \leq x \leq 5$

B) $1 \leq x \leq 5$

C) $-5 \leq x \leq -1$

D) $-5 \leq x \leq 1$

4

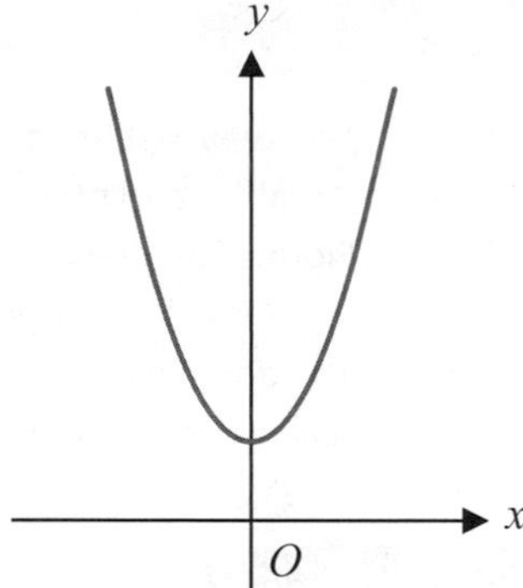

Which of the following equations could have the graph shown above?

A) $y = 2x + 2$

B) $y = x^2 + 2$

C) $y = x^2 - 2$

D) $y = (x + 2)(x - 2)$

CONTINUE

5

$$y = \frac{x^2 - 2x - 15}{x + 3}$$

Which of the following statements describes the domain of the equation above?

A) $x > 0$

B) $x < 0$

C) $x = -3$

D) $x \neq -3$

6

If $2^4 \times 8^x = 2^{16}$, what is the value of x?

A) 1

B) 2

C) 3

D) 4

7

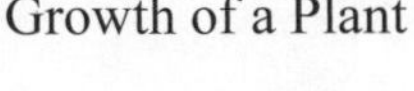

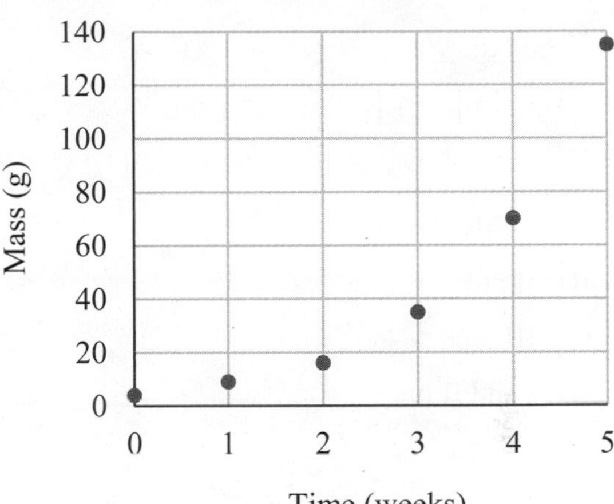

A botanist is researching the growth of a type of plant. He measures the mass of the plant over five weeks. The scatterplot above shows his data. Which of the following best describes the plant's growth over time?

A) The plant's mass increases at a constant rate.

B) The plant's mass increases by approximately 50% each week.

C) The plant's mass approximately doubles every week.

D) The plant's mass is inversely related to time.

CONTINUE

8

If $x < 0$ and $y > -1$, which of the following must be true?

I. $\frac{x}{y} > 0$

II. $|x| + |y| > 0$

III. $x < y$

A) I only

B) II only

C) III only

D) I and II only

9

Two cruise boats follow the same route up a river. Boat A is moving at 10 miles per hour, and Boat B is moving at 12 miles per hour in the same direction. If Boat A is 40 miles ahead of Boat B, how many hours will it take for Boat B to catch up to Boat A?

A) 5

B) 10

C) 15

D) 20

10

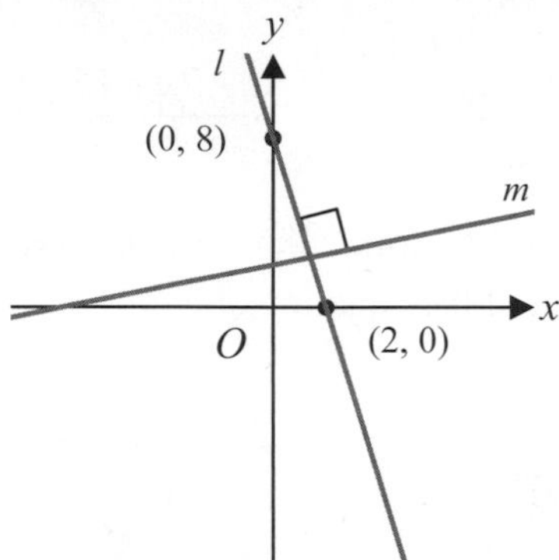

In the xy-coordinate plane above, line l is perpendicular to line m. What is the slope of line m?

A) $\frac{1}{4}$

B) 4

C) $-\frac{1}{4}$

D) -4

CONTINUE

11

If b and c are positive integers, which of the graphs below represents $y = -x^2 - 2cx + b^2$?

A)

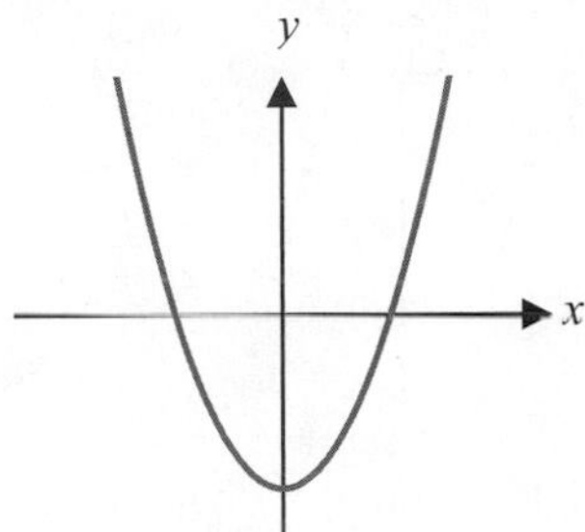

B)

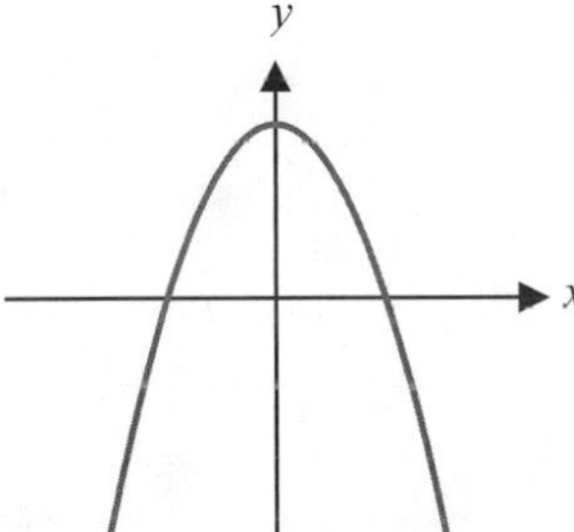

C)

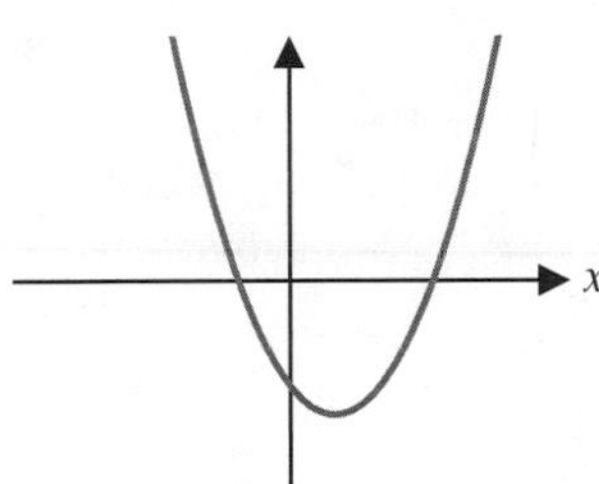

D)

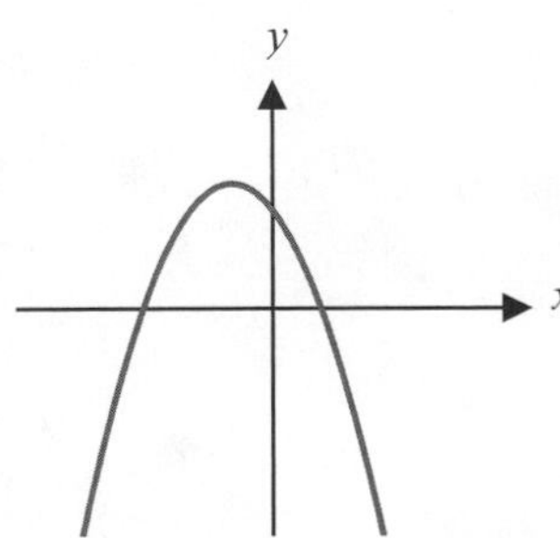

12

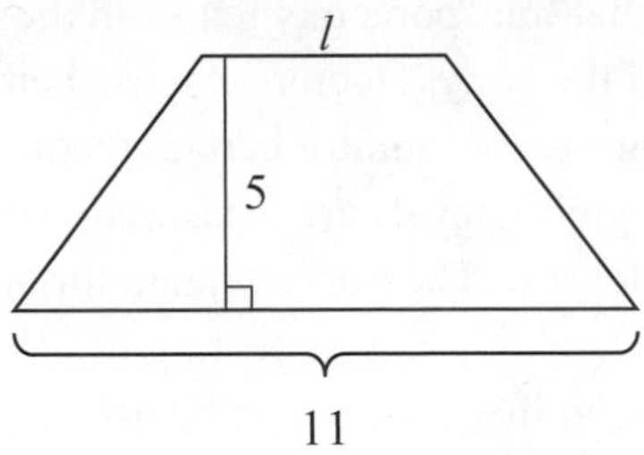

The trapezoid above has an area of 35. What is the value of l?

A) 1

B) 2

C) 3

D) 4

13

For $i = \sqrt{-1}$, which of the following expressions is equivalent to $\sqrt{-9}$?

A) $3i$

B) $3i^2$

C) $9i$

D) $9i^2$

CONTINUE

14

Hemoglobin is a protein molecule in red blood cells that transports oxygen from the lungs to the rest of the body. Doctors can use hemoglobin tests to diagnose or monitor certain medical conditions. Hemoglobin levels are measured in grams, g, per deciliter, dL. The normal range for hemoglobin levels in children is 11 to 13 g/dL. Which of the following inequalities can be used to determine if a child's hemoglobin level, l, is in the normal range?

A) $|l - 1| \leq 12$

B) $|l - 12| \leq 1$

C) $|l - 1| \geq 12$

D) $|l - 12| \geq 1$

15

If $\cos(x) = -\frac{3}{4}$, what is the value of $\cos(x + \pi)$?

A) $-\frac{3}{4}$

B) 0

C) $\frac{3}{4}$

D) $\frac{4}{3}$

CONTINUE

DIRECTIONS

Questions **16-20** ask you to solve a problem and enter your answer in the grid provided on your answer sheet. When completing grid-in questions:

1. You are required to bubble in the circles for your answers. It is recommended, but not required, that you also write your answer in the boxes above the columns of circles. Points will be awarded based only on whether the circles are filled in correctly.
2. Fill in only one circle in a column.
3. You can start your answer in any column as long as you can fit in the whole answer.
4. For questions 16-20, no answers will be negative numbers.
5. **Mixed numbers,** such as $4\frac{2}{5}$, must be gridded as decimals or improper fractions, such as 4.4 or as 22/5. "42/5" will be read as "forty-two over five," not as "four and two-fifths."
6. If your answer is a **decimal** with more digits than will fit on the grid, you may round it or cut it off, but you must fill the entire grid.
7. If there are **multiple correct solutions** to a problem, all of them will be considered correct. Enter only **one** on the grid.

5/11 | 8.4 | 3/7

.422 | .326 | .125

CONTINUE

16

If $3x - 4z = 0$, what is the value of $\frac{z}{x}$?

17

$$y = 2x - 2$$
$$z = 2x^2 - 2x$$

If $y = z$, what is the value of x in the system of equations above?

18

A company ordered \$400 worth of promotional magnets and hats. Magnets cost \$2 each, and hats cost \$4 each. If the company ordered twice as many hats as magnets, how many total items did the company order?

19

What is the product of the solutions of x in the equation $(2x + 10)(x - 2) = -20$?

20

$$\frac{6}{x+4} + 1 = \frac{6}{x+1}$$

If $x > 0$, what is the value of x in the equation above?

STOP

If you complete this section before the end of your allotted time, check your work on this section only. Do NOT use the time to work on another section.

Section 4

Math Test – Calculator

55 MINUTES, 38 QUESTIONS

Turn to Section 4 of your answer sheet to answer the questions in this section.

DIRECTIONS

Questions **1-30** ask you to solve a problem, select the best answer among four choices, and fill in the corresponding circle on your answer sheet. Questions **31-38** ask you to solve a problem and enter your answer in a grid provided on your answer sheet. There are detailed instructions on entering answers into the grid before question 31. You may use your test booklet for scratch work.

NOTES

1. You **may** use a calculator.
2. Variables and expressions represent real numbers unless stated otherwise.
3. Figures are drawn to scale unless stated otherwise.
4. Figures lie in a plane unless stated otherwise.
5. The domain of a function f is defined as the set of all real numbers x for which $f(x)$ is also a real number, unless stated otherwise.

REFERENCE

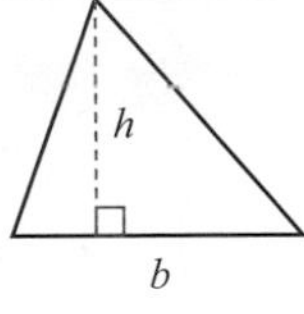

$A = \frac{1}{2}bh$

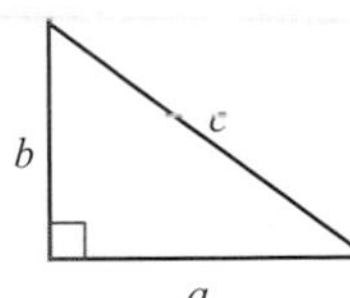

$a^2 + b^2 = c^2$

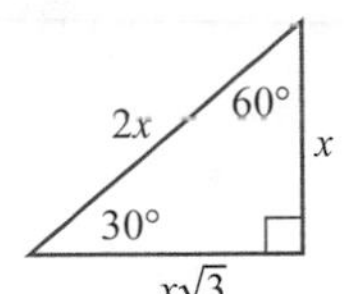

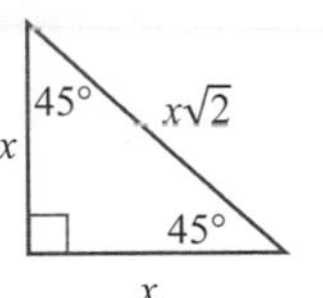

Special Triangles

h
w
l

$V = \frac{1}{3}lwh$

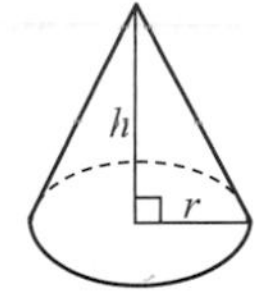

$V = \frac{1}{3}\pi r^2 h$

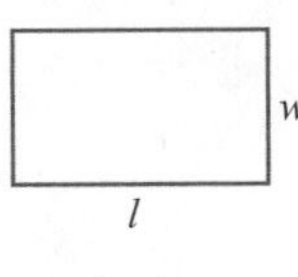

$A = lw$

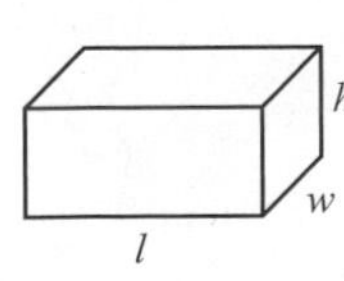

$V = lwh$

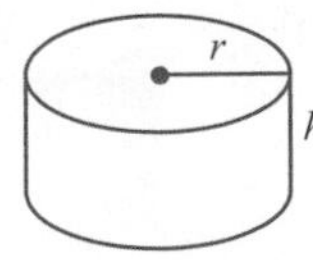

$V = \pi r^2 h$

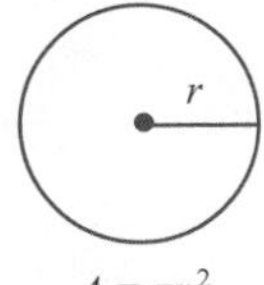

$A = \pi r^2$

$C = 2\pi r$

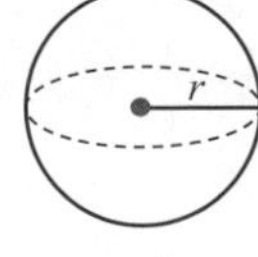

$V = \frac{4}{3}\pi r^3$

There are 360° in a circle.

The sum of the angles in a triangle is 180°.

The number of radians of arc in a circle is 2π.

CONTINUE

1

If $m = \frac{5k}{3}$, what is k in terms of m?

A) $\frac{3m}{4}$

B) $\frac{4m}{3}$

C) $\frac{3m}{5}$

D) $\frac{5m}{4}$

2

A machine can cut 36 sheets of tin in 30 minutes. How many sheets of tin can it cut in two hours?

A) 18

B) 36

C) 72

D) 144

3

x	–2	0	2
$f(x)$	7	3	–1

Based on the table above, which of the following equations could represent $f(x)$?

A) $f(x) = -2x + 3$

B) $f(x) = -4x + 3$

C) $f(x) = 2x + 3$

D) $f(x) = 4x + 3$

4

The lines $y = 2x + 6$ and $y = -\frac{1}{2}x + 4$ intersect at point (j, k) in the xy-plane. What is the value of j?

A) $\frac{3}{2}$

B) $\frac{2}{3}$

C) $-\frac{4}{5}$

D) $-\frac{3}{2}$

CONTINUE

Questions 5 and 6 refer to the following information.

Akiko competes in the long jump for her track and field team. During her practice, she records the distance of each jump in the table below.

Jump Distances (m)			
5.21	4.85	5.34	4.76

5

What is the average of Akiko's distances for the practice?

A) 4.73 m

B) 4.98 m

C) 5.04 m

D) 5.34 m

6

What is the median distance for the practice?

A) 4.85 m

B) 5.03 m

C) 5.10 m

D) 5.21 m

7

If $f(x) = x^2 + 7$ and $g(x) = -f(x) + 3$, what is $g(4)$?

A) 26

B) 19

C) –1

D) –20

8

Monthly Budget	
Expenses	Percent of Budget
Rent	37.5
Entertainment	25
Food	25
Other	12.5

The chart above shows the breakdown of Diego's budget. If Diego spends \$350 on food each month, which of the following is the best estimate for the amount Diego spends on rent each month?

A) \$175

B) \$400

C) \$525

D) \$700

CONTINUE

9

Which of the following is the equation of a line that is parallel to $5y = -6x + 10$?

A) $y = -\frac{5}{6}x - \frac{9}{10}$

B) $y = \frac{5}{6}x - \frac{5}{12}$

C) $y = -\frac{6}{5}x + \frac{1}{2}$

D) $y = -\frac{6}{5} + \frac{13}{10}$

10

The outermost layer of the Earth's surface is made up of tectonic plates that shift very slowly. Scientists determine that the plates move apart at an average rate of 8 mm per year. At the beginning of the study, two of the plates are 3 mm apart. Which of the following functions represents the distance, D, in millimeters, between the plates y years after the start of the study?

A) $D(y) = 3 + 8y$

B) $D(y) = 3 + 0.8y$

C) $D(y) = 3 + 0.08y$

D) $D(y) = 3 + 0.008y$

11

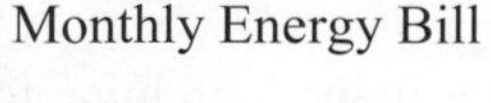

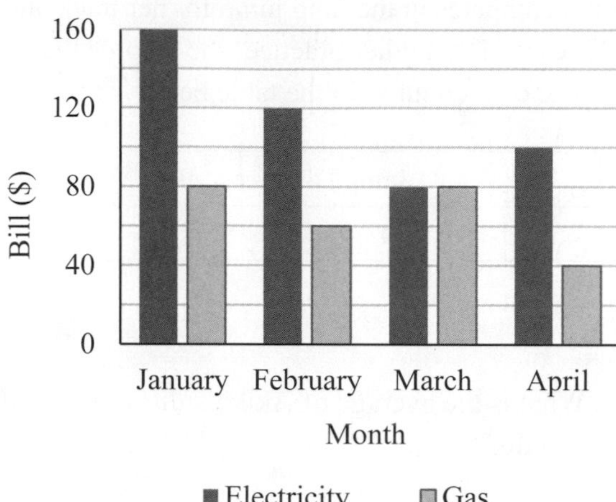

The bar graph above shows a family's monthly energy bill for electricity and gas. For the four months shown, what is the ratio of the total electricity bill to the total gas bill?

A) 23:13

B) 21:12

C) 13:23

D) 12:21

12

A line passes through the points $(-3, 0)$ and $(0, 3)$. Which of the following points lies on the line?

A) $(-6, 0)$

B) $(-6, 3)$

C) $(3, 0)$

D) $(3, 6)$

CONTINUE

13

$$f(x) = 2x + 6$$

The function $f(x)$ is defined above. If $2f(k) = 24$, what is the value of $f(3k)$?

A) 12

B) 24

C) 36

D) 48

14

$$2k + 3n < 2k$$

Based on the inequality above, which of the following must be true?

A) $k > \frac{2}{3}n$

B) $k = 0$

C) $n < 0$

D) $k = 0$ and $n < 0$

15

$$h = -(t - 5)^2 + 3$$

The equation for the height h of a toy rocket above the top of its launch platform at time t is shown above. At what time will the rocket attain its maximum height?

A) 3

B) 5

C) 8

D) 10

16

Alex drove 20 km to work at an average speed of 80 km/hour. On the way back, he drove at an average speed of 60 km/hour along the same route. What was his average speed for the round trip?

A) 74.6 km/hour

B) 71.4 km/hour

C) 70.0 km/hour

D) 68.6 km/hour

CONTINUE

17

Which of the following graphs represents the equation $y = |x + 2| + 1$?

A)
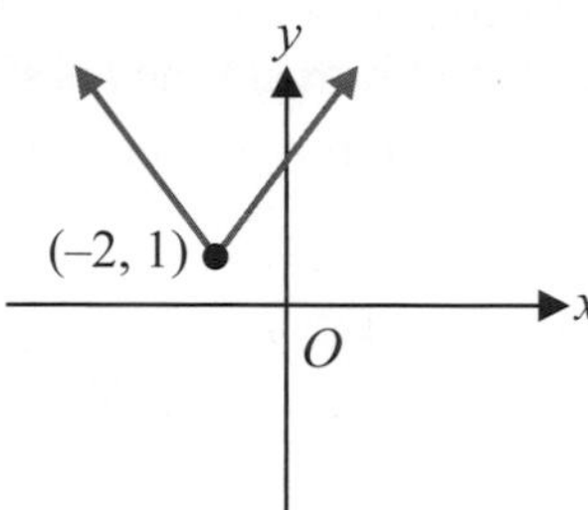

B)
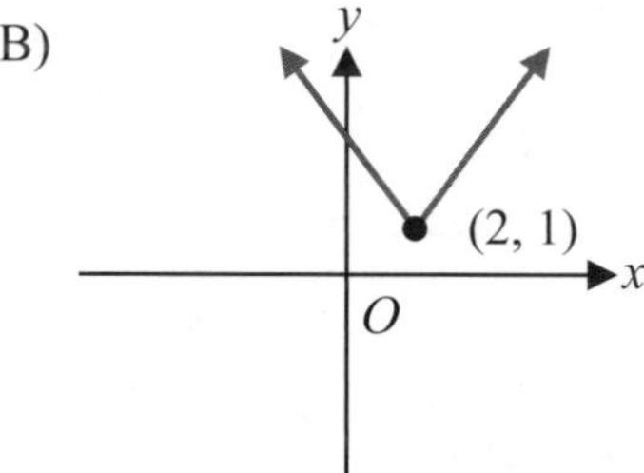

C)
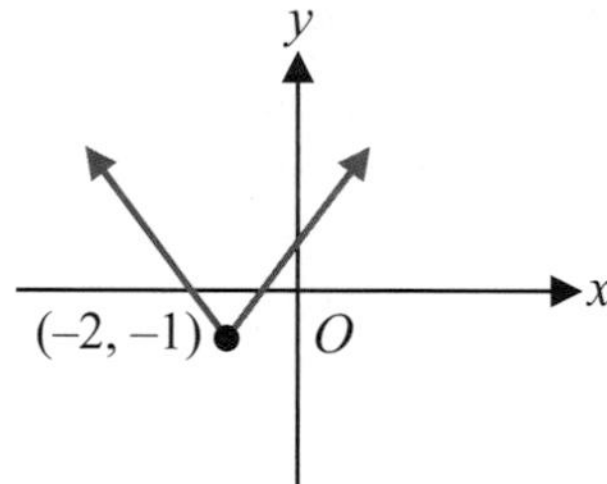

D)
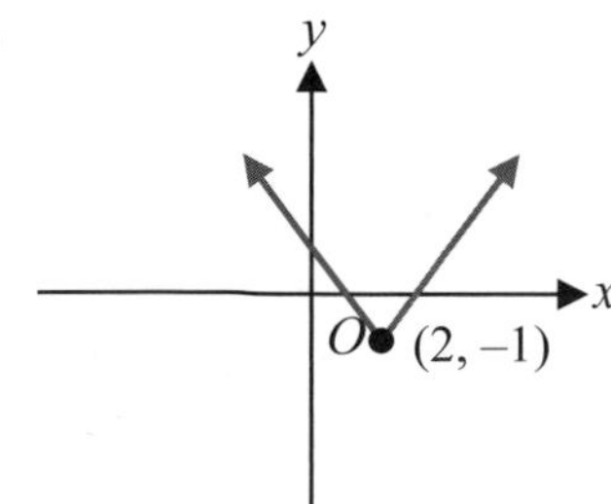

18

A weather station measures the outdoor temperature, in degrees Fahrenheit, between 8:00 PM and 8:00 AM. Researchers use this data to create a model for overnight temperature patterns. They find the temperature T for one night's data was related to the number of hours after 8:00 PM, h, according to the equation $T = h^2 - 12h + 46$. Based on this model, at what time did the temperature reach its minimum?

A) 12:00 AM

B) 2:00 AM

C) 4:00 AM

D) 6:00 AM

19

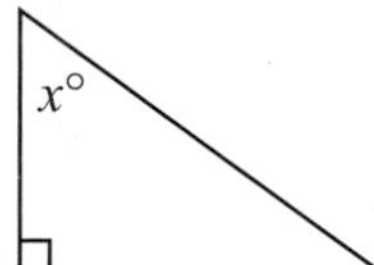

If $\sin(x) = \frac{4}{5}$, what is $\cos(x)$?

A) $\frac{1}{5}$

B) $\frac{3}{5}$

C) $\frac{3}{4}$

D) $\frac{4}{3}$

CONTINUE

20

Popularity of New Songs		
Day	Number of Hits (thousands)	
	Song A	Song B
1	2.0	2.0
2	5.1	4.2
3	8.3	7.9
4	11.2	16.4

A band releases two songs on the same day. They record the number of hits each song receives at the end of each day after the release. The data is shown in the table above. Which of the following best describes the trends for the two songs?

A) Song A's hits show a linear increase while Song B's hits show an exponential increase.

B) Song A's hits show an exponential increase while Song B's hits show a linear increase.

C) Both Song A's hits and Song B's hits show a linear trend.

D) Both Song A's hits and Song B's hits show an exponential trend.

21

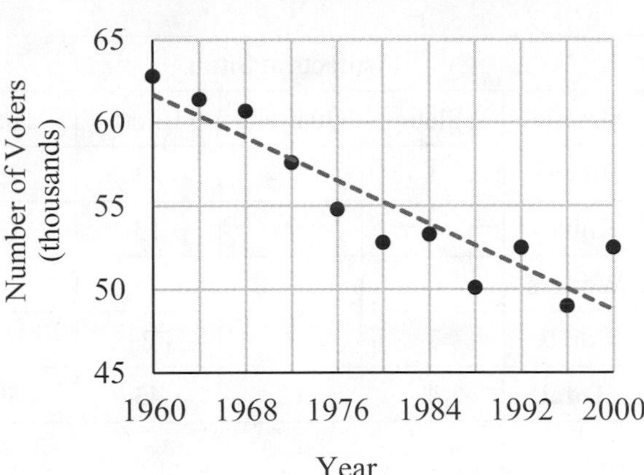

The scatterplot above shows the number of voters who participated in a municipal election from the year 1960 to 2000. Based on the line of best fit, which of the following is the best estimate for the annual decrease in voters between 1960 and 2000?

A) 250

B) 325

C) 2,500

D) 3,250

CONTINUE

Questions 22 and 23 refer to the following information.

Artifacts at Site 1				
Material	Slate	Quartzite	Chert	**Total**
Bifaces	1	5	23	**29**
Knives	0	2	13	**15**
Wedges	0	3	5	**8**
Points	3	2	2	**7**
Total	**4**	**12**	**43**	**59**

Archaeologists studying a region in the arctic recorded the types of artifacts they found and the material of each artifact. The table above lists the artifacts found at one of the archaeological sites.

22

Which tool type had the highest percentage of quartzite artifacts?

A) Bifaces

B) Knives

C) Wedges

D) Points

23

The archaeologists expand the area of Site 1 by 40%. If the artifacts are distributed in the same ratio in the new area as in the original area, how many additional chert wedges should the archaeologists expect to find in the new area?

A) 2

B) 3

C) 6

D) 7

24

How many times do the graphs of $y = 4x^2 - 16x - 20$ and $y = 5x + 6$ intersect in the xy-plane?

A) 0

B) 1

C) 2

D) 3

CONTINUE

25

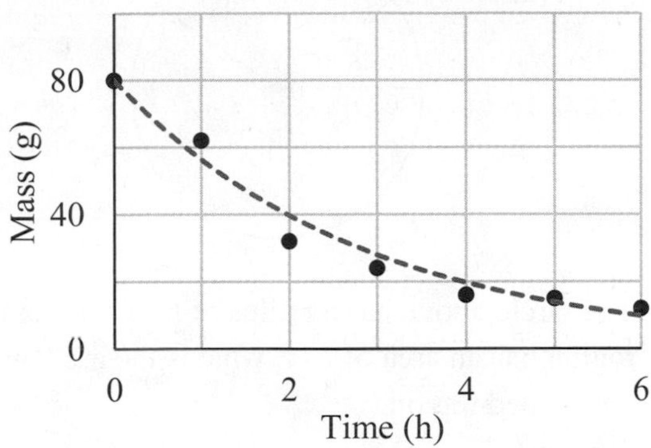

The half-life is the point at which radioactive material degrades to half its original mass. Based on the graph above, what is the approximate half-life of the radioactive material?

A) 2.0 hours

B) 2.5 hours

C) 4.0 hours

D) 6.0 hours

26

If the expression $\frac{x^2 + 2x - 3}{x^2 + 3}$ is equal to $\frac{C}{x^2 + 3} - 1$, what is C in terms of x?

A) $x + 4$

B) $x^2 + 3$

C) $2x^2 + x$

D) $2x^2 + 2x$

27

$$\text{Population density} = \frac{\text{Population}}{\text{Area}}$$

Coastal watershed areas, which account for about 500,000 square miles in the U.S., have three to four times the national average population density. In 2010, the population density in coastal watershed regions was approximately 320 people per square mile. Researchers estimate that the population in coastal watershed areas will grow by 20 million people between 2010 and 2020. Based on this estimate, which of the following is the best prediction for the population density in coastal watershed areas in 2020?

A) 330

B) 340

C) 350

D) 360

CONTINUE

28

A data set has a standard deviation equal to 4. If each number in the data set is multiplied by 6, which of the following statement is true?

A) The standard deviation of the data set increases.

B) The standard deviation of the data set doesn't change.

C) The standard deviation of the data set decreases.

D) It is impossible to determine with the information given.

29

A chemist needs to make a solution that is 8% acetic acid by volume. She does this by adding water to a solution that is 50% acetic acid and 50% water. Which of the following will give her 200 mL of the 8% acetic acid solution?

A) She adds 92 mL water to 8 mL of the stock solution.

B) She adds 84 mL water to 16 mL of the stock solution.

C) She adds 184 mL water to 16 mL of the stock solution.

D) She adds 168 mL water to 32 mL of the stock solution.

30

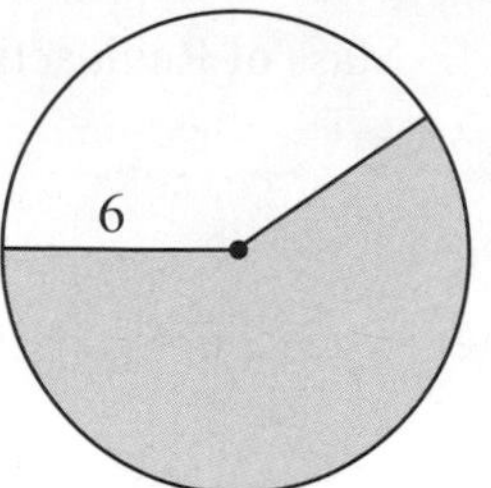

The circle above has a radius of 6. If the shaded region has an area of 24π, what is the arc length of the shaded region?

A) 4π

B) 8π

C) 9π

D) 12π

CONTINUE

DIRECTIONS

Questions **31-38** ask you to solve a problem and enter your answer in the grid provided on your answer sheet. When completing grid-in questions:

1. You are required to bubble in the circles for your answers. It is recommended, but not required, that you also write your answer in the boxes above the columns of circles. Points will be awarded based only on whether the circles are filled in correctly.
2. Fill in only one circle in a column.
3. You can start your answer in any column as long as you can fit in the whole answer.
4. For questions 31-38, no answers will be negative numbers.
5. **Mixed numbers,** such as $4\frac{2}{5}$, must be gridded as decimals or improper fractions, such as 4.4 or as 22/5. "42/5" will be read as "forty-two over five," not as "four and two-fifths."
6. If your answer is a **decimal** with more digits than will fit on the grid, you may round it or cut it off, but you must fill the entire grid.
7. If there are **multiple correct solutions** to a problem, all of them will be considered correct. Enter only **one** on the grid.

5/11	8.4	3/7
.422	.326	.125

CONTINUE

31

$$\sqrt{x+1} - 5 = x - c$$

If the solutions for x in the equation above are 0 or -1, what is the value of c?

32

Two miniature solar cars pass each other on a circular track with a circumference of 100 meters. Car 1 travels at a speed of 1 m/s along the track and Car 2 travels at a speed of 3 m/s in the opposite direction along the same track. If they both continue travelling at constant speeds, how many seconds will it take them to pass each other again?

33

$$\frac{y}{4} + \frac{x}{2} = 1$$

$$y - 2 = 2x$$

Based on the system of equations above, what is the value of $4x$?

34

On Monday the mean age of the employees of a bakery is 43 years. After hiring a new 19-year-old employee on Tuesday, the mean age of the bakery employees is now 41 years. How many employees did the bakery have on Monday?

35

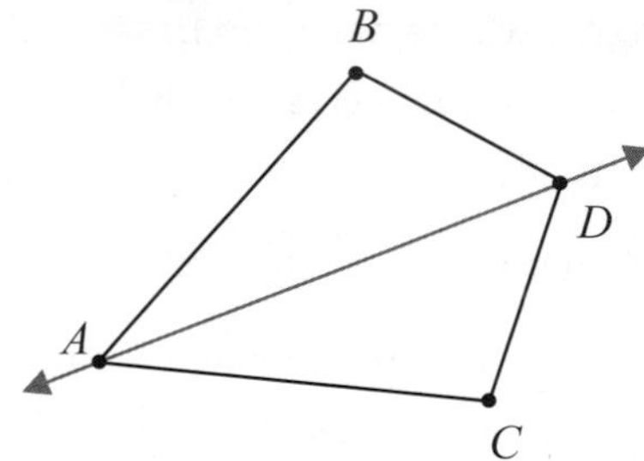

In the diagram above, $\overline{AD}$ bisects $\angle BAC$ and $\angle BDC$. $\angle BAC = 50°$ and $\angle BDC = 110°$. What is the measure, in degrees, of $\angle ABD$?

36

$$x^2 + px + q = 0$$

If the only solution for x in the equation above is 5, what is the value of $p + q$?

CONTINUE

Questions 37 and 38 refer to the following information.

A machine that shapes water bottles can be adjusted to produce bottles at different rates. A faster rate produces more water bottles per minute but, if the rate is too high, the machine produces defective bottles that cannot be sold. The manufacturer models the relationship between the machine's output efficiency, E, and its rate, r, as $E = -r(r - 20)$. The rate is measured in bottles produced per minute.

37

According to the manufacturer's model, the machine will produce no useable water bottles when it operates at a rate of b bottles per minute or higher. What is the value of b?

38

The machine is run at a rate of 8 bottles per minute for 8 hours. How many more water bottles would the machine produce in 8 hours if it were set to the rate with the maximum efficiency?

STOP

If you complete this section before the end of your allotted time, check your work on this section only. Do NOT use the time to work on another section.

Essay

Essay (Optional)

50 MINUTES

Turn to the lined pages of your answer sheet to write your essay.

DIRECTIONS

This essay is optional. It is a chance for you to demonstrate how well you can understand and analyze a written passage. Your essay should show that you have carefully read the passage and should be a concisely written analysis that is both logical and clear.

You must write your entire essay on the lines in your answer booklet. No additional paper will be provided aside from the Planning Page inside your answer booklet. You will be able to write your entire essay in the space provided if you make use of every line, keep tight margins, and write at a suitable size. Don't forget to keep your handwriting legible for the readers evaluating your essay.

You will have 50 minutes to read the passage in this booklet and to write an essay in response to the prompt provided at the end of the passage.

REMINDERS

- What you write in this booklet will not be evaluated. Write your essay in the answer booklet only.
- Essays that are off-topic will not be evaluated.

As you read the passage below, consider how Lindsey Lusher Shute and Benjamin Shute use

- evidence, such as facts or examples, to support claims.
- reasoning to develop ideas and to connect claims and evidence.
- stylistic or persuasive elements, such as word choice or appeals to emotion, to add power to the ideas expressed.

Adapted from Lindsey Lusher Shute and Benjamin Shute, "Keep Farmland for Farmers." Originally published September 20, 2013.

1 When we went looking in upstate New York for a home for our farm, we feared competition from deep-pocketed developers, a new subdivision or a big-box store. These turned out to be the least of our problems. Though the farms best suited for our vegetables were protected from development by conservation easements, we discovered that we couldn't compete, because conserved farmland is open to all buyers—millionaires included.

2 Few bankers farm; long days with little pay lack appeal. A new report by the National Young Farmers Coalition, a group we helped start, reveals that one-quarter of the land trusts that oversee these conservation easements have seen protected land go out of production. Why? A nonfarmer had bought it.

3 Still, tax incentives in New York encourage nonfarmers to rent their land to farmers, so you would think suitable land would be easy to find. Most landlords, however, offer only short-term leases. They want peace and quiet; they don't want vegetable or livestock operations that bring traffic, workers, noise and fences. But long-term land tenure is essential for vegetable and livestock growers, who need years to build soil fertility, improve pasture and add infrastructure. Only farms that grow low-value animal feed crops like hay, corn or beans are attracted to one-year leases.

4 Once well-off city residents who are looking for second homes buy the land, farmer ownership is over. After they've added an air-conditioned home, a heated pool and an asphalt drive, the value increases so much that no working farmer can afford it. The farm, and its capacity to feed a community, is lost.

5 Thankfully, there is a solution. The Vermont Land Trust and the State of Massachsuetts are keeping farmland in the hands of farmers through stricter conservation easements that limit who can own it, which keeps farms affordable and deters farm sales to nonfarmers.

6 In the next 20 years, 70 percent of the nation's farmland will change hands. Farmers do not live forever, and most farm kids do not choose to carry on the family business. An eager generation of young Americans is motivated to farm but, like us, they need land and few will be able to secure it without help.

7 The federal government and states spend hundreds of millions of dollars on farmland conservation each year, which can do much more than protect pastoral views for the wealthy. Those dollars must also be used to shore up rural economies and national food security with productive farms.

8 Eighty percent of us live in or near cities. It's critical that farms ring those cities, and that farmers in the ring be protected. The United States Department of Agriculture spends money to preserve farms, but matching funds are required, and there aren't enough.

9 Smart, self-interested cities would be wise to do their part. New York City needs to think about the land beyond the boroughs. The need is well documented: a recent study identified 614 vital unprotected farms in the Hudson Valley. New York City invested in the protection of its watershed in the Catskills; it needs to do the same with farmland to assure fresh food. It must come up with the money and leadership to help regional land trusts protect farms.

10 As water resources dwindle in the West, and as transportation and fuel costs climb and research shows that fresh, clean food is the key to a healthy life, isn't it the job of every city and town to secure the land and the farmers necessary to grow the food they need? Locking up land for farmers is the first step.

11 We started our Hearty Roots Community Farm nine years ago but quickly realized that we needed more stability than we were getting with the 20 acres we had rented in Dutchess County. After a grueling four-year search, a land trust came to our aid: with help from Scenic Hudson, we were able to buy a 70-acre farm in Clermont, a town of 2,000 people, just five miles north of where we'd been renting.

12 This land is protected only by a traditional conservation easement, but because it never made the transition to an estate and the previous landowner felt strongly that it be sold to a farmer, we got lucky. But what happens after us? We want to pass our stewardship of this land on to future farmers. We are now working with the land trust to tighten our easement and make sure that on our land, an American farm family will always have a chance to succeed.

Write an essay in which you explain how Lindsey Lusher Shute and Benjamin Shute build an argument to persuade their audience that the government should make it easier for farmland to stay with farmers. In your essay, analyze how Shute and Shute use one or more of the features listed in the box above (or features of your own choice) to strengthen the logic and persuasiveness of their argument. Be sure that your analysis focuses on the most relevant features of the passage.

Your essay should not explain whether you agree with Shute and Shute's claims, but rather explain how Shute and Shute build an argument to persuade their audience.

Answers

Chapter 7

Reading Chapter Answers

Part 1

Section 2: Approaching the Reading Test

Part 1: Marking Up a Passage (Pages 39-40)

Check how you did by comparing your marked-up passage to a fully marked-up version of the passage below. Don't worry if you did not underline your passage in exactly the same way. There can be more than one way to capture an idea. For example, in the fourth paragraph you may have underlined "shortly after 1285" rather than "late-medieval" to indicate when the Aracoeli fresco was painted. As long as you identified the same main ideas, you are on the right track.

Tommaso Strinati clambers to the top of the rickety scaffold and laughs. "It's a good thing that all this Baroque work is so unimpressive," he says, pointing at the clumsy trompe l'oeil painting covering the wall in front of him. "Otherwise, we might not have been allowed to scrape it off!"

A 28-year-old art historian, he is standing 16 feet above the marble floor of San Pasquale Baylon chapel, a long-neglected nook of Santa Maria in Aracoeli, a Franciscan basilica in the center of Rome. Last year, Mr. Strinati, who is still a graduate student, began studying the church's history. Records suggested that the Roman artist Pietro Cavallini—a painter and mosaicist whose greatest works have been destroyed—spent years decorating Aracoeli toward the end of the 13th century. Yet only one small Cavallini fresco, in the church's left transept, remained visible. Mr. Strinati wondered: had other Cavallini frescoes been painted over with inferior work? And if so, could modern restorers uncover them?

"The answer to both questions was yes," Mr. Strinati says. A close-up examination of the chapel's walls last summer revealed ghostly images lying beneath the surface. The entire chapel, it seemed, was a painted palimpsest. And when a heavy altarpiece was removed from one wall, a remarkably tender portrait of the Madonna and Child was found hidden behind it.

After months of careful paint-peeling, what has been uncovered are dazzling fragments of a late-medieval masterpiece completed shortly after 1285. Although the Aracoeli fresco is not signed, the figures strongly resemble those in a surviving Cavallini work, the resplendent "Last Judgment" fresco at nearby Santa Cecilia.

Mr. Strinati has grand ambitions for his discovery. He hopes that in a few yearsthe fully restored fresco will not only rescue Cavallini's name from obscurity, but also upend the widespread notion that the first flowers of the Renaissance budded in Florence, not Rome. For the fresco's lifelike figures—in particular, an impish Christ child with charmingly flushed cheeks—suggest to Strinati that Cavallini may have anticipated some of the extraordinary naturalistic innovations that have long been credited to the Florentine artist Giotto.

Moreover, the Aracoeli fragments may provide a critical new clue in a decades-old battle concerning the "St. Francis

Legend," the 1296 fresco cycle at Assisi, universally recognized as one of the foundations of the Renaissance. For centuries, the 28-scene cycle—which recounts the life of the saint with a narrative zest and compositional depth that leave the flat tableaus of the Byzantine era far behind—was attributed to Giotto. But since the 1930's, various scholars have questioned this judgment, claiming that the Assisi cycle doesn't resemble Giotto's other work. Now, the Aracoeli discovery is ammunition for Italian art historians who believe that Cavallini might actually be the primary creative force behind the "St. Francis Legend."

The growing debate about Cavallini's importance was the occasion for a symposium in Rome in November. *La Republicca*, an Italian daily, has cast the debate as "War Between Rome and Florence." Mr. Strinati is enjoying the ruckus. "I had a hunch that there was more Cavallini lurking around here," he says of the Aracoeli basilica. "But I didn't expect to find an exquisite work that could shake up the history of art."

Part 1: Summarizing (Pages 41-42)

- Paragraph 1: T.S. glad remove Baroque
- Paragraph 2: T.S. thinks hidden P.C. frescos
- Paragraph 3: Found P.C. frescoes
- Paragraph 4: Resemble other P.C. work
- Paragraph 5: P.C. maybe anticipated Giotto/Renaissance
- Paragraph 6: P.C. maybe painted "St. F"
- Paragraph 7: P.C. causing art history debates

Part 1: Reading a Passage (Pages 42-43)

Unemployment down; labor force same

The unemployment rate, the figure that dominates reporting on the economy, is the fraction of the labor force (those working or seeking work) that is unemployed. This rate has declined slowly since the end of the Great Recession. What hasn't recovered over that same period is the labor force participation rate, which today stands roughly where it did in 1977.

L.F. had increased, now stopped

Labor force participation rates increased from the mid-1960s through the 1990s, driven by more women entering the workforce, baby boomers entering prime working years in the 1970s and 1980s, and increasing pay for skilled laborers. But over the past decade, these trends have leveled off. At the same time, the participation rate has fallen, particularly in the aftermath of the recession.

In one view, this decline is just a temporary, cyclical result of the Great Recession. If so, we should expect workers to come back as the economy continues to expand. Some research supports this view. A 2013 study by economists at the Federal Reserve Bank of San Francisco found that states with bigger declines in employment saw bigger declines in labor-force participation. It also found a positive relationship between these variables in past recessions and recoveries.

Could be recession (temporary)

But structural changes are plainly at work too, based in part on slower-moving demographic factors. A 2012 study by economists at the Federal Reserve Bank of Chicago estimated that about one-quarter of the decline in labor-force Other

Could be demograph (structura

participation since the start of the Great Recession can be traced to <u>retirements</u>.

economists have attributed about half of the drop to the <u>aging of baby boomers</u>.

Part 2: Reading the Questions (Pages 46-47)

1. A 2. B 3. B 4. C

Part 3: Selecting Your Answers (Pages 52-53)

1. C 2. D 3. A

Part 4: Practice Set (Pages 54-58)

1. C	6. C	11. D	16. D	21. A
2. A	7. A	12. A	17. A	
3. A	8. D	13. A	18. B	
4. C	9. A	14. A	19. B	
5. D	10. A	15. C	20. B	

Section 3: SAT Passage Types

Part 1: Literature Passages (Pages 64-65)

1. B 2. D 3. C

Part 2: Science Passages (Pages 70-71)

1. B 2. D 3. C

Part 3: Social Studies and Historical Passages (Pages 74-75)

1. C 2. B 3. D

Section 4: Understanding the Facts

Part 1: Words in Context (Pages 79-81)

1. C	3. A	5. A
2. C	4. C	6. A

Part 2: Explicit and Implicit Meaning (Page 85-86)

1. D 2. A 3. B 4. B

Part 3: Central Ideas and Relationships (Pages 91-92)

1. A 2. A 3. C

Part 4: Command of Evidence (Pages 96-97)

1. B 2. A 3. C 4. C

Part 5: Analogical Reasoning (Pages 100-101)

1. C	2. B	3. A

Part 6: Practice Set (Pages 102-106)

1. C	5. D	9. C	13. B	17. C
2. B	6. C	10. A	14. B	18. A
3. B	7. C	11. B	15. A	19. A
4. B	8. D	12. A	16. C	

Section 5: Persuasive Language

Part 1: Analyzing Word Choice (Page 111)

1. C	2. D

Part 2: Analyzing Text Structure (Pages 115-116)

1. B	2. D	3. A

Part 3: Point of View and Analyzing Purpose (Pages 119-120)

1. A	2. B

Part 4: Analyzing Arguments (Pages 125-126)

1. B	2. D	3. B

Part 5: Practice Set (Pages 127-132)

1. C	5. D	9. D	13. C	17. D
2. A	6. B	10. A	14. B	
3. C	7. D	11. B	15. C	
4. A	8. C	12. C	16. D	

Section 6: Combining Ideas

Part 1: Paired Passages (Pages 138-139)

1. B	2. D	3. A

Part 2: Passages with Graphics (Pages 143-146)

1. C	2. B	3. D	4. A	5. B

Part 3: Practice Set (Pages 147-152)

1. C	4. C	7. B	10. D	13. D
2. A	5. B	8. D	11. A	14. C
3. D	6. A	9. B	12. C	15. B

Writing Chapter Answers

Part 2

Section 2: Approaching the Writing Test

Part 2: Reading the Questions (Pages 171-173)

1. A	2. B	3. C	4. D	5. D
1a. C	2a. B	3a. B	4a. A	5a. C

Part 3: Answering the Questions (Pages 177-179)

1. C	2. B	3. D	4. A	5. C
1a. B	2a. C	3a. A	4a. D	5a. C

Section 3: SAT Grammar

Part 1: Common Grammar Errors (Pages 190-191)

1. D	3. C	5. B	7. C
2. D	4. A	6. B	8. A

Part 2: Harder Grammar Errors (Pages 198-199)

1. D	3. D	5. B
2. A	4. C	6. B

Part 3: Practice Set (Pages 200-201)

1. B	3. D	5. A
2. C	4. C	6. C

Section 4: Expression of Ideas

Part 1: Development of Ideas (Pages 211-212)

1. A	2. B	3. A	4. C

Part 2: Organizing Ideas (Pages 217-218)

1. C	2. B	3. A

Part 3: Effective Language Use (Pages 223-224)

1. C	2. D	3. D	4. B

Math Chapter Answers

Part 3

Section 3: Heart of Algebra

Part 1: Algebraic Expressions (Pages 304-305)

1. A	3. A	5. B	7. B	9. 3
2. D	4. A	6. C	8. 25/3	10. 6

Part 2: Linear Equations (Pages 309-310)

1. B	3. A	5. D	7. B	9. 15/2 or 7.5
2. C	4. A	6. B	8. 4	10. 16

Part 3: Inequalities (Pages 315-316)

1. D	3. D	5. B	7. C	9. $x \geq 4$
2. A	4. D	6. D	8. 3.8 < GPA < 3.9	10. 2

Part 4: Absolute Value (Pages 319-321)

1. C	3. C	5. A	7. A	9. $8.8 \leq b \leq 9.2$
2. C	4. D	6. A	8. 2.7	10. 2

Part 5: Systems of Equations and Inequalities (Pages 325-326)

1. B	3. C	5. C	7. C	9. $5 < x \leq 6$
2. C	4. A	6. B	8. 5	10. 10

Part 6: Linear Functions (Pages 329-330)

1. D	3. B	5. D	7. A	9. 0
2. C	4. A	6. C	8. 3	10. 10

Part 7: Interpreting Equations (Pages 334-335)

1. B	3. B	5. A	7. C	9. 6
2. A	4. A	6. A	8. 13	10. 6

Part 8: Graphing Equations (Pages 344-347)

1. A	3. A	5. B	7. C	9. 2/5 or 0.4
2. D	4. B	6. D	8. $145 < x < 185$	10. 0

Section 4: Passport to Advanced Math

Part 1: Polynomial Expressions (Pages 355-356)

1. B	3. D	5. C	7. D	9. 111
2. A	4. C	6. D	8. 88	10. 48

Part 2: Factoring Polynomials (Pages 361-362)

1. A	3. B	5. B	7. C	9. 5
2. D	4. B	6. C	8. 10	10. 18

Part 3: Quadratic Equations (Pages 367-368)

1. A	3. B	5. B	7. C	9. 10
2. C	4. B	6. A	8. 5	10. 1 or 2

Part 4: Quadratic Functions and Graphs (Pages 374-376)

1. C	3. B	5. C	7. D	9. 4
2. B	4. C	6. A	8. 7	10. 8

Part 5: Advanced Equations (Pages 380-382)

1. D	3. C	5. A	7. D	9. 1.5
2. B	4. D	6. A	8. 6	10. 2012 or 2017

Part 6: Applications of Functions (Pages 386-388)

1. C	3. D	5. B	7. D	9. 5
2. C	4. A	6. D	8. 4	10. 0.2 or 1/5

Section 5: Problem Solving and Data Analysis

Part 1: Measurement and Units (Pages 394-395)

1. A	3. A	5. C	7. D	9. 1050
2. B	4. D	6. B	8. 5.5	10. 54.4

Part 2: Properties of Data (Pages 404-406)

1. D	3. B	5. C	7. D	9. 3.16
2. C	4. A	6. D	8. 3	10. 6000

Part 3: Ratios, Percentages, Proportions, and Rates (Pages 411-413)

1. B	3. C	5. C	7. B	9. 6/17
2. D	4. B	6. D	8. 8	10. 4

Part 4: Probability and Statistics (Pages 422-424)

1. A	3. C	5. D	7. D	9. 16
2. B	4. C	6. B	8. 33 or 33.3	10. 9

Part 5: Modeling Data (Pages 427-429)

1. B	3. D	5. C	7. A	9. 4
2. B	4. C	6. A	8. 2	10. 6

Part 6: Using Data as Evidence (Pages 435-437)

1. B	3. A	5. B	7. C	9. 300
2. C	4. C	6. B	8. 2	10. 930

Section 6: Additional Topics

Part 1: Angles and Volumes of Shapes (Pages 446-447)

1. D	3. C	5. B	7. C	9. 9
2. C	4. B	6. A	8. 20	10. 16

Part 2: Right Triangles (Pages 453-455)

1. C	3. A	5. B	7. D	9. 4
2. C	4. C	6. B	8. 12	10. 2

Part 3: Radians and the Unit Circle (Pages 463-464)

1. B	3. A	5. B	7. C	9. 3
2. B	4. A	6. A	8. 0.89	10. 2

Part 4: Circles (Pages 470-471)

1. B	3. A	5. B	7. C	9. 13
2. C	4. B	6. C	8. 229	10. 3

Part 5: Complex Numbers (Pages 475-476)

1. C	3. B	5. D	7. A	9. 1
2. C	4. B	6. A	8. 4	10. 24

Practice Test Chapter Answers

Part 4

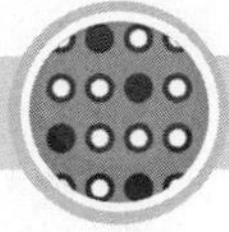

For live scoring and scaling, please visit **ivyglobal.com/study**.

Practice Test 1

Reading (Pages 491-508)

1. B	12. A	23. A	34. A	45. D
2. A	13. C	24. A	35. A	46. C
3. C	14. C	25. A	36. D	47. B
4. B	15. C	26. B	37. A	48. B
5. A	16. D	27. A	38. C	49. C
6. B	17. A	28. C	39. C	50. C
7. C	18. A	29. D	40. A	51. A
8. C	19. D	30. B	41. A	52. B
9. B	20. A	31. B	42. A	
10. A	21. C	32. D	43. D	
11. D	22. A	33. C	44. C	

Writing (Pages 509-526)

1. A	10. B	19. C	28. A	37. D
2. C	11. C	20. B	29. C	38. C
3. D	12. D	21. D	30. D	39. A
4. A	13. A	22. A	31. B	40. C
5. B	14. A	23. C	32. D	41. C
6. D	15. C	24. D	33. C	42. B
7. B	16. A	25. C	34. D	43. C
8. D	17. D	26. A	35. D	44. B
9. B	18. A	27. B	36. D	

Math: No-Calculator (Pages 527-536)

1. C
2. A
3. D
4. B
5. C
6. D
7. B
8. D
9. A
10. A
11. A
12. C
13. B
14. C
15. B
16. 14
17. 6
18. 120
19. 8
20. 6

Math: Calculator (Pages 537-551)

1. D
2. B
3. A
4. A
5. D
6. C
7. C
8. C
9. B
10. B
11. A
12. A
13. D
14. D
15. D
16. D
17. A
18. B
19. A
20. B
21. D
22. B
23. A
24. C
25. D
26. C
27. B
28. C
29. C
30. B
31. 8
32. 4425
33. $5/3 < x < 9/4$
34. .53
35. 400
36. 13.5
37. 13
38. 5

Practice Test 2

Reading (Pages 571-589)

1. C
2. D
3. B
4. A
5. B
6. C
7. C
8. D
9. A
10. B
11. B
12. D
13. A
14. B
15. D
16. B
17. C
18. C
19. C
20. B
21. A
22. D
23. C
24. D
25. A
26. A
27. D
28. A
29. B
30. A
31. C
32. A
33. C
34. B
35. D
36. D
37. B
38. D
39. A
40. C
41. B
42. D
43. D
44. A
45. B
46. D
47. A
48. B
49. C
50. A
51. D
52. C

Writing (Pages 591-605)

1. C
2. A
3. C
4. B
5. C
6. D
7. C
8. C
9. D
10. B
11. B
12. C
13. A
14. A
15. D
16. A
17. A
18. C
19. B
20. D
21. C
22. D
23. D
24. B
25. A
26. C
27. C
28. C
29. A
30. C
31. C
32. D
33. C
34. C
35. A
36. B
37. C
38. A
39. B
40. C
41. D
42. C
43. C
44. D

Math: No-Calculator (Pages 607-616)

1. B
2. B
3. D
4. B
5. C
6. C
7. A
8. C
9. D
10. C
11. D
12. A
13. B
14. A
15. C
16. 23
17. 6
18. 6
19. 4 or 5/4
20. 5 or 1.5 or 3/2

Math: Calculator (Pages 617-632)

1. A
2. B
3. D
4. C
5. B
6. B
7. B
8. A
9. D
10. B
11. D
12. C
13. A
14. D
15. A
16. B
17. C
18. D
19. D
20. C
21. A
22. B
23. D
24. C
25. B
26. C
27. C
28. D
29. B
30. A
31. 150
32. 80
33. 32
34. 33
35. 18
36. 141
37. 8833
38. 1553 or 1554

Practice Test 3

Reading (Pages 651-668)

1. D
2. C
3. D
4. A
5. D
6. A
7. B
8. C
9. D
10. D
11. A
12. A
13. A
14. A
15. D
16. A
17. A
18. C
19. A
20. C
21. B
22. C
23. A
24. A
25. A
26. B
27. C
28. B
29. A
30. C
31. A
32. A
33. D
34. B
35. C
36. C
37. D
38. A
39. D
40. D
41. B
42. B
43. B
44. A
45. B
46. B
47. D
48. A
49. C
50. B
51. C
52. C

Writing (Pages 669-684)

1. C
2. D
3. B
4. D
5. A
6. C
7. B
8. D
9. B
10. D
11. D
12. D
13. B
14. D
15. A
16. C
17. C
18. D
19. C
20. D
21. C
22. D
23. B
24. C
25. A
26. D
27. B
28. B
29. A
30. B
31. B
32. C
33. D
34. A
35. D
36. C
37. C
38. B
39. B
40. B
41. A
42. D
43. B
44. C

Math: No-Calculator (Pages 685-694)

1. C	5. D	9. D	13. A	17. 1
2. C	6. D	10. A	14. B	18. 120
3. A	7. C	11. D	15. C	19. 0
4. B	8. B	12. C	16. 3/4	20. 2

Math: Calculator (Pages 695-709)

1. C	9. C	17. A	25. A	33. 2
2. D	10. A	18. B	26. D	34. 11
3. A	11. A	19. B	27. D	35. 100
4. C	12. D	20. A	28. A	36. 15
5. C	13. B	21. B	29. D	37. 20
6. B	14. C	22. C	30. B	38. 960
7. D	15. B	23. A	31. 4	
8. C	16. D	24. C	32. 25	

PISSARRO'S PEOPLE

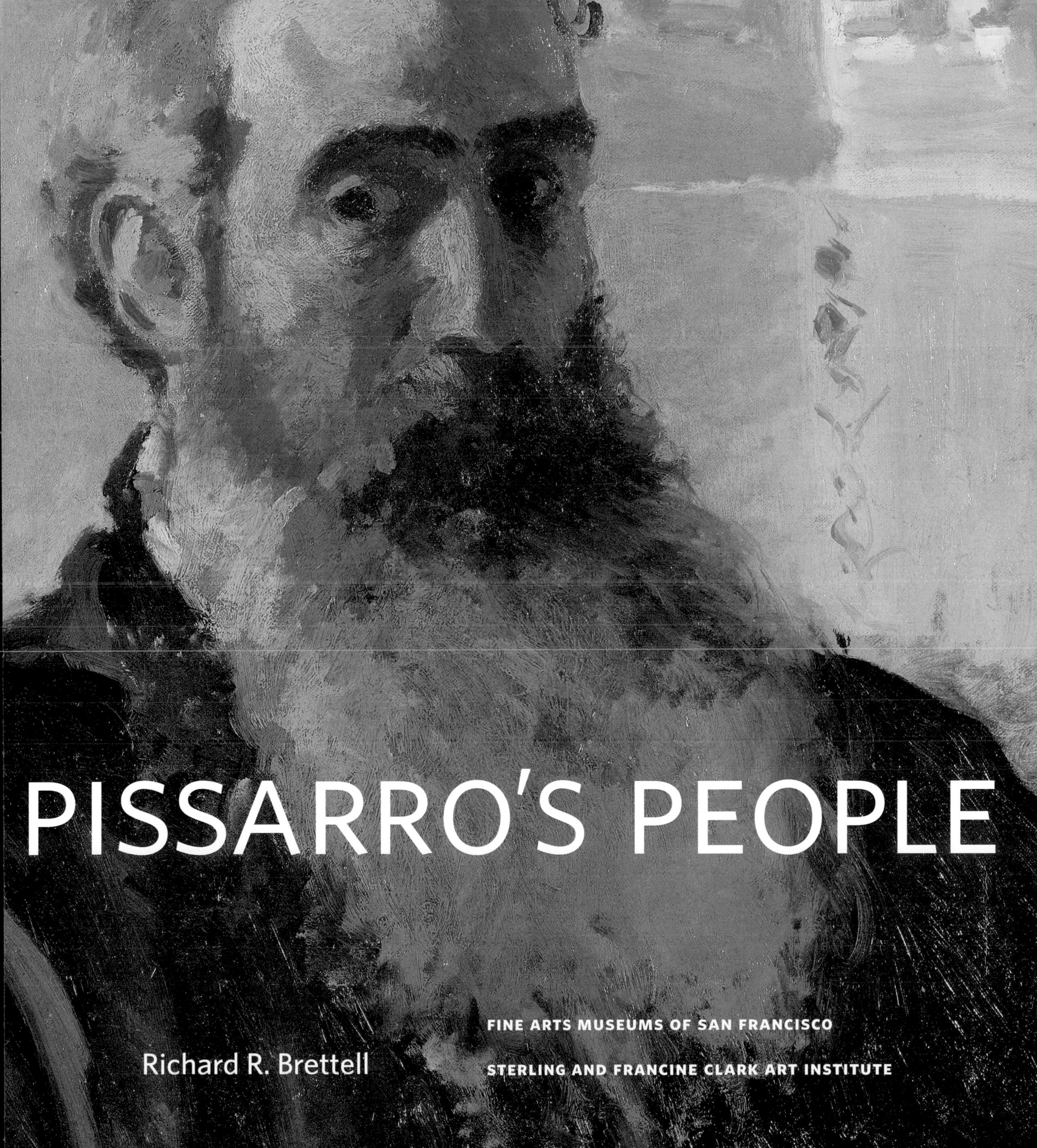

PISSARRO'S PEOPLE

Richard R. Brettell

FINE ARTS MUSEUMS OF SAN FRANCISCO

STERLING AND FRANCINE CLARK ART INSTITUTE

CONTENTS

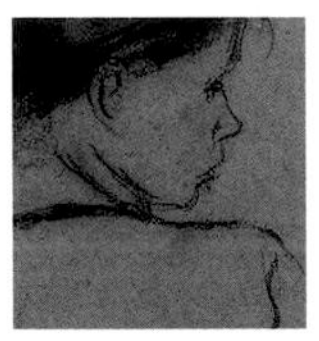

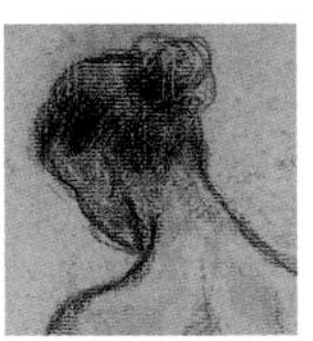

In memory of Françoise Cachin

DIRECTORS' FOREWORD

We are proud to introduce this perceptive investigation of the social philosophy and political ethics of the Impressionist painter Camille Pissarro. It has long been a commonplace to mention in passing both Pissarro's political radicalism and his commitment to the human figure, which is certainly unique among the Impressionist landscape painters. However, this exhibition and catalogue, conceived by the distinguished scholar Richard R. Brettell, represents the first in-depth examination of the family circumstances, life experiences, and personal motivations that promoted and sustained Pissarro's lifelong interest in the human form as reflective of the human condition.

Ranging from his earliest years in the Caribbean and Venezuela until his death in Paris in 1903, Pissarro's extensive output of figural works included more than two hundred paintings and some two thousand drawings and prints. Of crucial importance in this regard, Pissarro was a lifelong reader of social, political, and economic theory. The artist's knowledge of social philosophy ran deeper than that of any other significant painter of the nineteenth century. He was profoundly influenced by the writings of the French protoanarchist Pierre-Joseph Proudhon, and he counted among his friends the radical theorists Jean Grave and Élisée Reclus as well as the greatest anarchist writer of the period, the Russian émigré prince Peter Kropotkin. It is clear that Pissarro's careful study of social and economic philosophy colored his many depictions of rural and domestic workers.

1

Pissarro and his wife, Julie (montage of two photographs), ca. 1873

No less important for the evolution of Pissarro's figurative works was his identity as a member of a diasporic Sephardic Jewish family—a network of individuals living and working in Uruguay and Venezuela, Bordeaux and Paris, and even London and the United States. Dr. Brettell's long-standing friendships with Pissarro's descendants have aided in no small measure the veracity of his reconstruction of the artist's community of family and friends. For in addition to touching portraits of his nuclear family, Pissarro painted many tributes to the artists, merchants, neighbors, servants, and others who populated his world.

Building on existing scholarship, this project identifies key relationships and significant texts among the vast sociopolitical literature absorbed by Pissarro, taking advantage of newly discovered and largely unpublished letters located in private archives. Dr. Brettell's sophisticated analysis of Pissarro's social and historical context, intellectual milieu, and artworks offers, for perhaps the first time, a fully three-dimensional portrait of the artist. Without a doubt, Pissarro's commitment to family, friends, and novel ideas both ordered his life and permeated his art.

Pissarro's People is a joint project of the Fine Arts Museums of San Francisco and the Sterling and Francine Clark Art Institute, and many members of our respective staffs have been vital to the development of the exhibition. At the Clark, where the exhibition premiered, we especially wish to thank Sarah Hammond, Kathleen Morris, Richard Rand, Mattie Kelley, Paul M. Richardson, Curtis Scott, and Teresa O'Toole. At the Fine Arts Museums, Krista Brugnara, Therese Chen, Lynn Federle Orr, and James Ganz made important contributions. We recognize with particular thanks Karen Levine, director of publications at the Fine Arts Museums, who shepherded this volume through all of its stages with efficient professionalism and deceptive ease. This ambitious catalogue could not have been realized without the assistance of associate editor Danica Hodge and managing editor Leslie Dutcher, the careful copyediting of Jennifer Boynton, the wise counsel of Ed Marquand and his team at Marquand Books, and the enthusiastic partnership of Mary DelMonico and her colleagues at Prestel.

We extend warm appreciation to the many collectors, museums, galleries, and auction houses that furnished images for reproduction, and especially to Sandrine Pissarro for her magnificent selection of family photographs from the Archives L&S Pissarro in Paris. For their advice and information on the selection of artworks, Dr. Brettell is particularly indebted to Joachim Pissarro, Claire Durand-Ruel Snollaerts, and Barbara Stern Shapiro, who were continuously peppered with e-mails and phone calls in the final two years of this exhibition's long gestation period. He is also indebted to Marie-Christine Maufus at the Wildenstein Institute in Paris for help with photographs. Perhaps the greatest thanks for *Pissarro's People* goes to George Shackelford of the Museum of Fine Arts, Boston, who took Dr. Brettell's cumbersome draft titles and created a two-word masterpiece.

Every exhibition is indebted to the generous private collectors and museums that must part with their treasures for the duration of the tour. We would be remiss if we did not single out for special thanks the Ashmolean Museum at the University of Oxford. Its loan of twenty artworks makes it an essential partner in this exhibition, giving international recognition to its Pissarro collection and archive, which represent the single largest institutional holding of works by this artist. To each of our other lenders we extend our utmost gratitude. In addition, the support of the National Endowment for the Arts has become absolutely essential for such international exhibitions; we deeply appreciate the NEA's commitment to the nation's cultural programs. The San Francisco presentation of *Pissarro's People* is made possible by the generous support of Jeannik Méquet Littlefield, who has come on board as our grand patron. Education programs presented in conjunction with this exhibition are generously underwritten by Denise Littlefield Sobel. The catalogue is published with the assistance of the Fine Arts Museums' Andrew W. Mellon Endowment for Publications.

We cannot conclude without expressing profound thanks to our friend and colleague Rick Brettell. An art historian of amazing breadth, Rick continues to engage general audiences and scholars alike with his intellectual integrity, easy accessibility, and sharp wit. In the pages of this catalogue, he shares insights of the most detailed and nuanced sophistication as if in conversation with dear friends. We remain in his debt for his tireless efforts to bring this exhibition and publication to fruition—and for bringing Pissarro's people to light.

John E. Buchanan, Jr.
Director of Museums
Fine Arts Museums of San Francisco

Michael Conforti
Director
Sterling and Francine Clark Art Institute

FOREWORD

Camille Pissarro painted the first of his four major self-portraits (fig. 2) in 1873 in L'Hermitage, a hamlet outside Pontoise, just north of Paris. Given to the French state in 1930 by his youngest son, Paul-Émile, it entered the canonical collection of the Jeu de Paume in 1947 and was transferred to the Musée d'Orsay when that museum opened in 1986. As Joachim Pissarro has demonstrated, it was in the act of defining himself for others that Pissarro reflected upon himself as a man. What can we learn about Pissarro from this self-image? He presents us with a calm, self-possessed, yet modest man, age forty-three, already nearly bald and with untrimmed hair. His eyes and bushy eyebrows are almost black, and he has a prominent, aquiline nose; his mouth is all but completely covered by his mustache and great gray beard. He wears what appears to be a dark gray-brown overcoat, and a scarf peeks out above its collar. Pissarro does not include his hands or artist tools and, were it not for the two small landscape sketches pinned to the wallpapered wall behind him, we would have no clue about his occupation. The sketches have never been convincingly identified from the scores of watercolors, gouaches, and oils that survive to form Pissarro's oeuvre before 1874, but they are both landscapes of villages, and the white-washed buildings with red and blue tile roofs nestle among fields and trees that are decidedly French.

We don't learn whether the subject was married or single, where he came from, or where he lived. We only suspect that he was an artist and that he might be Jewish, although nothing about the painting encourages us to reach these conclusions. It is modest and utterly secular—a man alone in a simple, light-filled room. He appears to be seated near a window that illuminates the proper right side of his face, yet we see no chair. There is a darkened section to the painter's

2
Self-Portrait, 1873
Oil on canvas
22 × 18⁵⁄₁₆ in. (56 × 46.5 cm)
Musée d'Orsay, Paris, gift of Paul-Émile Pissarro, 1930, RF 2837 (PDR 283)

C. Pissarro. 1873.

INTRODUCTION

Writing a book about the figure paintings and drawings of Camille Pissarro is, at first glance, like writing a book about the landscapes of Édouard Manet, Edgar Degas, or Henri de Toulouse-Lautrec. Although no scholar has braved the waters with either Manet or Toulouse-Lautrec, Richard Kendall and George Shackelford together produced a fascinating exhibition, and Kendall alone a beautiful book, devoted to the landscapes of the figural artist Degas. When I saw *Degas Landscapes* in 1994 at the Museum of Fine Arts, Houston, I immediately scrolled through my mental data bank of Impressionism, asking, "What about the figure paintings of Monet? Pissarro? Sisley? Or the landscapes of Renoir?" Pierre-Auguste Renoir's landscapes have since been treated admirably by Christopher Riopelle at the National Gallery, London, but no one has attempted to deal seriously with the figure paintings and works on paper of any of the three great Impressionist landscape painters. The majority of Monet's figure paintings and drawings date from the first decade of his production and, of those in subsequent decades, most are difficult to love except by those who think that Monet never painted a bad painting. And Alfred Sisley just didn't do enough figure paintings to justify more than a "Shorter Notice" in the *Burlington Magazine* of old.

But Pissarro? He drew, painted, sketched, and etched human figures in every decade of his life and was, in addition, a devoted family man and a faithful friend to the hundreds of men and women who constituted his larger family. He was an avid reader of political, historical, social, and theoretical texts, both in book form and in the journals to which he subscribed. Most of these sources dealt frankly—and variably—with what we might call "the human condition" in a secular capitalist world. Indeed, his left-wing politics,

3
Pissarro and his wife, Julie, near the washhouse in Éragny, ca. 1897

and those of many of his friends and fellow artists, have long been known to scholars, forcing most to think about the problematic relationship between Pissarro's pictorial world and his politics (a subject that is discussed throughout this book).

Pissarro was also assiduous about documenting his life, writing thousands of letters and saving an equal number that arrived at the numerous houses and apartments in which he lived and worked. In this, he is all but unique among the Impressionists. Students of more "important" artists such as Degas, Cézanne, or Renoir would have been happy to have had a quarter of the correspondence that Pissarro left his biographers and art historians, and the late John Rewald, the first great historian of Impressionism, could not have written his pathbreaking 1946 book (*The History of Impressionism*) about the movement without the Pissarro family archives.

Pissarro is known as a landscape painter primarily because the majority of the 1,528 paintings recently catalogued by Joachim Pissarro (the artist's great-grandson) and his colleague Claire Durand-Ruel Snollaerts (the great-great-granddaughter of Paul Durand-Ruel, Pissarro's most important art dealer) are landscapes. The exhibition catalogues devoted to Pissarro that line the shelves of the art libraries of the world are filled with his landscapes; the plates of paintings by Pissarro in the voluminous books on Impressionism are virtually all landscapes; and on and on. If there is a Pissarro reproduced or discussed in dealers' catalogues, auction catalogues, books on rural France, etc., ninety-nine times out of a hundred, it is a landscape painting.

Several years ago, Joachim Pissarro and I decided to excise the cityscapes from Pissarro's landscape production and deal sensibly and thoroughly with his response to the modern capitalist city. This exhibition, *The Impressionist and the City: Pissarro's Series Paintings,* was designed to counter two prevailing notions among students of Impressionism: one, that Pissarro had made no serious contribution to urban painting when compared with Degas, Renoir, Manet, and even Claude Monet (all of whom painted Paris in the early years of the Third Republic); and two, that Pissarro's cityscapes were minor works created for art-market purposes at the end of his life, when his art had become irrelevant to avant-garde discourse. When the works of art Pissarro made in Paris, Rouen, Dieppe, and Le Havre were grouped in the book and, more importantly, in the galleries in Dallas, Philadelphia, and London, it became clear that Pissarro was a major painter of cityscapes rather than a detailed pictorial investigator of specific social interactions in urban contexts. He made what we might call "urban landscapes," in contrast to the urban figure painting of Manet, Degas, and Toulouse-Lautrec so often favored by art historians in their discussions of anomie and modernism. Pissarro was interested in what others have called the "spectacle" of urban life—

an idea of urbanism in which the individual is subsumed by the sheer vastness and ceaseless activity of the city.

From this, one might think that Pissarro's figure paintings are "figured landscapes," where the character and individuality of the human figure are less important than the creation of a generalized image in which figure and ground are treated so similarly that together they become a "landscape." But this is not the case at all. Although one could not mount as magisterial an exhibition of Pissarro portraits as Colin Bailey did of Renoir's, Pissarro practiced the art of portraiture seriously enough to make his oeuvre in this genre more important than those of other landscape painters such as Claude Lorrain, John Constable, J. M.W. Turner, Théodore Rousseau, Sisley, or Monet. When the more generic "figure pictures" painted by Pissarro from models or from memory are included, the oeuvre becomes large enough to investigate in both exhibition and book form. Like Degas, Pissarro's graphic production—his works on paper—exceeds his production of oil paintings and, within this large oeuvre, figures predominate over landscapes. So we have a *real* subject when we confront Pissarro's pictorial people.

Before one plunges into the body of the text, it is perhaps best to pause a moment and think about Pissarro's humanized *landscape* paintings. Unlike his younger colleague Cézanne, who omitted human figures from all but a few of his hundreds of landscape paintings (one of which is a copy of a Pissarro), Pissarro painted only a handful of unpopulated landscapes; indeed, one struggles to find a landscape by Pissarro *without* a human figure. Most of his landscapes and cityscapes have between three and thirty figures, many so carefully delineated that we know their approximate age, gender, and sometimes social class. Whether they trudge down a road, chat quietly by a rural path, fish, sow seeds in a field, sit listlessly on a riverbank, stare at the viewer, snooze at the base of a haystack, buy chickens in a market, wait to cross a busy street, saw wood, bake bread, climb onto the roof of an omnibus, carry a basket of eggs from market to an urban apartment—whether they are bourgeois, servants, workers, or peasants—Pissarro gives us enough information that we are tempted to understand the landscape *through* them. They not only make the *space* of the landscape accessible, they also make it socially accessible, even in fantasy, for the viewer.

Pissarro's first masterpieces were the six large landscapes he created in his attempt to enter the Paris Salon in the second half of the 1860s. These works—and the handful of similarly scaled paintings made at the same time—secured his reputation as a major artist; had he, like Frédéric Bazille, been killed in the Franco-Prussian War, his place in the history of French landscape painting would have been secured. Five of the six paintings depict the hamlet of L'Hermitage outside Pontoise, where the Pissarro family lived in the years 1866–1868; collectively,

they represent this tiny hamlet almost in its entirety. The two areas of flat, alluvial land are the subject of two landscapes that evoke the age-old world of vegetable and fruit gardens, tended by men and women well versed in the cycles of weather, plantings, insects, and harvests. Pissarro includes these rural workers as staffage in the paintings; they bend to weed or plant, walk with their baskets to gather, and look beneath trees for errant plums or apples. The figures are fully part of the landscape, although, because they are small, we are not encouraged to think of it as *their* landscape. Three more paintings represent the hills that form a kind of natural amphitheater around L'Hermitage. In two, we look down onto its houses and gardens, and in the third and largest work, we look up at a path with houses on the hill. In two of the landscapes, the figures are not rural workers. The famous *Jalais Hill, Pontoise* (fig. 4) includes two comparatively well-dressed bourgeois women, one of whom holds a parasol, rounding the corner on a walk up the hill. In *The Hermitage at Pontoise* (fig. 5)—Pissarro's largest painting—we see figures who are surely his wife, Julie, and daughter Jeanne stopping so that Madame Pissarro can chat with a neighbor while other rural workers walk along the path and children play in the fields. In each case, there is a profound sense that the figures belong in the landscape—something one doesn't feel when looking at a painting such as *Young Women from the Village* by Courbet (fig. 6), about which Pissarro was thinking a good deal when he painted these works.

It must be said—and this is an idea that will play an important part in this book—that Courbet and his sisters *did* belong in that landscape much more profoundly than the Pissarro family belonged in L'Hermitage. It was, for Pissarro, an act of will to belong in France at all, much less to become an accepted part of a tiny agricultural community, many of whose families had lived in the region for

4
Jalais Hill, Pontoise, 1867 (detail)
Oil on canvas
34¼ × 45¼ in. (87 × 114.9 cm)
The Metropolitan Museum of Art, bequest of William Church Osborn, 1951, 51.30.2 (PDR 116)

5
The Hermitage at Pontoise, ca. 1867 (detail)
Oil on canvas
59⅝ × 79 in. (151.4 × 200.6 cm)
Solomon R. Guggenheim Museum, New York, Thannhauser Collection, gift, Justin K. Thannhauser, 78.2514.67 (PDR 121)

6
Gustave Courbet
Young Women from the Village, 1852
Oil on canvas
76¾ × 102¾ in. (194.9 × 261 cm)
The Metropolitan Museum of Art, gift of Harry Payne Bingham, 1940, 40.175

centuries. And this very act of will must be seen as a primary aesthetic mission of Pissarro the painter. His landscapes are *primarily* figured, because they are worked by men and women who plant, weed, prune, and tend plants as well as keep, feed, and slaughter birds and animals. His paintings do more than evoke these worked landscapes—they promote them, by placing ordinary people in their ordinary environment, and they make a moral statement by representing them with a certain ambition. The paintings were not made to be viewed *in* the landscape they represented; rather, they were intended to make manifest for urban dwellers—for example, critics, collectors, connoisseurs, amateurs, and dealers—the profound harmony constituted by that landscape. Although landscape painters around Fontainebleau had been doing this for more than a generation, it in no way undercuts the originality and brilliance of Pissarro's work. Indeed, no earlier landscapes accomplished for the French working landscape what Pissarro did with these six paintings. What is most interesting about this act of pictorial promotion is that the cultural distance between Pissarro himself and these landscapes was more profound than the distance had been for earlier French landscape painters *or* for the intended urban viewers. And *this* will be an insistent theme of this book.

If it is, as we suspect, Madame Pissarro who occupies the center of the *Hermitage* landscape, her white parasol both protecting and bringing pictorial attention to her, and if she is also, perhaps with her sister or a friend, walking up the path in the *Jalais Hill* landscape, she made these pictures personally accessible for Pissarro simply by being there. It is less important that we recognize her than that *he* knew she was there. It was, in the end, for himself—and perhaps also for her—that she was included as a figure. When we begin to look specifically for Madame Pissarro, we find her, or a figure who might be her, often. She dominates her tiny front garden—again chatting with a neighbor and again with Jeanne—in *The Conversation (Road from Versailles to Louveciennes)* of 1870 (fig. 7). Surely it is she and Jeanne who trudge through the ruts of a recently plowed field outside Pontoise in *The Road to Rouen, the Slopes of L'Hautil, Pontoise* of 1872 (fig. 8). In both, she wears a sober black dress—scarcely the height of fashion but altogether respectable. In neither is she represented as a rural worker but as a bourgeoise, hardly grand but definitely a bourgeoise.

Is that Madame Pissarro at market in *The September Fair, Pontoise* of 1872 (PDR 266), with Jeanne holding her hand as they seem to pose for Pissarro, who signs the canvas directly to the right of these stiff familial figures? Is that Jeanne, with a little dog nearby, standing on a sunny day in *The Municipal Garden, Pontoise* of 1873 (PDR 309)? Is Jeanne shown yet again, near the end of her short life, wearing a pretty dress while she stands in the same garden looking at a ball, as Madame Pissarro holds the hand of three-year-old Georges nearby (PDR 347)? Is that Madame Pissarro in her flower garden as Georges rushes by on a tricycle in a painting of 1875 (PDR 404)? Is she knitting on a garden bench while her

7

The Conversation (Road from Versailles to Louveciennes), 1870
Oil on canvas
39⅜ × 31⅞ in. (100 × 81 cm)
Foundation E. G. Bührle Collection, Zurich (PDR 163)

8

The Road to Rouen, the Slopes of L'Hautil, Pontoise, 1872 (detail)
Oil on canvas
16½ × 21⅞ in. (42 × 55.5 cm)
Private collection, Texas (PDR 246)

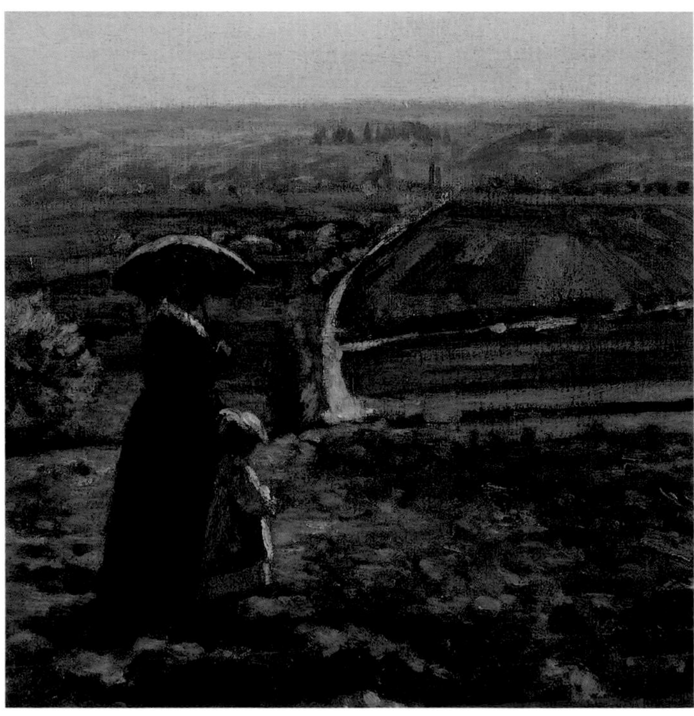

son Félix plays nearby in 1877 (PDR 502)? Is she peeling vegetables on another bench, having just gathered a bumper crop of fruit from the garden in 1878? The answer to all these questions is surely yes. Why does it surprise us? If the artist were Monet, we would think nothing of it. After all, he painted his wife, Camille, and their first son, Jean, countless times in the early and mid-1870s, as the Monet family struggled to find its place in French society. It is simply that we don't think that way about Pissarro. We don't think of him as sentimental, as painting in a personal way, as "using" art at the service of psyche. Yet surely we are wrong.

We will return to Pissarro's family, in both the nuclear and extended sense, but let us first consider the nameless or anonymous figures that populate his landscapes. How many of them did he know? It is likely that, when he was painting in or around Pontoise, Louveciennes, Osny, and Éragny, he knew almost all of them and probably by name. They also surely knew him—a bearded foreigner who spoke excellent but most likely accented French (accented in local terms, that is) and who walked to work and then worked all day, practically every day (including Sunday), on the same roads and paths that they did. In the afternoon, they walked home to lunch together and, at the end of the day, to dinner. Surely he asked polite permission to paint in their fields or to place his easel in their gardens? Surely they looked at his paintings and commented on them. His children knew their children and, although the Pissarros were among the most unusual families in any of the small places they called home during the last four decades of the nineteenth century, they did what they could to fit in. And Madame Pissarro was like many of them in her manner of speaking, her poor writing skills, her practicality, and her ambition for her children to better their lives.

We realize that Pissarro's representation of these several French rural landscapes was in a profound sense intimate. It was particular, specific to locale, and as variable as the place and its people. He was not simply painting *la France profonde* in a general way; rather, he was painting particular corners of rural France, and even a superficial study of the original titles of his paintings makes that clear. With virtually every landscape, we know *precisely* where we are. If an art collector had thought to visit the place represented by the painting, he or she would have met the same people who wandered down the path the days that Pissarro worked on the painting. Surely there were stories of his interaction with these people, for he stood working in the landscape almost every day of the year. Until the last fifteen years of his life, when it became difficult for him to paint outside because of persistent eye infections, only bad weather kept him indoors.

When we consider the paintings as intimate landscapes and their figures as part of the artist's social world, these works change profoundly. Far from being like Monet, Renoir, and Manet, who painted urban and suburban society without social access to the rural poor, the Pissarros lived amid and socialized with rural workers and the petite bourgeoisie (including merchants, construction workers, factory workers, shopkeepers, and repairmen). In this, the Pissarros were much more like the Sisley family, who tended to live away from the worlds of plenty painted by Monet and Renoir, in the socially and economically marginal landscape the Sisleys—like the Pissarros—could afford. They are not landscapes of upward mobility, but of men and women whom we would today call the permanent poor.

It is important to note that these landscapes are *not* like the traditional "peasant" landscapes evoked earlier in the century by Jean-François Millet. The agricultural world around Louveciennes, Pontoise, Osny, and to an extent Éragny was associated with a network of food production centered in the markets of the capital city. Its inhabitants were less timeless peasants who ate and wore what they themselves produced than they were protomodern rural workers who grew crops for sale and lived in a cash economy. Often, they owned their own homes and small garden plots or rented them for very little money from a local landlord. They did not work for anyone but themselves, paying their expenses with cash. They were *part* of the modern world, not apart from it.

We can see this clearly in one of Pissarro's most charmingly evocative paintings of Pontoise itself, *The Parc-aux-Charrettes, Pontoise* of 1878 (fig. 9). Pissarro walked about ten minutes from his rented home on the quai du Pothuis, set up his easel in the shade, and painted both the city of Pontoise and a proto-snapshot of the people who passed by. We see two bourgeois women (one with a parasol); a stray dog; a male worker carrying freshly sawn lumber on his shoulder; a female worker carrying a baby; and a young girl (whose smock and straw hat suggest that she might be a servant or the child of a servant) and a plainly dressed female servant, each pushing newfangled baby carriages they could never have afforded. Perhaps because it is a midday picture, there is only one male figure, but the variety of women and the fact that three of them care for children gives the picture a palpable sense of the future of this small place. In back of the wooden gate is the church of Saint-Maclou, with its wonderful spire by Pontoise native Jacques Lemercier, and the town's middle school, which one or two of the Pissarro children attended. How different this is from Monet's evocations of gardens, sailboats, flower-filled fields, and railroads that we associate with his years in Argenteuil. And there is not a single evocation by Monet of the town of Vétheuil (where he lived with his small family in semipoverty during 1878, the same year Pissarro painted this picture) that demonstrates any comparable degree of social interaction between artist and place. Although none of the figures in the painting turns toward Pissarro as if to greet him, there is no doubt that several of the people who *served* as figures did just that.

9

The Parc-aux-Charrettes, Pontoise, 1878
Oil on canvas
25⅝ × 21¼ in. (65.1 × 54 cm)
Private collection (PDR 545)

This sense of involvement and social intimacy is completely unique to Pissarro among Impressionist landscape painters. Sisley made a real contribution to the representation of suburban and rural labor in his landscapes of the 1870s and 1880s, in which we see dredging, canal work, woodworking, boatbuilding, and other work-for-hire. Yet we have little real sense of participation in the pictorial world of work. Sisley represents without giving a feeling that we could talk to or shake hands with his figures. Pissarro attempted something more specific and human in his representations of rural and small-town life.

Pissarro's figured rural landscape, however, was anything but "natural." He worked within distinct traditions of landscape painting, providing staffage figures to give scale to the space and grouping them in ways that evoke earlier European landscape painters, both northern and southern. When we look at a painting such as *Landscape in the Vicinity of Louveciennes (Autumn)* of 1870 (fig. 10), we find four figures, each of which is placed so as to render the space of this horizontally banded landscape painting more legible. The woman carrying a metal water bucket in the foreground stops to chat with a little boy of about

seven years old (her son?) who is carrying a satchel, most probably on his way to school. Behind them to the left is a woman working in the garden (picking berries perhaps?), and to the right we see a small patch of blue that represents the blouson of a male rural worker farther back in landscape. These figures perform two functions: they allow us to read the landscape's space in bodily terms, and they tell us about the social class of the landscape's inhabitants. By pairing two figures and separating the others, it also gives the landscape a social dimension while insisting on the individuality of the work.

When the figures play less obviously natural roles in the landscape, Pissarro struggles to make their placement appear unforced. Take, for example, the wonderful *Louveciennes with Mont Valérien in the Background* of the same year (fig. 11). While painting it, Pissarro stood in his front garden, looking across the route de Versailles to the small lawn opposite. There, a young woman sits under a sapling and chats with a French soldier, perhaps a recent enlistee given the painting's 1870 date and the obvious autumn season it represents, while an older gentleman with a cane walks nearby. This precise transcription of the landscape includes the church of Louveciennes behind the older man and what has been identified as the house of the town's blacksmith to the left. Monet painted a similar landscape populated by two members of the French infantry in the same

10

Landscape in the Vicinity of Louveciennes (Autumn), 1870 (detail)
Oil on canvas
35 × 45⅝ in. (88.9 × 115.9 cm)
The J. Paul Getty Museum, Los Angeles, 82.PA.73 (PDR 157)

year in nearby Bougival. In each case, the artists (Pissarro was forty years old, and Monet thirty) used the figures to measure their own attitudes toward the recently declared war between France and Prussia. Pissarro's attempt to enlist was rebuffed, perhaps because he was not a French citizen, while Monet fled France with his wife and son because of his family responsibilities. Pissarro's military figure, unlike Monet's pair of guards, is integrated into the landscape because he speaks to the young woman (who could be a lover or a young wife). The integration of figures into the landscape is essential for Pissarro, who makes a link between the local and the national in this simple picture. In Monet's case, the guards seem like temporary inhabitants who have wandered in and might soon leave forever.

One landscape from the 1870s, Pissarro's greatest and most problematic decade as an artist, might help shed light on his figured landscapes: *The Railway Crossing at Les Pâtis near Pontoise* (fig. 12). This now famous painting is signed and dated twice in the lower left corner, first in 1873 and again in 1874. Each signature and date is neatly applied, the earlier in dark black-brown and the later in a medium-value warm gray. (A curious viewer immediately begins to search for those hues in the painting, finding the black-brown in the pants of the male

11

Louveciennes with Mont Valérien in the Background, 1870
Oil on canvas
17¾ × 20⅞ in. (45 × 53 cm)
Nationalgalerie, Staatliche Museen, Berlin, Inv. NG 23/61 (PDR 149)

worker and several of the shadows and the warm gray in the vertical slats of wood in the fence behind the same figure.) The two dated signatures are a record of doubt and struggle and of what Pissarro wanted us to interpret as two separate campaigns on the painting, each of which resulted in a "finished" work and only the second of which we see completely. Pissarro struggled with the effect of industrial modernity in the landscape around Pontoise a good deal in 1873, when he first completed this painting. He returned to the same landscape dominated by the railroad a little later in the year to paint *The Road near the Railway, Effect of Snow, Osny* (PDR 286), now in the National Museum of Western Art, Tokyo. And he painted four works of the then new factory of Chalon et Cie across the Oise river from his own house in L'Hermitage (PDR 297–300). Pissarro represented the railroad bridge across the Oise in both a painting (PDR 305) and an etching (D 37) in the same year, while the slight chimneys of Monsieur Arneuil's paint factory, also on the Oise, feature prominently in two other landscapes (PDR 302–303).

Only three of these pictorial "analyses" of industrial modernism include figures, and just one—the present picture—gives them a prominent role. In the four factory landscapes, the only hints of human presence are tiny marks in the

12

The Railway Crossing at Les Pâtis near Pontoise, 1873–1874 (detail)
Oil on canvas
25⅝ × 31⅞ in. (65 × 81 cm)
The Phillips Family Collection (PDR 306)

péniches (barges) on the river. The railroad landscape now in Tokyo has tiny human figures walking down the rutted road that parallels the raised train embankment. But in Pissarro's painting of the barrier itself, the two figures—one male and one female, one facing the railroad and the other the viewer—play prominent roles. They are larger than the figures in any other painting of 1873 and have a greater affinity with the first true "figure-landscapes" painted by the artist in 1874, the year of the painting's second date. They also relate to one of Pissarro's first series of lithographs, executed, according to all students of his prints, in 1874. We know from documentary sources that Pissarro sold the painting privately in August of 1874, creating a *terminus ante quem* for his later reworking and suggesting that the related lithograph (fig. 13) was made during the reworking, perhaps to allow him to focus exclusively on that part of the larger composition. That the related graphic work is a print and not a drawing means that Pissarro wanted to record this composition rather than simply study it in a sketchbook. The integration of rural workers—of the people of Pontoise and its environs—into a landscape affected by industrial modernity was clearly a problem for Pissarro, more than it ever was for Monet, Renoir, or Sisley.

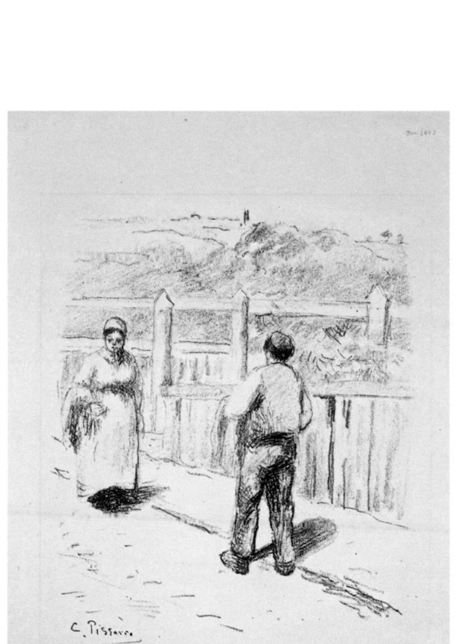

13
A Road through the Pastures in Pontoise, 1874
Lithograph
Image: 10⅜ × 8⅝ in. (26.5 × 22 cm); sheet: 14³⁄₁₆ × 10¾ in. (36 × 27.3 cm)
Print Collection, Miriam and Ira D. Wallach Division of Art, Prints, and Photographs, The New York Public Library, Astor, Lenox, and Tilden Foundations
(D 130)

It seems clear that Pissarro, as he restudied the painting he had completed in 1873, either added or significantly enlarged the figures early in 1874, and that, as he rethought the figures, he also rethought and repainted the barrier itself, making the figures and the barrier form their own composition within the landscape. The figures are deliberately elemental—one of each gender, both adults, and neither "modern" in any sense. Both wear workers' clothing, and the male holds a blue parcel or bundle in front of him so that we have no idea what it is. The female figure, facing us, has a shawl or cloth over her elbow. They are far enough apart from each other that we do not think of them as interacting. They go along, one already having negotiated the barrier and the other about to. In the lithograph, by contrast, they are closer together, although the female figure, who now has the facial features she lacks in the painting, looks straight at the viewer rather than at the male figure. The painting's first owner, a Monsieur Panis, referred to it as the "barrière du chemin de fer" without mentioning the figures, but it seems evident that there would be no need for a barrier if there were no one to stop. Clearly, the largest painting Pissarro had yet devoted to industrial modernism focused on the nexus between the modern and the premodern, between the absent rushing train (which never stops here) and the plodding rural movements that have animated the landscape, albeit slowly, for centuries.

It is interesting to think briefly about the chromatics of this crucial composition. Pissarro made a deliberate decision, probably in the repainting of 1874, to contrast the orange of the barrier and the trim on the house of its keeper with the equally bright blue of the woman's apron and the paler blue of the man's bundle. Orange and blue are a contrasting pair on the color wheel memorized by all nineteenth-century art students. Ever since Michel-Eugène Chevreul's famous lecture on color to students at the École des Beaux-Arts in 1839, painters had been taught that colors on opposite sides of the color wheel visually exaggerated one another when they were juxtaposed. Pissarro seems to have been fascinated by these binary chromatic pairs in 1874, for later in the year he painted a small figured landscape that abounds in them—*Harvesting Potatoes, Pontoise* (fig. 87). It is the sense of optical contrast that makes the other contrasts in the picture so strong: man-woman, urban-rural, industrial-agricultural, forward-backward. Clearly, in this case, Pissarro's figures play a greater role than they have heretofore in his oeuvre. They no longer play by the rules of staffage.

What exactly *are* the rules of staffage? The word itself, the same in French and English (and as euphonious in the former as it is ugly in the latter), is used frequently and hardly ever defined. It doesn't even appear in *Le Grand Robert,* the multivolume dictionary of the French language, and its definition in the *Oxford English Dictionary* is vague, tracing its origins to the German verb *staffiren,* which means "to fit out, garnish." In the large and varied bibliography of landscape painting, staffage refers to elements that are added to a picture to complete it, and it is used for human figures as well as animals, birds, carts, and other movable items that make the landscape believable and particular. Most often, staffage figures or forms allow the viewer to know the space of the landscape first by the absolute scale and then by the relative scale of the figures within its spaces. Staffage figures also compel viewers to explore parts of the landscape that they might otherwise have overlooked. Both painters and critics of landscape deal with what could be called the believability of the figures within the landscape. Their costumes should be appropriate; for example, a staffage figure would not wear a toga in a picture with a seventeenth-century subject. Most importantly, the figures must *not* relate to the viewer, either by gaze or by gesture. That would break the illusory world of the picture, involving the viewer in a way that might literally destroy the illusory rules of art.

I have written previously about a type of staffage figure introduced into French landscape painting by Corot, Pissarro's most often cited "teacher." These figures are in strictly frontal poses and seem to stare at the viewer, keeping us from effectively entering the landscape. Wherever our eyes might wander along the surface or into the space of the picture, these figures are always in front of us. (There are many examples: *Tivoli, Gardens of the Villa d'Este* in the Musée du Louvre or *View of Venice: The Piazzetta Seen from the Riva degli Schiavoni* in the Norton Simon Museum, Pasadena, California.) Like Corot, Pissarro used these frontal figures often in his paintings of the late 1860s and throughout the 1870s. Whether it's the bourgeois couple posing for us in the foreground of a painting

14
The Chemin de l'Ecluse and the Pontoise Bridge, 1867 (detail)
Oil on canvas mounted on panel
12¼ × 17⅞ in. (31 × 45.5 cm)
Tel Aviv Museum of Art, bequest of Lilli Schocken, TAMA 2462 (PDR 122)

15
The Côte des Boeufs at L'Hermitage, 1877 (detail)
Oil on canvas
45¼ × 34½ in. (114.9 × 87.6 cm)
National Gallery, London, presented by C. S. Carstairs to the Tate Gallery through the Art Fund, 1926, transferred, 1950, NG4197 (PDR 488)

of the quay in Saint-Ouen-l'Aumône (fig. 14) or the peasant woman and child who stare out from the tangled winter vegetation in his 1877 masterpiece *The Côte des Boeufs at L'Hermitage* (fig. 15), the figures both enforce our self-conscious recognition of our status of viewers and make us seem like interlopers in the real landscape. Their appearance in Pissarro's painting signals his own sense of "otherness" in the landscape—a sense we rarely have in the landscapes of fellow Impressionists Monet, Sisley, or Renoir, all of whom "belonged" in France.

Pissarro, as we can clearly see, thought deeply about his figured landscapes, sometimes questioning the status of the landscape by forcing us as viewers into a level of social consciousness rare in contemporary landscape painting. Whether they visually "belong" or are consciously "posed," the figures do more than activate or bring scale to their surroundings. Even the act of describing their social natures, ages, and relationships brings the landscapes to life and engages us, as viewers, in a conversation about the nature of the landscape as a human realm. This is equally true when one deals with Pissarro's cityscapes, although, in these cases, his social relationship with the figures was nonexistent. In the hundreds of views of the quays, gardens, bridges, avenues, plazas, factories, and ports of Paris, Rouen, Dieppe, and Le Havre, the figures are deliberately observed and placed, even though they appear to have been observed simultaneously in their present locations.

In *Place du Havre, the Omnibus, Sunlight* (fig. 231), one of Pissarro's earliest paintings in what would become a vast series, we find ourselves floating over one of the busiest intersections in Paris, just across from the east entrance to the Gare Saint-Lazare. The plaza itself stretches from the top to the bottom and to the left and right edges of the canvas and is, at first glance, a swirl of movement—the melee of the city on a wonderful, sunlit day. Centered in the lower part of the canvas is the circular traffic island with a lamppost; here, ten figures cling—with an eleventh about to step on—as if they were on a tiny island in the Pacific Ocean in a storm. Around them are nine hansom cabs, three open carriages, one immense and overfilled omnibus, an open cart loaded with stuff, and a very full wheelbarrow. There are more than thirty human figures, and in considerable variety. Two dots of blue paint in the upper left corner identify two male workers in their characteristic blousons, and two more stand on the traffic island. Two women wear flowing red skirts, and one woman in the lower foreground carries a full basket on her head. The picture literally quivers with life, but it is also alive with social observation. How different it is from any of the great paintings by Monet of the boulevards and streets of Paris of the 1870s, each of which treats the swarming masses of people in such visually summary terms that we are encouraged to think of it as just that—a mass of people. They are not socially specific individuals. For Pissarro, each hansom cab has a driver

PISSARRO'S PEOPLE

No historian of art could imagine a less likely life path for a French Impressionist than that of Camille Pissarro. Born in 1830 on the Danish colony of Saint Thomas in the Caribbean, Pissarro was never a French citizen; he died a Danish citizen in Paris in 1903. As if this were not enough to distance him from his mainly French colleagues, he was born into a Sephardic Jewish family, effectively doubling the distance. Though francophone, the painter's mother, Rachel Pomié Petit Pissarro, was a Creole who first traveled to France in middle age and lived there for the final forty-four years of her life. Although the Pissarros clearly viewed France as home, it was not a particularly welcoming one for this family of New World Jews.

Every serious study of Pissarro's oeuvre recognizes his New World and religious background, but few treat either as important to his career as an Impressionist painter. Because Pissarro himself became staunchly secular, repudiating the practice of Judaism in his immediate family, scholars have assumed that the painter quickly outgrew and discarded his Jewish childhood, making it irrelevant to his artistic production. Only scholars interested in the Jewish contribution to modern art explore Pissarro's religious background in detail, and their literature is easy to summarize: Pissarro was one of a growing number of secular artists with Jewish origins who gave shape to what might be called the cosmopolitan branch of Euro-American modernism. The best of these scholars, Stephanie Rachum, has done extensive research on the Pissarro family's beginnings in Portugal and France and has dealt seriously with the conditions of the Jew in postrevolutionary French society, all without making any convincing links to Pissarro's work. This type of research has convinced secular art historians that Pissarro's Jewish heritage is notable but not essential.

16

Pissarro in the apartment at 28, place Dauphine, Paris, photographed by his son Paul-Émile, ca. 1901. Among the paintings visible in the background are *The Little Country Maid* (cover and fig. 93) and *Woman Sewing* (fig. 147).

Nothing could be further from the truth. Like many Jews in the nineteenth century, Pissarro dropped or modified the practice of his religion. Nonetheless, he assiduously maintained contact with his numerous Jewish relatives throughout the world, and his attitude toward that world was not simply colored but shaped by his experiences as a Jew. The first letter in Bailly-Herzberg's magisterial five-volume compilation of the correspondence of Camille Pissarro was sent by him to his second cousin, Eugène Petit, to announce the death of Pissarro's father, Frédéric Abraham Gabriel. Composed from an address in Passy, then a suburb of Paris, on the last day of January 1865, the letter is heartfelt, beautifully written, and overtly religious. This last quality might surprise those who have read about Pissarro's disavowal of his Jewish faith and his adoption of a modern and secular life; however, a thorough study of Pissarro's correspondence, both sent and received, makes clear that his extended Jewish family—his personal diaspora, if you will—was a core part of his identity throughout his life.

Pissarro maintained close ties with the many branches of his family—named Pissarro, Petit, Manzana, Pomié, Nunes, Cardoze, Isaacson, Auzon, and Bensusan—despite the distances between their various homes in Haiti, Saint Thomas, Montevideo, Paris, London, and even Minneapolis. He also had close relationships with both parents. When Pissarro moved to Paris in 1855, his mother was already living there. Frédéric arrived later, after the American Civil War had disrupted shipping and wreaked havoc with their import-export business in the Caribbean. Although his mother, Rachel, was seven years older than his father, she outlived him by twenty-four years, passing away in 1889 at age ninety-four, surrounded by her family.

Pissarro's father was only sixty-three when he died; from the terrible nature and prolonged duration of his suffering, it is likely the cause was cancer. Pissarro's January 1865 letter tells us several other things about the importance of family. First, it entrusted the family's business interests in the New World to a second cousin with the surname Petit, which was the name of Pissarro's mother's first husband. It also discussed with complete honesty the surviving children of that earlier marriage, indicating that Pissarro's father intended to include them in the succession. Throughout his life, Pissarro corresponded with the family of his mother's first husband. Letters from his Isaacson cousins, including one written from the United States in English, were sent to Pissarro until the last year of his life.

It is evident that family mattered to Pissarro. Although he rarely practiced Judaism as an adult—he married a non-Jew and they raised their children in a thoroughly secular environment—his family ties trumped religious ideology. This diasporic family, which had no native land or language, lived in several countries, creating a distance between themselves and the people among whom they lived, and this enforced distance is essential to understanding Pissarro's life and art. For many Jewish families, the ties that bound them together included all Jews. The Pissarros, however, had a history of strained relations with the Jewish community that could be traced back to Saint Thomas, the painter's birthplace, and this was the basis for Pissarro's lifelong ambivalence about Jewish religious law.

Every biography of Pissarro begins with the contested union of his parents, which is rooted in the traditions of Jewish life in the diaspora. The Pissarro family had been in Bordeaux, France, for only two generations when Pissarro's father, Frédéric, was born there in 1802. Frédéric's father, Joseph Gabriel Pissarro (fig. 17), was the son of Pierre Rodriguez Alveraz Pizarro, whose Marrano (or Christianized Jewish) family had lived in the remote northern town of Braganza, Portugal, for several generations and, before that, in Spain, probably for hundreds of years. (It is likely that the Spanish conquistador of Peru, Francisco Pizarro, was a Marrano.) These Sephardic Jewish families in Spain have been well studied, with particular attention given to the continuous negotiation of their religion in eras under the rule of the Romans, the Visigoths, the Moors, and the Catholics. In the fifteenth century, Jews in Spain were forced either to convert to Christianity or leave, and many fled to North Africa or, like the Pizarros, to Portugal. The Pizarros lived as Jews in Braganza until the Inquisition came to Portugal in the sixteenth century. Even after the Inquisition, the Pizarros practiced their religion secretly until the eighteenth century, when the cruel pogroms of the Marquis de Pombal forced Jews to flee to more liberal France. One can belabor this with copious historical detail, but the point to be made is that Pissarro came from a family that moved frequently, that adapted to various foreign linguistic and cultural contexts, and that had, perhaps as a direct result, developed a strong sense of the importance of extended family in negotiating life's problems. Pissarro, the secular Jewish painter, never lost that sense.

Even when Pissarro's father (fig. 18) was born in Bordeaux in 1802, Jews had been recognized as French *and* Jewish for only seventy-five years—and this status was reserved for Bordeaux (*not* France in general) until the French Revolution. Spelling their surname as Pissarro, perhaps legally accomplished in Bordeaux by Pissarro's father, was important to the regularization of what became a tightly knit and self-regulating French Sephardic community in Bordeaux. It is clear that Pissarro was aware of the family's Spanish and Portuguese heritage as Jews. Interestingly, the painter was ambivalent about the spelling of his name. He had been recorded as Pizarro at birth in the Saint Thomas synagogue records, and he used that spelling when signing works of art early in his career and, indeed, for two years after arriving in France. In fact, it was not until 1882, when he was fifty-two years old, that Pissarro wrote to relatives in Saint Thomas, asking them

17
Pissarro's grandfather Joseph Gabriel Pissarro, ca. 1845

18

The artist's father, Frédéric Abraham Gabriel Pissarro, ca. 1855–1860

19

The artist's mother, Rachel Pomié Petit Pissarro, ca. 1850

to correct the spelling of the family name from Pizarro to Pissarro in the government and synagogue documents.

Rachel Pomié (fig. 19), Pissarro's mother, was what is often called a Creole in the Caribbean: a woman of European origins who was born in the New World. She was descended from a Jewish family that had settled in Santo Domingo in the eighteenth century; after the slave revolt and revolution in that region in 1791, the family fled to Saint Thomas, where Rachel was born in 1795. The Pomié name is fascinating; it appears to be a literal translation of the Sephardic Jewish name Manzano (which means apple in Portuguese) into an approximation of the French word for apple, or *pomme.* Both of Pissarro's parents, therefore, were Sephardic Jews.

The Jewish community on the island of Saint Thomas was, in the late eighteenth and nineteenth centuries, one of the largest and wealthiest in the New World. Saint Thomas, along with the nearby islands of Saint John and Saint Croix, was controlled by Denmark throughout the nineteenth century. The region's largest port, Charlotte Amalie in Saint Thomas, had been tax free since the late eighteenth century, and Jews with import-export businesses established an important presence there, building a new synagogue in 1824. This was also the year that twenty-two-year-old Frédéric Pissarro arrived in Saint Thomas to help his young aunt Rachel, then twenty-nine, with the family business after the early death (he was just fifty) of her husband, Isaac Petit, who was Frédéric's uncle (his mother's brother). In fact, Frédéric was the executor of his uncle's will.

Rachel Pomié Petit was well known in the Jewish community of Saint Thomas, having lived there since birth, while young Frédéric Pissarro had no immediate family in Charlotte Amalie. Because of the religious tolerance of Denmark, the Jews of Saint Thomas suffered little of the persecution that had been experienced in France, and they were prosperous pillars of the community. There was, however, a rift in the Sephardic Jew community: one group was French, from Bordeaux and Bayonne, and the other group was Dutch, from Curaçao, the earliest Jewish community in the New World. To further complicate matters, there was also a split between the Sephardic Jews and the Ashkenazi Jews from Denmark, and tensions between these three groups were played out in the marriage of Rachel and Frédéric.

We know that Frédéric developed a romantic relationship with his aunt, which resulted in the birth of a child in 1826 (Camille's mysterious older brother Félix, whose death date is not known). This birth truly shocked the senior members of the synagogue and instigated a battle that could be followed in the newspaper. The synagogue refused to sanction the marriage of Rachel and Frédéric, which had taken place in the home of a Jewish friend in the presence of ten Jewish men who had become b'nai mitzvah. The union was announced in the newspaper, and the synagogue elders denounced it in the same newspaper. Thus began a standoff between the elders, who had ties to both Curaçao and Denmark, and the French Pissarros that would simmer for eight years. The factions included the synagogue itself (the French, the Dutch, and the Danes), the civil government in Saint Thomas (which registered the marriage), the synagogue in Copenhagen (which was the ultimate authority in Jewish law), and the Petit family in Bordeaux. The latter two factions also denounced the marriage: the Danish Jews on religious grounds, and the Bordeaux Petits most likely for financial reasons.

Frédéric and Rachel had produced and registered three sons, including Camille in 1830, before the synagogue finally relented and sanctioned the marriage in 1833. The eight-year battle created a fissure in the Jewish community, in addition to making the Pissarro and Pomié families feel embattled and disavowed. However, it also laid the groundwork for the creation of a new family business in Saint Thomas—eventually called Auzon, Pissarro, and Isaacson—and this formed the basis of the Pissarro's prosperity. When the painter announced to his Petit cousins in 1865 that Frédéric had died, the business was incorporated in Montevideo, Saint Thomas, and Paris, and it included many of Isaac Petit's considerable business assets that Rachel had received at his death. For the Petit family in Bordeaux, denouncing Frédéric and Rachel's marriage had more to do with the Pissarro family gaining control of the Petit assets than it did with religion.

This controversy played a large role in the psychological makeup of the Pissarro children. Pissarro historians have long wondered why the children were sent to a Moravian school, where they were educated with Afro-Caribbeans, rather than to one of the European schools in Charlotte Amalie. In their important biography of the painter, *Pissarro: His Life and Work* (1980), Ralph Shikes and Paula Harper theorized that the Pissarro children attended the Moravian school to avoid being shunned or taunted by Jewish classmates; although there is no documentary evidence for this, it makes a good deal of sense. What is interesting, though, is the unexpected result of this decision—the painter was educated in an atmosphere of racial tolerance and followed a curriculum that was among the most socially progressive and morally driven in the New World.

When Pissarro's Moravian education ended at age twelve, he had already acquired many of his lifelong values. The Moravian school, together with the religious tolerance of Charlotte Amalie and the multilingual and multicultural aspects of this bustling small city, prepared Pissarro to confront a complex world with an ease essentially unknown to other artists of his generation in France (Gauguin being the only exception). We see evidence for this tolerance and inclusive humanism in Pissarro's earliest works of art, which include detailed portraits of Afro-Caribbean children; complex genre scenes with predominantly black figures; portraits of Danes and European Hispanics; drawings of churches, markets, and ports; and a wealth of social observations done in pencil, pen, brush and ink, watercolor, and oil. In this varied world, Pissarro clearly felt comfortable everywhere and with everybody. His particular emphasis on Afro-Caribbeans, the majority population in Saint Thomas then as today, surely stemmed not simply from their ubiquity but from his education, background, and personal affections.

Who else from this larger world appears in Pissarro's life as an artist? From the letters and other archival evidence, it is clear that the painter was never far from his extended family. It is fascinating to imagine the twenty-five-year-old Pissarro getting off the train in Paris on October 3, 1855, after a monthlong journey from Saint Thomas via London, to rush to the bedside of his dying half sister Delphine Petit. He made his way to 16, chaussée de la Muette in Passy, then a small village on the outskirts of Paris, in which lived his paternal grandparents from Bordeaux (who owned the house); his mother; his half sister Emma; her children (his nieces Amélie and Alice); and Delphine. He was surrounded by relatives, both French and Creole, forcing him to play a demanding familial role that severely undercut his independence as a young artist in the artistic capital of the world. Pissarro's life—and his experience of the city—was centered on his diasporic family: its dramas, tragedies, and particular forms of provincialism. No one in that suburban household was a Parisian (Passy was not annexed by Paris to form the sixteenth arrondissement until the 1860s, and only his grandparents were French. No one was equipped to help Pissarro assuage his protoprofessional anxieties or channel his excitement and desire for independence.

Pissarro, however, was familiar with Passy. His grandparents had owned a house there for several years, and his parents sent him to school there in the 1840s. At that time, Passy was inside the walls of Paris but outside the city proper, and it had the air of an independent place with its own religious establishments, markets, shops, and government. It had been a traditionally Jewish town since the early nineteenth century, and even today the neighborhood has a large Jewish population and an important synagogue. (In fact, several of Pissarro's descendents live in Passy today.) Clearly, the Pissarros sent young Camille there knowing that he would be carefully watched by friends and relatives in a suburban setting with a long-established tolerance of Jews. No one knows whether the school he attended, that of a Monsieur Savary, was specifically for French Jewish boys or simply a private school without religious affiliation. Pissarro had already received an education at the Saint Thomas Moravian school, and his parents likely sent him to Paris to ensure that French would become his dominant language. Although French seems to have been spoken in the Pissarro home in Charlotte Amalie, the language of business in Saint Thomas was English. (Pissarro would also learn a good deal of Spanish when he was in Caracas in the

1850s with his friend Fritz Melbye, and this trilingualism was useful, if it did undercut competence in the dominant language.)

Pissarro's Jewish roots were perhaps of primary importance in his early life, determining even the Parisian neighborhood in which he lived and the people with whom he associated, making his independence a form of interdependence. After he arrived in France in 1855, did he attend the last days of the Exposition Universelle alone or with his family? Did he look up school chums from his earlier days in Passy? Unfortunately, we can never know these personal details, because he was not yet writing and saving the letters that would document his daily life twenty-five years later. It is clear, however, that his world was primarily familial, and in this he was very like the Parisian artists Manet, Degas, and Berthe Morisot, none of whom he had yet met. His future colleagues who hailed from other parts of France or from other countries—Monet, Renoir, Cézanne, and, to the extent her gender allowed, Mary Cassatt—were essentially alone while they lived in Paris, able to meet whom they wanted and not give accounts of their activities to relatives. By contrast, family members were omnipresent in Pissarro's life, as they were for the utterly Parisian Degas—the difference being that Degas's family was Parisian while Pissarro's was at once either provincial or foreign and also Jewish. The crucible of family life was, in fact, a barrier to becoming a Parisian, which is why Pissarro never became one. Indeed, his ambivalence toward Paris was a somewhat constant aspect of his life, despite the luxurious apartments he rented in the capital to complete his late series of Parisian views between 1899 and his death in 1903. He knew the city well, but he experienced it always as a Jew and a foreigner. He also much preferred more intimate communities to large-scale urban societies.

Most of the letters in the family archives are to and from members of his family, with the majority being between his sons and himself, but there are also letters to his diasporic family, particularly the Isaacsons and the Cardozes. Now in the Ashmolean Museum, a sensitive early graphite drawing (done about 1860) of Jules Cardoze, his cousin, is perhaps among the few surviving portraits of such a family member, but there are numerous letters to Pissarro from Jules Cardoze and Louise Cardoze (Louise was married to a brother of Jules). Jules, a novelist who lived in France, was a member of Pissarro's extended family who, like the painter, had opted to pursue the arts rather than commerce. The last letter in the archives from Jules to Camille was sent on January 22, 1897, nearly forty years after Pissarro had sketched his portrait. In it, Jules admits that they had lost touch with each other and refers to two paintings by Pissarro in his collection—works from the earliest days of Pissarro's career. It also mentions other aged relatives—Pissarro was sixty-six at the time—as well as Cardoze's father, then eighty-seven years old and living in Auvergne. The surviving Cardoze letters to

Pissarro date from 1856 to 1897. Who can say that the secularized Pissarro forgot his Jewish origins and family?

The letters to the Isaacsons are also interesting. Pissarro's half sister Emma Petit married Phineas Isaacson, an English Ashkenazi Jew, in Saint Thomas. The couple (fig. 20) produced five children, the last of whom was born in 1861 and named Alfred after Pissarro's brother, before Emma's death in 1868. The archives include letters to Pissarro from three of these children—Amélie, Rodolphe, and Alfred—dating between 1870 and 1886, when Alfred writes his uncle alternately in English and French from Minneapolis, Minnesota. The letters from Amélie and Rodolphe were written in the 1870s, after the death of their mother. Each letter is in perfectly correct and fluent French, the language of their mother but not their father, who spoke English for most of his life. Pissarro, of course, was almost equally fluent in both languages, having spoken and written in English since the 1840s. But the children, recognizing that the painter was their mother's half brother, always took the opportunity to practice their French when corresponding with him. The final letter of the group, from Alfred, is worth quoting not simply because it was written in English but also because it reveals the continuous importance of diasporic family for the painter.

20

Pissarro's half sister Emma Petit with her husband, Phineas Isaacson, ca. 1865

> My dearest uncle,
> Many thanks for your letter of ___. Its length and interest have made ample amends for your long silence. It is so refreshing(ly) pleasant to read you that I hope you will give me that at least as often as you can.
>
> I quite understand what you write concerning socialism. The idea is logical and necessary. I am convinced thereof. As such, it [a social revolution] must come some day.

From there, the letter—which contains more grammatical mistakes in English than in French—veers into French and concentrates on the twenty-seven-year-old man's own political ideas as well as his reactions to American capitalism. This indicates that Pissarro felt truly responsible for educating the young members of both his immediate and extended families in the theories of anarchism and socialism that consumed him as a painter and as a modern man. The letter from Pissarro to Alfred does not survive, which is a pity, because it might have prepared us for what was to be Pissarro's most elaborate political statement as an artist—*Les turpitudes sociales* (figs. 190–221), a unique book of drawings begun in 1889 for his niece Esther Isaacson (who was soon to become his daughter-in-law as well) and her sister. It is clear both from Alfred's reply to his uncle and from *Les turpitudes sociales* (to be extensively discussed in section II of this volume) that Pissarro reserved his most overt and trenchant political communications for his own family. Within this world, he felt comfortable enough to be frank about views that became increasingly radical as he aged. This tells us that Pissarro, although a revolutionary as an old man, was a reluctant one, preferring to inculcate the young rather than engage with these issues himself in a public forum.

If Pissarro's life was largely determined by his New World and Jewish origins, he was quick to annex other territories to what we might call his birth society. His first act of independence was his love affair with a Catholic French girl, Julie Vellay, whom he eventually married and with whom he had eight children (see also section 2, this volume). From 1863, after the birth of Julie and Camille's first surviving child, Lucien, until the painter's death forty years later, Pissarro's life was dominated by his children. The uneven and widely spaced intervals of the births, between 1863 and 1884, suggest that Madame Pissarro may have suffered from undocumented miscarriages, although none that prevented her from continuing to get pregnant. Of the eight children, Jeanne-Rachel, born in 1865 and nicknamed Minette, died at seven years old; Adèle-Emma, born in 1870, died as an infant; and Félix, born in 1874, died at twenty-three of tuberculosis. (As if anticipating Jeanne's early death, Pissarro painted her more often and in more situations than he did any of his other children; see section 2, this volume.) The five surviving children were each represented two or three times in oil paintings. Like the paintings of Jeanne, many of these were neither signed nor dated and were obviously made as part of the family's daily life—worked up while the children were reading, painting, doing chores, eating, or sleeping in the increasingly crowded Pissarro household. Pissarro's friend, the Neo-Impressionist Maximilien Luce, made a wonderful lithograph of the Pissarro family around 1890 (fig. 21) in which the interdependence and independence of each member is clear. We see Camille twice, each time in his beret and the half-glasses he wore habitually. Near him are grouped separate portraits of sons Félix, Georges, and Ludovic-Rodolphe. Luce was aware of Pissarro's insistence that his children be treated always as individuals. Any sort of conformity was anathema to Pissarro, who actively encouraged his children to express themselves and pursue different paths, even as artists. In Luce's rendition of the family, the only identifiable activity is reading: both Félix and Georges are shown with books, while the others, Pissarro included, have downcast eyes as if concentrating on books that can't be seen by the viewer. If Jews are often called "People of the Book," the Pissarro family was a "Family of the Book." Reading is the single most common activity in Pissarro's portraits of his children, and many of the representations of Pissarro by his friends show him reading. The sharing of books and ideas—and the constantly expanding circle of subjects for discussion at family meals and on outings—was as vital to the idea of this artistic family as was making works of art.

21
Maximilien Luce
The Pissarro Family, ca. 1890
Lithograph
Sheet: 14³⁄₁₆ × 11⁷⁄₁₆ in. (36 × 29 cm)
Private collection, Paris

It is impossible to conceive of a single work of art, similar to Luce's private lithograph, to represent Pissarro's birth family. Indeed, in his diasporic childhood, parents and children were often separated and filial devotion was hardly the norm. As Camille and Julie's family grew, and as their antibourgeois and nontraditional character became clear, the artist became increasingly estranged from his older brother Alfred, who worked actively to cut his brother out of the will when Rachel, their mother, died in 1889. Pissarro did everything in his power to create a family that was interdependent, loving, and respectful—

22

Pissarro surrounded by his family at Éragny, ca. 1890. From left: Paul-Émile, Jeanne, Camille, Tommy, Ludovic-Rodolphe, Alice Isaacson, Julie, and the maid all qualities notably absent from his birth family, where competition for affection was the norm.

When Pissarro fled Saint Thomas for Caracas with his Danish friend Fritz Melbye, he left his birth family's bourgeois life behind. He didn't, however, leave behind all notions of family life, although Pissarro's conception of family came to be antibourgeois—based on shared beliefs, experiences, and affections rather than on money or a sense of loyalty that positioned the family against the rest of the world. Pissarro's new nuclear family was porous, linked in a thousand ways to the social world outside it. His children were separate but equal to him and his wife, and their relationships were constantly redefined as they aged, read, developed new ideas, had experiences, and grew. As we will see later, anarchism in any of its nineteenth-century variants was not particularly concerned with the family unit; however, anarchism's ideals of social leveling, the antihierarchical notion of engagement, and the theories of cooperation within a commune were, in a sense, models for what Pissarro created in his own family. The bourgeois family was replaced by the anarchist family (lowercase *a* for a reason), lacking large, fixed assets or capital but possessing a sense of shared labor and a commitment to collective development through the encouragement of individual development.

The "Frenchness" of the Pissarros and the increasing insistence on the French spelling of their name is another powerful force in determining the painter's makeup. Although Pissarro was never himself a French citizen, his father was born French, and the Manzana shift to Pomié and their marriage to the French-Jewish family of Petit made Pissarro a "French" Jew on both sides, even if only for two generations.

Pissarro's Friends

Except for Degas, few artists among the Impressionists had such a large and varied circle of friends as Pissarro. Degas, although he had no responsibilities to a family of his own, had a multinational family and a lifelong commitment to the frantically social city of Paris. Pissarro's background had prepared him for a different life, one dominated by his extended family. Befriending people outside the family was not the norm, and commerce was the glue linking relatives in multinational business efforts. Friendships for this family were essentially based on mercantile exchange rather than on shared emotional or intellectual interests. Although Pissarro remained an active and lifelong member of this diasporic family, he worked to create a family on a model emphatically different from that of his background. His household was open to others in a way unimaginable to his parents, and his wife presided over a modest but generous table and hosted weekend and weeklong guests easily by displacing a child or two from their beds and adding water to the soup.

Because the nineteenth century can perhaps be called *the* era of personal correspondence, and because Pissarro himself was an assiduous writer, we know a good deal about his friendships. His friends included men and women, Jews and gentiles, French and foreign, political conservatives and radicals, wealthy and impoverished, quiet and gregarious, nice and nasty. Indeed, his tolerance for others was so great that it is difficult to find in Pissarro's letters any truly negative passages about his friends, and those that do exist are about matters of principle or ideas, not about issues of personality or gossip. When Pissarro turned definitively against Gauguin, as he did in the late 1880s, it was because Gauguin had swerved so far from the radically secular aesthetic of Impressionism into the realms of symbolism and religion that Pissarro could no longer understand his former friend and colleague. Even at the height of French anti-Semitism in the late 1890s, during the Dreyfus Affair (see section 13, this volume), Pissarro persisted in writing affectionately about Degas, whose anti-Semitism was by then well known. For Pissarro, Degas's art was completely humanistic and even anarchist in its messages, and the older artist seems almost to have chosen to disregard the Parisian's prejudices.

Pissarro maintained particularly close relationships with a small number of artists. They worked alongside him, discussed their work together, and became fully involved in Pissarro's emotional life. Several of these relationships were effectively life-changing for the participants, and their number and depth are essentially unique in the history of modern art. One can contrast these relationships with those of other major Impressionists. Renoir (fig. 24), who was perhaps the most popular of the group, worked side by side with Monet in the late 1860s and early 1870s. He was chosen as the executor of the estates of both Gustave Caillebotte and Morisot and as the guardian of Morisot's only child with Eugène Manet, Julie; he also painted, subserviently, with Cézanne and had a transformative effect on the late style of Morisot. Yet none of these relationships had for him the depth and complexity of Pissarro's. Monet, who became more personally generous as he grew older and established himself as the first Impressionist, in terms of his financial position, was treated with equal generosity by artists such as Cassatt and Cézanne, but he never had an effect on their work, nor did he work with them in protracted pictorial experiments in the fields or studios of Giverny. Monet did have a fascinating and underexplored relationship with the young American painter John Singer Sargent. He allowed Sargent to paint with him in the fields and spend long periods in Giverny, and Sargent introduced Monet to Auguste Rodin. These encounters, however, were more useful for both artists than they were transformative for either.

Joachim Pissarro, the artist's great-grandson, has written extensively about the transformative intersubjectivity in Pissarro's pictorial and personal

23
From left: the photographer Martinès, the amateur painter and medical student Alphonso, Paul Cézanne, Lucien Pissarro, the Cuban Aguiar, and Camille Pissarro in the garden at Pontoise, ca. 1877

relationships, particularly stressing the Cézanne-Pissarro relationship of the 1870s and 1880s. Using language and analytical techniques derived from philosophy, he explored these relationships in "dialogical" terms, assessing their structure and interdependence and creating a model very different from that of the so-called teacher-student or the larger model of the school of art instruction. His dissertation, "Cézanne/Pissarro, Johns/Rauschenberg: Comparative Studies on Intersubjectivity in Modern Art," combined theory with what could be termed old-fashioned art history, critiquing the progressive theory of modernism as a series of invented pictorial movements and creating a new framework for the study of art in intersubjective terms. Unfortunately for us, the dissertation applied the model in only two cases. This, along with the fact that the examples are widely separated by time and cultural context, makes it difficult to extend the model to additional examples.

24

Pierre-Auguste Renoir, ca. 1886

Pissarro's life was filled with intersubjective relationships. Some of these were dialogical, while others were more complex in their triangulations and even more baroque forms of intersubjectivity. Pissarro's most important dialogical relationships were with Fritz Melbye, Ludovic Piette, Cézanne, Cassatt, Degas, and Gauguin, but there are many other relationships of either shorter duration or more limited utility to either person (for example, with the Danish painter David Jacobsen, the Puerto Rican master Francisco Oller, Armand Guillaumin, and Francis Picabia as well as Georges Seurat, Paul Signac, Henri Matisse, Renoir, Monet, Sisley, Morisot, and Luce). Indeed, this second list could be much longer. It is kept short here to recognize that there were relationships of two types: those of a long-term nature that effectively transformed both parties, and those with more focused impact, either pictorial or personal. It is no accident that many of these relationships resulted in technical shifts in the artists' works. For example, Cézanne and Gauguin worked with Pissarro to transform their respective pictorial "factures," or the way each artist lay paint on the surface. Degas and Cassatt were involved in technical experimentation in various printmaking methods, while Piette had a profound effect on Pissarro's use of gouache and, later, tempera media, many of which Pissarro adopted after the early death of Piette in 1878, as if to memorialize his friend through artistic practice.

Because these friend/artists were central to Pissarro's enterprise as an artist and had a profound effect on his humanized or figural art, several of them need to be discussed in detail. The earliest friendship—with the Danish painter Melbye—has often been treated in the biographical literature devoted to Pissarro, but it has rarely been seen as the model for later variants of Pissarro's professional/personal relationships. What do we know about Melbye? We know that he was Pissarro's first experience of an "other"—a balding, blond Dane with blue eyes and a thoroughly Protestant family history. He also belonged to a family of "brother artists," again a contrast to Pissarro's "brother businessmen." He was an adept traveler and had commenced an almost vagabond professional life. He thought nothing of leaving suddenly for somewhere new or of returning just as suddenly to a place he had already been. He was not intimidated by the vagaries of language, simply launching into his own versions of French or Spanish with little regard for his linguistic foibles or embarrassments. He would default into English when matters got tough, knowing that Danish was not a universal language.

Melbye met Pissarro in Charlotte Amalie, Saint Thomas, having traveled there simply because it was a Danish colony; he used the Danish West Indies as places to collect mail and receive money, supplies, and information. There is considerable variance in the dates given by historians for this meeting, but it was no later than 1850. Melbye apparently recognized Pissarro's talent and provided an outlet for him both to make and talk about art. Melbye was also sufficiently independent from his family, and his example gave Pissarro the courage to flee the bourgeois life and set out on his own. Melbye was, in Pissarro's terms, basically free to do what he wanted and go where he wanted. While Pissarro felt constrained by his family's desire for him to work in their business, Melbye's family business *was* art, and no one seemed to be telling him how to live his life. No letters from Pissarro to Melbye survive, but one from Melbye to Pissarro made a dramatic entrance into the Pissarro literature in 1980, in Shikes and Harper's still definitive biography. We learn that, by early 1852, the two had decided to leave Saint Thomas together and embark on a shared adventure. Melbye does not mention their intended destination, but his charmingly stilted English makes clear that the two artists used this language with each other and that they shared a vision in the making of art. Melbye asks Pissarro not about his family, his love affairs, or his friends but specifically about his artistic progress since their parting some months before. The letter also alludes to Alfred (Pissarro's brother) and his visit to France, inquiring about the date of his return, after which, presumably, the two young artists would depart, leaving the Pissarro family business in the hands of Alfred and his father. There were undoubtedly more letters, all unfortunately lost or inaccessible, but it was not in writing that these two young men developed their friendship—it was in working, eating, drinking, talking, and sharing leisure time.

The completeness of Pissarro's relationship with Melbye—its totally devoted and reciprocal character—cannot be exaggerated. Theirs was probably not a sexual relationship, or even an erotically charged homosocial one. Rather, it was completely focused on the making of art as a way of creating a rich and varied life. Each presumably felt that the other had some ability or experience or quality that he lacked, and each yearned for the freedom to work and experiment

25

Pissarro in gaucho costume, before 1860

together. Many young men leave home to be with a loved one: Pissarro left for the sake of art. He chose to go with an artist who had already experienced monetary success, and there is no doubt that Pissarro hoped his mercantile father might release him from the family business and allow him to succeed as an artist. Fortunately, a good deal of material from Melbye and Pissarro's early collaboration survives, scattered among public and private collections in England, France, the United States, and Venezuela.

The inclusion of Venezuela might seem surprising until it is revealed that the two young painters went to Caracas after leaving Saint Thomas in November of 1852 (following Alfred's return from France). Pissarro became a famous artist, while Melbye died in obscurity in China in the late 1860s, and attempts to collect their work have tended to focus on that of Pissarro. Only in Venezuela, where the two worked side by side, has there been equal interest in both artists. Fortunately, Melbye entrusted the contents of his studio to the American landscape painter Frederic Edwin Church before his ultimate departure for China, and there is a large collection of Melbye's work in Church's home and studio, Olana, in upstate New York. It is evident when comparing this material with Pissarro's early works that both young artists had almost equal abilities when they were together, making it difficult to attribute unsigned works to one or the other with any confidence. It is in itself remarkable that a French-speaking Sephardic Jew educated in France and a Danish artist five years his senior, trained as an artist in Denmark, could make art so similar and with such shared goals. Theirs was truly a collectivity—a true artistic interdependence—in which they transcribed the world around them in graphite, pen and ink, wash, watercolor, and oil and began to conceive of larger composite works of art incorporating their studies. There is evidence that they were also successful financially. Pissarro and Melbye's representations of their workplace in Caracas (see fig. 79) depict an impressive studio, and it is known that they were fully part of the cultural life of this growing city, participating in readings and musicales and, thus, promoting themselves to the cultural elite. Clearly, their facility in Spanish improved, and Pissarro seems to have maintained a lifelong familiarity with the language. It is likely, however, that they continued to converse with each other in English, which they spoke almost fluently (their written English was another matter). This skill in English, acquired at the docks and in the shops of Saint Thomas, was to be important throughout Pissarro's life. As late as 1885, the art dealer Paul Durand-Ruel invited Pissarro, rather than Renoir, Monet, or Degas, to dinner with visiting Americans because he knew that Pissarro could speak creditable English and decrease the apparent distance between the worlds of the American capitalist art collector and the French vanguard artist.

Pissarro's fluency in what might be called cultural translation is another quality that surely aided him throughout life. He had had diverse cross-cultural and transracial experiences growing up, making him unafraid of those different from himself and teaching him how to communicate across various borders. We see this with Pissarro and Melbye in Venezuela, where neither man was a native or part of the dominant Hispanic or Venezuelan Indian culture. When we look at the surviving works by both artists done in Venezuela, we see a formidable visual analysis of those cultures. They studied Hispanic colonial and vernacular architecture, vegetation, small communities, Indian communities, markets, agriculture, cooking, husbandry, and the like, and the sheer volume of the surviving production clearly indicates that they were hard workers, not dilettantes. There are also a handful of portraits, demonstrating that they each achieved skill in this financially rewarding genre. Their pencil and watercolor portraits of the bourgeoisie of Caracas, in addition to local landscapes and genre scenes, were most likely their bread and butter, although it is certain that they were actually making these works for themselves, realizing that they might use them in the future. Both possessed the clear belief that art was "work," and that practice was a necessary part of lifelong artistic learning. The now ubiquitous Cézanne comment that Pissarro had had the good fortune to learn "sans maîtres" (without masters) is surely true when it is applied to the Melbye-Pissarro relationship. Melbye was not Pissarro's master but his colleague, perhaps only serving to goad him toward an independent—and an interdependent—life of art.

It is evident that the social and environmental reality was the raw material for Pissarro's art. When Pissarro and Melbye worked together, each conceived of and represented the landscape as socialized or humanized, anticipating the tradition of the *géographie humaine* later developed by the French geographer (and future friend of Pissarro) Élisée Reclus, which in turn led to modern cultural anthropology. The idea of the world as inhabited by diverse peoples who coexist with one another and with nature is central to Pissarro's practice as an artist, and its origins clearly stem from his early years with Melbye, who shared this humanized idea of art. Although it is easy to decry this notion as purely descriptive, that is not the case. Indeed, a work of art that re-creates a socialized realm in representation does so, by definition, in an analytical manner—choices are made about what to include and how to include it. This creates patterns of what is experienced, and when that socialized realm is reexperienced in representation, the viewer comes away with a new sense of an ordered world.

Melbye and Pissarro's experience of living and working together was to be the model for many, though not all, of Pissarro's future artist/friendships. With Piette, Cézanne, Gauguin, Guillaumin, or Luce, Pissarro re-created this live-work situation during which the artists shared so much time together that their professional lives entered a personal domain. This model has a long tradition in Western art—and it was rethought by groups of traveling artists who lived and worked together on trips away from the city or in the nationally oriented collective studios of Rome, Paris, and Munich—but there was an intensity to and focus in Pissarro's artist/friendships that was truly remarkable. None of his encounters was with an artist whom he regarded as a student or a teacher—with perhaps one exception, and that is Degas. In his letters, Pissarro reserved his highest and most frequent praise for the difficult Parisian artist. Degas and Pissarro were alike in two important ways—both had large, non-French families, and both were fascinated by technique. Degas frequently visited friends and family in Italy and spoke the language fluently, and he often helped visiting Italian artists and critics find their way through the artistic maze of Second Empire and Third Republic Paris. And Pissarro did the same for artists and writers from England, Denmark, and the Caribbean.

26

Portrait of Cézanne, 1874
Oil on canvas
28¾ × 23½ in. (73 × 59.7 cm)
National Gallery, London, on loan from Graff Diamonds Ltd. (PDR 326)

Degas and Pissarro also shared an almost scientific interest in technical experimentation. Each would try—and then experiment with each other—to attempt something new with the materials and processes of art. This took Degas increasingly away from easel painting—his production of printed works and autograph works on paper rose, while that of oils on canvas fell, throughout his long working life. Pissarro never ceased exploring the graphic arts, and he tended to work on series of prints in various media, trading the fields and the painting studio for the printing press and its chemicals and plates. Unlike Degas, he experimented with the earliest print medium, woodblock printing, and he extended his investigations into the realm of easel painting. Degas became progressively bored with oils and canvas, while Pissarro experimented endlessly with pigments, thinners, and brushes so that his application of paint would create new and different factures. For these types of projects, he worked with other artist/friends, notably Cézanne, Gauguin, and the young Seurat.

The prolonged and intense encounters of Cézanne and Pissarro have been extensively studied, and Cézanne even consented to serve as a model for an important portrait by Pissarro in the early 1870s (figs. 26, 81). This work of art, first analyzed brilliantly by Theodore Reff in a 1967 article, is in many senses an ideological portrait; that is, a portrait not so much of a particular painter as of the conditions of modern painting at the time. Cézanne *was* the model, and as he sat stolidly in his winter coat to be painted by Pissarro, he did so not to be immortalized for his appearance but rather as an individual embodiment of an engaged and activist kind of art. Reff worked as diligently to identify the images on the wall behind Cézanne as Pissarro did to select and arrange them. In an important sense, these images are what make the portrait interesting. The sitter, Cézanne, is primarily interesting because he is *not* represented as a painter and *not* represented as successful. He is shown almost as if listening to their hero, Courbet, an artist whom neither appears to have met but whose career is central to theirs. (For more about this portrait, see section 3, this volume.) Pissarro's intentions here seem directly analogous to those of Manet in his 1866–1867 portrait of Zola (Musée d'Orsay, Paris)—painting the condition of being a realist artist. But Manet's painting is a highly polished and reference-filled work that, by its scale and eventual ambitions at the official Salon, resulted in an image of material and social success, whereas Pissarro's painting is abject—smaller, thicker, cruder, and aggressively uglier than Manet's urbane representation of the young realist. *This* is my friend, Pissarro tells us, and we are together in our enterprise, and that enterprise is intended not to *please* but to *engage* the viewer with its power, honesty, and clarity. It proves that Pissarro had indeed left the bourgeois world to become a friend of a young rebel.

Pissarro's self-portrait of the same period (fig. 2) might be called a kinder, gentler version of the Cézanne picture. Behind him are not political cartoons arranged to shock and surprise, but rather tiny, handmade paintings seemingly tacked on or pinned to the wall, without frames or the trappings of luxury commonly associated with art. Pissarro was projecting an idea of art—and of life—without gilt frames, luxurious interior spaces, or excessive leisure.

Several of Pissarro's dearest and, to him, most important artist/friends were not celebrated artists and are often absent in the discussion of the painter's artistic relationships. The names of Cézanne, Degas, Gauguin, Seurat, and Matisse roll off the tongue of the art historian with greater ease than do those of Jacobsen, Piette, Guillaumin, or Luce, but it was these men who were in many senses more significant to Pissarro. Their friendship was primary, and they gave the painter and his family the chance to interact with greater intimacy and personal depth. Of these, we know most about Pissarro's deep friendship with Ludovic Piette (fig. 27), an artist from Brittany who had met Pissarro by 1861, possibly through another then important and now little-studied landscape painter, Antoine Chintreuil. After Melbye, Piette was the only artist/friend of Pissarro's who was older than the painter. Pissarro, like Gauguin, preferred the company of younger men and women, seemingly always endeavoring to keep up with the latest developments in art, politics, society, and culture. Piette was the exception, being four years older than Pissarro, and was an artist with an independent income derived both from Paris real estate and a substantial family farm. Despite this relative comfort, Piette was active in politics throughout his life, serving as counselor in Melleray, the town nearest the family's property at Montfoucault in Brittany. Interestingly, Piette married a Jewish woman, Adèle Lévy, in 1862, shortly after meeting Pissarro (did Pissarro introduce them?), and the Pissarros and Piettes were in important senses analogous, though opposite in

27
Ludovic Piette, ca. 1865

gender, in being a union of a Jew and a Catholic in religion and an urbanite and a country person in birthplace. Piette lived in Paris almost exclusively until his marriage, after which he retired to his large farm in Montfoucault. The Pissarros, who had an open invitation to the Piette farm, visited six times, and several of their stays were quite long. In fact, it was in Montfoucault that Pissarro made his earliest significant group of figure paintings dealing with rural life.

Pissarro seems to have encouraged Piette artistically, including him at an early stage in the planning for the Société Anonyme of artists that morphed into Impressionism. (Pissarro, however, did not ask Piette to join initially, only including him in 1877 and posthumously in 1879.) But Piette, in turn, seems to have had a profound effect on two aspects of Pissarro's later work: his interest in rural markets, which Piette made a major subject of his art earlier than Pissarro, and his extensive use of gouache and tempera, which Piette preferred already in the 1860s and which gradually assumed an important role in Pissarro's career in the 1880s and 1890s, after his friend's death. The correspondence between the two families was intimate, and there exists in the Pissarro family archives in Paris a powerful letter from Madame Piette detailing the last days of her husband, who suffered from cancer, in 1878. The Pissarros were so devastated by the loss of Piette, who died in April, that they named their fourth son, born that November in Paris, after him. Piette often worked while staying with the Pissarro family in Pontoise, and what little is known about his artistic production has been learned from the assiduous collecting of the Musée de Pontoise.

It is fascinating to wonder if Pissarro showed Piette the works of art he brought with him to France from Saint Thomas and Venezuela. Pissarro's work with Melbye is almost always discussed *only* in terms of the painter's own early years. Even though Cézanne spoke about Pissarro's origins "sans maîtres," it has never been speculated whether or not Pissarro shared his early work with his later artist/friends. The most compelling case to be made for this having taken place is surely Piette, who worked closely with Pissarro beginning in 1861, only six years after Pissarro's arrival in France. There are, for example, many sheets from the early sketchbooks, as well as loose sheets, that record the markets in Saint Thomas, Saint Croix, and Caracas, and these drawings have always been used by scholars as precedents for Pissarro's later representations of markets. Yet what if Pissarro reviewed all of this material with Piette, providing the older artist with examples that Piette soon followed when he represented the markets of Pontoise while visiting the Pissarros in the 1870s? If this was indeed the case, it would make sense that Pissarro might also have shared his early works on paper with other artist/friends, thus creating and reinforcing a kind of mythology about his independent and free art education that was so essential to his later work, and also for the redirection of the careers of Cézanne and Gauguin when they worked with Pissarro. Although there is no positive evidence for this in the letters, it seems likely that Pissarro *did* base a good deal of his collaborative work with others on his first artist/friendship, with Melbye. It is easier to explain the "constructivist stroke" of Cézanne by finding exactly the same marks in Pissarro's drawings of the early 1850s. The same is true for the markets of Piette, which seem to have migrated from Pissarro to Piette and then back to Pissarro (see section 10, this volume).

The artist/friendships with Degas and Cassatt are among the most important in Pissarro's life, although they play little role in the vast Pissarro bibliography, largely because they were confined to printmaking rather than painting. Pissarro, Degas, and Cassatt worked together intently in the late 1870s, and students of Pissarro's prints have long known that Degas was, in some ways, the finest printer of Pissarro's etched plates, teaching the older artist by example rather than by explanation. Pissarro, always scrupulously honest, was the first to admit this, writing on the impression itself that it had been printed by Degas. This intense printmaking interaction included Cassatt in the late 1870s, but it took another turn when Pissarro first saw her extraordinary color prints in 1891. This pushed Pissarro into color printmaking and instigated another deeply experimental phase in his own graphic production, a phase that would not have occurred without Cassatt. The mutual respect of these two artists was remarkable, especially because they were so different in so many ways. Pissarro was a committed feminist and deeply familiar with feminist ideas, particularly from the mid-1870s onward, when he spent a good deal of time with his neighbor in Pontoise, the "bourgeois" feminist Maria Deraismes. His beliefs were reinforced from the late 1870s through the early 1880s, when he became acquainted with the feminist ideas of Flora Tristan, Gauguin's grandmother. Of all the male Impressionists, Pissarro had the shortest ideological distance to traverse in accepting a woman as a professional equal and working on a basis that would have been unheard of in earlier generations. His work with Cassatt was profoundly different, in the degree of its sheer, nonhierarchical professionalism, from what might initially be considered comparable contemporary relationships: Manet-Morisot, Renoir-Morisot, Rodin-Claudel, or even Degas-Cassatt.

Interestingly, of his friends, Pissarro painted oil portraits of only Cézanne and Eugène Murer, and the latter was commissioned by the sitter (fig. 83). Renoir painted portraits of Sisley several times, as well as Monet, Caillebotte, Pissarro, and Morisot. But Pissarro rarely asked his closest artist/friends to sit for portraits, and even his most intimate and long-term relationships (for example, with Gauguin) are recorded only in drawings. Degas, the artist Pissarro most admired among his contemporaries, does not appear in Pissarro's art; neither do Cassatt or Seurat. This absence does not mean that these friendships were unimportant to Pissarro's art. Rather, it tells us that portraiture was not a central part of his aesthetic investigations and that he practiced it only occasionally. Portraiture assumes a larger place in the works of almost all of his artist/friends, particularly Degas, Renoir, Cézanne, and even Gauguin. For Pissarro, art was less about his own personal world than about the larger world of social experience. With the exception of his portraits of Cézanne and members of his immediate family, his most distinguished painted portraits represent either anonymous sitters or people Pissarro knew but did not correspond with or befriend.

Pissarro's Reading

Pissarro's circle of family and friends was large and mutually reinforcing, but it was not the most important instigator of his pictorial humanism. Rather, it was his lifelong practice of reading that formed the intellectual and aesthetic basis of his figural art. Pissarro read every day, subscribed to important periodicals, dashed through contemporary novels, and devoured social and political tracts. His reading was as necessary to his life as eating, sleeping, drawing, and painting; indeed, it seems to have trumped even conversation in the division of "labor" in his day. Pissarro's children, too, read obsessively, and mealtimes were as much the occasion for almost seminar-like exchanges as they were for nutrition. The origins of Pissarro's obsession with reading are not clear; neither of his parents was an intellectual, and it appears that the homes in Saint Thomas and Paris were not book-filled. It is likely that Pissarro's habit of reading came from his evolving friendships with writers and intellectuals in France, and we learn a good deal about these friendships from reading his letters. Pissarro's correspondents included Zola, Théodore Duret, Octave Mirbeau, Gustave Geffroy, J. K. Huysmans, Georges Lecomte, Félix Fénéon, Jean Grave, Bernard Lazare, Louise Michel, and Julius Meier-Graefe. If we search the letters themselves for references to other writers, the textual world of Pissarro expands even more.

He was not primarily a reader of literature. Although Pissarro quoted Charles Baudelaire in *Les turpitudes sociales,* the poet is never mentioned in the published correspondence, and Stéphane Mallarmé's appearances are connected not to his advanced (and probably, to Pissarro, decadent and incomprehensible) poetry but to his art criticism and friendships with Manet and Renoir. So too Huysmans, whose critical writing Pissarro followed closely, although there is no evidence that he read either Huysmans's early realist novels or his masterpiece, *À rebours* (Against nature). Pissarro did read Zola's novels, some of which he was sent by the author, and he commented on several of his texts, particularly Zola's *L'oeuvre,* but the passages that survive suggest that the painter's readings were neither refined nor subtle, and that he corresponded with the writer more out of friendship than because of any literary bent.

For that reason, those familiar with important French poetry and fiction from 1860 to 1900 would be disappointed if they attempted to mine the index of Bailly-Herzberg's five-volume *Correspondance de Camille Pissarro* searching for the contemporary reactions of Pissarro to these great texts. For Pissarro, comparatively minor writers such as Duret, Mirbeau, Geffroy, and Lecomte—few of whom are read any longer by students of French literature—trumped Baudelaire, Maupassant, Flaubert, Verlaine, and Huysmans. Indeed, Gauguin was much better read in French poetry and fiction than was his mentor, Pissarro. Monet, too, was a more sophisticated reader of French literature, and Renoir was more assiduous in keeping abreast of what we might call literary society in Paris through his friend the literary publisher Georges Charpentier.

So what *did* Pissarro read? The simplest answer is texts produced in connection with homeopathic medicine and anarchist political and economic theory. In this, he was very much a "modern" person, for whom adherence to any form of tradition was antithetical to progress in human civilization. An enemy of traditional medicine, he befriended several homeopathic physicians and read the voluminous literature—both theoretical and practical—that emanated from homeopathy. There is no need to go much further into the theories of homeopathic medicine to gain a better understanding of Pissarro's representations of human figures. All we need to do is to recognize that for Pissarro, the human body was a whole organism composed of highly complex, interrelated parts that functioned on both a cellular and an organic level. He was thoroughly familiar with the underlying idea of homeopathy (similar, in a sense, to the modern medical concept of vaccines)—that small quantities of a substance that *causes* illness can, when introduced to the body, enable the body to apply its vital force to combat the substance and, hence, cure the disease. The basic idea is that the body is able to heal itself if minimally encouraged to do so. Also central to homeopathy in both the nineteenth and twentieth centuries was the devotion to natural medicines—that is, compounds derived not from chemical synthesis in the laboratory but rather from plants and animals. In this, it is like many so-called traditional or vernacular systems of medicine.

Pissarro spent his life searching for homeopathic remedies to treat the health problems of his family and friends. There are two stories describing Pissarro's introduction to the French homeopathic physician Dr. Paul Gachet, with whom Pissarro maintained a professional friendship from at least 1872. One story claims that the introduction came from Armand Gautier, a mediocre academic painter known to both Pissarro and Gachet from the early 1860s. Another traces the introduction back to Pissarro's mother, Rachel, who was treated successfully by Gachet for her illnesses in the late 1860s. Whoever made the introduction, the relationship was formed, and through Gachet Pissarro met other homeopathic doctors and patients, all of whom kept up a fascinatingly technical correspondence through the last decades of the nineteenth century.

We must remember that medicine in the nineteenth century was not the dominant medico-pharmaceutical industry it would become in the twentieth century. Homeopathy, now considered an alternative mode of medicine, had much greater claim on the public's attention in Pissarro's lifetime than it does today in the United States. Even now, homeopathic pharmacies abound in France, and it is impossible to go through any large French town or city without encountering one. This was not the case in Pissarro's time, when homeopathy was essentially a private rite practiced within a small and highly educated circle. For Pissarro and his fellow homeopathic devotees, the body was not merely a skin-covered collection of organs and systems of exchange and transmission. It was, instead, the seat of the *élan vital,* the vital force that is, for a modern and secular Frenchman, the scientific equivalent of religion's "soul." To be a homeopath was to be modern and secular, and this tells us a great deal about Pissarro's aesthetic. It also tells us that, in painting the human figure, Pissarro thought differently about the body than most earlier European artists. It was *itself,* for him, the seat of health and vitality. As he studied the body through figure drawing, posing, and painting, he treated it as a temple of homeopathic vitalism.

Although homeopathy occupied much of Pissarro's reading, it definitely took a backseat to anarchism, which was, for the artist, a dominating and lifelong quest. Unlike many of his contemporaries, Pissarro was an advocate of anarchism well before the movement took on almost a mythic status in the last two decades of the nineteenth century. He had been attracted to anarchist ideas and writings in his early life, and his earliest close friend in France, Ludovic Piette, was involved in left-wing and even radical French politics by the late 1850s. For those of us in early twenty-first-century America, it is difficult to recapture a vivid sense of the possibility of sociopolitical transformation that was alive in nineteenth-century France. Not having experienced a political revolution since the eighteenth century and possessing a firm suspicion of radicalism of any kind, Americans have trouble accepting the idea that someone whose political ideology called for the complete reformation of society could be a functioning member of that society. In nineteenth-century France, with its cycles of revolution and retrenchment, it was considerably easier to put one's faith in the next—or, with hope, the *final*—revolution and its aftermath, a new society formed on principles of individual equality and fraternity among all men, women, and children. Throughout his life, Pissarro was an idealist who actually believed that society could—and would—be completely transformed, and that such a transformation would come as the result of cooperative action following a large-scale revolution. This revolution would result in a situation so catastrophic to the old order that it would be possible to break the cycle of small-scale revolutions followed by retrenchment, a cycle that had characterized nineteenth-century French society and politics to that point.

Pissarro made paintings in and for an imperfect world that he believed could never last because of the very depth of those imperfections. Although he denied any direct connections between specific political ideas and specific works of art throughout his career, it is impossible to understand his art without a meaningful assessment of his political and moral ideology. Pissarro was a lifelong anarchist. This word was used initially by philosophers and political writers at mid-century in a neutral fashion. It meant, quite simply, a world without hierarchy and rules or, more practically, a world without government. Initially, the words *anarchy, anarchism,* and *anarchist* had few of the negative connotations of violent lawlessness and disorder that they had acquired by the 1890s. These negative meanings persist to this day, and it is only an act of intellectual will that allows us to accept the original or neutral meanings of *anarchy,* which, in Greek, means simply "without ruler" or "without authority."

In France, the first important philosopher of anarchism was Pierre-Joseph Proudhon, who called himself an anarchist and created, for the French at least, the earliest theoretical definitions of the movement. Born in 1809, Proudhon was almost a generation older than Pissarro, but he entered the public realm as a major force in the late 1840s, shortly before Pissarro's final arrival in France. His most famous work, *Qu'est-ce que la propriété?* (What is property?), was published in 1840 and quickly became a founding text for anarchism throughout the remainder of nineteenth century. Like the painter Gustave Courbet, whom he befriended, Proudhon became active in the Revolution of 1848 in France and attempted to play a role in the revolutionary government that ensued. The lifelong friendship with Courbet, who twice painted his portrait, made him more aware than most anarchist theorists of the role of the arts in revolutionary politics, and his final book, published posthumously in 1865, was entitled *Du principe de l'art et de sa destination sociale* (The principle of art and its social destiny).

Although there is no documentary proof, there is little doubt that Pissarro read this book, and it is even possible that he knew Proudhon, who died in a house in Passy not far from that of Pissarro's grandparents. Like many of Proudhon's writings, *Du principe de l'art* is rambling and filled with arcane digressions, but its core points were as important to Pissarro as those of any later text. Not only did the book transform Pissarro's idea of painting, it also enabled him to produce at least one work of overtly revolutionary art, innocently entitled *Donkey Ride at La Roche-Guyon* (fig. 45). After lengthy and admittedly dreary chapters that deal with the entire history of Western art, Proudhon announces that only the art of the ancient Egyptians, the classical Greeks, and the seventeenth-century

moment o
1871 living
political u
viving lette
Ludovic Pi
left-wing p
Herzberg's
to the "ass
who were t
to underst
teenth cent
well on far
ideas— into
Pissarro fle
his attempt
because he
dren. In fa
thus declari
always resis

We n
ues as so m
their thirtie
realizing th
the imperfe
made perfe
linked to Pr
cal theorists
a country t
also no dou
in Geneva a
whom Pissar
younger thar
of the elite I
to his length
to England a
anarchist cir
though offici
With an apa
more easily t
towns he pre

29
Pissarro's wife, Julie, and son Paul-Émile, 1884

28
Pissarro's son Lucien, ca. 1890

Dutch are worthy models for a moral art in the future. Of the rest, he decries art tied to any form of power (one wonders how he overlooked that in the ancient Egyptians), whether religious or secular, and he exhorts modern artists to follow the example of Courbet and engage with the moral character of actual human experience. In a wonderful series of adjectives, he calls most living artists "distinguished, elegant, sensual, filled with cupidity, capricious, vain" and then contrasts these amoral traits with those of artists who are truly participants in their own societies but who transform contemporary life in representation because of their profoundly moral and humanitarian character. An important artist must "continuously struggle to maintain an equilibrium within himself" and, by implication, with the larger society, and this equilibrium is particularly difficult to achieve because the artist works alone rather than in a collective. Proudhon himself struggled to reconcile the conventional idea of an artist as an isolated genius with his notions of social responsibility and collective work, and it is precisely this struggle, expressed in anguished sentences in his posthumous book, that became Pissarro's struggle: how to be true to oneself while contributing to the larger collective progress of society.

Although Pissarro most likely read this book in 1865, and perhaps again in 1875, when it was republished as part of the *Oeuvres complètes* (Complete works) of Proudhon, nothing he wrote about it survives. It is more the numerous connections between Proudhon's ideas about art and both his and Pissarro's reliance on Courbet as a "model artist" that proves Proudhon's importance for Pissarro. It is also Proudhon's sense of the importance of collective action that underlay Pissarro and Monet's work in planning the collective project of Impressionism. The Société Anonyme they formed, based on a union of bakers, attempted simultaneously to preserve individuality and promote collective aims. Much later in his life, Pissarro wrote about a Proudhon text in a long, unusually ruminative letter to his son Lucien (fig. 28), composed over two days, July 7 and 8, in 1891. The text Pissarro read in 1891 was a booklet by Proudhon originally printed in 1860 (and therefore already thirty-one years old when Pissarro picked it up) and entitled *De la justice dans la révolution et dans l'église* (Justice in the revolution and in the church). It was, in turn, the condensation of arguments made in a three-volume work of 1858. Pissarro had already completed both an essay-length letter (now lost) outlining his social philosophy and his own revolutionary book, *Les turpitudes sociales,* when he reread this seminal anarchist text, indicating that he was a sophisticated and lifelong student of anarchism, not a casual reader of the contemporary literature that swirled around that decentralized political movement.

The ideas of Proudhon that survived in Pissarro's thinking are simple: that the then current forms of social organization are unjust and, hence, unsustainable;

that a social revolution is necessary to create
system to provide a basis for long-term chan
must be based on the idea that all humans
equally entitled to the fruits of the earth and
them; that, because of this principle, there
individual or familial hoarding of material goc
erty, no government is necessary, because th
from others; and that all decisions about col
with collectives and associations of people kr

These ideas were expressed in Proud
along with the ideas of many others, for the c
lective meeting called First International in
tions or collectives. It is important to remen
the major anarchist thinkers, over whom
Mikhail Bakunin, were united only in their re
communism. Indeed, there was a major sch
their "anarcho-communism," and the Marxist
revolutionary government would own all col
dispersal and use. For Bakunin and the anarc
sive and thus fundamentally like all previous
based on religious ideology, aristocratic linea
the very idea of the state or any form of gover
repressive *by definition.* Hence, all social orgar
the individuals in society acting in consort wi
rule. Even the Anglo-American concept of th
anarchist ideology, whether that of Proudhon,

It is difficult today to document Pissarr
ing the 1860s and 1870s, the seminal decades c
movement was illegal in France during that per
exception of the Paris Commune of 1871, Fren
political rallies, and any antistate publications
nents of the anarchist Commune were sent ei
France before their pardon in 1878. All anarchis
and publications were repressed during those y
largely underground, working primarily from Sv
the United States. Perhaps only because Prou
republish his anarchist texts in 1875. For these
time have to be surmised rather than tidily do

It is also difficult to discuss Pissarro's ana
1870s, because he was out of the country for tl

1

RACE AND GENDER
SAINT THOMAS AND VENEZUELA

When Pissarro lived in Saint Thomas, as today, the majority population was Afro-Caribbean, and it was significantly poorer than the Caucasian community, indeed economically marginal. We know that Pissarro was educated with Afro-Caribbeans at a Moravian school from 1835 or 1836 until 1842, when he was sent to Passy, outside Paris, for a proper French education. Unfortunately, we know almost nothing about this schooling except what can be found in the archives of the Moravian Missionaries in Winston-Salem, North Carolina. We do know that English was used in the classroom, a language that Pissarro used all his life and the primary language of business throughout the Danish West Indies in the eighteenth and nineteenth centuries. It also appears that many of the teachers in the Moravian school were American Mennonites who spoke only English or German, the latter of which had limited utility in Saint Thomas. What is important is that Pissarro and his brothers had direct contact with Afro-Caribbean children in the school and, by extension, with their families, although one must not think that Pissarro, because of his educational background and the vaunted tolerance of the Danish colony, was raised free of racial prejudice or stereotyping. Records indicate that, at the death of Isaac Petit (Pissarro's mother's first husband) in 1824, his estate included not only two houses and their contents but also two slaves. Records also show that his mother's Creole family was attended by Afro-Caribbean slaves or servants, who were viewed with the same mixture of intimacy and superiority found in the American South in the same period.

What do we see in Pissarro's pictorial world that can help us sort out his attitudes toward race? The first drawing in the catalogue of the largest collection of Pissarro's drawings extant (in the Ashmolean Museum at the University

32
Two Women Chatting by the Sea, Saint Thomas, 1856 (detail of fig. 43)

of Oxford) is a careful study of an Afro-Caribbean woman sitting on her washing board on the ground, apparently sewing or repairing a garment that she has washed (fig. 33). The drawing, on the back of a ledger sheet from Pissarro's father's business, was no doubt made in 1852, when he was working at the family store. It is incredibly careful in technique, the artist having first outlined the figure in pencil before completing the study in pen and ink. The woman is seated in a way that indicates that she was most likely unaware she was being drawn; that is, she was *not* a model. But the stability and duration of her pose gave the young proto-artist the time he needed to render her completely. The folds of her heavy cotton skirt and long-sleeved blouse are carefully noted, as is her almost turbanlike headdress. We see only a hint of her face, but it is notably dark, making her race obvious. We do not know how she was originally placed on the page because the verso is a fragment and was obviously cut later from the ledger sheet. As she is currently shown, we look *at* her from some distance rather than *down* at her. It seems that, already in his career, Pissarro was attracted to images of work and seated poses with no chairs or other means of support. We will remember this woman later, less for her race than for her social class, when we consider Pissarro's images of female rural workers in the early 1880s (see section 7, this volume).

33
Study of a Seated Female Figure Sewing, ca. 1852
Pen and brown ink over pencil
4³⁄₁₆ × 4¾ in. (10.7 × 12 cm)
Ashmolean Museum, University of Oxford, Pissarro Family Gift, 1952, WA1952.6.20 (BL 1)

34–35
Studies of Two Young Boys with Faint Indications of a Female Figure (recto); *Whole-Length Study of a Small Boy with Faint Studies of His Face and His Left Leg Seen from the Back*, 1852
Pencil with pen, India ink, and brown ink
7 13/16 × 11 1/8 in. (19.9 × 28.2 cm)
Ashmolean Museum, University of Oxford, Pissarro Family Gift, 1952, WA1952.6.22 (BL 3)

The next group of images, from a dismembered sketchbook, records three Afro-Caribbean boys about six or seven years old. The recto of the sketchbook sheet (fig. 34) represents two boys who must have been willing to serve as models for Pissarro, because they remained motionless long enough for the artist to complete complex pen-and-ink drawings over a scaffolding of pencil lines. Perhaps the artist negotiated with the boys for these studies by first befriending them and then giving one a piece of candy and paying the other to carry something? Yet there is no visual evidence of pity or condescension in the drawings. Both boys are treated individually, and Pissarro obviously planned to make two drawings because he placed each boy on his own half of the sheet. The "portrait" of the seated boy is a nest of fine pen lines that define his round head and chubby cheeks with precision. He seems at first to be sticking his tongue out at us, but he may instead be sucking on something; it is impossible to tell because the head is so small. The boy looks slightly sideways rather than at the artist who represents him; thus, he is not allowed the seeming equality of the mutual gaze that would be present in a true portrait. His body is defined only in pencil, as if the little boy left before Pissarro could finish the sheet. The smaller and thinner boy on the other side is bare-chested and wears ragged clothes. On his head he carries a carefully described slatted wooden bucket with two smaller objects.

On the verso (fig. 35) is a remarkably vivid graphite portrait of a little boy. Pissarro identifies him as Frederick David and dates the drawing to the day, as if for future use. We see him in hand-me-down or stolen clothes—a man's vest over a long cotton shirt, likewise possibly a man's. His frayed straw hat appears to have been "recycled" for his use as well. He seems to be an Afro-Caribbean street urchin: one who makes do, most likely begs, and is sure of his own identity. This same boy, with his name annotated, is also represented on a sheet in a private collection, suggesting that Pissarro developed a relationship with him and wanted to remember his name. All of these drawings depict the experience of growing up black in Saint Thomas, and they are sufficiently precise that we know they represent specific boys rather than types. Did they remind Pissarro of the boys who had gone to school with him fifteen years earlier?

When we turn to images of dark-skinned women, we are confronted with a conundrum: several of the most powerful and important of these works do not seem to represent Afro-Caribbean women but instead deal forcefully with mixed-race people or with the descendents of native South Americans or indigenous peoples. Saint Thomas had no history of either Hispanic or Indian populations, and indigenous peoples were much more common in Caracas. The Caribs themselves had long since been eradicated, and Pissarro was not introduced to dark-skinned South Americans until he arrived in Venezuela late in 1852.

The next four works represent these variably dark-skinned women, and they reveal a more complex and problematic visual cipher of race. The first (fig. 36) is from one of Pissarro's Venezuelan sketchbooks, and it represents a woman whose long, straight hair betrays no African blood. She is fully clothed and reclines seductively on a sofa, resting on a pillow that supports her elbow and head. There is no doubt that the drawing eroticizes her, and she is given

the hint of a smile and a seductive, slightly sideways glance. Yet she seems in no way vulnerable and is in possession of her charms. Pissarro struggled throughout his life with the erotic—both in art and in life. He was obviously perfectly competent at procreation, but he is not known to have had any affairs. And he never represented women as sexualized beings more strongly than he does in this sheet. Here, the woman is utterly aware that she is being drawn; she is, in fact, posing. Whether the pose was self-assumed or suggested to her we will never know, but the drawing *does* raise awkward questions of both sexual and racial superiority—of the "politics" of representation much discussed in recent years.

The next sheet (fig. 37) is altogether different. Found among the works left behind by Fritz Melbye, Pissarro's first artist/friend, it represents a woman who is seemingly without clothing although we only see her shoulders. Her head is carefully delineated with fine lines and then "colored" with a brush and ink. She is, thus, deliberately dark, but her hair, while an important aspect of the drawing, is not given in sufficient detail to allow us to know whether she is Afro-Caribbean. Her large eyes, full lips, and canted head lend the drawing an emotional focus lacking in other graphic works. She seems, to many viewers, to be afraid, of what or whom we do not know, and the drawing possesses an intensity that one rarely sees in Pissarro's future work. Clearly the image is "racialized," and the woman's darkness is a large part of the meanings we impart to the sheet. Is she a victim? Of what?

Another study of a racialized female (fig. 39) seems to have been made in Paris after Pissarro's arrival there in the fall of 1855. The model was posed in a slightly suggestive yet nonsexual manner. The sleeve of her loose chemise is pulled down, allowing us to see her bare shoulder and lack of undergarments, suggesting, perhaps, her availability. She wears a kerchief very like those seen often

36
Study of a Reclining Female Figure Leaning on Her Left Elbow, 1852–1855
Pencil
8 1/16 × 11 5/16 in. (20.4 × 28.8 cm)
Ashmolean Museum, University of Oxford, Pissarro Family Gift, 1952, WA1952.6.40 (BL 21)

37
Bust of Figure, 1854
Ink, brown wash, and watercolor
3 3/4 × 6 3/4 in. (9.5 × 17.1 cm)
Olana State Historic Site, New York, OL.1982.363

38

The Negress, 1867
Etching
Plate: 12¾ × 9⅜ in. (32.2 × 24 cm);
sheet: 19¼ × 13⅞ in. (48.7 × 35.2 cm)
Private collection (D 6)

in Pissarro's representations of Afro-Caribbean women from Saint Thomas, but the style of this study is utterly academic, evoking less the grittiness of the multiracial streets than the atmosphere of the artist's studio. Although the sheet itself had been badly damaged and the drawing remounted at the Ashmolean Museum, its quality and beauty are still evident. Many viewers interpret this study as the representation of resignation, of the model's simple acceptance of her status as a black woman seen and depicted by a white man. Unlike the slightly coquettish Indian woman who is fully aware of her charms, this model has no complicity in our fantasies. She allows them, but she does not encourage them.

Pissarro made a number of drawings of women of African origin in the fifteen years after he arrived in Paris from Saint Thomas, and the similarity of features among the women suggests that it was in fact one woman—his mother's West Indian maid, who remained in the Pissarro household for many years—rather than a paid model. The drawings of this woman vary in size and function: some are seemingly independent works, while others have the air of studies made for later use in the creation of composite works of art. In fact, one is a study for an etching of an African woman that Pissarro is known to have made in 1867 and is his first figural print (fig. 38). Called simply *The Negress,* the print exists in

39
Study of a Negress, ca. 1860
Charcoal
7 13/16 × 8 5/8 in. (19.9 × 21.9 cm)
Ashmolean Museum, University of Oxford, Pissarro Family Gift, 1952, WA1952.6.61 (BL 42)

two states and in only a handful of impressions, suggesting that it was an experimental work. It represents a seated black woman wearing a simple dress and a patterned scarf and kerchief reminiscent of Saint Thomas. Pissarro himself had not been in Saint Thomas for twelve years when he made this etching, and he never returned before his death in 1903. This print is, in fact, the final racialized work of art in his oeuvre, and it was made before he turned his attention to the representation not of race but of class. The subject of the print is at once the woman herself and the large shadow she casts on a pale, featureless wall, and the work has an undeniable melancholia. Her face and hands are in shadow to such an extent that we cannot read any expression. It is, instead, her body and position that suggest resignation and sorrow. She is, above all, utterly alone and lost in her thoughts, to which we can never have access. It is, in a sense, a farewell.

Pissarro included dark-skinned people of both African and indigenous South American origin in many composite works of art designed for sale or for later translation into oils, and three will suffice here to show the range of this material. Perhaps the earliest is a large graphite drawing finished with elaborate ink washes that represents a market scene in Saint Thomas or possibly Saint Croix (fig. 40). There are at least fifty figures in the scene, giving a crowded feel to a setting that includes both masonry and wooden buildings, deciduous trees and palm trees, raised wooden platforms, and quite possibly a well or source of water. All of the figures represented with any detail are Afro-Caribbeans; Europeans are either so tiny or peripheral they are invisible. Although the work is definitely racialized, there is an attempt to contrast racial experiences: the Afro-Caribbeans essentially own the space—and the commerce—of the work of art. This is also true of Pissarro's market study in Caracas (Consejo Municipal de Caracas), which he made in pen and ink over pencil and which represents a completely Indian market with no visible Europeans. The "freedom" of the market—to which we will return later—fascinated Pissarro even in his earliest years as an artist. He persisted in the representation of what one might call monoracial multifigural compositions, as one can see from an elaborate graphite genre scene (fig. 41) now at Frederic Edwin Church's Olana in New York. Here, Afro-Caribbean women and children seem to live completely outdoors, without architecture or running water but in a way that suggests the contented simplicity that Pissarro was to contrast with his representations of bourgeois life at the same period.

Perhaps the most powerfully racialized work of art from his early career is a large, multifigure composition in ink wash that is said to represent a carnival celebration (fig. 42). A dark room, bathed in brilliant daylight from three openings, serves as the "set" for a frenzied dance. We see a group of Europeans dancing, surrounded mostly by figures who are clearly Afro-Caribbean, only

40

Market Scene, 1852–1853
Ink wash over traces of graphite
10⅝ × 14¾ in. (27 × 37.5 cm)
Olana State Historic Site, New York, OL.1982.294

41

Figures along a Shore, 1852–1853
Graphite
10¼ × 13½ in. (26 × 33.7 cm)
Olana State Historic Site, New York, OL.1982.295

Melly

Melly

2

PISSARRO'S FAMILY

The Women in His Life Born in Charlotte Amalie, Saint Thomas, in 1795, Rachel Pissarro née Pomié, Pissarro's mother, died ninety-four years later in Paris. She was a tenacious and tragic figure throughout her life, a woman who used her influence over her sons long after the death of their father, Frédéric, in 1865. The painter's early life was deeply affected—in an oddly positive way—by the fallout from his parents' contested marriage. Yet if the Pissarro boys endured the harassment of other Jewish children over this scandal, most of the suffering was experienced by their mother, who was essentially considered to be a loose woman both by the elders of the synagogue and, because the situation played out in the local newspaper, by the literate public of Saint Thomas. The scandal, which endured for eight years, was surely a major contributing factor in the strong-mindedness and determination of Rachel, who played a central role in Pissarro's life. Her convictions were both hard fought and hard won, and she was true to these convictions to such an extent as to be inflexible. Although few letters between mother and son survive, there is a good deal of evidence in family lore and in other family letters of her indomitable maternal force. She was a pervasive influence throughout the lives of her children, and we learn this early on, particularly after the death of her last son by Frédéric, Gustave, which was announced to the absent Pissarro by his older brother Alfred in a letter dated August 30, 1853: "Maman walks up and down in front of the room where he died as if she hoped he would appear there again. Torrents of tears run down her cheeks and the most poignant sobs rack her. Yes, dear Camille, our mother must go through a profound emotional crisis before she accepts the death of our poor brother." The same letter treats their father so summarily that he clearly played

46

Pissarro surrounded by his family, Éragny, ca. 1886. Georges and Félix stand at top, Lucien and Ludovic-Rodolphe sit at center, and the maid Juliette[?], Camille, Julie, Paul-Émile, Jeanne, and Eugénie Estruc are seated below.

little role in the psychology of the household; he was a distant figure associated by all of the brothers with the family business and not with the family's emotional dynamic.

We know nothing of the cause of Gustave's death at age twenty; their first son, Félix, had either already died or did so the next year, 1854, at the age of twenty-eight. No family letter survives to tell us of Madame Pissarro's response to this other premature death, and there is no surviving document that confirms the death date of Félix. Perhaps he preceded Gustave in death, thus magnifying Madame Pissarro's grief the second time. In addition, Delphine, Madame Pissarro's first child and daughter from her first marriage to Isaac Petit, died in Paris in 1855, meaning that she lost three of her eight children as young adults over a period of three or four years. Two sons from her first marriage, Joseph and Isaac Petit, seem to have died in childhood, leaving her in 1855 with three adult children—Emma, Alfred, and Camille—only two of whom survived her. It is difficult to exaggerate the importance of loss in the life of a mother. She may not have been permanently scarred by the loss of her first sons: they do not seem to have survived into her marriage to Frédéric and the birth of four additional sons. But the loss of children as young adults is considerably more challenging for any mother. When her last daughter, Emma, died in 1868, she had only two sons remaining. She greatly desired grandchildren, and it appears that Alfred, her eldest surviving son, fathered only two children. Although her daughter Emma had five children, Emma's family, the Isaacsons, lived in London, and Rachel, who lived in France, saw little of them. This left her third son by her second marriage, the painter Camille Pissarro, who fathered eight children, to be the major source of grandchildren, forcing an even greater burden of familial responsibility on the artist.

The diasporic families of Pissarro's youth and the terrible battle for marital legitimacy suffered by his parents were defining aspects of the painter's social and emotional life. The fact that his mother lived to ninety-four cannot be forgotten when we think about Pissarro and his own "nuclear" family. She played an enormous role in the raising of her grandchildren and was, in bad economic times, the principal source of financial support for the family. All accounts of her treat her as highly emotional, even unstable, and prone to extreme mood shifts that affected everyone around her. She was, in some senses, the classic "Jewish mother," and she embodied almost every cliché associated with that stereotype. Nothing was ever good enough. If you were with her, you weren't supportive enough; if you were not with her, you had forgotten her. If you tried to intervene in a crisis, you were rebuffed; if you decided not to intervene, you were callous. And on and on. We cannot, of course, know her with any degree of completeness from the scant historical record, but all sources agree on her severe emotional

swings and her indomitable character. For Julie Vellay, who would marry Pissarro, she was certainly "the mother-in-law from hell."

As we shall see, she at once disapproved of and played a decisive role in her son's marriage. That Julie was not Jewish (Rachel's other children chose partners who were Jewish) and that she had been Madame Pissarro's servant was never forgotten by Madame Pissarro *mère*, even after Camille and Julie married in 1871. Although it was sheer coincidence, it is fascinating to see that Pissarro's own marriage came eight years after his first attachment to Julie and after the birth of two children, just as his parents' marriage had occurred eight years after the birth of their first son. These parallels seem not to have been noticed by Madame Pissarro *mère*, who for nearly two decades accepted her grandchildren without actually recognizing the existence of their mother. Pissarro's mother was never to experience the aching poverty that the painter's family knew all too well in the 1870s and 1880s, but her frequent and long separations from her husband and children, as well as the early deaths of six of her eight children, meant that she had her own share of personal traumas to counter her daughter-in-law's poverty.

47
Study of the Artist's Mother with Her Maid, ca. 1880–1885
Charcoal on off-white paper
11⅛ × 8⅝ in. (28.4 × 21.9 cm)
Ashmolean Museum, University of Oxford, Pissarro Family Gift, 1952, WA1952.6.202 (BL 152)

We know little about the real attitude of Madame Pissarro toward her artist son. She seems never to have allowed him to paint her, although she appears in his drawings and prints (see fig. 47) and seems to have stayed with his family for extended periods in the years before her death in 1889. She lived near them in a rented house outside London in 1871, so that she could see her son and grandchildren without being in the presence of her daughter-in-law. It also appears, from circumstantial evidence, that he left his large paintings of the late 1860s with her—her living spaces were larger—so that they were spared damage when the painter's suburban Paris house was ransacked by Prussian troops in the Franco-Prussian War. Indeed, from all indications, Pissarro was closely involved with his mother from 1855, when they were first together in Paris, until her death thirty-four years later.

Although her centrality to the painter's life cannot be denied, the tensions involved in his relationship with her, like so many aspects of family life for artists, were not overtly expressed in his art. What we know of her comes from letters and secondary biographical studies. Yet if she is largely absent from the painter's oeuvre, he seems to have been fascinated with her in the last years of her life, recording her as she aged and in her death throes. In fact, one of Pissarro's greatest and most complex etchings represents his dying mother alone in her bed at night, an empty armchair next to the bed (fig. 48). This haunting print has been compared by many to Rembrandt's etched evocations of night and, thus, to the history of the medium in the work of its first true genius. Pissarro worked

48
Grandmother (The Artist's Mother), 1889
Etching and aquatint on cream laid paper
Plate: 6¾ × 10⅛ in. (17.1 × 25.7 cm); sheet: 715⁄16 × 12¼ in. (20.1 × 31.1 cm)
Museum of Fine Arts, Boston, fund in memory of Horatio Greenough Curtis, 62.482 (D 80)

very hard on the print, and seven states were recorded by Delteil. Fascinatingly, Pissarro himself inscribed the words *La grand'mère (effet de lumiere)* on several of the impressions, detaching himself from the work and suggesting that it was made less for him than for his children—her grandchildren. The inclusion of the article *la* further depersonalizes the work, as if his mother, in art, had been transformed into The Grand Mother rather than his children's grandmother. He also separated the two words and left out the necessary *e* at the end of *grand*. Surely this was intentional, a linguistic device of distancing what was, for the painter, a death that must have been as much a relief as a tragedy.

In spite of her difficulties, Rachel was, in many ways, the defining person in Pissarro's life, and shortly after her death in 1889 he began work on his only printed self-portrait (fig. 49), an etching most likely completed in 1890. Its inclusion at this point in the essay is easy to understand, because its haunted, Rembrandtesque dark ground is so clearly similar to that of the masterful etching of his mother. In all likelihood, Pissarro worked on both plates at the same

49
Portrait of the Artist, ca. 1890
Etching on beige laid paper
Plate: 7 3/16 × 6 7/8 in. (18.3 × 17.4 cm); sheet: 13 7/16 × 9 13/16 in. (34.2 × 25 cm)
Museum of Fine Arts, Boston, Lee M. Friedman Fund, 60.249 (D 90)

time, particularly because his correspondence makes clear that he continued to redo and reprint the "grand'mère" print well into 1891. The death of his mother can have been nothing less than life-changing for Pissarro—as important as his friendship with Cézanne, which was the instigating factor for his first painted self-portrait. Here we see him looking dispassionately at himself over his half-glasses in what seems almost to be the same dark room in which his mother died.

In written inscriptions and letters, Pissarro decided to refer to his mother as *grand'mère* after the birth of Lucien in 1863. This decision is not without precedence in the lives of other nineteenth-century people, yet it seems to have been so strong in Pissarro that it must also have had psychological origins. The distancing of *grand'mère* from himself was certainly sought. His earliest surviving pencil drawing of her (BL 39) has often been interpreted as a portrait of Pissarro's French grandmother (his father's mother), but this is not the case. Although the inscription was initially thought to have been written by her grandson Lucien, we now know that Pissarro himself called his mother *grand'mère* and inscribed the drawing himself. This conflation of generations was convenient for Pissarro, who could keep his needy, meddlesome, and loving mother at a linguistic distance.

The relationship between Julie Vellay and Camille Pissarro evidently began in his mother's home, where Julie served as the cook's assistant in a large household with several servants. We don't know how she got the job or even precisely what she did in the kitchen, but she was "in service," a condition of modern life that fascinated Pissarro and became the primary subject for several important figure paintings and many drawings. Julie was born in Burgundy in a village not far from Dijon, where her mother owned vineyards and her family was part of a respectable and independent class that could be called the landowning peasantry. In many respects, the Vellays were precisely the type of people whom Pissarro would use as the subjects of his major figure paintings in the last decades of his life. Although his own family owned property, the Pissarros were strictly mercantile in origin—that is, completely bourgeois. This social contrast between Pissarro and his mother's servant was joined by an equally powerful religious contrast. He was raised as a Jew, she as a Catholic. In addition, Julie lacked any upper-level education and was only partially literate. In her own letters and in her addenda to later letters of her husband to their children, she used often-hilarious phonetic spellings. Some of the more egregious passages were actually blacked out after her death to shield her faults of spelling and grammar from archival readers.

We know more about Julie than we do about Pissarro's mother. The correspondence in the Pissarro archives is largely familial, and she is mentioned often. We know that she was an equal partner in her husband's life, that her opinions and ideas were taken seriously by everyone, and that she endured poverty, contentiousness, and various tragedies with skill, determination, and fortitude. She was, in many important senses, as strong-minded and stubborn as her mother-in-law—and both of these mutually distrustful women attained their indomitable character through their hardships. Julie Pissarro was most often called *mère* (mother) by her husband, who linguistically associated the two women in his life with his children rather than himself. Her maternal role was so important for Pissarro that there was surely a desire on his part to create a family that had greater cohesion than that of his mother's family. And indeed the Pissarro household was run by Julie with utter competence and imagination. Because she had rural origins, she always kept a plentiful kitchen garden as well as chickens, ducks, and sometimes even a cow. She cooked both healthfully and knowledgeably and, when the family could afford its own maids and servants, supervised others with a skill the origins of which surely lay in her own experience of service. She also was very good with children, worrying about them but not excessively, unlike Pissarro's mother. Indeed, Pissarro's fidelity to Julie and his decision to marry her formally in 1871 was surely because she was, in almost every sense, his mother's opposite.

Julie was also very open to Pissarro's many friends and seems to have been perfectly willing to include them at family meals, often at the last minute, and to advise them and their wives and girlfriends about practical matters. She was the registered godmother of Monet's first son, Jean, although neither of the young couples was married at the time, and she became very involved with the intertwined lives of Cézanne, his girlfriend (and eventual wife), and their child. She kept up with the various locals wherever the family lived, negotiated for credit in the shops, and generally ran interference for her often-absent husband. She outlived him by twenty-three years, dying in 1926, the same year as her friend Monet, to whom she had secretly written years before asking for a loan to buy the Pissarro family farm in Éragny. She was successful in this too, despite her husband's theoretical contempt for property ownership. Indeed, she tolerated many aspects of his social, political, and health ideas, although they were not at all in accord with her own practical nature. She seems never to have experienced marital infidelity, although she is known to have watched Pissarro carefully around younger maids and models, particularly after he started painting and drawing from the figure in the late 1870s. Some scholars have identified her hefty, middle-aged body in certain of Pissarro's female nudes of the mid-1890s, and, although she was pretty as a young woman, she was more concerned about the appearance of respectability than about fashion or conventional beauty.

We know from family anecdote that it was an early pregnancy in 1861 that forced their relationship into the open, causing the beginning of the long rupture between Julie and Rachel, who resolutely refused to permit the marriage. That

50
Julie Pissarro, 1874
Oil on canvas
45⅝ × 34⅞ in. (116 × 88.5 cm)
Musée du Petit Palais, Paris, gift of Ambroise Vollard to the city of Paris for the Petit Palais, 1930, Inv854 (PDR 363)

51
Jeanne-Rachel Pissarro Seated at a Table, ca. 1872–1874
Watercolor over black chalk on off-white paper
9⅝ × 7½ in. (24.5 × 19.2 cm)
Ashmolean Museum, University of Oxford, Pissarro Family Gift, 1952, WA1952.6.97 (BL 70)

52
Portrait of Félicie Vellay Estruc, ca. 1874
Pastel
18⅛ × 11⁷⁄₁₆ in. (46 × 29 cm)
Private collection, courtesy of Moeller Fine Art, New York–Berlin (PV 1521)

pregnancy ended in miscarriage, giving Pissarro a natural way out of the relationship had he cared for one. Yet like Monet, who remained faithful to Camille Doncieux when she became pregnant (even after being told by his father to desert her), Pissarro remained faithful to Julie, becoming deliriously happy at the birth of their first child, Lucien, on February 20, 1863. Julie and Camille remained together until his death, celebrating the births of eight children at irregularly spaced intervals between 1863 and 1884, when Julie was forty-five years old. In 1865, after the death of Camille's father and the birth of Camille and Julie's first daughter, Jeanne-Rachel, his mother moved to Paris's ninth arrondissement, where Pissarro had rented various studios and small apartments for nine years, to be nearer to her son and grandchildren, thus beginning the dance of criticism and reconciliation between the two generations that lasted until 1889. With the birth of Jeanne-Rachel, who was named after both grandmothers, Madame Pissarro merely accepted the relationship of Julie and Camille as a fact—without budging on the issue of marriage.

It is perhaps a little odd that Pissarro painted Julie so rarely. She is, as we have seen, more often present as a figure in his landscape paintings than as the subject of a proper portrait. Indeed, only six portraitlike painted representations

53
Bust-Length Portrait of Madame Pissarro Seen in Three-Quarters Profile Facing Right, early 1880s
Copying pencil with clear wash on off-white paper
$8\frac{1}{8}$ × 5 in. (20.5 × 12.5 cm)
Ashmolean Museum, University of Oxford, Pissarro Family Gift, 1952, WA1952.6.249 (BL 175B)

54
Portrait of Madame Pissarro, 1882
Black chalk on off-white paper
$5\frac{11}{16}$ × $3\frac{7}{8}$ in. (14.5 × 9.8 cm)
Ashmolean Museum, University of Oxford, Pissarro Family Gift, 1951, WA1952.6.205 (BL 155A)

55
Madame Pissarro Sewing beside a Window, ca. 1877
Oil on canvas
$21\frac{1}{4}$ × $17\frac{3}{4}$ in. (54 × 45 cm)
Ashmolean Museum, University of Oxford, Pissarro Family Gift, 1951, WA1951.225.3 (PDR 534)

of her survive, none of them finished and none exhibited during the painter's lifetime. He did make one large and accomplished pastel portrait of her in the early 1880s, which perhaps succeeds best in capturing her plump and pleasant features. Indeed, she seemed unwilling to sit for prolonged periods and, instead, bustled around their various houses, gardens, and neighborhoods, maintaining the households and dealing with an increasingly large family. The later painting of her in the present exhibition (fig. 55) is the most satisfying and complete. From 1877 or even 1878, it has been given a different title in the recent catalogue raisonné that conclusively situates it in the Pissarros' house in L'Hermitage, La Maison Rouge (The Red House). Earlier scholars had theorized that the painting was done in Pissarro's Parisian pied-à-terre on rue des Trois Frères in the eighteenth arrondissement, which he rented in January of 1878; both the wrought-iron balcony and the fact that the view from the window is dominated by architecture supported this theory. Yet Julie rarely came to Paris, particularly because she had to stay with the children, for whom there was no room in the tiny apartment.

Wherever she is, Madame Pissarro is intent on her sewing and seems blissfully unaware that she is being painted. The work is a loving study of domestic tranquility in a premodern era, and her simple profile, full red cheeks, and lack of adornment evoke a modesty that is somewhat at odds with the swooping curves of the expensive wrought-iron balcony against which she is juxtaposed. The hint of tree branches at the left edge suggests that the painting was made in the winter of 1877–1878, and the contrast of the chilly scene outside the window and the warmth and sheer physical accessibility of Madame Pissarro—we feel we can touch her—gives the painting an inexpressible charm. No painting by Renoir or Cézanne of their wives shares this quality of loving intimacy, which is never better expressed in Pissarro's oeuvre. The painting contrasts with the rather cool—one might even say Cézannian—quality of a somewhat earlier oil portrait of 1874 (fig. 50). Its surface is aquiver with delicate strokes, and the scumbling in the passages that describe her simple, collarless blouse suggests that it was made over several days. Perhaps Madame Pissarro got tired of sitting or the weather improved, for Pissarro never returned to finish the picture. By then, the very concept of "finish" had faded, and his paintings were intended to evoke the process of their making. He painted as she sewed.

56

Portrait of Jeanne Pissarro, Called Minette,
ca. 1872
Oil on canvas
7⅝ × 6⅞ in. (19.5 × 17.5 cm)
Private collection (PDR 237)

The Life and Death of Minette Jeanne-Rachel Pissarro was nicknamed Minette when still a baby. Born in 1865, a little less than two years after her older brother, Lucien, she was named after her two grandmothers, one of whom—Pissarro's mother, Rachel—was so set against her son's relationship with Minette's mother that surely the choice of names was an effort at conciliation. Minette makes her earliest appearance as a two- or three-year-old toddler, clutching her mother's skirt and looking up for attention, in Pissarro's largest Salon painting, *The Hermitage at Pontoise* (fig. 5) from about 1867. She appears again a few years later—also behind her mother's skirts—in *The Conversation (Road from Versailles to Louveciennes)* of 1870 (fig. 7). As the first girl and the only one yet to survive (Adèle-Emma, her younger sister, died as an infant in 1870), she was a favored child. She was also fair, inheriting her looks from her mother's side of the family, and Pissarro was so smitten that he painted her more often in a shorter period than any of his children. Joachim Pissarro and Claire Durand-Ruel Snollaerts unearthed what they consider to be his first oil portrait of her (fig. 56), published for the first time in the catalogue raisonné. It is one of four portraits of Minette from 1872 alone, and it may well have been painted on May 13, her seventh birthday. She stands stiffly, almost as if posing for a photograph, in front of a daintily papered wall in the Pissarros' rented house in Pontoise. Perhaps because of its tiny size, the portrait is at once unaffected and deeply moving, as Pissarro's little girl stared simply into her father's eyes while he painted her for the first time.

Later that year, he painted her sitting on a wooden chair placed on a garden path, as she looks intently at a red-and-white toy or doll that she holds with both hands (fig. 58). It is a study of quiet absorption and, because of its profile pose, outdoor setting, and large scale, it is literally the opposite of her father's tiny, earlier portrait. Neither of these portraits is signed or dated; indeed, both were stamped with the initials of the painter after his death in 1903, and both remained in the family. His widow, Julie, kept the garden portrait, and her niece and nephew, the LeBoeufs, who had known Minette, received the smaller one.

The wonderful small painting now in the Wadsworth Atheneum Museum of Art (fig. 57), perhaps the greatest of the four works, shows Minette standing in her blue smock, her hands held together, fiddling with her thumbs and looking away from the painter/viewer she faces. Under her smock she wears a jaunty red plaid dress with a white collar, dark bloomers, stockings, and red socks, suggesting that it is chilly in the house. The painting is fascinating because it is at once a portrait, an interior genre scene, and a still life, and all of these make clear the relative comfort of the Pissarro household. Directly behind Minette is an expandable dining table. Four of its six turned legs are visible and, in a witty pictorial touch, Minette provides the missing two. On the table, Pissarro has lined up a crystal decanter, a Chinese painted porcelain vessel (for tea), and an

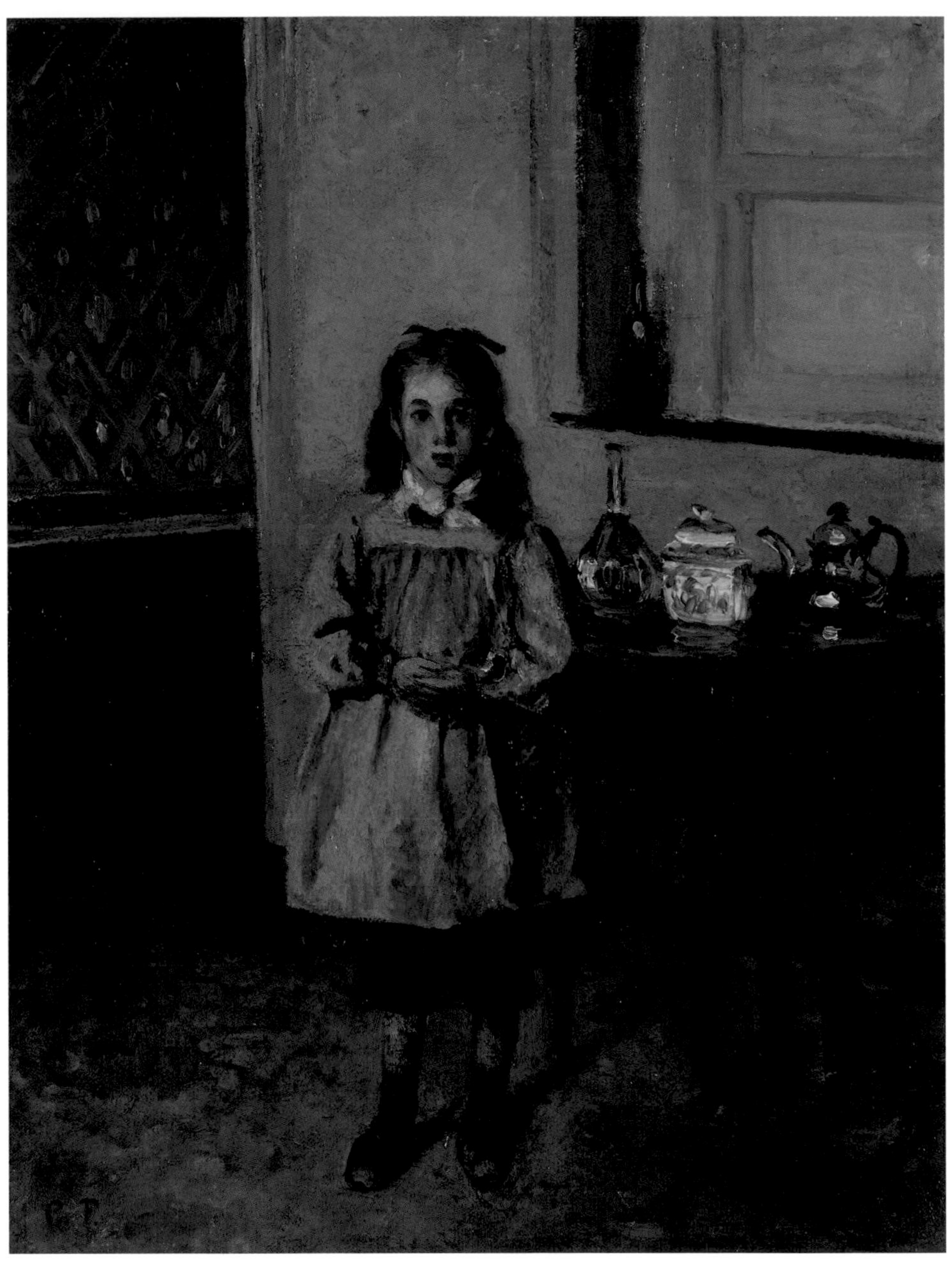

57
Minette, ca. 1872
Oil on canvas
18$\frac{1}{16}$ × 14 in. (46 × 35 cm)
Wadsworth Atheneum Museum of Art, Hartford, Connecticut, the Ella Gallup Sumner and Mary Catlin Sumner Collection Fund, 1958.144 (PDR 282)

58
Jeanne Pissarro, Called Minette, Sitting in the Garden, Pontoise, ca. 1872
Oil on canvas
28¾ × 23⅝ in. (73 × 60 cm)
Private collection (PDR 256)

expensive silver teapot or coffeepot with an ebony handle and top knob. These were surely chosen both as symbols of prosperity and as a pictorial revelation of the painter's skill at rendering surfaces that were reflective, transparent, and opaque. A lone wine bottle rests in the corner on a shelf, perhaps a visual metaphor for the painter himself.

Joachim Pissarro perhaps followed family precedents by identifying this painting as the one given by Pissarro to Adèle, the wife of his best friend, Ludovic Piette, in December of 1872. Apparently Pissarro decided to rescind the gift because he didn't feel the painting was finished, and Piette scolded his wife for allowing its return. The portrait appears finally to have entered the Piettes' collection in the summer of 1873, when Piette wrote to Pissarro so touchingly:

> I come to the little portrait, I didn't dare speak to you about it, it's a great pleasure for me to have it: the little girl, the recollection of your stay here, everything . . . retraced for us; and also the painter's ragout, those wan, somewhat sickly tones, that transparent skin, that ash-blond hair of the little one, what a feast for the eyes you have made them: a sketch no doubt, and one that is all the more delightful to me, a mere sketcher.

Reading this passage today, one wonders whether Piette was in fact describing the Wadsworth picture. It is perhaps easier for us to think of the first tiny painting that eventually entered the LeBoeuf collection, or—were it not for Piette's use of the phrase "la petite étude d'après Minette" (translated above as "the little portrait," but literally, "the little study after Minette")—the larger *Artist's Daughter* (fig. 59), the only one of the four that is signed and dated to 1872.

In this canvas, the same size as the garden scene, Pissarro seated his beautifully dressed young daughter in what looks like a mahogany dining chair for her first conventional portrait. She wears what is surely the same straw hat she wore in the garden, this time trimmed with pale blue ribbons, and she holds a bunch of freshly cut flowers. The portrait is comparatively broadly painted with large brushes and confident strokes like the *ébauche* or "painted sketch" described by Piette. Minette also has the "wan, somewhat sickly tones, that transparent skin, that ash-blond hair" he so touchingly evoked, none of which comes to mind when looking at the Wadsworth painting. Piette's letter has the quality of a prediction, because the sickly young girl began to deteriorate dramatically by October of 1873, when Pissarro wrote to his friend, the homeopathic physician Dr. Paul Gachet, about the gravity of the situation, describing the family as half dead with worry and concern.

Pissarro painted two more portraits of her, both of which are undated and unfinished and, therefore, difficult to place with precision in the arc of her illness. In what seems to be the earlier of them (fig. 60), Minette sits on a

59
The Artist's Daughter, 1872
Oil on canvas
28⅝ × 23⁷⁄₁₆ in. (72.7 × 59.5 cm)
Yale University Art Gallery, John Hay Whitney (B.A. 1926, M.A. [Hon.] 1956) Collection, 1982.111.4 (PDR 281)

C. Pissarro. 1872

60

Jeanne Holding a Fan, ca. 1874
Oil on canvas
22 × 18¼ in. (56 × 46.5 cm)
Ashmolean Museum, University of Oxford, Pissarro Family Gift, 1951, WA1952.6.2 (PDR 325)

61

Jeanne Pissarro, Called Minette, Holding a Doll, ca. 1874
Oil on canvas
28¾ × 23⅝ in. (73 × 60 cm)
Private collection, on loan to the Ashmolean Museum, University of Oxford, LI209.1 (PDR 366)

C.P.

backless chair (the same one she had used in the garden) in a dark interior, looking wanly at the painter/viewer and listlessly holding a large white Asian fan. She is simply dressed, and her hair has been cut very short and has darkened to a reddish brown. There is a cast-iron stove and what appears to be a shuttered window behind her. Nothing feels comfortable or prosperous, and Minette seems shut inside, away from the sun and the flowers with which she had always been associated.

The final oil portrait (fig. 61), recently discovered in the collection of the painter's British descendents, is searing. Her ash-blond hair has darkened even more and been so severely cut, likely due to her illness, that she almost looks like a little boy. She holds a blond doll and wears a red shawl for warmth. And she looks directly into her father's eyes with an unnerving combination of intensity and passive acceptance. Was this painted before Pissarro's lithograph of her lying alone in bed as if dead (fig. 62)? The lithograph, dated on the stone to February 2, 1874, two full months before Minette died, is eerily prescient of the much later etching of the painter's mother on her deathbed and was Pissarro's first representation of the process of dying. Pissarro's second daughter, Adèle-Emma, had died three short weeks after her birth, before he could represent her, but Minette was another matter. He recorded suffering as few other Impressionists did. The fact that all of these pictures were private and remained in the family does little to undercut their pathos. Few painters have dealt with the short life and death of a child more sensitively and dispassionately.

62

Dead Child, 1874
Lithograph on off-white wove paper
Image: 8⁹⁄₁₆ × 10¹¹⁄₁₆ in. (21.7 × 27.2 cm); sheet: 12⅛ × 15⅝ in. (30.8 × 39.7 cm)
The Art Institute of Chicago, gift of Celia and David Hilliard, 2007.652 (D 129)

Pissarro's Children

When Minette died on April 6, 1874, Julie and Camille Pissarro had lost two of their four children and both of their daughters. They had endured a major scare when their fourth child, Georges, born in 1871, suffered terrible convulsions and nearly died early in 1872. Their fifth child, Félix, was born in Pontoise just four months after the death of Minette, and the Pissarros named him after the painter's oldest brother, who had himself died before Camille came to France. Indeed, the heavy hand of death seemed to lie too often on the Pissarros. Félix was to die of tuberculosis at the age of twenty-three in what must have seemed a dreadful parallel to the short life of the uncle for whom he was named. Yet if death and tragedy were frequent visitors to the Pissarro household in the first years of their marriage, they came less often throughout the rest of the nineteenth century. Julie gave birth to three more children after Félix—Ludovic-Rodolphe, Jeanne-Marguerite, and Paul-Émile—all of whom lived long lives and joined their older brothers, Lucien and Georges, to attend their father's funeral in 1903. Of the five children who survived Pissarro, all but one—Jeanne-Marguerite, nicknamed Cocotte—became artists, and their budding professional lives and that of their ever-experimental father took many twists and turns.

Despite his frequent stays in Paris, Pissarro was a quintessential family man. He doted on his children and their education, teaching them to draw, to develop intellectually, and to question the received values of French civilization of the period. Without Julie, he could never have managed to raise such a large family on such a limited income and, as we know from the voluminous literature on Impressionism, Pissarro struggled with his finances well into his sixties. Indeed, the short periods of relative comfort that interrupted his life were but respites from longer bouts of poverty, made bearable principally by the thrift and industriousness of his wife. Fortunately, Pissarro never developed the taste for lavish living that his family had inculcated in him as symbolic of success. Although he produced works of art—what we would consider luxury goods—he did not himself desire such things, and his family ate plentifully and lived comfortably but frugally. Their produce, meats, poultry, and cheeses were almost all locally produced and raised, sometimes by Madame Pissarro herself, and the family often consumed their own chickens and rabbits while the pigs and lambs came from local farmers. Perhaps only the books and journals that the Pissarros bought or subscribed to would have been considered luxuries by their rural neighbors.

In this familial context, Pissarro was unlike most of his artist colleagues. Vincent van Gogh, Caillebotte, Cassatt, and Degas neither married nor had children; Seurat married secretly and had no children; both Cézanne and Morisot had one child each, as did Manet, *if* Léon Lenhoff was his son; Monet and Sisley each had but two children; and Renoir waited until he was in his forties to marry and father children. (Pissarro was thirty-three when his first son was

born in 1863, and fifty-four when his eighth and final child, also a son, was born in 1884. Renoir's first child was born in 1885.) Only Gauguin, who began first to collect works by Pissarro and then to paint with him in the late 1870s, had as many surviving children, but he was, as we shall see below, the opposite of the quintessential family man. Indeed, of all the major Impressionists, Pissarro was the only one for whom his children were central throughout his long professional career (1860–1903).

Oddly, while the Impressionists themselves avoided traditional family life, children play an extraordinarily large role in Impressionist iconography. Some of the most moving and important representations of children in the history of Western art were produced by Degas, Renoir, Cassatt, and Morisot, two of whom were childless. Pissarro's children, by contrast, were more important to his life than to his art, and this short essay is adequate to explore his portraits of them. It is fascinating to compare Pissarro's representations of his own children with those of his colleagues. There is no doubt that his many paintings, drawings, and prints exceed, for example, the representations of Monet's or Sisley's children.

63
Portrait of Lucien Pissarro as a Young Boy, 1868–1870
Brush drawing in dark ink heightened with Chinese white on dark-green paper prepared with brown wash
10 × 13⅞ in. (25.4 × 35.2 cm)
Ashmolean Museum, University of Oxford, Pissarro Family Gift, 1951, WA1952.6.64 (BL 45)

Monet did represent his first son, Jean, quite often in paintings, most of which seem to have been done to mark the young boy's birthdays. Jean also appears with his mother in numerous Monet landscapes, just as Madame Pissarro and Minette appear in Pissarro's. Sisley represented his children studying at home in one wonderful double portrait, but they rarely appear in his landscapes. By contrast, Morisot was all but obsessed with her only child, Julie Manet, who may be the best documented of the Impressionists' children. We see her throughout the life that mother and daughter led together—as a baby, a toddler, a child, a budding adolescent, and a young woman. She appears alone and with her father (Eugène Manet), servants, visitors, and friends in such a wide variety of pictorial contexts that she was surely her mother's principal muse, and Morisot didn't hesitate to include her paintings, pastels, and watercolors of her daughter in the group Impressionist exhibitions. (Renoir was also assiduous in his representation of his children in the last decades of his life.)

64
Lucien Pissarro, 1883
Pastel
21¾ × 14$^{13}/_{16}$ in. (55.2 × 37.6 cm) (framed)
Ashmolean Museum, University of Oxford, Pissarro Family Gift, 1952, WA1952.6.208 (BL 157)

Of the artists closest to Pissarro, both Cézanne and Gauguin are worth discussing in this context. Cézanne's son, also named Paul, appears in small-scale portraits in the 1870s and early 1880s and was used as a model by his father in elaborate figural allegories when he was a teenager (Renoir pulled the same trick with his son later in life). Pissarro probably would have seen few of these portraits and would have considered the latter works as contrived and artificial. Gauguin, however, actually used his children as part of a pictorial investigation of childhood that began shortly after the birth of his first child and continued even after he deserted his family. Gauguin included several paintings of his children in the Impressionist exhibition of 1882 and a single wonderful portrait of one of his sons reading in the final group exhibition. In contrast to this public "use" of personal images, Pissarro included only one work representing his children among the hundreds he sent to the Impressionist exhibitions between 1874 and 1886.

Most people with a casual knowledge of Pissarro can recall only one of his children, his firstborn son, Lucien. Lucien was alone among Pissarro's artist children to have an internationally recognized career during his father's lifetime and, as the oldest son, he took responsibility for a good deal of his father's legacy. There is little doubt that Lucien was also Camille's favored correspondent: not only was he the first to leave home and to marry, but he also was away from home for long stretches of the last two decades of his father's life. Yet, for all this biographical favoritism, Pissarro was not interested pictorially in his son. Only two oil paintings of Lucien survive, and neither is of the quality of the paintings of Minette already discussed, and perhaps only a large pastel (fig. 64) embodies Pissarro's pride in his handsome young son. There is a wonderful lithograph of Lucien from 1874 (fig. 65), but it too was produced in such a small edition that it is more often published than seen. A late lithograph of Lucien, from the time

he suffered one of his frequent bouts of illness, is also so rare that it does not appear in the great print collections of the world, all of which have numerous other prints by Pissarro.

The younger children fared better in the number of times Pissarro painted, drew, or printed them. Georges, born in 1871, had the reddish-blond hair of his mother's side of the family, and Pissarro allowed him to keep his long tresses well past the age of five, when most French boys wore their first trousers and had their hair cut. In drawings and two paintings, Georges's wonderfully luxuriant hair exceeds in both length and beauty that of his late older sister Minette. One small portrait (PDR 580), known only from a black-and-white photograph, was painted in 1878, when Georges was seven; it is rare among Pissarro's representations of his children in being both signed and dated, and its first owner was the art dealer Ambroise Vollard. Another more formal portrait, probably from the same year, was kept by Georges, who retouched it to make it appear more finished and sold it (probably with the former portrait) to Vollard for some quick cash. Both of these paintings are as much about Georges's hair as they are about the facial features of the child, and both, too, are visual documents of an unconventional childhood. Since he treated all his children as individuals with their own wills (being a true anarchist), he would never have imposed a haircut on an unwilling child, and his paintings of a seven-year-old boy with long hair would have broken the unspoken codes of gendered behavior in bourgeois France.

65

Portrait of the Artist's Son, Lucien, 1874
Lithograph on blued white wove paper
Image: 8¼ × 11 in. (21 × 28 cm); sheet: 9⁵⁄₁₆ × 11¹³⁄₁₆ in. (23.7 × 30 cm)
Museum of Fine Arts, Boston, Stephen Bullard Memorial Fund, 1972.54 (D 128)

66

Portrait of Lucien Pissarro, 1882
Black chalk on off-white paper
5¹¹⁄₁₆ × 3⅞ in. (14.5 × 9.8 cm)
Ashmolean Museum, University of Oxford, Pissarro Family Gift, 1951, WA1952.6.206 (BL 155B)

67
Child with Drum, 1877
Oil on canvas
21⅝ × 18⅛ in. (55 × 46 cm)
Collection of Diane B. Wilsey (PDR 505)

The most enchanting of Pissarro's portraits of Georges (fig. 67) was signed and dated in 1877. It shows the five-year-old Georges in the spring of that year, wearing his trousers, a dresslike jacket, and a jaunty straw hat, banging with martial authority on a small drum. The little boy dominates this private landscape, which is aquiver with dancing strokes of paint. Was the drum a birthday present for the boy, who had turned five in November of the previous year? If so, Georges still reveled in it months later, for the painting was surely made in March or April of 1877, when the small fruit trees in the Pissarro garden had burst into bloom. This portrait has never been shown before the present exhibition, and it was most likely a gift from Pissarro to his wife, who in turn gave it to its subject after Pissarro's death.

Georges's younger brother Félix was born in 1874, and Pissarro also delighted in his long brown hair, blue eyes, and delightfully upturned nose. In one portrait (fig. 68), we see him seated in a dining chair in a red beret with a topknot, a pink bow tied at his neck, and a black overblouse. Like Georges's, his long hair was nonconformist for a child of his age. The little boy looks shyly sideways at the painter/viewer, almost as if to ask permission to leave. The painting is unusual among Pissarro's family portraits for being highly finished, and the artist clearly worked on it over several sittings, most likely on the weekends (when Félix was not at school) or in inclement weather (otherwise, he would paint outdoors). Also unlike most of the other portraits of Pissarro's children, this one is simply a posed child rather than a genre-like painting of children reading or drawing in which the subjects have no apparent consciousness that they are being painted. Its formality almost suggests that it marked an important moment for Félix, who was seven years old on July 24, 1881. This painting was exhibited in the painter's lifetime—rare for Pissarro's portraits of his children—in a group exhibition held at the prestigious Galeries Georges Petit in the late spring of 1887. Perhaps fortunately for the Pissarro family, it failed to sell and remained in the family collections until Lucien, Félix's oldest brother, bequeathed it to the Tate, London, in 1944 (it has since been transferred to the National Gallery).

By the time the 1881 portrait of Félix was painted, the little boy had long since been called Titi, one of the numerous endearing nicknames used by the Pissarro family. He grew into a talented artist, and some family members believe that, had he lived, he might have become the finest painter in the next generation of Pissarros. He was also a bit rakish and was known as a ladies' man as a teenager, prompting his mother to recommend that he be taken away from Éragny (where he must have become involved improperly with a local girl) to go with his parents to Belgium in 1894. Yet the year before, Pissarro painted one of his most delightful small portraits of Félix reading (fig. 69). He is shown with legs crossed, seated in a comfortable armchair in a room with patterned wall-to-wall carpet and dark wallpaper, suggesting it was a hotel room or a rented apartment rather than the family's spartan home in Éragny. (Joachim Pissarro thinks it might have been the painter's rented suite of rooms in the Hôtel du Rome in Paris, where Pissarro was forced to stay from late February until mid-May of 1893 while being treated for an eye abscess.) This small painting records a father's love and a son's maturity, as Félix is well dressed, beautifully groomed,

68
Portrait of Félix Pissarro, 1881
Oil on canvas
21¾ × 18¼ in. (55.2 × 46.4 cm)
Tate: Bequeathed by Lucien Pissarro, the artist's son, 1944, N05574 (PDR 663)

69
Portrait of Félix Reading, 1893
Oil on canvas
18⅛ × 15 in. (46 × 38 cm)
Private collection (PDR 988)

70

Portrait of Ludovic-Rodo Pissarro,
ca. 1883–1884
Black chalk on off-white paper
8¾ × 6½ in. (21.1 × 16.7 cm)
Ashmolean Museum, University of Oxford, Pissarro Family Gift, 1951, WA1952.6.203 (BL 153)

71

Young Man Writing, Portrait of Rodo; Paul-Émile Pissarro, ca. 1895
Lithograph on wove paper
Image: 4¹³⁄₁₆ × 4¹¹⁄₁₆ in. (12.2 × 12 cm) and 3¾ × 4⁹⁄₁₆ in. (9.5 × 11.5 cm); sheet: 14⅛ × 10½ in. (35.9 × 26.7 cm)
Print Collection, Miriam and Ira D. Wallach Division of Art, Prints, and Photograph, The New York Public Library, Astor, Lenox, and Tilden Foundations (D 145/D 146)

and apparently engrossed in his small, red-covered book. What was the book? It is small enough that it might well have been an anarchist publication, perhaps even one of Peter Kropotkin's or Élisée Reclus's new books, and its red cover might well have been a pictorial allusion to the red flag of the anarchist Paris Commune. Félix visited the exiled anarchist Reclus in Belgium in 1894 with both his parents. None of them could have known that Félix was to die painfully of tuberculosis in three years.

Pissarro's last three children—Ludovic-Rodolphe (born in 1878 and nicknamed Rodo, Piton fleuri, and Tiolo), Jeanne (born in 1881 and nicknamed Cocotte), and Paul-Émile (born in 1884 and called Pitou, Guingasse, and Bébé)—were painted more often than their elder siblings. Pissarro was increasingly successful in the 1890s and spent longer periods at home in Éragny. He was also now an older father, who was more relaxed about his role and delighted by the antics of his brood. Twenty-three such portraits survive; as one might suspect, many of these are slight, were left unfinished, and cannot be considered important works. For this discussion, we have selected only four of them. But these four give an added dimension to Pissarro's visualization of his children. The earliest of them (fig. 72) represents Ludovic-Rodolphe as a serious young man of fifteen at a small and rather elegant desk in the artist's home in Éragny. He sits in front of

an inkwell and an empty pen holder, patiently and intently reading what appears to be a letter; behind him is a paper-strewn "standing" desk used by his father. The fresh, apple-green landscape out the window indicates that it is early spring. The entire painting was made using what Theodore Reff has called (referring to Cézanne) "the constructivist stroke": parallel hatched marks that line up in martial rhythms. Rodo is intensely serious and absorbed as his father transcribes him, and it almost seems inevitable that this patient young man should be the one, among the five surviving children, to complete the enormous catalogue raisonné of his father's work, published a little more than a generation after this delightful portrait was completed.

72
Ludovic-Rodolphe Pissarro Reading,
1893
Oil on canvas
18⅛ × 15 in. (46 × 38 cm)
Private collection (PDR 990)

The Pissarros' last child, Paul-Émile, is the subject of two completely contrasting portraits, painted in 1898 and 1899, respectively. The earlier (fig. 73) represents the boy as a busy young painter of fourteen, working in his father's studio in Éragny, his board or panel on his lap while his box of paints rests on a child's chair in front of him. The studio is filled with light, and one can see both the fronts and backs of his father's canvases piled against the wall in the background. It is informal and altogether delightful, quite in contrast to the earnest portrait of Paul-Émile painted in the winter of 1898–1899 and signed and dated in the latter year (fig. 74). This stiffly posed boy seems shy and at odds with his father's pictorial project. The painting is essentially a symphony in the chromatic

73
Paul-Émile Pissarro Painting (Sketch),
1898
Oil on canvas
21¾ × 18¼ in. (55.2 × 46.4 cm)
Courtesy of Giraud Pissarro Segalot
(PDR 1244)

varieties of gray: fifteen-year-old Paul-Émile not only wears a tailored gray coat but sits in the corner of a room in which everything is "grayed." He is seated in front of a table laden with books, and we can count at least fourteen of them. He himself is not reading but rather holding a paperbound booklet, the author and title of which are withheld from us. He casts a sidelong glance at his father, as if wondering just how long he has to wait until the painting is finished. And finished the painting is—highly worked and patiently completed over all its surface before being signed and dated. Yet Pissarro never exhibited it in his lifetime, and the painting remained in the family of the sitter until Paul-Émile's death in 1972 at the age of eighty-eight.

The final portraits in this section represent Pissarro's only surviving daughter, Jeanne-Marguerite. Raised carefully by her mother so that she would *not* become an artist, Jeanne stayed at home until her marriage in 1908, five years after her father's death. For that reason, Pissarro painted her often, in part because he was largely confined inside in the last decades of his life due to persistent eye infections. In 1899 Pissarro rented an apartment in Paris at 204, rue de Rivoli. Located on the fourth floor (although in France it is considered the third floor), it had large windows overlooking the Tuileries gardens and one superb room, which Pissarro turned into a temporary studio. He decorated it with his works in progress and painted the view out the window. When he was tired of the view, he turned to his daughter or flowers for a pictorial change of pace. Surely the best of the paintings made in the apartment is *Jeanne Pissarro, Called Cocotte, Reading* (fig. 77). We see Jeanne, her hair in a chignon, wearing a printed blouse

74
Portrait of Paul-Émile Pissarro, 1899
Oil on canvas
25 9/16 × 21 1/4 in. (65 × 54 cm)
Collection of Joel and Carol Honigberg, Chicago (PDR 1248)

75
Ludovic-Rodolphe Pissarro Reading, ca. 1899
Oil on canvas
7 1/8 × 9 5/8 in. (18.2 × 24.4 cm)
Collection of Cheryl A. Chase and Stuart Bear (PDR 1247)

and a black skirt covered by a pale-pink ruffled pinafore for housework. She reads a red-covered paperback book—again a chromatic allusion to anarchism—in the ample light from the windows. On the wall behind her, Pissarro placed one of the large views of the Tuileries on which he was working (probably PDR 1312) and a somewhat earlier canvas, *Gardener Standing by a Haystack, Overcast Sky, Éragny* (PDR 1278), which he had begun the year before in the country and brought with him to complete in Paris.

The painting is a symphony of reds, pinks, russets, and oranges in a range of values, with highlights of brilliant green. It seems oddly to contradict the testimony of Signac, who visited Pissarro in the rue de Rivoli apartment and complained about the dullness and monotony of his current work. Pissarro himself had already relinquished the Neo-Impressionist technique that Signac had perfected, and he had been none too impressed by the younger artist's attempt to justify his own painting method and, thus, discredit the Impressionists with his now famous essay *D'Eugène Delacroix au néo-impressionisme* (From Eugène Delacroix to Neo-Impressionism). Indeed, Pissarro's superb painting combines

76
Jeanne Pissarro, Called Cocotte, with Her Hair in a Chignon, ca. 1899
Oil on canvas
22 × 18½ in. (56 × 47 cm)
Sammlung Rau für UNICEF (PDR 1246)

77
Jeanne Pissarro, Called Cocotte, Reading, 1899
Oil on canvas
22 × 26⅜ in. (56 × 67 cm)
Collection of Ann and Gordon Getty
(PDR 1297)

an intimacy of subject, surely prompted by the young Nabi painters Édouard Vuillard and Pierre Bonnard, with a chromatic technique that, despite the absence of "dots," owes a good deal to his experiments with Neo-Impressionism.

Pissarro's children were so central to his life that any reading of his letters or any biography of the artist is filled with their presence—his pride in them, his worries about their health, his attempts to convince them to work in their own way, his encouraging them to read and think more ambitiously. He became the kind of father he never had, less a restraining force on the lives of his children than an anxiously patient guide to life. The paradox of this is that the pressure Pissarro's own father exerted on him to turn from art to business had not worked. By contrast, Pissarro was much more successful at keeping his sons "in the family business"—of art.

C. Pissarro Cézanne

3

PISSARRO'S FRIENDS

As discussed in the opening essay, Pissarro had a very large and diverse circle of friends or, more accurately, a series of partially overlapping circles of friends: friends who were artists, collectors, dealers, neighbors, anarchists, revolutionaries, political theorists, writers, and on and on. What is remarkable is that Pissarro juggled these friends with such ease and skill, able to maintain simultaneous relationships with Degas (in his most virulent phases of anti-Semitism) and the anarchist writer Bernard Lazare, who was, like Pissarro, Jewish. It was, in the end, the radical respect for the individual that was at the heart of anarchism that fueled Pissarro's tolerance, allowing him to find what he considered to be the good in people who had egregious qualities. Pissarro's tolerance was also made possible by the grounding of his life in his family, which was always there and always paramount.

Pissarro was not particularly interested in representing his friends. We have but two drawings of Gauguin, with whom the painter shared an intimate relationship for almost a decade. Even though Gauguin was a frequent houseguest in Pontoise and Osny, Pissarro was more interested in painting *with* him than he was in painting or drawing him. This is also true for other good friends—Degas, Cassatt, Sisley, Monet, Renoir, Signac, and Seurat—none of whom leave a trace in Pissarro's oeuvre despite their importance in his life. For every one representation of a friend, there are twenty of members of his family, both nuclear and extended. But a few of his friends made a major impact on his oeuvre, and we shall consider only those.

78
Pissarro and Paul Cézanne, ca. 1873

The first was, of course, Fritz Melbye, with whom Pissarro shared a studio in Caracas in 1852–1855 and a good deal more, artistically and personally, and who

appears in various drawings and watercolors by Pissarro. Although numerous, these representations are not what we would consider important works either in Pissarro's emotional life—he did not come to a new understanding of Melbye through the act of drawing him—or in his oeuvre. In fact, if one were to select the thirty most important works on paper from the several hundred that survive from the three years the two worked together, only one would include Melbye: the large sepia sheet representing Pissarro's Venezuelan studio, signed and dated 1854 (fig. 79).

By contrast, when we turn to the second painter who played an analogously important role in Pissarro's life and career, Cézanne, we have a major portrait, an important etching, one drawing, and what appear to be commissioned photographs. Clearly Pissarro felt that the time he spent with Cézanne was crucial to both artists, and he explored this relationship through representation. Cézanne, however, never painted Pissarro, although two wonderfully sensitive drawings survive in the collection of the Musée du Louvre, now on deposit at the Musée d'Orsay. Pissarro's outpouring of Cézanne representations occurred in 1874, toward the end of almost a year-and-a-half period in which the two painters

79
The Artist's Studio, Caracas, Venezuela, 1854
Sepia and pencil
14⅛ × 20⅞ in. (36 × 53 cm)
Banco Central de Venezuela, Caracas

worked together in and around Pontoise (from late December 1872 until April 1874). It is impossible to put the works in order, but it is likely that the painting and the etching were made at the same time. They are fascinatingly different; in fact, they almost seem to represent two different people. In the etching (fig. 80), Cézanne is a commanding, indeed magisterial figure, seated in a formal, three-quarter pose. Dressed in a hat, a cape, a long coat, trousers, and a scarf, he thrusts his chin forward purposefully and rests one hand on his lap. Like Jean-Auguste-Dominique Ingres's Monsieur Bertin, Pissarro's Cézanne dominates his portrait without props or artifice: there is no evidence of either a chair or a setting. What

80

Portrait of Paul Cézanne, 1874
Etching on beige laid paper
Plate: 10½ × 8⁷⁄₁₆ in. (26.6 × 21.5 cm); sheet: 17½ × 13⅝ in. (44.5 × 34.6 cm)
Museum of Fine Arts, Boston, gift of Henri M. Petiet, confirmed by his estate, 2001, 2001.704 (D 13)

he is *not*, however, is an artist; he is a man, dressed for the outdoors, ready and prepared to deal with anything and anyone.

Unsurprisingly, Cézanne wore the same hat and coat (if not the cape) when he posed for Pissarro's powerful small oil portrait (fig. 81). Although undated, the painting was made the same winter as the etching, which Pissarro had printed in Paris early in 1874. If one were to reverse the etching, as the original was when Pissarro drew it in the ground on the copper plate, it would be in the same orientation as the painting. Given the large number of photographs commissioned by Pissarro from this period that included Cézanne, it is even possible that the two portraits were made from photographs rather than from life. There is precedent for this. A Cézanne drawing of Pissarro was made from a photograph, and Pissarro made at least one figure painting during the mid-1870s from a photograph.

The portrait has been extensively analyzed since it was first decoded by Theodore Reff in 1967. Behind the stiffly posed Cézanne (who lacks the powerfully assertive quality seen in the etching), Pissarro arranged two political cartoons from identifiable issues of left-wing periodicals published respectively on June 13, 1867, and August 4, 1872. The earlier and more prominent of these cartoons, over Cézanne's left shoulder, represents Gustave Courbet as the hero of both Pissarro and Cézanne, standing assertively amid his paintings, holding a palette, smoking, drinking a beer, and talking. He seems almost to shout at Cézanne, exhorting him to continue in the radical path Courbet began in the 1840s. Courbet himself was already living in exile in Switzerland when the painting was made, and both young artists felt his absence and were inflamed to continue his work. Here again, Cézanne is not represented as a painter but as a humble, nonbourgeois man dressed as if for a journey or at least a brisk walk in the cold, winter countryside of the north of France. It is the very contrast between Cézanne's humility and his strength that allows him to compete with the lively and strongly political background conceived by both Courbet and Pissarro. Together with *Donkey Ride at La Roche-Guyon* (fig. 45) and *Les turpitudes sociales* (figs. 190–221), this forms the triumvirate of Pissarro's overtly political artworks.

Two additional portraits will complete this brief digression into the aesthetics of Pissarro's friendships. The subject here is not a painter but the working pastry cook and art collector Eugène Murer, a pseudonym for Hyacinthe-Eugène Meunier, who was born illegitimate in Pontoise in 1841 and recognized by his father only in 1872. Murer was self-educated and self-made, a perfect model for the anarchist Pissarro, and he put a good deal of the small income he eked out from his pastry shop on the boulevard Voltaire into the purchase of art. When Pissarro painted an oil portrait of him in 1878 (fig. 83), Murer already owned important paintings not only by Pissarro but also by Guillaumin, Cézanne,

81

Portrait of Cézanne, 1874
Oil on canvas
28¾ × 23½ in. (73 × 59.7 cm)
National Gallery, London, on loan from Graff Diamonds Ltd. (PDR 326)

L'ECLIPSE

Renoir, and Sisley, and he was particularly attracted to the paintings of Renoir and Pissarro. This portrait of Murer, in which he is dressed as if for a costume party or celebration, has a rococo quality reinforced by its oval format, and it was commissioned as a mate to an almost identically sized oval portrait of Murer's sister Marie by Renoir (fig. 82). A pointed series of letters exists regarding the price of this painting, but they do not explain or give a context for the sitter's unusual attire. Does the scarf indicate the Murer was playing a gypsy, a troubadour, or a generic bon vivant? It is an unconventional portrait of an unconventional man

82

Pierre-Auguste Renoir
Marie Murer, 1877
Oil on canvas
26⅝ × 22½ in. (67.6 × 57.1 cm)
National Gallery of Art, Washington, Chester Dale Collection, 1963.10.59

83

Portrait of Eugène Murer, 1878
Oil on canvas
25⅜ × 21⅜ in. (64.4 × 54.3 cm)
Michele and Donald D'Amour Museum of Fine Arts, Springfield, Massachusetts, the James Philip Gray Collection, 52.01
(PDR 582)

84

Murer as a Pastry Cook, 1877
Pastel
$25\frac{9}{16} \times 18\frac{15}{16}$ in. (65 × 48 cm)
Private collection (PV 1538)

whom Pissarro admired deeply and with whom he maintained a friendship for nearly three decades. Its anomalous place in Pissarro's oeuvre has more to do with the circumstances of its commission and its facture and oval format than with Pissarro's own notions of portraiture. Never exhibited in Pissarro's lifetime, it is a record of a double friendship—of Pissarro and Renoir and of Pissarro and Murer.

Pissarro's first portrait of Murer is a large pastel of 1877 (fig. 84), and it is as unusual in the artist's oeuvre as the oval portrait. Called simply *The Pastry Cook* in the catalogue of the 1879 Impressionist group show, it was the sole work in an exhibition of more than 250 to represent a proletarian urban laborer. As such, it makes a contribution to a small subgenre of Impressionist painting inaugurated by the wealthy bourgeois artist Caillebotte, who had sent his paintings of floor scrapers at work to the 1876 exhibition and a single work depicting house painters to the 1877 exhibition. For the portrait, Pissarro used a sheet of paper of the same dimensions as many of the canvases he painted that year, and he represented the handsome young Murer in his pastry shop, either taking something from or putting something in the oven. For Pissarro, the picture is unique in several ways. It is his only interior representation of labor, his only genre-portrait in pastel, his only representation of an urban occupation, and the only work of this type he ever exhibited. It was, in addition, one of six works—five by Pissarro and one by Monet—loaned by Murer to the 1879 Impressionist exhibition.

The very idea of work was central to life and thus to representation for Pissarro. Yet it was difficult for him to study workers in urban settings, a subject that required careful negotiation and insider knowledge. Pissarro was able to gain that knowledge through his friendship with Murer and, because of that, he could paint a pictorial hymn to male proletarian labor that is rare in the history of Impressionism. That these four portraits suffice in a discussion of Pissarro's representations of friendship is a testament to the fact that he did not exploit his friends for pictorial purposes.

4

PAINTING MILLET AFTER NATURE

The critical reactions to the first Impressionist exhibition in 1874 were considerable—and not all positive. Although Pissarro proclaimed it a "success" in a letter to his friend the critic Théodore Duret, his use of the word was in all likelihood edged with irony, as both the critical notices and the sales were disappointingly bland or bad. The artists lost money, and Pissarro's work was not selling at all. Duret advised the artists to maintain, even to develop, their own individual styles, and he suggested that Pissarro concentrate on rural landscapes with animals to separate himself from the modernist and urban imagery and aesthetic of Monet, Renoir, and Degas (or their suburban corollary). Pissarro took Duret's advice to heart and, by October of 1874, accepted his old friend Ludovic Piette's invitation to spend several months working deep in the countryside in Montfoucault, Brittany, where Piette owned a large farm. The entire Pissarro family left Pontoise and went to Montfoucault, where the artist began an intermittent, three-year investigation of "rural life with animals." For guidance, he looked to the works of Millet, who was, for Pissarro, the only artist who painted rural life seriously and, indeed, the only conceivable model for his own "modern" investigation of rural life.

Millet was in failing health throughout 1874 and died in January of 1875, while Pissarro was in Montfoucault. Yet Pissarro well understood the differences between their aesthetic and personal struggles. Unlike Millet, Pissarro had bourgeois origins, and only through his wife could he come to understand modern rural peoples. In addition, Madame Pissarro's family of cash-crop landowners were, in effect, less landless peasants than petit-capitalist farmers. Pissarro was also beginning to develop ideas about agrarian reform and work that were rooted

85
The Sower and the Plowman, Montfoucault, 1875 (detail of fig. 90)

in his utterly modern political ideas. Pissarro looked to Millet for ideas about composition and imagery and for techniques to integrate figures into the landscape. He himself wanted to create works that were current and without sentimentality, using the latest and most innovative pictorial and chromatic strategies. Unfortunately for Pissarro, most of those who wrote about his Millet-inspired series of paintings and prints saw only the similarities between the young Pissarro and the great master of French rural life.

How well did Pissarro know the work of Millet? He had seen Millet's Salon paintings regularly since his arrival in France in 1855, and he was later able to study the artist's more important paintings in the intimate setting of Durand-Ruel's Paris gallery. Interestingly, Durand-Ruel was showing his stock of works by Millet regularly in the gallery by 1872, and he had recently purchased a large and significant group of Millet paintings from the artist's biographer, Alfred Sensier, early in 1873. The works that Pissarro in all likelihood saw at Durand-Ruel's gallery in 1872 and 1873 include some of the master's greatest paintings—*The Sower, The Angelus, Seated Shepherdess,* and many others. In Paris, shortly after Millet's death in 1875, there were two massive sales of his work, both of which received a good deal of publicity and both of which were held during months in which Pissarro was often in Paris: the Millet studio sale took place on May 10–11, and the Gavet sale of ninety-three Millet drawings and pastels on June 11–12. Although more than a decade passed before the French state presented an official retrospective of Millet's work at the École des Beaux-Arts in 1887, there were many opportunities for Pissarro to study the earlier master's work in the original, and the numerous prints by and after Millet were another important source of knowledge about that artist's compositions and techniques.

For this volume we have selected a small number of paintings from these years, largely because Pissarro was struggling with his own pictorial identity when making these works. The earliest, *Woman Herding a Cow* of 1874 (fig. 86), was bought in December of that year by the person who had done more than any other to ensure its production, the critic Duret. In the summer of 1874, Pissarro took a short walk to the fertile alluvial plains that line the Oise river near Pontoise. Because of Duret's influence, he selected a prominent figural motif—a young rural worker with her dairy cow, kept on a lead as it eats the sweet grasses in a flowering field. Behind her, a man and woman weed the adjacent field of crops, and a basket with lunch sits between the two fields. The painting immediately suggests Millet, who represented male and female peasants with cattle several times in his life, yet the lack of a precise prototype suggests that Pissarro internalized Millet without referring to any particular work.

What distinguishes this painting from a work by Millet? First, its quivering landscape setting is beautifully evoked with intense greens, blues, and

86

Woman Herding a Cow, 1874
Oil on canvas
18 × 22 in. (45.7 × 55.9 cm)
Private collection (PDR 355)

yellows, creating a chromatic presence that would, in a painting by Millet, be too forceful for its background role. Also, it was the precise phrase used by Duret in his letter—"rural life with animals"—that was uppermost in Pissarro's mind, not Millet's work, when he began this superb painting. Because the young woman and her cow would return to the field at the same time daily, Pissarro could easily have worked on the painting over the lengthy period of observation and composition required for such a finished work. Pissarro himself selected the painting for Duret, charging him a modest one hundred francs and sending it to his Parisian dealer/paint-supplier, Père Martin.

Later the same year, Pissarro began work on one of his boldest and most experimental figure paintings of the mid-1870s, *Harvesting Potatoes, Pontoise* (fig. 87). He selected a small canvas and again represented an agricultural scene

87
Harvesting Potatoes, Pontoise, 1874
Oil on canvas
13 × 16⅛ in. (33 × 41 cm)
Private collection (PDR 360)

on the alluvial plains. The painting is powerful and rather crudely painted, and its bold combination of brilliant oranges, greens, yellow, violet, and red gives it a chromatic intensity that anticipates later landscapes by Gauguin, Van Gogh, and the Fauves. It is also compact and tightly composed, the figures placed with the precision of pieces on a chessboard. The subject suggests Millet, who represented a potato harvest in one of his most famous paintings, *The Angelus* (Musée d'Orsay, Paris), which Pissarro had probably seen at Durand-Ruel's gallery. Millet had also painted a monumental scene of potato planting that had been shown in Paris at the Exposition Universelle of 1867.

Yet these works by Millet are in no way compositional or chromatic proto types for Pissarro's little masterpiece. Instead of the paired male and female peasant couples favored by Millet, Pissarro posed six rural workers, four women and two men, in the potato field. He also made clear that they are field hands rather than peasants who grow crops only for themselves. The two men dig the potatoes, leaving them on the ground, while two women pick them up in small baskets and carry them over to be placed in sacks. Two other women stand and fill a large sack of potatoes, while in the background two filled sacks are ready to be taken to market. It is, in many senses, an almost industrial scene of divided labor, and we must not forget that Pissarro had painted the Chalon sugar beet factory (PDR 300), which had opened the year before across the Oise in Saint-Ouen-l'Aumône. For Pissarro, this painting embodied the modernity of rural life rather than any links to Millet; it almost has the air of a small *ébauche* for a large Salon painting that Pissarro never attempted.

Pissarro was at Piette's Montfoucault farm on December 11, 1874, when he wrote to Duret about his new kind of painting, and he spent considerable time in that rural environment for the next three years. It is tempting to think that his rural aesthetic was actually a response to this traditional peasant environment, but as we have seen with the last two pictures, that was not the case at all. It was Duret, not Piette's farm, that led Pissarro to rural subjects and to paint a large series of pictures that collectively form a modern "reworking" of Millet for Impressionism. Pissarro had begun to use paint more aggressively and to experiment with textured pictorial surfaces. He even adopted Courbet's palette-knife technique for certain of these pictures, which are rough and primitive in both style and subject, and, in doing so, he eschewed the refinements of Millet's style for Courbet's tactile, handmade aesthetic. Few scholars and connoisseurs of Impressionism have valued these aggressively painted works of the mid-1870s, preferring Pissarro's Impressionist paintings of the early and later 1870s. Indeed, an almost unspoken consensus has developed that actually mirrors the Pissarro critics of his time—that these works are too linked to Millet to be as original and important as the "modern" painting of Renoir, Monet, and Degas. In many ways,

90

The Sower and the Plowman, Montfoucault, 1875
Oil on canvas
18⅛ × 22 in. (46 × 56 cm)
Jorge Eljuri Antón Collection
(PDR 425)

of the sower (Museum of Fine Arts, Boston; Yamanashi Prefectural Museum of Art, Japan; National Museum Wales), none can be proven to have been accessible to Pissarro. It is *possible,* although unlikely, that he could have seen the National Museum Wales version at Durand-Ruel before it was sent to London in the spring of 1872. We do think, however, that Pissarro saw the ninety-three drawings and pastels in the Gavet sale in June of 1875, and one is clearly a prototype for Pissarro's scene juxtaposing a sower in the foreground and a plowman farther back. In all likelihood, however, it was Millet's print that Pissarro used.

Again, it is fascinating to see the changes Pissarro made to Millet. The sower is literally reversed in pose, facing away from the viewer. He is older and moves less steadily in his wooden shoes. His clothing is precisely observed, and he is set in a field that is alive with Courbet-like palette-knife work in which yellows, browns, and greens commingle in subtle rows defined by the plowman. Pissarro also provided a tree-lined edge to the field and a thick slap of green that brings attention to the plowman and his white horse. It is the wonderfully vibrant color and the thick paint that modernize Millet's immemorial sower, placing him securely in the 1870s. Pissarro also made a direct link between his own work and that of the rural workers, and this link is, in the end, what is radical about these seemingly traditional rural scenes. Pissarro was thinking about the very nature of labor, not just the physical work of the field, and about the relationships among workers, be they artists or agriculturalists.

5

MAIDS AND DOMESTIC SERVICE

Any true anarchist in nineteenth-century France would have frowned on inequality among individuals. Anarchists, including Pissarro, believed that all men, women, and children were equal, if not in abilities and appearance than in having the equal right to live without shame, on the same footing as every other person. This view would seemingly have little room for domestic service in its ideal society of the future. Yet, as we have seen, Pissarro's wife, Julie, had been in service in his mother's household and had, like many young women of rural origin in Second Empire France, come to Paris looking for such work. The lives of domestic workers in France tended not to be as miserable as those of other working-class people. They were often provided with free, if modest, housing in the comparatively elegant neighborhoods of their employers and were also usually given free board. Their salaries were modest when compared to those of factory workers, shop girls, milliners, and the like, but so too were their expenses.

Perhaps because of this combination of political ideals and personal history, it comes as a surprise to know that Pissarro made a small series of paintings and drawings that represent female domestic workers at the job and in uniform. Of his fellow Impressionist colleagues, only those from the upper class included domestic workers in their painterly world. The maids of Manet, Degas, and Caillebotte are hardly surprising, and on rare occasions even Monet hints at the presence of domestic workers in his summery suburban garden landscapes. But Pissarro was the only Impressionist who made figure paintings in which a single domestic worker is the motif. The earliest—and one of Pissarro's most masterful—is *The Maidservant* (fig. 92). This painting—large by the standards of Pissarro—represents a uniformed maid wearing her starched cap and white apron

91
Julie Pissarro and the maid at Pontoise, 1873 or 1874

over a plain, fitted, orange-brown dress. On what appears to be a ceramic plate, she carries a crystal-stemmed glass in which a silver spoon is prominently placed. Rather than being represented from the front or in a frontally oriented three-quarter pose, she is turned away from the viewer, facing an empty greenwood garden bench with wrought-iron legs. The pose, costume, garden location, and props of the painting are exactly the same as those seen in a photograph taken in 1873 or 1874 in the Pissarros' garden (fig. 91), one of a series commissioned by the family and made in a single photographic session in what appears to be the summer. The photograph shows Madame Pissarro seated on the garden bench, positioned as the recipient of the maid's offering. Either Pissarro used this photograph as the basis for the painting, omitting his wife and making changes in the maid's garment for compositional reasons, or he used another photograph that has been lost. However, the sheer number of similarities between the painting and the existing photograph make the former highly likely.

If this were his only painting of domestic servitude, it might be supposed that Pissarro wanted, for reasons we can only suspect, to project through representation an air of success and prosperity. However, had that truly been his aim (as it often was for Monet in the same years), Pissarro would have accomplished more by including his wife in the painting. Instead, he not only omitted her but isolated the maid, forcing us to accept the mere fact of her servitude without any narrative. How, one must ask, can one have a server if there is no one to serve? In this, Pissarro differs from the painter he admired most and who painted servants the eighteenth century artist Jean-Siméon Chardin. Chardin painted the conditions of service in a kind of "upstairs-downstairs" manner, representing servants in their kitchens and sculleries rather than in uniform attending to their masters. Two paintings by Chardin may well have been known to Pissarro—*Woman Drawing Water from a Cistern* (private collection, Paris), which was included in an exhibition held in Paris in 1874, and *Kitchen Maid with Provisions,* purchased by the Musée du Louvre in 1867. Had he seen these paintings, Pissarro would instantly have admired and studied them, but did he have either in mind when he painted his masterpiece in the summer of 1875? The answer is decidedly negative. In an important sense, Pissarro's singular representation of service as service injects a modernist vitality—and ambiguity—into this painting, separating him from his brilliant ancien régime progenitor.

Although there is another small painting of 1877 in which Madame Pissarro and a maid sit near each other on a nice day, one indoors, the other outside, and both sewing, it was not until two paintings of 1882 that Pissarro reprised this subject. Both are in British collections, one through the generosity of the artist's eldest son, Lucien. *The Little Country Maid* (fig. 93) was signed and dated by Pissarro in 1882 but was probably not exhibited until 1896, when it

92
The Maidservant, 1875
Oil on canvas
35 × 27 in. (88.9 × 68.6 cm)
Chrysler Museum of Art, Norfolk, Virginia, gift of Walter P. Chrysler, Jr., 71.530 (PDR 418)

C. Pissarro
1882

her mother until the 1890s. There is no doubt, however, that the Pissarro family could scarcely afford to pay a maid in the 1870s, when he painted the first work, and likely relied on help from family members and neighbors in the early 1880s, when the second picture was painted.

Nini probably also served as the model for a wonderful picture entitled *In the Garden at Pontoise: A Young Woman Washing Dishes* (fig. 95), which represents a maid wearing a simple cap and apron, washing dishes on a makeshift table outside the Pissarro kitchen in 1882. This work was snapped up by Durand-Ruel in June of that year and sold to Pissarro's friend Mary Cassatt three years later. It represents a moment of simple domestic work, the repetitive nature of which must have appealed to Pissarro. In both paintings of 1882, Pissarro follows more clearly the example of Chardin by showing domestic work being performed without a sense of service or hierarchy. In this, they differ from the profoundly ambiguous paintings of 1875, in which Pissarro included domestic service among the many menial tasks being performed by rural workers. There is little suggestion in either of these paintings of bourgeois opulence or class division. Rather, the little maids are family members who work—whether doing household chores or modeling—for their hosts in an easy, reciprocal manner, and, because of this, the paintings are subtly but profoundly anarchist. Indeed, anarchist Peter Kropotkin and others did allow for domestic work in their anarchist utopias, particularly for large families or groups of families. Individuals could choose among many types of labor as part of their lifetime of work—industrial, agricultural, artisanal, scientific, intellectual, or domestic.

Was there a personal dimension to these paintings? Did Pissarro want to confront artistically the servitude experienced by his wife? Most likely not. Instead, he turned domestic service from a class-based system of perpetual servitude into healthy, clean, and comfortable work. Nothing in these pictures suggests social tension. Indeed, like Chardin's maids and cooks, Pissarro's are attractive, well fed, and seemingly contented. And in no case are these workers shown being supervised or commanded to perform tasks. Instead, they perform the menial tasks necessary for any clean and comfortable life. We suspect, as we look at the subjects, that they do many other tasks, and that they are agreeably pitching in to help rather than constantly sweeping, washing clothes, cooking, and setting the table. That was for Madame Pissarro, who was too busy to be painted!

95
In the Garden at Pontoise: A Young Woman Washing Dishes, 1882
Oil on canvas
32¼ × 25¹¹⁄₁₆ in. (81.9 × 65.3 cm)
The Syndics of the Fitzwilliam Museum, Cambridge, acquired with the assistance of the National Art Collections Fund, 1947, PD.53-1947 (PDR 685)

6

DRAWING THE FIGURE

Life Drawing The history of Western art is, in many important senses, based on figure drawing. Since the Renaissance, the nude was the most elevated subject for artistic study, and anyone who wanted to make a contribution to the history of art needed to learn to draw the human figure. It is well known that the avant-garde painters of the last half of the nineteenth century rejected academic practice for both political and aesthetic reasons, yet one cannot imagine the oeuvres of many of the greatest members of that avant-garde without figure drawing. Manet, Degas, Cézanne, Renoir, Seurat, and Gauguin all left superb figure drawings. Because of their gender, Cassatt and Morisot found it more difficult to draw from the nude while studying. And although Monet made wonderful caricatures, his figure drawings are few and far between. So too Sisley. Pissarro, being the oldest and most experienced among the Impressionists, drew the figure before receiving formal instruction. He was properly taught to do what we now call *académies* when he arrived in Paris in 1855 for formal training, during which he drew from both male and female nude models. Although none of these drawings would set the world on fire or raise a record price at auction, they are better than competent. They also prepared him for his "conversion" to figure painting in the mid-1870s and early 1880s, giving him a technical armature on which he built his ambitious figural compositions.

Pissarro's earliest figure drawings can easily be compared with those of Cézanne, Degas, and Seurat, against which they fall a bit short. Pissarro did not, like his three more talented contemporaries, put a personal stamp on these drawings; rather, they have an air of duty about them. His studies of a middle-aged male model from the Académie Suisse (in the Ashmolean Museum) are

96
The Harvest, 1882 (detail of fig. 116)

97
Study of Two Female Harvesters, 1881–1882 (detail of fig. 118)

routine (see fig. 98). Only in a frontal pencil drawing of a female nude (fig. 99), made shortly after his arrival in France in 1855, does he rise to a higher level. Here one sees a beautifully drawn model of ample but not excessive proportions, her arms raised in a formal pose (she was probably holding onto a strap for support). Pissarro recorded all aspects of her skin and body, including small pockets of fat and dimples. He also gave her face an almost portraitlike specificity, rare in studio drawings after the nude. When we compare her to early figure drawings by Cézanne, Degas, or Seurat, she just barely holds her own. Pissarro was too concerned with being successful at his task to be original or even eloquent. Yet he did have stamina and ability, and when he approached the figure again in the 1870s, he was ready to develop his work to a considerably higher technical and aesthetic level.

Surely his example in this was Degas, whose figural works on paper, including charcoal and pastel drawings, Pissarro had seen numerous times, even in the Impressionist exhibitions. These powerful works provided a level of traditional skill and experimentation that Pissarro rose to as he applied Degas's lessons of eccentric composition, and his interest in clothed or partially clothed figures, to rural models. Fascinatingly, many, perhaps even the majority, of Pissarro's figure drawings represent standing subjects, many of whom perform some kind of activity associated with work. This too has its origins not in the atelier, with its posed figures, but in Degas's studies of laundresses, dancers, and horseback riders as they exercised or worked. These "modern" bodies were as important to Pissarro as they were to Degas. As Pissarro worked increasingly with rural models in Pontoise and Montfoucault (they were less expensive to hire, compared to urban models), he began to represent them with an increasing confidence and élan.

This is the first group of Pissarro's figure drawings ever assembled for exhibition. It is also a decidedly provisional one, chosen from published works in accessible collections, and while it will not have the extraordinary strength of a comparable selection of Degas's figure drawings of the same period, neither will it be an embarrassment to Pissarro's memory. Indeed, as a landscape painter for whom figures were intended to enliven and give scale to composed natural views, their sheer quality is extraordinary. Pissarro was never trained with the rigor of Degas, who knew Old Master drawings so well. As a result, Pissarro struggled to work on large sheets of paper, transcribing heads, limbs, muscles, and draped bodies with a sense that, with each drawing, he would move imperceptibly forward as an artist. None of these drawings was exhibited in his lifetime. Indeed, he did not think of them as works for either exhibition or sale. They were part of his lifelong work as an artist.

98

Study of a Male Nude Posed against a Wall Seen in Profile Facing Right, 1856–60
Charcoal with traces of highlighting in white chalk on blue paper
18 7/16 × 11 5/8 in. (46.8 × 29.5 cm)
Ashmolean Museum, University of Oxford, Pissarro Family Gift, 1952, WA1952.6.56 (BL 37)

99

Nude, ca. 1855
Conté crayon and white chalk on blue laid paper
23 5/8 × 17 11/16 in. (60 × 45 cm)
Collection of Joachim Pissarro

100

Woman Seen from Behind; Three-Quarter Length, Head in Profile to Right, Arms in Front, Wearing an Apron, 1881
Black, blue, and white chalk on gray paper
17½ × 12⁵⁄₁₆ in. (44.5 × 31.3 cm)
The British Museum, London, 1920,0712.3

101

Three Studies of Women Dressing,
ca. 1895–1900
Colored chalks on pink paper
18⅛ × 23 15/16 in. (46.1 × 60.8 cm)
The British Museum, London,
1920,0712.2

102

Nearly Whole-Length Study of a Female Peasant with a Detailed Study of the Foreshortening of the Right Forearm and Hand Above, ca. 1879
Black chalk on pink paper prepared with a thin layer of Chinese white
18⅛ × 10⅞ in. (46.2 × 27.6 cm)
Ashmolean Museum, University of Oxford, Pissarro Family Gift, 1951,
WA1952.6.152 (BL 106)

103

Study of a Female Peasant Cleaning a Saucepan, ca. 1879
Black chalk heightened in places with gouache on pink paper prepared with a thin layer of Chinese white
18⅜ × 12⅜ in. (46.8 × 31.6 cm)
Ashmolean Museum, University of Oxford, Pissarro Family Gift, 1952,
WA1952.6.151 (BL 105)

104

Young Female Peasant Leaning against a Tree (The Shepherdess), ca. 1884
Chalk and watercolor on paper
19 15/16 × 15 5/16 in. (50.6 × 39 cm)
The Whitworth Art Gallery, The University of Manchester, D.1946.11

105

Young Woman Standing, Holding a Stick in Her Hands, or *Peasant Woman in a Blue Apron; Study for* Apple-Picking, ca. 1885
Pastel over charcoal sketch on cream laid paper
24⅛ × 18½ in. (61.2 × 47 cm)
Musée d'Orsay, Paris, kept in the Department of Graphic Arts, Musée du Louvre, RF 29537

106

Study of a Young Woman Standing with Left Hand on Hip Leaning against a Window, ca. 1895–1900
Pastel on blue paper
17¾ × 10³⁄₁₆ in. (45.1 × 25.9 cm)
Ashmolean Museum, University of Oxford, Pissarro Family Gift, 1952, WA1952.6.378 (BL 276)

107

Full-Length Standing Nude of a Woman, from Behind, 1890s
Pastel on pink paper
18 13/16 × 9 9/16 in. (47.5 × 24.3 cm)
The Syndics of the Fitzwilliam Museum, Cambridge, PD.51-1947

108

Two Studies of a Girl, ca. 1895
Black chalk and pastel on pink paper
18 3/4 × 24 15/16 in. (47.6 × 61.8 cm)
Amgueddfa Cymru—National Museum Wales, NMWA 1697

109–110

Three Studies of a Male Harvester (recto); *Four Studies of Male Harvesters* (verso), 1881
Gray wash over graphite; graphite heightened with gray wash on off-white paper
5⅞ × 7$\frac{7}{16}$ in. (14.9 × 18.9 cm)
Ashmolean Museum, University of Oxford, Pissarro Family Gift, 1951, WA1952.6.165 (BL 119)

111–112

Studies of a Male and Female Harvester (recto); *Study of a Female Harvester with a Study of a Female Peasant Emptying a Wheelbarrow* (verso), 1881
Gray wash over graphite; graphite heightened with gray wash on off-white paper
5⅞ × 7⅞ in. (14.9 × 20 cm)
Ashmolean Museum, University of Oxford, Pissarro Family Gift, 1951, WA1952.6.166 (BL 120)

113–114

Four Studies of a Male Peasant Flailing (recto); *Three Studies of Male Harvesters* (verso), ca. 1881
Charcoal on faded blue paper
12 × 9 in. (30.5 × 23 cm)
Ashmolean Museum, University of Oxford, Pissarro Family Gift, 1951, WA1952.6.167 (BL 121)

Making a Figure Painting In the Impressionist exhibition of 1882, Pissarro included one of his largest and most ambitious paintings in tempera, *The Harvest* (fig. 116). The work is more than four feet wide, and he had most likely worked on it for at least a year before signing and dating it in February or March of 1882, just before the April exhibition. Unlike the other figure paintings in the exhibition, which represent one or two figures in relaxed, "natural" poses, this composition contains eight figures set in a panoramic landscape. It also represents a subject familiar in French rural genre painting since Millet: the grain harvest. Pissarro's is set in the plains of Saint-Ouen-l'Aumône across the Oise from Pontoise, and particularly from its hamlet of L'Hermitage, where the painter had lived for a decade. While its subject is clearly traditional, its mode of representation is decidedly modern. First, Pissarro chose a long, horizontal format similar to that being used by Degas for a large series of friezelike compositions of horse races and ballerinas. Pissarro knew these compositions (he had seen *The Dance Lesson* [fig. 115] at the 1880 Impressionist exhibition), although none of them can be considered a "source" for his own study of rural work. Like Degas in his horse-race friezes, Pissarro created an almost generic setting with a completely flat plain and a high horizon line, all of which act as a visually consistent background for the figures. Also like Degas, Pissarro placed the figures eccentrically, with the largest at the edge of the composition and the rest arranged in a directional movement appropriate for a frieze.

Pissarro did, however, veer from the prototype. Where Degas rigorously separated the genders, Pissarro included equal numbers of both in this scene of collective work. Also unlike Degas, whose works were all oil on canvas, Pissarro experimented with tempera, a medium that was relatively new to him. His frieze is also substantially larger than even the largest of Degas's. Although, in the complex negotiations for the 1882 Impressionist exhibition in which *The Harvest* was included, Degas elected not to submit, Pissarro was clearly tipping his hat to his

115

Edgar Degas
The Dance Lesson, ca. 1879
Oil on canvas
14 15/16 × 34 5/8 in. (38 × 88 cm)
National Gallery of Art, Washington, collection of Mr. and Mrs. Paul Mellon, 1995.47.6

116 (PAGES 158–159)

The Harvest, 1882
Tempera on canvas
27 11/16 × 49 9/16 in. (70.3 × 126 cm)
The National Museum of Western Art, Tokyo, donated by the heirs of Mr. Kojiro Matsukata, P.1984-3 (PV 1358)

1882

doctrinaire friend, who refused to exhibit with artists who had themselves sent work to the official Salon. As we shall see later, Pissarro wanted to have it both ways, engaging through his submissions to the 1882 exhibition with both the Salon artist Renoir and the anti-Salon Degas. (For a more in-depth discussion of the 1882 exhibition, see section 8, this volume.)

Fortunately, an accident of history has meant that most or all of the preparatory drawings for *The Harvest* were kept together by the artist's eldest son, Lucien, and are now in the collection of the Ashmolean Museum, which received the bulk of Lucien's collection of his father's work. They are shown for the first time in the present exhibition with the complex work of art for which they were made, answering many questions about Pissarro's technique that were resolved for Degas by George Shackelford in the 1985 exhibition *Degas: The Dancers* (National Gallery of Art, Washington). Until *The Harvest* recently entered a public collection (in Tokyo), it had been known to scholars only from photographs. This marks its first inclusion in decades in a Pissarro exhibition. Its publication in color by Joachim Pissarro in 1993 made clear the painting's quality, yet it is among a large number of major works by Pissarro in tempera, gouache, and pastel that remain uncatalogued since 1939. This is, with his drawings, the

117

Study of Harvesters Working in a Field near Pontoise, ca. 1881–1882
Brush drawing in gray wash on squared off-white paper printed in brown ink
10¹³⁄₁₆ × 18⁷⁄₈ in. (27.5 × 47.8 cm)
Ashmolean Museum, University of Oxford, Pissarro Family Gift, 1951, WA1952.6.168 (BL 122)

118

Study of Two Female Harvesters, 1881–1882
Black chalk on pink paper prepared with a thin layer of Chinese white
16⁷⁄₈ × 25¹⁄₈ in. (42.8 × 63.8 cm)
Ashmolean Museum, University of Oxford, Pissarro Family Gift, 1952, WA1952.6.169 (BL 123)

7

RURAL WORKERS

The Male Worker Pissarro, like most nineteenth- and twentieth-century painters of the human figure, had a much easier time finding female models, and he therefore tended to favor the female figure in his paintings, drawings, and prints. It was difficult for a modern man to "sit," unless it was for a commissioned portrait signifying his power (after all, whatever his class, he was supposed to be working). Those men who did pose tended to be close friends of the artists, artists themselves, or rare paid models specializing in historical and classical poses, and this was not a sufficiently broad pool of subjects to interest many artists. Pissarro, in his collective portrait of small-town rural workers, tried, at least at the beginning of that project, to integrate the genders, and his rural paintings of the 1870s contain a larger percentage of male figures than later works. But as time went on he diminished their presence, perhaps for market reasons. The quality of his first great study of a male figure working, *Père Melon Sawing Wood* of 1879 (fig. 121), makes us wish he had continued his project.

The large painting was already in Gauguin's collection when it was loaned to the fifth Impressionist exhibition of 1880, the year after it was signed and dated. Its scale makes it Pissarro's most ambitious figure painting to date, and its heavily worked surface suggests that it consumed the painter's attention for at least a year. The Père Melon (Father Melon) of the title was a source of curiosity among Impressionist scholars until Joachim Pissarro, the artist's great-grandson, pointed out that he was named for his *chapeau melon* (bowler hat). This must have lent an air of rural jocularity to the picture, because any contemporary Frenchman would have understood the joke. Pissarro took no real care with the composition in this work, placing the figure and his saw in the direct center of the

120
Pissarro in the garden at Éragny, ca. 1895

exhibition's dramatic confrontation of male urban work (Degas) and urban leisure (Caillebotte). And although perceived by Pissarro as minor artists, Armand Guillaumin and Jean-François Raffaëlli both included male figure paintings and works on paper, mostly representing the urban underclass. Eugène Vidal and Federico Zandomeneghi also submitted male portraits to the exhibition. If it was a comparative failure according to the press—largely because Renoir, Monet, and Sisley deserted the group—it must have been among the most intellectually and politically engaging of any of the group exhibitions.

Although Pissarro did include a large male rural worker in the 1882 Impressionist exhibition, this work, *Shepherd and Laundresses at Montfoucault,* was not painted from life but, rather, was an enlargement of an earlier work painted in Montfoucault. It was not until 1883 that Pissarro hired another model and commenced an easel painting of male rural labor. This work, *The Gardener—Old Peasant with Cabbage* (fig. 126), was nothing short of a labor of love for Pissarro.

124
Père Melon Resting, ca. 1879
Oil on canvas
21¼ × 25⅝ in. (54 × 65 cm)
Courtesy of Giraud Pissarro Segalot
(PDR 609)

The painting was begun and largely finished in 1883, but it was not submitted to the 1883 Durand-Ruel retrospective for which it clearly had been intended. Instead Pissarro kept it, reworking it sporadically until a final bout in 1895, twelve years after its earliest "completion." It must nonetheless have disappointed both Pissarro and his dealers, because the painting was never exhibited in Pissarro's lifetime. It was inherited as part of his widow's collection, which contained all the most important paintings remaining in his studio as well as key paintings Pissarro had given his wife throughout their long life together. The model here is not the younger man used for the Père Melon canvases; his jowls and wrinkled face reveal his physical maturity. He is intently occupied in sorting and cutting the outer leaves from cabbages, a large pile of which is in the middle ground, ready for market. As with Père Melon, Pissarro represented a male figure working at a task appropriate to his age. He also again used the subject of physical work as the occasion for an extended—*very* extended—visual investigation of pictorial work. Fascinatingly, the outer leaves of the cabbages to the right of the figure are painted with comparatively crude brushstrokes, while the already sorted cabbages are defined with thousands of tiny painted marks. In this way, Pissarro's "work" is linked directly with the rural worker he paid to model. Pissarro was always efficient in the use of his models, and the same man appears as a figure in at least two important representations of markets, *The Poultry Market at Pontoise* (fig. 174) and a large gouache work with a completely different composition (fig. 178). He also made a large tempera painting with the same general composition as *The Gardener*, but with female figures rather than cabbages in the middle ground (PV 1381).

We know from Pissarro's decision to change the gender of a large figure in his 1882 *The Harvest* from male to female that male models were more difficult to engage—and possibly more expensive—than female models. We also know that Pissarro used Eugénie (Nini) Estruc, his niece, as a model for many of the young rural women, because she would pose in exchange for room and board. For these reasons, as his career continued, Pissarro's male figures diminished both in number and in size, and individualized men gave way completely to generic men in his oeuvre. The hayworkers and shepherds in his later work are sufficiently small that he never needed to hire a model to study the particularities of clothing and appearance. In addition, the figures appear in a context that so dominates them as to render such detailed study unnecessary. In only two later works (figs. 224, 226) were the male figures large enough to demand a model, and these are quite decidedly "figures in a landscape" rather than portraits of rural men working.

125
Five Studies of a Male Peasant Working, early 1880s
Black chalk on off-white paper
9 × 6 13/16 in. (22.9 × 17.3 cm)
Ashmolean Museum, University of Oxford, Pissarro Family Gift, 1952, WA1952.6.158 (BL 112)

Rural Leisure Pissarro entered a completely new phase of his career in 1880 when he began what would become a large series of figure paintings devoted to rural females—either at work or, more often, at rest during the day. These works are a major contribution to Impressionist figure painting and are, in effect, a critical part of the collective Impressionist portrait of contemporary French society started by Manet and furthered mainly by Degas, Renoir, and Caillebotte. Pissarro's notion in painting them was to move rural figural art decisively beyond the fatalist formulae adopted by painters of peasant life following the lead of Millet. In Millet's world, peasants were part of a millennial population of men and women whose lives were essentially fatalist and who toiled in ways little different from their ancestors. If these peasants rest at all, it is after backbreaking premodern work; as if in acceptance of this, their features are often generic and animal-like, even when they were sympathetically represented by Millet.

Although routinely compared to Millet's peasants in both the contemporary press and most modern art history, Pissarro's figures are, in fact, essentially a critique of that rural image. Rather than peasants, they are more accurately rural workers whose labor in the fields is balanced both by plentiful leisure time and by their participation in the small-scale capitalist economy of French agricultural markets (see section 10, this volume). We never see gleaners taking the dregs of the harvest after the master has housed the grain, nor do we see bodies broken down by work. Instead, they are strong and hardy rather than graceful and conventionally beautiful. Pissarro was perhaps the first great painter of French rural life who actually revealed a kind of relaxed beauty in fieldwork, which he associated with women as much as with men. By the time he started this series in 1880, he had essentially banished male rural workers from his pictorial realm. Although this was partly based on the difficulty of finding male models, it was surely not exclusively for that reason. Pissarro in fact preferred to represent the work of women to that of men, and the "image" of rural labor that he formed over the next two decades is largely female. Pissarro seems to have been searching for a completely new kind of rural beauty, and he found it easier to embody these aesthetic yearnings in female figures. It is also distinctly possible that the rural workers in and around Pissarro's homes in L'Hermitage near Pontoise *were* mostly women, because an increasing number of men were employed in the local industries, which Pissarro had also painted.

The year 1881 saw an outpouring of finished canvases representing female rural workers. Most of these paintings, many of which no doubt had been begun the year before and completed in 1881, study female workers seated, leaning, or lying on the ground. They are suffused with a sense of ease in the rural landscape, and Pissarro's placement of the figures in highly complex settings filled with light and warmth adds to this sense of a modern rural pastorale. There is nothing in

126

The Gardener—Old Peasant with Cabbage, 1883–1895
Oil on canvas
32 1/16 × 25 9/16 in. (81.5 × 65 cm)
National Gallery of Art, Washington, collection of Mr. and Mrs. Paul Mellon, 1994.59.6 (PDR 710)

the work of Millet or his disciples to prepare us for these pictures. Some figures sit naturally on the grassy slopes of the Pontoise landscape, while others relax against tree trunks. Some have tasks—gathering grass to feed to animals, watching over a pretty white goat, knitting, weeding, walking to market with baskets of produce—but most simply sit alone or, if shown with other figures, chat idly. Their lives seem relaxed, contented, and, in the best sense, simple. Marie-Antoinette herself could scarcely have imagined such rural ease in Le Hameau, her Rousseau-induced fantasy rustic retreat at Versailles.

Yet, as if in sympathy with the notion of pastorale articulated with a political verve by the English literary critic William Empson, Pissarro's paintings are designed to counter the "realist" notion that rural labor was difficult, demeaning, and without leisure. These images introduced rural workers into a modern, anarchist world in which work is confined to certain times during the day and leisure can be taken without compromising one's living. This sense of plenty surely came from Pissarro's reading of anarchist literature, particularly early articles by Élisée Reclus and Peter Kropotkin dealing with modern agriculture. Pissarro, like these men, was a modern, progressive citizen who believed that advances in human knowledge can change the ways we live. With fertilizers, crop rotations, and fallow periods, the land in areas such as Normandy and the region surrounding Paris could be made to produce more than enough food to feed not only the rural community but all French citizens. And, according to the writings of the anarchists, this production could be accomplished with the part-time labor of those citizens. When considered in this light, Pissarro's idle women were making a political statement about work, sharing, and leisure that, in a certain sense, was so subtle that it easily infiltrated the minds of his early viewers. Indeed, these works were—and are—so successful in their evocation of rural leisure that they have routinely been misinterpreted as apolitical.

127

Two Peasants Resting by the Side of a Path, ca. 1880
Pastel
16⁹⁄₁₆ × 20½ in. (42 × 52 cm)
Private collection (PV 1549)

We know, of course, that even the pastorale—with its shepherds and laundresses, its women at the well, its men idling by small ponds—is a politically inflected world designed as a counterideology to urban life. Yet little in Pissarro's life allows us to interpret these modern rural images as a part of what might be called the literary pastorale. Pissarro's reading and thinking were not poetically directed and were certainly not historical. He concentrated instead on the world in which he lived and on the portions of it that held the potential for a viable and politically just future. In an important sense, Pissarro used his methods of analysis—confined primarily to representation—to study modern rural work and rural life in ways startlingly similar to the economically and socially inflected statistical studies of Reclus and Kropotkin. As he befriended a series of young women and persuaded them to pose for him, his representations were emphatically not redolent of François Boucher or Jean-Honoré Fragonard's

128

Two Young Peasant Girls Chatting under Trees, Pontoise, 1881
Oil on canvas
31⅞ × 25⁹⁄₁₆ in. (81 × 65 cm)
Private collection (PDR 654)

129

Peasants Resting, 1881
Oil on canvas
32 × 25¾ in. (81 × 65 cm)
The Toledo Museum of Art, Ohio, purchased with funds from the Libbey Endowment, gift of Edward Drummond Libbey, 1935.6 (PDR 655)

eighteenth-century shepherdesses or rural laundresses. Nor were they exactly akin to Renoir's simultaneous representations of urban working-class women at leisure. Indeed, for Renoir, although the figures were paid "models," they were posed to sit in ways contrived to transport the viewer to a contemporary reality in which their existence as models was minimized. Pissarro was unable to pay more than a pittance to his rural neighbors for their services (he often complained about the expense of models), and there were not enough artists in Pontoise to create a ready clientele for modeling work, unlike the artist-towns of Barbizon or Pont-Aven, places shunned by Pissarro.

Charles Durand-Ruel bought what might be interpreted as a triptych of figural pictures by Pissarro in 1881 and 1882. The two "side panels" (figs. 128–129) are identically dimensioned vertical compositions representing rural workers at rest—one in sunlight and the other under cloudy skies. The cloudy panel, exhibited only twice in Norway in the twentieth century, represents a standing female worker who is knitting as she chats with a companion seated on the ground beside her. The sunlit composition depicts two women in conversation, seated on the ground on either side of a shady rural path, while a small boy looks on in the middle distance and a figure trudges along carrying something in the background.

131

Peasant Women Weeding, Pontoise, 1882
Oil on canvas
24 13/16 × 30 5/16 in. (63 × 77 cm)
Private collection, Switzerland (PDR 671)

132

Study of a Female Peasant Lying on the Ground Seen from the Back, 1882
Black chalk with charcoal and some pastel heightened in places with gouache
13 11/16 × 21 1/8 in. (34.8 × 53.7 cm)
Ashmolean Museum, University of Oxford, Pissarro Family Gift, 1952, WA1952.6.171 (BL 125)

All of Pissarro's female figures wear very simple clothing—blouses, dresses, skirts, aprons, stockings, and scarves or fabric caps. The range of color varies from seemingly naturally dyed blues, deep browns, purples, brown-blacks, and tans to whites and factory-dyed oranges and reds. The cloth falls in heavy folds around the figures, indicating that it may have been spun, woven, and sewn by hand, but each of the blouses and dresses fits snugly and conforms well to the contours of the body, suggesting that the clothing was made for or fitted to each woman. Some of the blouses appear striped and certain of the headcloths are printed textiles, but the main effect is of homemade apparel. In contrast to urban

133
The Goat Girl, 1881
Oil on canvas
32 × 25¾ in. (81.3 × 65.4 cm)
Private collection (PDR 656)

134
The Shepherdess, 1881
Oil on canvas
31⅞ × 25½ in. (81 × 64.7 cm)
Musée d'Orsay, Paris, RF 2013
(PDR 653)

135
The Conversation, 1881
Oil on canvas
25¾ × 21¼ in. (65.3 × 54 cm)
National Museum of Western Art,
Tokyo, P.1959-165 (PDR 658)

136

Peasant Woman Lying in the Grass, Pontoise, 1882
Oil on canvas
25⅜ × 30¾ in. (64.5 × 78 cm)
Kunsthalle Bremen—Der Kunstverein in Bremen, 960-1967/8 (PDR 683)

figures of the same period, none of the women wear ruffles, collars, decorative trim, or luxury weaves. Only in the case of the girl in *Peasant Woman Gathering Grass* is there a suggestion of fringe or anything ornamental. There is also no hint of undergarments such as the chemises or slips often seen on Renoir's models. This was clearly intentional—and meaningful. Pissarro was giving pictorial form to a sociopolitical future in which handmade clothing, as well as baskets, furniture, and so on, would again replace machine-made items. Yet his very choice of young and vital women as models made it clear that their simple clothing constituted what might be called an alternative "fashion," beautifully made and worn because of—not in spite of—its simplicity.

Surely it is necessary to address the relative absence of eroticism in these images. In this, Pissarro departs forcefully from the pastorale tradition to which he otherwise pays court. In the rococo pastorales of Boucher and Fragonard, rural women are at once sexually provocative and, for social reasons, aesthetically and actually available to the urban viewer. Indeed, one of the primary functions of pastorale imagery in the eighteenth and nineteenth centuries was erotic, and figures of the rural working class were portrayed both as beautiful and as sexually active. Pissarro's young women were selected by the aging painter (he was fifty in 1880) because they were beautiful, but he represented them as modestly dressed and, though sometimes supine, emphatically not erotically available to any presumed painter/viewer. Instead, they are purposeful, strong, self-determined, and evidently happy in their setting. There are no broken ceramic vessels suggesting lost virginity or staged scenes with erotic implications as seen in the contemporary rural paintings of Breton, Bouguereau, and others.

The simple pleasures and ease of rural life stand at the fore of Pissarro's rural images of the 1880s and 1890s. His was, in every sense, the opposite of the realist current in French rural imagery that runs its course from the fatalistic lifelong toil of Millet to the lusty bestiality of Zola, whose *La terre,* published in 1887, is the antithesis of Pissarro's paintings in its representation of rural life.

137
Woman and Child at the Well, 1882
Oil on canvas
32⅛ × 26⅛ in. (81.5 × 66.4 cm)
The Art Institute of Chicago, Potter Palmer Collection, 1922.436 (PDR 688)

The Rural Portrait Pissarro's rural figure paintings are remarkable for the relatively large number of portraits and portraitlike representations of men and women who were socially outside the world of portraiture in Third Republic France. Those with sufficient income to commission a portrait were either former aristocrats or members of the haute bourgeoisie, and it is impossible to imagine an active market in nineteenth-century France for portraitlike representations of the rural poor. Yet this is precisely what Pissarro painted, beginning with a series of portraits of women executed in Brittany in the mid-1870s and concluding with a wonderful group of color-suffused rural portraits from the 1880s and 1890s. Some of the sitters' names are known to us today. In none of the cases, however, was the portrait owned by the sitter. Pissarro portrayed these people for undoubtedly sociopolitical reasons—to enfranchise the rural individual using the tools of art.

Two of these portraits date from 1874, when Pissarro spent a little more than three months with his family in Montfoucault. They stayed, as they had earlier, with the painter's closest friend, Ludovic Piette, whose family owned a large farm on which several peasant families worked. Pissarro immediately threw himself into this project and completed one very large and two standard-size portraits of peasant women at their labor. *Mother Jolly Darning* (PDR 368) is the largest of the twenty-two paintings completed by Pissarro in Montfoucault in 1874. It represents a woman whose name is known to us only from family tradition; she joins Mère Presle, who appears in *Mother Presle Carrying Buckets in the Courtyard of the Piette House, Montfoucault* (PDR 369), and Mère Jousse, who works in a substantial peasant interior in *Mother Jousse Spinning, Montfoucault* (PDR 381). Unsurprisingly, considering their subject, only one of these rural portraits sold in the painter's lifetime, and none was exhibited early enough for us to know conclusively the source of the titles they now bear. Of the three portraits, only one, that of the woman carrying buckets, looks as if it might represent the artist's wife, Julie, posing as Mère Presle, a peasant woman like herself. Because the picture represents an outdoor scene with blooming flowers, it suggests that it was not painted in November and December, when Pissarro was in Montfoucault in 1874. The other two portraits, however, not only have traditional rural names but also represent women who bear no resemblance to each other or to Madame Pissarro, suggesting that they are contextualized portraits of particular peasant women, wearing their daily dress and doing what they would normally do. In painting them, Pissarro took the peasant image from the generic to the specific in ways very different from artists such as Breton, Lhermitte, or Bastien-Lepage. For him, the motifs of the paintings *are* the particular woman, and including their names in the titles only increases the sense that these are not generic genre scenes but representations of individual women at their work.

138
Peasant Girl Warming Herself by a Hearth, 1883
Oil on canvas
28¾ × 23⅝ in. (73 × 60 cm)
Private collection (PDR 739)

The earliest signed and dated painting in Pissarro's greatest series of rural genre paintings (fig. 140) is, in every sense of the word, a portrait. According to family tradition (it remained in the collection of the Pissarro family until 1948), it represents a woman called Mère Larchevêque (Mother Archbishop), who has recently been identified as Marie Adeline Larchevêque (née Duquesne), who lived near the Pissarros and was fifty-six years old when this sympathetic portrait was painted. Interestingly, when Pissarro exhibited the picture he chose a generic title, *Washerwoman, Study,* instead of identifying it as a portrait. But we really don't need a title to tell us that a particular woman sat for this signed and dated portrait; when we compare it to any similar work in Millet's oeuvre, this becomes obvious. In the two closest comparisons, *Woman Feeding Her Child* of 1861 (Musée des Beaux-Arts, Marseilles) and *Woman Sewing by Lamplight* of the early 1870s (Frick Collection, New York), Millet gives his figures a specific domestic task to ensure that we view these as genre scenes rather than as portraits. In both cases, the women's faces and bodies are generic, even if the figures were based on specific women (often in composite for Millet). Pissarro, by contrast, depicts the woman as she sits quietly in the half-light of an open door; we *know* that she is not a generic but a specific washerwoman, who is resting in the sun before or after her work. In a sense, she is ennobled as she becomes

139

Mère Gaspard, Pontoise, 1876
Oil on canvas
22 × 18 in. (55.9 × 45.7 cm)
Private collection (PDR 480)

140

Washerwoman, Study, 1880
Oil on canvas
28¾ × 23¼ in. (73 × 59.1 cm)
The Metropolitan Museum of Art, gift of Mr. and Mrs. Nate B. Spingold, 1956, 56.184.1 (PDR 640)

the subject of an oil portrait that defines her individuality for others. And to know not only her name but also that the Pissarros were her neighbors in the L'Hermitage quarter of Pontoise makes her specificity all the more clear. The Pissarros, in fact, used her address for their mail when they moved a year later, demonstrating not just neighborliness but also trust. As viewers of Pissarro's portrait, we participate in her individuality—and in her particular form of middle-aged rural beauty.

From the "Mother" portraits that cling with this word to traditional rural stereotypes, Pissarro moved on to a succession of portraits of rural workers with no such association. They punctuate the rest of his career, beginning with the so-called *Portrait of a Peasant Woman* of 1880–1881 (fig. 141). Although signed and

141

Portrait of a Peasant Woman, 1880–1881
Oil on canvas
28¾ × 23¾ in. (73 × 60.4 cm)
National Gallery of Art, Washington, Chester Dale Collection, 1963.10.199 (PDR 620)

142

Peasant Girl with a Straw Hat, 1881
Oil on canvas
28⅞ × 23½ in. (73.4 × 59.6 cm)
National Gallery of Art, Washington, Ailsa Mellon Bruce Collection, 1970.17.52 (PDR 661)

plausibly dated 1880, one of the artist's sons, Ludovic-Rodolphe, said that the painting was unsigned and undated at his father's death, suggesting that another son (Georges, who once owned it) forged both to make the painting more salable. Regardless of its date, it is a masterpiece by Pissarro. It appears to represent his wife, Julie, in a simple rural costume; we see her familiar features, and she was the painting's first owner. Yet perhaps for that reason, Pissarro never exhibited the painting in his lifetime, and the rather crude painted lines that define her left hand and the delightful chaos of the background suggest that he left it unfinished.

Peasant Girl with a Straw Hat (fig. 142), however, was painted from a hired model whose name we will never know. She is seated on a grassy hillside in a classic three-quarter portrait pose. The only deterrent to reading this as a portrait is the fact that the girl looks forthrightly away from the viewer and therefore expresses no awareness that she is being painted—a quality required for a formal portrait. Pissarro exhibited this work in the 1882 Impressionist exhibition and, under the aegis of Durand-Ruel, in London the following year. The Durand-Ruels loved the painting, and they retained ownership until 1963.

From 1882 on, single-figure "portraits" of rural women, though rare, punctuate the remainder of the artist's career, and they constitute a subgenre of such

143
Young Peasant Woman Drinking Her Café au Lait, 1881
Oil on canvas
25¹¹⁄₁₆ × 21⁹⁄₁₆ in. (65.3 × 54.8 cm)
The Art Institute of Chicago, Potter Palmer Collection, 1922.433 (PDR 662)

144
Young Peasant Woman Drinking Her Café au Lait, 1881
Black chalk on tan laid paper, laid down on cream wove paper
24⅛ × 18¾ in. (61.3 × 47.5 cm)
The Art Institute of Chicago, Regenstein Endowment Fund, 2010.540

rigorous quality that few other sequences of paintings in his oeuvre can match it. In 1885 Pissarro posed a model in front of another green hillside, asking her to assume a comfortable, seated position, her hands folded together. Durand-Ruel purchased this brilliant painting (fig. 145) the year it was made, and the savvy dealer selected it to be shown in his 1892 Pissarro exhibition—the first after the disastrous exhibition of 1883. Perhaps in response to seeing it again, Pissarro posed another rural worker in a simple interior made alive with his dancing touches of paint (fig. 146). This painting appealed to no less a Pissarro connoisseur than the American artist Mary Cassatt, who loaned it to the 1893 Durand-Ruel exhibition of Pissarro's recent work. In 1895 Pissarro posed a housemaid named Rosa in a simple interior, darning. So occupied, she sat patiently for the hours and days it took Pissarro to complete a superb canvas (fig. 147), which,

145
Seated Peasant Woman, 1885
Oil on canvas
28¾ × 23½ in. (73 × 59.7 cm)
Yale University Art Gallery, collection of Mr. and Mrs. Paul Mellon, B.A. 1929, 1983.7.13 (PDR 798)

146
Woman with a Green Headscarf, 1893
Oil on canvas
25¾ × 21½ in. (65.5 × 54.5 cm)
Musée d'Orsay, Paris, RF 1972 30 (PDR 972)

C. Pissarro

unlike the previous two, remained in the family's private collection, unexhibited, until shortly after World War II.

This rural portraiture project, begun in earnest in 1874, occupied Pissarro for more than twenty years and produced paintings of such quality and aesthetic monumentality that they are among his greatest works. When we see them today in museums and private collections, they retain their quality but have lost the sense of radical experimentation—of political engagement—that made them so extraordinary when they were made. We are now accustomed to seeing portraits of dispossessed people of the underclass, and we no longer experience the aesthetic edge that these pictures once had. What is particularly interesting and important about these works is that they make ordinary people as compelling as any countess or capitalist. We long to know their names and never will.

At the very end of Pissarro's life, he went to visit his son Georges, then living in the picturesque town of Moret-sur-Loing (about fifty miles southeast of Paris), where Pissarro's friend Sisley had spent the last decade of his life. Because the weather in May was cold and rainy, and because of his own increasing age and infirmity, Pissarro had to work indoors, and he painted three portraits of elderly peasants at home. Too old to work, they nonetheless occupied themselves every day. The male peasant—an old wine grower, as we learn from the title—spends his time drinking, while his wife simply sits and another woman sews. The paintings of the man and his wife (PDR 1427–1428) are not, oddly, a pair, despite their similar compositions and nearly monochromatic palettes. The third, *Old Peasant Woman Sewing* (PDR 1429), is richly painted and full of color. Again, Pissarro found it easier and more psychologically comfortable to paint women than men. These works, tributes to the working life, are Pissarro's final figure paintings. Although none of them was sold, all three were included in the Berlin Secession exhibition held in April of 1903, just months before the painter's death.

147
Woman Sewing, 1895
Oil on canvas
25⅝ × 21⅜ in. (65.4 × 54.4 cm)
The Art Institute of Chicago, gift of Mrs. Leigh B. Block, 1959.636
(PDR 1098)

UNE VISITE AUX IMPRESSIONNISTES
PAR DRANER
vol d'oiseau
Femme à l'Eventail
Femme Epouvantail plutôt !
Notre Dame de la Fluxion
Chemin montant... par les têtes
Etude de figure en plein air — Temps gris
Par une aimable attention, l'auteur a supprimé les figures
Le Café au Laid
Soeurs" dit le Catalogue
Ta Soeur ! dit le Public
Cette peinture faisant suer dans le salon on a mis le poele à roulettes au Balcon
Jeune fille endormie pas de danger qu'on en abuse
Le Berger et les Laveuses — C'est le tableau qui sera difficile à laver
Rêverie non, cauchemar
Un jardin qui a ses plumeaux peints par un peintre qui a son plumet.
Jeune fille au chat — Fi, Mademoiselle, cachez ça tout de suite.
Une marine
Jusqu'au Rocher qui fait la grimace, et il s'y connait.
Jeux de mains, Jeu de bien Vilains
Pourquoi pas deux pigeons, cela aurait mieux représenté les visiteurs refaits de 1 livre vingt sous.

8

PISSARRO EXHIBITS THE FIGURE PAINTINGS

The Impressionist exhibition of 1882 was, for the purposes of this investigation, of crucial importance, because it was Pissarro's "debut" as a figure painter. Although he had included figure paintings in the 1880 exhibition, never before had he shown such a large number of these works in a context that, with one important exception, was ideal for them. Pissarro's fourteen figure paintings were shown in an exhibition that also included six figure paintings by Caillebotte, five by Gauguin, four by Morisot, and ten by Renoir. These appeared with a bumper crop of landscapes by Monet (who submitted thirty-two) and Sisley (twenty-seven), while Pissarro submitted only eight. Whereas the work of minor artists had lowered the quality of most of the earlier Impressionist exhibitions, only Victor Vignon was present in this one. The lacuna that must have mattered most to Pissarro was the absence of Degas, the artist he perhaps admired most among his contemporaries. No amount of negotiation could convince Degas to exhibit with Renoir and Monet, each of whom submitted to the Salon that year and were, to Degas, forever traitors to the avant-garde. As was often the case in his personal and professional life, Pissarro was the only one who spoke equally to those on both sides of the controversy, and, had he succeeded with Degas, he would have been overjoyed to debut his figural works with those by all the artists with whom he competed most actively.

The exhibition of more than two hundred Impressionist paintings was held in the Salon du panorama Reichshoffen (fig. 149) in the eighth arrondissement, an unusual place, unassociated with Impressionism and far from the rented gallery and even apartment spaces of the second arrondissement where they had previously shown. The building had been designed by Charles Garnier, the

148
Draner, "A Visit with the Impressionists," from *Le Charivari*, March 9, 1882

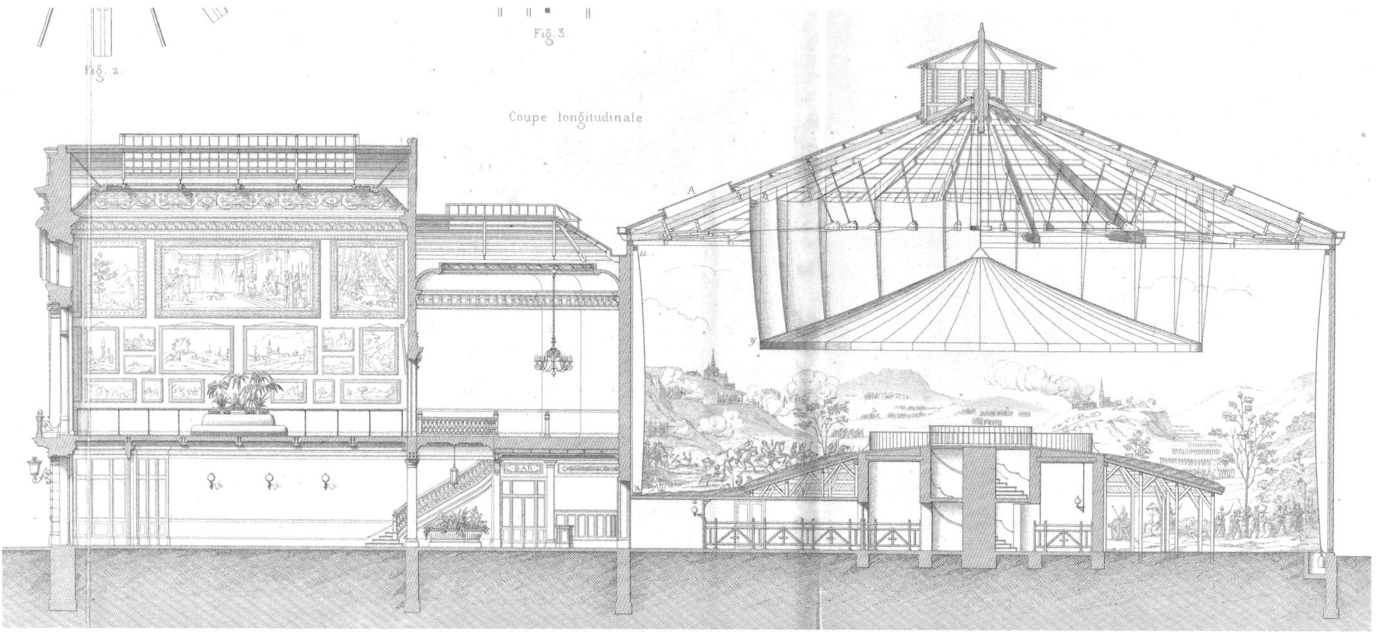

preeminent architect of the spectacle in nineteenth-century France. The exhibition room (a floor above the entrance to the adjacent panorama devoted to a battle of the Franco-Prussian War in Alsace) was enormous. Above its large walls were hung Gobelins tapestries, and a huge skylight was overhead. The room was also lit by electricity, making it utterly modern and allowing it to remain open until eleven o'clock at night (as was the panorama). The penultimate Impressionist exhibition was therefore associated with the culture of urban spectacle, which was a dramatic difference from the earlier installations, held in intimate, domestically scaled rooms with conventional windows. If there was ever an "Impressionist Salon," it was the exhibition of 1882.

Pissarro submitted more works to the exhibition than any other artist except Monet and, from the evidence of his correspondence, played a large role in negotiating the terms of the show. He was aware of what the other artists had to submit before he selected his own submissions, making the 1882 exhibition what we might call utterly collective rather than an exhibition of discrete individuals. No single artist's work was isolated in its own space, allowing critics, dealers, and collectors to measure the larger aesthetic endeavor without leaving the single large room. Although many critics wrote about the landscapes of Monet, Sisley, Pissarro, and Renoir, it was the figure paintings that dominated the discourse of the exhibition. Indeed, a full-page cartoon in *Le Charivari* (fig. 148) included caricature images of at least twenty-two paintings in the exhibition and was dominated by figure paintings by Renoir (four), Pissarro (four), and Caillebotte (three). *The* painting of the exhibition was Renoir's *Luncheon*

149
Sectional drawing of the Salon du panorama Reichshoffen, site of the Impressionist exhibition of 1882, from *Revue de l'Architecture et des Travaux Publics*, vol. 39, 1882

of the Boating Party (fig. 150), but Pissarro fared the best of all the artists in the press. As usual, he seems to have been disappointed in the reception, saying in a letter to his friend Théodore Duret that no one came to the opening (Manet, on the contrary, thought the opening successful) and that the critic Philippe Burty had misunderstood his paintings by comparing them to Millet's. The postscript to his letter contains one of the most famous passages in the Pissarro literature, in which he calls Millet "biblical," in contrast to his own "Hebrew" background, and marvels that they would even be linked. What Burty wrote about Pissarro is in fact largely favorable.

None of the critics recognized the collective aspects of the exhibition, particularly its figure paintings. There is no doubt that in the nineteenth century, as in the early twenty-first century, group exhibitions of contemporary art tended to be reviewed in terms of an individual artist's contributions compared with those of other artists rather than in collective terms. Yet when one thinks about the figure paintings of Caillebotte, Renoir, Pissarro, and to a lesser extent Gauguin, the collectivity of their aims becomes clear. Had Degas joined the exhibition, it would have been the most important avant-garde "collective portrait" of contemporary French society in history. Caillebotte dealt almost exclusively with the urban bourgeoisie, concentrating on male figures (see figs. 151–152), while Renoir preferred to represent women of either the bourgeoisie or the working class, allowing wealthy operagoers and day-trippers to the country to

150
Pierre-Auguste Renoir
Luncheon of the Boating Party, 1880–1881
Oil on canvas
51¼ × 69⅛ in. (130.2 × 175.6 cm)
The Phillips Collection, acquired 1923

join working girls at toil and at rest (figs. 150, 153). Like Renoir, Pissarro focused on female figures, although he dealt with rural workers. Gauguin, ever the contrarian, dealt with the psychological tensions of bourgeois family life. If Degas's dancers, hatmakers, prostitutes, and laundresses, or the horse races on which he was working at the time, had been on view, the bright lights of the "New Painting" would have been cast into virtually every corner of French society except those of government and religion. The life that they represented was profoundly secular, balancing work and leisure, if concentrating on the latter. It was, thus, a collective representation of unregulated lives.

It is fascinating to make direct comparisons across the gender and class divisions revealed by the exhibition. With Renoir, "politics" can be found in his fundamentally equalizing aesthetic, in which "beauty" was located across the economic spectrum of the city (and, of course, urbanites in the country). Incapable of representing tension or misery, Renoir was the visual poet of bonhomie, of the easy moments in the lives of the young and the healthy. Even his underage female

151
Gustave Caillebotte
The Bezique Game, 1880
Oil on canvas
49⅝ × 63⅜ in. (121 × 161 cm)
Private collection, Paris

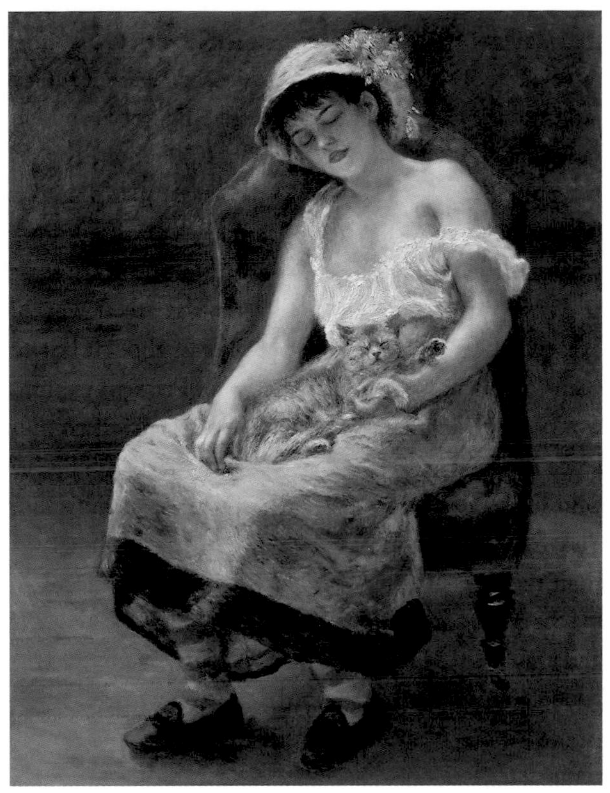

152
Gustave Caillebotte
A Balcony above Boulevard Haussmann, 1880
Oil on canvas
26¾ × 24 in. (68 × 61 cm)
Private collection, France

153
Pierre-Auguste Renoir
Sleeping Girl, 1880
Oil on canvas
47⅜ × 36³⁄₁₆ in. (120.3 × 91.9 cm)
Sterling and Francine Clark Art Institute, Williamstown, Massachusetts, 1955.598

circus performers look well fed, happy, and fulfilled. The "political" Pissarro was no less optimistic, although he confined himself exclusively to the lives of the rural working class where he, like Renoir, found abundant beauty and fulfillment. This might, in fact, explain his annoyance at being compared by Burty (and many others) to Millet. Yet the comparison was inevitable, even to critics such as Huysmans who thought, correctly, that Pissarro had finally transcended Millet's influence. If Pissarro "modernized" the rural worker, he did so with such respect and such an emphasis on ease that one can never think of these people as oppressed. The inhabitants of Pissarro's visual world, like those of Renoir, were youthful, and the one middle-aged peasant woman and the chubby, even homely, male shepherd must have looked discordant in this bevy of beautiful and well-nourished women. Interestingly, dreaming and sleeping occupied the attention of three artists in the exhibition—Gauguin, Renoir, and Pissarro—but only in the case of Gauguin is there a dark tinge to the subject, the slightest suggestion that dreams might become nightmares.

I have written elsewhere about the contrast of the three largest pictures in the exhibition, by Renoir, Caillebotte, and Gauguin. Surely these paintings dominated the upper middle-center of each large wall, while Pissarro's figure paintings were scattered about according to size, in a Salon-style arrangement. (It appears that Caillebotte and Pissarro—possibly with Gauguin—arranged the works themselves. Renoir was sick in Marseilles, and Monet refused to attend.) Two of these large paintings group several life-size figures around a table, representing camaraderie and togetherness in the city (Caillebotte) and the country (Renoir). Only Gauguin dealt with tension in his largest painting to date. The portraits of men (Caillebotte) and women (Renoir and Pissarro) are all respectful and honest, whatever the gender or social position of the sitter, and the genre scenes stress the ease of life, even when the subjects are at work. Several critics missed the presence of the visually acerbic Degas, though less for his difficult personality than for his tour-de-force technique. Pissarro exhibited both oil paintings and works in gouache and tempera under glass, which must have been a visual challenge for daytime viewers in a skylighted room. This befuddled at least one critic, who found it confusing to have works in oils installed as if they were pastels. Pissarro had long ago eschewed varnish, and he glazed his paintings to protect their rough, matte surfaces. So too were there small grumblings about the framing, because some artists, particularly Pissarro and Morisot, elected to use white and gray painted frames with gilded accents rather than the standard carved and gilded frames. And the fact that all the works were installed in the same room (some on easels, after the walls were filled up) exacerbated these differences in their presentation.

Despite the aesthetic and critical success of the exhibition, the proceeds from ticket sales and sales of works of art were not sufficient to pay its costs, even with a complete subvention by Henri Rouart of the expensive rent; an exhibition that might have taken the Impressionist cause to another level in public recognition failed, as had earlier such joint ventures with varying combinations of artists in various locations. To address this failure, their dominating dealer, Durand-Ruel (who played a large role in the selection of works by Monet and Renoir in the 1882 exhibition), decided that it was time to mount individual monographic exhibitions devoted to the stable of artists at his gallery. This was intended to give the art-buying public the opportunity to become aware of two important facts: first, that each of these vanguard artists had had a long and important career; and second, that each artist's work could stand on its own. Durand-Ruel elected to mount exhibitions of Eugène Boudin, Monet, Renoir, Pissarro, and Sisley at the gallery, hoping to transfer the gallery's success with earlier artists such as Corot, Millet, Rousseau, Delacroix, Charles Daubigny, and even Honoré Daumier by showing the younger artists in the same prestigious locations and with the same seriousness.

Pissarro's exhibition was held in May of 1883. The painter himself selected the works, assumed responsibility for their presentation, and installed them in ample rented spaces at the prestigious address used for all five exhibitions—

9, boulevard de la Madeleine. The work of Boudin provided the "transition" between the two generations in Durand-Ruel's stable, and Pissarro followed Renoir, in recognition of the increasing importance of the figure in his work. If Pissarro had succeeded in the critical press in 1882, he failed miserably in 1883. In fact, his career was actually set back by his first important monographic exhibition in a quarter century. Durand-Ruel must have encouraged him to choose a wide range of works, and Pissarro seems to have taken his advice up to a point. Perhaps unfortunately, he omitted entirely his greatest paintings of the 1860s but selected among a wide variety of paintings and pastels from the 1870s. Because he had shown so many works of the rural laborer genre in the 1882 exhibition and had sent others to a major exhibition organized by Durand-Ruel in London earlier in the year, he had to think carefully about the representation of his recent work. Alas, although a list of the exhibition survives, it contains only numbers and titles (and occasionally an owner, if it is not Durand-Ruel or Pissarro) and no information about media or size. We know from letters and reviews that it was much more a "multimedia" exhibition than the 1882 Impressionist show had been, undoubtedly because the comparatively smaller spaces encouraged this variety. Pissarro also was clear in his sense that—unlike Boudin, Monet, and Renoir, all of whom were primarily painters—he (like Degas) had worked in pastel, gouache, tempera, chalk, charcoal, lithography, and etching for more than a decade, and this multimedia achievement was central to his career as an artist. Yet he seems not to have included any prints or simple drawings, because these were not the kind of works sold by Durand-Ruel.

Pissarro included a greater number of works representing rural markets in the 1883 retrospective, and he took it as the opportunity to display for the first time his most important market painting, *The Poultry Market at Pontoise* (fig. 174). He had probably not yet finished his only other full-scale oil painting of a market, *The Pork Butcher* (fig. 175), so *The Poultry Market,* his most elaborate figural composition yet, made a major debut along with five gouaches and watercolors representing various markets. What was to be of central significance to Pissarro's anarchist vision and to his future pictorial achievement went unrecognized in 1883: not a single critic noticed either the painting or the group of market works, proving that they were installed in the same scattered way in which they appear in the exhibition list. It is clear when one "reads" the 1883 exhibition that Pissarro was giving greater importance to small-scale paintings and works on paper than he had in 1882, and also that landscapes dominated, rather than the figures of the past year.

The last appearance of Pissarro's figural work in a major exhibition of the 1880s was in the final Impressionist exhibition, held on rue Lafitte from May 15 through June 15, 1886. Here, Pissarro continued to stress his work in gouache, pastel, and, for the first time since the Impressionist exhibition of 1880, printmaking. He also took the cue of his young protégé, Seurat, and selected a single very large canvas, *Apple-Picking* (fig. 155), to dominate the exhibition. Pissarro had begun this painting in 1881, worked it almost to completion before the May 1883 retrospective at Durand-Ruel, and then extensively repainted it in 1885–1886, when he began to work with Seurat and Signac. Thus, it is a work in literal opposition to the large-scale Impressionist paintings made by Monet and Renoir between 1867 and the early 1880s. Where the two younger artists tended to work on large compositions outdoors, in the same conditions, until they were almost completed, thus preserving an Impressionist spontaneity and immediacy, Pissarro refined, altered, repainted, and again repainted this work, largely in the studio. It has, thus, the same highly worked qualities as the two paintings with which it was shown in 1886: Seurat's *A Sunday on La Grande Jatte—1884* (fig. 154) and Signac's *The Milliners* (fig. 156). Although we know all the paintings shown by Seurat, Signac, and the Pissarros (Lucien, his oldest son, joined his father in this exhibition), the precise way in which the works were installed is impossible to re-create. Yet the three large works were surely thought of as an ensemble that defined the ambitions of what was to become known as Neo-Impressionism. What is of importance for this discussion is that all three were figure paintings, works of such scale that they almost required comparison to the other comparably scaled works in the great art of museums to be understood. Although Pissarro himself had shown figure paintings in quantity since 1882, he had never managed one of this size. Indeed, his instinctive decision *not* to include it in the

154
Georges Seurat
A Sunday on La Grande Jatte—1884, 1884–1886
Oil on canvas
81¾ x 121¼ in. (207.5 x 308.1 cm)
The Art Institute of Chicago, Helen Birch Bartlett Memorial Collection, 1926.224

155
Apple-Picking, 1886
Oil on canvas
49½ x 50⅛ in. (125.8 x 127.4 cm)
Ohara Museum of Art, 1008 (PDR 824)

1883 exhibitions is evidence of his doubts and suggests that no one goaded him to do so. Now that he had seen Seurat's masterpiece and been intimately involved in both the choice of subjects and the composition of Signac's work, he had little choice but to complete and submit his most ambitious figure painting to date.

The scholarship devoted to Seurat, Signac, and Pissarro deals with the individual achievements of their great paintings of 1886, but rarely is their collective significance discussed. In many ways, the juxtaposition of Pissarro's rural workers with Signac's urban workers and Seurat's bourgeois and well-off workers at leisure was ideal for the older artist. For this first time in his career, he shared social and political views with the other exhibitors in the room, and

156
Paul Signac
The Milliners, 1885/1886
Oil on canvas
43⅞ × 35 in. (111.6 × 89 cm)
Foundation E. G. Bührle Collection, Zurich

several critics recognized their political radicalism. If Seurat's painting was about a secular Sunday ritual—strolling and resting in the park (as opposed to going to church), Signac and Pissarro's were "workday" paintings dealing with what we might call "real" work—picking fruit and making clothing, both essential to the maintenance of civilization. Indeed, Signac's milliners are making hats of the precise type worn by four of the larger female figures in Seurat's painting. Looking carefully, one might even claim that the red-orange hat in the center of Signac's painting is the same hat on the young woman holding her parasol in the middle of Seurat's. The connections between Seurat's and Pissarro's paintings have more to do with shadows and light-struck areas and with their respective observations of natural light falling over human bodies. Pissarro's standing rural worker is nonetheless almost the same size as the counterpart figures in Seurat's frieze, and each of the works was painted with a full knowledge of the other.

These three exhibitions effectively launched Pissarro as a figure painter—as an artist who wanted to transcend the limitations of landscape and create a truly modern art in which all of the bourgeois genres (landscape, portraiture, still life, and genre scenes) were explored in every available medium, combining the ambitions of Monet, Renoir, and Degas. Pissarro continued in all of these arenas after the 1886 Impressionist exhibition—and added urban views to his arsenal. Yet he was never again to reach the level of recognition as a figural artist that he attained in the early and mid-1880s. While he never stopped painting, drawing, and etching figures, particularly rural laborers, these works no longer dominated his oeuvre to the extent they had before 1886. When combined with Pissarro's increasingly public profile as an anarchist, this issue is forced more fully into the foreground when we interpret his oeuvre. Pissarro came to accept the inevitability of a large-scale European revolution, and there is little doubt that he prepared himself for it. His figural representations stray more from direct observation of rural life and tend, instead, to be artificial creations of ideal—postrevolutionary—pictorial worlds.

9

RURAL SUBJECTS

Apple-Picking It is difficult to imagine a more symbolically laden rural subject than apple-picking. Somehow, the grain harvest, animal herding, and vegetable gardening pale into insignificance when one thinks of the religious and pastorale ramifications of picking apples. Millet avoided the subject, even though Pissarro himself had called the earlier artist "biblical," but blooming and fruit-filled apple trees play an important role in the rural landscape painting of Daubigny. For Pissarro, it was, as we have seen, the subject for his first truly monumental rural genre painting, *Apple-Picking* (fig. 155), which appeared in the 1886 Impressionist exhibition. In 1881 Pissarro had completed a smaller, vertical canvas of the same subject with similar figures and the same juxtaposition of the tree trunk and the shadows of an unseen building off to the left (fig. 158). But this marvelous picture, made famous by its inclusion as a color plate in John Rewald's 1954 monograph on Pissarro, must not have pleased the painter or his dealer, Durand-Ruel, sufficiently for it to be included with the many other figure paintings from the same year in the 1882 Impressionist exhibition or the 1883 retrospective. Perhaps his wife, Julie, who was often allowed to choose whatever she wanted from her husband's recent efforts for her own collection, refused to share it with the public. Sadly, we will never know.

The subject of apple-picking was of paramount importance to Pissarro in 1881, when he not only completed one canvas but also began work on the large picture not exhibited until 1886. We know from a letter Pissarro wrote to Lucien, his oldest son, on July 22, 1883, that he had mulled over the picture for a long time and that he hoped to complete it by April of 1884, nearly a year later. He may have arrived at a suitable finish by that point but had no exhibition to which

157
Pissarro heading outside to paint, pushing a special easel built to roll through the fields of Éragny, ca. 1895

to submit it. When he met the young Seurat in October of 1885, he found yet another opportunity to rework the painting's surface (just as Seurat was reworking that of *A Sunday on La Grande Jatte—1884* [fig. 154]). Pissarro's earliest monumental rural figure painting therefore occupied him intermittently for five full years. Because Pissarro dated it only to 1886 on the canvas, it is clear that he had never finished it earlier. When he reworked an already completed painting, he either signed and dated it twice to record both campaigns or indicated a date range directly on the canvas. That he didn't is evidence that the artist wanted the public and, more importantly, the critics to interpret *Apple-Picking* as new rather than reworked.

It is worth noting that, in the letter to Lucien cited above, Pissarro referred to the painting not as *Apple-Picking* but as *Apple Eaters.* Although this was perhaps just a slip, it is a significant one, because it is not so much the picking of apples that has biblical significance for Jews, Christians, and Muslims, it is the eating of the apple. Interestingly, Pissarro's 1881 painting of apple pickers has three figures, none of whom eat an apple. In rethinking the figural aspect of the composition and adapting it to the large, square format, Pissarro introduced the figure in the left foreground who has selected an apple from her basket and is taking her first bite. She is shown behind the trunk of a very small tree onto which three branches have been grafted. This young experiment in plant husbandry has yet to bear fruit, and Pissarro contrasted it pictorially with the older tree, whose branches fringe the upper edge of the composition and are laden with apples. The two other women perform tasks—the standing rural worker pokes at the apples with a stick, dislodging the ripe ones, and her kneeling companion bends over, picks them off the ground, and puts them in a basket. As with *The Harvest* (fig. 116), Pissarro effectively divided the activities of apple-picking into specialties performed by different kinds of rural workers, again linking rural work to the new division of industrial and production-assembly labor in Europe.

The one crucial observation to make is this: whereas biblical references to fruit-picking require only two figures, a male (tempted) and a female (temptress), both of the compositions begun by Pissarro in 1881 include only female figures, visually undercutting any attempt to read religious significance into the subject. Pissarro's secularism was so complete that he must have worked diligently to drain the subject of biblical associations and lend it a "modern" quality. Interestingly, he did include a male figure in one of his rare paintings on earthenware from the mid-1880s, replacing the three women performing tasks in the two paintings with three women and a man. Instead of using a stick to dislodge the apples from the tree, the figure steadies a ladder, high up on which a woman, whose shoes and lower skirt penetrate the pictorial format from the top, picks the apples and drops them to the ground. They are then gathered into a basket

158
Apple-Picking, 1881
Oil on canvas
25 9/16 × 21¼ in. (65 × 54 cm)
Collection of Mr. and Mrs. Klaas H. Hummel (PDR 659)

159

The Pea Stakers, 1890
Gouache with traces of black chalk on gray-brown paper
15⅜ × 23¾ in. (39 × 60.2 cm)
Ashmolean Museum, University of Oxford, Pissarro Family Gift, 1952, WA1952.6.310 (BL 219)

by another woman, while a male figure returns with two empty baskets, having just unloaded them into a larger container for market. Indeed, the male figure in the ceramic work actually completes the cycle of picking, gathering, loading, and packing that would end, ultimately, in one of Pissarro's market scenes, concluding two intertwining agricultural and market cycles.

Pissarro's final painting of an apple harvest (fig. 224) consumed a good deal of his time at the end of the 1880s and was finally signed and dated in 1888. With its four figures arranged in a decorative frieze beneath the spreading branches of an apple tree, this work relates less to Pissarro's figural concerns of the years 1880–1886 than to his developing series of anarchist rural decorations (and, thus, will be discussed in section 12 of this volume). Here, it is only worth noting that none of its four figures is precisely derived from any figure in the earlier group. Pissarro instead had completely rethought the subject, creating the first canvas in a series of agricultural paintings that would occupy him intermittently for the rest of his life.

The Peasant Dance

If Degas was the great visual poet of classical dance and if Renoir created almost totemic images of urban and rural dance, Pissarro was, in most ways, their opposite. His rural figures tend either to rest or to work, and their movement is pictorially confined to walking, sewing, washing, sweeping, leaning, pulling, digging, and pushing—activities in which there is almost always resistance. Yet in representing even these plebian actions, Pissarro took many cues from Degas's dancers, creating a visual repertoire of carefully studied rural movements that was intended to contrast with that master's urban world. Interestingly, there are a handful of works that counter this discourse. After liberating himself from what he considered the stylistic tyranny of Neo-Impressionist technique around 1890, Pissarro followed the lead set by Seurat in turning—however briefly—to dance and rhythmic motion. Although he had made a large pastel of a rural woman dressed up for the evening and riding a wooden carousel horse in Osny around 1883 (Albright-Knox Art Gallery, Buffalo, New York), this was to prove anomalous until 1890, when he began two closely related pairs of compositions of rural rhythm during and after work.

The earliest and most ambitious of this subseries is a fan-shaped composition representing a group of young, shapely female workers setting up long stakes on which to train pea plants in a rural garden (fig. 159). The four women (most likely a single female model viewed from four perspectives and placed rhythmically along the surface) hold the wooden stakes, which are taller than they are, and push them firmly into the earth. The curving rhythms of their bodies and the gentle curves of the stakes are, in effect, a rural dance. Pissarro almost immediately began an oil version of the composition on a small, vertical canvas,

switching the positions of two of the figures (fig. 160). When it was completed in 1891, Pissarro gave the painting as a gift to his wife. She in turn presented it to their friend Monet, as a token of appreciation for the substantial loan he had made to the Pissarros, enabling them to buy the small farm they rented in Éragny. Surely the fact that the painting was used twice as a gift proves that, for Pissarro and his wife, these female figures had a celebratory content. As he worked on these figures, Pissarro also began a watercolor (fig. 161) and a tempera painting representing an actual harvest celebration, where rural workers held hands and swayed in circular dance as their husbands and fellow workers watched. A letter indicates that he intended to create an oil painting of this subject but shied away from its difficulties. In Pissarro's elegiac rural dances, the bodies of young rural workers are ideally proportioned—plump enough to suggest prosperity and strong enough to convey a healthy vitality. In his rural world, both work and leisure are a sort of dance.

160

Peasant Women Planting Poles into the Ground, 1891
Oil on canvas
21⅝ × 18⅛ in. (55 × 46 cm)
Private collection, on loan to the Sheffield Galleries and Museums Trust, UK (PDR 922)

161

The Round, 1892
Watercolor over black chalk on pink paper
18 × 23½ in. (46 × 60 cm)
Private collection (PV 1392)

These works are most compelling not simply for their relationship to Symbolist and other antirealist aesthetics but also because they make us look at Pissarro's other paintings as representations of rhythmic motion rather than as representations of work. The coalescence of labor and dance and the sense of harmonious individual and collective movement fill Pissarro's production of the 1880s and 1890s.

Japanese collections ever since. It was not published in color until 1993 (where the label was switched with the other large oil version of the composition), and its first compelling analysis was in *Pissarro, Neo-Impressionism, and the Spaces of the Avant-Garde,* Martha Ward's 1996 book that was read mostly by academic art historians. It is fascinating to think that both of Pissarro's conscious masterpieces of rural figure painting are in Japan, a country he admired but never visited. Most of the artist's other great works seen in this volume are part of important European or American public collections.

In conceiving of this composition, Pissarro replaced the middle-aged male rural worker of the 1870 drawing with an attractive young female and switched the fuel from dung to wood—both decisions made for obvious market reasons. This section of the book has been dominated by paintings that deal with the interaction of rural workers and wood, and this series of compositions adds to

163
Hoarfrost, Peasant Girl Making a Fire, 1888
Oil on canvas
36½ × 36⅜ in. (92.8 × 92.5 cm)
Musée d'Orsay, Paris, RF 2000 83
(PDR 857)

that larger rhythmic theme. In a certain sense, these long poles or sticks are Pissarro's vertical, rural equivalents to the horizontal barres in Degas's representations of dance. They are, however, supple: they bend and move, quite unlike the stationary barre. The subject here is a young rural woman and a small boy of about eight, out on a brisk winter morning watching their dairy cows munch contently on grasses. The woman and the cows are in strict profile while the little boy is frontal, reminiscent of Seurat's chessboard figures in *A Sunday on La Grande Jatte.* Where Seurat's earlier painting was about the interaction of various figures in sun and shade on a bright summer day, Pissarro's painting evokes a cold morning landscape made to vibrate in light from the interaction of the fire and heat.

The convincing representation of fire, smoke, and cold air is anything but easy for a painter, even an Impressionist who had long practiced similar effects by representing frost, fog, and snow, and no other work by any of the artists with whom Pissarro worked can equal it in this way. Pissarro's friend, the critic Gustave Geffroy, gushed about the canvas "shot with luminous beams, while the pale meadow, the bare trees, the frosty distances, the fire flaring up and smoking, the wind ruffling the girl's rough wool skirt, the little boy's garment, all the details of the work making up one of the most extraordinary effects of cold ever produced in painting." Other critics added equally poetic descriptions. It was, indeed, the tour-de-force subject about which Pissarro had written in 1870 and finally realized after twenty years of hard work as a painter.

164

Study of a Young Female Peasant Kindling a Fire, 1888
Black chalk on squared paper printed in blue ink
6 × 3¼ in. (15.2 × 8.2 cm)
Ashmolean Museum, University of Oxford, Pissarro Family Gift, 1952, WA1952.6.215 (BL 160B)

While he worked on the larger painting, he completed two smaller square oil versions, one of which was an unsigned Neo-Impressionist sketch of 1886–1887 for a larger, finished work signed and dated 1888. The latter (fig. 163) was much admired by artist Félix Bracquemond and was shown in Brussels at the avant-garde Salon des XX in 1889, after having been acquired by Durand-Ruel. The dealer failed to sell the picture until 1930, and it, like its larger and later counterpart, remained little known in the Pissarro literature until its acquisition by the Musée d'Orsay in 2000. It is likely that Pissarro made a large gouache of the female figure before he sold the Orsay canvas, referring to it and his own new observations of the landscape near his studio when completing it in 1889–1890, after the Orsay picture left his studio. All of these elaborate works seem to have been based on a small but beautifully observed and rhythmic black chalk drawing preserved today in the Ashmolean Museum (fig. 164), which surely records the original "sensation" later formalized in the planar compositions of 1887–1890. This small study was cut from a sketchbook, the only datable sheet from which was made in 1884, when Pissarro was traveling, searching for new places to live after the Osny house in which the family had been for a year proved unsatisfactory.

10

THE MARKET ECONOMY

What did an avowed anarchist such as Pissarro make of capitalist markets? A long, theoretical essay could be written on this subject, dealing with the anarchist critique of the concept of capital and of capital markets such as the stock market or bank lending. This would probably lead us to suspect that a doctrinaire anarchist would despise the very concept of currency and market exchange, preferring to return to the blissful state of barter to negotiate the exchange of goods. Yet this was far from the truth, as the increasingly subtle and realistic branch of anarchism gained ascendancy over the doctrinaire theorists of the movement's early decades. As less was written about the revolution itself and more about how to reconstruct during and after the revolution, anarchist thinkers focused more on keeping what was desirable about human interaction—including economics—and even about the sacred cow of private property. Increasingly after the death in 1865 of French anarchist philosopher Pierre-Joseph Proudhon, anarchist thinkers began to soften their absolute ban on private property, realizing that the home and garden of the worker or working family, if earned, could be considered valid as property, if all nondomestic property was kept in common. This extended as well to monetary exchange and their markets, which, as long as they were of an intimate or collective nature, could permit negotiating for goods and services using currency.

Labor was the basic concept central to all of this theory—that is, the value of a commodity was related to the labor required to produce (or harvest) it. When thinking in this way, the "ideal" market is agricultural: producers sell their commodities at a fair price (with haggling) directly to the consumers who need those commodities. In capitalism of this scale, no hoarding of capital is

165
The Marketplace, 1882 (detail of fig. 178)

required and the exchange is direct, taking place without middlemen. These kinds of simple, unregulated markets were, in fact, central to the anarchist idea of postrevolutionary economic behavior and, by representing them, Pissarro began increasingly to engage in a form of pictorial anarchism. From small beginnings in the 1870s, Pissarro brought the image of the small-town and rural market into the center of his production by 1883, where it remained until shortly before his death. Indeed, if the peasant image of realist and naturalist artists stressed the production of agricultural products, Pissarro was the first to balance this with numerous representations of the marketing and consumption of those products. For every peasant of Millet, who eats what he or she grows, raises, and gathers, Pissarro created a rural worker who both consumed *and* sold what she or he grew, raised, and gathered. The very notion of this is that, with intelligence, each human being or each family could easily produce a superfluity of food that could then be sold to others who produced a superfluity of garments, crockery, furniture, and other goods. This concept of plenty or superfluity is central to the anarchism of Peter Kropotkin, Élisée Reclus, and Jean Grave, the three writers who were most important for Pissarro.

This basic reading of the place of market scenes in Pissarro's oeuvre can lead us to Pissarro's own personal notion of markets, particularly those in which he himself worked—the art markets. For most theorists of art, this type of product was classified as a luxury accessible only to those who had attained the highest levels of wealth and social status. It was conceived of not as work but rather as production to decorate lifelong leisure. Needless to say, Pissarro and many left-wing artists of the nineteenth century had a very different idea of art. For Pissarro, the very life of the artist was a liberation from bourgeois life—or life in league with money or capital. Like many artists of his time, including Renoir, Van Gogh, and Gauguin, Pissarro believed that the artist should live simply, without luxury, and devote herself or himself to the production of what one might call basic beauty—beauty to decorate ordinary life. Yet in the art markets of the late nineteenth century, art was so aligned with luxury that it was necessary even for the anarchist artist to survive by producing work for the haute bourgeoisie. Pissarro attempted to do this without compromising either his style or his imagery, and this attitude meant that he led a life of near-constant material struggle until the decade before his death in 1903. What is fascinating, however, is that Pissarro understood that there were many levels to the art market in nineteenth-century Paris and myriad ways to produce for diverse consumers. The Parisian markets catered to tourists, to eccentric middle-class collectors of certain types of objects, to the very wealthy, to new money, to the professional classes, and so on. To succeed in these overlapping markets, artists needed to produce works at many different price points.

166
The Market on the Grand-Rue, Gisors,
1885
Oil on canvas
18⅛ × 15 in. (46 × 38 cm)
Private collection (PDR 816)

Pissarro's representations of rural food markets can be read as a metaphor for his own marketing of art. Markets had the greatest range for representation in Pissarro's oeuvre, and there is scarcely a scale or a medium—save one—that he did not explore using markets as a subject. Pissarro produced preparatory and salable drawings, watercolors, gouaches, fans, temperas, pastels, etchings, lithographs, and oil paintings of markets, and in each of these media there was an equal range of scales. Hence, Pissarro "marketed markets." Interestingly, the only format left unexplored by Pissarro as a "marketer" was large-scale oil painting. Although he painted many large-scale rural figures and landscapes, presumably for the luxury class, only one large canvas of a market survives, *The Poultry Market at Pontoise* of 1882 (fig. 174). At a little more than two and a half feet by two feet, this painting is so physically complex and was evidently so time-consuming to produce that Pissarro was unable to complete it before the opening of the 1882 Impressionist exhibition, where he made his debut as a figure painter. Indeed, even *looking* at the painting is exhausting. Each square inch of it is a layered compilation of tiny chromatic gestures, each of which needed to dry before an overlayer could be added. Producing a complex, multifigure representation of a market in slow-drying oil paint took much more time than if an artist used quicker-drying media such as tempera, pastel, or especially gouache. As if proof of this, Pissarro's largest market representation is a thirty-two-inch square sheet of paper mounted on canvas in gouache and black chalk (fig. 177). One wonders whether it was a full-scale cartoon for a large-format square painting such as *Apple-Picking* (fig. 155) or *Woman Breaking Wood* (fig. 162).

167
Woman Selling Chestnuts, 1878
Drypoint on beige laid paper
Plate: 8⅛ × 6⅜ in. (20.6 × 16.2 cm); sheet: 11¾ × 8⁷⁄₁₆ in. (29.9 × 21.5 cm)
Museum of Fine Arts, Boston, fund in memory of Horatio Greenough Curtis, 60.1459 (D 15)

It seems clear that the major impetus for Pissarro to tackle the subject of rural markets came from his first close friend in France, Ludovic Piette. Piette, as we know, was a lifelong anarcho-communist and was married to a Jewish woman from Passy, Adèle Lévy, who may have been introduced to Piette by Pissarro. The marriages of both Piette and Pissarro (Jew and non-Jew, urban and rural) were as much a factor in their friendship as their politics and their art, and the two men spent hours discussing social and economic issues as they affected art, its production, and its sale. It seems that Piette preceded Pissarro in his investigation of markets, and the timing of Pissarro's adoption of the subject suggests that he veered away from it while Piette was alive. After Piette's tragic early death in 1878, Pissarro felt free to explore a subject that had, in effect, belonged to his friend. Indeed, Piette had sent ten paintings and gouaches of markets to the 1877 Impressionist exhibition, where he made his debut as an Impressionist. These were discussed by more than one critic and were the first market scenes in any Impressionist exhibition. Pissarro's first important market print, *Woman Selling Chestnuts* (fig. 167), was made in the autumn or winter of 1878, after Piette's death on April 15 of that year. It is worth contrasting the market scenes of the two men because, although Pissarro's markets were clearly made as a form of homage to his dear friend, they differ markedly. The largest and most important of these representations is an immense 1876 oil on canvas of the poultry market in front of the town hall in Pontoise (fig. 168), the masterpiece among the thirty works submitted by Piette to the 1877 Impressionist exhibition. This painting encapsulates a sizable area of the town and includes detailed renderings of six large buildings and a cobblestone plaza with at least sixty figures and assorted arrangements of market goods. It is suffused with light and a generosity of urban pictorial space unknown in works by Pissarro of the same period. When compared with Pissarro's largest urban market, *The Poultry Market at Pontoise,* the differences abound—Piette horizontal, Pissarro vertical; Piette's space filled, Pissarro's packed with figures; Piette's distant, Pissarro's proximate; Piette's open, Pissarro's closed; and so on.

Pissarro surely felt that Piette's views of small-town markets were essentially descriptive and conventional rather than modern and experimental, and he also must have known that his own market scenes needed both to contrast and complement his rural agricultural representations. Indeed, among the Pissarro market scenes in various media gathered in this exhibition, none are horizontal and few have any real indicators of place besides their titles. Even the titles have often proven to be wrong, and modern cataloguers have learned that many of the so-called Pontoise markets are actually representations of Gisors—and vice versa. (One might well ask, "Who cares?") This is because it didn't fundamentally matter to Pissarro precisely where the markets were. What *did* matter was that these were represented places in which specific people

168

Ludovic Piette
The Poultry Market, Place de l'Hôtel-de-Ville, Pontoise, 1876
Oil on canvas
43¾ × 73¼ in. (111 × 186 cm)
Musée de Pontoise, Inv. P.1981.4.0

169

The Maid Shopping, 1888
Etching and drypoint printed in brown-black on off-white wove paper
Plate: 7½ × 5³⁄₁₆ in. (19 × 13.2 cm); sheet: 7¹³⁄₁₆ × 5½ in. (19.8 × 14 cm)
Sterling and Francine Clark Art Institute, Williamstown, Massachusetts, 1962.90 (D 74)

170

Poultry Market at Gisors, 1891
Etching on cream laid paper
Plate: 9¹³⁄₁₆ × 7⅜ in. (25 × 18.8 cm); sheet: 12⅝ × 8 in. (32.1 × 20.3 cm)
Museum of Fine Arts, Boston, Lee M. Friedman Fund, 1981.135 (D 98)

sell their own products directly to other specific people, many of whom they know. These representations negate the anonymity of modern urban industrial shopping (department stores), and because of that they tap into a deep well of French sentiment about the intimacy of food shopping. Even today, Parisians and inhabitants of other large French cities shop daily or many times a week in small, family-owned food shops grouped together in the urban equivalent of village and small-town markets. For Piette, marketing was part of the spectacle of modern life. For Pissarro, it was a place of specific encounters, odors, and sounds. It must be remembered that Pissarro's market representations were made in the same historical period in which the vast Second Empire central food market in Paris, Les Halles, was thriving, and a decade after Zola published his sensual evocations of that place in *Le ventre de Paris* (The belly of Paris) of 1873. The markets represented by Pissarro were at once the opposite of this huge, centralized (and government-controlled) urban market and also the sources of many of the products sold there. For Pissarro, however, it was the sheer fact of the superfluity of food production by rural workers and the directness and simplicity of exchange in the small-town markets that made such places proper anarchist subjects.

Perhaps the most remarkable aspect of Pissarro's various market scenes is that they are his first systematic study of the crowd. Many of the works have such a great number of figures crammed onto their small surfaces that one has no

171
The Market at Gisors, Rue Cappeville, ca. 1894
Etching printed in grayish black, red, blue, and yellow on ivory laid paper
Plate: 7 7/8 × 5 1/2 in. (20 × 14 cm); sheet: 10 11/16 × 7 13/16 in. (27.1 × 19.9 cm)
Sterling and Francine Clark Art Institute, Williamstown, Massachusetts, 1962.93 (D 112)

172
The Market at Gisors (Rue Cappeville), mid-1890s
Etching and drypoint, colored with crayon on white paper
Plate: 7 3/4 × 5 1/2 in. (19.8 × 14.1 cm); sheet: 11 × 8 1/8 in. (27.8 × 20.5 cm)
Ashmolean Museum, University of Oxford, presented by Miss Orovida Pissarro, 1953, WA1953.88.1 (BL 299)

desire even to try to count them. They chat, jostle, bargain, call out, gossip, and look at one another; more often than not, it is difficult to gauge any real social difference between buyers and sellers. Rarely does Pissarro include obviously bourgeois figures such as purchasers, suggesting that his markets are meeting places of social and economic equals. They are also dominated by women, who, in nineteenth-century France, were largely responsible for meals and prided themselves on their ability to buy the best for the least. Again, one senses the example of the eighteenth-century artist Jean-Siméon Chardin, whose cooks and maids occasionally are represented as they return from market or as they purchase food from the vendors who stopped at the major houses of Paris. It is perfectly possible to read many of Pissarro's female figures as maids or cooks in bourgeois households, sent to procure food in the local markets. This was the world not of Pissarro himself but of his wife, Julie, who had undoubtedly marketed in Paris for Pissarro's mother and who continued to negotiate good prices—and occasionally credit—from her friends in the markets of Pontoise and Gisors.

173
The Market at Pontoise, ca. 1895
Lithograph on ivory chine collé on ivory laid paper
Image: 11⅞ × 8¹¹⁄₁₆ in. (30.1 × 22.1 cm); sheet: 17¹¹⁄₁₆ × 12⁵⁄₁₆ in. (44.8 × 31.2 cm)
Sterling and Francine Clark Art Institute, Williamstown, Massachusetts, 1962.95
(D 147)

C. Pissarro. 82

174

The Poultry Market at Pontoise, 1882
Oil on canvas
32⅞ × 25⅝ in. (81 × 65.1 cm)
Norton Simon Art Foundation, M.1984.2.P (PDR 682)

175

The Pork Butcher, 1883
Oil on canvas
25⅝ × 21⅜ in. (65.1 × 54.3 cm)
Tate: Bequeathed by Lucien Pissarro, the artist's son, 1944, N05576 (PDR 706)

176

Market at Pontoise, 1895
Oil on canvas
18¼ × 15⅛ in. (46.3 × 38.4 cm)
The Nelson-Atkins Museum of Art, Kansas City, Missouri, purchase: The William Rockhill Nelson Trust, 33-150 (PDR 1097)

177

Poultry Market at Gisors, 1885
Gouache and black chalk on brown paper mounted on canvas
32⅜ × 32⅜ in. (82.2 × 82.2 cm)
Museum of Fine Arts, Boston, bequest of John T. Spaulding, 48.588 (PV 1400)

C. Pissarro. 1885

178

The Marketplace, 1882
Gouache on paper
31¾ × 25½ in. (80.6 × 64.8 cm)
Courtesy of The Metropolitan Museum of Art, private collection, L.1984.54.1 (PV 1361)

179

Poultry Market at Gisors, ca. 1890
Gouache and tempera
18⅛ × 14¹⁵⁄₁₆ in. (46 × 38 cm)
Private collection (PV 1453)

180

Horse Market, Saint-Martin Fair, Pontoise, 1883
Tempera on fine canvas
6 5⁄16 × 11 5⁄8 in. (16 × 29.5 cm)
Private collection, France (PV 1372)

181

The Gisors Market, 1887
Black ink, gouache, and watercolor heightened with lead white on paper
12 1⁄4 × 9 1⁄2 in. (31 × 24 cm)
Columbus Museum of Art, Ohio, gift of Howard D. and Babette L. Sirak, the Donors to the Campaign for Enduring Excellence, and the Derby Fund, 1991.001.051 (PV 1413)

C. Pissarro. 1887

188

The Market at Gisors, 1887
Watercolor on cream paper
12⅜ × 9⁷⁄₁₆ in. (31.4 × 24 cm)
Museum of Fine Arts, Boston,
M. and M. Karolik Fund, 1973.144

189

Market Scene, ca. 1893
Black crayon with pen and black ink, gray wash, and white body color on tracing paper, laid down on stiff white paper
12 9/16 × 8 7/8 in. (31.9 × 22.5 cm)
Ashmolean Museum, University of Oxford, presented anonymously, 1989, WA1989.120

TURPITUDES SOCIALES.

1890

11

LES TURPITUDES SOCIALES

In 1889 Pissarro made a series of twenty-eight identically scaled drawings in pen and ink over pencil intended to educate two of his nieces, Esther and Alice Isaacson, about what he considered to be the horrors of modern capitalist society. He grouped the drawings in an order that encompasses several rhymed narratives of economic and social exploitation and the resulting despair and death. Each drawing was given an explicit title, and many were accompanied by short paragraphs extracted from the anarchist press. Pissarro's most common source was *Le Révolté,* the premier anarchist journal in French, which commenced publication in Geneva in 1879, moved to France in 1885, and changed its name to *La Révolte,* which persisted until the censors closed it in 1894. Pissarro was listed in police reports as a subscriber to this and other anarchist or socialist journals and was closely watched by authorities, who were aware not only of his prominence as an artist but also of his friendship with well known political activists such as the exiled Reclus and Grave. The overt expression of his political beliefs in *Les turpitudes sociales* is unique in Pissarro's oeuvre, and the work was made to be hand-delivered to the recipients rather than to be risked being sent by mail.

What is inexplicable—indeed, even tragic—is that this series of drawings has never before been included in an important Pissarro exhibition and, until recently, was known only in an expensive facsimile edition of 999 copies produced in 1972 by Éditions Skira. What had been created as a personal educational crusade against the evils of capitalism became, paradoxically, an *objet de luxe* in the book trade. In 2009 a more readily accessible and affordable version with a preface by Henri Mitterand appeared in France, but Pissarro's most overtly political work of art is nonetheless almost invisible in the Pissarro

190
Front cover of *Les turpitudes sociales,* 1889–1890, designed by Pissarro's son Lucien

bibliography. Joachim Pissarro mentioned it, without publishing a single sheet, in his otherwise splendid monograph, *Camille Pissarro* (1993), and Kathleen Adler's *Camille Pissarro: A Biography* (1978) notes it in the index but omits reference to it on the indicated page or anywhere else in the book. Only Ralph Shikes and Paula Harper, in their excellent biography *Pissarro: His Life and Work* (1980), published five drawings from the series and discussed it at some length. But even they fell prey to indecision when they insisted that "some of the drawings are crude," and linked them to the caricatures of Daumier, William Hogarth, and George Cruickshank. Yet when *Les turpitudes sociales* is read and its drawings interpreted seriously, their emotional power and intensity are extraordinary. In many important senses, an understanding of Pissarro without *Les turpitudes* is like an understanding of Goya without *The Disasters of War*—a misunderstanding.

Les turpitudes sociales is difficult to translate, perhaps deliberately so. The word *turpitude* is the same in French and English and, because the recipients of the book were English, may have been chosen by the artist for that reason. Although the word was used for centuries in both languages, its precise meanings are elusive, and his title has most often been translated as "social disgraces." The essential meanings of *turpitude* are negative, which prepare us for a relentless visual onslaught on modern capitalist economies. Pissarro added a frontispiece (fig. 191) that represents a bearded middle-aged man, wearing sandals, sitting on a hill outside Paris (probably near Passy in the west of the city), looking down into the heart of the metropolis with its belching smokestacks (one wonders where Pissarro found them in Paris) and Eiffel Tower, which had just been completed for the 1889 Exposition Universelle. Above this symbol of the "New Paris," the word *anarchie* vibrates in the rays of a rising sun, and an hourglass in the foreground tells us that time is relentlessly passing. So Pissarro set the stage for what we soon learn will be a revolution.

The table of contents (fig. 192) is announced by a worker who carries a banner that reads *Table des matières,* while a bourgeois tries to stop his progress—scarcely subtle. The twenty-eight episodes of the story then commence with a savage sheet (fig. 193) displaying a bald, fat bourgeois on a circular platform in the middle of the 1889 Exposition Universelle holding a bag labeled *Capital.* Its text, taken from *La Révolte,* sets the book's tragic but defiant tone: "It is the War of the dispossessed against their dispossessors, the war of the hungry against the fat, the war of the poor against the rich, the war of life against death." Despite this strident text, it seems as if the crowd that surrounds the capitalist is at once worshipping and defying him. In the letter he wrote to the Isaacsons to accompany the book, Pissarro identified the figure with the well-known Jewish bankers of the world, "a portrait of a Bischoffsheim or an Oppenheim, a Rothschild or any old Gould; it is without distinction, vulgar and ugly." Perhaps only a Jewish artist could be anti-Semitic in this way.

The remainder of the book (figs. 194–220) chronicles bourgeois marriages for money, the anonymity and horror of the stock market, the suicide of a ruined broker, the sumptuous burial of a cardinal, the horrible working conditions in factories, the long hours of factory workers, the suicide by hanging of an impoverished man, the crowded dormitories of young female workers, the suicide by drowning of an abandoned woman, the starvation of an artist's family, the begging of officials, begging on the street, the violent robbery of a wealthy man, domestic violence, the drunkenness of the miserable, the unsafe working conditions in the city and a resulting injury, the horrors of a modern hospital for the poor, the funeral of a worker, and, finally, the immense insurrection that results from the combined greed of the bourgeoisie and the misery of the urban working class. The insurrection is violent and the victims are from every walk of life—an upheaval as terrible as any war but, for Pissarro, a necessary upheaval that will be the ultimate revolution.

When they received *Les turpitudes* early in 1890, Alice Isaacson was thirty-six years old and her younger sister, Esther, was thirty-three; both were unmarried. They were the daughters of Pissarro's half sister Emma Petit and Phineas Isaacson (fig. 20), with whom Pissarro had stayed as a boy while at school in Paris. Pissarro felt responsible for the political education of his nieces, as he had felt responsible for that of their younger brother, Alfred (named after Pissarro's older brother), to whom he had already written about the necessity for revolution. In December of 1892, Esther would become the wife of her first cousin, Pissarro's son Georges, who was fourteen years her junior. Thus, the two families of Isaacson and Pissarro were bound together by multigenerational ties.

How long had Pissarro been at work on *Les turpitudes* before he sent it on December 29, 1889? All evidence suggests that it was anything but a quickly thrown together project. Pissarro had to conceive of the twenty-eight scenes, choose appropriate texts, make compositional studies (a few of which survive in the Ashmolean Museum), and negotiate with his oldest son, Lucien, about producing a box and binding for the drawings. And, in the midst of his struggles with the techniques of Neo-Impressionism, Pissarro had to find a graphic style appropriate to the grand sweep of his narrative. He had worked for several years on his own graphism, largely the result of reading Champfleury's *Histoire de la caricature moderne* in 1884 but also because of Lucien's links to English illustrators during the mid- and later 1880s. Pissarro was well versed in the history of caricature, and it formed a major strand in his graphic—and political—aesthetic. Indeed, his figure of Capital on the first page of *Les turpitudes* recalls nothing less than Henri Monnier's full-scale caricatural "sculpture" of his character-type,

191–220

Les turpitudes sociales, 1889–1890
Thirty pen and brown ink over graphite drawings
on paper pasted in an album
Album: 12¼ × 9½ in. (31 × 24 cm)
Collection of Jean Bonna, Geneva

DES
N°1. Le Capital
2 – Le Mariage de raison –
3 – Le temple du Veau d'or.
4 – Les Boursicotières
5 – Le suicide du boursier
6 – Enterrement d'un Cardinal.
7 – Le bagne
8. – Les esclaves au repos
9 – Le bagne St. Honoré
10. – Le pendu.
11 – Jean misère
12 – L'asphixie
13 Suicide de l'abandonné
14 – Plus de pain
15 – La bouchée de pain
16 – La misère en chapeau noir
18 – Sophie Grande
19 – Le mendiant
21. – La vertu récompensée
22 – Petite scène de la vie conjugale
23 – Les ivrognes.
24 – Avant l'accident.
25 après l'accident.
26 l'Hopital.
27 Le convoi du pauvre.
28 Insurrection.

1. Capital

2. The Marriage of Reason

3. The Temple of the Golden Calf

4. Dabblers in the Stock Market

5. The Suicide of a Stockbroker

6. Burial of a Cardinal

7. Penal Servitude

8. Slaves at Their Meal

9. The "Prison" of Saint-Honoré

10. The Hanged Millionaire

11. Jean Misery

12. Asphyxiation

13. Suicide of an Abandoned Woman

14. No More Bread

15. For Next to Nothing

16. Misery in a Black Hat

17. Art in Stagnation

18. Sophie's Choice

19. The Beggar

20. Struggle for Life!

21. Virtue Rewarded

22. Little Scene of Married Life

23. The Drunkards

24. Before the Accident

25. After the Accident

26. The Hospital

27. The Cortege of a Poor Man

28. Insurrection

ANARCHIE
ERAGNY
1890

12

AFTER THE REVOLUTION

There is little doubt that Pissarro expected a European revolution to occur in the relatively near future, and that he made works of art in an attempt, like Peter Kropotkin, to "model" the new anarchist world as it would be after the revolution. To call this new world a utopia is to misunderstand it. Pissarro was too much of a realist to think that a new, nongovernmental world of equal citizens would be easy and problem-free. Rather, he thought that, without private property, inherited wealth, and disparate social classes, human society could have a chance gradually to ameliorate and to become harmonious. He knew that humans themselves would not completely change, but he felt that, if wealth was eradicated, a more moral society would result. Pissarro actively read Kropotkin and Élisée Reclus, the two anarchist writers who were the most practical and concrete in their ideas about what must occur during and after the revolution to build the just society of the future. Like many other members of the anarchist movement, Pissarro was painfully aware of the failings of earlier revolutions in France, from 1789 through the Paris Commune of 1871. This time, the practical anarchists wanted to get it right.

Between the late 1880s and 1901, Pissarro made a series of highly finished, multifigure rural genre scenes that seem almost mythic. None of them is as large as *Apple-Picking* (fig. 155) or *Woman Breaking Wood* (fig. 162), but all of them put their figures into vast landscapes that seem to stretch for miles into the distance. None has a quality of being observed from life; rather, they were patiently constructed, their compositions devised first after careful study of various harvests or plantings and then after drawings from posed models in the manner seen with *The Harvest* (fig. 116). All of them are highly worked, almost obsessive in their

221 (PAGE 255)

Back cover of *Les turpitudes sociales*, 1889–1890, designed by Pissarro's son Lucien

222

Pissarro in his studio at Éragny, ca. 1890–1895

13

THE FIGURE IN THE CITY

The Melee of Urban Life Early in 1893, Pissarro discovered the modern city as a subject for art. Suffering from the chronic eye infections that were to plague him the rest of his life, Pissarro went to Paris to consult with a physician and was told that, for the health of his eyes, he must not venture out into the dusty and polluted Paris streets. He was forced to remain in his hotel for more than two months while the infection slowly healed. From rooms in the utterly unglamorous Hôtel du Rome across from the Gare Saint-Lazare, he received visitors, wrote letters, and visited with family. Most importantly, he painted the streets around the hotel, one of the many in Paris that had been constructed near major railroad stations for provincial visitors arriving in the metropolis. Three of the four urban paintings that survive from this extended stay are hampered by Pissarro's pictorial struggles with technique. Since renouncing pointillism nearly three years before, he had attempted to create a looser and more confident facture while retaining the idea of the picture as the compilation of individual strokes of paint—as "work." Although his small gestural technique worked well for the representation of moving traffic, it was less successful for architecture, and these early urban pictures have a visually "wobbly" character. One of them, however, eschews architecture altogether and is simply a view of pedestrians and horse-drawn vehicles encircling a *rond-point* in the place du Havre in front of the hotel (fig. 231).

There is simply nothing quite like this picture in Impressionism. Monet, Caillebotte, and to a lesser extent Renoir had painted the new Parisian streets and boulevards from above in arresting images of the 1870s and early 1880s. Monet and Renoir stressed the spectacle of the streets, while Caillebotte evoked the urban ennui and alienation of these vast new spaces planned in the Second

230
Pissarro in the apartment at 204, rue de Rivoli, Paris, ca. 1900. Among the paintings visible in the background are *Jeanne Pissarro, Called Cocotte, Reading* (fig. 77) and *Woman Sewing* (fig. 147).

as a stream of fish, as Monet did in his two "revolutionary" urban views of the rue Montorgueil (Musée d'Orsay) and rue Saint-Denis (Musée des Beaux-Arts, Rouen) of 1878. Pissarro *had* to describe a blue blouson, a worker's lunch pail, a bowler hat on a bourgeois with a black-collared beige coat, a bright-red scarf on the omnibus driver, and on and on. Quickly but deftly applied, each stroke carries information about gender, class, and age. His is truly an anarchist capital of individuals moving on their own to their own destinations, or to their own loitering, or to their own purposelessness. They are, in a way, simultaneously lost in what could be called a sea of humanity and placed specifically—targeted, one might say—by the painter who "composes with people." They are, of course, the opposite of Pissarro's country scenes, in which there is a rhythmic compositional unity among the figures and between the figures and their landscape settings. Here, the city is a vast stone set for the human comedy. Indeed, if any paintings by Pissarro have wit, it is these great urban series from the last decade of his life.

232
The Place du Théâtre Français, 1898
Oil on canvas
28½ × 36½ in. (72.4 × 92.7 cm)
Los Angeles County Museum of Art, Mr. and Mrs. George Gard De Sylva Collection, M.46.3.2 (PDR 1208)

The Dreyfus Affair On December 15, 1897, Pissarro moved into a suite of rooms in the Hôtel du Louvre, where he remained until April 26, 1898. That period of more than four months was in some ways a refuge for the painter, who had spent much of the early part of 1897 in London nursing his son Lucien (who had suffered a stroke), and had learned of the death from tuberculosis of his son Félix later that year, on November 25. Pissarro scoured Paris for a new motif, even returning to Passy, on the western outskirts of the city, where he had been sent to school in 1842 and spent his early Parisian period as an artist. He had painted two of the grand boulevards, Montmartre and des Italiens, and had found, one block from the Musée du Louvre, a hotel with a panoramic view of three types of urban space—an old street (rue du Faubourg Saint-Honoré), a new "avenue" (de l'Opéra), and a tree-filled urban plaza (place du Théâtre Français)—from the windows of one suite. Known today as "la suite Pissarro," the rooms were the artist's sole place of peace and safety during the Dreyfus Affair, one of the most tumultuous periods in the history of France—and one particularly crucial for Pissarro.

Joachim Pissarro has already written at some length about Pissarro's reaction to the Dreyfus Affair, relating it to his views from the Hôtel du Louvre, so this discussion will merely mention the major points. Pissarro, as both a secular Jew and an anarchist, was fully capable of railing against the evils of Jewish bankers, as we have seen in *Les turpitudes sociales* (figs. 190–221). Yet, for him, systematic anti-Semitism was as evil as capitalism, and when Émile Zola's letter "J'accuse!" appeared in the newspaper *L'Aurore* on January 13, 1898, his earlier ambivalence about Dreyfus crystallized into the same defiant anger felt by his friend Zola. Unlike Zola, however, Pissarro was a Jew who not only looked Jewish but was living in the center of Paris during the months of the worst anti-Semitic street rallies in French history. Whereas his confinement at the Hôtel du Rome in 1893 had been due to his eye infection, his confinement this time was ethnic and religious in nature. After his personal tragedies of 1897, the sociocultural ones of 1898 piled insult onto injury.

Pissarro was in real physical danger when he left the hotel, as is evident from his letter of January 19, 1898. (It was written only a week after the appearance of Zola's "J'accuse!" Pissarro, obviously in a state of shock, misdated it November 19, 1898.) At five o'clock in the afternoon, Pissarro was walking to Durand-Ruel's when he found himself in the middle of a gang of youths shouting, "Death to the Jews! Down with Zola!" He stayed there, "tranquilly," as he puts it, with no seeming irony, until he reached the rue Lafitte and entered the safety of Durand-Ruel's gallery. Although later letters are sanguine about how much better it became in the coming weeks, it is clear that the white-bearded, hook-nosed Pissarro was an obvious Jew in a city brimming with anti-Semitic street demonstrations that have been horrifically quantified by Pierre Birnbaum in *The Anti-Semitic Moment: A Tour of France in 1898,* his definitive study of late nineteenth-century French anti-Semitism (translated by Jane Marie Todd). They did *not* stop in a week, as Pissarro suggests in his letters, and he remained indoors for some time. Never in the painter's life had his religious origins been subjected to such an assault, and no explanation about his *personal* religious and political beliefs would stop a mob from hurting or insulting him.

The pictures painted from the windows of the Hôtel du Louvre have always been read as a disavowal of or a retreat from these personal and social pressures—art as a refuge from life. Even Signac, who visited him on February 11, found that Pissarro worked with total absorption, even as he discussed Zola and Dreyfus with what the younger painter called "fire." Art, in this reading, was a release from the tumult of life. But is this really true? Pissarro hurled himself pictorially into the very streets and boulevards that were closed to him. He roamed above and across the crowds in all kinds of weather—indeed, he reveled in rain, fog, sleet, and snow, and he did so knowing well the tensions and hatreds of the city. It was, in the end, the sheer otherness of Paris, its *inaccessibility* to him, that the paintings embody. To us they are beautiful and full of life, but to him they represented a city that was unsafe and, in a sense, evil. This is brought into focus in a little-known self-portrait (fig. 233) painted by Pissarro in his suite in the Hôtel du Louvre. Pissarro, who was not prone to introspection, had little to look at while he was confined to the suite except the view out the window—and himself.

Although Joachim Pissarro and Claire Durand-Ruel Snollaerts dated this portrait to about 1896 and identified the view out the window as the rue Saint-Lazare, where the artist was confined because of his eye ailments in late 1896 and early 1897, surely they are mistaken. A careful examination of the faintly described architecture makes it clear that the buildings (though reversed in the mirror) are across the place du Théâtre Français from the Hôtel du Louvre; the distinctive silhouette of Garnier's great roof at the Opéra was carefully depicted by Pissarro to the left. Indeed, the painter was restricted to his rooms in both instances, but in the case of the Hôtel du Louvre, it had a good deal more emotional resonance. Interestingly, as Pissarro painted himself in 1897–1898, he decided to do something he had never done before and would never do again: represent himself in the act of painting, with his palette in his left hand and his right hand "exiting stage right" to put a mark on the portrait. Pissarro worked on the portrait over several sessions, repositioning the palette at least once and lengthening his brown painter's smock before abandoning the painting and leaving it unfinished. Surely, we are not surprised that this work—created under such emotionally charged circumstances—was left in its arrested state.

233
Self-Portrait, ca. 1898
Oil on canvas
20⅞ × 12 in. (53 × 30.5 cm)
Dallas Museum of Art, the Wendy and Emery Reves Collection, 1985.R.44
(PDR 1129)

14

THE BATHERS

REMEMBERING CÉZANNE

All artists, regardless of their strength of character and openness to the world around them, entertain doubts, and Pissarro was no exception. For him, the year 1895 brought two reasons to question his own career: the two exhibitions of the work of his friends and colleagues Monet and Cézanne. In the spring of 1895, Pissarro viewed the exhibition of Monet's final series, devoted to the Rouen cathedral. Pissarro had initially dismissed the notion of series of works when he learned about Monet's *Grainstacks* series before its 1891 exhibition at Durand-Ruel; he had thought of them as market-driven, as being less about temporal shifts than about sales to American millionaires. He changed his mind, however, in the presence of the actual paintings. By 1895 he had completely accepted the series idea, adapting it in his own particular way to his sequence of urban views, which he commenced in earnest in 1897.

But in November and December of 1895, Pissarro was, like most other artists, completely blindsided by the enormous Cézanne exhibition mounted by Ambroise Vollard. For the first time in his career, Cézanne parted with 150 paintings, which were installed sequentially in Vollard's galleries on the rue Lafitte. Unfortunately for scholars, there was no catalogue, and the paintings were rotated at least twice in the course of the two months to ensure that serious viewers would return to see the new works. All of the major Impressionists not only visited the exhibition but also acquired works by Cézanne. Monet, Degas, and Renoir were doing well financially and could buy what they wanted. Pissarro, not yet having reached the financial plateau that secured the last five years of his life, was forced to trade an early Louveciennes picture for two works by Cézanne, one of bathers and the other a self-portrait. Of the many works by Cézanne known

234
Paul Cézanne, ca. 1873

to have been owned by Pissarro, there were two self-portraits and three bather compositions, and it is impossible to know which were acquired through trade in 1895 and which he had already acquired through direct exchange with Cézanne when the two artists worked together extensively in the 1870s and early 1880s. There had been a long silence between the two good friends, exacerbated by Cézanne's basically permanent move to Provence and by Pissarro's decision to relocate to Éragny, which was much farther from Paris. The chance to see such a large number of paintings by Cézanne at one time was, for Pissarro, particularly charged and important.

We know from Pissarro's letters that he was upset by the fact that very few people in 1890s Paris were aware of the crucial role he had played in Cézanne's career—and vice versa. Pissarro, however, was a proud man who rarely expressed jealousy or felt the effects of a personal slight for very long. But when he saw the landscapes, still lifes, portraits, and figure paintings by Cézanne in quantity—and had sufficient time to study them—he began seriously to question his own career and its twists and turns. The Cézanne exhibition presented works by an artist who had remained true to his convictions and followed no one else. It is easy to understand why Pissarro might have winced when he heard this view expressed. It represented the seemingly hermetic development of a lone genius, Cézanne, against the legendary openness and experimentation of Pissarro. And all of this becomes relevant as we flip through the pages of the brilliant catalogue raisonné by Joachim Pissarro and Claire Durand-Ruel Snollaerts to find two clusters of Pissarro's bather paintings dated 1895 and 1896, and when we look at his drawings and, more pointedly, at his prints as catalogued by Loys Delteil and again by Barbara Stern Shapiro.

In light of this, it is tempting to interpret Pissarro's sudden output of bather paintings, drawings, and prints as a direct response to the 1895 Cézanne exhibition. With a more careful look at the evidence, it becomes clear that Pissarro had already created three rural bather paintings in 1894 and that at least one of the group of 1895 paintings, *Bather in the Woods* (fig. 236), had been sold to a collector by mid-October of that year, weeks before the Cézanne show opened. We also know that Pissarro owned at least two Cézanne bather compositions well before 1895, and that he was interested enough in Cézanne's investigations of these erotically charged subjects to buy, or more likely trade for, these paintings. We can make a more subtle argument by saying that Pissarro had reached a point in his own figural practice that he needed new subjects, and that the bather came to his attention before his reexposure to Cézanne's own treatment of the theme. Many Pissarro scholars have pointed to the link between *Bather in the Woods* and a delightful oil of a single rural bather by Millet painted in the late 1860s (Baltimore Museum of Art). It is also relevant to point to the links between

235

Three Bathers Stepping Out of the Water,
1896
Oil on canvas
29⅛ × 36¼ in. (74 × 92 cm)
Private collection (PDR 1108)

the bather compositions of the late 1880s and early 1890s by Degas and Renoir, both artists Pissarro followed much more closely than Cézanne.

Yet surely the sight of the works by Cézanne had the same effect on Pissarro that Monet's cathedrals had on Sisley. Sisley felt so overwhelmed by the sheer confidence of Monet's serial work that he—rather ill-advisedly, one thinks today—began a comparable series of paintings representing the large, late Gothic church in Moret-sur-Loing, where he lived. Such enterprises tend to be doomed to failure, and one suspects that Pissarro realized this before it was too late. No important scholar of Pissarro has expressed admiration for his 1894–1896 bather paintings. Even Joachim Pissarro, his most loving historian and his great-grandson, includes only a few in his 1993 monograph, *Camille Pissarro,* and his discussion of them is brief. And one scours the pages of other monographs and exhibition catalogues to find them. Perhaps the only one that has become canonical is *Woman Bathing Her Feet in a Brook* (fig. 237), a larger, clothed version of the nude in *Bather in the Woods.* Even this painting has often been interpreted as an homage by Pissarro to Goya's nude and clothed *majas,* but, to counter that, it must be noted that the pictures are different sizes, were never conceived as a pair, and have never been exhibited together—before or after Pissarro's death. Again, Pissarro both courted and veered from his sources.

Few of Pissarro's bather paintings could hang in the same gallery with any of the major paintings of bathers by Cézanne. They become sentimental rural

236
Bather in the Woods, 1895
Oil on canvas
23¾ × 28¾ in. (60.3 × 73 cm)
The Metropolitan Museum of Art, H. O. Havemeyer Collection, bequest of Mrs. H. O. Havemeyer, 1929, 29.100.126 (PDR 1062)

237
Woman Bathing Her Feet in a Brook, 1894/1895
Oil on canvas
28½ × 36 in. (73 × 92 cm)
The Art Institute of Chicago, a Millennium Gift of Sara Lee Corporation, 1999.364 (PDR 1061)

238
Study of a Young Woman Bathing Her Legs, 1895
Colored chalks highlighted with touches of pastel
20⅞ × 15⅜ in. (53.1 × 39.1 cm)
Ashmolean Museum, University of Oxford, Pissarro Family Gift, 1952, WA1952.6.360

narratives with restrained erotic content rather than Cézanne's assured posing of mythic women. And eroticism and Pissarro seem to have been born on different planets, for these pictures, as promising as they might be to the student of Pissarro's erotic life, actually send one back to the letters for our material, which is mostly confined to mentions of Madame Pissarro's worries about dalliances with models. The largest and most ambitious of the 1896 series—a picture that might actually have been conceived as a pair with *Woman Bathing Her Feet*—is *Three Bathers Stepping Out of the Water* (fig. 235), which was listed as number one in the catalogue of the large Durand-Ruel Pissarro exhibition held in the spring of 1896. The date of this exhibition suggests that all the bather compositions were begun in 1894–1895 and brought to completion gradually over the 1895–1896 season. *Woman Bathing Her Feet* had already been exhibited twice in Germany by March of 1895, months before the Cézanne exhibition, and it is clear that Pissarro worked carefully on the series before seeing that show. How sad it must have been for him that viewers of the 1896 Durand-Ruel exhibition had little choice but to feel that the most important bather composition in that exhibition of thirty-five works had been made as an homage to Cézanne.

In the end, Pissarro was much more successful with his printed bathers. The etchings and lithographs dated to 1895 by Delteil cling rather closely to the painted compositions, as if he had not been liberated by the printmaking technologies in his bather compositions. Yet the pair of friezes of bathers struggling with one another (see fig. 239), conventionally dated around 1896, are at once stronger and much more interestingly and confidently related to Cézanne's bathers. The wrestling bather prints have a quality completely lacking in the paintings, no matter how influenced by Cézanne. And when Pissarro made his last bather lithograph in 1897, he inscribed it with a title unique in his oeuvre, *The Theory of Bathers.* With this verbal sleight of hand, he distanced himself from the subject and from Cézanne, letting both go without a struggle.

239

Wrestling Bathers, ca. 1896
Lithograph (zinc) with wash
Image: 7 1/16 × 10 3/8 in. (18 × 26.3 cm); sheet: 10 11/16 × 14 15/16 in. (27.2 × 37.9 cm)
National Gallery of Art, Washington, Rosenwald Collection, 1944.5.129
(D 160)

240

Interior with Nude from the Back, 1895
Oil on canvas
16 5/16 × 13 1/8 in. (41.4 × 33.3 cm)
Private collection (PDR 1064)

15

LES TRAVAUX DES CHAMPS

Pissarro actively encouraged the artistic endeavors of his sons, from the beginning of Lucien's career in the early 1880s until his own death in 1903. This encouragement took many forms, from suggestion-filled letters to actual collaboration on works, and between these extremes was an entire middle ground of introductions to dealers, nudges to powerful friends, and the like. Pissarro's oldest son, Lucien, received the bulk of this encouragement, and his collaborations with his father have been the most closely studied. For the purposes of this investigation, it is critical that we learn something about the longest-term collaboration between father and son—an illustrated book with prints by Lucien made from drawings by Camille and entitled *Les travaux des champs* (Field work, or, more eloquently, The work of the fields).

In England, Lucien had learned a good deal about the hand-produced illustrated book, both from the well-known example of William Morris and from the more experimental and less well-funded projects of his friends Charles Ricketts and Charles Shannon. Pissarro was interested in fostering this medium for Lucien for many reasons, not the least being that he wanted his sons to have their own niches as artists and not imitate or compete with their father. Yet Lucien's name was not nearly as well known in France or England as his father's, and both realized that a true collaboration would have a better chance of commercial success than would an individual project by Lucien. Many such projects were mooted in letters, but the most persistent and important was *Les travaux des champs,* about which they exchanged letters, drawings, and prints from 1886 until Pissarro's death in 1903. This seventeen-year collaboration has been dissected and analyzed for some time, but because all the works from it are drawings in

241
Pissarro with his sons Félix and Lucien at 62 Bath Road, London, 1897

242

Compositional Study for Women Weeding the Grass, ca. 1893
Pen and India ink with watercolor over charcoal
9⅛ × 5⅞ in. (23.2 × 15 cm)
Ashmolean Museum, University of Oxford, Pissarro Family Gift, 1952, WA1952.6.443 (BL 325)

243

Compositional Study of Four Female Peasants Working in an Orchard (Spring), ca. 1894
Red-brown and India ink over charcoal on blue paper
9 5/16 × 11¾ in. (23.6 × 29.9 cm)
Ashmolean Museum, University of Oxford, Pissarro Family Gift, 1952, WA1952.6.450 (BL 332)

the Ashmolean Museum, it has not been integrated into the larger Pissarro literature. For us it is key because, in all its phases, it attempted to link Pissarro's representations of rural workers in systematic ways and to consider them in terms of texts.

Briefly, the collaboration on *Les travaux des champs* had three phases, the first of which (see figs. 242–243) lasted from 1886 until 1895 and resulted in a finished product, the portfolio *Travaux des champs* (Vale Press, 1895), which consisted of six wood-engravings by Lucien from drawings by Camille. This series might have been made in partial response to ten blocks produced from drawings by Millet, cut by Adrien Lavieille, and published with an unrelated text unpromisingly titled "Revue agricole" (Agricultural review) in an issue of *L'Illustration* on February 5, 1853. This was to be the only systematic assembly of Millet's rural images, and although it has certain similarities with Pissarro's later series, the differences, once again, are more noticeable, which comes as no surprise to anyone who studies Pissarro's "sources." Millet isolated his traditional peasant workers, whose labor is represented as physically demanding. Pissarro, by contrast, was interested in the comparative ease of rural work in the new anarchist society and also by the dominance of women as workers. Lucien and Camille went back and forth anxiously about the prints, and Pissarro, though always encouraging his son, was also capable of rather severe criticism. It is for this reason that the series took a long time to complete.

A concern with quality led father and son to begin almost immediately on a second phase (see figs. 244–245). They had already discussed a second collaboration in January of 1895 for an illustrated book with an English translation of a

244
Compositional Study of Female Peasants Harvesting Apples, 1895
Pen and India ink over pencil on gray paper prepared with a Chinese white ground
6³⁄₁₆ × 8 in. (15.7 × 20.3 cm)
Ashmolean Museum, University of Oxford, Pissarro Family Gift, 1952, WA1952.6.456 (BL 338)

245
Compositional Study for Women Carrying Bundles of Sticks, ca. 1895
Pen and India ink with Chinese white over pencil on tracing paper laid down on card
6 × 6⅞ in. (15.2 × 17.4 cm)
Ashmolean Museum, University of Oxford, Pissarro Family Gift, 1952, WA1952.6.458 (BL 340)

Greek pastoral romance, *Daphnis and Chloe,* by the third-century author Longus. Pissarro was to complete a dozen drawings to be engraved by Lucien. The technique chosen was more complex than that used for the first series of *Les travaux des champs* and, probably because they had already identified a text, it forced father and son to revive the earlier project and to think seriously about an appropriate text. Yet the second *Travaux,* like *Daphnis and Chloe,* languished. Camille completed only seven drawings, none of which were translated into print by Lucien. Of these seven themes (weeding, hay harvest, watching cattle, gathering apples, carrying wood, wheat harvest, and the mechanical thresher), all had been subjects of earlier paintings by Pissarro. It is likely that the project was aborted because neither Camille nor Lucien could identify an appropriate text, and the avant-garde Camille was clearly nervous about attempting classical subjects with ancient texts.

The third series (see figs. 246–249) began with real gusto in the fall of 1900, after a fallow period of five years. This time, father and son had agreed upon an author and commenced a long-term, if ultimately failed, relationship with the anarchist poet-journalist Benjamin Guinaudeau, who wrote regularly for Georges Clemenceau's radical journal *L'Aurore,* which had become famous for publishing Émile Zola's "J'accuse!" in January of 1898. Guinaudeau worked with the Pissarros to create a tripartite scheme for the illustrations, each of which would be a "series" of prints with a text. These were almost anthropological in nature: for example, "in the fields," "in the home," and "social relations." Although concentrating on subjects already painted or drawn by Camille between 1874 and 1900, they included some new subjects, two of which, "at the café" and "the wedding" seem far from Pissarro's aesthetic. Guinaudeau was involved in this conception and had described a series of three illustrated volumes of twenty-four pages, each with four poems by Guinaudeau and four prints by Lucien from drawings by Camille. Pissarro made thirty-six drawings for this project, many of them double and even triple studies of the same subject, giving Lucien a range of values to translate into print. These comprise twenty-two separate subjects, ten more than envisioned by Guinaudeau in the correspondence of 1900. From the evidence of the letters, we know that these occupied Pissarro for about a year, during which both father and son worked to secure a formal agreement with Guinaudeau. When, for various reasons, this was not forthcoming, Lucien suggested that they use Latin texts by Virgil, which Camille vetoed.

For those of us who yearn to know more specifically about the anarchist "content" of Pissarro's rural vision, the failure of this final collaboration is particularly tragic. Pissarro's willingness to work with an anarchist poet-journalist to create a totally modern view of rural work and leisure is surely not surprising. Yet, since no text survives, we have no way to gauge Pissarro's specific relationship to

246

Compositional Study of a Milking Scene, 1900
Pen and India ink with gray wash and Chinese white over black chalk
$5\frac{15}{16} \times 4\frac{7}{16}$ in. (15.1 × 11.3 cm)
Ashmolean Museum, University of Oxford, Pissarro Family Gift, 1952, WA1952.6.484 (BL 367)

247

Compositional Study of a Female Peasant Making Butter, 1900
Gray wash and Chinese white over black chalk
$6 \times 4\frac{5}{8}$ in. (15.2 × 11.7 cm)
Ashmolean Museum, University of Oxford, Pissarro Family Gift, 1952, WA1952.6.485 (BL 368)

AFTERWORD

250
Pissarro's studio at Éragny, ca. 1901. Among the paintings visible in the background is *Portrait of Cézanne* (fig. 81).

We end with Pissarro's final self-portrait (fig. 251), painted the year of his death while he stayed in an apartment on the tip of the Île de la Cité. Behind him, a north-facing window looks across the Seine to a row of modest, vernacular buildings he had depicted many times in his large series of urban landscapes painted from that rented apartment at 28, place Dauphine. Pissarro had returned to this apartment briefly, at the end of September of 1903, before moving to a newly rented apartment in the fourth arrondissement to paint his final series of urban views of Paris. Most scholars date this self-portrait to those final days in a favorite Parisian apartment. Pissarro was to die less than two months later, but, as he looked at himself in the mirror in Paris, he seemed a relatively healthy seventy-three-year-old. This last portrait remained with Madame Pissarro after the painter's death, and she gave it to their oldest child, Lucien, who in turn presented it to the Tate Gallery in London the year after his younger brother gave the painter's first self-portrait (fig. 2) to the French state. Hence, Pissarro's two "pendant" self-portraits can be found in the two cities to which he devoted most of his time in the last three decades of his life. The Tate and Orsay self-portraits were painted almost exactly thirty years apart, as Pissarro assessed himself at the ages of forty-three and seventy-three.

Interestingly—and not accidently—the 1903 self-portrait is slightly smaller than the 1873 one, which is already of modest dimensions. He turns the other way, almost as if he wished it to be a pendant to his earlier effort. He had just returned from a summer spent in Le Havre, painting its seaport and the bustling economic and industrial life of its quays. There can be no doubt that he remembered his first sight of that port in 1842, when he arrived

251
Self-Portrait, 1903
Oil on canvas
16⅛ × 13⅛ in. (41 × 33.3 cm)
Tate: Presented by Lucien Pissarro, the artist's son, 1931, N04592 (PDR 1528)

in France from the Caribbean for proper French schooling. As in 1873, Pissarro reveals remarkably little about himself in this painting. There are no clues to tell us about the interior of the apartment, its furnishings or decoration. There is no chair. His beard is now completely white, his mouth still almost completely covered by facial hair, and his bald head covered by an unblocked felt hat of a sort that any proper Parisian bourgeois would have avoided. He is, in an odd way, anonymous as he presents himself, with no hints of family or friends or social status. He wears eyeglasses, as he had in his two intervening self-portraits, and even these tell us little about the suffering he endured from persistent tear-duct infections that led eventually and inexorably to his death—an ironic way for an artist to die.

There had been no revolution, and Pissarro's ideas about the world that would be reformed after its chaotic birthing process were now much better formed than they were in 1873. In the earliest self-portrait, he was in the country; he is now in the very center of the great city of Paris, which had been the locus of his life since his arrival sixty-one years before. How odd—and apt, for this transnational, modern, secular man—that the Pontoise self-portrait should today be in Paris, while the Paris self-portrait is in London. When he painted this final self-image, three of his children had died and he had almost lost another, and his wife, Julie, was most likely in Éragny airing the house after the long absence in Le Havre. Hence, he was alone when he looked this one last time in the mirror—alone in an almost empty apartment. What is fascinating in this last self-portrait is that it represents in a profound way the same man Pissarro had painted in 1873—calm, modest, and clear-eyed. He had changed styles of painting more than any other major artist of the Impressionist circle. He had opened and altered his attitude toward both the human figure and the city. He had developed as a social thinker. He had been transformed by the experiences of fatherhood and of loss. He had repaid the only loan that had ever had been taken in his name, and he was, truth be told, a stolidly middle-class property owner—the last thing he could ever have imagined he would be. Despite all of this, he simply looks at himself in the mirror as if accepting his state and his appearance completely.

We now know that Pissarro was clear-headed and accepting of the whirl of ideas, births, deaths, and activities that had formed his fabled life. What we must remember is that he didn't paint that life; rather, he painted what he wanted *preserved* from that life. For him, the decent world that would happen after the upheaval of a global revolution was already at hand. He had tried—and succeeded remarkably well—to live *as if* that revolution had occurred, and he did that by working—daily and without a schedule—at representing the world that he saw and admired. Only in *Les turpitudes sociales* (figs. 190–221) did he allow his zeal to educate to politicize the repetitive and work-oriented realm of his art. If there were admirable people in the world in which he lived, he painted them. No matter where he was, he painted what he *could* paint. What he omitted from his art is the world of money and possessions and business that his parents admired and had sought for their children. He pursued his own path and, although he took many others on this journey, finally he pursued it alone.

CAMILLE PISSARRO

A BIBLIOGRAPHIC ESSAY

When the Wildenstein Institute published its massive three-volume catalogue raisonné of the paintings of Camille Pissarro in 2005, the bibliography alone occupied thirty-three large pages, each set in four columns in very small type. The persistent and detailed work of the painter's great-grandson Joachim Pissarro, his colleague Claire Durand-Ruel Snollaerts, and their assistants, Alexia de Buffévent and Annie Champié, had produced a cornucopia of references, many from the painter's lifetime. Indeed, it would take almost a lifetime simply to read the works cited in that bibliography. For many who study Impressionism, the sheer size of the bibliography came as a surprise given Pissarro's secondary status among the Impressionists. The bibliography is nonetheless considerably smaller than those devoted to his friends and colleagues Monet, Renoir, Degas, Cézanne, and Gauguin. For the purposes of this investigation of the painter's representations of human figures, there are a few works that are essential for an interested English-speaking reader.

The primary documents for a study of Pissarro's life, art, and thought are found in his massive correspondence. Ranking in scale and range with the correspondence of Van Gogh, Pissarro's letters, both published and unpublished, are the most important period documents for the study of Impressionism. Since the appearance in 1980 of the first of five volumes of Pissarro's correspondence, edited and scrupulously annotated by Janine Bailly-Herzberg, these letters have been easily accessible to scholars with a working knowledge of French. There is only one available resource in English, a selection of letters written by Pissarro to his oldest son, Lucien, edited by the first great scholar of Impressionism, John Rewald, originally published in 1943 and recently rereleased by the Museum of

Fine Arts, Boston. Entitled *Camille Pissarro: Letters to His Son Lucien,* this collection is somewhat awkwardly translated but remains the best single source for Pissarro's own ideas in English. Unfortunately, the large groups of letters written *to* Pissarro by a wide variety of men and women have never been published or digitized; they are in the Bibliothèque Nationale in Paris, the Ashmolean Museum at Oxford, and other public and private archives.

Perhaps because of his exotic non-European origins and his fascinating life, Pissarro has been the subject of several biographies. Indeed, his life is almost as interesting as his art, which is not true of his contemporaries Monet, Renoir, Sisley, and Cézanne. Among his friends, perhaps only Degas and Gauguin lived lives of comparable interest and complexity. Irving Stone's *Depths of Glory: A Biographical Novel of Camille Pissarro* (New York: Doubleday, 1985), although the most widely read biography of Pissarro and based extensively on the artist's life, is not included in the catalogue raisonné's vast bibliography, undoubtedly because it is, in the end, a work of historical fiction. Two biographies in English are noteworthy. Although published in 1978, before Bailly-Herzberg's five-volume *Correspondance,* Kathleen Adler's *Camille Pissarro: A Biography* (New York: St. Martin's Press) is a superbly paced and clearly written life. It was, however, surpassed in 1980 by Ralph Shikes and Paula Harper's *Pissarro: His Life and Work* (New York: Horizon Press). Harper worked with archival sources unavailable to Adler, and she was allowed access to many of the letters gathered by Bailly-Herzberg, thus giving this longer biography a real grounding in Pissarro's own thought. But the principal advantage of this book is the left-wing credentials of Shikes, who was the first among Pissarro's many students to give full sway to his anarchist philosophy and his political thought. Its chapter on Pissarro's anarchism was a particular inspiration for the present book.

The best source of biographical material for Pissarro is the superb chronology compiled for the catalogue raisonné by Alexia de Buffévent, which completely revolutionizes our idea of the painter's life, rendering the two earlier biographies and Stone's biographical novel obsolete. It should be read by everyone interested in modern painting because of its record of Pissarro's densely packed family and professional life.

Before the lengthy critical essay by Joachim Pissarro in the catalogue raisonné, there is little doubt that the best general study of the artist was written by the same author. Titled simply *Camille Pissarro* (New York: Abrams, 1993), this book is at once a biography and a critical study of Pissarro's art, and it is worthwhile just for its generous selection of color plates, many of which show works in private collections, little known to scholars and general readers interested in Impressionism. It firmly supplanted Rewald's earlier monograph of 1963 as well as Christopher Lloyd's monographs of 1979 and 1981.

Except in Japan, where his work resonates, Pissarro has not been very well served by international exhibitions. Indeed, the last major retrospective held in museums in Paris, London, and Boston closed in August of 1981, although smaller retrospective exhibitions have since been held in Tokyo, Stuttgart, Tel Aviv, and Sydney. None of these has produced a catalogue with any substantial contribution to scholarship. Specialized exhibitions dealing with Pissarro's cityscapes as well as his early landscapes have produced catalogues with new insights and material. *The Impressionist and the City: Pissarro's Series Paintings* (New Haven: Yale University Press, 1992), written by Joachim Pissarro and the present author, was the first attempt to consider this major body of work independently of Pissarro's career as a landscape painter and was, in important senses, a model for *Pissarro's People.* Katherine Rothkopf's exhibition *Pissarro: Creating the Impressionist Landscape* was accompanied by a slender catalogue (London: Philip Wilson, 2006) with sensitive readings of individual paintings.

Although Pissarro makes an appearance in every general history of Impressionism, his seminal role in the training of the next generation of painters—most notably Cézanne, Gauguin, Seurat, and Van Gogh—is rarely adequately recognized, and, as he himself predicted, he remains quite far back in the line of Impressionists, with Monet, Renoir, and Degas struggling through their historian and critic surrogates to be at the front. The exceptions to this, while major, are limited to explorations of the relationship between Pissarro and Cézanne, as seen in a superb exhibition held in New York, Los Angeles, and Paris and organized by Joachim Pissarro. Professor Pissarro also dealt with this relationship in greater depth in the book based on his brilliant doctoral dissertation and related book, *Cézanne/Pissarro, Johns/Rauschenberg: Comparative Studies in Intersubjectivity in Modern Art* (Cambridge: Cambridge University Press, 2006).

Pissarro's intensely productive and creative role in the development of Impressionist painting, theory, and exhibition practice began to be recognized seriously in 1986 with the publication of *The New Painting: Impressionism, 1874–1886* (Fine Arts Museums of San Francisco) by Charles S. Moffett et al., which was the first scholarly attempt to reconstruct each of the eight Impressionist exhibitions held in Paris during those years. This book and its immensely detailed two-volume documentation, published ten years later (Fine Arts Museums of San Francisco, 1996), place Pissarro and his oeuvre securely at the center of Impressionist exhibition practice. Indeed, it was this intensely detailed documentary study that proved the centrality of Pissarro's art to the movement, even if he received comparatively short shrift in the critical press during his lifetime. The two volumes of documentation of those eight exhibitions, edited by Ruth Berson, complete this work and bring a wealth of contemporary art criticism to the attention of French-speaking scholars.

Students interested in Pissarro's own extensive reading in anarchist literature can refer to a wealth of material in print; however, these publications can also be found on an extraordinary website compiled and edited by Professor Dana Ward of Pitzer College. Ward's Anarchy Archives (http://dwardmac.pitzer.edu/anarchist_archives) includes all major texts by the nineteenth-century anarchists read by Pissarro, many in English translation. For those who want to dip their toes into this fascinating literature, it is best to begin with the writings of Pierre-Joseph Proudhon and Peter Kropotkin. The website also contains fascinating biographies, bibliographies, and discussions of the works of lesser-known anarchists close to Pissarro, including Élisée Reclus, Jean Grave, and Bernard Lazare.

LENDERS TO THE EXHIBITION

Amgueddfa Cymru—National Museum Wales
The Art Institute of Chicago
Ashmolean Museum, University of Oxford
Jean Bonna, Geneva
The British Museum, London
Cheryl A. Chase and Stuart Bear
Chrysler Museum of Art, Norfolk, Virginia
Columbus Museum of Art
Dallas Museum of Art
Mr. Jorge Eljuri Antón Collection
The Fitzwilliam Museum, Cambridge
Ann and Gordon Getty
Giraud Pissarro Segalot
Mr. and Mrs. J. Honigberg, Chicago
Mr. and Mrs. Klaas H. Hummel
Joslyn Art Museum, Omaha, Nebraska
Kunsthalle Bremen
The Metropolitan Museum of Art, New York
Michele and Donald D'Amour Museum of Fine Arts, Springfield, Massachusetts
Musée d'Orsay, Paris
Museum of Fine Arts, Boston
National Gallery of Art, Washington, D.C.
The National Museum of Western Art, Tokyo
The Nelson-Atkins Museum of Art, Kansas City, Missouri
Ohara Museum of Art
Philadelphia Museum of Art
Joachim Pissarro
Lionel and Sandrine Pissarro
Private collections
Sir Tim Rice
Barbara Stern Shapiro
Sterling and Francine Clark Art Institute, Williamstown, Massachusetts
Tate
The Tia Collection
Toledo Museum of Art
Bruce and Robbi Toll
Wadsworth Atheneum Museum of Art, Hartford, Connecticut
The Whitworth Art Gallery, The University of Manchester
Diane B. Wilsey

WORKS IN THE EXHIBITION

All works in this exhibition are by Camille Pissarro (1830–1903). Unless otherwise indicated below, all artworks will be presented at both the Sterling and Francine Clark Art Institute, Williamstown, Massachusetts, and the Legion of Honor, San Francisco.

PDR numbers [and titles or dates, if different from those provided by lenders] correspond to: Pissarro, Joachim, and Claire Durand-Ruel Snollaerts. *Pissarro: Critical Catalogue of Paintings*. 3 vols. Milan: Skira; Paris: Wildenstein Institute, 2005.

PV numbers [and titles or dates, if different from those provided by lenders] correspond to: Pissarro, Ludovic-Rodo, and Lionello Venturi. *Camille Pissarro: Son art, son oeuvre*. 2 vols. Paris: Paul Rosenberg, 1939.

D numbers [and titles or dates, if different from those provided by lenders] correspond to: Delteil, Loys. *Le peintre-graveur illustré*. Vol. 17, *Camille Pissarro, Alfred Sisley, Auguste Renoir*. Paris: Chez l'auteur, 1923.

BL numbers [and titles or dates, if different from those provided by lenders] correspond to: Brettell, Richard, and Christopher Lloyd. *A Catalogue of the Drawings by Camille Pissarro in the Ashmolean Museum, Oxford*. Oxford: Clarendon Press; New York: Oxford University Press, 1980.

PAINTINGS

Two Women Chatting by the Sea, Saint Thomas, 1856 (fig. 43)
Oil on canvas
10⅞ × 16⅛ in. (27.7 × 41 cm)
National Gallery of Art, Washington, collection of Mr. and Mrs. Paul Mellon, 1985.64.30
PDR 23 [*Two Women Chatting by the Sea*]

Donkey Ride at La Roche-Guyon, ca. 1865 (fig. 45)
Oil on canvas
13¹³⁄₁₆ × 20⅜ in. (35 × 51.7 cm)
Collection of Sir Tim Rice
PDR 105

Jeanne Pissarro, Called Minette, Sitting in the Garden, Pontoise, ca. 1872 (fig. 58)
Oil on canvas
28¾ × 23⅝ in. (73 × 60 cm)
Private collection
PDR 256

Minette, ca. 1872 (fig. 57)
Oil on canvas
18¹⁄₁₆ × 14 in. (46 × 35 cm)
Wadsworth Atheneum Museum of Art, Hartford, Connecticut, The Ella Gallup Sumner and Mary Catlin Sumner Collection Fund, 1958.144
PDR 282 [*Portrait of Jeanne Pissarro, Called Minette*]

Self-Portrait, 1873 (fig. 2)
Oil on canvas
22 × 18⁵⁄₁₆ in. (56 × 46.5 cm)
Musée d'Orsay, Paris, gift of Paul-Émile Pissarro, 1930, RF 2837
PDR 283

Harvesting Potatoes, Pontoise, 1874 (fig. 87)
Oil on canvas
13 × 16⅛ in. (33 × 41 cm)
Private collection
PDR 360

Jeanne Holding a Fan, ca. 1874 (fig. 60)
Oil on canvas
22 × 18¼ in. (56 × 46.5 cm)
Ashmolean Museum, University of Oxford, Pissarro Family Gift, 1951, WA1952.6.2
PDR 325 [*Jeanne Pissarro Called Minette Holding a Fan*]

The Maidservant, 1875 (fig. 92)
Oil on canvas
35 × 27 in. (88.9 × 68.6 cm)
Chrysler Museum of Art, Norfolk, Virginia, gift of Walter P. Chrysler, Jr., 71.530
PDR 418 [*The Maid at Pontoise*, ca. 1875]

The Sower and the Plowman, Montfoucault, 1875 (fig. 90)
Oil on canvas
18⅛ × 22 in. (46 × 56 cm)
Jorge Eljuri Antón Collection
PDR 425

Child with Drum, 1877 (fig. 67)
Oil on canvas
21⅝ × 18⅛ in. (55 × 46 cm)
Collection of Diane B. Wilsey
PDR 505

Madame Pissarro Sewing beside a Window, ca. 1877 (fig. 55)
Oil on canvas
21¼ × 17¾ in. (54 × 45 cm)
Ashmolean Museum, University of Oxford, Pissarro Family Gift, 1951, WA1951.225.3
PDR 534 [*Julie Pissarro Sewing, the "Red House," Pontoise*]

Portrait of Eugène Murer, 1878 (fig. 83)
Oil on canvas
25⅝ × 21⅜ in. (64.4 × 54.3 cm) (oval)
Michele and Donald D'Amour Museum of Fine Arts, Springfield, Massachusetts, the James Philip Gray Collection, 52.01
PDR 582

Père Melon Resting, ca. 1879 (fig. 124)
Oil on canvas
21¼ × 25⅝ in. (54 × 65 cm)
Courtesy of Giraud Pissarro Segalot
PDR 609

Washerwoman, Study, 1880 (fig. 140)
Oil on canvas
28¾ × 23¼ in. (73 × 59.1 cm)
The Metropolitan Museum of Art, gift of Mr. and Mrs. Nate B. Spingold, 1956, 56.184.1
PDR 640 [*Mère Larchevêque*]

Apple-Picking, 1881 (fig. 158)
Oil on canvas
25 9/16 × 21¼ in. (65 × 54 cm)
Collection of Mr. and Mrs. Klaas H. Hummel
PDR 659

Peasant Woman Gathering Grass, 1881 (fig. 130)
Oil on canvas
45 11/16 × 35 7/16 in. (116 × 90 cm)
Private collection, United States
PDR 657

Peasants Resting, 1881 (fig. 129)
Oil on canvas
32 × 25¾ in. (81 × 65 cm)
The Toledo Museum of Art, Ohio, purchased with funds from the Libbey Endowment, gift of Edward Drummond Libbey, 1935.6
PDR 655 [*Peasant Women Resting*]

Portrait of Félix Pissarro, 1881 (fig. 68)
Oil on canvas
21¾ × 18¼ in. (55.2 × 46.4 cm)
Tate: Bequeathed by Lucien Pissarro, the artist's son, 1944, N05574
PDR 663 [*Félix Pissarro Wearing a Red Beret*]

Young Peasant Woman Drinking Her Café au Lait, 1881 (fig. 143)
Oil on canvas
25 11/16 × 21 9/16 in. (65.3 × 54.8 cm)
The Art Institute of Chicago, Potter Palmer Collection, 1922.433
PDR 662 [*The Breakfast, Young Peasant Girl Having Café au Lait*]

The Harvest, 1882 (fig. 116)
Tempera on canvas
27 11/16 × 49 9/16 in. (70.3 × 126 cm)
The National Museum of Western Art, Tokyo, donated by the heirs of Mr. Kojiro Matsukata, P.1984-3
PV 1358

In the Garden at Pontoise: A Young Woman Washing Dishes, 1882 (fig. 95)
Oil on canvas
32¼ × 25 11/16 in. (81.9 × 65.3 cm)
The Syndics of the Fitzwilliam Museum, Cambridge, acquired with the assistance of the National Art Collections Fund, 1947, PD.53-1947
PDR 685 [*Washing Up*]

The Little Country Maid, 1882 (fig. 93)
Oil on canvas
25 × 20⅞ in. (63.5 × 53 cm)
Tate: Bequeathed by Lucien Pissarro, the artist's son, 1944, N05575
PDR 681 [*The Young Country Servant*]

Peasant Woman Lying in the Grass, Pontoise, 1882 (fig. 136)
Oil on canvas
25⅜ × 30¾ in. (64.5 × 78 cm)
Kunsthalle Bremen—Der Kunstverein in Bremen, 960-1967/8
PDR 683 [*The Nap, Peasant Woman Lying in the Grass, Pontoise*]
Clark only

Peasant Women Weeding, Pontoise, 1882 (fig. 131)
Oil on canvas
24 13/16 × 30 5/16 in. (63 × 77 cm)
Private collection, Switzerland
PDR 671

Woman and Child at the Well, 1882 (fig. 137)
Oil on canvas
32⅛ × 26⅛ in. (81.5 × 66.4 cm)
The Art Institute of Chicago, Potter Palmer Collection, 1922.436
PDR 688 [*Woman and Child at a Well*]

Horse Market, Saint-Martin Fair, Pontoise, 1883 (fig. 180)
Tempera on fine canvas
6$\frac{5}{16}$ × 11$\frac{5}{8}$ in. (16 × 29.5 cm)
Private collection, France
PV 1372

The Pork Butcher, 1883 (fig. 175)
Oil on canvas
25$\frac{5}{8}$ × 21$\frac{3}{8}$ in. (65.1 × 54.3 cm)
Tate: Bequeathed by Lucien Pissarro, the artist's son, 1944, N05576
PDR 706 [*The Charcutière*]

The Gardener—Old Peasant with Cabbage, 1883–1895 (fig. 126)
Oil on canvas
32$\frac{1}{16}$ × 25$\frac{9}{16}$ in. (81.5 × 65 cm)
National Gallery of Art, Washington, collection of Mr. and Mrs. Paul Mellon, 1994.59.6
PDR 710 [*Sorting Cabbages*]

Apple-Picking, 1886 (fig. 155)
Oil on canvas
49½ × 50⅛ in. (125.8 × 127.4 cm)
Ohara Museum of Art, 1008
PDR 824

Apple Harvest, 1888 (fig. 224)
Oil on canvas
24 × 29⅛ in. (61 × 74 cm)
Dallas Museum of Art, Munger Fund, 1955.17.M
PDR 850 [*Apple-Picking, Éragny*, 1887–1888]

Haymakers, Evening, Éragny, 1893 (fig. 228)
Oil on canvas
21⅜ × 25¾ in. (54 × 65 cm)
Joslyn Art Museum, Endowment Fund Purchase, JAM1946.28
PDR 1005

Portrait of Félix Reading, 1893 (fig. 69)
Oil on canvas
18⅛ × 15 in. (46 × 38 cm)
Private collection
PDR 988 [*Félix Pissarro Reading*]
Clark only

Market at Pontoise, 1895 (fig. 176)
Oil on canvas
18¼ × 15⅛ in. (46.3 × 38.4 cm)
The Nelson-Atkins Museum of Art, Kansas City, Missouri, purchase: The William Rockhill Nelson Trust, 33-150
PDR 1097 [*Gisors Market*]

Woman, Called "La Rosa," Pulling Up Her Stocking, 1895
Oil on canvas
15 × 18½ in. (38.1 × 47 cm)
The Tia Collection
PDR 1099

Paul-Émile Pissarro Painting (Sketch), 1898 (fig. 73)
Oil on canvas
21¾ × 18¼ in. (55.2 × 46.4 cm)
Courtesy of Giraud Pissarro Segalot
PDR 1244

Self-Portrait, ca. 1898 (fig. 233)
Oil on canvas
20⅞ × 12 in. (53 × 30.5 cm)
Dallas Museum of Art, the Wendy and Emery Reves Collection, 1985.R.44
PDR 1129 [*Self-Portrait with Palette*, ca. 1896]

Jeanne Pissarro, Called Cocotte, Reading, 1899 (fig. 77)
Oil on canvas
22 × 26⅜ in. (56 × 67 cm)
Collection of Ann and Gordon Getty
PDR 1297

Portrait of Paul-Émile Pissarro, 1899 (fig. 74)
Oil on canvas
25$\frac{9}{16}$ × 21¼ in. (65 × 54 cm)
Collection of Joel and Carol Honigberg, Chicago
PDR 1248 [*Paul-Émile Pissarro Holding a Book*]

Ludovic-Rodolphe Pissarro Reading, ca. 1899 (fig. 75)
Oil on canvas
7⅛ × 9⅝ in. (18.2 × 24.4 cm)
Collection of Cheryl A. Chase and Stuart Bear
PDR 1247
Clark only

Self-Portrait, 1903 (fig. 251)
Oil on canvas
16⅛ × 13⅛ in. (41 × 33.3 cm)
Tate: Presented by Lucien Pissarro, the artist's son, 1931, N04592
PDR 1528 [*Self-Portrait with Hat*]

PRINTS AND DRAWINGS (INCLUDING PASTELS, WATERCOLORS, AND GOUACHES)

Nude, ca. 1855 (fig. 99)
Conté crayon and white chalk on blue laid paper
23⅝ × 17 11/16 in. (60 × 45 cm)
Collection of Joachim Pissarro

Portrait of Lucien Pissarro as a Young Boy, 1868–1870 (fig. 63)
Brush drawing in dark ink heightened with Chinese white on dark-green paper prepared with brown wash
10 × 13⅞ in. (25.4 × 35.2 cm)
Ashmolean Museum, University of Oxford, Pissarro Family Gift, 1951, WA1952.6.64
BL 45

Jeanne-Rachel Pissarro Seated at a Table, ca. 1872–1874 (fig. 51)
Watercolor over black chalk on off-white paper
9⅝ × 7½ in. (24.5 × 19.2 cm)
Ashmolean Museum, University of Oxford, Pissarro Family Gift, 1952, WA1952.6.97
BL 70

Dead Child, 1874 (fig. 62)
Lithograph on off-white wove paper
Image: 8 9/16 × 10 11/16 in. (21.7 × 27.2 cm); sheet: 12⅛ × 15⅝ in. (30.8 × 39.7 cm)
The Art Institute of Chicago, gift of Celia and David Hilliard, 2007.652
D 129, only state

Portrait of the Artist's Son, Lucien, 1874 (fig. 65)
Lithograph on blued white wove paper
Image: 8¼ × 11 in. (21 × 28 cm); sheet: 9 5/16 × 11 13/16 in. (23.7 × 30 cm)
Museum of Fine Arts, Boston, Stephen Bullard Memorial Fund, 1972.54
D 128, only state [*Portrait: Lucien Pissarro*]

Portrait of Paul Cézanne, 1874 (fig. 80)
Etching on beige laid paper
Plate: 10½ × 8 7/16 in. (26.6 × 21.5 cm); sheet: 17½ × 13⅝ in. (44.5 × 34.6 cm)
Museum of Fine Arts, Boston, gift of Henri M. Petiet, confirmed by his estate, 2001, 2001.704
D 13, only state [*Paul Cézanne*]

Woman Selling Chestnuts, 1878 (fig. 167)
Drypoint on beige laid paper
Plate: 8⅛ × 6⅜ in. (20.6 × 16.2 cm); sheet: 11¾ × 8 7/16 in. (29.9 × 21.5 cm)
Museum of Fine Arts, Boston, fund in memory of Horatio Greenough Curtis, 60.1459
D 15 i/ii

Nearly Whole-Length Study of a Female Peasant with a Detailed Study of the Foreshortening of the Right Forearm and Hand Above, ca. 1879 (fig. 102)
Black chalk on pink paper prepared with a thin layer of Chinese white
18⅛ × 10⅞ in. (46.2 × 27.6 cm)
Ashmolean Museum, University of Oxford, Pissarro Family Gift, 1951, WA1952.6.152
BL 106

Study of a Female Peasant Cleaning a Saucepan, ca. 1879 (fig. 103)
Black chalk heightened in places with gouache on pink paper prepared with a thin layer of Chinese white
18⅜ × 12⅜ in. (46.8 × 31.6 cm)
Ashmolean Museum, University of Oxford, Pissarro Family Gift, 1951, WA1952.6.151
BL 105

Peasant Woman Lying on the Grass, ca. 1880
Pastel on paper
10⅛ × 15½ in. (25.5 × 39.5 cm)
Courtesy of Giraud Pissarro Segalot

Bust-Length Portrait of Madame Pissarro Seen in Three-Quarters Profile Facing Right, early 1880s (fig. 53)
Copying pencil with clear wash on off-white paper
8⅛ × 5 in. (20.5 × 12.5 cm)
Ashmolean Museum, University of Oxford, Pissarro Family Gift, 1951, WA1952.6.249
BL 175B

Five Studies of a Male Peasant Working, early 1880s (fig. 125)
Black chalk on off-white paper
9 × 6 13/16 in. (22.9 × 17.3 cm)
Ashmolean Museum, University of Oxford, Pissarro Family Gift, 1951, WA1952.6.158
BL 112

Study of a Female Figure Examining a Market Stall, early 1880s (fig. 184)
Black chalk on off-white paper
8½ × 6¼ in. (21.5 × 16 cm)
Ashmolean Museum, University of Oxford, Pissarro Family Gift, 1951, WA1952.6.232
BL 168H

Study of the Artist's Mother with Her Maid, ca. 1880–1885 (fig. 47)
Charcoal on off-white paper
11⅛ × 8⅝ in. (28.4 × 21.9 cm)
Ashmolean Museum, University of Oxford, Pissarro Family Gift, 1951, WA1952.6.202
BL 152

Compositional Study of the Market at Pontoise, 1881 (fig. 185)
Black chalk and gray wash on off-white paper
12 × 7½ in. (30.4 × 19.3 cm)
Ashmolean Museum, University of Oxford, Pissarro Family Gift, 1951, WA1952.6.173
BL 127

Studies of a Male and Female Harvester (recto); *Study of a Female Harvester with a Study of a Female Peasant Emptying a Wheelbarrow* (verso), 1881 (figs. 111–112)
Gray wash over graphite; graphite heightened with gray wash on off-white paper
5⅞ × 7⅞ in. (14.9 × 20 cm)
Ashmolean Museum, University of Oxford, Pissarro Family Gift, 1951, WA1952.6.166
BL 120

Three Studies of a Male Harvester (recto); *Four Studies of Male Harvesters* (verso), 1881 (figs. 109–110)
Gray wash over graphite; graphite heightened with gray wash on off-white paper
5⅞ × 7 7/16 in. (14.9 × 18.9 cm)
Ashmolean Museum, University of Oxford, Pissarro Family Gift, 1951, WA1952.6.165
BL 119

Woman Seen from Behind; Three-Quarter Length, Head in Profile to Right, Arms in Front, Wearing an Apron, 1881 (fig. 100)
Black, blue, and white chalk on gray paper
17½ × 12 5/16 in. (44.5 × 31.3 cm)
The British Museum, London, 1920,0712.3

Young Peasant Woman Drinking Her Café au Lait, 1881 (fig. 144)
Black chalk on tan laid paper, laid down on cream wove paper
24⅛ × 18¾ in. (61.3 × 47.5 cm)
The Art Institute of Chicago, Regenstein Endowment Fund, 2010.540

Four Studies of a Male Peasant Flailing (recto); *Three Studies of Male Harvesters* (verso), ca. 1881 (figs. 113–114)
Charcoal on faded blue paper
12 × 9 in. (30.5 × 23 cm)
Ashmolean Museum, University of Oxford, Pissarro Family Gift, 1951, WA1952.6.167
BL 121

Study of Two Female Harvesters, 1881–1882 (fig. 118)
Black chalk on pink paper prepared with a thin layer of Chinese white
16⅞ × 25⅛ in. (42.8 × 63.8 cm)
Ashmolean Museum, University of Oxford, Pissarro Family Gift, 1952, WA1952.6.169
BL 123

Study of Harvesters Working in a Field near Pontoise, ca. 1881–1882 (fig. 117)
Brush drawing in gray wash on squared off-white paper printed in brown ink
10^13/16 × 18⅞ in. (27.5 × 47.8 cm)
Ashmolean Museum, University of Oxford, Pissarro Family Gift, 1951, WA1952.6.168
BL 122

The Marketplace, 1882 (fig. 178)
Gouache on paper
31¾ × 25½ in. (80.6 × 64.8 cm)
Courtesy of The Metropolitan Museum of Art, private collection, L.1984.54.1
PV 1361 [*Poultry Market, Pontoise*]

Portrait of Lucien Pissarro, 1882 (fig. 66)
Black chalk on off-white paper
5^11/16 × 3⅞ in. (14.5 × 9.8 cm)
Ashmolean Museum, University of Oxford, Pissarro Family Gift, 1951, WA1952.6.206
BL 155B

Portrait of Madame Pissarro, 1882 (fig. 54)
Black chalk on off-white paper
5^11/16 × 3⅞ in. (14.5 × 9.8 cm)
Ashmolean Museum, University of Oxford, Pissarro Family Gift, 1951, WA1952.6.205
BL 155A

Study of a Female Peasant Arranging Her Scarf, ca. 1882–1883
Pastel on paper mounted on canvas
21⅝ × 17¾ in. (55 × 45 cm)
Courtesy of Giraud Pissarro Segalot
PV 1562 [*Peasant Woman in a Blue Apron Arranging Her Scarf in a Field*]

Portrait of Ludovic-Rodo Pissarro, ca. 1883–1884 (fig. 70)
Black chalk on off-white paper
8¾ × 6½ in. (21.1 × 16.7 cm)
Ashmolean Museum, University of Oxford, Pissarro Family Gift, 1951, WA1952.6.203
BL 153

Young Female Peasant Leaning against a Tree (The Shepherdess), ca. 1884 (fig. 104)
Chalk and watercolor on paper
19^15/16 × 15^5/16 in. (50.6 × 39 cm)
The Whitworth Art Gallery, The University of Manchester, D.1946.11

Poultry Market at Gisors, 1885 (fig. 177)
Gouache and black chalk on brown paper mounted on canvas
32⅜ × 32⅜ in. (82.2 × 82.2 cm)
Museum of Fine Arts, Boston, bequest of John T. Spaulding, 48.588
PV 1400

Young Woman Standing, Holding a Stick in Her Hands, or *Peasant Woman in a Blue Apron; Study for* Apple-Picking, ca. 1885 (fig. 105)
Pastel over charcoal sketch on cream laid paper
24⅛ × 18½ in. (61.2 × 47 cm)
Musée d'Orsay, Paris, kept in the Department of Graphic Arts, Musée du Louvre, RF 29537

Marketplace in Pontoise, 1886 (fig. 187)
Graphite and pen and black-gummed ink on buff wove paper; right margin torn from notebook
6⅝ × 5 in. (16.8 × 12.7 cm)
The Metropolitan Museum of Art, Robert Lehman Collection, 1975, 1975.1.679

Pig Market, Saint-Martin Fair—Pontoise, ca. 1886 (fig. 186)
Pen and ink on chine over traces of graphite
6⅞ × 5 in. (17.5 × 12.7 cm)
Musée d'Orsay, Paris, gift of Max Kaganovitch, 1970, kept in the Department of Graphic Arts, Musée du Louvre, RF 36502

Tending Cattle, Éragny, 1887
Gouache on paper
$21\frac{1}{4} \times 25\frac{9}{16}$ in. (54 × 65 cm)
Private collection
PV 1416

The Gisors Market, 1887 (fig. 181)
Black ink, gouache, and watercolor heightened with lead white on paper
$12\frac{1}{4} \times 9\frac{1}{2}$ in. (31 × 24 cm)
Columbus Museum of Art, Ohio, gift of Howard D. and Babette L. Sirak, the Donors to the Campaign for Enduring Excellence, and the Derby Fund, 1991.001.051
PV 1413 [*The Market at Pontoise*]

The Market at Gisors, 1887 (fig. 188)
Watercolor on cream paper
$12\frac{3}{8} \times 9\frac{7}{16}$ in. (31.4 × 24 cm)
Museum of Fine Arts, Boston, M. and M. Karolik Fund, 1973.144

Picking Peas, 1887
Gouache on paper
$20\frac{7}{16} \times 24\frac{13}{16}$ in. (52 × 63 cm)
Private collection
PV 1408 [*Pea Harvest*]

The Maid Shopping, 1888 (fig. 169)
Etching and drypoint printed in brown-black on off-white wove paper
Plate: $7\frac{1}{2} \times 5\frac{3}{16}$ in. (19 × 13.2 cm);
sheet: $7\frac{13}{16} \times 5\frac{1}{2}$ in. (19.8 × 14 cm)
Sterling and Francine Clark Art Institute, Williamstown, Massachusetts, 1962.90
D 74 i/iv

The Maid Shopping, 1888
Drypoint on beige laid paper
Plate: $7\frac{13}{16} \times 5\frac{7}{16}$ in. (19.8 × 13.8 cm);
sheet: 11 × 9 in. (28 × 22.8 cm)
Museum of Fine Arts, Boston, gift of Mr. and Mrs. Peter A. Wick, 61.1179
D 74 iv/iv

Grandmother (The Artist's Mother), 1889 (fig. 48)
Etching and aquatint on cream laid paper
Plate: $6\frac{3}{4} \times 10\frac{1}{8}$ in. (17.1 × 25.7 cm);
sheet: $7\frac{15}{16} \times 12\frac{1}{4}$ in. (20.1 × 31.1 cm)
Museum of Fine Arts, Boston, fund in memory of Horatio Greenough Curtis, 62.482
D 80 vii/vii [*Grandmother: The Artist's Mother*]

Les turpitudes sociales, 1889–1890 (figs. 190–221)
Thirty pen and brown ink over graphite drawings on paper pasted in an album
Album: $12\frac{1}{4} \times 9\frac{1}{2}$ in. (31 × 24 cm)
Collection of Jean Bonna, Geneva

Portrait of the Artist, ca. 1890 (fig. 49)
Etching on beige laid paper
Plate: $7\frac{3}{16} \times 6\frac{7}{8}$ in. (18.3 × 17.4 cm);
sheet: $13\frac{7}{16} \times 9\frac{13}{16}$ in. (34.2 × 25 cm)
Museum of Fine Arts, Boston, Lee M. Friedman Fund, 60.249
D 90 ii/ii [*Camille Pissarro, a Self-Portrait*]

Full-Length Standing Nude of a Woman, from Behind, 1890s (fig. 107)
Pastel on pink paper
$18\frac{13}{16} \times 9\frac{9}{16}$ in. (47.5 × 24.3 cm)
The Syndics of the Fitzwilliam Museum, Cambridge, PD.51-1947

The Marketplace, Gisors, 1891 (fig. 182)
Gouache over traces of charcoal on fabric mounted to thin cardboard
$14 \times 10\frac{1}{4}$ in. (35.6 × 26 cm)
Philadelphia Museum of Art, The Louis E. Stern Collection, 1963, 1963-181-55
PV 1465 [*The Gisors Market, with a Peasant Woman Sitting on a Basket in the Foreground*]

Peasants and Peasant Woman Arranging Her Scarf, 1891
Gouache on paper
$11\frac{7}{8} \times 22\frac{7}{8}$ in. (30 × 58 cm)
Courtesy of Giraud Pissarro Segalot
PV 1655

Poultry Market at Gisors, 1891 (fig. 170)
Etching on cream laid paper
Plate: 9 13/16 × 7 3/8 in. (25 × 18.8 cm);
sheet: 12 5/8 × 8 in. (32.1 × 20.3 cm)
Museum of Fine Arts, Boston, Lee M. Friedman Fund, 1981.135
D 98 i/ii

The Market at Gisors, Rue Cappeville, ca. 1894 (fig. 171)
Etching printed in grayish black, red, blue, and yellow on ivory laid paper
Plate: 7 7/8 × 5 1/2 in. (20 × 14 cm);
sheet: 10 11/16 × 7 13/16 in. (27.1 × 19.9 cm)
Sterling and Francine Clark Art Institute, Williamstown, Massachusetts, 1962.93
D 112 vii/vii, proof

The Market at Pontoise, ca. 1895 (fig. 173)
Lithograph on ivory chine collé on ivory laid paper
Image: 11 7/8 × 8 11/16 in. (30.1 × 22.1 cm);
sheet: 17 11/16 × 12 5/16 in. (44.8 × 31.2 cm)
Sterling and Francine Clark Art Institute, Williamstown, Massachusetts, 1962.95
D 147 iii/iii, proof

Two Sudies of a Girl, ca. 1895 (fig. 108)
Black chalk and pastel on pink paper
18 3/4 × 24 15/16 in. (47.6 × 61.8 cm)
Amgueddfa Cymru—National Museum Wales, NMWA 1697
Clark only

Young Man Writing, Portrait of Rodo; Paul-Émile Pissarro, ca. 1895 (see fig. 71 for alternate impression)
Lithograph on wove paper
Image: 4 3/4 × 4 5/8 in. (12.1 × 11.7 cm)
and 3 3/4 × 4 1/2 in. (9.5 × 11.4 cm);
sheet: 14 1/8 × 10 5/8 in. (35.9 × 26.2 cm)
Collection of Barbara Stern Shapiro
D 145, only state / D 146, only state

The Market at Gisors (Rue Cappeville), mid-1890s (fig. 172)
Etching and drypoint, colored with crayon on white paper
Plate: 7 3/4 × 5 1/2 in. (19.8 × 14.1 cm);
sheet: 11 × 8 1/8 in. (27.8 × 20.5 cm)
Ashmolean Museum, University of Oxford, presented by Miss Orovida Pissarro, 1953, WA1953.88.1
BL 299

Three Studies of Women Dressing, ca. 1895–1900 (fig. 101)
Colored chalks on pink paper
18 1/8 × 23 15/16 in. (46.1 × 60.8 cm)
The British Museum, London, 1920,0712.2

The Plow (frontispiece for *Les temps nouveaux*), 1898
Lithograph printed in olive green, red, blue, and yellow on ivory wove paper
Image: 8 13/16 × 5 7/8 in. (22.4 × 15 cm);
sheet: 15 11/16 × 11 7/16 in. (39.8 × 29.1 cm)
Sterling and Francine Clark Art Institute, Williamstown, Massachusetts, 1962.96
D 194 ii/iii, proof

INDEX

Page numbers in *italics* refer to illustrations. All artworks are by Camille Pissarro unless otherwise indicated.

PHOTOGRAPHY CREDITS

Frontispieces, pages 2–3: photo by Lars Lohrisch, courtesy of Kunsthalle Bremen—Der Kunstverein in Bremen (detail of fig. 136); 4: Archives L&S Pissarro; 5: photo by Hervé Lewandowski, Réunion des Musées Nationaux / Art Resource, NY (detail of fig. 2).

Table of contents, pages 6–7 (left to right): courtesy of Archives L&S Pissarro; courtesy of the Ashmolean Museum, University of Oxford (detail of fig. 63); photography © The Art Institute of Chicago (detail of fig. 147); courtesy of the Ashmolean Museum, University of Oxford (detail of fig. 102); © The Trustees of the British Museum (detail of fig. 100); courtesy of the Ashmolean Museum, University of Oxford (detail of fig. 51); © Fitzwilliam Museum, Cambridge (detail of fig. 107); image courtesy of the Board of Trustees, National Gallery of Art, Washington (detail of fig. 126); courtesy of the Ashmolean Museum, University of Oxford (detail of fig. 132); photo by René-Gabriel Ojéda, Réunion des Musées Nationaux / Art Resource, NY (detail of fig. 146); courtesy of the Ashmolean Museum, University of Oxford (detail of fig. 34); courtesy of the Ashmolean Museum, University of Oxford (detail of fig. 60); photography © The Art Institute of Chicago (detail of fig. 237); photography © The Art Institute of Chicago (detail of fig. 143); courtesy of the Ashmolean Museum, University of Oxford (detail of fig. 61); photograph © 2011 Museum of Fine Arts, Boston (detail of fig. 49).

Figs. 1, 3, 16–25, 27–31, 46, 73, 78, 91, 120, 124, 157, 222, 230, 234–235, 241, 250: courtesy of Archives L&S Pissarro; 2, 123: photo by Hervé Lewandowski, Réunion des Musées Nationaux / Art Resource, NY; 4, 6, 187, 236: image copyright © The Metropolitan Museum of Art / Art Resource, NY; 5: courtesy of the Solomon R. Guggenheim Museum, New York; 7, 88, 156: courtesy of the Foundation E. G. Bührle Collection; 8, 44, 56, 128, 166, 231: courtesy of Archives du Wildenstein Institute, Paris; 9, 38: courtesy of Sotheby's Picture Library; 10: courtesy of The J. Paul Getty Museum, Los Angeles; 11: photo by Jörg P. Anders, Bildarchiv Preussischer Kulturbesitz / Art Resource, NY; 12: courtesy of the Phillips Family Collection; 26, 81: © Graff Diamonds Ltd., courtesy of National Gallery Picture Library; 13, 71: courtesy of the New York Public Library; 14: Tel Aviv Museum of Art, Israel / The Bridgeman Art Library; 15: National Gallery, London / The Bridgeman Art Library; 32, 43, 82, 115, 126, 141–142, 239: image courtesy of the Board of Trustees, National Gallery of Art, Washington; 33–36, 39, 47, 51, 53–55, 60–61, 63–64, 66, 70, 97–98, 102–103, 106, 109–114, 117–118, 125, 132, 159, 164, 172, 184–185, 189, 238, 242–249: courtesy of the Ashmolean Museum, University of Oxford; 37, 40–41: courtesy of the Olana State Historic Site, New York; 42: Snark / Art Resource, NY; 45, 84, 87, 130: courtesy of private collections; 48–49, 65, 80, 167, 170, 177, 188: photograph © 2011 Museum of Fine Arts, Boston; 50: Réunion des Musées Nationaux / Art Resource, NY; 52: courtesy of Moeller Fine Art, New York–Berlin; 57: Wadsworth Atheneum Museum of Art / Art Resource, NY; 58: © Christie's Images Limited 2011; 59, 145: courtesy of the Yale University Art Gallery; 62, 137, 143–144, 147, 154, 237: photography © The Art Institute of Chicago; 67: courtesy of Diane B. Wilsey; 68, 93, 175, 251: © Tate, London 2010; 69: photo by Malcolm Varon, N.Y.C., © 2010; 72, 86, 161–162: The Bridgeman Art Library; 74: courtesy of Joel and Carol Honigberg, Chicago; 75: courtesy of Cheryl A. Chase and Stuart Bear; 76: © GRUPPE Köln, Hans G. Scheib, courtesy of Sammlung Rau für UNICEF; 77: courtesy of Ann and Gordon Getty; 79, 119, 152: Erich Lessing / Art Resource, NY; 83: photo by David Stansbury, courtesy of the Michele and Donald D'Amour Museum of Fine Arts, Springfield, Massachusetts; 85, 90, 133, 223: courtesy of Sotheby's; 89, 153, 169, 171, 173: © Sterling and Francine Clark Art Institute, Williamstown, Massachusetts (photo by Michael Agee); 92: courtesy of the Chrysler Museum of Art, Norfolk, Virginia; 94: Ole Haupt, courtesy of Ny Carlsberg Glyptotek, Copenhagen; 95, 107: © Fitzwilliam Museum, Cambridge; 96, 116, 135: courtesy of the National Museum of Western Art, Tokyo; 99: photo by Kenny Komer; 100–101: © The Trustees of the British Museum; 104: courtesy of The Whitworth Art Gallery, The University of Manchester; 105: photo by Thierry Le Mage, Réunion des Musées Nationaux / Art Resource, NY; 108: © Amgueddfa Genedlaethol Cymru—National Museum of Wales; 121: photo © Christie's Images / The Bridgeman Art Library; 122: photo by Gérard Blot, Réunion des Musées Nationaux / Art Resource, NY; 127: courtesy of Galerie Schmit, Paris; 129: Photography Incorporated, Toledo, courtesy of the Toledo Museum of Art; 131: photo by Patrick Goetelen; 134, 146: photo by René-Gabriel Ojéda, Réunion des Musées Nationaux / Art Resource, NY; 136: photo by Lars Lohrisch, courtesy of Kunsthalle Bremen—Der Kunstverein in Bremen; 138: courtesy of Gallery Itsuraku Co., Ltd.; 139, 232: digital image © 2009 Museum Associates / LACMA / Art Resource, NY; 140: photo by Malcolm Varon, image copyright © The Metropolitan Museum of Art / Art Resource, NY; 148–149: Bibliothèque nationale de France; 150: Phillips Collection, Washington, D.C. / The Bridgeman Art Library; 151: Giraudon / The Bridgeman Art Library; 155: Bridgeman-Giraudon / Art Resource, NY; 158: courtesy of Richard Green Gallery, London; 160: Sheffield Galleries and Museums Trust, UK / photo © Museums Sheffield / The Bridgeman Art Library; 163: photo by Patrice Schmidt, Réunion des Musées Nationaux / Art Resource, NY; 165, 178: private collection, image © The Metropolitan Museum of Art; 168: courtesy of the Musée de Pontoise; 174: © Norton Simon Art Foundation; 176: photo by John Lamberton, courtesy of the Nelson-Atkins Museum of Art, Kansas City, Missouri; 179: courtesy of Noortman Master Paintings; 180: private collection, courtesy of the Musée de Pontoise; 181: courtesy of the Columbus Museum of Art, Ohio; 182: courtesy of the Philadelphia Museum of Art; 183: © Culture and Sport Glasgow (Museums); 186: photo by Jean-Gilles Berizzi, Réunion des Musées Nationaux / Art Resource, NY; 190–221: photo by Patrick Goetelen, Geneva, courtesy of Jean Bonna; 224, 233: courtesy of the Dallas Museum of Art; 225: Kunstmuseum Basel, Martin P. Bühler; 226: Albright-Knox Art Gallery / Art Resource, NY; 227: © McNay Art Museum / Art Resource, NY; 228: courtesy of the Joslyn Art Museum, Omaha, Nebraska; 229: © National Gallery of Canada, Ottawa; 240: photo © Boltin Picture Library / The Bridgeman Art Library.

Published by the Fine Arts Museums of San Francisco and the Sterling and Francine Clark Art Institute on the occasion of the exhibition *Pissarro's People.*

Sterling and Francine Clark Art Institute
Williamstown, Massachusetts
June 12–October 2, 2011

Legion of Honor
San Francisco
October 22, 2011–January 22, 2012

Pissarro's People was organized by the Fine Arts Museums of San Francisco and the Sterling and Francine Clark Art Institute. It is supported in part by a grant from the National Endowment for the Arts.

NATIONAL
ENDOWMENT
FOR THE ARTS

The San Francisco presentation of *Pissarro's People* is made possible by the generous support of Jeannik Méquet Littlefield. Education programs presented in conjunction with this exhibition are generously underwritten by Denise Littlefield Sobel.

The catalogue is published with the assistance of the Andrew W. Mellon Foundation Endowment for Publications.

Photography credits appear on pages 318–319.

Library of Congress Cataloging-in-Publication Data
Brettell, Richard R.
Pissarro's people / Richard R. Brettell.
p. cm.
Published on the occasion of an exhibition held at the Sterling and Francine Clark Art Institute, Williamstown, Mass., June 12–Oct. 2, 2011 and at the Legion of Honor, San Francisco, Calif., Oct. 22, 2011–Jan. 22, 2012.
Includes bibliographical references and index.
ISBN 978-3-7913-5118-6 (hardcover) —
ISBN 978-0-88401-133-0 (pbk.)
1. Pissarro, Camille, 1830–1903—Themes, motives—Exhibitions. 2. Human beings in art—Exhibitions. I. Pissarro, Camille, 1830–1903. II. Sterling and Francine Clark Art Institute. III. Legion of Honor (San Francisco, Calif.). IV. Title.
ND553.P55A4 2011
759.4—dc22 2010047718

Pissarro's People was produced through the Publications Department of the Fine Arts Museums of San Francisco:

Karen A. Levine, Director of Publications
Leslie Dutcher, Managing Editor
Golden Gate Park
50 Hagiwara Tea Garden Drive
San Francisco, CA 94118-4502

Edited by Jennifer Boynton
Proofread by Carrie Wicks
Index by Susan G. Burke
Designed by Jeff Wincapaw
Typeset in Hoefler, with captions in Whitney, by Brynn Warriner
Color management by iocolor, Seattle
Produced by Marquand Books, Inc., Seattle
Printed and bound in China by C&C Offset Printing Co., Ltd.

The hardcover edition of this catalogue was published in 2011 in association with DelMonico Books, an imprint of Prestel Publishing:

Prestel, a member of Verlagsgruppe Random House GmbH

Prestel Verlag
Neumarkter Strasse 28
81673 Munich Germany
Tel: 49 89 4136 0
Fax: 49 89 4136 2335
www.prestel.de

Prestel Publishing Ltd.
4 Bloomsbury Place
London WC1A 2QA
United Kingdom
Tel: 44 20 7323 5004
Fax: 44 20 7636 8004

Prestel Publishing
900 Broadway, Suite 603
New York, NY 10003
Tel: 212 995 2720
Fax: 212 995 2733
E-mail: sales@prestel-usa.com
www.prestel.com

Frontispieces:
Pages 2–3: *Peasant Woman Lying in the Grass, Pontoise,* 1882 (detail of fig. 136)
Page 4: Pissarro, ca. 1895
Page 5: *Self-Portrait,* 1873 (detail of fig. 2)

Endsheets, front to back (hardcover edition only):
From left: Alfred Isaacson, Julie Pissarro, Camille Pissarro, and their children Jeanne, Georges, Félix, Ludovic-Rodolphe, and Lucien, ca. 1884
Pissarro in the apartment at 28, place Dauphine, Paris, ca. 1895
Pissarro and his son Félix, Paris, 1893
Pissarro's studio at Éragny, ca. 1901

Carnegie Learning Integrated Math III

Student Edition

Volume 2

4th Edition

David Dengler
Sandy Bartle Finocchi
William S. Hadley
Mary Lou Metz

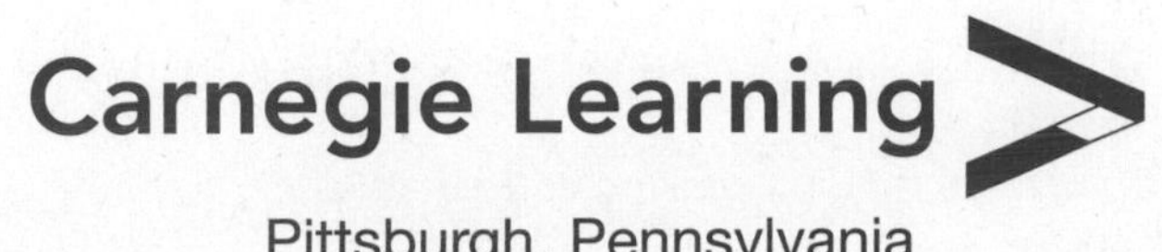

Pittsburgh, Pennsylvania

Carnegie Learning

501 Grant St., Suite 1075
Pittsburgh, PA 15219
Phone 888.851.7094
Customer Service Phone 888.851.7094, option 3

www.carnegielearning.com

Printing History
First Edition 2013
Second Edition 2014
Third Edition 2015
Fourth Edition 2016

ISBN: 978-1-60972-669-0
Set ISBN: 978-1-60972-234-0

Printed in the United States of America by Sinclair Printing Palmdale
4 5 6 7 8 SPP 22 21 20 19 18

Dear Student,

You are about to begin an exciting endeavor using mathematics! To be successful, you will need the right tools. This book is one of the most important tools you will use this year. Throughout this book there is space for note-taking, sketching, and calculating. You will be given opportunities to think and reason about various mathematical concepts and use tools such as tables, graphs, and graphing calculators.

This year you will face many new challenges both in and outside of the classroom. While some challenges may seem difficult, it is important to remember that effort matters. You must realize that it may take hard work and perseverance to succeed—and your hard work will pay off!

Connections in mathematics are important. Throughout this text, you will build new knowledge based upon your prior knowledge. It is our goal that you see mathematics as relevant because it provides a common and useful language for discussing and solving real-world problems.

I bet the folks at home would like to know what we're going to do this year!

Don't worry—you will not be working alone. Working with others is a skill that you will need throughout your life. When you begin your career, you will most likely work with all sorts of people, from shy to outgoing, from leaders to supporters, from innovators to problem solvers—and many more types of people! Throughout this book, you will have many opportunities to work with your classmates. You will be able to discuss your ideas and predictions to different problem situations; present your calculations and solutions to questions; and analyze, critique and suggest, or support your classmates' answers to problem situations.

Today's workplace demands teamwork and self-confidence. At Carnegie Learning, our goal is to provide you with opportunities to be successful in your math course. Enjoy the year and have fun Learning by Doing™!

—The Carnegie Learning Curriculum Development Team

Acknowledgments

Carnegie Learning Curriculum Development Team

- Michael Amick
  Math Editor
- Joshua Fisher
  Math Editor
- Allison Dockter
  Math Editor
- John Fitsioris
  Curriculum Developer
- Danielle Kandrack
  Math Editor
- Beth Karambelkar
  Curriculum Developer
- David "Augie" Rivera
  Math Editor
- Lezlee Ross
  Curriculum Developer

Vendors

- Cenveo Corporation
- Mathematical Expressions
- Bookmasters, Inc.
- Mind Over Media
- Lapiz
- eInstruction

Special Thanks

- Carnegie Learning Managers of School Partnerships for their content review
- Teacher reviewers and students for their input and review of lesson content
- Carnegie Learning Software Development Team for their contributions to research and content
- Jaclyn Snyder for being a mentor to the development team, her leadership, and her pedagogical pioneering in mathematics education
- Amy Jones Lewis for her review of content
- Colleen Wolfe for project management

Photograph Credits

Chapter 9 © iStockphoto.com/samxmeg; Chapter 10 © iStockphoto.com/blackred; Chapter 11 © iStockphoto.com/EpicStockMedia; Chapter 12 © iStockphoto.com/bartvdd; Chapter 13 © iStockphoto.com/Ivan Bliznetsov; Chapter 14 © iStockphoto.com/greatpapa; Chapter 15 © iStockphoto.com/mbbirdy; Chapter 16 © Luca Parmitano/ISS Expedition 36, Volare;

9 Rational Functions 647

10 Solving Rational Equations 709

11 Radical Functions 769

12 Graphing Exponential and Logarithmic Functions 845

Table of Contents

Exponential and Logarithmic Equations 917

Table of Contents

14

Modeling with Functions 989

Trigonometric Functions 1067

Trigonometric Equations 1131

The Crew

The Crew is here to help you throughout the text. Sometimes they will remind you about things you have already learned. Sometimes they will ask you questions to help you think about different strategies. Sometimes they will share fun facts. They are members of your group—someone you can rely on!

Teacher aides will guide you along your way. They will help you make connections and remind you to think about the details.

Mathematical Representations

Introduction

During this course, you will solve problems and work with many different representations of mathematical concepts, ideas, and processes to better understand the world. Each lesson will provide you with opportunities to discuss your ideas, work within groups, and share your solutions and methods with your class. These process icons are placed throughout the text.

Discuss to Understand

- Read the problem carefully.
- What is the context of the problem? Do we understand it?
- What is the question that we are being asked? Does it make sense?
- Is this problem similar to some other problem we know?

Think for Yourself

- Do I need any additional information to answer the question?
- Is this problem similar to some other problem that I know?
- How can I represent the problem using a picture, a diagram, symbols, or some other representation?

Work with Your Partner

- How did you do the problem?
- Show me your representation.
- This is the way I thought about the problem—how did you think about it?
- What else do we need to solve the problem?
- Does our reasoning and our answer make sense to each other?
- How will we explain our solution to the class?

Share with the Class

- Here is our solution and the methods we used.
- Are we communicating our strategies clearly?
- We could only get this far with our solution. How can we finish?
- Could we have used a different strategy to solve the problem?

Academic Glossary

Key Terms of the Course

There are important terms you will encounter throughout this book. It is important that you have an understanding of these words as you get started through the mathematical concepts. Knowing what is meant by these terms and using these terms will help you think, reason, and communicate your ideas. The Graphic Organizers shown display a definition for a key term, related words, sample questions, and examples.

You will see these terms throughout each lesson.

Academic Glossary

Definition

To study or look closely for patterns.

Analyzing can involve examining or breaking a concept down into smaller parts to gain a better understanding of it.

Related Words

- examine
- evaluate
- determine
- observe
- consider
- investigate
- what do you notice?
- what do you think?
- sort and match
- identify

Ask Yourself

- Do I see any patterns?
- Have I seen something like this before?
- What happens if the shape, representation, or numbers change?
- What is the question asking me to accomplish?
- What is the context?
- What does the solution mean in terms of this problem situation?

Analyze

Example

PROBLEM 1 Feeling a Little Congested

City planners consider building a new stadium on several acres of land close to the downtown of a large city. They monitored the number of cars entering and exiting downtown from a major highway between 1:00 PM and 7:00 PM to determine current traffic conditions.

1. Analyze the table of values that represent the average number of cars entering and exiting downtown during the given hours of a typical weekday. The value for time represents the start-time for the full hour over which the vehicles were monitored.

Time (PM)	Average Number of Vehicles on a Typical Weekday (thousands)
1:00	7.0
2:00	10.8
3:00	14.5
4:00	21.1
5:00	23.9
6:00	19.0
7:00	10.0

When entering the data into your calculator, enter 1:00 as 1, 2:00 as 2, 3:00 as 3, etc.

a. Describe any patterns you notice. Explain the patterns in the context of this problem situation.

The number of cars increase, reach a maximum at 5:00 PM, and then decrease again. This pattern makes sense in the context of this problem because rush hour occurs around 5:00 PM.

b. Predict the type of polynomial that best fits the data. Explain your reasoning.

Answers will vary.

The data increases and then decreases. The curve appears to be quadratic.

Academic Glossary

Definition

To give details or describe how to determine an answer or solution.

Explaining your reasoning helps justify conclusions.

Related Words

- show your work
- explain your calculation
- justify
- why or why not?

Ask Yourself

- How should I organize my thoughts?
- Is my explanation logical?
- Does my reasoning make sense?
- How can I justify my answer to others?
- Did I use complete sentences in my answer?

Don't forget to check your answers!

Explain Your Reasoning

Example

12. Circle the function(s) shown that could describe the given graph. Explain your reasoning.

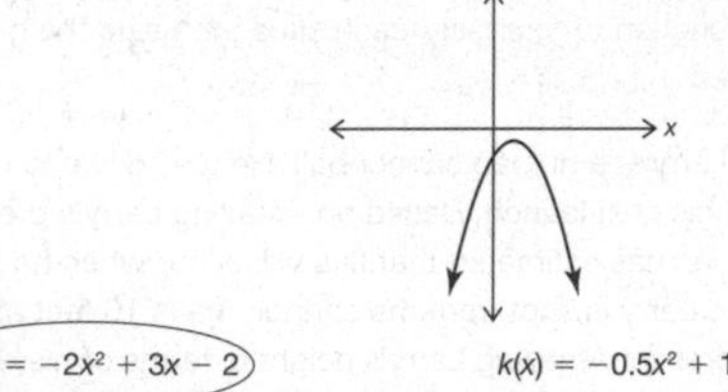
y
x

$h(x) = -2x^2 + 3x - 2$ (circled) $\qquad k(x) = -0.5x^2 + 1.5x + 1$

$t(x) = -\frac{1}{2}x^2 + 3x - \frac{9}{2} \qquad w(x) = 2x^2 - 4x - 10$

Only $h(x)$ could describe the function whose graph is shown. The discriminant of $h(x)$ is -7, so it does not intersect the x-axis.

The discriminant of $k(x)$ is 4.25, so it intersects the x-axis twice. Also, $k(x)$ has a positive y-intercept.

The discriminant of $t(x)$ is equal to 0, so it intersects the x-axis one time.

The discriminant of $w(x)$ is 96, so it intersects the x-axis twice. Also, $w(x)$ is concave up.

Definition

To display information in various ways. Representing mathematics can be done using words, tables, graphs, or symbols.

Related Words

- show
- sketch
- draw
- create
- plot
- graph
- write an equation
- complete the table

Ask Yourself

- How should I organize my thoughts?
- How do I use this model to show a concept or idea?
- What does this representation tell me?
- Is my representation accurate?
- What units or labels should I include?
- Are there other ways to model this concept?

Represent

Example

PROBLEM 4 Just Another Day at the Circus

Write a quadratic function to represent each situation using the given information. Be sure to define your variables.

1. The Amazing Larry is a human cannonball. He would like to reach a maximum height of 30 feet during his next launch. Based on Amazing Larry's previous launches, his assistant DaJuan has estimated that this will occur when he is 40 feet from the cannon. When Amazing Larry is shot from the cannon, he is 10 feet above the ground. Write a function to represent Amazing Larry's height in terms of his distance.

   Let $h(d)$ represent Amazing Larry's height in terms of his distance, d.

   $$h(d) = a(d - 40)^2 + 30$$
   $$10 = a(0 - 40)^2 + 30$$
   $$10 = 1600a + 30$$
   $$-20 = 1600a$$
   $$-\frac{1}{80} = a$$
   $$h(d) = -\frac{1}{80}(d - 40)^2 + 30$$

Academic Glossary

Predict

Definition

To declare or tell in advance based on the analysis of given data.

Predicting first helps inform reasoning.

Related Words

- estimate
- approximate
- expect
- about how much?

Ask Yourself

- What do I know about this problem situation?
- What predictions can I make from this problem situation?
- Does my reasoning make sense?
- Is my solution close to my estimation?

Example

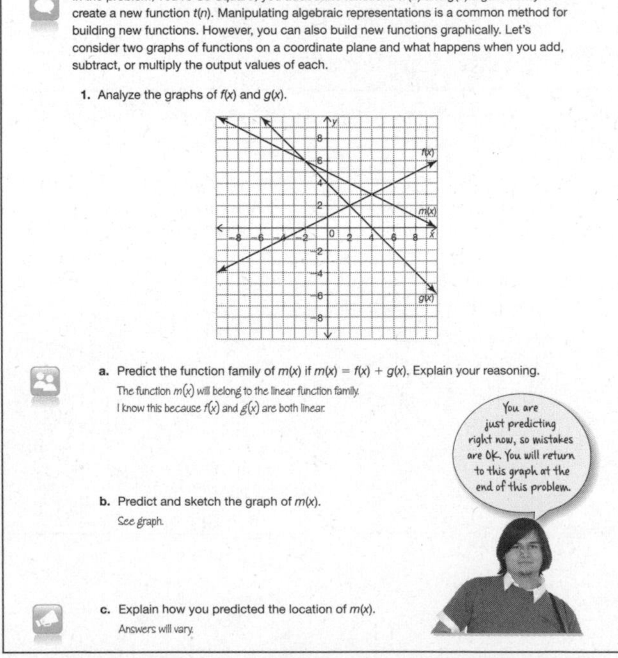

In the problem, *You're So Square*, you added the functions $w(n)$ and $g(n)$ algebraically to create a new function $t(n)$. Manipulating algebraic representations is a common method for building new functions. However, you can also build new functions graphically. Let's consider two graphs of functions on a coordinate plane and what happens when you add, subtract, or multiply the output values of each.

1. Analyze the graphs of $f(x)$ and $g(x)$.

a. Predict the function family of $m(x)$ if $m(x) = f(x) + g(x)$. Explain your reasoning.

The function $m(x)$ will belong to the linear function family.
I know this because $f(x)$ and $g(x)$ are both linear.

b. Predict and sketch the graph of $m(x)$.

See graph.

c. Explain how you predicted the location of $m(x)$.

Answers will vary.

You are just predicting right now, so mistakes are OK. You will return to this graph at the end of this problem.

Definition

To represent or give an account of in words. Describing communicates mathematical ideas to others.

Related Words

- demonstrate
- label
- display
- compare
- define
- determine
- what are the advantages?
- what are the disadvantages?
- what is similar?
- what is different?

Ask Yourself

- How should I organize my thoughts?
- Is my explanation logical?
- Did I consider the context of this situation?
- Does my reasoning make sense?
- Did I use complete sentences in my answer?
- Did I include appropriate units and labels?
- Will my classmates understand my reasoning?

Describe

Example

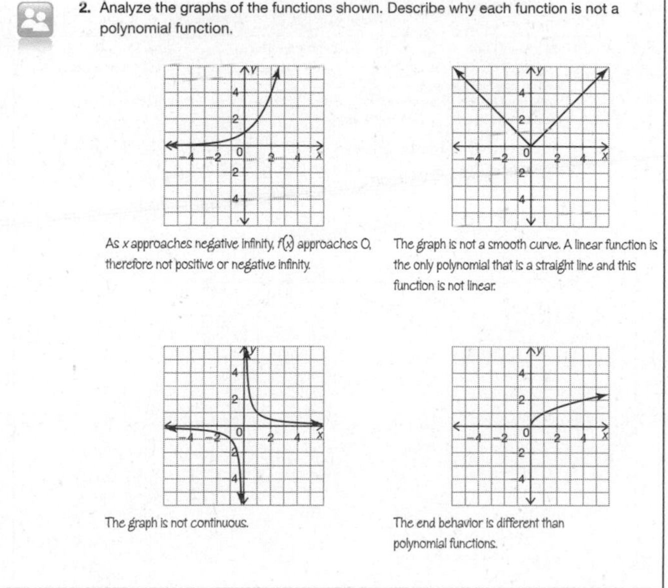

2. Analyze the graphs of the functions shown. Describe why each function is not a polynomial function.
As x approaches negative infinity, f(x) approaches 0, therefore not positive or negative infinity.
The graph is not a smooth curve. A linear function is the only polynomial that is a straight line and this function is not linear.
The graph is not continuous.
The end behavior is different than polynomial functions.

Academic Glossary

Problem Types You Will See

Worked Example

WHEN YOU SEE A WORKED EXAMPLE

- Take your time to read through it,
- Question your own understanding, and
- Think about the connections between steps.

ASK YOURSELF

- What is the main idea?
- How would this work if I changed the numbers?
- Have I used these strategies before?

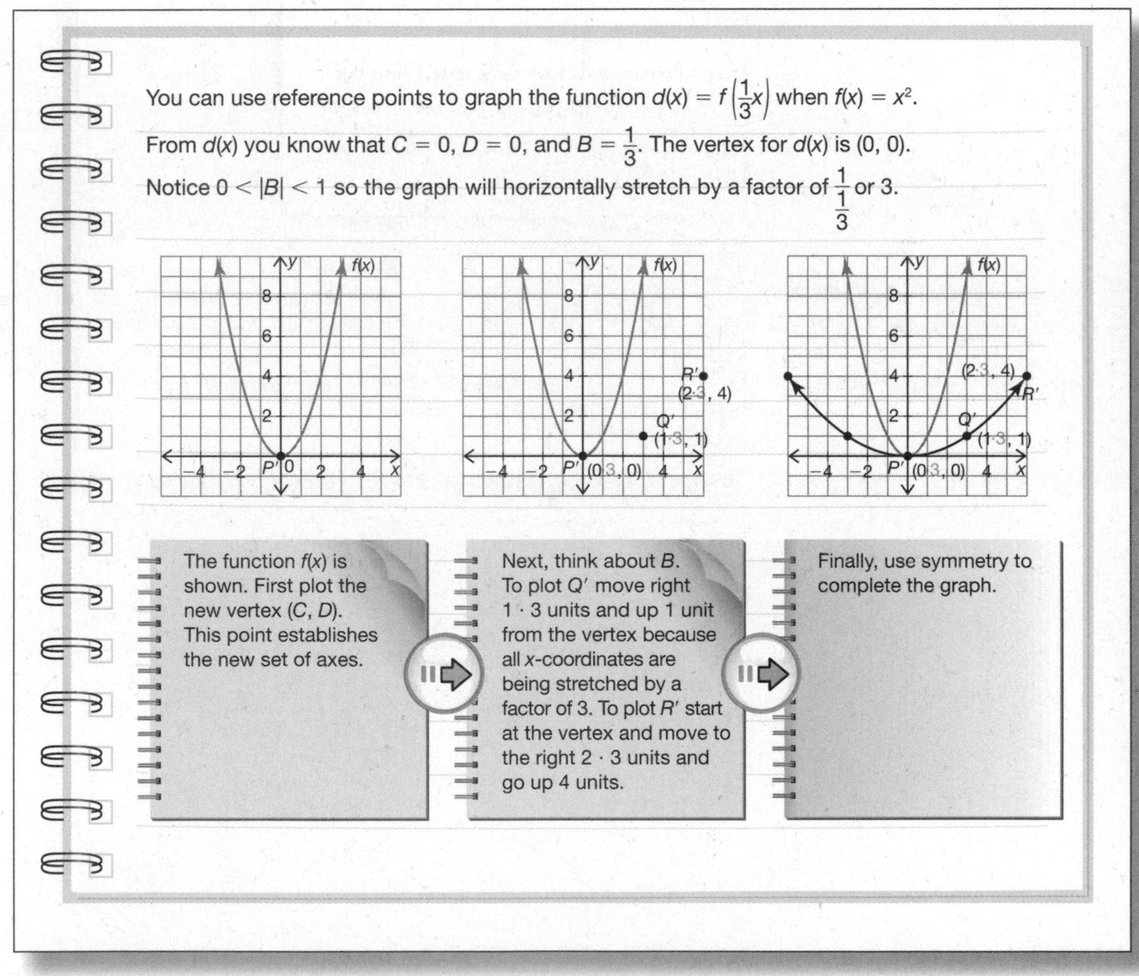

You can use reference points to graph the function $d(x) = f\left(\frac{1}{3}x\right)$ when $f(x) = x^2$.
From $d(x)$ you know that $C = 0$, $D = 0$, and $B = \frac{1}{3}$. The vertex for $d(x)$ is (0, 0).
Notice $0 < |B| < 1$ so the graph will horizontally stretch by a factor of $\frac{1}{\frac{1}{3}}$ or 3.
The function $f(x)$ is shown. First plot the new vertex (C, D). This point establishes the new set of axes.
Next, think about B. To plot Q' move right $1 \cdot 3$ units and up 1 unit from the vertex because all x-coordinates are being stretched by a factor of 3. To plot R' start at the vertex and move to the right $2 \cdot 3$ units and go up 4 units.
Finally, use symmetry to complete the graph.

Thumbs Down

WHEN YOU SEE A THUMBS DOWN ICON

- Take your time to read through the *incorrect* solution.
- Think about what error was made.

ASK YOURSELF

- Where is the error?
- Why is it an error?
- How can I correct it?

5. Emily makes an observation about the number of imaginary zeros a cubic function may have.

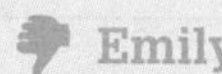

Emily

A cubic function must have three zeros. I know this from the Fundamental Theorem. However, the number of real and imaginary zeros can vary. The function may have 0, 1, 2, or 3 imaginary zeros.

Explain the error in Emily's reasoning.

If a cubic function has imaginary roots, those imaginary roots come from the quadratic function that builds the cubic function. The imaginary roots will appear only in pairs when the quadratic function never intersects the x-axis. Therefore, the number of imaginary zeros a cubic function may have is 0 or 2 imaginary roots.

Problem Types

Thumbs Up

WHEN YOU SEE A THUMBS UP ICON

- Take your time to read through the *correct* solution.
- Think about the connections between steps.

ASK YOURSELF

- Why is this method correct?
- Have I used this method before?

4. Christine and Kate were asked to determine the vertex of two different quadratic functions each written in different forms. Analyze their calculations.

 **Christine**

$f(x) = 2x^2 + 12x + 10$

The quadratic function is in standard form. So I know the axis of symmetry is $x = \frac{-b}{2a}$.

$x = \frac{-12}{2(2)}$

$= -3.$

Now that I know the axis of symmetry, I can substitute that value into the function to determine the y-coordinate of the vertex.

$f(-3) = 2(-3)^2 + 12(-3) + 10$

$= 2(9) - 36 + 10$

$= 18 - 36 + 10$

$= 8$

Therefore, the vertex is (3, 8).

 **Kate**

$g(x) = \frac{1}{2}(x + 3)(x - 7)$

The form of the function tells me the x-intercepts are −3 and 7. I also know the x-coordinate of the vertex will be directly in the middle of the x-intercepts. So, all I have to do is calculate the average.

$x = \frac{-3 + 7}{2}$

$= \frac{4}{2} = 2$

Now that I know the x-coordinate of the vertex, I can substitute that value into the function to determine the y-coordinate.

$g(2) = \frac{1}{2}(2 + 3)(2 - 7)$

$= \frac{1}{2}(5)(-5)$

$= -12.5$

Therefore, the vertex is (2, −12.5).

a. How are these methods similar? How are they different?

Both methods require that you determine the axis of symmetry, and then substitute that value into the function to determine the *y*-coordinate of the vertex.

The methods are different in the ways the axis of symmetry was determined. Christine used $x = \frac{-b}{2a}$ and Kate used $x = \frac{r_1 + r_2}{2}$.

b. What must Kate do to use Christine's method?

Kate knows the *a*-value from the form of her quadratic equation. She must multiply the terms together and combine like terms. She would then have a quadratic function in standard form to determine the *b*-value.

c. What must Christine do to use Kate's method?

Christine must factor the quadratic function or use the quadratic formula to determine the *x*-intercepts. Once she determines the *x*-intercepts, she can use the same method as Kate.

Problem Types

Who's Correct?

WHEN YOU SEE A WHO'S CORRECT? ICON

- Take your time to read through the situation.
- Question the strategy or reason given.
- Determine which solution is correct and which is not correct.

ASK YOURSELF

- Does the reasoning make sense?
- If the reasoning makes sense, what is the justification?
- If the reasoning does not make sense, what error was made?

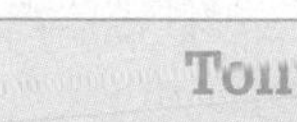

7. Tonya and Alex came up with different expressions to represent the number of gray tiles in each pattern. Their expressions are shown.

Tonya	Alex
$4n^2 + (2n + 1)(2n + 1)$	$(4n + 1)^2 - 4n(2n + 1)$

Tonya claims that they are the same expression written different ways. Alex says, "One expression has addition and the other has subtraction. There is no way they are equivalent!"

Who is correct? Justify your reasoning using algebraic and graphical representations.

Tonya is correct.

Tonya's expression

$4n^2 + (2n + 1)(2n + 1)$

$4n^2 + 4n^2 + 4n + 1$

$8n^2 + 4n + 1$

Alex's expression

$(4n + 1)^2 - 4n(2n + 1)$

$16n^2 + 8n + 1 - 4n^2 - 4n$

$8n^2 + 4n + 1$

Both expressions are equivalent to $8n^2 + 4n + 1$.

When I graph both expressions as equations, they produce the same graph which guarantees equivalence.

Problem Types

Habits of Mind

The Standards for Mathematical Practice

Effective communication and collaboration are essential skills of a successful learner. With practice, you can develop the habits of mind of a productive mathematical thinker.

Make sense of problems and persevere in solving them.

I can:

- explain what a problem "means" in my own words.
- analyze and organize information.
- keep track of my plan and change it if necessary
- always ask myself, "does this make sense?"

Attend to precision.

I can:

- calculate accurately and efficiently.
- use clear definitions when I talk with my classmates, my teacher, and others.
- specify units of measure and label diagrams and other figures appropriately to clarify the meaning of different representations.

Reasoning and Explaining

Reason abstractly and quantitatively.

I can:

- create an understandable representation of a problem situation.
- consider the units of measure involved in a problem.
- understand and use properties of operations.

Construct viable arguments and critique the reasoning of others.

I can:

- use definitions and previously established results in constructing arguments.
- communicate and defend my own mathematical reasoning using examples, drawings, or diagrams.
- distinguish correct reasoning from reasoning that is flawed.
- listen to or read the conclusions of others and decide whether they make sense.
- ask useful questions in an attempt to understand other ideas and conclusions.

Modeling and Using Tools

Model with mathematics.

I can:

- identify important relationships in a problem situation and represent them using tools such as, diagrams, tables, graphs, and formulas.
- apply mathematics to solve problems that occur in everyday life.
- interpret mathematical results in the contexts of a variety of problem situations.
- reflect on whether my results make sense, improving the model I used if it is not appropriate for the situation.

Use appropriate tools strategically.

I can:

- use a variety of different tools that I have to solve problems.
- use a graphing calculator to explore mathematical concepts.
- recognize when a tool that I have to solve problems might be helpful and also when it has limitations.

Habits of Mind

Seeing Structure and Generalizing

Look for and make use of structure.

I can:

- look closely to see a pattern or a structure in a mathematical argument.
- can see complicated things as single objects or as being composed of several objects.
- can step back for an overview and can shift my perspective.

Look for and express regularity in repeated reasoning.

I can:

- notice if calculations are repeated.
- look for general methods and more efficient methods to solve problems.
- evaluate the reasonableness of intermediate results.
- make generalizations based on results.

Each lesson provides opportunities for you to think, reason, and communicate mathematical understanding. Here are a few examples of how you will develop expertise using the Standards for Mathematical Practice throughout this text.

PROBLEM 1 Business Is Growing

The Plant-A-Seed Planter Company produces planter boxes. To make the boxes, a square is cut from each corner of a rectangular copper sheet. The sides are bent to form a rectangular prism without a top. Cutting different sized squares from the corners results in different sized planter boxes. Plant-A-Seed takes sales orders from customers who request a sized planter box.

Reason abstractly and quantitatively. You will move from real-life context to t mathematics and back the context througho problems.

Each rectangular copper sheet is 12 inches by 18 inches. In the diagram, the solid lines indicate where the square corners are cut and the dotted lines represent where the sides are bent for each planter box.

It may help to create a model of the planter by cutting squares out of the corners of a sheet of paper and folding.

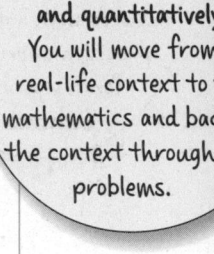

18 inches

12 inches

h h h h h h h h

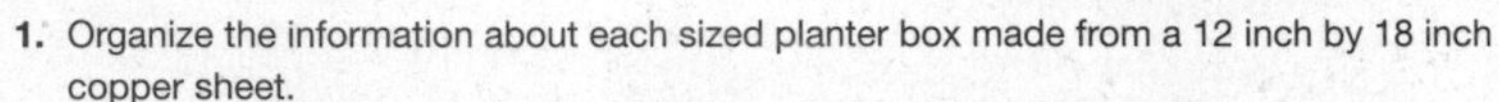

1. Organize the information about each sized planter box made from a 12 inch by 18 inch copper sheet.

   a. Complete the table. Include an expression for each planter box's height, width, length, and volume for a square corner side of length h.

Model with mathematics. You will identify relationships and represent them using diagrams, tables, graphs, and formulas.

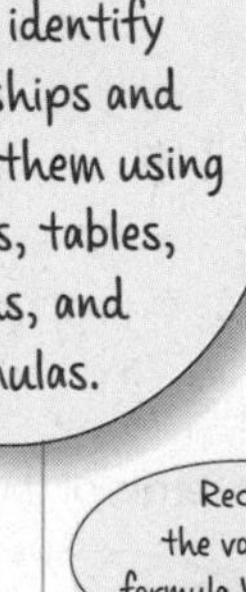

Recall the volume formula $V = lwh$.

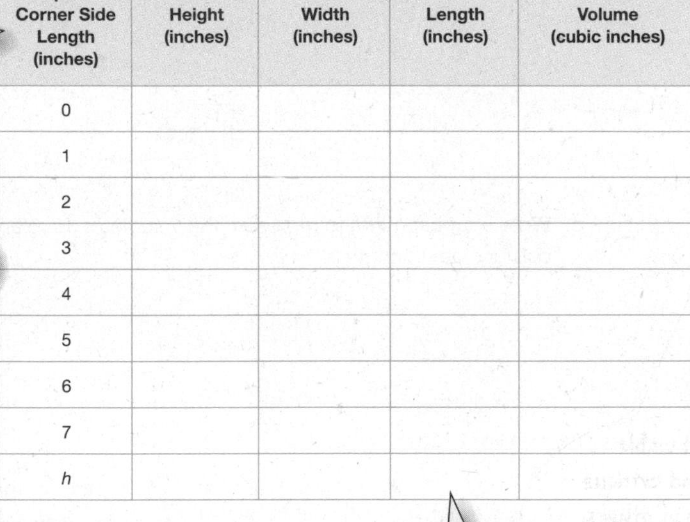

Square Corner Side Length (inches)	Height (inches)	Width (inches)	Length (inches)	Volume (cubic inches)
0				
1				
2				
3				
4				
5				
6				
7				
h				

Look for and make use of structure. You will look for patterns in your calculations and use those to write formal expressions and equations.

b. What patterns do you notice in the table?

Attend to precision. You will specify units of measure and express answers with a degree of precision appropriate for the problem context.

2. Analyze the relationship between the height, length, and width of each planter box.

   a. What is the largest sized square corner that can be cut to make a planter box? Explain your reasoning.

   b. What is the relationship between the size of the corner square and the length and width of each planter box?

   c. Write a function $V(h)$ to represent the volume of the planter box in terms of the corner side of length h.

Model with mathematics. You will identify important quantities and map their relationships using functions.

Construct viable arguments and critique the reasoning of others. You will share your answers with your classmates and listen to their responses to decide whether they make sense.

Habits of Mind

Rational Functions

9

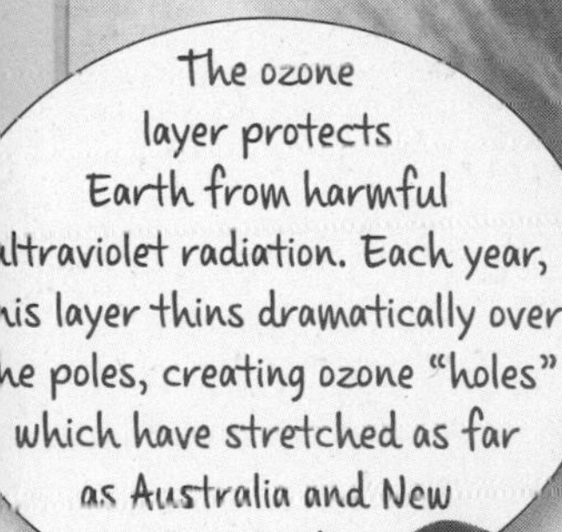
The ozone
layer protects
Earth from harmful
ltraviolet radiation. Each year,
is layer thins dramatically over
e poles, creating ozone "holes"
which have stretched as far
as Australia and New
Zealand.

A Rational Existence

9.1

Introduction to Rational Functions

LEARNING GOALS

In this lesson, you will:

- Graph rational functions.
- Compare rational functions in multiple representations.
- Compare the basic rational function to various basic polynomial functions.
- Analyze the key characteristics of rational functions.

KEY TERMS

- rational function
- vertical asymptote

Consider the following mathematical explanation that 1 is equal to 2. Yes, you read that correctly–you will analyze a proof of $1 = 2$.

Let's start by noting that any number multiplied by 0 is equal to 0, correct? Therefore,

$$1 \times 0 = 0$$
$$2 \times 0 = 0.$$

Since the expressions 1×0 and 2×0 both equal zero, then they must be equal to each other by the transitive property. Therefore,

$$1 \times 0 = 2 \times 0.$$

Dividing both sides of an equation by the same value preserves equality. Therefore, you can divide both sides of the equation by 0.

$$\frac{1 \times 0}{0} = \frac{2 \times 0}{0}$$

Anything divided by itself is 1, so $\frac{0}{0} = 1$. This leaves

$$1 \times 1 = 2 \times 1$$
$$1 = 2.$$

There weren't any sneaky tricks or magical sleights of hand in this proof. In fact, all steps were justified according to the rules of algebra . . . so then what's wrong with this proof?

PROBLEM 1 My World Is Turned Upside Down

Recall from previous math courses that the reciprocal of any number x is $\frac{1}{x}$.
For example, the reciprocal of 5 is $\frac{1}{5}$ and the reciprocal of 0.5 is $\frac{1}{0.5}$, or 2.
Throughout this course you have studied many connections between polynomial functions and real numbers. Does it follow then that polynomial functions also have reciprocals? Is the reciprocal also a polynomial? Is it a function? How would the graph and table of values of $\frac{1}{f(x)}$ compare to the original function $f(x)$?

To begin answering these questions, consider the reciprocal of the basic linear function $f(x) = x$. The reciprocal can be defined as $g(x) = \frac{1}{f(x)}$, or simply $g(x) = \frac{1}{x}$.

1. Consider the graph and table of values for $f(x) = x$. The domain of $f(x)$ is $(-\infty, \infty)$. The points $(-1, -1)$ and $(1, 1)$ are shown and used to create three intervals for analysis.

x	1	2	3	4	5	6
$f(x) = x$	1	2	3	4	5	6
$g(x) = \frac{1}{x}$						

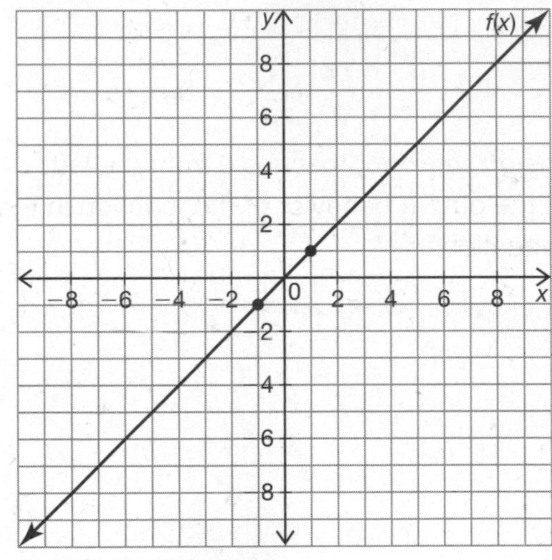

−6	−5	−4	−3	−2	−1	x
−6	−5	−4	−3	−2	−1	$f(x) = x$
						$g(x) = \frac{1}{x}$

x	−1	$-\frac{1}{2}$	$-\frac{1}{10}$	$-\frac{1}{100}$	0	$\frac{1}{100}$	$\frac{1}{10}$	$\frac{1}{2}$	1
$f(x) = x$	−1	$-\frac{1}{2}$	$-\frac{1}{10}$	$-\frac{1}{100}$	0	$\frac{1}{100}$	$\frac{1}{10}$	$\frac{1}{2}$	1
$g(x) = \frac{1}{x}$									

a. Complete the table of values for $g(x) = \frac{1}{x}$. Then plot the points and draw a smooth curve to graph $g(x)$ on the coordinate plane.

b. Describe the graph of $g(x)$. How is it similar to the graphs of other functions that you've studied? How is it different?

9

c. Describe the end behavior of $g(x)$. Explain your reasoning in terms of the graph, equation, and table of values.

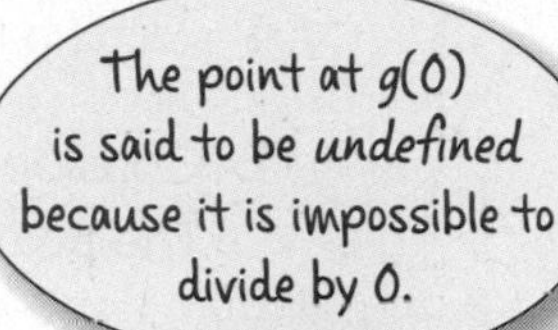
The point at g(0)
is said to be undefined
because it is impossible to
divide by 0.

d. Describe $g(x)$ as x approaches 0 from the left. Explain the output behavior of the function in terms of the equation.

e. Describe $g(x)$ as x approaches 0 from the right. Explain the output behavior of the function in terms of the equation.

9

2. Henry and Rosie disagree about $g(x) = \frac{1}{x}$.

Henry
The graph and table both clearly show that it is a function.

Rosie
It is not a function. Every input doesn't have an output.

Who is correct? Explain your reasoning.

3. Analyze the key characteristics of $g(x) = \frac{1}{x}$.

   a. Will the graph ever intersect the horizontal line $y = 0$? Explain your reasoning in terms of the graph, table, and equation.

   b. Will the graph ever intersect the vertical line $x = 0$? Explain your reasoning in terms of the graph, table, and equation.

   c. Describe the domain and range of $g(x)$.

The function $g(x) = \frac{1}{x}$ is an example of a *rational function*. A **rational function** is any function that can be written as the ratio of two polynomials. It can be written in the form $f(x) = \frac{P(x)}{Q(x)}$ where $P(x)$ and $Q(x)$ are polynomial functions, and $Q(x) \neq 0$. You have already seen some specific types of rational functions. Linear, quadratic, cubic, and higher order polynomial functions are types of rational functions.

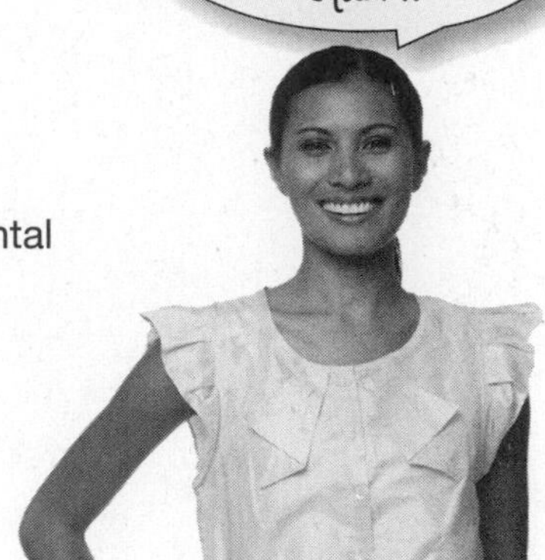

All polynomials are rational functions. Remember $Q(x)$ can equal 1.

Recall from your study of exponential functions that a horizontal asymptote is a horizontal line that a function gets closer and closer to, but never intersects. In this problem, the function $g(x)$ has a horizontal asymptote at $y = 0$.

The function $g(x) = \frac{1}{x}$ has a *vertical asymptote* at $x = 0$. A **vertical asymptote** is a vertical line that a function gets closer and closer to, but never intersects. The asymptote does not represent points on the graph of the function. It represents the output value that the graph approaches. An asymptote occurs for input values that result in a denominator of 0.

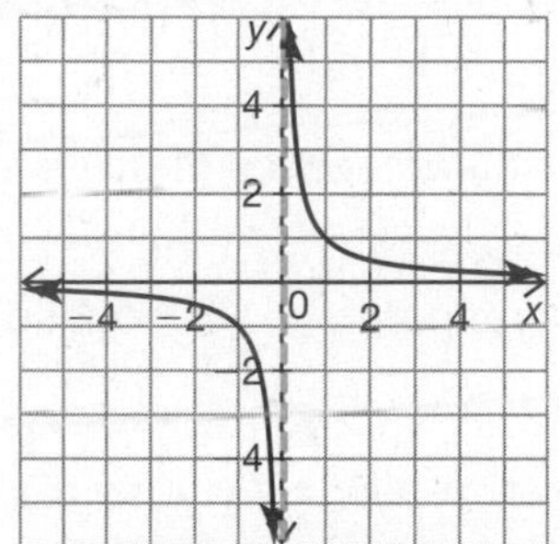

The vertical asymptote is often represented in textbooks and graphing calculators as a dashed or solid line. The convention used in this textbook is to represent asymptotes as dashed lines.

Changing the mode to "dot" on many calculators removes the asymptote from the screen. Asymptotes are often more easily viewed with a smaller viewing window. Try $[-5, 5] \times [-5, 5]$ for $g(x)$.

9

4. Analyze each function.

$f(x) = x$	$g(x) = \frac{3x}{2}$	$h(x) = \frac{\sqrt{x}}{2x}$
$p(x) = \frac{3}{x} + 2$	$k(x) = 12$	$n(x) = \frac{2^x}{5}$
$j(x) = \frac{4x^2 + 3x + 2}{6x^3 + 10}$	$m(x) = \frac{1}{(x + 2)(x - 3)}$	

a. Circle the rational functions.

b. Explain why the remaining functions are not rational.

c. Do you think the graphs of all rational functions will have a vertical asymptote? Explain your reasoning.

5. Use a graphing calculator to explore various rational functions of the form $p(x) = \frac{a}{x}$ where a is a constant.

a. Describe changes in the function for various a-values. Make as many conjectures as you can about the key characteristics of functions in this form.

Consider domain, range, intercepts, end behavior, asymptotes, etc. Remember that a does not have to be an integer. Explore values between −1 and 1.

b. Abby and Natasha disagree about functions of the form $p(x) = \frac{a}{x}$ where a is a constant.

Abby
The horizontal asymptote will vary depending on the a-value.

Natasha
All rational functions of this form will have a horizontal asymptote at $y = 0$.

Who is correct? Explain your reasoning.

c. List several rational functions that do not have a horizontal asymptote at $y = 0$.

6. If $g(x)$ is the reciprocal function of $f(x)$, what is $f(x) \cdot g(x)$ where $g(x) \neq 0$ for any input value? Explain your reasoning.

7. The opener to this lesson provides a proof that $1 = 2$. Describe the error in the proof in terms of what you learned in this problem.

9

PROBLEM 2 Power in Rational Behavior

Recall that power functions are any functions of the form $y = x^n$ for $n \geq 1$. In Problem 1, *My World Is Turned Upside Down*, you discovered that the graph of the function $g(x) = \frac{1}{x}$ looks very different than the linear function $f(x) = x$. How will the graphs of the other power functions compare to their reciprocals? Will they all have the same shape? Will they all have asymptotes?

1. Analyze the graph of the quadratic power function $q(x) = x^2$.

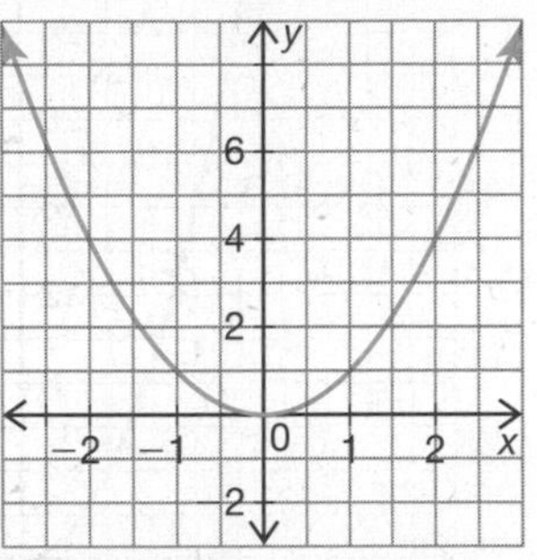

Predict the graph of $r(x) = \frac{1}{x^2}$. Sketch it on the coordinate plane. Explain your reasoning.

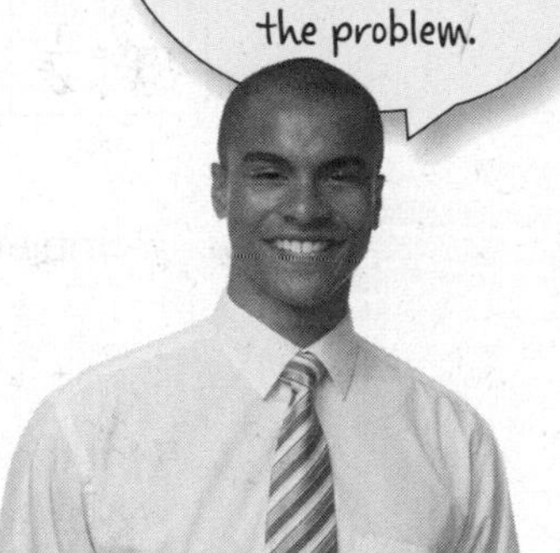

You are just making a prediction based on what you know up to this point. We will return to the problem.

2. Consider the graph and table of values for $q(x) = x^2$. The domain of $q(x)$ is $(-\infty, \infty)$. The tables represent three intervals of the domain.

-5	-4	-3	-2	-1	x
		9	4	1	$q(x) = x^2$
					$r(x) = \frac{1}{x^2}$

x	1	2	3	4	5
$q(x) = x^2$	1	4	9		
$r(x) = \frac{1}{x^2}$					

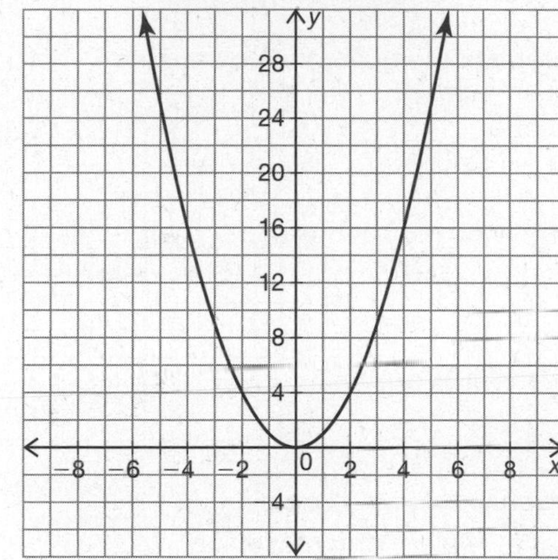

x	-1	$-\frac{1}{2}$	$-\frac{1}{10}$	$-\frac{1}{100}$	0	$\frac{1}{100}$	$\frac{1}{10}$	$\frac{1}{2}$	1
$q(x) = x^2$									
$r(x) = \frac{1}{x^2}$									

a. Complete the table of values for $r(x) = \frac{1}{x^2}$.

b. Plot the points and sketch the reciprocal function $r(x)$ on the coordinate plane.

c. Describe the shape of the graph of $r(x) = \frac{1}{x^2}$.
How is it similar to $g(x) = \frac{1}{x}$? How is it different?

3. Analyze the key characteristics of $r(x)$.

a. Describe the domain and range of $r(x)$.

b. Describe the end behavior of $r(x)$.

9

c. Describe the horizontal and vertical asymptotes of $r(x)$. How can you determine the asymptotes from the graph, table, and equation?

4. Use a graphing calculator to explore the key characteristics of the reciprocals of all power functions. Consider the general shape of the graphs, domain, range, end behavior, horizontal asymptotes, and vertical asymptotes.

a. List your conjectures about the even-powered functions $\left\{\frac{1}{x^2}, \frac{1}{x^4}, \frac{1}{x^6}, \ldots\right\}$. Justify your conjectures.

b. List your conjectures about the odd-powered functions $\left\{\frac{1}{x^3}, \frac{1}{x^5}, \frac{1}{x^7}, \ldots\right\}$. Justify your conjectures.

c. Summarize the similarities and differences between the groups of reciprocal power functions by describing the key characteristics in the Venn diagram. Characteristics that are shared should go in the overlapping space.

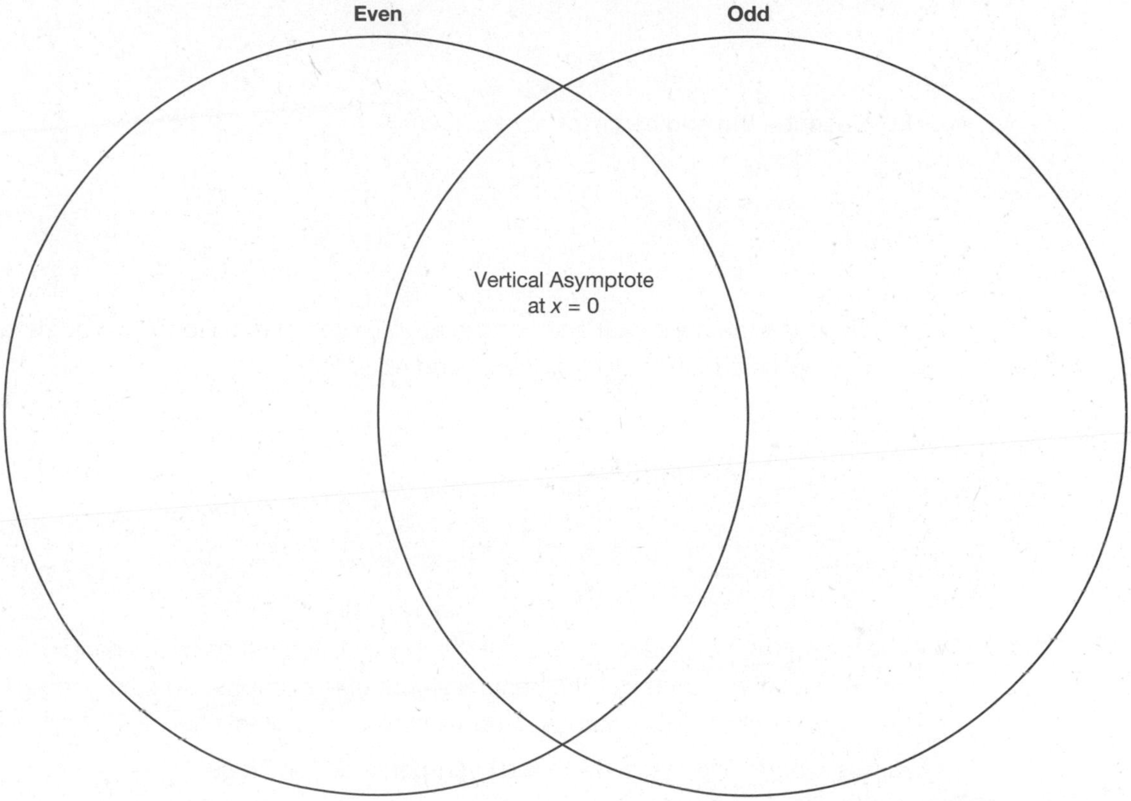

Even

Odd

Vertical Asymptote at $x = 0$

An example is provided. What other characteristics are shared? Which ones are different? How would you describe them?

9

Be prepared to share your solutions and methods.

9

A Rational Shift in Behavior

Translating Rational Functions

9.2

LEARNING GOALS

In this lesson, you will:

- Analyze rational functions with a constant added to the denominator.
- Compare rational functions in different forms.
- Identify vertical asymptotes of rational functions.

When cars were first built, they all had manual transmissions. This means the drivers had to press on a clutch and shift gears when starting the car, accelerating, or going up an incline. In the 1940's automatic transmission cars were introduced. The transmission was designed so that the gears shift automatically for the driver as the car accelerates or decelerates. Today, automatic transmission cars make up more than 90% of the cars on the road. Ten percent is a pretty small number, but that still amounts to millions of drivers who choose to manually shift gears while driving. Why would they choose a manual transmission?

Manual transmissions are in less demand, so the lower price tag often attracts drivers. They generally get better gas mileage than automatics, adding to the savings over time. Repairs are usually cheaper, too, as the transmission is less complicated. Some drivers also prefer the control that the manual transmission cars offer, especially having the ability to choose the gear when in poor weather or road conditions.

Have you driven a car? Was it an automatic or manual transmission?

PROBLEM 1 Shifty Behavior, Take 1

Recall from *A Rational Existence* that the reciprocal of power functions have a vertical asymptote at $x = 0$ and a horizontal asymptote at $y = 0$. The domain is all real numbers except for 0, because division by 0 is undefined.

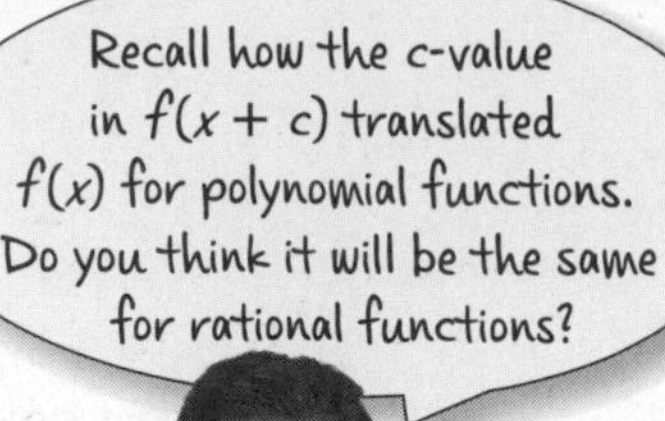
Recall how the c-value in f(x + c) translated f(x) for polynomial functions. Do you think it will be the same for rational functions?

9

In this problem you will use a graphing calculator to explore rational functions of the form

$g(x) = \frac{1}{x - c}$ for a constant value c.

1. Consider the table shown.
   a. Identify the vertical asymptote, horizontal asymptote, domain, and range for the given c-values. Then choose different positive and negative c-values to complete the table.

c-value	$g(x) = \frac{1}{x - c}$	Vertical Asymptote(s)	Horizontal Asymptote(s)	Domain	Range
1	$g(x) = \frac{1}{x - 1}$				
−2	$g(x) = \frac{1}{x + 2}$				

Compare your answers to your classmates' and discuss the behavior of the rational functions before making a conjecture.

b. Determine the general formula to identify the vertical asymptote of a rational function in the form $g(x) = \frac{1}{x - c}$. Explain your reasoning.

c. What generalization(s) can you make about the c-value and the domain? The range?

d. What effect does changing the c-value have on the function's end behavior? Explain your reasoning.

2. Without using a graphing calculator, determine the domain, range, and vertical and horizontal asymptotes of each rational function.

a. $f(x) = \frac{10}{x}$

Domain:

Range:

Vertical Asymptote:

Horizontal Asymptote:

b. $g(x) = \frac{1}{x + 10}$

Domain:

Range:

Vertical Asymptote:

Horizontal Asymptote:

c. $j(x) = 10x$

Domain:

Range:

Vertical Asymptote:

Horizontal Asymptote:

d. $g(x) = \frac{1}{x - 10}$

Domain:

Range:

Vertical Asymptote:

Horizontal Asymptote:

3. Write the rational function(s) from the graph, table, or description provided. Explain your reasoning.

a. 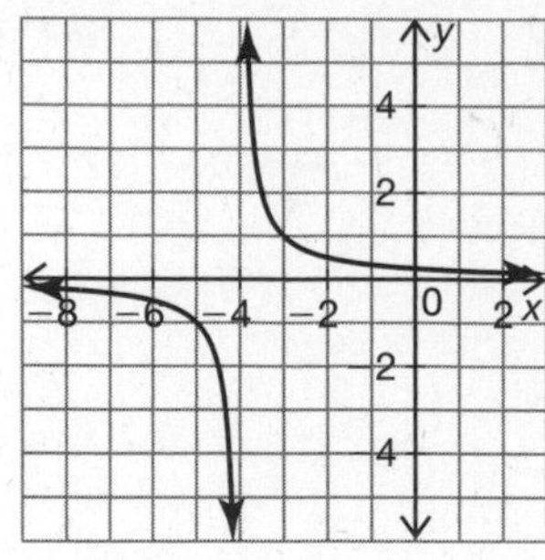

Function: ________________

Explanation:

9

b. Vertical asymptote at $x = 3$ and a horizontal asymptote at $y = 0$.

You are asked to determine 2 functions. How many functions exist that fit the description given?

Function 1: ________________

Function 2: ________________

Explanation:

c. Domain: All Real Numbers except $x = 7$
Range: All Real Numbers except $y = 0$

Function 1: ________________

Function 2: ________________

Explanation:

d.

x	y
−2	−0.5
−1	$-\frac{2}{3}$
0	−1.0
1	−2.0
2	undefined
3	2.0
4	1.0

Function: ________________

Explanation:

e.

x	y
−2	−3.0
−1	undefined
0	3.0
1	1.5
2	1
3	0.75
4	0.60

Function: ________________

Explanation:

4. Compare the effect that changing the c-value has on the reciprocal function to the effect that changing the C-value has on any polynomial function $f(x)$ to form $g(x) = f(x - C)$.

PROBLEM 2 Shifty Behavior, Take 2

Recall that rational functions are any functions of the form $f(x) = \frac{P(x)}{Q(x)}$ where $P(x)$ and $Q(x)$ are polynomial functions, and $Q(x) \neq 0$. So far you have only studied a small subset of all rational functions. Let's consider the structure of the rational functions that you have explored so far.

9

1. Why have the horizontal asymptotes occurred at $y = 0$? Do you think all rational functions will have a horizontal asymptote at $y = 0$? Explain your reasoning.

2. What determines a vertical asymptote? Do you think that a rational function could have more than one vertical asymptote?

3. Without using a graphing calculator, sketch each function.

a. $y = \frac{1}{x}$

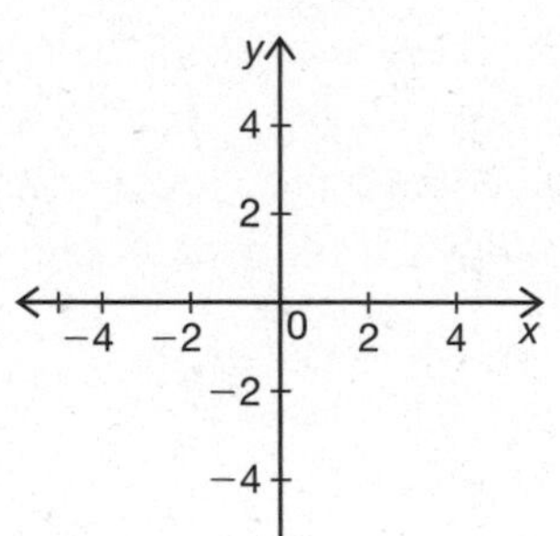

b. $y = \frac{1}{x - 2}$

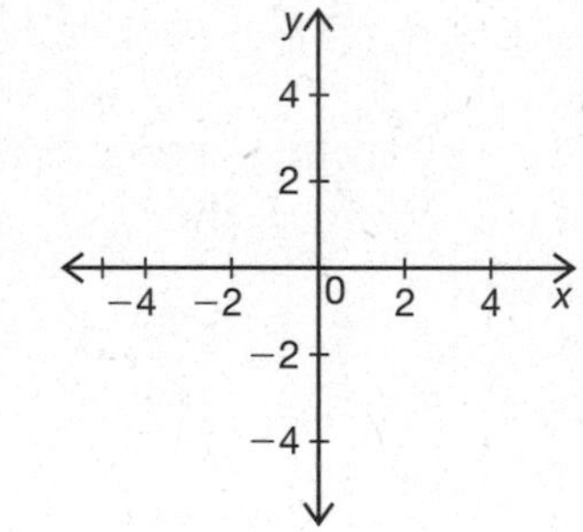

c. $y = \frac{1}{(x - 2)^2}$

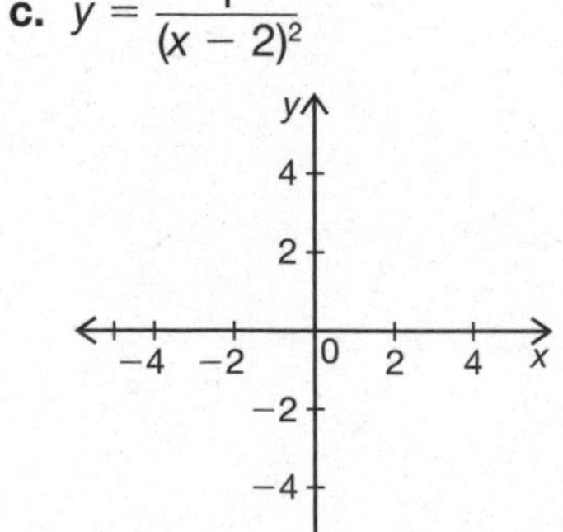

d. $y = \frac{-1}{(x - 2)^2}$

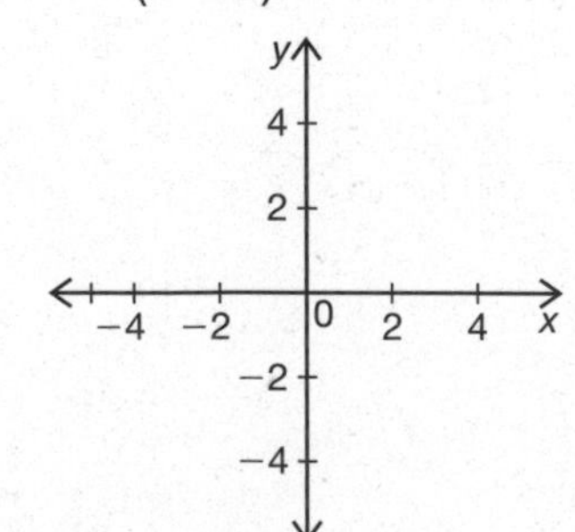

You haven't done anything exactly like part (d), but think about what you already know about functions and transformations.

4. Without using a graphing calculator, sketch each function.

a. $y = \frac{1}{x}$

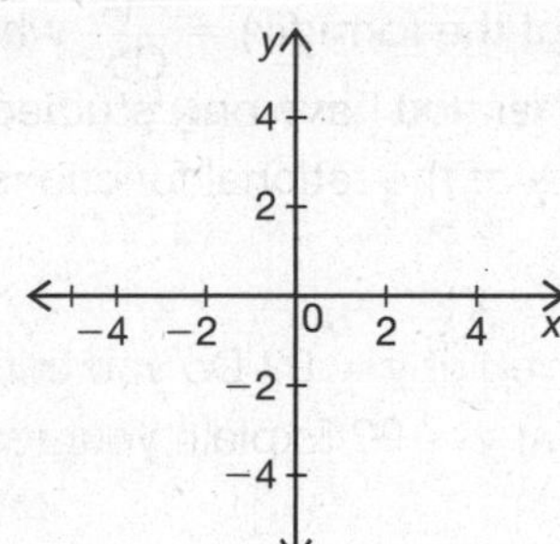

b. $y = \frac{1}{x^3}$

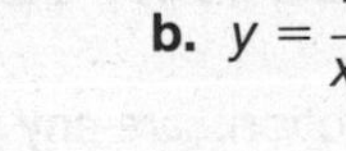

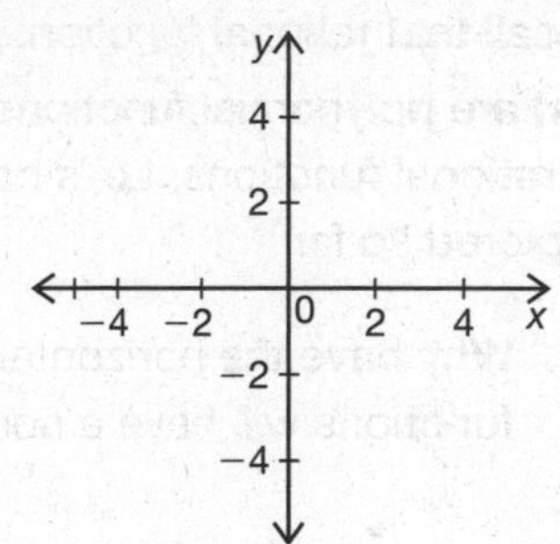

c. $y = \frac{1}{(x + 3)^3}$

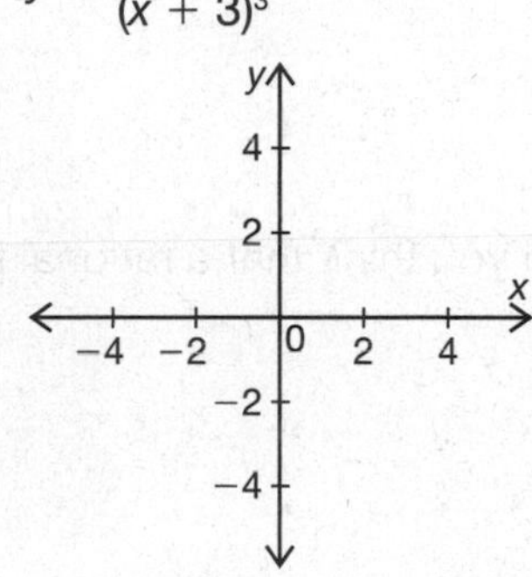

d. $y = \frac{-1}{(x + 3)^3}$

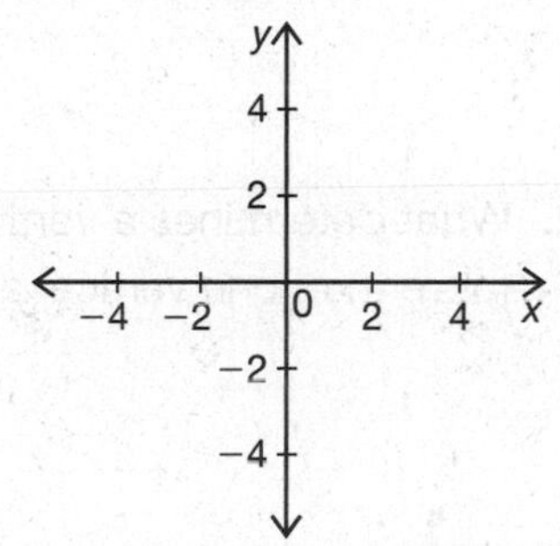

5. How would the graphs in Question 3 change for a greater even power? Explain your reasoning.

6. How would the graphs change in Question 4 for a greater odd power? Explain your reasoning.

PROBLEM 3 Shifty Behavior, Take 3

In the previous problems in this chapter, you analyzed rational functions with just 1 vertical asymptote. The vertical asymptote occurred at the value for which the denominator was zero.

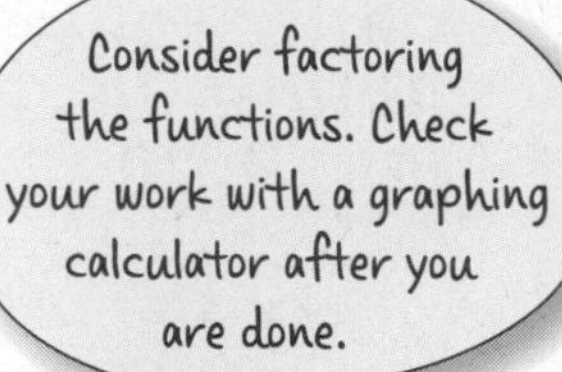

Consider factoring the functions. Check your work with a graphing calculator after you are done.

1. Without graphing, determine the number of vertical asymptotes for each function. Show all work and explain your reasoning.

   a. $f(x) = \dfrac{4}{x^2 + 4}$

   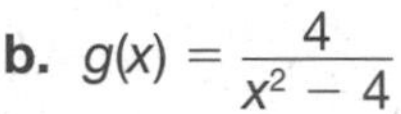

   b. $g(x) = \dfrac{4}{x^2 - 4}$

   c. $h(x) = \dfrac{4}{x^2 + 4x + 4}$

Recall from the Fundamental Theorem of Algebra that a function of degree *n* has *n* zeros. Some of the zeros may be imaginary. Therefore, it follows that the reciprocal of a function of degree *n* can have at most *n* vertical asymptotes.

2. Sarah determines the vertical asymptotes for the function $f(x) = \dfrac{1}{2x^2 - 14x - 16}$.

Sarah

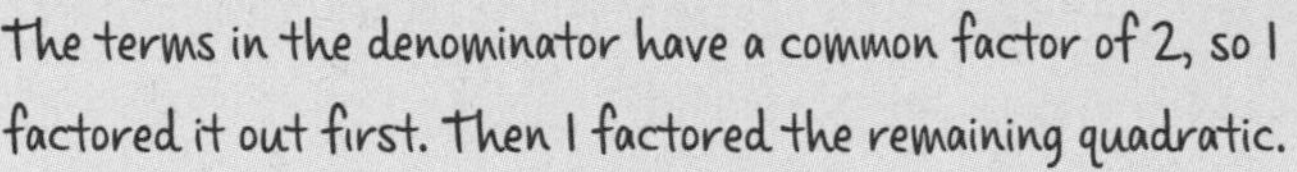

The terms in the denominator have a common factor of 2, so I factored it out first. Then I factored the remaining quadratic.

$$f(x) = \frac{1}{2(x^2 - 7x - 8)} = \frac{1}{2(x - 8)(x + 1)}$$

Vertical asymptotes occur when the denominator is zero. So, the asymptotes will occur when $x - 8 = 0$ and when $x + 1 = 0$.

Therefore, the asymptotes occur at $x = 8$ and $x = -1$.

Is Sarah correct? Explain your reasoning.

3. Analyze each rational function. Use algebra to determine the vertical asymptotes.

a. $f(x) = \dfrac{5}{7x - 35}$

b. $g(x) = \dfrac{1}{x(x - 2)(2x + 3)}$

c. $h(x) = \dfrac{10}{x^2 - 3x - 10}$

d. $h(x) = \dfrac{x}{2x^2 + 9x + 4}$

e. $h(x) = \dfrac{7}{x^4 - 1}$

f. $f(x) = \dfrac{2}{x^2 + 2}$

g. $h(x) = \dfrac{x - 2}{x - 2}$

h. $g(x) = \dfrac{x + 2}{(x + 2)(x - 5)}$

Hmmm . . . something interesting is going on with the functions in parts (g) and (h). We'll explore this concept later in the chapter, but for now consider why their asymptotic behavior might be different.

i. Use a graphing calculator to check your answers to Questions 3 by graphing and then by analyzing the table of values.

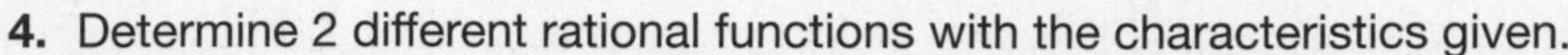

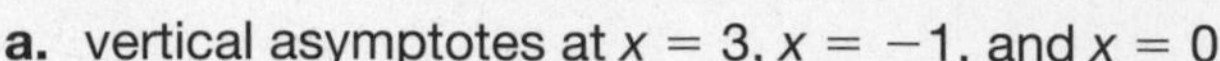

4. Determine 2 different rational functions with the characteristics given.

a. vertical asymptotes at $x = 3$, $x = -1$, and $x = 0$

9

b. vertical asymptotes at $x = \frac{1}{2}$ and $x = 2$

Be prepared to share your solutions and methods.

A Rational Approach

9.3

Exploring Rational Functions Graphically

LEARNING GOALS

In this lesson, you will:

- Graph rational functions.
- Determine graphical behavior of rational functions from the form of the equation.
- Translate rational functions.

The word "rational" means to be sensible or reasonable. Humans are said to be rational beings for our ability to use logic to move from a problem to its solution. Most definitions for the word "rational" are subjective. What might seem rational to one person may seem completely irrational to another. A person or group may come up with an idea that seems perfectly reasonable to them, but may seem eccentric to another group. This sometimes makes coming to a decision, or devising a solution path, very difficult for large groups of people.

Have you ever come up with an idea that you thought was perfectly rational, but others didn't quite agree with your rationale? Were you able to use logic to convince them that your idea made sense?

PROBLEM 1 Slow Down, Asymptotic Curves Ahead!

1. Analyze the methods Jodi, Theresa, and Jin each used to graph the rational function $j(x) = \frac{1}{x^2 - 4}$.

9

Jodi

I created a table and plotted the points.

-6	-5	-4	-3	-2	-1	0	1	2	3	4	5	6
$\frac{1}{32}$	$\frac{1}{21}$	$\frac{1}{12}$	$\frac{1}{5}$	undefined	$-\frac{1}{3}$	$-\frac{1}{4}$	$-\frac{1}{3}$	undefined	$\frac{1}{5}$	$\frac{1}{12}$	$\frac{1}{21}$	$\frac{1}{32}$

I see that vertical asymptotes occur at $x = -2$ and $x = 2$, where the denominator is 0 and the output is undefined.

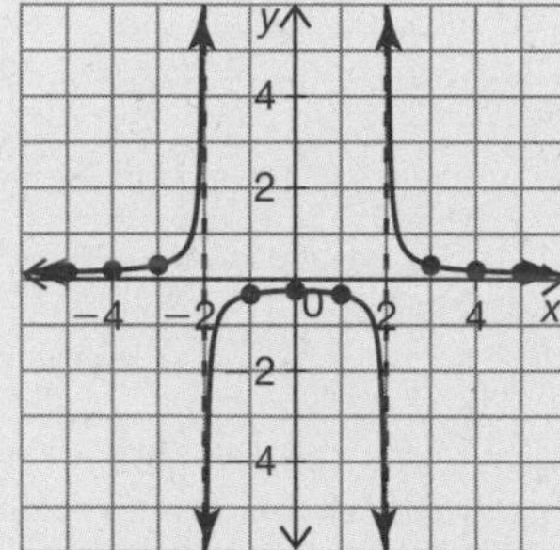

Theresa

I graphed the function $f(x) = x^2 - 4$. The function $j(x)$ is the reciprocal of $f(x)$, so I took the reciprocal of several key points and sketched the graph.

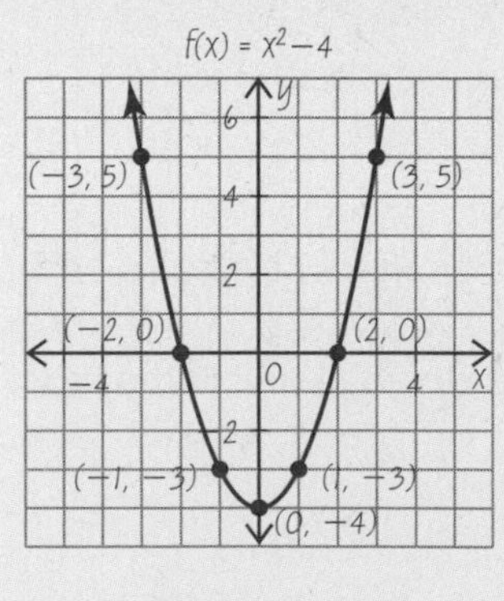

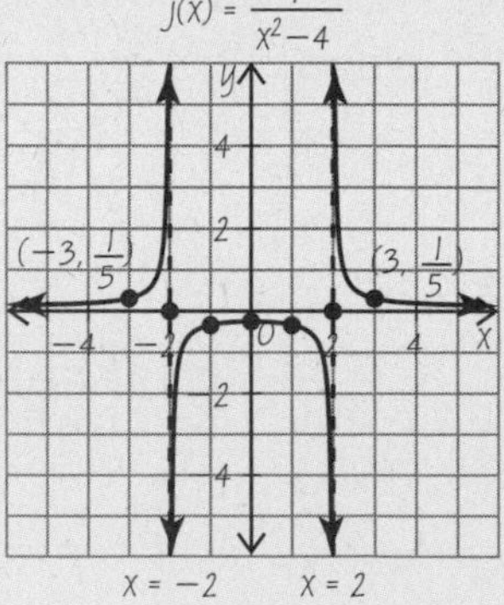

The zeros of the function $f(x) = x^2 - 4$ are $(-2, 0)$ and $(2, 0)$ that become asymptotes at $x = -2$ and $x = 2$ in the function $j(x) = \frac{1}{x^2 - 4}$. The y-intercept shifts from $(0, -4)$ in $f(x)$ to $\left(0, \frac{-1}{4}\right)$ in $j(x)$. By plotting a couple key points and recognizing that a horizontal asymptote is at $y = 0$, I can sketch the function.

Note that these aren't really "new" methods. Each student is applying previous knowledge to a new situation.

Jin

I used what I know about rational functions and function-building. Since the function $f(x) = \frac{1}{x^2 - 4}$ can be rewritten as two separate factors, $f(x) = \left(\frac{1}{x+2}\right)\left(\frac{1}{x-2}\right)$, I graphed each factor separately and multiplied their outputs to determine the graph of their product.

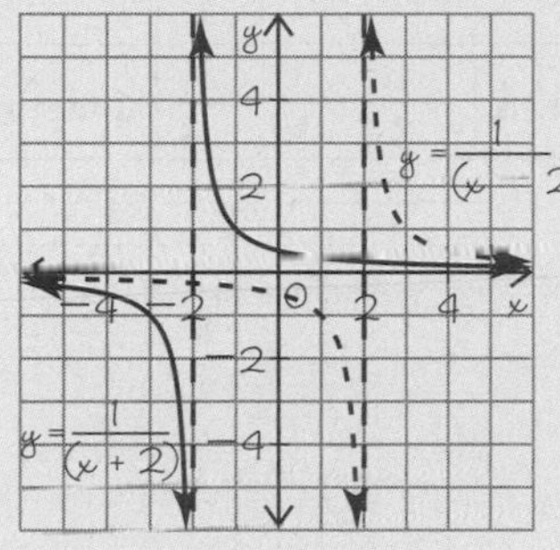

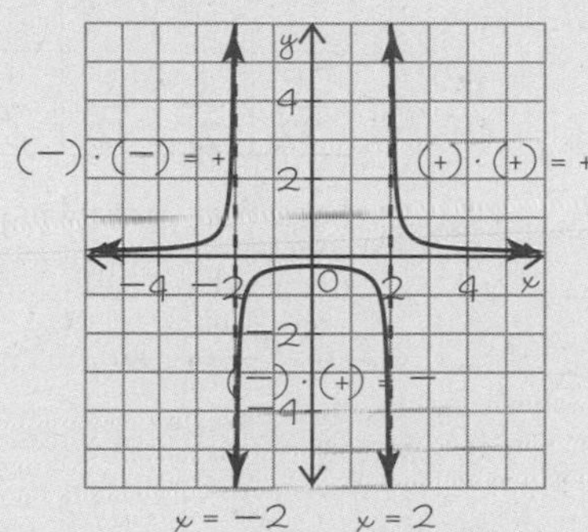

The asymptotes are at $x = -2$ and $x = 2$. Analyzing each function, I saw that the outputs were both negative for the interval $(-\infty, -2)$. Their product will always be positive so $f(x)$ will be above the x-axis for this region. Similarly, a positive and a negative output for the interval $(-2, 2)$ will always be negative. Two positive outputs multiplied together will be positive for the interval $(2, \infty)$.

a. Which method do you think is most efficient? Explain your reasoning.

b. Which method do you think is the most accurate? Explain your reasoning.

c. How does a vertical asymptote affect the domain of a function?

2. Without using a graphing calculator, sketch each function. Indicate the domain, range, vertical and horizontal asymptotes, and the y-intercept for each function.

a. $f(x) = \dfrac{1}{(x - 2)(x + 4)}$

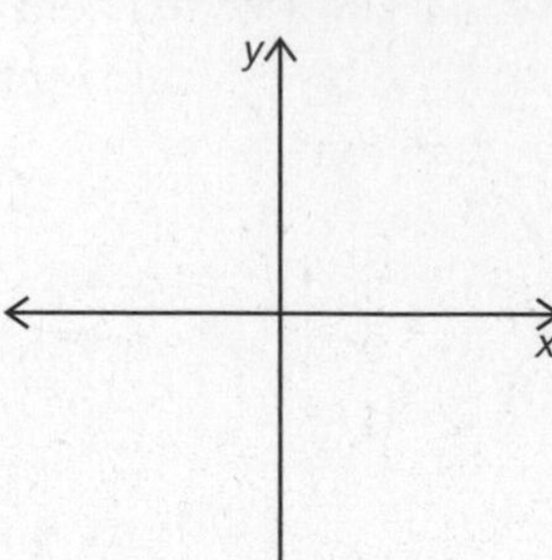

Domain:

Range:

Asymptote(s):

y-intercept:

b. $f(x) = \dfrac{2}{x^2 - 2x - 8}$

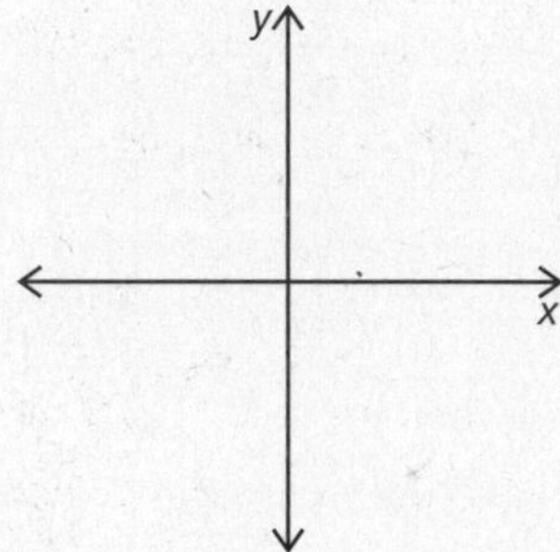

Domain:

Range:

Asymptote(s):

y-intercept:

c. $h(x) = \dfrac{1}{x^2 + 3x - 10}$

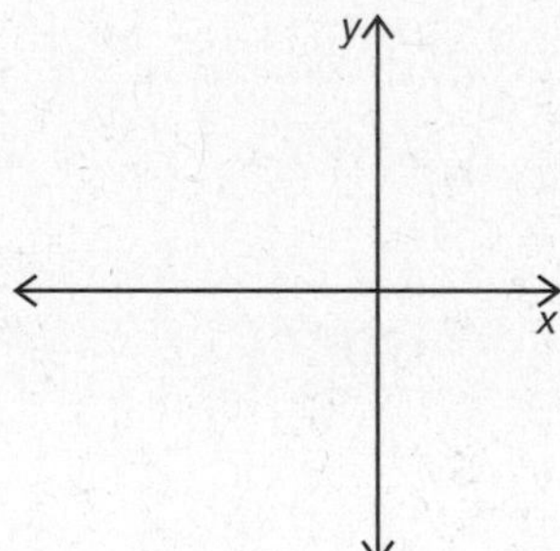

Domain:

Range:

Asymptote(s):

y-intercept:

d. $h(x) = \dfrac{1}{x^3 - 1}$

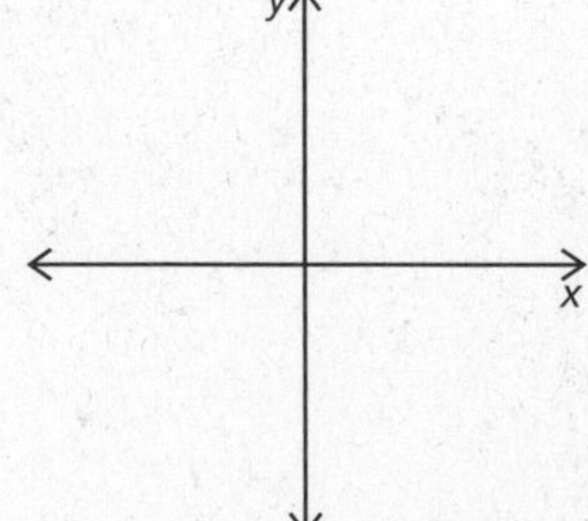

Domain:

Range:

Asymptote(s):

y-intercept:

PROBLEM 2 Ctrl-Alt-Shift

Consider the functions $y = f(x)$ and $g(x) = Af(B(x - C)) + D$. Recall that adding a constant D translates $f(x)$ vertically, while adding a constant C translates $f(x)$ horizontally. Multiplying by the constant A dilates $f(x)$ vertically, while multiplying by the constant B dilates $f(x)$ horizontally. Rational functions are transformed in the same manner.

1. The function $f(x) = \frac{1}{x}$ is shown in black on each coordinate plane. Determine whether the second function on each graph is $j(x) = \frac{1}{x + 2}$, $m(x) = \frac{2}{x}$, or $k(x) = \frac{1}{x} + 2$. Explain your reasoning.

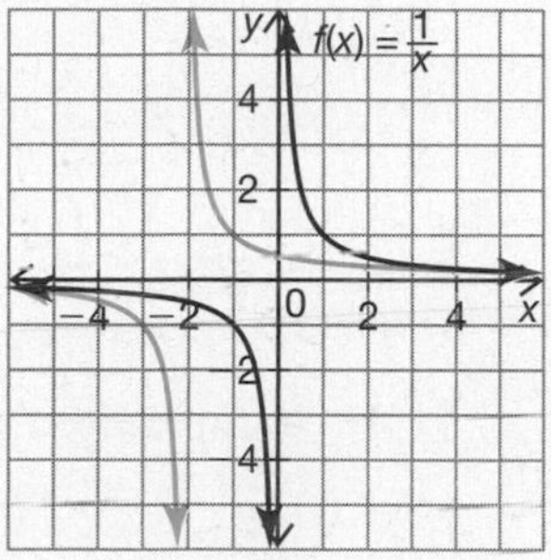 $f(x) = \frac{1}{x}$	Function: Explanation:
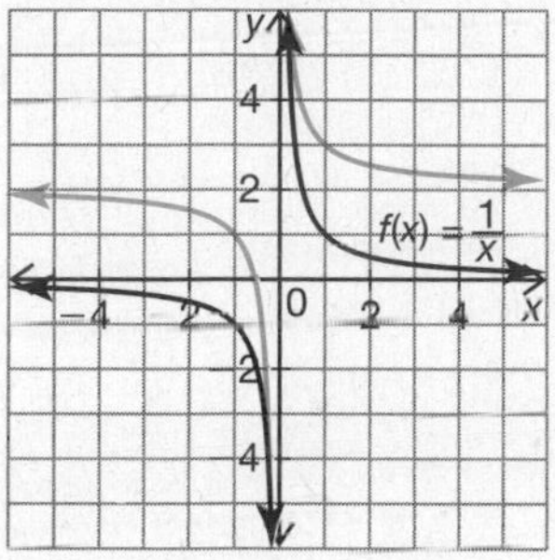 $f(x) = \frac{1}{x}$	Function: Explanation:
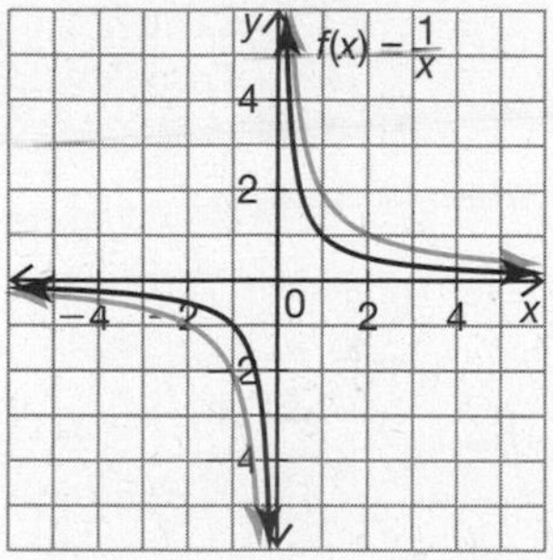 $f(x) = \frac{1}{x}$	Function: Explanation:

2. Given $f(x) = \frac{1}{x}$.

a. Sketch $g(x) = f(x) + 5$

b. Sketch $h(x) = f(x + 5)$.

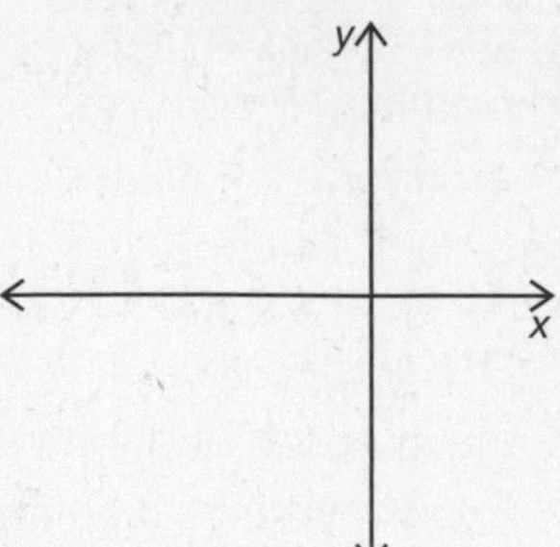

Explanation:

Explanation:

3. Write a rational function $g(x)$ that matches the given characteristics. Sketch the function on the coordinate plane.

a. Vertical asymptote at $x = 2$
Horizontal asymptote at $y = 1$

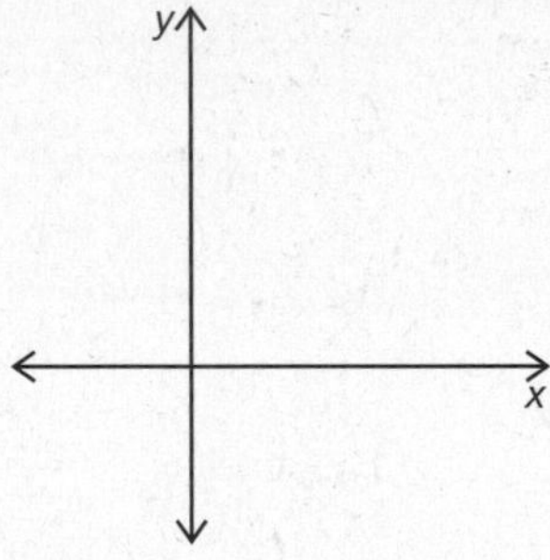

$g(x) =$

b. Vertical asymptote at $x = 1, x = -5$
Horizontal asymptote at $y = -3$

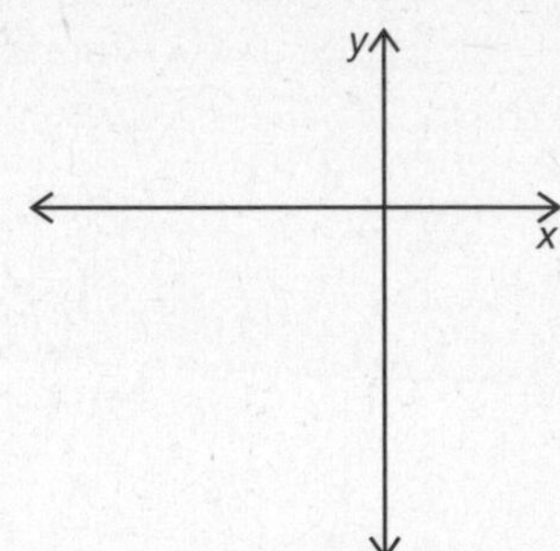

$g(x) =$

c. For $f(x) = \frac{1}{x}$, $g(x) = f(x - 2) - 4$

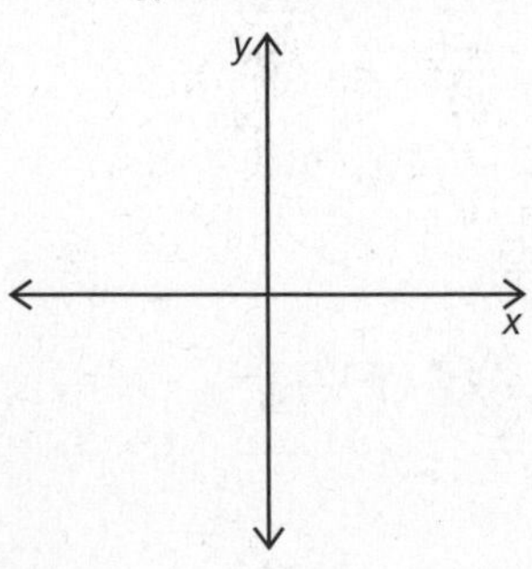

$g(x) =$

d. For $f(x) = \frac{1}{x}$, $g(x)$ shifts $f(x)$ up and to the left.

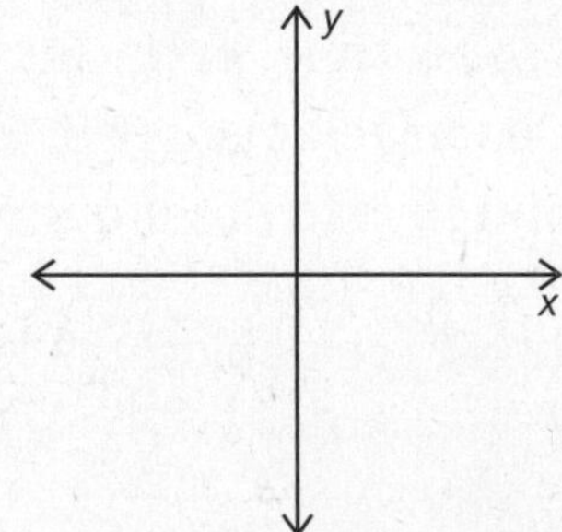

$g(x) =$

Be prepared to share your solutions and methods.

9.4

There's a Hole In My Function, Dear Liza

Graphical Discontinuities

LEARNING GOALS

In this lesson, you will:

- Sketch rational functions with removable discontinuities.
- Rewrite rational expressions.
- Compare removable discontinuities to vertical asymptotes.
- Identify domain restrictions of rational functions.

KEY TERM

- removable discontinuity

There's a Hole In My Bucket is an old children's song. Henry and Liza are two characters in the story.

The ozone layer is a part of the atmosphere that contains high levels of ozone. Ozone absorbs the UV radiation from the sun that might otherwise be harmful to life on Earth. Recently, some experts believe that the ozone levels have been depleting over time. In particular, areas around the North and South poles have developed "ozone holes" which are allowing the harmful rays to enter our atmosphere.

Why is the ozone depleting? What effects will this have on our environment?

PROBLEM 1 Mend Your Function, Dear Henry!

1. Without using a graphing calculator, match each rational function provided with the correct graph. Write the function below the graph.

$y = \dfrac{1}{x - 2}$	$y = \dfrac{1}{x}$	$y = \dfrac{x^2}{x}$	$y = \dfrac{x - 2}{x - 2}$
$y = \dfrac{x^3}{x}$	$y = \dfrac{(x - 2)^2}{x - 2}$	$y = \dfrac{x}{x}$	$y = \dfrac{(x - 2)^3}{x - 2}$

You may want to match the ones you know first. Consider the exponent rules and how the functions may reduce to a simpler form.

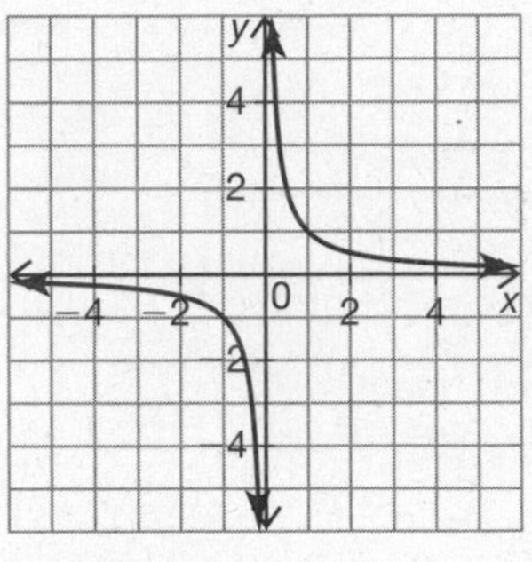

Function:

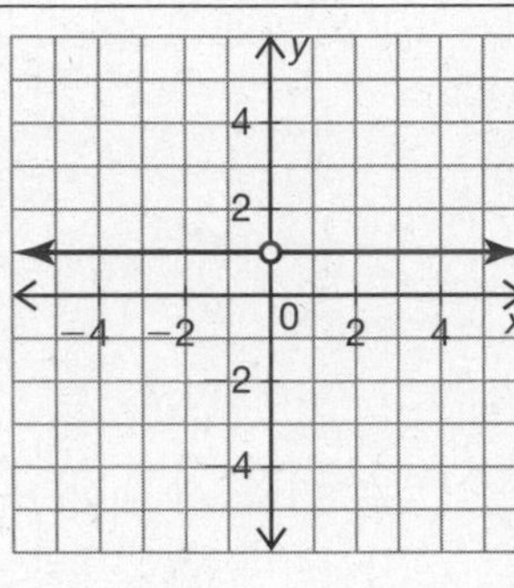

Function:

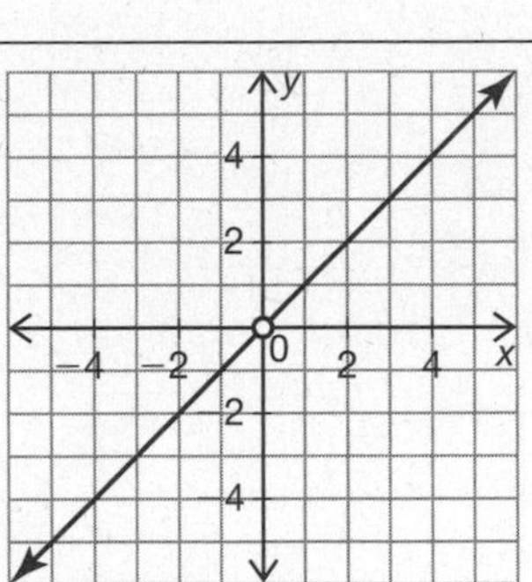

Function:

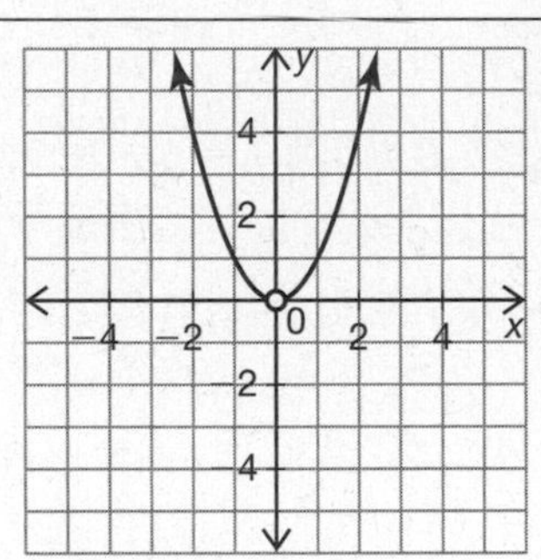

Function:

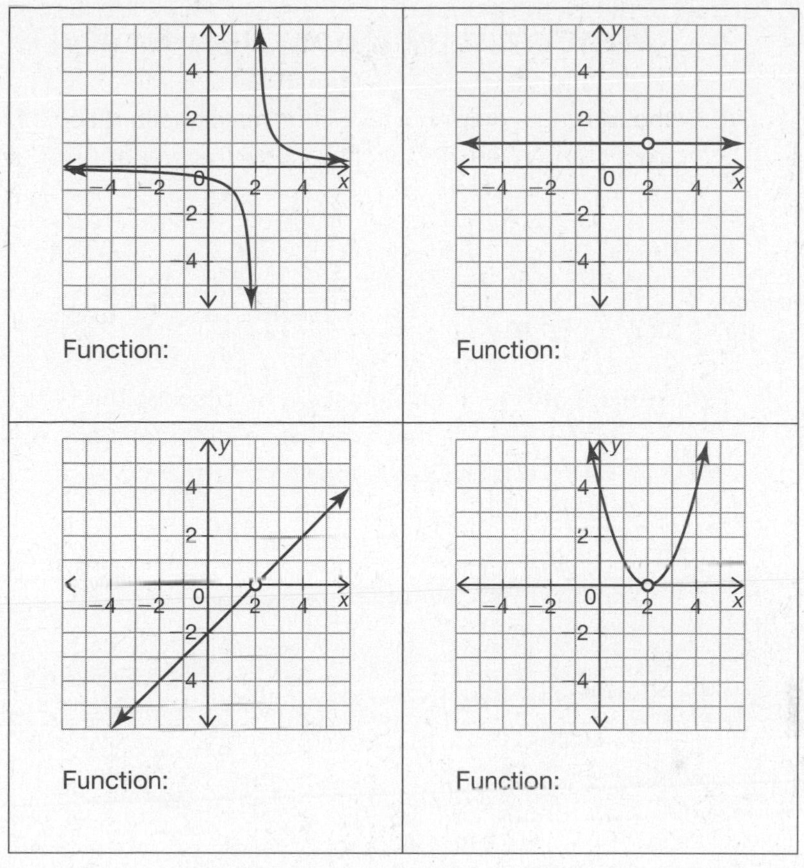

9

a. Which functions have asymptotes and which functions have "holes" in their graphs? Describe how the structure of the equation determines whether the function will have an asymptote or a "hole."

b. Compare the graphs of $y = \frac{1}{x - 2}$ and $y = \frac{x - 2}{x - 2}$. How are they the same? How are they different? Describe how the structure of the equation determines these differences.

When comparing the graphs, consider the general shape of the graph, domain, range, asymptotes, end behavior, etc.

c. Compare the graphs of $y = \frac{x}{x}$ and $y = \frac{x-2}{x-2}$. How are they the same? How are they different? Describe the similarities and differences in the domain and range in terms of the structure of their equations.

d. Without using a graphing calculator, describe the similarities and differences between the graphs of $y = \frac{x^3}{x^2}$ and $y = x$. Explain your reasoning in terms of the structure of the equations.

Many rational functions have "holes," or breaks, in the graphs instead of asymptotes. Let's analyze the structure of the function $y = \frac{x}{x}$ to determine why this function has a "hole" in the graph rather than a vertical asymptote at $x = 0$.

The function $y = \frac{x}{x}$ can be rewritten as the product of two factors: $y = (x)(\frac{1}{x})$. Looking at these reciprocal factors as separate functions reveals important characteristics.

x	-4	-3	-2	-1	0	1	2	3
$y = (x)\left(\frac{1}{x}\right)$	$(-4)\left(-\frac{1}{4}\right)$ 1	$(-3)\left(-\frac{1}{3}\right)$ 1	$(-2)\left(-\frac{1}{2}\right)$ 1	$(-1)\left(-\frac{1}{1}\right)$ 1	$(0)\left(\frac{1}{0}\right)$ und	$(1)\left(\frac{1}{1}\right)$ 1	$(2)\left(\frac{1}{2}\right)$ 1	$(3)\left(\frac{1}{3}\right)$ 1

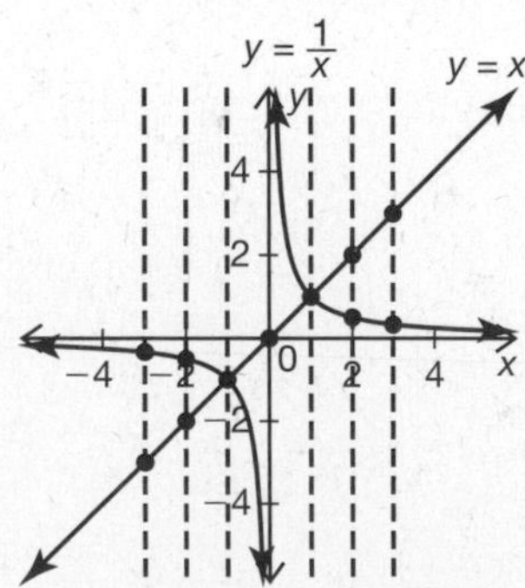

Graphical representation of each factor

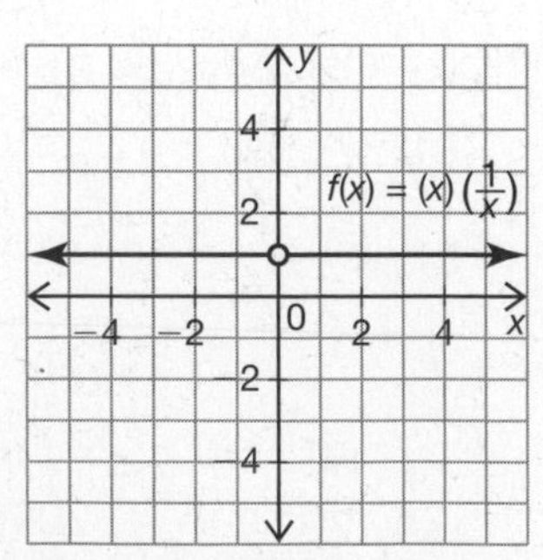

Graphical representation of the product

Multiplying the outputs for each input reveals that $(x)\left(\frac{1}{x}\right) = 1$. This graph is a horizontal line that is undefined at $x = 0$. It is undefined at $x = 0$ because this is the value for which an asymptote exists for the factor $\frac{1}{x}$. Similar reasoning can be used to show that for any function $f(x)$, $f(x) \cdot \frac{1}{f(x)} = 1$, with breaks in the graph for all undefined values where $f(x) = 0$. These breaks, or "holes," in the graph are called *removable discontinuities*. A **removable discontinuity** is a single point at which the graph is not defined. Vertical asymptotes and removable discontinuities must be listed as domain restrictions.

This shows graphically why common factors divide to 1. This is why it is not mathematically correct to say that terms "cancel."

2. Henry and Liza each describe a different way to graph $y = \frac{x^3}{x^2}$.

Henry

I know any function multiplied by its reciprocal is 1.

I can rewrite the function as $y = \frac{x^3}{x^2} = x \cdot \left(\frac{x^2}{x^2}\right)$.

This means that the output of $y = x$ is multiplied by $y = 1$ with a discontinuity at $x = 0$. The result is the line $y = x$ with a removable discontinuity at $(0, 0)$, so $x \neq 0$.

Liza

A removable discontinuity will exist anywhere that the denominator is 0 for the original function. In this case it is $(0, 0)$. I can use the exponent rules to simplify the function

$$y = \frac{x^3}{x^2}$$
$$= x^{3-2}$$
$$= x^1.$$

Then I can just graph $y = x$ with a hole at $(0, 0)$, so $x \neq 0$.

Which method do you prefer? Explain your reasoning.

9

3. Without using a graphing calculator, sketch the graph of each function. Be sure to note any asymptotes or holes in the graph.

a. $y = \frac{2x^2}{x^2}$

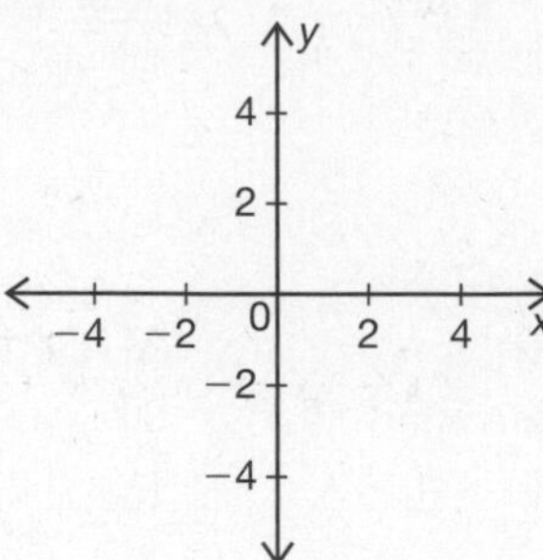

Think about the domain of each original function. Any domain restrictions should be visible in your sketch.

b. $y = \frac{x^2}{x^3}$

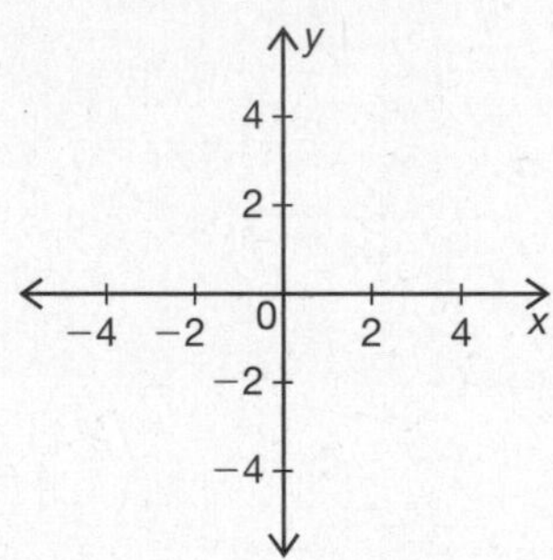

c. $y = \frac{x^4}{x^1}$

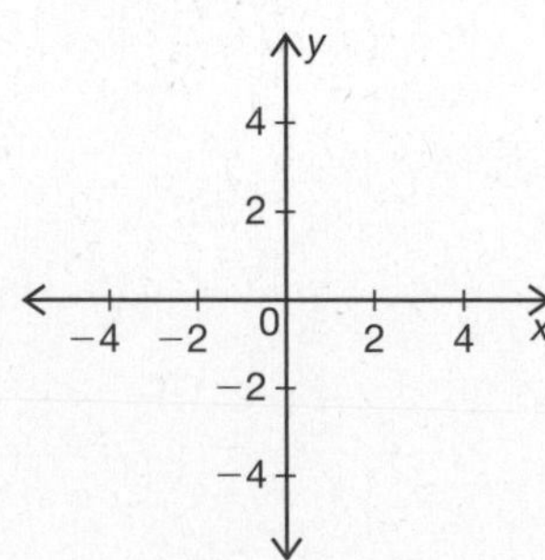

d. $y = \frac{-x^2}{x^4}$

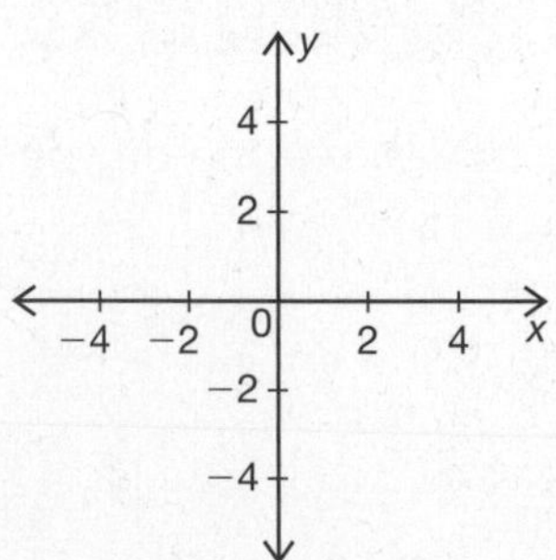

PROBLEM 2 With What Shall I Mend The Function, Dear Liza?

1. Henry graphed the rational function $f(x) = \frac{x^2 + x - 6}{x - 2}$. Analyze his work.

 **Henry**

I know there is a domain restriction, so $x \neq 2$.
I'm not sure if this is a vertical asymptote or a removable discontinuity, so I'm going to factor the numerator, if possible, to see if a common factor exists.

$$f(x) = \frac{x^2 + x - 6}{x - 2} = \frac{(x - 2)(x + 3)}{x - 2}$$
$$= \frac{1(x + 3)}{1} = x + 3$$

I know the output values of $\frac{(x - 2)}{(x - 2)} = 1$ with a discontinuity at $x = 2$. Therefore I can simply graph $f(x) = x + 3$. The removable discontinuity is at $(2, 2 + 3)$ and appears as a "hole" in the graph.

Note that the common factors do not "cancel." Many people use this term incorrectly to describe when factors divide to equal 1.

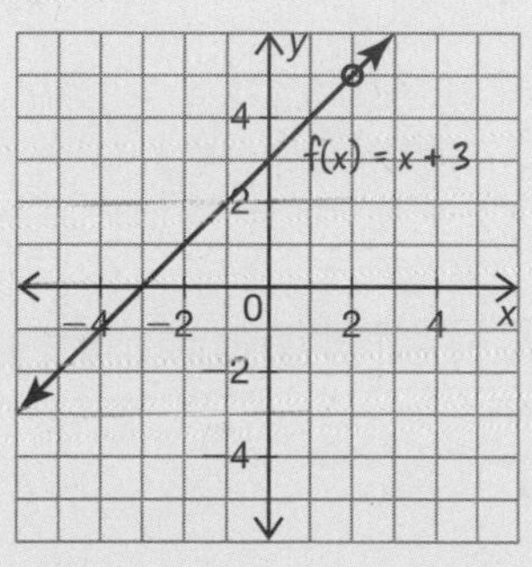

9

a. Why did Henry include an open circle at (2, 5) and *not* a vertical asymptote at $x = 2$?

b. Explain why $f(x) = \frac{x^2 + x - 6}{x - 2}$ can be rewritten as $f(x) = x + 3$.

The graphs of rational functions will have either a removable discontinuity or a vertical asymptote for all domain values that result in division by 0. Simplifying rational expressions is similar to simplifying rational numbers: common factors divide to 1.

2. Analyze the table that shows similarities between rational numbers and rational functions.

		Rational Numbers	**Rational Expressions**
A common numerator and denominator divide to equal 1.	**Examples**	$\frac{5}{5} = 1$	$\frac{x}{x} = 1$
		$\frac{10.7}{10.7} = 1$	$\frac{5x}{5x} = 1$
		$\frac{0.025 + 0.016}{0.025 + 0.016} = 1$	$\frac{x + 5}{x + 5} = 1$
Common monomial factors divide to equal 1.	**Examples**	$\frac{5 \cdot 3}{5} = \frac{1 \cdot 3}{1}$ $= 3$	$\frac{5x}{5} = \frac{1 \cdot x}{1} = x$
		$\frac{4}{4 \cdot 6} = \frac{1}{1 \cdot 6} = \frac{1}{6}$	$\frac{x}{xz} = \frac{1}{1 \cdot z} = \frac{1}{z}$
Common binomial factors divide to equal 1.	**Examples**	$\frac{(5 + 3)(16 - 7)}{(5 + 3)} = \frac{1 \cdot (16 - 7)}{1}$ $= 16 - 7$	$\frac{(x + 5)(x - 4)}{(x + 5)} = \frac{1(x - 4)}{1}$ $= (x - 4)$
		$\frac{(9 - 4)}{(9 - 4)(9 + 5)} = \frac{1}{(9 + 5)}$	$\frac{x - 4}{(x - 4)(x + 5)} = \frac{1}{(x + 5)}$

a. Describe how simplifying rational numbers is similar to simplifying rational expressions.

b. Why is there a 1 in the numerator after simplifying $\frac{x}{xz} = \frac{1}{z}$?

c. For each example in the rational expressions column, list any restrictions on the domain.

3. Liza rewrites the rational expression as shown.

Liza

$$\frac{x^2 + 4x + 3}{4x + 3} = x^2$$

I divided out the common factors. The numerator and denominator each have a 4x and a 3, so I am left with the squared term.

9

Describe the error in Liza's reasoning.

4. Simplify each rational expression. List any restrictions on the domain.

a. $\dfrac{2x^2 - 8}{x - 2}$

b. $\dfrac{3xy - 3y}{x^2 - 1}$

c. $\dfrac{x^2 - 5x + 6}{3x - 9}$

d. $\dfrac{x^3 - 7x^2 - 18x}{3x^2 - 9x}$

e. $\dfrac{25x^2 - 9}{5x^2 - 12x - 9}$

f. $\dfrac{x^3 - 5x^2 - x + 5}{x^2 - 6x + 5}$

PROBLEM 3 Use Your Head, Dear Henry!

9

1. Determine whether the graph of the rational function has a vertical asymptote, a removable discontinuity, both, or neither. List the discontinuities and justify your reasoning.

   a. $j(x) = \frac{x + 2}{x(x + 2)}$

   b. $h(x) = \frac{x}{x + 5}$

   c. $j(x) = \frac{5}{5(x + 2)}$

   d. $j(x) = \frac{x + 2}{x^2 - 2x - 15}$

2. Write two examples of rational functions with one or more removable discontinuities. Explain your reasoning.

3. Write a unique function that has a vertical asymptote and a removable discontinuity. Explain your reasoning.

4. Liza graphed the rational function $h(x) = \frac{x - 1}{x^2 + x - 2}$. Analyze her work.

Liza

I'm not sure where the asymptotes are, so I'm going to factor the denominator if possible.

$$h(x) = \frac{x - 1}{x^2 + x - 2} = \frac{x - 1}{(x - 1)(x + 2)}$$
$$= \frac{1}{x + 2}.$$

I know there are domain restrictions at $x = 1$ and $x = -2$. The common factor $(x - 1)$ is in the numerator so $\frac{x - 1}{x - 1} = 1$. Therefore $x = 1$ is a removable discontinuity, while $x = -2$ is a vertical asymptote. I can quickly sketch $h(x) = \frac{1}{x + 2}$ as a horizontal shift of $h(x) = \frac{1}{x}$ two units to the left. I know a discontinuity will exist at $\left(1, \frac{1}{1 + 2}\right)$, or $\left(1, \frac{1}{3}\right)$. A horizontal asymptote is at $y = 0$ and the y-intercept is $\left(0, \frac{1}{2}\right)$.

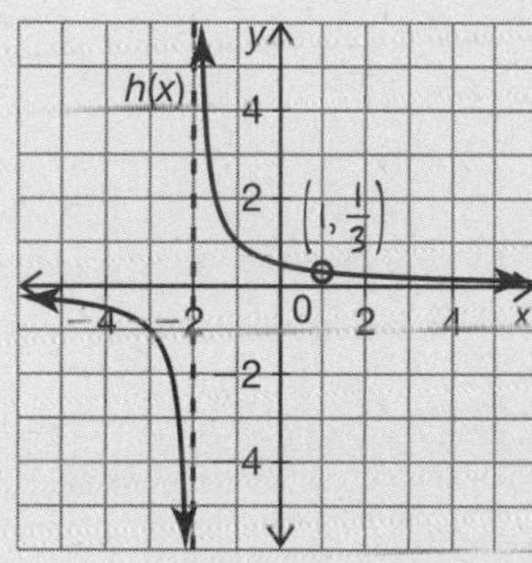

a. Summarize why $x = -2$ is a vertical asymptote while $x = 1$ appears as a "hole" in the graph.

b. Explain why the graph has a horizontal asymptote at $y = 0$.

5. Sketch each function without the use of a graphing calculator. Identify any restrictions.

a. $f(x) = \dfrac{x + 2}{x^2 + 4x + 4}$

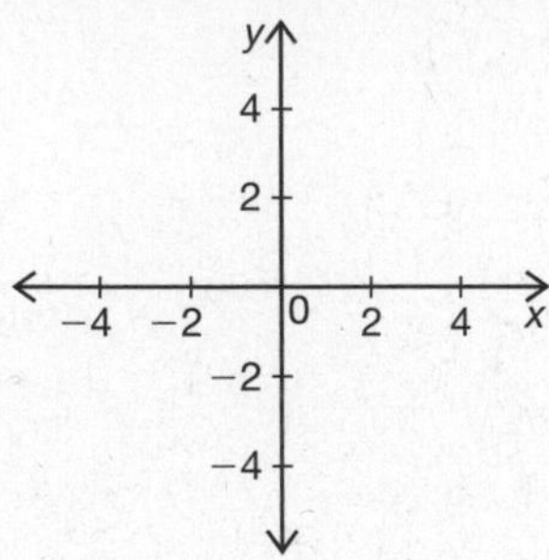

b. $g(x) = \dfrac{x}{x^2 + 3x}$

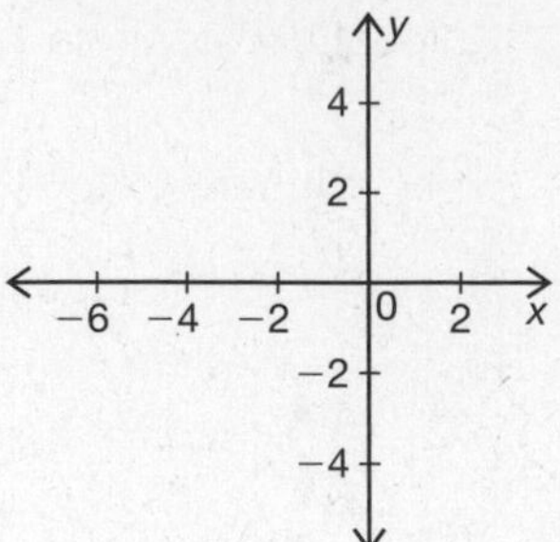

c. $h(x) = \dfrac{x}{x^3 - x}$

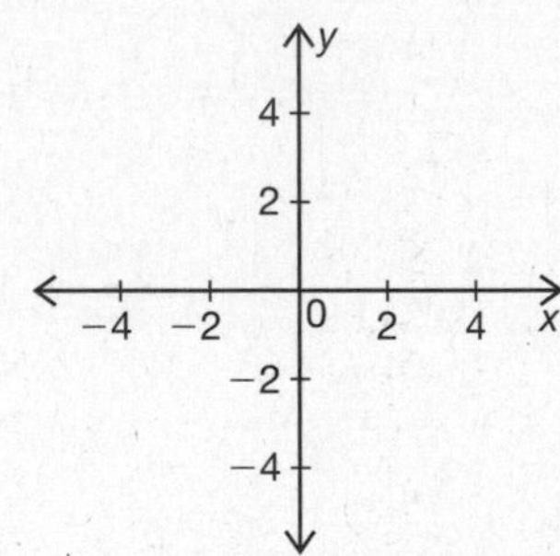

d. $m(x) = \dfrac{x^2 + 5x + 6}{x^2 + 5x + 6}$

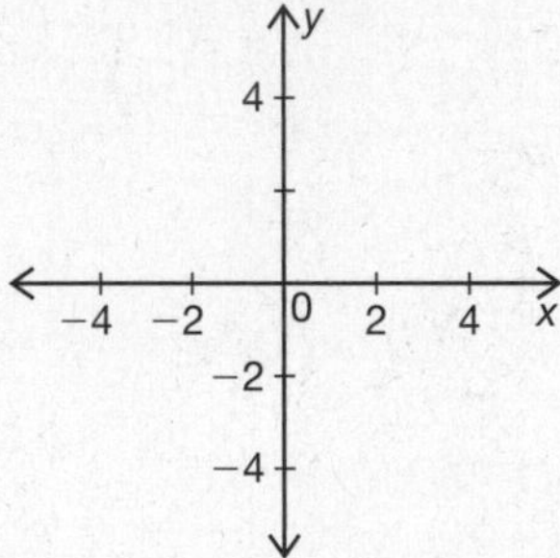

e. $k(x) = \dfrac{x^2 - 2x - 15}{x - 5}$

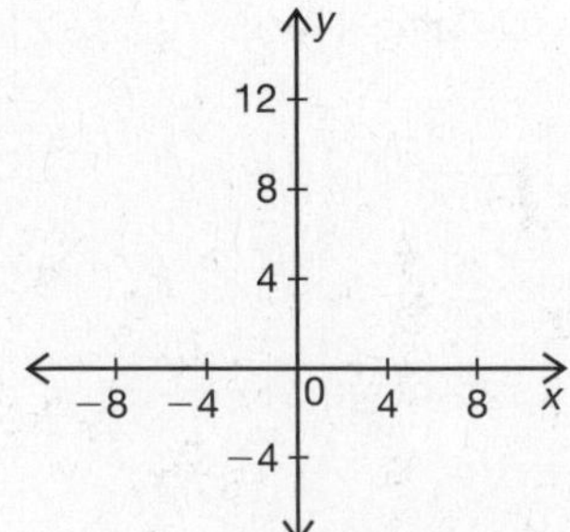

f. $k(x) = \dfrac{x^3 + x^2 + 2x + 2}{x + 1}$

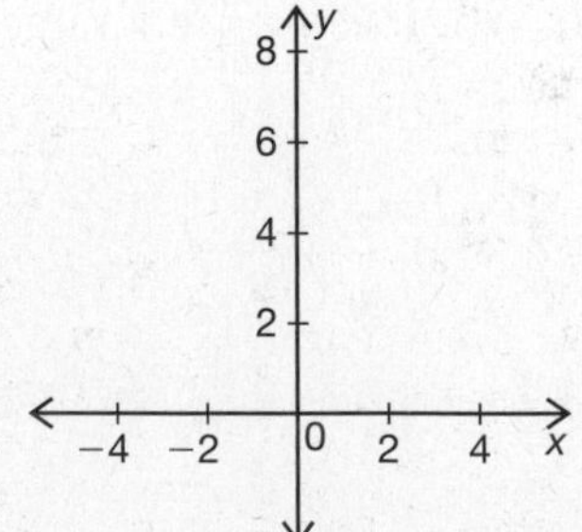

Talk the Talk

1. Describe the similarities and differences between rational numbers and rational expressions.

2. Describe the similarities and differences between vertical asymptotes and removable discontinuities.

3. Why is it incorrect to describe division by a common factor as "canceling out"?

Be prepared to share your solutions and methods.

9

9

The Breaking Point

9.5

Using Rational Functions to Solve Problems

LEARNING GOALS

In this lesson, you will:

- Model situations with rational functions.
- Use rational expressions to solve real-world problems.

In Psychology, the term *breaking point* refers to a traumatic moment when a person breaks down. This may happen because of emotional or physical stress, and often ends up being the point at which there must be some sort of resolution to a problem.

Television and movies regularly use this as the moment of climax or resolution to their stories. A criminal may break down because of intense feelings of guilt during a police interrogation. Two characters in a story may try to avoid a conflict over something until their bad feelings reach a breaking point where they must somehow resolve their conflict. During an intense sports competition, often one team struggles to win while the other team hits a breaking point that is too much to overcome.

Can you think of any specific movies where a character reaches a breaking point? How was this moment used in the story?

9

PROBLEM 1 Start Applying Yourself, Rational Function!

Recall that a rational expression is the ratio of two polynomials. Rational expressions can be used to solve problems that involve comparing two quantities of the same unit of measure.

1. Delilah is making her own salad dressing out of red vinegar and olive oil. It's a new recipe so she has to determine the correct proportions. She mixes 10 teaspoons of vinegar and 16 teaspoons of olive oil. After she stirs the mixture, she realizes it's not the consistency she wants, so she adds more olive oil.

   a. What is the ratio of red vinegar to olive oil if she adds 6 teaspoons more of olive oil?

   b. What is the ratio of red vinegar to olive oil if she adds 10 teaspoons more of olive oil?

   c. Write an expression to represent the ratio of red vinegar to olive oil. Let x represent the number of additional teaspoons of olive oil added to the recipe.

   d. Describe the behavior of the ratio as the number of additional teaspoons of olive oil increases. Show all of your work and explain your reasoning.

   e. The recommended ratio of vinegar to olive oil is 1:7. Determine the amount of olive oil that she must add to the mixture. Show all of your work and explain your reasoning.

Remember to use your proportional reasoning skills.

   f. What are the domain and range of the function? Explain your reasoning.

2. A door-to-door salesperson for TV Bonanza Cable Company offers cable television for only $55.95 per month. However, there is a one-time installation cost of $180.

   a. Determine the total cost of cable for the first two months. What is the average cost per month over the first two months?

Don't forget about the upfront charges.

9

   b. Determine the total cost of cable for the first year. What is the average cost per month over the first year?

   c. Write an equation to represent the total cost of cable for x months.

   d. Write an equation to represent the average monthly cost of cable for x months.

   e. A competitor offers a similar product for $65 per month and no installation charges. Who is offering the better deal? Show all work and explain your reasoning.

9

3. Tracy and Adrian model the following problem with a rational function.

Crunchy College Kid Snack Company manufactures a new brand of trail mix containing peanuts, almonds, and chocolate. Each package contains 400 grams of trail mix, with 50% peanuts, 35% almonds, and 15% chocolate. Herbert loves chocolate. When he gets the bag home, he wants to add enough chocolate so that the mixture is 50% chocolate. How many grams of chocolate should he add?

> Tracy
>
> I must first determine the amount of chocolate in the bag.
>
> $(0.15) \cdot (400) = 60g$
>
> The ratio of chocolate to total trail mix must increase to 50%. Adding chocolate increases the total amount of trail mix, so the new ratio is $\frac{60 + x}{400 + x}$. I can set up the proportion $\frac{60 + x}{400 + x} = 0.50$.
>
> The x-value represents the amount of additional chocolate.

> Adrian
>
> The current chocolate to trail mix ratio is $\frac{15}{100}$. Adding chocolate to get a mixture with 50% chocolate, add x to the percent chocolate as well as the total, so the rational equation becomes $\frac{15 + x}{100 + x} = 0.50$. The x-value of the intersection point represents the amount of chocolate Herbert must add.

a. Who is correct? Explain your reasoning. If necessary, include the error in the student's reasoning.

b. Determine the grams of chocolate that Herbert must add to the trail mix to get a mixture that is 50% chocolate.

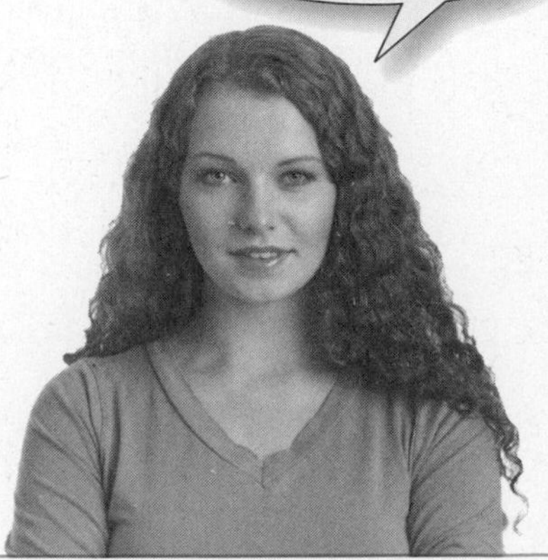
Use proportional reasoning to solve each equation.

4. A common misconception is that you can determine how far away a storm is by measuring the time between thunder and lightning. In reality, though, the time between seeing lightning and hearing thunder is a function of both distance and temperature. The time between seeing lightning and hearing thunder is represented by the function $Time = \frac{d}{1.09t + 1050}$, where d is the distance (feet) between the observer and the lightning, and t is the temperature (Fahrenheit).

   a. If the temperature outside is 70 degrees and you count 3 seconds between the thunder and the lightning, approximately how far away is the storm? Show all of your work and explain your reasoning.

9

   b. If the temperature is 80 degrees and you estimate half a second between thunder and lightning, how far away is the storm? Show all of your work and explain your reasoning.

   c. On a 60-degree day, what is the time between thunder and lightning when the storm is directly overhead? Show all work and explain your reasoning.

PROBLEM 2 For The Record

1. In football, a quarterback's completion percentage is the ratio of the number of complete passes to the total number of pass attempts. The current record holder for highest completion percentage is Chad Pennington who completed 66% of his passes over the course of his career in the National Football League. The quarterback in second place completed 3843 passes out of 5853 attempts. Estimate the number of consecutive complete passes the second place quarterback must throw in order to break the record. Show all of your work and explain your reasoning

9

2. Josie compares two different refrigerators at the local hardware store. The sales tags are shown.

ICY COLD
- Crushed Ice Dispenser
- Price $699.00
- Uses 75 Kilowatt hours of electricity per month

COOL AS A CUCUMBER
- Gold Star EPA efficiency rating
- Price: $825
- Uses 30 kilowatt hours of electricity per month

Josie does some research online and learns that a kilowatt hour costs approximately $0.06. She also learns that the average refrigerator lasts about 10 years.

a. Write a function to represent the average cost of each refrigerator per month.

b. Which refrigerator will have a lower average monthly cost over the next ten years? Show all of your work and explain your reasoning.

3. What is the least possible positive value for the sum of an integer and its reciprocal? Show all of your work and explain your reasoning.

9

4. Scott is taking a test that has two different parts to it. His goal is to get a 90%. He finished Part 1, and a quick scan by the teacher reveals that he got 18 out of the 23 questions correct. He begins Part 2. If he answers each consecutive question correctly, how many must he answer correctly for his grade to be higher than a 90%? Show all of your work and explain your reasoning.

5. Manuel enjoys racquetball, so he is considering joining a local gym. Joining the gym costs $30 each month, and they charge $2 per hour for using the racquetball courts. They also allow people who are not members of the club to use the courts for $7 per hour. If he joins the gym, how many hours would he have to play before the average cost is less than $7 per hour? Show all work and explain your reasoning.

6. The ancient Greeks felt as though certain rectangles in art and architecture were much more pleasing to the eye than others. When the ratio of the sum of the length and width to the length is approximately 1.618, they felt the rectangle was perfectly proportionate. This ratio came to be known as the *Golden Ratio*. Determine the length and width of several rectangles with dimensions that are in the *Golden Ratio*.

Many buildings today are constructed with windows that are in the golden ratio. In studies, people today still find rectangles with dimensions in this ratio most pleasing to look at.

Be prepared to share your solutions and methods.

Chapter 9 Summary

KEY TERMS

- rational function (9.1)
- vertical asymptote (9.1)
- removable discontinuity (9.4)

9

9.1 Determining Whether a Function Is or Is Not a Rational Function

A rational function is any function that can be written as the ratio of two polynomials.

It can be written in the form $f(x) = \frac{P(x)}{Q(x)}$ where $P(x)$ and $Q(x)$ are polynomial functions, and $Q(x) \neq 0$.

Example

$f(x) = \frac{x}{x + 7}$

The function $f(x)$ is a rational function because it is the ratio of two polynomials.

$g(x) = \frac{2^x}{x - 3}$

The function $g(x)$ is not a rational function because the numerator of the function has a variable in the exponent. The term 2^x is not a polynomial.

9.1 Determining the Domain and Range of a Rational Function

The domain of a rational function $f(x) = \frac{P(x)}{Q(x)}$ is the set of all real numbers that can be input as that variable x such that $f(x)$ is a real number. The range is the set of all values that the rational function can output when x is a value from the domain.

Example

$f(x) = \frac{-2}{x^3}$

The domain of $f(x)$ is the set of real numbers excluding 0. The range of $f(x)$ is the set of real numbers excluding 0.

9.1 Describing Vertical and Horizontal Asymptotes of a Rational Function

A vertical asymptote is a vertical line that a function gets closer and closer to, but never intersects. A horizontal asymptote is a horizontal line that a function gets closer and closer to, but never intersects. These asymptotes do not represent points on the graph of the function. They represent the output value that the graph approaches. In particular, a vertical asymptote generally occurs for input values that result in a denominator of 0.

9

Example

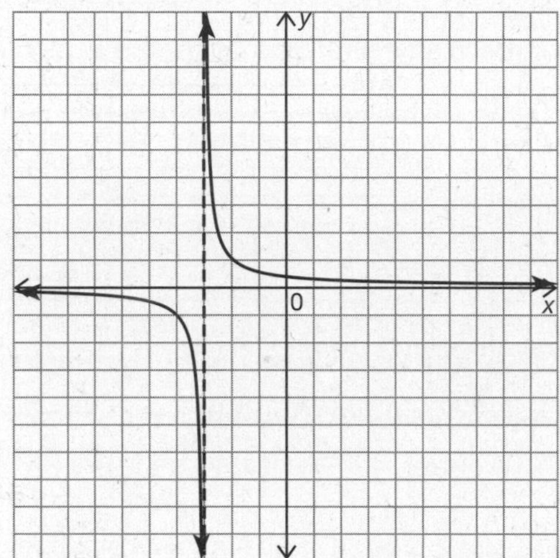

The vertical asymptote is the line $x = -3$. The horizontal asymptote is the x-axis or the line $y = 0$.

9.1 Describing the End Behavior of a Rational Function

The end behavior of a rational function is the characteristics of the function as the values of *x* approach positive and negative infinity.

Example

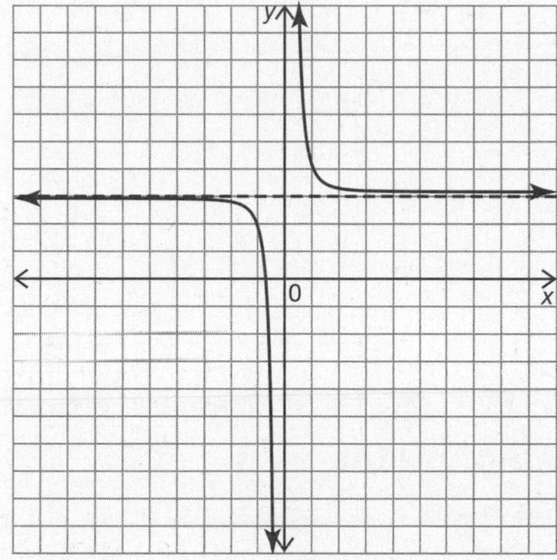

In this graph the end behavior of the rational function can be stated as follows. As *x* approaches negative infinity, *y* approaches 3. As *x* approaches positive infinity, *y* approaches 3.

9.1 Describing the Behavior of a Rational Function as *x* Approaches Zero From the Left and as *x* Approaches Zero From the Right

The behavior of a rational function on the left and right side of zero is the characteristics of the function as the values of *x* approach zero from the left and right.

Example

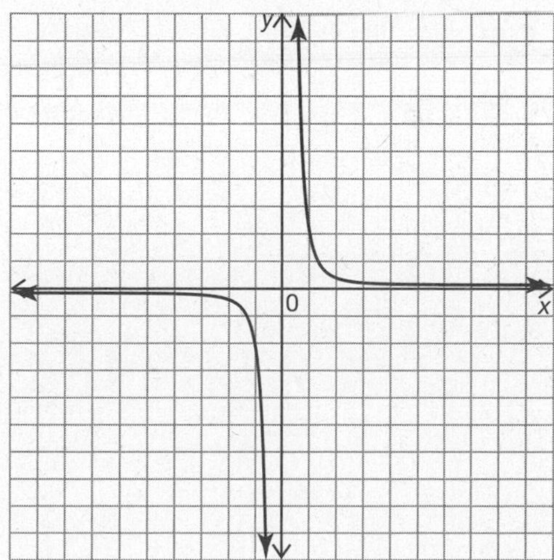

In this graph the behavior of the rational function as the values of *x* approach zero from the left and right can be stated as follows. As *x* approaches zero from the left, the *y* values approach negative infinity. As *x* approaches zero from the right, the *y* values approach infinity.

9

9.2 Determining the Domain, Range, and Vertical and Horizontal Asymptotes for a Rational Function

Just like all of the other functions previously studied, it is important to identify the domain and range of a rational function. Since the graph of rational function often has vertical and horizontal asymptotes it is equally important to identify them also.

Example

$f(x) = \dfrac{3}{x + 5}$

Domain: All real numbers except -5.

Range: All real numbers except 0.

Vertical Asymptote: $x = -5$

Horizontal Asymptote: $y = 0$

9.2 Analyzing Rational Functions Using Algebra to Determine Vertical Asymptotes

Vertical asymptotes for a rational function occur at the value(s) for which the denominator is zero. Sometimes algebra is needed to help identify the vertical asymptote(s).

Example

$f(x) = \dfrac{1}{x^2 + 2x - 8}$

$$x^2 + 2x - 8 = 0$$

$$(x + 4)(x - 2) = 0$$

$$x = -4, x = 2$$

Vertical asymptotes exist at $x = -4$ and $x = 2$.

9.2 Putting the Pieces Together and Using Them to Sketch a Rational Function Given Its Equation

Once the domain, range, and vertical and horizontal asymptotes are known a sketch of the rational function can be made.

Example

$f(x) = \frac{-1}{x + 2}$

Domain: All real numbers except -2.

Range: All real numbers except 0.

Vertical Asymptote: $x = -2$

Horizontal Asymptote: $y = 0$

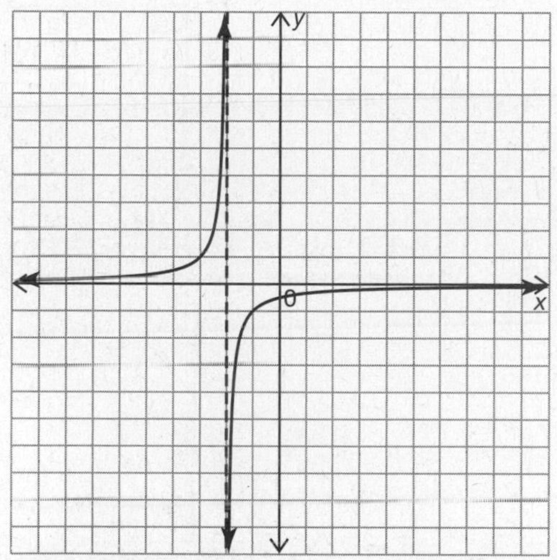

9

9.2 Writing a Rule for a Rational Function Given Its Description

If enough characteristics of a rational function are known, an equation modeling these characteristics can be written. Be aware that there are many correct answers implying different rational functions can share similar characteristics.

Example

Vertical asymptote at $x = 4$. The range is all real numbers except $y = 0$.

Sample answer: $f(x) = \frac{3}{x - 4}$

The denominator cannot be 4 so there will be a vertical asymptote at $x = 4$. The function has a constant in the numerator and a variable in the denominator, so the output will approach 0 as x increases or decreases, creating a horizontal asymptote at $y = 0$.

9.3 Translating and Dilating a Rational Function

Consider the functions $y = f(x)$ and $g(x) = Af[B(x - C)] + D$. Recall that adding a constant D translates $f(x)$ vertically, while adding a constant C translates $f(x)$ horizontally. Multiplying by the constant A dilates $f(x)$ vertically, while multiplying by the constant B dilates $f(x)$ horizontally. Rational functions are transformed in the same manner.

9

Example

The function $f(x) = \frac{1}{x}$ is shown in black on the coordinate plane. Determine whether the second function on the coordinate plane is the graph of $g(x) = \frac{1}{x - 1}$, $p(x) = \frac{1}{x + 1}$, or $q(x) = \frac{1}{x} + 1$. Explain your reasoning.

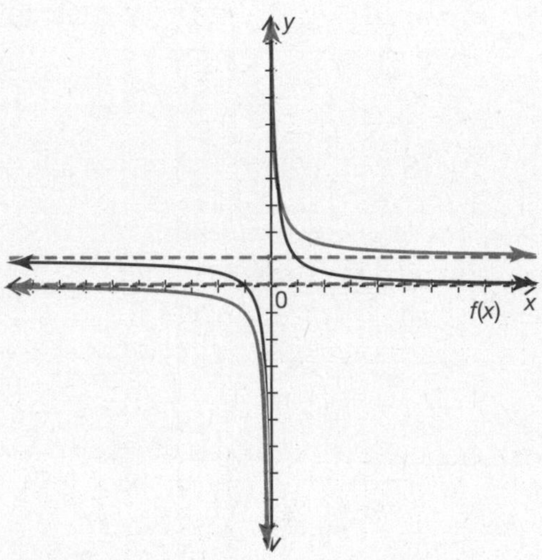

Function: $q(x) = \frac{1}{x} + 1$

Explanation: The original function $f(x) = \frac{1}{x}$ has been translated 1 unit up. This results from a change in the D-value.

9.3

Sketching a Rational Function in Detail

Given the equation of a rational function and having developed the tools to analyze its characteristics, a detailed sketch of the function can be made.

Example

$f(x) = \frac{1}{x^2 - x - 6}$

$\frac{1}{x^2 - x - 6} = \frac{1}{(x + 2)(x - 3)}$

$(x + 2)(x - 3) = 0$

$x = -2, x = 3$

Domain: All real numbers except $x = -2$ and 3.

Range: All real numbers except 0.

Vertical Asymptotes: $x = -2$ and $x = 3$

Horizontal Asymptote: $y = 0$

y-intercept: $\left(0, -\frac{1}{6}\right)$

9

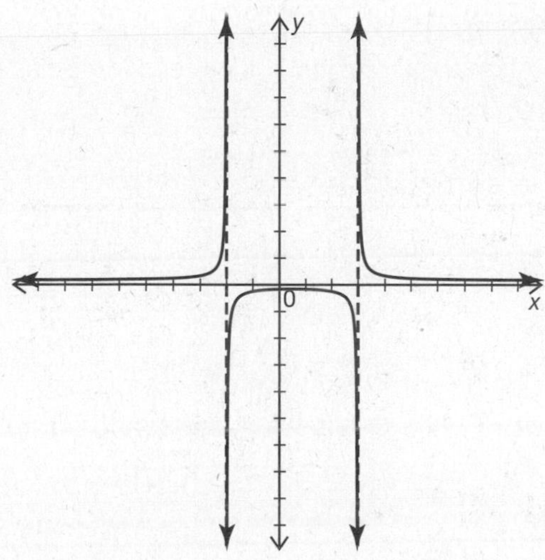

9.3

Writing the Equation of a Rational Function that Matches the Given Characteristics

The more that is known about the characteristics of a rational function, the easier it is to write an equation modeling the given characteristics. Be aware that there are many correct answers implying different rational functions can share similar characteristics.

Example

Given $f(x) = \frac{1}{x}$ and $g(x) = f(x - 4) + 3$, write a rational equation modeling $g(x)$.

Sample answer: $g(x) = \frac{1}{x - 4} + 3$

9

9.4 Comparing Removable Discontinuities to Vertical Asymptotes

A removable discontinuity is a single point at which the graph of a function is not defined. A vertical asymptote is a vertical line that a function gets closer and closer to, but never intersects. When looking for removable discontinuities, look for common factors in the numerator and denominator of the rational function. The zeros of these common factors, if they exist, represent removable discontinuities.

Example

$$f(x) = \frac{x(x + 7)}{(x - 3)(x + 7)}$$

The function $f(x)$ has a removable discontinuity at $x = -7$ and a vertical asymptote at $x = 3$. Notice that $x + 7$ is a common factor in both the numerator and denominator of the rational function.

9.4 Simplifying Rational Expressions

When simplifying a rational expression it is necessary to list all restrictions on the variable along with the answer.

Example

$$\frac{x^2 + 6x - 7}{x - 1}$$

$$\frac{x^2 + 6x - 7}{x - 1} = \frac{\overset{1}{\cancel{(x - 1)}}(x + 7)}{\underset{1}{\cancel{(x - 1)}}}$$

$$= x + 7; x \neq 1$$

9.4 Sketching Rational Functions with Removable Discontinuities

A removable discontinuity is a single point at which the graph is not defined.

Example

$$f(x) = \frac{(x - 2)}{(x + 4)(x - 2)}$$

$$f(x) = \frac{(x - 2)}{(x + 4)(x - 2)}$$

$$= \frac{\overset{1}{\cancel{(x - 2)}}}{(x + 4)\underset{1}{\cancel{(x - 2)}}}$$

$$= \frac{1}{x + 4}; x \neq -4, 2$$

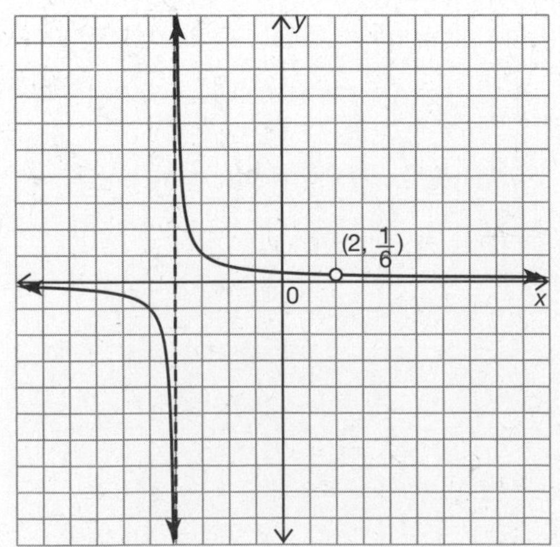

9.5 Modeling Situations with Rational Functions

Rational expressions can be used to solve problems that involve comparing two quantities of the same unit of measure.

Example

Television Land is a media service provider. They advertise that you can buy a monthly plan for as low as \$75 per month as long as you buy a DVR from them costing \$150. If you buy the monthly plan along with the DVR, how many months will it take for your average monthly cost of owning the DVR and the plan to be less than \$100?

In the 6th month the average monthly cost will be less than \$100. The average monthly cost of buying the plan along with the DVR for x months is $\frac{150 + 75x}{x}$.

$$100 = \frac{150 + 75x}{x}$$

$$100x = 150 + 75x$$

$$25x = 150$$

$$x = 6$$

9.5 Solving Rational Functions Graphically

Equations of the form $f(x) = g(x)$, where $f(x)$ and $g(x)$ are rational functions, can be solved by graphing $y = f(x)$ and $y = g(x)$ on the same coordinate plane and identifying their intersection.

Example

$$\frac{-1}{x - 2} = -1$$

$$f(x) = \frac{-1}{x - 2}$$

$$g(x) = -1$$

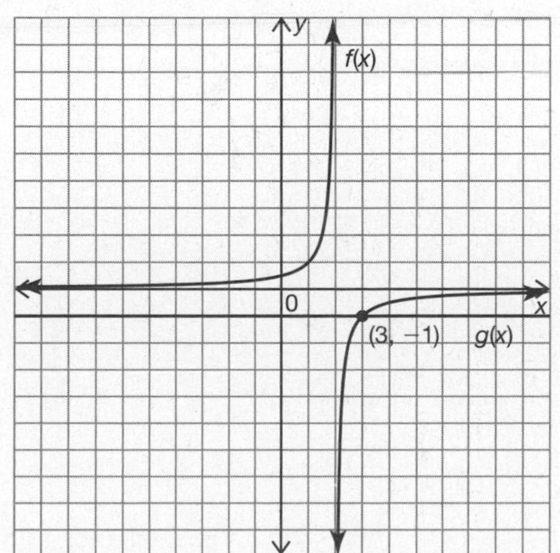

$f(x) = g(x)$ at $x = 3$.

The solution is $x = 3$.

Solving Rational Equations

10

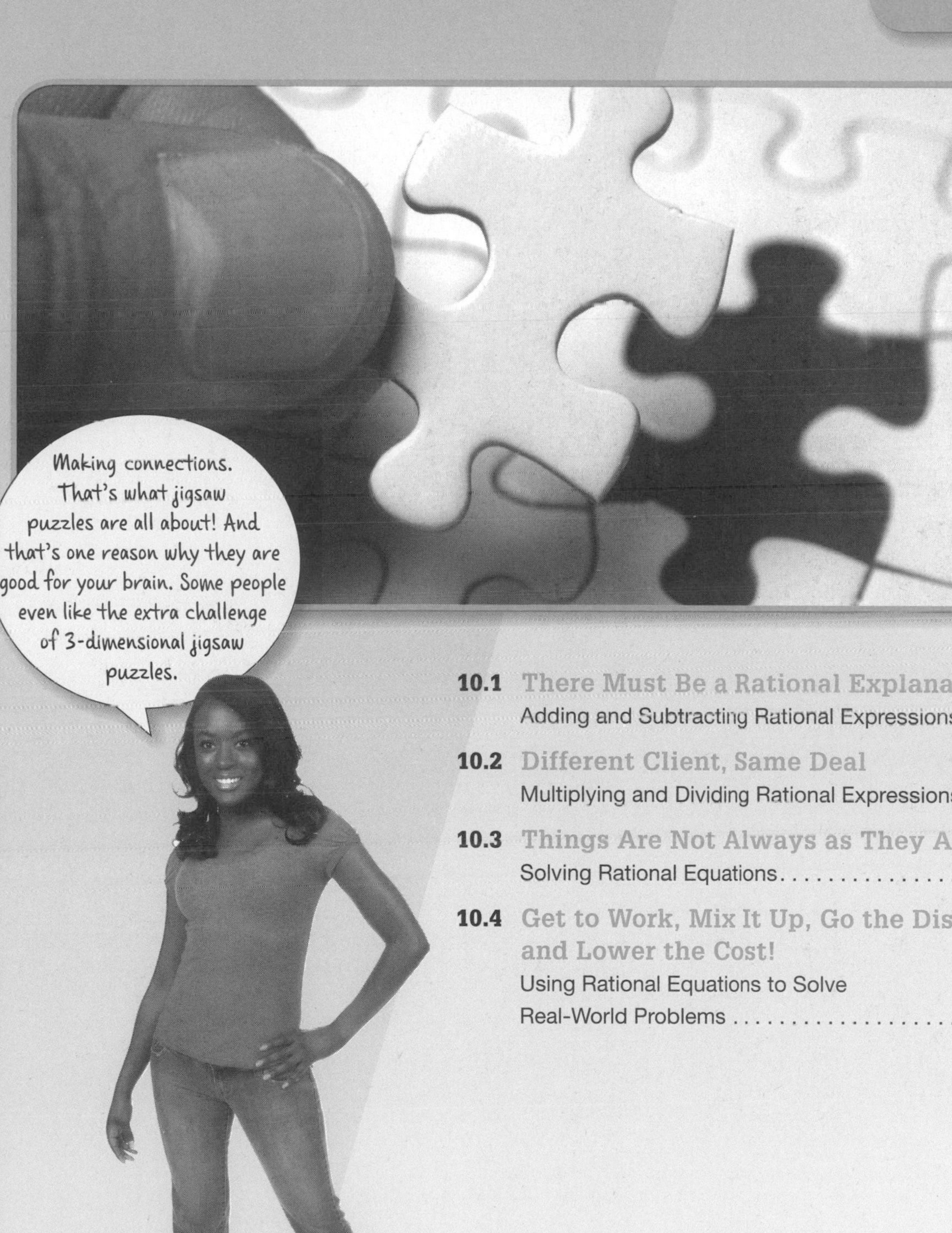
Making connections. That's what jigsaw puzzles are all about! And that's one reason why they are good for your brain. Some people even like the extra challenge of 3-dimensional jigsaw puzzles.

There Must Be a Rational Explanation

Adding and Subtracting Rational Expressions

10.1

LEARNING GOALS

In this lesson, you will:

- Add and subtract rational expressions.
- Factor to determine a least common denominator.

At some point in most people's lives, the task of putting together a jigsaw puzzle is just one of the things everyone seems to do. In a jigsaw puzzle, small, interlocking pieces with colors or designs fit together to make a larger picture. The pieces can only fit together one way, so various strategies are employed to determine which pieces fit together. Younger children are often encouraged to work on jigsaw puzzles as a way of developing problem-solving skills. Jigsaw puzzles are popular among adults, too, and some of them can get quite complicated. Sometimes, complex designs, a large number of pieces, or even 3-dimensional platforms can make puzzles very challenging. A lot of time, skill, and patience are required to put these puzzles together. One particular puzzle has 24,000 pieces! That certainly isn't child's play!

People who are serious about puzzles can qualify to be on a national puzzling team and compete in international competitions. The most prestigious competition is held every year in Belgium. What types of puzzles or board games do you like? Do you know anybody who is really good at putting puzzles together?

PROBLEM 1 Oh Snap . . . Look at the Denominator on that Rational

Previously, you learned that dividing polynomials was just like dividing integers. Well, performing operations on rational expressions involving variables is just like performing operations on rational numbers.

	Rational Numbers	Rational Expressions Involving Variables in the Numerator
Example 1	$\frac{1}{6} + \frac{5}{6} - \frac{1}{6} = \frac{5}{6}$	$\frac{1x}{6} + \frac{5x}{6} - \frac{1x}{6} = \frac{5x}{6}$
Example 2	$\frac{3}{2} + \frac{2}{5} - \frac{3}{4} = \frac{3(10)}{2(10)} + \frac{2(4)}{5(4)} - \frac{3(5)}{4(5)}$ $= \frac{30}{20} + \frac{8}{20} - \frac{15}{20}$ $= \frac{23}{20}$	$\frac{3x}{2} + \frac{2y}{5} - \frac{3x}{4} = \frac{3(10)x}{2(10)} + \frac{2(4)y}{5(4)} - \frac{3(5)x}{4(5)}$ $= \frac{30x}{20} + \frac{8y}{20} - \frac{15x}{20}$ $= \frac{15x + 8y}{20}$
Example 3	$\frac{3}{5} + \frac{2}{3} - \frac{2}{15} = \frac{3(3)}{5(3)} + \frac{2(5)}{3(5)} - \frac{2}{15}$ $= \frac{9}{15} + \frac{10}{15} - \frac{2}{15}$ $= \frac{17}{15}$	$\frac{3x}{5} + \frac{2y}{3} - \frac{2}{15} - \frac{2x + 3y}{5} = \frac{3(3)x}{5(3)} + \frac{2(5)y}{3(5)} - \frac{2}{15} - \frac{(2x + 3y)(3)}{5(3)}$ $= \frac{9x}{15} + \frac{10y}{15} - \frac{2}{15} - \frac{6x + 9y}{15}$ $= \frac{9x + 10y - 2 - (6x + 9y)}{15}$ $= \frac{9x + 10y - 2 - 6x - 9y}{15}$ $= \frac{3x + y - 2}{15}$

1. Analyze the examples.

   a. Explain the process used to add and subtract each expression.

   b. In Example 2, why is $\frac{3}{2} = \frac{3(10)}{2(10)}$ and why is $\frac{3x}{2} = \frac{3(10)x}{2(10)}$?

   c. In Example 3, explain how $-\frac{(2x + 3y)(3)}{5(3)} = \frac{-6x - 9y}{15}$.

2. Analyze Noelle's work.

> *Noelle*
>
> $$\frac{3x}{3} + \frac{2x}{8} - \frac{1}{2}$$
>
> *To determine a common denominator, I multiply all the denominators together:* $3 \cdot 8 \cdot 2 = 48$
>
> $$\frac{3x(16)}{3(16)} + \frac{2x(6)}{8(6)} - \frac{1(24)}{2(24)} = \frac{48x}{48} + \frac{12x}{48} - \frac{24}{48}$$
> $$= \frac{60x - 24}{48}$$
> $$= \frac{5x - 2}{4}$$

Explain how Noelle could have added the rational expressions more efficiently.

10

3. Calculate each sum and difference.

a. $\frac{3}{6} + \frac{5x}{4} - \frac{y}{8}$

b. $\frac{x - 2y}{3} + \frac{x}{12} - \frac{z}{4}$

c. $\frac{4x}{6} - \frac{2x}{9} - \frac{x}{18}$

4. Is the set of rational expressions closed under addition and subtraction? Explain your reasoning.

5. Notice that all the variables in the right column of the table are in the numerator. If there were variables in the denominator, do you think the process of adding and subtracting the expressions would change? Explain your reasoning

PROBLEM 2 Umm, I Think There Are Some Variables in Your Denominator . . .

10

When rational expressions contain variables in the denominator, the process remains the same—you still need to determine the least common denominator (LCD) before adding and subtracting.

It will save time and effort if you determine the LCD and use it to add and subtract rational expressions.

All your factoring skills will come in handy.

1. Consider Method A compared to Method B in both columns of the table.

	Rational Numbers	Rational Expressions Involving Variables in the Denominator
Method A	$\frac{1}{3}+\frac{1}{3^2}=\frac{1(3^2)}{3(3^2)}+\frac{1(3)}{3^2(3)}$ $=\frac{3^2}{3^3}+\frac{3}{3^3}$ $=\frac{3^2+3}{3^3}$ $=\frac{3(3+1)}{3(3^2)}$ $=\frac{3+1}{3^2}$	$\frac{1}{x}+\frac{1}{x^2}=\frac{1(x^2)}{x(x^2)}+\frac{1(x)}{x^2(x)}$ $=\frac{x^2}{x^3}+\frac{x}{x^3}$ $=\frac{x^2+x}{x^3}$ $=\frac{x(x+1)}{x(x^2)}$ $=\frac{x+1}{x^2}$ $\frac{1}{x}+\frac{1}{x^2}=\frac{x+1}{x^2}$ for $x \neq 0$
Method B	$\frac{1}{3}+\frac{1}{3^2}=\frac{1(3)}{3(3)}+\frac{1}{3^2}=\frac{4}{3^2}$	$\frac{1}{x}+\frac{1}{x^2}=\frac{1(x)}{x(x)}+\frac{1}{x^2}$ $=\frac{x+1}{x^2}$ $\frac{1}{x}+\frac{1}{x^2}=\frac{x+1}{x^2}$ for $x \neq 0$

a. Explain the difference in the methods.

How are these restriction(s) shown in the graph of the function?

Which method do you prefer?

b. Explain why the statement $\frac{1}{x} + \frac{1}{x^2} = \frac{x+1}{x^2}$ has the restriction $x \neq 0$.

10

2. Ruth and Samir determine the LCD for the expression: $\frac{1}{x^2 - 1} + \frac{1}{x + 1}$.

Ruth

$\frac{1}{x^2 - 1} + \frac{1}{x + 1}$

$(x^2 - 1)(x + 1)$

LCD: $x^3 + x^2 - x - 1$

Samir

$\frac{1}{x^2 - 1} + \frac{1}{x + 1}$

$\frac{1}{(x - 1)(x + 1)} + \frac{1}{x + 1}$

$(x - 1)(x + 1)$

LCD: $x^2 - 1$

a. Who is correct? Explain your reasoning.

b. Describe any restriction(s) for the value of x.

3. Calculate the least common denominator for each pair of rational expressions.

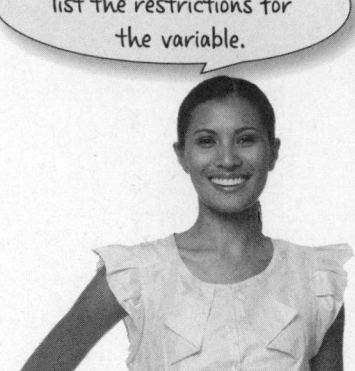

a. $\frac{3}{x+4}, \frac{7x}{x-4}$

LCD:

b. 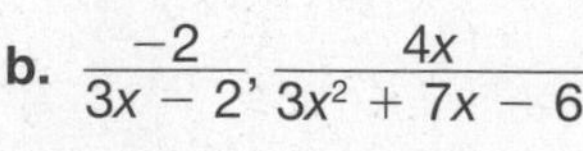 $\frac{-2}{3x-2}, \frac{4x}{3x^2+7x-6}$

LCD:

c. 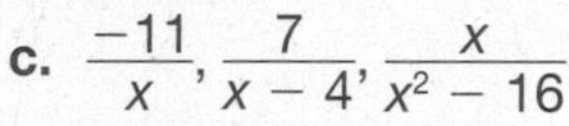 $\frac{-11}{x}, \frac{7}{x-4}, \frac{x}{x^2-16}$

LCD:

d. 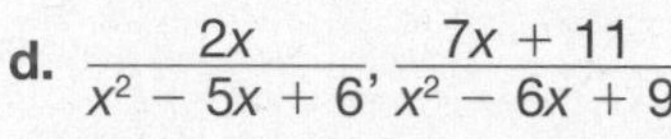 $\frac{2x}{x^2-5x+6}, \frac{7x+11}{x^2-6x+9}$

LCD:

Notice that even though there are binomials in the denominator, adding two rational expressions is similar to adding two rational numbers.

Rational Expressions Involving Binomials in the Denominator
$\frac{1}{x^2-1} - \frac{1}{x+1} = \frac{1}{(x+1)(x-1)} - \frac{1}{x+1}$
$= \frac{1}{(x+1)(x-1)} - \frac{1(x-1)}{(x+1)(x-1)}$
$= \frac{1}{(x+1)(x-1)} - \frac{x-1}{(x+1)(x-1)}$
$= \frac{1-x+1}{(x+1)(x-1)}$
$= \frac{-x+2}{(x+1)(x-1)}$

4. Marissa and Salvatore add $\frac{2x+2}{x+1} + \frac{1}{x}$.

Marissa

$$\frac{2x+2}{x+1} + \frac{1}{x} = \frac{(2x+2)(x)}{(x+1)(x)} + \frac{1(x+1)}{x(x+1)}$$
$$= \frac{2x^2+2x}{(x+1)(x)} + \frac{x+1}{x(x+1)}$$
$$= \frac{2x^2+2x+x+1}{x(x+1)}$$
$$= \frac{2x^2+3x+1}{x(x+1)}$$
$$= \frac{(2x+1)\cancel{(x+1)}}{x\cancel{(x+1)}}$$
$$= \frac{2x+1}{x}$$

Salvatore

$$\frac{2x+2}{x+1} + \frac{1}{x} = \frac{2\cancel{(x+1)}}{\cancel{(x+1)}} + \frac{1}{x}$$
$$= 2 + \frac{1}{x}$$
$$= \frac{2(x)}{(x)} + \frac{1}{x}$$
$$= \frac{2x+1}{x}$$

Explain the difference in the methods used.

5. Randy says the only restriction on the variable x in Marissa and Salvatore's problem is $x \neq 0$. Cynthia says $x \neq 0, -1$. Who is correct? Explain your reasoning.

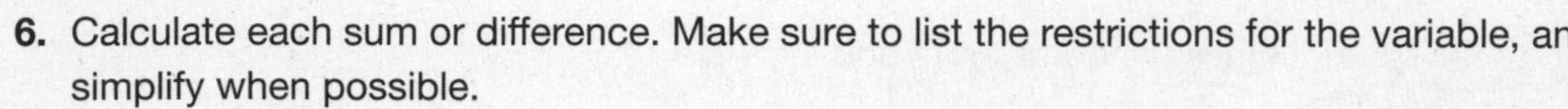

6. Calculate each sum or difference. Make sure to list the restrictions for the variable, and simplify when possible.

a. $\frac{5x - 6}{x^2 - 9} - \frac{4}{x - 3}$

b. $\frac{x - 7}{x^2 - 3x + 2} + \frac{4}{x^2 - 7x + 10}$

c. $\frac{2x - 5}{x} - \frac{4}{5x} - 4$

d. $\frac{3x - 5}{4x^2 + 12x + 9} + \frac{4}{2x + 3} - \frac{2x}{3}$

PROBLEM 3 Can You Spot the Difference?

Consider the worked examples.

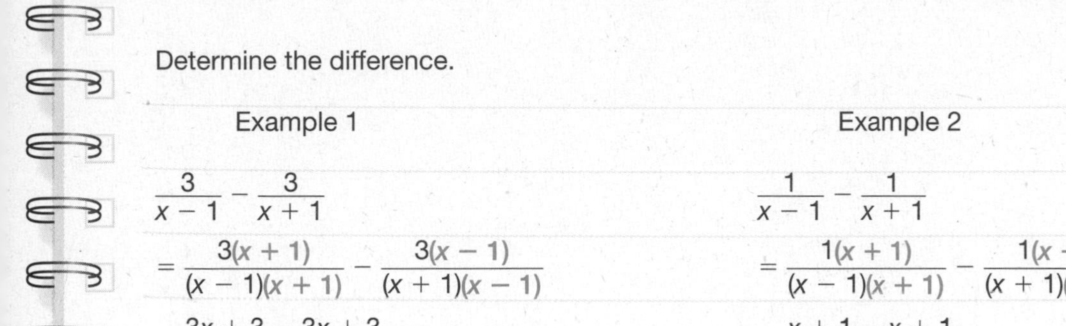

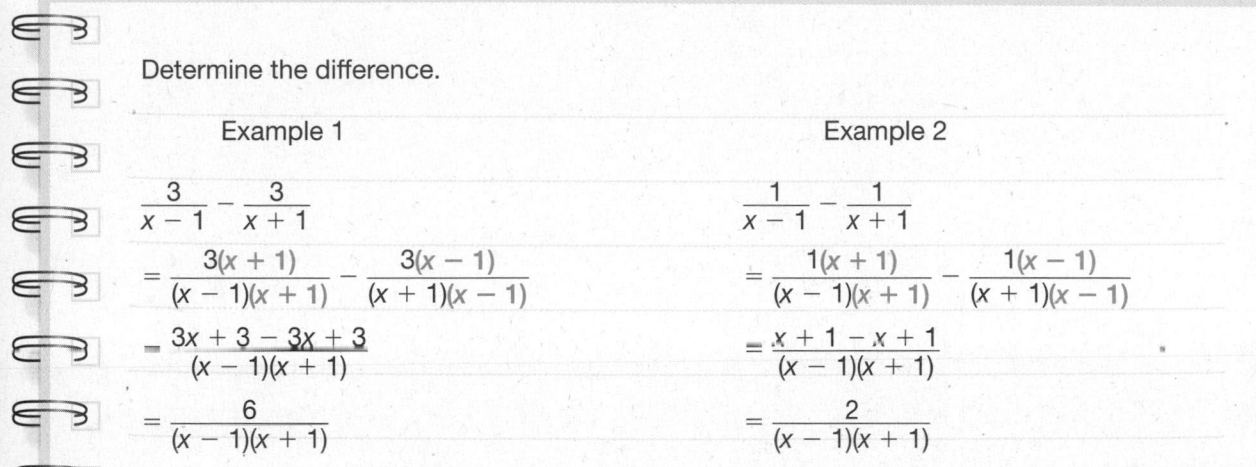

Determine the difference.

Example 1

$$\frac{3}{x-1} - \frac{3}{x+1}$$

$$= \frac{3(x+1)}{(x-1)(x+1)} - \frac{3(x-1)}{(x+1)(x-1)}$$

$$= \frac{3x+3-3x+3}{(x-1)(x+1)}$$

$$= \frac{6}{(x-1)(x+1)}$$

Example 2

$$\frac{1}{x-1} - \frac{1}{x+1}$$

$$= \frac{1(x+1)}{(x-1)(x+1)} - \frac{1(x-1)}{(x+1)(x-1)}$$

$$= \frac{x+1-x+1}{(x-1)(x+1)}$$

$$= \frac{2}{(x-1)(x+1)}$$

1. Describe the similarities and the differences in the structure of each example.

2. Consider the given expression and the resulting difference. What pattern do you notice?

3. If the numerators in Example 1 of the worked example were doubled, what would be the new answer?

4. Can you use this pattern to determine $\frac{4}{(x-2)} - \frac{4}{(x+2)}$? Explain your reasoning.

5. How would the pattern in the worked examples change if you added the terms together?

Be prepared to share your solutions and methods.

Different Client, Same Deal

10.2

Multiplying and Dividing Rational Expressions

LEARNING GOALS

In this lesson, you will:

- Multiply rational expressions.
- Divide rational expressions.

Imagine that 6 adults order a 12-slice pizza for delivery. Simple division will tell you that each adult gets 2 slices in order to divide the pizza fairly. Consider a situation where a parent brings home a big bag of marbles for her 3 children. If the bag contains 108 marbles, the simple number equation $108 \div 3 = 36$ allows the parent to determine how to fairly divide the marbles up so that each of her children is happy. Have you ever thought that this type of division may not always be the best way to fairly divide resources? Consider the following problem:

Five animals share the resources in a wooded region of land. They all eat fruit, berries, and nuts, and must store an adequate amount of food to get them through the winter. They live on several acres of land that contains exactly 50 pounds of food. How much food should each animal receive? Does your answer change when you learn that the five animals are a squirrel, a mouse, a bird, a deer, and a bear? How would you divide the 50 pounds of food so that each animal gets a "fair" amount? Does it make sense that they all receive the same amount of resources? Is dividing 50 by 5 a fair way to go about this problem?

The mathematical concept "fair division" is an interesting mathematical concept. What criteria do you think should be used to determine whether resources are divided fairly?

PROBLEM 1 Take Advantage of the Clearance on Expressions

Previously, you learned that adding and subtracting rational expressions involved the same process as adding and subtracting rational numbers. Now, you will see that multiplying rational expressions involves the same steps as multiplying rational numbers.

Remember that when you multiply rational numbers, you can simplify at the beginning or the end, and the product is the same; however, simplifying earlier saves time and will keep the numbers smaller.

1. Consider Method A compared to Method B in both columns of the table.

	Rational Numbers	Rational Expressions Involving Variables
Method A	$\frac{2}{15} \cdot \frac{5}{8} = \frac{10}{120}$ $= \frac{1}{12}$	$\frac{2x}{15x^2} \cdot \frac{5x^2}{8} = \frac{10x^3}{120x^2}$ $= \frac{1x}{12}$
Method B	$\frac{\overset{1}{\cancel{2}}}{\underset{3}{\cancel{15}}} \cdot \frac{\overset{1}{\cancel{5}}}{\underset{4}{\cancel{8}}} = \frac{1}{12}$	$\frac{\overset{1}{\cancel{2}}x}{\underset{3}{\cancel{15}}\cancel{x^2}} \cdot \frac{\overset{1}{\cancel{5}}\cancel{x^2}}{\underset{4}{\cancel{8}}} = \frac{1x}{12}$

   a. Explain the difference in the methods.

   b. Which method do you prefer?

2. Brody says $x \neq 0$ for the equation in the table, $\frac{2x}{15x^2} \cdot \frac{5x^2}{8} = \frac{1x}{12}$. Damiere says that there are no restrictions because the answer is $\frac{x}{12}$ and there are no variables in the denominator. Who is correct? Explain your reasoning.

3. Analyze Isha's work.

Isha

$$\frac{12xyz^2}{11} \cdot \frac{33x}{8z} = \frac{\overset{9}{\cancel{396}}x^2y\overset{z}{\cancel{z^2}}}{\underset{2}{\cancel{88}}\cancel{z}}$$

$$= \frac{9x^2yz}{2}$$

Explain how Isha could have multiplied the rational expressions more efficiently.

4. Shaheen multiplies $\frac{5x^2}{3x^2 - 75} \cdot \frac{3x - 15}{4x^2}$ without simplifying first.

Shaheen

$$\frac{5x^2}{3x^2 - 75} \cdot \frac{3x - 15}{4x^2} = \frac{15x^3 - 75x^2}{12x^4 - 300x^2}$$

$$= \frac{15x^2(x - 5)}{3x^2(4x^2 - 100)}$$

$$= \frac{\overset{5}{\cancel{15x^2}}(x - 5)}{\underset{1}{\cancel{3x^2}}(4x^2 - 100)}$$

$$= \frac{5(x - 5)}{4(x^2 - 25)}$$

$$= \frac{5\cancel{(x - 5)}}{4\cancel{(x - 5)}(x + 5)}$$

$$= \frac{5}{4(x + 5)}$$

Complete the same problem as Shaheen, simplifying first, and then list the restrictions.

5. Multiply each expression. List the restrictions for the variables.

a. $\frac{3ab^2}{4c} \cdot \frac{2c^2}{27ab}$

b. $\frac{3x}{5x - 15} \cdot \frac{x - 3}{9x^2}$

c. $\frac{x + 5}{x^2 - 4x + 3} \cdot \frac{x - 3}{4x + 20}$

d. $\frac{7x - 7}{3x^2} \cdot \frac{x + 5}{9x^2 - 9} \cdot \frac{x^2 - 5x - 6}{x^3 + 6x^2 + 5x}$

6. Is the set of rational expressions closed under multiplication? Explain your reasoning.

PROBLEM 2 Topsy Turvy World

Dividing rational expressions is similar to the process you use when dividing rational numbers.

Notice that when you multiply $\frac{4}{5}$ by a form of 1, in this case $\frac{3}{3}$, you maintain equivalent fractions:

$$\frac{4}{5} \cdot \frac{\boxed{3}}{\boxed{3}} = \frac{12}{15}$$

$$\frac{4}{5} = \frac{12}{15}$$

What is the product of any nonzero number and its multiplicative inverse?

This same process works when the numerator and denominator are fractions. Consider $\frac{\frac{4}{5}}{\frac{3}{7}}$.

When you multiply by a form of 1, in this case $\frac{\frac{7}{3}}{\frac{7}{3}}$, you maintain equivalent fractions:

$$\frac{\frac{4}{5} \cdot \boxed{\frac{7}{3}}}{\frac{3}{7} \cdot \boxed{\frac{7}{3}}} = \frac{\frac{28}{15}}{\frac{21}{21}} = \frac{\frac{28}{15}}{1} = \frac{28}{15}$$

$$\frac{\frac{4}{5}}{\frac{3}{7}} = \frac{28}{15}$$

1. What is special about the form of 1 used to multiply $\frac{\frac{4}{5}}{\frac{3}{7}}$?

Remember, reducing first could save a lot of time and effort later.

10

You may recall that, to divide fractions, you multiply the dividend by the multiplicative inverse of the divisor.

	Rational Numbers	Rational Expressions Involving Variables
Example 1	$\frac{1}{5} \div \frac{3}{10} = \frac{1}{\cancel{5}_1} \cdot \frac{\cancel{10}^{2}}{3}$ $= \frac{2}{3}$	$\frac{xy^2}{5z} \div \frac{3xy}{10z^2} = \frac{\cancel{xy^2}^{y}}{{}_1\cancel{5z}} \cdot \frac{\cancel{10z^2}^{2z}}{3\cancel{xy}}$ $= \frac{2yz}{3};\ x, y, z \neq 0$
Example 2	$\frac{6}{7} \div 4 = \frac{\cancel{6}^{3}}{7} \cdot \frac{1}{\cancel{4}_2}$ $= \frac{3}{14}$	$\frac{6a^3}{7b} \div 4a = \frac{\cancel{6a^3}^{3a^2}}{7b} \cdot \frac{1}{\cancel{4a}_2}$ $= \frac{3a^2}{14b};\ a, b \neq 0$

10

2. Analyze the examples shown in the table.

a. Explain the process for dividing rational expressions.

b. In Example 2, explain why $\frac{1}{4a}$ is the multiplicative inverse of $4a$.

3. Ranger calculates the quotient of $\frac{4x^2 - 4x}{5x^2} \div \frac{x^2 - 16}{x + 6} \div \frac{x^2 - 7x + 6}{x^2 + x - 12}$.

Ranger

$$\frac{4x^2 - 4x}{5x^2} \div \frac{x^2 - 16}{x + 6} \div \frac{x^2 - 7x + 6}{x^2 + x - 12} = \frac{4x(x - 1)}{5x^2} \div \frac{(x + 4)(x - 4)}{(x + 6)} \div \frac{(x - 6)(x - 1)}{(x + 4)(x - 3)}$$

$$= \frac{4\cancel{x}\cancel{(x - 1)}(x + 6)\cancel{(x + 4)}(x - 3)}{5\cancel{x^2}_{x}(x - 4)\cancel{(x + 4)}(x - 6)\cancel{(x - 1)}}$$

$$= \frac{4x^2 + 12x - 72}{5x^3 - 50x^2 + 120x}$$

List the restrictions for the variables.

4. Determine the quotients of each expression.

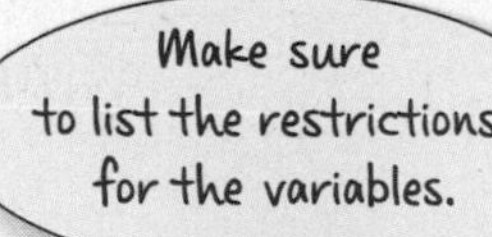
Make sure
to list the restrictions
for the variables.

a. $\dfrac{9ab^2}{4c} \div \dfrac{18c^2}{5ab}$

b. $\dfrac{7x^2}{3x^2 - 27} \div \dfrac{4x^2}{3x - 9}$

10

c. $\dfrac{3x^2 + 15x}{x^2 - 3x - 40} \div \dfrac{5x^2}{x^2 - 64}$

d. $\dfrac{4x}{x^2y^2 - xy} \div \dfrac{x^2 - 4}{3x^2 + 19x - 14} \div \dfrac{x - 2}{xy}$

5. Is the set of rational expressions closed under division? Explain your reasoning.

Be prepared to share your solutions and methods.

10

10.3

Things Are Not Always as They Appear

Solving Rational Equations

LEARNING GOAL

In this lesson, you will:

- Solve rational equations in one variable.

KEY TERMS

- rational equation
- extraneous solution

A paradox is a statement that leads to a contradiction. Consider the following statements:

"Don't go near the water until you have learned how to swim!"

"Nobody shops at that store anymore, it's always too crowded."

They involve faulty logic. You couldn't actually learn to swim if you never got near water, and obviously a lot of people must still shop at that store if it's always crowded. Some paradoxes use mathematics that lead you to a solution path that does not necessarily make sense in real life. A famous example is Zeno's paradox, which involves traveling a distance approaching a specific value, but never quite getting there. Here is an example of Zeno's paradox:

Suppose you are walking to catch a parked bus that is 20 meters away. You decide to get there by going half the distance every few seconds. This means that you walk 10 meters, then 5 meters, 2.5 meters, 1.25 meters, and so on, until you reach the bus.

The paradox is that if you continually halve the distance between you and the bus, you will never actually reach the bus.

Have you ever followed the correct steps to solve a problem, but then your answer didn't make sense?

Method Mayhem

A **rational equation** is an equation that contains one or more rational expressions. You have already solved simple rational equations with a single variable as a denominator and performed simple operations using rational expressions. You will follow the same rules and guidelines when solving more involved rational equations.

There are multiple methods you can use to solve rational equations. Depending on the structure of the equation, some methods will be more efficient than others.

1. Randall and Sully solved the equation $\frac{x + 5}{x + 2} = \frac{x + 1}{x - 5}$.

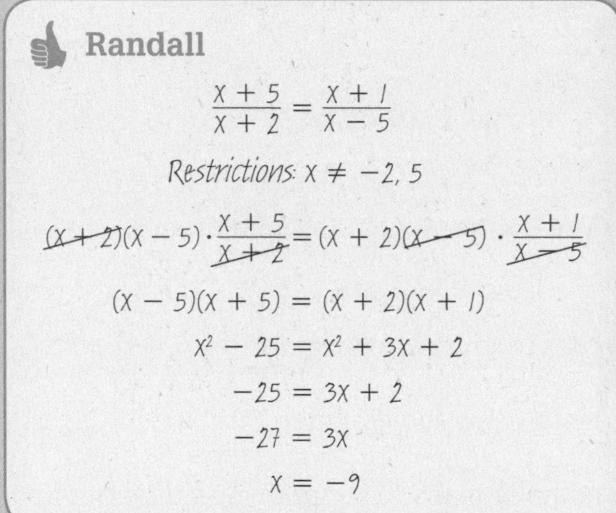

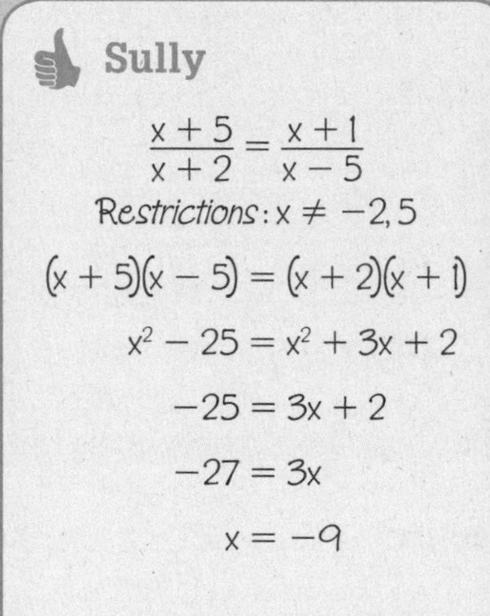

a. Explain Randall's method of solving.

b. Sully used proportional reasoning to solve the equation. Explain how he solved the equation.

c. Which method do you prefer for this problem? Explain your reasoning.

2. Sully was presented with a slightly different equation to solve. Notice that a new factor appears in one of the denominators. Again, he uses proportional reasoning to solve.

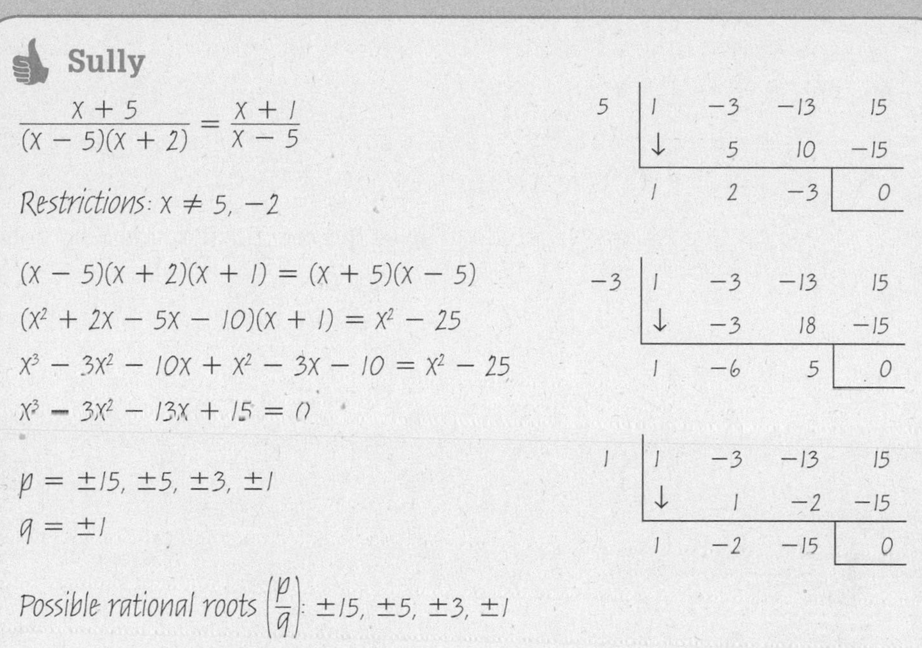

Sully

$$\frac{x + 5}{(x - 5)(x + 2)} = \frac{x + 1}{x - 5}$$

Restrictions: $x \neq 5, -2$

$(x - 5)(x + 2)(x + 1) = (x + 5)(x - 5)$

$(x^2 + 2x - 5x - 10)(x + 1) = x^2 - 25$

$x^3 - 3x^2 - 10x + x^2 - 3x - 10 = x^2 - 25$

$x^3 - 3x^2 - 13x + 15 = 0$

$p = \pm 15, \pm 5, \pm 3, \pm 1$

$q = \pm 1$

Possible rational roots $\left(\frac{p}{q}\right)$: $\pm 15, \pm 5, \pm 3, \pm 1$

5	1	−3	−13	15
	↓	5	10	−15
	1	2	−3	0

−3	1	−3	−13	15
	↓	−3	18	−15
	1	−6	5	0

1	1	−3	−13	15
	↓	1	−2	−15
	1	−2	−15	0

Using synthetic division, I realize the three roots are 5, −3, and 1. However, from my list of restrictions, I know that $x \neq 5$. So, my solutions to the equation can only be $x = -3$ or $x = 1$. I will check to see if they work.

Check $x = -3$

$$\frac{-3 + 5}{(-3 - 5)(-3 + 2)} \stackrel{?}{=} \frac{-3 + 1}{-3 - 5}$$

$$\frac{2}{(-8)(-1)} \stackrel{?}{=} \frac{-2}{-8}$$

$$\frac{2}{8} = \frac{2}{8}$$

Check $x = 1$

$$\frac{1 + 5}{(1 - 5)(1 + 2)} \stackrel{?}{=} \frac{1 + 1}{1 - 5}$$

$$\frac{6}{(-4)(3)} \stackrel{?}{=} \frac{2}{-4}$$

$$-\frac{6}{12} \stackrel{?}{=} -\frac{2}{4}$$

$$-\frac{1}{2} = -\frac{1}{2}$$

Thus, $x = -3$ or $x = 1$.

a. What is different about the structure of this equation compared to the equation in Question 1?

10

b. Prior to checking his solution, explain why Sully identified three possible roots to the equation.

c. Use Randall's method to solve the second equation Sully solved.

10

d. Which method is more efficient based on the structure of the original equation? Explain your reasoning.

There is a mathematical reason why Sully identified an extra solution to his equation. Recall that one of the basic principles of algebra is that you can multiply both sides of an equation by a non-zero real number or expression, as long as you maintain balance to the equation. When you multiply both sides of the equation by an expression that contains a variable, you may introduce solutions that are not solutions of the original equation. Notice Sully multiplied by $x - 5$. By doing so, he introduced an additional solution. These extra solutions are called *extraneous solutions*. **Extraneous solutions** are solutions that result from the process of solving an equation, but are not valid solutions to the original equation.

3. Sully wanted to graph the equation using a graphing calculator. He rewrote the equation so that one side of the equation equaled zero. Then, he graphed:

$y_1 = \frac{x+1}{x-5} - \frac{x+5}{(x-5)(x+2)}$. Consider the graph:

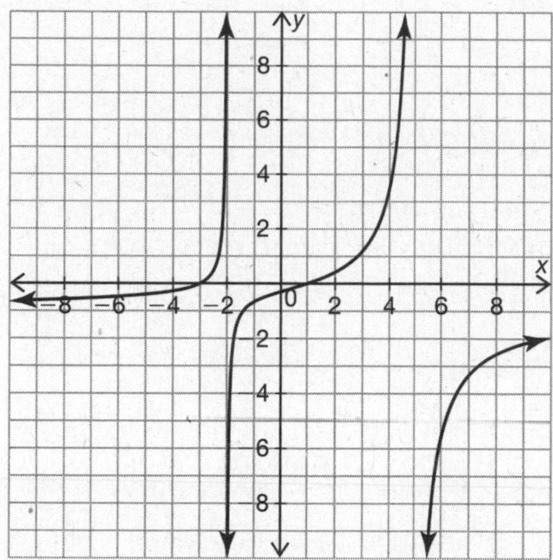

Use the graph to explain why $x \neq 5$ and why $x = -3$ and $x = 1$.

4. Mike used a graphing calculator to solve the same equation:

$y_1 = \frac{x+1}{x-5}$

$y_2 = \frac{x+5}{(x-5)(x+2)}$.

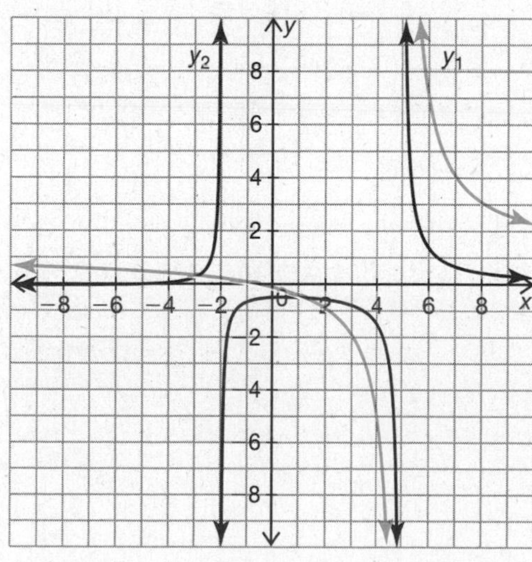

How does Mike's graph represent the solutions to the equation?

5. Analyze the methods Jake and Sasha used to solve $\frac{2x + 4}{x^2 - 2x - 8} = \frac{x + 1}{x - 4}$.

Sasha

$$\frac{2x + 4}{(x - 4)(x + 2)} = \frac{x + 1}{x - 4} \quad x \neq 4, -2$$

$$\frac{2x + 4}{(x - 4)(x + 2)} = \frac{x + 1}{x - 4} \cdot \frac{(x + 2)}{(x + 2)}$$

$$\frac{2x + 4}{(x - 4)(x + 2)} = \frac{x^2 + 3x + 2}{(x - 4)(x + 2)}$$

$$\cancel{(x - 4)(x + 2)}\left[\frac{2x + 4}{\cancel{(x - 4)(x + 2)}} = \frac{x^2 + 3x + 2}{\cancel{(x - 4)(x + 2)}}\right]$$

$$2x + 4 = x^2 + 3x + 2$$

$$x^2 + x - 2 = 0$$

$$(x + 2)(x - 1) = 0$$

$$x = -2, 1$$

I know that $x \neq -2$, so I just need to check $x = 1$.

Check $x = 1$

$$\frac{2(1) + 4}{(1 - 4)(1 + 2)} \stackrel{?}{=} \frac{1 + 1}{1 - 4}$$

$$\frac{6}{(-3)(3)} \stackrel{?}{=} \frac{2}{-3}$$

$$-\frac{2}{3} = -\frac{2}{3}$$

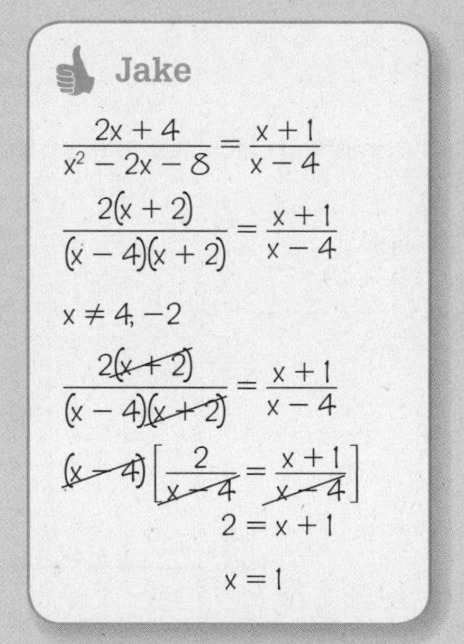

Jake
$\frac{2x + 4}{x^2 - 2x - 8} = \frac{x + 1}{x - 4}$
$\frac{2(x + 2)}{(x - 4)(x + 2)} = \frac{x + 1}{x - 4}$
$x \neq 4, -2$
$\frac{2\cancel{(x + 2)}}{(x - 4)\cancel{(x + 2)}} = \frac{x + 1}{x - 4}$
$\cancel{(x - 4)}\left[\frac{2}{\cancel{x - 4}} = \frac{x + 1}{\cancel{x - 4}}\right]$
$2 = x + 1$
$x = 1$

a. Describe how Jake and Sasha's methods are similar and different.

b. What would happen if you tried to solve this problem using proportional reasoning?

6. Analyze the methods Seth, Damiere, and Sidonie each used to solve the equation $\frac{6}{x^2 - 4x} + \frac{4}{x} = \frac{2}{x - 4}$.

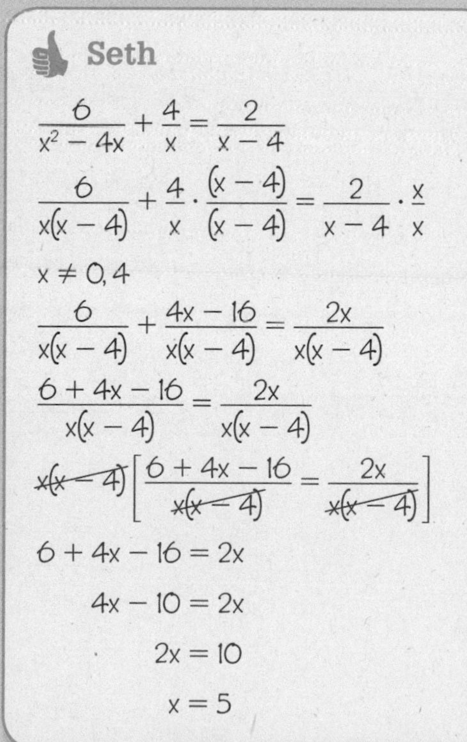

Seth

$$\frac{6}{x^2 - 4x} + \frac{4}{x} = \frac{2}{x - 4}$$

$$\frac{6}{x(x - 4)} + \frac{4}{x} \cdot \frac{(x - 4)}{(x - 4)} = \frac{2}{x - 4} \cdot \frac{x}{x}$$

$x \neq 0, 4$

$$\frac{6}{x(x - 4)} + \frac{4x - 16}{x(x - 4)} = \frac{2x}{x(x - 4)}$$

$$\frac{6 + 4x - 16}{x(x - 4)} = \frac{2x}{x(x - 4)}$$

$$\cancel{x(x - 4)}\left[\frac{6 + 4x - 16}{\cancel{x(x - 4)}} = \frac{2x}{\cancel{x(x - 4)}}\right]$$

$6 + 4x - 16 = 2x$

$4x - 10 = 2x$

$2x = 10$

$x = 5$

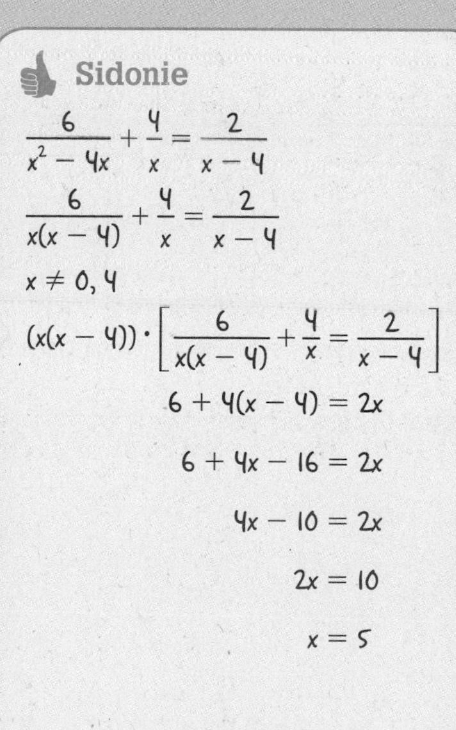

Sidonie

$$\frac{6}{x^2 - 4x} + \frac{4}{x} = \frac{2}{x - 4}$$

$$\frac{6}{x(x - 4)} + \frac{4}{x} = \frac{2}{x - 4}$$

$x \neq 0, 4$

$$(x(x - 4)) \cdot \left[\frac{6}{x(x - 4)} + \frac{4}{x} = \frac{2}{x - 4}\right]$$

$6 + 4(x - 4) = 2x$

$6 + 4x - 16 = 2x$

$4x - 10 = 2x$

$2x = 10$

$x = 5$

 **Damiere**

$$\frac{6}{x(x-4)} + \frac{4}{x} = \frac{2}{x-4}$$

$x \neq 0, 4$

$$\frac{6}{x^2-4x} + \frac{4}{x} = \frac{2}{x-4}$$

$$\frac{(x)(x-4)}{(x)(x-4)} \cdot \frac{6}{x^2-4x} + \frac{(x^2-4x)(x-4)}{(x^2-4x)(x-4)} \cdot \frac{4}{x} = \frac{2}{x-4} \cdot \frac{(x^2-4x)(x)}{(x^2-4x)(x)}$$

$$\frac{6x^2-24x}{x^4-8x^3+16x^2} + \frac{4x^3-16x^2-16x^2+64x}{x^4-8x^3+16x^2} = \frac{2x^3-8x^2}{x^4-8x^3+16x^2}$$

$$\cancel{x^4-8x^3+16x^2} \cdot \frac{6x^2-24x+4x^3-16x^2-16x^2+64x}{\cancel{x^4-8x^3+16x^2}} = \cancel{x^4-8x^3+16x^2} \cdot \frac{2x^3-8x^2}{\cancel{x^4-8x^3+16x^2}}$$

$6x^2 - 24x + 4x^3 - 16x^2 - 16x^2 + 64x = 2x^3 - 8x^2$

$4x^3 - 26x^2 + 40x = 2x^3 - 8x^2$

$2x^3 - 18x^2 + 40x = 0$

$2x(x^2 - 9x + 20) = 0$

$2x(x-4)(x-5) = 0$

$x = 0, 4, 5$

I know that $x \neq 0, 4$, so I will just check $x = 5$.

Check:

$x = 5$

$$\frac{6}{5^2-4(5)} + \frac{4}{5} \stackrel{?}{=} \frac{2}{5-4}$$

$$\frac{6}{25-20} + \frac{4}{5} \stackrel{?}{=} \frac{2}{1}$$

$$\frac{6}{5} + \frac{4}{5} \stackrel{?}{=} 2$$

$$\frac{10}{5} \stackrel{?}{=} 2$$

$$2 = 2$$

a. Describe the methods Seth, Sidonie, and Damiere each used to solve the rational equation.

b. Prior to checking his solution, explain why Damiere identified three possible roots to the equation.

10

7. Solve the equation $\frac{10}{x^2 - 2x} + \frac{1}{x} = \frac{3}{x - 2}$. Explain why you chose your solution method.

Think about the structure of this equation before you start solving.

10

PROBLEM 2 Seeing Structure

1. Cut out each of the equations on the following three pages. Before solving each equation, think about how the structure of the equation informs your solution method. Then, sort the equations based on the solution method you intend to use. Finally, solve each equation. Be sure to list the domain restrictions.

a. $\frac{12}{x + 5} = -2$	b. $\frac{x - 5}{3} = \frac{x - 38}{12} - \frac{x}{4}$
c. $\frac{x^2 - 5x}{4} = \frac{8x}{2}$	d. $\frac{1}{x - 5} = \frac{5}{x^2 + 2x - 35}$

10

10

e. $\frac{3}{x-1} + \frac{2}{5x+5} = \frac{-3}{x^2-1}$

f. $\frac{x-5}{x-2} = \frac{8}{9}$

g. $\frac{5}{x} = 25 + \frac{5}{x}$

h. $\frac{1}{x^2} + \frac{1}{x} = \frac{1}{2x^2}$

10

i. $\frac{-2}{x+3} + \frac{3}{x-2} = \frac{5}{x^2+x-6}$

j. $\frac{7}{x+3} = \frac{8}{x-2}$

k. $\frac{x+3}{x^2-1} + \frac{-2x}{x-1} = 1$

l. $\frac{3}{x^2+2x} = \frac{6}{x^2}$

10

Paste your solved rational equations in the space provided.

10

10

10

2. Did you solve the equations using the method you first intended?

10

Be prepared to share your solutions and methods.

Get to Work, Mix It Up, Go the Distance, and Lower the Cost!

10.4

Using Rational Equations to Solve Real-World Problems

LEARNING GOALS

In this lesson, you will:

- Use rational equations to model and solve work problems.
- Use rational equations to model and solve mixture problems.
- Use rational equations to model and solve distance problems.
- Use rational equations to model and solve cost problems.

If you haven't noticed, learning is not limited to the classroom, but is part of everyday life. In fact, there's the old adage that confirms this: You learn something new everyday.

But learning alone does not equate to success. You need to apply that knowledge and gain experience. In many ways, the classroom sets the foundation for success, but by applying your knowledge, you can shine!

Mathematics is no different. When you gain a deep understanding of the mathematics you use in the classroom and can relate it to real-world situations, you are able to do your own problem-solving and gain success.

How have you used mathematics in your everyday life? How do you think you will use math in the future?

PROBLEM 1 This Is Quite a Work-Out

A work problem is a type of problem that involves the rates of several workers and the time it takes to complete a job. For example, the rate at which two painters work and the total time it takes them to paint a house while working together is an example of a work problem.

Anita and Martin are the assistant managers for the marketing department of the Snarky Larks Hockey Team. This hockey season is fast-approaching, and the rink board ads need to be mounted to the rink boards before the season begins.

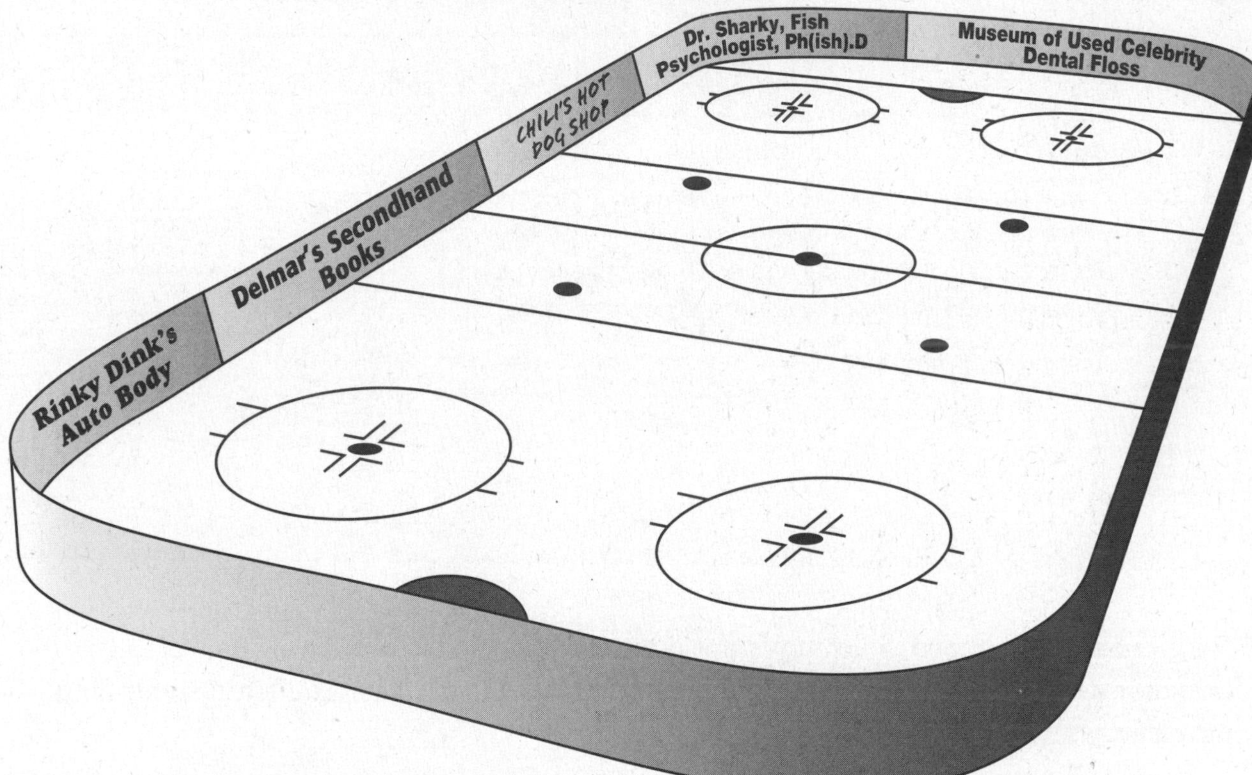

Each ad is like a giant vinyl sticker that is stuck to each rink board along the inside of the hockey rink. It takes a team of three people to attach each ad: two people hold the ad while a third person carefully presses it to the rink board, being careful that it does not wrinkle.

Up until last year, Anita's team and Martin's team have taken turns doing this job—Anita's team attached the rink boards for the first season, Martin's team attached them for the next season, the following season Anita's team attached them, and so on.

1. It takes Anita's team 20 hours to attach all of the rink boards, and it takes Martin's team 30 hours to attach all of the rink boards. This year, however, their boss has asked them to work together to get the job done faster.

a. Determine the portion of the rink each team completes in the given number of hours.

<u>Anita's Team</u>

1 hour:

5 hours:

10 hours:

10

<u>Martin's Team</u>

1 hour:

5 hours:

10 hours:

b. Consider the amount of the rink that each team can complete in x hours.

i. Write an expression to represent the portion of the rink that Anita's team can complete in x hours.

ii. Write an expression that represents the portion of the rink that Martin's team can complete in x hours.

c. Each team's rate of work is defined as number of jobs completed per hour. In this case, the rate of work is the number of rinks completed per hour.

i. Determine Anita's team's rate of work.

ii. Determine Martin's team's rate of work.

d. Complete the table.

10

	Portion of the Rink Completed	Time Spent Working	Rate of Work
	Rinks	Hours	$\frac{\text{Rinks}}{\text{Hour}}$
Anita's Team		x	
Martin's Team		x	
Entire Job, or 1 Rink		x	

e. Consider the expression from the table that represents the portion of the rink that Anita's and Martin's teams can complete when working together. If you want to determine the total time it takes the two teams to complete one rink while working together, what should you set this expression equal to?

f. Write and solve an equation to determine the total time it takes the two teams to complete the rink.

Make sure you are using the appropriate units of measure.

g. Suppose that the two teams work together attaching rink board ads for 4 hours each day. How many days will it take them to complete the job?

Maureen is a community volunteer. She volunteers by watering the large vegetable garden in her neighborhood. Sometimes, Maureen's friend Sandra also volunteers.

2. It takes Maureen 90 minutes to water the garden. When Maureen and Sandra are working together, they can complete the job in 40 minutes.

a. Complete the table. Let x represent the time it takes Sandra to water the garden if she works alone.

	Portion of the Garden Watered	Time Spent Watering	Rate of Watering
	Gardens	Minutes	$\frac{\text{Gardens}}{\text{Minute}}$
Maureen		40	
Sandra		40	
Entire Job, or 1 Garden		40	

10

b. Write and solve an equation to determine the total time it would take Sandra to water the garden if she were working alone.

PROBLEM 2 Shhh! The Mixmaster Needs Complete Concentration

A mixture problem is a type of problem that involves the combination of two or more liquids and the concentrations of those liquids.

1. Manuel is a taking a college chemistry course, and some of his time is spent in the chemistry lab. He is conducting an experiment for which he needs a 2% salt solution. However, all he can find in the lab is 120 milliliters (mL) of 10% salt solution.

   a. How many milliliters of salt and how many milliliters of water are in 120 mL of 10% salt solution?

10

   b. What would the concentration of the salt solution be if Manuel added 80 mL of water? 180 mL of water?

   c. Write and solve an equation to calculate the amount of water Manuel needs to add to the 120 mL of 10% salt solution to make a 2% salt solution. Let x represent the amount of water Manuel needs to add.

2. Keisha is working on a chemistry experiment. She has 20 mL of a 20% sulfuric acid solution that she is mixing with a 5% sulfuric acid solution.

   a. Describe the range of possible concentrations for the new solution.

   b. Suppose that the 20 mL of 20% sulfuric acid solution is mixed with 10 mL of the 5% sulfuric acid solution. What is the concentration of the resulting solution? Explain your reasoning.

   c. Write and solve an equation to calculate the amount of 5% sulfuric acid solution Keisha added it the resulting solution is a 12% sulfuric acid solution. Let x represent the amount of 5% sulfuric acid that Keisha added.

PROBLEM 3 Are We There Yet?

A distance problem is a type of problem that involves distance, rate, and time.

1. A river barge travels 140 miles from a loading dock to a warehouse to deliver supplies. Then the barge returns to the loading dock. The barge travels with the current to the warehouse and against the current from the warehouse. The barge's total travel time is 20 hours, and it travels in still water at an average speed of 15 miles per hour.

   a. Use the given information to complete the table. Let x represent the average speed of the current.

	Distance Traveled	Time Traveled	Average Speed
	Miles	Hours	$\frac{\text{Miles}}{\text{Hours}}$
With the Current			$15 + x$
Against the Current	140		
Round Trip		20	

   b. You are given that the barge's total travel time is 20 hours. Write an algebraic expression, in terms of the number of hours the barge travels with the current and the number of hours it travels against the current, that is equivalent to 20 hours.

   c. Write and solve an equation to calculate the average speed of the current.

2. Calculate each value.

   a. What is the barge's average speed during its trip to the warehouse?

   b. What is the barge's average speed during its trip back to the loading dock?

   c. How long does it take the barge to get from the loading dock to the warehouse?

   d. How long does it take the barge to return to the loading dock from the warehouse?

   e. Use your answers to parts (a) and (b) to calculate the average speed of the barge in still water. Verify that your answer matches the given information.

   f. Use your answers to parts (c) and (d) to calculate the barge's total travel time. Verify that your answer matches the given information.

PROBLEM 4 How Much Is It?

A cost problem is a type of problem that involves the cost of ownership of an item over time.

Melinda has decided that it is time to replace her old refrigerator. She purchases a new Energy Star certified refrigerator. Energy Star certified refrigerators use less electricity than those that are not certified. In the long run, the Energy Star refrigerator should cost Melinda less to operate.

1. Melinda purchases a new Energy Star refrigerator for $2000. The refrigerator costs $46 per year to operate.

a. Assume that the refrigerator is reliable and its only costs of ownership are the purchase price and the cost of operation. Determine Melinda's average annual cost of owning the new refrigerator for the given number of years.

10

1 year:

5 years:

10 years:

b. Write an expression to represent Melinda's average annual cost of owning the new refrigerator for x years.

c. When Melinda's average annual cost of owning the refrigerator is less than $400, she plans to shop for a new television. When can Melinda shop for a new television?

2. Melinda is curious to know how much money the Energy Star certified refrigerator will save her, compared to one that is not certified. A comparable non-certified model costs $1900 to purchase and $60 per year to operate.

   a. Assume that this non-certified refrigerator's only costs of ownership are the purchase price and the operation costs. Determine the average annual cost of owning this refrigerator in the given number of years.

      1 year:

      5 years:

      10 years:

   b. Write an expression to represent the average annual cost of owning the non-certified refrigerator for x years.

3. In how many years will the average annual cost of owning the Energy Star certified refrigerator be less than the average annual cost of owning the non-certified refrigerator? Show all of your work.

Be prepared to share your solutions and methods.

10

Chapter 10 Summary

KEY TERMS

- rational equation (10.3)
- extraneous solutions (10.3)

10.1 Determining the Least Common Denominator (LCD)

To add or subtract rational numbers, a common denominator is needed. To add or subtract rational expressions, a common denominator is also needed. Determining a common denominator is done in much the same way for both rational numbers and rational expressions.

Example

Rational Numbers	Rational Expressions
$\frac{5}{6} + \frac{3}{4} = \frac{5}{2(3)} + \frac{3}{2(2)}$ $= \frac{5(2)}{2(3)(2)} + \frac{3(3)}{2(2)(3)}$ $= \frac{10}{12} + \frac{9}{12}$ $= \frac{19}{12}$ The least common denominator is 12.	$\frac{7}{2x} + \frac{5}{6x^2} = \frac{7}{2x} + \frac{5}{2(3)x^2}$ $= \frac{7(3)x}{2x(3)x} + \frac{5}{2(3)x^2}$ $= \frac{21x}{6x^2} + \frac{5}{6x^2}$ $= \frac{21x + 5}{6x^2}$ The least common denominator is $6x^2$.

10.1 Determining Restrictions for the Value of x

When there are variable(s) in the denominator of a rational expression, the value of the variable cannot equal a value that will produce a zero in the denominator.

Example

$$\frac{6x + 1}{5x^2 - 10x} = \frac{6x + 1}{5x(x - 2)}$$

$5x(x - 2) = 0$

$5x = 0, x - 2 = 0$

$x = 0, x = 2$

The restrictions on the value of x are $x \neq 0$ or $x \neq 2$, since the value of the denominator in the rational expression $\frac{6x + 1}{5x^2 - 10x}$ would equal zero.

10

10.1 Adding Rational Expressions

To add rational expressions, determine a common denominator and then add. Identify any restrictions on the value of the variable and simplify when possible.

Example

$$\frac{2}{x} + \frac{5}{x+2} = \frac{2(x+2)}{x(x+2)} + \frac{5(x)}{x(x+2)}$$
$$= \frac{2x+4}{x(x+2)} + \frac{5x}{x(x+2)}$$
$$= \frac{7x+4}{x(x+2)}; x \neq -2, 0$$

10.1 Subtracting Rational Expressions

To subtract rational expressions, determine a common denominator and then subtract. Identify any restrictions on the value of the variable and simplify when possible.

Example

$$\frac{4x}{2x+6} - \frac{3}{x+3} = \frac{4x}{2(x+3)} - \frac{3}{x+3}$$
$$= \frac{4x}{2(x+3)} - \frac{3(2)}{2(x+3)}$$
$$= \frac{4x}{2(x+3)} - \frac{6}{2(x+3)}$$
$$= \frac{4x-6}{2(x+3)}$$
$$= \frac{\cancel{2}(2x-3)}{\cancel{2}(x+3)}$$
$$= \frac{2x-3}{x+3}; x \neq -3$$

10.2 Multiplying Rational Expressions

Multiplying rational expressions is similar to multiplying rational numbers. Factor each numerator and denominator, simplify if possible, and then multiply. Finally, describe any restriction(s) on the variable(s).

Example

$$\frac{4x^3}{9} \cdot \frac{3}{2x} = \frac{\overset{2}{\cancel{4}}\,\overset{x^2}{\cancel{x^3}}}{\underset{3}{\cancel{9}}} \cdot \frac{\overset{1}{\cancel{3}}}{\underset{1}{\cancel{2}}\,\underset{1}{\cancel{x}}}$$
$$= \frac{2x^2}{3}; x \neq 0$$

10.2 Dividing Rational Expressions

Dividing rational expressions is similar to dividing rational numbers. Rewrite division as multiplication by using the reciprocal, factor each numerator and denominator, simplify if possible, and then multiply. Finally describe any restriction(s) for the variable(s).

Example

$$\frac{x-2}{x^2-9} \div \frac{2x-4}{x-3} = \frac{x-2}{x^2-9} \cdot \frac{x-3}{2x-4}$$

$$= \frac{\overset{1}{\cancel{x-2}}}{\underset{1}{\cancel{(x-3)}}(x+3)} \cdot \frac{\overset{1}{\cancel{x-3}}}{2\underset{1}{\cancel{(x-2)}}}$$

$$= \frac{1}{2(x+3)}; x \neq -3, 2, 3$$

10.3 Solving Rational Equations Using Proportional Reasoning

A rational equation is an equation containing one or more rational expressions. If a rational equation is in the form of a proportion with only one factor in the denominator on either side of the equation, it can be solved by using proportional reasoning. After using proportional reasoning and solving, describe any restrictions for the value of the variable, check each solution, and identify any extraneous solutions should they occur.

Example

$$\frac{2}{x} = \frac{1}{x-4}$$

Restrictions: $x \neq 0, 4$

$$2(x-4) = x(1)$$
$$2x - 8 = x$$
$$x - 8 = 0$$
$$x = 8$$

Check $x = 8$.

$$\frac{2}{8} \stackrel{?}{=} \frac{1}{8-4}$$
$$\frac{1}{4} = \frac{1}{4}$$

10.3 Solving Rational Equations by Multiplying Both Sides of the Equation by the Least Common Denominator

One method of solving a rational equation is to multiply both sides of the equation by the least common denominator and then solve the resulting equation for the variable. After solving, describe any restrictions for the variable, check each solution, and identify any extraneous solutions should they occur.

Example

$$\frac{7}{x-3} = \frac{3}{x-4} + \frac{1}{2}$$

Restrictions: $x \neq 3, 4$

$$2(x-3)(x-4)\left(\frac{7}{x-3}\right) = 2(x-3)(x-4)\left(\frac{3}{x-4} + \frac{1}{2}\right)$$

$$14x - 56 = (6x - 18) + (x^2 - 7x + 12)$$

$$14x - 56 = x^2 - x - 6$$

$$x^2 - 15x + 50 = 0$$

$$(x-5)(x-10) = 0$$

$$x = 5 \text{ or } x = 10$$

Check $x = 5$.

$$\frac{7}{5-3} \stackrel{?}{=} \frac{3}{5-4} + \frac{1}{2}$$

$$\frac{7}{2} \stackrel{?}{=} 3 + \frac{1}{2}$$

$$3\frac{1}{2} = 3\frac{1}{2}$$

Check $x = 10$.

$$\frac{7}{10-3} \stackrel{?}{=} \frac{3}{10-4} + \frac{1}{2}$$

$$\frac{7}{7} \stackrel{?}{=} \frac{3}{6} + \frac{1}{2}$$

$$1 = 1$$

10.3 Solving Rational Equations Using a Graphing Calculator

A graph can also be used to solve a rational equation. Rewrite the equation so that one side of the equation equals zero. Then set the non-zero side, $f(x)$, equal to y and graph $y = f(x)$. The vertical asymptotes indicate restrictions on the variable x. The x-intercept(s) of the graph are solution(s) to the original equation.

Example

$$\frac{x}{x-1} + \frac{x-5}{x^2-1} = 1$$

Rewrite the equation so that one side equals 0, then graph $y = \frac{x}{x-1} + \frac{x-5}{x^2-1} - 1$.

The graph shows that $x = -1$ and $x = 1$ are vertical asymptotes and thus represent restrictions on the variable. The graph also shows that $x = 2$ is a possible solution to the original rational equation.

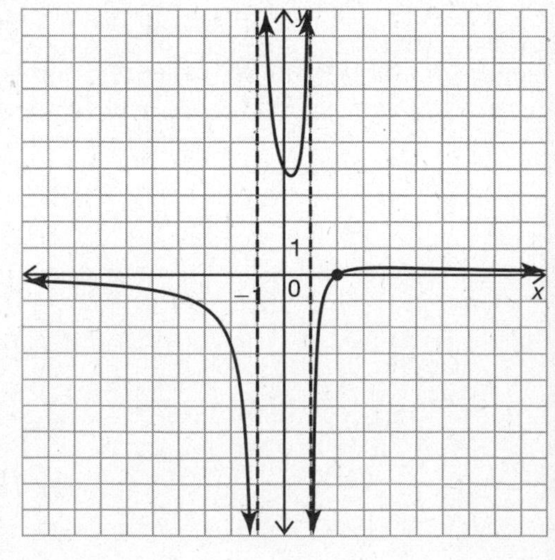

Check $x = 2$.

$$\frac{2}{2-1} + \frac{2-5}{2^2-1} \stackrel{?}{=} 1$$

$$2 + \frac{-3}{3} \stackrel{?}{=} 1$$

$$2 + (-1) \stackrel{?}{=} 1$$

$$1 = 1$$

10.3 Identifying Extraneous Roots

When both sides of a rational equation are multiplied by an expression that contains a variable, additional solutions may be introduced. These additional solutions are called extraneous solutions. Extraneous solutions are solutions that result from the process of solving an equation, but are not valid solutions to the original equation.

Example

$$\frac{5}{x-1} = \frac{10}{x^2-1}$$

Restriction: $x \neq -1, 1$

$$\frac{5}{x-1} = \frac{10}{x^2-1}$$

$$\frac{5}{x-1} = \frac{10}{(x-1)(x+1)}$$

$$(x-1)(x+1)\left[\frac{5}{x-1}\right] = (x-1)(x+1)\left[\frac{10}{(x-1)(x+1)}\right]$$

$$5(x+1) = 10$$

$$x+1 = 2$$

$$x = 1$$

However $x \neq 1$ since it is a restriction on the variable and thus is an extraneous solution. Therefore, this equation has no solution.

10.4 Writing and Solving an Equation that Best Models a Work Problem

A work problem is a type of problem that involves the rates of several workers and the time it takes to complete a job. To solve a work problem, define an appropriate variable, set up an equation that best models the situation, and solve the equation.

Example

Ramiro can rake a lawn in 2.5 hours; Zelda can rake the same lawn in 2 hours. If they rake the lawn together, how long will it take them to rake the lawn?

Let x represent the number of hours it will take to rake the lawn while working together.

$$\frac{x}{2.5} + \frac{x}{2} = 1$$

$$5\left(\frac{x}{2.5} + \frac{x}{2}\right) = 5(1)$$

$$2x + 2.5x = 5$$

$$4.5x = 5$$

$$x = 1\frac{1}{9} \text{ hours}$$

Working together, it will take Ramiro and Zelda $1\frac{1}{9}$ hours to rake the lawn.

10.4 Writing and Solving an Equation that Best Models a Mixture Problem

A mixture problem is a type of problem that involves the combination of two or more liquids and the concentration of these liquids. To solve a mixture problem, define an appropriate variable, set up an equation that best models the situation, and solve the equation.

Example

A chemist has 5 liters of a 30% brine solution. She needs to create a solution containing 25% brine by mixing the 5 liters with a second solution containing 20% brine. How much of the second solution should she use?

Let x represent the number of liters of the 20% brine solution needed.

$$\frac{0.3(5) + 0.2x}{5 + x} = 0.25$$

$$1.5 + 0.2x = 1.25 + 0.25x$$

10

$$0.25 = 0.05x$$

$$x = 5 \text{ liters}$$

The chemist needs to add 5 liters of the 20% brine solution to obtain the desired mixture.

10.4 Writing and Solving an Equation that Best Models a Distance Problem

A distance problem, is a type of problem that involves distance, rate, and time. To solve a distance problem, define an appropriate variable, set up an equation that best models the situation, and solve the equation.

Example

When there is no wind, Sierra rides her bike at a rate of 15 miles per hour. Last Monday she rode her bike for 6 miles into a headwind and then returned home with the wind at her back. If the entire trip took 1.5 hours, what was the speed of the wind?

Let r represent the speed of the wind.

$$\frac{6}{15 + r} + \frac{6}{15 - r} = 1.5$$

$$(15 + r)(15 - r)\left(\frac{6}{15 + r} + \frac{6}{15 - r}\right) = 1.5(15 + r)(15 - r)$$

$$6(15 - r) + 6(15 + r) = 1.5(225 - r^2)$$

$$180 = 1.5(225 - r^2)$$

$$120 = 225 - r^2$$

$$105 = r^2$$

$$r \approx \pm 10.247; \text{ choose } 10.247 \text{ miles per hour}$$

The speed of the wind was approximately 10.247 miles per hour.

10.4 Writing and Solving an Equation or Inequality that Best Models a Cost Problem

A cost problem is a type of problem that involves the cost of ownership of an item over time. To solve a cost problem, define an appropriate variable, set up an equation or inequality that best models the situation, and solve the equation or inequality.

Example

Tobias purchased a new electric range for $1100 and was told by the salesperson that the yearly average operating cost of the range was approximately $110. In what year of ownership will Tobias's average annual cost of owning the range be $210?

Let x be the year in which Tobias's average annual cost of owning the range is $210.

$$\frac{1100 + 110x}{x} = 210$$

$$1100 + 110x = 210x$$

$$1100 = 100x$$

$$x = 11 \text{ years}$$

In the 11th year of ownership, the average annual cost of owning the range will be $210.

10

Radical Functions

This picture
shows a surfer in a
"barrel ride"—one of
fing's most sought-after
xperiences. Given the
ght conditions, a surfer
can ride inside a wave
as it breaks.

With Great Power . . .

11.1

Inverses of Power Functions

LEARNING GOALS

In this lesson, you will:

- Graph the inverses of power functions.
- Use the Vertical Line Test to determine whether an inverse relation is a function.
- Use graphs to determine whether a function is invertible.
- Use the Horizontal Line Test to determine whether a function is invertible.
- Graph inverses of higher-degree power functions.
- Generalize about inverses of even- and odd-degree power functions.

KEY TERMS

- inverse of a function
- invertible function
- Horizontal Line Test

The word *transpose* means to switch two or more items. The word combines the Latin prefix *trans-*, meaning "across" or "over" and *ponere*, meaning "to put" or "place." The word *interchange* means the same thing as *transpose*.

Like many words, *transpose* is used in different ways in different fields:

- In music, the word *transpose* is most often used to mean rewriting a song in a different key—either higher or lower.
- In biology, a *transposable element* is a sequence of DNA that can move from one location to another in a gene.
- Magicians use transposition when they make two objects appear to switch places.

Keep an eye out for the word *transpose* in these lessons! What different ways can you use the word *transpose*?

PROBLEM 1 Strike That, Invert It

Recall that a power function is a polynomial function of the form $P(x) = ax^n$, where n is a non-negative integer.

The graphs at the end of this lesson show these 6 power functions.

$$L(x) = x,\ Q(x) = x^2,\ C(x) = x^3,\ F(x) = x^4,\ V(x) = x^5,\ S(x) = x^6$$

Cut out the graphs.

1. The graph of the linear function $L(x) = x$ models the width of a square as the independent quantity and the height of the square as the dependent quantity.

What part or parts of this graph don't make sense in terms of the quantities in this situation?

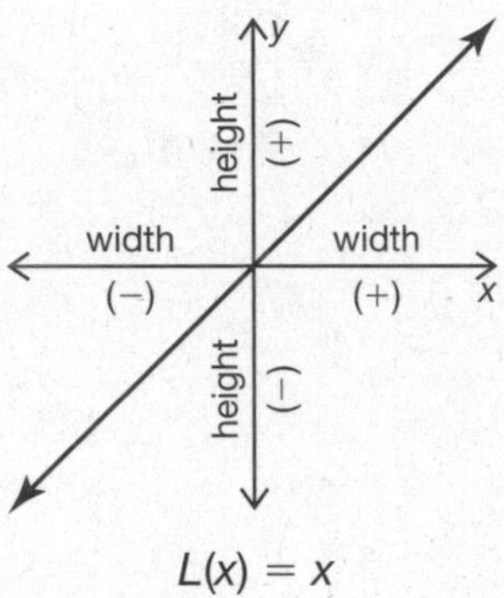

$L(x) = x$

11

a. Transform the cutout so that it shows the height as the independent quantity on the horizontal axis and the width as the dependent quantity on the vertical axis. Then sketch the resulting graph and label the axes.

How do I know when I've got the right graph?

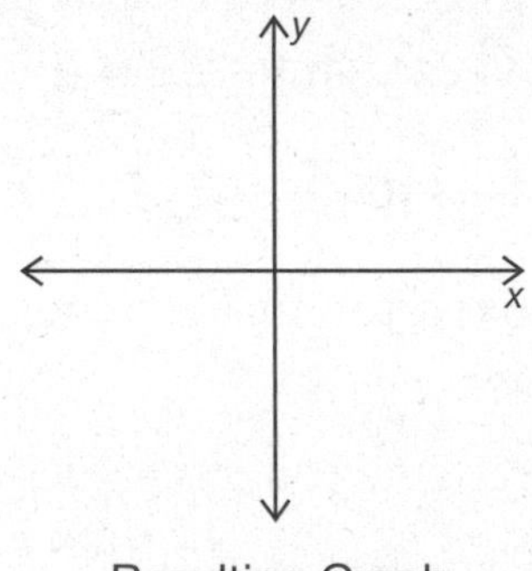

Resulting Graph

b. Describe the transformations you used to transpose the independent and dependent quantities.

c. Is the resulting graph a function? Explain your reasoning.

11

d. Compare the graph of $L(x) = x$ to the resulting graph. Interpret both graphs in terms of the width and height of a square.

2. The graph of the quadratic function $Q(x) = x^2$ models the side length of a square as the independent quantity and the area of the square as the dependent quantity.

What part or parts of this graph don't make sense in terms of the quantities in this situation?

a. Transform the cutout so that it shows the area as the independent quantity on the horizontal axis and the side length as the dependent quantity on the vertical axis. Then sketch the resulting graph and label the axes.

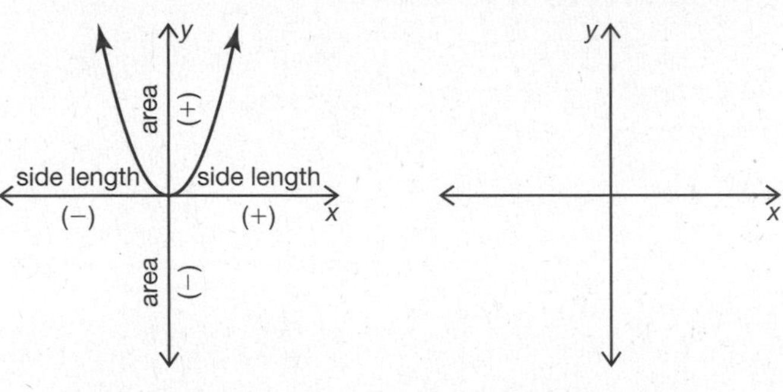

$Q(x) = x^2$ Resulting Graph

b. Describe the transformations you used to transpose the independent and dependent quantities.

11

c. Is the resulting graph a function? Explain your reasoning.

d. Cole used an incorrect strategy to transpose the independent and dependent quantities.

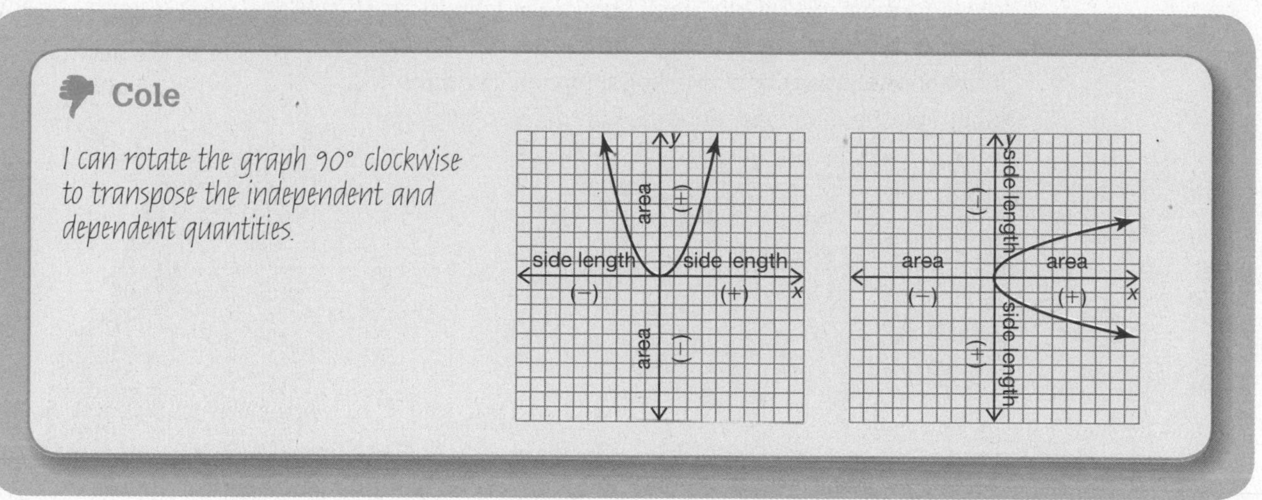

Describe why Cole's strategy is incorrect.

11

e. Compare the graph of $Q(x) = x^2$ to the resulting graph you sketched. Interpret both graphs in terms of the side length and area of a square.

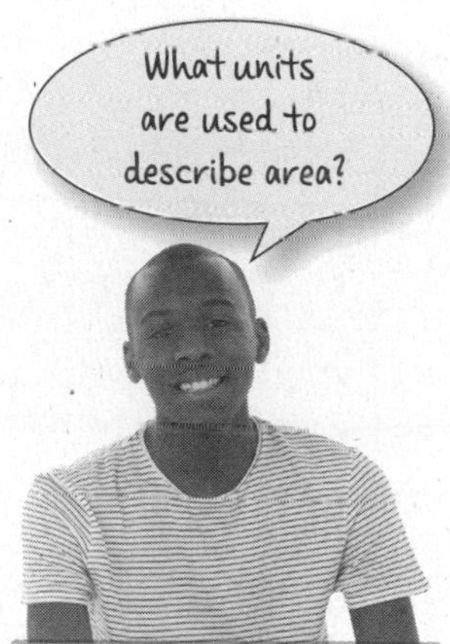

3. The graph of the cubic function $C(x) = x^3$ models the side length of a cube as the independent quantity and the volume of the cube as the dependent quantity.

   a. Transform the cutout so that it shows the volume as the independent quantity on the horizontal axis and the side length as the dependent quantity on the vertical axis. Then sketch the resulting graph and label the axes.

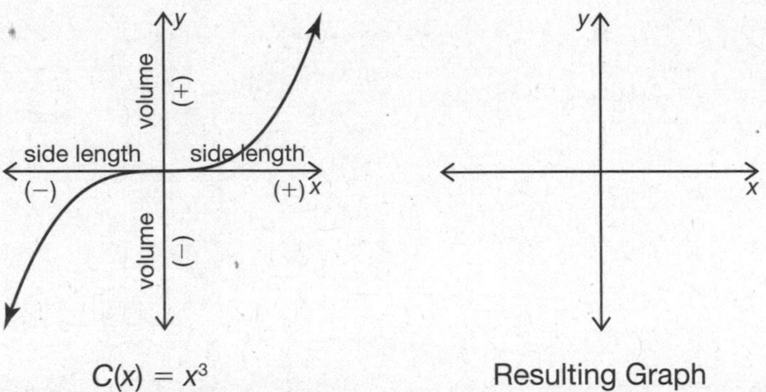

   b. Describe the transformations you used to transpose the independent and dependent quantities.

11

   c. Is the resulting graph a function? Explain your reasoning.

   d. Compare the graph of $C(x) = x^3$ to the resulting graph. Interpret both graphs in terms of the side length and volume of a cube.

PROBLEM 2 Across the Line

Recall that a function f is the set of all ordered pairs (x, y), or $(x, f(x))$, where for every value of x there is one and only one value of y, or $f(x)$. The **inverse of a function** is the set of all ordered pairs (y, x), or $(f(x), x)$.

By transforming the cutouts in Problem 1, you were able to see and sketch the inverses of the functions $L(x) = x$, $Q(x) = x^2$, and $C(x) = x^3$.

1. Deanna discovered a way to use just one reflection to transpose the independent and dependent quantities.

Deanna

I can reflect the graph across the line $y = x$ by folding it diagonally to switch the independent and dependent quantities.

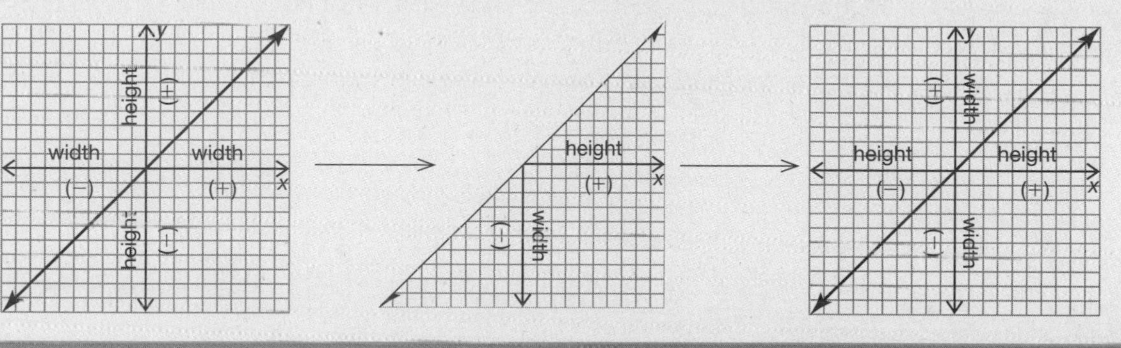

Use your cutouts and Deanna's strategy to sketch the graphs of the inverses of $F(x) = x^4$, $V(x) = x^5$, and $S(x) = x^6$.

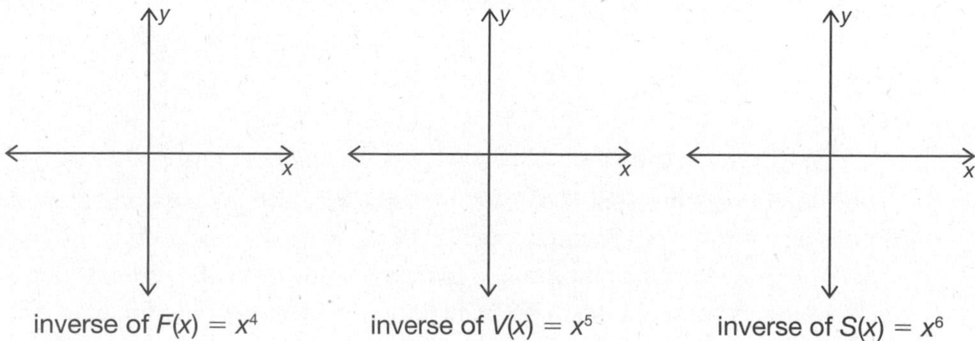

inverse of $F(x) = x^4$ inverse of $V(x) = x^5$ inverse of $S(x) = x^6$

If the inverse of a function f is also a function, then f is an **invertible function**, and its inverse is written as $f^{-1}(x)$.

2 Which of the 6 power functions that you explored are invertible functions? Explain your reasoning.

3. You used the Vertical Line Test to determine whether or not the inverse of a power function was also a function. What test could you use on the original power function to determine if its inverse is also a function? Explain your reasoning.

11

Talk the Talk

1. How does the graph of a power function and the graph of its inverse demonstrate symmetry? Explain your reasoning.

The **Horizontal Line Test** is a visual method to determine whether a function has an inverse that is also a function. To apply the horizontal line test, consider all the horizontal lines that could be drawn on the graph of the function. If any of the horizontal lines intersect the graph of the function at more than one point, then the inverse of the function is not a function.

2. If a graph passes both the Horizontal Line Test and the Vertical Line Test, what can you conclude about the graph?

3. If a graph passes the Vertical Line Test but not the Horizontal Line Test, what can you conclude about the graph?

4. Given any point (x, y) on a graph, use a single transformation to transform the point to its inverse location. What do you notice?

11

Be prepared to share your solutions and methods.

11

$L(x) = x$

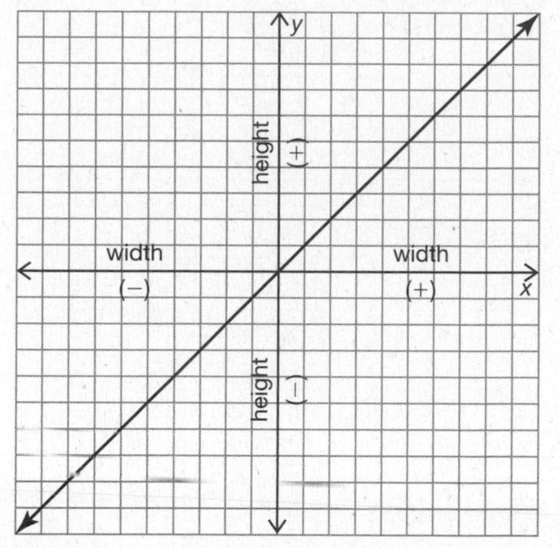

$Q(x) = x^2$

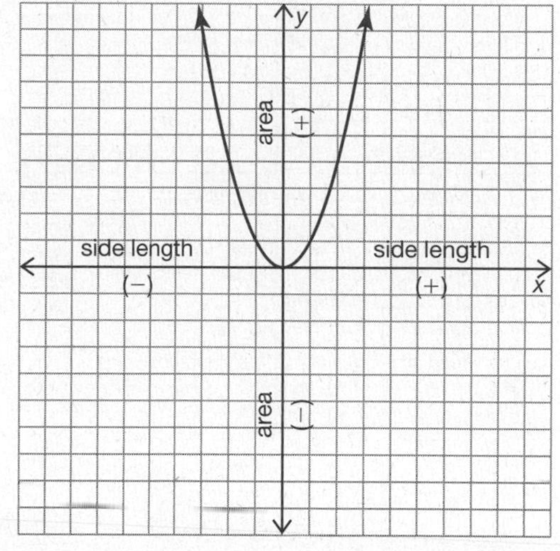

$C(x) = x^3$

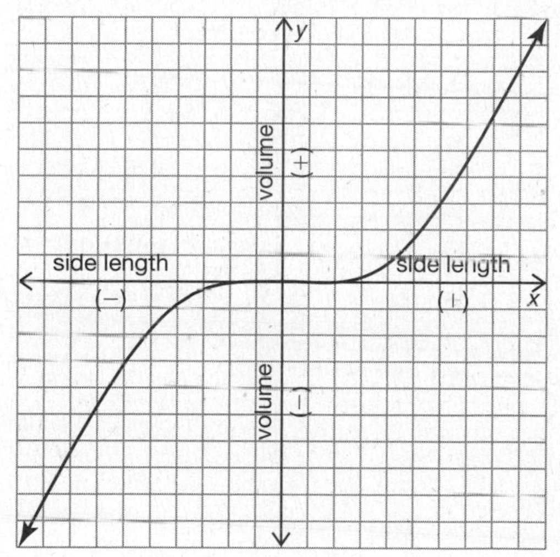

$F(x) = x^4$

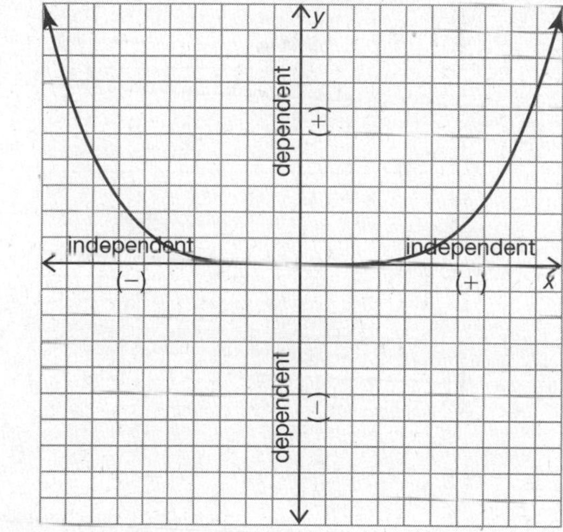

$V(x) = x^5$

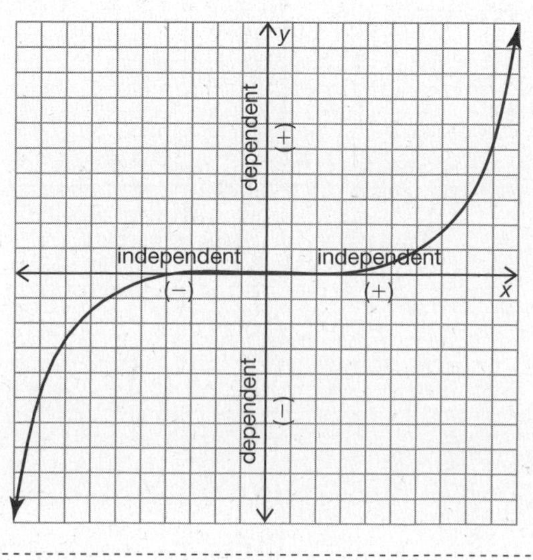

$S(x) = x^5$

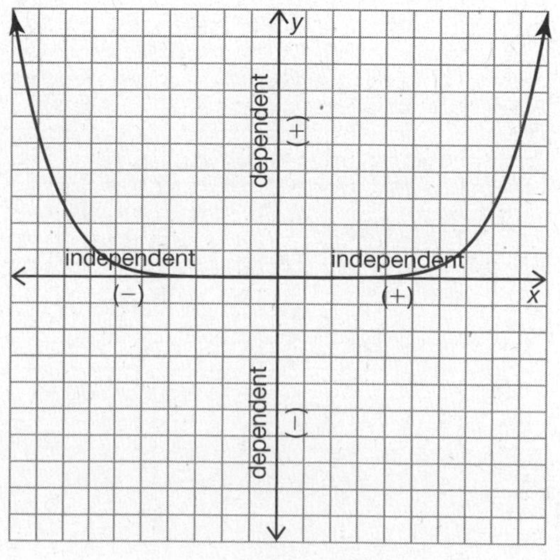

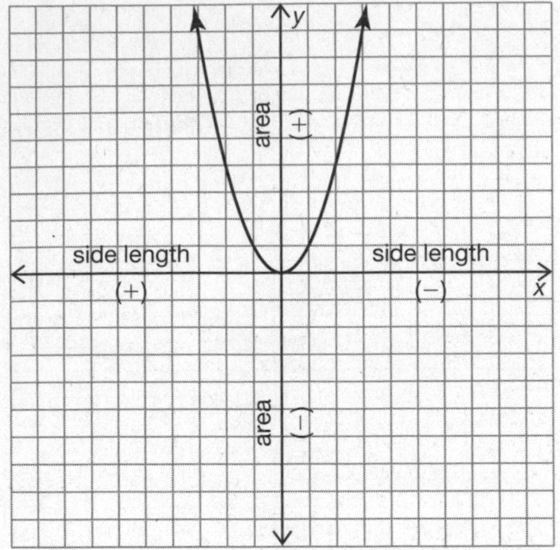
y
area
(+)
side length
(+)
side length
(−)
x
area
(−)

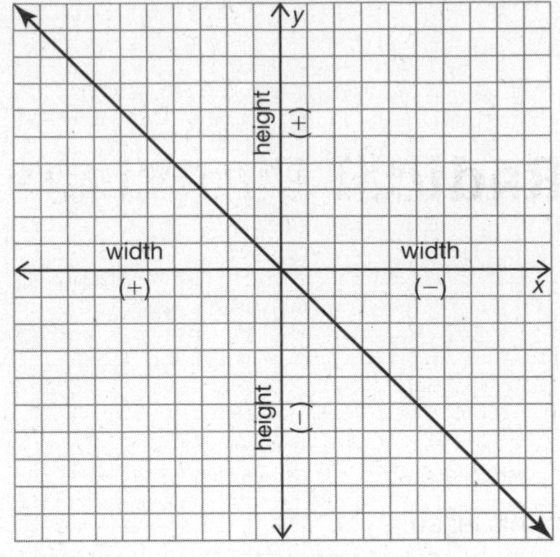
y
height
(+)
width
(+)
width
(−)
x
height
(−)

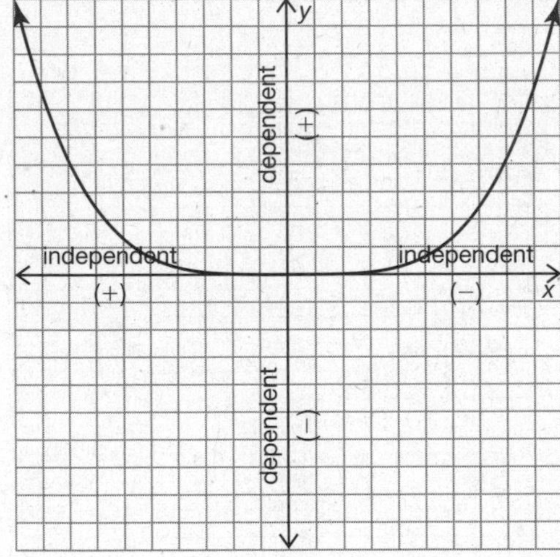
y
dependent
(+)
independent
(+)
independent
(−)
x
dependent
(−)

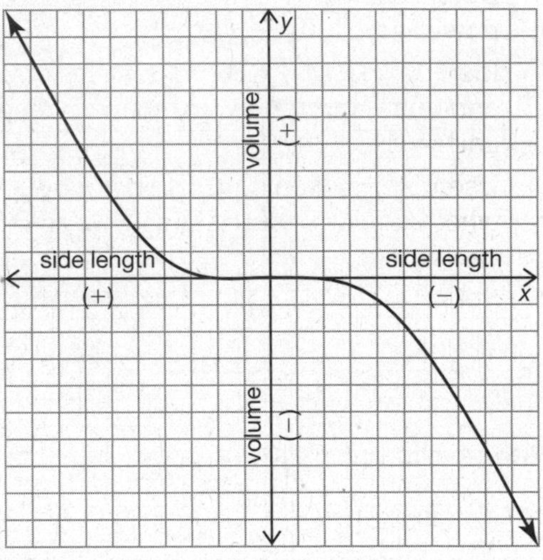
y
volume
(+)
side length
(+)
side length
(−)
x
volume
(−)

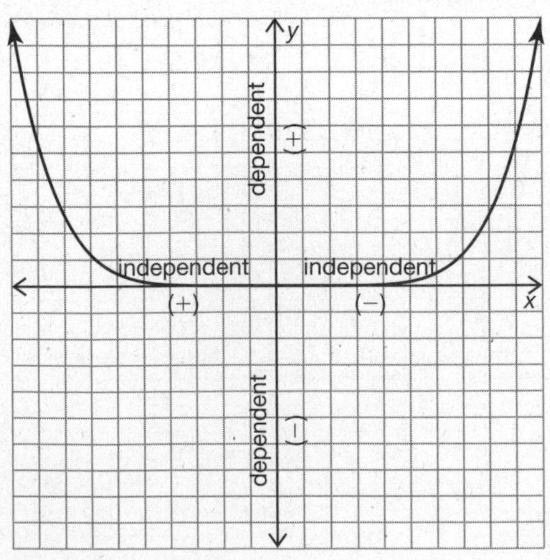
y
dependent
(+)
independent
(+)
independent
(−)
x
dependent
(−)

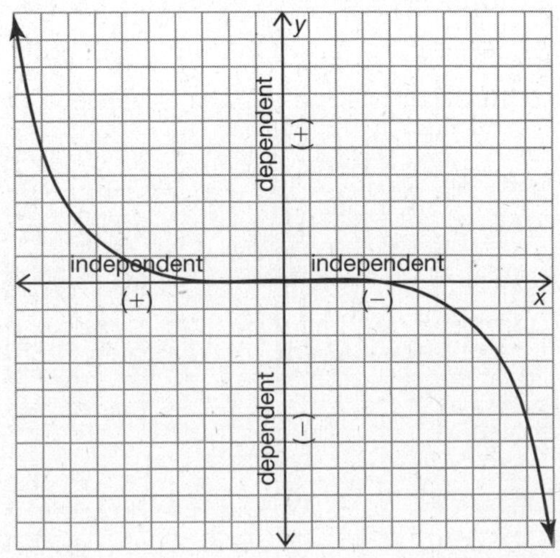
y
dependent
(+)
independent
(+)
independent
(−)
x
dependent
(−)

11

The Root of the Matter

Radical Functions

11.2

LEARNING GOALS

In this lesson, you will:

- Restrict the domain of $f(x) = x^2$ to graph the square root function.
- Determine equations for the inverses of power functions.
- Identify characteristics of square root and cube root functions, such as domain and range.
- Use composition of functions to determine whether two functions are inverses of each other.
- Solve real-world problems using the square root and cube root functions.

KEY TERMS

- square root function
- cube root function
- radical function
- composition of functions

Many science museums display what is known as a Foucault pendulum. French physicist Léon Foucault used a device like this to demonstrate in 1851 that the Earth was rotating in space—although it was known long before that the Earth rotated on its axis.

As a Foucault pendulum swings back and forth throughout the day, the Earth's rotation causes it to appear to move in a circular direction. At the North Pole, a Foucault pendulum would appear to move clockwise during the day. At the South Pole, it would appear to move counterclockwise.

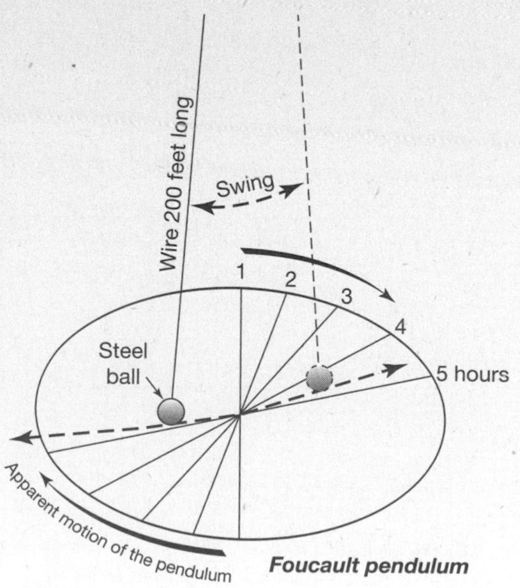

Foucault pendulum

The time it takes for one swing of a pendulum can be modeled by the inverse of a power function.

PROBLEM 1 The Square Root Function

In the previous lesson, you learned that the inverse of a power function defined by the set of all points (x, y), or $(x, f(x))$ is the set of all points (y, x), or $(f(x), x)$.

Thus, to determine the equation of the inverse of a power function, you can transpose x and y in the equation and solve for y.

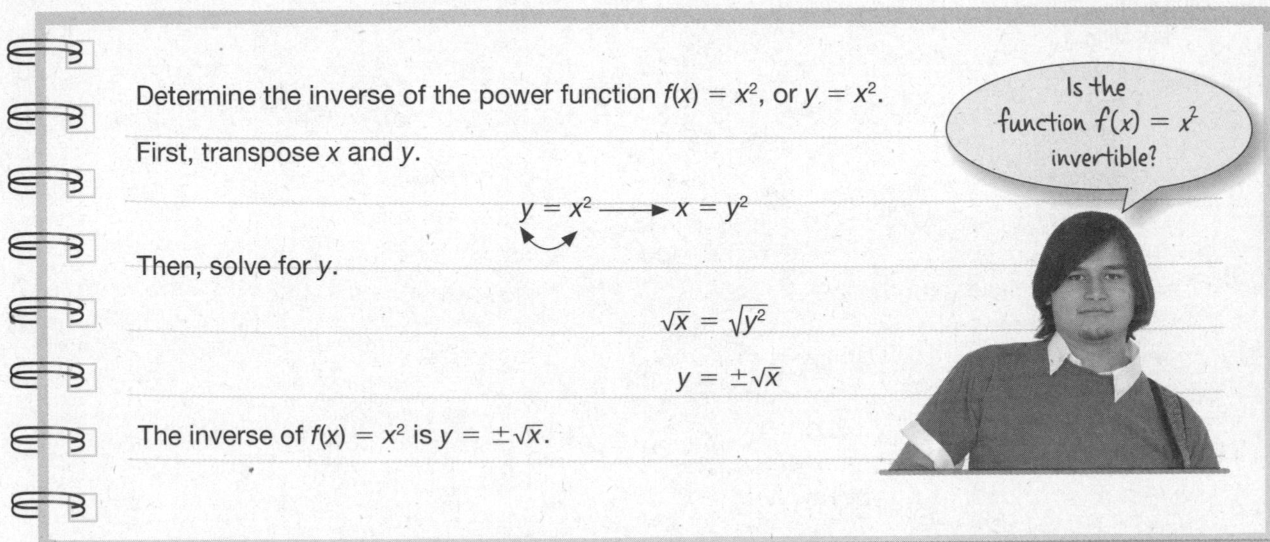

Is the function $f(x) = x^2$ invertible?

Determine the inverse of the power function $f(x) = x^2$, or $y = x^2$.

First, transpose x and y.

$$y = x^2 \longrightarrow x = y^2$$

Then, solve for y.

$$\sqrt{x} = \sqrt{y^2}$$

$$y = \pm\sqrt{x}$$

The inverse of $f(x) = x^2$ is $y = \pm\sqrt{x}$.

11

1. Why must the symbol $\pm$ be written in front of the radical to write the inverse of the function $f(x) = x^2$?

2. Why is the inverse of the function $f(x) = x^2$ not written with the notation $f^{-1}(x)$? Explain your reasoning.

3. The table shows several coordinates of the function $f(x) = x^2$.

a. Use the ordered pairs in the table and what you know about inverses to graph the function and the inverse of the function, $y = \pm\sqrt{x}$. Explain your reasoning.

Now the function and its inverse will be on one coordinate plane. How does each point (x, y) of the function map to the inverse?

x	$f(x) = x^2$
−3	9
−2	4
−1	1
0	0
1	1
2	4
3	9

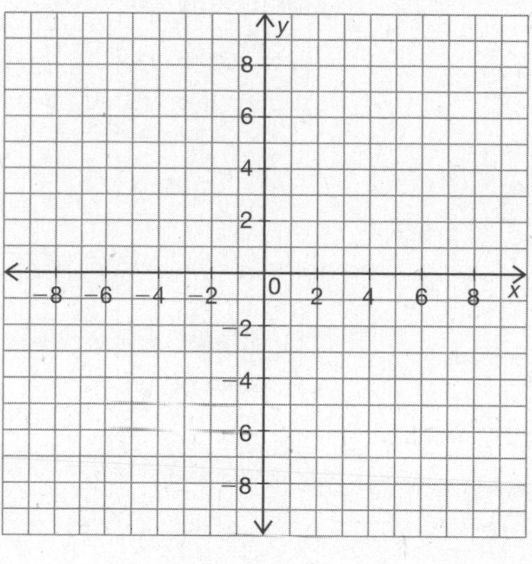
y
8
6
4
2
−8
−6
−4
−2
0
2
4
6
8
x
−2
−4
−6
−8

b. What point or points do the two graphs have in common? Why?

The graph in Question 3 shows that every positive real number has 2 square roots—a positive square root and a negative square root. For example, 9 has 2 square roots, because $(-3)^2 = 9$ and $3^2 = 9$. The two square roots of 9 are 3 and −3.

When you restrict the domain of the power function $f(x) = x^2$ to values greater than or equal to 0, the inverse of the function is called the **square root function** and is written as:

$$f^{-1}(x) = \sqrt{x}, \text{ for } x \geq 0.$$

4. Draw dashed line segments between the plotted points on the function for the restricted domain $x \geq 0$ and the corresponding inverse points.

a. List the ordered pairs of the points you connected.

b. List the ordered pairs of the points that you did not connect. Explain why these points are not connected.

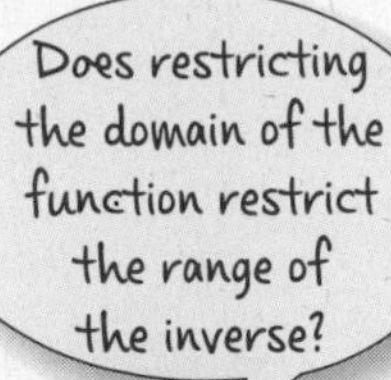

Does restricting the domain of the function restrict the range of the inverse?

5. Graph the square root function $f^{-1}(x) = \sqrt{x}$ by restricting the domain of $f(x) = x^2$.

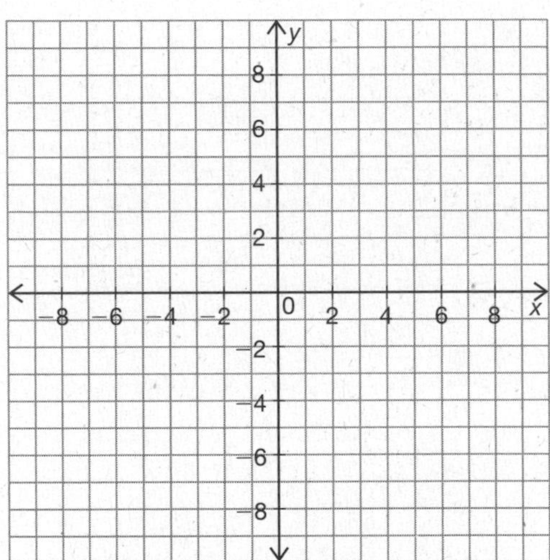

6.

Explain why Brent's equation is incorrect.

11

7. Describe the key characteristics of each function:

Function: $f(x) = x^2$, for $x \geq 0$	Inverse function: $f^{-1}(x) = \sqrt{x}$
Domain: ____________	Domain: ____________
Range: ____________	Range: ____________
x-intercept(s): ____________	x-intercept(s): ____________
y-intercept(s): ____________	y-intercept(s): ____________

Keep in mind the restrictions placed on $f(x)$ to produce $f^{-1}(x)$.

8. Does the inverse function $f^{-1}(x) = \sqrt{x}$ have an asymptote? Explain your reasoning.

PROBLEM 2 The Cube Root Function

The **cube root function** is the inverse of the power function $f(x) = x^3$ and can be written as $f^{-1}(x) = \sqrt[3]{x}$.

1. The table shows several coordinates of the function $c(x) = x^3$.

   a. Use these points to graph the function and the inverse of the function, $c^{-1}(x)$.

x	$c(x) = x^3$
−2	−8
−1	−1
0	0
1	1
1	8

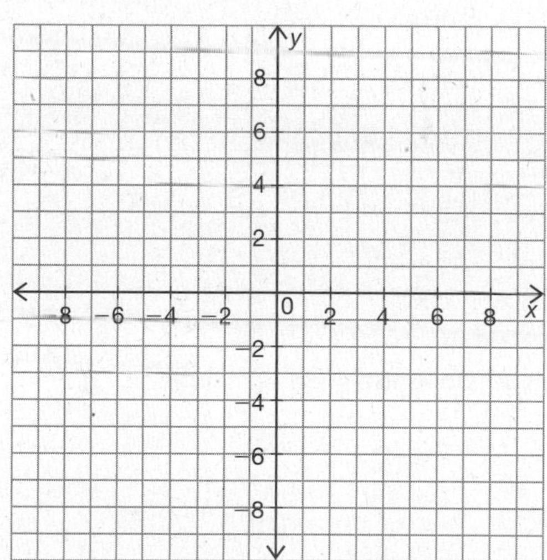

   b. Explain how you determined the coordinates for the points on the inverse of the function.

   c. What point or points do the two graphs have in common? Why?

2. Why is the symbol $\pm$ not written in front of the radical to write the inverse of the function $c(x) = x^3$?

3. Why do you not need to restrict the domain of the function $c(x) = x^3$ to write the inverse with the notation $c^{-1}(x)$?

4. Describe the key characteristics of each function:

Function: $c(x) = x^3$	Inverse function: $c^{-1}(x) = \sqrt[3]{x}$
Domain: ____________	Domain: ____________
Range: ____________	Range: ____________
x-intercept(s): ____________	x-intercept(s): ____________
y-intercept(s): ____________	y-intercept(s): ____________

11

5. Does the inverse function $c^{-1}(x) = \sqrt[3]{x}$ have an asymptote? Explain your reasoning.

The inverses of power functions with exponents greater than or equal to 2, such as the square root function and the cube root function, are called **radical functions**. Radical functions are used in many areas of science, including physics and computer science.

PROBLEM 3 Inverse by Composition

You know that when the domain is restricted to $x \geq 0$, the function $f(x) = \sqrt{x}$ is the inverse of the power function $g(x) = x^2$. You also know that the function $h(x) = \sqrt[3]{x}$ is the inverse of the power function $q(x) = x^3$.

The process of evaluating one function inside of another function is called the **composition of functions**. For two functions f and g, the composition of functions uses the output of $g(x)$ as the input of $f(x)$. It is notated as $(f \circ g)(x)$ or $f(g(x))$.

To write a composition of the functions $g(x) = x^2$ and $f(x) = \sqrt{x}$ when the domain of $g(x)$ is restricted to $x \geq 0$, substitute the value of one of the functions for the argument, x, of the other function.

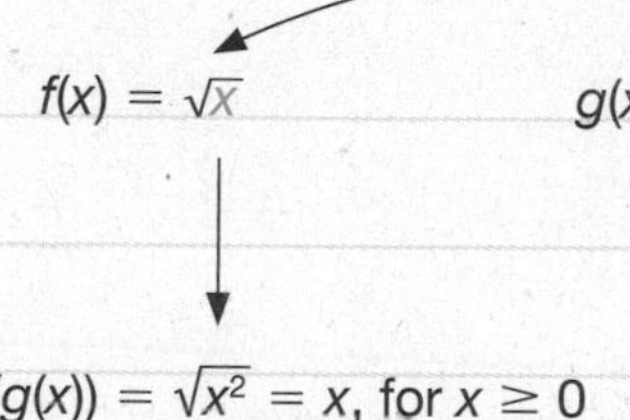

$f(g(x)) = \sqrt{x^2} = x$, for $x \geq 0$

You can write the composition of these two functions as $f(g(x)) = x$ for $x \geq 0$.

11

1. Determine $g(f(x))$ for the functions $g(x) = x^2$ and $f(x) = \sqrt{x}$ for $x \geq 0$.

If $f(g(x)) = g(f(x)) = x$, then $f(x)$ and $g(x)$ are inverse functions.

2. Are $f(x)$ and $g(x)$ inverse functions? Explain your reasoning.

3. Algebraically determine whether each pair of functions are inverses. Show your work.

a. Verify that $h(x) = \sqrt[3]{x}$ is the inverse of $q(x) = x^3$.

b. Determine if $k(x) = 2x^2 + 5$ and $j(x) = -2x^2 - 5$ are inverse functions.

11

4. Mike said that all linear functions are inverses of themselves because $f(x) = x$ is the inverse of $g(x) = x$.

Is Mike correct? Explain your reasoning.

PROBLEM 4 Pendula

The time it takes for one complete swing of a pendulum depends on the length of the pendulum and the acceleration due to gravity.

The formula for the time it takes a pendulum to complete one swing is $T = 2\pi\sqrt{\frac{L}{g}}$, where T is time in seconds, L is the length of the pendulum in meters, and g is the acceleration due to gravity in meters per second squared.

1. If the acceleration due to gravity on Earth is 9.8 m/s², write a function $T(L)$ that represents the time of one pendulum swing.

2. Graph the function $T(L)$.

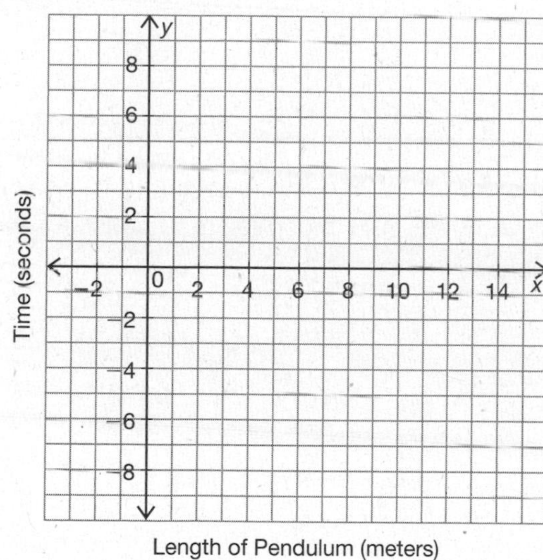

Use a calculator to determine the approximate locations of the points.

3. Describe the characteristics of the function, such as its domain, range, and intercepts. Explain your reasoning.

4. How long does it take for one complete swing when the length of the pendulum is 0.5 meter?

5. A typical grandfather clock pendulum completes a full swing in 2 seconds. Use your graph to determine the approximate length of a grandfather clock pendulum.

Talk the Talk

11

1. How can knowing the domain, range, intercepts, and other key characteristics of a power function help you determine those characteristics for the function's inverse? Explain your reasoning.

2. When a function has an asymptote, will its inverse have an asymptote? If so, describe the location of the asymptote for the function's inverse.

Be prepared to share your solutions and methods.

Making Waves

11.3

Transformations of Radical Functions

LEARNING GOALS

In this lesson, you will:

- Graph transformations of radical functions.
- Analyze transformations of radical functions using transformational function form.
- Describe transformations of radical functions using algebraic, graphical, and verbal representations.
- Generalize about the effects of transformations on power functions and their inverses.

Some people think that they won't need math if they choose to work in an artistic career. Not so! Much of the graphic and animation work you see on television, in movies, and even in print and art galleries is done on the computer, using sophisticated graphic design software.

To use many graphic design programs, a knowledge of transformations, like reflections and rotations, coordinate systems, ratios, and on and on, is essential to working efficiently and accurately—and to get just the right effect.

How do you think knowledge about power functions and radical functions can be used in graphic design?

PROBLEM 1 Shifting Sands

Recall that transformations performed on a function $f(x)$ to form a new function $g(x)$ can be described by the transformational function:

$$g(x) = Af(B(x - C)) + D$$

A group of art students had the idea to use transformations of radical functions to create a logo for the Radical Surfing School.

To start, they graphed the function $f(x) = \sqrt{x}$, for $0 \leq x \leq 14$, and shifted copies of the curve to create the waves $g(x)$, $h(x)$, and $k(x)$.

The square root function has a restricted domain. Now the dimensions of the logo will restrict it even more!

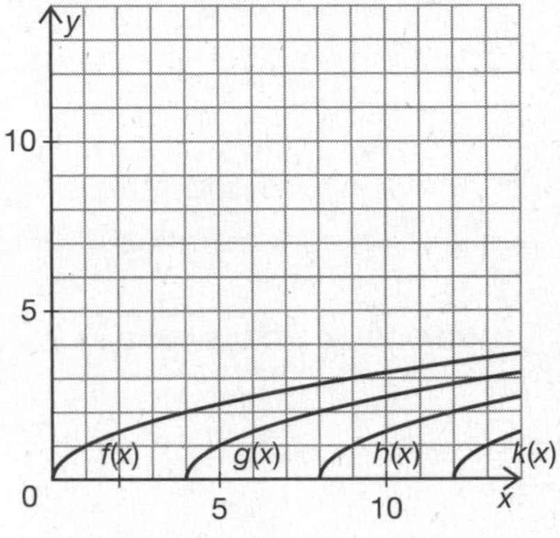

11

1. Do the transformations of $f(x)$ shown on the graph take place inside the function or outside the function? Explain your reasoning.

2. What value or values in the transformation function were changed to create these curves? Explain your reasoning.

3. Write the domain of each transformed function as an inequality statement using the dimensions of the logo.

4. Devin, Stuart, and Kristen each wrote an equation for a function that was added to the graph first using the transformational function form of $f(x)$, and then in terms of x.

- Devin's equation: $g(x) = f(x) - 4$
  $= \sqrt{x} - 4$
- Stuart's equation: $h(x) = f(x - 8)$
  $= \sqrt{x - 8}$
- Kristen's equation: $k(x) = f(x + 12)$
  $= \sqrt{x + 12}$

a. Describe whether each student's equation is correct or incorrect. Explain your reasoning.

11

b. Write the correct equations to describe the 3 new functions shown in the graph first using transformational function form of $f(x)$, and then in terms of x. Finally, write their domains as inequality statements.

$f(x) = \sqrt{x}$ Domain: ____________

$g(x) =$ ____________ $=$ ____________ Domain: ____________

$h(x) =$ ____________ $=$ ____________ Domain: ____________

$k(x) =$ ____________ $=$ ____________ Domain: ____________

5. The students decide that reflecting each curve, $g(x)$, $h(x)$, and $k(x)$, across the respective lines where $x = C$ will make them look more like waves crashing on the beach.

a. Graph the resulting functions $f'(x)$, $g'(x)$, $h'(x)$, and $k'(x)$. Write each function first in terms of their transformations of $f(x)$, $g(x)$, $h(x)$, and $k(x)$, and then in terms of x. Finally, state the domain of each.

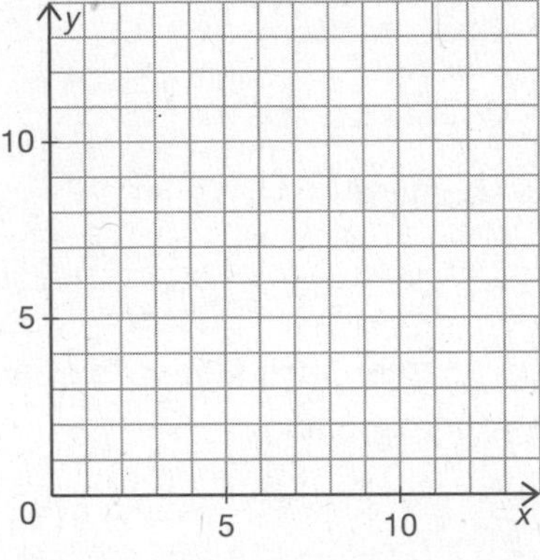

You can use the prime symbol (') to indicate that a function is a transformation of another function.

11

b. Describe how you used the transformation function to determine the equations of the new functions.

c. How did the domain of each transformed function change as a result of the reflection across $x = C$?

d. Why does your graph show only 3 curves when the original graph had 4? Explain your reasoning.

6. Suppose the students wanted to reflect the 3 new waves $g'(x)$, $h'(x)$, and $k'(x)$ across the line $y = 0$.

   a. Describe how you can use the transformational function to determine the equations of the reflected functions.

   b. Write three new functions using transformational form to represent each reflection of $g'(x)$, $h'(x)$, and $k'(x)$, and then each in terms of x. Use the double prime symbol (″) to indicate each transformed function. Finally, write the domain of each transformed function.

7. Jamal wants to add waves below the 3 waves as shown. These waves should be copies of $g'(x)$, $h'(x)$, and $k'(x)$, except half as high and shifted to the left 2 units.

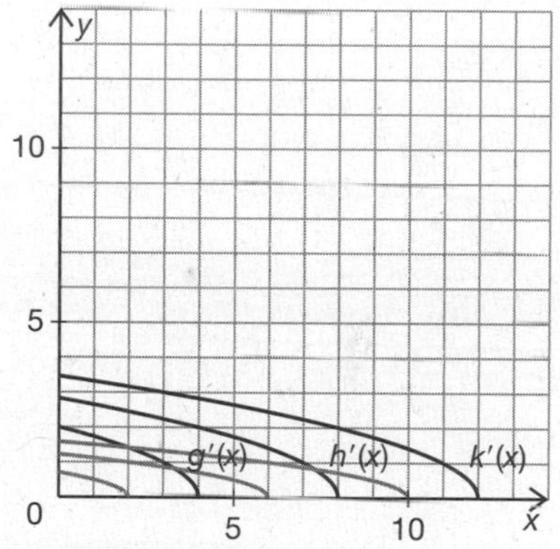

   a. Write 3 new functions $q(x)$, $r(x)$, and $s(x)$ in terms of $g'(x)$, $h'(x)$, and $k'(x)$ to create the waves that Jamal wants. Make sure to write the domains of each transformed function.

   b. Describe how you used what you know about transformational function form to determine your answer to part (a).

11

8. The art students want to add some clouds to the top of the logo. For the clouds, they will use the inverses of cubic functions. They start with the function $c(x) = -\sqrt[3]{x} + 14$.

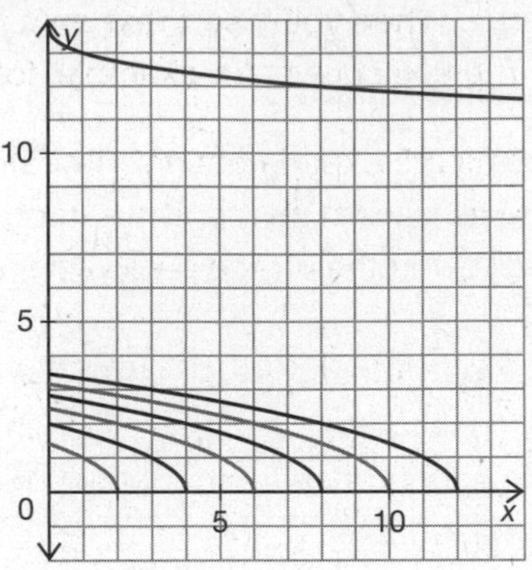

a. Transform this function and write 2 more equations to create the clouds the students want. Graph the results.

11

b. Color the graph to show the waves and the clouds on the logo.

In many graphic design programs, a trace path can be created. A trace path is an invisible line or curve that acts as the baseline of text that is added to the design. When you insert text on a trace path, the text follows the line or curve. The text shown, for example, follows the curve $f(x) = -x^2$.

9. The art students are experimenting with different square root and cube root function graphs to use as trace paths for the surfing school's name: Radical Surfing School. They have narrowed their trace paths down to 2 choices. The graphs of the functions are shown.

$h(x) = \sqrt[3]{2(x - 1)}$ $\qquad$ $j(x) = 2\sqrt[3]{x - 1}$

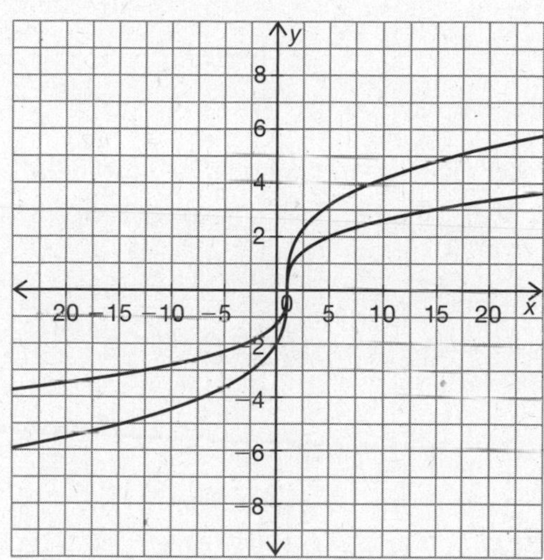

a. Compare and contrast the graphs of the functions and their equations. What do you notice?

b. Compare the effects of increasing the *A*-value with increasing the *B*-value in a radical function. What do you notice?

c. Label each graph with the correct equation and include the domain restrictions.

11

10. Choose one of the cube root functions as a trace path for the title of the surfing school. Or, write a different radical function to use as a trace path. Graph the function on the coordinate plane in Question 8, and write the title of the school on the trace path.

11

Be prepared to share your methods and solutions.

11.4

Keepin' It Real

Extracting Roots and Rewriting Radicals

LEARNING GOALS

In this lesson, you will:

- Extract roots from radicals.
- Rewrite radicals as powers that have rational exponents.
- Rewrite powers that have rational exponents as radicals.

Radicals can produce imaginary results. For example, the square root of -4 is equal to $2i$, $\sqrt{-4} = 2i$. But, in this chapter we are not going to talk about imaginary numbers. We are going to keep it real!

PROBLEM 1 Root of the Problem

Previously, you have rewritten radicals by extracting roots involving numbers. In this lesson you will explore how to extract roots for expressions of the form $\sqrt[n]{x^n}$. To determine how to extract a variable from a radical, let's consider several different values of n.

1. For each value of n for the expression $\sqrt[n]{x^n}$, complete the table and sketch the graph. Then identify the function family associated with the graph and write the corresponding equation.

   a. Let $n = 2$.

x	$x^n = x^2$	$\sqrt[n]{x^n} = \sqrt[2]{x^2}$
−2		
−1		
0		
1		
2		

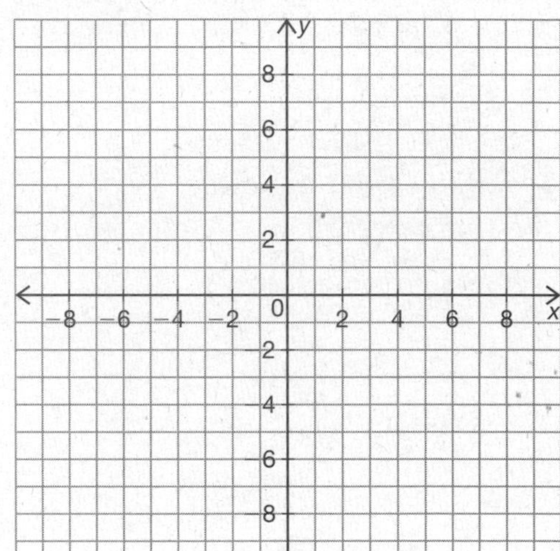

11

Function family of the graph: ________________

Equation of the graph: ________________

   b. Let $n = 3$.

x	$x^n = x^3$	$\sqrt[n]{x^n} = \sqrt[3]{x^3}$
−2		
−1		
0		
1		
2		

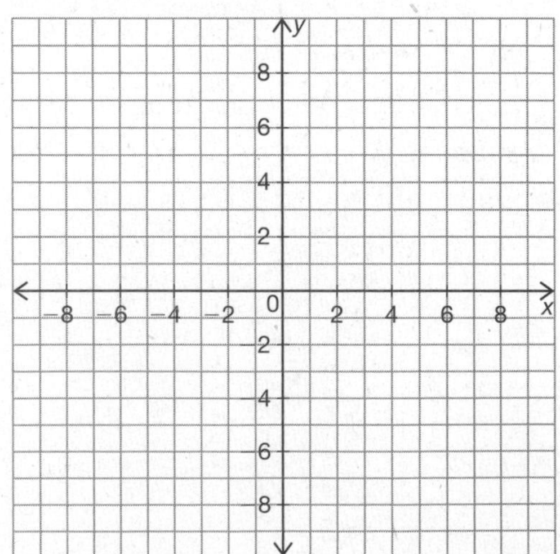

Function family of the graph: ________________

Equation of the graph: ________________

c. Let $n = 4$.

x	$x^n = x^4$	$\sqrt[n]{x^n} = \sqrt[4]{x^4}$
−2		
−1		
0		
1		
2		

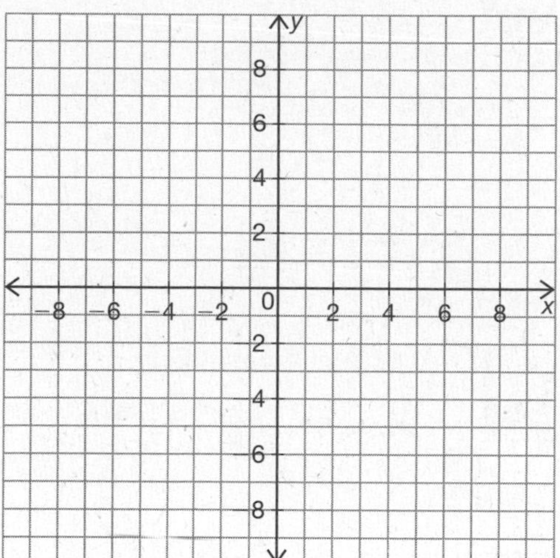

Function family of the graph: ____________________

Equation of the graph: ____________________

d. Let $n = 5$.

x	$x^n = x^5$	$\sqrt[n]{x^n} = \sqrt[5]{x^5}$
−2		
−1		
0		
1		
2		

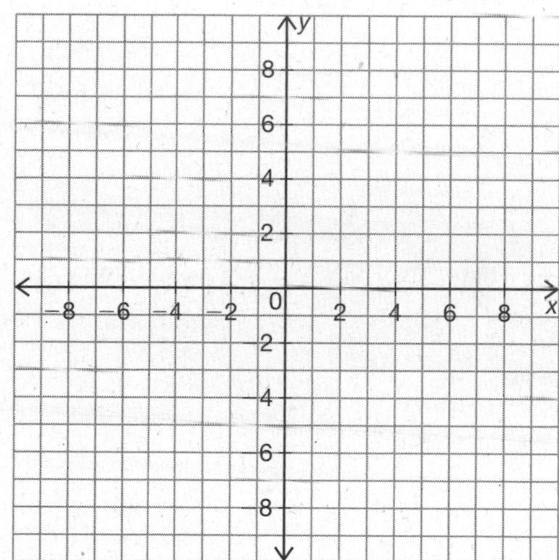

Function family of the graph: ____________________

Equation of the graph: ____________________

e. Analyze your representations for each value of n. What do you notice?

To extract a variable from a radical, the expression $\sqrt[n]{x^n}$ can be written as:

$$\sqrt[n]{x^n} = \begin{cases} |x|, & \text{when } n \text{ is even} \\ x, & \text{when } n \text{ is odd} \end{cases}$$

2. Explain why $\sqrt[7]{x^7} = |x|$ is incorrect, for real values of x.

One way to say $\sqrt[7]{x^7}$ is "the seventh root of x to the seventh."

3. Asia and Melissa shared their work for extracting the root from $\sqrt{x^4}$, for real values of x.

Asia	Melissa
$\sqrt{x^4} = \lvert x^2 \rvert$	$\sqrt{x^4} = x^2$

Who's correct? Explain your reasoning.

PROBLEM 2 Sort It Out

Let's review the properties of powers.

1. Write an explanation for each property to complete the table.

Property of Powers	Rule	Written Explanation
Product of Powers	$a^m \cdot a^n = a^{m+n}$	
Quotient of Powers	$\frac{a^m}{a^n} = a^{m-n}$	
Power to a Power	$(a^m)^n = a^{mn}$	
Product to a Power	$(a^m \cdot b^n)^p = a^{mp} \cdot b^{np}$	
Quotient to a Power	$\left(\frac{a^m}{b^n}\right)^p = \frac{a^{mp}}{b^{np}}$	
Zero Power	$a^0 = 1$, if $a \neq 0$	
Negative Exponent In Numerator	$a^{-m} = \frac{1}{a^m}$, if $a \neq 0$ and $m > 0$	
Negative Exponent In Denominator	$\frac{1}{a^{-m}} = a^m$, if $a \neq 0$ and $m > 0$	

11

11

2. Cut out the items and tape each item into the appropriate group on the next page.

a^0	$\frac{a^6}{a^6}$
$(-a)^4$	$\frac{a^3}{a^7}$
$a^3 \cdot a$	$\frac{a^6}{a^2}$
$a^0 \cdot a^4$	$\left(\frac{1}{a^2}\right)^2$
$a \cdot a^{-5}$	$\left(a^{\frac{1}{2}}\right)^8$
$a^{-4} \cdot a^0$	$(a^{-12})^{\frac{1}{3}}$
$a^4 \cdot a^{-4}$	$\left(\frac{b^{12}}{a^{-6}}\right)^{\frac{1}{3}}$
$(a^2)^2$	$\left(\frac{b}{a^{-2}}\right)^2$
$(ab^2)^2$	$\frac{1}{a^4}$
$(a^8b^4)^{\frac{1}{2}}$	$\frac{1}{a^{-4}}$

11

1

a^4

a^{-4}

a^2b^4

a^4b^2

11

PROBLEM 3 The Power of Radicals!

You can rewrite a radical as a power with a rational exponent, and rewrite a power with a rational exponent as a radical.

Solve the equation $\sqrt{x} = x^a$ for a, given $x \geq 0$, to determine the exponential form of $\sqrt{x}$.

$$\sqrt{x} = x^a$$

Square each side of the equation. $(\sqrt{x})^2 = (x^a)^2$

Because the bases are the same, you can set the exponents equal to each other.

$$x = x^{2a}$$

$$1 = 2a$$

Divide by 2 to solve for a. $a = \frac{1}{2}$

The exponential form of the square root of x given $x \geq 0$, is x to the one-half power.

$$\sqrt{x} = x^{\frac{1}{2}}, \text{ given } x \geq 0$$

11

1. Why was the restriction "given $x \geq 0$" stated at the beginning of the worked example?

2. How do you know when the initial x-value can be any real number or when the initial x-value should be restricted to a subset of the real numbers?

3. Determine the power that is equal to the radical.

   a. Write and solve an equation to determine the power that is equal to the cube root of x.

   b. Write and solve an equation to determine the power that is equal to the cube root of x squared.

4. Complete the cells in each row. In the last column, write "$x \geq 0$" or "all real numbers" to describe the restrictions that result in equal terms for each row.

11

Radical Form	Radical to a Power Form	Exponential Form	Restrictions
$\sqrt[4]{x^2}$	$(\sqrt[4]{x})^2$		
		$x^{\frac{3}{4}}$	
		$x^{\frac{2}{5}}$	
$\sqrt[5]{x}$			

You can rewrite a radical expression $\sqrt[n]{x^a}$ as an exponential expression $x^{\frac{a}{n}}$:

- For all real values of x if the index n is odd.
- For all real values of x greater than or equal to 0 if the index n is even.

PROBLEM 4 Extracting Roots and Rewriting Radicals

You can extract roots to rewrite radicals, using radicals or powers.

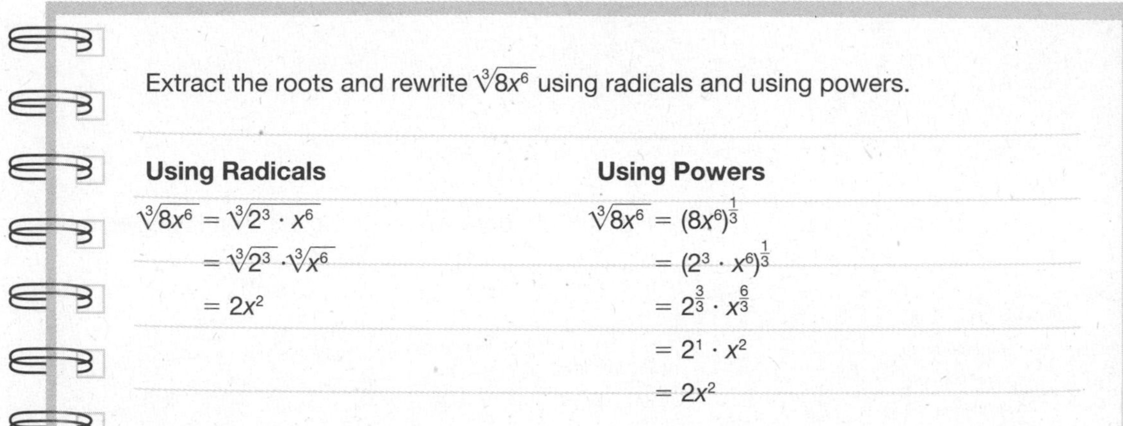

Extract the roots and rewrite $\sqrt[3]{8x^6}$ using radicals and using powers.

Using Radicals

$$\sqrt[3]{8x^6} = \sqrt[3]{2^3 \cdot x^6}$$
$$= \sqrt[3]{2^3} \cdot \sqrt[3]{x^6}$$
$$= 2x^2$$

Using Powers

$$\sqrt[3]{8x^6} = (8x^6)^{\frac{1}{3}}$$
$$= (2^3 \cdot x^6)^{\frac{1}{3}}$$
$$= 2^{\frac{3}{3}} \cdot x^{\frac{6}{3}}$$
$$= 2^1 \cdot x^2$$
$$= 2x^2$$

1. Which method do you prefer?

11

My motto is, when in doubt rewrite radicals using radical form!

2. Devon and Embry shared their work for extracting roots from $\sqrt[4]{f^8g^4}$.

Embry

$$\sqrt[4]{f^8g^4} = \sqrt[4]{f^8} \cdot \sqrt[4]{g^4}$$
$$= \sqrt[4]{(f^2)^4} \cdot \sqrt[4]{g^4}$$
$$= f^2|g|$$

Devon

$$\sqrt[4]{f^8g^4} = (f^8g^4)^{\frac{1}{4}}$$
$$= (f^8)^{\frac{1}{4}}(g^4)^{\frac{1}{4}}$$
$$= f^{\frac{8}{4}}g^{\frac{4}{4}}$$
$$= f^2|g|$$

a. Explain why it is not necessary to use the absolute value symbol around f^2.

b. Explain why it is necessary to use the absolute value symbol around g.

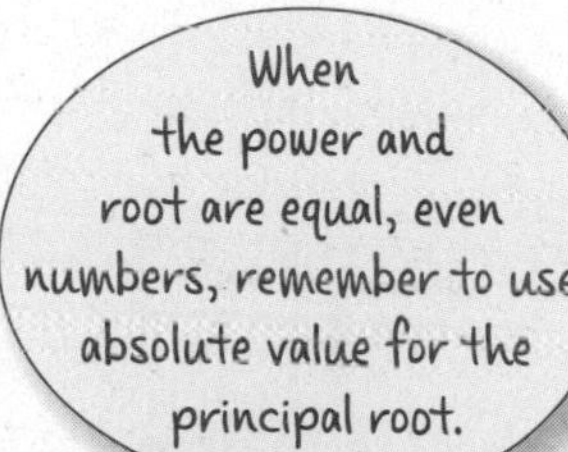

When the power and root are equal, even numbers, remember to use absolute value for the principal root.

In Question 2, Embry extracted the root from $\sqrt[4]{f^8g^4}$ using radical form because the root of a product is equal to the product of its roots, $\sqrt[p]{a^mb^n} = \sqrt[p]{a^m} \cdot \sqrt[p]{b^n}$.

That concept applies to quotients also. The root of a quotient is equal to the quotient of its roots, $\sqrt[p]{\frac{a^m}{b^n}} = \frac{\sqrt[p]{a^m}}{\sqrt[p]{b^n}}$.

For some radicals, you may not be able to extract the entire radicand.

3. Angelo, Bernadette, and Cris extracted the roots from $\sqrt[3]{16x^8}$.

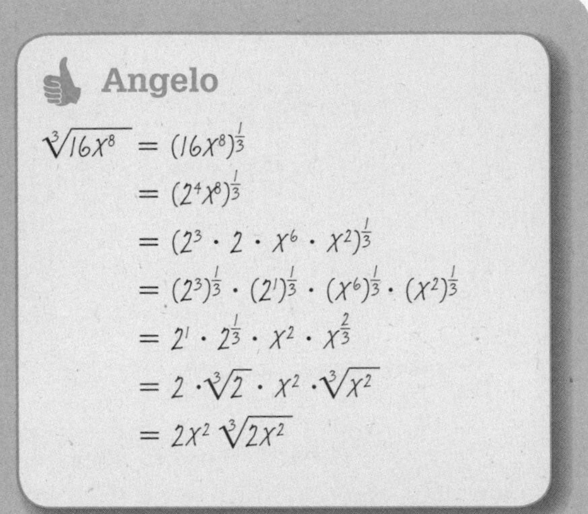

Angelo

$$\begin{aligned}\sqrt[3]{16x^8} &= (16x^8)^{\frac{1}{3}}\\ &= (2^4x^8)^{\frac{1}{3}}\\ &= (2^3 \cdot 2 \cdot x^6 \cdot x^2)^{\frac{1}{3}}\\ &= (2^3)^{\frac{1}{3}} \cdot (2^1)^{\frac{1}{3}} \cdot (x^6)^{\frac{1}{3}} \cdot (x^2)^{\frac{1}{3}}\\ &= 2^1 \cdot 2^{\frac{1}{3}} \cdot x^2 \cdot x^{\frac{2}{3}}\\ &= 2 \cdot \sqrt[3]{2} \cdot x^2 \cdot \sqrt[3]{x^2}\\ &= 2x^2\sqrt[3]{2x^2}\end{aligned}$$

Bernadette

$$\begin{aligned}\sqrt[3]{16x^8} &= 2^{\frac{4}{3}} \cdot x^{\frac{8}{3}}\\ &= 2^{\frac{3}{3}} \cdot 2^{\frac{1}{3}} \cdot x^{\frac{6}{3}} \cdot x^{\frac{2}{3}}\\ &= 2 \cdot \sqrt[3]{x} \cdot x^2 \cdot \sqrt[3]{x}\\ &= 2x^2\sqrt[3]{2x^2}\end{aligned}$$

Cris

$$\begin{aligned}\sqrt[3]{16x^8} &= \sqrt[3]{2^4 \cdot x^8}\\ &= \sqrt[3]{2^3x^6} \cdot \sqrt[3]{2x^2}\\ &= 2x^2\sqrt[3]{2x^2}\end{aligned}$$

11

a. In the last line of work, why was $2x^2$ not extracted from the radical?

b. Compare and contrast the methods.

4. Betty, Wilma, and Rose each extracted roots and rewrote the radical $\sqrt{x^2y^2}$.

Betty

$$\sqrt{x^2y^2} = \sqrt{x^2 \cdot y^2}$$
$$= \sqrt{x^2} \cdot \sqrt{y^2}$$
$$= |x| \cdot |y|$$

Wilma

$$\sqrt{x^2y^2} = \sqrt{x^2 \cdot y^2}$$
$$= \sqrt{x^2} \cdot \sqrt{y^2}$$
$$= |xy|$$

Rose

$$\sqrt{x^2y^2} = \sqrt{x^2 \cdot y^2}$$
$$= \sqrt{x^2} \cdot \sqrt{y^2}$$
$$= xy$$

Who's correct? Explain you reasoning.

11

5. Rewrite each radical by extracting all possible roots, and write the final answer in radical form.

a. $\sqrt{16x^6}$

b. $-\sqrt{8v^3}$

c. $\sqrt{d^3f^4}$

d. $\sqrt{h^4j^6}$

e. $\sqrt{25a^2b^8c^{10}}$

f. $\sqrt[4]{81x^5y^{12}}$

g. $\sqrt[3]{(x + 3)^9}$

h. $\sqrt{(x + 3)^2}$

Be prepared to share your solutions and methods.

11.5

Time to Operate!

Multiplying, Dividing, Adding, and Subtracting Radicals

LEARNING GOALS

In this lesson, you will:

- Rewrite radicals by extracting roots.
- Multiply, divide, add, and subtract radicals.

The word radical can describe something that is cool, something that is extreme or very different from the usual, something related to the root or origin in a non-mathematical context, and of course a mathematical function.

The origin or the word radical is related to the Latin word *radix*, meaning "*root*."

PROBLEM 1 Multiplying and Dividing Radicals

1. Arianna and Heidi multiplied $\sqrt{18a^2} \cdot 4\sqrt{3a^2}$ and extracted all roots.

Arianna

$$\begin{aligned}\sqrt{18a^2} \cdot 4\sqrt{3a^2} &= 4\sqrt{54a^4} \\ &= 4\sqrt{9 \cdot 6 \cdot a^4} \\ &= 4 \cdot \sqrt{9} \cdot \sqrt{6} \cdot \sqrt{a^4} \\ &= 4 \cdot 3 \cdot \sqrt{6} \cdot a^2 \\ &= 12a^2\sqrt{6}\end{aligned}$$

Heidi

$$\begin{aligned}\sqrt{18a^2} \cdot 4\sqrt{3a^2} &= \sqrt{9 \cdot 2 \cdot a^2} \cdot 4 \cdot \sqrt{3 \cdot a^2} \\ &= \sqrt{9} \cdot \sqrt{2} \cdot \sqrt{a^2} \cdot 4 \cdot \sqrt{3} \cdot \sqrt{a^2} \\ &= 3 \cdot \sqrt{2} \cdot |a| \cdot 4 \cdot \sqrt{3} \cdot |a| \\ &= 12a^2\sqrt{6}\end{aligned}$$

Compare Arianna's and Heidi's solution methods. Explain the difference in their solution methods.

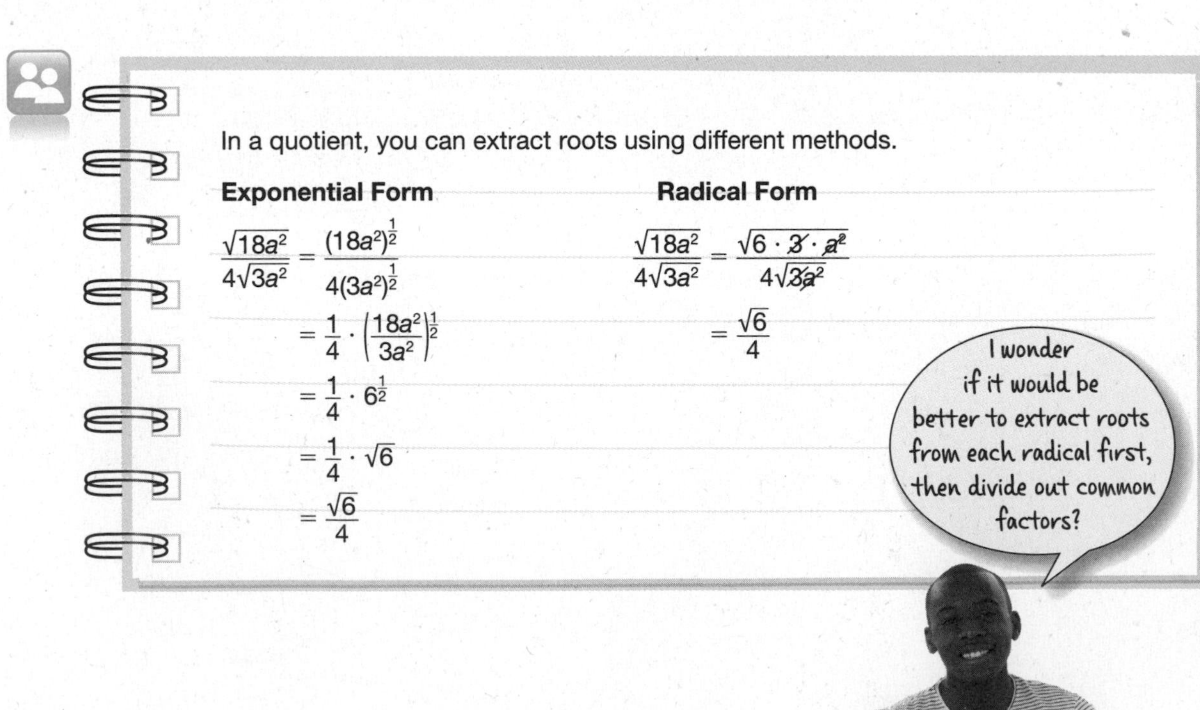

In a quotient, you can extract roots using different methods.

Exponential Form

$$\begin{aligned}\frac{\sqrt{18a^2}}{4\sqrt{3a^2}} &= \frac{(18a^2)^{\frac{1}{2}}}{4(3a^2)^{\frac{1}{2}}} \\ &= \frac{1}{4} \cdot \left(\frac{18a^2}{3a^2}\right)^{\frac{1}{2}} \\ &= \frac{1}{4} \cdot 6^{\frac{1}{2}} \\ &= \frac{1}{4} \cdot \sqrt{6} \\ &= \frac{\sqrt{6}}{4}\end{aligned}$$

Radical Form

$$\begin{aligned}\frac{\sqrt{18a^2}}{4\sqrt{3a^2}} &= \frac{\sqrt{6 \cdot \cancel{3} \cdot \cancel{a^2}}}{4\sqrt{\cancel{3a^2}}} \\ &= \frac{\sqrt{6}}{4}\end{aligned}$$

I wonder if it would be better to extract roots from each radical first, then divide out common factors?

2. Which method do you think is more efficient?

3. Jackie shared his solution for extracting roots and rewriting the quotient $\frac{\sqrt{25bc}}{\sqrt[3]{b^2c^2}}$, given $b > 0$ and $c > 0$.

Jackie

$$\frac{\sqrt{25bc}}{\sqrt[3]{b^2c^2}} = \frac{\sqrt{25\cancel{bc}}}{\sqrt[3]{b^{\cancel{2}\,1}c^{\cancel{2}\,1}}}$$

$$= \frac{\sqrt{25}}{\sqrt[3]{bc}}$$

$$= \frac{5}{\sqrt[3]{bc}}$$

a. Why are the restrictions $b > 0$ and $c > 0$, instead of $b \geq 0$ and $c \geq 0$?

b. Explain why Jackie's work is incorrect.

c. Robert and Maxine also shared their solutions for extracting roots and rewriting the quotient $\frac{\sqrt{25bc}}{\sqrt[3]{b^2c^2}}$, given $b > 0$ and $c > 0$.

Robert

$$\frac{\sqrt{25bc}}{\sqrt[3]{b^2c^2}} = \frac{\sqrt{25} \cdot \sqrt{bc}}{\sqrt[3]{b^2c^2}}$$

$$= \frac{5\sqrt{bc}}{\sqrt[3]{b^2c^2}}$$

$$= \frac{5\sqrt{bc}}{\sqrt[3]{b^2c^2}} \cdot \frac{\sqrt[3]{bc}}{\sqrt[3]{bc}}$$

$$= \frac{5\sqrt{bc}\,\sqrt[3]{bc}}{\sqrt[3]{b^3c^3}}$$

$$= \frac{5(bc)^{\frac{1}{2}}(bc)^{\frac{1}{3}}}{bc}$$

$$= \frac{5(bc)^{\frac{5}{6}}}{bc}$$

$$= \frac{5(b^5c^5)^{\frac{1}{6}}}{bc}$$

$$= \frac{5\sqrt[6]{b^5c^5}}{bc}$$

Maxine

$$\frac{\sqrt{25bc}}{\sqrt[3]{b^2c^2}} = \frac{\sqrt{25} \cdot \sqrt{bc}}{\sqrt[3]{b^2c^2}}$$

$$= \frac{5\sqrt{bc}}{\sqrt[3]{b^2c^2}}$$

Who's correct? Explain your reasoning.

11

4. Perform each operation and extract all roots. Write your final answer in radical form.

   a. $2\sqrt{x} \cdot \sqrt{x} \cdot 5\sqrt{x}$, given $x \geq 0$

   b. $2\sqrt[3]{k}(\sqrt[3]{k})$

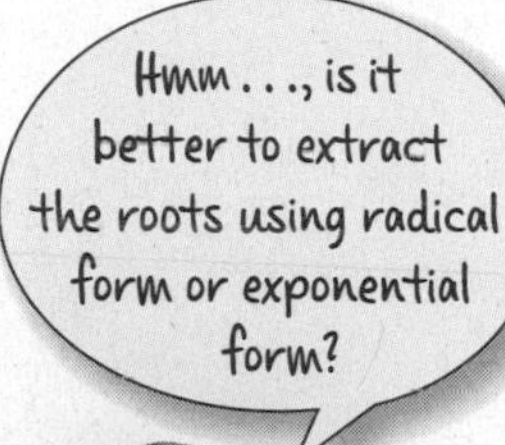

   c. 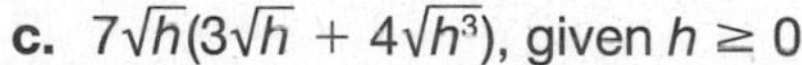 $7\sqrt{h}(3\sqrt{h} + 4\sqrt{h^3})$, given $h \geq 0$

   d. 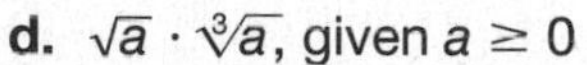 $\sqrt{a} \cdot \sqrt[3]{a}$, given $a \geq 0$

   e. 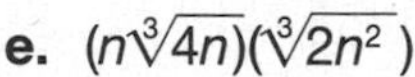 $(n\sqrt[3]{4n})(\sqrt[3]{2n^2})$

   f. 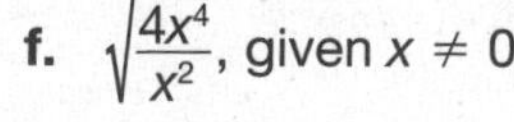 $\sqrt{\frac{4x^4}{x^2}}$, given $x \neq 0$

5. Perform each operation, extract all roots, and write your final answer in radical form, without radicals in the denominator.

a. $\frac{2\sqrt{a}}{5\sqrt[3]{a}}$, given $a > 0$

b. $\frac{2\sqrt{2a^5}}{5\sqrt[3]{16a^2}}$, given $a > 0$

Multiplying by
a form of one
helps to eliminate
the radical from
the denominator.

c. $\frac{-5\sqrt{4j^2k^5}}{\sqrt{75jk^2}}$, given $j > 0$ and $k > 0$

PROBLEM 2 Adding and Subtracting Radical Terms

To add and subtract terms, it is important to identify like terms.

1. Use the symbols to identify six groups of like terms. The first group has been started for you.

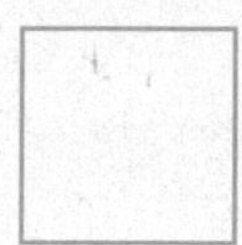

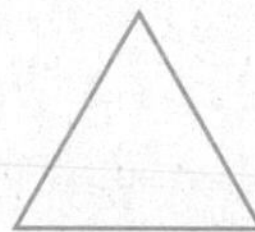

$4x$	$\sqrt{x}$	$\frac{1}{3}x^{\frac{1}{5}}$	$2x^3$	$0.2x$
$-8\sqrt{x}$	$10\sqrt[3]{x^2}$	x^3	$\sqrt[3]{x}$	$x^{\frac{1}{5}}$
$-7\sqrt[3]{x^2}$	$-6x^{\frac{1}{5}}$	$-5x^3$	$-3x$	$-\sqrt{x}$
$-\sqrt[3]{x}$	$\frac{1}{3}\sqrt{x}$	$10\sqrt{x}$	$\sqrt[3]{x^2}$	x

In some cases, you can rewrite the sum or difference of two terms as one term.

2. Explain why Grace and Diane were able to rewrite their original expression as one term.

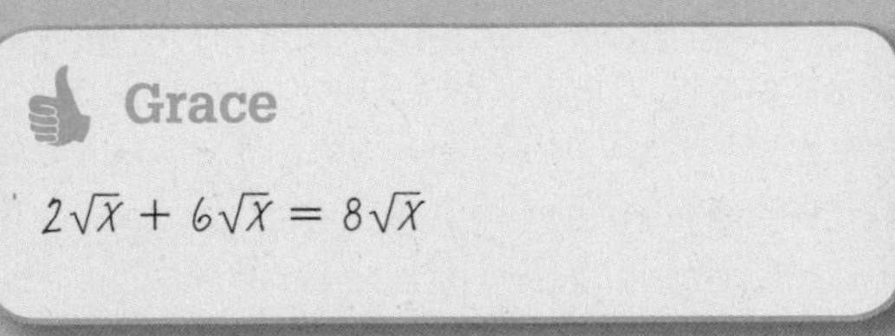

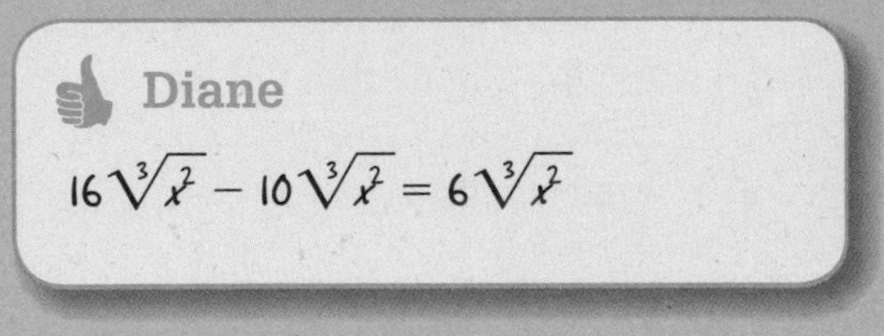

Diane
$16\sqrt[3]{x^2} - 10\sqrt[3]{x^2} = 6\sqrt[3]{x^2}$

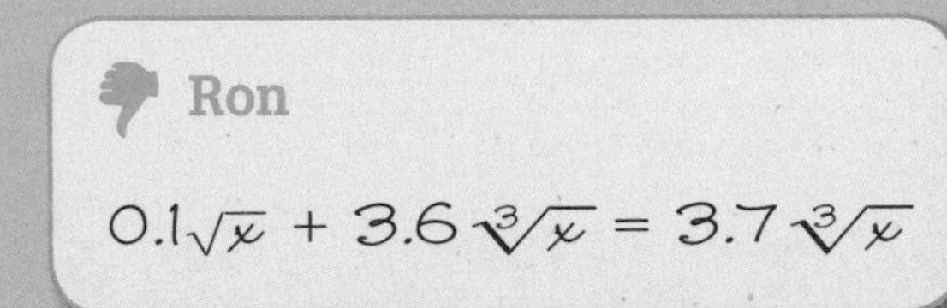

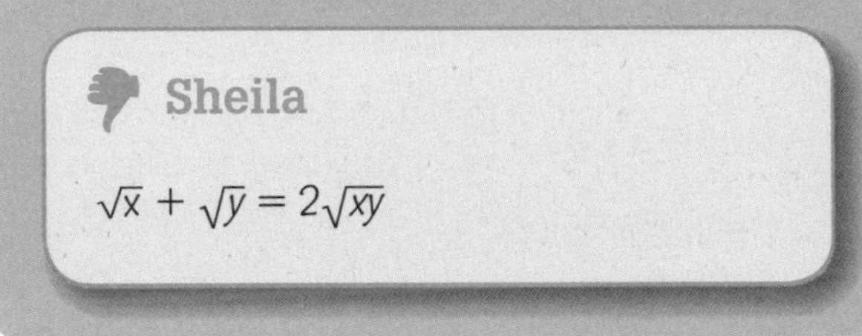

3. Explain why Ron's answer is incorrect.

4. Explain why Sheila's answer is incorrect.

When adding or subtracting radicals, you can combine like terms and write the result using fewer terms.

For example, the two terms, $3\sqrt{x}$ and $\sqrt{x}$ are like terms because their variable portions, $\sqrt{x}$, are the same. The coefficients do not have to be the same.

On the other hand, the terms $-8\sqrt[3]{x^4}$ and $7\sqrt[3]{x}$ are not like terms because their variable portions, $\sqrt[3]{x^4}$ and $\sqrt[3]{x}$, are different. The indices are the same but the radicands are different. In exponential form, $x^{\frac{4}{3}}$ and $x^{\frac{1}{3}}$, notice that the bases are the same, the denominators in the exponent are the same, but the numerators in the exponents are different.

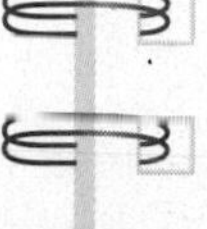

To determine the sum or difference of like radicals, add or subtract the coefficients.

$$3\sqrt{x} + \sqrt{x} = 4\sqrt{x}, \text{ given } x \geq 0$$

You can also write an equivalent expression using powers.

$$3x^{\frac{1}{2}} + x^{\frac{1}{2}} = 4x^{\frac{1}{2}}, \text{ given } x \geq 0$$

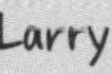

5. Larry and D.J. discussed whether or not $4\sqrt{x}$ and $-5x^{\frac{1}{2}}$ are like terms, given $x \geq 0$.

Larry	DJ
They are not like terms because their variable parts are different.	They are like terms. Their variable parts look different, but they are actually the same.

Who's correct? Explain your reasoning.

6. Combine like terms, if possible, and write your final answer in radical form.

a. $\sqrt{y} - \sqrt{y}$, given $y \geq 0$

b. $9\sqrt{a} + 5\sqrt{b}$, given $a \geq 0$, $b \geq 0$

c. $2\sqrt{x} + \sqrt{x} + 5\sqrt{x}$, given $x \geq 0$

11

d. $7\sqrt{h} - 4.1\sqrt{h} + 2.4\sqrt{h}$, given $h \geq 0$

e. $3\sqrt{t}(\sqrt{t} - 8\sqrt{t}) + 4t$, given $t \geq 0$

f. $5\sqrt{g} + 2\sqrt[3]{g}$, given $g \geq 0$

Talk the Talk

Complete the graphic organizer. Write two radicals whose sum, difference, product, and quotient are each equivalent to $6\sqrt[3]{x}$.

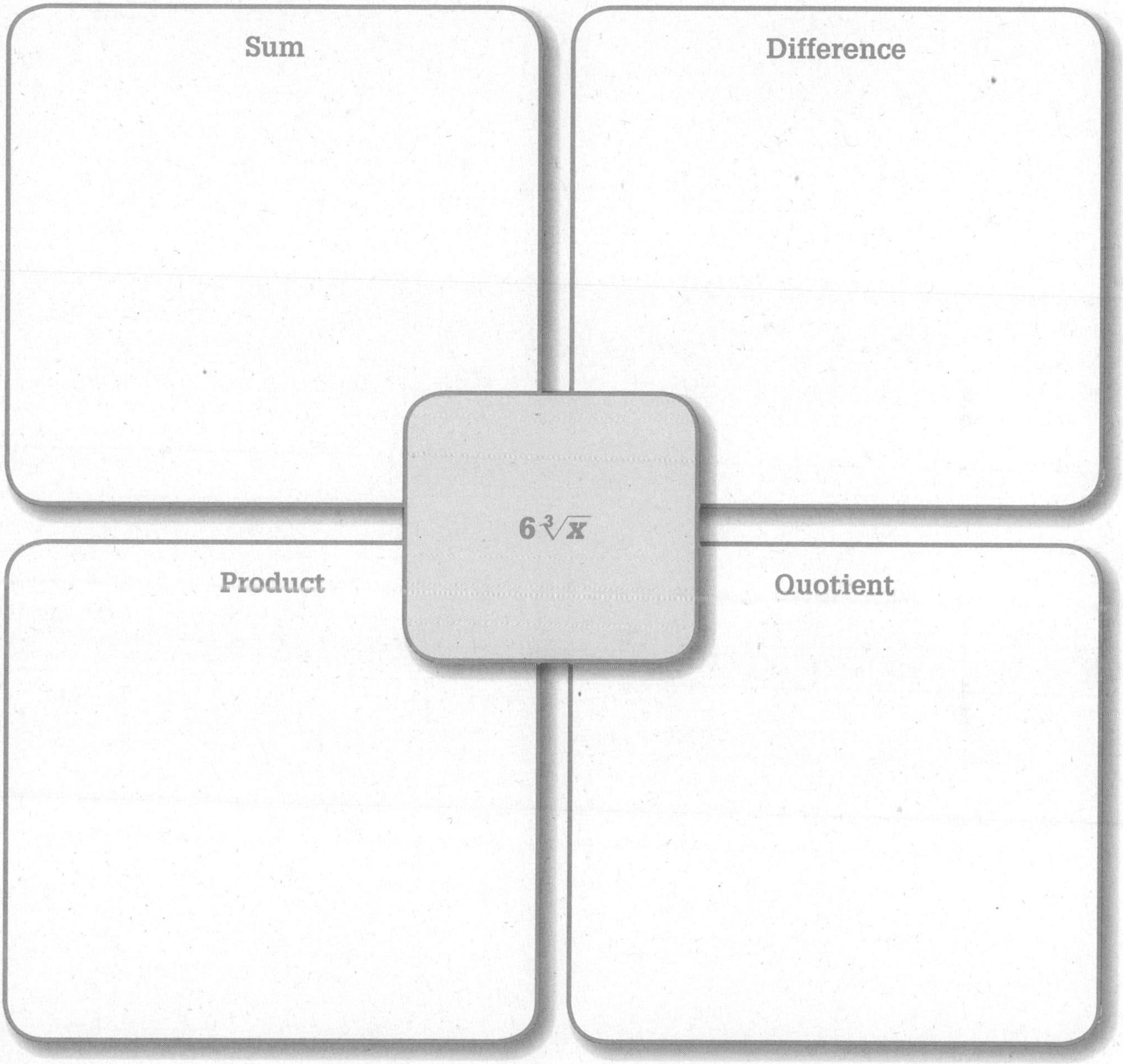

Sum	Difference

$6\sqrt[3]{x}$

Product	Quotient

Be prepared to share your solutions and methods.

11

Look to the Horizon

Solving Radical Equations

11.6

LEARNING GOALS

In this lesson, you will:

- Use algebra to solve radical equations.
- Write the solution steps of a radical equation using radical notation.
- Write the solution steps of a radical equation using exponential notation.
- Identify extraneous roots when solving radical equations.

So, you have been wondering whether there is a system to measure wind speed and describe conditions at sea and on land, right? The answer is the Beaufort scale. It was developed in the early 1800's and is still in use today.

Beaufort Scale			
Beaufort Number	**Description**	**Wind Speed (miles per hour)**	**Wave Height (feet)**
0	calm	< 1	0
1	light air	1–3	0–1
2	light breeze	4–7	1–2
3	gentle breeze	8–13	2–3.5
4	moderate breeze	13–17	3.5–6
5	fresh breeze	18–24	6–9
6	strong breeze	25–30	9–13
7	near gale	31–38	13–19
8	gale	39–46	18–25
9	strong gale	47–54	23–32
10	storm	55–63	29–41
11	violent storm	64–73	37–52
12	hurricane	74	46

PROBLEM 1 Analyzing Solution Paths for Radical Equations

Strategies for solving equations such as maintaining balance and isolating the term containing the unknown are applicable when solving radical equations.

Let's compare the algebraic solution of a two-step quadratic equation to a two-step radical equation.

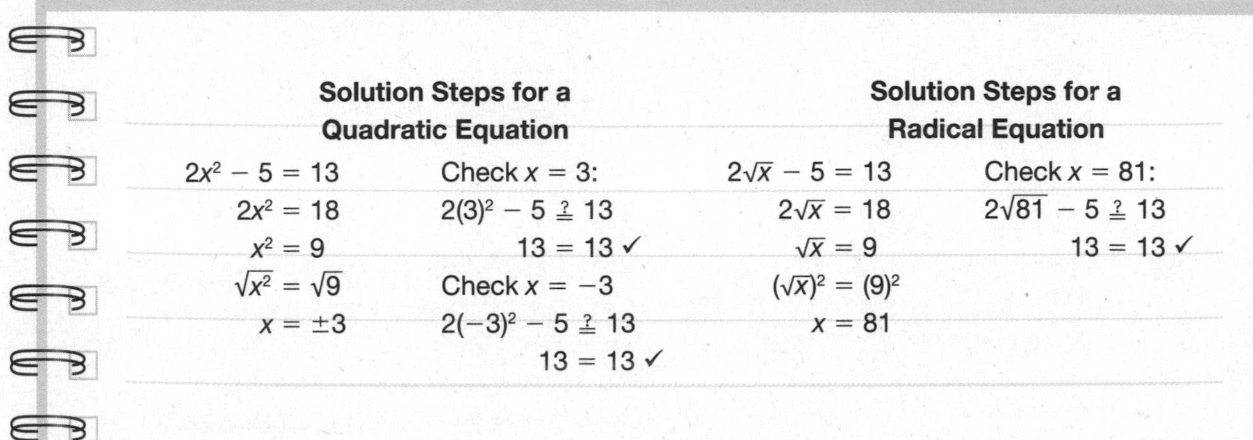

Solution Steps for a Quadratic Equation		Solution Steps for a Radical Equation	
$2x^2 - 5 = 13$	Check $x = 3$:	$2\sqrt{x} - 5 = 13$	Check $x = 81$:
$2x^2 = 18$	$2(3)^2 - 5 \stackrel{?}{=} 13$	$2\sqrt{x} = 18$	$2\sqrt{81} - 5 \stackrel{?}{=} 13$
$x^2 = 9$	$13 = 13$ ✓	$\sqrt{x} = 9$	$13 = 13$ ✓
$\sqrt{x^2} = \sqrt{9}$	Check $x = -3$	$(\sqrt{x})^2 = (9)^2$	
$x = \pm 3$	$2(-3)^2 - 5 \stackrel{?}{=} 13$	$x = 81$	
	$13 = 13$ ✓		

1. Analyze the examples.

   a. Describe the similarities in the first two steps of each solution.

   b. Describe the differences in the remaining steps of each solution.

2. Franco, Theresa, Dawnelle, and Marteiz shared their work for solving $3\sqrt{x} + 7 = 0$, given $x \geq 0$.

Franco

$$\begin{aligned}
3\sqrt{x} + 7 &= 25 \\
(3\sqrt{x} + 7)^2 &= (25)^2 \\
9x + 42\sqrt{x} + 49 &= 625 \\
9x + 42\sqrt{x} - 576 &= 0 \\
3(3x + 14\sqrt{x} - 192) &= 0 \\
3(3\sqrt{x} + 32)(\sqrt{x} - 6) &= 0
\end{aligned}$$

$$3\sqrt{x} + 32 = 0 \quad \text{or} \quad \sqrt{x} - 6 = 0$$

$$\begin{aligned}
3\sqrt{x} &= -32 & \sqrt{x} &= 6 \\
\sqrt{x} &= \frac{-32}{3} & (\sqrt{x})^2 &= (6)^2 \\
(\sqrt{x})^2 &= \left(\frac{-32}{3}\right)^2 & x &= 36 \\
x &= \frac{1024}{9}
\end{aligned}$$

Theresa

$$\begin{aligned}
3\sqrt{x} + 7 &= 25 \\
(3\sqrt{x} + 7)^2 &= (25)^2 \\
9x + 42\sqrt{x} + 49 &= 625 \\
9x + 42\sqrt{x} - 576 &= 0 \\
3(3x + 14\sqrt{x} - 192) &= 0 \\
3(3\sqrt{x} + 32)(\sqrt{x} - 6) &= 0
\end{aligned}$$

$$3\sqrt{x} + 32 = 0 \quad \text{or} \quad \sqrt{x} - 6 = 0$$

$$\begin{aligned}
3\sqrt{x} &= -32 & \sqrt{x} &= 6 \\
\sqrt{x} &= \frac{-32}{3} & (\sqrt{x})^2 &= (6)^2 \\
(\sqrt{x})^2 &= \left(\frac{-32}{3}\right)^2 & x &= 36 \\
x &= \frac{1024}{9}
\end{aligned}$$

Check:

$$\begin{aligned}
3\sqrt{\left(\frac{1024}{9}\right)} + 7 &\stackrel{?}{=} 25 & 3\sqrt{(36)} + 7 &\stackrel{?}{=} 25 \\
3\left(\frac{32}{3}\right) + 7 &\stackrel{?}{=} 25 & 3(6) + 7 &\stackrel{?}{=} 25 \\
39 &\neq 25 & 25 &= 25 \checkmark
\end{aligned}$$

There is one solution, $x = 36$.

Dawnelle

$$\begin{aligned}
3\sqrt{x} + 7 &= 25 \\
(3\sqrt{x} + 7)^2 &= (25)^2 \\
3x + 7 &= 625 \\
3x &= 618 \\
x &= 206
\end{aligned}$$

Marteiz

$$\begin{aligned}
3\sqrt{x} + 7 &= 25 \\
3\sqrt{x} &= 18 \\
\sqrt{x} &= 6 \\
(\sqrt{x})^2 &= (6)^2 \\
x &= 36
\end{aligned}$$

Check:

$$\begin{aligned}
3\sqrt{(36)} + 7 &\stackrel{?}{=} 25 \\
3(6) + 7 &\stackrel{?}{=} 25 \\
25 &= 25 \checkmark
\end{aligned}$$

11

a. Theresa and Marteiz each solved the equation correctly. Explain the difference between their solution methods.

b. Explain the error in Franco's work.

c. Explain the error in Dawnelle's work.

11

3. Solve and check each equation.

a. $\sqrt{2x} = 3$

Increasing the power of the variable may introduce an extraneous solution . . . So, remember to check your answers.

b. $\sqrt[3]{2x - 3} = 2$

c. $4\sqrt{x - 6} = 8$

d. $\sqrt{2x + 1} = 5$

e. $2\sqrt[3]{x} + 16 = 0$

f. $\sqrt{3x - 1} + 9 = 8$

11

g. $x - \sqrt{x} = 2$

h. $x - 1 = \sqrt{x + 1}$

PROBLEM 2 Read, Interpret, and Solve

1. The Beaufort scale is a system that measures wind speed and describes conditions at sea and on land. The scale's range is from 0 to 12. A zero on the Beaufort scale means that the wind speed is less than 1 mile per hour and the conditions at sea and on land are calm. A twelve on the Beaufort scale represents hurricane conditions with wind speeds greater than 74 miles per hour, resulting in greater than 50-foot waves at sea and severe damage to structures and landscape.

   Consider the equation $V = 1.837B^{\frac{3}{2}}$ that models the relationship between wind speed in miles per hour V and the Beaufort numbers B. Determine the Beaufort number for a wind speed of 20 miles per hour.

11

2. In medicine, Body Surface Area BSA is used to help determine proper dosage for medications. The equation $BSA = \frac{\sqrt{W \cdot H}}{60}$ models the relationship between BSA in square meters, the patient's weight W in kilograms, and the patient's height H in centimeters. Determine the height of a patient who weighs 90 kilograms and has a BSA of 2.1.

3. Big Ben is the nickname of a well-known clock tower in London, England, that stands 316 feet tall. The clock is driven by a 660-pound pendulum in the tower that continually swings back and forth. The relationship between the length of pendulum L in feet and the time it takes for a pendulum to swing back and forth one time, or its period T, is modeled by the equation $T = 2\pi\sqrt{\frac{L}{32}}$. If the pendulum's period is 4 seconds, determine the pendulum's length.

11

4. A pilot is flying a plane high above the earth. She has clear vision to the horizon ahead.

   a. Use the diagram to derive an equation to show the relationship between the three sides of the triangle. Then, solve the equation for the plane's altitude, p.

      Note: The variable r represents the Earth's radius (miles), p represents the plane's height above the earth, or altitude (miles), and h represents the distance from the pilot to the horizon (miles).

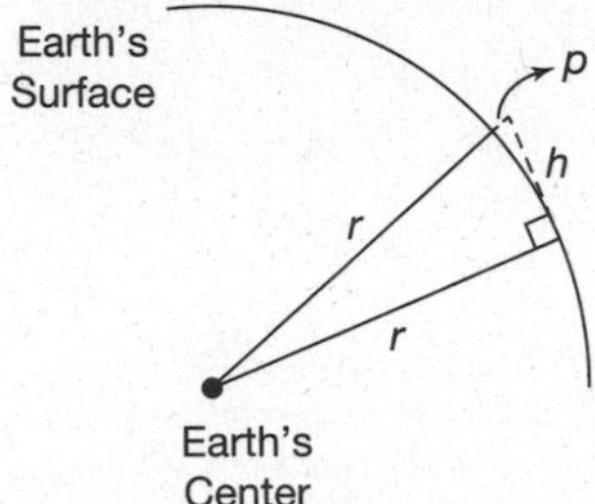

The Earth is not actually a perfect sphere, but it's very close. Our work will give us a very good estimate of the distance from the pilot to the horizon.

11

b. Use your equation from part (a) to calculate the plane's altitude, if the distance from the pilot to the horizon is 225 miles. The earth's radius is 3959 miles.

11

Be prepared to share your solutions and methods.

11

Chapter 11 Summary

KEY TERMS

- inverse of a function (11.1)
- invertible function (11.1)
- Horizontal Line Test (11.1)
- square root function (11.2)
- cube root function (11.2)
- radical function (11.2)
- composition of functions (11.2)

11.1 Graphing Inverses of Power Functions

A function f is the set of all ordered pairs (x, y) or $(x, f(x))$, where for every value of x, there is one and only one value of y, or $f(x)$. The inverse of a function is the set of all ordered pairs (y, x), or $(f(x), x)$. To graph the inverse of a function, simply reflect the function over the line $y = x$.

Example

Graph $f(x) = x^3$, and then graph its inverse.

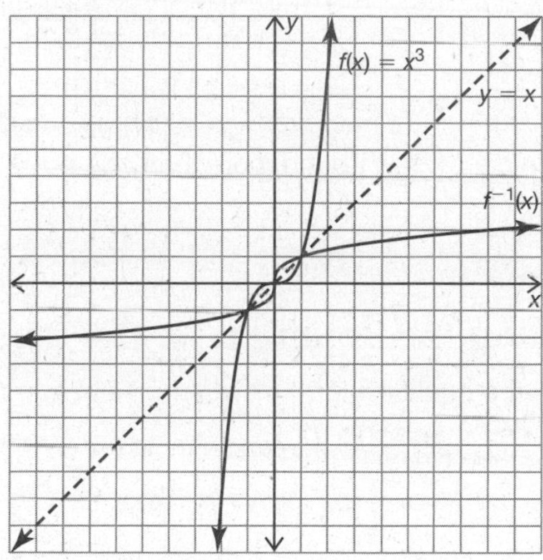

11

11.1 Determining Whether or Not Functions are Invertible

To determine whether or not a function is invertible, graph the function and apply the Horizontal Line Test. If the graph of the function passes the Horizontal Line Test, then it is invertible.

Example

Determine whether or not $f(x) = \frac{x^4}{56}$ is invertible.

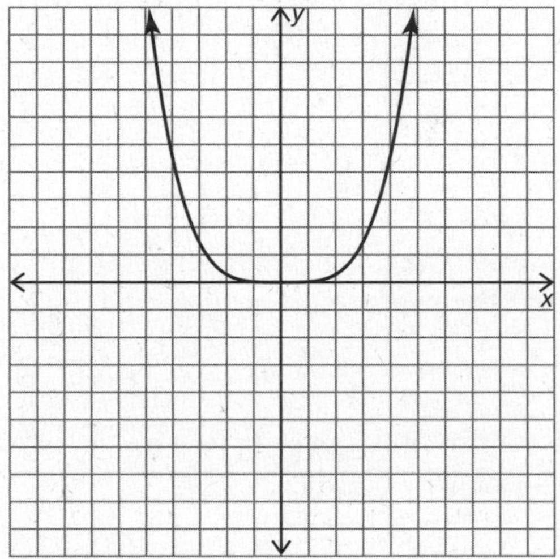

11

The function $f(x) = \frac{x^4}{56}$ is not invertible, because it fails the Horizontal Line Test. That is, a horizontal line can pass through more than one point on the graph at the same time.

11.2 Determining the Equation for the Inverse of a Power Function

To determine the equation for the inverse of a power function, transpose the x and the y in the equation and then solve for y.

Example

Determine the equation for the inverse of the function $y = \frac{2}{3}x^5$.

$$y = \frac{2}{3}x^5$$

$$x = \frac{2}{3}y^5$$

$$\frac{3}{2}x = y^5$$

$$\sqrt[5]{\frac{3}{2}x} = y$$

$$\frac{\sqrt[5]{48x}}{2} = y$$

Therefore, the equation for the inverse of the function $y = \frac{2}{3}x^5$ is $y = \frac{\sqrt[5]{48x}}{2}$.

11.2 Describing the Characteristics of Square Root and Cube Root Functions

The characteristics of square root and cube root functions include the domain, range, and x- and y-intercepts.

Example

Describe the characteristics of the function $f(x) = \sqrt{5 - x}$

Domain: $(-\infty, 5]$

Range: $[0, \infty)$

x-intercept: $(5, 0)$

y-intercept: $(0, \sqrt{5})$

11.3 Describing Transformations of Radical Functions

Transformations performed on a function $f(x)$ to form a new function $g(x)$ can be described by the transformational function:

$$g(x) = Af(B(x - C)) + D$$

Translating a Radical Function Horizontally: If a number, C, is added under the radical, the graph of the function is shifted C units to the left. If a number, C, is subtracted under the radical, the graph of the function is shifted C units to the right.

Translating a Radical Function Vertically: If a number, D, is added outside the radical, the graph of the function is shifted D units up. If a number, D, is subtracted outside the radical, the graph of the function is shifted D units down.

Vertically Stretching and Compressing a Radical Function: Multiplying the function by a number, A, that is greater than one vertically stretches the function. Multiplying the function by a number, A, that is greater than zero but less than one vertically compresses the function.

Reflecting a Radical Function: Multiplying the function by a negative one reflects the graph across the x-axis. Multiplying by a negative one under the radical reflects the graph across the y-axis.

Example

Describe how the graph of the function $f(x) = \sqrt[3]{x}$ would be transformed to produce the graph of the function $g(x) = 2f(x - 4) + 1$.

The graph of $f(x)$ would be vertically stretched by a factor of two, translated 4 units to the right and up 1 unit.

11

11.3 Graphing Transformations of Radical Functions

Transformations that take place inside the radical shift the function left or right. Transformations that take place outside the radical shift the function up or down.

Example

The graph of $f(x) = \sqrt{x}$ is shown. Graph the transformation of $f(x)$ as represented by the equation $g(x) = f(x + 5) + 3$. Then, list the domain for each function.

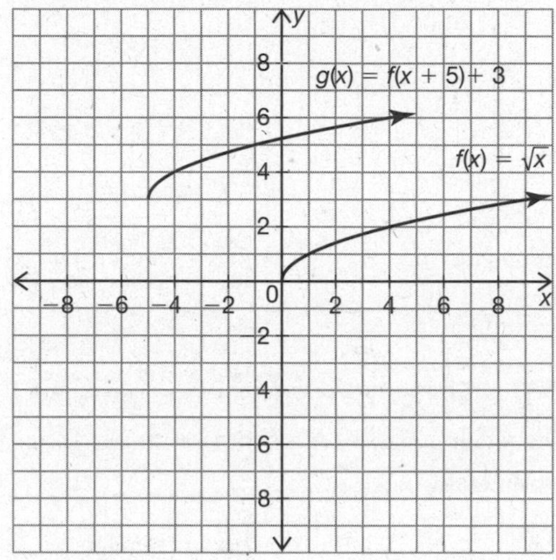

Domain of $f(x)$: $[0, \infty)$

11

Domain of $g(x)$: $[-5, \infty)$

11.4 Rewriting Radical Expressions

To rewrite a radical expression, extract the roots by using the rational exponents and the properties of powers. To extract a variable from a radical, the expression $\sqrt[n]{x^n}$ can we written as $|x|$ when n is even, and x when n is odd.

Example

Rewrite the expression $\sqrt[4]{625x^6y^5z}$.

$$\sqrt[4]{625x^8y^5z} = \sqrt[4]{625 \cdot x^8 \cdot y^4 \cdot y \cdot z}$$

$$= \sqrt[4]{625} \cdot \sqrt[4]{x^8} \cdot \sqrt[4]{y^4} \cdot \sqrt[4]{y} \cdot \sqrt[4]{z}$$

$$= 5x^2|y|\sqrt[4]{yz}$$

11.5 Operating with Radicals

To operate on radicals, follow the order of operations and properties of powers. Remember to extract all roots.

Example

Perform the indicated operations and extract all roots for $x \geq 0$ and $y \geq 0$. Write your final answer in radical form.

$$
\begin{aligned}
(-3x\sqrt{x^5y^6})(2\sqrt{x^3}) - 5\sqrt[4]{81x^{20}y^{12}} &= \left(-3x(x^5y^6)^{\frac{1}{2}}\right)\left(2(x^3)^{\frac{1}{2}}\right) - 5(81x^{20}y^{12})^{\frac{1}{4}} \\
&= (-3 \cdot x \cdot x^{\frac{5}{2}} \cdot y^{\frac{6}{2}})(2 \cdot x^{\frac{3}{2}}) - (5 \cdot 81^{\frac{1}{4}} \cdot x^{\frac{20}{4}} \cdot y^{\frac{12}{4}}) \\
&= (-3 \cdot x^{\frac{7}{2}} \cdot y^3)(2 \cdot x^{\frac{3}{2}}) - (5 \cdot 3 \cdot x^5 \cdot y^3) \\
&= (-3 \cdot x^{\frac{7}{2}} \cdot y^3)(2 \cdot x^{\frac{3}{2}}) - (15 \cdot x^5 \cdot y^3) \\
&= -6 \cdot x^5 \cdot y^3 - 15 \cdot x^5 \cdot y^3 \\
&= -6x^5y^3 - 15x^5y^3 \\
&= -21x^5y^3
\end{aligned}
$$

11.6 Solving Radical Equations

To solve a radical equation, isolate the radical term if possible. Then, raise the entire equation to the power that will eliminate the radical. Finally, follow the steps necessary to solve the equation. Check for extraneous solutions.

Example

$$
\begin{aligned}
\sqrt{x+2} + 10 &= x \\
\sqrt{x+2} &= x - 10 \\
(\sqrt{x+2})^2 &= (x-10)^2 \\
x + 2 &= x^2 - 20x + 100 \\
0 &= x^2 - 21x + 98 \\
0 &= (x-14)(x-7) \\
x &= 14 \text{ or } \cancel{x = 7}
\end{aligned}
$$

Check:

$$
\begin{aligned}
\sqrt{14+2} + 10 &\stackrel{?}{=} 14 \\
\sqrt{16} + 10 &\stackrel{?}{=} 14 \\
14 &= 14 \checkmark
\end{aligned}
$$

Check:

$$
\begin{aligned}
\sqrt{7+2} + 10 &\stackrel{?}{=} 14 \\
\sqrt{9} + 10 &\stackrel{?}{=} 14 \\
13 &\neq 14
\end{aligned}
$$

Extraneous solution

There is one solution, $x = 14$.

11.6 Problem Solving with Radical Equations

To solve a problem with radical equations, identify what the problem is asking. Then, determine how to use the given equation to solve the problem. Finally, follow the process for solving radical equations.

Example

The distance between any two points on a coordinate plane can be calculated by using the equation $d = \sqrt{(x_2 - x_1)^2 + (y_2 - y_1)^2}$, where (x_1, y_1) represents the coordinates of one point and (x_2, y_2) represents the coordinates of the other point. Determine the point(s) on the line $y = 1$ that is (are) exactly 5 units from the point $(1, -2)$. Use the point $(x, 1)$ to represent a point on the line $y = 1$.

$$d = \sqrt{(x_2 - x_1)^2 + (y_2 - y_1)^2}$$

$$5 = \sqrt{(1 - x)^2 + (-2 - 1)^2}$$

$$5 = \sqrt{(1 - 2x + x^2 + 9)}$$

$$25 = 1 - 2x + x^2 + 9$$

$$0 = x^2 - 2x - 15$$

$$0 = (x + 3)(x - 5)$$

$$x = -3 \text{ or } x = 5$$

The points $(-3, 1)$ and $(5, 1)$ are on the line $y = 1$ and are exactly 5 units from the point $(1, -2)$.

Graphing Exponential and Logarithmic Functions

12

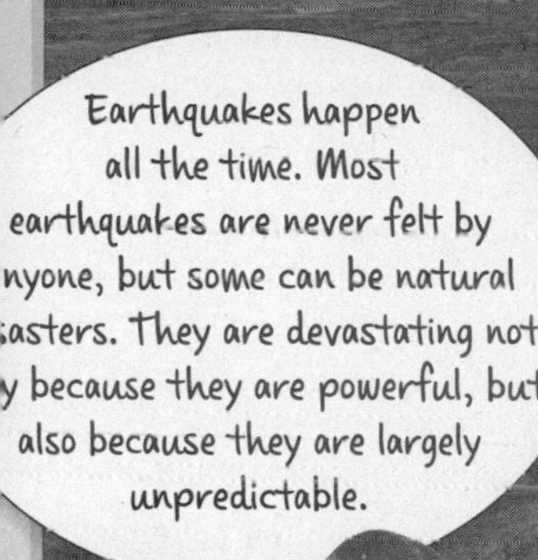
Earthquakes happen
all the time. Most
earthquakes are never felt by
nyone, but some can be natural
asters. They are devastating not
y because they are powerful, but
also because they are largely
unpredictable.

Small Investment, Big Reward

Exponential Functions

12.1

LEARNING GOALS

In this lesson, you will:

- Construct an exponential function from a geometric sequence.
- Classify functions as exponential growth or decay.
- Compare tables, graphs, and equations of exponential functions.

KEY TERM

- half-life

Have you ever seen a funny picture or video online, and then it suddenly seems like everyone is talking about it? Social media and the internet have made it really easy to pass things along from person to person. You can pin, post, and share anything that you find interesting, thought-provoking, or funny with your friends all over the world. Your friends can in turn share it with their own friends, who share it with their friends, and before you know it, it seems like everyone in the world is exposed to it.

When something becomes extremely popular on the internet in a very short amount of time, it's known as "going viral." Trends can spread across the country or around the world in a matter of days. Some "viral" videos and pictures have produced overnight celebrities and inspired spin-offs in the form of books or TV shows.

What is your favorite "viral" video or picture that you've seen online?

PROBLEM 1 Big Things Come to Those Who Wait!

Allison and Beth each receive $10 per week for doing chores for their neighbor. One day, Allison decides to try and increase her income using her knowledge of exponential growth. She proposes that her payment be changed to a penny, and then doubled each week thereafter.

1. Complete the table to represent the amount that Allison and Beth will earn each week.

Hmmm, there seems to be a pattern here . . .

Week	Allison's Income (dollars)	Beth's Income (dollars)
1	0.01	10.00
2		
3		
4		
5		
6		
7		
8		

2. How does Allison's income change as the number of weeks increases?

12

3. Does Allison's income represent an arithmetic or geometric sequence or series? Explain your reasoning and state the general formula.

4. Write an equation to represent Allison's income after n weeks.

5. What is the value of g_n for $n = 0$? Does this value make sense in this problem situation?

6. If the pattern were to continue, how many weeks would it take for Allison to have a larger weekly income than Beth? Complete the table to show your answer.

Week	Allison's Income (dollars)	Beth's Income (dollars)

You can write the explicit formula for the geometric sequence $g_n = 0.01 \cdot 2^{(n-1)}$ in function notation using the properties of powers.

Statement	**Reason**
$g_n = 0.01 \cdot 2^{(n-1)}$	Explicit formula for a geometric sequence
$f(n) = 0.01 \cdot 2^{(n-1)}$	Rewrite in function notation
$f(n) = 0.01 \cdot 2^n \cdot 2^{-1}$	Product Rule
$f(n) = 0.01 \cdot 2^n \cdot \frac{1}{2}$	Definition of negative exponents
$f(n) = 0.01 \cdot \frac{1}{2} \cdot 2^n$	Commutative Property of Multiplication
$f(n) = 0.005 \cdot 2^n$	Associative Property of Multiplication

So, $g_n = 0.01 \cdot 2^{(n-1)}$ written in function notation is $f(n) = 0.005 \cdot 2^n$.

Recall that a geometric sequence, when written in function notation, is called an exponential function. The function gets its name from the variable in the exponent.

12

7. Calculate the income that Allison would earn per week in the:

   a. 15th week.

   b. 20th week.

   c. 24th week.

8. Predict the shape and characteristics of the graph that will model Allison's income as a function of the number of weeks.

12

PROBLEM 2 The Tortoise and the Hare

1. Beth is amazed at how quickly Allison was able to make a lot of money and decides that she wants in on the action. She asks her two friends, Quinton and Alisha, to help her come up with a plan.

Quinton

You could start with a dollar and ask for 50% more each week.

Alisha

You could start with a dollar and add another dollar each week.

Whose plan should Beth choose? Complete the table and graph to justify your reasoning. Round to the nearest hundredth.

Week	Quinton's Plan (dollars)	Alisha's Plan (dollars)
0		
1		
2		
3		
4		
5		
6		
7		

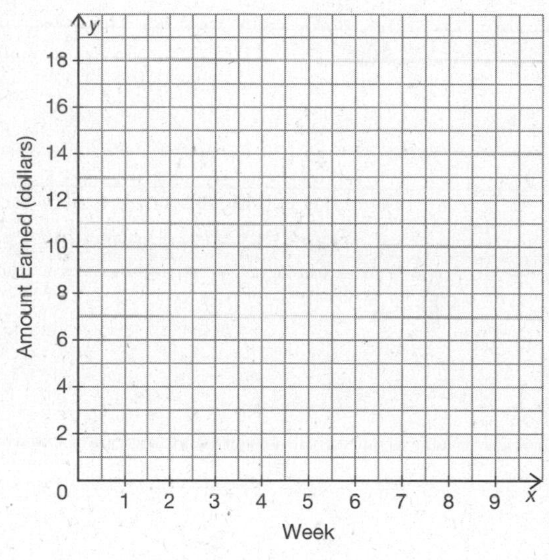

12

2. Write functions to represent Quinton's plan, $q(x)$, and Alisha's plan, $a(x)$.

3. Use your choice from Question 1 to determine how much Beth will earn in Week 10.

4. If Beth and Allison both start using their exponential model to earn income at the same time, who will earn a higher income in Week 12?

5. Use a graphing calculator to determine when Allison's and Beth's incomes will be equal. Does this make sense in this problem situation? Explain your reasoning.

12

6. Compare Allison's and Beth's function models.

   a. As the number of weeks continues to increase, whose model will earn them more per week?

The general form of an exponential equation is $a \cdot b^x$.

   b. Consider the a- and b-values of the exponential functions if $y = ab^x$. How do they further support your claim?

PROBLEM 3 Half-Life of Caffeine

Simeon is studying for a big test and is trying to stay awake. He drank a 12-ounce can of Big Buzz Energy Drink that contains 80 milligrams of caffeine. He is wondering how long the caffeine will stay in his system if the caffeine has a *half-life* of 5 hours.

A **half-life** is the amount of time it takes a substance to decay to half of its original amount.

1. How much caffeine remains in Simeon's system after 5 hours? After 10 hours? Explain your reasoning.

12

2. Complete the table to determine the amount of caffeine in Simeon's system at each time interval.

Time Elapsed (hours)	0	5	10	15	20
Caffeine in System (mg)					
Number of Half-Life Cycles					

3. What is the initial amount of caffeine in Simeon's system? What is the rate of decay?

4. Emily, Tyler, and Renee were asked to write an exponential function $A(t)$ to represent the amount of caffeine remaining in Simeon's system after t hours.

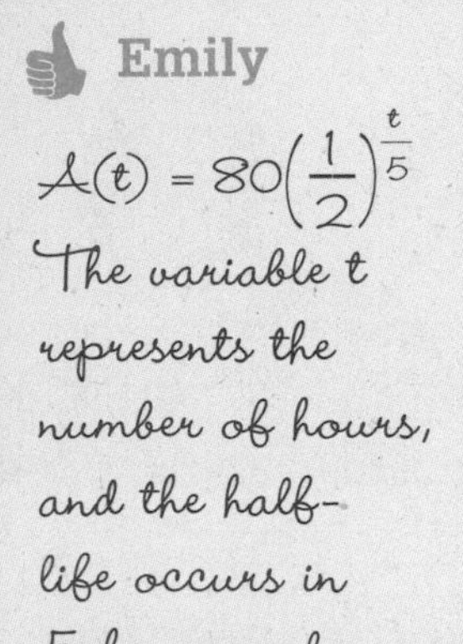

Emily
A(t) = 80(1/2)^(t/5)
The variable t represents the number of hours, and the half-life occurs in 5 hour cycles, so I divided my exponent by 5.

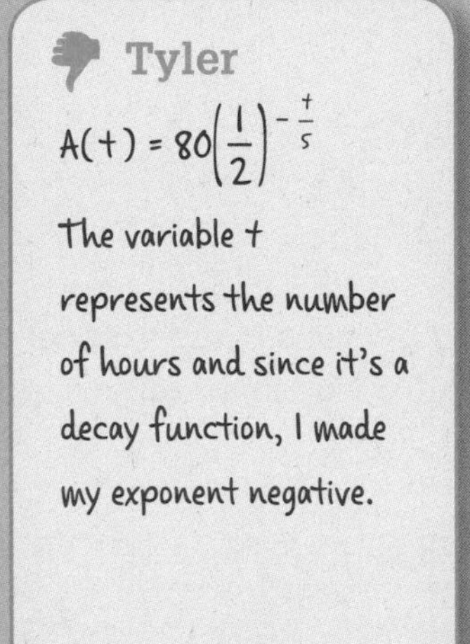

Tyler
A(t) = 80(1/2)^(-t/5)
The variable t represents the number of hours and since it's a decay function, I made my exponent negative.

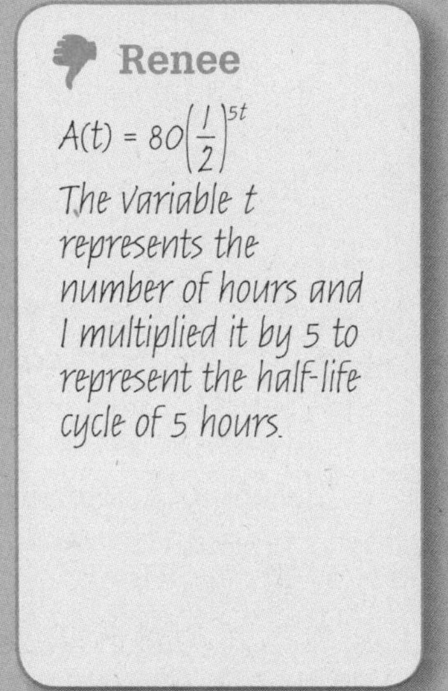

Renee
A(t) = 80(1/2)^(5t)
The variable t represents the number of hours and I multiplied it by 5 to represent the half-life cycle of 5 hours.

a. Why is Tyler's reasoning incorrect?

It may be helpful to substitute the values from the table to check each student's function.

b. Why is Renee's reasoning incorrect?

5. How much caffeine remains in Simeon's system after 2 hours?

6. Kendra suggests that she can calculate the amount of caffeine remaining by rewriting the equation as $A(t) = 40^{\frac{t}{5}}$. Is Kendra correct? Explain your reasoning.

7. Use the table function of a graphing calculator to predict when the caffeine will be completely out of Simeon's system. Does this make sense, given what you know about exponential functions? Explain your reasoning.

8. Approximately when will the amount of caffeine remaining in Simeon's system be less than 1 milligram?

12

9. Use the properties of exponents to rewrite your function so that only the variable t is in the exponent. What percentage of caffeine remains after each hour?

10. Suppose Simeon is taking an antibiotic that extends the half-life of caffeine to 8 hours. Write a function $B(t)$ that models the amount of caffeine remaining under these new conditions.

11. Complete the table for the new half-life. Round to the nearest hundredth.

Time Elapsed (hours)	0	5	10	15	20
Caffeine in System (mg)					
Number of Half-Life Cycles					

12. How does the medication affect the amount of caffeine remaining in Simeon's system?

13. Under these new conditions, approximately when will the amount of caffeine remaining in Simeon's system be less than 1 milligram?

12

14. What generalization can you make about the effect of larger or smaller half-lifes on substances?

Be prepared to share your solutions and methods.

We Have Liftoff!

12.2

Properties of Exponential Graphs

LEARNING GOALS

In this lesson, you will:

- Identify the domain and range of exponential functions.
- Investigate graphs of exponential functions through intercepts, asymptotes, intervals of increase and decrease, and end behavior.
- Explore the irrational number *e*.

KEY TERM

- natural base *e*

Have you ever tried to remember a long list of things and ended up getting mixed up along the way?

There are lots of tried-and-true ways of memorizing things, and it all depends on what you're trying to memorize. Some people like to make mnemonic devices, where the first letter in each word corresponds to something in the list they're trying to memorize. You may have used one of these when you were learning the order of operations—Please Excuse My Dear Aunt Sally is a great way to help you remember parentheses, exponents, multiplication, division, addition, and subtraction. Some people try doing some sort of movement as they recite their list, so that they can use their muscle memory to help them. Some people like to use rhymes, some people use visualization, and some people rely on good old-fashioned repetition.

But there are some people who are just naturally skilled at remembering things. In fact, there are competitions held around the world to see who can memorize the most digits of pi. In 2005, Chao Lu of China set a world record by memorizing an incredible 67,890 digits of pi! It took him 24 hours and 4 minutes to accurately recite the digits, with no more than 15 seconds between each digit.

Do you have any memory tricks to help you remember things?

12

PROBLEM 1 I've Got the Power

1. Cut out the exponential graphs and equations and match them. Sort them into "growth" or "decay" functions and tape them onto the graphic organizer in this lesson. Finally, complete each table.

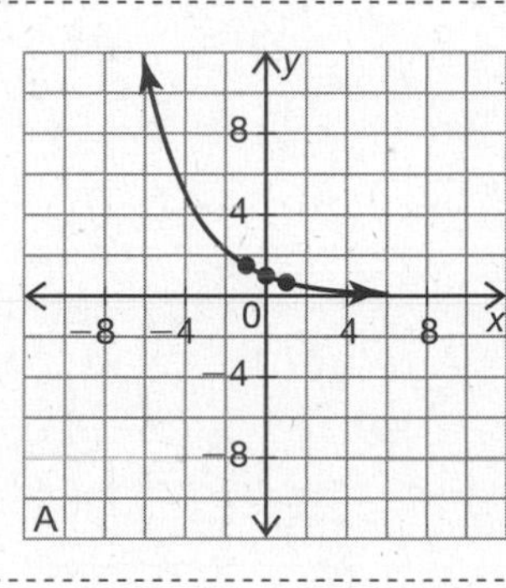	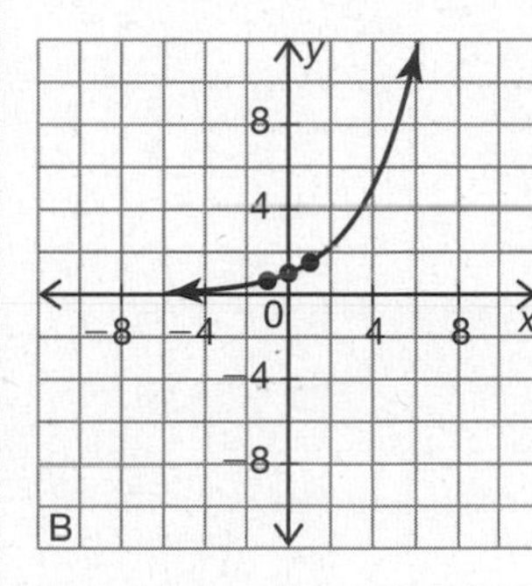	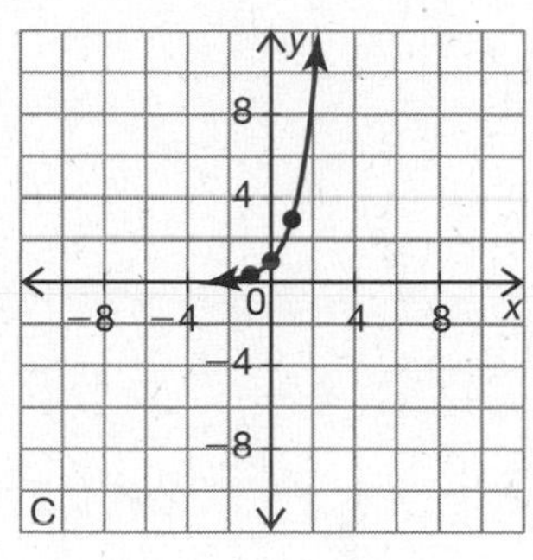
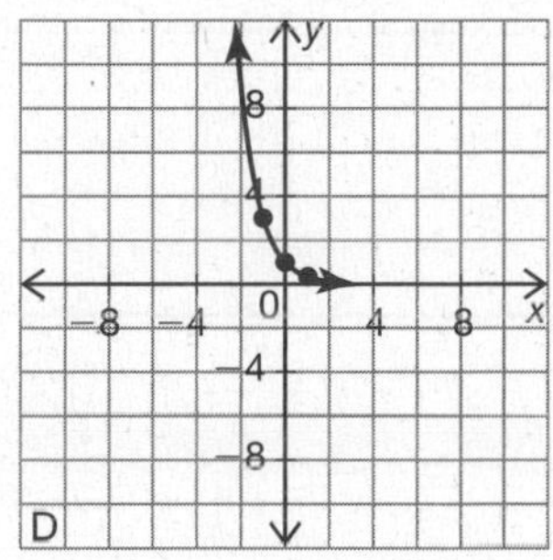	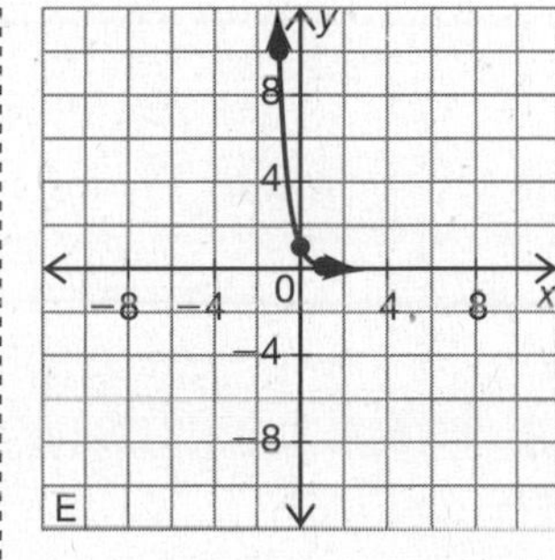	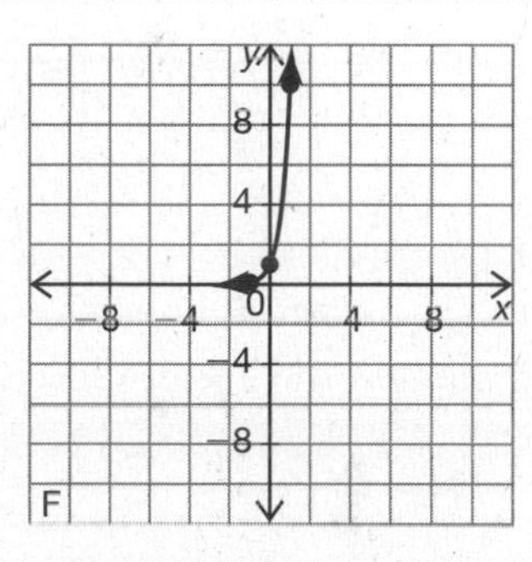
$f(x) = \left(\frac{2}{3}\right)^x$	$f(x) = 10^x$	$f(x) = 1.5^x$
$f(x) = 0.1^x$	$f(x) = 3^x$	$f(x) = \left(\frac{1}{3}\right)^x$

Think about how the base affects the graph of an exponential function!

12

12

Growth

x	f(x)
−1	
0	
1	

Decay

x	f(x)
−1	
0	
1	

Growth

x	f(x)
−1	
0	
1	

Decay

x	f(x)
−1	
0	
1	

Growth

x	f(x)
−1	
0	
1	

Decay

x	f(x)
−1	
0	
1	

2. Analyze the exponential growth and decay functions.

   a. What point do the graphs have in common? Why?

   b. Compare the equations of the six functions you just sorted. What differentiates an exponential growth from an exponential decay?

3. Sarah and Scott's teacher asked them to each write a rule that would determine whether a function was exponential growth or decay, based on its equation.

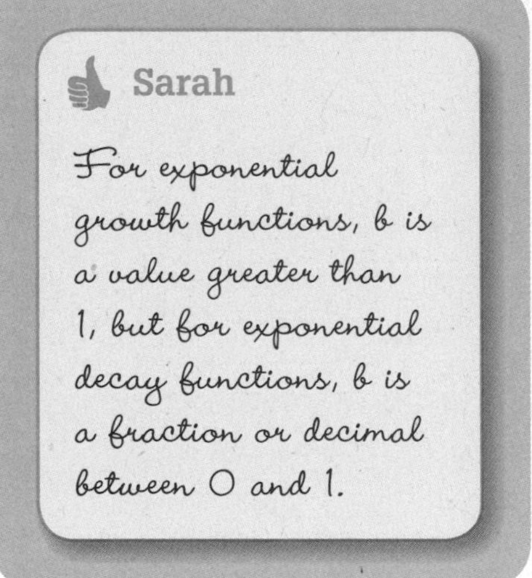

Sarah
For exponential growth functions, b is a value greater than 1, but for exponential decay functions, b is a fraction or decimal between 0 and 1.

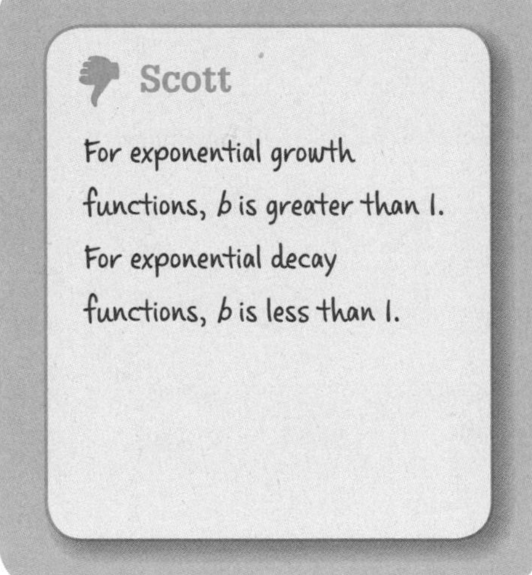

Scott
For exponential growth functions, b is greater than 1. For exponential decay functions, b is less than 1.

Why is Scott's reasoning incorrect? Provide a counterexample that would disprove his claim and explain your reasoning.

12

4. What b-values in exponential functions produce neither growth nor decay? Provide examples to support your answer.

5. Write an exponential function with the given characteristics.

   a. Increasing over $(-\infty, \infty)$
   Reference point (1, 6)

   b. Decreasing over $(-\infty, \infty)$
   Reference point (−1, 4)

   c. End behavior As $x \to -\infty$, $f(x) \to 0$
   As $x \to \infty$, $f(x) \to \infty$
   Reference point (2, 6.25)

6. Summarize the characteristics for the basic exponential growth and exponential decay functions.

	Basic Exponential Growth	Basic Exponential Decay
Domain		
Range		
Asymptote		
Intercepts		
End Behavior		
Intervals of Increase or Decrease		

12

PROBLEM 2 Let's Compound Some Dough

Helen is opening her first savings account and is depositing \$500. Suppose she decides on a bank that offers 6% annual interest to be calculated at the end of each year.

1. Write a function $A(t)$ to model the amount of money in Helen's savings account after t years.

2. Calculate the amount of money in Helen's savings account at the end of 1 year?

3. How much money will be in Helen's savings account at the end of 5 years?

12

4. Suppose that the bank decides to start compounding interest at the end of every 6 months. If they still want to offer 6% per year, how much interest would they offer per 6-month period?

5. John, Betty Jo, and Lizzie were each asked to calculate the amount of money Helen would have in her savings at the end of the year if interest was compounded twice a year. Who's correct? Explain your reasoning.

John	Betty Jo	Lizzie
1st 6 months: $A(t) = 500(1 + 0.03)$ $A(t) = 515$ 2nd 6 months: $A(t) = 515(1 + 0.03)$ $A(t) = 530.45$	$A(t) = 500\left(1 + \frac{0.06}{2}\right)^2$ $A(t) = 530.45$	$A(t) = 2(500(1 + 0.03))$ $A(t) = 1030$

12

6. Write a function to model the amount of money in Helen's savings account at the end of t years, compounded n times during the year.

7. Determine the amount of money in Helen's account at the end of 3 years if it is compounded:

   a. twice a year.

   b. monthly.

   c. daily.

12

8. What effect does the frequency of compounding have on the amount of money in her savings account?

PROBLEM 3 Easy "e"

Recall that in Problem 2 the variable n represented the number of compound periods per year. Let's examine what happens as the interest becomes compounded more frequently.

Even though we are working with money, in order to see the pattern, it will be helpful to compute the compound interest to at least six decimal places.

1. Imagine that Helen finds a different bank that offers her 100% interest. Complete the table to calculate how much Helen would accrue in 1 year for each period of compounding if she starts with $1.

Period of Compounding	$n =$	Formula	Amount
Yearly	1	$1\left(1+\frac{1}{1}\right)^{1\cdot 1}$	2.00
Semi-Annually	2	$1\left(1+\frac{1}{2}\right)^{2\cdot 1}$	2.25
Quarterly	4	$1\left(1+\frac{1}{4}\right)^{4\cdot 1}$	
Monthly	12		
Weekly			
Daily			
Hourly			
Every Minute			
Every Second			

2. Make an observation about the frequency of compounding and the amount that Helen earns. What is it approaching?

12

The amount that Helen's earnings approach is actually an irrational number called e.

$$e \approx 2.718281828459045\ldots$$

It is often referred to as the **natural base *e***.

In geometry, you worked with π , an irrational number that was approximated as 3.14159265 . . . and so on. Pi is an incredibly important part of many geometric formulas and occurs so frequently that, rather than write out "3.14159265 . . . " each time, we use the symbol π.

The number e goes on forever with no repetition. There are even competitions to see who can memorize the most digits of e. In 2007, Bhaskar Karmakar from India set a World Record for memorizing 5002 digits!

Similarly, the symbol e is used to represent the constant 2.718281 . . . It is often used in models of population changes as well as radioactive decay of substances, and it is vital in physics and calculus.

The symbol for the natural base e was first used by Swiss mathematician Leonhard Euler in 1727 as part of a research manuscript he wrote at age 21. In fact, he used it so much, e became known as Euler's number.

The constant e represents continuous growth and has many other mathematical properties that make it unique, which you will study further in calculus.

3. The following graphs are sketched on the coordinate plane shown.
   $f(x) = 2^x$, $g(x) = 3^x$, $h(x) = 10^x$, $j(x) = \left(\frac{3}{5}\right)^x$, $k(x) = 1.3^x$.

   a. Label each function.

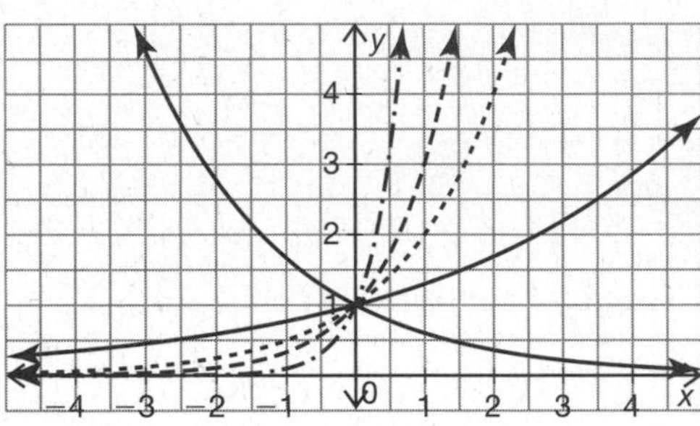

   b. Consider the function $m(x) = e^x$. Use your knowledge of the approximate value of e to sketch its graph. Explain your reasoning.

c. Using the functions $f(x) = 2^x$, $g(x) = 3^x$, $m(x) = e^x$, approximate the values of $f(2)$, $g(2)$, and $m(2)$ on the number line. Explain your reasoning.

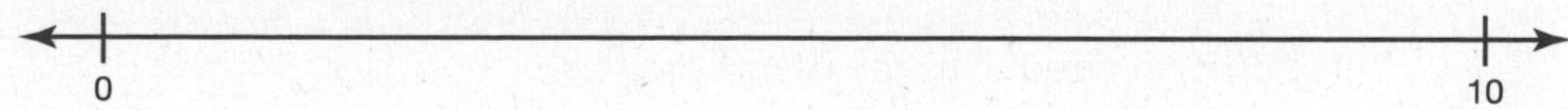

PROBLEM  4 It Keeps Growing and Growing and Growing...

1. The formula for population growth is $N(t) = N_0e^{rt}$. Complete the table to identify the contextual meaning of each quantity.

Quantity	Contextual Meaning
N_0	
r	
t	
$N(t)$	

2. Why is e used as the base?

3. How could this formula be used to represent a decline in population?

4. The population of the city of Fredericksburg, Virginia, was approximately 19,360 in 2000 and has been continuously growing at a rate of 2.9% each year.

   a. Use the formula for population growth to write a function to model this growth.

   b. Use your function model to predict the population of Fredericksburg in 2013.

   c. What value does your function model give for the population of Fredericksburg in the year 1980?

12

5. Use a graphing calculator to estimate the number of years it would take Fredericksburg to grow to 40,000 people, assuming that the population trend continues.

Be prepared to share your solutions and methods.

12.3

I Like to Move It

Transformations of Exponential Functions

LEARNING GOALS

In this lesson, you will:

- Dilate, reflect, and translate exponential functions using reference points and transformational function form.
- Investigate graphs of exponential functions through intercepts, asymptotes, intervals of increase and decrease, and end behavior.
- Describe how transformations of exponential functions affect their key characteristics.

Andy Warhol was an American pop artist whose work explored the relationship between artistic expression, celebrity culture, and advertisement. A recurring theme throughout Warhol's art is the transformation of the mundane and commonplace into art. His most renowned images are silk-screened reproductions of Campbell's soup cans and publicity photographs of pop culture icons like Marilyn Monroe and Elvis Presley.

Have you ever seen any of Andy Warhol's work?

PROBLEM 1 It's the Same . . . But Different!

1. The two tables show four exponential functions and four exponential graphs.
   a. Match the exponential function to its corresponding graph, and write the function under the graph it represents.
   b. Explain the method(s) you used to match the functions with their graphs.

Exponential Functions	
$f(x) = 10^x$	$g(x) = 10^{-x}$
$h(x) = -10^x$	$j(x) = -10^{-x}$

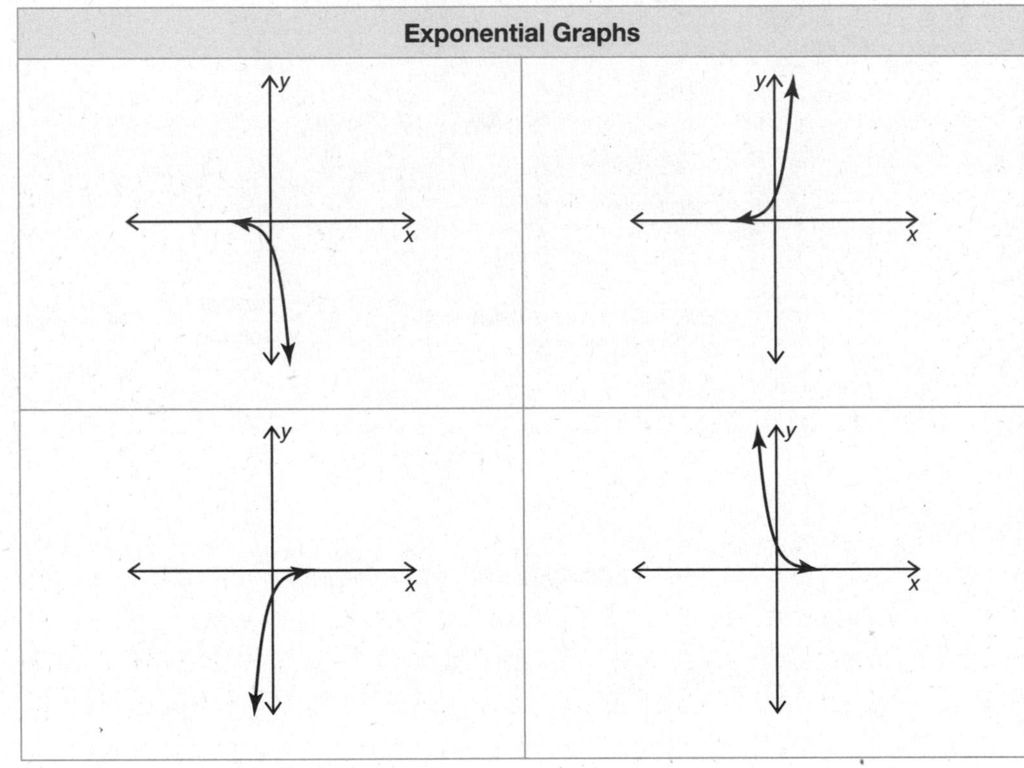

2. Analyze the graphs.

   a. Write an equation for $h(x)$ in terms of $f(x)$. Describe the transformation on $f(x)$.

   b. Write an equation for $g(x)$ in terms of $f(x)$. Describe the transformation on $f(x)$.

   c. Write an equation for $j(x)$ in terms of $f(x)$. Describe the transformation on $f(x)$.

3. Determine the asymptotes, intervals of increase and decrease, and end behavior for each exponential function.

Function	Asymptotes	Intervals of Increase and Decrease	End Behavior
$f(x) = 10^x$			
$g(x) = 10^{-x}$			
$h(x) = -10^x$			
$j(x) = -10^{-x}$			

4. How would the graph of $k(x) = \left(\frac{1}{10}\right)^x$ compare to the graph of $g(x) = 10^{-x}$?

12

5. How do the transformations on $f(x)$ affect the asymptotes, intervals of increase and decrease, and end behavior?

PROBLEM 2 Keep On Moving

Consider the functions $y = f(x)$ and $g(x) = Af(B(x - C)) + D$. Recall that the D-value translates $f(x)$ vertically, the C-value translates $f(x)$ horizontally, the A-value vertically stretches or compresses $f(x)$, and the B-value horizontally stretches or compresses $f(x)$. Exponential functions are transformed in the same manner.

The function $f(x) = 3^x$ is shown. Recall the key characteristics of basic exponential functions, including a domain of all real numbers, a range of positive numbers, and a horizontal asymptote at $y = 0$.

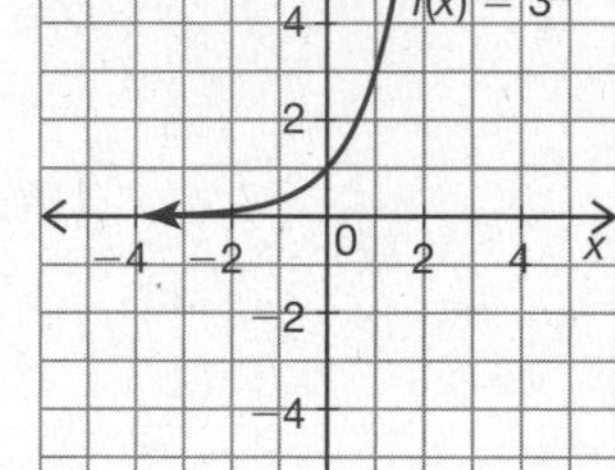

1. Suppose that $a(x) = f(x + 1)$.

   a. Describe the transformation on the graph of $f(x)$ that produces $a(x)$.

12

   b. Complete the table to determine the corresponding points on $a(x)$, given reference points on $f(x)$. Then, graph and label $a(x)$.

Reference Points on $f(x)$	Corresponding Points on $a(x)$
$\left(-1, \frac{1}{3}\right)$	
(0, 1)	
(1, 3)	

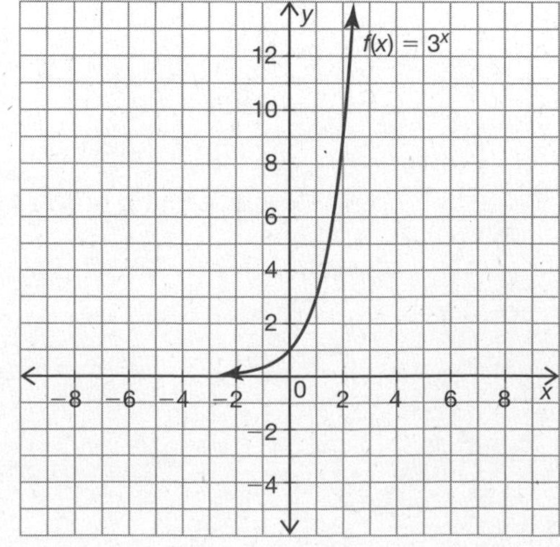

c. Determine the domain, range, and asymptotes of $a(x)$.

2. Suppose that $b(x) = f(x) + 1$.

a. Describe the transformation on the graph of $f(x)$ that produces $b(x)$.

b. Complete the table to determine the corresponding points on $b(x)$, given reference points on $f(x)$. Then, graph and label $b(x)$.

Reference Points on $f(x)$	Corresponding Points on $b(x)$
$\left(-1, \frac{1}{3}\right)$	
(0, 1)	
(1, 3)	

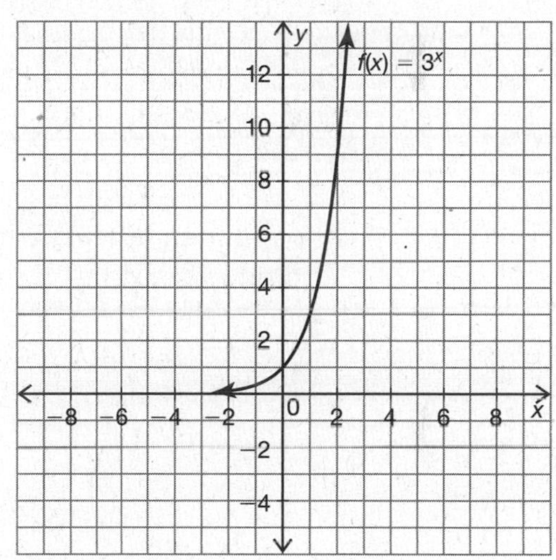

c. Determine the domain, range, and asymptotes of $b(x)$.

3. Suppose that $c(x) = f(x) - 5$.

a. Describe the transformation on the graph of $f(x)$ that produces $c(x)$.

b. Complete the table to determine the corresponding points on $c(x)$, given reference points on $f(x)$. Then, graph and label $c(x)$.

Reference Points on $f(x)$	Corresponding Points on $c(x)$
$\left(-1, \frac{1}{3}\right)$	
(0, 1)	
(1, 3)	

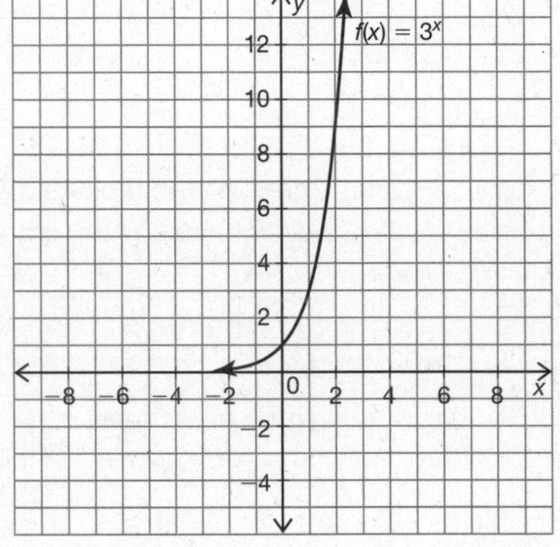

c. Determine the domain, range, and asymptotes of $c(x)$.

12

4. Suppose that $d(x) = f(2x)$.

a. Describe the transformation on the graph of $f(x)$ that produces $c(x)$.

b. Complete the table to determine the corresponding points on $d(x)$, given reference points on $f(x)$. Then, graph and label $d(x)$.

Reference Points on $f(x)$	Corresponding Points on $d(x)$
$\left(-1, \frac{1}{3}\right)$	
(0, 1)	
(1, 3)	

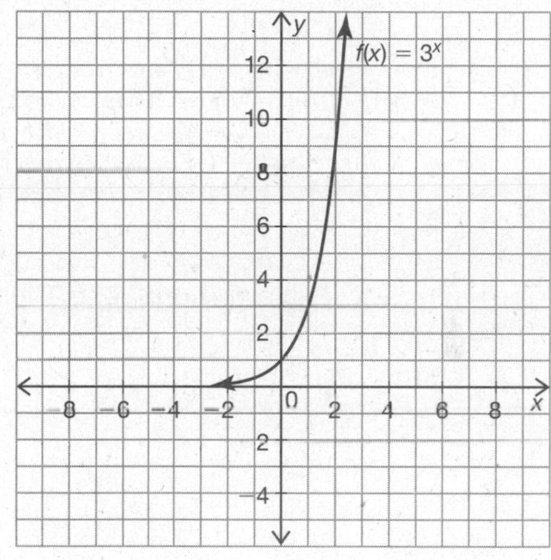

c. Determine the domain, range, and asymptotes of $d(x)$.

12

5. Analyze the transformations performed on $f(x)$ in Questions 1 through 4.

a. Which, if any, of these transformations affected the domain, range, and asymptotes?

b. What generalizations can you make about the effects of transformations on the domain, range, and asymptotes of exponential functions?

6. Andres and Tomas each described the effects of transforming the graph of $f(x) = 3^x$, such that $p(x) = 3f(x)$.

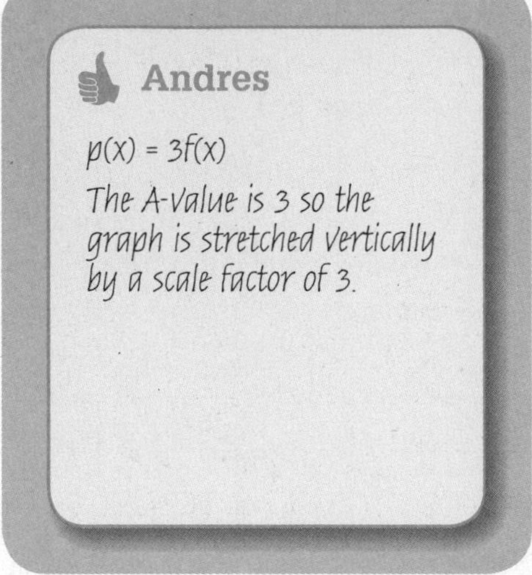

Andres
p(x) = 3f(x)
The A-value is 3 so the graph is stretched vertically by a scale factor of 3.

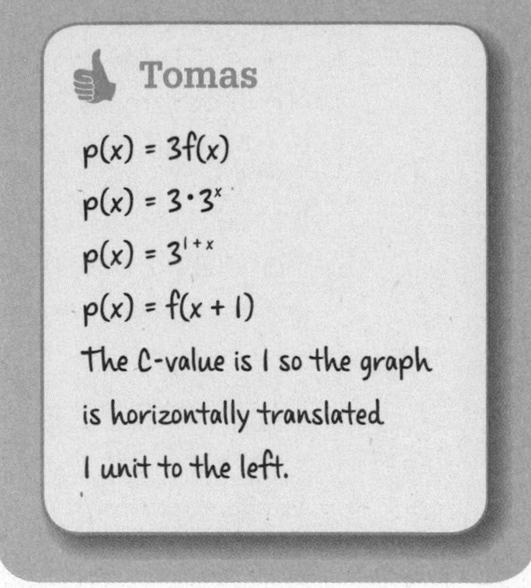

Tomas
p(x) = 3f(x)
p(x) = 3·3^x
p(x) = 3^(1+x)
p(x) = f(x + 1)
The C-value is 1 so the graph is horizontally translated 1 unit to the left.

a. Explain Andres' and Thomas' reasoning.

12

b. Determine the domain, range, and asymptotes of $p(x)$.

c. What generalizations can you make about the effects of vertical dilations on the domain, range, and asymptotes of exponential functions?

PROBLEM 3 Multiple Transformations

1. Analyze the graphs of $f(x)$ and $g(x)$. Describe the transformations performed on $f(x)$ to create $g(x)$. Then, write an equation for $g(x)$ in terms of $f(x)$. For each set of points shown on $f(x)$, the corresponding points are shown on $g(x)$.

a. $g(x) =$ ____________________

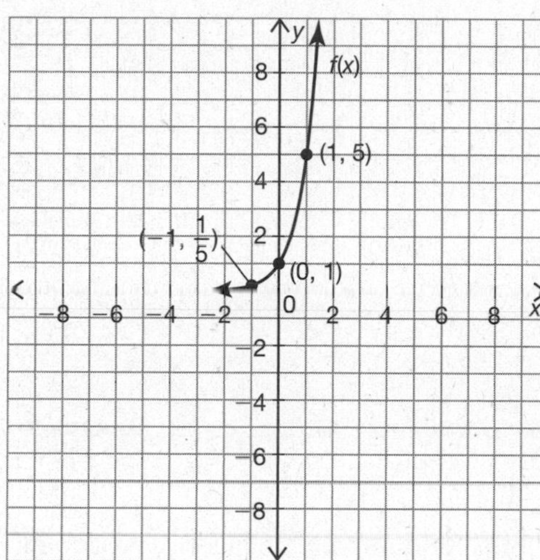

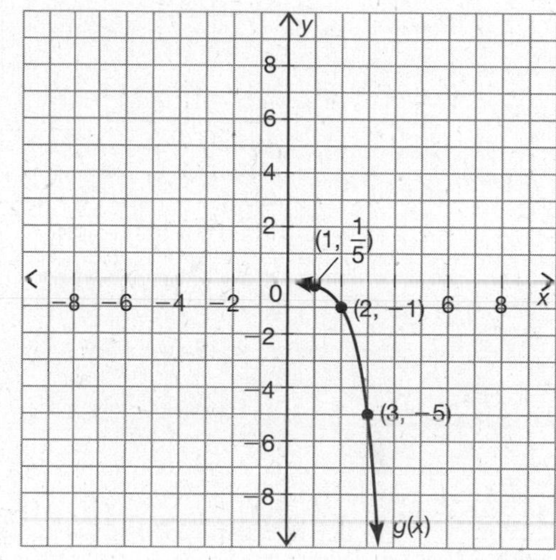

b. $g(x) =$ ____________________

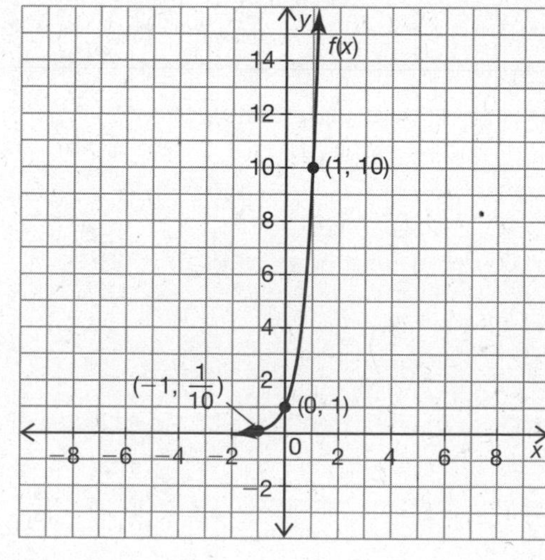

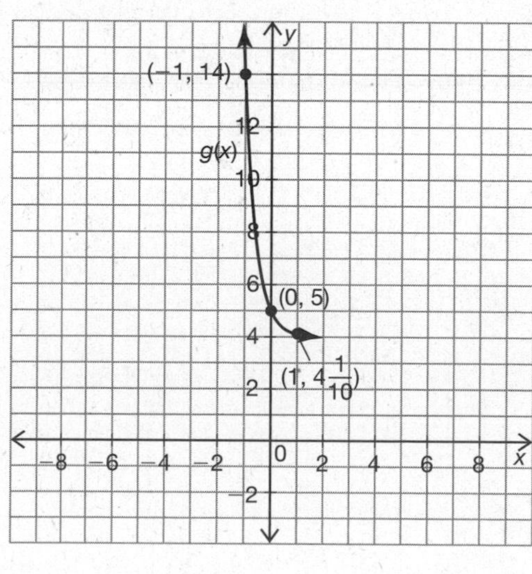

12

c. $g(x) =$ ____________________

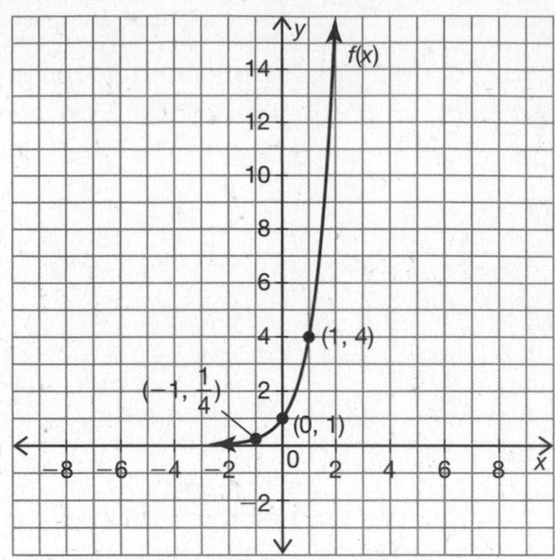

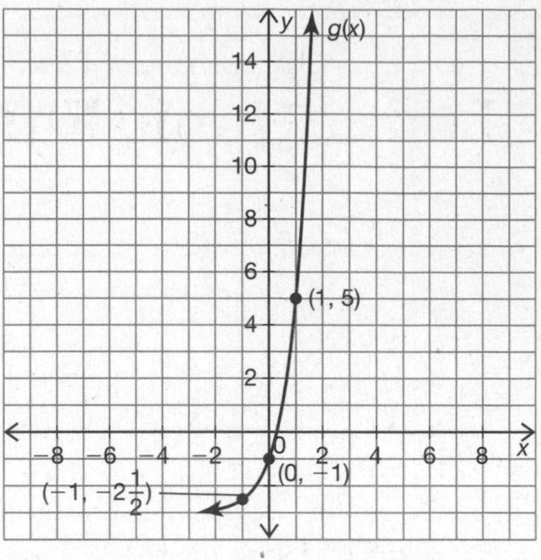

2. The equation for an exponential function $m(x)$ is given. The equation for the transformed function $t(x)$ in terms of $m(x)$ is also given. Describe the graphical transformation(s) on $m(x)$ that produce(s) $t(x)$. Then, write an exponential equation for $t(x)$.

a. $m(x) = 2^x$
$t(x) = 0.5m(x + 3)$

12

b. $m(x) = e^x$
$t(x) = -m(x) - 1$

c. $m(x) = 6^x$
$t(x) = 2m(-x)$

Be prepared to share your solutions and methods.

I Feel the Earth Move

12.4

Logarithmic Functions

LEARNING GOALS

In this lesson, you will:

- Graph the inverses of exponential functions with bases of 2, 10, and *e*.
- Recognize the inverse of an exponential function as a logarithm.
- Identify the domain and range of logarithmic functions.
- Investigate graphs of logarithmic functions through intercepts, asymptotes, intervals of increase and decrease, and end behavior.

KEY TERMS

- logarithm
- logarithmic function
- common logarithm
- natural logarithm

You may have heard about the Richter scale rating. The Richter scale was developed in 1935 by Charles F. Richter of the California Institute of Technology. The Richter scale is used to rate the magnitude of an earthquake—the amount of energy it releases. This is calculated using information gathered by a seismograph.

The Richter scale is logarithmic, meaning that whole-number jumps in the rating indicate a tenfold increase in the wave amplitude of the earthquake. For example, the wave amplitude in a Level 4 earthquake is ten times greater than the amplitude of a Level 5 earthquake, and the amplitude increases 100 times between a Level 6 earthquake and a Level 8 earthquake.

Most earthquakes are extremely small, with a majority registering less than 3 on the Richter scale. These tremors, called microquakes, aren't even felt by humans. Only a tiny portion, 15 or so of the 1.4 million quakes that register above 2 each year, register at 7 or above, which is the threshold for a quake to be considered major.

PROBLEM 1 Return of the Inverse

Consider the table and graph for the basic exponential function $f(x) = 2^x$.

x	$f(x) = 2^x$
-3	$\frac{1}{8}$
-2	$\frac{1}{4}$
-1	$\frac{1}{2}$
0	1
1	2
2	4
3	8

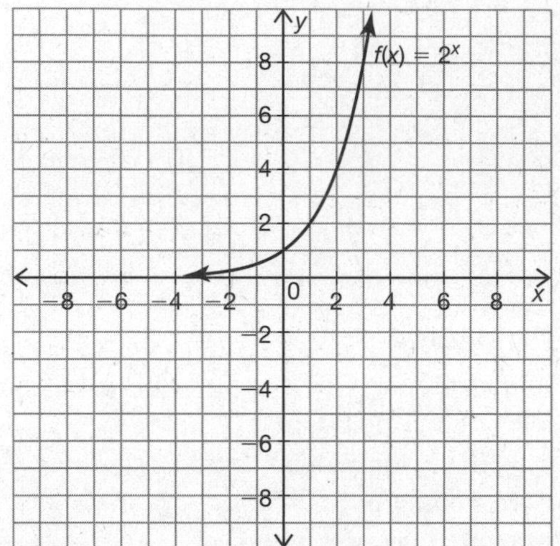

You learned that the key characteristics of basic exponential functions are:

- The domain is the set of all real numbers.
- The range is the set of all positive numbers.
- The y-intercept is (0, 1).
- There is no x-intercept.
- There is a horizontal asymptote at $y = 0$.
- The function increases over the entire domain.
- As x approaches negative infinity, $f(x)$ approaches 0.
- As x approaches positive infinity, $f(x)$ approaches positive infinity.

12

Recall that for any function f with ordered pairs (x, y), or $(x, f(x))$, the inverse of the function f is the set of all ordered pairs (y, x), or $(f(x), x)$.

1. Graph the inverse of $f(x) = 2^x$ on the same coordinate plane as $f(x)$. Complete the table of values for the inverse of $f(x)$.

x	*y*

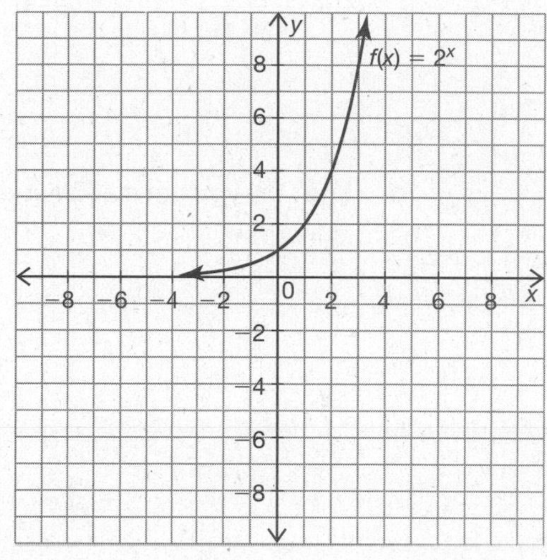

2. Analyze the key characteristics of the inverse of $f(x) = 2^x$.

   a. Is the inverse of $f(x) = 2^x$ a function? Explain your reasoning.

   b. Identify the domain, range, intercepts, asymptotes, intervals of increase and decrease, and end behavior of $f^{-1}(x)$.

We reserve using function notation, such as f⁻¹(x), for inverse relations that are also functions.

12

c. What do you notice about the domain and range of the exponential function and its inverse?

d. What do you notice about the asymptotes of the exponential function and its inverse?

e. What do you notice about the intervals of increase and decrease of the exponential function and its inverse?

f. What do you notice about the end behavior of the exponential function and its inverse?

12

g. Write the equation for the inverse of $y = 2^x$. Explain your reasoning.

It is necessary to define a new function in order to write the equation for the inverse of an exponential function. The **logarithm** of a number for a given base is the exponent to which the base must be raised in order to produce the number. If $y = b^x$, then x is the logarithm and can be written as $x = \log_b(y)$. The value of the base of a logarithm is the same as the base in the exponential expression b^x.

For example, the number 3 is the logarithm to which base 2 must be raised to produce the argument 8. The base is written as the subscript 2. The logarithm, or exponent, is the output 3. The argument of the logarithm is 8.

$$3 = \log_2(8)$$

(logarithm, or exponent → 3; argument → 8; base → 2)

You can write any exponential equation as a logarithmic equation and vice versa.

Example	Exponential Form	⇔	Logarithmic Form
A	$y = b^x$	⇔	$x = \log_b(y)$
B	$16 = 4^2$	⇔	$2 = \log_4(16)$
C	$1000 = 10^3$	⇔	$3 = \log_{10}(1000)$
D	$32 = 16^{1.25}$	⇔	$1.25 = \log_{16}(32)$
E	$a = b^c$	⇔	$c = \log_b(a)$

3. Rewrite your equation in Question 2, part (g), in logarithmic form. Label the graph from Question 1 with your equation.

In words, the exponential form of Example B is, "The number 2 is the *exponent* to which the base 4 must be raised to produce 16," whereas the logarithmic form is, "The number 2 is the *logarithm* to which the base 4 must be raised to produce 16."

Think about the key characteristics of the exponential function to make connections to the logarithmic function.

4. Analyze the exponential equation $y = b^x$ and its related logarithmic equation, $x = \log_b(y)$. State the restrictions, if any, on the variables. Explain your reasoning.

$y = b^x \Leftrightarrow x = \log_b(y)$		
Variable	**Restrictions**	**Explanation**
x		
b		
y		

PROBLEM 2 A Logarithm by Any Other Name . . .

1. The graph of $h(x) = b^x$ is shown. Sketch the graph of the inverse of $h(x)$ on the same coordinate plane. Label coordinates of points on the inverse of $h(x)$.

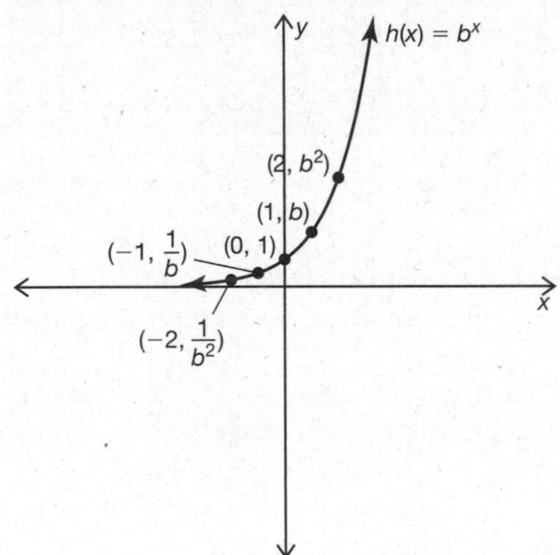

2. Write the equation for the inverse of $h(x) = b^x$. Label the graph.

3. Do you think all exponential functions are invertible? If so, explain your reasoning. If not, provide a counterexample.

Recall that the logarithm of a number for a given base is the exponent to which the base must be raised in order to produce the number. If $y = b^x$, then the logarithm is written as $x = \log_b y$, where $b > 0, b \neq 1$, and $y > 0$. A **logarithmic function** is a function involving a logarithm.

Logarithms were first conceived by a Swiss clockmaker and amateur mathematician Joost Bürgi but became more widely known and used after the publication of a book by Scottish mathematician John Napier in 1614. Tables of logarithms were originally used to make complex computations in astronomy, surveying, and other sciences easier and more accurate. With the invention of calculators and computers, the use of logarithm tables as a tool for calculation has decreased. However, many real-world situations can be modeled using logarithmic functions.

Two frequently used logarithms are logarithms with base 10 and base *e*. A **common logarithm** is a logarithm with base 10 and is usually written *log* without a base specified.

$$c(x) = \log_{10}(x) \quad \Leftrightarrow \quad c(x) = \log x$$

A **natural logarithm** is a logarithm with base *e*, and is usually written as *ln*.

$$n(x) = \log_e(x) \quad \Leftrightarrow \quad n(x) = \ln x$$

4. The functions $p(x) = \log_2(x)$ and $q(x) = \log_3(x)$ have been graphed for you.

   a. Sketch and label the functions $c(x) = \log x$ and $n(x) = \ln x$.

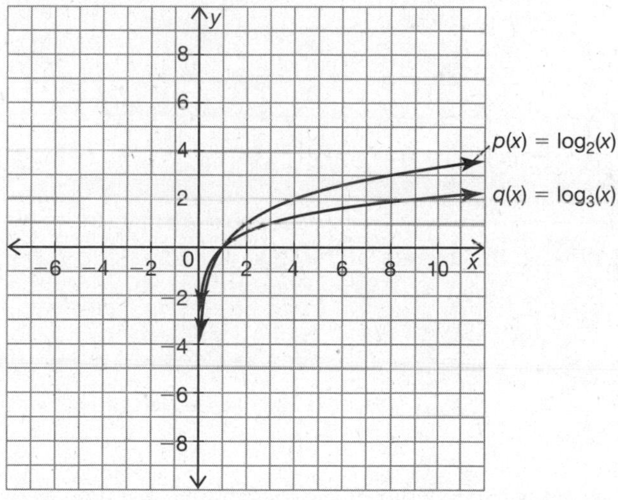

   b. Explain how you determined the graphs of $c(x)$ and $q(x)$.

12

c. Analyze the key characteristics of $p(x)$, $q(x)$, $c(x)$, and $n(x)$. Describe the similarities and differences.

Some of the graphs grow more quickly than others before $x = 1$, but then more slowly after that.

d. What is the inverse of the logarithmic function $c(x) = \log x$?

12

e. What is the inverse of the logarithmic function $n(x) = \ln x$?

PROBLEM 3 Ground Shaking

The Richter scale is used to rate the magnitude of an earthquake, or the amount of energy released. An earthquake's magnitude, M, is determined using the equation, $M = \log\left(\frac{I}{I_0}\right)$, where I is the intensity of the earthquake being measured (measured by the amplitude of a seismograph reading taken 100 km from the epicenter of the earthquake), and I_0 is the intensity of a standard earthquake or "threshold quake" whose seismograph amplitude is 10^{-4} cm.

1. Determine the magnitude of a standard earthquake.

2. An earthquake in California measured 6.8 on the Richter scale, while an earthquake in Japan measured 7.2. How many times more intense was the Japanese earthquake?

12

3. Early in the century an earthquake in Indonesia registered 8.3 on the Richter scale. In the same year, another earthquake was recorded in Chile that was 4 times stronger. What was the magnitude of the Chilean earthquake?

12

Talk the Talk

1. Complete the graphic organizer for the exponential function and the logarithmic function at the end of this lesson.

   a. Cut out each key characteristic on this page.

   b. Tape each key characteristic to its corresponding function.

a. (0, 1)	**b.** As $x \to 0$, $y \to -\infty$. As $x \to +\infty$, $y \to +\infty$.
c. All real numbers	**d.** 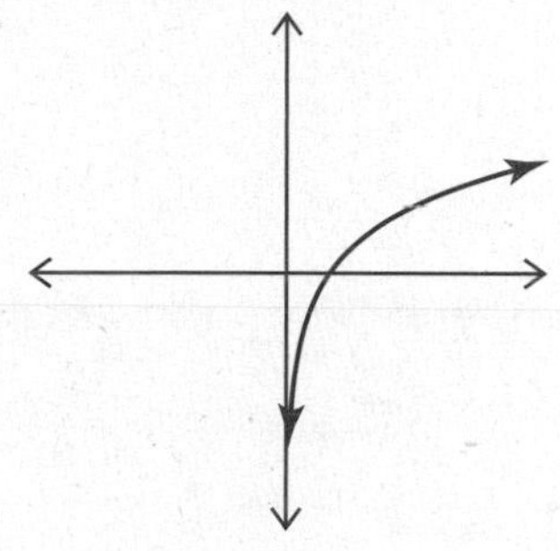
e. $f(x) = b^x$	**f.** $x > 0$
g. $y = 0$	**h.** All real numbers
i. As $x \to -\infty$, $y \to 0$. As $x \to +\infty$, $y \to +\infty$.	**j.** (1, 0)
k. 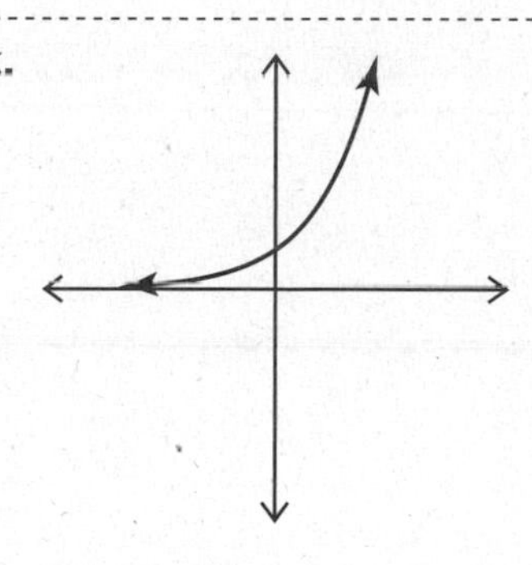	**l.** $g(x) = \log_b(x)$
m. $x = 0$	**n.** $y > 0$

12

12

	Basic Exponential Function	Basic Logarithmic Function
Function:		
Graph:		
Domain:		
Range:		
Intercepts:		
Asymptotes:		
End behavior:		

Be prepared to share your solutions and methods.

12

More Than Meets the Eye

Transformations of Logarithmic Functions

12.5

LEARNING GOALS

In this lesson, you will:

- Dilate, reflect, and translate logarithmic functions using reference points.
- Investigate graphs of logarithmic functions through intercepts, asymptotes, intervals of increase and decrease, and end behavior.

'Practice makes perfect'!

When you practice the same motion over and over, you are building up procedural memory in your brain that instructs your muscles to perform a task. The more often your muscles receive those same instructions, the more quickly and efficiently they are able to carry them out until they become like second nature to you. Athletes use this idea of "muscle memory" when conditioning their bodies to perform, and musicians use it to train their fingers to hit the correct keys or strings accurately.

The best way to train your body and mind when learning a new skill is to practice it slowly at first to be sure that your technique is perfect, and then repeat that same quality practice as often as possible. Break the skill or information up into pieces and work on it, a piece at a time, until it is committed to memory. Once you've learned all of the parts, continue to practice, practice, practice until your new skill becomes an ingrained habit.

What skills do you like to practice?

PROBLEM 1 Don't Flip Out! It's Just a Reflection

1. The two tables show four logarithmic functions and four logarithmic graphs. Match the logarithmic function to its corresponding graph, and write the function under the graph it represents.

Logarithmic Functions	
$f(x) = \log_2(x)$	$g(x) = -\log_2(x)$
$h(x) = \log_2(-x)$	$j(x) = -\log_2(-x)$

Logarithmic Graphs

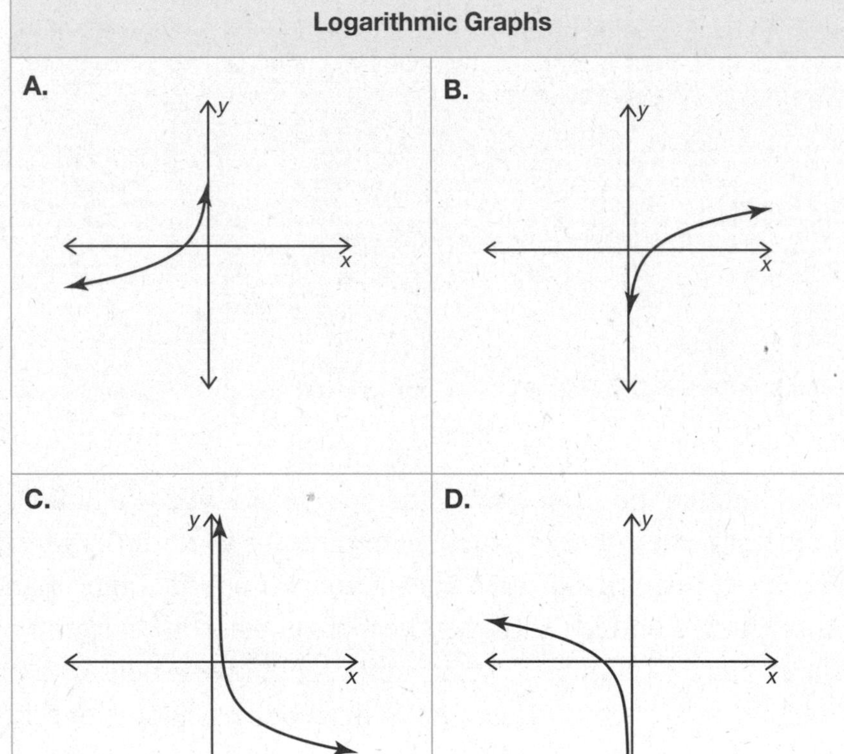

12

2. Analyze the graphs of $f(x)$, $g(x)$, $h(x)$, and $j(x)$. Write an equation for each function $g(x)$, $h(x)$, and $j(x)$ in terms of $f(x)$. Describe each transformation on $f(x)$.

Logarithmic Function	Transformation on $f(x)$
$g(x) =$	
$h(x) =$	
$j(x) =$	

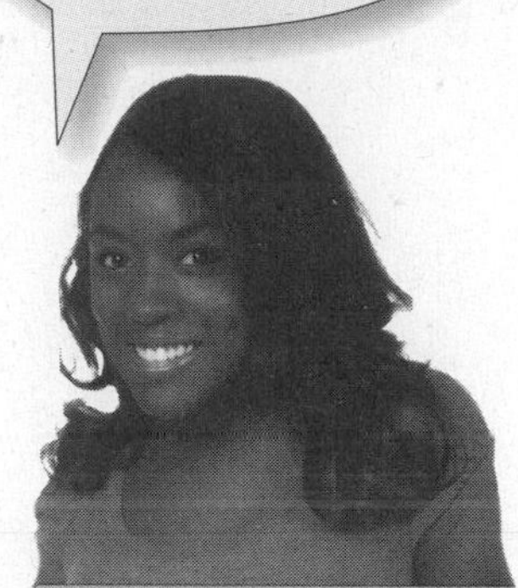

Recall that all transformations can be written in transformational function form in terms of f(x).

3. Analyze the key characteristics of each logarithmic function. What similarities exist among the four functions?

12

4. What generalizations can you make about the effects of these transformations on the domain and range of a logarithmic function?

PROBLEM 2 You've Got Some Moves!

1. Analyze the graphs of $f(x)$ and the transformed function. Describe the transformations produced on $f(x)$ to create the transformed function. Then, write an equation for the transformed function in terms of $f(x)$. For each set of points shown on $f(x)$, the corresponding points are shown on the transformed function.

   a. Describe the transformation:

   $m(x) =$ ____________________

   b. Describe the transformation:

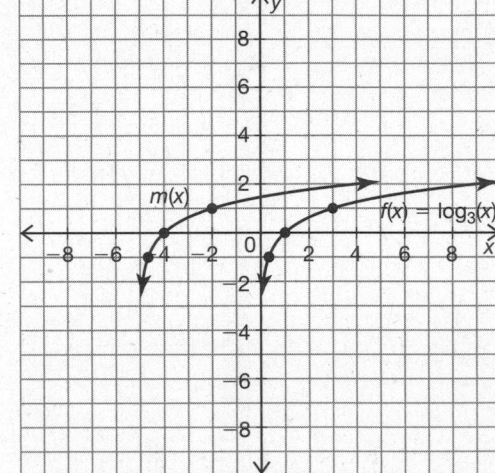

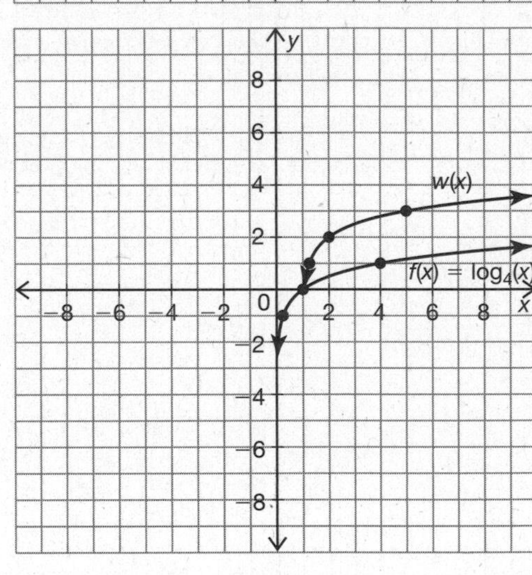

   $w(x) =$ ____________________

   c. Describe the transformation:

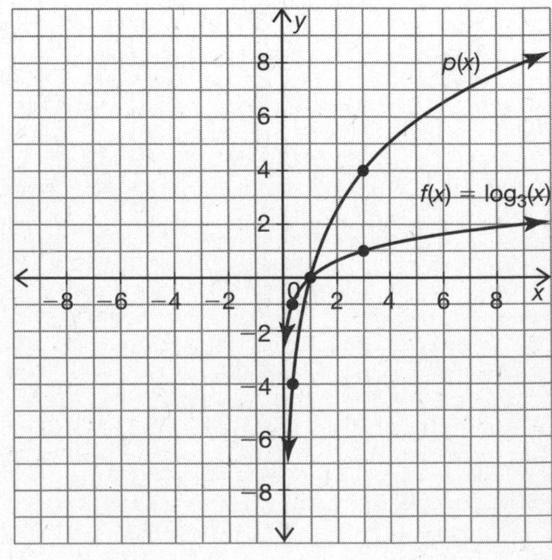

   $p(x) =$ ____________________

2. The graph of a basic logarithmic function *f(x)* is shown. Graph each transformation of *f(x)*. State the domain, range, and asymptotes of your graph.

a. $c(x) = f(x - 2) - 6$

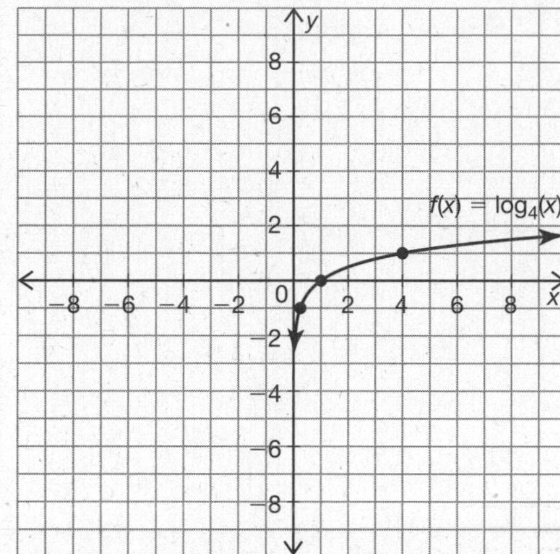

Domain of $c(x)$:

Range of $c(x)$:

Asymptote of $c(x)$:

b. $n(x) = -f(x) + 3$

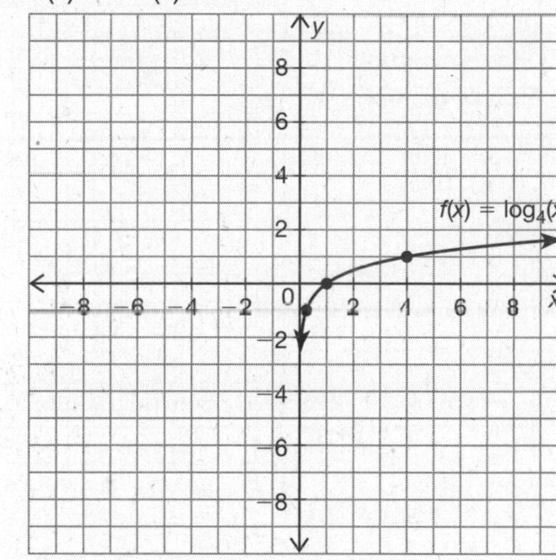

Domain of $n(x)$:

Range of $n(x)$:

Asymptote of $n(x)$:

c. $z(x) = f\left(\frac{x}{2}\right)$

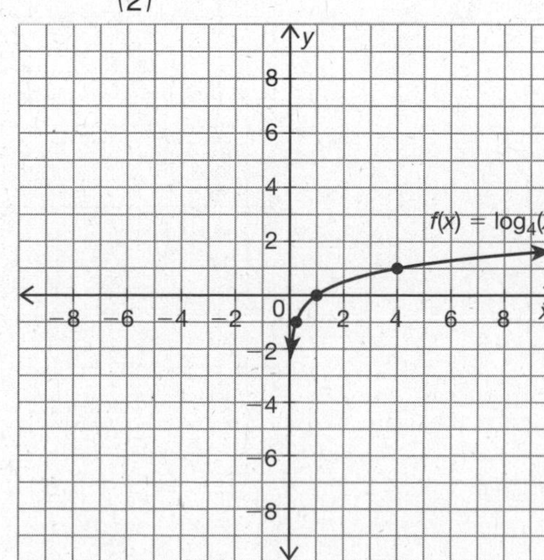

Domain of $z(x)$:

Range of $z(x)$:

Asymptote of $z(x)$:

12

3. Write a transformed logarithmic function in terms of $f(x)$ with the characteristic(s) given. Then, graph the transformed function.

a. $f(x) = \log_2 (x)$

vertical asymptote at $x = -3$

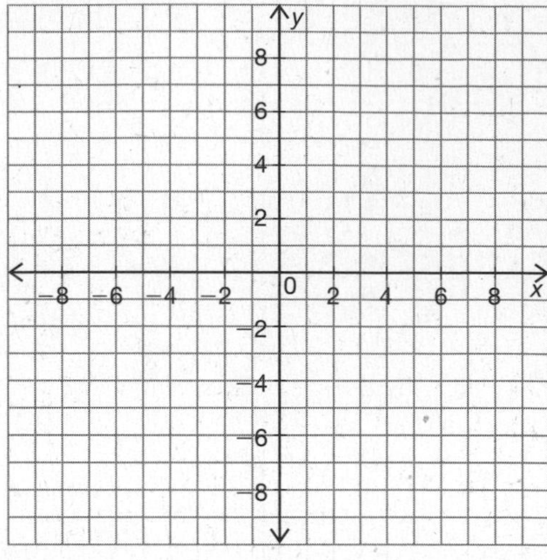

$m(x) =$ ____________________

b. $f(x) = \log_3 (x)$

Reference Points on $f(x)$	→	Corresponding Points on $h(x)$
$\left(\frac{1}{3}, -1\right)$	→	$\left(\frac{1}{3}, -\frac{1}{2}\right)$
(1, 0)	→	(1, 0)
(3, 1)	→	$\left(3, \frac{1}{2}\right)$

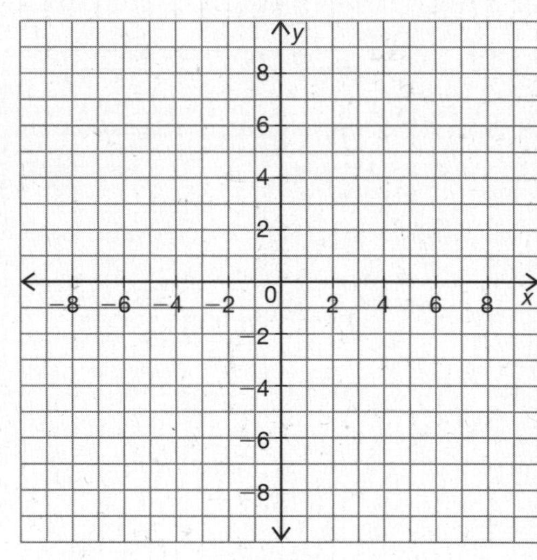

$h(x) =$ ____________________

12

c. $f(x) = \log_5 (x)$

Domain: $(-\infty, 2)$

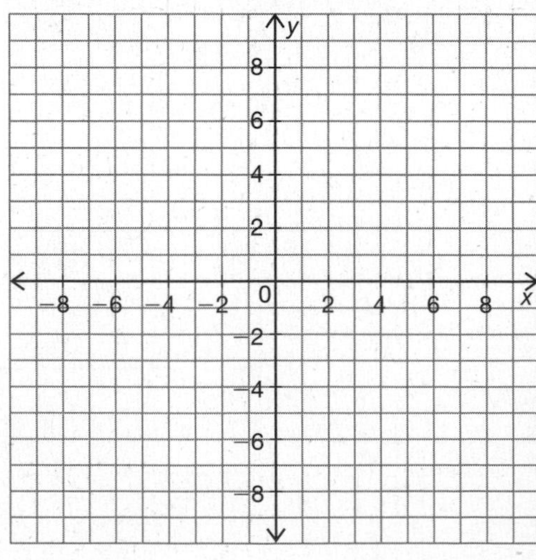

$k(x) =$ ____________________

12

PROBLEM 3 Makin' Moves

1. Consider the functions $f(x) = 2^x$ and $g(x) = f^{-1}(x)$, or $\log_2(x)$. The graphs of $f(x)$ and $g(x)$ are shown.

   a. Cut out the four grids. Use the graphic organizer in this lesson to organize your information.

   b. On each of your cut outs, graph and label the transformed function A, B, C, or D. Describe the transformation(s) performed on $f(x)$.

   c. Use your cut out to graph the inverse of the transformed function.

   d. Describe and label the graph of the inverse of the transformed function as a transformation on $g(x)$.

Don't forget you can fold the cut outs to determine the inverse graph.

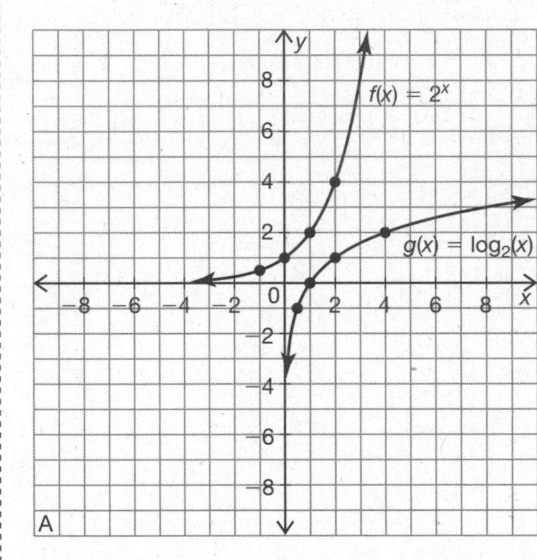

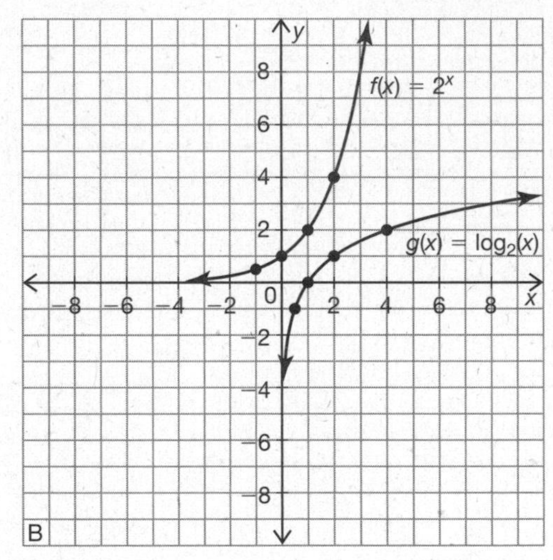

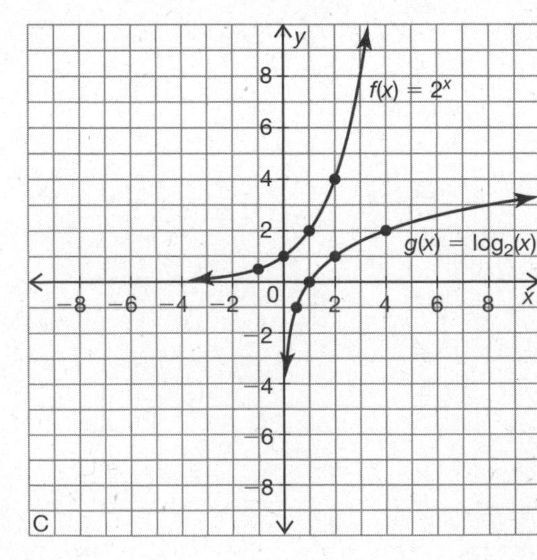

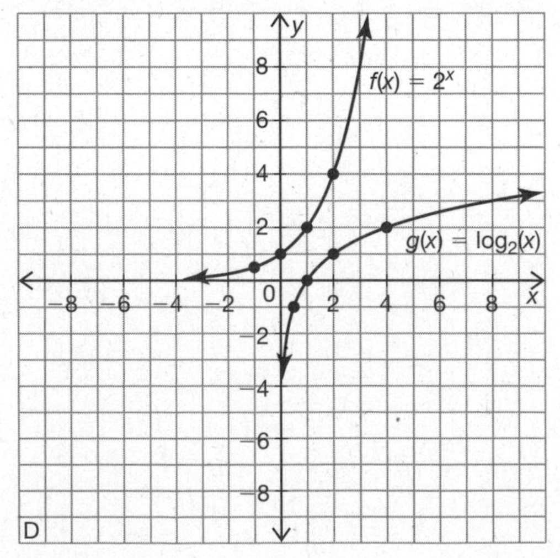

12

A. $f(x + 4)$ Transformation(s) on $f(x)$: Transformation(s) on $g(x)$:	**B.** $f(x) + 5$ Transformation(s) on $f(x)$: Transformation(s) on $g(x)$:
C. $f(x - 3) + 6$ Transformation(s) on $f(x)$: Transformation(s) on $g(x)$:	**D.** $f(x + 1) + 1$ Transformation(s) on $f(x)$: Transformation(s) on $g(x)$:

12

2. Generalize the effects of transformations on $f(x)$ and its inverse function, $f^{-1}(x)$. Complete the table to organize your results.

	Transformation on $f(x)$	Effect of Transformation on $f^{-1}(x)$
$f(x + C)$		
$f(x - C)$		
$f(x) + D$		
$f(x) - D$		

3. Consider the function $y = f(x)$ and the transformed function $g(x)$. Write an equation for $g^{-1}(x)$ in terms of $f^{-1}(x)$.

   a. $y = f(x)$
   $g(x) = f(x - 1)$ $g^{-1}(x) =$ ____________

   b. $y = f(x)$
   $g(x) = f(x) - 2$ $g^{-1}(x) =$ ____________

   c. $y = f(x)$
   $g(x) = f(x + 5)$ $g^{-1}(x) =$ ____________

   d. $y = f(x)$
   $g(x) = f(x - 4) + 3$ $g^{-1}(x) =$ ____________

12

PROBLEM 4 Here We Go Again . . .

The function $f(x) = 2^x$ and its inverse function $f^{-1}(x) = \log_2(x)$ are shown in the table.

$f(x)$	$f^{-1}(x)$
$\left(-1, \frac{1}{2}\right)$	$\left(\frac{1}{2}, -1\right)$
(0, 1)	(1, 0)
(1, 2)	(2, 1)

1. Complete each table. Write the inverse of the transformed function in terms of $f^{-1}(x)$ and identify the effect of the transformation on the inverse.

a.

$3f(x)$	________

Transformation on $f(x)$:

Effect on the inverse:

12

b.

$\frac{1}{2}f(x)$	________

Transformation on $f(x)$:

Effect on the inverse:

c.

$f\left(\frac{x}{4}\right)$	________

Transformation on $f(x)$:

Effect on the inverse:

d.

$f(2x)$	________

Transformation on $f(x)$:

Effect on the inverse:

12

2. How does a vertical dilation on a function affect its inverse?

3. How does a horizontal dilation on a function affect its inverse?

4. Given the function $f(x)$, write the equation for the inverse function, $f^{-1}(x)$. Then graph the inverse function.

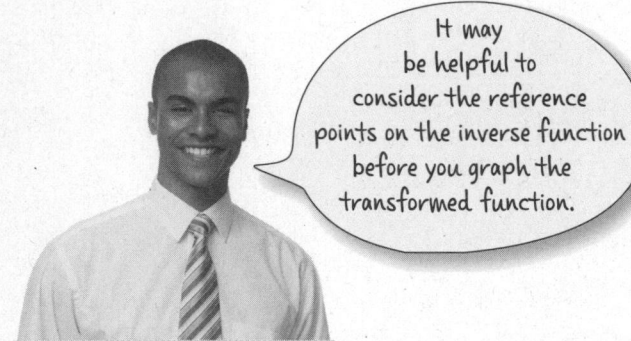

a. $f(x) = 2 \cdot 3^x$

$f^{-1}(x) =$ ____________________

b. $f(x) = \log_4\left(\frac{x}{2}\right)$

$f^{-1}(x) =$ ____________________

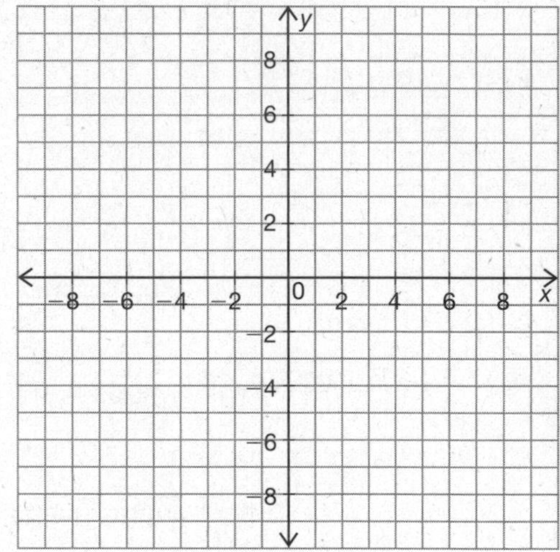

12

c. $f(x) = -5^x$

$f^{-1}(x) =$ ____________________

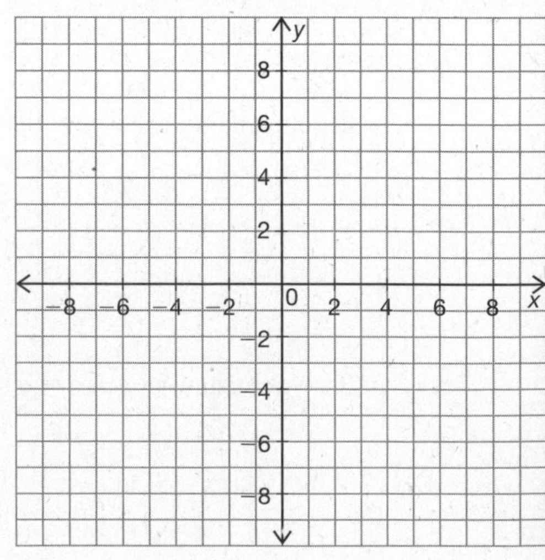

Be prepared to share your solutions and methods.

Chapter 12 Summary

KEY TERMS

- half-life (12.1)
- natural base *e* (12.2)
- logarithm (12.4)
- logarithmic function (12.4)
- common logarithm (12.4)
- natural logarithm (12.4)

12.1 Constructing an Exponential Function from a Geometric Sequence

The general formula for a geometric sequence is $a_n = a_1 \cdot r^{(n-1)}$. This formula can be written as an exponential function by using properties of exponents and multiplication.

Example

$a_n = 20 \cdot 5^{(n-1)}$

$f(n) = 20 \cdot 5^n \cdot 5^{-1}$

$f(n) = 20 \cdot \frac{1}{5} \cdot 5^n$

$f(n) = 4 \cdot 5^n$

12

12.1 Using an Exponential Function to Solve Half-Life Problems

Half-life refers to the amount of time it takes a substance to decay to half of its original amount. An exponential function can be used to solve problems about half-life.

Example

An exponential function $A(t)$ represents the amount of a drug in a person's system, where t represents elapsed time. If the half-life of the drug occurs in multiple-hour cycles—for example, every 3 hours—divide the exponent t by that amount: $\frac{t}{3}$.

Elapsed Time (Hours)	0	2	4	6	8	20
Drug in System (mg)	160	80	40	20	10	?
Number of Half-Life Cycles	0	1	2	3	4	10

$$A(t) = 160\left(\frac{1}{2}\right)^{\frac{t}{2}}$$

$$A(20) = 160\left(\frac{1}{2}\right)^{\frac{20}{2}}$$

$$A(20) = 160\left(\frac{1}{2}\right)^{10}$$

$$A(20) \approx 160(0.00098)$$

$$A(20) \approx 0.15625$$

After 20 hours, there will be about 0.15625 mg of the drug remaining in the person's system.

12.2 Investigating Exponential Growth and Decay

For exponential growth functions, b is a value greater than 1. For exponential decay functions, b is a fraction or decimal between 0 and 1.

Example

$f(x) = 15^x$	$f(x) = \left(\frac{2}{3}\right)^x$
growth	decay

12.2 Investigating Graphs of Exponential Functions

Every basic exponential function has the point (0, 1) in common. The x-value represents the exponent, and any base raised to the power of 0 will equal 1. Basic functions of exponential growth and decay can be identified by their domain, range, asymptotes, and end behavior as described in the table below.

	Basic Exponential Growth	Basic Exponential Decay
Domain	$(-\infty, \infty)$	$(-\infty, \infty)$
Range	$(0, \infty)$	$(0, \infty)$
Asymptote	$y = 0$	$y = 0$
Intercepts	(0, 1)	(0, 1)
End Behavior	As $x \to -\infty$, $f(x) \to 0$ As $x \to \infty$, $f(x) \to \infty$	As $x \to -\infty$, $f(x) \to \infty$ As $x \to \infty$, $f(x) \to 0$
Intervals of Increase or Decrease	Increasing over $(-\infty, \infty)$	Decreasing over $(-\infty, \infty)$

Examples

$f(x) = 4^x$

x	$f(x)$
−1	$\frac{1}{4}$
0	1
1	4

Increasing over $(-\infty, \infty)$.

End behavior: As $x \to -\infty$, $f(x) \to 0$
As $x \to \infty$, $f(x) \to \infty$

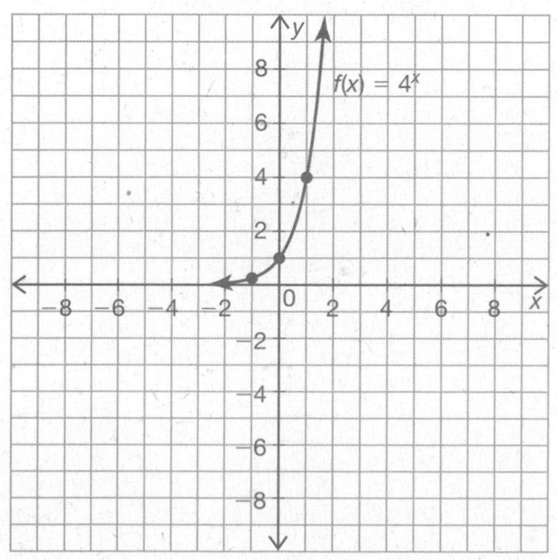

$f(x) = 0.5^x$

x	$f(x)$
−1	2
0	1
1	0.5

Decreasing over $(-\infty, \infty)$.

End behavior: As $x \to -\infty$, $f(x) \to \infty$
As $x \to \infty$, $f(x) \to 0$

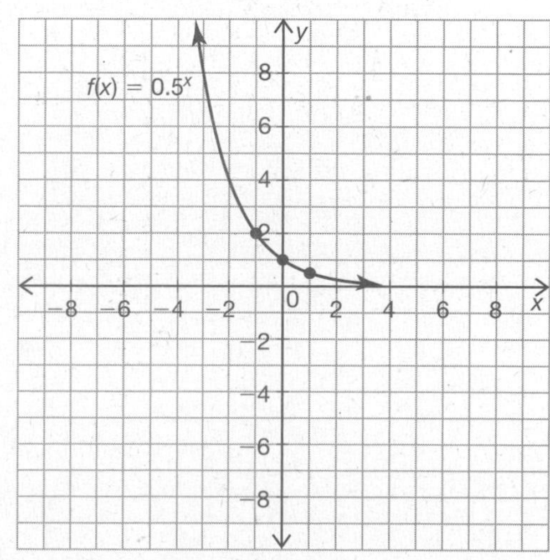

12

12.2 Using Exponential Equations to Solve Compound Interest Problems

The formula for compound interest is $A = P(1 + r)^t$, where A is the amount earned, P is the original amount, or principal, r is the rate, and t is the time in years. If interest is compounded more than once per year, then the formula is: $A(t) = \left(1 + \frac{1}{n}\right)^{n \cdot t}$.

Example

Sarah invests $500 in the bank. Her bank compounds interest 4 times a year at a rate of 4%. How much money will she have in her account after 10 years?

$$A(10) = 500\left(1 + \frac{0.04}{4}\right)^{4 \cdot 10}$$

$$= 500(1.01)^{40}$$

$$\approx 500(1.4889)$$

$$\approx 744.43$$

Sarah will have $744.43 in her account after 10 years.

12.2 Using the Natural Base, *e*

The constant *e* represents continuous growth and is often referred to as the natural base *e*. The symbol *e* is used to represent the constant 2.718281. . . and so on. The natural base *e* is used in the formula for population growth: $N(t) = N_0e^{rt}$.

Example

Miami's population in 2005 was 216,500 people and is growing at a rate of about 3%. According to the population growth model, what would be the approximate population of Miami in 2020?

$$N(15) = 216{,}500e^{(0.03 \cdot 15)}$$

$$= 216{,}500e^{0.45}$$

$$\approx 339{,}540$$

Miami's population in 2020 would be approximately 339,540 people.

12

12.3 Dilating, Reflecting, and Translating Exponential Functions Using Reference Points

Consider the functions $y = f(x)$ and $g(x) = Af(B(x - C)) + D$. Recall that the D-value translates $f(x)$ vertically, the C-value translates $f(x)$ horizontally, the A-value vertically stretches or compresses $f(x)$, and the B-value horizontally stretches or compresses $f(x)$. Exponential functions are transformed in the same manner.

Example

$f(x) = 2^x$

$a(x) = f(x) - 4$

Reference Points on $f(x)$	Corresponding Points on $a(x)$
$\left(-1, \frac{1}{2}\right)$	$\left(-1, -\frac{7}{2}\right)$
(0, 1)	(0, −3)
(1, 2)	(1, −2)

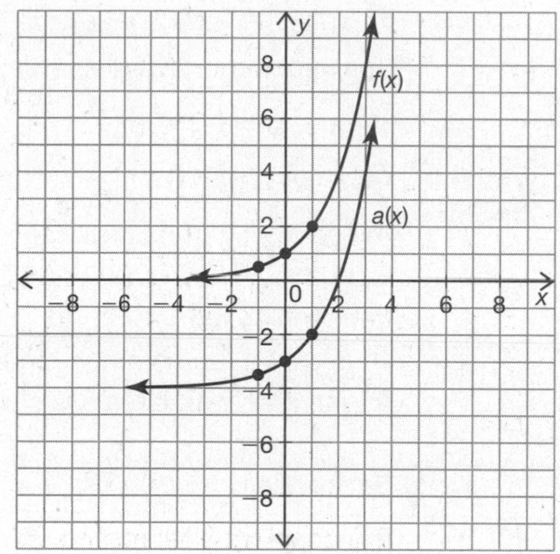

Domain: All real numbers

Range: $y > -4$

Horizontal asymptote: $y = -4$

12.3 Describing Transformations Performed on Exponential Equations

Using the functions $y = f(x)$ and $g(x) = Af(B(x - C)) + D$, you can describe the transformations to the graph of an exponential function.

Example

$m(x) = 4^x$

$t(x) = -m(x) + 3$

The graph of the function $m(x)$ is translated vertically up 3 units and is reflected across the x-axis to produce $t(x)$.

$t(x) = -4^x + 3$

12

12.4 Writing Exponential Equations as Logarithmic Equations

The inverse of an exponential equation can be written as a logarithmic equation. The logarithm of a number for a given base is the exponent to which the base must be raised in order to produce the number. If $y = b^x$, then the logarithm is x, and can be written as $x = \log_b y$. The value of the base of a logarithm is the same as the base in the exponential expression b^x.

Examples

$4^3 = 64$ $\qquad$ $\log_5\left(\frac{1}{625}\right) = -4$

$\log_4(64) = 3$ $\qquad$ $5^{-4} = \frac{1}{625}$

12.4 Graphing the Inverse of an Exponential Function

A logarithmic function is the inverse of an exponential function. It is a function involving a logarithm. Many real-world situations can be modeled using logarithmic functions. Two frequently used logarithms are logarithms with base 10 and base *e*. A logarithm with base 10 is called the common logarithm and is usually written *log* without a base specified. A logarithm with base e is called the natural logarithm and is usually written as *ln*.

Example

$f(x) = 10^x$

$f^{-1}(x) = \log x$

x	$f(x)$
−1	0.1
0	1
1	10

x	$f^{-1}(x)$
0.1	−1
1	0
10	1

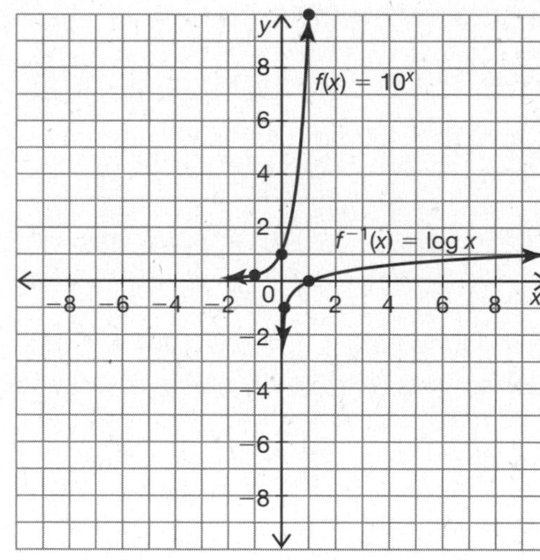

12

12.5 Describing Transformations Performed on Logarithmic Functions

Using the functions $y = f(x)$ and $g(x) = Af(B(x - C)) + D$, you can describe the transformations to a logarithmic function.

Example

$f(x) = \log_4(x)$

$g(x) = -f(x + 3)$

$g(x) = -\log_4(x + 3)$

horizontally translated left 3 units and reflected across the x-axis

Domain of $g(x)$: $(-3, \infty)$

Range of $g(x)$: $(-\infty, \infty)$

Asymptote of $g(x)$: $x = -3$

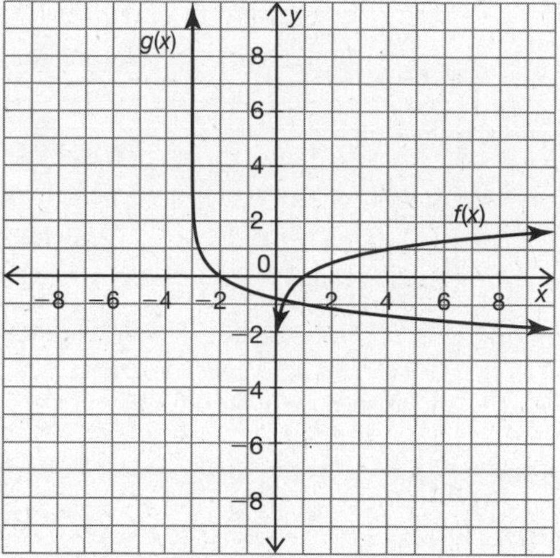

12

12.5

Describing the Effects of Transformations on Inverse Functions

Transformations performed on a function and its inverse will have inverse effects.

	Transformation on $f(x)$	Effect of Transformation on $f^{-1}(x)$
$f(x + C)$	Translate horizontally left C units	Translate vertically down C units
$f(x - C)$	Translate horizontally right C units	Translate vertically up C units
$f(x) + D$	Translate vertically up D units	Translate horizontally right D units
$f(x) - D$	Translate vertically down D units	Translate horizontally left D units
$Af(x)$	Vertical dilation of 3	Horizontal dilation of 3
$f(Bx)$	Horizontal dilation of $\frac{1}{B}$	Vertical dilation of $\frac{1}{B}$

Example

Consider the transformation on the function $f(x) = 2^x$ and its inverse function $f^{-1}(x) = \log_2(x)$.

$m(x) = \frac{1}{3}f(x)$	$m^{-1}(x) = f^{-1}(3x)$
$\left(-1, \frac{1}{6}\right)$	$\left(\frac{1}{6}, -1\right)$
$\left(0, \frac{1}{3}\right)$	$\left(\frac{1}{3}, 0\right)$
$\left(1, \frac{2}{3}\right)$	$\left(\frac{2}{3}, 1\right)$

12

Transformation on $f(x)$: vertical dilation of $\frac{1}{3}$

Effect on the inverse: horizontal dilation of $\frac{1}{3}$

Exponential and Logarithmic Equations

13

Logarithmic equations
can be used to describe
the intensity of sounds
d the amount of medication
n a patient's bloodstream.
They can even be used
to help solve crimes!

All the Pieces of the Puzzle

13.1

Exponential and Logarithmic Forms

LEARNING GOALS

In this lesson, you will:

- Convert exponential equations into logarithmic equations.
- Convert logarithmic equations into exponential equations.
- Solve exponential and simple logarithmic equations.
- Estimate the values of logarithms on a number line.
- Evaluate logarithmic expressions.

KEY TERM

- logarithmic equation

In the past, logarithms helped mathematicians and other scientists save a lot of time. Astronomers especially benefited from logarithms because of the enormous numbers—representing distances to other bodies in the solar system—they were required to calculate with.

The advantage to using logarithms was that they could essentially turn multiplication into addition and division into subtraction.

For example, what's 4×16? If you know (or can look up) some logarithms, you can turn this multiplication, $2^2 \cdot 2^4$, into addition: $2 + 4 = 6$.

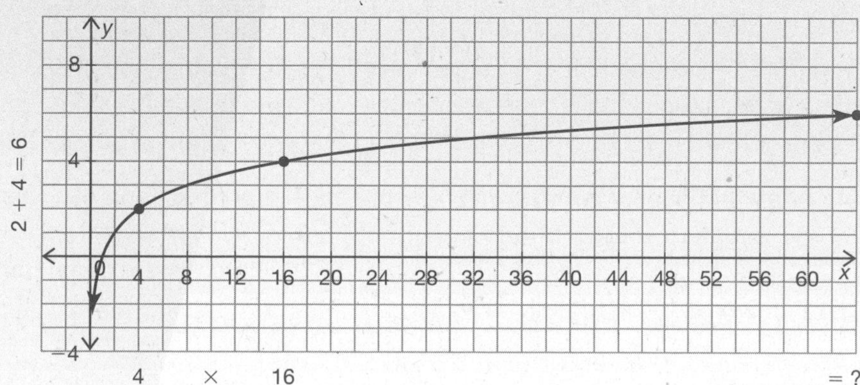

The graph above shows the function $\log_2(x)$. What other multiplications can you turn into additions on this graph? What divisions can you turn into subtractions?

PROBLEM 1 It's All Coming Together . . .

Recall that a logarithmic function is the inverse of an exponential function.

1. Write the equivalent form of the given exponential or logarithmic expression.

Exponential Form $y = b^x$	$\Leftrightarrow$	Logarithmic Form $x = \log_b (y)$
$12^2 = 144$	$\Leftrightarrow$	
	$\Leftrightarrow$	$\log_{16} (4) = \frac{1}{2}$
$10^5 = 100{,}000$	$\Leftrightarrow$	
	$\Leftrightarrow$	$\ln 20.086 \approx 3$
$\left(\frac{2}{3}\right)^3 = \frac{8}{27}$	$\Leftrightarrow$	
	$\Leftrightarrow$	$\log_9 (27) = \frac{3}{2}$
	$\Leftrightarrow$	$\log_2 (x) = 8$
$6^x = 36$	$\Leftrightarrow$	
$n^5 = 243$	$\Leftrightarrow$	$\log_n (243) = 5$

When you evaluate a logarithmic expression (logarithm), you are determining the value of the exponent in the corresponding exponential expression.

$$\text{base}^{\text{exponent}} = \text{argument} \Leftrightarrow \log_{\text{base}} (\text{argument}) = \text{exponent}$$

13

The variables of the logarithmic equation have the same restrictions as the corresponding variables of the exponential equation. The base, b, must be greater than 0 but not equal to 1; the argument must be greater than 0; and the value of the exponent has no restrictions.

It is important to become familiar with how the base, argument, and exponent fit into a *logarithmic equation*. A **logarithmic equation** is an equation that contains a logarithm. To write a logarithmic equation, sometimes it is helpful to consider the exponential form first and then convert it to logarithmic form.

2. Arrange the given terms to create a true logarithmic equation.

a. 49, 2, 7

b. $-3, 6, \frac{1}{216}$

Remember, it
may be helpful to think
of a true exponential
equation first!

c. 4, 4, 1

d. 256, 4, 4

Let's consider the relationship between the base, argument, and exponent. You can use that relationship to solve for any unknown in a logarithmic equation.

To solve for any unknown in a simple logarithmic equation, begin by converting it to an exponential equation.

Argument Is Unknown	Exponent Is Unknown	Base Is Unknown
$\log_4 (y) = 3$	$\log_4 (64) = x$	$\log_b (64) = 3$
$4^3 = y$	$4^x = 64$	$b^3 = 64$
$64 = y$	$4^x = 4^3$	$b^3 = 4^3$
	$x = 3$	$b = 4$

It is important to note that you can convert a logarithmic equation to an exponential equation regardless of which term is unknown.

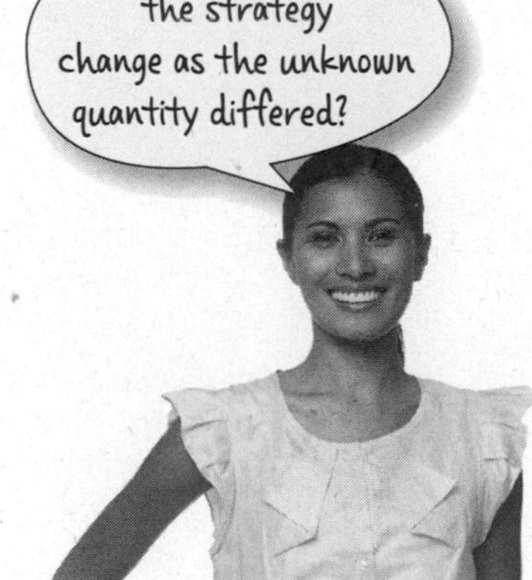
How did
the strategy
change as the unknown
quantity differed?

3. Justify the last step of each case in the worked example.

a. If $4^3 = y$, why does $y = 64$?

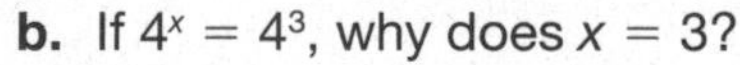

13

b. If $4^x = 4^3$, why does $x = 3$?

c. If $b^3 = 4^3$, why does $b = 4$?

4. Solve for the unknown in each logarithmic equation.

a. $\log_8 (64) = n$

b. $\log_n \left(\frac{1}{16}\right) = -2$

c. $\log_{\frac{1}{2}} (64) = n$

d. $\log n = -3$

e. $\log_n (\sqrt[3]{49}) = \frac{2}{3}$

f. $\log_9 (27) = n$

5. Write three logarithmic expressions that are equivalent to each given expression. Explain your strategy.

a. $\log_5 (625)$

13

b. $\log_7\left(\frac{1}{7}\right)$

c. $\log_{64}(8)$

d. $\log_2(-2)$

13

PROBLEM 2 Estimating Logarithms

In Problem 1, each logarithm was a rational number. However, a logarithm can be any real number, even an irrational number.

1. Label each number line using logarithmic expressions with the indicated base.

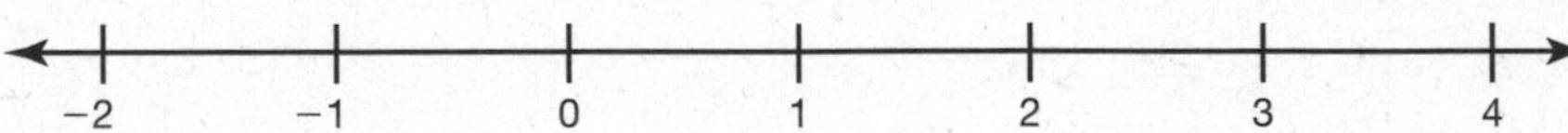

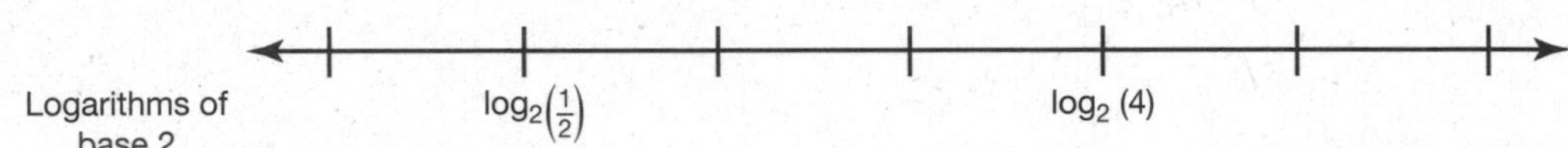

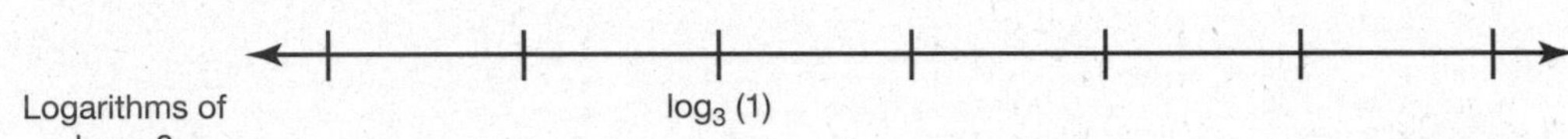

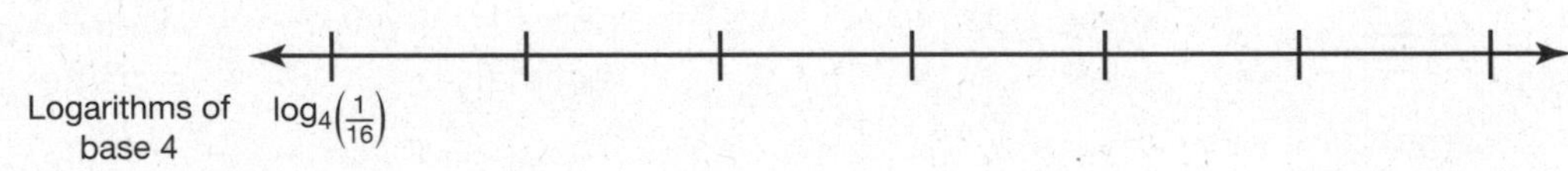

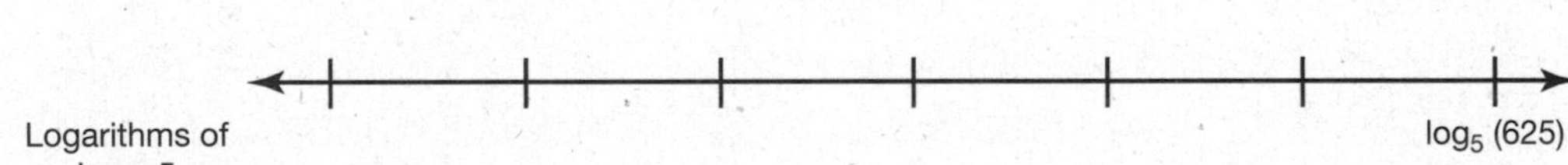

2. Compare the logarithms on the number lines.

   a. Analyze all the logarithms that are equivalent to 0. Write a general statement using the base b to represent this relationship.

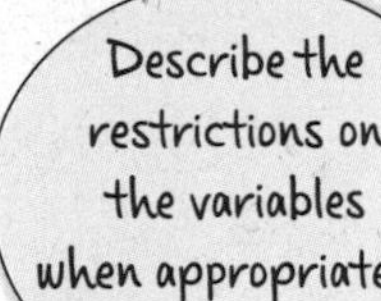

Describe the restrictions on the variables when appropriate.

   b. Analyze all the logarithms that are equivalent to 1. Write a general statement using the base b to represent this relationship.

c. Rewrite the general statements from parts (a) and (b) in exponential form. Use exponent rules to verify that each statement is true.

You can estimate the value of a logarithm that is not an integer by using a number line as a guide.

Estimate the value of $\log_3 (33)$.

To estimate $\log_3 (33)$ to the tenths place, identify the closest logarithm whose argument is less than 33 and the closest logarithm whose argument is greater than 33 on the number line that represents base 3.

The closest logarithm whose argument is less than 33:	The logarithm you are estimating:	The closest logarithm whose argument is greater than 33:
$\log_3 (27)$	$\log_3 (33)$	$\log_3 (81)$

You know that $\log_3 27 = 3$ and $\log_3 81 = 4$. This means the estimate of $\log_3 33$ is between 3 and 4.

$$\log_3 (27) < \log_3 (33) < \log_3 (81)$$

$$3 < x < 4$$

Next, estimate the decimal digit.

Because 33 is closer to 27 than to 81, the value of $\log_3 33$ is closer to 3 than to 4.

log3 (33)
3
log3 (27)
4
log3 (81)

Remember, this is just an estimate, so 3.1 and 3.2 are both good answers.

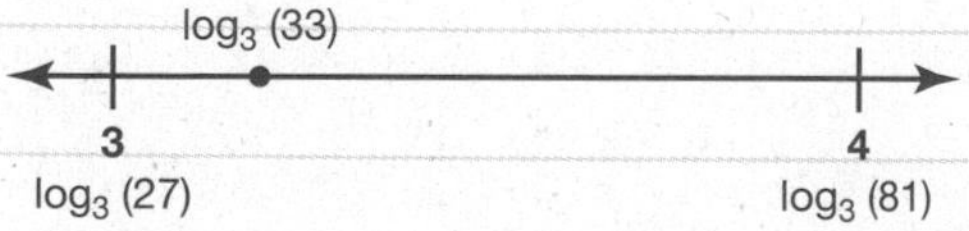

In this case, 3.2 is a good estimate for $\log_3 (33)$.

3. Sutton and Silas were each asked to estimate $\log_4 (28)$.

Sutton

I estimated $\log_4 (28)$ by using the number line.

−2	−1	0	1	2	3	4
$\log_4\left(\frac{1}{16}\right)$	$\log_4\left(\frac{1}{4}\right)$	$\log_4 (1)$	$\log_4 (4)$	$\log_4 (16)$	$\log_4 (64)$	$\log_4 (256)$

$$\log_4 (16) < \log_4 (28) < \log_4 (64)$$

$$2 < x < 3$$

$$\log_4 (28) \approx 2.3$$

Silas

I estimated $\log_4 (28)$ by converting the log into exponential form and estimating based on powers of 4.

$$\log_4 (28) = x$$

$$4^x = 28$$

I know that $4^2 = 16$ and $4^3 = 64$ so the estimate of $\log_4 (28)$ must be between 2 and 3.

$$\log_4 (28) \approx 2.4$$

Silas did not use the number line, but his estimate was about the same as Sutton's. Will Silas's method always work?

13

4. Estimate each logarithm to the tenths place and explain your reasoning.

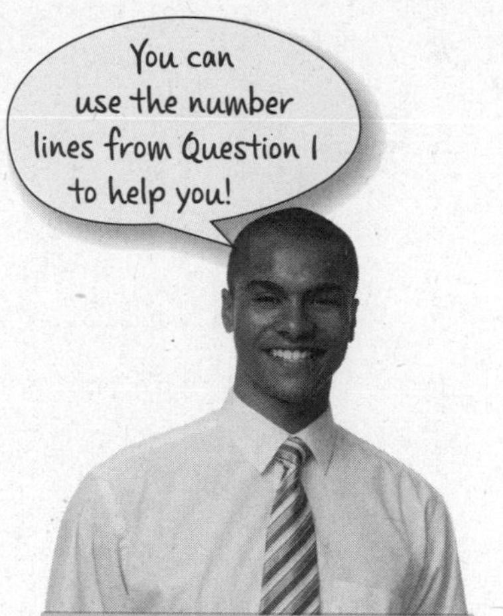

You can
use the number
lines from Question 1
to help you!

a. $\log_2 (10)$

b. $\log_5 (4)$

c. $\log_4 (300)$

d. $\log 2500$

13

5. Mark and Scotty were each asked to determine which base was used to estimate the value of $\log_b(58) = 2.9$.

Mark

The log of 58 falls between 2 and 3 when the base is 4.

$\log_4(16) < \log_b(58) < \log_4(64)$

$2 < 2.9 < 3$

So, $b \approx 4$.

Scotty

The log of 58 falls between 2 and 3 when the base is 5.

$\log_5(25) < \log_b(58) < \log_5(125)$

$2 < 2.9 < 3$

So, $b \approx 5$.

Who is correct? Explain your reasoning.

13

6. Use the number lines from Question 1 to determine the appropriate base of each logarithm.

a. $\log_b (108) = 2.9$

b. $\log_b (0.4) = -1.3$

c. $\log_b (74) = 3.1$

13

7. For a fixed base greater than 1, as the value of the argument gets larger, what happens to the value of the logarithm? Provide an example to illustrate your statement.

8. Plot $\log_2 (18)$, $\log_3 (18)$, $\log_4 (18)$, and $\log_5 (18)$ on the appropriate number lines in Question 1. Then use the number lines to estimate the numeric value of each logarithm to the tenths place. Verify your answers in exponential form.

9. For a fixed argument, when the value of the base is greater than 1 and increasing, what happens to the value of the logarithm?

10. How could you use the number lines from Question 1 to predict the value of ln 18?

11. Make a prediction for the value of ln 18.

Talk the Talk

Choose a word from the box that makes each statement true. Explain your reasoning.

always	sometimes	never

1. The value of a logarithm is ____________ equal to the exponent of the corresponding exponential equation.

2. The argument of a logarithmic expression is ____________ a negative number.

3. The value of a logarithm is ____________ equal to a negative number.

4. The base of a logarithm is ____________ a negative number.

5. A logarithm is ____________ a value that is not a whole number.

6. For a base greater than 1, if $b > c$ then the value of $\log_a b$ is ____________ greater than $\log_a c$.

7. If $a > b$, then the value of $\log_a 1$ is ____________ less than $\log_b 1$.

8. The base of a logarithm is ____________ equal to 1.

Be prepared to share your solutions and methods.

Mad Props

13.2

Properties of Logarithms

LEARNING GOALS

In this lesson, you will:

- Derive the properties of logarithms.
- Expand logarithmic expressions using the properties of logarithms.
- Rewrite multiple logarithmic expressions as a single logarithmic expression.

KEY TERMS

- Zero Property of Logarithms
- Logarithm with Same Base and Argument
- Product Rule of Logarithms
- Quotient Rule of Logarithms
- Power Rule of Logarithms

Dimitri Mendeleev is best known for his work on the periodic table—arranging the 63 known elements into a periodic table based on atomic mass, which he published in *Principles of Chemistry* in 1869. His first periodic table was compiled on the basis of arranging the elements in ascending order of atomic weight and grouping them by similarity of properties. He predicted the existence and properties of new elements and pointed out accepted atomic weights that were in error. His table did not include any of the noble gases, however, which had not yet been discovered. Dmitri Mendeleev revolutionized our understanding of the properties of atoms and created a table that probably embellishes every chemistry classroom in the world.

PROBLEM 1 Setting Ground Rules

Logarithms by definition are exponents, so they have properties that are similar to those of exponents and powers. In this lesson, you will develop logarithmic rules and properties that correspond to various exponential rules and properties you already know.

Look back at your number line representations. How did you use your number lines to verify this property?

1. Let's consider the Zero Property of Powers to develop a corresponding logarithmic property.
   a. Write a sentence to summarize the Zero Property of Powers, $b^0 = 1$.

   b. Write the Zero Property of Powers in logarithmic form. This is a corresponding logarithmic property called the *Zero Property of Logarithms*.

   c. State the Zero Property of Logarithms in words.

2. Let's consider the exponent rule that says that any number raised to the first power is equal to the base.
   a. Write an exponential equation to represent this rule. Use b as the base.

   b. Write your exponential equation from part (a) in logarithmic form.

   c. State this logarithmic relationship in words.

3. Let's consider the Product Rule of Powers to derive a corresponding logarithmic property.

   a. Write a sentence to summarize the Product Rule of Powers, $b^m \cdot b^n = b^{m+n}$.

You can start with a substitution to make the property easier to derive.

   b. Analyze the steps that begin with the Product Rule of Powers to derive a corresponding logarithmic property called the *Product Rule of Logarithms*. Complete the last line of the diagram.

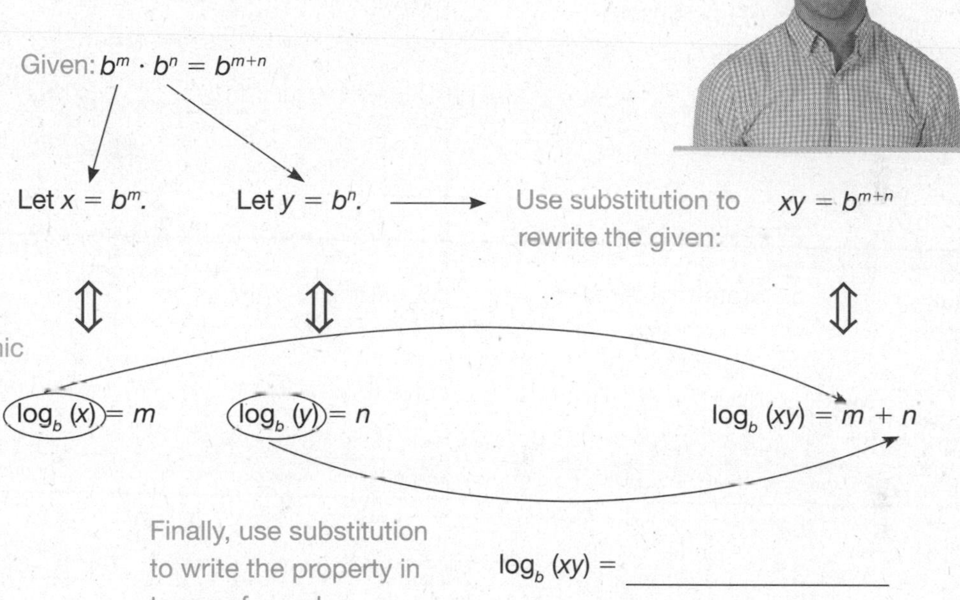

Given: $b^m \cdot b^n = b^{m+n}$
Let $x = b^m$.
Let $y = b^n$.
Use substitution to rewrite the given:
$xy = b^{m+n}$
Rewrite each exponential equation as a logarithmic equation.
$\log_b(x) = m$
$\log_b(y) = n$
$\log_b(xy) = m + n$
Finally, use substitution to write the property in terms of x and y:
$\log_b(xy) =$ ______

   c. State the Product Rule of Logarithms in words.

13

4. Let's consider the Quotient Rule of Powers to derive a corresponding logarithmic property.

a. Write a sentence to summarize the Quotient Rule of Powers, $\frac{b^m}{b^n} = b^{m-n}$, if $b^n \neq 0$.

Look at your derivation of the Product Rule of Logarithms to help you get started.

b. Complete the steps that begin with the Quotient Rule of Powers to derive a corresponding logarithmic property called the *Quotient Rule of Logarithms.*

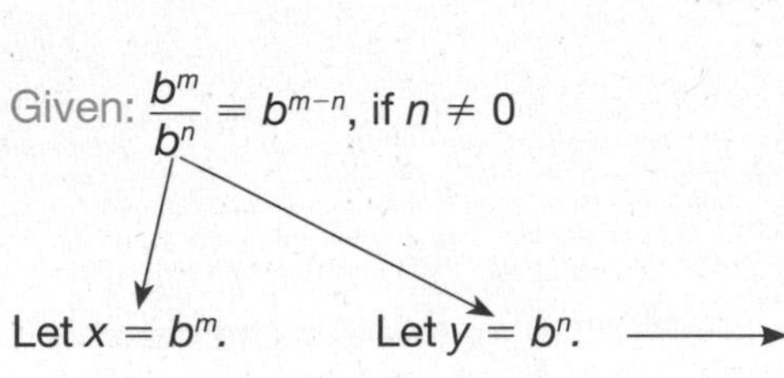

Given: $\frac{b^m}{b^n} = b^{m-n}$, if $n \neq 0$

Let $x = b^m$. Let $y = b^n$. ⟶ Use substitution to rewrite the given: ____________

Rewrite each exponential equation as a logarithmic equation.

⇕ ⇕ ⇕

$\log_b x = m$ $\log_b y = n$ ____________

Finally, use substitution to write the property in terms of x and y: $\log_b \left(\frac{x}{y}\right) =$ ____________

c. Summarize the Quotient Rule of Logarithms in words.

13

5. Let's consider the Power to a Power Rule to derive a corresponding logarithmic property.

a. Write a sentence to summarize the Power to a Power Rule, $(b^m)^n = b^{mn}$.

b. Complete the steps that begin with the Power to a Power Rule to derive a corresponding logarithmic property called the *Power Rule of Logarithms*.

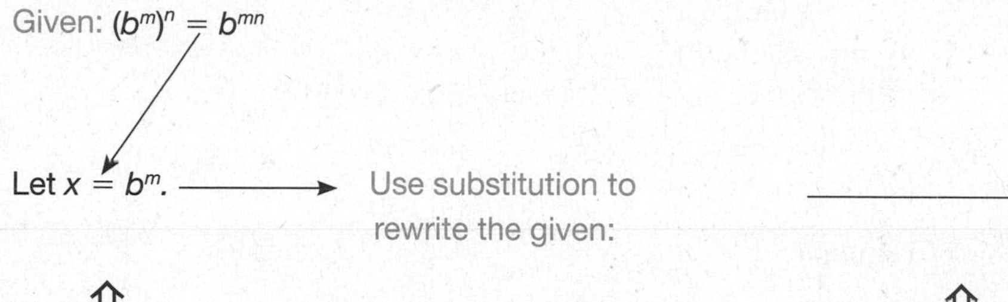

Given: $(b^m)^n = b^{mn}$

Let $x = b^m$. → Use substitution to rewrite the given: ____________

Rewrite each exponential equation as a logarithmic equation.

⇕ ⇕

____________ ____________

Finally, use substitution to write the property in terms of x: $\log_b x^n =$ ____________

c. State the Power Rule of Logarithms in words.

13

6. In this problem, you derived different properties of logarithms. Complete the tables to define each exponential and logarithmic property verbally and symbolically. Provide examples for each property.

Exponential Property	Logarithmic Property
Zero Property of Powers	**Zero Property of Logarithms**
Verbal:	**Verbal:**
Symbolic:	**Symbolic:**
Examples:	**Examples:**
Base Raised to First Power	**Logarithm with Same Base and Argument**
Verbal:	**Verbal:**
Symbolic:	**Symbolic:**
Examples:	**Examples:**
Product Rule of Powers	**Product Rule of Logarithms**
Verbal:	**Verbal:**
Symbolic:	**Symbolic:**
Examples:	**Examples:**

Exponential Property	Logarithmic Property
Quotient Rule of Powers	**Quotient Rule of Logarithms**
Verbal:	**Verbal:**
Symbolic:	**Symbolic:**
Examples:	**Examples:**
Power to a Power Rule	**Power Rule of Logarithms**
Verbal:	**Verbal:**
Symbolic:	**Symbolic:**
Examples:	**Examples:**

PROBLEM 2 Don't Break the Rules!

1. Use the properties of logarithms to rewrite each logarithmic expression in expanded form.

   a. $\log_4 (6x^5)$

   b. $\log_7 \left(\frac{3y^4}{x^3}\right)$

   c. $\ln (3xy^3)$

The logarithm properties apply to both natural logarithms and common logarithms!

13

2. Use the properties of logarithms to rewrite each logarithmic expression as a single logarithm.

a. $\log_2 (10) + 3 \log_2 (x)$

b. $4 \log (12) - 4 \log (2)$

c. $3(\ln 3 - \ln x) + (\ln x - \ln 9)$

3. Suppose $\log_a (5) = p$, $\log_a (3) = q$, and $\log_a (2) = r$. Write an algebraic expression for each logarithmic expression.

a. $\log_a (50)$

b. $\log_a (0.3)$

13

c. $\log_a \left(\frac{1}{27}\right)$

Be prepared to share your solutions and methods.

13.3

What's Your Strategy?

Solving Exponential Equations

LEARNING GOALS

In this lesson, you will:

- Solve exponential equations using the Change of Base Formula.
- Solve exponential equations by taking the log of both sides.
- Analyze different solution strategies to solve exponential equations.

KEY TERM

- Change of Base Formula

It may seem like everyone you know is online. But of course not everyone in the world is online—yet. Here's a glimpse of how fast internet use was growing among the Earth's 7 billion people in June of 2012:

Region	Population (2012)	Internet Users (2000)	Internet Users (2012)
Africa	1,073,380,925	4,514,400	167,335,676
Asia	3,922,066,987	114,304,000	1,076,681,059
Europe	820,918,446	105,096,093	518,512,109
Middle East	223,608,203	3,284,800	90,000,455
North America	348,280,154	108,096,800	273,785,413
Latin America	593,668,638	18,068,919	254,915,745
Oceania/Australia	35,903,569	7,620,480	24,287,919

World Internet Usage and Population Statistics, June 30, 2012

How long do you think it will take before everyone on Earth is using the internet?

PROBLEM 1 Don't Burst My Bubble

The newest online game is Bubblez Burst, a highly addictive game that runs on social media. On the first day of its release, 50 people subscribe. The creators estimate that everyone who subscribes will then send 3 more people to subscribe.

1. Write a function using the creator's estimate to model the total number of subscribers P who will be playing Bubblez Burst after t number of days.

2. How many days will it take for Bubblez Burst to have 4050 subscribers?

3. How many days will it take for Bubblez Burst to reach 20,000 subscribers?

13

4. How did your methods in Question 2 and Question 3 differ?

So far, you have used estimation to determine the value of logarithms whose values were not integers. The *Change of Base Formula* allows you to calculate an exact value for a logarithm by rewriting it in terms of a different base. First, you will use the Change of Base Formula and then you will derive it.

Most calculators
can only evaluate
common logs and natural logs.
So, the Change of Base Formula
can be helpful to evaluate
logs of other bases.

The **Change of Base Formula** states:

$\log_b(c) = \dfrac{\log_a(c)}{\log_a(b)}$, where $a, b, c > 0$ and $a, b \neq 1$.

5. Rewrite the exponential equation you wrote in Question 3 as a logarithmic equation.

6. Use the Change of Base Formula to evaluate the logarithmic expression using common logs. Round to the nearest thousandth.

7. Compare your estimate in Question 3 with the calculated value in Question 6 by substituting each value back into the original equation. What do you notice?

Do a few
decimal places really
make that much of a
difference?

13

8. Use a calculator to determine how many days it will take for Bubblez Burst to reach one million subscribers.

9. Tammy was asked to approximate how many days it would take Bubblez Burst to reach 30,000 subscribers. Describe the calculation error Tammy made. Then, use your knowledge of estimation to explain why x could not equal 2.3.

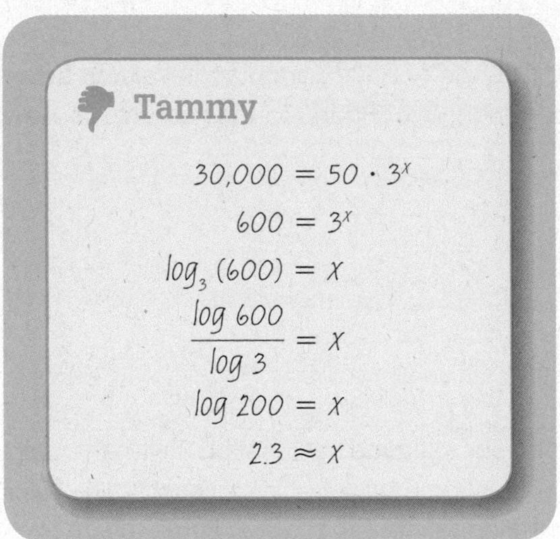
Tammy
$30{,}000 = 50 \cdot 3^x$
$600 = 3^x$
$\log_3(600) = x$
$\frac{\log 600}{\log 3} = x$
$\log 200 = x$
$2.3 \approx x$

10. In 2012, there were approximately 314 million people in the United States. In that year, how long would it take for everyone in the country to subscribe to Bubblez Burst?

PROBLEM 2 Log of Both Sides

Previously you solved exponential equations with common bases as well as exponential equations with common exponents.

1. Solve each exponential equation.

   a. $2^x = 64$

   b. $y^3 = 125$

2. Explain the strategy you used to solve each exponential equation in Question 1.

3. Solve each logarithmic equation.

   a. $\log_3 (w) = \log_3 (20)$

   b. $\log_m (9) = \log_4 (9)$

4. Explain the strategy you used to solve each logarithmic equation in Question 3.

13

You just derived the relationship that if $\log_b(a) = \log_b(c)$, then $a = c$. The converse is also true. If $a = c$, then $\log_b(a) = \log_b(c)$. You can use this knowledge to now derive the Change of Base Formula.

Taking the log of both sides of an equation keeps the equation balanced.

5. Todd and Danielle each solved the exponential equation $4^{x-1} = 50$.

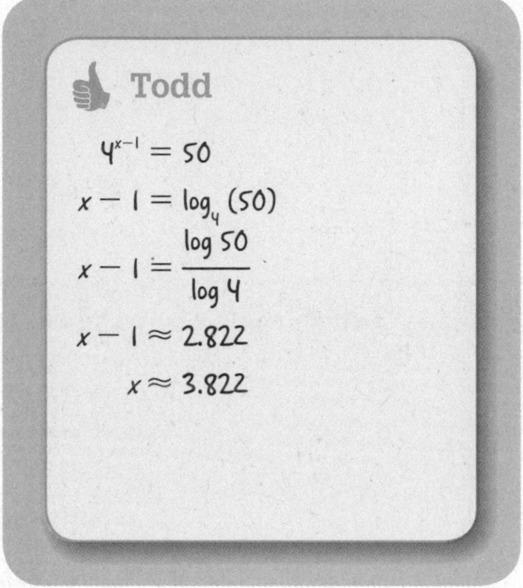

Todd

$$4^{x-1} = 50$$
$$x - 1 = \log_4(50)$$
$$x - 1 = \frac{\log 50}{\log 4}$$
$$x - 1 \approx 2.822$$
$$x \approx 3.822$$

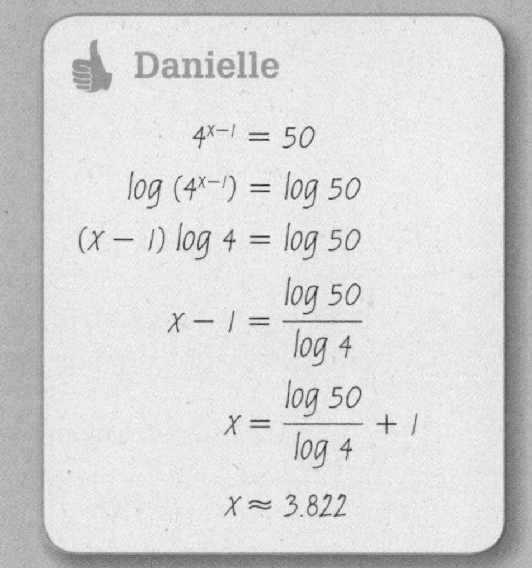

Danielle

$$4^{x-1} = 50$$
$$\log(4^{x-1}) = \log 50$$
$$(x - 1)\log 4 = \log 50$$
$$x - 1 = \frac{\log 50}{\log 4}$$
$$x = \frac{\log 50}{\log 4} + 1$$
$$x \approx 3.822$$

Describe how Todd's and Danielle's methods are different.

6. Consider the exponential equation $a^x = c$, where x is the unknown in the exponent and a and c are constants.

   a. Solve the exponential equation for x by rewriting it in logarithmic form.

   b. Solve the exponential equation for x by taking the log of both sides.

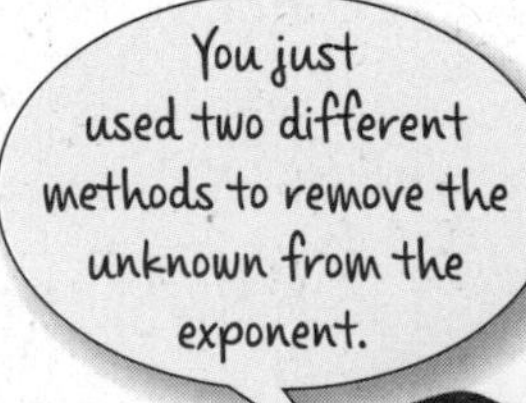
You just used two different methods to remove the unknown from the exponent.

13

c. How do the results from these two methods demonstrate the Change of Base Formula?

7. Solve the exponential equation $8^x = 38.96$ using both Todd's and Danielle's methods. Round to the nearest thousandth and check your work.

Remember that when solving equations, it's important to isolate the term with the variable first before solving.

13

8. John, Bobbi, and Randy each solved the equation $9^{x+4} = 27$.

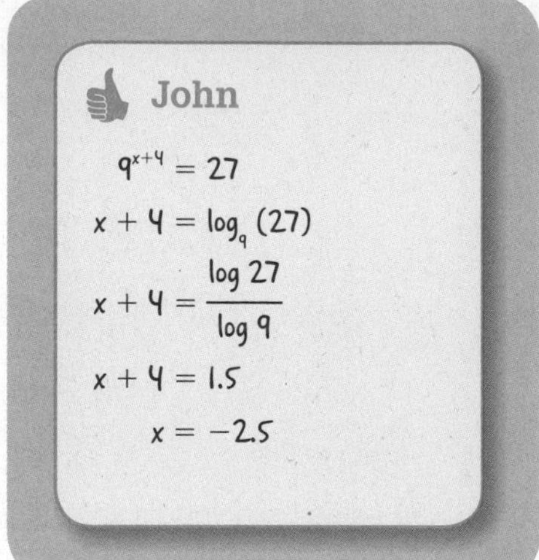
John
9^(x+4) = 27
x + 4 = log_9 (27)
x + 4 = log 27 / log 9
x + 4 = 1.5
x = −2.5

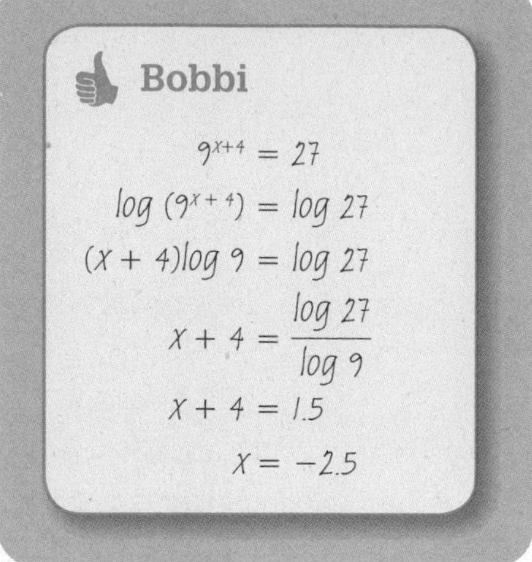
Bobbi
9^(x+4) = 27
log (9^(x+4)) = log 27
(x + 4)log 9 = log 27
x + 4 = log 27 / log 9
x + 4 = 1.5
x = −2.5

Randy
9^(x+4) = 27
(3^2)^(x+4) = 3^3
3^(2(x+4)) = 3^3
2(x + 4) = 3
2x + 8 = 3
2x = −5
x = −2.5

a. Describe each method used.

b. Will each method work for every logarithmic equation? Describe any limitations of each method.

9. Ameet and Neha each took the logarithm of both sides to solve $24^x = 5$.

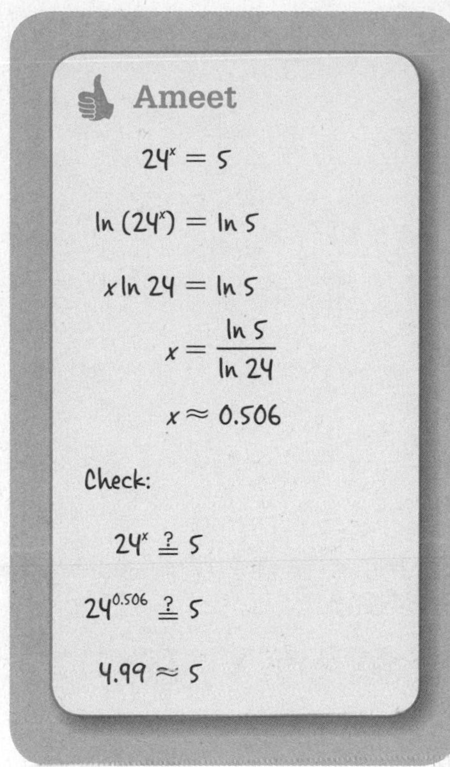
Ameet
$24^x = 5$
$\ln(24^x) = \ln 5$
$x \ln 24 = \ln 5$
$x = \frac{\ln 5}{\ln 24}$
$x \approx 0.506$
Check:
$24^x \stackrel{?}{=} 5$
$24^{0.506} \stackrel{?}{=} 5$
$4.99 \approx 5$

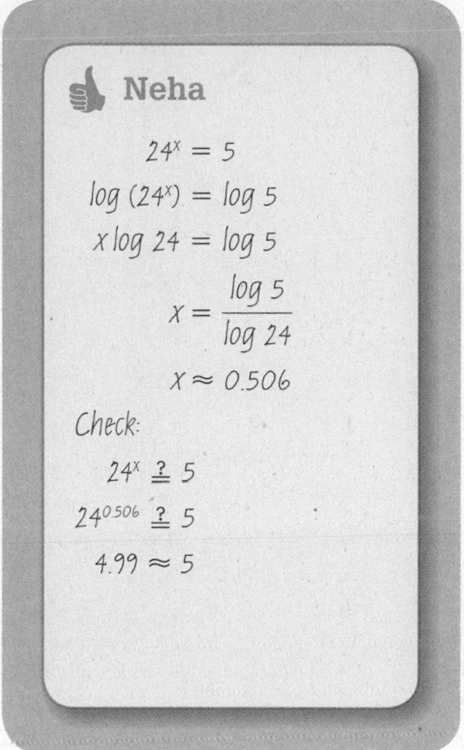
Neha
$24^x = 5$
$\log(24^x) = \log 5$
$x \log 24 = \log 5$
$x = \frac{\log 5}{\log 24}$
$x \approx 0.506$
Check:
$24^x \stackrel{?}{=} 5$
$24^{0.506} \stackrel{?}{=} 5$
$4.99 \approx 5$

Describe the similarities and differences in their methods. Explain why each student's method is correct.

13

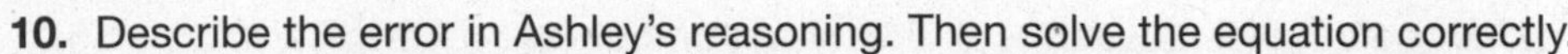

10. Describe the error in Ashley's reasoning. Then solve the equation correctly.

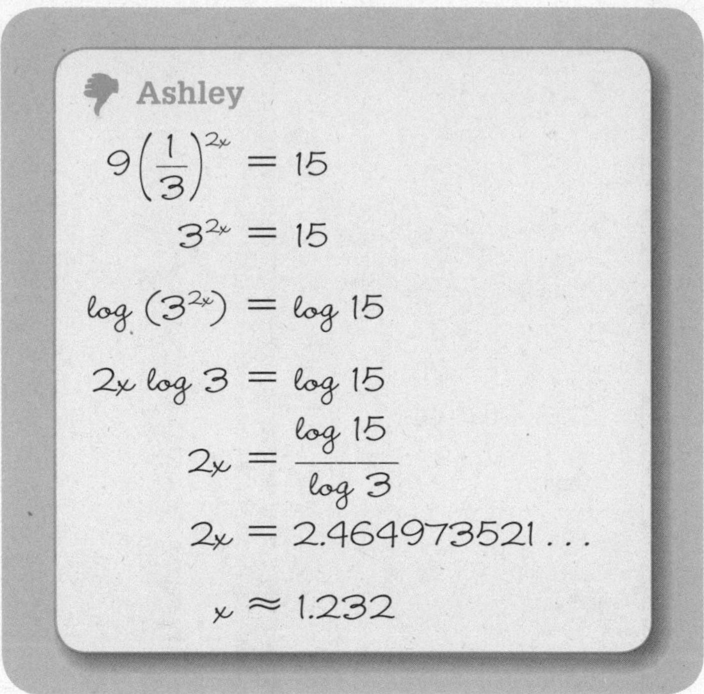
Ashley
$9\left(\frac{1}{3}\right)^{2x} = 15$
$3^{2x} = 15$
$\log(3^{2x}) = \log 15$
$2x \log 3 = \log 15$
$2x = \frac{\log 15}{\log 3}$
$2x = 2.464973521\ldots$
$x \approx 1.232$

11. Solve each exponential equation. Explain why you chose the method that you used.

a. $4^{x-3} - 5 = 16$

13

b. $10 \cdot \left(\frac{3}{2}\right)^{2x} = 360$

c. $2 \cdot 3^{5x} + 1 = 55$

13

Be prepared to share your solutions and methods.

13.4

Logging On

Solving Logarithmic Equations

LEARNING GOALS

In this lesson, you will:

- Solve for the base, argument, and exponent of logarithmic equations.
- Solve logarithmic equations using logarithmic properties.
- Solve logarithmic equations arising from real-world situations.
- Complete a decision tree to determine efficient methods for solving exponential and logarithmic equations.

Have you ever been asked to change your password?

Password strength is a measure of the effectiveness of a password in resisting guessing and brute-force attacks. In its usual form, it is an estimate of how many trials an attacker who does not have direct access to the password would need, on average, to guess it correctly. The strength of a password is a function of its length, complexity, and unpredictability.

Passwords are there to protect your private information, so make sure your password follows some common guidelines:

- A minimum password length of 12 to 14 characters, if permitted.
- Avoid passwords that use repetition, dictionary words, letter or number patterns, usernames, relative or pet names, or other biographical information.
- Include numbers, symbols, and capital and lowercase letters if allowed by the system.
- Avoid using the same password for multiple sites.

Can you recognize the difference between a strong and a weak password?

PROBLEM 1 Keep It Down!

A decibel is a unit used to measure the loudness of sound. The formula for the loudness of a sound is given by

$$\text{dB} = 10 \log\left(\frac{I}{I_0}\right)$$

where dB is the decibel level. The quantity I_0 is the intensity of the threshold sound—a sound that can barely be perceived. The quantity I is the number of times more intense a sound is than the threshold sound.

1. The sound in a quiet library is about 1000 times as intense as the threshold sound: $I = 1000I_0$. Calculate the decibel level of a quiet library.

2. The sound of traffic on a city street is calculated to be 500 million times as intense as the threshold sound. Calculate the decibel level for city traffic.

13

3. The sound of a crying baby registers at 115 decibels. How many times more intense is this sound than the threshold sound?

Each equation you wrote in Questions 1 through 3 is a logarithmic equation. To solve for an unknown in a simple logarithmic equation, you consider the relationship between the base, argument, and exponent.

Previously, you developed two strategies to solve for any unknown in a simple logarithmic equation:

- Rewrite the logarithmic equation as an exponential equation.
- Apply the Change of Base Formula.

When solving equations with a certain method, it is important to consider the number of steps involved. The more steps there are, the more chances you have to introduce an error in your calculations. Methods with fewer steps can be more accurate and efficient.

13

4. Solve each logarithmic equation using two different methods.

	Example	First rewrite as an exponential equation. Then solve for x.	First apply the Change of Base Formula. Then solve for x.
Argument Is Unknown	$\log_5(x) = 3.1$		
Exponent Is Unknown	$\log_8(145) = x$		
Base Is Unknown	$\log_x(24) = 6.7$		

13

5. Consider the position of the unknown for each logarithmic equation in Question 4. Circle your preferred method for solving. Explain your choice.

6. When might it be more efficient to solve a simple logarithmic equation by rewriting it in exponential form?

7. When might it be more efficient to solve a simple logarithmic equation by applying the Change of Base Formula?

13

8. Circle the logarithmic equations that can be solved more efficiently when rewritten as exponential equations. Box the equations that can be solved more efficiently by applying the Change of Base Formula. Explain your choice.

a. $\log_4 (x + 3) = \frac{1}{2}$

b. $\log_{4.5} (9) = x - 1$

c. $\log_{x+2} (7.1) = 3$

d. $\log_3 (4.6) = 2 - x$

e. $\ln (x + 4) = 3.8$

f. $\log_{11} (12) = x - 7$

13

g. $\log_{1-x} (8) = 14.7$

h. $\log (4 - x) = 1.3$

9. Solve each logarithmic equation. Check your work.

   a. $\log_2 (x^2 - 6x) = 4$

   b. $\log_6 (x^2 + x) = 1$

13

PROBLEM 2 Doctor, Doctor!

While most medications have guidelines for dosage amounts, doctors must also determine how long a medication will last when they write prescriptions. The amount of medicine left in a patient's body can be predicted by the formula

$$t = \frac{\log\left(\frac{C}{A}\right)}{\log(1 - r)}$$

where t is the time in hours since the medicine was administered, C is the current amount of medicine left in the patient's body in milligrams, A is the original dose of the medicine in milligrams, and r is the rate at which the medicine leaves the body.

1. A patient is given 10 milligrams of medicine which leaves the body at the rate of 20% per hour. How long will it take for 2 milligrams of the medicine to remain in the patient's body?

2. Six hours after administering a 20-milligram dose of medicine, 5 milligrams remain in a patient's body. At what rate is the medicine leaving the body?

3. A patient is undergoing an 8-hour surgery. If 4 milligrams of medicine must be left in the patient's body at the end of surgery, and the medicine leaves the body at the rate of 15% per hour, how much medicine must be administered at the start of surgery?

13

If a logarithmic equation involves multiple logarithms, you can use the properties of logarithms to rewrite the equation in a form you already know how to solve.

4. Analyze Georgia's, Santiago's, and Lorenzo's work.

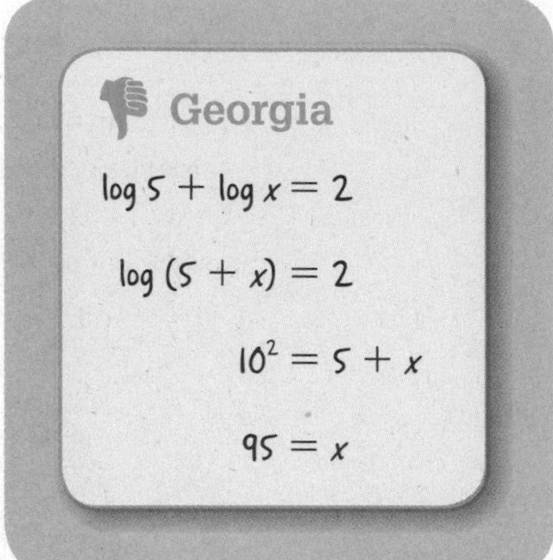

Georgia
$\log 5 + \log x = 2$
$\log(5 + x) = 2$
$10^2 = 5 + x$
$95 = x$

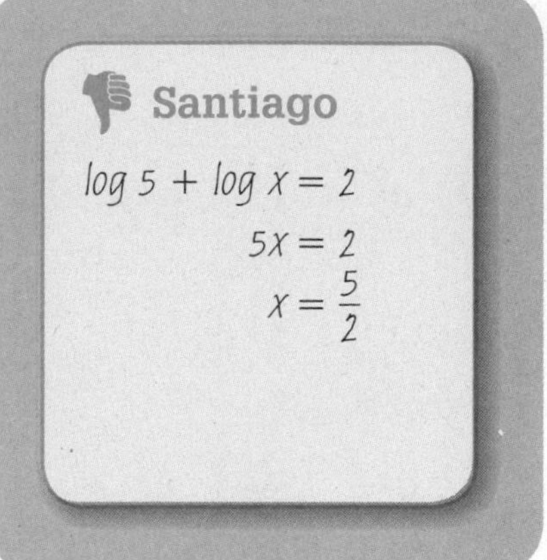

Santiago
$\log 5 + \log x = 2$
$5x = 2$
$x = \frac{5}{2}$

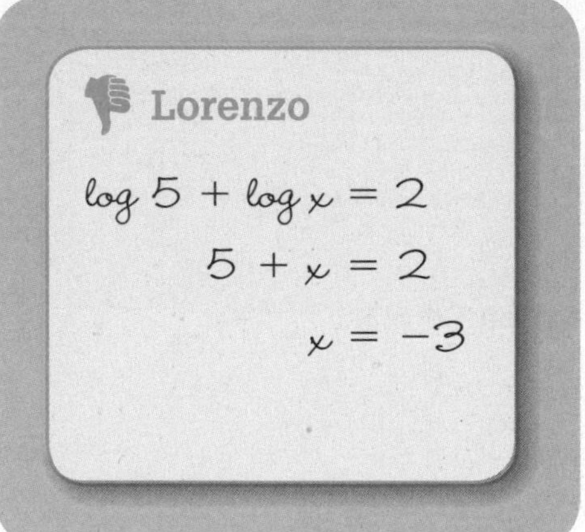

Lorenzo
$\log 5 + \log x = 2$
$5 + x = 2$
$x = -3$

a. Explain the error in each student's reasoning.

b. Solve $\log 5 + \log x = 2$. Check your work.

5. Solve each logarithmic equation. Check your work.

a. $\log_5 (45x) - \log_5 (3) = 1$

Don't forget the restrictions on the variables for the logarithmic equation, $y = \log_b x$. The variable y can be any real number, the base b must be greater than 0 and not equal to 1, and the argument x must be greater than zero.

b. $\log_2 (8) + 3 \log_2 (x) = 6$

13

6. Pippa and Kate disagree about the solution to the logarithmic equation $\log_5 x^2 - \log_5 4 = 2$.

Kate

$\log_5 (x^2) - \log_5 (4) = 2$

$\log_5 \left(\frac{x^2}{4}\right) = 2$

$5^2 = \frac{x^2}{4}$

$25 = \frac{x^2}{4}$

$100 = x^2$

$x = 10, -10$

Pippa

$\log_5 (x^2) - \log_5 (4) = 2$

$\log_5 \left(\frac{x^2}{4}\right) = 2$

$5^2 = \frac{x^2}{4}$

$25 = \frac{x^2}{4}$

$100 = x^2$

$x = 10, \cancel{-10}$

Reject −10 because the argument of a logarithm must be greater than zero.

Who is correct? Explain your reasoning.

13

7. Solve $\log_3 (x - 4) + \log_3 (x + 2) = 3$. Check your work.

8. Elijah and Zander each solved the logarithmic equation $2 \log 6 = \log x - \log 2$.

Elijah

$2 \log 6 = \log x - \log 2$

$\log (6^2) = \log \left(\frac{x}{2}\right)$

$36 = \frac{x}{2}$

$72 = x$

Check: $2 \log 6 \stackrel{?}{=} \log 72 - \log 2$

$\log (6^2) \stackrel{?}{=} \log \left(\frac{72}{2}\right)$

$\log 36 = \log 36$

Zander

$2 \log 6 = \log x - \log 2$

$\log (6^2) - \log x + \log 2 = 0$

$\log \left(\frac{36}{x}\right) + \log 2 = 0$

$\log \left(\frac{72}{x}\right) = 0$

$10^0 = \frac{72}{x}$

$1 = \frac{72}{x}$

$x = 72$

Check: $2 \log 6 \stackrel{?}{=} \log 72 - \log 2$

$\log (6^2) \stackrel{?}{=} \log \left(\frac{72}{2}\right)$

$\log 36 = \log 36$

Explain why each student's method is correct.

9. Solve each logarithmic equation. Check your work.

a. $2 \log (x + 1) = \log x + \log (x + 3)$

13

b. $2 \log (x - 3) = \log 4 + \log \left(x - \frac{15}{4}\right)$

c. $\ln (x - 3) + \ln (x - 2) = \ln (2x + 24)$

d. $2 \log_3 x = \log_3 4 + \log_3 16$

13

Talk the Talk

You have solved a variety of exponential and logarithmic equations. When doing so, you have had to consider the structure and characteristics of each equation.

The list shown contains an example of each type of exponential and logarithmic equation you have solved.

- $2^{x+2} = 32$
- $\log_6 (x + 7) = \log_6 31$
- $4^{5.1} = x$
- $\log_3 (x) - \log_3 (9) = 5$
- $5^x = 17$
- $\log x + \log 2 = \log 24 - \log 3$
- $x^{5.5} = 22$
- $\log_8 (x) = 0.3$

1. Complete the decision tree on the following pages to demonstrate the most advantageous strategy to solve each type of equation.
   a. For each branch of the decision tree, write the appropriate example equation from the list.
   b. Describe the first step you would use to solve each equation.

13

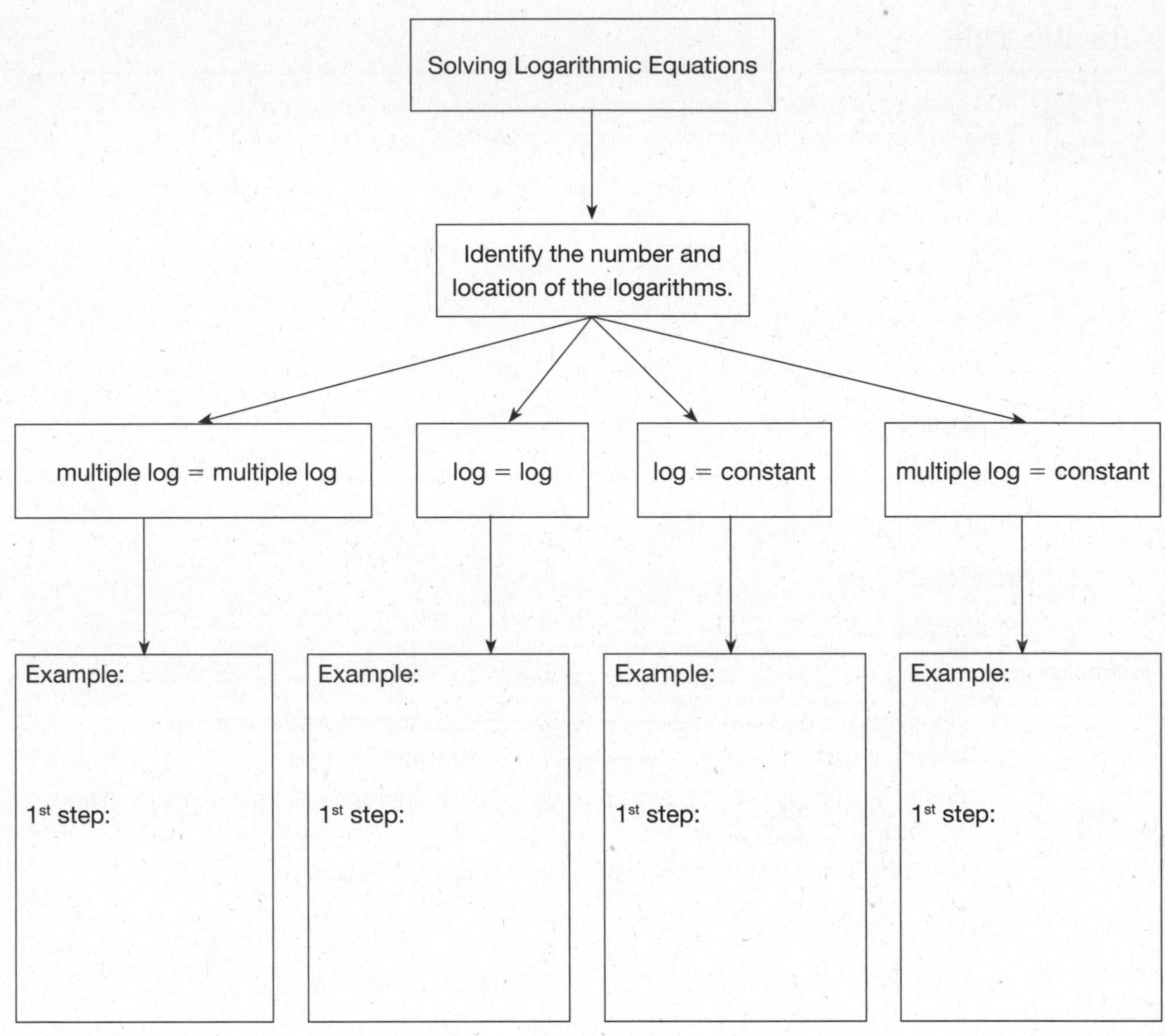
Solving Logarithmic Equations
Identify the number and location of the logarithms.
multiple log = multiple log
log = log
log = constant
multiple log = constant
Example:
1st step:
Example:
1st step:
Example:
1st step:
Example:
1st step:

13

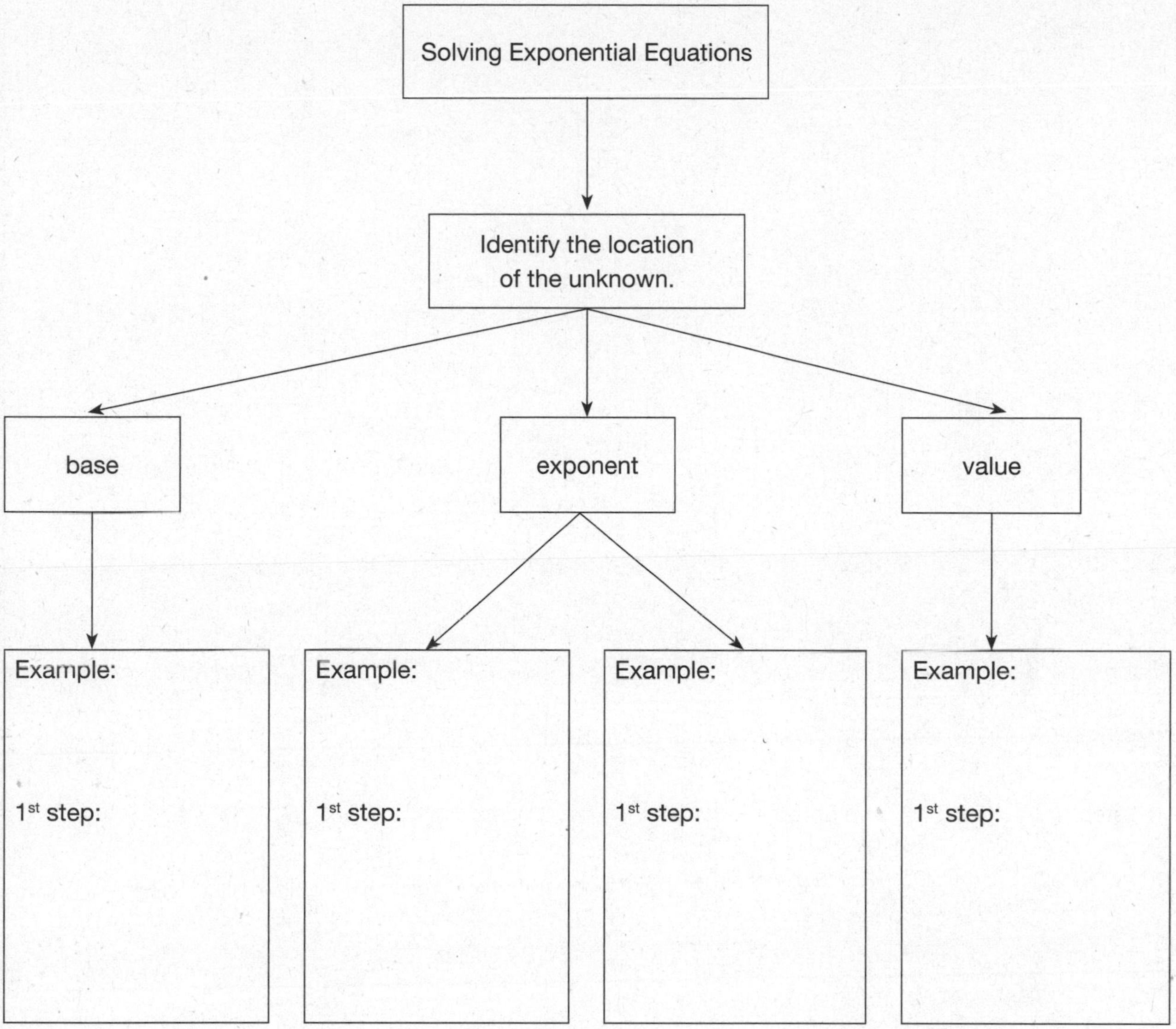

Solving Exponential Equations

Identify the location of the unknown.

base	exponent		value
Example:	Example:	Example:	Example:
1st step:	1st step:	1st step:	1st step:

Be prepared to share your solutions and methods.

13.5

So When Will I Use This?

Applications of Exponential and Logarithmic Equations

LEARNING GOALS

In this lesson, you will:

- Use exponential models to analyze problem situations.
- Use logarithmic models to analyze problem situations.

Crime investigators use logarithmic equations to estimate a body's time of death based on two temperature readings of the body. Specifically, investigators use what's known as Newton's Law of Cooling, which states that an object cools down at a rate that is proportional to the temperature difference between the object and the environment.

Coroners—government officials who are responsible for verifying deaths—often use a rule of thumb to estimate the time of death: subtract 2 degrees from normal body temperature for the first hour after death and then 1 degree for each hour after that.

PROBLEM 1 Efficient pHarming

The pH scale is a scale for measuring the acidity or alkalinity of a substance, which is determined by the concentration of hydrogen ions. The formula for pH is

$$pH = -\log H^+$$

where H^+ is the concentration of hydrogen ions in moles per cubic liter. Solutions with a pH value less than 7 are acidic. Solutions with a pH value greater than 7 are alkaline. Solutions with a pH of 7 are neutral. For example, plain water has a pH of 7.

1. The H^+ concentration in orange juice is 0.000199 mole per cubic liter. Determine the pH level of orange juice, and then state whether it is acidic or alkaline.

2. The concentration of hydrogen ions in baking soda is 5.012×10^{-9} mole per cubic liter. Determine the pH level of baking soda, and then state whether it is acidic or alkaline.

The "p" in "pH" stands for "power."

3. Vinegar has a pH of 2.2. Determine the concentration of hydrogen ions in vinegar.

13

4. Lime water has a pH of 12. Determine the concentration of hydrogen ions in lime water.

The pH level of soil is used to determine which plants will grow best in an area. Different types of plants and vegetables require varying degrees of soil acidity. Generally, the soil tends to be acidic in moist climates and alkaline in dry climates.

The chart shows the optimal pH soil levels for a variety of fruits and vegetables.

Asparagus 6.5 – 7.5	**Avocados** 6.0 – 7.0	**Beets** 5.6 – 6.6
Carrots 5.0 – 6.0	**Garlic** 5.0 – 6.0	**Lettuce** 6.5 – 7.0
Mushrooms 7.0 – 8.0	**Onions** 6.2 – 6.8	**Peanuts** 5.0 – 6.0
Peppers 6.0 – 8.0	**Potatoes** 5.8 – 6.5	**Raspberries** 6.0 – 6.5
Spinach 5.0 – 7.0	**Sweet Corn** 6.0 – 7.0	**Yams** 6.0 – 8.0

5. A farmer measures the hydrogen ion concentration of the soil to be 6×10^{-7} mole per cubic liter. List the crops that the farmer can grow in this type of soil.

13

6. Determine the range of the soil's optimal hydrogen ion concentration for growing onions.

7. The farmer wants to plant spinach, carrots, and beets. She measures the hydrogen ion concentration of the soil to be 3.16×10^{-6} mole per cubic liter. Is her plan feasible? Explain your reasoning.

13

PROBLEM 2 Follow Me!

Gina, a social media manager, uses the model for continuous population growth to project the monthly increase in the number of followers on her clients' social media sites.

1. Recall that the formula for continuous population growth is $N(t) = N_0e^{rt}$. State what each quantity represents in terms of this problem situation.

2. Gina claims that when she started working with an up-and-coming boy band, they had 18,450 online followers and she was able to increase their followers by 26% per month.

   a. Use Gina's claim to write a function to represent the number of online followers that the boy band had after t months.

   b. If Gina started working with the band on May 1st, how many online followers did they have by September 1st?

   c. How long did it take for the band to surpass 100,000 online followers?

Don't round your decimals until the very end! Instead, use the "ANS" feature on your calculator to recall the previous step.

13

3. Gina's top client is a pro football quarterback. On her website, Gina claims that since she began managing his account three years ago, his online followers have grown to 105,326.

   a. If he had 4125 online followers when he hired Gina, at what monthly rate did his number of online followers grow?

   b. Write an exponential function to represent the number of online followers the quarterback will have in any given month, assuming the number of followers continues to grow at the same rate.

   c. How long would it take the quarterback to double his current online following of 105,326?

13

4. Gina also manages a running back on the same team who currently has 62,100 online followers. If he has seen a 14% increase in his followers, how many people followed him when he hired Gina 15 months ago?

5. Will the running back ever have the same number of online followers as the quarterback? If so, when? If not, explain your reasoning.

6. Gina acquires a talk show host as a new client. The host currently has 5200 online followers.

   a. Gina claims that she can triple the host's number of online followers in 6 months. Determine the rate per month of increased online following.

13

b. Josh decides to check Gina's work.

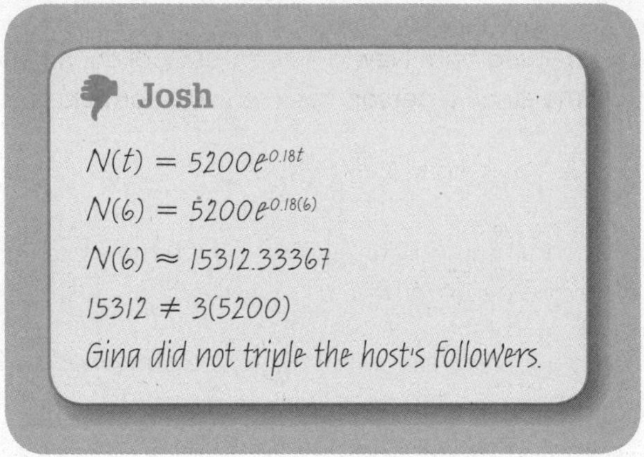

Josh
$N(t) = 5200e^{0.18t}$
$N(6) = 5200e^{0.18(6)}$
$N(6) \approx 15312.33367$
$15312 \neq 3(5200)$
Gina did not triple the host's followers.

What is the error in Josh's method? Check Gina's work correctly.

c. Assuming that Gina's promised rate of growth is true, project how many followers the talk show host will have in a year.

PROBLEM 3 Cracking the Case

A coroner uses a formula derived from Newton's Law of Cooling, a general cooling principle, to calculate the elapsed time since a person has died. The formula is

$$t = -10 \ln\left(\frac{T - R}{98.6 - R}\right)$$

where T is the body's measured temperature in °F, R is the constant room temperature in °F, and t is the elapsed time since death in hours.

1. At 8:30 AM a coroner was called to the home of a person who had died. The constant temperature of the room where the body was found is 70°F.

   a. At 9:00 AM the body's measured temperature was 85.5°F. Use this body temperature to estimate the time of death.

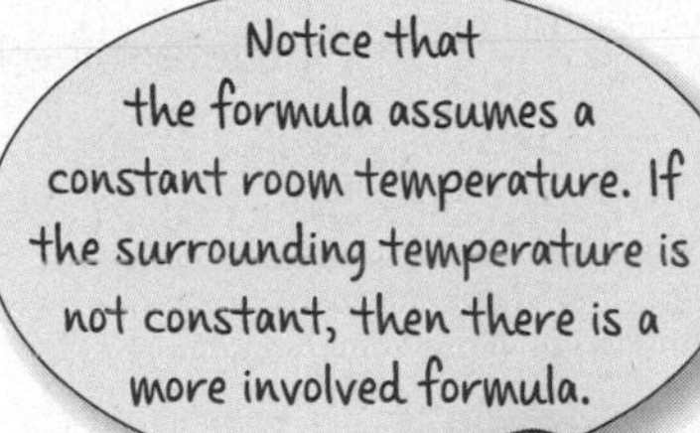

Notice that the formula assumes a constant room temperature. If the surrounding temperature is not constant, then there is a more involved formula.

A more accurate estimate of the time of death is found by taking two or more readings and averaging the calculated times of death.

   b. At 9:30 AM the body's measured temperature was 82.9°F. Use this body temperature to estimate the time of death.

c. Compare the estimated time of death from part (a) and (b). Are your answers fairly close? Determine a more accurate estimated time of death.

d. Assuming the body remains in a room with a constant temperature of 70°F, determine the temperature of the body after 24 hours.

e. When will the temperature of the body drop to 60°F? Explain your reasoning.

13

2. At 6:00 PM, a coroner was called to the home of a person who had died. The body was found at the bottom of the stairs in a hallway, where the constant temperature is 65°F. At 6:30 PM the body's measured temperature was 95.9°F, and at 7:00 PM the body's measured temperature was 93.7°F.

A witness claims that the person fell down the stairs around 5:30 pm, and she immediately called for an ambulance. Is her statement consistent with the forensic evidence?

13

Be prepared to share your solutions and methods.

13

Chapter 13 Summary

KEY TERMS

- logarithmic equation (13.1)
- Zero Property of Logarithms (13.2)
- Logarithm with Same Base and Argument (13.2)
- Product Rule of Logarithms (13.2)
- Quotient Rule of Logarithms (13.2)
- Power Rule of Logarithms (13.2)
- Change of Base Formula (13.3)

13.1 Writing Exponential and Logarithmic Equations

A logarithmic function is the inverse of an exponential function. The diagram below shows the relationship between the base, argument, and exponent of logarithmic and exponential equations.

$\text{base}^{\text{exponent}} = \text{argument} \quad \Leftrightarrow \quad \log_{\text{base}} (\text{argument}) = \text{exponent}$

Example

Arrange the terms 3, 4, and 81 to create a true exponential equation and a true logarithmic equation.

Exponential equation: $3^4 = 81$

Logarithmic equation: $\log_3 (81) = 4$

13.1 Solving Logarithmic Equations

To solve a logarithmic equation, begin by converting it to an exponential equation. If the argument is unknown, writing the equation in exponential form will isolate the argument and make it simpler to solve. If the exponent is unknown, you will need to rewrite both sides of the exponential equation so that they have the same base. If the base is unknown, you will need to rewrite both sides of the exponential equation so that they have the same exponent.

Example

Solve the logarithmic equation.

$$\log_n (\sqrt[3]{25}) = \frac{2}{3}$$

$$n^{\frac{2}{3}} = \sqrt[3]{25}$$

$$n^{\frac{2}{3}} = 25^{\frac{1}{3}}$$

$$n^{\frac{2}{3}} = (5^2)^{\frac{1}{3}}$$

$$n^{\frac{2}{3}} = 5^{\frac{2}{3}}$$

$$n = 5$$

13.1 Estimating Logarithms

To estimate the value of a logarithm, identify the closest logarithm whose argument is less than the given argument and the closest logarithm whose argument is greater than the given argument. If the argument is closer to the lower limit, the value of the given logarithm will also be closer to the value of the logarithm of the lower limit. Similarly, if the argument is closer to the upper limit, the value of the given logarithm will also be closer to the value of the logarithm of the upper limit.

Example

Estimate the value of $\log_6 (210)$ to the nearest tenth.

$$\log_6 (36) < \log_6 (210) < \log_6 (216)$$

$$2 < n < 3$$

Because 210 is closer to 216 than 36, the approximation should be closer to 3 than 2. Therefore, $\log_6 (210) \approx 2.9$.

13.2 Writing Logarithmic Expressions in Expanded Form

To write a logarithmic expression in expanded form, use the properties of logarithms.

Example

Write the logarithmic expression $\log_3 \left(\frac{5x^2}{2y^5}\right)$ in expanded form.

$$\log_3 \left(\frac{5x^2}{2y^5}\right) = \log_3 (5) + 2 \log_3 (x) - \log_3 (2) - 5 \log_3 (y)$$

13.2 Writing Logarithmic Expressions as a Single Logarithm

To write a logarithmic expression as a single logarithm, use the properties of logarithms.

Example

Write the logarithmic expression $4 \log_6 (x) + 2 \log_6 (y) - 7 \log_6 (x)$ as a single logarithm.

$$4 \log_6 (x) + 2 \log_6 (y) - 7 \log_6 (x) = \log_6 \left(\frac{x^4 y^2}{x^7}\right)$$

$$= \log_6 \left(\frac{y^2}{x^3}\right)$$

13

13.3 Solving Exponential Equations Using the Change of Base Formula

The Change of Base Formula states that $\log_b(c) = \frac{\log_a(c)}{\log_a(b)}$, where $a, b, c > 0$ and $a, b \neq 1$. To solve an exponential equation using the Change of Base Formula, first write the equation using logarithms. Next, write the logarithm as the quotient of the common log of the argument and the common log of the base. Use your calculator to determine that quotient. Finally, solve for the variable.

Example

Solve the exponential equation by using the Change of Base Formula.

$$8^{3x-4} = 257$$

$$3x - 4 = \frac{\log 257}{\log 8}$$

$$3x - 4 \approx 2.669$$

$$3x \approx 6.669$$

$$x \approx 2.223$$

13.3 Solving Exponential Equations by Taking the Log of Both Sides

To solve an exponential equation by taking the log of both sides, first isolate the variable term on one side. Next, take the common log of both sides. Use your calculator to determine the common logs. Then, solve for the variable.

Example

Solve the exponential equation by taking the log of both sides.

$$6^{x-5} + 7 = 259$$

$$6^{x-5} = 252$$

$$\log(6^{x-5}) = \log 252$$

$$(x - 5)\log 6 = \log 252$$

$$x - 5 = \frac{\log 252}{\log 6}$$

$$x - 5 \approx 3.086$$

$$x \approx 8.086$$

13

13.4 Solving Logarithmic Equations

To solve a logarithmic equation, rewrite the equation using exponents or rewrite the equation using the properties of logarithms. Then, solve.

Example

Solve the logarithmic equation. Check your answer.

$$\log_6 x + \log_6 (x + 5) = 2$$

$$\log_6 (x(x + 5)) = 2$$

$$\log_6 (x^2 + 5x) = 2$$

$$x^2 + 5x = 6^2$$

$$x^2 + 5x - 36 = 0$$

$$(x + 9)(x - 4) = 0$$

$$x = \cancel{-9}, 4$$

Check: -9 is an extraneous solution.

$$\log_6 4 + \log_6 (4 + 5) \stackrel{?}{=} 2$$

$$\log_6 (4(9)) \stackrel{?}{=} 2$$

$$\log_6 (36) \stackrel{?}{=} 2$$

$$6^2 \stackrel{?}{=} 36$$

$$36 = 36$$

13

13.5 Using Exponential Models to Analyze Problem Situations

Some problem situations can be modeled with exponential equations. To solve these problems, identify what the question is asking and then use the given model to determine the answer.

Example

The given exponential equation models the appraised value of a vehicle over time. Use the model to answer the question.

Given $V = 47{,}000(10^{-0.0499t})$, where t represents the time in years, determine how old the vehicle is if its appraised value is \$21,028.

$$V = 47{,}000(10^{-0.0499t})$$

$$21{,}028 = 47{,}000(10^{-0.0499t})$$

$$0.4474042553 \approx 10^{-0.0499t}$$

$$\log 0.4474042553 \approx \log 10^{-0.0499t}$$

$$\log 0.4474042553 \approx -0.0499t \log 10$$

$$-0.3492998896 \approx -0.0499t$$

$$6.999997787 \approx t$$

The vehicle is about 7 years old.

13

13.5 Using Logarithmic Models to Analyze Problem Situations

Some problem situations can be modeled with logarithmic equations. To solve these problems, identify what the question is asking and then use the given model to determine the answer.

Example

The number of monthly payments a person must make to repay a car loan or a home mortgage can be determined by the formula $n = \frac{-\log\left(1 - \frac{I \cdot P_0}{p}\right)}{\log(1 + I)}$, where P_0 represents the original value of the loan, p represents the amount of the monthly payment, and I is the interest rate per payment period in decimal form.

Calculate the number of payments of $540 per month that would need to be made on a $79,000 mortgage loan at 4.2% interest.

$$n = \frac{-\log\left(1 - \frac{I \cdot P_0}{p}\right)}{\log(1 + I)}$$

$$= \frac{-\log\left(1 - \frac{\left(\frac{0.042}{12}\right)(79{,}000)}{540}\right)}{\log\left(1 + \frac{0.042}{12}\right)}$$

$$\approx \frac{-\log(1 - 0.512037037)}{\log(1 + 0.0035)}$$

$$\approx \frac{-\log 0.487962963}{\log 1.0035}$$

$$\approx \frac{0.3116131403}{0.0015173768}$$

$$\approx 205.3630583$$

A little more than 205 monthly payments would need to be made to pay off the loan.

13

Modeling with Functions

14

You are
looking at a
picture of a cat looking at
a picture of a cat looking at a
cture of a cat . . . But you are
lso looking at a mathematical
process of repetition and
self-similarity called
recursion.

14

It's Not New, It's Recycled

Composition of Functions

14.1

LEARNING GOALS

In this lesson, you will:

- Perform the composition of two functions graphically and algebraically.
- Use composition of functions to determine whether two functions are inverses of each other.
- Add, subtract, multiply, and divide with functions.
- Determine the restricted domain of a composite function.

KEY TERM

- identity function

A lot of people use coupons to save money on all kinds of items, especially groceries. And a few people really get into saving money with coupons. These strategic shoppers put a great deal of time and effort into spending as little money as possible.

How much can they save? Try $1100 in groceries for only $40.

But this is just a rare and extreme example. And it has been found that such "extreme couponing" isn't worth the time required to make it extremely successful—especially when that time could be spent earning income at a job instead. Yet, the allure of saving money has led some to harmful habits and even criminal behavior!

PROBLEM 1 Extreme Couponing

1. Betty is in the market for a new flat screen TV. She has two coupons that she can use to purchase the television. One coupon is for 20% off the original price and the other coupon is for $100 off the original price.

   a. Write a function $p(x)$ to represent the discounted price of the television after the 20% off coupon is applied.

   b. Write a function $d(x)$ to represent the discounted price of the television after the $100 off coupon is applied.

   c. Which coupon should Betty use? Justify your answer.

Is one
choice always
better than the other?
Are they ever the same?

2. Suppose Betty is able to use both coupons. If the television that she wants costs $350, in which order should Betty apply the coupons to yield the lowest final price? Show your work.

14

3. Suppose Betty uses the 20% off coupon first, followed by the $100 off coupon. Write the function $t(x)$ that represents the discounted price of a television that costs x dollars.

4. Suppose Betty uses the $100 off coupon first, followed by the 20% off coupon. Write the function $m(x)$ that represents the discounted price of a television that costs x dollars.

Recall that the process of evaluating one function inside of another function is called composition of functions. For two functions f and g, the composition of functions uses the output of $g(x)$ as the input of $f(x)$. It is notated as $(f \circ g)(x)$ or $f(g(x))$. The resulting function is called a composite function.

The two functions $t(x)$ and $m(x)$ that you wrote in Questions 3 and 4 can also be written as compositions of the original functions $p(x)$ and $d(x)$.

5. Rewrite $t(x)$ as $d(p(x))$ and $m(x)$ as $p(d(x))$.

6. Based on the functions $t(x)$ and $m(x)$, what can you conclude about the order to apply a percentage off coupon and a flat rate coupon? Explain your reasoning.

14

7. Determine the meaning of the composition of the two functions, $(f \circ g)(x)$. Give a possible real-life example for each.

   a. $f(x)$ = volume is a function of depth
      $g(x)$ = depth is a function of time

   b. $f(x)$ = cost is a function of consumption
      $g(x)$ = consumption is a function of appetite

   c. $f(x)$ = area is a function of radius
      $g(x)$ = radius is a function of time

14

Just as the composition function $f(g(x))$ can also be written as $(f \circ g)(x)$, you can write all function operations with similar notation.

8. In each row of the table, write the equivalent notation and describe what the notation means.

Equivalent Function Notation		Description in Words
$f(x) + g(x)$	$(f + g)(x)$	
$f(x) - g(x)$	$(f - g)(x)$	
$f(x) \cdot g(x)$	$(fg)(x)$	
$\frac{f(x)}{g(x)}$	$\left(\frac{f}{g}\right)(x)$	
$f(g(x))$	$(f \circ g)(x)$	

9. Consider the graphs of the functions $f(x)$ and $g(x)$. Determine each value. Explain your reasoning.

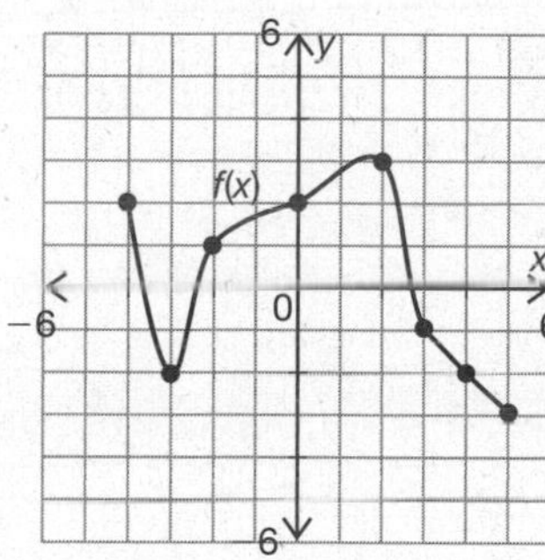

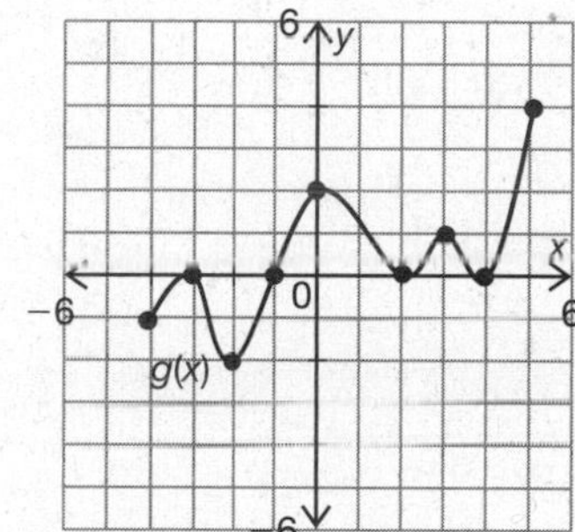

a. $f(3)$

b. $g^{-1}(4)$

c. $f(g(4))$

d. $g(f(4))$

14

e. $g(f^{-1}(-3))$

f. $(fg)(3)$

g. $(f - g)(5)$

h. $f(g^{-1}(0))$

i. $f(f^{-1}(3))$

j. $(f + g)(0)$

10. Consider the expressions in Question 9 that represent function composition.

a. Describe the similarities.

b. What distinguished them from the functions that were not composition?

14

PROBLEM 2 Calm, Cool, and Composed

1. Consider the functions $f(x) = 3x - 1$ and $g(x) = x^2 + 4$. Evaluate each composition of functions.

   a. $f(g(-2))$

   b. $g(f(-2))$

   c. $g(g(0))$

   d. $f(g(2x))$

   e. $f(g(x))$

   f. $g(f(x))$

2. Jess was asked to determine the composite function $(m \circ p)(x)$ given the functions $m(x) = 5 - x$ and $p(x) = 3x^2 + x$.

a. Describe the error in Jess's method.

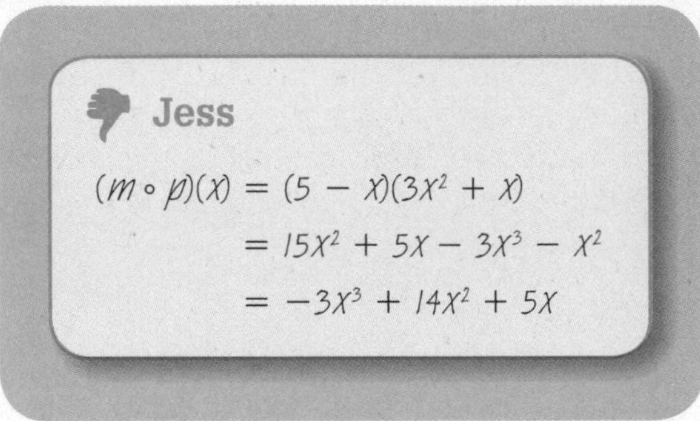

Jess
$(m \circ p)(x) = (5 - x)(3x^2 + x)$
$= 15x^2 + 5x - 3x^3 - x^2$
$= -3x^3 + 14x^2 + 5x$

b. Determine the correct composite function $(m \circ p)(x)$.

c. Is $(p \circ m)(x)$ equivalent to $(m \circ p)(x)$? Explain your reasoning.

3. Determine $(f \circ g)(x)$ and $(g \circ f)(x)$ for each pair of functions $f(x)$ and $g(x)$.

a. $f(x) = 5^{x-1}$

$g(x) = x + 3$

b. $f(x) = 5^{x-1}$

$g(x) = \log_5 x + 1$

c. $f(x) = 0.5x + 1.5$

$g(x) = 2x - 3$

d. $f(x) = 2x^2 - x$

$g(x) = \sqrt{x}$

14

4. Compare the compositions $(f \circ g)(x)$ and $(g \circ f)(x)$ from Question 3.

   a. Identify the pairs of functions in which $f(g(x))$ and $g(f(x))$ are equivalent functions. Describe the similarities.

   b. Determine the relationship between the functions you identified in part (a).

Consider these two statements:

- The additive identity is 0. It results when two quantities that are additive inverses are added.
- The multiplicative identity is 1. It results when two quantities that are multiplicative inverses are multiplied.

5. How would you describe the composition identity? Provide an example to support your claim.

14

The *identity function* is the function that maps every real number x to the same real number x. The composition identity, also known as the **identity function**, is defined as $f(x) = x$.

6. Use composition of functions to determine whether the given functions are inverses of each other.

a. $c(x) = \frac{1}{x} - 6$

$d(x) = \frac{1}{x + 6}$

b. $z(x) = \frac{5}{4}x + 3$

$w(x) = \frac{4}{5}x - 3$

c. $r(x) = 2e^{x+4}$

$t(x) = \ln\left(\frac{x}{2}\right) - 4$

14

7. Maggie is asked to determine whether $f(x) = x^3 + 1$ and $g(x) = \sqrt[3]{x} + 1$ are inverse functions.

Maggie

The two functions are equivalent at the value $x = 0$, so they must be inverse functions.

$$\begin{aligned}(f \circ g)(0) &= f(g(0)) \\ &= f(\sqrt[3]{0} + 1) \\ &= f(1) \\ &= 1^3 + 1 \\ &= 2\end{aligned}$$

$$\begin{aligned}(g \circ f)(0) &= g(f(0)) \\ &= g(0^3 + 1) \\ &= g(1) \\ &= \sqrt[3]{1} + 1 \\ &= 2\end{aligned}$$

Explain why Maggie's method is insufficient, and provide a counterexample.

8. For each composite function, determine two functions $h(x)$ and $k(x)$ that when composed will generate $(h \circ k)(x)$.

a. $(h \circ k)(x) = \sqrt{7x - 5}$

b. $(h \circ k)(x) = \dfrac{11}{x - 9} + 3$

c. $(h \circ k)(x) = 3^{2x} + 5$

PROBLEM 3 Domain Restrictions

Consider the functions $a(x) = \sqrt{x + 3}$ and $b(x) = x^2 - 4$.

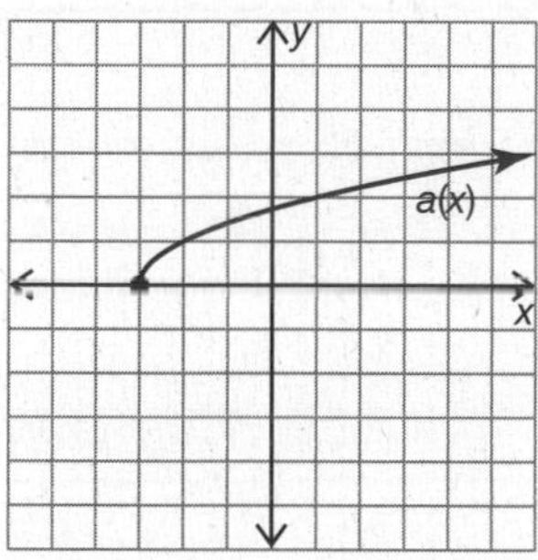

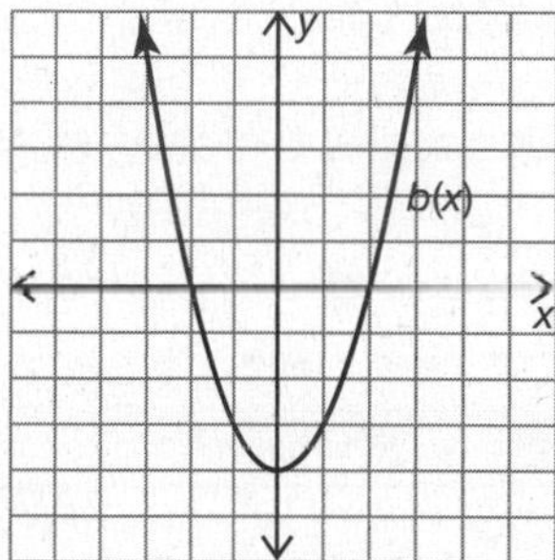

1. State the domain of $a(x)$ and of $b(x)$.

2. Write the composite function $(b \circ a)(x)$ and state the domain using interval notation.

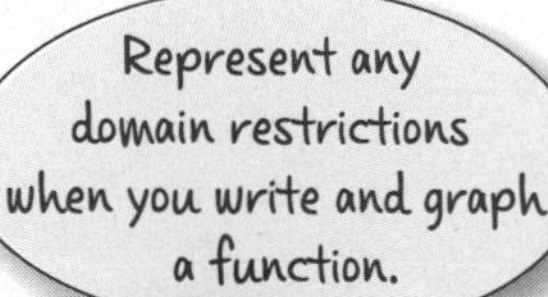

Represent any domain restrictions when you write and graph a function.

14

3. Jacob simplified the composition function algebraically and then graphed the result. Describe the error Jacob made.

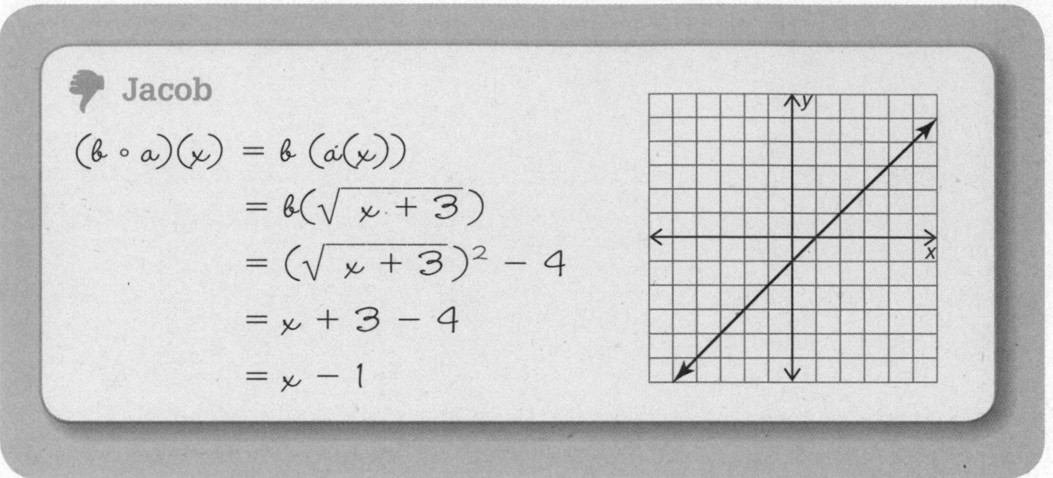
Jacob
$(b \circ a)(x) = b(a(x))$
$= b(\sqrt{x + 3})$
$= (\sqrt{x + 3})^2 - 4$
$= x + 3 - 4$
$= x - 1$
y
x

4. Sketch a graph of the function $(a \circ b)(x)$. Show your work.

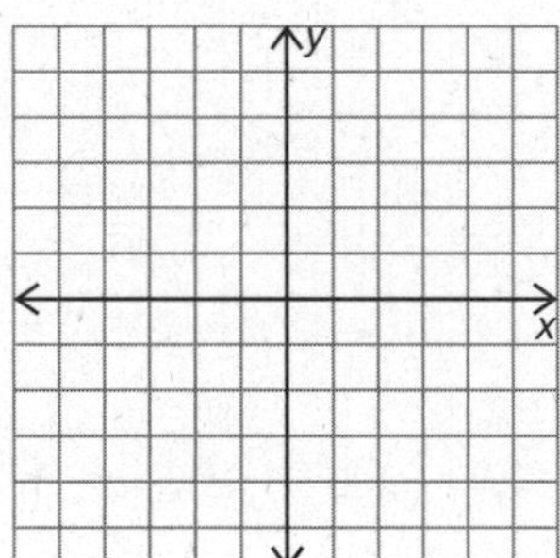
y
x

5. State the domain of $(a \circ b)(x)$. Is it the same as the domain of $(b \circ a)(x)$? Explain your reasoning.

The domain of $(f \circ g)(x)$ is the set of all real numbers x in the domain of g such that $g(x)$ is in the domain of f. In order for an element to be in the domain of the function $(f \circ g)(x)$, it must first be defined in the domain of $g(x)$.

You can graph the unsimplified version of a composition function in your graphing calculator to help you see domain restrictions.

6. Elise and Camden were given the functions $m(x) = \frac{1}{x}$ and $n(x) = \sqrt{x + 5}$ and asked to determine the domain of $m(n(x))$. Determine whose method is correct and explain your reasoning.

Elise

I know that $m(n(x))$ means that $n(x) = \sqrt{x + 5}$ is the input function and it has a domain of $[-5, \infty)$.

The output function is $m(x) = \frac{1}{x}$ and I know that the denominator can't be 0.

Therefore, the domain of $m(n(x))$ is $x \geq -5, x \neq 0$.

Camden

I know that $m(n(x))$ means $m(\sqrt{x+5}) = \frac{1}{\sqrt{x+5}}$.

The input function is $n(x) = \sqrt{x+5}$ and it has a domain of $[-5, \infty)$, but because it's in the denominator and the denominator can't be zero, -5 is not a part of the domain.

Therefore, the domain of $m(n(x))$ is $(-5, \infty)$.

14

7. Use the functions $f(x) = 4x - 3$, $g(x) = x^2 - 5$, $h(x) = \sqrt{x + 1}$ and $j(x) = \frac{1}{x + 2}$ to evaluate each composition. Then state the domain of the composite function. Explain your reasoning.

a. $(g \circ f)(x)$

b. $(h \circ g)(x)$

14

c. $(j \circ f)(x)$

d. $(g \circ h)(x)$

14

e. $(j \circ j)(x)$

14

PROBLEM 4 Can I Still Eat This?

The number of bacteria B in a refrigerated food is given by $B(c) = 20c^2 - 80c + 500$, where c is the temperature of the food in degrees Celsius. When the food is removed from refrigeration, the temperature of the food is given by $c(t) = 4t + 2$, where t is time in hours.

1. Calculate the number of bacteria that are in the food at each time interval.

   a. 30 minutes after removing the food from refrigeration

   b. 2 hours after removing the food from refrigeration

14

2. Refrigerated food that has been removed long enough to reach a temperature of 14 degrees Celsius is considered unsafe to eat.

   a. Determine the number of hours it takes for a food to become unsafe to eat.

   b. Determine the domain of the function $c(t) = 4t + 2$ in the context of this situation.

3. Write a function to determine the number of bacteria that are in a food that has been removed from refrigeration for t hours and is safe to eat.

Which function is the input function in this composition?

4. Determine the domain of the composite function.

14

5. Determine the range of the composite function. What does this mean in terms of this problem situation?

6. When will the number of bacteria reach 2000?

7. Write a function $F(t)$ to determine the temperature in degrees Fahrenheit of a food that is safe to eat and has been left out of refrigeration for t hours. State the domain and range and explain what they mean in the context of this problem situation.

Remember that the formula to convert Celsius to Fahrenheit is
$F = \frac{9}{5}C + 32$.

Be prepared to share your solutions and methods.

Paint by Numbers

Art and Transformations

14.2

LEARNING GOALS

In this lesson, you will:

- Use transformations of functions and other relations to create artwork.
- Write equations for transformed functions and other relations given an image.

Here's a picture that should make you smile:

$$y = -\sqrt{-x^2 + \frac{1}{2}}$$

$$\left(x - \frac{1}{2}\right)^2 + \left(y - \frac{1}{2}\right)^2 = \frac{1}{32}$$

$$\left(x + \frac{1}{2}\right)^2 + \left(y - \frac{1}{2}\right)^2 = \frac{1}{32}$$

Adorable, right?

Many contemporary artists like Helaman Ferguson and George Hart not only use mathematics to create their art but also use mathematics as a subject of their art.

Want to try your hand at creating some mathematical art?

PROBLEM 1 It's Van Gogh Time!

You have studied many types of relations throughout your high school mathematics career. Now it's time to use all of them to create some art.

Recall the seven basic functions and the basic equation for a circle shown.

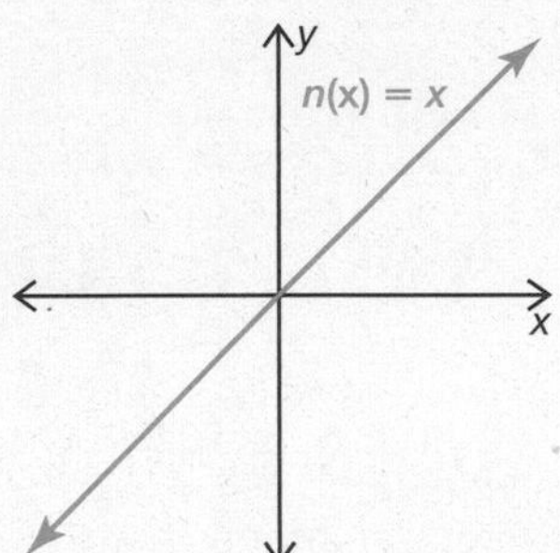

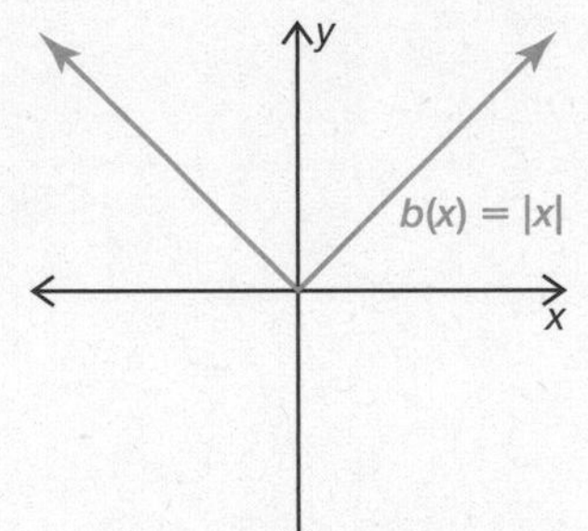

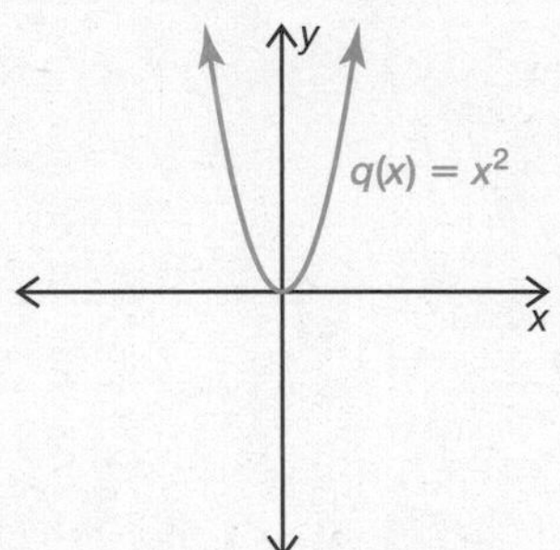

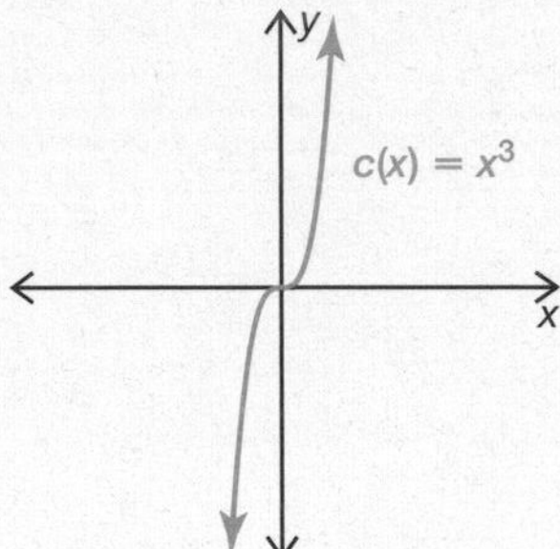

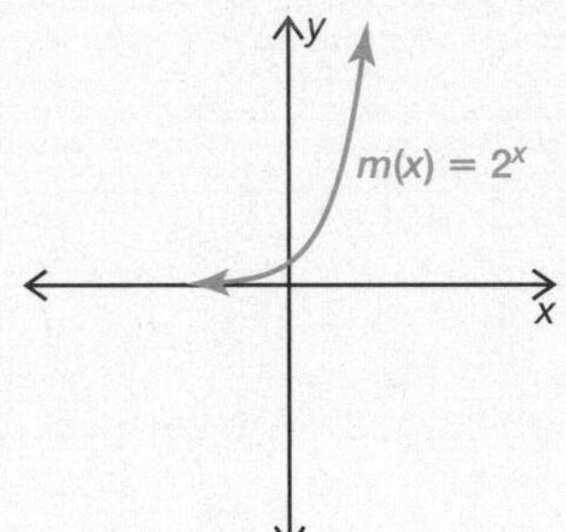

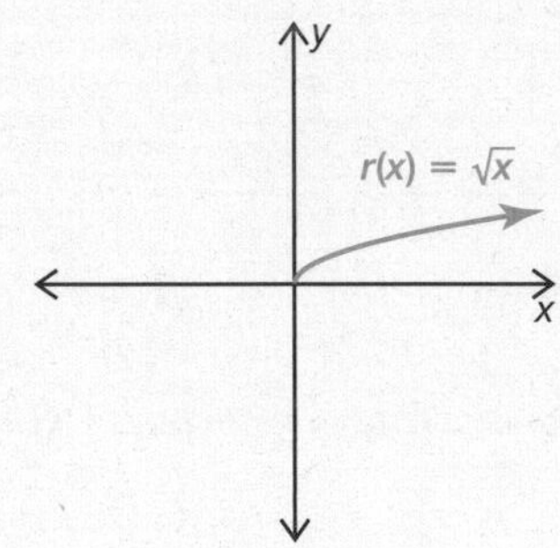

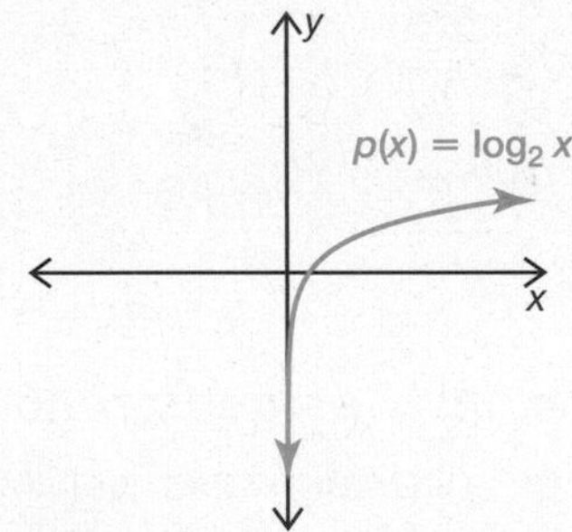

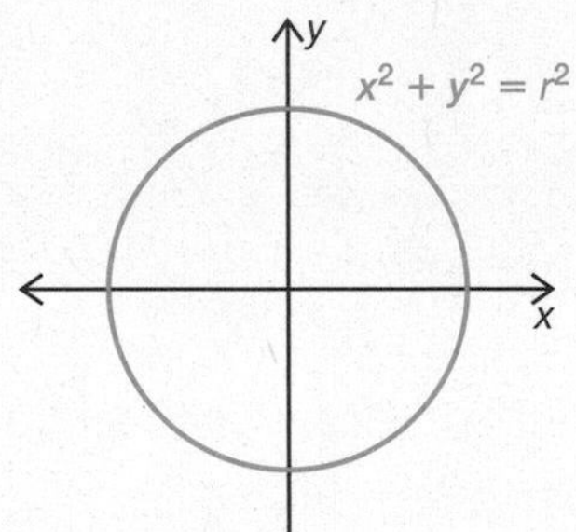

14

Recall the effect of each transformation on the graph of $y = f(x)$.

Function Form	Equation Information	Description of Transformation of Graph
$y = f(x) + D$	$D > 0$	Vertical shift up D units
	$D < 0$	Vertical shift down D units
$y = f(x - C)$	$C > 0$	Horizontal shift right C units
	$C < 0$	Horizontal shift left C units
$y = Af(x)$	$\|A\| > 1$	Vertical stretch by a factor of A units
	$0 < \|A\| < 1$	Vertical compression by a factor of A units
	$A < 0$	Reflection across the x-axis
$y = f(Bx)$	$\|B\| > 1$	Horizontal compression by a factor of $\frac{1}{\|B\|}$
	$0 < \|B\| < 1$	Horizontal stretch by a factor of $\frac{1}{\|B\|}$
	$B < 0$	Reflection across the y-axis

14

1. Use the seven basic functions, the basic equation for a circle, and your knowledge of the transformational function form to graph the given equations. What image do you see?

Equations	Restrictions
$y = -\frac{1}{10}q(x - 8) + 14$	$2 \leq x \leq 14$
$y = -3b(x - 4) + 16$	$2 \leq x \leq 5$
$y = -3b(x - 12) + 16$	$11 \leq x \leq 14$
$y = m(-x + 5) + 2$	$2 \leq x \leq 8$
$y = m(x - 11) + 2$	$8 \leq x \leq 14$
$(x - 6)^2 + (y - 10)^2 = 1$	
$(x - 10)^2 + (y - 10)^2 = 1$	
$y = q(x - 8) + 6$	$7 \leq x \leq 9$
$y = 7$	$7 \leq x \leq 9$
$y = -\frac{1}{4}n(x - 8) + 6.5$	$-1 \leq x \leq 7$
$y = -\frac{1}{4}n(x - 8) + 6.5$	$9 \leq x \leq 17$
$y = 6.5$	$-1 \leq x \leq 7$
$y = 6.5$	$9 \leq x \leq 17$
$y = \frac{1}{4}n(x - 8) + 6.5$	$-1 \leq x \leq 7$
$y = \frac{1}{4}n(x - 8) + 6.5$	$9 \leq x \leq 17$

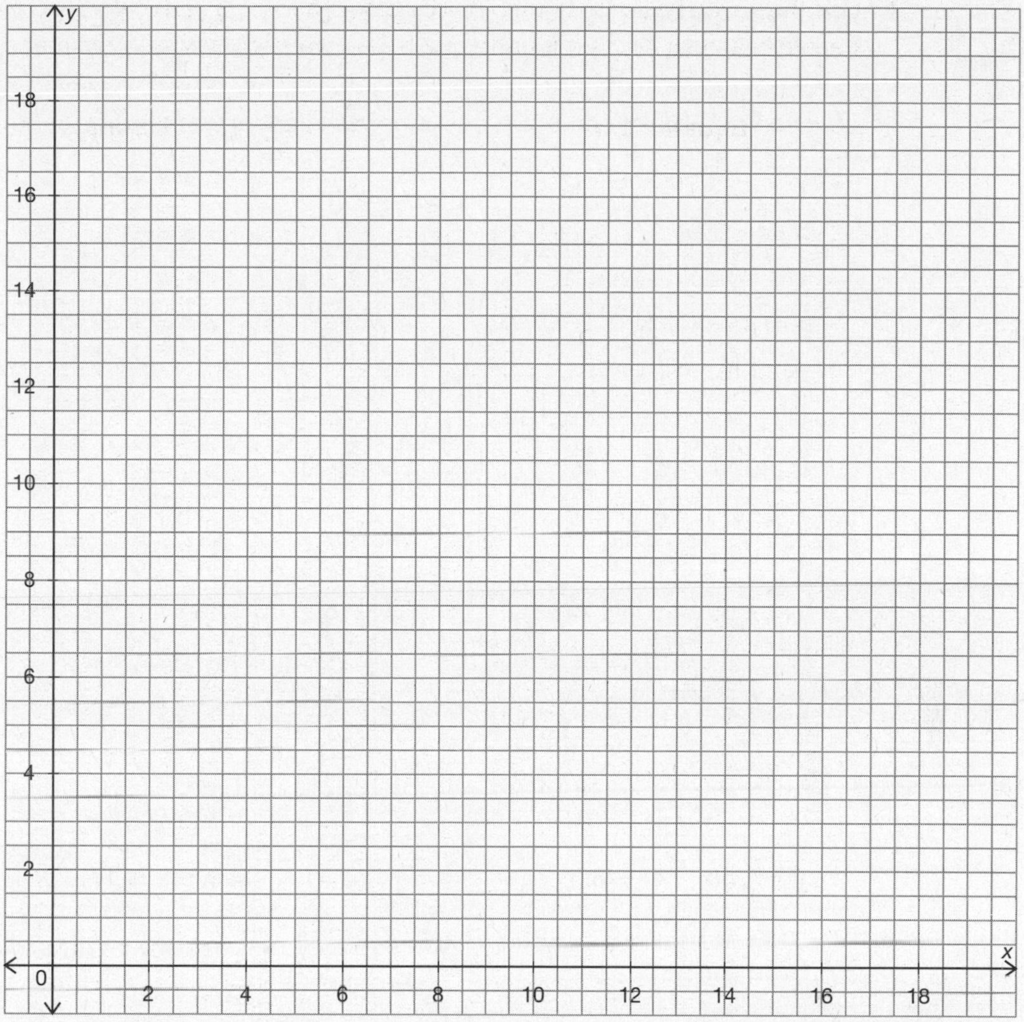

y

18

16

14

12

10

8

6

4

2

0

2 4 6 8 10 12 14 16 18

x

14

2. Use the seven basic functions, the equation of a circle, and your knowledge of the transformational function form to determine the equation of each graph in the picture. Include corresponding domain restrictions where necessary. When possible, write each equation in terms of one of the basic functions or equations given at the beginning of this problem.

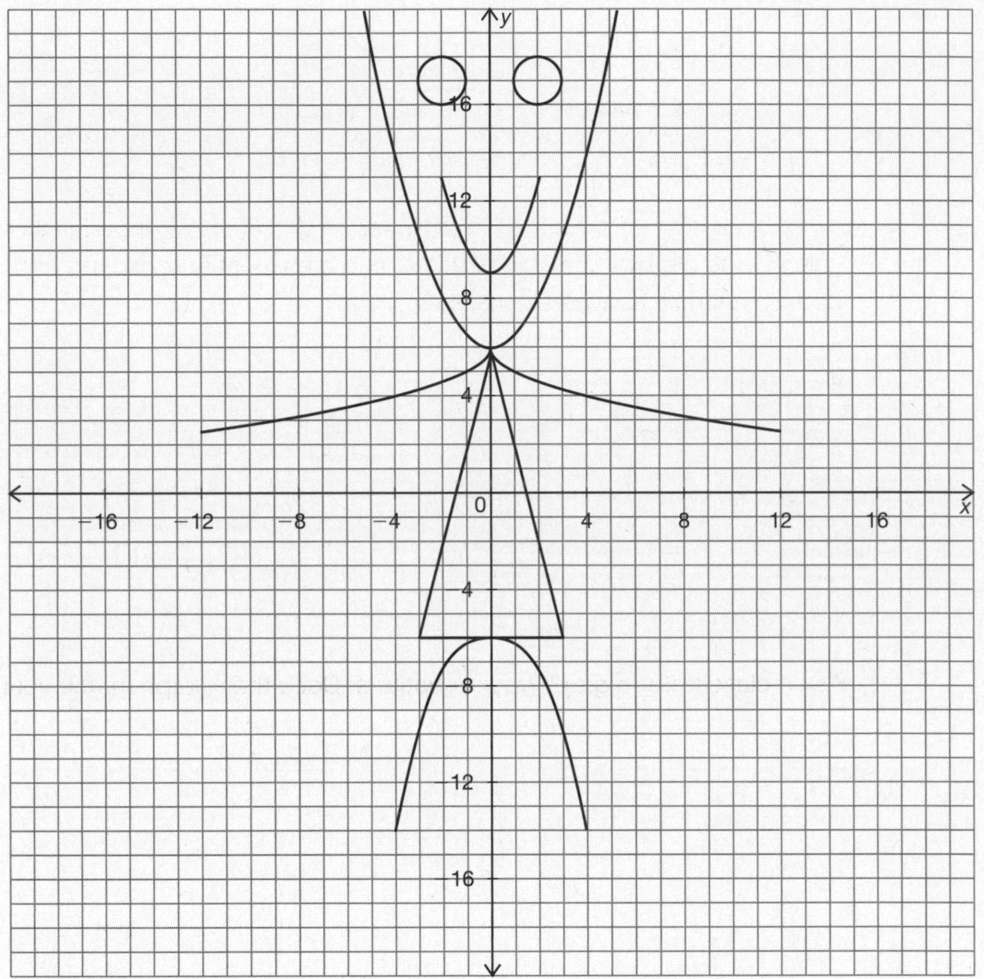

Equation(s) of a circle:

Exponential Equation(s):

Quadratic Equation(s):

Absolute Value Equation(s):

Radical Equation(s):

Linear Equation(s):

14

3. Create a picture or design using at least five transformed functions or equations. The transformations should include at least one stretch or compression, one translation, and one reflection. You must also include one of each of the following:

   - linear equation
   - absolute value equation
   - quadratic equation
   - exponential equation
   - radical equation

   When possible, write each equation in terms of one of the basic functions or equations given at the beginning of this problem, and then identify each type. Include corresponding domain restrictions where necessary.

   Equation: **Type:**

4. Ask a classmate to graph your equations. Does their graph match yours?

Be prepared to share your solutions and methods.

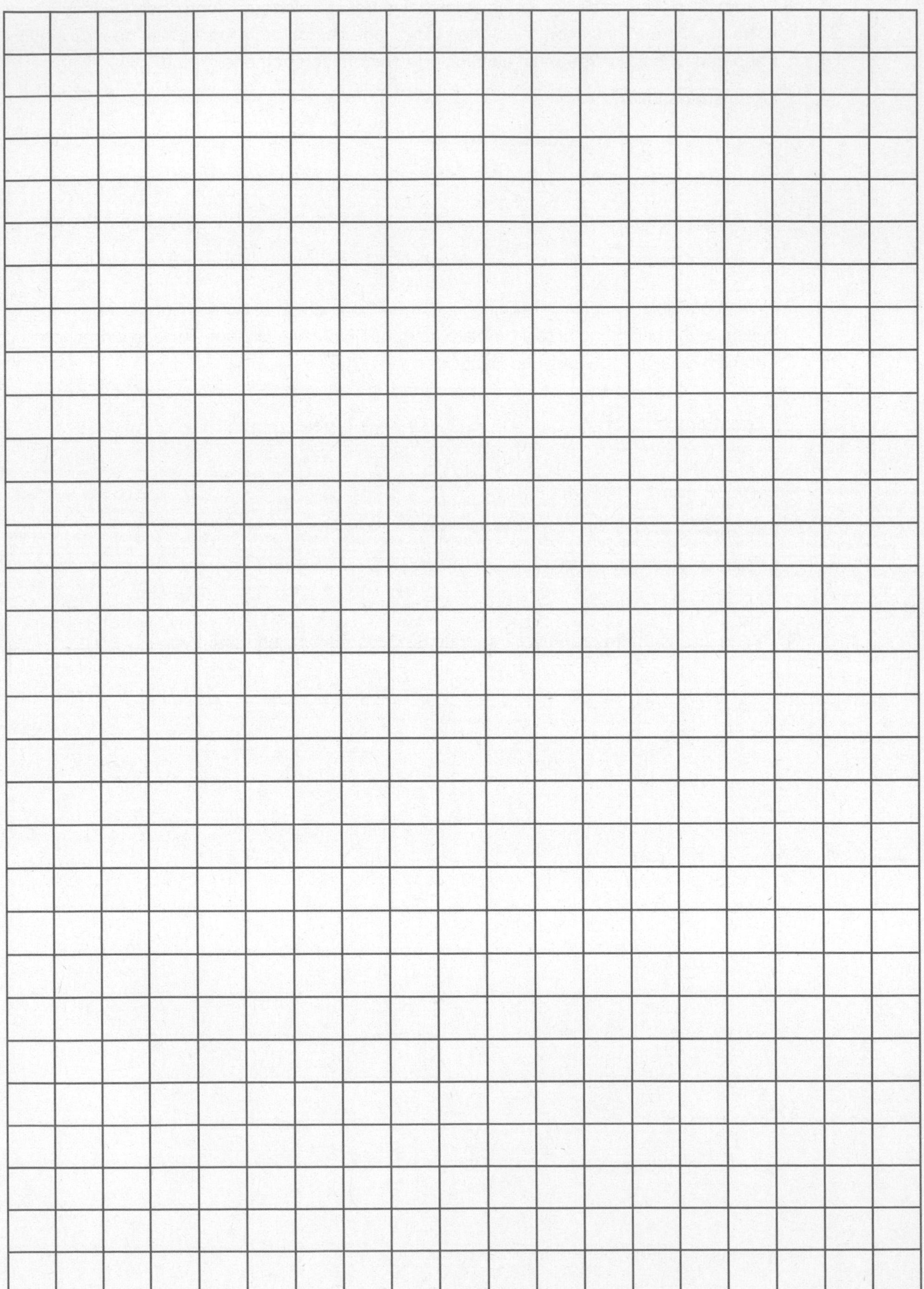

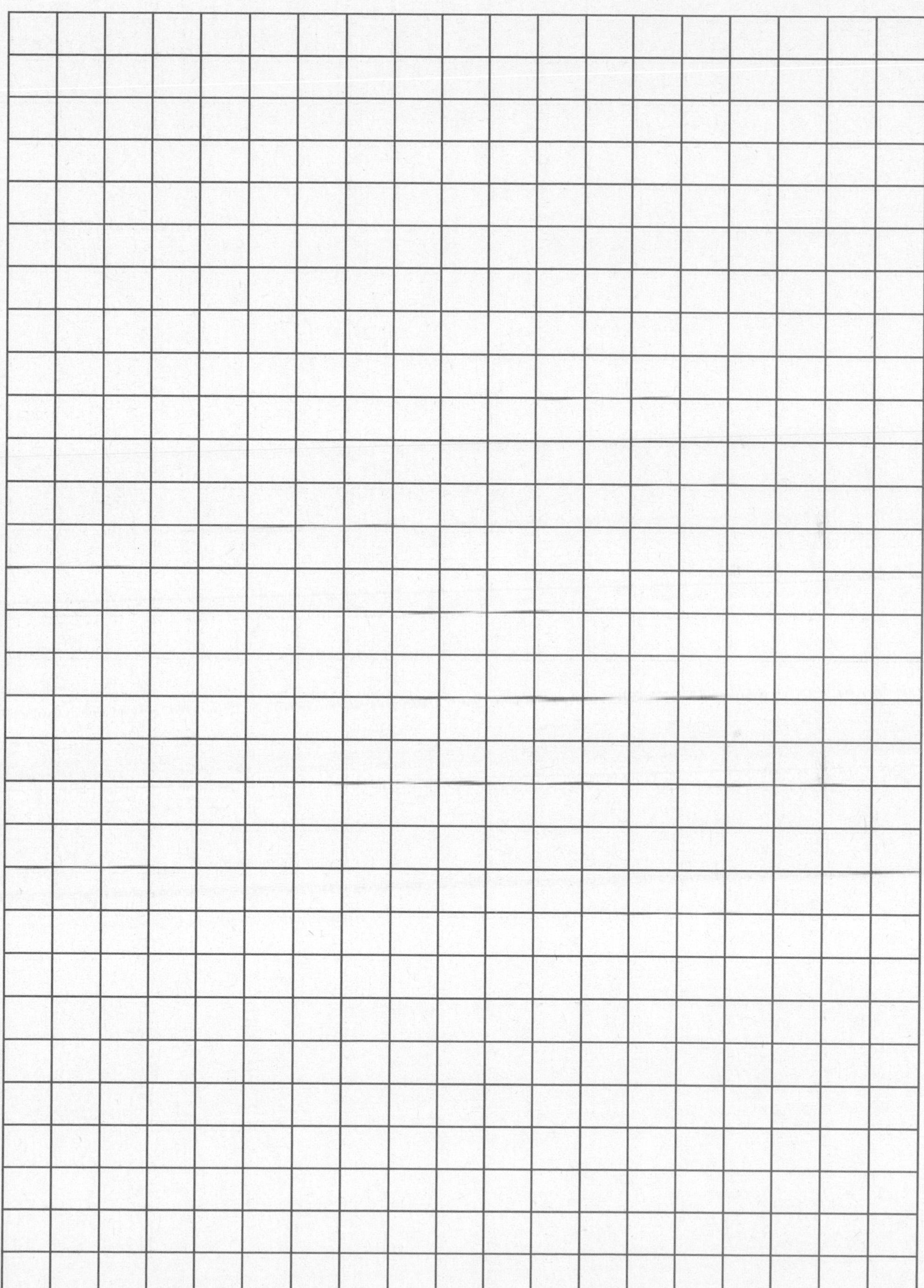

14

14

14.3

Make the Most of It

Optimization

LEARNING GOALS

In this lesson, you will:

- Determine constraints from a problem situation.
- Analyze a function to calculate maximum or minimum values.

Optimization problems involve finding the best solution from a choice of solutions given the objective. One of the most famous optimization problems in mathematics is the Traveling Salesman Problem. This problem can be stated as follows:

> Given a number of cities connected by roads, describe the shortest route that can be taken by a traveling salesman in order to visit every city once and then return to his starting place.

Work on problems like these has potential applications in computer science and other fields. But a solution may forever remain elusive. In 1972, a computer scientist named Richard Karp showed that a solution to the Traveling Salesman problem might not even be possible!

PROBLEM 1 Getting in Shape

Brad is a distance runner who wants to design the most effective workout plan to prepare for his next race. To adequately prepare for the race, Brad must run between 3 and 6 hours per week, but he knows that he must also spend some time strength training to reduce the risk of injury. Brad wants to devote at least twice as much time to running as to strength training, but he can spend no more than 8 hours at the gym each week.

1. Write a system of inequalities to represent the constraints of this problem situation. Be sure to define your unknowns.

2. Graph the system of inequalities on the coordinate plane shown. Shade the region that represents the solution set.

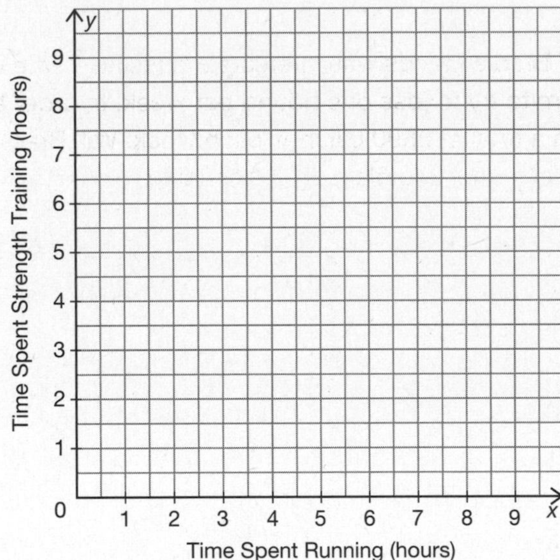

14

3. Running burns 600 calories per hour, while strength training burns 250 calories per hour. How many hours should Brad devote to each in order to maximize his weekly workout?

4. One of Brad's friends was interested in losing a little weight. He follows Brad's training program to try to lose one pound per week. In order to lose a pound a week, he needs to burn a total of 3500 calories each week. Will Brad's friend meet his goal of losing one pound per week? Explain your reasoning.

PROBLEM 2 It's Prom Time!

Last year, tickets to the prom cost $50 per student and 120 students attended. A student survey found that for every $5 reduction in price, 30 more students would attend.

1. Write a function to model the revenue generated from the sale of prom tickets for every x reduction in price.

2. Calculate the x- and y-intercept and explain what each means within the context of this problem situation.

14

3. Determine the ticket price that will maximize revenue.

What is the shape of the graph? How can I determine the maximum?

4. Calculate the amount of revenue that the new ticket price will generate.

14

5. The venue for the prom charges the school a flat rate of $2000 for up to 150 students, and then $15 for every additional student.

   a. Calculate the profit that the prom made for the school last year.

   b. Determine the profit that the school will make if they use the new ticket price.

6. Compare the profit that the prom made for the school last year with the profit that it will make this year if it uses the new ticket price. Is it worth it to change the ticket price? Explain your reasoning.

Be prepared to share your solutions and methods.

14.4

A Graph Is Worth a Thousand Words

Interpreting Graphs

LEARNING GOALS

In this lesson, you will:

- Interpret the contextual meaning of a graph and analyze it in terms of a problem situation.
- Write a logistic growth function to model a data set.
- Use technology to generate random numbers in order to conduct an experiment modeling logistic growth.

KEY TERMS

- logistic functions
- carrying capacity

Suppose that you were given the choice between an instant gift of $100 or flipping a coin for a chance to win $200 or nothing. Which would you choose?

Now imagine another choice. Either you can lose $100 instantly, or you can flip a coin for a chance of losing $200 or nothing. Which would you choose?

Many studies have shown that people would choose to gamble in the second situation but not the first, even though the situations are mathematically equivalent. The results point to a general tendency known as loss aversion. Psychologists Daniel Kahnemann and Amos Tversky first demonstrated that this tendency can be modeled by a function similar to what is known as a logistic function.

PROBLEM  The Hum Bug

Over the summer you noticed strange, noisy bugs in the field near your house. Each day, there seem to be more and more bugs in the field. You do a little research and find out that this insect is called a hum bug because of the humming sound it makes. You also find someone who has studied hum bug population growth in your area. The data they provide are summarized in the table shown.

Time (Days)	Population (Hum Bugs)
0	50
1	100
2	250
3	500
4	1200
5	2500
6	5250
7	10000
8	18000

Time (Days)	Population (Hum Bugs)
9	28000
10	37000
11	43000
12	46500
13	48500
14	49250
15	49750
16	49850
17	49950

1. Create a scatter plot for the data and sketch a curve through the points.

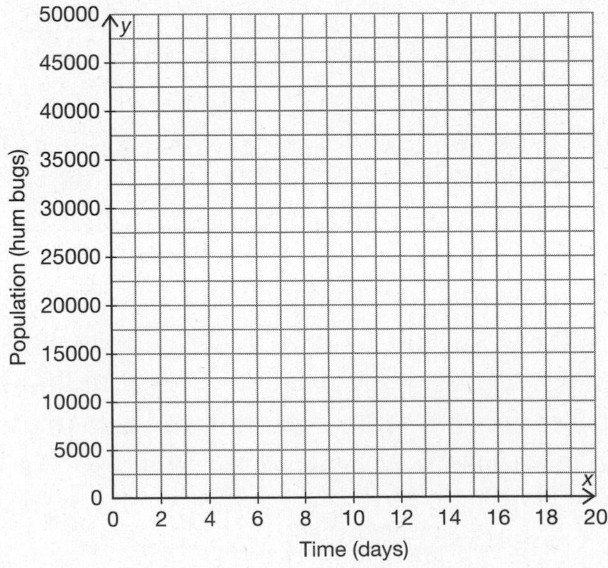

14

2. Describe the overall shape of your graph.

3. Where on the graph is the greatest increase in the hum bug population?

4. Where on the graph does the hum bug population growth seem to slow down?

5. Where on the graph does the hum bug population seem to level off?

6. What factors in the environment might have caused the hum bug population to grow as it did?

7. If insect populations can grow very quickly, why have they not just taken over the world?

14

The function graphed in this situation is closely modeled by the equation $f(x) = \frac{50{,}000}{1 + 1000e^{-0.8x}}$, which is part of the family of *logistic functions*.

Logistic functions are functions which can be written in the form $y = \frac{C}{1 + Ae^{-Bx}}$.

The S-shaped graph of a logistic function has four distinct intervals: the initial growth stage, the exponential growth stage, the dampened growth stage, and the equilibrium stage. The value the graph approaches in the equilibrium stage is called the **carrying capacity**.

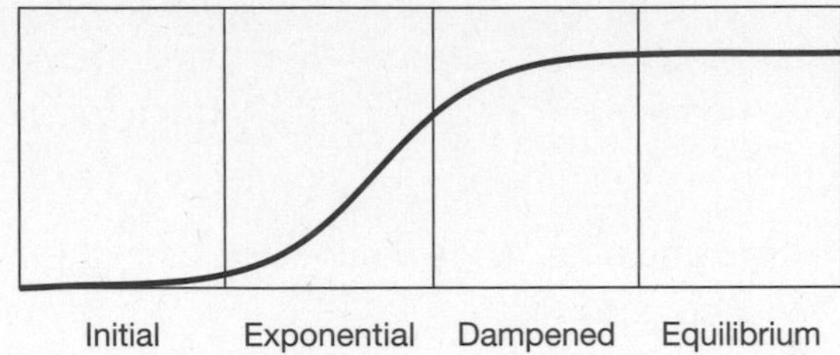

Logistic functions are good models of biological population growth, the spread of diseases, the spread of information, and sales of new products over time.

9. Enter the function $f(x) = \frac{50{,}000}{1 + 1000e^{-0.8x}}$ into a graphing calculator and view the graph.

   a. Change the numerator of the function so that it becomes $f(x) = \frac{40{,}000}{1 + 1000e^{-0.8x}}$. How did the graph change?

   b. Change the numerator again so the function becomes $f(x) = \frac{30{,}000}{1 + 1000e^{-0.8x}}$. How did the graph change?

10. What does the value of a in the logistic function $y = \frac{a}{1 + be^{-cx}}$ represent on the graph?

14

PROBLEM 2 Sick of School

Logistic functions can be used to model the spread of disease. The data you collect in this experiment will model the spread of a disease. After collecting the data, you will be able to analyze it by using a logistic function.

In a small school, there are 100 students. One day, Zelda Zero, a student, comes to the school infected with a virus that causes mild cold-like symptoms. On the first day that he has the virus, he has the potential to transmit the virus to one other person. On subsequent days, each infected person has the potential to transmit the virus to one other person. If the virus is transmitted to someone who has already had the virus, the person will not become ill again.

Before starting the experiment, take a few minutes to think about what will happen in the situation and answer each question.

1. How long will it take before most of the school is infected with the virus? Why?

2. Is there a limit to the number of people who can be infected? Explain your reasoning.

To keep things simple for the experiment, you will represent the 100 students in the school with numbers from 0 to 99. Using the list of numbers on the next page, you can keep track of students infected with the virus by crossing off their number. You'll notice that 0 is already crossed off because Zelda Zero is already infected.

To simulate students getting infected with the virus, you can use the random number generator on a graphing calculator. Generate a random number between 0 and 99 by typing int(rand*100) and pressing ENTER. After getting the first random number, you can get more random numbers simply by pressing ENTER.

On the first day, you will potentially infect one more person by choosing one random number. On subsequent days, you will generate an amount of random numbers equal to the number of people already infected. If a random number that is generated is not already crossed off, cross it off on the list.

Conduct the experiment following these directions.

- Use a graphing calculator to generate random numbers indicating who gets infected.
- Keep track of infected students by crossing out numbers as they are randomly selected. If a number is already crossed out, do not generate an alternate number.
- For each day, generate as many random numbers as there are currently infected students.
- At the end of each round of random numbers that represent one day, record the total number infected (crossed out numbers) in the table.
- Repeat the process. Work until most students are infected (you have most of your numbers crossed off).

3. Conduct the experiment.

~~0~~	1	2	3	4	5	6	7	8	9
10	11	12	13	14	15	16	17	18	19
20	21	22	23	24	25	26	27	28	29
30	31	32	33	34	35	36	37	38	39
40	41	42	43	44	45	46	47	48	49
50	51	52	53	54	55	56	57	58	59
60	61	62	63	64	65	66	67	68	69
70	71	72	73	74	75	76	77	78	79
80	81	82	83	84	85	86	87	88	89
90	91	92	93	94	95	96	97	98	99

Time (Days)	Total Number of Infected Students (Students)
0	1
1	
2	
3	
4	
5	
6	
7	
8	

4. Create a scatter plot of your data.

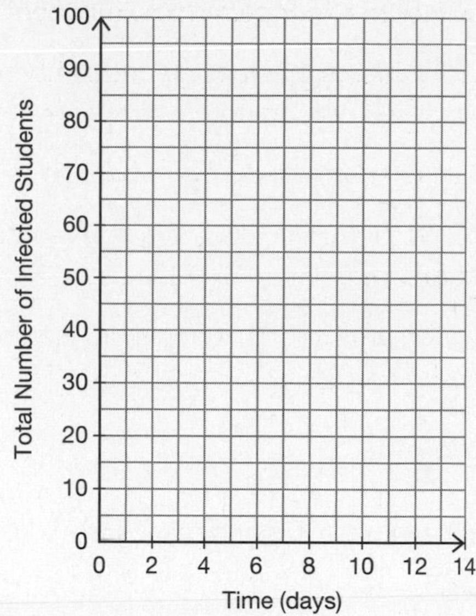

5. Using your graph and table, identify:

   a. the initial growth stage.

   b. the exponential growth stage.

   c. the dampened growth stage.

   d. the equilibrium stage.

6. Identify the carrying capacity for this function. Explain your reasoning.

14

7. Use a calculator to determine the equation of a logistic function that will model the data you collected for this problem. Determine the equation by performing a logistic regression.

8. How do you think the experiment and results would be different if there were 200 people in the school?

9. Could you model the spread of the virus with another type of function (e.g. linear, quadratic, or exponential)? Why or why not?

Be prepared to share your solutions and methods.

This Is the Title of This Lesson

Fractals

14.5

LEARNING GOALS

In this lesson, you will:

- Build expressions and equations to model the characteristics of self-similar objects.
- Write sequences to model situations and use them to identify patterns.
- Analyze the counterintuitive aspects of fractals.

KEY TERMS

- fractal
- self-similar
- iterative process

If you like looking at pictures of cats, then the internet is for you. And if you like looking at pictures of cats looking at pictures of cats on the internet, then look into looking at the Infinite Cat Project.

As of late 2013, the project showcased about 1800 pictures of cats looking at pictures of cats looking at . . . you get the (very simple) idea.

Recursion like that featured on the Infinite Cat Project is an interesting mathematical topic, and a source of inspiration for self-referential lesson titles.

PROBLEM 1 The Sierpinski Triangle

A **fractal** is a complex geometric shape that is constructed by a mathematical pattern. Fractals are infinite and *self-similar* across different scales. A **self-similar** object is exactly or approximately similar to a part of itself. Many objects in the real world, such as coastlines, are self-similar, in that parts of them look roughly the same on any scale. Fractals often appear in nature. Examples of phenomena known to have fractal features include river networks, lightning bolts, ferns, snowflakes, and crystals.

The first fractal you will study is the Sierpinski Triangle, first described by Polish mathematician Wacław Sierpiński in 1915.

To construct the Sierpinski Triangle:

Stage 0: Begin with an equilateral triangle.

Stage 1: Connect the midpoints of the sides and remove the center triangle by shading it.

Stage 2: Repeat Stage 1 on the remaining triangles.

1. Complete each equilateral triangle to represent each stage of the Sierpinski Triangle.

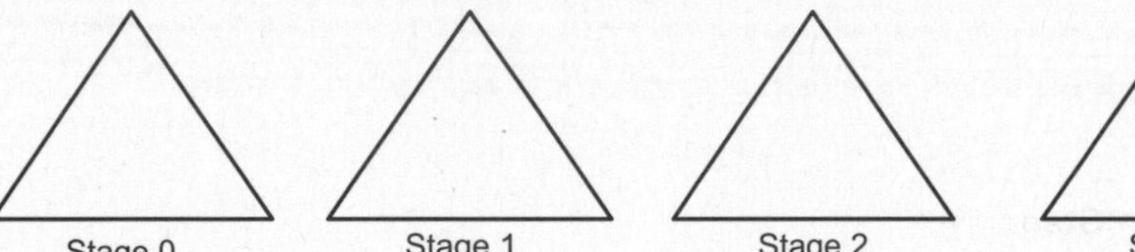

Fractals are formed by an **iterative process**. The output from one iteration is used as the input for the next iteration. In many situations, this is also known as recursion.

2. Describe the iterative process to create the Sierpinski Triangle.

3. Determine the number of unshaded triangles at each stage and complete the table.

Stage (n)	0	1	2	3	4	5	n
Number of Unshaded Triangles	1						

14

4. Identify the type of sequence represented by the number of unshaded triangles.

5. As the iterative process continues, what happens to the number of unshaded triangles in Sierpinski's Triangle?

6. Let the unshaded area at Stage 0 equal x square units. Determine the total area of unshaded triangles at each stage and complete the table.

Stage (n)	0	1	2	3	4	5	n
Area of Unshaded Triangles (square units)	x						

7. Identify the type of sequence represented by the area of unshaded triangles.

8. As the iterative process continues, what happens to the area of unshaded triangles in Sierpinski's Triangle?

9. Complete the table to determine the perimeter of the Sierpinski Triangle through each iteration. Let s equal the side length of the equilateral triangle in Stage 0.

Stage	Image	Number of Sides Added	Length of Added Side	Total Length Added	Total Perimeter
0		0	N/A	N/A	$3s$
1		3	$\frac{s}{2}$	$\frac{3s}{2}$	$3s + \frac{3s}{2}$
2					
n	N/A				

10. Write a formula using sigma notation for the perimeter of the Sierpinski Triangle at stage n.

PROBLEM  The Menger Sponge

The next fractal you will study is the Menger Sponge, first described by Austrian mathematician Karl Menger in 1926.

To construct the Menger Sponge:

Stage 0: Begin with a cube.

Stage 1: Divide every face of the cube into 9 squares. This will subdivide the cube into 27 smaller cubes. Remove the smaller cube in the middle of each face, and remove the smaller cube in the very center of the larger cube, leaving 20 smaller cubes.

Stage 2: Repeat Stage 1 for the remaining squares on each face.

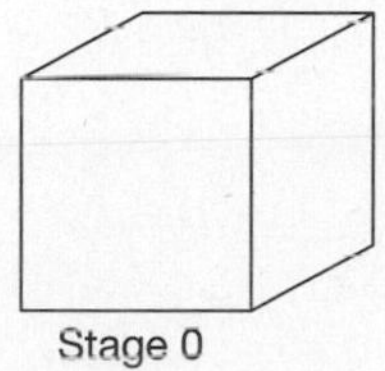

Stage 0

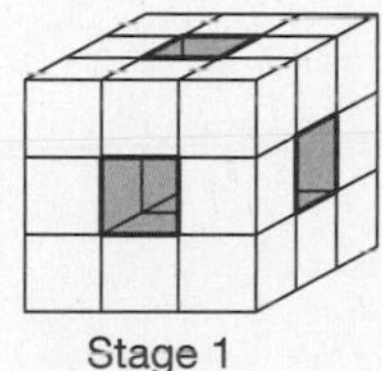

Stage 1

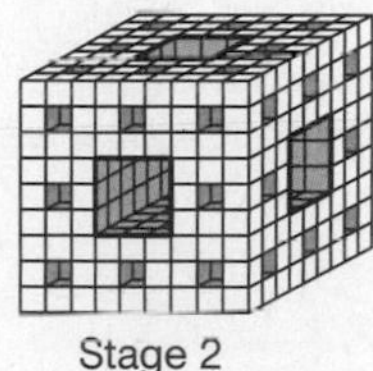

Stage 2

1. Describe the iterative process to create the Menger Sponge.

2. Determine the number of filled cubes at each stage and complete the table.

Stage (n)	0	1	2	3	4	5	n
Number of Filled Cubes							

3. Identify the type of sequence represented by the number of filled cubes.

4. As the iterative process continues, what happens to the number of filled cubes in the Menger Sponge?

5. Let the volume at Stage 0 equal 1 cubic unit. Determine the total volume of filled cubes at each stage and complete the table.

Stage (n)	0	1	2	3	4	5	n
Volume (cubic units)							

6. Identify the type of sequence represented by the volume of filled cubes.

7. As the iterative process continues, what happens to the volume of filled cubes in the Menger Sponge? Does this situation seem possible? Explain your reasoning.

14

PROBLEM 3 The Koch Snowflake

The Koch Snowflake is a fractal that is created by using equilateral triangles. It is based on the Koch curve, first mentioned in a 1904 paper by the Swedish mathematician Helge von Koch.

In Stage 0, you begin with an equilateral triangle, such as the one shown. This is the first step in the creation of the Koch Snowflake.

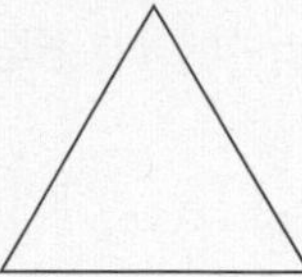

In Stage 1, each side of the triangle is divided into thirds. Then, each middle segment becomes the base of a new equilateral triangle as shown. Finally, the middle segment is removed.

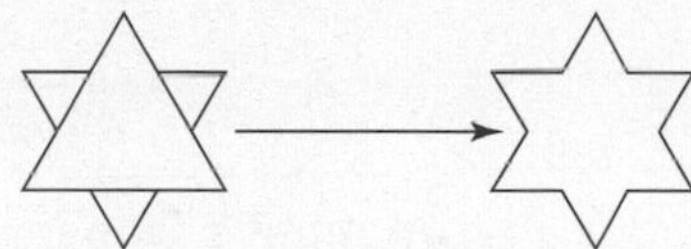

1. How does a side length of a new triangle compare to a side length of the Stage 0 triangle?

2. If a side length of the Stage 0 figure is 1 unit, what is a side length of the Stage 1 figure?

In Stage 2, each side of the figure from Stage 1 is divided into thirds, and the middle segments become the bases of new equilateral triangles. Then, the middle segments are removed.

This process is repeated on the remaining sides.

3. Describe the iterative process to create the Koch Snowflake.

4. Let the side length at Stage 0 equal s units. Complete the table.

Stage (n)	Length of a Side	Number of Sides	Total Perimeter
0	s	3	$3s$
1			
2			
3			
4			
5			
n			

5. Identify the type of sequence represented by:

   a. the length of a side.

   b. the number of sides.

   c. the total perimeter.

14

6. As the iterative process continues, what happens to:

   a. the length of a side.

   b. the number of sides.

   c. the total perimeter.

7. Does this situation seem possible? Explain your reasoning.

8. Consider the equilateral triangle in Stage 0.

   a. Calculate the altitude. (Hint: Use the fact that the altitude divides the triangle into two special right triangles.) Leave your answer in radical form.

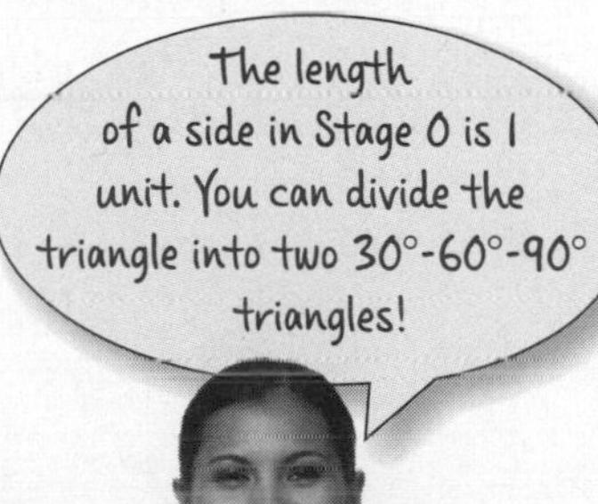

The length of a side in Stage 0 is 1 unit. You can divide the triangle into two 30°-60°-90° triangles!

   b. Calculate the area of the equilateral triangle. Show all of your work and leave your answer in radical form.

   c. What is the total area of the Stage 0 figure rounded to the nearest hundredth?

14

9. Consider one of the smaller triangles that was added to the Stage 0 figure.

   a. Calculate the altitude. Leave your answer in radical form.

   b. Calculate the area of this triangle. Show all of your work and leave your answer in radical form.

   c. Calculate the total area of the Stage 1 figure. Show all of your work and round your answer to the nearest hundredth.

10. Consider one of the smaller triangles that was added to the Stage 1 figure.

a. Calculate the altitude. Leave your answer in radical form.

b. Calculate the area of this triangle. Show all of your work and leave your answer in radical form.

c. Calculate the total area of the Stage 2 figure. Show all of your work and round your answer to the nearest hundredth.

11. Complete the table shown for Stage 0 through Stage 2.

Stage	Number of New Triangles	Area of One New Triangle	Total Area in Radical Form	Total Area (nearest hundredth)
0				
1				
2				

a. Predict the number of new triangles in the Stage 3 figure, the area of one new triangle, and the total area of the figure. Explain your reasoning. Record your results in the table.

b. What happens to the number of new triangles as the stage number increases?

c. What happens to the area of one new triangle as the stage number increases?

d. What happens to the total area as the stage number increases? Does this situation seem possible? Explain your reasoning.

14

Be prepared to share your solutions and methods.

14.6

Grab Bag

Choosing Functions to Model Situations

LEARNING GOALS

In this lesson, you will:

- Use technology to determine regression equations that model data.
- Choose functions to model problem situations.
- Graph and analyze function characteristics in terms of problem situations.

At some amusement parks, rotor rides can spin you around fast enough to make you stick to the wall. The same force—centrifugal force—can also help to get your clothes dry.

In some clothes dryers, a combination of heat and spin "sucks" away the moisture from your clothes during the spin cycle. Because there are holes in the rotating tube inside the dryer, the water is able to exit the tube or be evaporated, leaving your clothes dry.

So, being in the rotor ride at the amusement park is like being stuck in a giant clothes dryer!

PROBLEM 1 Stretch That Dollar

The table shows the purchasing value of the dollar, or the consumer price index, for consumers in the United States from 1955 to 2010. The table uses the year 1982 as a base period, so the consumer price index written in dollars and cents in 1982 is 1.00.

In 1955, the consumer price index was 3.73. This means that a dollar in 1955 was worth 3.73 times what it was worth in 1982. Similarly, a dollar in 2010 was worth 0.46 times what it was worth in 1982.

Year	Consumer Price Index	Year	Consumer Price Index
1955	3.73	1985	0.93
1960	3.37	1990	0.77
1965	3.17	1995	0.66
1970	2.57	2000	0.58
1975	1.86	2005	0.51
1980	1.22	2010	0.46

The scatter plot shows the data in the table where x represents the number of years since 1955 and y represents the consumer price index.

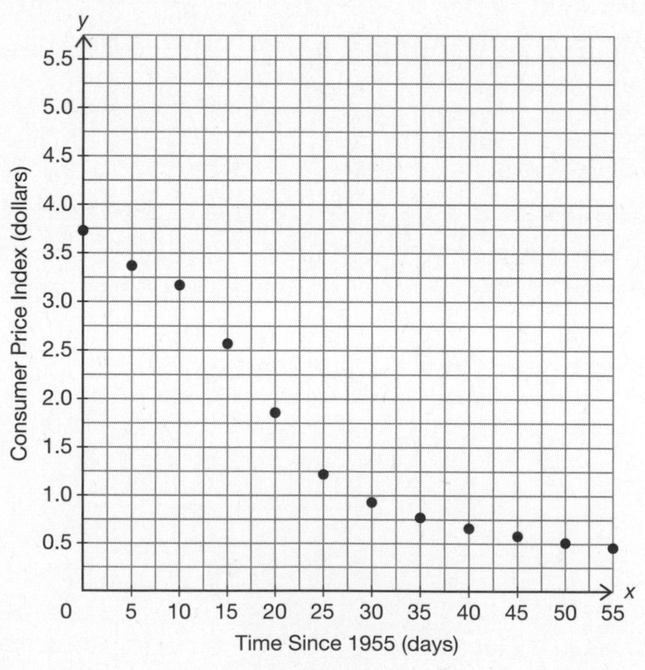

1. Determine the regression equation for the model that best represents the data. Explain how you determined your answer. Then, graph the model on the same coordinate plane as the scatter plot.

2. Predict the consumer price index in 2025. Explain what your answer means in terms of this problem situation.

3. Mr. Kratzer asks his students to calculate what model predicts the consumer price index was in 1950. Melina says that you must evaluate the function at $x = 5$ to determine the consumer price index in 1950. Dominique argues you must evaluate the function at $x = -5$ to determine the consumer price index in 1950. Who is correct? Explain your reasoning.

4. Calculate the consumer price index for 1950.

5. The consumer price index in 1950 was actually 4.15. Compare this to the answer you calculated in Question 4. Explain why these answers differ.

14

PROBLEM  The Rotor

The Rotor is a popular amusement park ride shaped like a cylindrical room. Riders stand against the circular wall of the room while the room spins. When The Rotor reaches the necessary speed, the floor drops out and centrifugal force leaves riders pinned up against the wall.

The minimum speed (measured in meters per second) required to keep a person pinned against the wall during the ride can be determined with the function $s(r) = 4.95\sqrt{r}$, where r is the radius of The Rotor measured in meters.

1. An amusement park designed a rotor ride with a radius of 2 meters. At what speed does it need to spin?

2. The same park decided to build a larger rotor ride with a radius of 4 meters. At what speed does it need to spin?

3. Designers at another park have a motor that could spin a rotor ride at 6 meters per second. How big can they make the ride?

4. Algebraically determine the inverse of the function used to determine the speed of The Rotor.

14

5. Create a graph of the function and its inverse on coordinate plane shown.

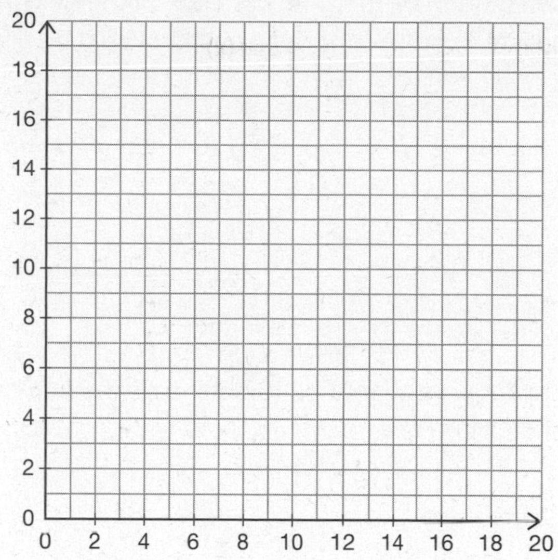

6. Write a paragraph to describe the initial function, $s(r) = 4.95\sqrt{r}$.

Be sure to include information about the basic function, domain, range, and behavior of the function.

7. Write a paragraph to describe the inverse function.

Be sure to include information about the parent function, domain, range, and behavior of the function.

8. The designers estimate that they must allow 60 cm (0.6 meter) of space along the wall for each person on the ride. For each of the designs from Questions 1 and 2, determine the maximum number of people who should be allowed on the ride at one time.

9. Write an algebraic function to determine the number of people a rotor ride can hold based on its radius.

10. Determine the inverse of your function from Question 9 algebraically.

11. Graph your functions from Questions 9 and 10 on the coordinate plane shown.

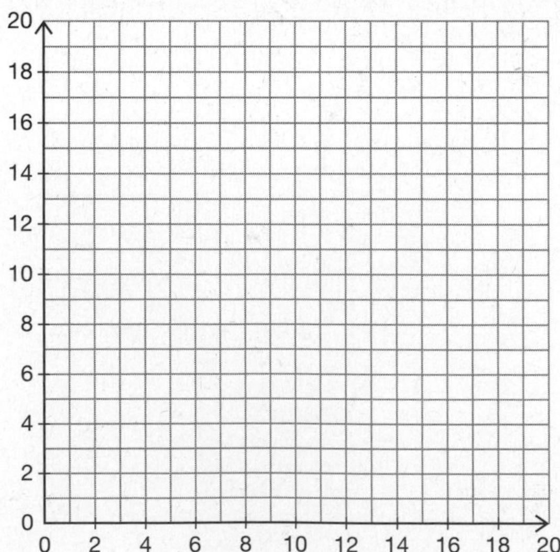

12. The ride designers at an amusement park want to create a rotor ride that can accommodate 25 riders at a time.

a. Would you use the function given at the start of the problem or its inverse to determine the size of the ride? Why?

b. How big must they make the ride?

13. Write a paragraph to describe your function from Question 9.

Be sure to include information about the parent function, domain, range, and behavior of the function.

14. Write a paragraph to describe the inverse function from Question 10.

Be sure to include information about the parent function, domain, range, and behavior of the function.

PROBLEM 3 It's Electric!

In an electrical circuit, when resistors are connected in parallel, the total resistance R_T of the circuit in ohms is given by:

$$\frac{1}{R_T} = \frac{1}{R_1} + \frac{1}{R_2} + \cdots + \frac{1}{R_n}$$

where n is the number of resistors and R_1 through R_n are the resistances of each resistor in ohms.

1. Determine the total resistance of an electrical circuit having two resistors connected in parallel if their resistances are 5 ohms and 8 ohms.

2. Three resistors connected in parallel have resistances of 4 ohms, 6 ohms, and 10 ohms. What is the total resistance in this electric circuit?

14

3. The total resistance in a parallel wiring circuit is 12 ohms. If the resistance of one branch is 30 ohms, what is the resistance in the other branch?

4. A three-resistor parallel wiring circuit has a total resistance of 10 ohms. If two of the branches of the circuit have resistances of 20 ohms and 30 ohms, what is the resistance in the third branch?

PROBLEM 4 Cool It Down

Andre bought several 2-liter bottles of soda, but he did not have enough room in his refrigerator. He left the bottles outside to cool. Before he put each bottle outside, they were at room temperature, 72°F.

The outside temperature was 25°F. After 30 minutes, he brought one bottle of soda inside and measured the temperature. The temperature of the bottle of soda was 60°F.

A bottle of soda will freeze at 28°F. How long can Andre leave the bottles of soda outside before they will freeze?

Different liquids freeze at various temperatures because of the difference in their molecular structure.

1. List everything you know about the function to model the temperature of a bottle of soda over time.

14

2. Write a function to model the temperature of a bottle of soda over time.

Think about transformational function form to determine the function that models this problem situation.

14

3. How long can Andre leave the bottles of soda outside before they freeze?

Be prepared to share your solutions and methods.

Chapter 14 Summary

KEY TERMS

- identity function (14.1)
- logistic functions (14.4)
- carrying capacity (14.4)
- fractal (14.5)
- self-similar (14.5)
- iterative process (14.5)

14.1 Writing Composition Functions

In a composition of two functions f and g, written as $(f \circ g)(x)$, the output of $g(x)$ becomes the input of $f(x)$. That is, the function $g(x)$ is substituted for x into the function $f(x)$.

Example

Consider the functions $f(x) = 2x - 3$ and $g(x) = x^2 + 3x - 7$. Determine $(f \circ g)(x)$.

$$\begin{aligned}(f \circ g)(x) &= f(g(x)) \\ &= f(x^2 + 3x - 7) \\ &= 2(x^2 + 3x - 7) - 3 \\ &= 2x^2 + 6x - 14 - 3 \\ &= 2x^2 + 6x - 17\end{aligned}$$

14.1 Determining Inverse Functions

Two functions f and g are inverses of each other if the composite functions $(f \circ g)(x)$ and $(g \circ f)(x)$ both yield the identity function. That is, $(f \circ g)(x) = x$ and $(g \circ f)(x) = x$.

Example

Use function composition to determine whether the functions $q(x) = \sqrt{x - 1}$ and $h(x) = x^2 + 1$, $x \geq 0$, are inverses of each other.

$$\begin{aligned}(q \circ h)(x) &= q(h(x)) \\ &= q(x^2 + 1) \\ &= \sqrt{(x^2 + 1) - 1} \\ &= \sqrt{x^2} \\ &= x\end{aligned}$$

$$\begin{aligned}(h \circ q)(x) &= h(q(x)) \\ &= h(\sqrt{x - 1}) \\ &= (\sqrt{x - 1})^2 + 1 \\ &= (x - 1) + 1 \\ &= x\end{aligned}$$

The functions $q(x) = \sqrt{x - 1}$ and $h(x) = x^2 + 1$, $x \geq 0$, are inverses of each other, because $(q \circ h)(x) = x$ and $(h \circ q)(x) = x$.

14.1 Determining the Domain of Composite Functions

The domain of $(f \circ g)(x)$ is the set of all real numbers x in the domain of g such that $g(x)$ is in the domain of f. In order for an element to be in the domain of the function $(f \circ g)(x)$, it must first be defined in the domain of $g(x)$.

Example

Let $r(x) = \frac{3}{6 - x}$ and $s(x) = \sqrt{x - 4}$. State the domain of $(r \circ s)(x)$. Explain how you determined your answer.

The composition of the functions $r(x)$ and $s(x)$ is $(r \circ s)(x) = \frac{3}{6 - \sqrt{x - 4}}$. The domain of the input is $[4, \infty)$, but because the denominator cannot be equal to zero, the domain of the composite function must be $[4, \infty)$, $x \neq 40$.

14.2 Reviewing Transformations of Functions

The function $y = f(x)$ is transformed when the function or its argument is multiplied, divided, increased, or decreased by a constant.

Example

Describe how the graph of the function $f(x) = x^2$ would be transformed to be the graph of the function $g(x) = -3(x - 2)^2 - 4$. Then, graph both functions.

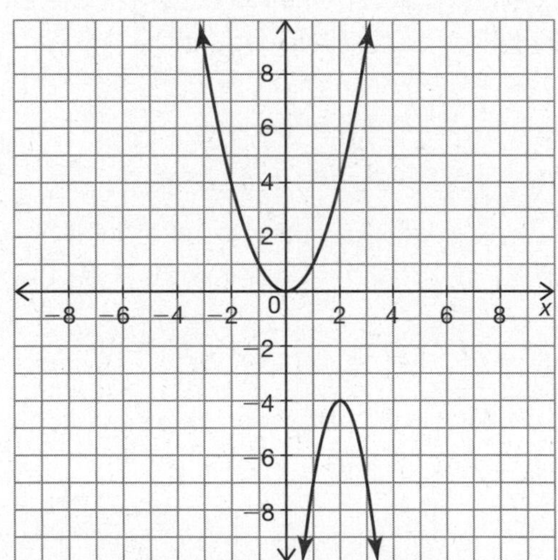

The −3 indicates that the function would be stretched vertically by a factor of 3 and reflected across the x-axis. The 2 indicates that the function would be shifted to the right 2 units. The 4 indicates that the function would be shifted down 4 units.

14

14.3 Analyzing Functions to Maximize or Minimize a Value

Functions can be written and analyzed to determine the maximum or minimum in a real-world situation. To do this, write a function to model the situation and then determine the input value that will yield the maximum or minimum output value.

Example

The dimensions of a rectangular garden in feet are given by the expressions $27 - x$ and $x + 3$. Write an equation for the area of the garden. Then, determine the actual dimensions of the garden that would produce that greatest area. What is that area?

$$\begin{aligned} A &= bh \\ &= (27 - x)(x + 3) \\ &= 27x + 81 - x^2 - 3x \\ &= -x^2 + 24x + 81 \end{aligned}$$

So, the area can be represented by the function $A = -x^2 + 24x + 81$.

$$\begin{aligned} x &= -\frac{b}{2a} \\ &= \frac{24}{2(-1)} \\ &= 12 \end{aligned}$$

The maximum area will occur when $x = 12$ feet. So, the dimensions that will produce the maximum area are $27 - 12$ or 15 feet and $12 + 3$ or 15 feet. A rectangular garden that is 15 feet by 15 feet will have an area of 225 square feet.

14

14.4 Modeling with Logistic Functions

Logistic functions are functions that can be written in the form $y = \frac{C}{1 + Ae^{-Bx}}$. They can be used to model biological population growth, the spread of diseases, the spread of information, and sales of new products over time. To model data with a logistic function, enter the data in a graphing calculator and then run a logistic regression on the data.

Example

On Monday, Alexa told several of her friends a secret. On Tuesday, each of her friends told a friend or two. The secret continued to spread over the following 10 days. The data representing the spread of the secret is shown in the table. Use a graphing calculator to run a logistic regression on the data. Write the function and identify the carrying capacity. Then, identify the initial growth stage, the exponential growth stage, the dampened growth stage, and the equilibrium stage.

Time (days)	Number of People who Know the Secret
0	4
1	8
2	16
3	35
4	49
5	64
6	85
7	103
8	119
9	130
10	134
11	135
12	137

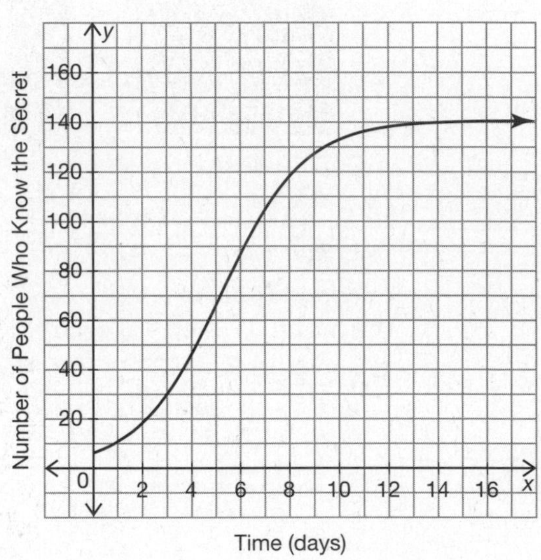

The function that represents this relationship is $f(x) = \frac{140.6514}{(1 + 21.7768e^{-0.5923x})}$, and the carrying capacity is approximately 141. The initial growth stage occurs from Day 0 to Day 2. The exponential growth stage occurs from Day 2 to Day 5. The dampened growth stage occurs from Day 5 to Day 10, and the equilibrium stage occurs from Day 10 to Day 12.

14

14.5 Understanding the Iterative Process Using Fractals

An iterative process is one in which the output of one iteration becomes the input of the next iteration. Relationships between the iterations and the area and perimeter of the fractal can often be represented as an infinite geometric sequence.

Example

The Sierpinski Carpet is formed in a manner that is similar to that of the Sierpinski Triangle. Begin with a square, and then divide it into 9 congruent squares. Remove the center square. Repeat this process. The initial stage and three additional stages of the Sierpinski Carpet are shown. Write a geometric sequence that represents the relationship between the stage and the number of shaded squares in the figure. Then, use the sequence to determine the number of shaded squares in the Stage 6 figure.

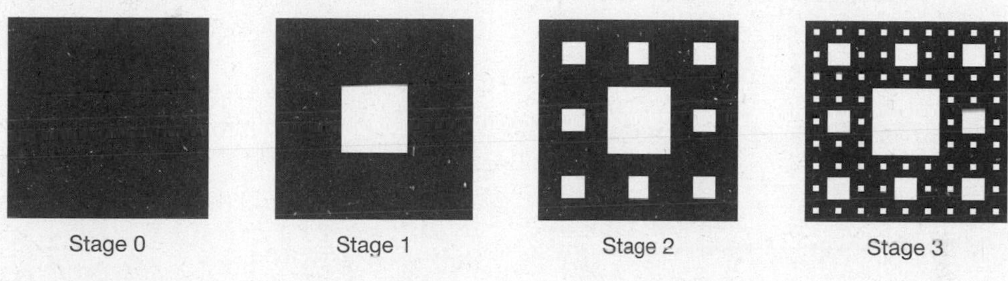

Stage (n)	0	1	2	3	n
Shaded squares	2^0 or 1	2^3 or 8	2^6 or 64	2^9 or 512	2^{3n}

The number of shaded squares in each figure represents an infinite geometric sequence. To determine the number of shaded squares in the Stage 6 figure, use the expression 2^{3n}.

$$\begin{aligned} 2^{3n} &= 2^{(3)(6)} \\ &= 2^{18} \\ &= 262{,}144 \end{aligned}$$

There are 262,144 shaded squares in the Stage 6 figure of the Sierpinski Carpet.

14

14.6 Choosing a Mathematical Model for a Real-World Situation

Real-life data can often be represented by a mathematical model. However, it can be difficult to determine which model works best. Plotting data on a scatter plot and then calculating and graphing regression equations on the same scatter plot can help determine which model is the best fit.

Example

The cell phone use of Americans has increased dramatically since 1985. The data table shows the number of cell phone subscribers in the small town of Springfield.

Time Since 1985 (years)	Number of Cell Phone Users
0	285
1	498
3	1527
4	2672
6	8186
7	14,325
8	25,069

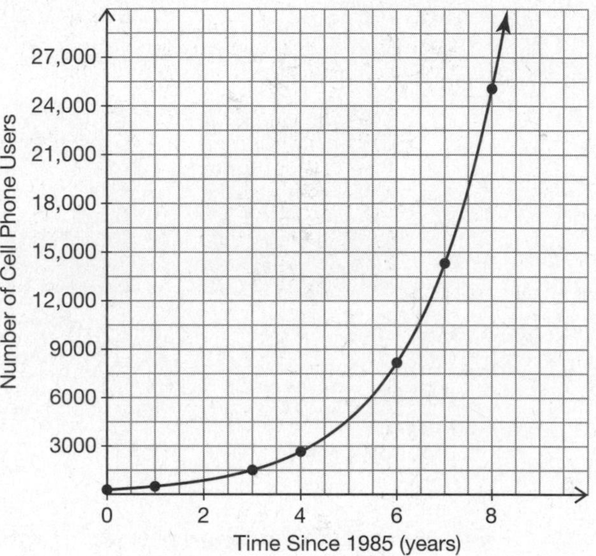

The number of cell phone users increases with the increase of each year. Increasing functions can be modeled by a linear or exponential function. However, because the number of cell phone users does not increase at a constant rate, the data cannot be modeled by a linear function. The exponential regression equation for the data is $f(x) = 284.938e^{0.55964x}$. This function when graphed closely models the data.

14

Trigonometric Functions

15

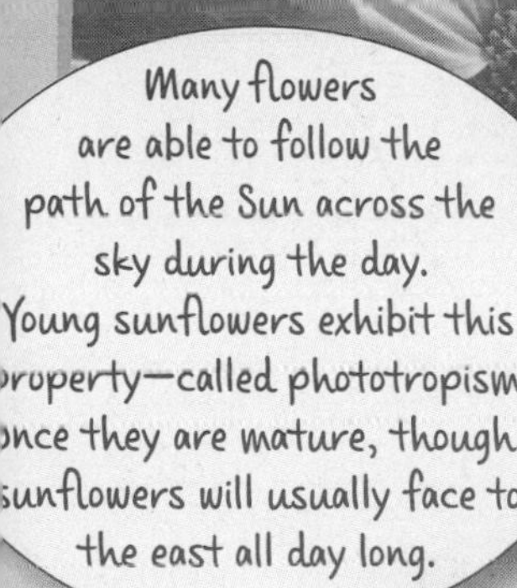

Many flowers
are able to follow the
path of the Sun across the
sky during the day.
Young sunflowers exhibit this
roperty—called phototropism.
nce they are mature, though,
unflowers will usually face to
the east all day long.

15.1

A Sense of Déjà Vu

Periodic Functions

LEARNING GOALS

In this lesson, you will:

- Model a situation with a periodic function.
- Analyze the period and amplitude of a periodic function.
- Determine the period, amplitude, and midline of a periodic function.

KEY TERMS

- periodic function
- period
- standard position
- initial ray
- terminal ray
- amplitude
- midline

The Ferris Wheel is named after George Washington Gale Ferris, Jr., a Pittsburgh bridge-builder. The first Ferris Wheel was designed and constructed by Ferris for the World's Columbian Exposition in Chicago in 1893. It stood 264 feet tall, contained 36 cars, took 20 minutes to complete 2 revolutions, and cost 50 cents per ride.

The record for the world's tallest Ferris Wheel has been broken many times since 1893. As of 2008, the Singapore Flyer, in Singapore holds the record. It stands a whopping 541 feet, over twice as tall as Ferris' original wheel.

PROBLEM 1 Who's Ready for a "Wheel" Good Time?

One of the most popular amusement park rides is the Ferris wheel. One Ferris wheel has a diameter of 50 feet. Riders board the cars at ground level and the wheel moves counterclockwise. Each ride consists of four revolutions and you can assume that the Ferris wheel rotates at a constant rate.

1. Create a sketch to model the height of a rider above ground with respect to the number of revolutions of the Ferris wheel. Include 4 revolutions.

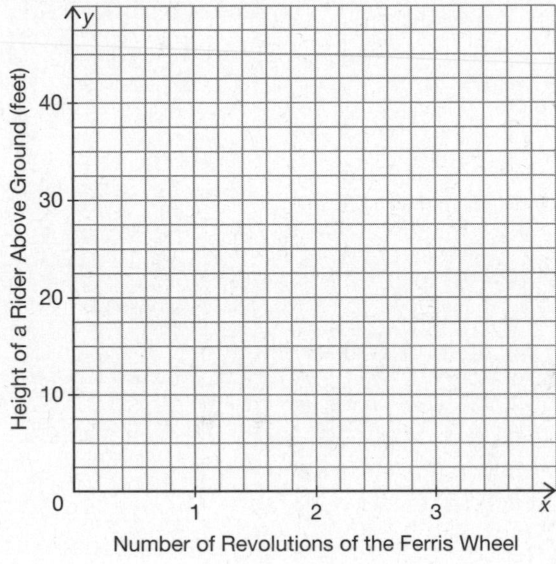

Imagine yourself on this Ferris Wheel. When will you be on the ground and when will you be 50 feet above the ground?

2. Compete the table to represent the height of a rider above ground as a function of the number of revolutions of the Ferris wheel.

Revolutions of the Ferris Wheel	Height of a Rider Above Ground (feet)
0	
$\frac{1}{8}$	
$\frac{1}{4}$	
$\frac{3}{8}$	
$\frac{1}{2}$	
$\frac{5}{8}$	
$\frac{3}{4}$	
$\frac{7}{8}$	
1	

3. Describe the characteristics of your graph.

4. What do you notice about the shape of the graph for each revolution?

To model the height of a rider above ground on the Ferris wheel, you used a *periodic function*. A **periodic function** is a function whose values repeat over regular intervals. The **period** of a periodic function is the length of the smallest interval over which the function repeats.

5. Describe the period of the function that models the height of a rider above ground on the Ferris wheel.

PROBLEM 2 The Underground Ferris Wheel

At a different amusement park, a Ferris wheel was designed so that half of the wheel is actually below the ground. The diameter of this underground Ferris wheel is still 50 feet. The top of the ride reaches 25 feet above ground and the bottom of the ride reaches 25 feet below ground. Riders board the cars at ground level to the right and the Ferris wheel moves counterclockwise.

1. Create a sketch to model the height of a rider above ground with respect to the number of revolutions of the underground Ferris wheel. Include 4 revolutions.

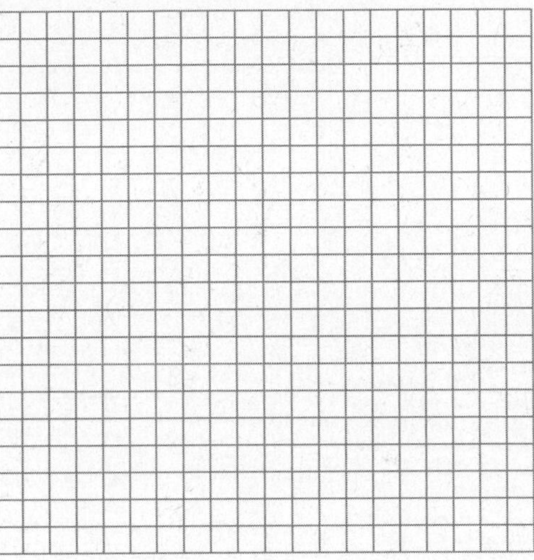

2. Complete the table to represent the height of a rider above ground as a function of the number of revolutions of the underground Ferris wheel.

Revolutions of the Ferris Wheel	Height of a Rider Above Ground (feet)
0	
$\frac{1}{8}$	
$\frac{1}{4}$	
$\frac{3}{8}$	
$\frac{1}{2}$	
$\frac{5}{8}$	
$\frac{3}{4}$	
$\frac{7}{8}$	
1	

3. Describe the characteristics of your graph.

4. Describe the period of the function that models the height of a rider above ground on the underground Ferris wheel.

15

PROBLEM 3 Periodic Functions

In the last two problems, you modeled the height of a rider above ground as a function of the number of revolutions of two different Ferris wheels. You can also model the height of a rider as a function using angle measures.

An angle is in **standard position** when the vertex is at the origin and one ray of the angle is on the x-axis. The ray on the x-axis is the **initial ray** and the other ray is the **terminal ray**.

1. Use a protractor, a straightedge, and the graph on the following page. Complete the steps shown to build a periodic function to model the height of a rider above ground on the underground Ferris wheel as a function of the measure of an angle in standard position. The position of the car is the intersection of the terminal ray and the circle.

Step 1: Analyze each axis label.

Step 2: Measure a 45° angle in *standard position*. Mark and label a point on the Ferris Wheel as shown.

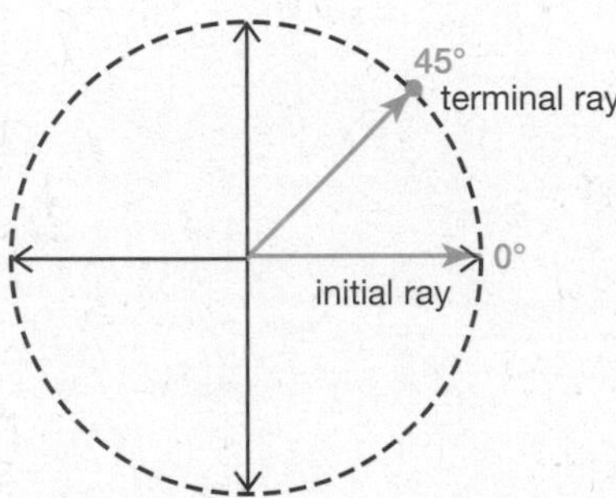

The measure of an angle in standard position is the amount of rotation from the initial ray to the terminal ray. When the rotation is counterclockwise, the angle measure is positive. When the rotation is clockwise, the angle measure is negative.

Step 3: Use a straightedge to line up the point on the Ferris wheel with the appropriate location on the coordinate plane. Plot the point.

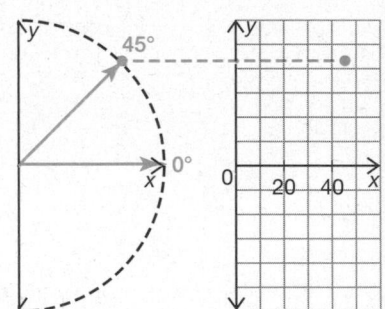

Step 4: Repeat Steps 2 and 3 for each angle measure:

0°, 30°, 60°, 90°, 180°, 270°, 360°

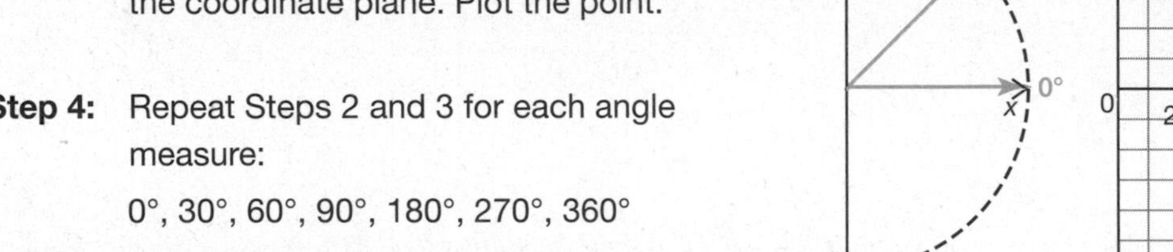

Step 5: Draw a smooth curve to connect the points of your graph.

Step 6: Continue the curve to represent angle measures greater than 360°.

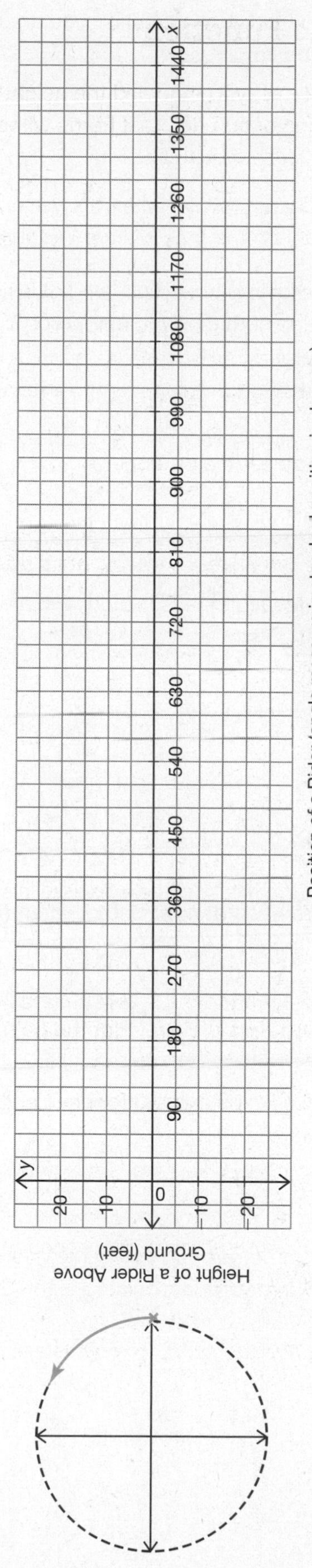

Height of a Rider Above Ground (feet)
Position of a Rider (angle measure in standard position in degrees)
y
x
20
10
0
−10
−20
90
180
270
360
450
540
630
720
810
900
990
1080
1170
1260
1350
1440

15

2. Determine the period of the function you graphed. What does this value represent in terms of this problem situation?

3. Determine any maximum or minimum values of your graph. What does each value represent in terms of this problem situation?

4. At certain angle measures, a rider is at its highest or lowest point.

   a. List 4 angle measures associated with a rider being at its highest point.

Remember, you can describe angle measures greater than 360°!

   b. List 4 angle measures associated with a rider being at its lowest point.

5. Describe the symmetries you see in the graph of the function. Explain how these are related to the symmetries associated with the Ferris wheel.

The graphs of periodic functions have characteristics that are given special names, such as *amplitude* and *midline*.

15

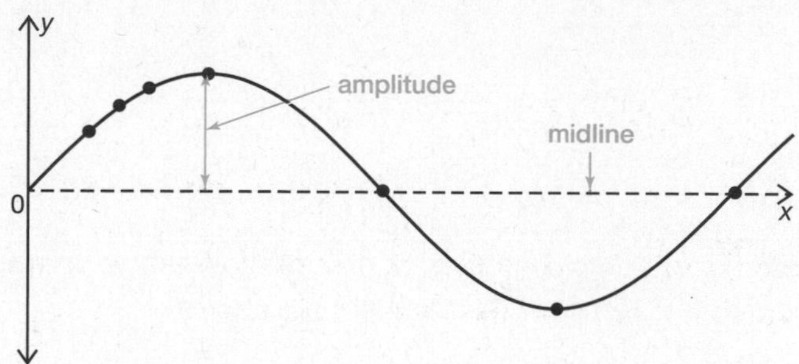

The **amplitude** of a periodic function is one-half the absolute value of the difference between the maximum and minimum values of the function.

The **midline** of a periodic function is a reference line whose equation is the average of the minimum and maximum values of the function.

6. Determine the amplitude of each function you graphed in Problems 1 through 3. Show your work.

7. Determine the midline of each function you graphed in Problems 1 through 3.

Be prepared to share your methods and solutions.

15.2

Two Pi Radii

Radian Measure

LEARNING GOALS

In this lesson, you will:

- Determine the radian measure of angles.
- Convert between angle measures in degrees and angle measures in radians.
- Estimate the degree measure of central angle measures given in radians.
- Identify reference angles in radians.

KEY TERMS

- theta (θ)
- unit circle
- radians

There are many issues associated with using degrees as units for angle measures. For starters, angles measured in degrees can't tell you anything about the distance of a rotation. The speed of the orbiting International Space Station, for example, is understood in miles per hour, rather than degrees per hour.

Secondly, the number 360—representing the number of degrees in a circle—is an arbitrary number which has no logical relationship to circle measures.

Finally, computing with a logical angle measure, like the one you'll learn about in this lesson, is often more efficient—once you get the hang of it!

Can you think of another way to measure central angles?

PROBLEM  1 An Angle Measure by Another Name

Recall that the measure of an arc of a circle is equal to the degree measure of the central angle that intercepts the arc.

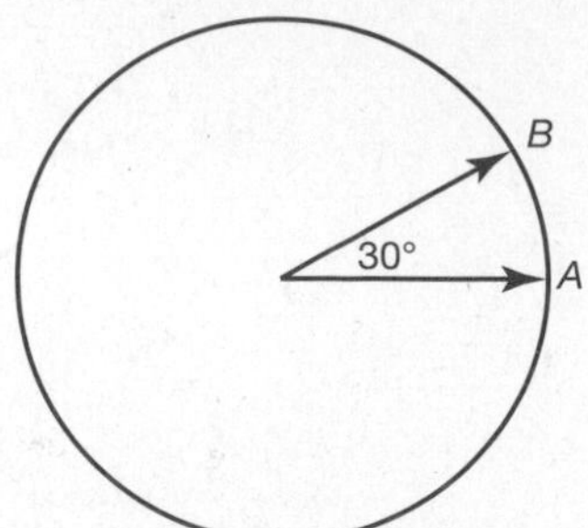

$$m\widehat{AB} = 30°$$

The length of the intercepted arc is given by the expression:

$$\text{arc length} = 2\pi r \cdot \frac{\text{measure of central angle}}{360°}$$

You can identify the central angle measures of a circle in standard position using the symbol **theta**, written as θ. For example, a central angle measure of 30° can be written as $\theta = 30°$.

The central angles you will discuss in this lesson are all angles in standard position.

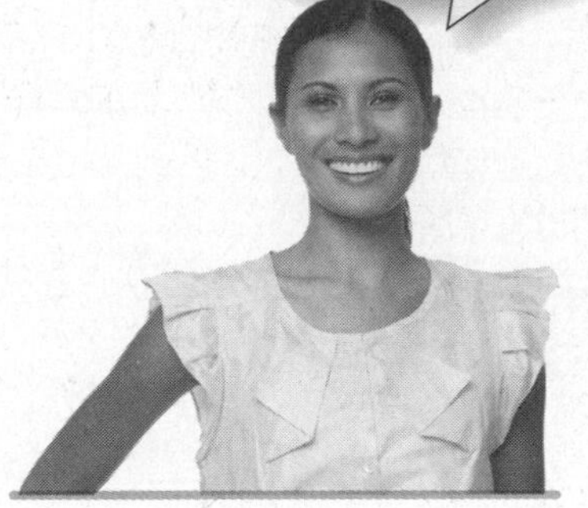

1. Given any circle with a radius of r units:

   a. Write an expression in terms of r to describe the arc length for a central angle measure of $\theta = 30°$.

   b. Write an expression in terms of r to describe the arc length for a central angle measure of $\theta = 45°$.

A powerful way to measure central angles of a circle is to identify arc lengths of the circle in terms of the radius of a *unit circle*. A **unit circle** has a radius of 1 unit.

2. Consider the unit circle shown.

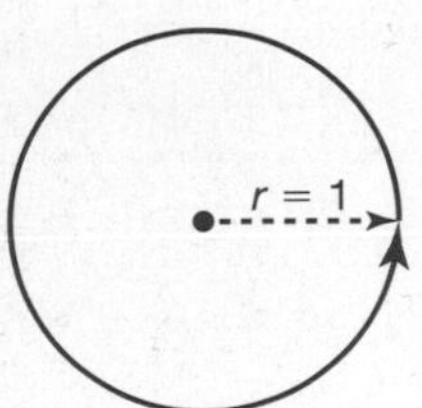

$r = 1$

a. Identify a central angle measure, θ, that represents a complete revolution of the terminal ray around the unit circle.

15

b. Identify a is the arc length of this central angle?

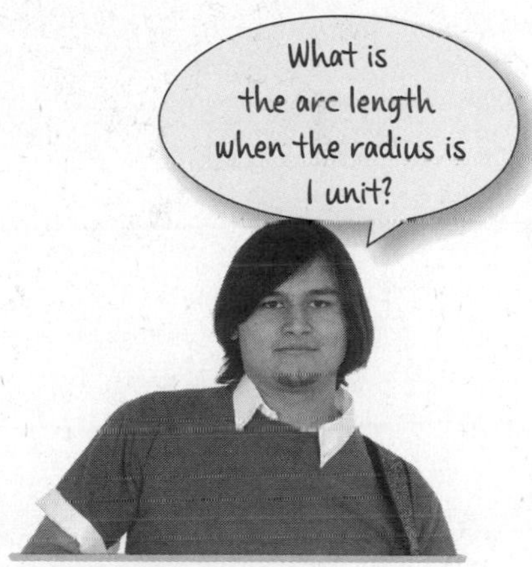

What is the arc length when the radius is 1 unit?

c. Identify a central angle measure, θ, and arc length that represent half of a revolution of the terminal ray around the unit circle.

3. Use a protractor to determine each central angle measure, θ, in the unit circle. Then label the angle measures and their corresponding arc lengths in units. Explain how you determined your answers.

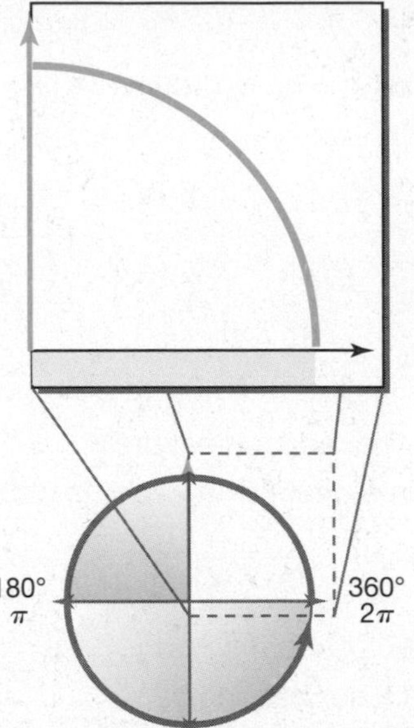

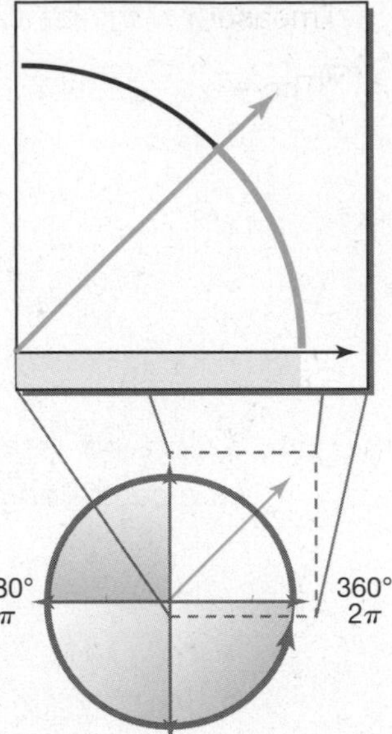

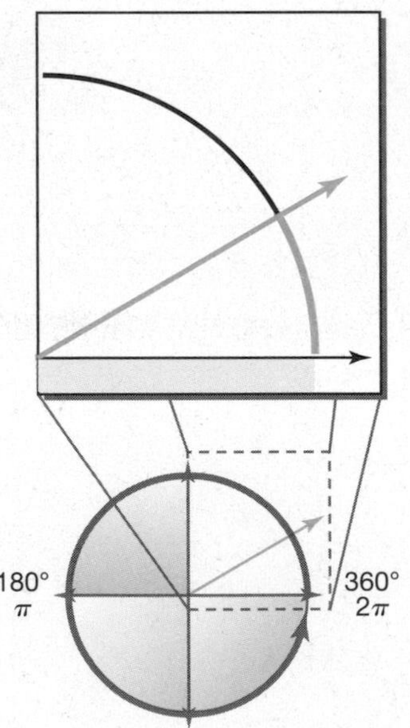

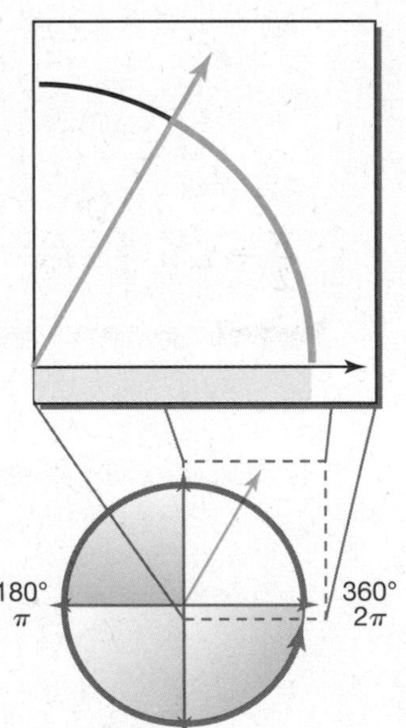

The unit that describes the measure of an angle theta, θ, in terms of the radius and arc length of a unit circle is called a *radian*. The ratio of the intercepted arc length of a central angle to the radius is the measure of the central angle in **radians**.

There are $\frac{2\pi r}{r}$, or 2π, radians in 360° and $\frac{\pi r}{r}$, or π, radians in 180°.

Radians are angle measures, not linear measures.

4. Sandy and Josh each determined the radian measure for a central angle measuring 45° in a circle with a radius of 2 units.

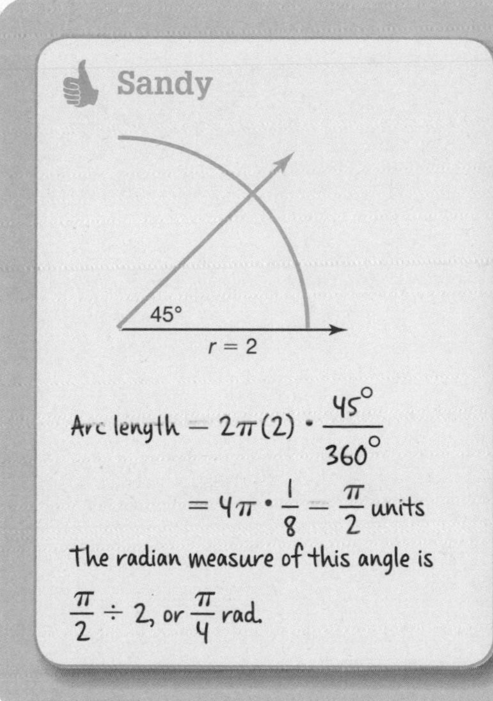

Sandy
45°
r = 2
Arc length = 2π(2) · 45°/360°
= 4π · 1/8 = π/2 units
The radian measure of this angle is
π/2 ÷ 2, or π/4 rad.

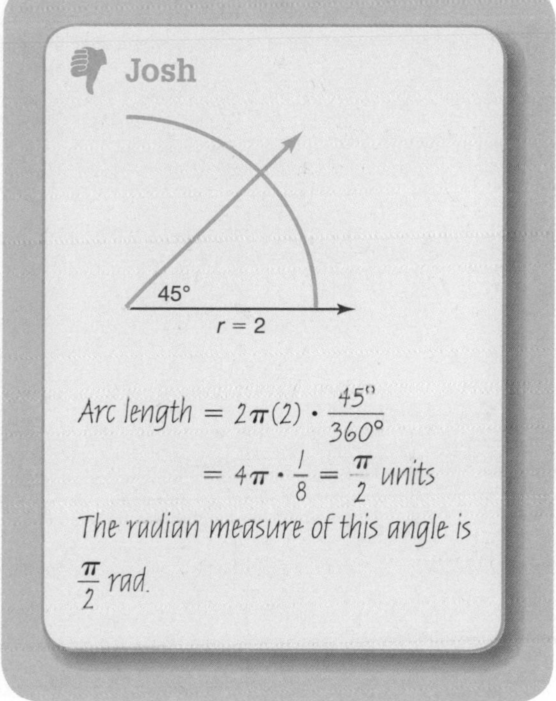

Josh
45°
r = 2
Arc length = 2π(2) · 45°/360°
= 4π · 1/8 = π/2 units
The radian measure of this angle is
π/2 rad.

Explain why Josh's reasoning is incorrect.

5. Use what you know about the symmetry of a circle to label each central angle measure in degrees and radians on the unit circle on the next page. Explain how you determined the measures and show your work.

Use your protractor to verify your angle measures.

Degrees and Radians

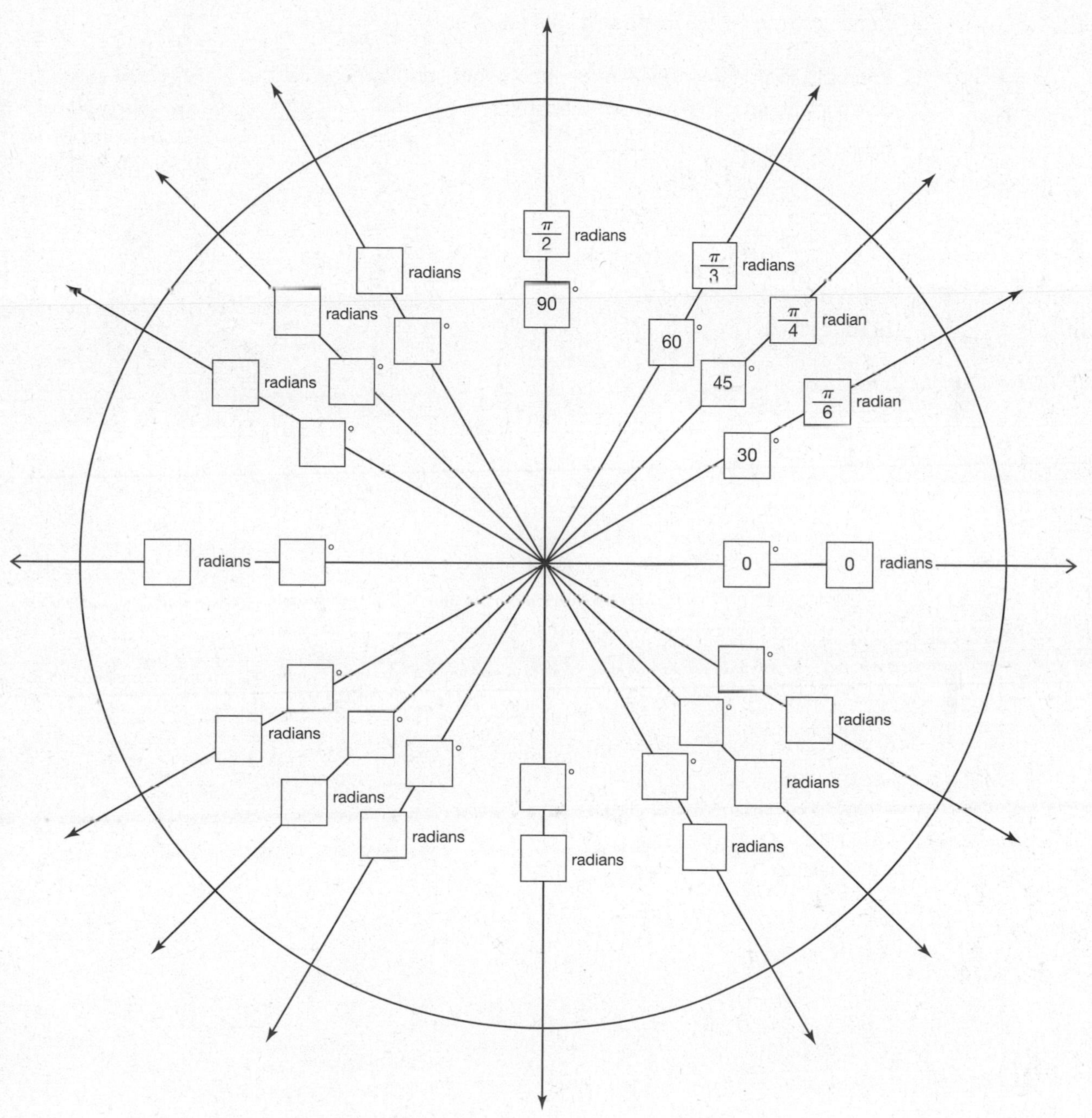

PROBLEM 2 Pin the Tail on the Radian

It is important to keep in mind that values such as $\frac{\pi}{4}$ and $\frac{7\pi}{6}$ are constants. Each of these irrational numbers can be rewritten as non-terminating, non-repeating decimals.

$$\frac{\pi}{4} \approx \frac{3.14}{4} \approx 0.785 \quad \frac{7\pi}{6} \approx \frac{7(3.14)}{6} \approx 3.6633\ldots.$$

You can also write whole-number values for radians.

1. Estimate the degree measure of each central angle measure given in radians. Explain your reasoning.

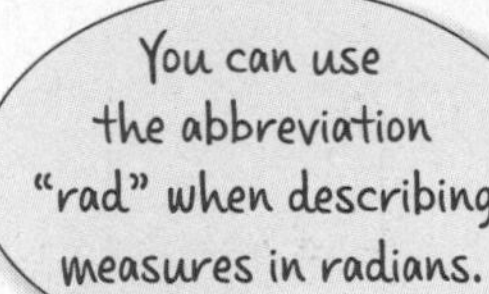

You can use the abbreviation "rad" when describing measures in radians.

   a. 3 radians

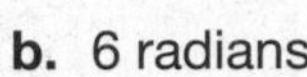

   b. 6 radians

   c. 2 radians

   d. 4 radians

   e. 1 radian

   f. 5 radians

2. What is the arc length of a central angle that has a measure of 1 radian on the unit circle? Explain your reasoning.

The formulas you can use to convert from radians to degrees and degrees to radians are shown.

Radians to Degrees: $x \text{ radians} \cdot \frac{180^\circ}{\pi \text{ radians}}$

Degrees to Radians: $x \text{ degrees} \cdot \frac{\pi \text{ radians}}{180^\circ}$

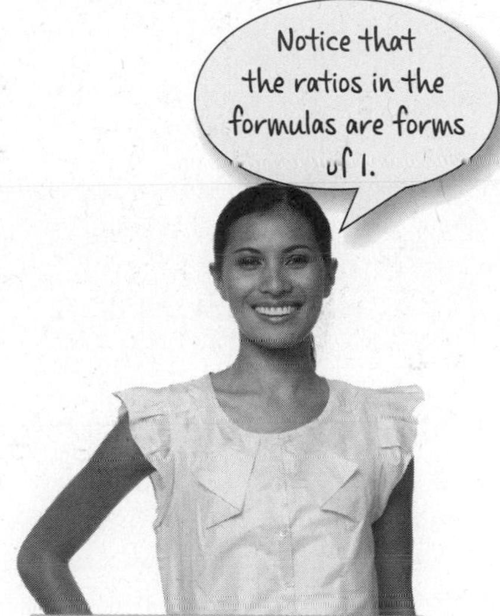

Notice that the ratios in the formulas are forms of 1.

3. Use the formulas to convert each angle measure in Question 1 to degrees.
   How close were your estimates?

4. Explain why Corinne is correct. Write a similar statement using degrees.

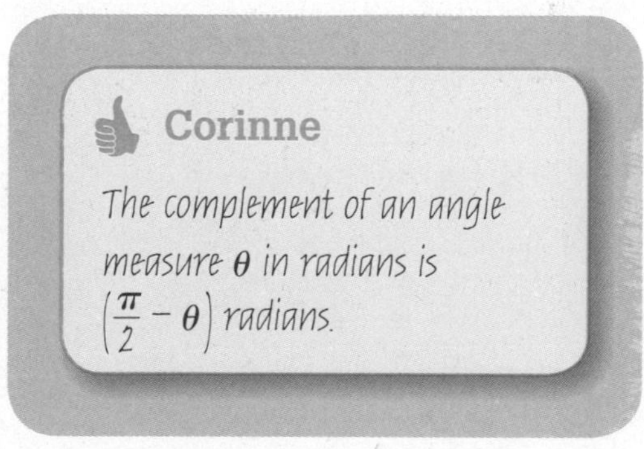

Corinne
The complement of an angle measure θ in radians is $\left(\frac{\pi}{2} - \theta\right)$ radians.

Be prepared to share your methods and solutions.

15

Triangulation

The Sine and Cosine Functions

15.3

LEARNING GOALS

In this lesson, you will:

- Define the sine and cosine functions.
- Calculate values for the sine and cosine of reference angles.
- Define the sine and cosine of an angle as a coordinate of a point on the unit circle.
- Graph and compare the sine and cosine functions.

KEY TERMS

- sine function
- cosine function
- trigonometric function
- periodicity identity

Triangulation is a method that involves using triangles to identify the coordinates of an object or the distance of an object from a point. It is used in astrometry—a branch of astronomy involved in precisely measuring the locations and distances of astronomical bodies—navigation, and meteorology.

And of course, triangulation can be used to determine the coordinates of points on the unit circle!

PROBLEM 1 Now You Will Determine the Right Triangle Connection

Recall that the sine ratio (sin) is the ratio of the length of the opposite side to the hypotenuse in a right triangle.

$$\sin(\theta) = \frac{\text{opposite side}}{\text{hypotenuse}}$$

The cosine ratio (cos) is the ratio of the length of the adjacent side to the hypotenuse.

$$\cos(\theta) = \frac{\text{adjacent side}}{\text{hypotenuse}}$$

The side-length relationships for a 30°–60°–90° triangle and a 45°–45°–90° triangle are shown.

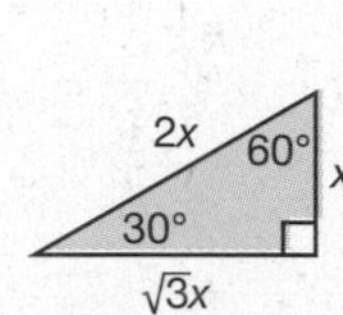

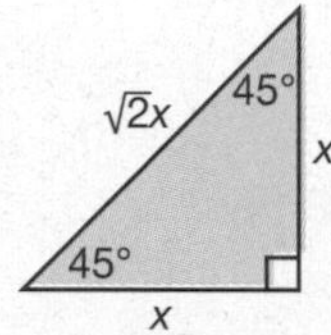

The diagram shows a right triangle *ABC* placed on a unit circle centered at the origin. The central angle measures $\theta = 30°$, $\theta = 45°$, and $\theta = 60°$ are shown.

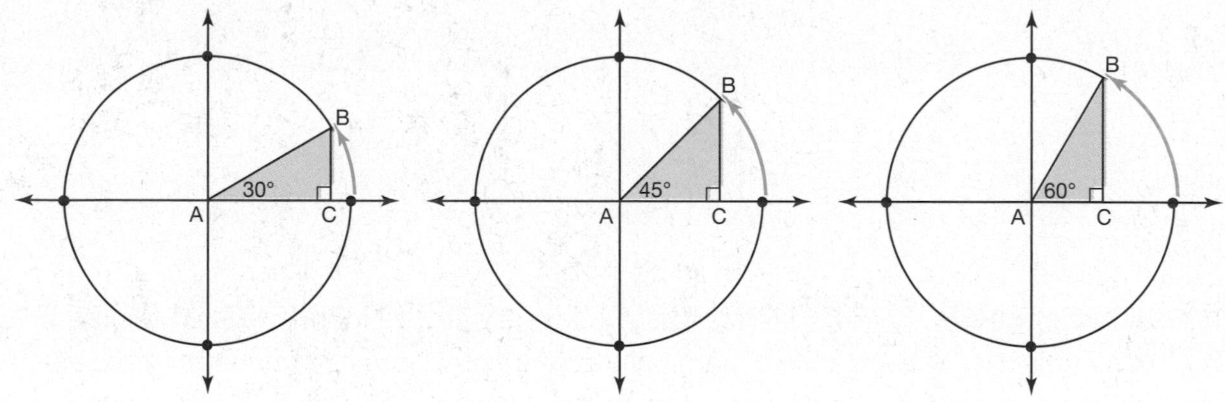

1. What is the length of the hypotenuse *c* in each circle? Label the measures on each triangle.

2. Label the side lengths of the triangles in each diagram in radical form.

3. The hypotenuse of each right triangle represents the terminal ray of a central angle which intersects the unit circle at point B.

   a. Complete the table to record the sine and cosine of each angle measure, θ, and the coordinates of the point where the terminal ray intersects the unit circle. Explain your reasoning.

θ	$\cos(\theta)$	$\sin(\theta)$	Coordinates of point B, Intersection of Terminal Ray and Unit Circle
30°			
45°			
60°			

   b. Write the coordinates of the intersection of the terminal ray and the unit circle at 0°.

   c. Write the coordinates of the intersection of the terminal ray and the unit circle at 90°.

15

4. Jorge conjectured that the coordinates of the point where the terminal ray of a central angle θ intersects the unit circle can always be written as $(\cos(\theta), \sin(\theta))$.

Do you think Jorge's conjecture is correct? Explain your reasoning.

5. Use your answers in Questions 1 through 3 to determine the coordinates of the points in the first quadrant on the unit circle on the next page. Label the coordinates.

You will label the first quadrant now. Then you will be able to determine the coordinates of the points in the other quadrants in Problem 2.

Sine and Cosine on the Unit Circle

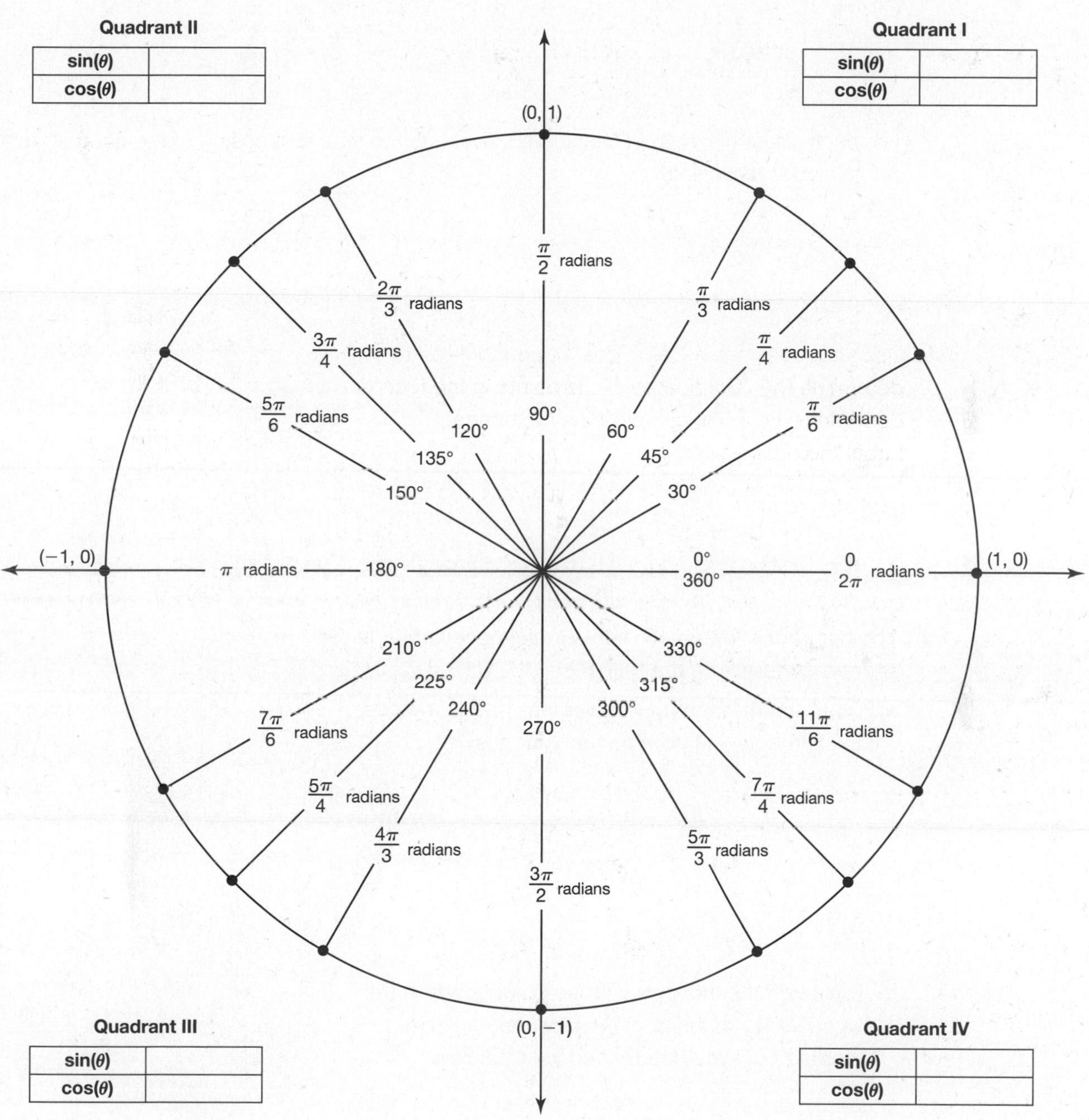

15

6. Use the unit circle to evaluate each measure.

- $\sin\left(\frac{\pi}{6} \text{ radian}\right) =$ ______________________
- $\cos\left(\frac{\pi}{6} \text{ radian}\right) =$ ______________________
- $\sin\left(\frac{\pi}{4} \text{ radian}\right) =$ ______________________
- $\cos\left(\frac{\pi}{4} \text{ radian}\right) =$ ______________________

7. For each angle measure in Question 6, evaluate the sine and cosine of the complement. Explain your reasoning.

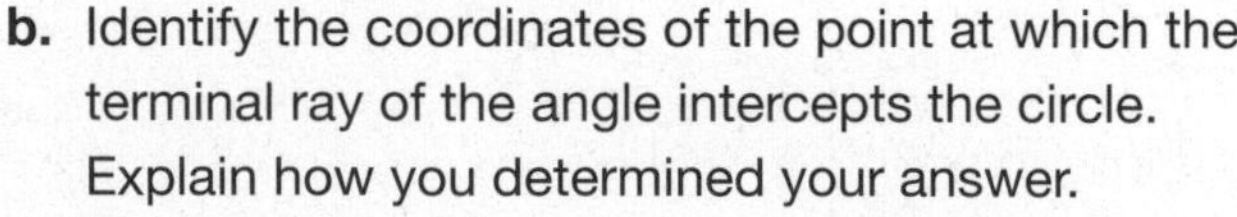

PROBLEM 2 To Infinity and Beyond the First Quadrant

1. The diagram shows a 45° central angle positioned in the second quadrant on the unit circle.

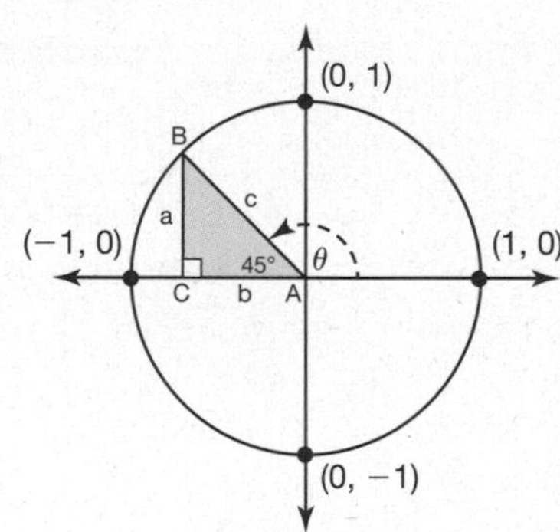

   a. State the measure of θ in degrees and in radians. Explain how you determined your answer.

   b. Identify the coordinates of the point at which the terminal ray of the angle intercepts the circle. Explain how you determined your answer.

The cosine is a negative value because the x-coordinate is negative.

15

c. What do you notice about the coordinates of this point and the coordinates of the symmetrical point in the first quadrant?

2. Use what you know about symmetry to label the coordinates of the remaining points on your Sine and Cosine on the Unit Circle diagram from Problem 1.

3. Look back at Jorge's conjecture in Problem 1, Question 4. Is his conjecture correct? Explain your reasoning.

4. Describe when the values of sine and cosine are positive and negative in the unit circle. Label this information on your Sine and Cosine on the Unit Circle diagram in Problem 1.

5. Give examples to support Ray's conclusion.

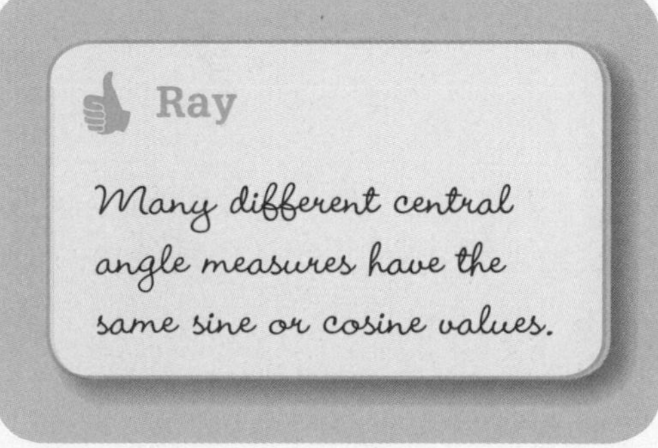

Ray
Many different central angle measures have the same sine or cosine values.

PROBLEM 3 Orbiting Back to the Functions

1. Use your completed unit circle from Problem 1 to graph the function $y = \sin(x)$.

   a. As the terminal ray traverses the unit circle counterclockwise in standard position, plot the output value, $\sin(\theta)$, that corresponds to the input value, θ, which is the radian measure of the central angle, from 0 to 2π radians.

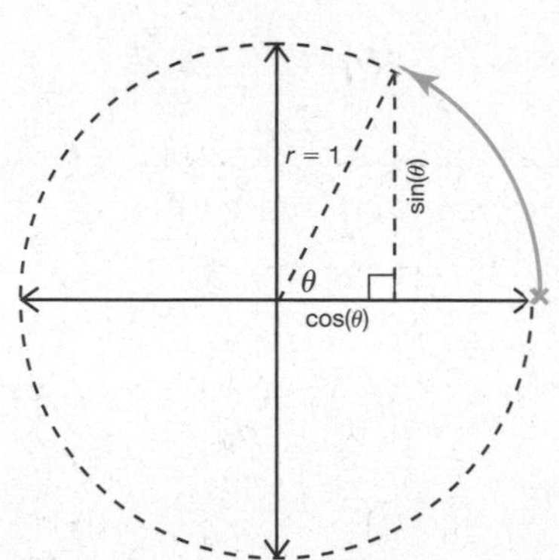

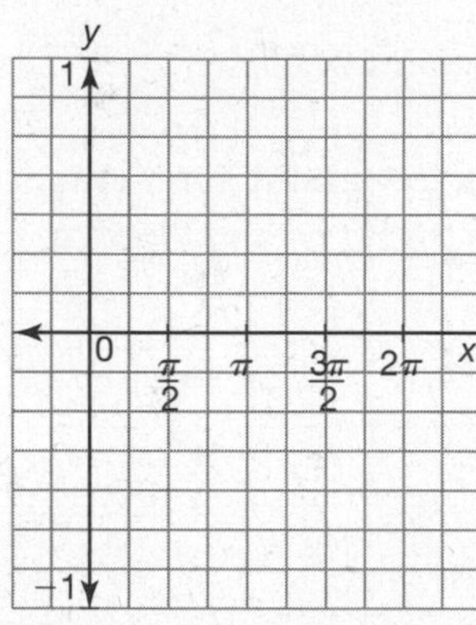

Plot the output values from left to right on the graph as you move counterclockwise around the unit circle.

   b. What coordinate values on the unit circle did you use to create the graph of $y = \sin(x)$?

2. Use your completed Sine and Cosine on the Unit Circle diagram from Problem 1 to graph the function $y = \cos(x)$.

   a. As the terminal ray traverses the unit circle counterclockwise in standard position, plot the output value, $\cos(\theta)$, that corresponds to the input value, θ, which is the radian measure of the central angle, from 0 to 2π radians.

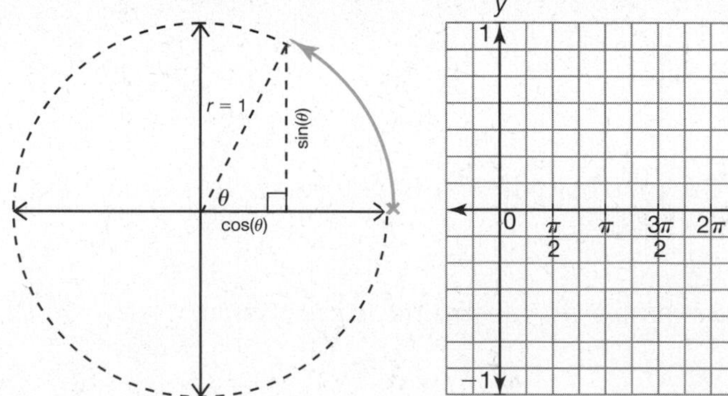

   b. What coordinate values on the unit circle did you use to create the graph of $y = \cos(x)$?

You have graphed the *sine function* and *cosine function*. The **sine function** and **cosine function** are periodic **trigonometric functions**. Each of these trigonometric functions takes angle measures (θ values) as inputs and outputs real number values, which correspond to coordinates of points on the unit circle.

3. Extend the graphs of the functions $y = \sin(x)$ and $y = \cos(x)$ to $x = 8\pi$ radians.

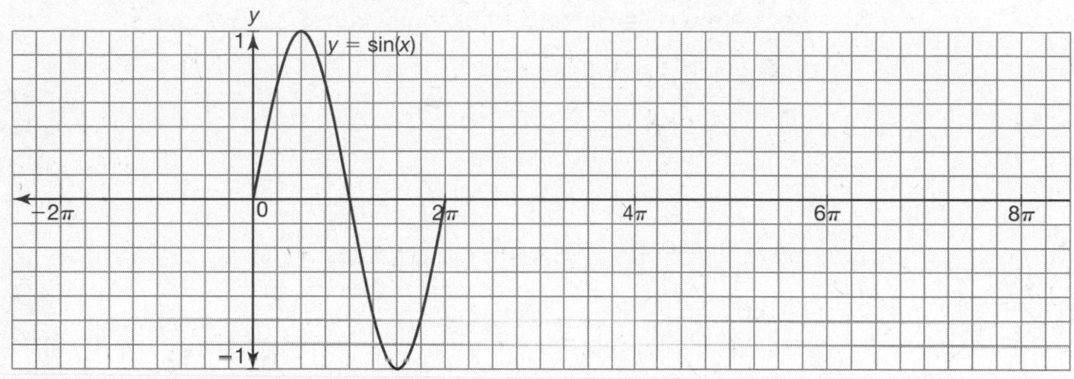

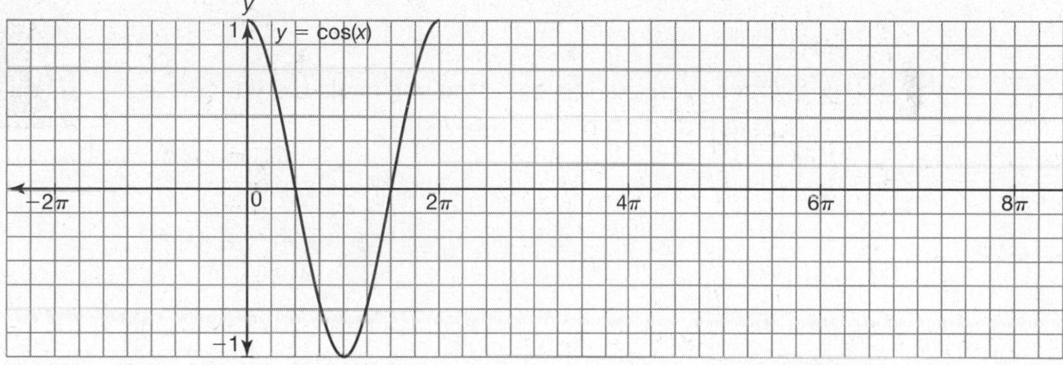

a. Determine the values of $\sin(x)$ and $\cos(x)$ at 4π, 6π, and 8π radians.

b. Describe how you can determine each value from part (a) on the unit circle for each function.

15

4. Extend the graphs of the functions $y = \sin(x)$ and $y = \cos(x)$ in Question 3 through $x = -2\pi$.

   a. Determine each sine value.

   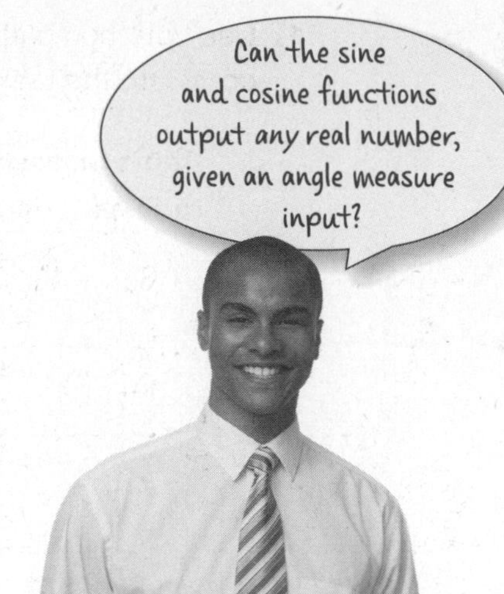

Can the sine and cosine functions output any real number, given an angle measure input?

   - $\sin\left(-\frac{\pi}{2}\right) =$ ____________
   - $\sin(-\pi) =$ ____________
   - $\sin\left(-\frac{3\pi}{2}\right) =$ ____________
   - $\sin(-2\pi) =$ ____________

   b. Determine each cosine value.

   - $\cos\left(-\frac{\pi}{2}\right) =$ ____________
   - $\cos(-\pi) =$ ____________
   - $\cos\left(-\frac{3\pi}{2}\right) =$ ____________
   - $\cos(-2\pi) =$ ____________

5. Consider the values of $\sin(x + 2\pi)$. How do these values compare to the values of $\sin(x)$?

6. Consider the values of $\cos(x + 2\pi)$. How do these values compare to the values of $\cos(x)$?

The period of the sine function is 2π radians, and the period of the cosine function is 2π radians. Thus, you can write two *periodicity identities*:

- $\sin(x + 2\pi) = \sin(x)$
- $\cos(x + 2\pi) = \cos(x)$

Each of these is called a **periodicity identity** because they are each based on the period of the function, 2π.

Talk the Talk

1. Use your completed Sine and Cosine on the Unit Circle diagram from Problem 1 to complete the table.

Angle Measure (θ) radians	Angle Measure (θ) degrees	$\cos(\theta)$	$\sin(\theta)$
0	0°	1	0
$\frac{\pi}{6}$	30°		
$\frac{\pi}{4}$	45°		
$\frac{\pi}{3}$	60°		
$\frac{\pi}{2}$	90°		
$\frac{2\pi}{3}$	120°		
$\frac{3\pi}{4}$	135°		
$\frac{5\pi}{6}$	150°		
π	180°		

Angle Measure (θ) radians	Angle Measure (θ) degrees	$\cos(\theta)$	$\sin(\theta)$
$\frac{7\pi}{6}$	210°		
$\frac{5\pi}{4}$	225°		
$\frac{4\pi}{3}$	240°		
$\frac{3\pi}{2}$	270°		
$\frac{5\pi}{3}$	300°		
$\frac{7\pi}{4}$	315°		
$\frac{11\pi}{6}$	330°		
2π	360°		

2. Compare and contrast the functions $y = \sin(x)$ and $y = \cos(x)$. Describe the similarities and differences between the two functions.

3. Identify each of the characteristics for $y = \sin(x)$ and $y = \cos(x)$.

	$y = \sin(x)$	$y = \cos(x)$
y-intercept(s)		
Domain		
Range		
Period		
Minimum Output Value		
Maximum Output Value		
Amplitude		
Midline		

4. Describe the intervals of increase and decrease for both the sine and cosine functions. Explain your reasoning.

5. Determine x-intercepts of the functions $y = \sin(x)$ and $y = \cos(x)$.

   a. x-intercepts for $y = \sin(x)$:

   b. x-intercepts for $y = \cos(x)$:

6. Use the language of transformations to explain how the sine and cosine functions are related.

How can I write this relationship mathematically?

Be prepared to share your solutions and methods.

15.4

Pump Up the Amplitude

Transformations of Sine and Cosine Functions

LEARNING GOALS

In this lesson, you will:

- Transform the graphs of the sine and cosine functions.
- Determine the amplitude, frequency, and phase shift of transformed functions.
- Graph transformed sine and cosine functions using a description of the period, phase shift, and amplitude.

KEY TERMS

- frequency
- phase shift

The word *frequency* is used in many different ways—inside and outside of mathematics. When it comes to sound, a greater frequency means a higher pitch and a lesser frequency means a lower pitch. Higher pitch sound waves vibrate faster than lower pitch sound waves.

The frequencies of sound waves are measured in a unit called a Hertz (Hz). One Hertz is equal to 1 vibration per second. Humans can typically hear sounds with frequencies in the range of 20 Hz to 20,000 Hz.

Dogs, cats, bats, and dolphins can all hear sounds with very high frequencies—45,000 Hz, 85,000 Hz, 120,000 Hz, and 200,000 Hz, respectively. Elephants, on the other hand, can hear low-frequency sounds down to 5 Hz.

15

PROBLEM 1 Amplitude

The table shows the characteristics of the graphs of the sine and cosine functions.

	$y = \sin(x)$	$y = \cos(x)$
y-intercept	(0, 0)	(0, 1)
Domain	$(-\infty, \infty)$	$(-\infty, \infty)$
Range	$[-1, 1]$	$[-1, 1]$
Period	2π	2π
Minimum Output Value	-1	-1
Maximum Output Value	1	1
Amplitude	1	1
Midline	$y = 0$	$y = 0$

Recall that transformations performed on any function $f(x)$ to form a new function $g(x)$ can be described by the transformational function form:

$$g(x) = Af(B(x - C)) + D$$

where A, B, C, and D represent constants.

1. In general, what effect does multiplying a function $y = f(x)$ by a constant, A, have on the graph of the function?

2. Which characteristics of the transformed function $y = A\sin(x)$ will differ from those of the basic function $y = \sin(x)$ if $|A| > 0$? Which characteristics will remain the same? Explain your predictions.

	$y = A\sin(x)$	
	Will Change	**Won't Change**
***y*-intercept**		
Domain		
Range		
Period		
Minimum Output Value		
Maximum Output Value		
Amplitude		
Midline		

3. A graph of the function $f(x) = \sin(x)$ is shown. Sketch the graphs of the functions $g(x) = 2\sin(x)$ and $h(x) = \frac{1}{2}\sin(x)$ on the same coordinate plane.

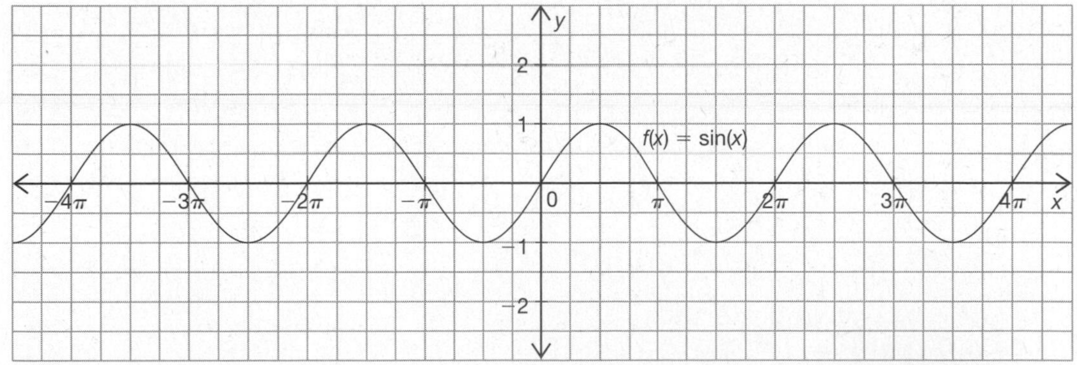

How is each value of the basic function affected by the transformation?

15

4. What similarities and differences do you notice about the three functions with respect to their periods, intercepts, and maximum and minimum values?

5. How do your graphs of the transformed functions compare with your predictions in Question 2?

Recall that the amplitude of a sine or cosine function is one-half the absolute value of the difference between the maximum and minimum values of the function.

6. Determine the maximum, minimum, and amplitude of each function you graphed.

   a. $g(x) = 2\sin(x)$

   b. $h(x) = \frac{1}{2}\sin(x)$

7. Determine the maximum, minimum, and amplitude of each cosine function.

   a. $f(x) = \cos(x)$

   b. $g(x) = 3\cos(x)$

   c. $h(x) = \frac{1}{4}\cos(x)$

PROBLEM 2 Period and Frequency

Let's consider what effect multiplying the argument of a sine or cosine function by a constant, B, has on the graph of the function. The transformed function can be written as $y = \sin(Bx)$ or $y = \cos(Bx)$.

What if $|B|$ is greater than 1? What if $|B|$ is greater than 0 but less than 1?

1. In general, what effect does multiplying the argument of a function $y = f(x)$ by a constant, B, have on the graph of the function?

2. Which characteristics of the transformed function $y = \cos(Bx)$ will differ from those of the basic function $y = \cos(x)$ if $|B| > 0$? Which characteristics will remain the same? Explain your predictions.

	$y = \cos(Bx)$	
	Will Change	**Won't Change**
***y*-intercept**		
Domain		
Range		
Period		
Minimum Output Value		
Maximum Output Value		
Amplitude		
Midline		

15

3. A graph of the function $f(x) = \cos(x)$ is shown. Sketch the graphs of the functions $g(x) = \cos(4x)$ and $h(x) = \cos\left(\frac{1}{2}x\right)$ on the same coordinate plane.

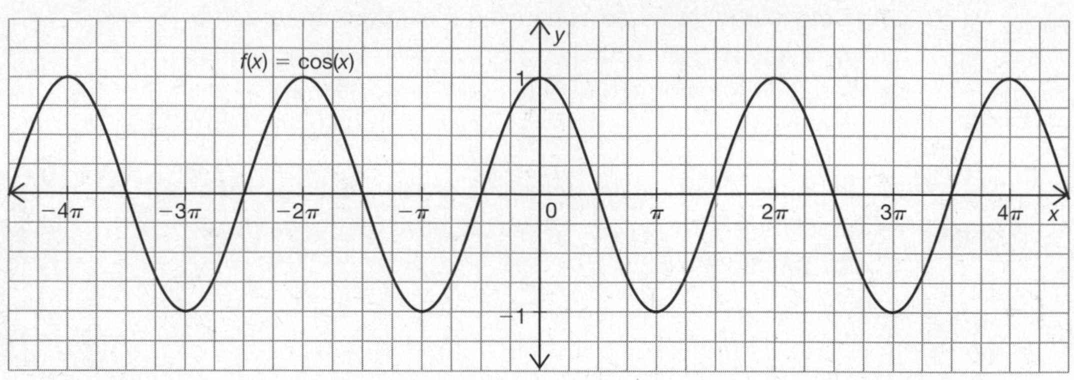

4. What similarities and differences do you notice about the three functions with respect to their periods, intercepts, and maximum and minimum values?

5. How do your graphs of the transformed functions compare with your predictions in Question 2?

6. How do the equations of the functions you graphed relate to the similarities and differences in the graphs?

Recall that the period of a periodic function is the length of the smallest interval over which the function repeats.

15

7. Determine the period of each function from the graph.

a. $f(x) = \cos(x)$

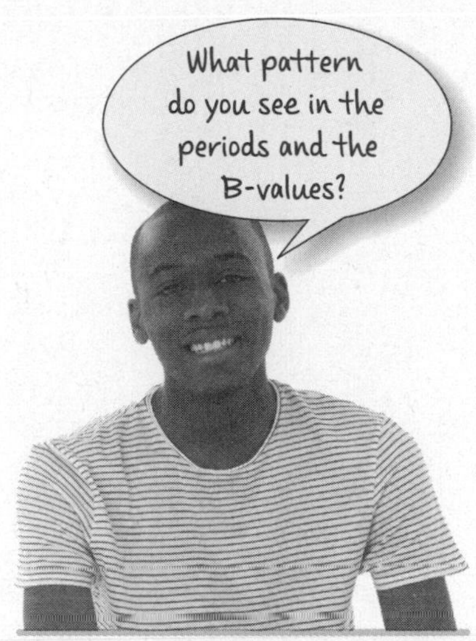
What pattern do you see in the periods and the B-values?

b. $g(x) = \cos(4x)$

c. $h(x) = \cos\left(\frac{1}{2}x\right)$

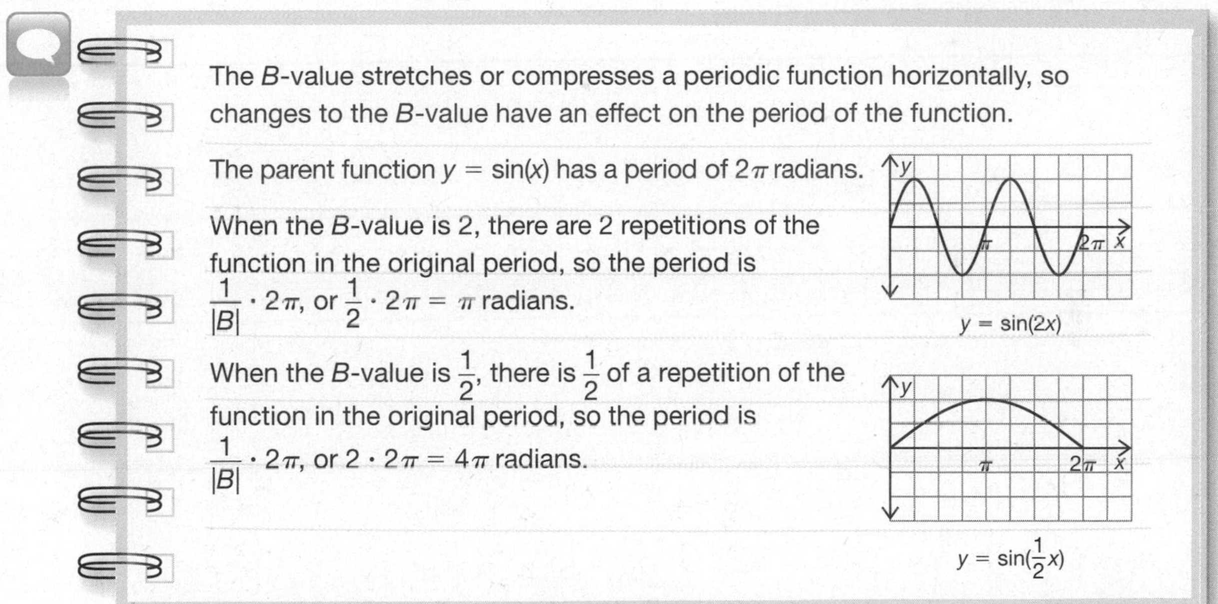

The *B*-value stretches or compresses a periodic function horizontally, so changes to the *B*-value have an effect on the period of the function.

The parent function $y = \sin(x)$ has a period of 2π radians.

When the *B*-value is 2, there are 2 repetitions of the function in the original period, so the period is $\frac{1}{|B|} \cdot 2\pi$, or $\frac{1}{2} \cdot 2\pi = \pi$ radians.

y
π
2π
x

$y = \sin(2x)$

When the *B*-value is $\frac{1}{2}$, there is $\frac{1}{2}$ of a repetition of the function in the original period, so the period is $\frac{1}{|B|} \cdot 2\pi$, or $2 \cdot 2\pi = 4\pi$ radians.

y
π
2π
x

$y = \sin(\frac{1}{2}x)$

8. Write an expression to describe the period of the functions $y = \sin(Bx)$ and $y = \cos(Bx)$.

15

Frequency is related to the period of the function. The **frequency** of a periodic function is the reciprocal of the period and specifies the number of repetitions of the graph of a periodic function per unit.

9. Write an expression to describe the frequency of the functions $y = \sin(Bx)$ and $y = \cos(Bx)$. Explain your reasoning.

10. Determine the period and frequency of each sine function.

a. $f(x) = \sin(3x)$

b. $g(x) = \sin\left(\frac{2}{3}x\right)$

c. $h(x) = \sin\left(\frac{1}{4}x\right)$

PROBLEM 3 Phase Shift

Now consider what effect subtracting a constant, C, to the argument of a sine or cosine function has on the graph of the function. The transformed function can be written as $y = \sin(x - C)$ or $y = \cos(x - C)$.

1. Sketch graphs of the functions shown over the domain $-4\pi \le x \le 4\pi$.

   a. $f(x) = \sin(x)$ **b.** $g(x) = \sin\left(x + \frac{\pi}{2}\right)$ **c.** $h(x) = \sin(x - \pi)$

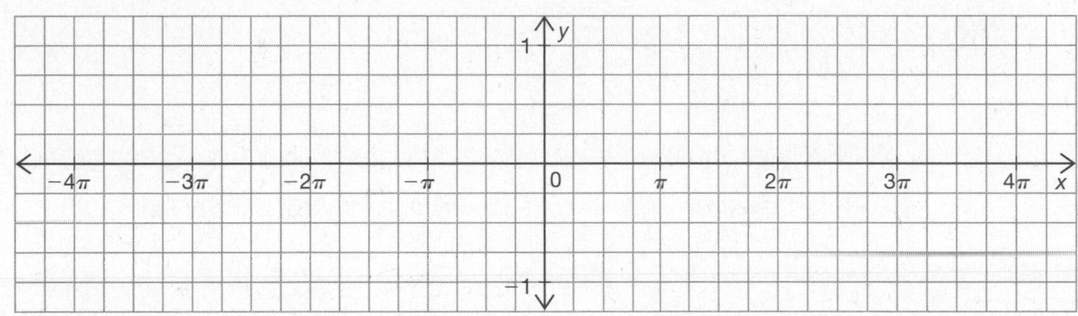

2. What similarities and differences do you notice about the three functions in terms of their maximums, minimums, periods, and amplitudes?

3. How do the equations of the functions you graphed relate to the similarities and differences in the graphs?

15

Transforming a periodic function by subtracting a C-value from the argument of the function results in horizontal translations of the function. These transformations act just as they have on other functions you have studied. For periodic functions, horizontal translations are called **phase shifts**.

Talk the Talk

1. Predict the effect of adding a constant, D, to a sine or cosine function $y = f(x)$.

2. Use what you know about transformations to sketch the graph of each function.

a. $y = -\sin(x)$

b. $y = \sin(-x)$

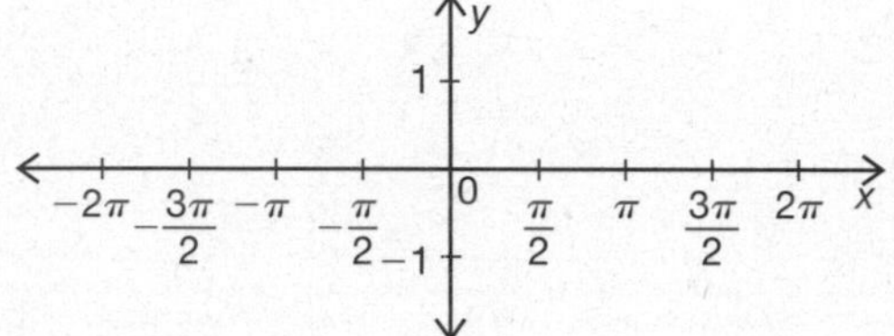

c. $y = -\cos(x)$

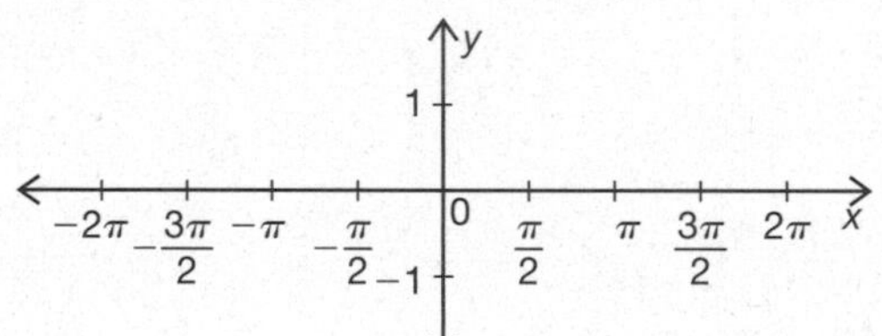

d. $y = \cos(-x)$

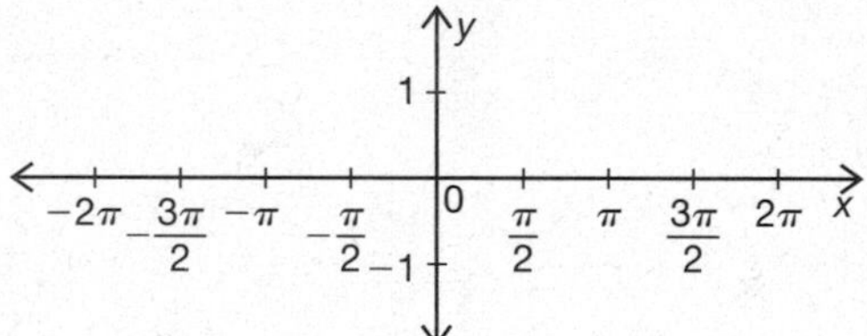

3. Compare and contrast the graphs you sketched. What do you notice?

15

4. Complete the table to describe the graph of each function as a transformation on $y = f(x)$.

Sine or Cosine Function	Equation Information	Description of Transformation of Sine or Cosine Graph	Effect on Period, Amplitude, Midline, Phase Shift
$y = f(x) + D$	$D > 0$		
	$D < 0$		
$y = f(x - C)$	$C > 0$		
	$C < 0$		
$y = Af(x)$	$\lvert A\rvert > 1$		
	$0 < \lvert A\rvert < 1$		
	$A < 0$		
$y = f(Bx)$	$\lvert B\rvert > 1$		
	$0 < \lvert B\rvert < 1$		
	$B < 0$		

Be prepared to share your methods and solutions.

15

15.5

Farmer's Tan

The Tangent Function

LEARNING GOALS

In this lesson, you will:

- Build the graph of the tangent function using the ratio $\frac{\sin(\theta)}{\cos(\theta)}$.
- Analyze characteristics of the tangent function, including period and asymptotes.
- Calculate values of the tangent function for common angles.
- Identify transformations of the tangent function.

KEY TERM

- tangent function

Farming is all about cycles. Producing crops requires—among many other things—preparing the soil, seeding, watering, and harvesting. And this process is repeated over and over again.

Sometimes crops are rotated to help the soil. When the same crop occupies the same land for a long period of time, the crop often depletes the soil of a specific nutrient. When crops are rotated, different nutrients are taken from and returned to the soil, making the land usable for a longer period of time.

Agricultural cycles often depend on other cycles, such as cyclical patterns in the weather and the Sun.

PROBLEM 1 Phototropism

Many plants have evolved the ability to track sunlight as the Sun moves across the sky during the day. This movement is called phototropism.

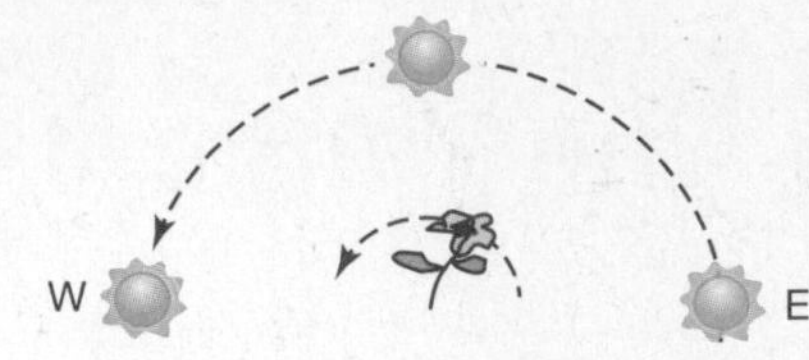

Imagine that flowers face due east in the morning where the Sun rises, and they track the sunlight throughout the day as the Sun moves directly overhead and then to the west.

1. Suppose you track the slope of the angle that a flower makes with the ground over the course of a day. Create a visual interpretation of the changing slope on the graph as you answer each question.

   a. What is the value of the slope at $\theta = 0$ radians, $\frac{\pi}{4}$ radian, and $\frac{\pi}{2}$ radians on the unit circle? Explain your reasoning.

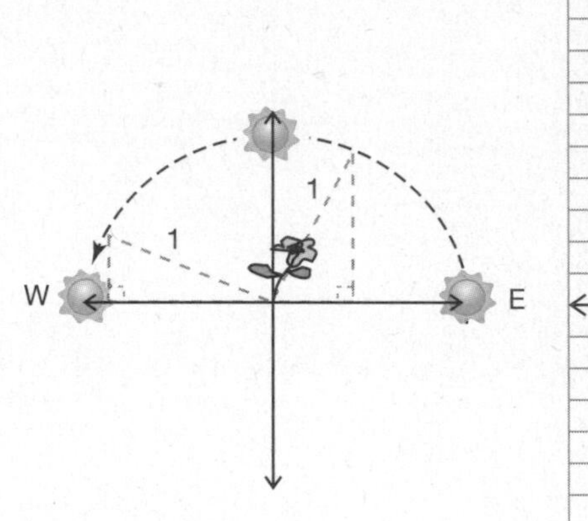

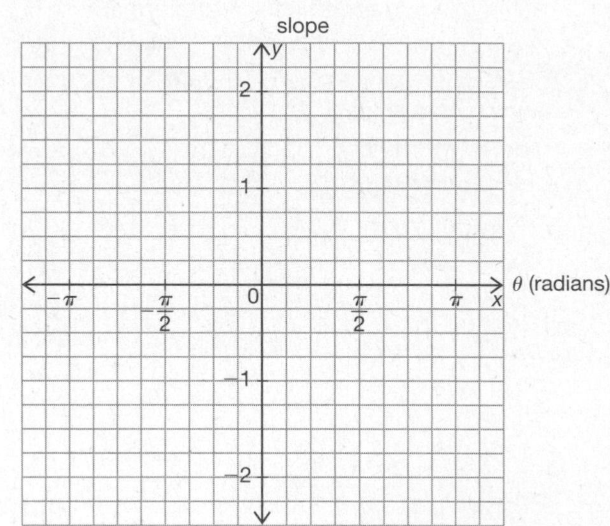

Is the slope defined for all values of theta?

15

b. Describe the value of the slope as θ increases from 0 radians and approaches $\frac{\pi}{2}$ radians.

c. What is the value of the slope at $\theta = \frac{3\pi}{4}$ radians and π radians? Explain how you determined each value.

Can you use symmetry to determine other slope values?

d. Describe the value of the slope as θ decreases from π radians and approaches $\frac{\pi}{2}$ radians.

At night, flowers do not continue to follow the Sun after it sets.

But suppose the flower represents the terminal ray of a central angle in standard position. Let's continue to model the change in the slope of the terminal ray as it traverses the unit circle.

2. Use your answers to Question 1 and what you know about symmetry to answer each question and complete the graph of the slope values from $-\frac{\pi}{2}$ radians to 2π radians.

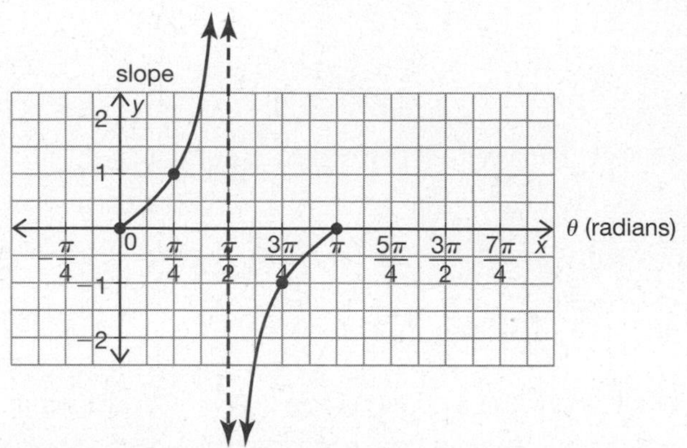

a. For what value(s) of θ is the slope equal to 0?

b. For what value(s) of θ is the slope undefined?

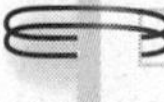
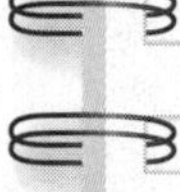
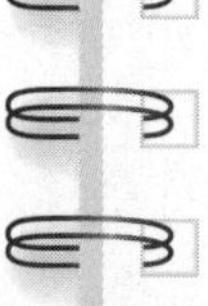

To help you think about slope values, you can remember that the terminal ray is a part of a line.

The triangles shown in the diagram are congruent. The hypotenuse of each triangle represents a terminal ray of a central angle with measure θ.

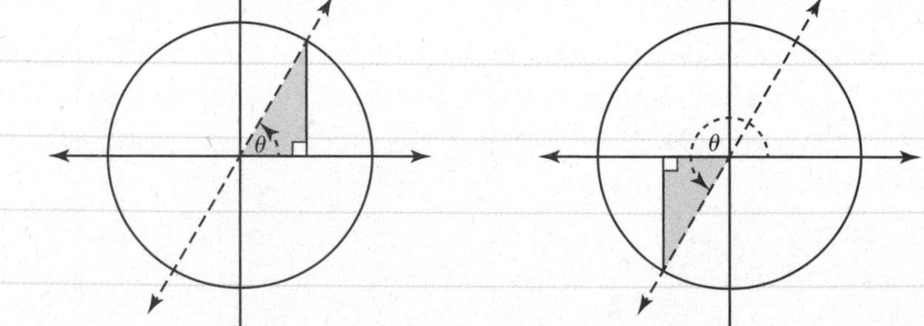

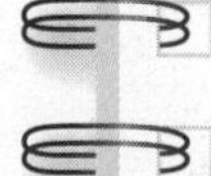
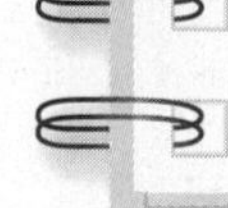

The slope of the terminal ray shown in Quadrant I is the same as the slope of the terminal ray shown in Quadrant III, because both rays are part of the same line. Both slopes are positive.

15

3. Use the worked example to help you answer each question and your completed graph in Question 2.

What special
triangle has a "rise"
and "run" each equal
to 1?

   a. For what value(s) of θ is the slope equal to 1?

   b. For what value(s) of θ is the slope equal to -1?

4. Use your completed graph to answer each question.

   a. Explain why the relation you graphed is a function.

   b. Is the function periodic? If so, determine the period of the function. If not, explain why not.

5. James said that the period of the tangent function is 2π radians because the graph starting at 2π radians repeats the same values as it does starting at 0 radians. Juli says that the period of the tangent function is $\frac{\pi}{2}$ radians, because there is an asymptote at multiples of $\frac{\pi}{2}$ radians.
   Who is correct? Explain your reasoning.

PROBLEM 2 Tangent Waves of Grain

The function that you graphed in the previous problem is the **tangent function**. Recall that the tangent ratio (tan) is the ratio of the lengths of the opposite side and the adjacent side in a right triangle. The tangent ratio is equal to the slope of the hypotenuse, which represents the terminal ray of the central angle on the unit circle.

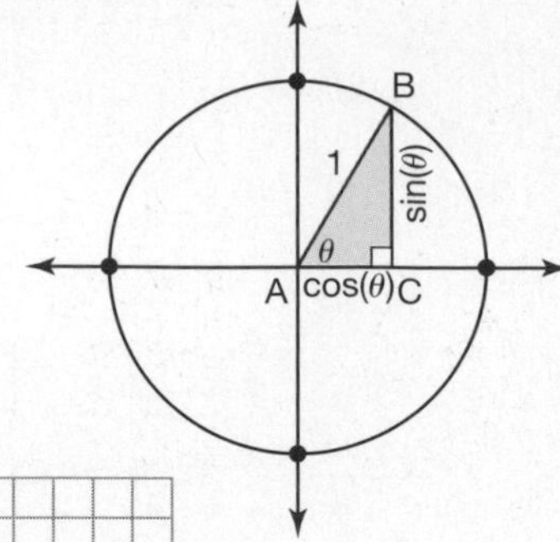

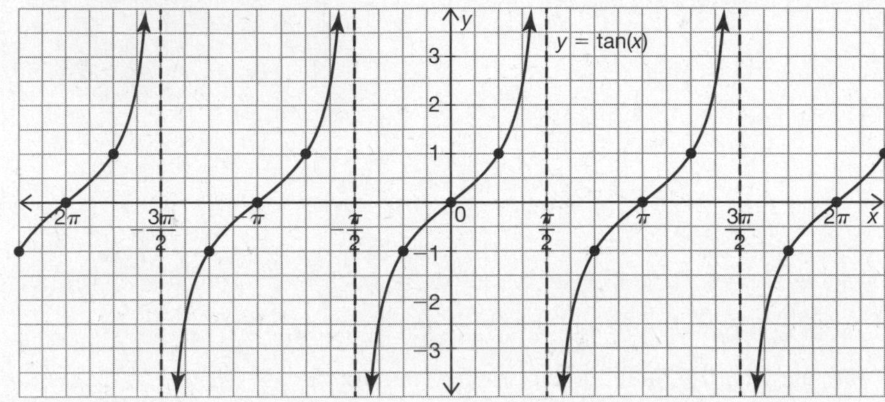

1. How can you write the tangent function in terms of sine and cosine, using the unit circle?

2. In which quadrants is the tangent function positive and negative? Explain your reasoning. Record this information on the Sine, Cosine, and Tangent on the Unit Circle diagram at the end of this Problem.

3. Use what you know about rational functions to describe the discontinuities in the graph of the tangent function.

15

4. What is the value of $\tan\left(\frac{n\pi}{2}\right)$ for any odd integer value of n?

5. In previous lessons, you identified periodicity identities for both the sine function and cosine function. What is the periodicity identity for the tangent function? Explain your reasoning.

6. The table shows some of the characteristics of the sine and cosine functions that you have identified. Complete the table for the tangent function.

	$y = \sin(x)$	$y = \cos(x)$	$y = \tan(x)$
y-Intercept	(0, 0)	(0, 1)	
Domain	$(-\infty, \infty)$	$(-\infty, \infty)$	
Range	$[-1, 1]$	$[-1, 1]$	
Period	2π	2π	
Minimum Output Value	-1	-1	
Maximum Output Value	1	1	
Amplitude	1	1	
Midline	$y = 0$	$y = 0$	

7. Complete the Sine, Cosine, and Tangent on the Unit Circle diagram by labeling the tangent values for each of the angle measures.

Sine, Cosine, and Tangent on the Unit Circle

Quadrant II

sin(θ)	+
cos(θ)	–
tan(θ)	

Quadrant I

sin(θ)	+
cos(θ)	+
tan(θ)	

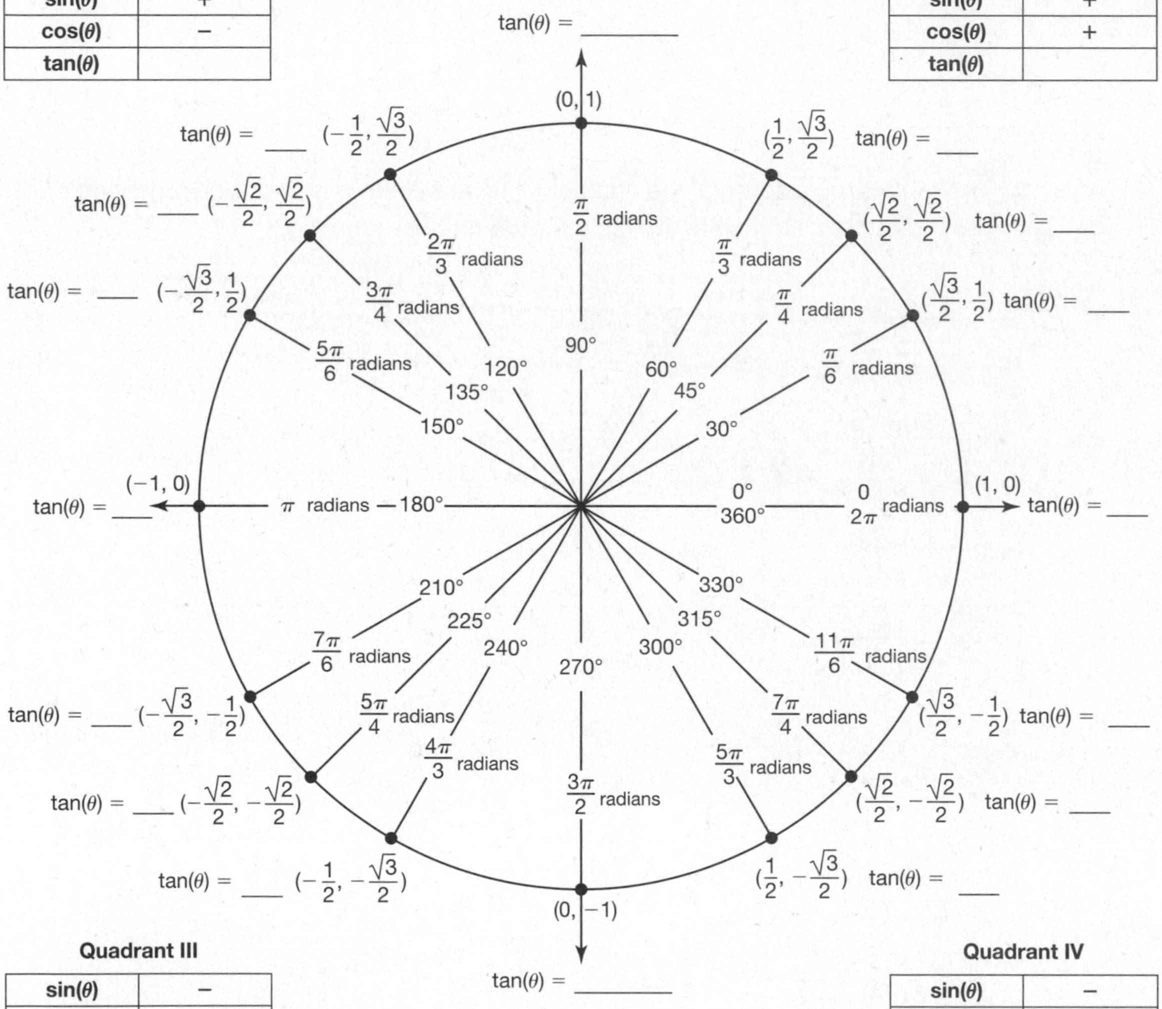

tan(θ) = ________

(0, 1)

$\frac{\pi}{2}$ radians 90°

tan(θ) = ___ $(-\frac{1}{2}, \frac{\sqrt{3}}{2})$ $\frac{2\pi}{3}$ radians 120°

tan(θ) = ___ $(-\frac{\sqrt{2}}{2}, \frac{\sqrt{2}}{2})$ $\frac{3\pi}{4}$ radians 135°

tan(θ) = ___ $(-\frac{\sqrt{3}}{2}, \frac{1}{2})$ $\frac{5\pi}{6}$ radians 150°

$(\frac{1}{2}, \frac{\sqrt{3}}{2})$ tan(θ) = ___ $\frac{\pi}{3}$ radians 60°

$(\frac{\sqrt{2}}{2}, \frac{\sqrt{2}}{2})$ tan(θ) = ___ $\frac{\pi}{4}$ radians 45°

$(\frac{\sqrt{3}}{2}, \frac{1}{2})$ tan(θ) = ___ $\frac{\pi}{6}$ radians 30°

(−1, 0) tan(θ) = ___ π radians 180°

0° 360° 0 2π radians (1, 0) tan(θ) = ___

210° $\frac{7\pi}{6}$ radians tan(θ) = ___ $(-\frac{\sqrt{3}}{2}, -\frac{1}{2})$

225° $\frac{5\pi}{4}$ radians tan(θ) = ___ $(-\frac{\sqrt{2}}{2}, -\frac{\sqrt{2}}{2})$

240° $\frac{4\pi}{3}$ radians tan(θ) = ___ $(-\frac{1}{2}, -\frac{\sqrt{3}}{2})$

270° $\frac{3\pi}{2}$ radians

330° $\frac{11\pi}{6}$ radians $(\frac{\sqrt{3}}{2}, -\frac{1}{2})$ tan(θ) = ___

315° $\frac{7\pi}{4}$ radians $(\frac{\sqrt{2}}{2}, -\frac{\sqrt{2}}{2})$ tan(θ) = ___

300° $\frac{5\pi}{3}$ radians $(\frac{1}{2}, -\frac{\sqrt{3}}{2})$ tan(θ) = ___

(0, −1)

tan(θ) = ________

Quadrant III

sin(θ)	–
cos(θ)	–
tan(θ)	

Quadrant IV

sin(θ)	–
cos(θ)	+
tan(θ)	

PROBLEM 3 Tan-sformations

1. Use what you know about transformations to sketch each graph.

   a. $f(x) = -\tan(x)$

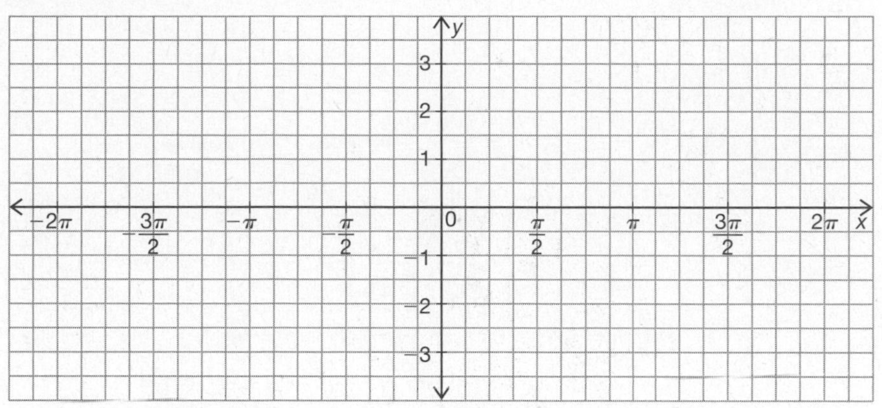

   b. $g(x) = \tan(-x)$

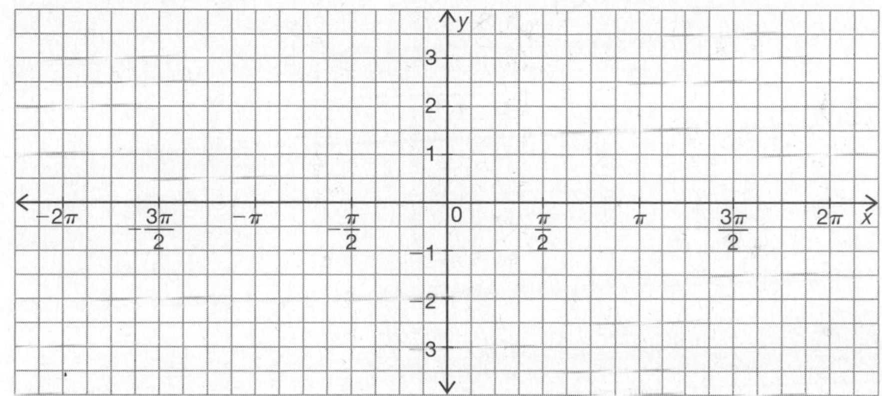

   c. What do you notice about the graphs in parts (a) and (b)?

What happens to the slope of a line when you reflect it across the x-axis or the y-axis?

15

2. Match each equation with its corresponding graph. Explain your reasoning.

a. $y = \tan\left(\frac{1}{2}x\right)$

b. $y = \tan\left(x + \frac{\pi}{2}\right)$

c. $y = \frac{1}{20}\tan(x) + 1$

d. $y = 2\tan(x)$

______

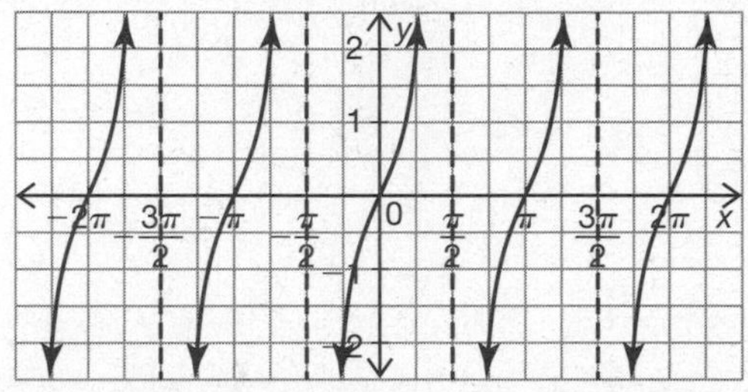

______

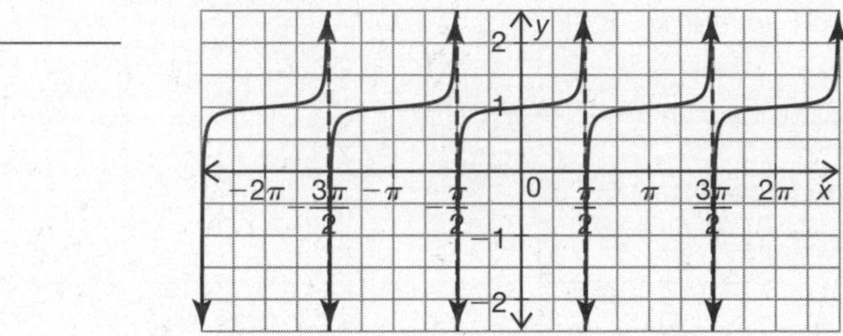

______

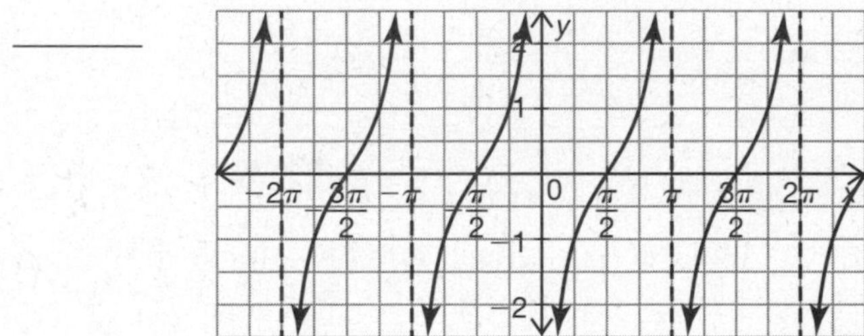

______

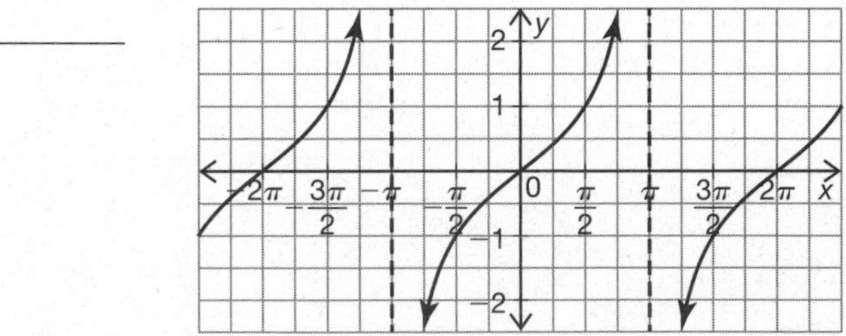

Be prepared to share your methods and solutions.

Chapter 15 Summary

KEY TERMS

- periodic function (15.1)
- period (15.1)
- standard position (15.1)
- initial ray (15.1)
- terminal ray (15.1)
- amplitude (15.1)
- midline (15.1)
- theta (θ) (15.2)
- unit circle (15.2)
- radians (15.2)
- sine function (15.3)
- cosine function (15.3)
- trigonometric function (15.3)
- periodicity identity (15.3)
- frequency (15.4)
- phase shift (15.4)
- tangent function (15.5)

15.1 Identifying Periodic Functions and their Periods

A periodic function is a function whose values repeat over regular intervals. To identify a periodic function's period, determine the length of the smallest interval over which the function repeats.

Example

Determine whether the graph represents a periodic function over the interval shown. If so, identify the period.

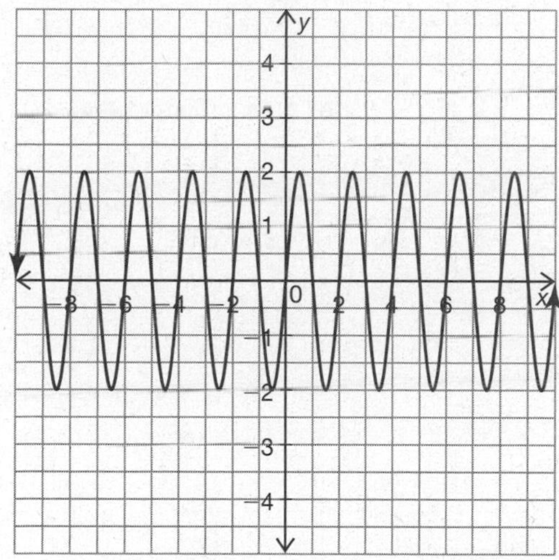

The smallest interval over which this function repeats is 2. So, the period of the function is 2.

15

15.1 Determining the Amplitude and Midline of Periodic Functions

To determine the amplitude of a periodic function, calculate one-half of the absolute value of the difference between the maximum and minimum values of the function. The midline of a periodic function is a reference line whose equation is the average of the maximum and minimum values of a function.

Example

Determine the amplitude and midline of the given function.

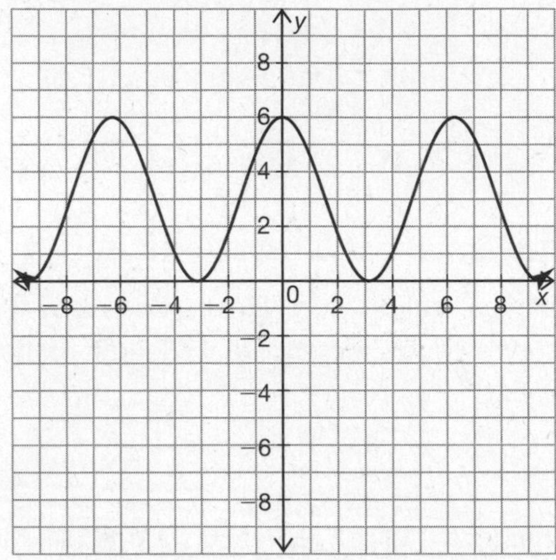

The maximum value of the function is 6 and the minimum value is 0. So, the amplitude is $\frac{1}{2}|6 - 0|$ or 3. The midline is $y = \frac{6 + 0}{2} = 3$.

15

15.2 Converting Radian Measures to Degree Measures of Central Angles in a Unit Circle

To convert radian measures to degree measures of central angles in a unit circle, use the formula $x \text{ radians} \cdot \frac{180°}{\pi \text{ radians}}$.

Example

Convert 3 radians to degrees.

$$x \text{ radians} \cdot \frac{180°}{\pi \text{ radians}} = 3 \text{ radians} \cdot \frac{180°}{\pi \text{ radians}}$$
$$= \frac{540°}{\pi}$$
$$\approx 171.89°$$

The degree measure of an angle with a radian measure of 3 radians is approximately 171.89°.

15.2 Converting Degree Measures to Radian Measures of Central Angles in a Unit Circle

To convert degree measures to radian measures of central angles in a unit circle, use the formula $x \text{ degrees} \cdot \frac{\pi \text{ radians}}{180°}$.

Example

Convert $\theta = 225°$ to radians.

$$x \text{ degrees} \cdot \frac{\pi \text{ radians}}{180°} = 225° \cdot \frac{\pi \text{ radians}}{180°}$$
$$= \frac{225\pi}{180} \text{ radians}$$
$$\approx \frac{5\pi}{4} \text{ radians}$$

The radian measure of an angle with a degree measure of 225° is $\frac{5\pi}{4}$ radians.

15.3 Using the Unit Circle to Determine the Sine and Cosine of an Angle

In a unit circle, the ordered pair of the point where the terminal ray of an angle intersects the circle is the value of the cosine and sine of the angle.

Example

Use the unit circle to determine the sine and cosine of a central angle whose radian measure is $\frac{7\pi}{6}$.

The ordered pair of the point where the terminal ray intersects the circle for a central angle with a measure of $\frac{7\pi}{6}$ radians is $\left(-\frac{\sqrt{3}}{2}, -\frac{1}{2}\right)$. Therefore, the sine of the angle is $-\frac{1}{2}$, and the cosine of the angle is $-\frac{\sqrt{3}}{2}$.

Quadrant II

sin(θ)	+
cos(θ)	–

Quadrant I

sin(θ)	+
cos(θ)	+

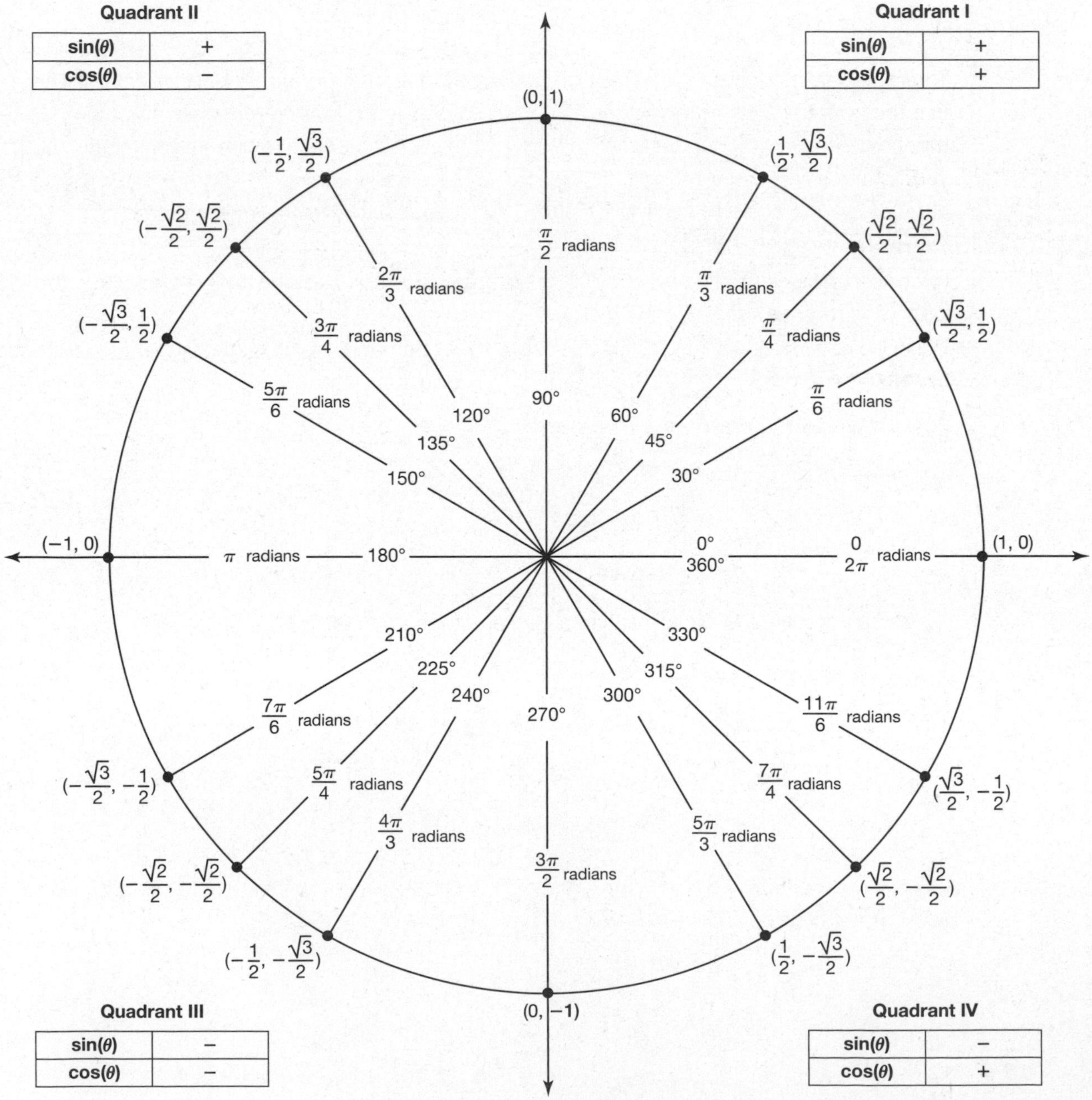

(0, 1) — $\frac{\pi}{2}$ radians — 90°

$(\frac{1}{2}, \frac{\sqrt{3}}{2})$ — $\frac{\pi}{3}$ radians — 60°

$(\frac{\sqrt{2}}{2}, \frac{\sqrt{2}}{2})$ — $\frac{\pi}{4}$ radians — 45°

$(\frac{\sqrt{3}}{2}, \frac{1}{2})$ — $\frac{\pi}{6}$ radians — 30°

(1, 0) — 0 / 2π radians — 0° / 360°

$(-\frac{1}{2}, \frac{\sqrt{3}}{2})$ — $\frac{2\pi}{3}$ radians — 120°

$(-\frac{\sqrt{2}}{2}, \frac{\sqrt{2}}{2})$ — $\frac{3\pi}{4}$ radians — 135°

$(-\frac{\sqrt{3}}{2}, \frac{1}{2})$ — $\frac{5\pi}{6}$ radians — 150°

(−1, 0) — π radians — 180°

$(-\frac{\sqrt{3}}{2}, -\frac{1}{2})$ — $\frac{7\pi}{6}$ radians — 210°

$(-\frac{\sqrt{2}}{2}, -\frac{\sqrt{2}}{2})$ — $\frac{5\pi}{4}$ radians — 225°

$(-\frac{1}{2}, -\frac{\sqrt{3}}{2})$ — $\frac{4\pi}{3}$ radians — 240°

(0, −1) — $\frac{3\pi}{2}$ radians — 270°

$(\frac{1}{2}, -\frac{\sqrt{3}}{2})$ — $\frac{5\pi}{3}$ radians — 300°

$(\frac{\sqrt{2}}{2}, -\frac{\sqrt{2}}{2})$ — $\frac{7\pi}{4}$ radians — 315°

$(\frac{\sqrt{3}}{2}, -\frac{1}{2})$ — $\frac{11\pi}{6}$ radians — 330°

Quadrant III

sin(θ)	–
cos(θ)	–

Quadrant IV

sin(θ)	–
cos(θ)	+

15

15.4 Determining the Frequency of Sine and Cosine Functions

The frequency of a periodic function specifies the number of repetitions of the graph of a periodic function per unit. It is equal to the reciprocal of the period of the function or $\frac{|B|}{2\pi}$, where B is the coefficient of the argument.

Example

Determine the frequency of the function $y = 2\sin(4\pi) + 5$.

$$\begin{aligned}\text{frequency} &= \frac{|B|}{2\pi}\\ &= \frac{|4|}{2\pi}\\ &= \frac{2}{\pi}\end{aligned}$$

15.4 Graphing Transformations of Sine and Cosine Functions

To graph a transformation of a sine or cosine function, first graph the basic function. Then, use the equation of the transformed function to determine how to transform the basic function. For periodic functions of the form $g(x) = Af(B(x - C)) + D$, the A-value indicates the vertical stretch or compression, the B-value indicates the horizontal stretch or compression, the C-value indicates the phase shift, and the D-value indicates the vertical shift of the function.

Example

Describe how the basic function, $y = \cos(x)$, would be transformed to create the function $y = 3\cos\left(x - \frac{\pi}{2}\right)$. Then, graph the function.

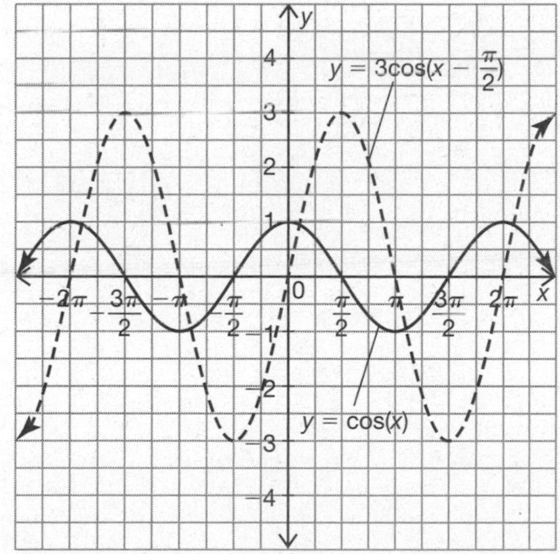

The 3 indicates that the basic function, $y = \cos(x)$, must be vertically stretched by 3, and the $\frac{\pi}{2}$ indicates a phase shift to the right by $\frac{\pi}{2}$ units.

15.5 Evaluating the Tangent Function Using the Sine and Cosine Functions

The tangent function is the ratio of the sine to the cosine, or $\tan(x) = \frac{\sin(x)}{\cos(x)}$. To evaluate a tangent function for a given angle, use the unit circle to determine the sine and cosine of the angle. Then, calculate the ratio.

Example

Evaluate the tangent of $\frac{2\pi}{3}$ radians by using the relationship between the tangent function and the sine and cosine functions.

$$\sin\left(\frac{2\pi}{3}\right) = \frac{\sqrt{3}}{2}$$

$$\cos\left(\frac{2\pi}{3}\right) = -\frac{1}{2}$$

$$\begin{aligned}\tan\left(\frac{2\pi}{3}\right) &= \frac{\sin\left(\frac{2\pi}{3}\right)}{\cos\left(\frac{2\pi}{3}\right)} \\ &= \frac{\frac{\sqrt{3}}{2}}{-\frac{1}{2}} \\ &= \frac{\sqrt{3}}{2} \cdot \left(-\frac{2}{1}\right) \\ &= -\sqrt{3}\end{aligned}$$

So, the tangent of $\frac{2\pi}{3}$ radians is $-\sqrt{3}$.

15

15.5 Graphing Transformations of the Tangent Function

To graph a transformation of a tangent function, first graph the basic function. Then, use the equation of the transformed function to determine how to transform the basic function. For periodic functions of the form $g(x) = Af(B(x - C)) + D$, the A-value indicates the vertical stretch or compression, the B-value indicates the horizontal stretch or compression, the C-value indicates the phase shift, and the D-value indicates the vertical shift of the function.

Example

Describe how the basic function, $y = \tan(x)$, would be transformed to create the function $y = 2\tan(x) + 1$. Then, graph the function.

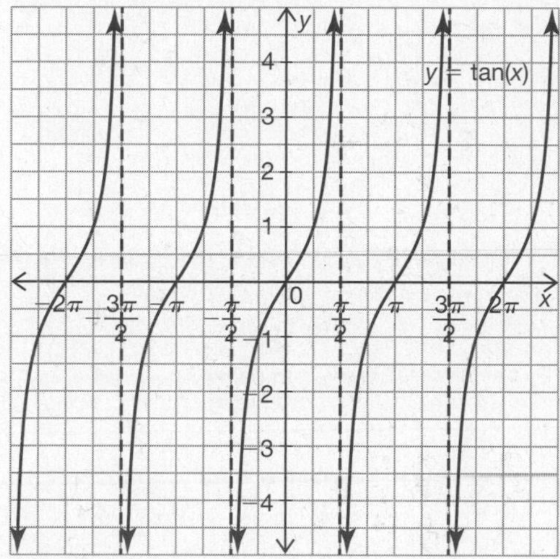

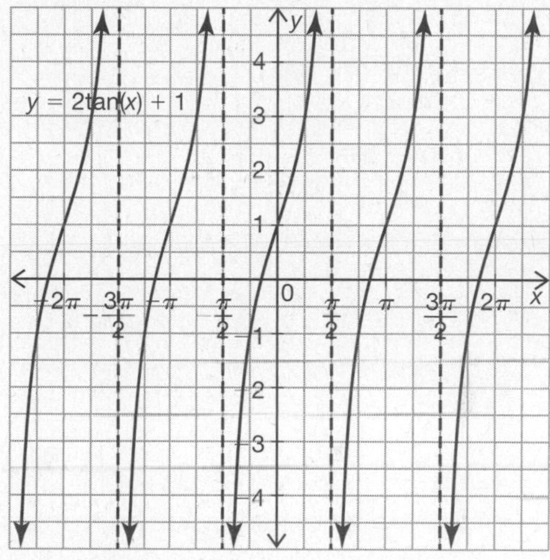

The 2 indicates that the basic function, $y = \tan(x)$, must be vertically stretched by 2, and the 1 indicates a vertical shift up of 1 unit.

Trigonometric Equations

16

$d(t) = 6800 \cos \frac{4}{3}\pi + 6400$

On October 14, 2013, astronaut Luca Parmitano sent us this picture from aboard the International Space Station (ISS). uring his mission, Luca became the first Italian astronaut to take part in a spacewalk. The trigonometric function he is holding represents the position of the ISS in orbit over time.

16.1

Chasing Theta

Solving Trigonometric Equations

LEARNING GOALS

In this lesson, you will:

- Write and solve trigonometric equations.
- Use periodicity identities to identify multiple solutions to trigonometric equations.
- Solve trigonometric equations using inverse trigonometric functions.
- Solve second-degree trigonometric equations.
- Prove the Pythagorean identity $\sin^2(\theta) + \cos^2(\theta) = 1$.
- Use the Pythagorean identity to determine other trigonometric values.

KEY TERMS

- trigonometric equation
- inverse sine ($\sin^{-1}$)
- inverse cosine ($\cos^{-1}$)
- inverse tangent ($\tan^{-1}$)
- Pythagorean identity

A ground track, or ground trace, is a path that can be created by an orbiting satellite, like the International Space Station, mapped onto the surface of the Earth. Ground tracks are useful to engineers—and amateur astronomers—in tracking the locations of these satellites.

Because orbits are circular, ground tracks are usually in the shape of the graphs of periodic functions.

However, if a satellite has what is called a geostationary orbit, its ground track will be a single point, because it rotates at the same rate as the Earth. That means that it is above the same place on Earth at all times.

PROBLEM 1 You Know A Lot!

A **trigonometric equation** is an equation in which the unknown is associated with a trigonometric function. The number of solutions of a trigonometric equation can vary depending on how the domain of the function is restricted.

You can solve trigonometric equations using what you already know.

16

Consider the equation $\sin(x) = \frac{1}{2}$.

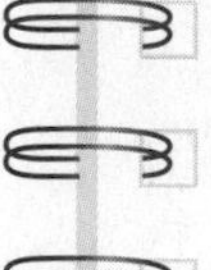

On the unit circle, you can see that $\sin\left(\frac{\pi}{6}\right) = \frac{1}{2}$ and $\sin\left(\frac{5\pi}{6}\right) = \frac{1}{2}$. So, $x = \frac{\pi}{6}$ or $\frac{5\pi}{6}$.

When the domain is restricted to $0 \le x \le 2\pi$, these are the only 2 solutions to the equation.

When there are no domain restrictions, the equation has an infinite number of solutions.

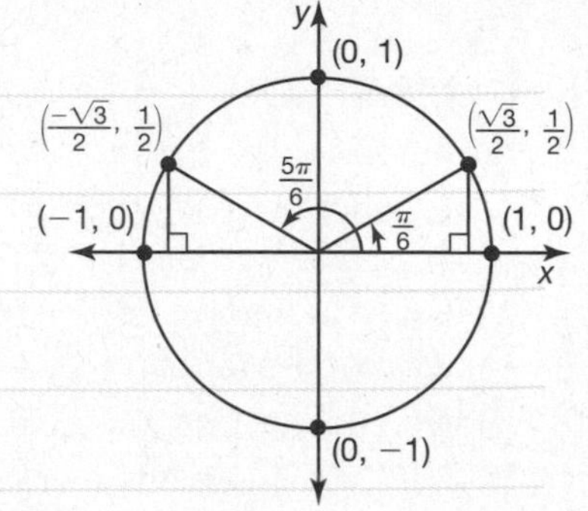

1. Explain what error(s) Caleb made in his reasoning.

Caleb

I can just keep adding or subtracting $\frac{2\pi}{3}$ to one solution to determine another solution to $\sin(x) = \frac{1}{2}$.

2. List the solution(s) of the trigonometric equation $\sin(x) = \frac{1}{2}$, given each of the domain restrictions.

   a. $0 \le x \le \frac{\pi}{2}$

   b. $0 \le x \le 4\pi$

   c. $-\pi \le x \le 0$

You can also use what you know about the graphs of trigonometric functions to solve trigonometric equations.

Let's consider the equation $\cos(x) = \frac{1}{2}$.

The equations $y = \cos(x)$ and $y = \frac{1}{2}$ are graphed on the coordinate plane.

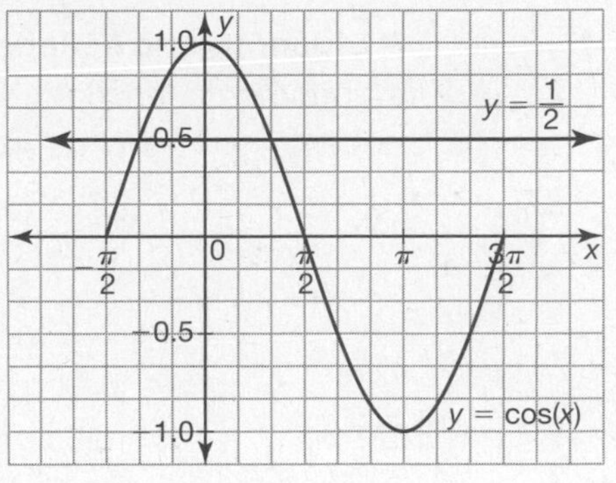

3. Study the graph of $y = \cos(x)$.

   a. Over what domain is the function graphed?

   b. Write the solution(s) to the equation $\cos(x) = \frac{1}{2}$, given the domain restrictions. Then, plot and label the solution(s) on the coordinate plane.

4. Write the solution(s) to each equation, given the same domain restrictions in Question 3.

   a. $\cos(x) = 1$

   b. $\cos(x) - 0$

   c. $\cos(x) = -\frac{1}{2}$

   d. $\cos(x) = -1$

Remember to think about reference angles on the unit circle!

16

5. Use the graph of $y = \tan(x)$ over the domain $-\frac{\pi}{2} \le x \le \frac{5\pi}{2}$ to solve each equation.

a. $\tan(x) = 0$

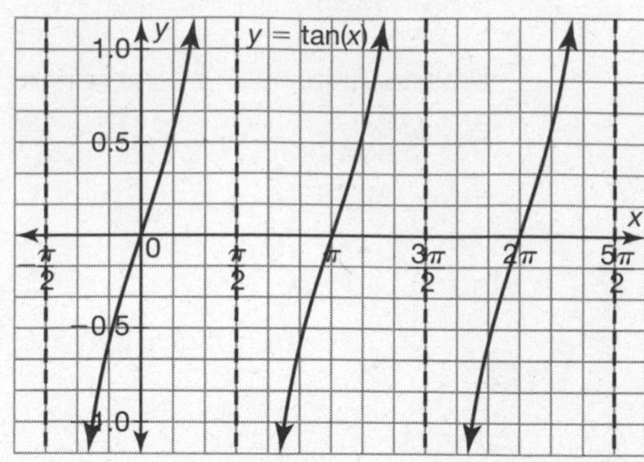

b. $\tan(x) =$ undefined

You can use what you know about the periods of trigonometric functions to solve trigonometric equations. The periodicity identities you have learned are shown. Adding or subtracting integer multiples, n, of the period for each function generates solutions to trigonometric equations.

Periodicity Identities	
Sine	$\sin(x + 2\pi n) = \sin(x)$
Cosine	$\cos(x + 2\pi n) = \cos(x)$
Tangent	$\tan(x + \pi n) = \tan(x)$

6. Use a periodicity identity to list 4 solutions to each equation.

a. $\cos(x) = \frac{\sqrt{2}}{2}$

I can use the reference angles to identify one of the solutions. Then I can go from there.

b. $\tan(x) = \sqrt{3}$

PROBLEM 2 Same Ol', Same Ol'

When a trigonometric equation involves transformations on the basic function, solving the equation requires the same techniques you have used to solve other equations.

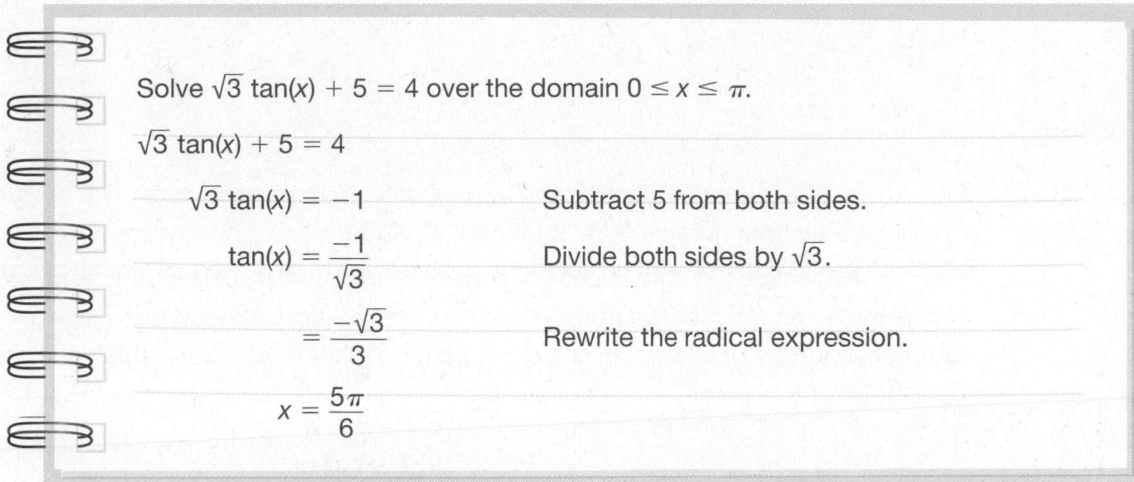

Solve $\sqrt{3}\tan(x) + 5 = 4$ over the domain $0 \le x \le \pi$.

$\sqrt{3}\tan(x) + 5 = 4$

$\sqrt{3}\tan(x) = -1$ Subtract 5 from both sides.

$\tan(x) = \frac{-1}{\sqrt{3}}$ Divide both sides by $\sqrt{3}$.

$= \frac{-\sqrt{3}}{3}$ Rewrite the radical expression.

$x = \frac{5\pi}{6}$

16

1. List all of the solutions to the equation in the worked example over the domain of all real numbers. Show your work.

2. Explain why Amy is incorrect.

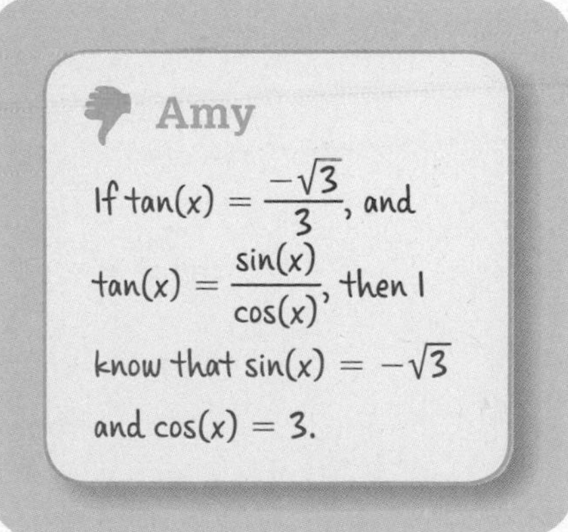

Amy
If $\tan(x) = \frac{-\sqrt{3}}{3}$, and
$\tan(x) = \frac{\sin(x)}{\cos(x)}$, then I
know that $\sin(x) = -\sqrt{3}$
and $\cos(x) = 3$.

3. Solve the equation $2\sin(x) + \sqrt{3} = 0$ over the domain $-\frac{\pi}{2} \le x \le \frac{\pi}{2}$.

16

You can use the inverse of each of the trigonometric functions to determine solutions to equations. The **inverse sine ($\sin^{-1}$), inverse cosine ($\cos^{-1}$),** and **inverse tangent ($\tan^{-1}$)** functions are used to determine solutions to sine, cosine, and tangent equations, respectively.

4. Use the steps shown to solve the equation $\sin(x) = \frac{1}{2}$ on a calculator.

Step 1:	*Press MODE and make sure it is set to RADIANS, not DEGREES.*
Step 2:	*Press 2ND and SIN^{-1}. Type the value of sin(x) inside parentheses and press ENTER.*

What value did the calculator return as the answer? Explain whether this value is or is not the correct answer and why.

Does your calculator give you a complete answer?

5. Solve each equation over the domain of all real numbers.

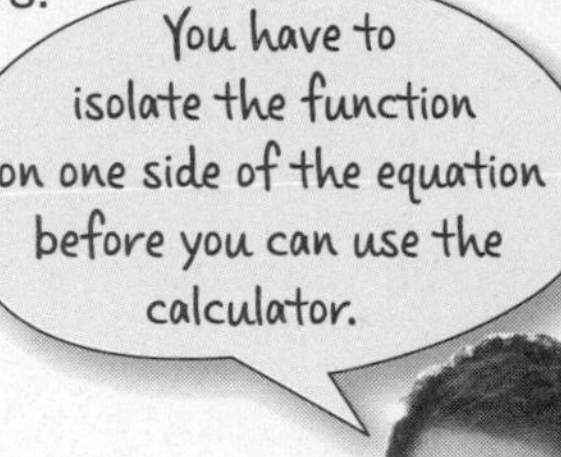

You have to
isolate the function
on one side of the equation
before you can use the
calculator.

a. $-5 + 2\sqrt{3}\cos(x) = -8$

b. $5\sin(x) + 9 = 3$

c. $6\tan(x) - 4 = -19$

d. $5 - 8\cos(x) = 3$

16

When the B-value is changed from a basic trigonometric function, you must take the change in period into account when determining solutions.

Let's consider the equation $\cos(x) = \frac{1}{2}$ over the domain $0 \le x \le 2\pi$.

The equations $y = \cos(x)$ and $y = \frac{1}{2}$ are graphed on the coordinate plane.

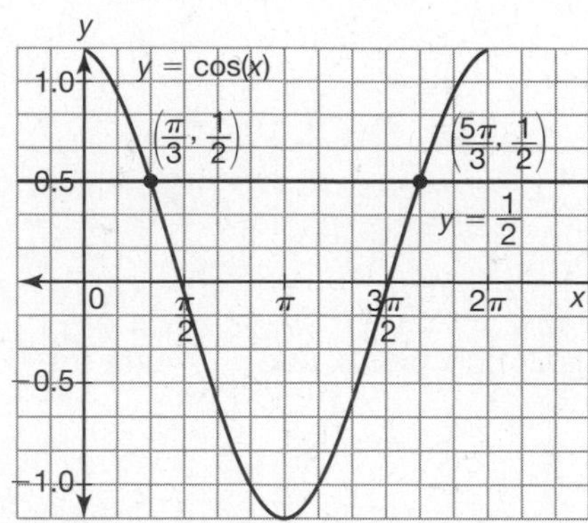

The solutions for $\cos(x) = \frac{1}{2}$ over the domain $0 \le x \le 2\pi$ are $x = \frac{\pi}{3}$ or $\frac{5\pi}{3}$.

The solutions for $\cos(x) = \frac{1}{2}$ over the domain for all real numbers are $x = \frac{\pi}{3} + 2\pi n$ or $\frac{5\pi}{3} + 2\pi n$.

6. Now, let's consider the equation $\cos(2x) = \frac{1}{2}$ over the domain $0 \le x \le 2\pi$.

a. Determine the period of this function.

b. The period of $y = \cos(2x)$ is different than $y = \cos(x)$. How does your answer to part (a) affect the number of possible solutions for $\cos(2x) = \frac{1}{2}$ over the domain $0 \le x \le 2\pi$?

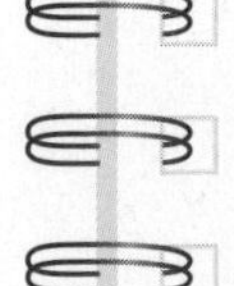

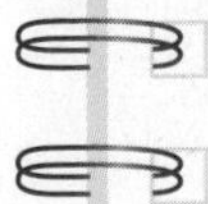

You can use what you know about reference angles to determine solutions for x.

To solve $\cos(2x) = \frac{1}{2}$, you know $\cos\left(\frac{\pi}{3}\right) = \frac{1}{2}$. So, to begin, let $\frac{\pi}{3} = 2x$ and solve for x.

$$2x = \frac{\pi}{3}$$
$$x = \frac{\pi}{6}$$

Because the period of $\cos(2x)$ is π, $x = \frac{\pi}{6}$ or $\frac{7\pi}{6}$ for $0 \le x \le 2\pi$.

c. Determine the remaining solutions for $\cos(2x) = \frac{1}{2}$ over the domain $0 \leq x \leq 2\pi$ given $\cos\left(\frac{5\pi}{3}\right) = \frac{1}{2}$.

16

d. Write the solution for $\cos(2x) = \frac{1}{2}$ over the domain for all real numbers.

7. Solve the equation $2 \sin(4x) + 1 = -1$ over the set of real numbers.

PROBLEM 3 Power Trig

If an equation that can be written in the form $ax^2 + bx + c = 0$ has x replaced with a trigonometric function, the result is a trigonometric equation in quadratic form. These equations can be solved as you would solve other quadratic equations, by factoring or by using the Quadratic Formula.

> Note that $(\sin(x))^2$ is usually written as $\sin^2 x$.

16

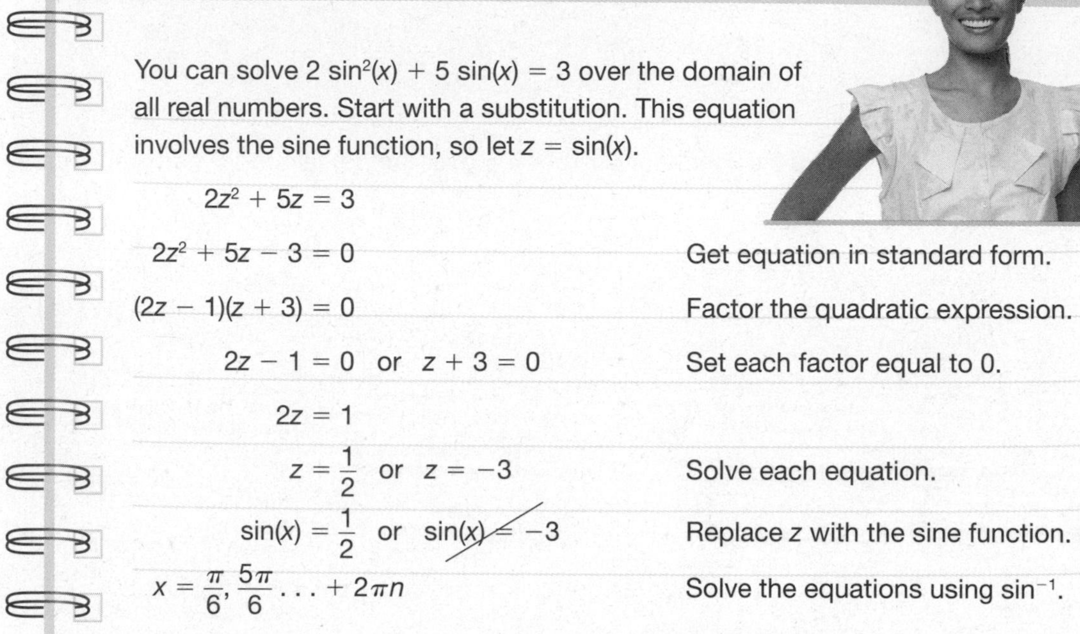

You can solve $2\sin^2(x) + 5\sin(x) = 3$ over the domain of all real numbers. Start with a substitution. This equation involves the sine function, so let $z = \sin(x)$.

$2z^2 + 5z = 3$	
$2z^2 + 5z - 3 = 0$	Get equation in standard form.
$(2z - 1)(z + 3) = 0$	Factor the quadratic expression.
$2z - 1 = 0$ or $z + 3 = 0$	Set each factor equal to 0.
$2z = 1$	
$z = \frac{1}{2}$ or $z = -3$	Solve each equation.
$\sin(x) = \frac{1}{2}$ or ~~$\sin(x) = -3$~~	Replace z with the sine function.
$x = \frac{\pi}{6}, \frac{5\pi}{6} \ldots + 2\pi n$	Solve the equations using $\sin^{-1}$.

1. Explain why $\sin(x) = -3$ is crossed off in the worked example.

2. Solve $4\sin^2(x) - 1 = 0$ over the domain of all real numbers.

3. Solve $2\cos^2(x) + \cos(x) = 1$ over the domain of all real numbers.

16

4. Solve $2\tan^2(z) + 3\tan(z) - 1 = 0$ over the domain of all real numbers.

5. Solve $6\sin^2(z) - 16\sin(z) - 33 = 0$ over the domain of all real numbers.

PROBLEM 4 A Pythagorean Identity

You have learned about the periodicity identities, but there is another identity in trigonometry that can also help you solve trigonometric equations. A **Pythagorean identity** is a trigonometric identity that expresses the Pythagorean Theorem in terms of trigonometric functions. The Pythagorean identity states $(\sin(\theta))^2 + (\cos(\theta))^2 = (1)^2$.

You can prove this Pythagorean identity using your knowledge of the unit circle and the Pythagorean Theorem.

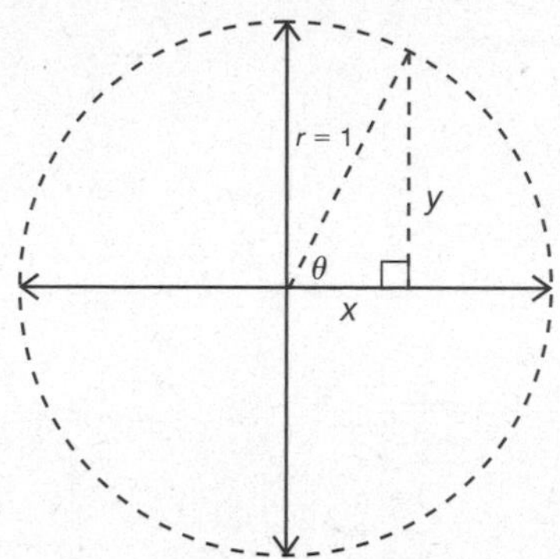

1. Demonstrate how the Pythagorean identity follows from the Pythagorean Theorem.

   a. Given the unit circle and the angle θ, label the side lengths of the right triangle in terms of $\sin(\theta)$ and $\cos(\theta)$.

You know that if the length of the hypotenuse of a right triangle is 1, then the lengths of the legs are the sine and cosine of one of the angles.

   b. State the Pythagorean Theorem.

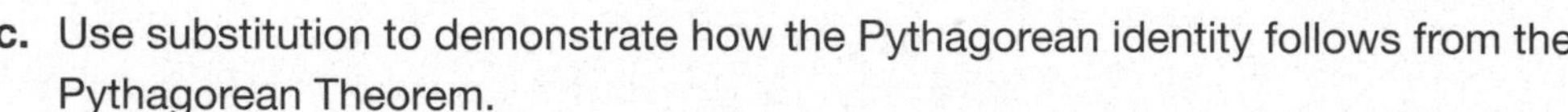

   c. Use substitution to demonstrate how the Pythagorean identity follows from the Pythagorean Theorem.

2. Write the Pythagorean identity $\sin^2(\theta) + \cos^2(\theta) = 1$ in two other forms.

   a. Solve for $\sin^2(\theta)$.

   b. Solve for $\cos^2(\theta)$.

You can use the Pythagorean identity $\sin^2(\theta) + \cos^2(\theta) = 1$ and what you know about solutions in different quadrants to determine values of trigonometric functions.

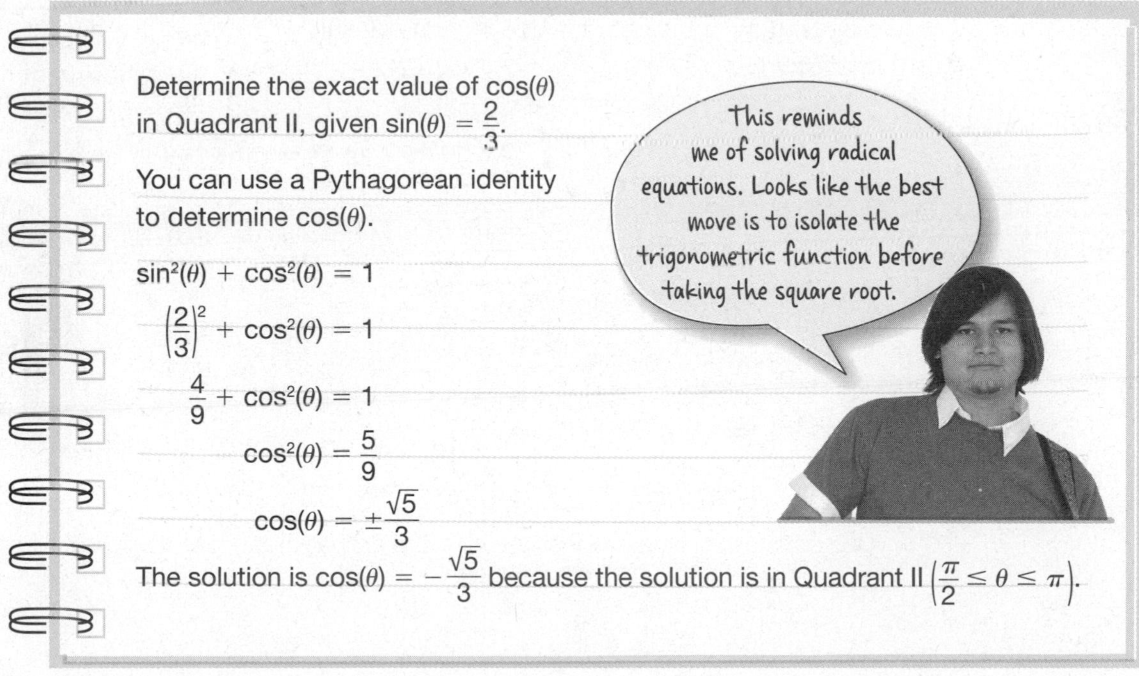

This reminds me of solving radical equations. Looks like the best move is to isolate the trigonometric function before taking the square root.

Determine the exact value of $\cos(\theta)$ in Quadrant II, given $\sin(\theta) = \frac{2}{3}$.

You can use a Pythagorean identity to determine $\cos(\theta)$.

$$\sin^2(\theta) + \cos^2(\theta) = 1$$
$$\left(\frac{2}{3}\right)^2 + \cos^2(\theta) = 1$$
$$\frac{4}{9} + \cos^2(\theta) = 1$$
$$\cos^2(\theta) = \frac{5}{9}$$
$$\cos(\theta) = \pm\frac{\sqrt{5}}{3}$$

The solution is $\cos(\theta) = -\frac{\sqrt{5}}{3}$ because the solution is in Quadrant II $\left(\frac{\pi}{2} \le \theta \le \pi\right)$.

3. Given $\sin(\theta) = \frac{3}{5}$ in Quadrant II, determine $\cos(\theta)$.

16

4. Given $\cos(\theta) = -\frac{12}{13}$ in Quadrant III, determine $\sin(\theta)$.

5. Given $\cos(\theta) = \frac{1}{4}$ in Quadrant IV, determine $\sin(\theta)$.

6. Given $\sin(\theta) = -\frac{1}{10}$ in Quadrant IV, determine $\cos(\theta)$.

16

Be prepared to share your methods and solutions.

16

16.2

Rabbits and Seasonal Affective Disorder

Modeling with Periodic Functions

LEARNING GOALS

In this lesson, you will:

- Model real-world situations with periodic functions.
- Interpret key characteristics of periodic functions in terms of problem situations.

Seasonal changes can affect a person's mood. You may have heard someone say that they have "the winter blues." Some people are so strongly affected by a lack of daylight that they experience a severe depression when the hours of daylight are shortest. This condition is called seasonal affective disorder (SAD).

A person with SAD experiences depression for several months when daylight hours are short. In general, the occurrence of SAD increases as the location gets farther from the equator. Symptoms of SAD include disruption of sleep patterns, feeling fatigued, overeating, craving carbohydrates, depression, and avoidance of social activity.

PROBLEM 1 Rabbits, Rabbits Everywhere!

16

The rabbit population in a national park rises and falls throughout the year. The population is at its approximate minimum of 6000 rabbits in December. As the weather gets warmer and food becomes more available, the population grows to its approximate maximum of 16,000 rabbits in June.

The function describing the rabbit population is

$$f(x) = 5000 \sin\left(\frac{\pi}{6}x - \frac{\pi}{2}\right) + 11,000$$

where x is the time in months and $f(x)$ is the rabbit population.

1. Complete the table to show the rabbit population through one year.

Month	Time (months)	Rabbit Population (rabbits)
December		
January		
February		
March		
April		
May		
June		
July		
August		
September		
October		
November		
December		

2. Sketch a graph of the function to show at least two periods of the function.

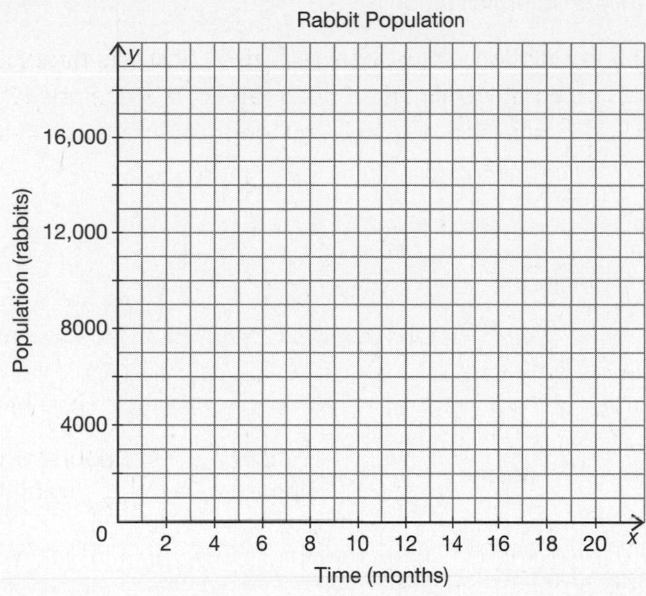

3. How has the function been translated vertically from the basic sine function?

4. Determine the amplitude of the function.

5. Determine the period of the function.

6. Determine the phase shift of the function.

7. How is the vertical translation related to the algebraic function? What does it represent in terms of this problem situation?

16

8. How is the amplitude related to the algebraic function? What does it represent in terms of this problem situation?

16

9. How is the period related to the algebraic function? What does it represent in terms of this problem situation?

10. How is the phase shift related to the algebraic function? What does it represent in terms of this problem situation?

16

11. If the rabbit population cycle occurred over six months instead of one year, how would the graph and equation change?

12. If the rabbit population has a minimum of 4000 and a maximum of 20,000, how would the graph and equation change?

13. Describe the time(s) in months when the rabbit population is equal to 12,000. Show your work.

PROBLEM 2 Seasonal Affective Disorder

Patterns of daylight are related to seasonal affective disorder (SAD). The amount of daylight varies in a periodic manner and can be modeled by a sine function. The table shows the number of approximate daylight hours in Chicago, Illinois, which has latitude of 42° N.

16

Date	Day	Daylight Hours
Dec. 31	0	9.2
Jan. 10	10	9.3
Jan. 20	20	9.6
Jan. 30	30	9.9
Feb. 9	40	10.3
Feb. 19	50	10.7
Mar. 1	60	11.4
Mar. 11	70	11.7
Mar. 21	80	12.2
Mar. 31	90	12.7
Apr. 10	100	13.1
Apr. 20	110	13.6
Apr. 30	120	14.0
May 10	130	14.4
May 20	140	14.7
May 30	150	15.0
June 9	160	15.2
June 19	170	15.2
June 29	180	15.2

Date	Day	Daylight Hours
July 9	190	15.1
July 19	200	14.8
July 29	210	14.5
Aug. 8	220	14.2
Aug. 18	230	13.7
Aug. 28	240	13.3
Sept. 7	250	12.9
Sept. 17	260	12.4
Sept. 27	270	12.0
Oct. 7	280	11.5
Oct. 17	290	11.0
Oct. 27	300	10.6
Nov. 6	310	10.2
Nov. 16	320	9.8
Nov. 26	330	9.5
Dec. 6	340	9.2
Dec. 16	350	9.2
Dec. 26	360	9.1

1. Plot the points from the table using the day of the year for your independent variable and hours of daylight for your dependent variable.

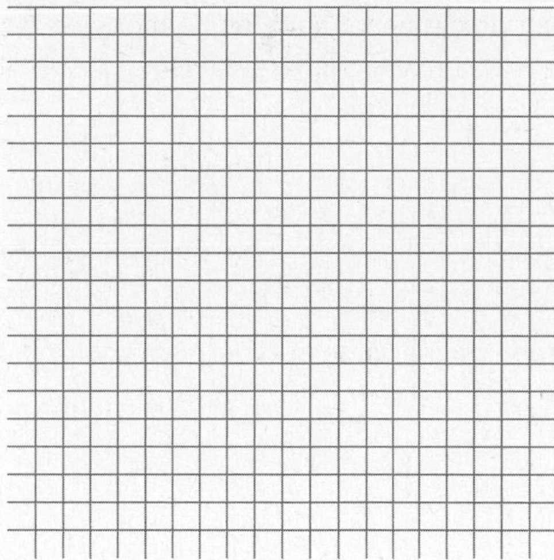

2. Describe any minimum and maximum values on your graph.

3. Determine the amplitude of the function.

4. Determine the period of the function.

5. Determine the phase shift of the graph.

6. Determine the vertical shift of the graph.

7. To model this situation with a sine function of the form $f(x) = A \sin B(x - C) + D$, you need to calculate the values of A, B, C, and D.

   a. Determine the value of A. What does it represent in terms of this situation?

16

   b. Determine the value of B. Explain your reasoning.

   c. Determine the value of C.

   d. Determine the value of D. What does it represent in terms of this situation?

   e. Write an algebraic function to model the data for the amount of daylight hours in Chicago, Illinois.

8. Enter the data from the table into a calculator. Use the calculator to perform a sinusoidal regression for this data. Write the regression equation from the calculator. How does it compare to your equation?

16

9. Use your function to describe times of the year when there are exactly 12 hours of daylight. Show your work.

10. Seasonal affective disorder appears to vary according to latitude. The farther a location is from the equator, the more prevalent cases of SAD become. Why might this happen?

16

11. Anchorage, Alaska, is located at a latitude of 61° N. This is considerably farther north than Chicago. If we created a graph to model the daylight hours in Anchorage, how do you think it would compare to the graph for daylight hours in Chicago? In what ways would it be the same? In what ways would it be different?

12. In locations like Chicago and Anchorage, SAD is most likely to occur around the month of January. In locations in the southern hemisphere, like Santiago, Chile (latitude 33.5° S), SAD occurs around the month of July. Why does this happen?

Be prepared to share your methods and solutions.

Behind the Wheel

Modeling Motion with a Trigonometric Function

16.3

LEARNING GOALS

In this lesson, you will:

- Interpret characteristics of a graph of a trigonometric function in terms of a problem situation.
- Construct a trigonometric function to model a problem situation.

The invention of the wheel is something that can sometimes come up in everyday conversation. "Reinventing the wheel," for example, is a phrase used to refer to coming up with a solution that already exists.

The phrase is likely used because the wheel is one of humankind's oldest "inventions." Evidence for vehicles that used wheels dates back to 3000 BCE.

In fact, the oldest wooden wheel, found in Slovenia, was determined to be over 5000 years old.

16

PROBLEM 1 To Everything . . . Turn, Turn, Turn

Suppose a wheel with a radius of 0.2 meter rolls clockwise on a street at a rate of 2.4 m/s.

You can build a trigonometric function to model the height, h, from the street of a point, P, on the wheel as a function of time, t, in seconds. As the wheel rolls, the position of point P will move along the circle.

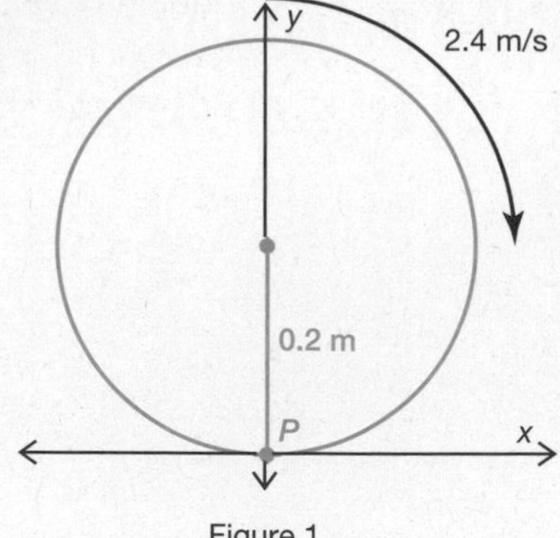

Figure 1

In order to build this trigonometric function, let's first think about point P from Figure 1 in standard position as point P' in Figure 2 moving counterclockwise. In essence, think about the basic sine function because you are trying to model the vertical distance of point P'.

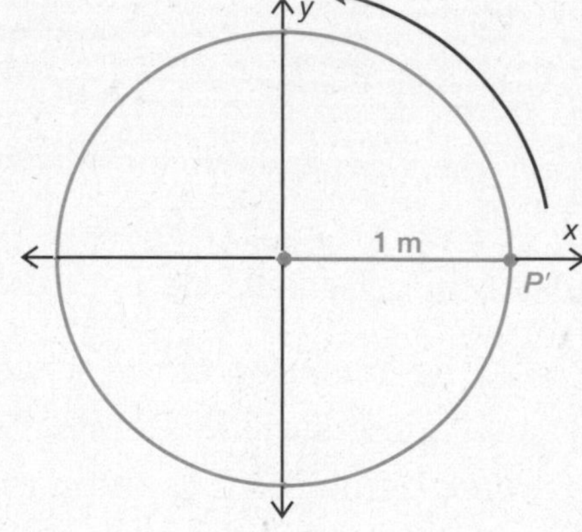

Figure 2

- Point P' is located where a terminal ray in standard position intersects the circle at 0 radians.
- The point is moving counterclockwise instead of clockwise.
- The wheel is rotating in place.
- The x-axis represents the ground.

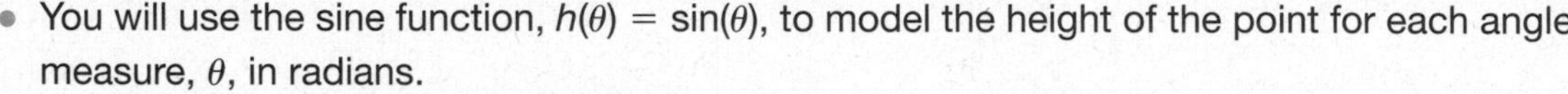

- You will use the sine function, $h(\theta) = \sin(\theta)$, to model the height of the point for each angle measure, θ, in radians.

Let's consider each piece of information in the original problem situation and how you can use transformations to build an equation to model Figure 1.

1. Use the given information to sketch the next figure and write the corresponding equation. Describe the transformation.

   a. Consider Figure 2 but the radius is 0.2 meter. Label point P' on your graph.

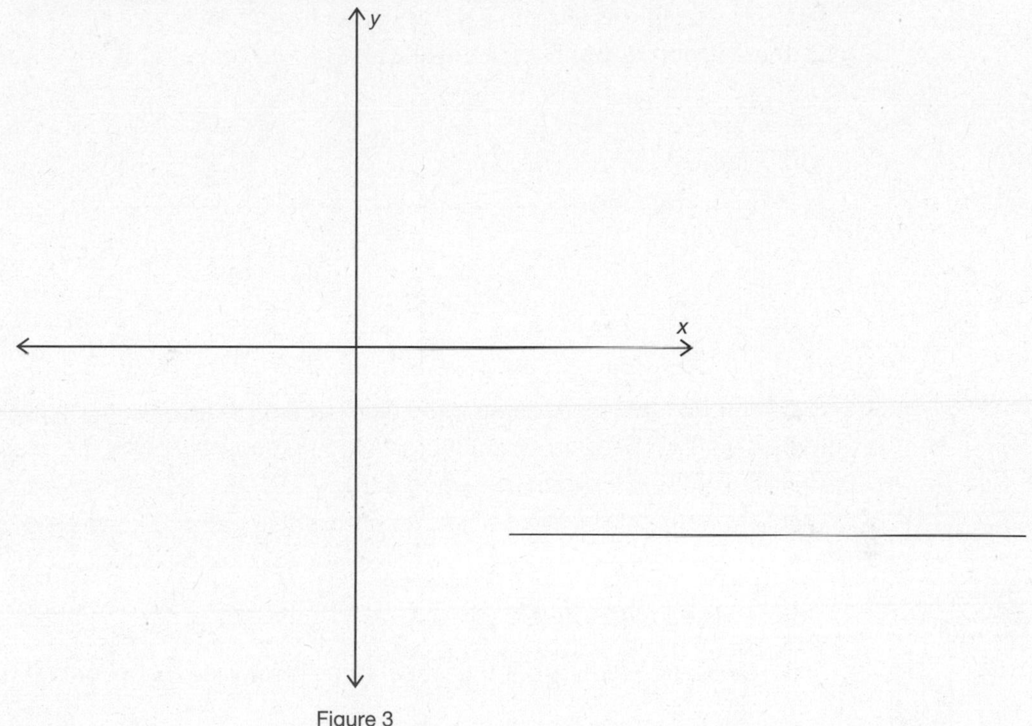

Figure 3

   b. Consider Figure 3 but the wheel rests on the ground. Label point P' on your graph.

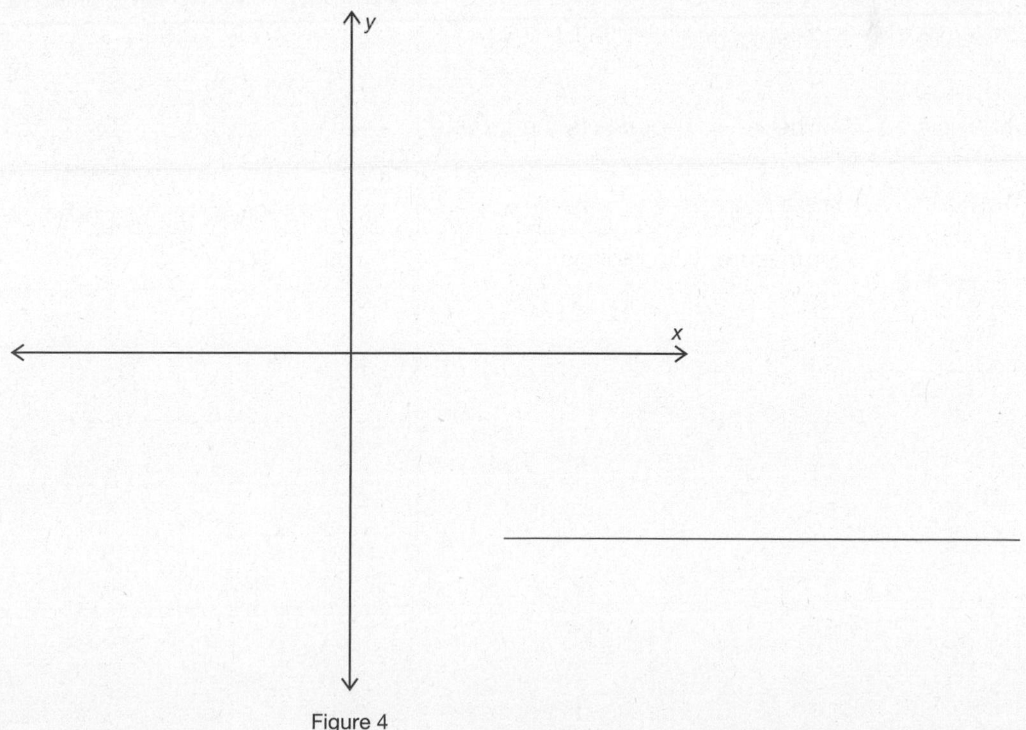

Figure 4

16

c. Consider Figure 4 but translate point P' to the original starting position, point P, in Figure 1. Label point P on your graph.

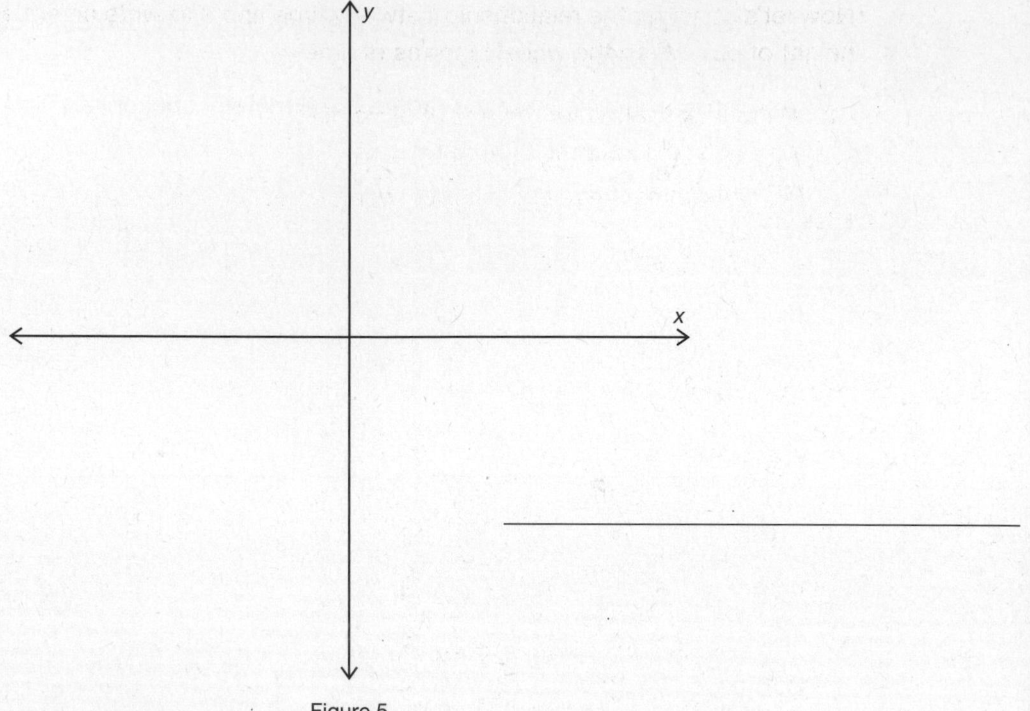

Figure 5

d. Consider Figure 5 but the wheel turns clockwise. Label point P on your graph.

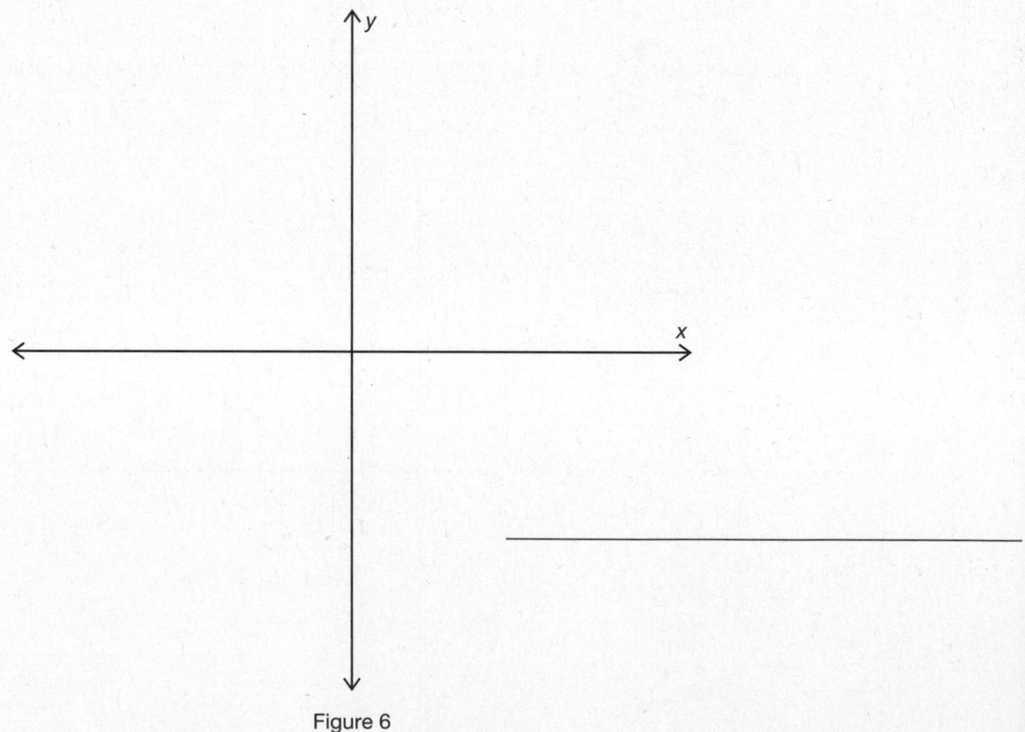

Figure 6

16

You have just written an equation that models the height of point P on the wheel with a radius of 0.2 meter in terms of θ.

Now let's consider the relationship between time and θ to write an equation for the height of point P on the wheel in terms of time.

2. Write an equation for the height of point P on the wheel in terms of time t.

a. Determine the relationship between time, t, and θ.

Use the relationship for distance in terms of rate and time to write distance as a function of θ.

16

b. Write the final equation in terms of time t.

16

3. Sketch a graph of your function in Question 2. Label the axes.

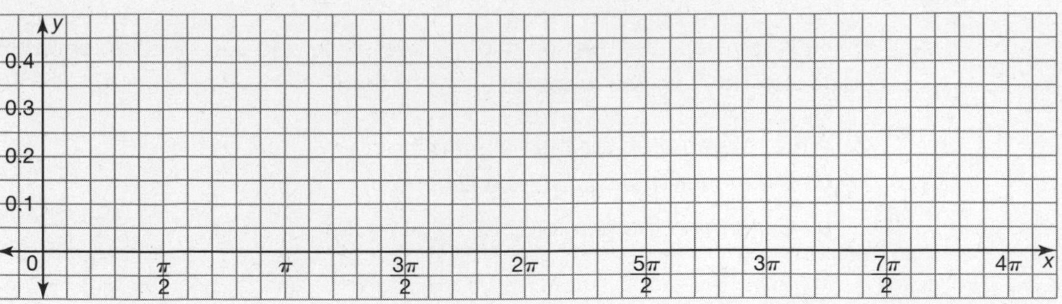

4. Determine the height of the point at 1 second.

5. Rewrite your function as a cosine function. Explain your reasoning.

6. What are the advantages of rewriting your function as a cosine function?

16

7. At what time(s) is the height of the point at 0.2 meter?

Be prepared to share your methods and solutions.

Springs Eternal

The Damping Function

16.4

LEARNING GOALS

In this lesson, you will:

- Choose a trigonometric function to model a periodic phenomenon.
- Determine the graphical attributes (amplitude, midline, frequency) of a periodic function from a description of a problem situation.
- Build a function that is a combination of a trigonometric function and an exponential function.

KEY TERM

- damping function

In this lesson, you will learn about a function that you probably use every day—to turn the volume of your music up or down. The volume dial alters the sound wave function by increasing or decreasing its amplitude.

Mathematical functions are often used to digitally modify sound waves, which can be encoded as periodic functions to be 'read' later by a sound-producing device. In fact, many digital sound effects—like the fade, which you will learn about in this lesson—are produced by mathematically adjusting sound wave functions.

PROBLEM 1 Bouncing Back

An object suspended from a spring is pulled 5 inches below its resting position and released, causing the object to bounce up and down once every second. At rest, the object's height above the ground is 16 inches.

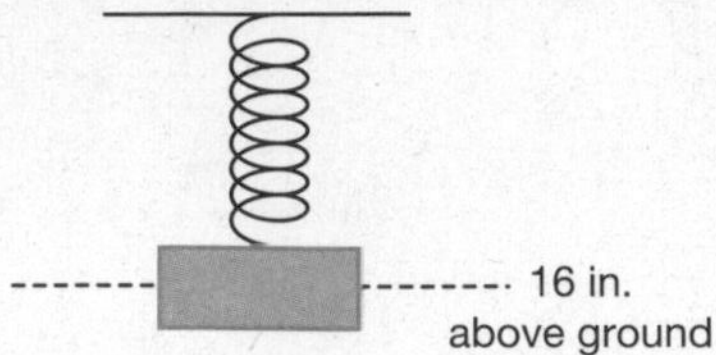

Suppose that the object bounces up 5 inches above its resting height and then back down to 5 inches below its resting height without stopping on every bounce. Let's build a periodic function to model the bouncing of the object on the spring over time.

1. Determine the independent and dependent quantities for this situation.

2. Sketch and label the graph of the function modeling the bouncing object over time $h(t)$, given what you know about the height of the object. Represent at least two bounces of the object on the graph.

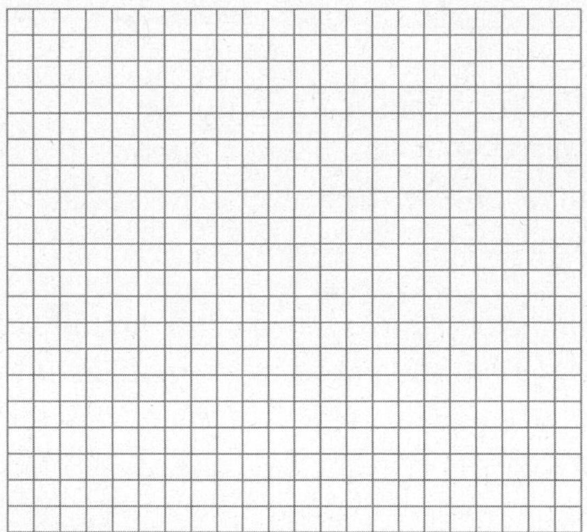

3. Use your graph to determine each characteristic of the periodic function that will model this situation. Explain your reasoning.

   a. Determine the equation of the midline of the graph.

16

   b. Determine the minimum, maximum, and amplitude of the function.

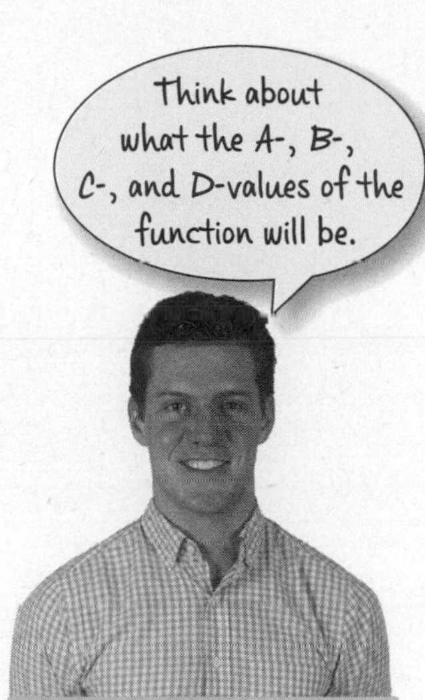

Think about what the A-, B-, C-, and D-values of the function will be.

4. Does your sketch model a sine curve or a cosine curve? Explain your reasoning.

5. Write the values of A, C, and D for the function $h(t)$. Explain how you determined each value.

6. Determine the period of the function $h(t)$. Then write the B-value of the function. Show your work.

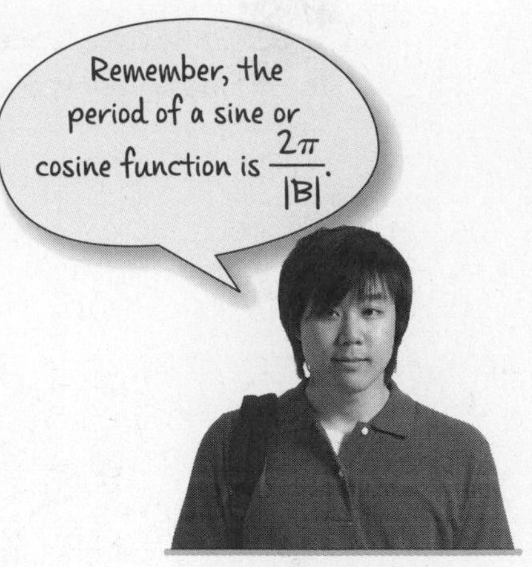
Remember, the period of a sine or cosine function is $\frac{2\pi}{|B|}$.

7. Write the equation for the function $h(t)$ to represent the height of the object over time.

8. Explain why the sign of the B-value in this function can be either positive or negative.

Think about cosine on the unit circle.

9. Solve an equation to determine when the object on the spring is at its minimum height. Show your work.

16

10. Solve an equation to determine when the object on the spring is at a height of 16 inches. Show your work.

Do your solutions represent every time the object is at the midline?

PROBLEM 2 And . . . Fade to Black

An object connected to a string and bouncing up and down the same amount forever is not realistic. Starting from when the object is released, the energy produced will eventually fade away. The object will bounce closer and closer to the midline until it once again comes to rest.

16

Let's consider the same situation from Problem 1. A more realistic model of the object's motion would look like this:

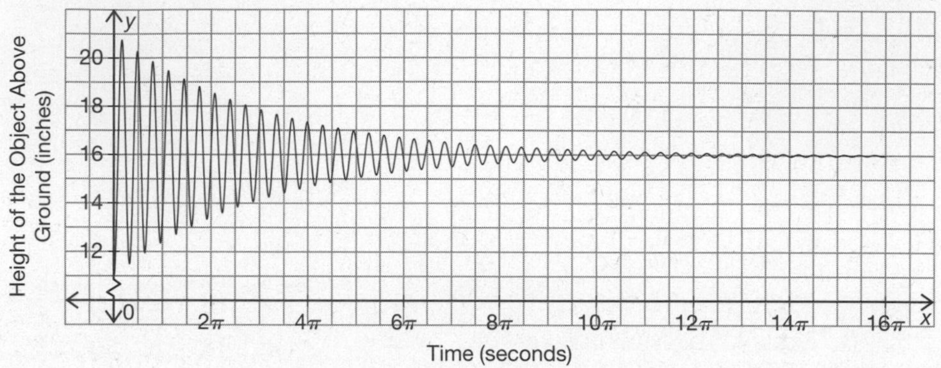

1. How do you think you can adjust the function $h(t)$ to create the shape of the graph shown? What is changing in each period of this function?

A graph of the function $h(t) - 16$ is shown. This is the function relative to its resting position. Suppose that the distance the object bounces from its resting position decreases at a rate of 10% each second.

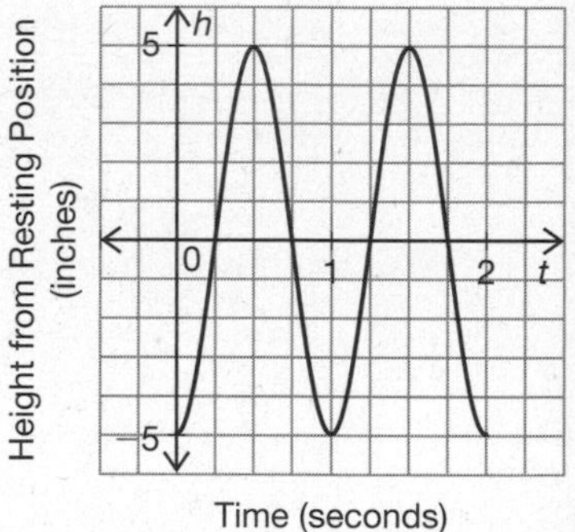

2. At $t = 0$, the object is at -5 inches from its resting position.

   a. Determine the object's new height at $t = 1$ second and $t = 2$ seconds.

   b. Write an equation to describe the object's new height, n, over time, t. Explain your reasoning.

c. Does your equation correctly describe the object's new height at $t = \frac{1}{2}$ second? at $t = 1\frac{1}{2}$ seconds? If not, what equation would be correct?

16

3. Explain why Kent is correct.

Kent

The equation $h(t) = |A| \cdot 0.9^t$ describes the change in the object's height over time, because $|A|$ represents the amplitude of the function.

4. Write the complete function that represents the height of the object on the spring over time.

5. After how many seconds is the maximum height of the object on the spring equal to 18 inches? Explain how you determined your solution.

16

The function that you multiplied to the periodic function to decrease its amplitude over time is called a **damping function**. A damping function can be linear, quadratic, exponential, and on and on!

6. Write a function $g(t)$ to model the height of an object connected to a spring with decreased amplitude over time given the conditions:

- At rest, the object's height is 10 inches above the ground.
- The object bounces up and down once every 2 seconds.
- At $t = 0$, the object's height is 14 inches.
- The distance the object bounces from its resting position decreases at a rate of 15% each second.

Be prepared to share your methods and solutions.

Chapter 16 Summary

KEY TERMS

- trigonometric equation (16.1)
- inverse sine ($\sin^{-1}$) (16.1)
- inverse cosine ($\cos^{-1}$) (16.1)
- inverse tangent ($\tan^{-1}$) (16.1)
- Pythagorean identity (16.1)
- damping function (16.4)

16

16.1 Solving Trigonometric Equations

Solutions to trigonometric equations can be determined using graphs, knowledge about periods and transformation, and inverses of the trigonometric functions. It is important to be aware of domain restrictions when solving trigonometric equations.

Example

Solve the equation over the domain of real numbers.

$$2\cos(x) + 5 = 6$$

$$2\cos(x) = 1$$

$$\cos(x) = \frac{1}{2}$$

$$x = \cos^{-1}\left(\frac{1}{2}\right)$$

$$x = \frac{\pi}{3} + 2\pi n \text{ or } \frac{5\pi}{3} + 2\pi n$$

Therefore, the values of x are $\frac{\pi}{3} + 2\pi n$ or $\frac{5\pi}{3} + 2\pi n$ for integer values of n.

16.1 Solving Trigonometric Equations in Quadratic Form

Trigonometric equations are in quadratic form when they are written in the form $ax^2 + bx + c = 0$, where x represents a trigonometric function. To solve trigonometric equations in quadratic form, use substitution and then follow the steps for solving quadratic equations.

16

Example

Solve the equation $4\sin^2(x) = 1$ over the domain of real numbers.

Let $a = \sin(x)$.

$$4a^2 = 1$$

$$4a^2 - 1 = 0$$

$$(2a - 1)(2a + 1) = 0$$

$$2a - 1 = 0 \quad \text{or} \quad 2a + 1 = 0$$

$$2a = 1 \quad \text{or} \quad 2a = -1$$

$$a = \frac{1}{2} \quad \text{or} \quad a = -\frac{1}{2}$$

$$\sin(x) = \frac{1}{2} \quad \text{or} \quad \sin(x) = -\frac{1}{2}$$

$$x = \sin^{-1}\left(\frac{1}{2}\right) \quad \text{or} \quad x = \sin^{-1}\left(-\frac{1}{2}\right)$$

$$x = \frac{\pi}{6}, \frac{5\pi}{6} \ldots + 2\pi n \quad \text{or} \quad x = \frac{7\pi}{6}, \frac{11\pi}{6} \ldots + 2\pi n$$

Therefore, the values of x are $\frac{\pi}{6}, \frac{5\pi}{6}, \frac{7\pi}{6}, \frac{11\pi}{6} + 2\pi n$ for integer values of n.

16.1 Using the Pythagorean Identity to Determine Trigonometric Values

The Pythagorean identity states that $\sin^2(\theta) + \cos^2(\theta) = 1$. It can be used to determine the values of trigonometric functions.

Example

Given $\cos(\theta) = -\frac{3}{4}$ in Quadrant III, determine $\sin(\theta)$.

$$\sin^2(\theta) + \cos^2(\theta) = 1$$

$$\sin^2(\theta) + \left(-\frac{3}{4}\right)^2 = 1$$

$$\sin^2(\theta) + \frac{9}{16} = 1$$

$$\sin^2(\theta) = \frac{7}{16}$$

$$\sin(\theta) = \pm\frac{\sqrt{7}}{4}$$

So, $\sin(\theta) = -\frac{\sqrt{7}}{4}$, because it is in Quadrant III.

16.2 Modeling with Periodic Functions

Periodic functions can be used to model real-world situations. Analyzing the functions in the context in which they are given can provide deeper understanding about the functions and the situation.

Example

As the tide changes over the course of the day, the depth of the water near the coast also changes. The change in the depth of the water in feet near the coast in Harbortown can be modeled by the function $d(t) = 4.8 \sin(0.5t + 1.4) + 5.8$, where t represents the number of hours after midnight. Graph the function. Then, identify and describe the amplitude, period, and vertical shift in terms of the situation.

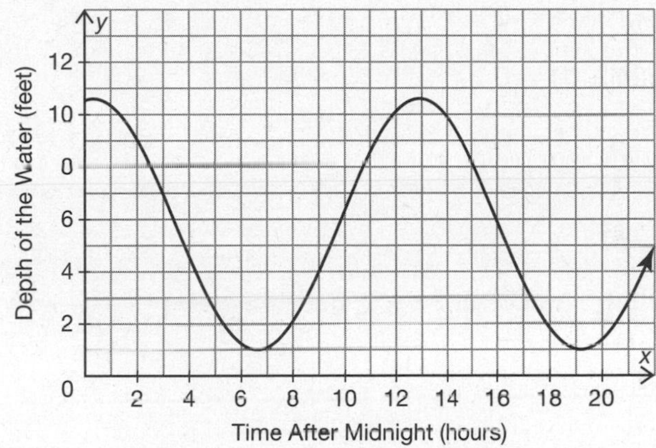

The amplitude is approximately $\frac{|10.6 - 1.0|}{2}$ or 4.8. This represents the average change in depth of the water in feet over the course of the day. The period is $\frac{2\pi}{|0.5|}$ or 4π, which is approximately 12 hours.

This represents the time it takes for the depth to return to its starting point. The vertical shift is 5.8, and it represents the average depth of the water over the course of the day.

16

16.4 Understanding a Damping Trigonometric Function

A damping trigonometric function is a function in which the amplitude changes as the input changes. In a damping function, A is not a constant.

Example

A ball is dropped from a height of 12 feet and allowed to bounce until it comes to a rest.

The function that represents the height of the ball over time, in seconds, is given by the function $h(t) = 6\left(\frac{1}{2}\right)^t \cos(2\pi t) + 6$. Calculate the height of the ball at 3 seconds.

$$h(t) = 6\left(\frac{1}{2}\right)^t \cos(2\pi t) + 6$$

$$h(3) = 6\left(\frac{1}{2}\right)^3 \cos(2\pi(3)) + 6$$

$$= 6\left(\frac{1}{8}\right) \cos(6\pi) + 6$$

$$= \frac{3}{4}(1) + 6$$

$$= 6.75$$

The height of the ball at 3 seconds is 6.75 feet.

Glossary

A

absolute maximum

A function has an absolute maximum if there is a point that has a y-coordinate that is greater than the y-coordinates of every other point on the graph.

Example

The ordered pair (4, 2) is the absolute maximum of the graph of the function $f(x) = -\frac{1}{2}x^2 + 4x - 6$.

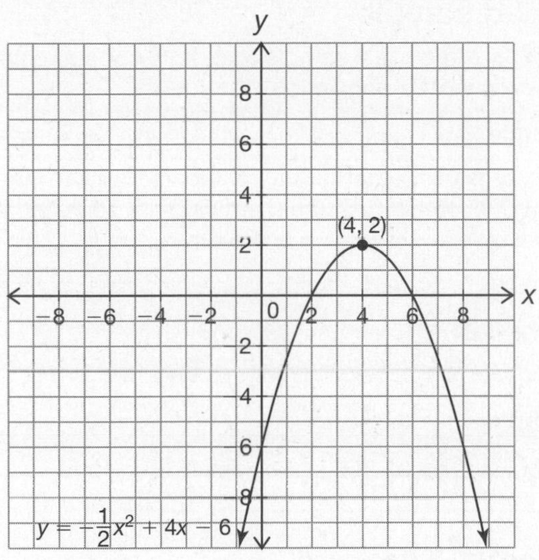

absolute minimum

A function has an absolute minimum if there is a point that has a y-coordinate that is less than the y-coordinates of every other point on the graph.

Example

The ordered pair (1, −4) is the absolute minimum of the graph of the function $y = \frac{2}{3}x^2 - \frac{4}{3}x - \frac{10}{3}$.

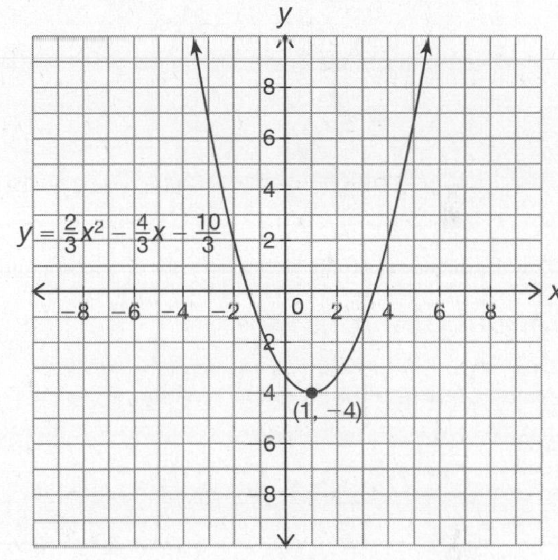

Glossary

amplitude

The amplitude of a periodic function is one-half of the distance between the maximum and minimum values of the function.

Example

The function $y = \sin(x)$ has a maximum of 1 and a minimum of -1. The distance between the maximum and minimum is 2. So, the amplitude of $y = \sin(x)$ is 1.

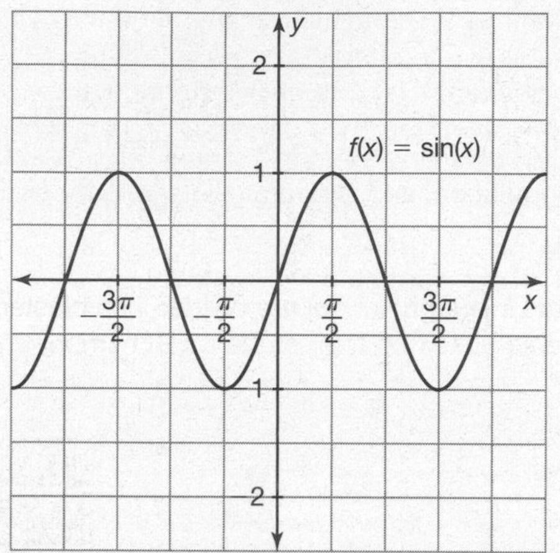

argument of a function

The argument of a function is the variable, term, or expression on which the function operates.

Example

In the function $f(x + 5) = 32$, the argument is $x + 5$.

arithmetic sequence

An arithmetic sequence is a sequence of numbers in which the difference between any two consecutive terms is a constant.

Example

The sequence 1, 3, 5, 7 is an arithmetic sequence with a common difference of 2.

arithmetic series

An arithmetic series is the sum of the terms of an arithmetic sequence.

Example

The arithmetic series corresponding to the arithmetic sequence 1, 3, 5, 7 is $1 + 3 + 5 + 7$, or 16.

average rate of change

The average rate of change of a function is the ratio of the independent variable to the dependent variable over a specific interval. The formula for average rate of change is $\frac{f(b) - f(a)}{b - a}$ for an interval (a, b). The expression $a - b$ represents the change in the input of the function f. The expression $f(b) - f(a)$ represents the change in the function f as the input changes from a to b.

Example

Consider the function $f(x) = x^2$.

The average rate of change of the interval (1, 3) is $\frac{3^2 - 1^2}{3 - 1} = \frac{9 - 1}{3 - 1} = \frac{8}{2} = 4$.

B

biased sample

A biased sample is a sample that does not accurately represent all of a population.

Example

A survey is conducted asking students their favorite class. Only students in the math club are surveyed. The sample of students is a biased sample.

binomial

A binomial is a polynomial with exactly two terms.

Example

The polynomial $3x + 5$ is a binomial.

Binomial Theorem

The Binomial Theorem is used to calculate any term of any binomial expansion. It is written in the form:

$$\begin{aligned}(x + y)^k &= \sum_{r=0}^{k} \binom{k}{r} x^{k-r} y^r \\ &= \binom{k}{0} x^k y^0 + \binom{k}{1} x^{k-1} y^1 + \binom{k}{2} x^{k-2} y^2 + \cdots \\ &\quad + \binom{k}{k-2} x^2 y^{k-2} + \binom{k}{k-1} x^1 y^{k-1} \\ &\quad + \binom{k}{k} x^0 y^k\end{aligned}$$

where k is the degree of the binomial exponent. Note that a given term is the $(r + 1)$th term.

Example

Use the Binomial Theorem to find the third term of $(x + y)^{20}$.

$$\begin{aligned}(x + y)^{20} &= \binom{20}{2} x^{20-2} y^2 = \frac{20!}{18!2!} x^{18} y^2 \\ &= \frac{20 \cdot 19}{2 \cdot 1} x^{18} y^2 = 190x^{18}y^2\end{aligned}$$

C

carrying capacity

The carrying capacity of a species is the maximum population size of the species that the environment can sustain. In logistic functions $f(x) = \frac{C}{1 + Ae^{-Bx}}$, C is the carrying capacity.

Example

The number of fish in a small pond is modeled by the logistic growth function $f(x) = \frac{150}{1 + 7e^{-0.06x}}$. The carrying capacity of the pond is 150 fish.

Change of Base Formula

The Change of Base Formula allows you to calculate an exact value for a logarithm by rewriting it in terms of a different base. It is especially helpful when using a calculator.

The Change of Base Formula states: $\log_b(c) = \frac{\log_a(c)}{\log_a(b)}$, where $a, b, c > 0$ and $a, b \neq 1$.

Example

$$\log_4(50) = \frac{\log 50}{\log 4} \approx 2.821928095$$

characteristic of interest

A characteristic of interest is the specific question that you are trying to answer or specific information that a study is trying to gather.

Example

In a sample survey to determine teenagers' online habits, a characteristic of interest is the amount of time that a teenager spends online per day.

closed under an operation

A set is closed under an operation if the operation is performed on any of the numbers in the set and the result is a number that is also in the same set.

Example

The set of whole numbers is closed under addition. The sum of any two whole numbers is always another whole number.

clusters

Clusters are area of the graph where data are grouped close together.

Example

A city manager randomly selects one block in the city and surveys all of the residents of that block. Each block is considered a cluster.

cluster sample

A cluster sample is a sample obtained by creating clusters, with each cluster containing the characteristics of the population, and randomly selecting a cluster.

Example

If students in a high school are divided into clusters of 20 students based on their student I.D. number and then one cluster is randomly selected, this is a cluster sample.

coefficient of determination

The coefficient of determination (R^2) measures the "strength" of the relationship between the original data and its regression equation. The value of the coefficient of determination ranges from 0 to 1 with a value of 1 indicating a perfect fit between the regression equation and the original data.

common logarithm

A common logarithm is a logarithm with a base of 10. Common logarithms are usually written without a base.

Example

$\log(10x)$ or $\log x$ are examples of a common logarithm.

complex conjugates

Complex conjugates are pairs of numbers of the form $a + bi$ and $a - bi$. The product of a pair of complex conjugates is always a real number.

Example

The expressions $(1 + i)$ and $(1 - i)$ are complex conjugates. The product of $(1 + i)$ and $(1 - i)$ is a real number: $(1 + i)(1 - i) = 1 - i^2 = 1 - (-1) = 2$.

composition of functions

Composition of functions is the process of substituting one function for the variable in another function.

Example

If $f(x) = 3x - 5$ and $g(x) = x^2$, then the composition of the functions $f(g(x))$ can be written as $f(g(x)) = 3(x^2) - 5 = 3x^2 - 5$.

The composition of functions $g(f(x))$ can be written as $g(f(x)) = (3x + 5)^2$.

concavity of a parabola

The concavity of a parabola describes the orientation of the curvature of the parabola.

Example

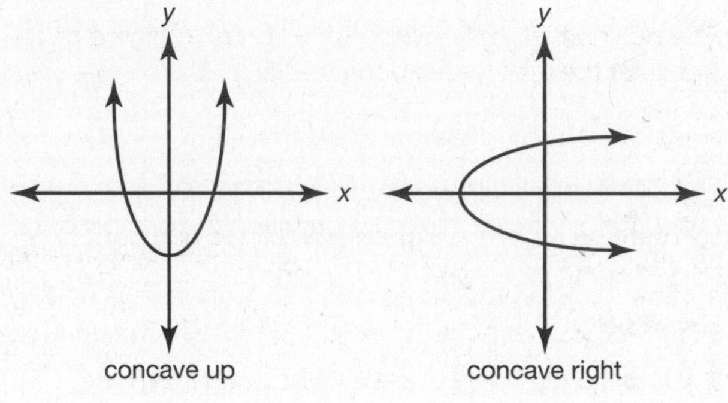

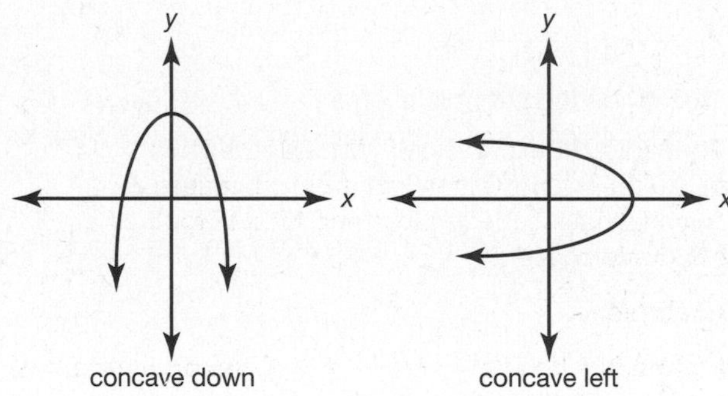

confidence interval

A confidence interval is an estimated range of values, based on the results of a sample survey, that will likely include the population proportion. Typically, a confidence interval of 95%, or 2 standard deviations from the mean, is used. The formula for calculating the confidence interval for proportions is $\sqrt{\frac{\hat{p}(1 - \hat{p})}{n}}$, where $\hat{p}$ is the sample population and n is the sample size. The formula $\frac{S}{\sqrt{n}}$, where S is the standard deviation of the sample and n is the sample size, is used for continuous data.

Example

A survey of 2000 teenagers reports that 42% have a part-time job.

$$\sqrt{\frac{0.42(1 - 0.42)}{2000}}$$

$$\sqrt{\frac{0.42(0.58)}{2000}}$$

≈ 0.011

The interval from 40.9% to 43.1% represents a 95% confidence interval for the population proportion.

confounding

Confounding is the process of overlooking factors and situations that distort the final results when seeking to gather information or data.

Example

Suppose that a study is conducted to determine if there is a link between a certain type of insulin that some diabetic patients use and cancer. Confounding can occur due to the fact that there are other potential causes of cancer that could be involved in the sample.

continuous data

Continuous data are data that have an infinite number of possible values.

Example

The heights of students is an example of continuous data.

convenience sample

A convenience sample is a sample whose data are based on what is convenient for the person choosing the sample.

Example

If you choose the students sitting closest to you in math class as your sample, you have a convenience sample.

convergent series

A convergent series is an infinite series that has a finite sum. The sum of a convergent series S can be calculated as $\frac{g_1}{1 - r}$ where g_1 is the first term of the series and r is the common ratio.

Example

The infinite geometric series $1 + \frac{1}{2} + \frac{1}{4} + \frac{1}{8} + \cdots$ can be calculated as $S = \frac{1}{1 - \frac{1}{2}} = \frac{1}{\frac{1}{2}} = 2$.

cosine function

A cosine function is a periodic function. It takes angle measures (θ values) as inputs and then outputs real number values based on coordinates of points on the unit circle.

Example

The function $h(\theta) = 4\cos(\theta + \pi)$ is a cosine function.

cube root function

The cube root function is the inverse of the power function $f(x) = x^3$.

Example

The cube root function is $g(x) = \sqrt[3]{x}$.

cubic function

A cubic function is a function that can be written in the standard form $f(x) = ax^3 + bx^2 + cx + d$ where $a \neq 0$.

Example

The function $f(x) = x^3 - 5x^2 + 3x + 1$ is a cubic function.

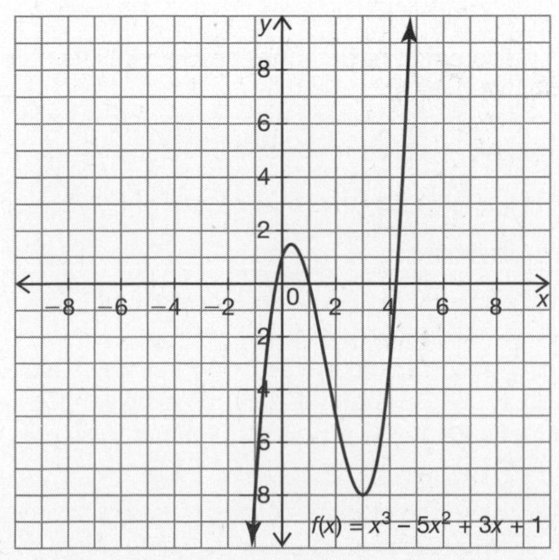

D

damping function

A damping function is a function that is multiplied to a periodic function to decrease its amplitude over time. It can be from a multitude of function families, including linear, quadratic, or exponential.

Example

In the function $f(x) = 2^x \cdot \sin(x) + 1$, the exponential function 2^x is the damping function.

degree of a polynomial

The degree of a polynomial is the greatest variable exponent in the expression.

Example

The polynomial $2x^3 + 5x^2 - 6x + 1$ has a degree of 3 because the greatest exponent is 3.

discrete data

Discrete data are data that have a finite number of possible values.

Example

If you roll a number cube 10 times and record the results, the results are discrete data.

discriminant

The radicand expression in the Quadratic Formula, $b^2 - 4ac$, is called the discriminant because it "discriminates" the number and type of roots of a quadratic equation.

Example

For the function $f(x) = 2x^2 - 5x + 1$, the discriminant is $(-5)^2 - 4(2)(1)$, or 17.

divergent series

A divergent series is an infinite series that does not have a finite sum.

Example

The infinite geometric series $1 + 2 + 4 + 8 + 16 + \cdots$ is a divergent series.

double root

A double root of an equation is a root that appears twice.

Example

The equation $x^2 + 2x + 1 = 0$ has a double root at $x = -1$.

$x^2 + 2x + 1 = 0$

$(x + 1)(x + 1) = 0$

$x + 1 = 0$ or $x + 1 = 0$

$x = -1$ or $x = -1$

E

Empirical Rule for Normal Distributions

The Empirical Rule for Normal Distributions states that:

- Approximately 68% of the area under the normal curve is within one standard deviation of the mean.
- Approximately 95% of the area under the normal curve is within two standard deviations of the mean.
- Approximately 99.7% of the area under the normal curve is within three standard deviations of the mean.

Example

For a data set that is normally distributed with a mean of 10 and a standard deviation of 1, the following are true:

- Approximately 68% of the data values are between 9 and 11.
- Approximately 95% of the data values are between 8 and 12.
- Approximately 99.7% of the data values are between 7 and 13.

end behavior

The end behavior of the graph of a function is the behavior of the graph as x approaches infinity and as x approaches negative infinity.

Example

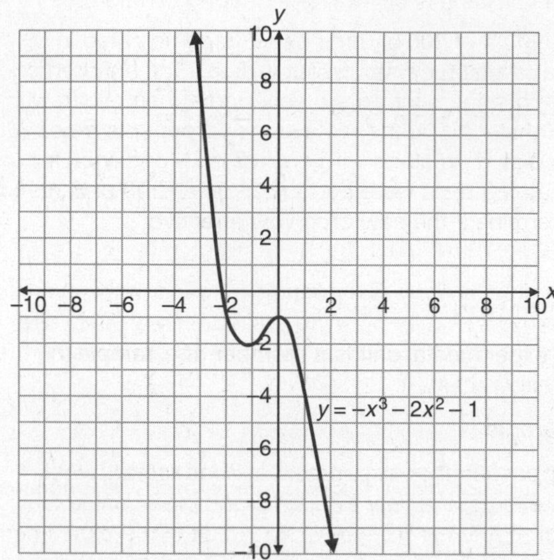

The end behavior of the graph shown can be described as follows:

As x approaches infinity, y approaches negative infinity.

As x approaches negative infinity, y approaches infinity.

Euclid's Formula

Euclid's Formula is a formula used to generate Pythagorean triples given any two positive integers. Given positive integers r and s, where $r > s$, Euclid's Formula is $(r^2 + s^2)^2 = (r^2 - s^2)^2 + (2rs)^2$.

Example

Let $r = 3$ and $s = 1$.

$(3^2 + 1^2)^2 = (3^2 - 1^2)^2 + (2 \cdot 3 \cdot 1)^2$

$10^2 = 8^2 + 6^2$

So, one Pythagorean triple is 6, 8, 10.

even function

An even function f is a function for which $f(-x) = f(x)$ for all values of x in the domain.

Example

The function $f(x) = x^2$ is an even function because $(-x)^2 = x^2$.

Glossary

experiment

An experiment gathers data on the effect of one or more treatments, or experimental conditions, on the characteristic of interest.

Example

The following is an example of an experiment.

A sample of 200 asthma patients participated in the clinical trial for a new asthma drug. One hundred of the patients received a placebo treatment along with an inhaler, while the remaining 100 patients received the new drug along with an inhaler. Monthly blood and breathing tests were performed on all 200 patients to determine if the new drug was effective.

experimental unit

An experimental unit is a member of a sample in an experiment.

Example

Suppose that an experiment is conducted to test the effects of a new drug on a sample of patients. Each patient is an experimental unit in the experiment.

extraneous solution

Extraneous solutions are solutions that result from the process of solving an equation; but are not valid solutions to the equation.

Example

$$\begin{aligned} \log_2(x) + \log_2(x+7) &= 3 \\ \log_2(x^2+7x) &= 3 \\ x^2+7x &= 2^3 \\ x^2+7x &= 8 \\ x^2+7x-8 &= 0 \\ (x+8)(x-1) &= 0 \\ x+8 = 0 \quad &\text{or} \quad x-1=0 \\ x = -8 \quad & \quad\quad\;\; x = 1 \end{aligned}$$

The solution $x = -8$ is an extraneous solution because the argument of a logarithm must be greater than zero.

extrema

Extrema are the set of all relative maxima and minima for a graph.

Example

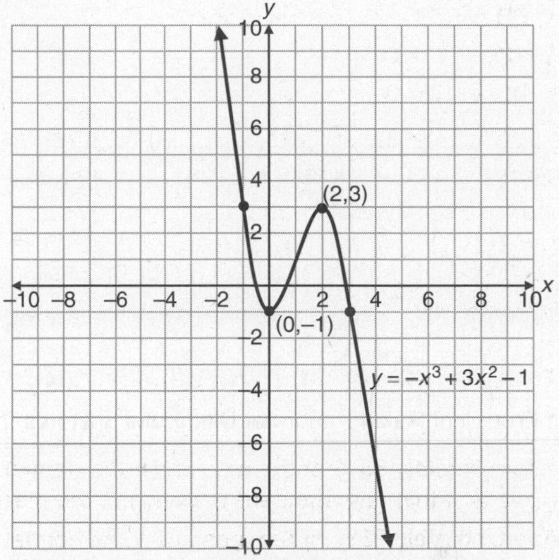

The graph shown has 2 extrema, a relative maximum at (2, 3) and a relative minimum at (0, −1).

F

Factor Theorem

The Factor Theorem states that a polynomial is divisible by $(x - r)$ if the value of the polynomial at r is zero.

Example

The polynomial $x^3 - 2x^2 + 2x - 1$ is divisible by $x - 1$ because $(1)^3 - 2(1)^2 + 2(1) - 1 = 0$.

factored form of a quadratic function

A quadratic function written in factored form is in the form $f(x) = a(x - r_1)(x - r_2)$, where $a \neq 0$.

Example

The function $h(x) = x^2 - 8x + 12$ written in factored form is $h(x) = (x - 6)(x - 2)$.

finite sequence

If a sequence terminates, it is called a finite sequence.

Example

The sequence 22, 26, 30 is a finite sequence.

finite series

A finite series is the sum of a finite number of terms.

Example

The sum of all of the even integers from 1 to 100 is a finite series.

fractal

A fractal is a complex geometric shape that is constructed by a mathematical pattern. Fractals are infinite and self-similar.

Example

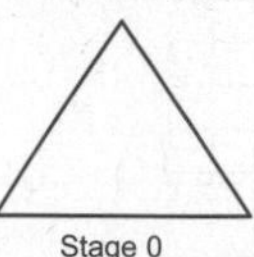
Stage 0

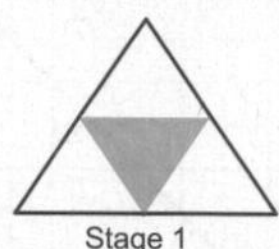
Stage 1

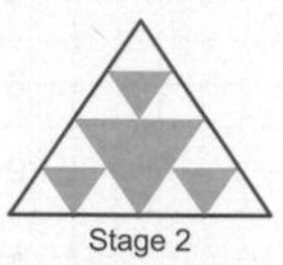
Stage 2

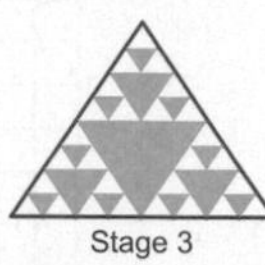
Stage 3

frequency

The frequency of a periodic function is the reciprocal of the period and specifies the number of repetitions of the graph of a periodic function per unit. It is calculated by the formula $\frac{|B|}{2\pi}$.

Example

The function $f(x) = 3\cos(2x)$ has a B-value of 2, so the frequency is $\frac{|2|}{2\pi}$ or $\frac{1}{\pi}$ units.

function

A function is a relation such that for each element of the domain there exists exactly one element in the range.

Example

The equation $y = 2x$ is a function. Every x-value has exactly one corresponding y-value.

function notation

Function notation is a way of representing functions algebraically. The function $f(x)$ is read as "f of x" and indicates that x is the input and $f(x)$ is the output.

Example

The function $f(x) = 0.75x$ is written using function notation.

Fundamental Theorem of Algebra

The Fundamental Theorem of Algebra states that any polynomial equation of degree n must have exactly n complex roots or solutions; also, every polynomial function of degree n must have exactly n complex zeros. However, any root or zero may be a multiple root or zero.

Example

The polynomial equation $x^5 + x^2 - 6 = 0$ has 5 complex roots because the polynomial $x^5 + x^2 - 6$ has a degree of 5.

geometric sequence

A geometric sequence is a sequence of terms in which the ratio between any two consecutive terms is a constant.

Example

The sequence 2, 4, 8, 16 is a geometric sequence with a common ratio of 2.

geometric series

A geometric series is the sum of the terms of a geometric sequence.

Example

The geometric series corresponding to the geometric sequence 2, 4, 8, 16 is $2 + 4 + 8 + 16$, or 30.

half-life

The half-life of a sample is the time it takes for half of the atoms in the sample to decay.

Example

The radioactive isotope strontium-90 has a half life of about 30 years. A 1000-gram sample of strontium-90 will decay to 500 grams in 30 years.

horizontal compression

Horizontal compression is the squeezing of a graph toward the y-axis.

Example

The graph of $g(x) = (2x)^2$ is a horizontal compression compared to the graph of $f(x) = x^2$.

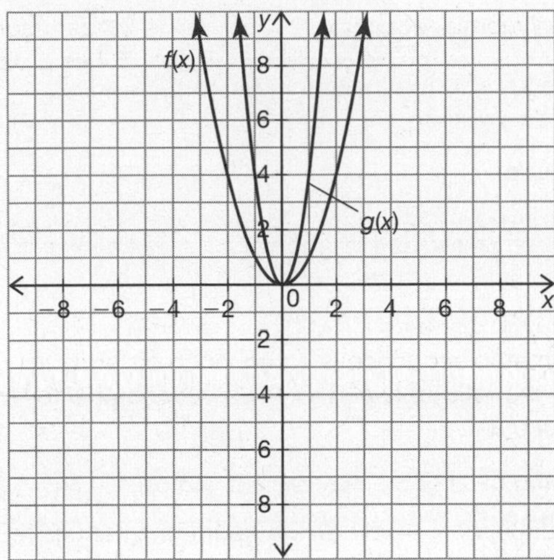

horizontal dilation

A horizontal dilation is a type of transformation that stretches or compresses the entire graph.

Example

The graphs of $g(x) = (2x)^2$ and $h(x) = \left(\frac{1}{2}x\right)^2$ are horizontal dilations of the graph of $f(x) = x^2$.

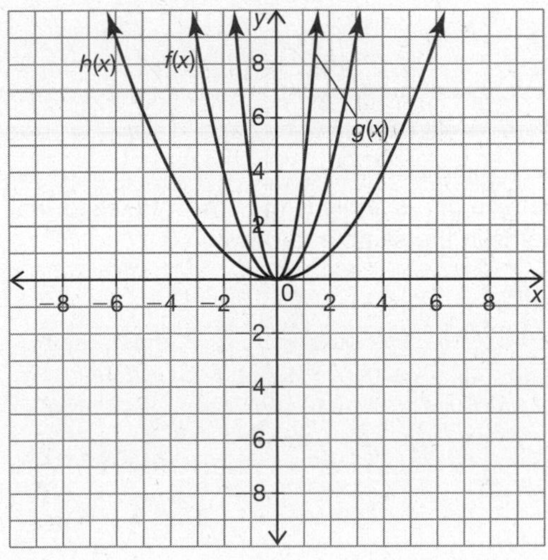

Horizontal Line Test

The Horizontal Line Test is a test to determine if a function is one to one. To use the test, imagine drawing every possible horizontal line on the coordinate plane. If no horizontal line intersects the graph of a function at more than one point, then the function is one to one.

Example

The function $y = x$ passes the Horizontal Line Test because no horizontal line can be drawn that intersects the graph at more than one point. So, the function is one to one.

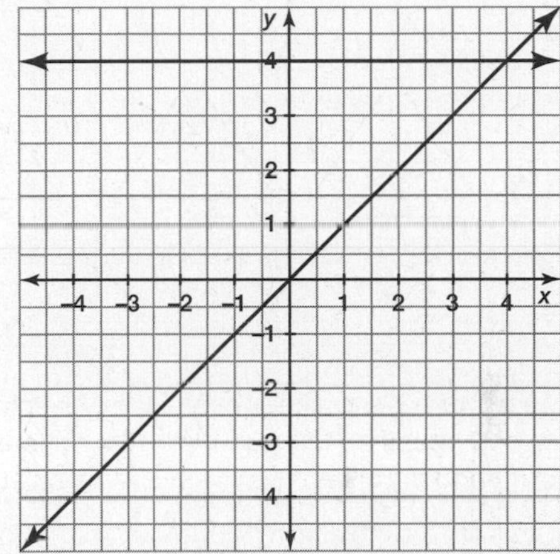

The function $y = x^2$ does not pass the Horizontal Line Test because a horizontal line can be drawn that intersects the graph at more than one point. So, the function is not one to one.

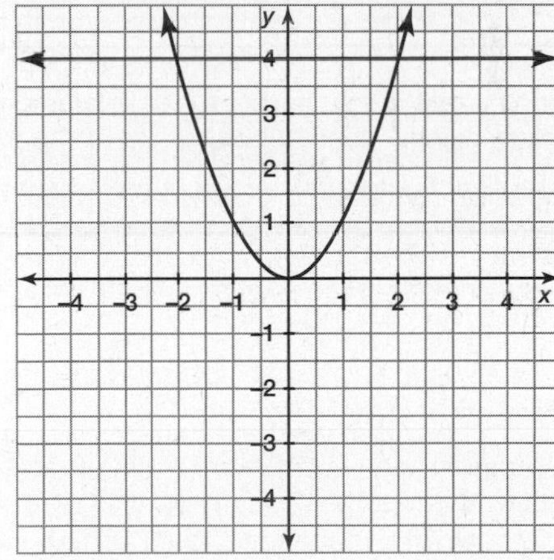

Glossary

horizontal stretching

Horizontal stretching is the stretching of a graph away from the y-axis.

Example

The graph of $g(x) = \left(\frac{1}{2}x\right)^2$ is a horizontal stretching compared to the graph of $f(x) = x^2$.

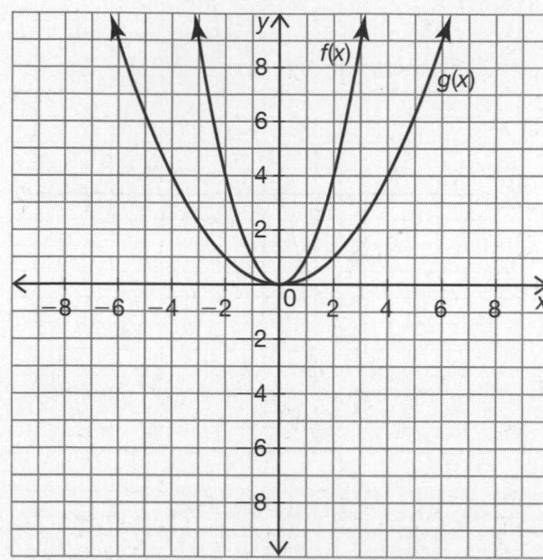

I

identity function

The identity function, also known as the composition identity, is defined as $f(x) = x$.

imaginary part of a complex number

In a complex number of the form $a + bi$, the term bi is called the imaginary part of a complex number.

Example

The imaginary part of the complex number $3 + 2i$ is $2i$.

imaginary roots

Imaginary roots are imaginary solutions to equations.

Example

The quadratic equation $x^2 - 2x + 2$ has two imaginary roots: $1 + i$ and $1 - i$.

infinite sequence

If a sequence continues forever, it is called an infinite sequence.

Example

The sequence 22, 26, 30, 34 . . . is an infinite sequence.

infinite series

An infinite series is the sum of an infinite number of terms.

Example

The sum of all of the even whole numbers is an infinite series.

initial ray of an angle

The initial ray of an angle in standard position is the ray with its endpoint at the origin and extending along the positive x-axis.

Example

The initial ray of the angle is labeled in the diagram.

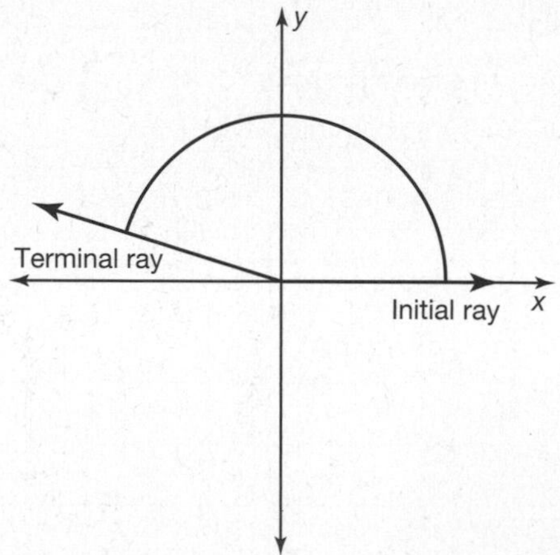

inverse cosine ($\cos^{-1}$)

The $\cos^{-1}$ function is the inverse of the cosine function. The inverse cosine function is written as arccos or $\cos^{-1}$.

Example

$\cos(60°) = \frac{1}{2}$ so $\cos^{-1}\left(\frac{1}{2}\right) = 60°$

inverse of a function

The inverse of a one-to-one function is a function that results from exchanging the independent and dependent variables. A function $f(x)$ with coordinates $(x, f(x))$ will have an inverse with coordinates $(f(x), x)$.

Example

The inverse of the function $y = 2x$ can be found by exchanging the variables x and y.

The inverse of $y = 2x$ is $x = 2y$.

inverse sine ($\sin^{-1}$)

The $\sin^{-1}$ function is the inverse of the sine function. The inverse sine function is written as arcsin or $\sin^{-1}$.

Example

$\sin(30°) = \frac{1}{2}$ so $\sin^{-1}\left(\frac{1}{2}\right) = 30°$

inverse tangent ($\tan^{-1}$)

The $\tan^{-1}$ function is the inverse of the tangent function. The inverse tangent function is written as arctan or $\tan^{-1}$.

Example

$\tan(45°) = 1$ so $\tan^{-1}(1) = 45°$

invertible function

An invertible function is a function whose inverse exists. It is one-to-one and passes the Horizontal Line Test, so its inverse will also be a function.

Example

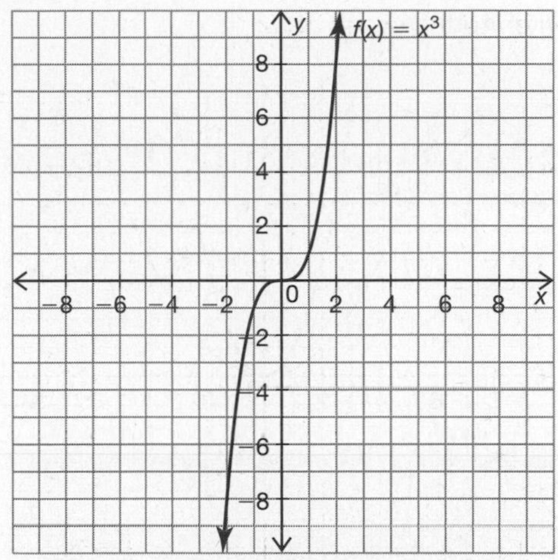

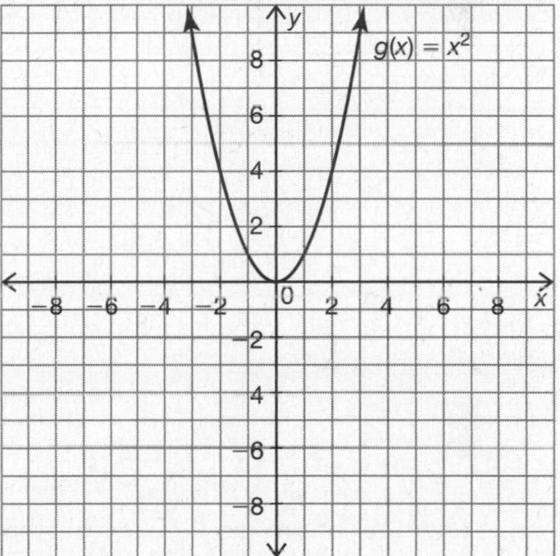

The graph of $f(x) = x^3$ is an invertible function because it is one-to-one and passes the Horizontal Line Test. Therefore its inverse will also be a function.

The graph of $g(x) = x^2$ is not an invertible function because it does not pass the Horizontal Line Test.

Glossary

iterative process

An iterative process is one in which the output from one iteration is used as the input for the next iteration.

Example

A recursive sequence uses an iterative process to generate its terms.

$a_n = 3a_{n-1} + 1$

$a_1 = 2$

Begin with the first term, which is 2, and substitute it into the sequence to get the next term.

$a_2 = 3a_1 + 1$

$= 3(2) + 1$

$= 7$

Then substitute a_2 into the sequence to produce a_3, and so on.

L

line of reflection

A line of reflection is the line that a graph is reflected about.

Example

The line of reflection for the graph of the function $f(x) = x^2$ is the y-axis, or the line $x = 0$.

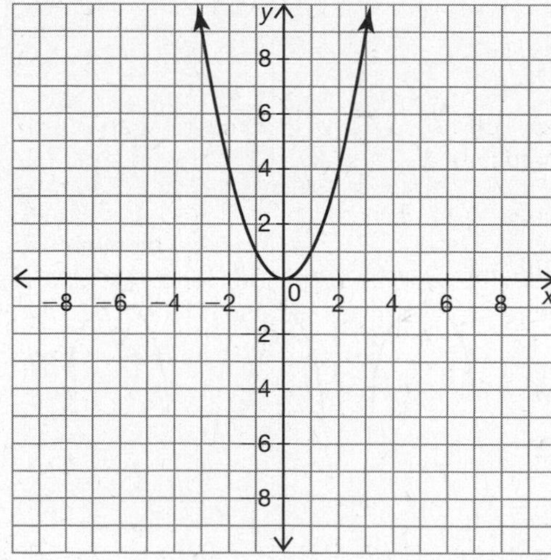

logarithm

The logarithm of a positive number is the exponent to which the base must be raised to result in that number.

Example

Because $10^2 = 100$, the logarithm of 100 to the base 10 is 2.

$\log 100 = 2$

Because $2^3 = 8$, the logarithm of 8 to the base 2 is 3.

$\log_2 (8) = 3$

logarithm with same base and argument

The logarithm of a number, with the base equal to the same number, is always equal to 1.

$$\log_b(b) = 1$$

Example

$\log_4(4) = 1$

logarithmic equation

A logarithmic equation is an equation that contains a logarithm.

Example

The equation $\log_2 (x) = 4$ is a logarithmic equation.

logarithmic function

A logarithmic function is a function involving a logarithm.

Example

The function $f(x) = 3 \log x$ is a logarithmic function.

logistic functions

Logistic functions are functions that can be written in the form $f(x) = \dfrac{C}{1 + Ae^{-Bx}}$. It is used to model population growth. The graph of a logistic growth function is shaped like an S-curve. The function appears to grow exponentially during the initial growth stage, but as it approaches the carrying capacity C, the growth slows and then stops when it reaches equilibrium.

Example

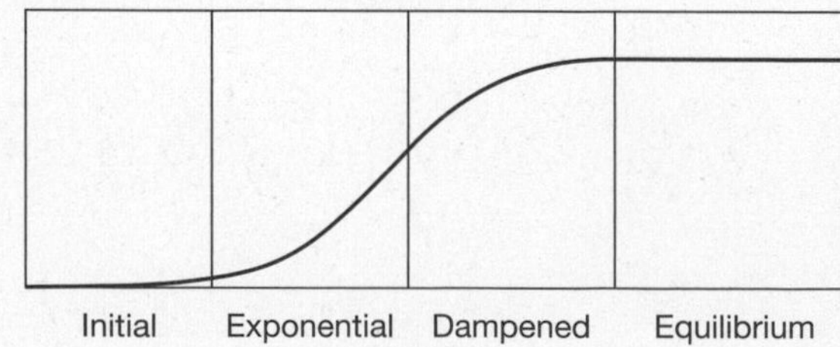

M

mean

The mean of a data set is the sum of all of the values of the data set divided by the number of values in the data set. With normal curves, the mean of a population is represented with the symbol μ, and the mean of a sample is represented with the symbol $\bar{x}$.

Example

The mean of the numbers 7, 9, 13, 4, and 7 is $\frac{7 + 9 + 13 + 4 + 7}{5}$, or 8.

The mean of a set of normally distributed data is aligned with the peak of the normal curve.

midline

The midline of a periodic function is a reference line whose equation is the average of the minimum and maximum values of the function.

Example

In the graph of $g(x) = -2\cos(x) + 3$ the midline occurs at $y = 3$ because the maximum value is 5 and the minimum value is 1.

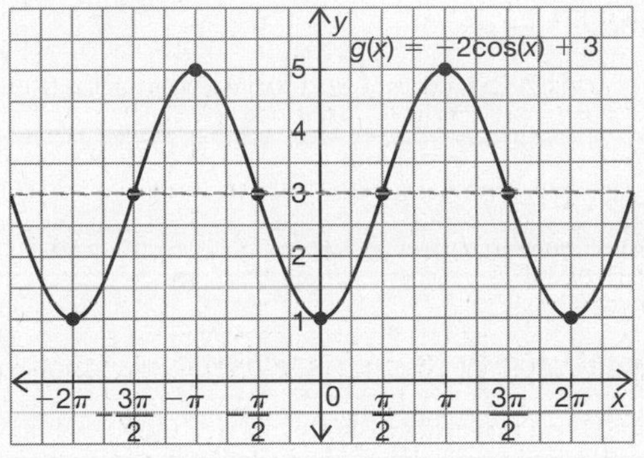

monomial

A monomial is a polynomial with exactly one term.

Example

The expressions $5x$, 7, $-2xy$, and $13x^3$ are monomials.

multiplicity

Multiplicity is how many times a particular number is a zero for a given function.

Example

The equation $x^2 + 2x + 1 = 0$ has a double root at $x = -1$. The root -1 has a multiplicity of 2.

$x^2 + 2x + 1 = 0$

$(x + 1)(x + 1) = 0$

$x + 1 = 0$ or $x + 1 = 0$

$x = -1$ or $x = -1$

N

natural base, e

The natural base e is an irrational number equal to approximately 2.71828.

Example

$e^2 \approx 2.7183^2 \approx 7.3892$

natural logarithm

A natural logarithm is a logarithm with a base of e. Natural logarithms are usually written as ln.

Example

$\log_e(x)$ or $\ln x$ is a natural logarithm.

normal curve

A normal curve is a curve that is bell-shaped and symmetric about the mean.

Example

A normal curve is shown.

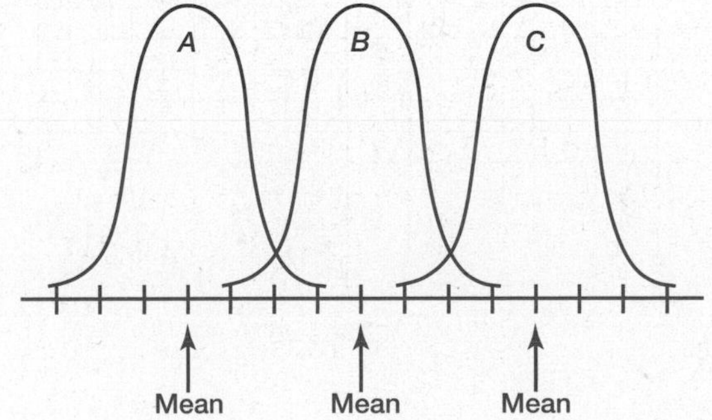

Glossary

normal distribution

A normal distribution, or normal probability distribution, describes a continuous data set that can be modeled using a normal curve.

Example

Adult IQ scores, gas mileage of certain cars, and SAT scores are all continuous data that follow a normal distribution.

observational study

An observational study gathers data about a characteristic of the population without trying to influence the data.

Example

The following is an example of an observational study.

New research funded by a pediatric agency found that nearly 70% of in-house day care centers show as much as 2.5 hours of television to the children in the center per day. The study examined 132 day care programs in 2 Midwestern states.

odd function

An odd function f is a function for which $f(-x) = -f(x)$ for all values of x in the domain.

Example

The function $f(x) = x^3$ is an odd function because $(-x)^3 = -x^3$.

parameter

When data are gathered from a population, the characteristic used to describe the population is called a parameter.

Example

If you wanted to find out the average height of the students at your school, and you measured every student at the school, the characteristic "average height" would be a parameter.

percentile

A percentile divides a data set into 100 equal parts.

period

A period of a periodic function is the length of the smallest interval over which the function repeats.

Example

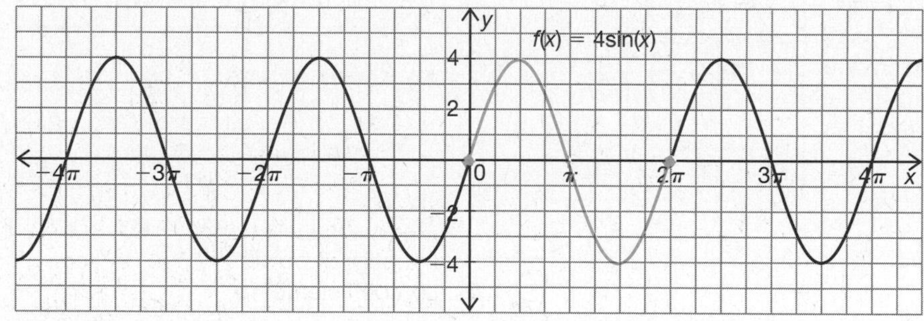

periodic function

A periodic function is a function whose graph consists of repeated instances of a portion of the graph.

Example

The function $f(x) = \sin(x)$ is a periodic function. The portion of the graph between $x = 0$ and $x = 2\pi$ repeats.

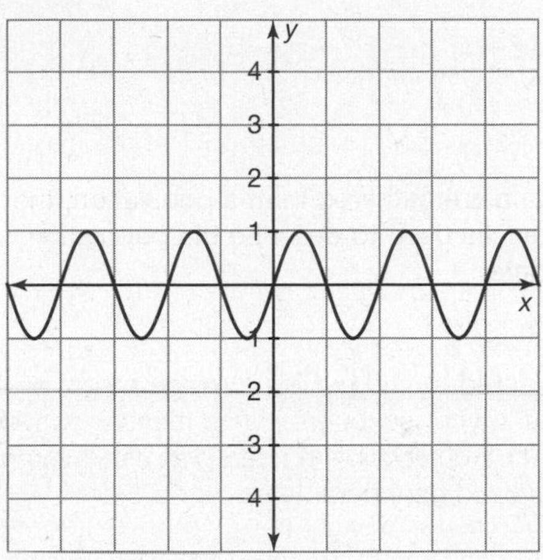

periodicity identity

A periodicity identity is a trigonometric identity based on the period of the trigonometric functions.

Example

The six periodicity identities are:
$\sin(x + 2\pi) = \sin(x)$; $\cos(x + 2\pi) = \cos(x)$
$\sec(x + 2\pi) = \sec(x)$; $\csc(x + 2\pi) = \csc(x)$
$\tan(x + \pi) = \tan(x)$; $\cot(x + \pi) = \cot(x)$

phase shift

A phase shift of a periodic function is a horizontal translation.

Example

The function $y = \sin(x - \pi)$ has a phase shift of π units from the basic function $y = \sin(x)$.

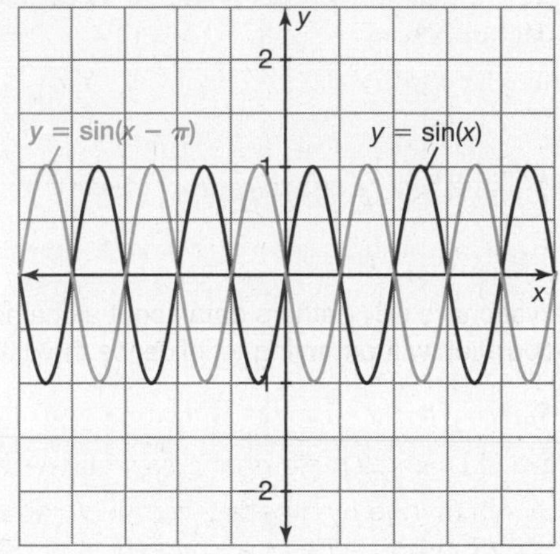

piecewise function

A piecewise function includes different functions that represent different parts of the domain.

Example

The function $f(x)$ is a piecewise function.

$$f(x) = \begin{cases} x + 5, & x \leq -2 \\ -2x + 1, & -2 < x \leq 2 \\ 2x - 9, & x > 2 \end{cases}$$

polynomial

A polynomial is a mathematical expression involving the sum of powers in one or more variables multiplied by coefficients.

Example

The expression $3x^3 + 5x^2 - 6x + 1$ is a polynomial.

Glossary

polynomial function

A polynomial function is a function that can be written in the form $p(x) = a_n x^n + a_{n-1}x^{n-1} + \cdots + a_2x^2 + a_1x + a_0$, where the coefficients $a_n, a_{n-1}, \ldots a_2, a_1, a_0$ are complex numbers and the exponents are nonnegative integers.

Example

The function $f(x) = 5x^3 + 3x^2 + x + 1$ is a polynomial function.

polynomial long division

Polynomial long division is an algorithm for dividing one polynomial by another of equal or lesser degree.

Example

$$\begin{array}{r|l} & 4x^2 - 6x + 3 \\ 2x + 3 & 8x^3 + 0x^2 - 12x - 7 \\ & -(8x^3 + 12x^2) \\ & -12x^2 - 12x \\ & -(-12x^2 - 18x) \\ & 6x - 7 \\ & -(6x + 9) \\ & \text{Remainder } -16 \end{array}$$

population

The population is the entire set of items from which data can be selected. When you decide what you want to study, the population is the set of all elements in which you are interested. The elements of that population can be people or objects.

Example

If you wanted to find out the average height of the students at your school, the number of students at the school would be the population.

population proportion

A population proportion is the percentage of an entire population that yields a favorable outcome in an experiment.

Example

In an election, the population proportion represents the percentage of people in the entire town who vote to re-elect the mayor.

power function

A power function is a function of the form $P(x) = ax^n$ where n is a non-negative integer.

Example

The functions $f(x) = x$, $f(x) = x^2$, and $f(x) = x^3$ are power functions.

Power Rule of Logarithms

The Power Rule of Logarithms states that the logarithm of a power is equal to the product of the exponent and the logarithm of the base of the power.

$$\log_b (x)^n = n \cdot \log_b (x)$$

Example

$\ln (x)^2 = 2 \ln x$

principal square root of a negative number

For any positive real number n, the principal square root of a negative number, $-n$, is defined by $\sqrt{-n} = i\sqrt{n}$.

Example

The principal square root of -5 is $\sqrt{-5} = i\sqrt{5}$.

Product Rule of Logarithms

The Product Rule of Logarithms states that the logarithm of a product is equal to the sum of the logarithms of the factors.

$$\log_b (xy) = \log_b (x) + \log_b (y)$$

Example

$\log (5x) = \log (5) + \log (x)$

pure imaginary number

A pure imaginary number is a number of the form bi, where b is not equal to 0.

Example

The imaginary numbers $-4i$ and $15i$ are pure imaginary numbers.

Pythagorean identity

A Pythagorean identity is a trigonometric identity based on the Pythagorean Theorem.

Example

The three Pythagorean identities are:
$\sin^2(x) + \cos^2(x) = 1$
$1 + \tan^2(x) = \sec^2(x)$
$1 + \cot^2(x) = \csc^2(x)$

Q

quartic function

A quartic function is a polynomial function with a degree of four.

Example

The function $f(x) = 3x^4 - 2x + 5$ is a quartic function.

quintic function

A quintic function is a polynomial function with a degree of five.

Example

The function $f(x) = 5x^5 + 3x^4 + x^3$ is a quintic function

Quotient Rule of Logarithms

The Quotient Rule of Logarithms states that the logarithm of a quotient is equal to the difference of the logarithms of the dividend and the divisor.

$$\log_b\left(\frac{x}{y}\right) = \log_b(x) - \log_b(y)$$

Example

$\log\left(\frac{x}{2}\right) = \log x - \log 2$

R

radians

A radian is a unit of measurement for an angle in standard position. It is equal to the length of its intercepted arc in the unit circle.

Example

The angle shown has a radian measure of π radians.

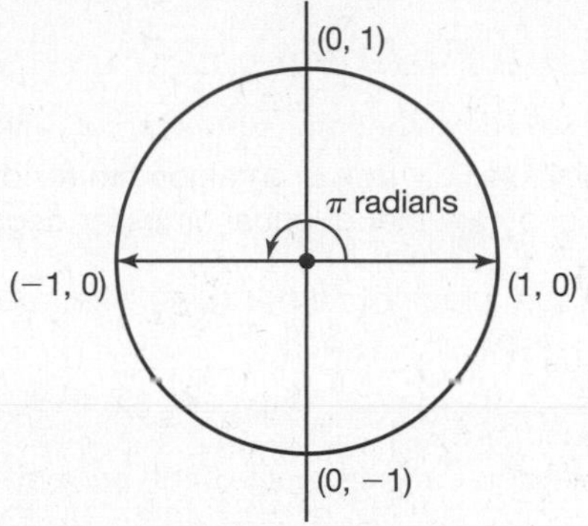

radical function

A radical function is a function that contains one or more radical expressions.

Example

The function $f(x) = \sqrt{3x + 5}$ is a radical function.

random sample

A random sample is a sample that is selected from the population in such a way that every member of the population has the same chance of being selected.

Example

Choosing 100 fans at random to participate in a survey from crowd of 5000 people is an example of random sample.

rational equation

A rational equation is an equation that contains one or more rational expressions.

Example

The equation $\frac{1}{x - 1} + \frac{1}{x + 1} = 4$ is a rational equation.

Glossary

rational function

A rational function is any function that can be written as the ratio of two polynomial functions. A rational function can be written in the form $f(x) = \frac{P(x)}{Q(x)}$ where $P(x)$ and $Q(x)$ are polynomial functions, and $Q(x) \neq 0$.

Example

The function $f(x) = \frac{1}{x - 1} + \frac{1}{x + 1}$ is a rational function.

Rational Root Theorem

The Rational Root Theorem states that a rational root of a polynomial $a_n x^n + a_{n-1} x^{n-1} + \cdots + a_2 x^2 + a_1 x + a_0 x^0$ must be of the form $\frac{p}{q}$, where p is a factor of the constant term and q is a factor of the leading coefficient.

Example

For the polynomial $2x^2 - x + 4$, $p = 4$, and $q = 2$.
So, the possible rational roots of the polynomial are ± 4, ± 2, ± 1, $\pm \frac{1}{2}$.

real part of a complex number

In a complex number of the form $a + bi$, the term a is called the real part of a complex number.

Example

The real part of the complex number $3 + 2i$ is 3.

reference points

Reference points are a set of key points that help identify the basic form of any function.

Example

The reference points of the basic quadratic function are (0, 0), (1, 1), and (2, 4).

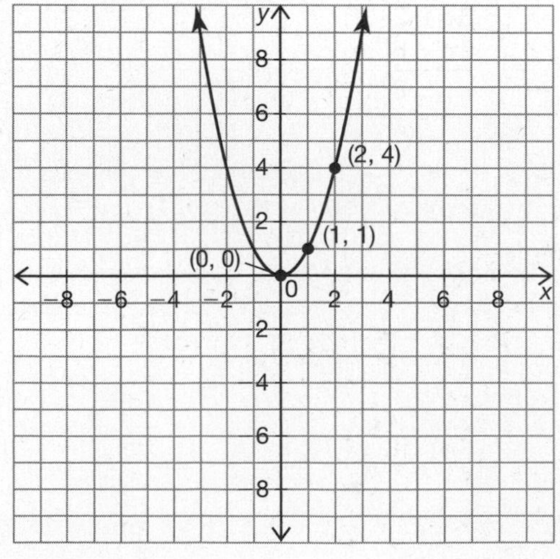

reflection

A reflection of a graph is a mirror image of the graph about a line of reflection.

Example

The triangle on the right is a reflection of the triangle on the left.

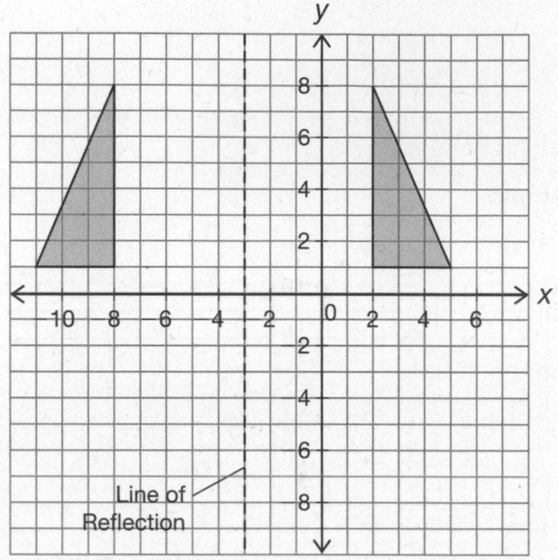

regression equation

A regression equation is a function that models the relationship between two variables in a scatter plot.

Example

The regression equation
$y = -0.41x^3 + 3.50x^2 - 4.47x + 8.44$ models the relationship between time and the number of vehicles.

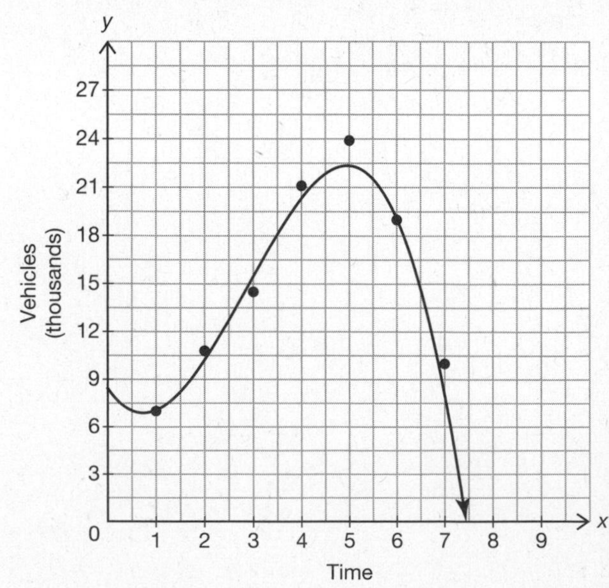

relation

A relation is the mapping between a set of input values called the domain and a set of output values called the range.

Example

The set of points {(0, 1), (1, 8), (2, 5), (3, 7)} is a relation.

relative maximum

A relative maximum is the highest point in a particular section of a graph.

Example

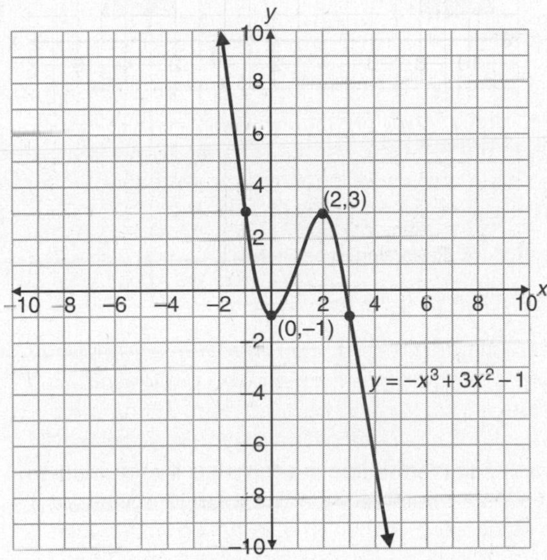

The graph shown has a relative maximum at (2, 3).

relative minimum

A relative minimum is the lowest point in a particular section of a graph.

Example

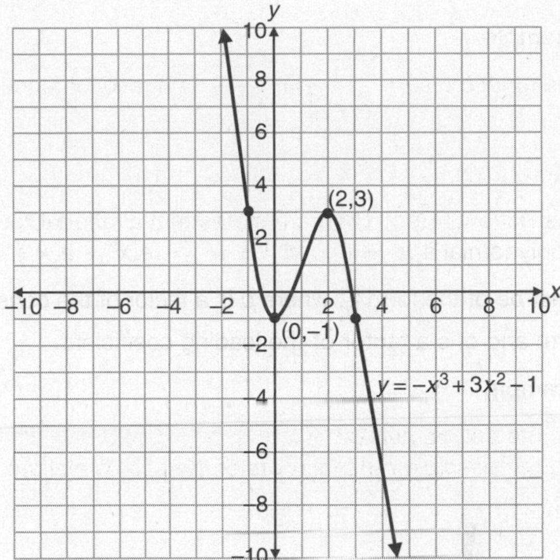

The graph shown has a relative minimum at (0, −1).

Remainder Theorem

The Remainder Theorem states that the remainder when dividing a polynomial by $(x - r)$ is the value of the polynomial at r.

Example

The value of the polynomial $x^2 + 5x + 2$ at 1 is $(1)^2 + 5(1) + 2 = 8$. So, the remainder when $x^2 + 5x + 2$ is divided by $x - 1$ is 8.

$$\begin{array}{r} x + 6 \\ x - 1 \overline{)x^2 + 5x + 2} \\ \underline{x^2 - x } \\ 6x + 2 \\ \underline{6x - 6} \\ 8 \end{array}$$

Glossary

removable discontinuity

A removable discontinuity is a single point at which the graph of a function is not defined.

Example

The graph of the function $f(x) = \frac{x^2}{x}$ has a removable discontinuity at $x = 0$.

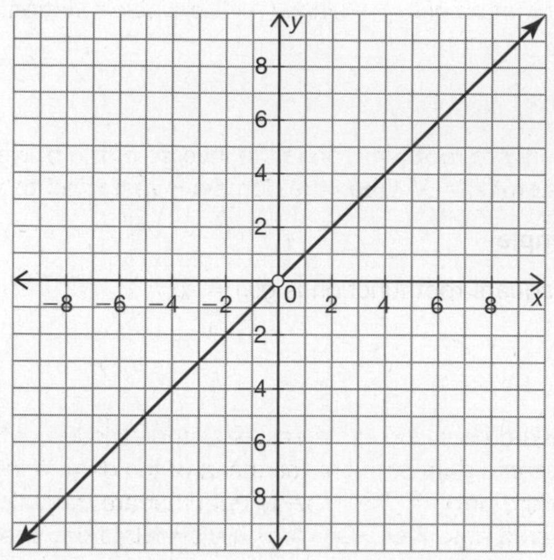

rigid motion

A rigid motion is a transformation that preserves size and shape.

Example

Reflections, rotations, and translations are examples of rigid motion.

S

sample

Where data are collected from a selection of the population, the data are called a sample.

Example

If you wanted to find out the average height of the students in your school, you could choose just a certain number of students and measure their heights.
The heights of the students in this group would be the sample.

sample proportion

A sample proportion is the percentage of a sample that yields a favorable outcome in an experiment. This is often used to make predictions about a population.

Example

In an election, a sample of townspeople is surveyed. The sample proportion represents the percentage of the survey results that indicate that they will vote to re-elect the mayor.

sample survey

A sample survey poses one or more questions of interest to obtain sample data from a population.

Example

The following is an example of a sample survey.

A recent survey of nearly 1200 young people from across the U.S. shows that 40% of 16- to 20- year-olds who have a driver's license admit to texting on a regular basis while they are driving.

sampling distribution

A sampling distribution consists of every possible sample of equal size from a given population.
A sampling distribution provides an estimate for population parameters. The mean or proportion of a sampling distribution is estimated by the mean or proportion of a sample. For categorical data, the standard deviation of a sampling distribution is estimated by calculating $\sqrt{\frac{\hat{p}(1-\hat{p})}{n}}$ where $\hat{p}$ (p-hat) is the sample proportion and n is the sample size.
For continuous data, the standard deviation of a sampling distribution is estimated by calculating $\frac{S}{\sqrt{n}}$ where S is the standard deviation of the original sample and n is the sample size.

Example

A sleep survey of 50 teens resulted in a sample mean of 7.7 hours and sample standard deviation of 0.8 hours.

The estimated mean of the sampling distribution is 7.7 hours. The estimated standard deviation of the sampling distribution is approximately 0.11 hours.

$$\frac{S}{\sqrt{n}} = \frac{0.8}{\sqrt{50}} \approx 0.11$$

self-similar

A self-similar object is exactly or approximately similar to a part of itself.

Example

A Koch snowflake is considered to be self-similar.

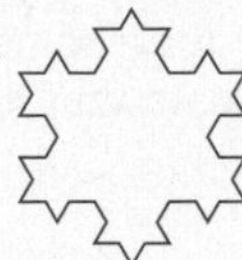

series

A series is the sum of the terms of a sequence. The sum of the first n terms of a sequence is denoted by S_n.

Example

The series corresponding to the sequence 1, 1, 2, 3, 5 is $1 + 1 + 2 + 3 + 5$, or 12.

set of complex numbers

The set of complex numbers is the set of all numbers written in the form $a + bi$, where a and b are real numbers. The set of complex numbers consists of the set of imaginary numbers and the set of real numbers.

Example

The numbers $1 + 2i$, 7, and $-3i$ are complex numbers.

set of imaginary numbers

The set of imaginary numbers is the set of all numbers written in the form $a + bi$, where a and b are real numbers and b is not equal to 0.

Example

The numbers $2 - 3i$ and $5i$ are imaginary numbers. The number 6 is not an imaginary number.

simple random sample

A simple random sample is a sample in which every member of the population has the same chance of being selected.

Example

Using a random number generator to select a sample is an example of simple random sampling.

sine function

A sine function is a periodic function. It takes angle measures (θ values) as inputs and then outputs real number values based on coordinates of points on the unit circle.

Example

The function $h(\theta) = -\sin(2\theta) + 1$ is a sine function.

square root function

The square root function is the inverse of the power function $f(x) = x^2$ when the domain is restricted to $x \geq 0$.

Example

The square root function is $g(x) = \sqrt{x}$.

standard deviation

Standard deviation is a measure of the variation of the values in a data set from the mean of the data. A lower standard deviation represents data that are more tightly clustered near the mean. A higher standard deviation represents data that are more spread out from the mean. Use the formula below to calculate standard deviation.

$$\text{standard deviation} = \sqrt{\frac{\sum_{i=1}^{n}(x_1 - \bar{x})^2}{n}}$$

where $\bar{x}$ is the mean and n is the number of data values in the data set $\{x_1, x_2, \ldots, x_n\}$.

Example

In the data set of test scores
60, 70, 80, 90, 100,
the mean $\bar{x}$ is 80 and the number of data elements n is 5. So, the standard deviation of the test scores is
standard deviation =

$$\sqrt{\frac{(60 - 80)^2 + (70 - 80)^2 + (80 - 80)^2 + (90 - 80)^2 + (100 - 80)^2}{5}}$$

$$= \sqrt{\frac{1000}{5}}$$

$$= \sqrt{200}$$

$$\approx 14.14.$$

standard form (general form) of a quadratic function

A quadratic function written in the form $f(x) = ax^2 + bx + c$, where $a \neq 0$, is in standard form, or general form.

Example

The function $f(x) = -5x^2 - 10x + 1$ is written in standard form.

Glossary

standard normal distribution

The standard normal distribution is a normal probability distribution with the following properties:

- The mean is equal to 0.
- The standard deviation is 1.
- The curve is bell-shaped and symmetric about the mean.

Example

A standard normal distribution curve is shown.

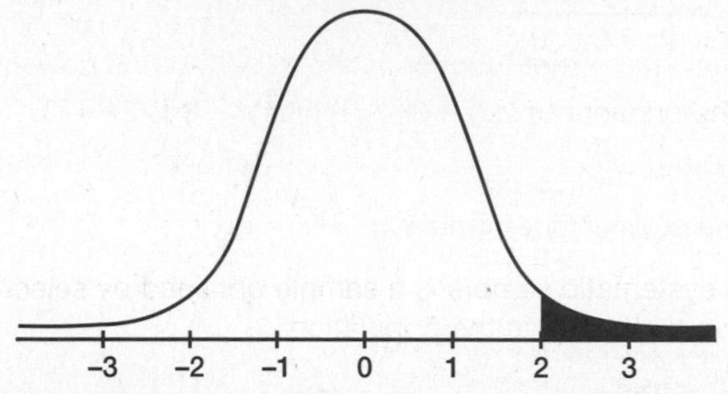

standard position of an angle

The standard position of an angle occurs when the vertex of the angle is at the origin and one ray of the angle is on the *x*-axis.

Example

The angle shown is in standard position.

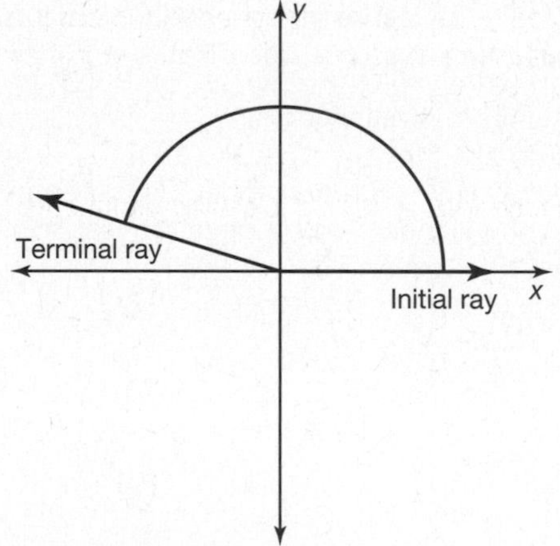

statistic

When data are gathered from a sample, the characteristic used to describe the sample is called a statistic.

Example

If you wanted to find out the average height of the students in your school, and you chose just a certain number of students randomly and measured their heights, the characteristic "average height" would be called a statistic.

statistically significant

A survey that has a result that is statistically significant indicates that the result did not likely occur by chance, but is likely linked to a specific cause. Typically, a result that is more than 2 standard deviations away from the mean is considered statistically significant.

Example

A survey of 2000 teenagers reports that 42% have a part-time job. The interval from 40.9% to 43.1% represents a 95% confidence interval for the population proportion. A survey that yields a report of 50% of teenager with a part-time job would be considered statistically significant.

stratified random sample

A stratified random sample is a sample obtained by dividing the population into different groups, or strata, according to a characteristic, and randomly selecting data from each group.

Example

If students in a high school are divided by class, and random samples are then taken from each class, the result is a stratified random sample.

subjective sample

A subjective sample is a sample that is chosen based on some criteria, rather than at random.

Example

From a set of students, "choosing five students you know" is a subjective sample. In contrast, "choosing five students at random" is a random sample.

symmetric about a line

If a graph is symmetric about a line, the line divides the graph into two identical parts.

Example

The graph of $f(x) = x^2$ is symmetric about the line $x = 0$.

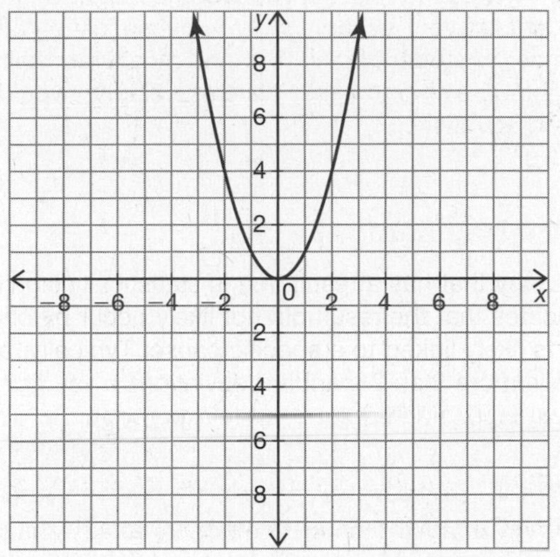

symmetric about a point

A function is symmetric about a point if each point on the graph has a point the same distance from the central point, but in the opposite direction.

Example

The graph of $f(x) = x^3$ is symmetric about the point (0, 0).

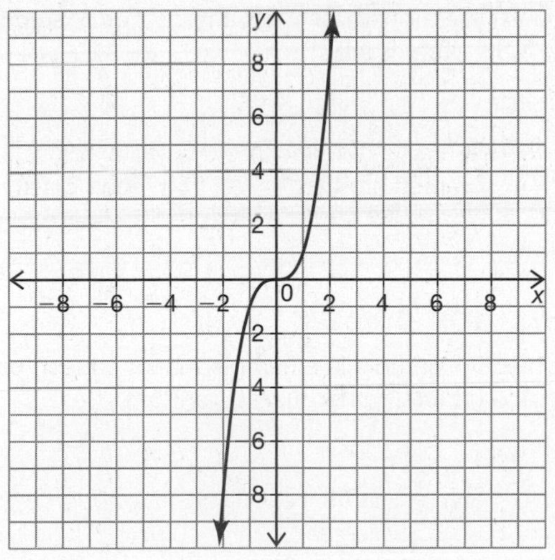

synthetic division

Synthetic division is a method for dividing a polynomial by a linear factor of the form $(x - r)$.

Example

The quotient of $2x^2 - 3x - 9$ and $x - 3$ can be calculated using synthetic division.

$$\begin{array}{r|rrr} 3 & 2 & -3 & -9 \\ & & 6 & 9 \\ \hline & 2 & 3 & 0 \end{array}$$

The quotient of $2x^2 - 3x - 9$ and $x - 3$ is $2x + 3$.

systematic sample

A systematic sample is a sample obtained by selecting every nth data in the population.

Example

If you choose every 12th student that walks into school, your sample is a systematic sample.

T

tangent function

A tangent function is a periodic function. It takes angle measures (θ values) as inputs and then outputs real number values based on coordinates of points on the unit circle.

Example

The function $f(\theta) = \tan\left(\frac{\theta}{2}\right)$ is a tangent function.

Glossary

terminal ray of an angle

The terminal ray of an angle in standard position is the ray with its endpoint at the origin that is not the initial ray.

Example

The terminal ray of the angle is labeled in the diagram.

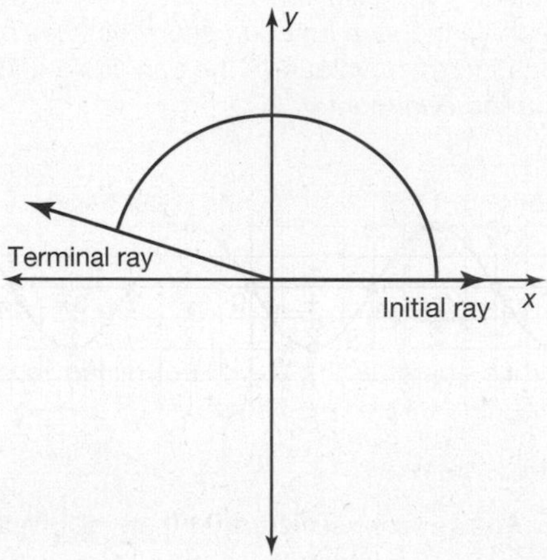

tessellation

A tessellation is created when a geometric shape is repeated over a two-dimensional plane such that there are no overlaps among the shapes and no gaps.

Example

A tessellation of diamonds is shown.

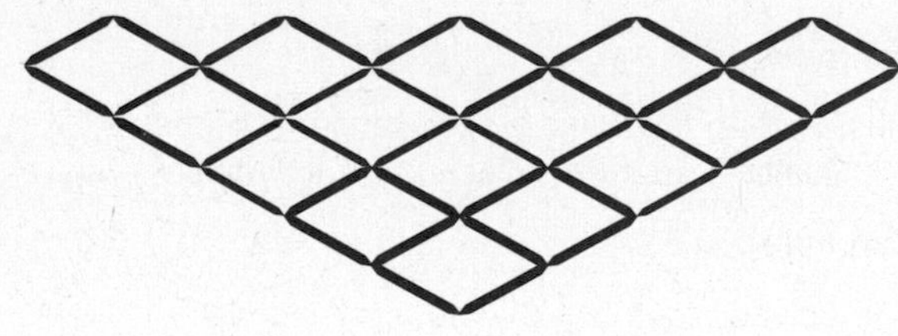

the imaginary number *i*

The number i is a number such that $i^2 = -1$.

theta (θ)

Theta is a symbol typically used to represent the measure of an angle in standard position.

Example

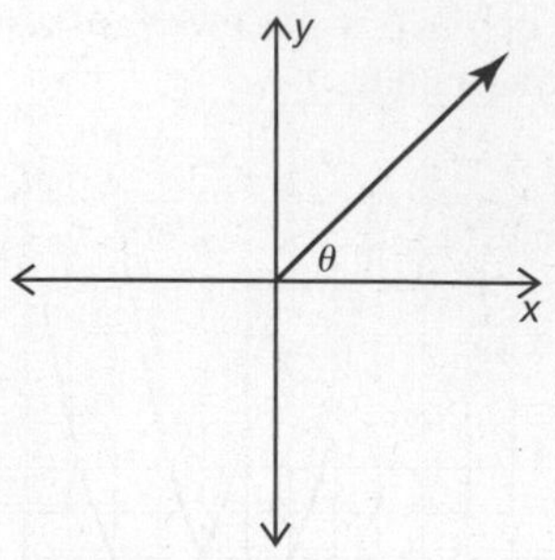

transformation

A transformation is the mapping, or movement, of all the points of a figure in a plane according to a common operation. Translations, reflections, rotations, and dilations are examples of transformations.

Example

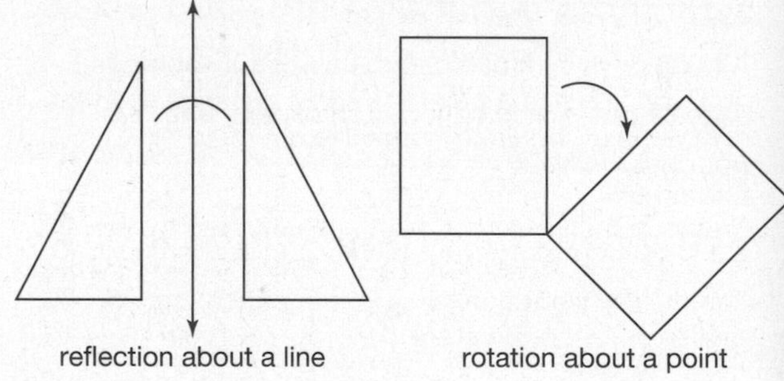

Glossary

translation

A translation is a type of transformation that shifts an entire figure or graph the same distance and direction.

Example

The graph of $g(x) = (x - 2)^2$ is a translation of the graph of $f(x) = x^2$ right 2 units.

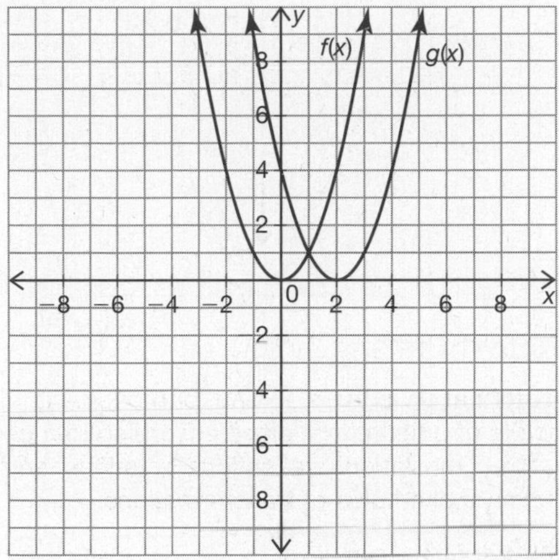

treatment

A treatment is a condition in an experiment.

Example

Suppose that an experiment is conducted to test the effects of a new drug on a sample of patients. The distribution of the drug to the patients is the treatment in the experiment.

trigonometric equation

A trigonometric equation is an equation that includes one or more trigonometric functions.

Example

The equation $\cos(x) = \frac{\sqrt{2}}{2}$ is a trigonometric equation.

trigonometric function

A trigonometric function is a periodic function that takes angle measures (θ values) as inputs and then outputs real number values based on coordinates of points on the unit circle.

Example

The function $g(x) = \sin(x)$ is a trigonometric function. The graph of the sine function $g(\theta) = \sin(\theta)$ is obtained by evaluating the θ values of the unit circle and graphing the coordinates.

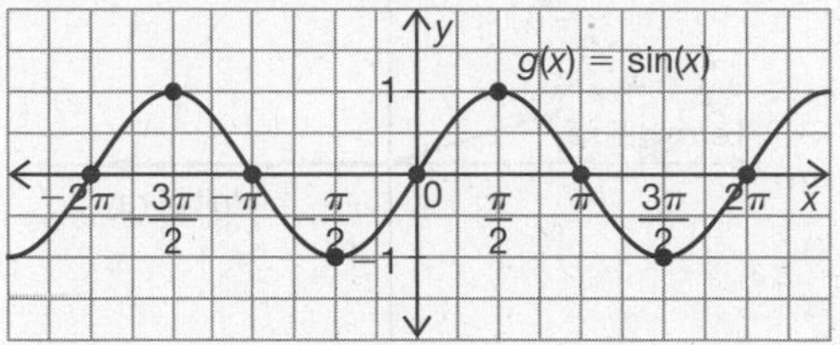

θ	$g(\theta) = \sin(\theta)$	$(\theta, g(\theta))$
0	$\sin(0) = 0$	(0, 0)
$\frac{\pi}{2}$	$\sin\left(\frac{\pi}{2}\right) = 1$	$\left(\frac{\pi}{2}, 1\right)$
π	$\sin(\pi) = 0$	$(\pi, 0)$
$\frac{3\pi}{2}$	$\sin\left(\frac{3\pi}{2}\right) = -1$	$\left(\frac{3\pi}{2}, -1\right)$
2π	$\sin(2\pi) = 0$	$(2\pi, 0)$

trinomial

A trinomial is a polynomial with exactly three terms.

Example

The polynomial $5x^2 - 6x + 9$ is a trinomial.

U

unit circle

A unit circle is a circle whose radius is one unit of distance.

Example

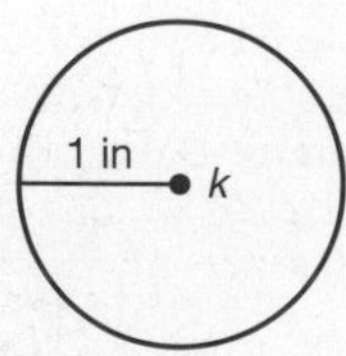

Circle K is a unit circle.

V

vertex form of a quadratic function

A quadratic function written in vertex form is in the form $f(x) = a(x - h)^2 + k$, where $a \neq 0$.

Example

The quadratic equation $y = 2(x - 5)^2 + 10$ is written in vertex form. The vertex of the graph is the point (5, 10).

vertical asymptote

A vertical asymptote is a vertical line that a function gets closer and closer to, but never intersects. The asymptote does not represent points on the graph of the function. It represents the output value that the graph approaches.

Example

The graph has two asymptotes: a vertical asymptote $x = 2$ and a horizontal asymptote $y = -1$.

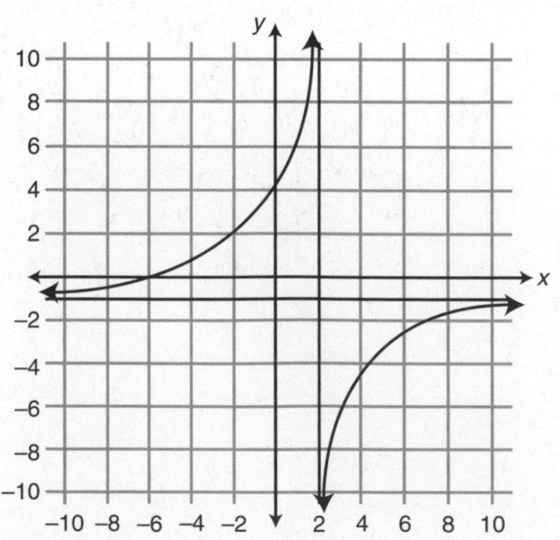

vertical compression

Vertical compression is the squeezing of a graph toward the x-axis.

Example

The graph of $g(x) = \frac{1}{2}x^2$ is a vertical compression compared to the graph of $f(x) = x^2$.

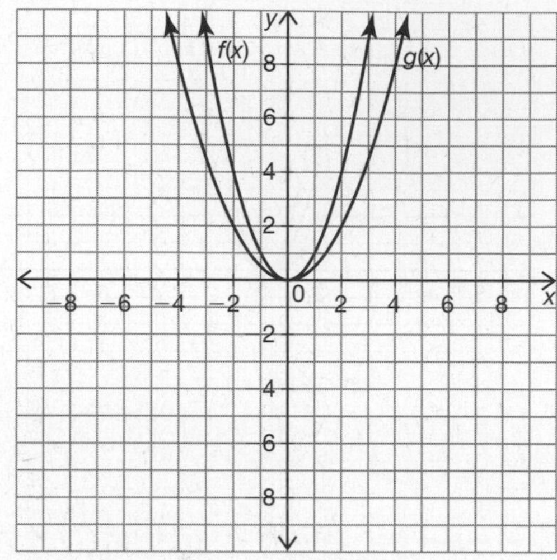

vertical dilation

A vertical dilation is a type of transformation that stretches or compresses an entire figure or graph. In a vertical dilation, notice that the y-coordinate of every point on the graph of a function is multiplied by a common factor, A.

Example

The graphs of $g(x) = 2x^2$ and $h(x) = \frac{1}{2}x^2$ are vertical dilations of the graph of $f(x) = x^2$.

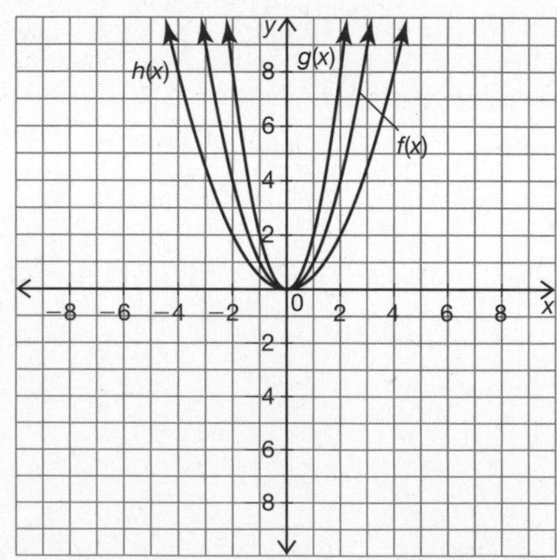

vertical stretching

Vertical stretching is the stretching of a graph away from the x-axis.

Example

The graph of $g(x) = 2x^2$ is a vertical stretching compared to the graph of $f(x) = x^2$.

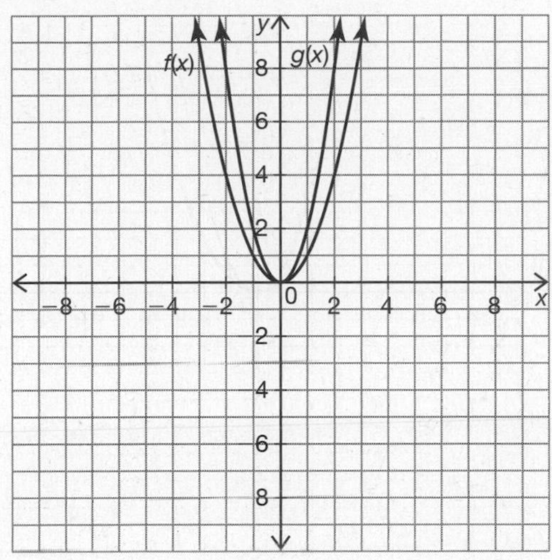

volunteer sample

A volunteer sample is a sample whose data consists of those who volunteer to be part of the sample.

Example

If you ask students in your school to complete and submit an optional survey so that you can collect data, your sample is a volunteer sample.

Z

z-score

A z-score is a number that describes how many standard deviations from the mean a particular value is. The following formula can be used to calculate a z-score for a particular value, where z represents the z-score, x represents the particular data value, μ represents the mean, and σ represents the standard deviation.

$$z = \frac{x - \mu}{\sigma}$$

Example

Suppose that a set of data follows a normal distribution with a mean of 22 and a standard deviation of 2.4.

The z-score for a data value of 25 is $z = \frac{25 - 22}{2.4} = 1.25$.

Zero Product Property

The Zero Product Property states that if the product of two or more factors is equal to zero, then at least one factor must be equal to zero. This is also called the Converse of Multiplication Property of Zero.

Example

According to the Zero Product Property, if $(x - 2)(x + 3) = 0$ then $x - 2 = 0$ or $x + 3 = 0$.

Zero Property of Logarithms

The Zero Property of Logarithms states that the logarithm of 1, with any base, is always equal to 0.

$$\log_b (1) = 0$$

Example

$\log_3 (1) = 0$

Glossary

Glossary

Index

A

Index

Index

D

Index

E

F

Index

Index

M

Index

N

O

P

Index

Index

Index

Q

R

S

T

U

V

W

X

Index